Creative PROFESSIONALS PRESS™

PHOTOSHOP 5
In Depth

DAVID XENAKIS AND **SHERRY LONDON**

Photoshop 5 In Depth
Copyright © 1998 by The Coriolis Group, Inc.
All rights reserved. This book may not be duplicated in any way without the express written consent of the publisher, except in the form of brief excerpts or quotations for the purposes of review. The information contained herein is for the personal use of the reader and may not be incorporated in any commercial programs, other books, databases, or any kind of software without written consent of the publisher. Making copies of this book or any portion for any purpose other than your own is a violation of United States copyright laws.

Limits of Liability and Disclaimer of Warranty
The author and publisher of this book have used their best efforts in preparing the book and the programs contained in it. These efforts include the development, research, and testing of the theories and programs to determine their effectiveness. The author and publisher make no warranty of any kind, expressed or implied, with regard to these programs or the documentation contained in this book.

The author and publisher shall not be liable in the event of incidental or consequential damages in connection with, or arising out of, the furnishing, performance, or use of the programs, associated instructions, and/or claims of productivity gains.

Trademarks
Trademarked names appear throughout this book. Rather than list the names and entities that own the trademarks or insert a trademark symbol with each mention of the trademarked name, the publisher states that it is using the names for editorial purposes only and to the benefit of the trademark owner, with no intention of infringing upon that trademark.

The Coriolis Group, Inc.
An International Thomson Publishing Company
14455 N. Hayden Road, Suite 220
Scottsdale, Arizona 85260

602/483-0192
FAX 602/483-0193
http://www.coriolis.com

Library of Congress Cataloging-In-Publication Data
Xenakis, David
   Photoshop 5 in depth/by David Xenakis and Sherry London.
      p. cm
   Includes index
   ISBN 1-57610-293-9
   1. Computer graphics.   2. Adobe Photoshop.
I. London, Sherry   II. Title
T385.X48   1998
006.6'869--dc21   98-8325
                                     CIP

Printed in the United States of America
10 9 8 7 6 5 4 3 2 1

Publisher
Keith Weiskamp

Acquisitions
Stephanie Wall

Project Editor
Don Eamon

Marketing Specialist
Dylan Zoller

Production Coordinator
Jon Gabriel

Cover Design
Anthony Stock
Additional art provided by Brandon Riza (www.101a.com)

Layout Design
April Nielsen

CD-ROM Development
Robert Clarfield

CORIOLIS
an International Thomson Publishing company

Albany, NY • Belmont, CA • Bonn • Boston • Cincinnati • Detroit • Johannesburg
London • Madrid • Melbourne • Mexico City • New York • Paris • Singapore
Tokyo • Toronto • Washington

ABOUT THE AUTHORS

David Xenakis is president of XRX, Inc., a corporation that produces *Knitter's Magazine*, *Weaver's Magazine*, Stitches Fair and Consumer Show, and operates Xenakis Design Services (specializing in corporate consulting, high-end color print preparation, and training for users of digital prepress systems).

The publications of XRX, Inc. began to use digital technology in 1987 with the purchase of Macintosh computers and then little-known software packages such as QuarkXPress and Adobe Illustrator. *Knitter's Magazine* was the first nationally distributed publication to be done entirely in QuarkXPress. Digital technology has evolved and XRX has benefited from an early lead in the field. Today, XRX produces more than 96 percent of its material on the computer and generates a significant number of its color separations.

David Xenakis was born 26 February 1944, in Mason City, Iowa. He attended public and secondary schools in Clear Lake, Iowa. At the University of South Dakota, Vermillion, South Dakota, he majored in Applied Piano and Composition with minors in History, English, and Mathematics.

After he left the University, David and two partners—Elaine Rowley and Alexis Xenakis—established two retail stores in South Dakota. From these, the first of two quarterly publications developed. David served as Executive Editor of *Weaver's Magazine* for the first four years of its existence.

With the advent of the second XRX, Inc. publication, *Knitter's Magazine*, David switched his role in the company, becoming the driving force that steered the publications toward digital methods. With his experience developed in real-world situations, David was increasingly called upon as a consultant to companies that were making the transition to digital methods. Eventually, his role became defined as an advisor standing between corporate purchasers and prepress equipment vendors, advisor for installation and workflow procedures, trainer for corporate staff, and consultant-on-retainer for the year following the installations. He continues on retainer for several large corporations, and as a troubleshooter for a number of regional clients.

David is recognized as a superb teacher and communicator who is readily able to make the most sophisticated concepts accessible to everyone. He has conducted his two-day seminar *Navigating Photoshop* in 35 cities across the nation with great success and with critical acclaim. More recently, he has added to his seminar activities with two additional classes, "Navigating Illustrator" and "Preparing Graphics for the World Wide Web." In addition to his teaching schedule, he has worked as an advisor for his clients' Web-site development.

David presently lives in Sioux Falls, South Dakota where he has been a guiding force in his region's prepress community.

Sherry London is an artist, a writer, and a teacher, which is exactly what a going-into-college aptitude test predicted. Sherry is the author of a number of books, including *Photoshop 4.0: An Interactive Course*, *Photoshop Textures Magic*, *Enhanced Photoshop 4*

About the Authors

(also with David Xenakis), *Painter 5 f/x* (with Rhoda Grossman and Sharon Evans), and *Photoshop 3 Special Effects How-To*. She teaches Photoshop and Prepress in the Continuing Education Department of Moore College of Art and Design in Philadelphia and has spoken at a number of conferences, including the Thunder Lizard Photoshop Conference and the Professional Photographers of America convention.

Sherry has worked as a social studies teacher, an instructional systems designer, a programmer, a fiber artist, and a graphic designer. She is the principal of London Computing: PhotoFX, a full-service design studio. She has designed needlework for the Philadelphia Museum of Art gift store and the *Horchow* catalog. Her fiber art has been exhibited in many group shows, including shows at the Delaware Museum of Art, Ormond Memorial Art Museum, and the Brevard Art Center. She was a contributing editor for *Computer Artist* magazine and has written for *Pre*, *MacWeek*, *MacUser*, *Digital Vision*, and the combined *MacWorld/MacUser* magazine.

Partial list of corporate attendees of David Xenakis' Navigating Photoshop™ seminars (individual attendee names available on request):

- 3M General Offices
- Anchor Hocking Packaging Company
- A G Edwards & Sons, Inc.
- Aegis Research Corporation
- Argonne National Laboratory
- AT&T
- Blue Cross/Blue Shield
- Boston University Medical School
- Busch Creative Services
- Cannon USA
- Colgate University
- College of William & Mary
- DAYNA Communications
- Dekalb Genetics
- Eli Lilly Company
- EMI Records
- Encyclopedia Britannica Education Corporation
- Exxon Company International
- Fedex
- Federal Reserve Bank/Chicago
- Federal Reserve Bank/San Francisco
- Franklin Mint
- Gateway 2000
- Graceland Division Elvis Presley Enterprises
- Harcourt Brace School of Publishing
- Iowa State University
- Kinney Shoe Corporation
- K-Mart Corporation
- Knight-Ridder Financial, Inc.
- Louisiana Lottery Corporation
- Lawrence Livermore National Laboratories
- Letraset
- Lockheed Martin
- Louisiana Department of Health & Hospitals
- McDonnell Douglas
- McGraw-Hill
- Midland National Life Insurance Company
- Mobil Oil Corporation
- Multi-Ad Services
- NC State University
- New York State Bar Association
- National Oceanic & Atmospheric Admin.
- New York Times
- Northwest Airlines
- PA School of Art & Design
- Parker Brothers
- Pratt Whitney
- Proctor & Gamble
- Purdue University
- Reynolds Metal Company
- Sather Companies
- Sears
- Smithsonian Institute
- The World Bank
- Unisys
- Viacom New Media
- Westinghouse Electric Company

ACKNOWLEDGMENTS

Despite the hours spent alone, looking at a computer screen, a book about a piece of software as large and as complex as Adobe's Photoshop is not written in a vacuum. I offer my gratitude to those who have helped me as I worked.

My partners Elaine Rowley and Alexis Xenakis took away the pressure of other duties so that I could concentrate on the task.

The staff at XRX, Inc. has been tremendously helpful and patient with me, taking over some of my work while I coped with deadlines.

My son Benjamin has become a genius at running interference, and at helping with the thousand small tasks that seem to get in the way of the work to be done.

My co-author Sherry London, who has proved to be a mine of esoteric knowledge as well as the possessor of one of the most interesting minds I've ever encountered, gave me the original opportunity to collaborate on this book. Sherry has become so dear to me that I can think of nothing more enjoyable than to work on another book project with her. Working with her through the intricacies of a program such as Photoshop 5 is an educational experience no one should miss!

To the staff at Coriolis—Stephanie Wall, Don Eamon, Jon Gabriel, Robert Clarfield, and those other hard-working folks who have had a hand in this large project—I would like to say: I'll never be able to adequately thank you for the kindness, helpfulness and encouraging words that have made this project a wonderful experience.

My agent, Margot Malley, deserves a medal for the treacherous territory she treads daily with great aplomb. As far as I can tell, she has never been flapped, nor has she ever been anything less than totally courteous, kind, helpful, and gracious.

Finally, thanks to Samantha and Christopher whose innocent, blue-eyed smiles can charm me out of thinking about Color Management strategies!

— David Xenakis
Sioux Falls, South Dakota

I need to add a few additional notes of thanks.

Margot Malley, my agent, was instrumental in the birth of this book. Although David has thanked her as well, I need to add a personal thanks.

I want to thank Chris Grams, of Ventana publications, for guiding this book so ably through its first version. Ventana is gone, but I will always remember Chris, and wish him well in whatever else he does.

I also want to thank the vendors who have contributed their products to this CD-ROM. You have helped to make the CD-ROM an even more useful part of the entire package, and you have enriched the Photoshop community with the creativity of your software.

ACKNOWLEDGMENTS

Words are inadequate to thank my co-author, David Xenakis. His breadth of knowledge about Photoshop is astounding. Finding a kindred spirit has been an amazing experience.

Finally, I need to thank my husband, Norm, for putting up with the phone ringing every time we sat down to dinner, and for being willing to eat whatever managed to get put on the table (even if it was only take-out—and it usually was!).

— *Sherry London*
Cherry Hill, New Jersey

TABLE OF CONTENTS

Introduction — XIII
- What's "In Depth" About This Book?   XIII
- What's In The Book   XIII
- The CD-ROM   XVI
- Other Resources   XVI
- How To Use This Book   XVII

Chapter 1
Optimizing Photoshop — 1
- Windows Or Mac?   1
- Built For Speed   2
- Other Hardware Goodies   8
- What's Your Preference?   9
- Special Issues   20
- Troubleshooting   28
- The History Palette   42
- Using Actions   52
- Moving On   68

Chapter 2
Acquiring Images — 69
- Resolution, Pixels, And Sampling Frequency   70
- Basic Scanning   75
- The Scanner's Controls, ArtScan Pro By Jetsoft   77
- Evaluating Images For Scanning   88
- Other Scanning Considerations   93
- Photo CD   109
- Moving On   118

Chapter 3
Toolbox Techniques — 119

    The Mouse With The Keyboard 119
    Go On, Type A Tool… 120
    Tools 139
    Type In Photoshop 190
    The Line, Paint Bucket, And Gradient Tools 201
    Moving On 224

Chapter 4
Paths And The Pen Tool — 227

    Beziér Curves 227
    Drawing Paths With The Pen Tool 230
    The Paths Palette 242
    Manipulating Paths In Photoshop 250
    Special Effects Using Strokes On Paths 263
    Moving On 293

Chapter 5
Using Channels — 295

    Channels: What They Can Do 296
    Manipulating Channels 318
    Moving On 355

Chapter 6
Using Layers — 357

    Layered Documents And The Layers Palette 358
    The Layers Palette 359
    The Layers Palette Menu And The Layer Menu 384
    Other Options Of The Layer Menu 398
    Moving On 420

Chapter 7
Calculations 423

- The Apply Image Command 424
- The Calculations Command 426
- Apply Image And Calculations Compared 436
- Calculating An Image—A Different Way To Work 439
- Classic CHOPs 450
- Moving On 452

Chapter 8
Filter Frolics 453

- Shortcuts 453
- Filters And RAM 454
- How Filters Work 454
- Native Filters 461
- Third-Party Filters 493
- Favorite Filter Tricks 509
- Creating Your Own Filters 513
- Managing Filters 515
- Moving On 516

Chapter 9
Photoshop Prepress 517

- Getting Good Printed Grays 518
- Duotones, Tritones, And Quadtones 575
- Spot Color 597
- Line Art And Bitmap Mode 625
- Moving On 651

Chapter 10
Calibration And Color Reproduction — 653

- Color Is Color, Isn't It? 653
- RGB Color 657
- Calibration And How It Works 659
- CMYK Setup: Built-In Options 665
- Separation Setup 669
- CMYK Setup: ICC Profiles 674
- Tables 687
- Preparing To Make A Color Separation 687
- Processing An RGB File Intended For Color Separation 688
- A Stochastic Screening Alternative 708
- Clipping Paths 712
- Saving Paths 714
- Trapping 723
- Ultra High-Fidelity Offset Color Reproduction 734
- Moving On 736

Chapter 11
Manipulating Images — 737

- Making Adjustments 738
- Transformations 763
- Grids And Positioning 776
- Putting It All Together 789
- Moving On 809

Chapter 12
Photoshop And The World Wide Web — 811

- Essentials Of Web Graphics 812
- Bit Depth, Two File Formats 820
- Bit Depth 820

The GIF Format   820
Converting To The GIF Format   820
The JPEG Format   839
PNG   842
A Nice Alternative To Interlacing   844
Background Basics   845
Assigning A Coded Background Color   845
Other Uses For The Hex Numbers   846
Background Tiles   846
Nonrectangular Graphics On The Web   868
Buttons, Arrows, And Display Type   875
Accessory Software   888
Moving On   900

Appendix A
What's On The CD-ROM   901

Practice Files   901
Third-Party Software   902

Appendix B
Common Prepress Terms And Definitions   905

Appendix C
Photoshop 5 Keyboard Shortcuts   919

Index   937

Photoshop 5
In Depth

INTRODUCTION

Hello! We haven't met yet, but perhaps we will become acquainted within the pages of this book.

You are probably a current user of Photoshop, or perhaps you want to become one. (Otherwise, there would be little reason for you to have picked up this very heavy book to see whether this might be the one—out of all the competing titles—that you need.) Is this the book you need? We would like to think so. We have spent a good deal of time putting concepts and ideas into words and figures. But how we have spent our time isn't your problem: Your problem is to decide if *this* book will give you the essentials of what you need to know about Photoshop 5. Therefore, it falls on us to tell you what we've done, and what we've assumed that you will want in a Photoshop book. After that, you can flip through the pages, look at the example illustrations, read some of the explanations, check to see what topics are included, and decide if we've done our job well enough to justify your investment and your time.

What's "In Depth" About This Book?

We have written this volume for the advanced user of Photoshop—or for an intermediate-level user who would like to *become* a power user of this application. We assume that you are familiar with the program and that you need a book that shows you the range of possibilities inherent in expert use of Photoshop. Although our explanations are clear, they do assume a prior general knowledge of the program. For this reason, we feel that we have written a book that enhances your depth of knowledge about Photoshop and builds on your previous accomplishments. If you are at this level, you don't need a book that explains how to save a file. You already know that! By starting at a higher level, we can cover the more critical and advanced skills. We've had fun writing this book; we hope you profit from reading it.

What's In The Book

This book is divided into 12 chapters. The order of the chapters is progressive. You'll learn the basics in the first few chapters, and then go on to explore increasingly advanced material. The following are short synopses of what you'll find in each of the chapters.

- Chapter 1, "Optimizing Photoshop." We begin with one of the most important topics—making the program perform at its best in your computer environment. You need to know about the important issues of RAM and drive space, environment settings, and the all-important Photoshop Preferences that make the program perform at its best. You'll learn to set up your system so that running Photoshop becomes a pleasure. System and configuration issues can then recede in importance as you concentrate on using the program.

- Chapter 2, "Acquiring Images." Because many people use Photoshop mainly as an editing program—where pre-existing data is manipulated and changed—rather than as a program in which new digital artwork is created, the next topic on your list of subjects to master is that of acquiring images. You'll be introduced to the pixel—really introduced!—and will learn the basics of scanning. We'll take a thorough look at what scanning software can do to eliminate some of the tedious aspects of acquiring your picture files, and how you can arrive at the best quality your scanner can give. You'll also learn how to clean up your scans, to remove dust, scratches, and other artifacts that interfere with the eventual use of the image. Finally, you will take a close look at Photo CD and how you can take advantage of this inexpensive source of digital images.

- Chapter 3, "Toolbox Techniques." Perhaps you have already experimented with Photoshop's superb collection of tools. If you have, we think this chapter will open your eyes to possibilities that you might not have suspected. This chapter—one of the largest in the book— shows you each tool in action (except for the Pen tool, which is so important that it merits its own chapter), looks at all the options associated with the tool, and suggests fast ways of choosing the tools and their options from the keyboard. This chapter also introduces a selection method called Quick Mask. You're going to love Quick Mask for the simple way it allows you to mask an image using both the Paint tools and the Selection tools. Two attractive photographs are furnished to give you an enjoyable, step-by-step look at some very different aspects of Quick Mask.

- Chapter 4, "Paths And The Pen Tool." This chapter is really the conclusion of Chapter 3 because its topic is the Pen tool (and the associated Paths palette). This tool will carry you into areas of special effects that you'll find easy to master and thrilling as possibilities for your own work. We're also going to sidestep Photoshop temporarily—as we do in many places in this book—to look at Adobe Illustrator's handling of paths and at how you can use these two amazing programs in tandem. As in Chapter 3, more practice files are provided so that you can get into doing useful things at once.

- Chapter 5, "Using Channels." You may have heard of the word *channel* connected with Photoshop and thought of it as a technical term. It certainly is technical, but it is far more than just a word. Channels, as you'll see in this chapter, are a way of displaying different kinds of information. Channels can be masks or selections, representations of color strength, an analog for transparency information, even a visual way of representing a way of controlling the effects of a command. Once you begin to understand channels, you'll have a behind-the-scenes look at some of Photoshop's most sophisticated inner mechanisms. Moreover, you'll have a foundation for some of Photoshop's most powerful editing functions. We will show you how to use the channels that are native to all Photoshop files, make new channels, and produce other channels that are the result of adding two channels together or subtracting one or more from another. The process will sound complex, at first, but with hands-on experience, you'll find that it is effortless and a good deal less challenging than rocket science.

- Chapter 6, "Using Layers." Layers amaze everyone who uses Photoshop. These really are Photoshop's most wonderful gift to the world of digital art. They are powerful and flexible and so easy to use! After you get past the surface delights of layers, you are going to find surprisingly interesting things that go beyond simply stacking up groups of pixels and playing with blends modes and changes in opacity. We'll show you how to use layer masks, clipping groups, and options that will allow you to make parts of your layer invisible based on its brightness or color or on the brightness or color of the pixels beneath it. This chapter includes a look at transformations of the pixels on a layer. You will learn how to subtly change the orientation of objects on a layer so that they seem to belong to the same reality as pixels on other layers. What else can we say about layers? If you like working in Photoshop—or think that you might—layers are just about the most fun you can have without laughing aloud.

- Chapter 7, "Calculations." This chapter deals with just two menu commands: *Apply Image* and *Calculations*. You've probably seen examples of the wild and wonderful photographic montages that are dominating the world of the graphic arts. If so, you've probably seen examples of images that flow together in ways that seem nearly impossible. High-level users of Photoshop make use of these two commands—as well as many other powerful Photoshop capabilities—to achieve such complex effects. To show you how these commands can be used in several situations, the Companion CD-ROM provides files on which you will apply our step-by-step instructions. After you've been through the basics and have seen how many possibilities you have at your disposal, you'll be in good shape to strike out on your own. Who knows? In a few months, maybe it will be *your* awesome photo montage that is furnishing amazement to the world of the graphic arts.

- Chapter 8, "Filter Frolics." No Photoshop book is complete without a look at filters. You'll see examples in use as they are applied to a photograph of a cat named Marmalade. Our hero the cat, as you will see, survives his encounters with altered reality in fine style. He, of course, remembers that removing the effects of an applied filter is as simple as the clicking one step up on the History palette.

- Chapter 9, "Photoshop Prepress." This is the first of two large-scale chapters that deal with the subject of Photoshop and prepress. If you need to prepare digital images for any kind of print reproduction, we think you'll appreciate both of these chapters as they cover just about every topic that you'll need to know about. Chapter 9 begins with a short course on press conditions and what you need to know when you are processing files. We then provide precise information for preparing halftones and duotones so they appear clean, clear, and beautifully balanced when they come from the press. Next, you'll learn about preparing line art and handling spot color. This chapter includes, among other topics, how-to information for using touch and bump plates—additional inks to augment black and process-color printing—that you'll find difficult to locate anywhere else.

- Chapter 10, "Calibration And Color Reproduction." Here is the second of our comprehensive chapters on using Photoshop to prepare images for printing. This chapter tackles calibration, color management, and making color separations. What have you read about color management? Or calibration? Did much of what you've read seem suspiciously as if it were being driven by marketing hype? We agree. Color management is simply a matter of understanding how what you see on the monitor relates to what you will get from the press. We'll introduce you to Photoshop's new support for ICC profiles and how you can use profiles to get the best color output. We employ a number of strategies to take away the mystery from Color Management. If knowledge is power, this chapter is going to make you a powerful producer of colored printing.

- Chapter 11, "Manipulating Images." In the two prepress chapters, you will have learned enough about editing your Photoshop files so that you end up with clear and pleasing images. Chapter 11 continues this process by showing you how to make corrections that can be revised as you go. This chapter also shows you how to use Photoshop's layout features. We will show you some clever ways to position your image layers with great precision.
- Chapter 12, "Photoshop And The World Wide Web." Since Photoshop was first introduced by Adobe Systems, it has become the best-selling image-editing software in the world. It is used for many purposes, but none have such far-reaching importance as the preparation of photographic material for the World Wide Web. We bring you a comprehensive look at what you can do to make your images look good, and how you can make sure that your digital files move from server to client as fast as possible. You'll hear about file formats for the Web, how to deal with Web color, and even a bit about what's involved with HTML code. If you are involved in Web or multi-media development work, this chapter will serve you well.

The CD-ROM

What else about the book should you find interesting? The CD-ROM disk. Many books of this type come with CD-ROMs, and many announce that they contain a selection of high-quality stock photos. How does ours differ from others? Read the fine print accompanying most CD-ROM stock images and you'll see that most of them are actually small, low-resolution demos/samples from stock photo companies, and that you can't actually *use* the images unless you pay a licensing fee. This book does not do that. The practice files that accompany this book are good-looking, high-resolution images of a size that you can use for many purposes. Most are absolutely royalty-free files. If you decide that you want to use any or all for a purpose of your own, go ahead and do it. Period. (If you come up with a good-looking photo presentation that uses one of this book's photos, we'd be happy to receive an email telling us where we might see it. It's a lot of fun for us to feel that we may have helped you in some small way.)

What else is on the CD-ROM? The usual stuff—mostly demos, and some resource files. Check these things out. The demo software will give you a good idea whether the product is going to work in the way that you expect and for the purpose that you expect. What better way to evaluate an interesting software title than to try it at no cost? For more information, see Appendix A in this book.

Other Resources

Some other useful resources are available to you simply because you have purchased the book. E-mail addresses, for example. Make a note of these two: **slondon@earthlink.com** and **xenakis.david@xrx-inc.com**. If you have a problem with anything that you find in the book, let us know. You will *not* get an automated response promising that we'll get back to you within the next 6-8 weeks. You may have to wait a day or two (sometimes we're not home), but we will respond with reasonable promptness with whatever help we can give you.

How To Use This Book

The simplest thing for us to tell you is this: Turn to page one and start reading. We know, this is a *software* book and hardly the sort of thing you'll want to read for entertainment. If this were a large paper on particle physics, perhaps we would be a little more hesitant about telling you to just get started. But this is Photoshop we're writing about. You're already interested in Photoshop, so you might as well just jump in. You can easily follow what's going on, even at the beginning stages. Just don't try to read in bed: The thing's too heavy.

If you know the basics, go ahead and jump around. But be aware that we've built up a sequence where one idea leads to the next. If you get lost, try backing up a few pages—or maybe to the previous chapter—and then move forward from there.

We have used a few conventions in the book that distinguish between the two platforms—Windows and Macintosh—on which Photoshop is most commonly used. If a piece of information is relevant to one platform over the other, we usually make this clear. Where key commands are used, we provide the Macintosh command first, followed by the Windows command. (For example: "…Command+E (*Command* is used on the Mac) or Ctrl+E (*Control* is used in Windows)." The Macintosh will always be the first modifier key listed, with the Windows modifier second. The ordering is alphabetical and indicates no preference for one platform over the other.) Beyond these small cautions, you can read this material without worrying that you are in the midst of information that might not apply to your platform.

We recommend keeping the CD-ROM disk handy so that you can get to the practice files whenever you need them. As we mentioned previously, nearly all of those files are high-resolution images. If you find that memory problems occur because of the sizes of the images, simply choose Image|Image Size, and change the resolution from 300 ppi down to 72 to 100 ppi. Doing so should give you the same image but with far less data with which to saddle your machine's memory.

Above all, have fun with this book. If an interesting idea comes to you as you work with the practice files, take a break and pursue it. It might come to nothing, it might turn out to be wonderful. Either way, you'll have learned something useful. And we'll always be waiting, ready to continue whenever you return from your side exploration.

PHOTOSHOP 5
IN DEPTH

OPTIMIZING PHOTOSHOP

A happy Photoshop system makes for a more contented artist. In this chapter, you will learn ways to keep your computer happy, make images easier to manage, and automate recurring procedures.

If you are going to work with Photoshop, it always helps to have the right equipment and the right configuration. Photoshop is the most powerful raster (i.e., pixel-based) graphics program available on Macintosh or Windows, but it can be ornery and recalcitrant if you do not know how to set it up correctly. Photoshop also stresses your computer more than almost any other application.

Photoshop is like the canary in the mineral mines (canaries are very sensitive to atmospheric changes and to gases that are undetectable to most humans; they were used—at least in tales—as an early warning system for miners). If your system configuration or hardware has a problem, Photoshop probably will find it before you notice it on any other program.

In this chapter, you will learn about setting up preferences, configuring your system, troubleshooting, working faster with Actions, and using the History palette—a new feature in Photoshop 5.

Windows Or Mac?

One of the most common questions asked about Photoshop performance is whether it runs better on a Macintosh or Intel machine. Although this is a simple question, there really isn't a simple answer—unless you are willing to accept "it doesn't matter" as an answer.

The program is identical in function on both platforms. The interface—except for some preferences and the physical appearance of the windows—is also identical. If you are looking for raw speed, most tests show that the latest chips (300 to 400MHz) on the Mac slightly outperform the latest versions of the Pentium chip, but that isn't the entire story.

The raw performance that you see in test suites is not always indicative of the performance that you will see when you work at *your* normal tasks. Many other factors are also involved—file size, the specific operation being performed, your disk speed, the amount of RAM, your hardware drivers, the operating system version, and sometimes, it seems, the phase of the moon! The latest Mac and Pentium chips are really close enough in performance that it makes little difference as the basis for selecting one over the other.

If you are thinking of changing platforms, try out the competing system carefully. Your final decision needs to be based on three things—cost, feel, and available software. Either platform can produce exceptional speed, and if one platform is ahead now, the other will soon catch up. Therefore, you need to select the system that feels "best" to you at the cost that you are able to spend. There is a difference in the physical sensation of working on Mac or Windows that might make you enjoy one platform over the other. It can be very subtle—sometimes the issue of menus staying down or flying back up on their own is the only thing that makes someone prefer Mac or Windows (although Mac OS 8 now provides "sticky" menus as well).

Software availability was originally a big concern. If you need specialized software that's only available on one platform, then your choice is made for you. There are still more options for third-party filters on the Mac, but this gap is narrowing every day. All of the major filter manufacturers such as Extensis, MetaCreations, and Alien Skin have versions for both platforms. Even Xaos Tools has finally ported their filters to the Windows platform.

Color-management software and controls are not as readily available on Windows 95 or NT 4, but Windows 98 and NT 5 have an embedded color-management system similar to Color Sync for the Mac. If video performance is vital to you, you need to look carefully at your options before switching platforms.

Except for these issues, however, you can be quite happy on either platform. If you work with a top-notch service bureau, either platform can produce excellent output.

Built For Speed

Production users of Photoshop are on a constant search for speed. In this section, we will look at some of the things that you can do to speed up Photoshop's performance. Some of them are easy—and others (also easy) only require large infusions of cash.

Photoshop And RAM

The following line is often attributed to Wallis Simpson, the Duchess of Windsor: "You can never be too rich or too thin." We could paraphrase that for Photoshop users and categorically state that you can never have too much RAM. RAM—*random access memory*—is the single most important thing that you can use to help Photoshop work faster.

The ideal scenario is to have enough RAM so that Photoshop can edit your file entirely in memory without needing to store much into temporary files on your hard drive (it always opens a temp file, regardless of whether it needs to use it a lot). Adobe has told us, over the years, that you need three to five times your file size in order to be able to edit images entirely in RAM.

If you edit files that are around 100MB in size (not uncommon if you prepare photographs for output to a film recorder), you need between 300MB and 500MB of RAM. This is a hefty financial investment—although much less hefty than it once was. (32MB DIMM chips purchased in the summer of 1995 cost $1,100 each.) However, it's still good to know whether you need to be closer to three times your file size or five times your file size (at this writing, the cost of a 32MB DIMM is approximately $50, and a 200MB difference translates to about $300—not a trivial amount of money for most users). The answer to how much RAM you need depends on what you do inside of Photoshop.

If you generally scan an image, color correct it, convert it to CMYK, and then save it for output from a page layout program, you will probably only need about twice the file size in RAM. This assumes that you are editing the image as a flat layer. If you tend to do a lot of image compositing and heavily use layers, then you will need much closer to the maximum of five times the file size.

Photoshop 5 has completely removed the Floating Selections (everything you do now creates a layer unless you select and drag within a single layer; then it simply moves pixels and doesn't float them). This helps to conserve RAM usage a bit, because the old Floating Selections were very wasteful of RAM resources. Using layers is a bit more sparing of your RAM, but not much. Layers that are mostly empty take up relatively little RAM, but the more data you place on them, the more memory they consume.

This is not to imply that you shouldn't use layers. On the contrary, layers are one of the best features of Photoshop, as they allow you to make compositing changes very easily and to edit those changes multiple times. You *should* use layers—but you will also need to purchase enough RAM to make working with Photoshop a pleasure rather than a penance. Few things are as discouraging as watching the Mac watch or the Windows hourglass cursor drain away minutes and hours that could be put to more profitable use.

Unless you are only using Photoshop to prepare small Web graphics, you really need a minimum of 32MB RAM allocated to the program on either platform for Photoshop to work reasonably well using medium-sized files (2 to 5MB).

Two Are Better Than One

Your operating system and the speed of your hardware also play a large part in the speed with which the program works. If adding RAM doesn't give you enough speed, make sure that you have the following:

- The most current version of Photoshop.
- The most current version of the operating system for your computer. Windows users, keep in mind that Microsoft makes upgrades available for Windows 95 and NT. These upgrades are called Service Packs, and you can download them directly from Microsoft (**www.microsoft.com/support**) or from an independent source (such as **www.winfiles.com**).

If you are still seeing pokey performance, it may be time to purchase a new machine. On both the Macintosh and Wintel platforms, the new chips are running at 400MHz and up. You can even purchase multiple-processor cards. These cards give you more than one computer chip with which to process your image. Photoshop on the Mac or under Windows NT can take advantage of these cards. They can almost double your speed on many of the accelerated functions. Quadruple processor cards can shorten the time even more.

Multiple processor cards work by handing off part of the processing task to each chip. This is similar to dumping your groceries on two checkout counters so that you finish almost twice as fast. Of course, not every graphics task can be divided up (nor can every task in real life—the "classic" example in computer literature is that it takes one woman nine months to give birth to a baby, and that time cannot be shortened to one month by employing nine women). Therefore, you only see an increase in speed when Photoshop can use all of the available chips.

Although we are not yet sure what speed improvements will be available in the forthcoming releases of Windows or NT or in any future release from Apple, as of this writing, you get the fastest speed from using the latest version of Macintosh System 8.1 (which has many of its system calls now written in native Power PC code) or from Windows NT.

Intel is in the process of phasing out the Pentium platform, replacing it with the Pentium II. The high end of the Pentium II line consists of the 350MHz and 400MHz CPUs—with faster speeds coming. The current top-of-the-line Mac chips are the G3 CPUs, and faster machines are rumored to be on the way.

A Semi-Scientific Comparison

We recently had the opportunity to conduct our own test to see whether it's better to get a faster chip, a multiprocessing card, or more RAM to increase Photoshop's performance. Although this test was only conducted on a Macintosh, its conclusion is valid for all flavors of machine.

The original machine was a Macintosh 9500 with 160MB of RAM that had been upgraded from its factory 120MHz chip to an Apple 180+ dual-processor card. This meant that the machine normally ran at 180MHz but could process at up to 360MHz when running an application that was "multiprocessor" aware. Photoshop is such a program, and some (but not all) of its functions and commands are accelerated for multiprocessing.

We were given the chance to replace this processor with a 275MHz G3 card on loan from Newer Technologies. At the same time, we upgraded the machine from 160 to 352MB RAM. We then did some timing tests. We discovered that the G3 chip was, in fact, faster—surprise—at most functions. The initial timings were done using 70MB RAM allocated to Photoshop and a 97MB file. Table 1.1 shows the times for both systems on the same file with RAM allocations to Photoshop of 70MB and 300MB.

The actual numbers are not as critical to examine as the pattern. With 300MB of RAM, all functions were much faster. The G3 chip outperformed the Dual 180 on all tasks except Unsharp Mask and Rotate Canvas. When the Dual 180 worked faster, the speed gain was apparent *only when enough RAM was present to keep the file in memory*. This was one of the major findings. Multiprocessing only helps when you have enough RAM. If you do not, the speed is slowed by the speed of your hard drive.

We made another major finding, this one by accident. One of the RAM chips that we had purchased was the wrong type of RAM for the machine, and caused errors. When we pulled the 32MB DIMM, there was only enough RAM to run Photoshop in a 270MB partition. When we

Table 1.1 Comparison of Dual 180+ and Macintosh G3 speeds (in seconds).

Task	Dual 180 +		275MHz G3	
	70MB	300MB	70MB	300MB
Open image	87.5 s	51.3 s	73.4 s	41.6 s
Flip vertical	315 s	75.5 s	287.3 s	52.9 s
Offset	160.6 s	62.5 s	151.5 s	57.4 s
Gaussian blur	238.4 s	75.3 s	203.2 s	64 s
Unsharp mask	209.7 s	47.5 s	190.5 s	79.9 s
Rotate canvas	157.6 s	12.6 s	125.9 s	33.4 s

ran the test again, we discovered that the time needed to flip the image vertically jumped from 52.9 seconds to 155.9 seconds. The RAM allocation only went down by 30MB, but the time increased dramatically. We realized that we were now below the critical "three times the file size." It really *does* make a difference.

Conserving RAM

You can work "smarter" in Photoshop to help conserve the RAM that you do have. One of the best ways to help Photoshop use less RAM is to keep the clipboard buffer as free of data as possible. This means that you should use the Copy and Paste commands as infrequently as possible.

How can you avoid Copy and Paste? It's actually fairly simple. Use the drag-and-drop capabilities of Photoshop to transfer images from one file to another. You can use the Move tool to drag entire layers from one document to another. You can use the Move tool to transfer selected areas from one image to another. (The transferred area will appear as a new layer in Photoshop 4 and later.)

If you need to duplicate part of a layer within a file, select the area and use the Layer|New|Layer via Copy or Layer|New|Layer via Cut commands (Mac: Command+J or Shift+Command+J; Windows: Ctrl+J or Shift+Ctrl+J). If you need to duplicate the entire layer, just drag the thumbnail for that layer onto the New Layer icon at the bottom of the Layers palette. None of these commands use the clipboard.

You can also use the Apply Image or Calculations commands in the Image menu. This is the best way to get image data into a channel without using the clipboard. Chapters 5 and 7 discuss these commands. If you are not familiar with them, read these chapters, as these commands add greatly to Photoshop's power.

The capability to take a snapshot of your image at a specific point in time is very useful but costly in RAM and in scratch disk space. Photoshop 5 now combines the snapshot feature with a user-selectable number of Undo levels in a new feature called the History palette. From the

History palette, you can take a virtually unlimited number of snapshots of either a single layer, a merged version of the image, or the entire image—layers and all. You can take snapshots of multiple open images, and the History palette records them for each image independently of the other. (However, snapshots only restore to their own images.) If you have multiple open images and like to use snapshots, you can easily tie up a large chunk of RAM and hard drive. We will discuss the History palette and its ramifications in RAM and hard drive usage a bit later in this chapter.

Sometimes, instead of creating a snapshot, it is less costly in RAM usage if you place a layer that you want to preserve into a new layer (by dragging it to the New Layer icon) and hide its visibility icon so that you have it there to restore when needed. You can easily do this with a merged layer copy as well. Create a new layer and press Shift+Option+Command+E (Mac) or Shift+Alt+Ctrl+E (Windows). This takes the contents of the image (merged) and places them in the active layer (which, because you just created it, is empty). If you want to do this using the menus, you need to hold down the Option key (Mac) or Alt key (Windows) as you select Layer|Merge Visible.

You can purge the Clipboard, Undo, Snapshot, History, and Pattern buffers when you need to free up RAM and scratch disk. This is a very handy feature that was new to version 4. Select Edit| Purge, as shown in Figure 1.1, and then select the extra storage area that you want to purge.

> **TIP**
>
> **If you allow the clipboard to be exported from Photoshop, you should purge the clipboard buffer before you transfer to another program if you do not need to use its contents. This allows your system to switch applications more quickly—especially if a large image exists in the clipboard.**

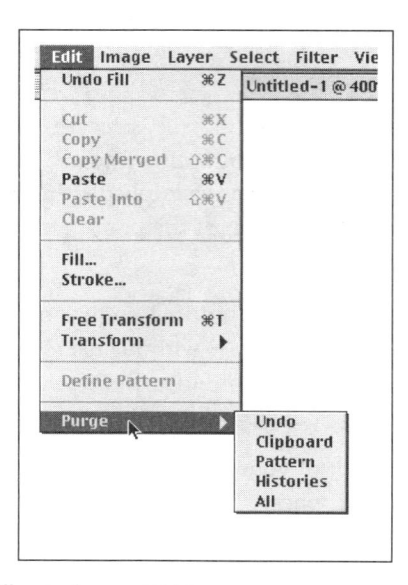

Figure 1.1 Purging Photoshop buffers to free up RAM.

Filters, RAM, And Speed

Filters aren't supposed to take up much RAM when they aren't running. However, we have discovered that loading every third-party filter known to man causes Photoshop to work more slowly—even with a lot of RAM. If you don't need certain filters very often, you may want to leave them in a folder/directory outside of Photoshop and only put them into the Plug-Ins folder when you need them. Alternately, you can organize your filters into "sets" and select a specific set as your Plug-Ins folder.

This strategy also avoids the "disappearing filter act." In what may be either a bug or a feature, if you have enough filters loaded, the last classes of filters on the native filter list start to appear in the Other category in the menu (along with the overflow from the third-party filter list). This means that if directions say "Choose Filter|Texture|Grain" and you are a third-party filter junkie, you may need to look in Filter|Other|Grain instead.

Scratch Disks

Photoshop always opens up a *scratch disk* for your image. This is a temporary file that stores your work in progress. Unfortunately for those of you who experience crashes, this Temp file—which is left on your disk in the event of a crash—is not salvageable. You cannot open it and continue editing. All you can do is move it to the trash and weep (and save early and often).

In order to open a file in Photoshop, you must have free disk space that is *at least as large as the file size*. If you don't have that amount available, you'll get an error message—but it won't always tell you what the real problem is. The usual error message that you see in this situation is "Unable to open file. Scratch disk is full." If you cannot load a file, always check to see if you have enough free space on the hard drive(s) that you have selected for your scratch disks.

You can select up to four volumes to use as scratch disks. If one fills up, then Photoshop will move on to the next one. Even if you have enough RAM to edit a file in memory, Photoshop will still write some data to disk. Obviously, the more RAM you have, the less Photoshop needs to use the hard drive, and the faster the program performs edits. However, if you don't have enough RAM, Photoshop will run more slowly, but it will edit the file as long as your scratch disk space holds out.

For those occasions when your file is too large to fit in RAM, it is helpful to have a disk that contains a large amount of contiguous storage. The best strategy is to devote an entire disk (or disk partition) to Photoshop to be used as a scratch disk. Resist the urge to use the disk for anything else! Defragment your hard disks (to put files in order) by using Norton Utilities or Central Point on the Mac or Disk Defragmenter, the utility that is part of Windows. Doing so makes disk access faster.

You can tell how well Photoshop is performing by reading the status windows. You will see an arrow that hides the five types of status readings. Clicking on the arrow (located on the image windows itself on the Mac, as shown in Figure 1.2a, and at the bottom of the application window in Windows, as shown in Figure 1.2b) reveals the choices of Document Sizes, Scratch Sizes, Efficiency, Timing, or Current Tool.

Figure 1.2a Macintosh Status menu.   **Figure 1.2b** Windows Status menu.

The Scratch Sizes show the RAM used by all open windows. The second number shows the amount of RAM available to the program to use for editing (your memory allocation, less the amount needed to run Photoshop itself). If the first number is larger than the second number is, then Photoshop has had to use the scratch disk to edit the image. When this happens, if you switch to the Efficiency indicator, you will notice that it falls below 100%. This also shows that Photoshop has had to use your scratch disks.

Other Hardware Goodies

If possible, invest in a fast hard drive. A fast and wide SCSI hard drive is a good solution. If you can afford it, a RAID disk array can also speed up access to your files. Both solutions are available in either platform flavor.

Although you can designate a removable disk (SyQuest, SyJet, Zip, Jaz, Magneto Optical, or Super Floppy) as your scratch disk, this is usually not a wonderful idea. Removable media is not usually as fast as fixed hard drives, although this might change in the future.

However, a Zip or Jaz drive (or Magneto Optical disk or other removable drive) is certainly a plus when you need to exchange files with someone or take your images to a service bureau. They are not cost-effective methods, however, for backup (or for archiving).

To work efficiently in Photoshop, you also need to keep current backups. Get the largest, fastest backup tape unit that you can afford and use it frequently. Keep at least three complete sets of backup tapes and store one of them off-site (at home, if you work in an office; at a friend's house; in a bank vault). If your data is critical to you, consider what would happen if a fire, flood, or other catastrophe destroyed your computer. Make certain that you have a recent backup somewhere else to get you started again. One backup plan that works well is to create a complete backup at the end of each week and then back up incrementally each day. At the end of the week, back up completely over your *oldest* set of backup tapes.

The most cost-effective method of archiving your data (keeping old projects, finished assignments, completed images, and so on) is a CDR unit. This is a CD-ROM burner (a recordable CD-ROM). Each CD-ROM costs between $2 and $8 and can store 650MB of data. Some models of CDR units let you rewrite data, but often the CD-ROMs are not reusable (the data image is burned onto them). Because of this, we do not recommend using these CD-ROMs for routine backups. However, we've found that a CDR unit is the best "luxury/necessity" that you can buy your computer.

If you want to purchase other enhancements for Photoshop, get a large monitor. If you need to create accurate prepress color, consider one of the Radius PressView monitors. They're available in 17" and 21" sizes. If your budget is really unlimited, look at a Barco monitor (which is all we've been able to do with one—look!). These monitors are very expensive, but they contain excellent facilities for producing accurate color.

The Colortron or other colorimeter is also a good investment. It helps to calibrate your monitor and to create profiles that help you match your scanner or printer colors to the colors displayed on your monitor.

What's Your Preference?

Another factor in working efficiently with Photoshop is setting your Preferences to reflect the way that you work. Figure 1.3 shows the File|Preferences menu on the Mac. (The menu is the same on Windows except for the Image Cache setting, which is called Memory and Image Cache under Windows.) Take a look at the Preferences settings that make a difference.

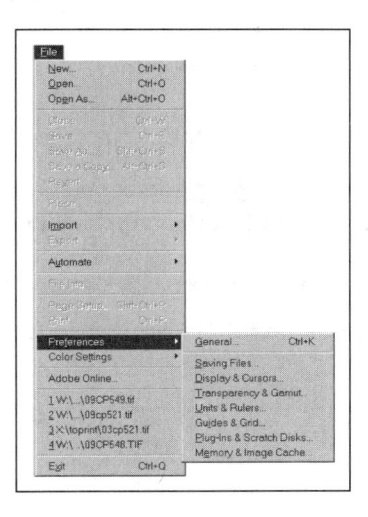

Figure 1.3 Preferences menu.

General Preferences

General Preferences is the first Preferences dialog box. You can access it by pressing Command+K (Mac) or Ctrl+K (Windows). Figure 1.4 shows the General Preferences dialog box.

Use the Photoshop Color Picker unless you have a good reason for not using it. A good reason might be to access one of the special Color Picker items on the Macintosh, such as the Pantone Web color set, or if you need values from the system Color Picker. The Mac System Color Picker, for example, returns different RGB numbers than Photoshop, because it uses a scale of 1 to 100 rather than a scale of 1 to 255. The Windows RGB picker produces the same values as Photoshop.

You should always leave your Interpolation method set to Bicubic unless you have a compelling reason not to. The Interpolation method controls the way in which Photoshop calculates new pixels when it increases or decreases the number of pixels in an image or selection. The Preferences setting determines the method used by the Transform commands and sets the default in the Image Size dialog box as well. There is no reason to ever use bilinear interpolation, but you will want to use Nearest Neighbor whenever you need to scale a selection or file without creating any anti-aliased (fuzzy) edges. Nearest Neighbor produces a very "blocky" resizing that works best in whole increments (200 percent, 300 percent, and so on) or in 50 percent and 25 percent reductions. It can get very ugly if you don't follow these guidelines. When you resize an image, Photoshop lets you choose the Interpolation method to be used. This is a wonderfully useful feature because it allows you to leave the preference set to Bicubic, but lets you resize using Nearest Neighbor when you need to. If you should change the actual Preferences setting, remember to *change it back* as soon as you are done.

You normally want to check the Anti-alias PostScript box. The only exception is during the probably infrequent times when you need to print at high resolution and want to import text or objects so that their edges do not blend towards transparent. Usually you are better off placing your image into a page layout program and setting type in that program rather than doing it in Photoshop—especially if the type is small. However, you might have to import objects from Illustrator and keep them sharp. In any case, you usually have the option to turn anti-alias on or off except when you drag Paths in from Illustrator. That's the one circumstance when you are not given a chance to switch the status of the Preferences setting.

Unless you need to paste a part of an image in another program, you might consider unchecking the Export Clipboard preference. You will switch applications much faster with it turned off.

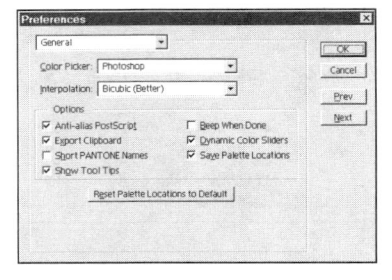

Figure 1.4 General Preferences dialog box.

You don't need Short PANTONE Names turned on unless you are trying to place a Duotone or EPS DCS 2 format image into an old copy of QuarkXPress. Otherwise, most programs use the same standard of naming that is used by Photoshop.

Show Tool Tips slows down the computer a bit. Use them or lose them, as you prefer. Some folks like them; they drive other folks up the wall.

We usually keep Beep When Done off. The sounds of silence are quite welcome, and co-workers do not really need to know when you've finished something—or when you make a mistake. However, if you like noise....

The Dynamic Color Sliders is a feature worth enabling. It shows you a preview of the colors that occurs if you move the sliders in the Color palette. Figure 1.5 shows the Color palette. If you were seeing it in color, you would see that the chosen color is a burgundy. If you move the red slider to the right, you obtain a stronger red. Moving the blue slider to the right gives a shade of purple. It's easier to mix your colors if you leave Dynamic Color Sliders turned on.

Unless you like to use the default settings for palette locations, keep the Save Palette Locations turned on. It saves a lot of time if you prefer your own arrangements. You can always return to the "factory" settings by clicking on the Reset Palette Locations to Default button. This is helpful if your Toolbox ever gets "stuck" under the menu bar at the top of the screen (an annoyance that seems limited to the Mac).

> **TIP**
>
> **Make sure that you can see the Toolbox when you quit out of Photoshop—especially on the Mac. This seems to be one of the things that causes the Toolbox to hide under the menu. If you have used the Tab key to hide the palettes, press it again to reveal all before leaving the application.**

Saving Files

The Saving Files Preferences is a bit different on the Mac and Windows. Figure 1.6a shows the Mac version and Figure 1.6b shows the Windows version.

The major difference in platforms is that the Mac is able to save small preview icons that the PC cannot. The icons are cute—and convenient—but are also capable of getting very scrambled

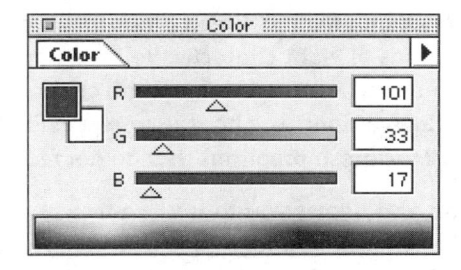

Figure 1.5 Color palette showing effect of Dynamic Color Sliders preference.

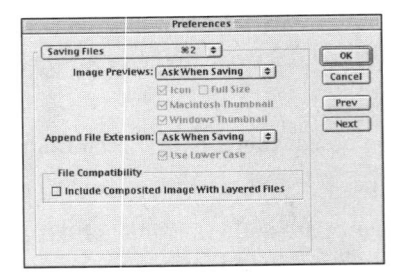

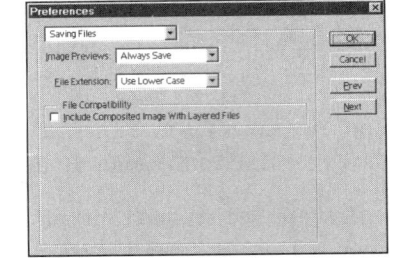

Figure 1.6a Mac Saving Files dialog box.

Figure 1.6b Windows Saving Files dialog box.

on your hard disk. Although the latest versions of the Mac operating system seem less subject to icon scramble, there have been times when every icon of the hard drive displayed the wrong picture (rebuilding the desktop usually fixes this, however). We recommend the Ask When Saving option for this preference—even on the PC. The Ask When Saving dialog box allows you to decide on a case-by-case basis whether to create a preview or, on the Mac, a thumbnail icon.

When you create an image preview, especially of a large file, it can take a very long time to save the image. Saving a full-size preview also adds to the time and disk space occupied by the file (although you don't have the option to save a full-size preview in Windows). The advantage to saving a full-size preview is that you get a better display in a page layout program, but this is not a necessity.

The Mac also gives you the option of saving a file extension automatically with the Append File Extension. The jury is out on this one—it totally depends on the way you work and where your files end up when you are done with them. The Macintosh opens PC files if there is an extension (Windows files always have file extensions) and if the PC File Exchange extension is loaded on your Mac. Win/Photoshop only opens a file *without* an extension if you use the Open As command. If you want to be able to use the Open command, you must attach the appropriate extension for the file to even appear in the file list.

> **TIP**
>
> **The Mac doesn't have an "Open As" command. If you need to open a file that came from Windows, but has no extension, you need to check the Show All Files box at the bottom of the Open dialog box.**

If you need to move files back and forth between platforms, it is usually safest to use "standard" DOS naming conventions of eight characters followed by a period and the correct file extension. It is really nice that you don't need to fuss with changing the Mac Type and Creator of a file imported from Windows as long as it has the correct extension. This is a welcome relief from the behavior of many Macintosh programs that do not read Windows files at all.

The Saving Files dialog box also allows you to save your images to allow for Photoshop 2.5 compatibility (a flattened, composited image that can be opened in programs that do not support Photoshop layers). This Photoshop 2.5 compatibility has been renamed in Photoshop 5 to "Include Composited Version With Layered Files." Unless you need to place a flattened file into a program that doesn't read the Photoshop 3 specification (but does accept 2.5), turn off this preference. Using this option is a major waste of disk space, and the authors can think of no good reason why you would need 2.5 compatibility. Most page layout programs will not import files saved in Photoshop format, nor—because of the large size of these files—would you want to. In order to save a file in 2.5 compatibility mode, Photoshop writes another (invisible) layer to the file; it then saves a flattened copy of the file that it can use when something asks for the 2.5 version. This can add a lot to the space used to save your file if you normally use layers in an image. Figure 1.7 shows two Info windows on the Mac. The files saved are identical, but one was saved with Include Composited Version With Layered Files turned on and the other one was not. Include Composited Version With Layered Files changed the saved file size from 2.4MB to 3.2MB. The image contains a Background layer, a copy of the Background layer in Overlay mode, and two selections floated in the image—one layer in Multiply mode and the other in Screen mode.

Display & Cursors

This preference, shown in Figure 1.8, allows you to set up the display characteristics of your system. It contains a number of options.

Do not select the Color Channels in Color option. While nothing dire results from selecting it, you need to train yourself to think of each color as simply the grayscale values in that channel.

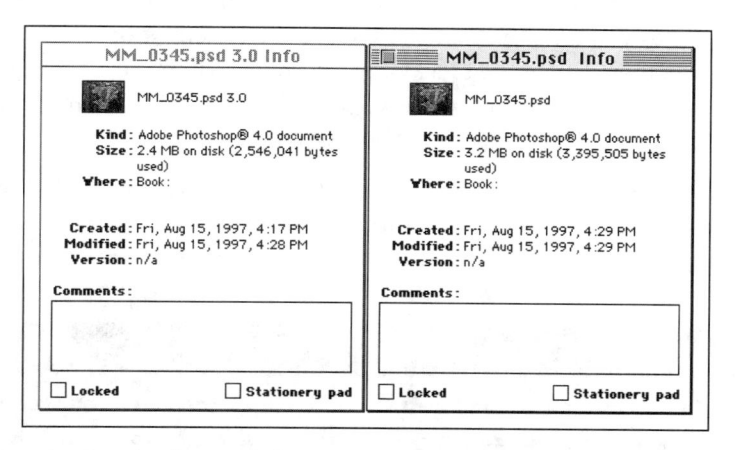

Figure 1.7 Files saved with and without Include Composited Version With Layered Files.

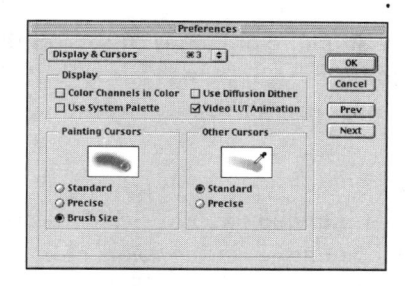

Figure 1.8 The Display & Cursors option in the Preferences dialog box.

Chapter 5 has an in-depth discussion of the relationship between the color channels and the grayscale values they contain. Because you really need to think "value and density" when you look at the contents of a specific channel, seeing the actual colors gets in the way.

If you own a decent color card (one that allows you to work in 24-bit color), then you don't need either of the next two options (and should not select them): Use System Palette or Use Diffusion Dither. If you don't own a 24-bit color card and you work with Photoshop for anything other than Web or multimedia, you need to get one.

However, you *do* want to select Use Video LUT Animation (assuming, once again, that you have a color card that supports it—and you should, at least on the Mac, if you have one that allows 24-bit color).Video LUT animation gives you some additional options—especially when you are using the Levels dialog box. The option uses your color card to do a "quick and dirty" calculation of the changes that you make in the dialog box. This allows you to work with Preview off in the dialog box and see a fast "before" version of your image by clicking the title bar of the image window while you are in the Levels or Curves dialog box. With Preview off, you don't see a totally accurate preview, but it is usually good enough until you have the correct settings. Then, you can click on the Preview button to make sure that you like your changes. However, it's really handy to be able to see a before-and-after image very quickly.

The other thing that Video LUT Animation allows you to do in the Levels dialog box is to find the lightest and darkest areas of the image very quickly. If you press the Option key (Mac) or Alt key (Windows) as you drag the White or Black point sliders (with Preview turned off in the dialog box), you can see where the black or white values will be clipped. If you haven't used this feature before, try it. It can save a lot of "poking about" with the Info palette to find the darkest or lightest areas in an image that need to color corrected.

Always select the Brush Size painting cursors (unless, of course, you like to be surprised about the size of the brush with which you are painting). This is one of Photoshop's best productivity features. It does have a price, however. It can slow down your drawing if you use a large brush—but that's probably when you also need to see your brush size the most.

> **TIP**
> If you should need to remove the Direct Cursors plug-in (because your cursor disappears when you place it over an image—see the Troubleshooting section below), you will not be able to see any brush size over 16 pixels.

It's your choice whether to use Standard or Precise cursors for the other tools such as the Marquee and the Eyedropper. Because you can change one type of cursor into the other by pressing the Caps Lock key, you can easily leave this option set to Standard.

Transparency & Gamut

The Transparency & Gamut settings allow you to pick the size of the grids that show through transparent areas of your image and to set the colors of both the transparency and gamut warnings. Figure 1.9 shows the dialog box.

Figure 1.9 Transparency & Gamut Preferences dialog box.

The Gamut warning is an option that you can turn on under the View menu to show you the out-of-gamut colors in an image (out-of-gamut colors are colors that cannot be printed using the standard CMYK inks). You can also change the opacity of the color displayed for the warning so that it does not totally obscure the out-of-gamut colors.

These settings come with no particular suggestions for use. The defaults usually work without problems. You might want to change the color of the Gamut warning indicator if you are using an image on which the warning isn't visible.

Units & Rulers

The Units & Rulers Preferences box, shown in Figure 1.10, allows you to pick the measuring system for the Rulers and to specify default column widths for setting text.

Select pixels as your default unit measure unless you have a really good reason not to. This setting controls the default unit when you choose File|New. Pixels are unambiguous. A pixel is a pixel is a pixel.... A document that is 800×800 pixels remains that size whether it is set to 10 pixels per inch or 5,000 pixels per inch—it still contains 800×800 pixels. If you create files of any other measurement, you need to know the output dimensions (resolution) or else your file will not be the "correct" size. Of course, you need to set physical dimensions (ppi) if you are going to print your image, but it's much easier to think and work in pixels. We usually always leave the settings at pixels—even if later we change the units on a new image to picas or inches.

Photoshop 5 has a new Units setting. You can now select Percent as a unit of measure. The new Photoshop documentation states that this setting has been designed to make it easier for you to

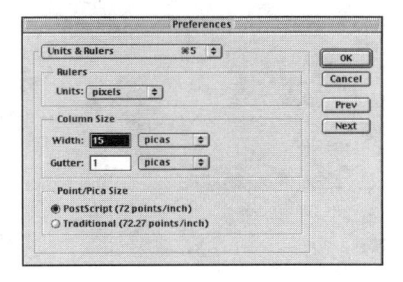

Figure 1.10 The Units & Rulers Preferences box.

script Actions. However, we are trying to think of a situation in which it can be used that didn't allow for it before.

> **TIP**
>
> You can change the Units Preferences quickly when you use Rulers by double-clicking on a ruler. This opens the Units & Rulers preference so that you can select a different ruler scale.

Because the authors do not recommend setting text in Photoshop, we leave the column settings alone because we never use them anyway. However, because we work in a digital world, we typically leave Point/Pica Size set at 72 points/inch.

Guides & Grids

This preference allows you set the color and style for Guides and Grids and to set the Grid dimensions. This preference dialog box is shown in Figure 1.11.

You can easily leave the default values for this preference. This is a preference that you will probably change fairly often, but the changes are specific to the needs of the image that you are editing rather than a general-purpose setting.

In most cases, you have little reason to view either Guides or Grids as dashed lines or dots, but you might need to change the color so that they stand out against your image.

Both authors are involved in the textile arts and would like to have the ability to use different Grid settings for the width and height, but Photoshop only permits you one dimension. However, you can subdivide your image into major and minor divisions, which is a useful feature to have.

Plug-Ins & Scratch Disk

The Plug-Ins & Scratch Disk Preferences settings allow you to select the Plug-In folder to use and to specify four locations where Photoshop can store its temporary files. Figure 1.12 shows this dialog box.

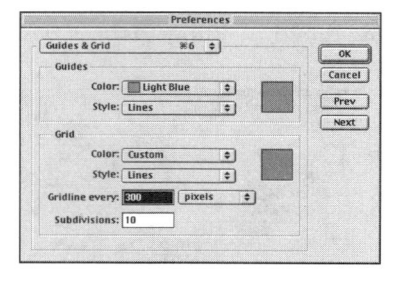

Figure 1.11 Guides & Grid Preferences dialog box.

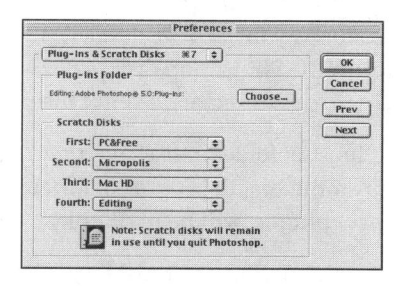

Figure 1.12 The Plug-Ins & Scratch Disk Preferences box.

Plug-ins are optional pieces of code (Photoshop doesn't need them in order to run). They are also pieces of code that add functionality to the original program. There are two "flavors" of plug-ins, and several places on the menu where they can appear.

Plug-ins come from either Adobe or a third party. They can appear on the Filter menu or on the File menu (as Import or Export options) or the Select menu. They can also appear as file type options when you open or save a file; some correction options, such as Variations (Image| Adjust|Variations) are also plug-ins.

You can have only one plug-in folder/directory active at a time. However, you can place aliases of plug-ins into the folder so that the actual plug-ins can be kept elsewhere. (In Windows, these aliases are known as "shortcuts.")

In versions of Photoshop earlier than 3, all the plug-ins needed to be "loose" inside the main folder/directory. You couldn't have subdirectories or embedded folders. In version 3, that changed. You can now nest folders and subdirectories, and we urge you to do that. It makes life much easier when you can organize your plug-ins, especially if you tend to collect a lot of third-party filters. The subfolders that are created when you install Photoshop are just for organization. Any filter can be placed in any subfolder or subdirectory.

> **TIP**
>
> **Keep all your third-party filters in a separate folder/directory. You can nest them with that folder as well. This makes applying upgrades or reinstalling the program much easier as you do not need to remember what came with the program and what pieces you need to reinstall.**

CSI (Cytopia Software) produces a filter that allows you to create different plug-in sets. It is available only on the Mac, but it's very useful. There had also been a plug-in manager from BeInfinite (also only for the Mac), but this company is now defunct and it's unlikely that you will be able to locate the plug-in.

On the Windows side, a shareware plug-ins manager called Plugin Manager is available. It even allows you to name the sets that appear in your Filters menu (a feature that we dearly wish Photoshop had).

If you have plug-ins that you don't want to keep loaded at all times, remove them not only from the Plug-Ins folder, but from the Photoshop directory as well. Photoshop sometimes loads any plug-in that it sees anywhere in its directory, even if the plug-in isn't in the Plug-Ins folder.

To add a new plug-in to the Plug-Ins folder, *make sure that Photoshop is not open*. Then either copy the file into the folder or run the Install program, if there is one for the plug-in. When you start Photoshop again, your new plug-in will be available.

If you need to change the Plug-Ins folder (or locate it), select the option in the Plug-Ins & Scratch Disk preference and locate the correct folder or directory on your disk (the folder is called Plug-Ins on both platforms).

You can also set up four scratch disks. As we mentioned previously, leave plenty of free disk space and, if possible, devote an entire disk or disk partition to Photoshop. Keep the scratch disk defragmented.

If you are running Windows, make sure that your scratch disks are not located on the same volume as the drive(s) that Windows uses for Virtual Memory.

Memory & Image Cache

The final preference setting is slightly different on the PC and on the Mac. It sets the Image Cache on both platforms, but controls the amount of RAM usage on Windows. Figure 1.13a shows the Mac dialog box and Figure 1.13b shows the Windows dialog box.

Take a look at the Memory setting first. In the preceding discussion, we already mentioned that Photoshop likes RAM. (You know that it has an insatiable appetite for it, don't you?) The way you satisfy Photoshop's appetite for RAM differs between the PC and the Mac. On the Mac, you need to offer Photoshop the specific amount of RAM for its meal by selecting the Photoshop program icon and pressing Command+I. This displays the Get Info dialog box shown in Figure 1.14. To change the Preferred amount of RAM for the program, enter the new amount in that field. It's rarely necessary to change the minimum amount of RAM needed (a few third-party plug-ins, such as the ones from Human Software, require this in order to work properly). *Do not ever give Photoshop all of your available RAM, or you will cause the system to crash.* Leave at least 1.5MB RAM free beyond the amount used by the system file.

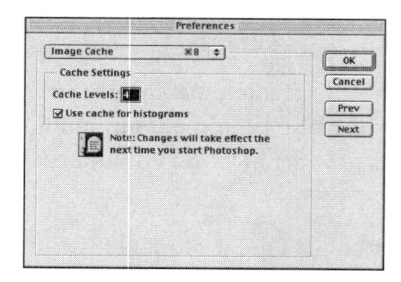

Figure 1.13a   Image Cache Preferences on the Mac.

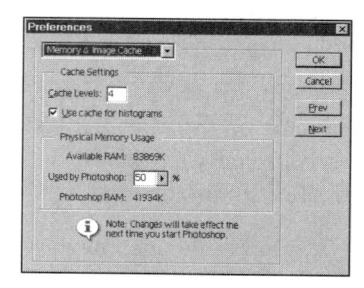

Figure 1.13b   Memory & Image Cache setting on Windows.

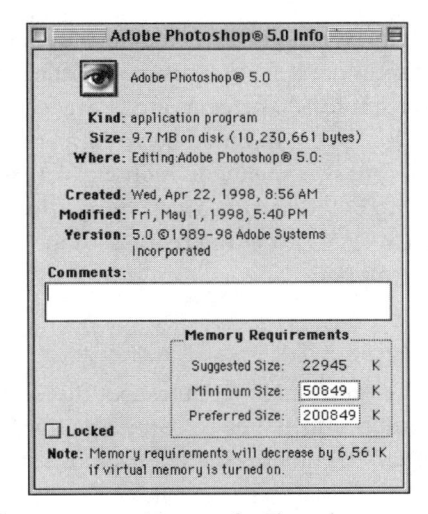

Figure 1.14 Setting Macintosh memory requirements for Photoshop.

If you are working on the Windows platform (or on Windows NT), you restrict Photoshop's appetite for RAM to a maximum percentage of RAM available (choose File|Preferences|Memory & Image Cache). Just as on the Mac, it is wrong to allow Photoshop to get greedy and grab it all. Although giving Photoshop all of your RAM will not cause as much trouble on Windows, it's still a bad idea. It is more reasonable to keep Photoshop "lean and mean" at 75 percent of available RAM. The program defaults to 50 percent of available RAM.

Additionally, if you are on Windows 95 and receive memory errors while trying to save a file, set both the minimum and maximum virtual memory settings to twice the size of your actual amount of RAM. If you have 64MB RAM in your system, set both the minimum and maximum amount to 128. According to Adobe, this allows Photoshop to do a better job of managing its own virtual memory system.

The Image Cache is a feature that was new in Photoshop 4. It's the magic that's responsible for the very fast screen redraws that you see. When you open an image, Photoshop now creates a screen resolution preview of the image at a variety of zoom levels (using a pyramid scheme of cached redraws). When you need to zoom in or out on your image, Photoshop pulls the new calculation from the cached views rather than reading the file or portion of the file from your hard drive. This makes the screen updates remarkably faster than they were in Photoshop 3 or earlier. It also allows Photoshop to anti-alias the edges more rapidly on the previews.

This wonderful speed increase also has a downside—of course. It's slower to open a file and takes more RAM. Therefore, you can set the optimum size of the Image Cache in the Image Cache preference. A setting of 1 disables the cache completely. Unless you always work at 100 percent magnification, you shouldn't use a setting of 1. You almost always benefit from the use of the Image Cache even if it uses a bit more RAM. The additional RAM needed is not proportional to the cache setting selected.

For example, changing the cache setting from 1 to 2 adds about one-third more RAM to an image, whereas changing the setting from 4 to 8 costs very little more. A setting of 8 caches all the preview sizes from 6.25 percent to 100 percent and is needed only if your file is very large. For most users, a setting of 4 is a good compromise between speed and RAM. If your images are small enough to open at 50 percent size, then you might be okay with a cache setting of 2. You should choose your cache setting based on the largest image that normally edit. If Photoshop seems too slow or uses too much RAM, lower the cache setting. You can experiment until you find the setting that works best for you.

Special Issues

Several topics do not fit into the upcoming "Troubleshooting" section because they aren't actual problems, but they are important issues to consider. One is the topic of installing the program and applying upgrades; the other is the Photoshop feature called "Big Data."

Installation And Upgrades

Many years ago, before CD-ROM drives became popular and Photoshop grew large enough to need one, the Photoshop application arrived with a number of installation disks. The directions stated that the program was to be installed with all extensions on the MAC or TSRs on the PC turned off. Now that the program ships with its installation code on CD-ROM, the warning is no longer given, in part, because you need to load the CD-ROM drivers before you can install Photoshop from the CD-ROM.

Photoshop should still be installed into a system that has as few other programs, extensions, and TSRs open as possible. Many problems that folks have with Photoshop stem from code that was corrupted by some other program that was in memory at the time that Photoshop was installed. Usually Photoshop's installation is not all that sensitive, but these corruption problems have occurred often enough that you need to be aware of the possibility. For safety's sake, if you can remove all unneeded memory-resident programs (especially on the Mac) when you install Photoshop, do so. The only extensions that should be running on the Mac when Photoshop is installed are the CD-ROM drivers and QuickTime. After you've checked the media for viruses (if you are so inclined), remove any virus software temporarily on either platform.

On Windows 95, you can start the machine in Safe mode. Here's how: When you turn on your machine, it will run a memory check. Right before Windows starts, a message appears at the bottom of the screen that says "Starting Win95." At this point, you have two or three seconds to press F8 to bring up a menu that has seven or eight options on it (depending on your machine). The third option in this menu is Safe Mode, which you should choose. A faster way to do this is to press and hold the Shift key at the "Starting Win95" message. That will take you directly to Safe mode. On Windows NT, there is no Safe mode.

Windows does a better job than the Mac does of installing a Photoshop version upgrade over an existing copy of Photoshop. On Windows, you can usually let the install program do what it wants, for example, if you are moving from Photoshop 3 to 4. On the Mac, a Photoshop 4 to 5 upgrade will *not* automatically replace the earlier version, although it *will* check for its presence and it can replace it, if you prefer. The upgrade version of the program not only needs a valid serial number, it must find evidence on your system that you have the previous version.

It is sometimes necessary to reinstall the program if you are having problems with it. In this case, Windows users should be able to install the program directly over the original install, but if this doesn't fix the problem, then you need to run the Uninstall program. *Mac users should not try to install one copy of the program over the other.* Drag the Photoshop program icon to the trash and also drag the Preferences file (actually, the entire Photoshop Settings Folder) to the trash. Your install may not work properly if you don't trash the Preferences file before you reinstall the software. Adobe also recommends that you remove the Adobe folder in the Application Support folder in the System file on the Mac.

Sometimes, Adobe releases interim upgrades. Adobe releases upgrades either by making a patch available online or by releasing a new CD-ROM of the program—depending on how extensive the changes are. Sometimes they release a patch and also make available a CD-ROM version for a nominal fee. We urge you to pay the additional fee (usually just a shipping and handling charge) whenever a new version is available on CD-ROM. Simply because it is larger, there are often unpublicized "goodies" on the CD-ROM that can add value to the program. If room is available, Adobe might also include the full version of the program on the CD-ROM instead of just the patch (it obviously cannot make the full program code available online, where it could be downloaded by folks who do not own the original). It is always better to have a full version of the program rather than just a patch (if you need to reinstall the program again, you only need one process rather than two—one to place the old version and the other to update it).

If you ever download a patch with which to upgrade your copy of Photoshop, here are a few useful suggestions:

- Back up your machine before you install anything new.
- If you have created custom gradients or Actions or you're fond of a custom Swatches palette, save these to disk before you upgrade.
- On the Mac, start the Mac without any extensions, trash your Photoshop Settings folder (or move it out of harm's way), and remove your Photoshop 5 installation (if you have third-party plug-ins, remember to get them out of the Plug-Ins folder before you trash the installation). Install a clean copy of Photoshop 5. Finally, install the patch updater.
- On Windows, it's usually unnecessary to operate in Safe mode and impossible if you are using Windows NT. Disable any virus-checking programs and exit all other applications before running the upgrade. Unless the instructions say otherwise, just run the Installer and let it take over.

Big Data

In version 3 and earlier in Photoshop, when you pasted data into your image that was larger than your document, the extra image area was removed and only the parts of the pasted data that could fit in your image were saved. Photoshop uses a data model called "Big Data." It can hold image data that doesn't fit inside the document—almost like the pasteboard in PageMaker or QuarkXPress. This is a wonderful new convenience because you can paste large images and recover the data that didn't fit in the image. Play with this for a while. (After all, you've done a lot of reading with no computer time yet!)

Working With Big Data

In this exercise, you will place some flowers inside of the knothole in a tree. The flowers image is larger than the tree image.

1. Open the files named KNOTHOLE.PSD and BOUQUET.PSD from the CD-ROM that accompanies this book. Figure 1.15 shows the knothole image, and Figure 1.16 shows the bouquet image.

2. Click on the flower image to make it active. Press the modifier key (Mac: Command, Windows: Ctrl) and the Shift key and drag the flower image on top of the tree image. Figure 1.17 shows the result. You can see by comparing that figure to Figure 1.16 how much larger the flower image really is.

3. The tree image contains a channel that selects the knothole. Load Channel 4 (Mac: Command+Option+4, Windows: Ctrl+Alt+4). Then create a layer mask by clicking on the Layer Mask icon at the bottom left of the Layers palette. Your mask automatically uses the selection, and the only area of the bouquet that is visible is in the knothole. Figure 1.18 shows this image.

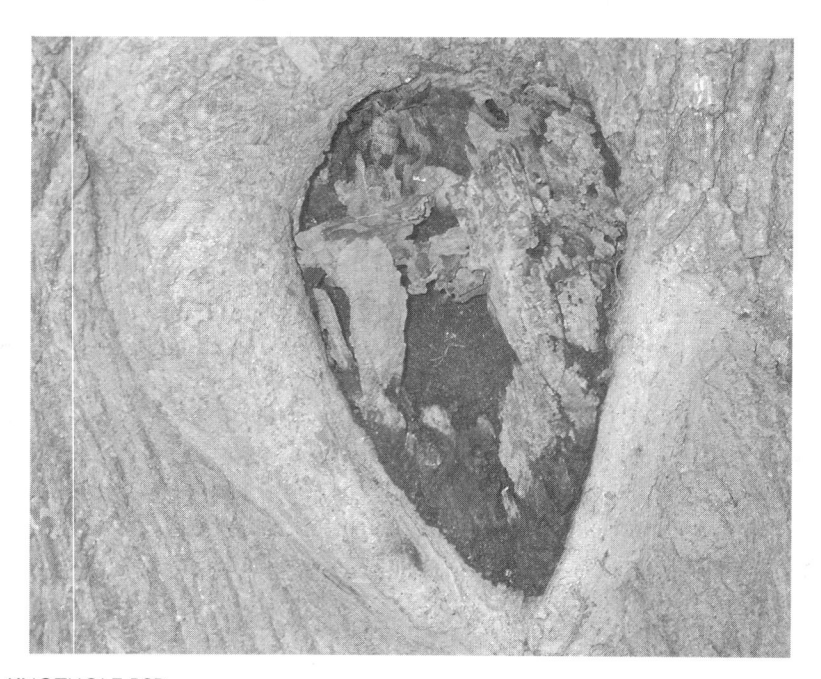

Figure 1.15 KNOTHOLE.PSD.

Figure 1.16 BOUQUET.PSD.

Figure 1.17 BOUQUET.PSD dragged onto KNOTHOLE.PSD and partially cut off.

4. Click on the Link icon between the thumbnail of the flowers and the flower layer mask on the Layers palette to unlink the layer and the layer mask. This allows you to move the layer while the masked area remains stationary.

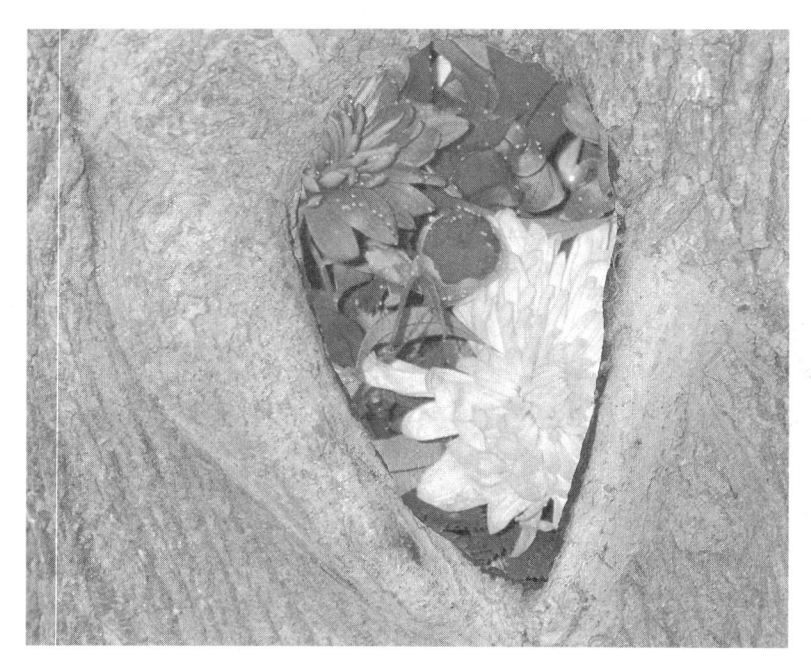

Figure 1.18 Flowers in the center of the knothole.

5. Click on the layer thumbnail to select it. Figure 1.19 shows the Layers palette as it should look—notice that you have a Paintbrush icon in the second column next to the flower layer. Select the Move tool (or press the Mac: Command or Windows: Ctrl key) and move the flower image around. You can even move it so that the side edge of the original image is visible, as you can see in Figure 1.20.

6. Use the Free Transform command (Mac: Command+T, Windows: Ctrl+T) to scale the flower image. The transform marquee appears inside the document window even though the data is larger than the document. Press the Shift key to constrain the aspect ratio and at the same time, press the Option key (Mac) or Alt key (Windows) to scale from the center of the image as you drag the upper left corner of the transform marquee toward the center of the image. Figure 1.21 shows the amount by which we scaled the image. Double-click inside of the marquee to complete the scaling operation.

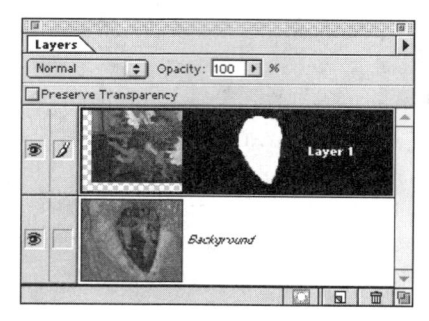

Figure 1.19 Layers palette with Paintbrush icon indicating that the layer, rather than the layer mask, is active.

Figure 1.20 Big Data keeps the image area larger than that which will fit into the image.

Figure 1.21 Scaling the flower image.

7. Move the flower image inside of the layer mask until you like the view. Notice as you move the image that the edges of the original flower image are still in the file and

have not been removed by the scaling that you did. You still have the entire original layer, even if it's now a bit smaller.

The flowers do not look as if they are inside of the knothole at all—which is a bit silly. So, although it has nothing to do with Big Data, let's create some shadows and texture to make the flowers look better.

8. Drag the Background layer to the New Layer icon at the bottom of the Layers palette. Move the layer up so that it's above the flower layer (Mac: Command+], Windows: Control+]).

9. Leave the new layer active. Drag the Layer Mask icon for the flower layer down to the Create Layer Mask icon at the bottom of the Layers palette. This is a new feature in Photoshop 5, and it will copy the layer mask of the flower layer into the layer mask of the new layer that you just created.

> **TIP**
>
> *Copying layer masks*—If you press the Option key on the Mac or the Alt key on Windows as you drag the layer mask that you want to copy down to the Layer Mask icon at the bottom of the Layers palette, Photoshop not only copies the layer mask into the active layer, but it also inverts it.

10. Change the Blend mode to Hard Light. Choose Filter|Stylize|Emboss, Angle: -153, Height: 3, and Amount: 122.

11. Make a new layer (click on the New Layer icon at the bottom of the Layers palette). Drag it to the top of the stack. Check your History palette to make sure that the History Brush icon is on the starting image of the knothole. Press Shift+Delete and fill from History. This image fills with the Background layer. Repeat Step 9 to place the layer mask into the layer. Change the Blend mode to Color and the layer Opacity to 50%. You have now added some texture and reduced the color intensity of the flower image.

12. Make a new layer (click on the New Layer icon at the bottom of the Layers palette). Load Channel 4 as you did in Step 3. Create a layer mask (click on the Add Layer Mask icon—the bottom left icon on the Layers palette). This is the "familiar" way to add a layer mask.

13. Click on the layer thumbnail to make the layer active. Load Channel 4 again. Reverse the selection (Select|Inverse or for the Mac: Shift+Command+I; for Windows: Shift+Ctrl+I). Press D to set the colors back to the default of black and white. Fill the area (Mac: Option+Delete, Windows: Alt+Delete). Your image still looks blank because you filled the area that is *masked*.

14. Deselect (Mac: Command+D, Windows: Ctrl+D).

15. Click on the Link icon between the layer and the layer mask to turn it off. If you do not, the Gaussian Blur filter softens both the image and mask. Apply a Gaussian Blur (Filter|Blur|Gaussian Blur) of 20.

16. The softness of the blurred edge creates a general shadow around the edges of the knothole. It is not quite dark enough, however. Drag the icon for the shadow layer to the New Layer icon (the center icon at the bottom of the Layers palette). This duplicates the shadow layer. Change the Blend mode to Multiply.

17. Duplicate the new second shadow layer by dragging it to the New Layer icon. This is too dark. Set the Opacity back to about 30% or to the setting that looks good on your monitor. If you want an uneven shadow, drag the first shadow layer slightly to your right (make sure that the Link icon is off when you drag). Figure 1.22 shows the finished image.

18. Now that the image looks okay, what has happened to the data that was too large to fit? Nothing. It's still there and makes a very large file. You have several ways to get rid of the extra image area. You can apply the mask: Make the layer mask active and click on the trash can icon at the bottom of the Layers palette. The dialog asks if you want to Apply or Discard the layer mask. Click on Apply. Notice that the Document Size status window shows a greatly decreased amount. You could select each mask and apply it—but don't.

19. Select Undo (Mac: Command+Z, Windows: Ctrl+Z).

20. Here is the other way to remove all of the extra image in the document. Select the entire image (Mac: Command+A, Windows: Ctrl+A). Choose Image|Crop. Once again, the Document Size decreases. Flattening the image also removes the pasteboard area.

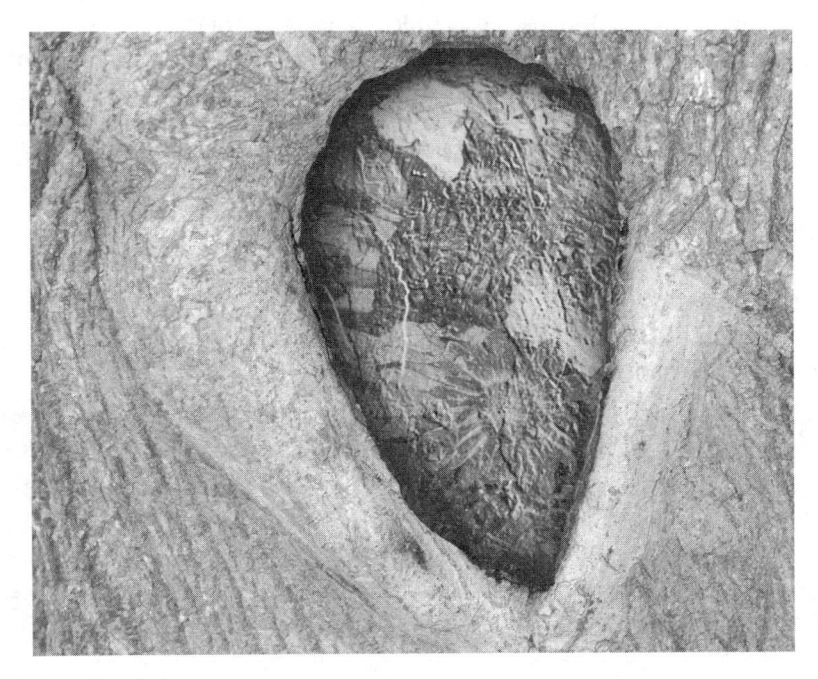

Figure 1.22 Finished knothole image.

Now you should have a good idea of how best to work with the Big Data feature. Remember, as long as you save your image in Photoshop format, you will keep the pasteboard data unless you crop your image to the document size first. It's possible to perform transformations that keep the large data but orphan it as well, so it is important that you trim your document to size once you know you no longer need the extra material.

You can incorporate some of the area of Big Data around the image if you crop the image beyond the image borders. When you use the Crop tool, it will automatically hug the perimeter of the image if you drag it from the top-left corner to the lower-right corner. However, after the Crop Marquee is finished, you can drag the Marquee into the pasteboard area of the image (if your window is sized to show it).

Troubleshooting

Photoshop is actually one of the most stable graphics applications. However, computers and operating systems have gotten very complex and problems can and do occur. This section discusses some of the issues that have surfaced most often on the CompuServe Adobe Photoshop Forum and reflects the advice given there. Although CompuServe is more expensive than many online services, the Adobe Forum is worth the price. It provides some of the fastest, and most complete, Photoshop advice available. It also attracts some of the best Photoshop users on the planet.

You can also obtain access to "prerecorded" technical advice on Adobe's Web site (**www.adobe.com**). You will find a large technical database that provides detailed information on a number of problem areas. When you encounter trouble with Photoshop that you cannot solve by yourself or with the advice given there, check the FAQ documents on Adobe's Web site. There are also Internet discussion groups on using Photoshop, for example, **www.dejanews.com**. If all else fails, call Adobe Technical Support. You can either purchase a yearly service contract, pay a fixed fee using a credit card for your call, or you can use a 900 number at $2 per minute (including waiting time).

Common Concerns

Troubleshooting Photoshop is usually quite platform-specific. However, several issues seem to be common across platforms. Let's look at these first.

> **WARNING**
>
> Here is the part where we need to include some legalese to tell you that neither Adobe, nor Coriolis, nor the authors take responsibility for any damage that might occur from following the troubleshooting advice. We strive to be accurate, but computers are quite complex and configurations (as well as user expertise) differ so much that what works on one machine might not behave the same way on another. So...proceed at your own risk.

Preference File Corruption

Have you ever looked at several-day-old food in your refrigerator and wondered if it was still good? Did you then hear a little voice say "When in doubt, throw it out?" Photoshop's preference file is like that. It turns bad in sneaky little ways that leave you wondering "Is it or isn't it?"

It never hurts the application to toss out the preference file. On the Mac, the preference file is called Adobe Photoshop 5 Prefs and is located in the Adobe application folder inside a folder named Adobe Photoshop Settings. Under Windows, the file is called Adobe Photoshop 5.0.PSP. It's located in the application folder (usually under Program Files) in the Adobe Photoshop Settings subdirectory. A separate color settings file and an Actions file are saved in the Adobe Photoshop Settings folder/directory as well. All these files are re-created the next time you launch Photoshop if you have removed them.

This is your first line of defense against program oddities. If something doesn't work correctly that used to, or you just get a "bad feeling" about something that is happening in the program, toss the prefs files. It's astonishing how much that simple action can help.

Just remember that you need to save your Actions, Gradients, and Swatches palette before you remove the prefs files, or else you will lose all of your custom settings.

Because the preferences file is so touchy, you might want to save a copy of it onto another hard drive when you have one that is configured to your liking (with all of the palettes where you want them to be, and all of your color settings in place). Do not use this copy of the file, and keep it in a safe place. Then, the next time you need a "clean" copy, you can simply duplicate your "spare" and replace the old, worn-out file with it. If you decide to make a duplicate of the preferences file, copy the entire Adobe Photoshop Settings folder as well.

Do not try to reuse a prefs file from an earlier version. That is not a safe thing to try. However, if your workgroup uses the same version of Photoshop and you are all on the same platform, you can give your preferences file to other users so that all your systems are set up the same way.

Just remember to ditch the prefs file at the first sign of trouble.

Old Filters

Another area of potential problem and conflict is with filters and plug-ins. They can sometimes cause the same havoc with one another that Mac extensions have been known to create. If you suspect a filter conflict, here's how to find it:

1. Remove all the third-party plug-ins from the Photoshop directory (remember, we told you to keep them in a separate subdirectory for easy removal).
2. Open Photoshop and see if the problem disappears (of course, it might disappear because the filter has also disappeared). However, if the problem *situation* can be re-created and the problem does not occur, you know that a filter conflict caused it.
3. Put back one-half of your third-party filters and try again. If the problem comes back, then one of the filters in the group is the culprit.

4. Remove half of the set that you just put back. Does the problem go away? If it doesn't, remove half of what's left. If it does, then you have a smaller set of culprits.

Continue to add or remove filters by half until you locate the problem filter. If you want to try a technique that isn't quite as random, *remove your oldest filters first*. They make the most likely suspects. Many filters were not updated for Photoshop 3 (when layers were first introduced), and they are quite likely to be the first ones to cause trouble. If these filters are valuable to you (and many of them are), then keep them outside of the Photoshop directory and load them (with as few other filters as possible) when needed. Also, check with the manufacturers to see if newer versions are available. As much as possible, you should keep your third-party filters up to date.

Known problem filters include Alien Skin Black Box 2, which doesn't run on Photoshop 4 on either platform (upgrade to 2.1 or Eye Candy 3) and, on the PC, early versions of Aldus Gallery Effects (you no longer need these because updated versions are included with version 5 of Photoshop). Version 3 of Kai's Power Tools needs to be updated to version 3.01 or later. Many filters also need to be updated for Photoshop 5 compatibility. Chroma Graphics MagicMask has been updated to version 2, because version 1 does not work. Extensis PhotoTools has an update available, because the icon bar doesn't work in Photoshop 5. TypeCaster 1.15 under Windows can cause Photoshop to crash. Get an update from Xaos Tools on their Web site, **www.xaostools.com**.

Adobe has also updated many of its native filters from Photoshop 4. With the exception of the QuickEdit plug-in (which has been dropped from Photoshop 5, but which still works), do not load any of your Photoshop 4 native filters. All of the filters in the Extensions folder have been updated, the Lighting Effects filter has been rewritten, and the Stained Glass filter has been updated. Also:

- *Digimarc folder*—All of the plug-ins in this folder have been updated.
- *File Formats*—The PNG, Kodak Photo CD, and CompuServe GIF plug-ins have been updated.
- *Filters*—The Radial Blur plug-in has been updated.
- *Import Export*—The GIF89a Export plug-in has been updated.
- *Parser Folder*—All files in this folder have been updated.
- *Filter*—The Emboss filter has changed and holds more color.

Scanner Noise

Another problem we see fairly often on the Adobe Forum is noise along the bottom edge of a scan or across an entire scanned image. We have seen reports of lines appearing randomly in images. *This is not a Photoshop problem.*

Photoshop doesn't cause this noise, even if you have used Photoshop as your scanning application; the noise is coming from the SCSI chain on your computer. All scanners on Macs and most scanners on Windows systems are attached to a SCSI adapter in the computer. SCSI devices are chained together on the computer. The first device in the chain is connected to the SCSI adapter using a SCSI cable. The second device in the chain connects to the first, and so on. Scanner noise is caused by a SCSI cable that is not in good condition and it can take a lot of work to figure out which one is bad. Please believe us. Even if Photoshop is the only program in which you see the problem, Photoshop is not at fault. We have never seen a case of this that wasn't caused by a defective SCSI cable.

Check all of your connections; the cable to the scanner might not be the one that is bad. Keep your SCSI cables very short. Buy the best cables that you can find from the most reputable manufacturer. Even if you end up spending a lot of money on SCSI cables, it's worth it in time saved.

Corrupt Fonts

Corrupt fonts are not the symptom of a problem so much as they can be the cause of a number of problems that are hard to solve on either Mac or Windows. On the Mac, you might get an "Unable to initialize" message. On Windows systems, a corrupt TrueType font is thought to be the cause of problems importing Adobe Illustrator files. If you have trouble, you need to test each font to see which one is causing the system to reject it. You can do this in Windows by double clicking on the Fonts icon in the Control Panel. Open each font by clicking on it. If the font doesn't open, it is corrupted and you need to reinstall it.

Under Photoshop 5, fonts may also cause problems even if they aren't corrupt. Because Photoshop scans all of the loaded fonts at startup, if you have a large number of fonts, your startup times might be unacceptably slow. Adobe unhelpfully recommends that you use fewer fonts!

General Troubleshooting Strategies

Some of the specifics to check are different on Mac and Windows, but what follows is an all-purpose "Before-I-throw-out-the-computer" guide to help you figure out what could be bugging a system and program that had previously been working just fine. If you suddenly notice a problem with Photoshop, here's a general list of things to try (from simple to drastic):

1. Toss out the prefs file and restart Photoshop.

2. Did you install or uninstall any software on your computer? If you did, see if you can figure out what it replaced or what changes it made to your system files (the Control Panels or Extensions on the Mac and the System Registry in Windows). Did it update any utilities such as ATM or QuickTime? If possible, revert back to the time before the changes. Programs available on the Windows platform—such as Uninstaller, Quarterdeck Clean Sweep, and others—can monitor software installations and allow you to easily see what has changed or temporarily back out the programs to see if your problems go away.

3. Have you changed anything in your system? Deleted any files? Moved anything? Had any children playing with your system? If so, check to see anything significant was not inadvertently deleted. Restore your system to the way it was and see if that works. Photoshop on Windows requires certain shared files (see the Photoshop README file on your Photoshop installation CD-ROM). If an uninstaller has deleted one of these files, Photoshop will not run.

4. Try running without extensions on the Mac. In Windows, exit all other applications.

5. If you are still having problems, check your RAM allocation and make sure that it's enough on the Mac (and not too much on Windows). Check to make sure that the *computer* thinks you have as much RAM as is actually installed in the computer. On a Mac, choose About This Macintosh in the Finder on the Apple Menu. On Windows systems, click on Start|Settings|Control Panel. Double-click on the System icon. Click on the Performance tab, and look at the Memory entry. The information you find here reveals the amount of physical RAM installed on the system.

6. Test your RAM with a diagnostic program—especially if you are getting random crashes.

7. Reinstall Photoshop.

8. If nothing helps after you have gotten to Step 7, call Adobe Tech Support and then call your hardware vendor. You *should not* perform Steps 9 or 10 unless requested to do so by Tech Support.

9. Reinstall your operating system. *Do not* perform this step unless you know *exactly* what you are doing. Depending on your operating system, you may need to reinstall every existing application following this step.

10. Reformat your hard drive and restore from backup tape—then reinstall your system software and the application software. This is a major hassle. Try everything else first!

Mac Troubleshooting

Troubleshooting the Mac is a topic all to itself. It's not that the Mac is unstable, but it's delicate. It is usually "plug and play"—much more so than the Wintel platform—but when things don't work, they can be even harder to fix because the Mac tries to be user-friendly and to protect you from technical matters. Therefore, when something goes wrong, it often takes a professional technician to fix what a technically savvy PC user could do without a technician. Luckily, things don't usually go that wrong.

A number of issues pertain only to the Macintosh (just as Windows has its own set of "gotchas").

Making The Mac Run Fast

When folks complain that their Mac runs Photoshop too slowly, here is the standard CompuServe Adobe Photoshop Forum response:

1. Turn off Virtual Memory. Even on a Power Mac, where Adobe says that you can use a small amount of Virtual Memory, don't. Photoshop uses its own memory scheme when it writes to temporary files on your scratch disks. Unless RAM is critically short for you, do not turn on VM. It only gets in the way.

2. Don't set your cache higher than 96K. Most graphics programs do not require a high cache setting. You should be able to get away with a cache setting of 32K if your system setup allows it (on some configurations, 96K is the minimum).

3. Although they are very useful, turn off the Layer palette and Channel palette thumbnails. They slow down the screen redrawing. *Do not do this unless you are having a problem*. Better yet, get more RAM.

4. Make sure that you have a large area of free disk space for your scratch disk and keep it defragmented.
5. Get more RAM.
6. Consider a multiprocessor card or a faster Mac.
7. Get more RAM.
8. Purchase a RAID disk array.
9. Get more RAM. (It's true; you can never have too much.)

Type 11 And Other System Errors

The dreaded Type 11 error message has plagued the Mac since the introduction of the Power Mac. It is not a very specific error—even though it indicates a memory error, all it really means is "You lose...system going down." You can get a Type 11 error from a buggy piece of software or from bad RAM or from a variety of other causes. The trick is to determine which it is. If you are getting constant Type 11 errors on a new computer, two causes are likely: You have noisy SCSI cables or bad RAM. Take the computer back to the vendor and have it checked out. Keep taking the machine back to the vendor until it's fixed.

It is not uncommon to get a Type 11 error several times a month; several times a day is too much. If you get frequent Type 11 errors that are totally random and not repeatable, then your RAM is the first thing that you should suspect. We have found the Mac to be quite temperamental, in general, about the quality of the RAM that it wishes to consume. It only wants the "good stuff." Newer Technology makes an excellent RAM for the Mac. It's more expensive than "no name" brands, but it always seems to work. Sometimes, the Mac's RAM seems to get bored with its location and just wants to be rearranged. You might be able to recover from Type 11 errors by changing the placement of the RAM in your machine. Do not use composite RAM SIMMs. Make sure that all of your RAM is the same speed. In some rare instances, you might also need to replace the computer's motherboard.

> **TIP**
>
> O/S 8.1 seems to be much more successful at avoiding constant Type 11 errors, so you might want to upgrade your operating system. Of course, once you switch to System 8, you might start seeing a lot of Type 2, Type 3, and Type 10 errors, so it's hard to tell if that is an improvement (a crash is still a crash, after all). In our experience, all of these "Error of Type whatever" messages are nonspecific and seem to come from the same thing (if one could ever figure out what that was). In general, however, System 8 does seem to be more stable.

If RAM is not the problem and your SCSI cables seem to be working just fine, here are some other steps that you can take in addition to the general troubleshooting steps already mentioned:

1. Check your RAM, Cache, and VM settings.
2. Start up the machine without extensions by holding down the Shift key after you see the Welcome to Macintosh message.

3. Remove the Fonts folder from the System folder. Sometimes a corrupt font can cause the problem and the system will create a new folder with the minimum fonts that it needs. You can then put the fonts back a few at a time or get one of the new font checker programs that verify the integrity of the fonts.

4. If this doesn't help, remove the Extensions, Control Panels, and Preferences folders from the System folder. They, too, will be re-created with the minimum needed to run. Don't trash the original folders—just drag them out of the System folder.

5. Make sure that you are using the latest disk drivers and that they are compatible with the system version you're using. Check your disk for bad media using Disk First Aid or Norton or Central Point Utilities.

6. Remove the Enable Asynch I/O plug-in folder from the Photoshop Plug-Ins/Extensions folder. This plug-in is no longer installed by default. You have to load it yourself. Read the README that comes with it. Don't use this plug-in unless you feel you need it, and pull it at the first sign of trouble.

7. Change your scratch disk so that it uses an internal hard drive (ideally, your boot drive) and locate Photoshop on the internal drive as well.

8. Make sure that you keep your graphics card drivers up to date. Out-of-date drivers may be incompatible with Photoshop 5 and cause serious or intermittent screen redraw problems.

Type 1 or Type 10 errors can be treated the same way, but they are neither as severe nor as prevalent as the Type 11 errors.

Extension Conflicts And The Usual Suspects

Mac extension conflicts are notorious and annoying. They can be hard to spot and there can also be conflicts between certain extensions and Mac plug-ins. Although we don't want to make disparaging remarks about specific pieces of software, what follows is a list of "suspect" extensions—extensions that are known to *sometimes* cause trouble. They work flawlessly for most users and cause other users major headaches. If you use one of the suspects and have no problems, then consider yourself fortunate. If you begin to have problems occur in Photoshop, these are the extensions that you should immediately remove (in this order) to see if the problems go away:

1. *Norton Directory Assistance*. This program is bad news. Do not use it. Norton has discontinued it in Version 3. Its work-alikes, such as Super Boomerang from NOW Utilities, are also troublesome, though not as buggy.

2. *RAM Doubler*. This works for most users, but if you have a problem, it should be one of the first programs you disable. If you use it, do not assign Photoshop any more RAM than the machine physically contains. If you have a 16MB machine, do not give Photoshop a RAM partition larger than 16MB.

3. *QuickKeys*. Usually okay, but disable if there is a problem. The CE Toolbox needed to run QuickKeys seems to cause the most trouble. Also, QuickKeys 3.5 is incompatible

with Adobe online registration software and can cause a system crash. Disable QuickKeys before you install Photoshop.

4. *Any form of disk compression.* In particular, do not use a compressed volume for your scratch disk: It's asking for trouble. You are better off buying more hard drive.

5. *True Finder Integration.* This feature, which comes with Stuffit Deluxe, can be another candidate for trouble.

6. *Older versions of ATM and ATR (Adobe Type Reunion) in conjunction with older versions of Suitcase.* This is a dangerous mix. Update them all. Tread warily with the new versions as well, although these are necessary extension categories.

7. *The clock that appears in the top menubar.* This feature has been found to cause problems on some systems that are still running earlier versions of System 7.

8. *Any version of OneClick.* This is a very badly behaved extension, which is a shame because it gives AutoF/X Power Pac most of its power (and you cannot run Power Pac without it).

9. *Norton File Saver.* This can cause Photoshop to crash or quit. If you are crashing whenever you leave Photoshop, then you are either running File Saver (or a similar program) or an old version of MetaCreations KPT 3. If KPT is the problem, an update is available.

10. *DOS Mounter Plus and DOS Mounter 95.* These applications seem to make the system a bit more crash-inclined. Don't stop using them, just be aware of the number of times that you crash and when the crashes happen. If they usually occur when you are opening or accessing files, try removing these Control Panels.

11. *The Adobe Gamma Utility, if you are using another Calibration program such as Color Synergy.* Don't run Adobe Gamma Utility and the older Gamma Control Panel at the same time.

12. *Master Juggler and some of the filters in Cytopia PhotoOptics.* These don't get along with one another. The system crashes.

Memory Leaks

One of the most troublesome and difficult-to-remove problems in Photoshop is the memory leak. It seems to affect users with a lot of RAM. The symptoms include a message "Unable to... because of insufficient RAM." This usually occurs after you've been working for a long time and have opened and closed a large number of windows. The message can appear when you have a tiny 1MB file open or even a 100K file. You look at your generous RAM allocation and wonder if Photoshop has lost its mind.

The problem seems to be caught somewhere between Photoshop and the Macintosh operating system. All systems perform an operation called "garbage collection," in which unused memory locations are reclaimed and recycled to give programs more space. Sometimes, the garbage collectors seem to go on strike. When this happens, you get a memory leak—and a message announces that you are out of RAM, even though you know that it should not be possible.

We haven't run into this problem using Photoshop 5 with System 8 yet, but we are also unwilling to claim that the problem will never happen. Sometimes, after Photoshop has run for a long time along with Microsoft Word, Claris Emailer claims that it does not have enough memory to launch its script. Because at that point no other program is running, and Claris Emailer has almost an entire 320MB of RAM in which to romp, we think that garbage collection is still somewhat problematic on the Mac.

Although the problem is hard to cure, it's easy to fix—quit Photoshop and restart it. The problem will disappear, at least for a while. Learn to anticipate this. Don't run Photoshop for three days without quitting from it. If new windows seem to appear very slowly, restart the program. Because you might not be able to save your image if there isn't enough RAM, it's better to quit Photoshop before you get into trouble. By the way, save early and often.

Lost Cursor

Another common problem that occurs for no reason that we can pinpoint is the "lost cursor" error. The symptoms are clear: When you drag your cursor over your image, you can no longer see it. That makes editing and painting very tricky!

The fix is easy. Remove the Direct Cursors plug-in from the Extensions folder inside of the Photoshop Plug-Ins folder. Unfortunately, you will no longer be able to see any painting tool that is larger than 16 pixels, but you *will* be able to see the cursor—which is more important in the scheme of things.

We've also seen a less serious version of this problem in Photoshop 5. With certain graphics cards (the ixmicro card seems to be one of the worst offenders), the Brush Size cursor flickers and vanishes if you hold down the mouse button for too long as you paint. "Too long" is not a precise measure, and its definition varies every time you paint. While removing the Direct Cursors plug-in would probably fix this, the price might be too high. If you can tolerate it (and you should be able to), just paint in smaller strokes.

Cannot Initialize Because Of A Disk Error

This error message is usually lying to you. Only very rarely is something actually wrong with your hard drive. The three most common causes of this message are a corrupt font, corrupted preferences file, or the presence or absence of the Macintosh Easy Open Control Panel.

Trash your prefs file. Remove the Fonts folder from the System folder. Check to see if Easy Open is loaded. If it is, remove it; if it is not; load it. One of these actions should fix the problem.

If a font is the problem, move your fonts back in one at a time until you locate the problem child.

In one case, this error message appeared after a system crash left the prefs file both corrupt and open. The system thought that the file was open, so it could not replace the prefs file. When we moved the prefs file to the trash and emptied it, it wasn't really removed and the new file still could not be created. Unfortunately, with the file gone, there was no way to close it either. We needed to restore the prefs file from a backup tape and then trash the restored copy in order to get the system up and running properly again. Bottom line: *Do not empty the trash until you can reopen Photoshop.*

Preview Icons Are Scrambled In The Finder Or Do Not Launch Photoshop

Sometimes the cute preview icons that Photoshop creates aren't worth the trouble. System 7.5 seemed to mangle them frequently, although the problem seems much better under System 7.5.3 and later, and we have seen the problem only infrequently on removables under System 8. However, if you look at the preview icon and it doesn't match the name of the file, you know that you've been hit. You're more likely to find this occurring on a removable drive than on a fixed disk.

This is unrelated to the problem of not being able to launch a file by double-clicking on it, but the fix is the same (we will get to it in a moment): Sometimes a program causes Photoshop's file creator to be incorrectly specified. Installing version 6 of Adobe Illustrator with the Gallery Effects filters turned all Photoshop documents into documents created by Gallery Effects. Double-clicking on an icon does not invoke Photoshop when the file creator is incorrectly set.

When this happens, you need to rebuild your desktop (or every so often even when it doesn't). To rebuild your desktop, hold down the Option and Command keys after your extensions have loaded, but before the hard drives are mounted. You then have the chance to rebuild all of the desktop files for hard drives (or to skip those volumes that you prefer), but you might lose the Get Info comments when you rebuild the desktop (depending on your operating system version).

For good measure, you might also want to reset your Parameter RAM. Reset the Parameter RAM (PRAM) by holding down the Command+Option+P+R keys when you restart the computer. Hold the keys until you hear two beeps, then release the keys. This resets the system preferences to the default.

Magnifier Keyboard Command Does Not Work

If you press the Command+spacebar keys and do not see the Zoom tool icon, you are probably not looking at an English language keyboard layout. Unfortunately, it's easy to accidentally change your language definition. Remove the WorldScript extension and the extra keyboard definitions and the problem will go away.

Windows Troubleshooting

Windows troubleshooting can get technical very quickly. Advice can differ depending on whether you're using Windows 95 or Windows NT. Photoshop 5 *will not run* under any flavor of Windows 3.1. Unless we specify, advice applies to all Windows flavors. Adobe provides FAXBACK and online support via the Web. They have many FAQs available that give detailed advice on configuring Windows. You should check the Web site (**www.adobe.com**) first to see if any documents deal with your problem. CompuServe's Adobe Forum is still the best way to ask specific questions and get customized advice.

Making Windows Run Fast

Here are some tips to make Photoshop run as fast as possible on a Windows machine:

1. Set up your Windows virtual memory file so that it's twice as large as the maximum amount of RAM that you have available in your system. In Windows, click on Start|Settings|Control Panel. Double-click on the System icon. Click on the Performance tab. The first line of the Performance Status tells you the amount of RAM installed on your system.
2. Leave at least three to five times the size of your largest file in free disk space on the disk that you specify as your scratch disk. If you can devote an entire disk partition to Photoshop for its scratch files, that is even better. Keep your scratch disk defragmented and optimized.
3. Although they are very useful, turn off the Layer palette and Channel palette thumbnails. They slow down the screen redrawing. *Do not do this unless you are having a problem.* Better yet, get more RAM.
4. Run the latest version of the operating system and the most current version of Photoshop. Run Windows NT in preference to Windows 95 if you want peak performance.
5. Get more RAM.
6. Consider a faster machine. Photoshop should run faster under NT than under Windows 95, especially if you have more than one processor or are running a Pentium II or MMX processor.
7. Get more RAM.
8. Purchase a RAID disk array running on a Fast-Wide SCSI 3 adapter.
9. Get more RAM. (It's true; you can never have too much.)
10. If you choose to upgrade to a new, faster machine, look for a machine that allows you to exceed 256MB of RAM. (High-end PCs typically allow less RAM expansion than high-end Macs.)

Testing To Find Windows 95 Errors

You have already been shown how to start your computer in Safe mode (refer to the section "Installation And Upgrades"). However, when you do, you cannot access all of the drivers and features that you need, and you cannot run Photoshop from Safe mode because it typically loads the standard VGA driver (16 colors), which is not sufficient for Photoshop. You can create a test configuration for Photoshop, however, that allows you to selectively add and remove drivers, or whatever you need to help you determine the problem. It requires that you start the computer in Step by Step Confirmation mode. You can get more detail by reading the Adobe document "Minimizing Windows 95 to Troubleshoot Errors in Photoshop 3.0.5 and Later." Follow this procedure ONLY if you are using 16-bit drivers in Config.Sys. If you can't tell, don't bother (and if you do not understand this paragraph, *definitely* don't bother unless an Adobe Technical Support person walks you through it). Briefly, you need to do the following:

1. Press F8 after you see the Starting Windows message.

2. Enable HIMEM.SYS, IFSHLP.SYS, all Windows drivers, and the Windows GUI. Also say "yes" to any devices that contain the word "double" in them. If you are using Doublespace to compress your disk, you need to have it running.

3. After all of the Windows drivers are loaded, Windows will start.

If this doesn't fix the problem, you can set up a test configuration that will allow you to turn off one device at a time until you discover the driver or device that is causing the problem.

Windows NT Troubleshooting

Here is a sequence of items for you to check if you have trouble with your Photoshop installation under Windows NT. Many of these items are also applicable to Windows. For details of how to do the specifics, you need to consult your Windows manuals or to call Adobe Technical support. In the meantime, here's what you should be looking for if you have trouble with your Photoshop installation under Windows NT:

1. Make sure you have the minimum amount of RAM that Photoshop requires to run (at least 48MB for Photoshop 5). In Windows NT 4.0, click on Start|Settings|Control Panel, then double-click on the System icon. On the Performance tab, the first line tells you the amount of physical RAM on the system. If you are using any RAM-doubling software, turn it off and try to re-create the error.

2. Update to the latest Windows NT 4.0 or Windows 95 Service Pack. Contact Microsoft for further information.

3. Trash and re-create Photoshop's preferences files.

4. Specify a different default printer. You might try to install Microsoft's PostScript printer driver as the default. Even if you have no PostScript printer (or any printer), you should specify a default printer. If that helps, and you have a different PostScript printer, then contact your printer manufacturer to see if an updated driver is available.

5. Remove Photoshop and then reinstall it from the installation disks or CD-ROM while in VGA mode. (Make sure that you have moved your third-party plug-ins to a different location before you do this. Otherwise, you will lose them all and have to reinstall them from the original disks.)

6. Ensure there's adequate free space on the hard disk to which Windows temporary (.tmp) variables are set. Exit all programs.

7. Ensure there's adequate free space on the hard disk to which Photoshop's scratch disks are set.

8. Change the location of and/or resize the Windows Virtual Memory Paging File. If not enough free space is available on the drive, consider changing the drive on which the Paging file is located. Set the Initial Size to twice the amount of physical RAM on your system. The maximum and minimum sizes should be the same.

9. If you have a dual-boot system, optimize and defragment your hard disk(s) using the ScanDisk and Disk Defragmenter utilities included with Windows 95. If you only use Windows NT 4.0, use an NT 4.0-compatible third-party utility to run disk scanning and defragmenting programs. Read the documentation before you do this!

10. Verify that all your device drivers are Windows NT 4.0 compatible and working correctly. Device drivers run things such as your scanner, video card, SCSI card, mouse, keyboard, and so on. Contact the hardware manufacturer for the latest Windows NT 4.0 drivers. Adobe cannot keep track of all of the drivers and doesn't supply them.
11. Change the number of colors and resolution of the video display adapter (but never while Photoshop is running). If your machine is set to 256 colors, try the millions of colors option; if it's set to millions, try setting it to 256 to see if the problem goes away. If it does, your drivers may be having trouble with Windows NT 4.0. If changing the video display driver fixes the problem, contact your video card manufacturer to see if updated drivers are available.
12. Disable hard drive compression or move the temporary files location and Photoshop's scratch disk to an uncompressed drive.
13. Use Event Manager to check for reports of damaged files or stopped drivers. These reports can sometimes give you valuable hints as to what system component is causing the problem. However, the messages tend to be cryptic.
14. Turn off Application Performance Boosting. To do this, click on Start|Settings|Control Panels. Double-click on the System icon. On the Performance tab, click on the Graphicx button. Move the slider from Full to None.
15. Make sure that all of your hardware drivers are compatible with the version of Windows you are using and are the most recent versions. SCSI adapters, video display adapters, sound cards, scanners, CD-ROMs, removable hard drives, removable media such as Syquest, Jaz, and Zip drives all need to have updated and compatible Windows drivers.
16. Make sure that your SCSI chain is terminated properly. When you check this, also make sure that your cables are connected properly and that they're in good condition.
17. Check the status of the SCSI Adapters. You can find this by clicking on Start|Settings|Control Panel. Double-click on SCSI Adapters. Click on each adapter listed on the Devices tab, and then, for each, click on the Properties button. The Cardinfo tab's Device Status section will tell you if the SCSI adapter is working correctly or not. You can find out what drivers are used by clicking on the Driver tab. If you suspect there's a problem with this device or driver, contact the manufacturer for updated drivers for further help.
18. Always shut down Windows properly. Don't simply flick the switch to Off—no matter how annoyed you get with the computer!
19. Reinstall Windows. **Warning**: This is a drastic step. Do not reinstall Windows unless you have been specifically instructed to do so and you know what you are doing! If you are not sure, hire someone to do it for you.

MMX

Because Photoshop 4 was released before the MMX machines were available, there were compatibility problems between Photoshop 4 and the MMX chip. These problems were fixed in the release of Photoshop 4.01. They shouldn't occur at all in Photoshop 5. This troubleshooting advice is included in case you need to deal with a leftover problem from Photoshop 4 for some reason. We hope that you will simply upgrade to Photoshop 5.

If you are using Windows NT 4 and an MMX-enhanced Pentium processor, Photoshop may return the Access violation error if the MMX plug-ins are out of date (that is, if they are not from version 4 of Photoshop). The FastCore plug-in included with Photoshop 4 can cause Photoshop to return an error when running on a computer with an MMX-enhanced Pentium processor. The updated FastCore and MMXCore plug-ins replace the FastCore plug-in included with Photoshop 4.

To solve this problem, disable the FastCore plug-in, then install the updated FastCore and MMXCore plug-ins as follows:

1. Make sure that Photoshop is not running.
2. In Windows Explorer, rename the FASTCORE.8BX file in the Adobe\Photoshp\Plugins\Extensns folder to FASTCORE.OLD.
3. You can download the FastCore and MMXCore plug-ins file (FAST.EXE) from Adobe's Web site (**www.adobe.com**), but we recommend that you purchase the Photoshop 4.0.1 Update CD-ROM from Adobe Customer Services (800-833-6687).

MMX technology adds major performance boosts to Intel processors. The FastCore plug-in included with Photoshop 4 and the updated FastCore and MMXCore plug-ins let Photoshop take advantage of MMX technology. Photoshop can run without these plug-ins, though some of the functions will be slower.

Color

You must install a video driver with at least 256 colors for Photoshop to be able to operate. Never change video drivers or color depth while Photoshop is running.

Page Fault Errors In Windows 95

If you get a message that you cannot open Photoshop because of a Page Fault error in module <unknown>, check your video drivers. A damaged or incorrect video driver usually causes this error. Install your video driver again using the original driver file either from the manufacturer or from the list in Windows. Sometimes, when Windows detects new hardware, it "helps" by loading a generic driver, even when the "real" thing is available. Generic drivers are rarely as good as or as reliable as the driver that is supposed to be working. A number of video drivers have experienced problems with Photoshop 5. Check the README file on your Photoshop installation CD-ROM for the latest list.

Problems With Deluxe Tutorial

A number of users have reported problems when installing the Deluxe Tutorial. The most common problem is that games that used to work no longer do. You might want to do a custom installation of Photoshop and not install the tutorial. The problem is that the installation program places a copy of QuickTime on your machine that might not be the one needed to run other applications. QuickTime and Windows are still trying to work together peaceably, but they're not quite there yet, and the results can sometimes be unpredictable with different versions of QuickTime.

Mouse Problems

This is another well-known area of problems. The symptoms are GROWSTUB errors in Module POINTER.DLL or mouse freezes. You need to check to make sure that you have only one MOUSE.DRV file installed. You also need to use a Microsoft mouse driver. This issue has been tricky because, while you need to make sure that your mouse driver is not corrupt, sometimes you need to replace the driver with an *earlier* one. If you cannot get your mouse to work properly, you might need to call Adobe Tech support and have them work through this one with you.

Double-Clicking On An Icon Starts The Wrong Program

Windows systems use the file extension to determine what program to launch. When an application is installed, it tells Windows what to do when an icon with that extension is double-clicked. Most applications don't bother looking to see if a different program already claims that extension. If you install two applications that register the same extension, such as Photoshop and Corel Draw—both register TIF files—the last program installed is the one that launches when the icon is double-clicked. Version 5 of Photoshop only registers the Photoshop file format (PSD) and all of the supplementary formats (ATN, ACV, and so on) that go with it. If you want to be able to launch Photoshop by double-clicking on a TIF file, you need to register it yourself.

If a newly installed application has grabbed an extension that you want processed by Photoshop, you have three choices:

- Reinstall Photoshop over your existing installation. This will do no harm as long as you are installing the same version and you can take back the vagrant extension.
- Live with it and open the files by first opening Photoshop and using the File Open dialog box.
- Modify the extension's owner by taking these steps:
    1. From the Desktop, use the mouse to select a file of the type you want to open.
    2. Press the Shift key and right-mouse-click on the file.
    3. Select the Open With option in the context menu that appears when you right-click the mouse.
    4. In the Open With dialog box, select Photoshop from the list of available applications. If you don't see Photoshop in the list, you can use the Other button to find it.
    5. Click on the Always Use This Program To Open This Type Of File checkbox.
    6. Click on OK.

The History Palette

It makes sense to discuss one of the major new features of Photoshop 5 next. Unlimited undos are finally here—Adobe style. In the context of this chapter about optimizing the way you work with Photoshop, the History palette is important because it impacts both your workflow and your storage needs.

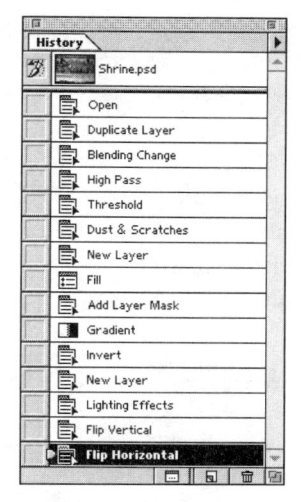

Figure 1.23 The History palette allows you to backtrack to a prior state in the creation of an image.

Why do we say "undos, Adobe-style?" Every other program that allows you to perform multiple undos lets you move back and forth between the states of the image. In no case can you pick and choose the states. The engineers at Adobe resisted the call for multiple undos until they could find a better way of doing it. This better way is the History palette. Figure 1.23 shows the History palette. As you can see, it records the basic commands used as you work. A bit later in this chapter, you will read about the Actions palette. It too can record commands as you work. The two palettes have nothing to do with one another and the recordings are for quite different purposes. Actions let you replay a sequence of events. The History palette lets you revert to prior steps in time. When you close an image, its history is lost forever. When you record an Action, you can always play it again.

The History Palette, Menus, And Options

A menu is attached to the History palette that gives you additional options. Figure 1.24 shows this menu. You can use the keyboard to step forward and backward through the History palette (using the menu to do this seems inefficient; if you don't remember the key commands, it's easier to just click on the History step that you want). You can make a new snapshot, delete a step (which you can also do by dragging the step to the History palette trashcan), clear all of the history, or make a new document from the selected state. You can also select the History Options, which let you specify the type of history record and the number of steps to keep.

Figure 1.24 The History palette menu.

> **TIP**
>
> You can drag a history step into any open document. It replaces whatever was in the image before with the newly dragged image.

Figure 1.25 shows the History Options dialog box. You can keep two types of History. The Non-Linear option (shown in Figure 1.26) can be recognized because it keeps all of the states in the image active when you select a prior state. In the example shown, if you revert the image back to the Dust & Scratches filter as shown, and then decide that you want to apply a few other

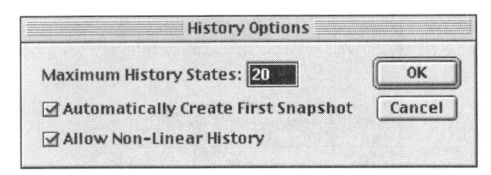

Figure 1.25 The History Options dialog box allows you to decide how many states you want to keep.

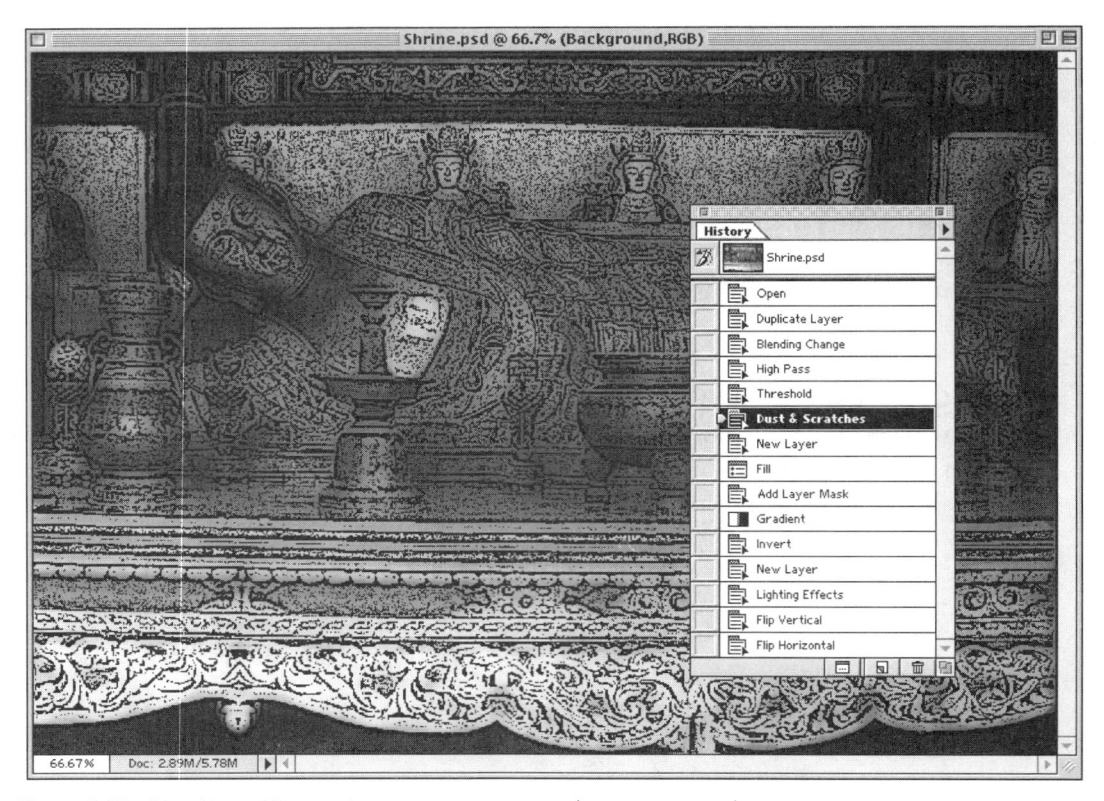

Figure 1.26 Non-Linear History gives you many ways to change your mind.

changes to the image, you can still bring the image back the way it looked after applying the Flip Horizontal command shown at the bottom of the History palette. If you select the Linear History option, as you can see in Figure 1.27, you will lose all of the changes past the currently selected state of the image (they're grayed out; if you perform another command, they will be lost permanently).

Figures 1.28 and 1.29 show exactly what happens when you revert to a prior state. In Figure 1.28, a Lighting Effects filter is applied to the image after it was brought back to the Dust & Scratches step in the History palette. Non-Linear History is on. You can still back up and go forward. Figure 1.29 picks up where Figure 1.27 stopped. Figure 1.29 shows what happens using Linear History. We brought the image back to the Fill command, and then applied a Lighting Effects filter. Notice that all of the steps that used to follow the Fill command are gone. It looks like Non-Linear History gives you more flexibility. It does, but because it has no clear sequence of linked steps, if you skip back and forth between steps, you may find it more confusing.

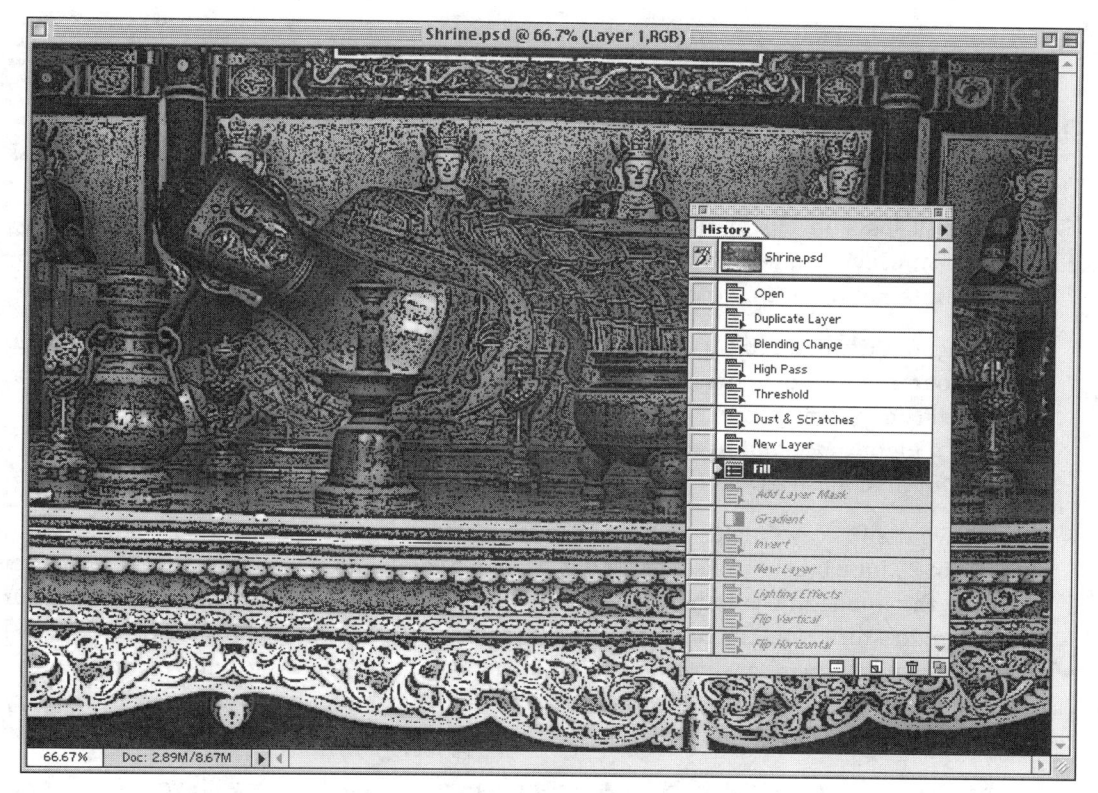

Figure 1.27 Linear History lets you revert, but will drop all of the steps after a command if you revert and then pick a command not already shown in the History list.

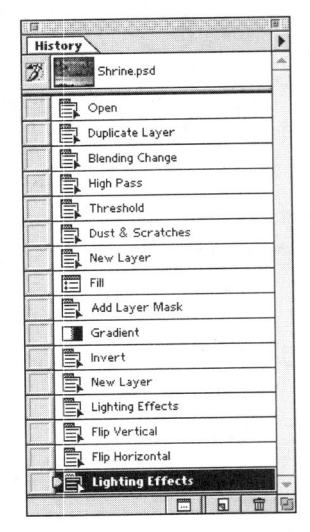

Figure 1.28 The Non-Linear History option allows you to keep sequences of changes.

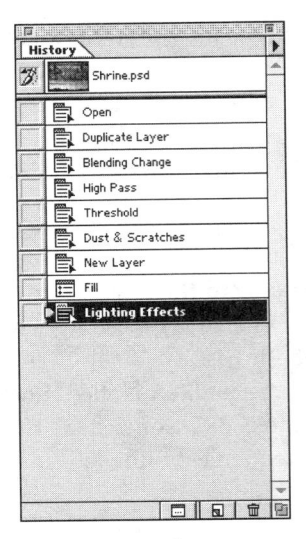

Figure 1.29 Linear History allows you to pursue only one set of possibilities.

History And Hard Drive

No significant difference (and in many cases, no difference at all) exists in the scratch disk space used by either method of keeping history. If you revert "up-the-chain" a lot, you might use less disk space in Linear History mode because the steps following your "revert-to" are tossed away, which can tend to keep the total list of steps shorter. However, both methods use the same internal storage method.

Certain actions are more costly in terms of hard disk space. Brush strokes, for example, eat up large amounts of storage space. Here is a record of the disk consumption taken by one editing session. The image being edited was an 8MB full-color photograph. Each brush stroke does not consume a lot of space, but in the aggregate they are costly and use up your "20 wishes" (or whatever number of steps you have elected to save).

If you have the History palette set to the default 20 steps, you could lose all of your previous changes in 20 little brush strokes. Therefore, when you are painting, you might want to either duplicate the image into another one so that you can keep the prior history active in your original image, turn Non-Linear History on and toss away some earlier brush strokes once you know that you like them, or save snapshots of your work at the points to which you think you might like to revert (do this before you start painting). As long as the step is in the History palette, you can click on it and either create a new image from it or make it into a snapshot.

When you are using the History palette, resist the nervous urge to play with your tools (especially the selection tools). One of the authors has the annoying habit of drawing totally unnecessary selection Marquees on the screen when she is thinking about something (so now you know which one of us is guilty!). When she finally looks up at the History palette, it is to say "Whoops! The History is all gone." All useful History was replaced by Select and Deselect.

Table 1.2 Hard drive usage by the History palette feature.

Action	New Free Space Amount
Open Photoshop	970.8MB
Open Image	956.2MB
18 brush strokes	912.6MB
Add Noise	911.3MB
Gaussian Blur	901.7MB
Find Edges/AutoLevels	873.5MB

Using The History Palette

The History palette can change the way you work with Photoshop. The more you use it, the more things you will discover to do. It's time to try an example and see for yourself. Let's jump-start this example by playing an Action—which will bring your file to a consistent state and

How Are The History Steps Stored?

Knowing how Photoshop stores data can help you make informed decisions about the number of History steps you can "afford" to save or how much scratch disk space you need to have available to the program. Photoshop stores its data in 128×128-pixel blocks. The smallest amount written to disk is a "snapshot" (our term—not a "Photoshop word") of an area of your image 128 pixels by 128 pixels. The data for that area of your image needs to be recorded for each channel in the image.

If you make a change to a 10-pixel-square area at the top-left of your image, then the History palette will need to save that change to scratch disk in the block where it stores the top-left 128-square-pixel area. If nothing else changes in that single step, then only that one changed block needs to be written. If your next activity in the file results in changed pixels in an area 100 pixels wide that starts about 100 pixels down from the top, then Photoshop needs to write two new blocks (because the change is over a boundary).

The amount of storage used, therefore, depends on the distribution and amount of pixels changed. Were you to change every 128th pixel in a grid pattern, Photoshop would need to resave the entire image. Resaving the entire image does not necessarily mean that an amount of disk space the same size as your image will be consumed. If you fill an image with a solid color, Photoshop only needs to record that one color was used and repeated for the length and width of your image. It compresses disk space when possible. On continuous-tone images (photographs), compression is rarely possible.

In addition to writing history to the scratch disk, Photoshop uses an area for Image Cache. The Image Cache is used to predraw previews of the image at various sizes so that you can quickly scroll, pan, and zoom through your image. Photoshop also deals with the overhead of opening the file itself; on a large file, this can be considerable. Each layer adds additional storage-space requirements. Luckily, the price of both hard drives and RAM has tumbled in recent years.

give you some known History steps as well. It will also act as a good segue into the discussion of Actions that follows this section:

1. Open the image SHRINE.PSD. Ed Scott, a California-based photographer and digital artist, took this image in China. Figure 1.30 shows the original.
2. In the Actions palette menu, select Load Actions and choose the Chapter1.ATN Action from the book's CD-ROM.
3. Play the Action "Lit Woodcut" in the Chapter1 folder. The Action performs one of our favorite Photoshop tricks. It makes a photograph look like a woodcut. Figure 1.31 shows the Lit Woodcut Action. Figure 1.32 shows the History palette that is produced when you play the Action.

Notice that the fifth Action statement, Select Background, has no matching History step. Selecting the Background layer (or any layer) causes no change in your image. You can click on a layer to your heart's content without losing any data. Therefore, it's a "free" command as far as the History palette is concerned. Figure 1.33 shows the image after the Action is finished.

Here's what the Action does: It duplicates the Background layer of your image and changes the newly added layer to Multiply mode. It then applies the High Pass filter at a setting of 1.6. High Pass removes the contrast from the image and allows the Threshold command (which is used next) to find more detail. Because the Blend mode was changed to Multiply, the white space introduced by the Threshold command drops out and the black lines that remain form a woodcut on the layer below. The Action then selects the Background layer and blurs using the Dust & Scratches filter at a much too high setting for normal use. However, this high setting keeps much stronger colors than would the Gaussian Blur filter.

Figure 1.30 Image of a shrine in China photographed by Ed Scott.

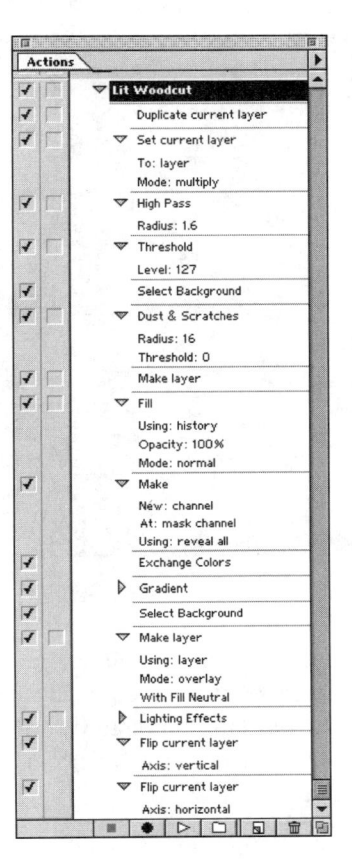

Figure 1.31 The Lit Woodcut Action.

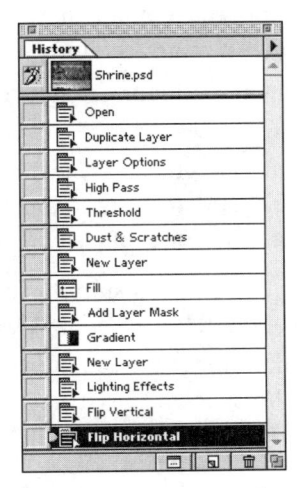

Figure 1.32 The History palette shows the steps that can be saved.

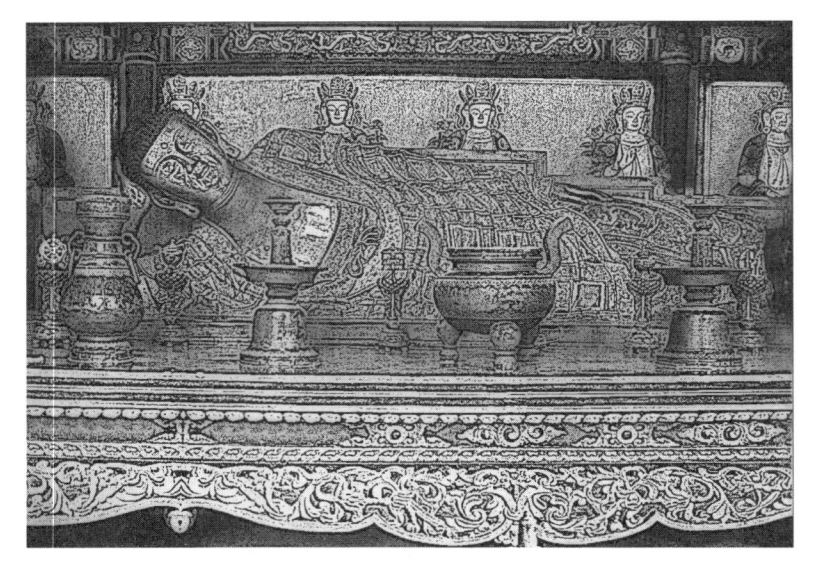

Figure 1.33 After the Lit Woodcut Action has finished.

After the Dust & Scratches filter, the Action makes a new layer above the Background layer and fills it from the History palette with the *original* image. It then creates a layer mask and adds a Gradient that shows more of the original image toward the bottom of the document than it does at the top (by applying the Gradient in the layer mask, the light areas reveal what is on the layer and the dark areas hide it).

One of the interesting things, then, that you can do with the History palette is use it to fill another layer. Instead of dragging the Background layer to copy it as many steps in this book suggest, you can fill from History with the original Background layer. You can fill with any step in the History palette, but keep these caveats in mind:

- The History brush icon must be next to the History state or the snapshot with which you want to fill the layer.
- The state or snapshot must be flat—either a state in which the file only contained the Background layer, the initial image snapshot (assuming that you opened an image with no layers), a Composite snapshot, or a snapshot of a single layer.

If you have the History brush symbol next to a snapshot or a history state that is layered, you can only Fill from History to the original layer. Follow these steps to see what we mean:

1. Click on the left-hand column in the History palette next to the first state (which says "Open") to move the History brush icon. The History brush icon denotes the state to be used either by the History brush (a new tool in the Toolbox) or with the Fill from History command.
2. Select the top layer in the image (Background copy). Make a new layer (click on the New Layer icon at the bottom of the Layers palette).

3. Select the History brush from the Toolbox (Y—either because it's the last letter in the word "History" or for "why not"). Press the Enter/Return key and change the Mode to Saturation. Leave the brush opacity at 100%. Choose a medium brush—the last brush in the second row of the default brushes works nicely for this.

4. Paint over the faces of the six small statues in the background. Change the Blend mode to Normal and paint over the face of the main statue in the image. Choose the Fade command under the Filter menu and set the opacity to 78%.

5. Click on the Dust & Scratches step in the History palette. The image reverts back to that point in the image's history.

6. Press the modifier key (Mac: Option, Windows: Alt) and click on the New Snapshot icon at the bottom of the History palette (it's the center icon and looks like the New Layer or New Channel icon). Figure 1.34 shows the dialog box that appears.

7. Select the Merged Layers option. Click on the first column next to the new snapshot to place the History brush icon.

8. Add a new Layer to the document at the top of the layer stack. Fill with the snapshot (Shift+Delete; From History, 100% opacity, Normal).

9. Change the layer Blend mode to Overlay.

10. Make Layer 1 the active layer. Press the modifier key (Mac: Option, Windows: Alt) and click on the New Layer icon at the bottom of the Layers palette. When the dialog box appears, select Overlay mode and check the box marked Fill with Overlay—Neutral Color 50% gray.

11. Choose Filter|Render|Lighting and change the light style to Omni. Leave the other settings alone. Drag the light into the center of the image and press OK. You will notice a slight highlight near where the light was placed.

12. Use the Move tool to drag the layer around until the light shows up in the center of the double-handled urn (second from the right).

13. Choose the Elliptical Marquee tool (press Shift+M until the Elliptical Marquee appears, which might take several key presses). Press the modifier keys (Mac: Shift+Option, Windows: Shift+Alt) and drag a perfect circle from the center of the urn so that it covers the urn completely. Choose Select|Feather, 15, and click on the Layer Mask icon at the bottom of the Layers palette. This cuts the light off so that you don't see any hard edges.

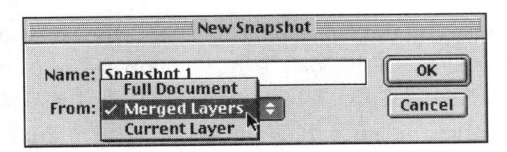

Figure 1.34 The Snapshot options dialog box.

14. Create a new snapshot as you did in Step 6, but choose Current Layer as the basis for the snapshot (the gray lighting layer, Layer 5, is still active). Move the History brush icon next to this snapshot.

15. Click on the top layer to make it active. Make a new layer (click on the New Layer icon at the bottom of the Layers palette). Press Shift+Delete and Fill with History. Change the Blend mode to Overlay. Now you need to re-create the layer mask.

16. Let the top layer remain active. Drag the thumbnail for Layer 5 to the Layer Mask icon at the bottom of the Layers palette. This step duplicates the layer mask in Layer 5 into the layer mask of Layer 6.

17. Use the Move tool to move the light wherever you want it to go. This is a wonderful trick that acts like a movable spotlight.

This has been a tour through many of the features of the History palette. You can also create a new document from any stage in the History palette. Either select the New Document option in the History palette menu or click on the leftmost icon at the bottom of the History palette (the one with the three dots in it).

Using Actions

In Photoshop 4, Adobe replaced the Commands palette with an Actions palette. While this was not a universally beloved change (the Commands palette allowed for quick access to frequently executed commands in a way that occupied much less screen real estate), the Actions facility adds a much-needed scripting environment to Photoshop and can be a real productivity assist. In Photoshop 5, the capability of Actions has been enhanced.

Actions allow you to save a series of steps and execute them again by clicking on the location where the steps are stored, as you saw in the exercise above. This is very useful if you perform repetitive sequences of commands in Photoshop (for production or for special effects). If, for example, you scan a roll of film into the computer and discover that you need to add the same Curves correction to each image, you can create an Action that applies the Curves setting, resizes the image to a specific size and resolution, and changes the image to CMYK. You can then drag all of the images for that roll of film into one folder and run your saved Action on all of the images at one time (using the Batch command under Automate in the File menu). Many of the grayscale images in this book were prepared in batch mode using an Action to change the original color images into grayscale images by changing the RGB mode to LAB color and then removing channels a and b, and finally, setting the color space to Grayscale.

Take a look at the Actions palette. Figure 1.35 shows the Actions palette with the default Actions and the Actions palette menu visible. As you can see, you can do all of the "usual" things to an Action—make a New Action, Save an Action, Delete an Action, and so forth. You can also Duplicate an Action, and, of course, Play an Action. The menu items are very straightforward and selecting them does exactly what you would expect (for example, Replace Actions takes the current Actions in your palette, deletes them, and loads another set of Actions).

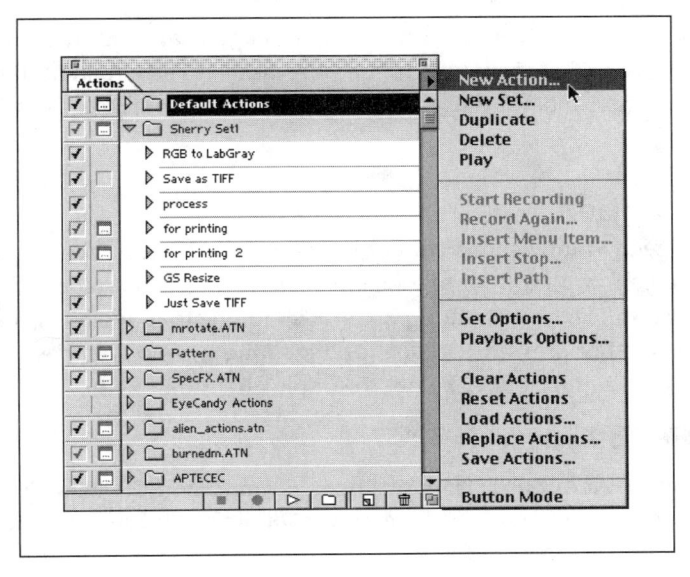

Figure 1.35 Actions palette and menu.

However, this tells only part of the story. We have two other tales to tell: what Actions *can't* do, and what Actions *can* do that you probably didn't think about.

Limitations Of Actions

To create an Action, you choose New Action and then simply perform the task that you want to record. The Actions palette "watches" what you do and writes a script that allows you to repeat that sequence of commands any time you want. If this sounds too good to be true, it is. Although you can record many more things in this version of Photoshop, you still cannot record the actions of the painting tools.

You can record most—but not all—of the commands found on the main menu and its submenus. On the File menu, for example, you cannot record options for the Page Setup dialog box. You can record all of the activities that you perform on the Layers and Channels palettes, including Opacity and Blend mode changes.

You can record the specific settings of all of Photoshop's built-in filters (including the Lighting Effects filter, which was just too complex for version 4—as you discovered previously). Many of the third-party filters, however, are still not recordable. If a filter is not recordable, the finished Action will show that a specific third-party filter was used, but not the settings for the filter. All filters need to be updated to at least the 4 standards for them to be recordable. Kai's Power Tools, if you have the KPT Actions pack, and Alien Skin Eye Candy are fully recordable.

The Paint tools in the Toolbox are not recordable. You cannot capture brush strokes. This means that you can't use the Actions palette to design a low-resolution version of your image and play it back at higher resolution to save time (as you can in Painter, for example) if you want to paint during the Action. However, you can record image transformations and movement of layers with the Move tool. A new unit of measure named Percent should let you record sequences that do not use the painting tools and then play them back from low resolution to high resolution.

Recording An Action

Now that you've read what Actions cannot do, you should know what they can do. In this exercise, we will create two fairly simple Actions, just to give you an idea of how this is done. The two Actions we will create are changing an RGB image to grayscale using Lab mode (this usually produces a better grayscale image) and creating a simple emboss without using the Emboss filter (which will turn out to be not so simple after all).

Converting RGB To Grayscale

1. Open the image PALACE.PSD from this book's companion CD-ROM. This is another one of Ed Scott's China images. Choose Image|Duplicate and click on OK. You will use this duplicate image to record the Action.

2. Click on the New Action icon at the bottom of the Actions palette (it looks just like the icons for New Layer, New Channel, and so on). Figure 1.36 shows the resulting dialog box. Name the Action RGB to Gray.

3. Select Image|Mode|Lab. The Actions palette records "Convert Mode".

4. Click on the Channels tab to view the Channels palette (this step is not recorded, but it doesn't need to be). Click on the Lightness channel so that it is the only selected channel. Figure 1.37 shows the Channels palette.

5. Finally, choose Image|Mode|Grayscale to convert the image into a Grayscale image. When asked, click on OK to remove hidden channels.

6. Click on the Stop button to the left of the Record button in the Actions palette. Figure 1.38 shows the completed Action expanded so that you can see exactly what was recorded.

7. Close the image that you used for the Action without saving it. In the History palette, click on the Duplicate step to bring the image back to its original form.

8. Click on the Play button on the Actions palette (it's the right-most button in the left group of buttons and looks like a right-pointing unfilled triangle). This tests your Action to make sure that it does what you *want* it to do (as well as what you *told* it to do—a common problem with any kind of programming).

This Action is typical of the type of Action that you would want to record so that you could batch-process a group of files at one time. The Action that you just created doesn't save your file. Therefore, if you were to batch a folder full of RGB images to convert, you have to think about what you want done to the file after it has been converted. We will discuss several different possibilities.

Figure 1.36 New Action dialog box.

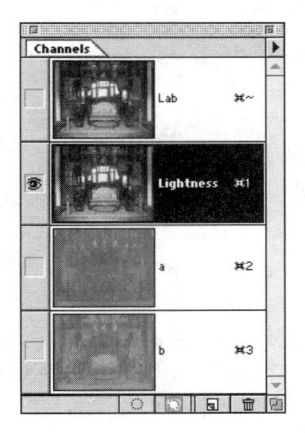

Figure 1.37 Channels palette in Lab mode.

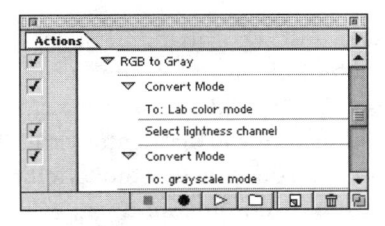

Figure 1.38 Completed Action showing all recorded commands.

Figure 1.39 shows the dialog box that results from selecting the File|Automate|Batch option. You can see that this box allows you to select your input method, the Action to run, and the output destination.

For input, you can select Folder or Import. Folder produces the standard File Open dialog box and allows you to select the folder or subdirectory that you want to process. The command can be recursive—you may have it open folders nested within the selected folder. The Import option allows you to process successive input from QuickEdit, a TWAIN source, or your attached scanner.

You have three output options: When the Action is finished, you can do nothing, Save and Close, or write the changed file to a specified folder. If you select Nothing as the option, the batch process ignores the file once the Action is completed. In the Action that you just created,

56 Chapter 1

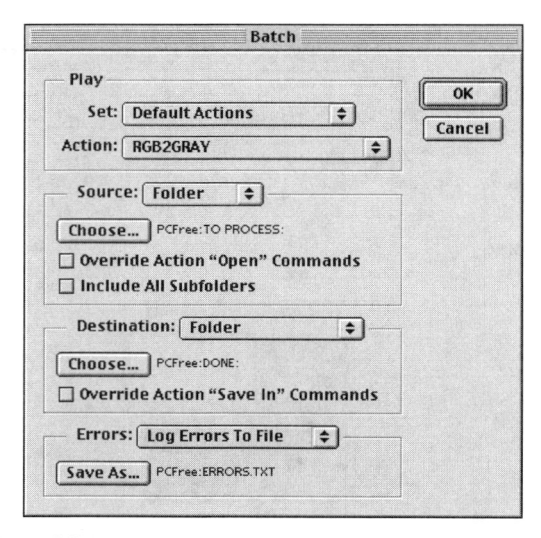

Figure 1.39 To process a folder of files at one time, select File|Automate|Batch.

this would leave all of the files open in Photoshop—which could lead you to run out of RAM if too many files are open, and then, you would still have to save the files if you wanted to keep the results (and if you didn't want to keep the results, why bother batching the files in the first place?). "Nothing" is a good option only when you have built into your Action the total number of steps needed to fully complete and save the file.

The Save and Close option does just what its name suggests. It saves the changes that the Action has made onto the original file in its original location. By doing so, it updates your original copy, and then closes it. This sounds like a wonderful option, but think for a moment about its implications. What happens if you accidentally run the wrong Action on it and walk away? Or if the Action does not quite do what you thought it would? You would lose all of your original images. This is a very dangerous option. If you want to use this option, *duplicate the folder and its contents before your run the batch process* and let Photoshop work with the copy.

The third option, Folder, allows you to select the location to which Photoshop will write the completed Action. It gives you a standard File dialog box and allows you to pick a folder or subdirectory. Usually, this is the best option. Create your subdirectory before you invoke the Batch command. Then your changes are written to a new location and your originals are safe. Maybe.

There is one major "gotcha" when you use this scenario. If you are preparing grayscale images for placement in a page layout program, as the Action that you have created seems to indicate, then you might want to change the file type to TIF to make it easier to place the files. The only way to change a file type when a file is saved is to use the Save As command. This writes the file to the location specified in the *Action*—not the location specified by the Folder choice in the Batch command. Unless you really understand what is happening, you will get unintended results:

- If "Save As" is placed in an Action on the Mac with "Never" as the Add file extension option in the Saving Files Preference, and you select the same folder as the original image when you record the Action, then you are likely to select Replace as the Save As option. When this happens, your batch will replace all of your original files with the grayscale ones and write the file again to the specified Folder location. This leaves you with two grayscale versions and no RGB originals.
- If you are working on the PC or if the Mac is set to append a file extension, you will not be writing over your original file. However, you will end up leaving a copy in the location specified in the Action and another copy in the batch folder. Now you have three versions—two grayscales and an RGB.

So what's the solution? You have two, equally valid. You can rerecord your Action and specify the new "Save As" folder for your grayscale files before you run each new batch. If you want to use this option, then add a Close command into the original Action as well. Choose Nothing as your option for the destination.

You can check the box that says Override Actions Save In Command. This then places the Save As file in the folder that you specify in the Batch command. Either way works.

Because there is real potential for damage, you must test any Action on a noncritical file. Remember, you are really writing a small computer program when you create an Action, and like any other computer program, it can have bugs (unfortunately). An ounce of prevention....

Sometimes, you might want to change an Action after it has been recorded. That is very easy to do. Follow along and give it a try.

Editing An Action

1. Open the image file PALACE.PSD on the accompanying CD-ROM. Choose Image| Duplicate|OK to make a copy.
2. Click on the twirly arrow next to the RGB to Gray Action to expand it (if it's closed). Then click to select the last step that says Convert Mode, as shown in Figure 1.40.
3. Click on the Record button of the Actions palette. You can add commands from the bottom of the list now.
4. Choose Image|Image Size. Make sure that Resample Image is not checked, and then change the image Resolution to 300 ppi.

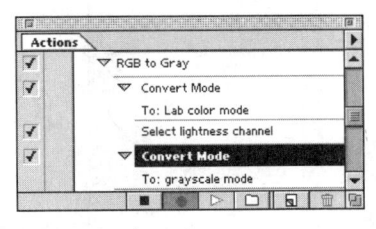

Figure 1.40 Expanded Action with last step selected.

5. Select File|Save As and choose TIF as the file type. If you are using the Mac, select a different directory so you don't have to replace the original or turn on the File Extension option in the Preferences. Otherwise, you can save the TIF file to any location you want (including the current directory). Figure 1.41 shows the two new steps that you have recorded.

6. Click on the Stop button.

7. Now you need to test the Action. Make another duplicate of the original image (Image|Duplicate|OK). You cannot use the History palette to revert now because your Save As command created a new file in the History palette. Place your cursor on the RGB to Gray Action and press the Play button. Everything should work properly. Close the image that you just converted to grayscale.

8. Examine Figure 1.41 very carefully. You should be able to see what looks like three little dots placed next to the Action title and next to the Image Size command in the second column. Click on the second column next to the Image Size command in the RGB to Gray Action on your Actions palette. You have just inserted a break point at that command. A break point allows you to stop the Action at a dialog box so that you can respond to the dialog and make changes to the way that the Action works. Figure 1.42 shows the Actions palette with the break point inserted.

9. Make another duplicate of the original file. Play the RGB to Gray Action again. This time, you actually have the opportunity to respond to the Image Size dialog box, and you can change the dimensions of the file as you resize. Click on the Resample image box and change the image size to 1,000 pixels wide.

10. You can also change the order in which commands are performed. If, for some reason, you wanted the image resizing done first, all you need to do is place the cursor on that command. It turns into a hand. Press the mouse and drag the command entry up until it is under the RGB to Gray title. Figure 1.43 shows the new order of the commands.

If you ever want to run the RGB to Gray Action in batches, you can remove the break point and set the Batch command to override the Save option in the Action.

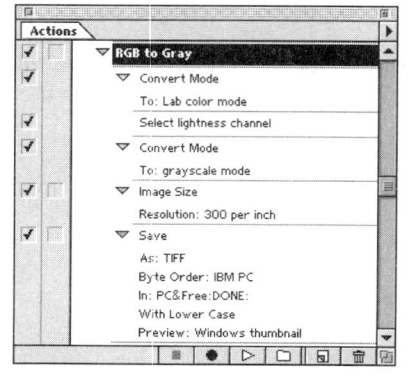

Figure 1.41 Additional steps added to the RGB to Gray Action.

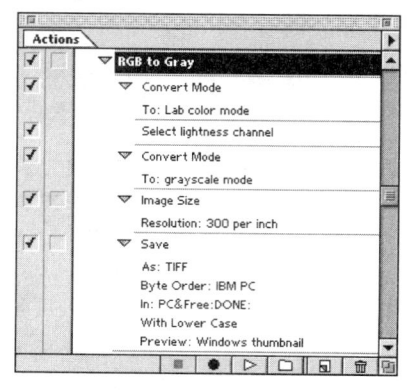

Figure 1.42 Inserting a Break Point into an Action.

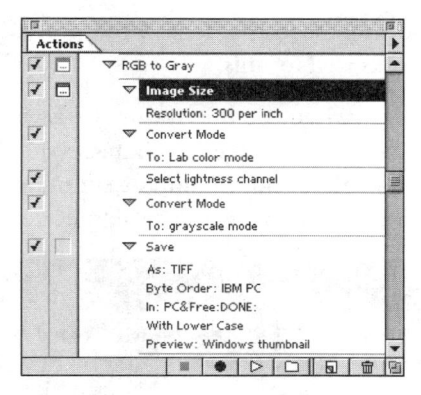

Figure 1.43 New order for RGB to Gray Action.

The Action that you just recorded should work beautifully in Photoshop 5. It wouldn't have been as easy in Photoshop 4. If, for some reason, you are still using Photoshop 4, you should be aware that it wasn't capable of recording the fact that the image resize to 300 ppi should occur with the Resample flag off. If you run this Action in Photoshop 4 with the Resample flag on, you will end up with a huge file.

Getting Complex

You can create very complex steps with Actions. In the Action you created while learning about the History palette, you used a number of complex features that were not possible in Photoshop 4. Photoshop 4 couldn't record either the Gradient tool or the Lighting Effects filter; Photoshop 5 can record both. For both of these processes, the Actions palette records an extensive group of settings.

In the first edition of this book (for Photoshop 4), we included an Action for an embossing technique by Kai Krause. Here are the steps to perform the embossing trick if you weren't scripting it:

1. Open the image to be embossed.
2. Drag the icon for the Background layer to the New Layer icon.
3. Invert the image (Mac: Command+I, Windows: Ctrl+I).
4. Press 5 to change the Layer Opacity to 50%. (If it doesn't work, select the Marquee tool and try again.) The image turns solid gray. Why? Because every pixel on the top layer is the inverse of the pixel on the bottom, and when you add the two values together and divide by 2 (which is what happens at 50% Opacity), you always get 128—which is middle gray.
5. Press the modifier key (Mac: Command, Windows: Ctrl) and, while holding the key, press the Left arrow key twice and the Down arrow key twice.

Under Photoshop 4, this thing was an absolute nightmare to script. In Photoshop 5, all of the keys in the instructions above work and cause the activity to be recorded. You can create an

Action for this simply by following the instructions. If you want to try it, the image TABLE1.PSD, on the enclosed CD-ROM, works well for this.

There will still be times, however, when you might want to use features that cannot be scripted. The next Action for you to record is a special effect that uses the Clouds filter to create a repeating pattern. In this Action, you will see how to handle situations where the user must perform some activities that cannot be scripted, or even referred to, in the Actions list.

> **TIP**
>
> You can refer to any command found in the menus, even if you cannot script its options, by choosing the Insert Menu Item command on the Actions palette menu. This lets you insert a reference to the command so that when the Action is played, the command is chosen for the user to select the desired options. You can add the Apply Image command or the File Info command to your Actions in this manner, but it means that you cannot run a batch Action and simply walk away from the computer—user interaction is always required.

Repeating Clouds Pattern

This Action creates a new document, runs the Clouds and Difference Clouds filter on it, Posterizes, Blurs, finds a Threshold, Offsets the image, and then lets you edit the image using the Pencil tool. It then reduces the image to a "reasonable" pattern tile size and blurs it, selects the image, and defines it as a pattern. The Action continues by creating a new document and allowing you to select a Background color. It fills the Background layer with the new color and creates a new layer that is set to Hard Light mode. It then fills the top layer with the previously defined pattern, and embosses and blurs it. That is quite a lot to happen almost automatically.

1. Click on the New Action icon on the Actions palette and name the Action "Cloud Repeat." Just follow the steps and let the Action record them.
2. Create a new document (Mac: Command+N, Windows: Ctrl+N), 400×400 pixels.
3. Press D to set the colors back to the default of black and white.
4. Select Filter|Render|Clouds. Figure 1.44 shows the image at this point.
5. Select Filter|Render|Difference Clouds. The Difference Clouds filter begins to build up complexity in the clouds structure. It is the basis for a number of wonderful special effects that don't belong in this book or in this chapter. However, the more times you apply this filter (within reason), the more interesting the structure is when you posterize it later or use the Find Edges filter on it. Figure 1.45 shows the clouds image with Difference Clouds applied once.
6. Select Filter|Clouds|Difference Clouds five more times (you will apply it a total of six times). Figure 1.46 shows the image after the Difference Clouds filter has been applied the sixth time.
7. Choose Image|Adjust|Posterize and select 4 levels in the dialog box. This begins to give you islands, as shown in Figure 1.47.
8. Choose Filter|Blur|Gaussian Blur; Radius 6.6.

Figure 1.44 Image filled with Clouds filter.

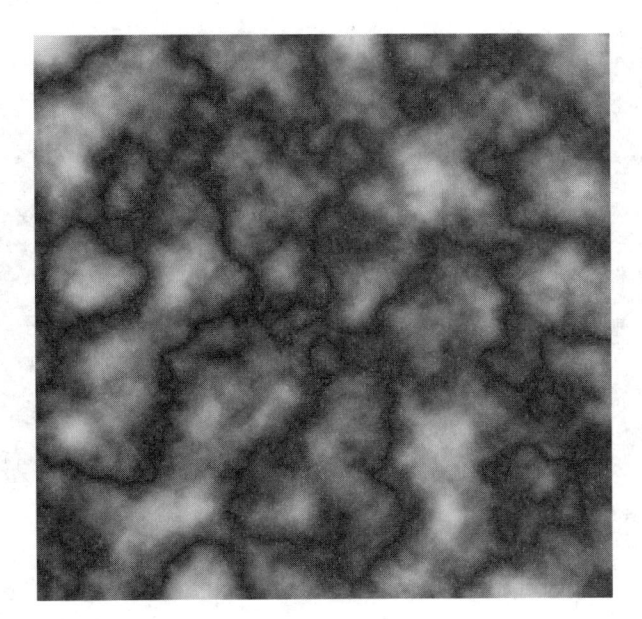

Figure 1.45 Difference Clouds filter applied once.

9. Select Image|Adjust|Threshold and select a Threshold of 84. Figure 1.48 shows the pattern-to-be at this point.
10. Select Filter|Other|Offset; 200 pixels right, 200 pixels down, Wrap around. This divides the image in half so you can see what the pattern seams will do. There will always be hard lines, as shown in Figure 1.49.

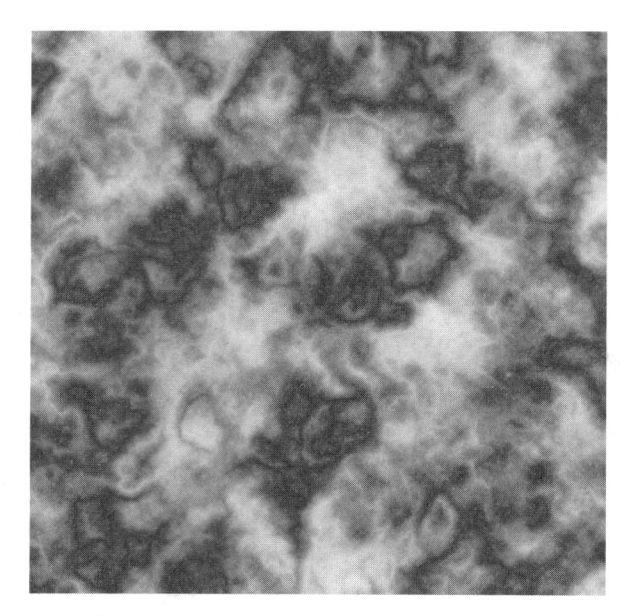

Figure 1.46 Difference Clouds filter applied six times.

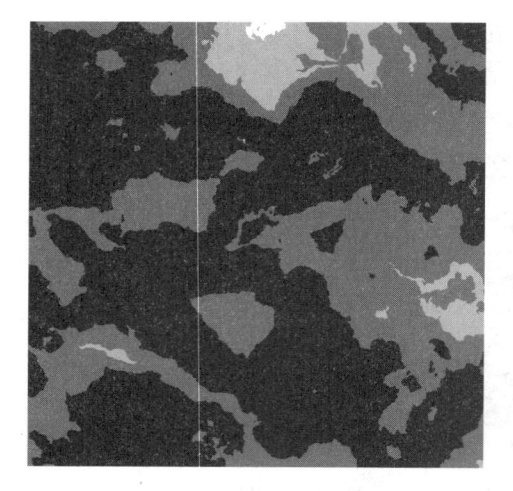

Figure 1.47 Difference Clouds posterized.

Figure 1.48 Image with Threshold command applied.

11. The next step is for the user to use the Pencil tool to color away the hard edges by adding black or white as desired to soften the edges along the seam line. This is the point at which the script gets very interesting. There is no way to create a script that shows the results of using the Paintbrush, and even if there were, the strokes need to be different for each image. So, how to do this? Try the following:

Choose Insert Stop from the Actions palette and enter the message shown in Figure 1.50. This will stop the Action from playing but will not reset the "play from" to the top of the Action. It allows the Action to be continued from the next instruction in the

Figure 1.49 Image offset by half in each direction.

list. You can click on the "Allow Continue" box if you feel that a hard-edged pattern is acceptable or should at least be an option. That box is very good for optional steps, because it allows users to click on Continue to ignore whatever action they were supposed to take. Do not place a Continue option into an Action unless you don't care if users follow the steps that they're supposed to do.

When the script is played, the message will be shown and the Action will stop. To finish performing the Action, the user needs to click on the Play button again. Figure 1.51 shows the result of making the tile seamless.

12. Choose Image|Image Size and set Resample Image on, Constrain Proportions On, and set the new dimensions to 100×100 pixels. This is a fairly common size for a repeat pattern. At 300 ppi, each repeat is one-third of an inch, which is large enough to see.

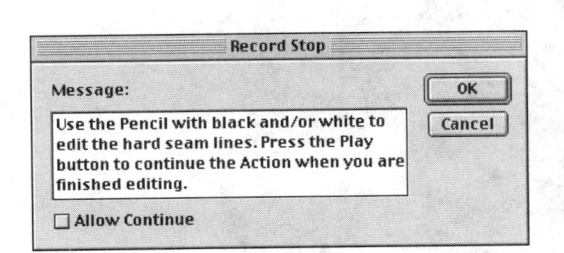

Figure 1.50 Enter this message to tell the user to stop the Action from playing.

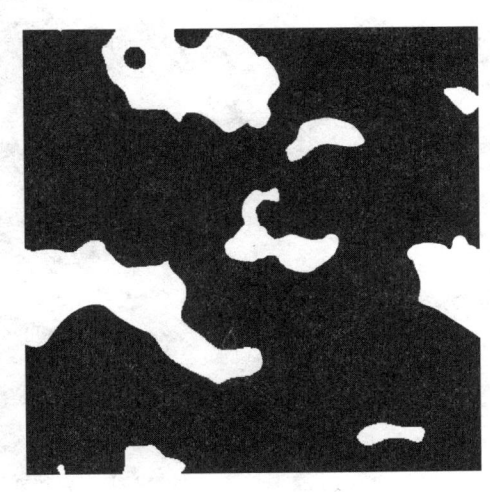

Figure 1.51 The seamless tile.

13. Select the entire image (Mac: Command+A, Windows: Ctrl+A). Define this as a pattern (Edit|Define Pattern).
14. You now need to create a new image for the pattern. Select File|New and create an image 1,000×1,000 pixels square.
15. You need to have the user pick a new color for the background of the image (the main color for the repeat pattern). Choose Insert Stop from the Action palette menu and enter the message "Pick a new Foreground color and click on Play to resume the Action". Do not allow Continue.
16. Fill the area (Mac: Option+Delete, Windows: Alt+Backspace).
17. Make a new layer (press the Option key for the Mac or the Alt key on Windows and click on the New Layer icon at the bottom of the Layers palette). In the dialog box that appears, set the Opacity to 100% and the Mode to Hard Light.
18. Fill the new layer with the pattern (Shift+Delete|Pattern, 100% Opacity, Normal).
19. Choose Filter|Stylize|Emboss (Angle: 129°, Height: 3 pixels, Amount: 100).
20. Select Filter|Blur|Gaussian Blur; Radius 2.5. Figure 1.52 shows the final pattern.
21. Click on the Stop button on the Actions palette. Believe it or not, you are actually finished creating the Action.
22. Close all of your open documents and play the Action to make sure it works correctly. Figure 1.53 shows the expanded steps in the Action.

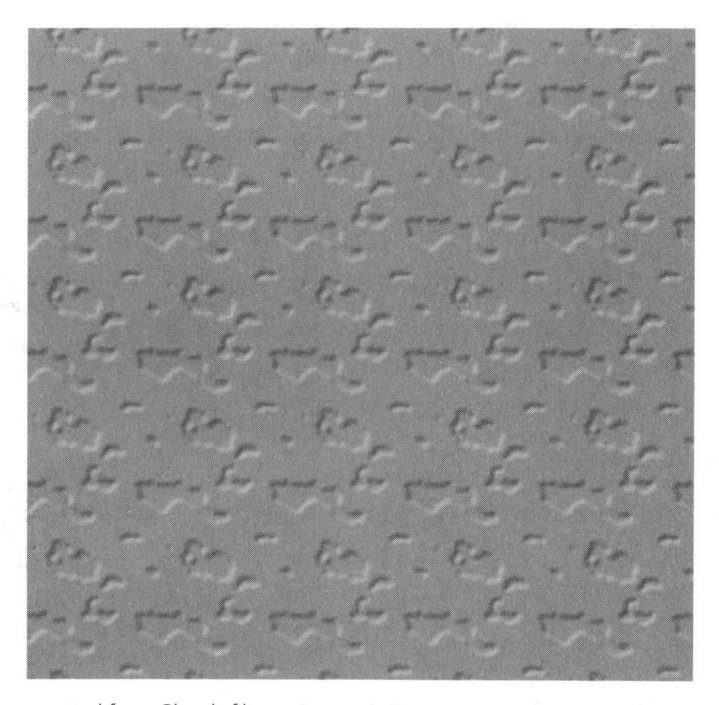

Figure 1.52 Pattern created from Clouds filter using an Action.

OPTIMIZING PHOTOSHOP 65

Clouds Repeat

- Make
  - New: document
  - Mode: RGB color mode
  - Width: 5.555 inches
  - Height: 5.555 inches
  - Resolution: 72.001 per inch
  - Fill: white
- Reset
  - colors
- Clouds
- Difference Clouds
- Difference Clouds
- Difference Clouds
- Difference Clouds
- Difference Clouds
- Difference Clouds
- Posterize
  - Levels: 4
- Gaussian Blur
  - Radius: 6.6
- Threshold
  - Level: 84
- Offset
  - Horizontal: 200
  - Vertical: 200
  - Fill: wrap
- Stop
  - Message: "Use the Pencil with black and/or white to edit the hard seam lines. Press the Play button to continue the Action when you are finished editing."

- Image Size
  - Width: 100 pixels
  - With Constrain Proportions
  - Interpolation: bicubic
- Set
  - selection
  - To: pixel all
- Define Pattern
- Make
  - New: document
  - Mode: RGB color mode
  - Width: 13.889 inches
  - Height: 13.889 inches
  - Resolution: 72.001 per inch
  - Fill: white
- Stop
  - Message: "Select a Foreground Color and click on Play to resume the Action."
- Fill
  - Using: foreground color
  - Opacity: 100%
  - Mode: normal
- Make
  - New: layer
  - Mode: hard light

- Fill
  - Using: pattern
  - Opacity: 100%
  - Mode: normal
- Emboss
  - Angle: 129
  - Height: 3
  - Amount: 100
- Gaussian Blur
  - Radius: 2.5

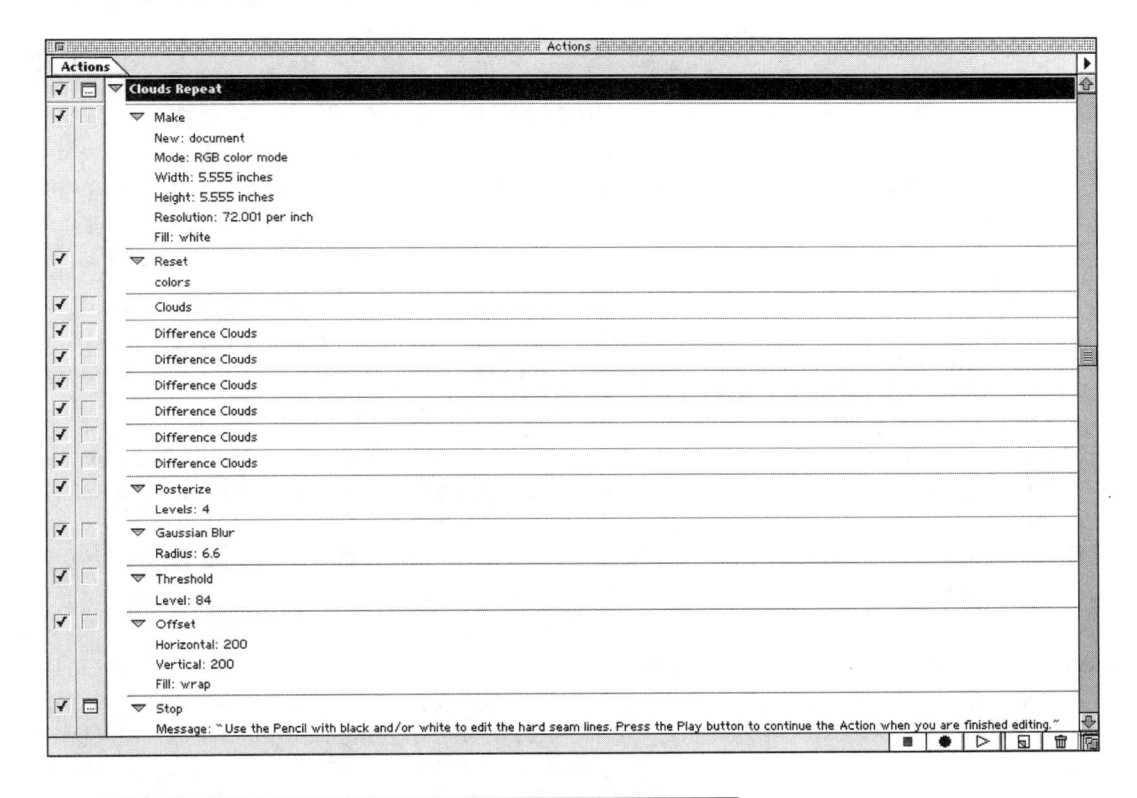

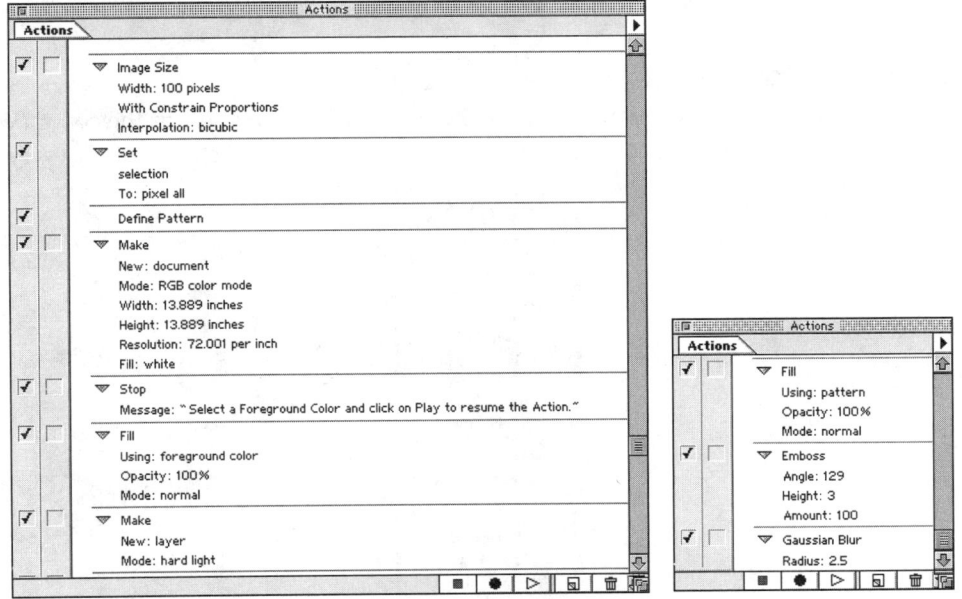

Figure 1.53 Steps in Clouds Repeat Action.

Should you decide that you want to change any of the steps in the Action, double-clicking on them will allow you to edit the Action step (if they have an attached dialog box). This is the same as selecting the Action step and choosing Record Again from the menu. If you use the menu, you must be careful that you are only re-recording that one step (which should be the default if you click to select the step first). For example, if you want to change the command that creates the 1,000-pixel-square image so that it creates an image of a different size, first click on the statement and then look at the menu as shown in Figure 1.54.

It's interesting to see what other options are also available. You can duplicate the single statement within the Action, delete it (of course), play only that step, or play the rest of Action starting with that step. In addition, you can also add additional steps after Make by selecting Start Recording, or you can insert a Stop or a Menu Item.

The ability to edit and fine-tune your Action after it has been recorded is one of the less obvious abilities of the Actions subsystem. However, it is a very powerful one. Another not-quite-obvious feature is that the checkmarks next to each step can be turned on or off. When the command is not checked, it is not executed—which gives you a very easy way to run an Action that is almost what you want, or to run part of an Action.

Saving And Recalling Actions

Actions can be saved and loaded. They are automatically saved in the Adobe Photoshop Settings folder unless you specifically save an Actions folder to another location (which you ought to do whenever you create Actions that you do not want to lose). When you click on an Action folder to save it, you save every Action stored within that folder.

Commands Palette R.I.P.

One of the more agonizing yelps heard when Photoshop 4 first shipped was the cry of "Where did the Commands palette go?" Many users really miss it, although Actions will do everything

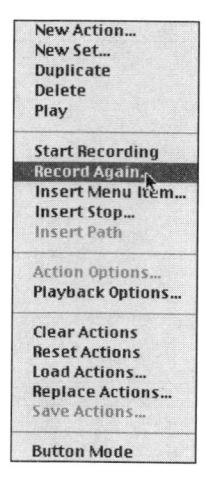

Figure 1.54 Editing options for recorded Action.

that the Commands palette did and more. If you want one-click access to certain commands, you can record those commands as Insert Menu Item commands.

You can change the Actions palette into Buttons if you want. This gives you the ability to play an Action simply by clicking on it. If you really miss the old Photoshop 3 Command palette for simple things like one-click access to Image Size, Convert to Grayscale, Define Pattern, and so forth, consider purchasing Extensis PhotoTools. Figure 1.55 shows the button bar that one of the authors created to replace the Commands palette. From left to right, the icons provide access to the following commands:

- File Info
- Page Setup
- Convert to Grayscale
- Image Size
- Save As
- Save
- Save a Copy
- Canvas Size
- Duplicate
- Define Pattern
- Select Similar (useful because its key command vanished in version 4)
- Apply Image
- Levels
- AutoLevels
- Threshold
- Select|Inverse
- Feather
- Multi-channel
- Gaussian Blur
- Add Noise
- High Pass
- Unsharp Mask
- Offset
- Find Edges
- Emboss
- Layer Mask with Hide All
- Merge Visible
- Color Table
- Flip Horizontal
- Flip Vertical
- Layer|Transform menu (pops down all of the options on that menu)
- Crop
- Flatten

As you can see, a button bar that takes a minimum of space at the top of the screen can add a wealth of access. It's a waste of the features of the Actions palette to try to make it duplicate single one-click commands. PhotoTools is a wonderful filter set with many more filters in it, and the button bar is only a small part of it (even though the set would be worth the price for many users even if the only thing the set did was to create the button bar).

Figure 1.55 Extensis PhotoTools button bar.

> **TIP**
>
> Have you ever produced a very complex image and then tried to re-create it? And you cannot remember what you did to produce those particular results? It has happened to us many times. Turn on Actions and then "play" it. Even if you don't get a fully usable Action from it, you should be able to reconstruct your steps when you are done.

Moving On

This chapter covered a lot of ground. We have discussed many ways to optimize your Photoshop system and to configure it. We've also looked at many ways to troubleshoot the most common problems. You learned the Preferences settings that the authors consider to be the best for professional Photoshop users. Finally, you learned—possibly more than you ever wanted to know—about Actions. Do master the Actions feature. It can prove very useful!

In the next chapter, you learn about acquiring images. You also learn how to make good scans, what to do if you are scanning a previously screened image, and how to work with PhotoCD.

ACQUIRING IMAGES

Before you can apply Photoshop's vast editing powers, you need an image. You can use a scanner or Kodak's Photo CD as a source for your image work.

To help you get the most from your scanner, this chapter will take an extensive look at how you can get the best possible scan from your equipment. You'll also learn about what you can do to make a Photo CD image look as good as it can.

A cartoon from a 10-year-old digital-graphics publication has proved to be prescient. Picture a prepress technician, his computer loaded into a child's toy wagon trailing a long extension cord, holding up his flatbed scanner to record an outdoor scene. The caption reads, "The trick is to hold it steady for four minutes."

Hand-held miniature scanners in the form of digital cameras are now commonplace. However, the technology of the digital camera has not progressed very far past that shown in the cartoon. Digital cameras exhibit a number of deficiencies:

- They share the problem detailed by the cartoon: exposure times, when compared to traditional cameras, are lengthy.
- Because of the way the sensing mechanism must operate, the more inexpensive models can capture only a small number of pixels. The captured image is suitable only for publication on the Web, or as an offset reproduction at a small size.
- Though they range in price from a few hundred dollars to many thousands of dollars, only the most expensive units capture data with a sufficient number of pixels to make them widely flexible in size prepress work. A scanner with a transparency attachment remains the most cost-effective method for capturing images of all sizes.

Digital cameras are one of the principal *digitizing* (converting images to digital form) devices in widespread use. The most widely used device is the scanner. Although it suffers some limitations, a scanner is still the most easily configured and easily used device. It also produces the highest-quality results.

Scanners are manufactured in two flavors: *charged-coupled device* (CCD) and *drum*. The differences between the two types lie mainly in the sensing mechanisms. Flatbed scanners use CCD sensors, whereas drum scanners rely on photomultiplier vacuum tubes. CCDs include digital cameras and the inexpensive desktop scanners in widespread use. The general scan quality of CCDs is not as high, nor is the optical resolution as great as that achieved by a drum scanner. This difference is reflected in the average prices of the devices. Drum scanners range from about $15,000 on the low end of the scale to as high as $200,000. The equivalent range for CCDs is from under $200 up to

$25,000 (the latter are exceptionally well-engineered transparency scanners used mostly by separation houses). Drum scanners, although used more widely now than in the past, are still marketed for the professional user. Such a user might be a publication house desiring to reduce commercial scanning costs, or a professional scanning house that furnishes high-quality digital files for the prepress world.

Another scanning device, although one that isn't available to the average consumer, is the Photo CD scanner, developed by Kodak. Photo CD scanners are operated as a film-processing service. They place reasonably good-quality scans into the hands of the consumer at a modest per-image cost, for as little as $.65 per image. Photo CD purchasers receive their scans on CD-ROM disks or floppy disks. Each scanned image is saved at six resolutions that can be read from disk and processed with a program such as Photoshop. Typical Photo CD images are scans of 35mm films. A more advanced scanner—called Photo CD Pro—is now available that can scan large-format material. Because of the relatively high cost of individual images, Photo CD Pro has not proven to be as successful as its predecessor. At this time, large-format Photo CD scans are not cost-competitive with commercial service bureau drum scans.

With the advent of high-speed microcomputers, digital images have become increasingly important. This advance in technology has led to an increasingly important role for Adobe Photoshop as the most widely used image-manipulation software. Photoshop now plays a pivotal role in the development of image material for the Web, for the multifaceted world of print reproduction, and for the increasingly important multimedia industry. With Photoshop's growth, scanners are also becoming vital equipment. To help you get the most from a scanner, this chapter gives you a complete understanding of concepts such as pixels and resolution, how to operate a scanner effectively, what to do to repair less-than-perfect images, and how to get the most from Photo CD.

Resolution, Pixels, And Sampling Frequency

The terms *resolution* and *pixel* are difficult—but important—to understand.

Resolution, by itself, is simply a way of assigning an arbitrary two-dimensional value—width and height—to that chimerical beast, the *pixel*. The pixel, believe it or not, has no intrinsic real-world size. It is simply a collection of three or four numbers tied to a location within a raster coordinate system. A pixel begins to have a life of its own only when you assign it a real-world size; it is however big *you* choose to make it.

The pixel receives its initial size at the time photographic material is digitized (scanned), or when other kinds of artwork are brought into Photoshop and converted to raster format. (Note: We discuss rasterizing—the operation of changing a file into the pixel-based image type Photoshop can process—later in this book. Our discussion here deals with the digitizing of information by means of a scanner.) The size of a pixel is part of an instruction to the scanning software that determines at what size an image is to be scanned and at what resolution you want the final file to be. The scanner then reads the object to be scanned at its native *sampling rate* and gives you the number of pixels you need based on its sampling.

The terms *sampling rate* and *sampling frequency* mean exactly what they seem to mean. The scanner aims a light at the scanned object. As the light passes through transparent objects or is reflected from opaque objects, its color is analyzed and stored as a single component of the scan. Every analysis of a single spot on the scanned material is called a *sample*. The number of samples in a given unit is the *sampling frequency*.

Scanners vary in the precision with which they can take samples. Some scanners can analyze the color of the scanned material only 300 times in every inch. Other scanners can analyze the color 6,000 to 10,000 times in every inch! The number of samples a scanner can take from the scanned material is a function of its optical assembly and its sensing hardware. In general, extremely high resolution is possible only with the more expensive scanning equipment. Figure 2.1 shows how the increase of the sampling rate results in ever-greater precision when the image is scanned. The original (a) is in the upper left corner. The sections marked *b-f* show a range of sampling rates from coarse to fine. By studying this figure, it is easy to see why a scanned image loses some of its clarity in the digitizing process: Fitting any contour to a raster grid inevitably makes the contour less smooth.

Every sample—or group of samples—represents a value that eventually becomes a pixel. When your file opens in Photoshop, you see a file that contains the requested physical dimensions and pixel density. It is important to recognize, however, that pixels and the sampling rate are not the same thing.

Your scans need not contain the largest number of pixels your scanner can deliver. Your file's pixel frequency can vary. A scan intended for the Web or for a multimedia presentation, for example, requires a relatively small number of samples such as 72 ppi (72 ppi is a common resolution for a computer monitor). For images that you plan to reproduce on an offset press at 150 line screen, a file of 300 ppi is appropriate.

Interpolated Sampling

The optical precision of the scanner is sometimes augmented by what is called *interpolated* resolution. Interpolated resolution amplifies the scanner's sensing mechanism. It does its job by taking the scanner's individual samples and making an educated guess about what samples the scanner *might have taken* if its sensing system were capable of more precision. In short, the scanner's software invents new values for what it could *not* see based on what it *could* see.

Interpolated samples are sometimes useful, but not universally so. When scanning for line art (see Chapter 9), interpolated samples help to give smooth edges to simple shapes such as display type and logos. When used for other purposes—halftones, duotones, color separations—interpolated samples are not a good idea. Although the scanning software might make extremely sophisticated guesses about the samples it invents, these samples are still nothing more than mathematical fiction. An image containing interpolated samples will always appear to be softened and blurred because its detail has been compromised.

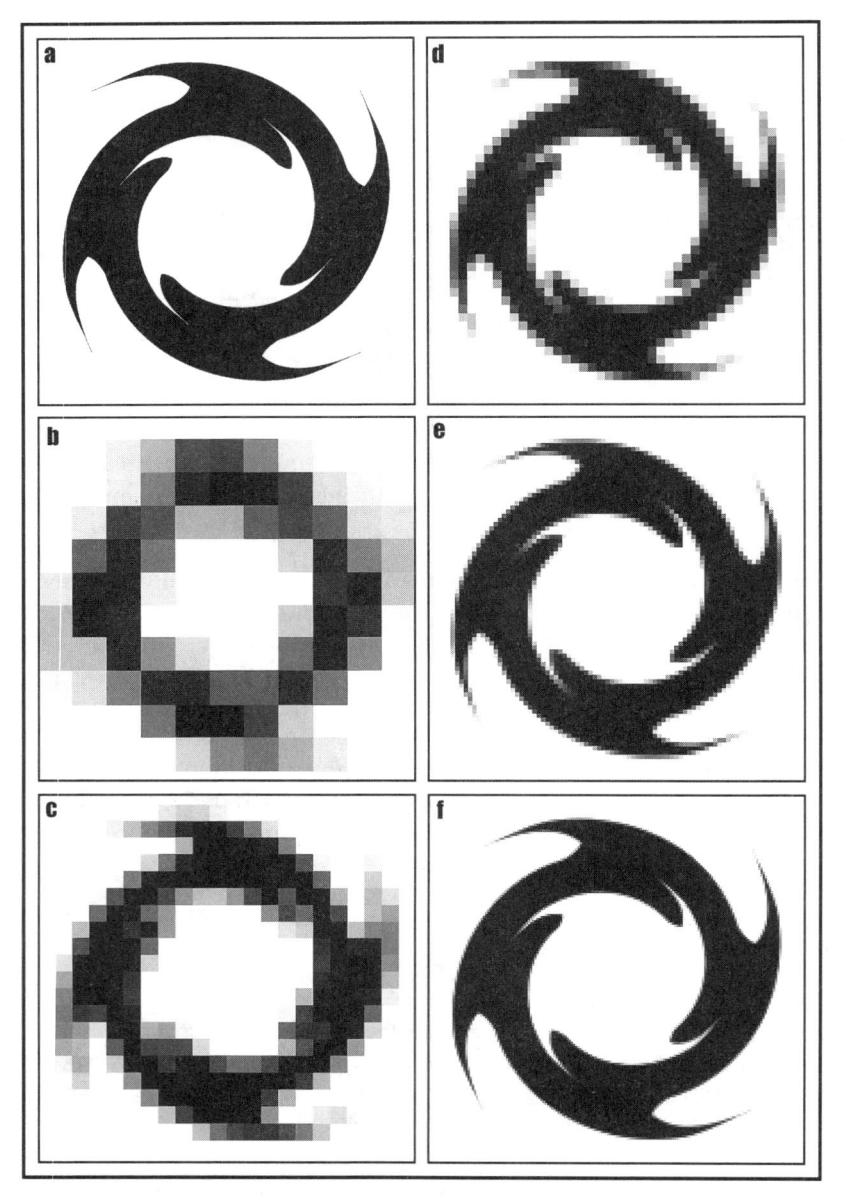

Figure 2.1 Increased sampling rates increase the precision of the scan.

> **TIP**
>
> For offset reproduction, the best results are achieved when the input file's ppi value is twice that of the line screen value.

As we discussed previously, the scanner's software furnishes you with controls that allow you to specify two input values: the pixel frequency you desire, and the physical dimensions of the file. To arrive at the file you desire, your scanner's software is going to do some behind-the-scenes calculations.

Assume for the moment that your scanner has an optical resolution of 600 samples per inch. If you request a scan of 300 ppi at 100 percent of the size of the original material, your scanner will do the scan sampling at 600/inch, its native frequency. It then combines groups of pixels—2 wide and 2 tall, averaging the values—to make one pixel that is 1/300 inches on a side. (Think about it: 2/600×2/600 = 1/300×1/300.)

If you desire to scan so that your file is 200 percent of the size of the original material, the scanner still samples at 600 samples per inch. When you open the file, all of the pixels will be twice the size—1/300 inches—of the sampling frequency. This doubles the linear dimensions of the original material and gives you the 200 percent size.

The idea of pixels changing sizes may be a little confusing. However, as we stated at the beginning of this chapter, the pixel is an abstraction. A pixel can be any size you want, as is illustrated in Figure 2.2. This figure is in six parts, labeled *a* through *f*. The upper part of the figure, *a*, shows a square, which represents a pixel. Because this is a grayscale image, we can describe this pixel's file value as equal to one byte. A group of similar pixels is shown at *b*. This group contains 16 pixels, which makes their combined file value equal to 16 bytes. In *c*, we can stipulate that we want the group of 16 to occupy an area twice as large in each dimension. The arbitrary size of each pixel enlarges, but each pixel remains equal to one byte. The *d* portion of the figure shows how pixels of the original size can be interpolated (see the sidebar, "Interpolated Sampling"). The pixels retain their original size, but new pixels need to be added to cover the area. Notice that the original pixels are outnumbered by the invented pixels by three to one. In *e*, the pixels are made to occupy half the original space. The pixels are smaller, but there are still 16 of them. The file size for this group remains 16 bytes. Finally, in *f*, the pixels of the original group are made to occupy half the area, but retain the original resolution, or pixel size. For this to happen, 75 percent of the pixels need to be discarded, which makes the file size 25 percent of the original. Note that discarding information also requires that pixels be interpolated. The difference between *d* and *f* is this: *d* contains invented values, while *f* contains only original information. Although *f* contains less information, what it does contain is accurate.

> **TIP**
>
> This whole system of scanning to size and causing the pixels to accommodate themselves seems wonderfully flexible. However, some limitations involve the sampling frequency of the scanner. Imagine that your scanner is capable of a sampling frequency of 600/inch. Now suppose that you want to scan so that your final file is 300 percent of the original material's size, and that the resolution needs to be 300 ppi. If you recall that the scanner can only sample 600 places in the linear inch, you'll see that this would deliver a maximum enlargement of only 200 percent at 300 ppi. Unless you want the scanning software to make use of interpolation, this scanner's sampling rate can deliver a 300 percent size only if the pixel density is changed to 200 ppi. To give 300 percent at 300 ppi, the scanner's sampling frequency would have to be 900/inch.

74 CHAPTER 2

> **TIP (CONTINUED)**
>
> You can easily calculate your scanner's capabilities. If you divide the maximum optical sampling frequency of the scanner by the resize percentage you desire, you will have the largest possible pixel density. In the case above, 600/300 percent = 200 ppi. Alternately, you can use this formula: 100 (sampling frequency/desired ppi) = largest percentage of enlargement. For the case in this tip, 100(600/300 ppi) = 200 percent.

The same kind of calculation takes place when you use Photoshop's Image|Image Size dialog box (see Figure 2.3). In the upper part of the figure, the Resample Image checkbox is turned on. When the dialog box is in this state, numerical information in any one of the five data entry fields can be changed. Changing the number of pixels—increasing or decreasing—doesn't af-

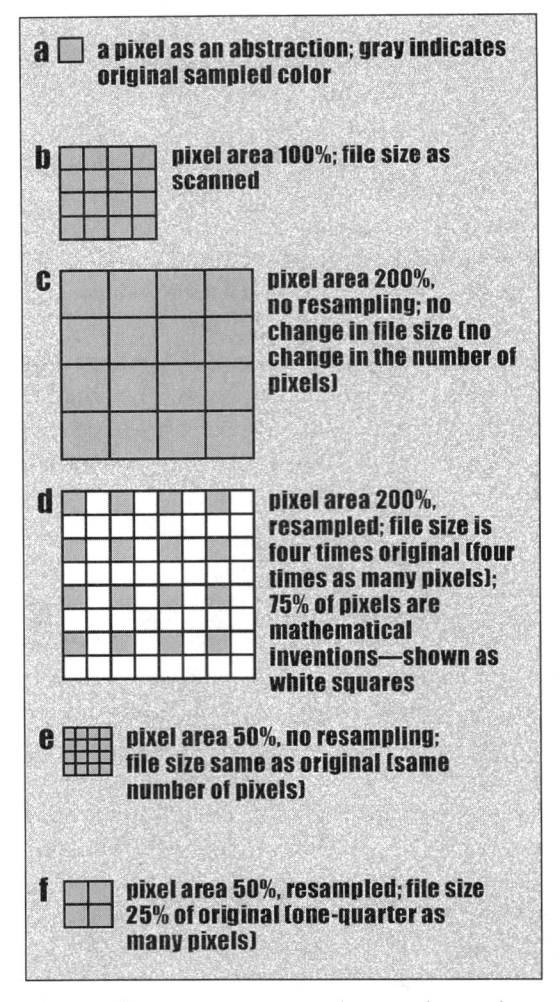

- **a** ☐ a pixel as an abstraction; gray indicates original sampled color
- **b** pixel area 100%; file size as scanned
- **c** pixel area 200%, no resampling; no change in file size (no change in the number of pixels)
- **d** pixel area 200%, resampled; file size is four times original (four times as many pixels); 75% of pixels are mathematical inventions—shown as white squares
- **e** pixel area 50%, no resampling; file size same as original (same number of pixels)
- **f** pixel area 50%, resampled; file size 25% of original (one-quarter as many pixels)

Figure 2.2 Pixel size and pixel interpolation are two commonly misunderstood concepts.

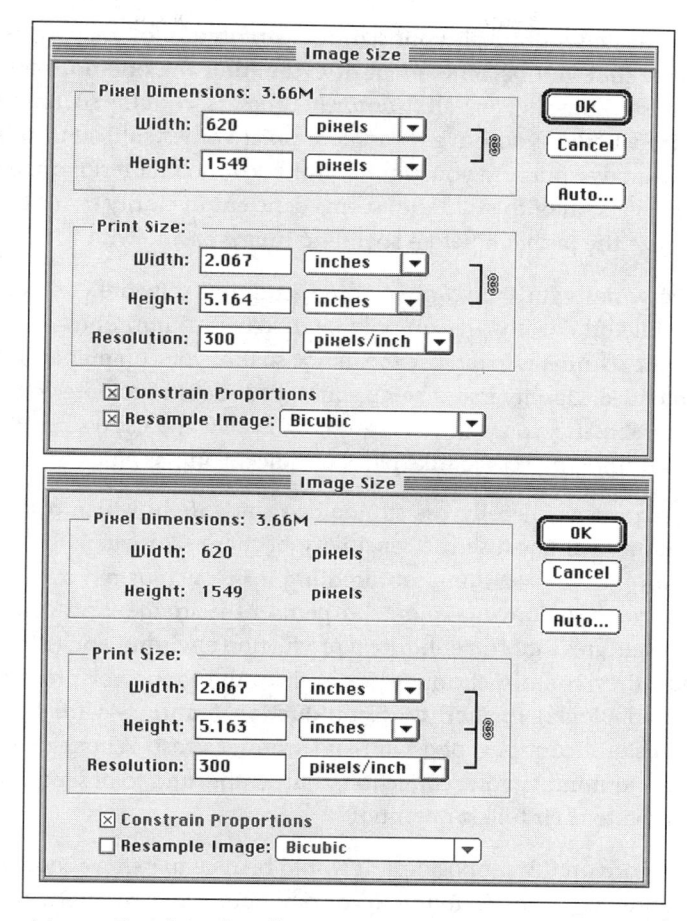

Figure 2.3 Photoshop's Image Size dialog box illustrates the difference between resampling (top) and resizing (bottom).

fect the values for Print Size or Resolution. Changing the Print Size values doesn't affect the Resolution, but it does change the number of pixels. In either case, the Image Size will be changed using Interpolation. In the lower part of the figure, the Resample Image checkbox has been turned off. Note that the Pixel Dimensions can no longer be altered, nor can the file size be changed. A change in any one of the three data entry fields will immediately alter the other two. (The pop-up menu at the bottom of the dialog box tells Photoshop which method—Bicubic, Bilinear, or Nearest Neighbor—it should use to interpolate the image. The merits of these three are not relevant to a discussion of the change in an image's size. For best results, when you're changing the size of a Photoshop file, leave this setting at its default, Bicubic. Bicubic is the slowest interpolation method of the three, but it also produces the best results.)

Basic Scanning

The technical aspects of scanning an image vary with the intended purpose of the image. In general, a scanner's controls should be adjusted so that after you scan, you can work in Photoshop with the most accurate set of pixels your scanner can obtain for you. Scanning isn't difficult, but it does require that you become adept at evaluating the original material for potential problems. You must also train yourself to accurately assess what the scanner delivers. You must learn to recognize whether you have a range of pixel values sufficient to be able to prepare your image for whatever purpose you require. If the scanned material appears to be adequate and your scanned version of the material seems deficient in clarity or tone range, you need to be able to recognize the problem before spending time working with it.

Scanner software varies with the scanner. Some scanning software contains controls of great sophistication, while other software can only be described—charitably—as adequate. The ultimate purpose of the scanner is to digitize the image so that you can prepare it to suit the purpose for which it is intended. Quality issues being equal, you should evaluate your scanning software with an eye to how it assists you with your workflow. Even if you use a scanner only occasionally, you'll want the scanning process to take place as quickly and as efficiently as possible.

Very expensive scanners generally use standalone software in which a variety of production tasks can be automated. Because the sensitivity of these scanners is usually more than adequate for general-purpose scanning, automating tasks such as removing screens and noise, correcting tonal range, balancing color, sharpening the image, and converting the scan to CMYK format are features that can enhance a production environment. (When files are changed to CMYK format, they contain channels for each of the four-color process inks—Cyan, Magenta, Yellow, and Black.) In fact, these production features—with the overall scanning sensitivity—are a significant part of a high-end scanner's cost. Whenever these kinds of automatic capabilities—automatic color correction, sharpening, and color separation—are available, they should be used to their fullest potential.

Low-end scanners are an iffy proposition. It would be nice to believe that cost alone would be sufficient to evaluate a scanner's ability to capture data. Unfortunately, cost seems to be only an approximate guide: In some cases, cost as a guide to a scanner's quality is totally unreliable. For example, one major manufacturer of imaging equipment markets CCD scanners with a cost range of $600 to $12,000. It is true that the less expensive units are smaller and are bundled with less sophisticated software. However, it is also true that the overall quality of scans from the most expensive units doesn't greatly differ from the quality of the least expensive. The difference in quality is certainly not great enough to compensate for the difference in cost, nor is that cost difference sufficiently offset by powerful scanning software.

Evaluating a scanner is made difficult by the fact that scanners need to capture data for many different purposes. If a scanner is going to be used for digitizing images to be placed on the Internet, it may be that a low-cost CCD scanner—no matter the manufacturer—will serve the need. For more demanding jobs such as scanning for offset printing, you'll need a better-quality scanner. Typical parameters for offset work require that large-scale editorial images—and images for high-quality four-color ads—be scanned by high-end machines. For this reason, much of the prepress industry makes use of service bureaus that specialize in custom scanning on drum machines.

Smaller images in the prepress world can usually be scanned in-house on less expensive equipment. These smaller images are probably the most demanding of performance in low-end machines because they must end up looking nearly as good as the high-end scans with which they are associated. These images also tend to be the most problem-laden. They are the ones that are reproduced at a small size because the original material is less than perfect. You can imagine the situation in the production room: "Okay, we've got this wretched Polaroid that is too dark, but we've got to use it. Let's scan it here, rather than wasting $75 on a scan that won't improve it that much anyway."

The Scanner's Controls, ArtScan Pro By Jetsoft

If your scanner doesn't have a standalone scanning program, chances are good that you were furnished with a plug-in that allows you to do your scanning from within Photoshop. You may be using a scanner that follows the *TWAIN* (or "Technology Without An Interesting Name") standard, or you may be using hardware-specific software. In either case, your scanner controls are selected from the File|Import submenu.

When the scanner controls open, you see an interface window that differs only in detail from that shown in Figure 2.4. Your scanner software, unless it comes in a package shipped with a

Figure 2.4 The interface window for the ArtScan Pro scanning software.

high-end model, will probably not have as many features as you see here, but its features will be similar to those we will discuss.

The window shown in the figure is that of a third-party scanning software package, ArtScan Pro by Jetsoft Development Software. We use ArtScan Pro here as an example because it is fairly generic, and because it is a package that has nearly all the features you are likely to encounter. It's also an excellent way to breathe new life into an older scanner that is no longer supported by the manufacturer. For example, the bundled software for the scanner that generated the figure is old enough that it doesn't operate under Macintosh system software version 7.5 or higher. The company that sold the scanner isn't interested in continuing to write updated software for a machine that, although perfectly serviceable, has been superseded by about a gazillion newer models. However, the scanner is still functioning perfectly and will continue to do so for at least several more years. (By the way, ArtScan is able to drive a great many older scanners made by companies such as Agfa, Avec, Canon, Epson, Hewlett-Packard, Microtek, Nikon, PixelCraft, Relisys, Ricoh, Sharp, Tamarack, and UMAX. It is available for Windows, Macintosh, and Power Macintosh, and costs less than $90. If you own one of these older scanners, investigate ArtScan. You can find the Jetsoft Web site at **www.dpi-scanner-authority.com**.)

After placing the material to be scanned on the bed of the scanner, your next task is to open the scanning software module from Photoshop's File|Acquire submenu. After the window opens, click on the Preview button. The scanner makes a preliminary, low-resolution scan of the entire bed area. You can then draw a cropping rectangle so that, on the final scan, you acquire only those pixels within the crop and not the entire area.

The image to be scanned is shown in the central area of the figure. This software has a shape-recognition feature that assigns a crop rectangle automatically. (ArtScan is intelligent enough to place the crop rectangle and then, if the image is not quite straight on the bed, to counter-rotate the scan to straighten it out while it is scanning.) ArtScan also allows you to zoom in to the area you have cropped. Click on the magnifying-glass icon on the vertical tool palette on the left site of the preview area. Another preview scan will take place automatically.

Figure 2.5 shows an expanded view of the interface window and several pop-up windows.

The ArtScan Interface Window

On the right side of the interface window, a series of pop-up menus and data-entry fields allow you to choose very precise settings for the new scan.

Units Of Measurement And Sample Preview

At the top of the preview image—to the right of the Art Scan logo—is a pop-up menu that lets you choose the units of measurement you want to use. Your settings in this pop-up affect the units of the rulers at the top and left of the preview, and the numeric fields to the left of the preview.

A smaller pop-up—without a label—is located next to the lower right corner of the logo. As you move your cursor around the preview of the scan, the logo disappears and becomes a small

Figure 2.5 Expanded view of the ArtScan Pro dialog box.

preview window in which you can see magnified details of the image. The small pop-up allows you to set the degree of magnification for the logo-area preview.

Scan Type

Scanning requires a fair amount of patience. Getting a good scan can be satisfying, but the scanning process is not one of those things that springs to mind when you think of fun. The items in this pop-up menu (upper left corner below the logo) take some of the more tedious details and automate them. The following list describes how each scanning method works:

- *Single Image with Current Settings*—Single Image is the generic method for most scans. You place the material to be scanned on the scanner, acquire the scanning software, request a preview, draw the crop rectangle, perform whatever adjustments you desire, and scan. To scan another image, follow the same procedure. When you need only a single scanned image, and if you scan relatively infrequently, this is a perfectly satisfactory way to do your scanning.

- *Multiple Pages with Same Settings*—The Multiple Pages setting is handy for scanning more than one item that requires the same basic scan settings and the same area of the flatbed. When this option is selected, you follow the same set of steps through the completion of the first scan. When the scan is complete, the software asks if you want to continue with another scan. If you answer yes, all you need to do is reload the scanner bed and click on OK.

For example, you might want to scan in four or five pages of a text document to be analyzed by OCR—Optical Character Recognition—software. On the other hand, you may want to scan one area on a number of originals that differ only within the area you want to scan. Using the Multiple Pages setting allows you to continue scanning without relinquishing the scanner controls until you are finished. Please note that this option can be used with automatic document feeders.

- *Batch Different Originals on One Page*—For those who are used to the Single method, batch capability will come as a wonderful surprise!

First, you need to load the scanner with as many images as will fit the scanning area. Acquire the ArtScan software from the File|Import submenu, and click on the Preview button. When the preview is complete, choose the Batch option. A set of controls (shown in Figure 2.6) appears at the top of the preview area.

The center of the Batch controls has an open area that contains some numbers. The first time you use the batch feature, it will read "1 of 1". Click on the button with the plus symbol (+) until the rightmost number is the same as the number of individual images in the preview window. Now, click on the left button (<<) until the reading says "1 of *xx*" (with *xx* reflecting the number of images).

At the left of the preview window, you see a small vertical tool palette (described in detail later in this chapter). Click on the eleventh tool from the top. With this tool, draw a crop rectangle on the first of the images in your batch. After you draw the crop, make whatever setting changes you want—size, resolution, color range adjustments, and so forth. You can even select from the pop-up menu directly below the Scan Type pop-up, Scan Mode, whether the designated image is to be scanned as color, grayscale, or line art. After you complete your settings for the first image, click on the right button (>>). Draw a new crop rectangle on the second image, and make selections for the scan. Continue in this way until all of your images are selected and settings specific to each are chosen.

As you cycle backward through the batch controls (<<), you'll see the settings shift with each click. You may have set some images as grayscale, some in color (transparency or reflective), some to be enlarged, some reduced, some at low resolution, some at high resolution, and some to be scanned as line art. After you approve all your choices, click on the Scan button, and find something else to do for a while. ArtScan scans your images one by one, using the settings that you chose for each. When the batch scan is complete, you will find each of the scans in an open window in Photoshop, ready for use. It isn't quite magic, but it's awfully close. As a production tool, having this feature on a relatively low-end scanner—most high-end scanners have been able to do batch scanning for years—is invaluable. (Note: Batch scanning requires more memory than acquiring a single image.)

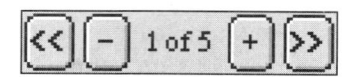

Figure 2.6 Batch scan controls from ArtScan Pro.

- *Auto Preview, Settings, and Scan*—This choice puts the ArtScan software into its default mode. When it is checked, almost all the other controls disappear, and you are left with only the Scan and Exit buttons and the bit depth pop-up to the right of the Scan Mode pop-up. When you check the Auto button, you are saying to the scanner, "Okay, you choose. Give me the best scan of whatever is on the flatbed." For some kinds of scanning—OCR, for example—this can be a valid option. Our opinion is that for nearly all other kinds of scanning, the quality of the image is far too important for the scanning software to perform the task with no thoughtful input from you.

Scan Mode

The pop-up menu beneath Scan Type gives the choice of scanning in CMYK, RGB, Gray Scale, Line Art, or Vector Line Art. Under most circumstances, you will be scanning in color or grayscale modes.

- *CMYK Color*—When a scan is intended to be reproduced on a press, it must first be converted from RGB to CMYK. Because scanners scan in RGB mode, the conversion of files to CMYK, at least with low-end scanners, is normally handled by Photoshop. In a production environment, this scanning option would provide exceptionally useful time savings because the conversion takes place as the scan data is being acquired. The final scan would appear in the document window already in CMYK mode. It can then be saved in any file format appropriate for importing into page layout programs such as QuarkXPress or Adobe PageMaker.

  Scanning directly to CMYK mode is not exactly a straightforward process with ArtScan because the software depends upon the use of *ICC (International Color Consortium) Device Profiles* to make accurate color transformations. (The use of device profiles is discussed more completely in Chapter 10.) For the software to work correctly and to generate the separation accurately, you'll need to open the ColorSync/ICC dialog box by clicking on the eighth button from the top of the vertical tool palette. The window with its pop-up menus is shown in Figure 2.7.

  As you can see from Figure 2.8, you will have some significant choices to make, and all of them must be appropriate for the system you use in order for the scanner's separation utility to function with the desired efficiency.

- *RGB Color*—RGB is the native scan method for scanners. This color scan mode allows you to capture the most image data in less time than for CMYK. You should use this mode if you need to do extensive corrective work on your scan, or if your scan is to be used for some purpose other than printing. Some examples of other purposes might include photo material on the Web or within a multimedia presentation.

- *Grayscale*—Grayscale mode will give you a scanned image containing nothing but gray values, even if your original material is in color. You can use this mode to prepare images for halftone reproduction. A more satisfactory way to prepare halftones from an RGB original is described in Chapter 9.

- *Line Art*—For very fast I-don't-care-if-it's-not-perfect line art scans, use the Line Art option from this pop-up. For higher-quality line art, scan in grayscale. Complete details on scanning for line art can be found in Chapter 9.

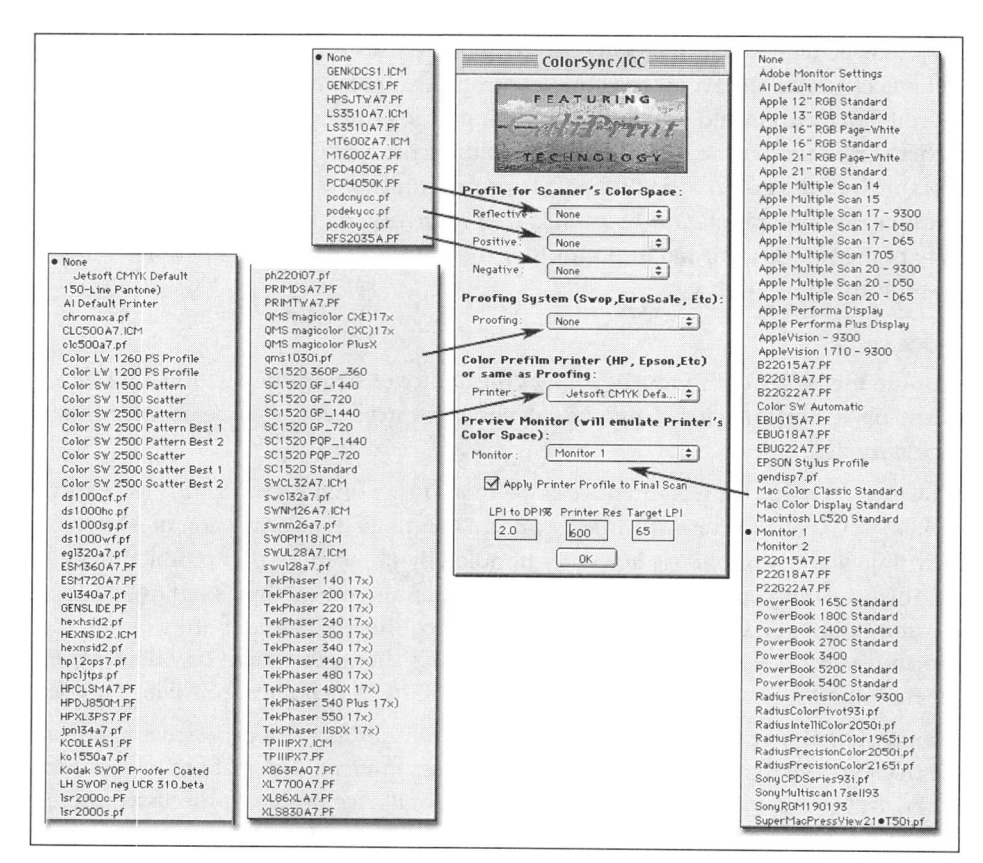

Figure 2.7 The ColorSync/ICC Profile dialog box from ArtScan Pro.

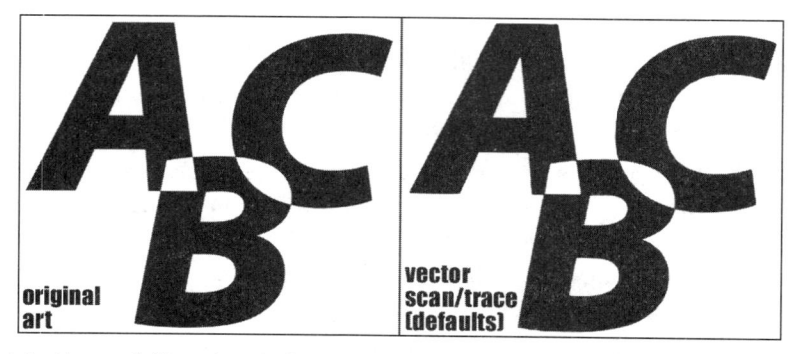

Figure 2.8 Original image (left), and an ArtScan Pro Vector Line Art autotraced image (right).

- *Vector Line Art*—The fifth option, Vector Line Art, is a spectacular bonus from an already impressive software package. When this option is selected, line art scans are autotraced, and then saved as EPS files. These files can then be edited in programs such as Adobe Illustrator or Macromedia FreeHand.

The impressive part of this option is the quality of the finished trace file, given that only a single tolerance setting is available. It doesn't compare to a full-featured program such as Adobe Streamline, which gives the ability to precisely tweak the settings that control the autotrace. However, for very fast work, this option does a very good job. Figure 2.8 displays an example of the quality of this ArtScan feature. On the left is a 300 ppi printout of a Photoshop file. On the left, the printout was scanned and autotraced using the software's default settings.

Sample Depth

The small pop-up to the left of the Scan Mode menu is visible whenever the Scan Mode is set to RGB or to Grayscale. With this button, you can choose the sample depth or bit depth of your scan. Eight bits per channel has been the default bit depth for scanning software for a number of years. Sixteen bits per channel is a relatively recent choice that is supported by Photoshop 5's 16-bit mode. For a more complete discussion of the implications of this option, please see "More-Than-8-Bit Digital Files" later in this chapter.

The three varieties of 256-color are this scanning software's equivalent to switching from RGB Mode to Index Color mode from within Photoshop. You might want to experiment with these settings, especially in a batch scan of images intended to be used on the Web.

Image Adjustment

After you have made a preview of the image to be scanned, the Image Adjustment slider allows you to make a few quick—but powerful—tweaks to the scan. The horizontal scroll bar and thumb button can be used to adjust any or all of seven combinations. The default is "Dark <-> Light". Move the slider to the left to make the image darker, and to the right to make it lighter. The same slider can adjust "Cyan <-> Red", "Magenta <-> Green", "Yellow <-> Blue", "Shadows", "Highlights", and "Saturation". Using these adjustment sliders is fast and efficient. Make a small change and you'll see the effects of the adjustment on the Preview Image. All the adjustments made by this slider also can be made in Photoshop after the scan has been made. However, a quick tweak of this kind is one of many time-saving capabilities that well-engineered scanning software can give you.

Type Of Original

The three radio buttons here inform the scanner whether to scan reflective material or transparency. If your scanner doesn't contain a transparency-scanning module, you won't be able to check the Positive or Negative buttons. The default is Print (reflective).

Speed Vs. Quality

You have three choices: HS (High Speed), S&Q (Speed and Quality), and HQ (High Quality). Under most circumstances, you want your scan to be the best it can be, and HQ will be your choice. In some cases, however—with OCR scanning, for example—you may want to choose speed over quality because OCR images don't require the same level of quality as a scan destined to be reproduced on an offset press. HS and S&Q give you two settings with which you can test the capabilities of the scanner against your need for fast throughput.

Numeric Input Fields And Pop-Ups

The center section on the left of the scanner interface window contains a set of nine data entry fields. These fields allow you to set the physical size of the crop rectangle, to change the post-scan dimensions, to see the size of the file at the dimensions you've requested, and to assign a Line Screen value.

The top row of three fields is an expression of the ratio of pixels per inch to the line screen. Any change to a number assigned to Line Screen automatically changes the Resolution value (the left side) based on the HT value. The reverse is also true: Any change to the Resolution value changes the Line Screen. For press reproduction purposes, you'll want your scan to have a resolution that is twice your line screen value: 2 is the correct choice for HT. Once this has been entered, simply enter the line screen you want to use. (Note that when Photoshop files are output for press reproduction, the pixel information is converted to lithographic dots. This is called *screening*. The size of the dots in an output image is based on the number of lines of dots in some unit of measurement. We could say, for example, that an image has been screened at 133 lpi, which means that there are 133 lines of screen dots in an inch. You may sometimes see measurements expressed as *lpc*—lines per centimeter. The *line screen*—another way of referring to the number of dot lines—is specified at the time of output.)

To the right of the top row of fields is a small, unmarked pop-up menu that allows you to set the target resolution of your scan. (You can also enter your desired resolution directly in the field to the left.) This pop-up is useful because it allows you to see just how much information you can obtain from your scanner. You should be aware, however, that the values in the pop-up are not always a true indication of your scanner's optical resolution. The scanner used to generate the figure, for example, has an optical resolution of 1,200 samples horizontally and 600 samples vertically. A desired scan resolution of 1200×1200 would mean that half of the vertical values would be interpolated. In some cases, as we have noted, interpolated values are quite useful. In other cases, they are not.

When you're scanning very high-resolution values, keep this in mind: Your files can quickly grow to vast proportions for no beneficial reason. Many new users of scanners believe that if they scan with the highest resolution possible, their scanned material will be cleaner. Beyond a certain point where the resolution should be appropriate for the end use of the scan, the reverse is actually true: More resolution makes the image progressively unclear. Also, just so you will know: If you try to do a CMYK scan at 19,200 ppi, you'll end up with a file that will be about 1.5 gigabytes per square inch!

The two data entry fields directly below the Line Screen field show the actual dimensions of the cropping rectangle in the Preview. To the right of these two fields is a box containing a number that expresses the relationship between the pairs of fields on the right and left. The number is a percentage figure. You can enter a number directly in this field that automatically updates the values on the right. You also can enter numbers on the right that update the percentage field.

The last data field (bottom right) displays the disk size of your final scan.

Control Buttons

The contents in the row of control buttons at the bottom of the controls are all fairly obvious. Please note the checkbox above the Preview button. By clicking on it, you will automatically load all of your current settings—and your current Preview image—the next time you open this software program.

Contextual Text Help

The blank area below the Control buttons is devoted to online assistance. As you move your cursor around the window, the text displayed in this area changes. If you locate your cursor over one of the tools in the tool palette, for example, the tool's name and a brief description of how the tool is used appears. You will also be informed of special options that are available for that tool or function.

The ArtScan Pro Tools Palette

Besides the functions provided by the controls at the left of the window, the tools palette provides a range of services that can be applied to the scan as it is being made. Two of the sets of tools give other ways of adjusting the image; other tools automate some routine tasks which, if not accomplished by the scanning software, need to be applied to the image by using Photoshop's controls. In a production setting, the automation of these tasks delivers a significant time savings. The following is a summary of the tools (which are redisplayed and captioned at the right of Figure 2.5).

- *Eyedropper tools*—The Eyedropper tools are used to set the highlight, midtone, and shadow values of the image manually. To set the shadow, click on the Sample Black Point tool and move the cursor into the preview window. As the cursor moves, the set of values directly below the preview window will change. Keep an eye on these values and move to a very dark area of the image. Locate the darkest point you can find, and click. To set the highlight, click on the Sample White Point tool. Move your cursor into the image and locate the lightest point you can find. Click. Set the midtone value by finding, if you can, a neutral area that gives a K value of about 50 percent. Click. For a more complete understanding of how Eyedropper tools function when you select the endpoints and midpoints of the tonal range, please see the sections "Understanding And Customizing Curves" and "Understanding And Customizing The Levels Controls" in Chapter 9.

- *Arbitrary Rotation*—Although ArtScan will rotate-to-straighten original material, you might want to rotate the material to be scanned for some other purpose. For example, the subject of the photograph might not be squared with the sides. If you would like the subject to be aligned so that it is straight, even if the edges of the photo are at an angle, you can use this button to rotate the rectangular crop.

- *Descreen*—If necessity forces you to scan original material that has been reproduced by a printing press, you will find that your scan is perfectly dreadful. Moiré patterns—interference patterns between the sampling of the scan and the screens used to reproduce the original—will make the image virtually unusable.

  You have a number of methods at your disposal that you can use to eliminate screen artifacts after scanning (we'll discuss one method that works well later in this chapter, and another is found in Chapter 8). However, ArtScan will attempt to remove the screens for you. You should try this function to see how well you think it works for your needs. If you find it satisfactory, it will prove to be a time-saving feature. If you do not like the results you get, check out the method discussed later in this chapter as an alternative.

- *Rotate 90°*—If you need to scan from source material that doesn't fit the scanner bed in the correct orientation, you may need to scan at 90° from the way you eventually want the image to be positioned. This button counter-rotates the material during the scanning, eliminating the need to rotate in Photoshop.

- *Magnify Image Preview*—When you decide to use the Eyedropper tools to set your own tone-range endpoints, it is very helpful to be able to see a larger version of the image. After you have done your preview and drawn the crop rectangle, click on this button. ArtScan will do a new preview and enlarge the image to fit the preview area.

- *Color Sync*—This tool opens the ColorSync/ICC Profile window (Figure 2.7), discussed in "Scan Mode" previously in this chapter.

- *Sharpen*—In a normal production situation, an image is sharpened slightly during the scan. The scan is then corrected, resized, and sharpened again at the last stage of preparation. Use this button to perform a modest amount of sharpening on the image while it is being scanned. The dialog box with which you assign Unsharp Mask parameters is shown in Figure 2.9. Please note that this dialog box gives more control over the sharpening than Photoshop's Unsharp Mask filter does.

  One especially useful feature is the Soften Blue Channel checkbox. You will find—particularly when you're scanning outdoor images and other photos containing large areas of blue tones—that sharpening often leaves visible noise in blue areas. This checkbox lets you apply sharpening selectively so that blue noise is not exaggerated in the scan.

- *Invert*—This button gives you the color-inverse version of the original material. You use this feature if you are scanning a transparency that would normally be used to produce a color

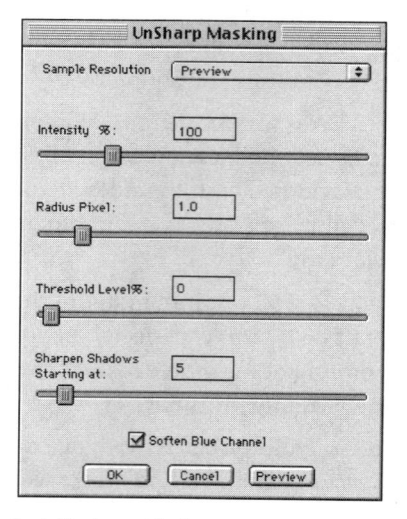

Figure 2.9 Dialog box for ArtScan Pro's Unsharp Mask settings.

print. This kind of transparency is called a *color negative*. It is the inverse of a transparency such as a 35mm slide.

- *Draw New Selection*—When you click on this button, the crop rectangle drawn by the scanner during the preview disappears. You can then draw a new rectangle in its place.
- *Line, Noise, Artifact Removal*—This button directs the program to attempt to remove lines, noise, and other artifacts from the shadow areas of the scanned image.
- *Save Settings, Load Settings*—If you find that your scanning tasks divide themselves into groups of similar scan types, it will be useful for you to use the Save Settings command for each group. For example, your color scans might all be intended for use in multimedia, or your grayscale scans might all be reproduced at 120 line screen. You can then use the Load Settings command and bypass making all of the scanning choices every time you need to do a scan.
- *Flip Image*—Clicking on this button is equivalent to taking a transparency you have previewed, and turning it over so that it is scanned from the flip side. You would use this option if your scanner requires that you scan with the emulsion side of the transparency up, but you want to have the image scanned as if the emulsion side were down. You may also encounter situations where, for aesthetic reasons, a photo needs to be presented flipped. You can accomplish this task in Photoshop, or you can have the scanning software do the task for you (see "Understanding And Customizing Curves" and "Understanding And Customizing Levels" in Chapter 9).
- *Histograms, Curves, and Levels*—Figure 2.10 shows ArtScan Pro's Histogram/Curves dialog box, in which you can make adjustments to your scan using controls similar to those in

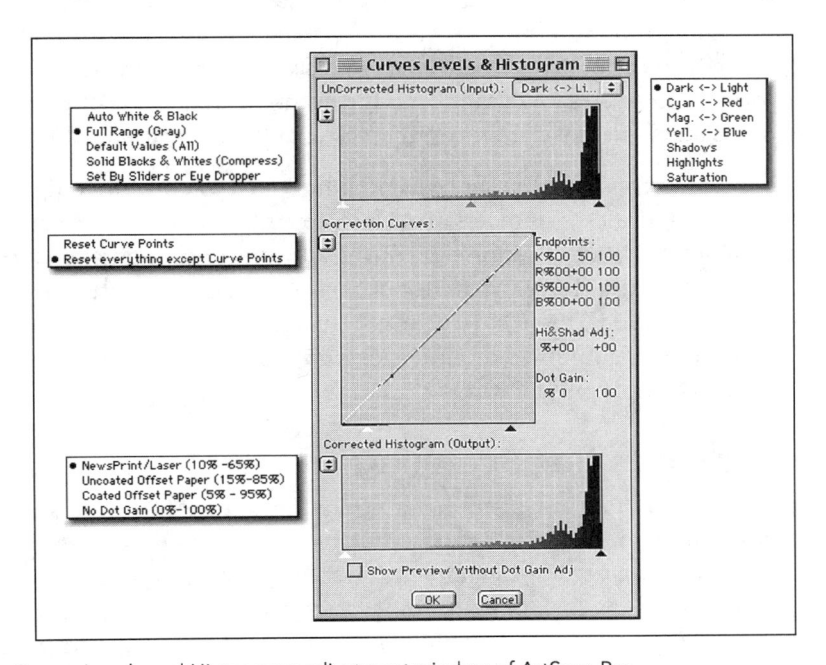

Figure 2.10 Curves Levels and Histograms adjustment window of ArtScan Pro.

Photoshop. Although these controls differ slightly from those in Photoshop, you can learn how to use them by referring to "Understanding And Customizing Curves" and "Understanding And Customizing The Levels Controls" in Chapter 9.

- *Auto Balance*—The Auto Balance tool is a choice that enables ArtScan to do much of your image adjustment work automatically. This option takes information from the prescan that tells what data is actually present in the original material—the range between dark and light values—and applies automatic adjustments. When you use the Auto Balance tool, ArtScan attempts to give you the best possible scanned image by using its own analysis of the image to be scanned. As with most automation routines, you need to evaluate the results you get. While the scanner software may be intelligent about the choices it makes, your scanner may not have the full-tone-range sensitivity to make the Auto adjustments worthwhile. In such cases, one of the other settings might be a better choice because you can then make use of Photoshop's capabilities to perform the same task.

- *Preferences*—The Preferences tool summons a dialog box in which you can make choices about how ArtScan Pro behaves under normal use. Choices include a toggle for Auto Zoom Of The Selection Rectangle, blurring the area outside of the crop rectangle, and the resolution of the scanned preview image.

A Few Points About Scanning Software

We have discussed in detail the features of a single multifaceted scanning software package. We don't intend to suggest that you need to use this software in order to get good scans (although it does a remarkable job). Instead, we want you to realize that the software that shipped with your scanner may be the type we would describe as barely adequate. If you do only a small amount of scanning, your bundled software may be all that you need—particularly because you have Photoshop to remedy many of the deficiencies of your scanning software. However, if you do a large amount of scanning, you should consider using a scanning package—this one or any other that does the same tasks—to make your scanning faster and more efficient.

Here's another point to consider, one that has nothing much to do with your own scanning. Rather, it has to do with the large numbers of older scanners that are sitting in corporate storage rooms all over the country simply because the driver software is out of date. Many graphic arts students would be thrilled to have a scanner of their own. When a software package is as inexpensive as ArtScan Pro is, these older scanners might be usable by students or as gifts to local artist centers, library multimedia centers, or rural schools where operating budgets are notoriously small. Why not consider it?

Evaluating Images For Scanning

Your scanner is simply a digitizing instrument. It may have a wide-ranging sensitivity to the tone values present in the material to be scanned, or it may be relatively insensitive. You also have Photoshop, which can accomplish miracles on fairly poor material. Even with these powerful tools, it is vital that you look at every image that you intend to scan. Try to assess how successful the scan will be based on the quality of the original. The better the quality of your input images, the better the quality of your scans.

ACQUIRING IMAGES   **89**

You can tell a lot just from looking at the image. Does it seem to be a good exposure? Can you see details in both the lightest and the darkest areas? Does the overall image look too light? Too dark? Does it have poor overall contrast? Your eyes, your common sense, and your increasing experience will be able to tell you a great deal. You can tell even more by doing a preliminary, low-resolution scan of the image, and looking at its histogram within Photoshop. By evaluating the histogram, you'll be able to tell what information the original image contains, and whether it can be sufficiently improved to be usable.

The image on the left in Figure 2.11 shows one kind of problem. The image is generally too light overall and has highlight areas where no detail remains. The wide spike at the highlight end of the histogram indicates a concentration of highlight values that have little to differentiate them. The lack of values showing above 70 percent on the histogram indicates that the image was probably overexposed.

Using the methods discussed in the sections titled "Processing A Grayscale Image" in Chapter 9 and "Processing An RGB File Intended For Color Separation" in Chapter 10, the scan can be made to look much better. The values present in the original have been redistributed over the entire range. The image now has better contrast in all areas except for the falling water. With respect to the highlights, there is really no way to redistribute image data when it does not

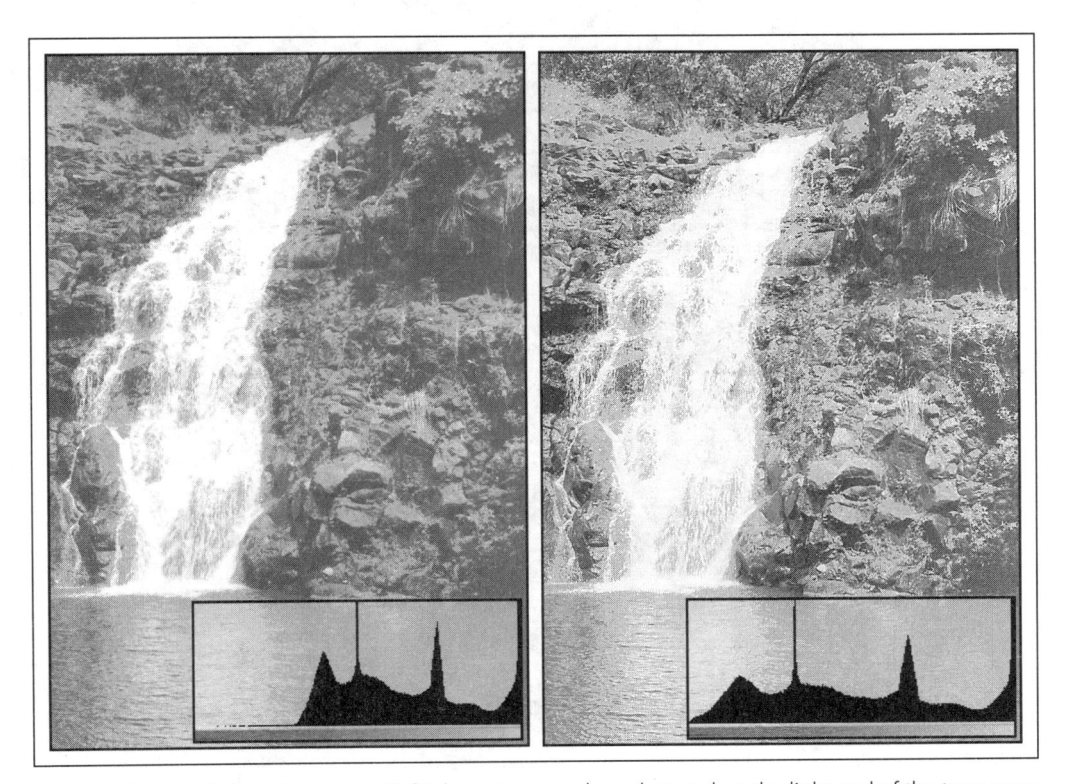

Figure 2.11 The preliminary histogram (left) shows image values clustered on the light end of the tone range. The redistributed histogram (right) is more satisfactorily arranged. Even with the better distribution, the highlight values are still blown out.

exist. As powerful as Photoshop's correction tools are, detail cannot be put back into the highlights. Consequently, although the image does look better, its usability is questionable.

The image in the upper part of Figure 2.12 illustrates a problem that is the inverse of that shown in Figure 2.11. This image contains no values lighter than about 55 percent. There is a large spike containing slightly-darker-than-midtone values that are probably the range of tones within the sky and the medium tones within the shingle texture. The recognizable shadow values in this image contain very little detail. This is not always a weakness: The high-contrast look of certain parts of the image can be graphically effective. It simply depends upon whether that effect is what is desired.

Figure 2.12 The preliminary histogram (upper image) shows image values clustered on the dark end of the tone range. The redistributed histogram (lower image) shows a better arrangement. The new arrangement has increased the overall contrast of the image.

The lower part of Figure 2.12 has the value range redistributed. As you can see, the histogram maintains its overall configuration. It has simply been stretched to fit nearly all of the available range. Had it been stretched further, the sky tones would have ended as highlights and made the high-contrast effects much more pronounced.

The upper image in Figure 2.13 is much the same as the image in Figure 2.11. The histogram clearly shows the result of an aimed exposure of a shadowed area that has included very brightly lit areas as well. The picture divides itself into three general zones: the upper right quadrant, containing the very bright values; the upper left-hand quadrant; containing most

Figure 2.13. A difficult image showing clearly defined areas of bright values, medium values, shadow values (upper image). The difficulty lies in lightening the shadows without bleaching out the medium and light tones (lower image).

of the tones in the middle range, and the lower half containing most of the shadow values. Any attempt to lighten the lower part of the picture results in too much brightening of the upper half.

You have a number of ways to make an image with these kinds of problems look even better than the corrected version in the lower part of Figure 2.13. Take a look at Chapter 11.

The left image in Figure 2.14 shows a histogram that is fairly satisfactory. There is a uniform distribution of values across the entire range. The single spike at the highlight end comes from the bright sky and the foaming water at the bottom. After corrective measures are taken, the image on the right shows good contrast and good detail information in both the highlights and the shadows.

A good histogram is shown in the upper image in Figure 2.15. As you can see, there is a complete range of values with no prominent spikes, other than that on the highlight end of the scale. This spike is specular because it is the result of sunlight flashing from very shiny leaves. The corrective work shown in the lower part of the figure has produced a picture that is clear, easy to grasp, and easy to reproduce.

Figure 2.14 The preliminary histogram (left) shows a wide distribution of values. Very little adjustment is required to make the image as open and clear as the one on the right.

Figure 2.15 A good initial histogram (upper image) that requires almost no change and that flattens out only slightly in the adjustment process (lower image).

Other Scanning Considerations

Beyond the mechanics of the scanner and the software that controls the hardware, we have a few other points to make that deal with the material you intend to scan. These points include simple housekeeping—advice about cleaning the scanner and the material it will digitize.

Cleaning The Original Material

Considering that a flatbed scanner is a low-end digitizer, its sensitivity is good enough to pick up dust and fingerprints on the material to be scanned. They are easily visible as blemishes in the picture image. Removing the traces of surface dirt from the digital file is a waste of time; you can easily to clean the image beforehand.

Handled with reasonable care—and properly stored—photographic prints and transparencies accumulate only small amounts of dust. You can purchase small aerosol cans with a plastic tube nozzle that spray bursts of inert gas for blowing away the dust. If the material is too contaminated for the aerosol, you can purchase solvents made especially for cleaning photographic transparencies and prints. You must also purchase the special wiping cloths used with these solvents. Never use tissues or paper towels, particularly on the emulsion side of a transparency. Common paper products are very abrasive—tissues included, and some of them contain skin-softener lotions that can make the whole problem worse—and will damage the surface of the transparency. Even the ultra-soft wipes used with the solvent must be totally saturated and applied with the lightest pressure you can manage.

The scanner bed must also be kept clean. This may mean that you have to disassemble the cover so that you can clean it inside and out with streakless cleaning solution and lint-free pads. While the scanner is open, you can use your inert-gas aerosol to blow away any dust that has accumulated on the inner surfaces.

Removing Artifacts From The Scanned File

No matter how carefully you treat your own photographic originals, at some time you will probably have to scan material that is scratched and on which cleaning solvents have no effect. When there is no alternative, you need to go ahead and do the scan in the hope that Photoshop's powerful tools will help you get rid of the artifacts without a lot of work.

Mounting With Oil

Oil-mount fluid can be purchased from any photo-supply or prepress supply retailer. It is a clear, light, volatile, oil-like substance that can be easily removed after scanning. It is very simple to use and does an amazingly good job on scratched transparencies. Place a few drops of the fluid onto the scan bed glass and push the transparency into the oil so that it spreads out to cover the surface. Place a few more drops on top of the transparency. Cover the transparency with a larger piece of clear base (or any kind of thin, transparent plastic or acetate). Push the clear base onto the transparency to spread the oil. Tape the edges of the clear base so that it's held tightly against the transparency. Scan as usual. When you're finished, remove the oil with photo-cleaning pads. You will find that the oil fills in the scratches and minimizes their visibility in the digital file.

Correction Filters

Four of Photoshop's bundled filters use blur methods that help eliminate scratches and dust spots. Depending upon the kind of artifacts to be removed and the subject matter of the image, these filters can only be described as partially successful. None of these filters works perfectly—although some work better than others do—and all have the effect of eliminating some of the detail from the image. You have, then, a trade-off: eliminate dust/scratch artifacts and lose picture detail or leave the artifacts to disfigure the image while retaining whatever detail can be captured by the scanner. The choice is always difficult and needs to be made on a case-by-case basis. It doesn't usually take a lot of time to try each of the four filters on a problem image. If they produce good results, then a good deal of manual work can be saved.

ACQUIRING IMAGES   **95**

To illustrate how each of the four filters affects a blemished image, we have applied them to the photo shown in Figure 2.16. At the top is the complete photo, and at the bottom is an enlargement of a section of the upper photo. The image contains dust speckling overall, as well as some serious scratches. The following list describes these four filters:

- *Despeckle*—The Despeckle filter is found under the Filter|Noise submenu. The filter has no parameters that can be set; it simply functions with built-in tolerances. (Note: You can moderate the effects of this filter—and all of the others discussed here—by using the Fade command.) As you can see in the two photos in Figure 2.17, the filter has a small effect on the scratch marks, but does very little to eliminate the dust spots. This filter is very effective when used on images in which emulsion graininess is a problem because it smoothes grainy textures without doing much harm to image detail. Despeckle is a filter best used on images

Figure 2.16 Every scanner operator's dream come true—a dusty image with scratches. The lower image is an enlargement of a section of the upper photo.

Figure 2.17 The Despeckle filter has almost no effect on this problem image.

where noise artifacts are very small. The dust spots in the figure are far too large for Despeckle to affect a change.

- *Gaussian Blur*—The Gaussian Blur (Filter|Blur|Gaussian Blur) is not usually considered to be a corrective filter. However, it can be used as such in some cases. The two photos in Figure 2.18 show the result of the filter at a Radius setting of 1. Although the resulting blur nearly eliminates all of the dust marks, the large scratch is still visible. The clarity of the image has also been reduced.

Sometimes, a very small setting of the blur Radius will do the job. For example, a setting of .5 might be used. When small Radius values are successful, some of the image details can be restored by using the Unsharp Mask filter (Filter|Sharpen|Unsharp Mask). Sharpening helps, but it isn't a perfect solution: You can never have the image as sharp and clear as it would have been without the Blur filter.

Figure 2.18 The Gaussian Blur filter eliminates the dust, but not the scratches. It also reduces the clarity of the image.

- *Median*—The Median filter (examples are shown in Figure 2.19) works by taking an average of pixel values for the distance of the Radius value. As the Radius value increases, so does the amount of blurriness in the image. The Median filter, as you can see from the figure, is more successful than Gaussian Blur or Despeckle at eliminating the scratches and all but the largest dust marks. It also retains more image detail if used at small Radius values. Because this filter generates small areas of average or similar tones, there is an all-over posterization. Sharpening tends to accentuate the posterization rather than restore image detail.
- *Dust & Scratches*—The Dust & Scratches filter works in much the same way as the Median filter, but with the additional Threshold control (Figure 2.20). The latter allows you to assign a value to the difference in pixel values below which the filter does not function. For ex-

Figure 2.19 The Median filter works moderately well to remove surface blemishes, but does not lend itself to resharpening to increase the photo's clarity.

ample, with the Threshold set to 20 levels, two pixels might have values of 128 and 147. Because the difference between these two numeric values is less than 20, the filter will not touch them. Where the difference is greater than 20, the filter will function using the Radius value in precisely the same way the Median filter does.

The Dust & Scratches filter is the most successful of the four correction filters. However, it also decreases the amount of image detail. With the Threshold control setting parameters over the pixels that will be affected, there is a less pronounced posterization effect. Unsharp Mask can be used more effectively after executing this filter.

- *The Rubber Stamp tool*—The Rubber Stamp tool is not a filter, but it will be your best friend, if none of the filters are satisfactory. You should learn to love this tool: If a photo is bad

Figure 2.20 The Dust & Scratches filter is the most successful of the four artifact-removal filters.

enough, you'll spend a lot of time with it. With the Rubber Stamp tool, you are able to clone pixels from one part of the image so that they cover up defective pixels in a different part of the image. You can find a complete look at this tool in Chapter 3.

Descreening

Scanning photographic material that has been reproduced on a printing press is one of the least rewarding scanning tasks. If the reproduction was in color, you will be able to capture only the limited color range offered by four-color printing, as opposed to the broader range of colors present in a continuous-tone photographic image. For both color and halftone scans, you will be capturing an image from which much of the detail has been eliminated by the output screening process. Still, scanning screened material—they are often called *rescreens*—is sometimes necessary.

Almost every Photoshop user has a pet method for eliminating screens from a scan. Some users like the Median filter. Others go to elaborate lengths to place the rescreen originals on the scanner bed at 15°. We have a method that we think works very well, and we hope you'll try it. It's based on the inverse of the process that originally produced the screens.

Unless your eyes are good enough—or experienced enough—to look at the material to be scanned and to tell the screen frequency used to produce it, you need a small piece of equipment to do this job correctly. Your extra equipment (shown in Figure 2.21) is a Gaebel Half-Tone Screen Determiner. You can purchase one of these determiners from most prepress-supply retailers at a cost of less than five dollars. The screen determiner is simply a piece of positive film or a thin sheet of clear plastic with some not-quite-parallel lines drawn on it. The lines are very close together at one end and diverge slightly toward the other end. A set of numbers runs along the sides of the lines. To use the screen determiner, put it down on top of the screened material. Begin to rotate the plastic sheet until you see a four-pointed interference star begin to form within the area of the lines. Continue to rotate the sheet until the side points of the star reach to the outer edges of the lines. The star will point to one of the numbers along the edge—the number it points to is the screen frequency used to produce the piece. Simple, huh? This thing is really clever!

After you determine the line screen that produced the piece, place the original on the scan bed, perform the preview scan, and crop the portion of the image you intend to use. Set the scan percentage to 100 percent of the original size and the pixel density to twice the measured line

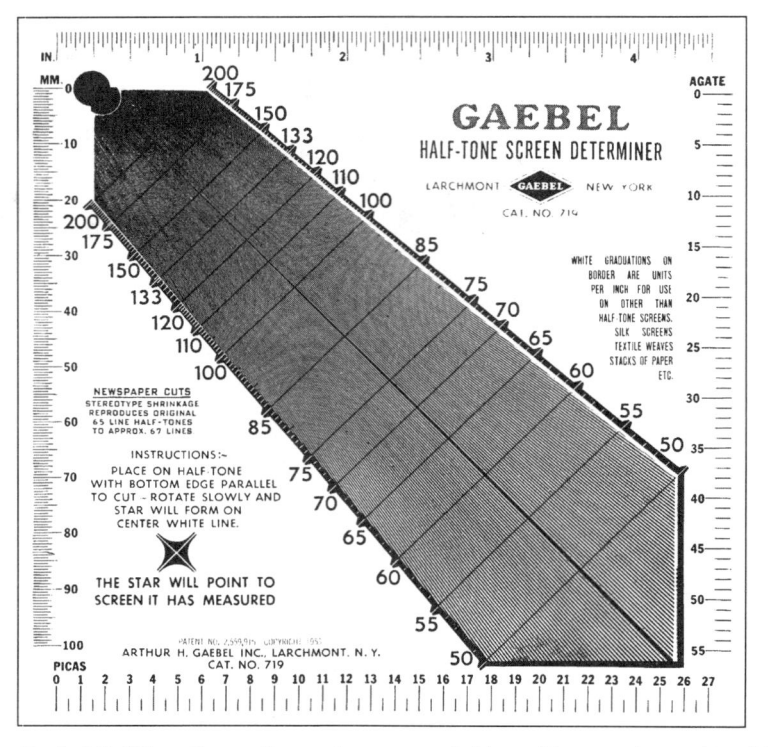

Figure 2.21 The Gaebel Half-Tone Screen Determiner, a remarkable and inexpensive gadget. No scanner user should be without one!

screen. These two values are crucial to the process. If, for example, you determined the line screen to be 133, set the requested ppi to 266 (2×133 = 266). Press the Scan button.

When the scan is complete, your image shows a screen interference pattern similar to that in Figure 2.22. From the Filter menu, choose Blur|Gaussian Blur. Set the Radius value to 1.5. With just this blur, your image loses all of its surface noise and appears as shown in Figure 2.23. Once the blur has been done, the scan can then be treated as any other scan.

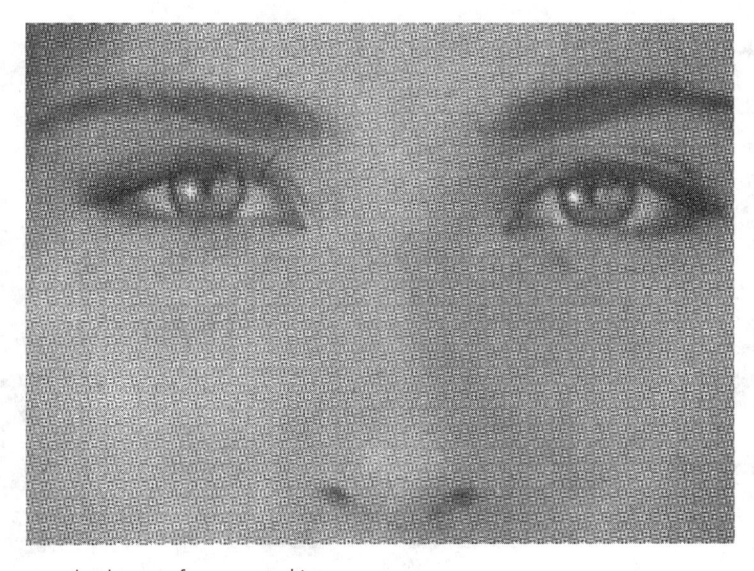

Figure 2.22 An untouched scan of a screened image.

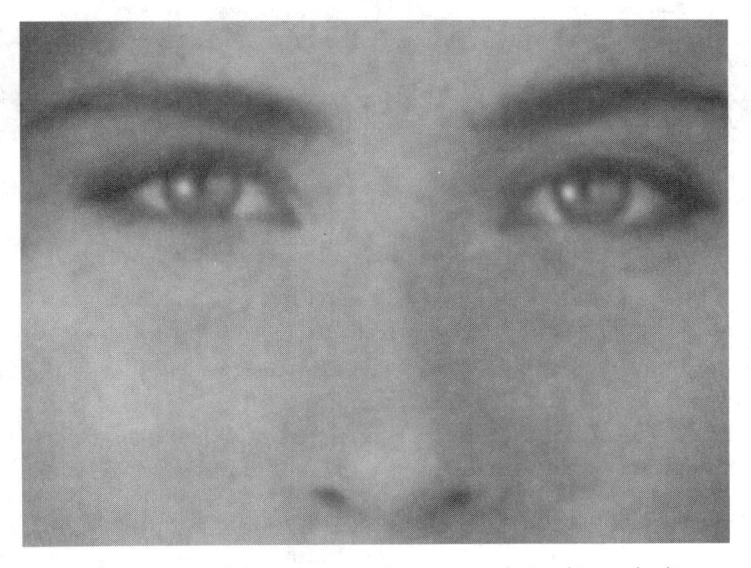

Figure 2.23 If the size and resolution of the scan are in the correct relationship to the line screen of the original, one application of the Gaussian Blur filter removes the screen artifacts.

Figure 2.24 It's difficult to imagine how the before (left) could result in the after (right). It is actually a very simple procedure.

The image in Figure 2.24 (Figures 2.22 and 2.23 are enlarged details of this photo) was determined to have been printed at a 150 line screen. It was scanned full size at 300 ppi and then subjected, on the right side, to the Gaussian Blur filter. The rightmost part of the image was then processed in the usual way, the image was resized, and then the right side was subjected to the Unsharp Mask filter. As you can see, this technique works very well indeed.

For other perspectives—and different kinds of solutions—on scanning material that has been screened, please see the section titled "Reducing A Moiré Pattern" in Chapter 8, and the section titled "Processing Line Art Scans" in Chapter 9.

More-Than-8-Bit Digital Files

Photoshop is internally geared to process digital files containing eight bits of information in each channel. For example, every pixel in an RGB file can be described with eight bits (one byte) for each of the channels—Red, Green, and Blue. Each RGB pixel, then, contains one of 256 possible values for each channel. The total number of colors this makes possible is 256^3, or 16,777,216. Many scanners have a sampling sensitivity that is able to describe each of a channel's pixel components with more than eight bits. Some scanners use 10 bits, some 12, and some 16 (full 16-bit scanners are fairly rare). With more bits come more values: a 16-bit scan, for example, represents a color range containing 2,858,455,254,310,656 values. That is a number that easily exceeds the human visual range.

Why scan with that many values? The explanation is really more theoretical than real, but to understand how such enormous numbers can affect your scan, you must first understand that all scanners have difficulty differentiating very dark values *and* very light values. (In fact, human eyes have much the same difficulty.) If you think about it, all of the problems that we typically associate with an imperfect scan have to do with shadows and highlights. Shadows become so dark that they merge into a single value and lose their details. Highlights wash out and leave us with only uniform areas of white. Perhaps you thought that these problems originated with the original photo material. Sometimes that is the case, but more often, the fault lies with the scanner. Less light is reflected from a dark area of a scan—or transmitted by a dark area on a transparency—and simple rounding errors occur. When a larger bit depth is used, there is a more precise differentiation simply because sampling areas can be very close to each other and can still be discerned by the scanner as different from each other.

After the scanner has sampled an area, the extra bits are usually discarded. However, having those extra bits means that the scanner software has made an intelligent choice with respect to the real value of a pixel. Reading the extra bits eliminates most of the rounding errors and makes the scan much more accurate than it would have been with only eight bits. You also end up with a much larger tonal range that gives you far more latitude when making corrections, especially drastic corrections.

Some scanners and scanning software allow Photoshop to retain a higher number of bits after the scan. (ArtScan Pro, described previously in this chapter, is one such software program.) The scanner delivers the information as a 16-bit file. You can confirm that this is so by choosing the Image|Mode submenu and looking to see that 16 Bits/Channel has a checkmark. Photoshop 5 can display only 8 bits per channel (the largest number your monitor can display), but it allows you to proceed with numerous functions, even though you cannot see all of the values you still have under your control.

Adjustment possibilities on a 16-bit file have been considerably expanded in Photoshop 5. Photoshop 4 allowed you to work with a 16-bit scan using only the Levels and Curves controls and 16-bit images were limited to RGB and grayscale files. With Photoshop 5, however, CMYK files have been added to the list for supported modes. You can also apply adjustments to a 16-bit scan using Hue/Saturation, Brightness/Contrast, Color Balance, Equalize, Invert, and the

Channel Mixer. (Explanations and directions for each of these controls can be found in other parts of this book.) Several of the tools are now functional with 16-bit scans: the Crop tool, the Rubber Stamp tool, and the History Brush (see Chapter 3). You can also use the Image|Image Size command and the six options found under the Image|Rotate Canvas submenu.

Why Use All Those Colors?

If you have a normal 8-bit scan which, after scanner-software adjustment, still looks to be too dark (Figure 2.25), you might want to use the Levels or the Curves controls to try to lighten it (Figure 2.26).

Using the Levels controls, the lightening would probably be accomplished by moving the midtone (gamma) slider of the Input scale to the left. This move, with the cutoff of the shadow tones, results in too few values in the range between 50 percent to 95 percent. Figure 2.27 shows an enlarged detail from Figure 2.26 in which the missing values result in severe posterization in the areas where dark tones are present. There are simply too few values present to represent a continuous range of tones. (This figure's posterization has been slightly exaggerated—with the Unsharp Mask filter—to make it easier to see.) The problem is fairly serious if this image is to be reproduced on an offset press. Some of the posterization will disappear because of the blurring

Figure 2.25 Scanner-adjusted scan is still too dark.

Figure 2.26 Gamma/midtone shift lightens the scan, but damages the image by leaving too few values to represent the dark tones.

that occurs due to dot gain, but enough of the posterization will remain as a visible defect in the image.

With a 16-bit image, you have considerably more latitude in your adjustments—in fact, you have a tonal range that is roughly 170,000,000 times as large as an equivalent 8-bit image. This range gives you a lot of space in which to maneuver. A lot!

Adjustments on 16-bit images bend all the rules you might have heard about a series of small adjustments being injurious to the data in the image. With a normal 8-bit scan, these rules should be taken seriously: Every adjustment that changes the image (Levels, Curves, Hue/Saturation, Color Balance, Selective Color, etc.) is destructive. Each adjustment, although it probably improves the appearance of the image, leaves you with less data than you had before the adjustment. This is the why the images in Figures 2.25 and 2.26 suffered: After a serious adjustment by the scanner software, further adjustments forfeited enough data to cause visible harm to the continuous tone range.

With 16-bit scans, a series of three or four smaller adjustments actually works better than one large-scale move. Small adjustments help to distribute the values present in the image so that

106 Chapter 2

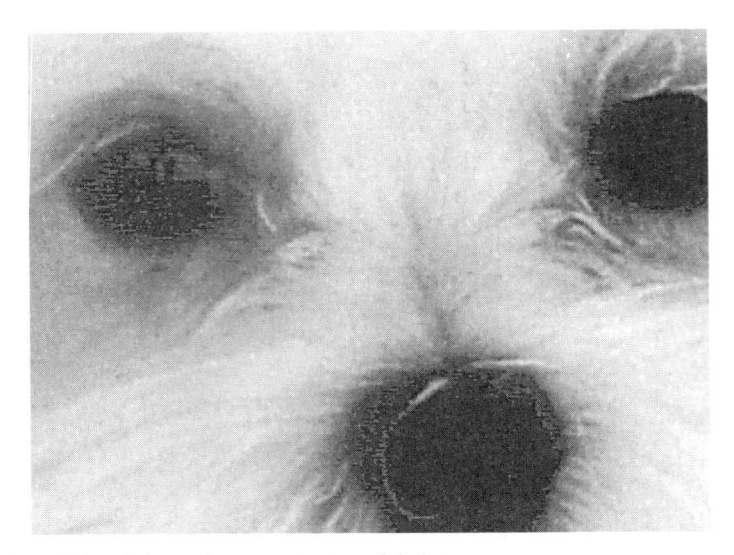

Figure 2.27 Enlarged detail shows the posterization of dark tones.

they are placed where they are needed. Figures 2.28, 2.29, 2.30, and 2.31 illustrate how this might work.

Figure 2.28 shows an image that seems so dark that it would normally be considered unusable. The initial histogram shows that the entire range of values is above 50 percent, with most of the tones concentrated above 70 percent.

In Figure 2.29, the first—and largest—set of changes was made to the image with the Levels controls. All three channels' highlight sliders were moved over to the left to point to the first

Figure 2.28 This 16-bit image seems too dark to be usable.

ACQUIRING IMAGES   **107**

Figure 2.29 Drastic shifts of the highlight sliders in all three channels as well as a shift of the midtone slider considerably lighten the image.

real values present in the image. The midtone slider was shifted to read 1.30. After this set of adjustments, the histogram at the upper right shows a much more satisfactory—though still far from perfect—distribution of values.

Figure 2.30 shows the shadow slider on the Levels Input scale moved to 22, and the midtone slider moved to read 1.24. The resulting histogram (upper left) now displays an even better distribution of tones.

Figure 2.30 Another, smaller, tweak of the midtone slider makes the image better yet.

Figure 2.31 One more midtone adjustment results in an image that is not merely usable, but is quite good. There is no degradation of the histogram because the image was a 16-bit file.

In the last figure, Figure 2.31, there is a small nudge of the midtone slider to 1.08. This further lightens the image and results in the final histogram, shown at the upper left. Notice that the image now has a full range of values. Notice, also, that despite making drastic moves with the Levels controls, the histogram has not degraded as it would have had this image been adjusted the same way in 8-bit mode.

The first and last stages of the photo shown in these figures can be seen in the color plate section of this book. The amount of change from first to last illustrates the vastness of the data you have at your disposal when you're working with a 16-bit scan. It also indicates how much corrective power you have. If you want, you can also perform these corrections on a copy of the file used in these figures. The file is titled GARDEN.PSD, and it's located in the Chapter 2 Practice Files folder on the In Depth CD-ROM.

After making tonal corrections in 16-bit mode by using any of the tools listed in the preceding paragraphs, you need to return to 8-bit mode (Image|Mode|8 Bits/Channel) in order to use the file for output. Please note that your scanner may not scan in 16-bit color and may have only 10-bit or 12-bit capability. The extra data still gives you a tremendous amount of flexibility when you run into problem images. If your scanner's software will allow it, you can still make use of the extra data by using Photoshop's 16-bit mode. A 10-bit or 12-bit file will work in 16-bit mode. You will not have the astronomical range of tones present in a true 16-bit file, but even a 10-bit file has 64 times as much data as an equivalent 8-bit file. (Note: If you're unsure whether your scanner uses more than 8 bits, you may want to check the manufacturer's Web site to obtain the information. In some cases, you may find that an upgrade to your existing scanning software is available, either free or at a small charge.)

Using 16-Bit Mode To Pull Inferior Originals Into Shape

Photoshop's 16-bit mode has a wonderfully useful bit of magic associated with it that makes use of the vastness of the 16-bit space and Photoshop's amazing interpolative abilities.

If you have an image that you consider unusable because it is too dark—and if you have a moderately sensitive 10-bit or 12-bit scanner that doesn't allow you to scan directly in 16-bit mode—go ahead and make your scan in 8-bit RGB mode. After you acquire the image, convert it to 16-bit mode and perform your corrections in the previously described manner. You will find that Photoshop's preservation of your data, even though it is accomplished by means of interpolation, is nothing short of miraculous. You will be able to bring the tones of your dark scans into a usable range. You'll find that when you convert back to 8-bit mode, your histogram displays no gaps, and that your image looks better than it has any right to look. Be sure to try this. It's incredible!

Photo CD

When Photo CD was introduced by the Eastman Kodak Company in 1993, it was marketed as an alternative to lab prints and slides. The basic idea was that consumers would purchase a home-television-compatible CD-ROM player. They would then, after having their film processed on a Kodak Photo CD scanner, be able to view snapshots and slides on the television screen. Despite formidable amounts of money thrown into marketing this system, consumers, as the saying goes, stayed away in droves.

Graphics professionals, however, saw the potential for Photo CD very early—far earlier than Kodak did. At a time when professional digital scans of questionable quality were being sold at three to five times the cost of the same scan today, Photo CD seemed a good alternative for many graphics purposes. The key to the desirability of Photo CD scans was, and still is, cost. Today, an average cost for a Photo CD scan is about $3. However, some vendors have pricing structures that bring the cost down as low as $1 for each roll of film. Even at the highest average cost, Photo CD scans are inexpensive. The fact that the scan quality is not as high as equivalent work done on a high-end drum scanner doesn't seem to be a deterring factor. The quality, in the opinion of many Photo CD consumers, is good enough for their purposes, and consumers include developers and technicians in multimedia, the Internet, CD-ROM authoring, and prepress. (Be aware that Photo CD costs include a fee that averages about $10 for the media. Once purchased, the media can be used repeatedly until it is filled to capacity.)

Photo CD scanners use CCD sensors in what is called a trilinear array. In common with most CCD scanners, Photo CD scanners are not as sensitive in very dark areas of the scanned material. This has been a conspicuous failing in many Photo CD scans. Figure 2.32 shows a typical example of a bright-light shot with deep shadows. All of the very dark areas in the figure have been clipped to the same digital value (in the lower half of the figure, all non-clipped pixels have been screened back to show how extensive the clipping problem really is). While problems with dark tones can be partially addressed by the Photo CD scanner operator, the dark tone clipping limit can be expanded only at the expense of highlight values. Recent changes in the scanner software have attempted to remedy this problem, but it remains one of Photo CD's most conspicuous drawbacks. Please note that dark clipped values of the kind shown in Figure 2.32 cannot be remedied by using the technique described in the preceding sidebar, "Using 16-Bit Mode To Pull Inferior Originals Into Shape."

Photo CD scans are stored in a Kodak-proprietary color model called YCC. YCC is somewhat analogous to the Lab color model in Photoshop. The Y channel of a YCC document carries luminance information, and the two C channels carry color. The YCC model is also associated with data compression, which makes it a good format for storing large-scale color scans. Pro-

Figure 2.32 Photo CD scans often exhibit dark tones that clip to the same value.

grams such as Photoshop access the YCC data through plug-ins that function as converters. Photo CD data is read by the plug-in and then translated from YCC to Photoshop's RGB, Lab, or Grayscale modes. The bundled Kodak CMS plug-in that ships with Photoshop is one example of a converter. Kodak also furnishes an Acquire module (chosen, if available, from the File|Import submenu) that furnishes more functionality than the bundled Photoshop plug-in. This plug-in can be downloaded for free from the Kodak site, at **ftp://ftp.Kodak.com/pub/photo-cd/drivers/dd0253.hqx**. Because Kodak's plug-in has more features than Photoshop's built-in converter, we recommend that you download and use it. (Note: While you are on the web, it's worth checking out Kodak's Web site for the latest information on Photo CD and Kodak's other imaging technologies.)

Beyond these two easily available utilities for opening Photo CD scans, Kodak also sells a modestly priced software package called Kodak Access. Access includes a set of generic profiles for output devices that are used for converting Photo CD files to CMYK mode. Kodak also sells custom profiles for color printers and proofing systems.

Photo CD scans are stored on a CD-ROM disk in Image Pack format, an amalgam of six related files all containing the same image, but at different resolutions. The typical Image Pack file has six files. (The more recent Photo CD Pro format has seven.) When a Photo CD scan is to be loaded, the plug-in gives you the choice of loading any one of the six Base Values (Photo CD's term for the six available resolutions you can open). The chart in Figure 2.33 shows the size of each of the six, the number of pixels in each dimension, and the real-world size of each at both 72 ppi and 300 ppi. Because loading the larger sizes takes more time, having the smaller versions of the same file allows you to open the size that is appropriate for your purpose. (Note: The Base/64 file size is the one used by the Photo CD scanning station to print the small dye-sub thumbnail of each image that appears on the printed cover insert of the disk.)

Despite whatever marketing hype you've been exposed to, Photo CD is a valuable and useful way of acquiring reasonably good-quality digital images. It is not, however, a poor man's answer to a drum scan. In fact, if you plan to use Photo CD, be prepared for the fact that, once you have the image loaded into Photoshop, you have to treat it as a raw scan. Automated translation software can be purchased for quantity users of Photo CD, but average users will

Photo CD Source Size	Pixels (1.5:1)	Dimensions @ 72 ppi	Dimensions @ 300 ppi
Base/64	96 × 64	1.333" × .889"	.32" × .213"
Base/16	192 × 128	2.667" × 1.778"	.64" × .427"
Base/4	384 × 256	5.333" × 3.556"	1.28" × .853"
Base	768 × 512	10.667" × 7.111"	2.56" × 1.707"
4 Base	1536 × 1024	21.333" × 14.222"	5.12" × 3.413"
16 Base	3072 × 2048	42.667" × 28.444"	10.240" × 6.827"

Figure 2.33 Table of Photo CD Base values, pixel dimensions, and actual sizes at two common file resolutions.

have to make use of one of the plug-in modules. Neither of the easily available plug-in modules can do very much in the way of correction beyond simple lightening, darkening, or a primitive variety of sharpening of the CD file as it is translated. The loaded image should be processed using basic corrective methods described in Chapters 10 and 11.

Loading A Photo CD Image

For best results, we recommend that you use version 3.0 of the Photo CD Acquire module. After you download this Photoshop add-on from the Kodak FTP site (the address is given in the preceding section) and mount a Photo CD in your computer, choose the module from the Photoshop File|Import submenu.

Figure 2.34 shows the initial file-locator window. Having selected the Photo CD, you will find that it contains three directories titled CDI, Photos, and Photo_CD. Choose the last of these. Within this directory/folder are two files—Overview and Startup—as well as another directory/folder titled Images. The Photo CD Image pack files are within this folder. From within this folder, locate the image you want to open: Use the number given on the cover thumbnail printout and then locate the file by using the two or three digits to the left of the part of the title that reads .PCD;1. Click on the Open button.

Another window then appears. An expanded view of this window is shown in Figure 2.35.

Thumbnail

In the upper left corner of the new window is a thumbnail of the image. If you move your cursor into the thumbnail, you can click and drag a crop marquee that will open only the part of the image within the selection. To eliminate the crop marquee, click once anywhere in the thumbnail window.

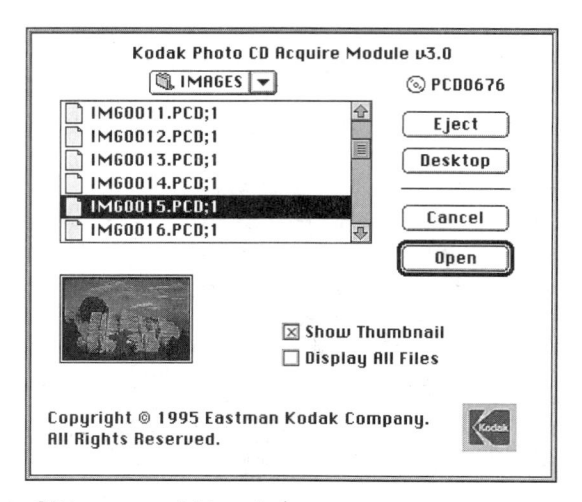

Figure 2.34 The first Photo CD image acquisition window.

ACQUIRING IMAGES   113

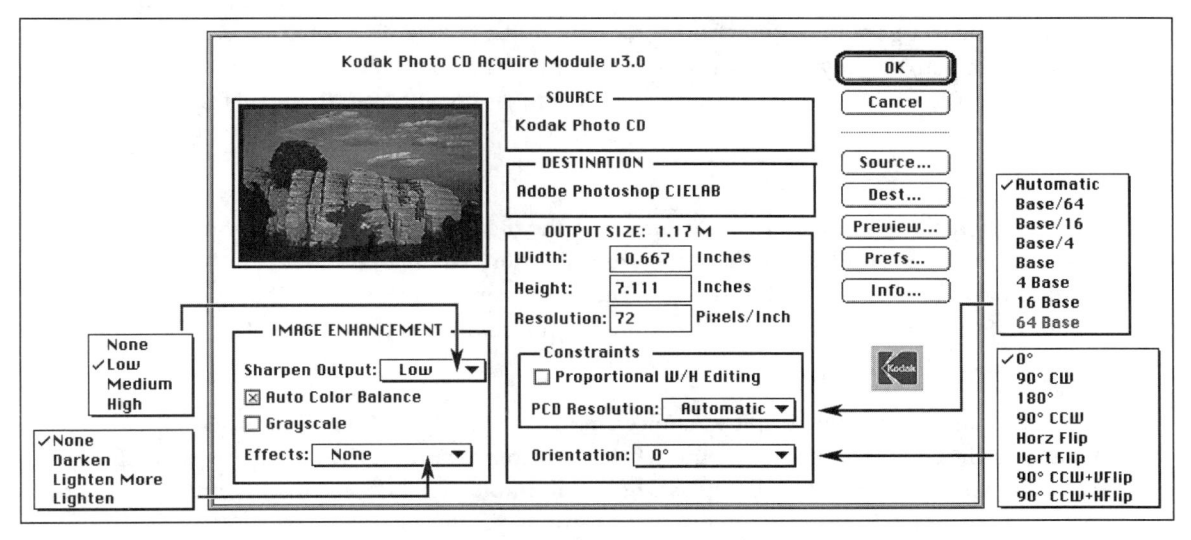

Figure 2.35 Expanded view of the main Photo CD image acquisition window.

Image Enhancement

Directly below the thumbnail, you see two pop-up menus and two checkboxes in a rectangular area. These elements, which is described in the following list, are devoted to image-enhancement features:

- *Sharpening*—The first pop-up allows you to sharpen the image as you open it. This sharpening method is inferior to the Unsharp Mask filter of Photoshop, however, and is probably not worth using.

- *Auto Color Balance*—The Auto Color Balance checkbox is a problematical choice. It has a noticeable effect on the image, but whether or not you will find this change desirable is something that you have to decide. If you are opening a photo of the outdoors, the Auto Color Balance checkbox will really jazz up the blues of the sky and the greens of the foliage. This will give a cool quality to everything else in the image. You may want to test this option by opening up two Base/16 versions of the file—one with Auto Color Balance checked, and one without—and make your choice based on the comparison. Our guess is that you will find the checked version almost surreal in the way its color enhancement affects the image.

- *Grayscale*—The Grayscale checkbox allows you to open the colored image directly into Grayscale mode. It doesn't work very well. If you need to use grayscale, you're better off translating the color image into Photoshop Lab mode and then retaining only the L channel for your grayscale file. To do this once the image is open in Photoshop, press Command+1 or Ctrl+1 to view the L channel. From the Image menu, choose Mode|Grayscale. Click on OK when you are asked if you want to discard the other channels. A comparison of the Acquire module's grayscale file and using the L channel of a Lab file will convince you of the superiority of the latter method.

- *Effects*—The last pop-up lets you darken or lighten the image. This selection is another choice that you will have to judge based on comparisons between small versions of the file with and without these options selected. Some images benefit from these effects and some do not.

Source

The Source rectangle displays choices made in the dialog box (Figure 2.36) that opens when you click on the Source button below the Cancel button. The scrolling window shows you what kind of original was scanned to the CD. The pop-up menu gives three choices shown at the bottom of the window. You should probably use the default, Kodak Photo CD.

Destination

The Destination rectangle displays choices made in the dialog box (Figure 2.37) that opens when you click on the Destination button below the Source button. The pop-up gives the choices. For color work, you should probably use the Adobe Photoshop RGB because it allows you to use many of the corrective techniques discussed throughout this book.

Output Size

The first important choice you need to make in this area of the dialog box is the resolution you want the translated file to have. Enter your choice in the Resolution data entry field. Next, make a selection from the PCD Resolution pop-up. The choices are shown at the side with Automatic as the default. The Base choices are explained in the chart in Figure 2.33. When you have made your choice, you'll find that the width and height have been entered for you. If you draw a crop marquee in the thumbnail window, the size of your crop will be shown as updated figures for both the Width and Height values.

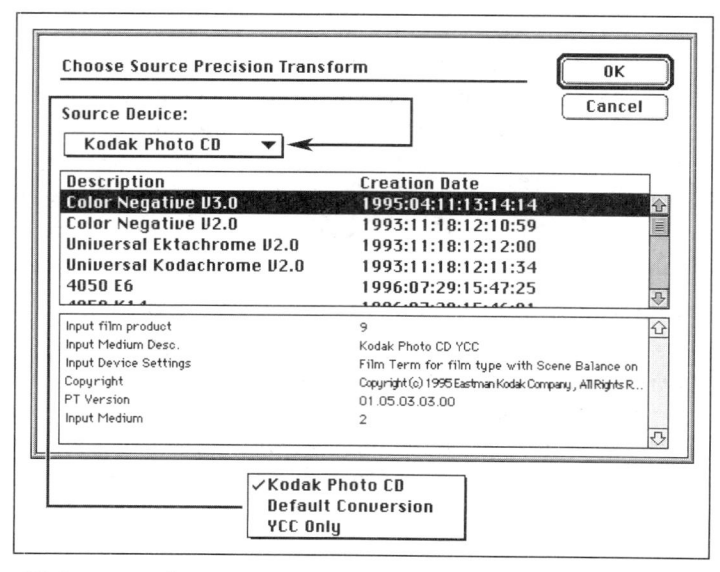

Figure 2.36 Photo CD Source window.

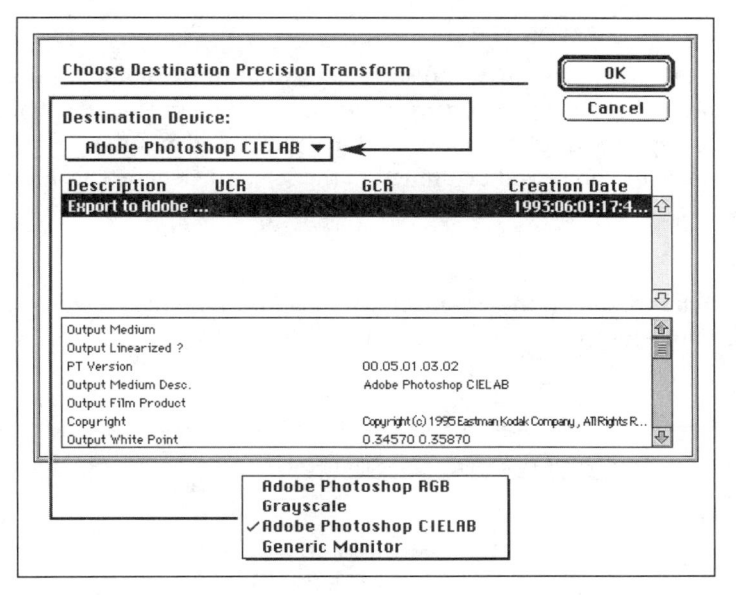

Figure 2.37 The Photo CD Destination box.

At the bottom of this dialog box, an Orientation pop-up lets you choose a variety of flip and rotate options. Because Photo CD scans are always done with the short axis of the image as vertical, an image taken with the long axis vertical will appear sideways in the thumbnail window. Of course, you can rotate the image in Photoshop. The Orientation selections, however, allow you to open the image already rotated, which is the way you want it.

Preview Button

Click on the Preview button to open a window with a larger thumbnail of the image (Figure 2.38). You can draw, if you want, your selection crop within this window.

Figure 2.38 Photo CD Preview window.

Prefs Button

The Prefs dialog box (Figure 2.39) gives you some choices for measurement units and resolution. Another button in this dialog box opens the window shown in Figure 2.40 that gives you the ability to choose a specific display. Unless you have purchased monitor profiles for use with this Acquire module, your choice will be limited to the selected Generic Display shown in the scrolling window.

Info Button

Clicking on the Info button opens the screen shown in Figure 2.41. In this window you will see details of the film from which the Photo CD file was made, the scanner, the disk name, and the file name.

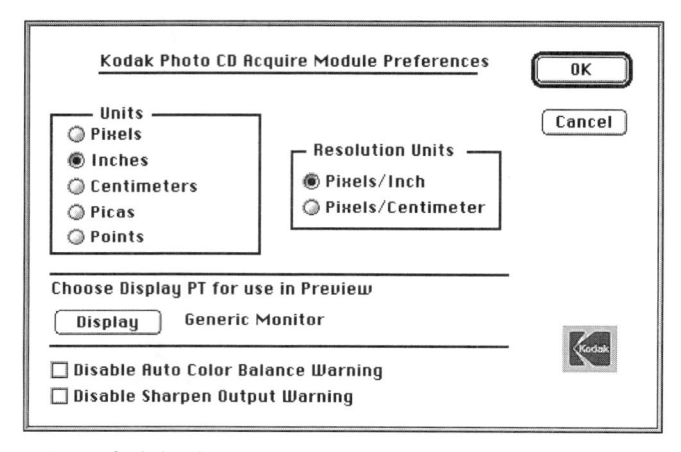

Figure 2.39 The Photo CD Prefs dialog box.

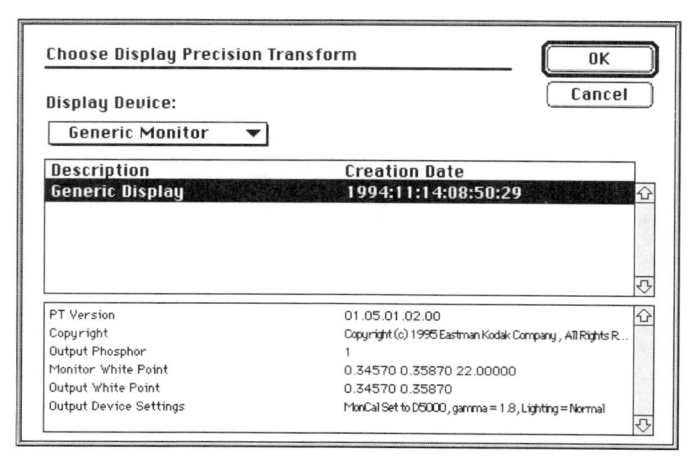

Figure 2.40 The Photo CD Display Device dialog box.

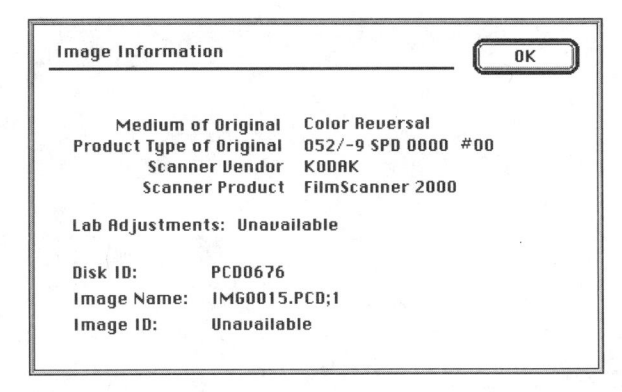

```
Image Information                    [ OK ]

       Medium of Original   Color Reversal
   Product Type of Original  052/-9 SPD 0000  #00
          Scanner Vendor    KODAK
          Scanner Product   FilmScanner 2000

Lab Adjustments: Unavailable

Disk ID:       PCD0676
Image Name:    IMG0015.PCD;1
Image ID:      Unavailable
```

Figure 2.41 Photo CD Info window.

Correcting The Photo CD Image

After you have loaded the image from this book's CD-ROM, you'll probably find that your image requires some modification before it can be used. The kinds of modifications you make depend on how you intend to use the picture. Please refer to the sections titled "Processing A Grayscale Image" in Chapter 9, and "Processing An RGB File Intended For Color Separation" in Chapter 10. Other correction information is available in Chapter 11.

Figures 2.42 and 2.43 show *before* and *after* versions of an image acquired by Photo CD. As you can see, the larger final image is very satisfactory, although it was cropped to eliminate most of the problem shadow values noted in Figure 2.32. After cropping, we used the Rubber Stamp tool to eliminate all traces of the shadows from the bottom of the picture. The resulting file is

Figure 2.42 Image acquired from Photo CD. The photo looks fairly good, but it requires correction.

Figure 2.43 Photo CD image after correction. The image is satisfactory in every imaginable way.

clear and shows very good fidelity of detail and tonal range. These same files are shown in this book's color section.

Moving On

In this chapter we've discussed the sometimes confusing terms *resolution*, *pixels*, and *scanning frequency*. You've also seen how a well-constructed scanning program can help you with the task of acquiring images. Finally, you've had an extensive look at Kodak's Photo CD, a service technology that puts reasonably good-quality scans into the hands of Photoshop users at an affordable price.

Our discussion of scanning isn't complete without a look at the eventual use of the scan. After you have acquired an image, you probably will want to work with it, edit it, or apply special procedures such as silhouetting, removing unwanted image details, and enhancing parts of the photo to show it to better advantage. For these tasks, you need familiarity with Photoshop's tools. In Chapter 3, we highlight a number of ways to make your image editing faster and more efficient.

TOOLBOX TECHNIQUES

Perfect pictures are the exception. From selections to painting to brush-on effects, Photoshop 5 provides you with a powerful set of tools to work on small parts of an image.

Whenever you open a file in Photoshop, chances are good that you'll be working on specific areas of the file rather than on the file as a single object. Certainly global edits—manipulations of the entire file—are one kind of Photoshop work; in many cases, however, you will need to resort to local edits—changing just part of the file. Perfect pictures, after all, are the exception rather than the rule. For local editing, you can use Photoshop's powerful set of paint and selection tools. The palette for these tools usually opens, by default, in the upper left corner of your computer screen.

The Tools palette is deceptively compact. It contains 46 separate tools (several of them variations of a single concept), two color selectors, controls for entering and leaving a fast masking mode called Quick Mask, and three buttons that control the way Photoshop displays your document on your monitor. Most of the tools have additional flexibility in the form of Options that allow you to control their behavior. Even if you are somewhat acquainted with the tools, you may be surprised at how powerful they really are.

In this chapter, you learn about the tools in detail. You'll see several uses for each of the tools and have the opportunity to follow along with several small projects. These projects will give you knowledge of the tools, insight into the way Photoshop works, and tips on which tools to use for specific situations. You'll also be shown a number of techniques that will help you to become a more efficient Photoshop user.

Before starting this chapter, you may find it useful to copy the files in the Chapter 3 Practice Files folder from the CD-ROM onto your hard drive so you have quick and easy access to them.

The Mouse With The Keyboard

Workplace studies have shown that up to 40 percent of a user's time is spent moving the cursor from one place on the screen to another—to menu, to image, to Toolbox, back to image, back to Toolbox, and so on. An efficient user with one hand on the keyboard and the other on the mouse can work circles around one who uses only the mouse.

Many Photoshop menu commands have keyboard equivalents. You can assign those that do not to the Actions palette (see Chapter 1). You can also assign keyboard commands with third-party macro/hot-key software such as CE Software's QuicKeys. Photoshop possesses another refinement that goes well beyond the capabilities of any other program—you can select most of the tools and many editing options using the keyboard. While you are working, you can select tools and discard them without moving the cursor from the working area. In like manner, you can select brush sizes, change opacity and pressure settings, switch around the foreground/background colors, change the magnification of the image within the window, and make use of a wide variety of options that can be performed without moving the cursor from its working position. These features give fluency to the program and make it one of the most efficient working environments of any graphics program.

Such fluency, however, has a cost: There is a good deal of memorizing to do. Learning all of the keyboard commands might seem an impossible task—especially because most users are pretty busy using the program—but the extra work will really pay off. One way to make the task seem less intimidating is to divide the commands into logical groups. Menu commands could be one group, tool commands another, palette commands a third, useful commands noted throughout this book might be a fourth. Once you begin to see what spectacular efficiency the program can bring you, it will be hard for you to be satisfied with old, slow work habits. For now, the Toolbox commands are a good place to begin.

Go On, Type A Tool...

Photoshop makes it easy to use the Toolbox. Simply press one of the alphabetical tool key commands and your tool is instantly selected. Most of the letter commands that select the tools are logical: G is for *Gradient*, B is for *Brush*, and so on. The illogical ones are easy to remember simply because they don't make mnemonic sense: Y for *Pencil*, O for *Dodge*, *Burn*, or *Sponge*. Some of the key commands fall into a different category; they are the ones that use one of the inner consonants of the tool name or—in one case—a bad pun: V for *Move tool*, K for *Paint Bucket*, and I for *Eyedropper* (get it?). The complete chart is shown here in Figure 3.1. (Note: You also can find a complete listing of keyboard commands for the Tools palette, and for other Photoshop commands as well, in Appendix C of this book.)

Ten of the tool rectangles contain small triangles in the lower right corner. These indicate a pop-up menu with other tool choices. Click and drag on the pop-up tool icon if you wish to select a tool with the mouse cursor. An alternative is to hold down Option or Alt and click repeatedly on a tool icon containing a pop-up triangle. This cycles through all of the pop-up's tools. If you hold down the Shift key, pressing the tool's letter command will cycle through the available choices. Press the letter P with the Shift key down, for example, and the Pen tool becomes selected. Press P again and the Magnetic Pen tool becomes selected. More keystrokes of the same letter (and Shift) cycle through the Freeform Pen tool, the Add Point, Delete Point, Direct Selection, and Convert Anchor Point tools in turn. Pressing M repeatedly cycles through the Rectangular, Elliptical, Single Row, and Single Column Marquee tools.

TOOLBOX TECHNIQUES **121**

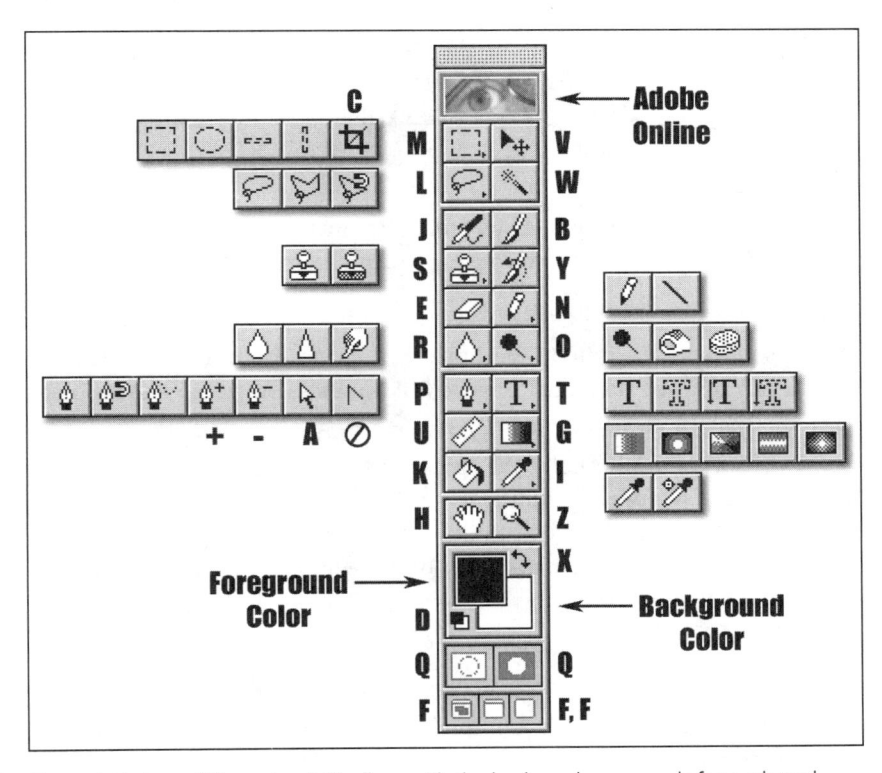

Figure 3.1 Expanded view of Photoshop's Toolbox with the keyboard commands for each tool.

> **TIP**
>
> While you're trying to memorize the letters for each tool, you might find it helpful to use the tiny balloon help windows that Photoshop furnishes. When you position the cursor over a tool, its name and command letter appears for a few moments within a small window. Eventually you can turn off the small balloons by selecting File|Preferences|General (press Command+K on the Mac or Ctrl+K in Windows) and removing the checkmark from the Show Tool Tips option.

Other Key Commands For The Toolbox

Located below the tools section of the palette, you'll find three areas that are not really tool selectors, but which control some important display and environment capabilities.

Foreground And Background Colors

The Foreground/Background colors are shown as two overlapping squares (see Figure 3.2). The Foreground color is uppermost square. There is no logical reason why these two active colors should use position names; they could just as easily be called color A and color B, upper and lower colors, and so on. I suspect that the names are a holdover from one of those graphics

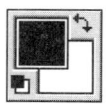

Figure 3.2 The Foreground/Background color square.

programs from remotest antiquity, such as MacPaint. In any case, the names are irrelevant as long as you understand how the two colors are acquired and used.

The following list describes how to use Foreground and Background:

- Click on either square to open the Photoshop Color Picker. From the Color Picker, select a new color. You can also select colors from the Color palette or the Swatches palette.
- You can use the Eyedropper tool to assign colors taken directly from an image window. A simple click makes the sampled color the Foreground color. Hold down the Option or Alt key and click in the image window to sample a new Background color. (The Eyedropper tool is also available while using six of the painting tools: Airbrush, Paintbrush, Pencil, Line, Gradient, and Paint Bucket. When you have any of these tools selected, press the Option or Alt key to temporarily access the Eyedropper tool.)
- The Paint tools paint with the *Foreground* color.
- The Eraser tool paints, on the background layer, with the *Background* color.
- When a selection is active on the Background layer, the selection can be filled with the Background color by pressing the Delete/Backspace key.
- Selections can be filled with the Foreground color by holding Option or Alt and pressing the Delete/Backspace key. Use Command+Delete (Mac) or Ctrl+Delete (Windows) to fill a selection with the Background color.

The default colors for Foreground and Background are black and white, respectively, unless you're working on a layer mask or in a channel, in which case the defaults are white and black. Even in extensive color work, these two are the most frequently used colors. The default colors can be restored by pressing the D (for default) key. The position of the two colors can be reversed by pressing the X key.

Quick Mask

Located below the Foreground/Background colors on the Toolbox is the pair of icons that you use to enter (click on the right icon) and exit (click on the left icon) Quick Mask mode. A faster way to enter and exit Quick Mask is to press Q.

You'll find that Quick Mask is a superbly useful way to construct masks using an overlay metaphor. The default color is a translucent red that is reminiscent of that not-quite-extinct (unfortunately) artifact known as *rubylith*. Rubylith consists of two transparent sheets of plastic—one red, one without color—lightly bonded to each other. To use it, a sheet of rubylith is taped over the material to be masked, red layer up. Then, with a very sharp blade, the area to be masked is traced with a cutting pressure that penetrates the red layer but does not cut entirely through the colorless layer. When the cut is complete, the red plastic is peeled away from the sheet in the non-masked areas. Quick Mask works in much the same way as rubylith did: Red areas are masked, and non-red, clear areas are not masked. To put it into Photoshop terms, any part of the image that is *not* painted red while in Quick Mask mode becomes selected after leaving Quick Mask. (See Figures 3.3 and 3.4.)

Sometimes the red of the Quick Mask may not be appropriate for the image. You may have, for example, an image with areas of red against which the Quick Mask color does not show up. If this is the case, it's easy to change the mask color. Simply double-click on either icon. In the resulting dialog box, click once on the Color rectangle. The Color Picker then appears and allows you to choose a new mask color (see Figure 3.5).

The Quick Mask dialog box shown in Figure 3.5 also has several other features that allow for adjustments, which are detailed in the following list:

- *Opacity*—Allows you to set how much of the image is visible through the masking color. The default is 50%. In Figure 3.5, it was changed to 70%. How much Opacity you choose depends on the way you like to work—and the nature of the project.
- *Color Indicates*—The default is Masked Areas. If, for some reason, you wish to reverse the color/non-color relationship, click on the other button, Selected Areas. Using this option is not as perverse as it may sound. You'll come across situations when it's easier to eliminate areas from all-over color than to add color to all-over non-color. However, to drastically understate

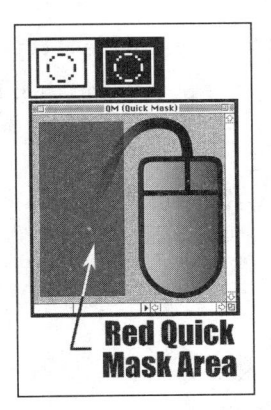

Figure 3.3 Red mask area in Quick Mask mode.

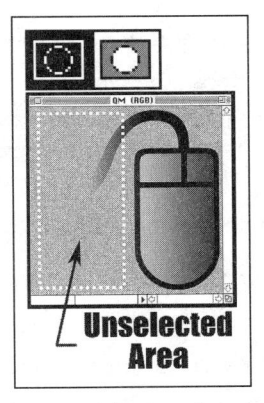

Figure 3.4 Selection outlining red masked area after leaving Quick Mask mode.

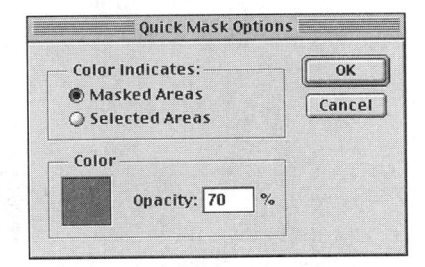

Figure 3.5 Color, selection, and transparency options for Quick Mask.

the case: It is really important that you remember which settings you're using. Switching them and then forgetting that you've done it can lead to a good deal of confusion.

You can also transpose the masked and unmasked areas by pressing Command+I or Ctrl+I. The mask/non-mask areas are instantly reversed, as shown in Figures 3.6 and 3.7.

You can use Quick Mask for a surprising number of tasks, some of which seem unrelated to each other. As you use Quick Mask, you'll think of more and more interesting possibilities. In the following section, "Quick Mask Tryout," you'll discover how Quick Mask works and learn a few useful tricks as well.

Quick Mask Tryout

For a tour of Quick Mask, first open the file QM_01.PSD, in the Chapter 3 Practice Files folder on this book's CD-ROM. Please note that the tryout file is of fairly high resolution (300 ppi). Some of the following instructions give specific numbers that are based on this file's resolution. If you wish to use a different tryout file, you'll need to make allowance for your file's resolution. For example, if your file is at a resolution of about 100 ppi, decrease the numbers given below by about two-thirds.

To enter Quick Mask mode, take these steps:

1. Press Q. You'll know you are in Quick Mask because the words appear in the window's title bar.
2. Set your Foreground/Background colors to the default (by pressing the D key).
3. Next, choose the rectangular Marquee tool by pressing the M key, and then make a rectangular selection in the shape of the darkened area, as shown in Figure 3.8. Hold down Option or Alt and press Delete.
4. Finally, press Command+D (Mac) or Ctrl+D (Windows) to Deselect Quick Mask. The image should look similar to Figure 3.8.

Try inverting the mask by pressing Command+I or Ctrl+I. The clear areas become red and the red areas become clear (see Figure 3.9).

Next, let's invert the mask again so that the inner rectangular area is again darkened. Exit Quick Mask by pressing Q. You now have two selection marquees—one around the outer edges of the window and one around the inner rectangle, as shown in Figure 3.10.

The selection you now see is the area outside the rectangle you first drew. Press Delete to fill the selection with the Background color (see Figure 3.11).

Figure 3.6 Shaded Quick Mask area; non-masked areas are white.

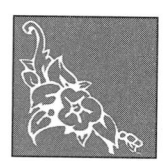

Figure 3.7 Quick Mask area inverted; non-masked areas are white.

Figure 3.8 Add a rectangular area of Quick Mask.

Figure 3.9 Invert the Quick Mask.

Figure 3.10 A selection marquee outlines your non-masked area when you exit Quick Mask.

Figure 3.11 Fill the selection with the background color.

Now try painting two edges of the mask with a soft Paintbrush. Here's how:

1. Press Command+Z (Mac) or Ctrl+Z (Windows) to undo the fill.
2. Press the Q key again to re-enter Quick Mask mode.
3. Press the B key to choose the Paintbrush tool and select the 200-pixel brush. If you don't have a brush this size, choose New Brush from the Brushes palette pop-up menu. Make the Size 200 pixels and the Hardness 0.
4. On the Options palette, set the Opacity to 100% by pressing 0 (zero) and the mode to Normal. Make sure that your Foreground/Background colors are set to the default because the colors can change when you move in and out of Quick Mask.
5. To actually paint two edges of the rectangle, center the brush over the upper left corner and click once.

6. Now, center the brush over the upper right corner, hold down the Shift key, and click again. Photoshop connects the two clicks with the Brush tool.

7. Continue to hold down the Shift key, center the brush over the lower right corner, and click again.

Your image should resemble that shown in Figure 3.12.

Press the Q key to exit Quick Mask, and then press Delete. You can see the difference in the selection edges since you've filled the new selection with white. The results are shown in Figure 3.13. Notice the difference in the edges between the painted and unpainted sides. Press Command+Z or Ctrl+Z to Undo the fill and re-enter Quick Mask mode.

Now let's paint the other two sides of the rectangle. Change the brush to 40% Opacity. This can be done on the Options palette, or you can press 4. Notice that the Opacity and Pressure settings on the Options palettes and the Layers palette can be changed in 10% increments by using any of the number keys: 1 for 10%, 2 for 20%, 0 for 100%.

Paint the area outside the rectangle with the 40% opaque brush, as shown in Figure 3.14.

Next, fill the new selection with white to see how a semi-opaque brush affects the selection. First, exit Quick Mask and press the Delete Key. Notice that in Figure 3.15, the edges of the image are screened back—by 60%—while the inner portion of the image is left untouched.

Let's see what happens when the Quick Mask window is filled with black. Undo the fill and return to Quick Mask mode. Hold down the Option or Alt key and press Delete. Your image fills with the masking color, as shown in Figure 3.16.

To eliminate part of the Quick Mask covering the image, press X to make your Foreground color white. Choose the 100-pixel soft-edged brush and then set the Opacity of the brush to 80% by pressing 8. Paint the area on the right side of the image, as shown in Figure 3.17.

Figure 3.12 Paint two edges of the mask with a soft Paintbrush.

Figure 3.13 Fill the new selection with white to see the difference in the selection edges.

Figure 3.14 Paint in the area around the rectangle with the Paintbrush set to 40% Opacity.

Figure 3.15 Fill the new selection with white to see how a semi-opaque brush affects the selection.

Figure 3.16 Fill the Quick Mask window with black. The window appears to be filled with a translucent red.

Figure 3.17 Paint with 80% white to eliminate part of the Quick Mask covering the image.

To eliminate part of the Quick Mask in a different area of the image, divide the area into three parts: upper, lower, and underarm. As you paint each area, continue to hold the mouse button. What you're doing here is removing part of the mask by painting it with 80% white. As long as the mouse button is depressed, you're able to paint over the same area without removing more of the mask. If you release the mouse button, more of the mask is removed, which results in a blotchy, uneven painted area.

Next, change the Opacity of the brush to 40% by pressing 4. Paint the other side of the image, as shown in Figure 3.18. Be certain to paint the entire area without releasing the mouse button. When you're finished, the model should be untouched, and the areas on each side will be masked with lesser densities.

Figure 3.18 Paint with 40% white to eliminate part of the Quick Mask in a different area of the image.

Figure 3.19 Outside of Quick Mask, fill the selection with white to screen back the areas around the model.

Fill the selection with white to screen back the areas around the model. First exit Quick Mask by pressing Q, and then press the Delete key. The model is now shown (see Figure 3.19) to be untouched, while the areas on either side are screened back by 60% (right) and 20% (left). The two percentages are the reciprocals of the Paintbrush Opacity settings.

Quick Mask offers an easy way to edit portions of an image. In cases where you're going to apply unusual editing effects, it is very helpful to use one of the large, soft-edged brushes so that there is a free and natural transition along the edges of the affected areas. The following set of directions shows how a somewhat romanticized background can be added to the Quick Mask Tryout image. When you see how easy and quick some of these effects are, you'll want to experiment with your own combinations.

Return to Quick Mask mode and fill the image with the mask color. You can do this by returning the Foreground/Background colors to their defaults by pressing either the D or the X key, then Option+Delete or Alt+Delete. Or you can fill the image with the background color—black— by pressing Command+Delete or Ctrl+Delete. Choose the 200-pixel brush and set its Opacity to 80%. Paint the area to the upper left of the model to partially remove its mask. The area to be painted is shown in Figure 3.20.

Now try the Watercolor filter on the selected area. To do that, exit Quick Mask. Then from the Filter menu, choose Artistic|Watercolor. Experiment, if you wish, with the settings for this filter. When you find one you like, allow the filter to execute. The result is shown in Figure 3.21.

The Watercolor filter can also be applied to a completely unmasked area as well as an area that has been masked at 20%. But this usually results in an overall darkening of the pixels to which it's applied. By using the partial mask, the darkening effect of the filter can be mitigated. Note: As an alternative way of doing the same thing, you could execute the filter on a completely unmasked area and then use the Filter|Fade command—20% Opacity setting—to accomplish the same effect.

Figure 3.20 Paint out part of the Quick Mask with a white Paintbrush set to 80% Opacity.

Figure 3.21 Use the Watercolor filter on the selected area.

Now return to Quick Mask mode and eliminate a different area of the Quick Mask with a white Paintbrush. First, fill the entire window with the mask color. Then, using the same 200-pixel brush—this time with 60% Opacity—paint the lower left part of the image, as shown in Figure 3.22. Don't waste time trying to get the edges painted perfectly; the final image will probably be more successful if you paint out the mask in a fairly casual manner. It doesn't really matter that the filter to be applied next slightly overlaps the central figure.

Next try the Pointillize filter on the new selection. With the mask complete, exit Quick Mask mode. From the Filter menu, choose Pixelate|Pointillize. Choose a cell size of 10 pixels and click on OK. The effect of the filter is shown in Figure 3.23.

Figure 3.22 Eliminate a different area of the Quick Mask with a white Paintbrush set to 60% Opacity.

Figure 3.23 Use the Pointillize filter on the new selection.

Now let's enter Quick Mask mode and fill the entire image with the mask color. Use the same brush size—Foreground color set to white—but with the Opacity to 20%. Paint out the entire right side of the image, as shown in Figure 3.24.

Exit Quick Mask mode. Because of the low Opacity setting for the Paintbrush, you may receive a message that reads, "Warning: No pixels are more than 50% selected. The selection edges will not be visible." Don't worry about the message. Simply click on OK and try to remember for the next few minutes that a selection is active even if you cannot see its edges.

Let's try the Retroscan filter (available on the companion CD-ROM) on the selection, to fill it with translucent horizontal lines. To do this, choose Deep Devices|Retroscan from the Filter menu. (Note: If you have a lot of filters installed, the Deep Devices submenu may not be present. If it isn't, look for Retroscan under the Other submenu.) Experiment with the settings if you wish, or accept the defaults. When the Retroscan filter has executed, the selected area will be filled with a set of narrow horizontal lines, as shown in Figure 3.25.

For another interesting effect, try using the Ripple filter on top of the Retroscan filter. Choose Distort|Ripple from the Filter menu. Experiment with the settings of the filter until the small preview window shows you a result you like. Allow the filter to execute. The results of the two filters are shown in Figure 3.26.

Let's try a more complex mask and make the sides of the unmasked area hard-edged, while leaving the top soft-edged, as shown in Figure 3.27. To do this, use the same brush with the Opacity set to 80%. Paint out the area of the model's slacks. Press X to reverse the Foreground/Background colors. Change the Opacity of the brush to about 20%. Then paint over the upper area of the slacks, working downward. Finally, lay new color over old color to build up the gradual change from dark to light shown in the figure.

To look at the final figure, exit Quick Mask. Choose Pixelate/Mosaic from the Filter menu. Use a cell size of 30 pixels. Click on OK to execute the filter. Press Command+D or Ctrl+D to

Figure 3.24 Paint out a different section of the Quick Mask with a white Paintbrush set to 20% Opacity.

Figure 3.25 Use the Retroscan filter on the selection to fill it with translucent horizontal lines.

Figure 3.26 The Ripple filter used on top of the Retroscan filter produces a fill with attractive waving lines.

Figure 3.27 Make a more complex unmasked area with the Paintbrush: The sides of the unmasked area are hard-edged, while the top is soft-edged.

deselect, and take a look at the final image (see Figure 3.28). You can also see the finished image in color in the color section of this book.

You can also use Quick Mask to create a variety of textured edges for your images. Try these fast effects using an untouched copy of the file QM_01.PSD.

Create a Quick Mask rectangle subjected to 15-pixel Gaussian Blur. To do that, enter Quick Mask mode. Now draw a rectangular selection similar in size to that shown in Figure 3.29. Next, fill the rectangle with the mask color. Deselect by pressing Command+D or Ctrl+D. Then choose Blur|Gaussian Blur from the Filter menu using a pixel radius of 15. With the blur, the preparation for the edge effect is complete. In order to try a number of different effects, use the

Figure 3.28 The final figure is realistically centered amid romantic special effects.

Figure 3.29 Quick Mask rectangle subjected to 15-pixel Gaussian Blur.

Image menu's Duplicate command to create a new image window. Perform the following steps on the duplicate of the image. If you wish to try more than one of these effects, continue to duplicate the original image and work from the copies.

The simplest edge effect, the vignette edge, can be accomplished at once. Simply exit Quick Mask mode after blurring the mask. With the Background color set to white, press the Delete key.

Applying filters of various kinds while you're in Quick Mask mode results in more interesting edges. Figure 3.30, for example, shows the Filter|Distort|Ripple effect—with settings of Large and 800—after it has been applied to the blurred rectangular mask area. To obtain another interesting border effect, simply exit Quick Mask and press Delete to fill the selection with white, as shown in Figure 3.31.

Figures 3.32 and 3.33 were made the same way. Figure 3.32 uses the Mosaic filter with a pixel value of 35. To get the edge effect shown in Figure 3.33, use the Filter|Pixelate|Color Halftone filter. Then set the Maximum Pixel Radius value to 20 and the value of Channel One to 45°.

Figure 3.34 uses Filter|Pixelate|Pointillize with a cell size value of 15. After executing this filter, you need to fill in the pixellated areas within the central figure. Use a Paintbrush with the Foreground color set to black. If you don't fill in the speckled areas within the figure, you will eliminate parts of the model when, after you exit Quick Mask, you fill the selection with white.

Finally, another edge effect combines several techniques you've already used along with a new one. Go back to the original masked image (Figure 3.29) and subject it to a heavier (Radius of 30) Gaussian Blur.

Open the file QM_01PAT.PSD shown in Figure 3.35 from the Chapter 3 Practice Files folder. Select All. Choose Edit|Define Pattern. Close the document.

Figure 3.30 The Ripple filter applied to the blur-edged Quick Mask.

Figure 3.31 Outside of Quick Mask, fill the selection with white for an interesting border effect.

Figure 3.32 A different edge effect uses the Mosaic filter.

Figure 3.33 You can create another edge effect with the Color Halftone filter.

Figure 3.34 You can create this edge effect with the Pixelate/Pointillize filter.

Figure 3.35 Use the contents of this small file to define a pattern. The letters, in the font New Berolina, are offset lines containing the name of a play by Alexandre Dumas, *The Lady of the Camellias*.

Work now on your original image. Select All, and press Shift+Delete. This command opens the Fill dialog box (which you can also select from the Edit menu). Make the settings as shown in Figure 3.36: Foreground Color, 20% Opacity, Normal. After you click on OK, your non-masked areas should be filled with a 20% screen of the mask color.

Your entire window should be selected. Press Shift+Delete again. This time, make the settings as shown in Figure 3.37: Pattern, 100% Opacity, Normal. Click on OK, and deselect. Your mask window should now look the way it does in Figure 3.38.

This edge effect is as simple as those you achieved earlier are. Just press the Q key to leave Quick Mask, and press Delete to fill the selection with white (see Figure 3.39). Considering the sophisticated look of this image, it's breathtakingly simple to create.

Here's another useful trick you can use with Quick Mask: By filling the Quick Mask window with various percentages of the masking color and then exiting Quick Mask, you have a quick way to modify—or mask—the results of a command or a filter. You can see one example of this in the application of the Watercolor filter to the upper left part of the Tryout image (see Figure 3.20). For another possibility, open the CD-ROM file titled QM_02.PSD.

This CMYK image lost some of its color intensity during the translation from RGB mode to CMYK. These colors can be brightened a number of ways, but we can use Quick Mask to give an effect that will brighten and intensify the central figure. Then, with the inverse of the same mask, we will make the area around the figure darker and duller. The overall effect will be a radical enhancement of the figure against the background. Follow these instructions:

1. When you open the file QM_02.PSD, you will already be in Quick Mask mode. The mask you see in Figure 3.40 will already be in place. Notice that the mask shape was made by simply cutting out the figure of the woman from the all-over fill of the window with the mask color. Making a mask of this sort, as you can imagine, is only a few moments' work.

Figure 3.36 Fill the entire window with the mask color set to 20% Opacity.

Figure 3.37 Use the Fill dialog box to fill your window with the pattern.

TOOLBOX TECHNIQUES **135**

Figure 3.38 After you've completed both fills, your Quick Mask window should look like this.

Figure 3.39 The final edge effect—a smooth amalgamation of type and image.

2. From the Filter menu, choose Blur|Gaussian Blur. Set the radius to a fairly high value. Figure 3.41 shows the setting for this image as 50.

3. Press the Q key to exit Quick Mask. From the Image menu, choose Adjust|Hue/Saturation. Move the Saturation slider (see Figure 3.42) to the right so that it reads 18. Notice how this brightens the central part of the image and makes the colors more intense. Click on OK.

Figure 3.40 When you open the practice file, you will already be in Quick Mask mode, with the mask of the background area already in place.

Figure 3.41 Blur the mask with a high radius setting. In this case, 50 was the setting.

4. From the Select menu, choose Inverse. The background of your image is now selected. Open the Hue/Saturation controls again and desaturate the selection by the amount shown in Figure 3.43 (the Saturation data field reads –25). With this adjustment, you make the figure of the woman stand out from the background by boosting the difference in saturation between the two areas. Although you have made the colors in the center of the image brighter by saturating them, you have made them appear even more vivid by muting the colors that surround them. Click on OK.

5. Press Q to return to Quick Mask. Press Command+F or Ctrl+F (your last-used filter was Gaussian Blur) four or five times to reapply the blur to the mask. This operation spreads the mask and further attenuates it (see Figure 3.44).

6. Exit Quick Mask and type Command+L or Ctrl+L to open the Levels controls. Move the gamma slider (the center slider on the upper scale) to the right until the center data entry field reads 0.80. Notice that the background becomes darker and that the colors in the background become richer (see Figure 3.45).

A comparison of the original and the altered image is shown in Figure 3.46. Even though the image is presented here in black and white, you can see how the woman on the right side is surrounded by a subtle halo of light. The image is more dramatic in color (see the Color Studio of this book), where the central part of the image seems to glow with the intensity of the colors. The effect is magical.

Figure 3.42 With the selection mask active, open the Hue/Saturation controls. Adjust the Saturation of the selection by the amount shown here.

Figure 3.43 After selecting the inverse, desaturate the background to boost the contrast between both areas.

TOOLBOX TECHNIQUES **137**

Figure 3.44 Return to Quick Mask. Apply the Gaussian Blur filter four or five times to attenuate the mask.

Figure 3.45 With the new selection of the background active, use the Levels controls to darken and enrich the colors.

Figure 3.46 The final image: Glowing light surrounds the figure.

Screen Mode Selectors

At the bottom of the Photoshop Toolbox are three icons that control the screen display. You can switch between the modes by clicking on the icons, or you can cycle through them by pressing the F key.

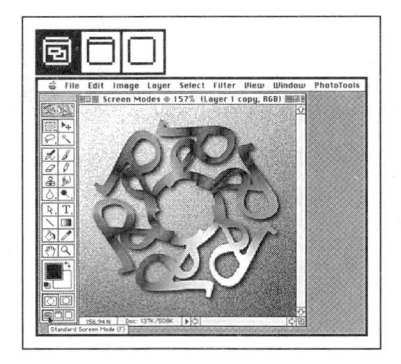

Figure 3.47 Photoshop's Standard window mode.

The first mode is the standard for Windows or Macintosh programs; in this mode, the desktop and other open windows are visible behind the active window (see Figure 3.47).

The second mode expands the image window to cover the desktop and all other open windows with a neutral gray. This mode is particularly handy in several situations. First, desktop patterns may be an enjoyable way of personalizing your computer, but they can sometimes interfere with your color perception as you make adjustments to an image. Covering the desktop with neutral gray is a good temporary solution. Second, when you're making selections—particularly on the far-left edge of the active window—it's sometimes difficult to avoid clicking outside the window. The operating system interprets a click outside the window as a command to go back to the desktop. With the second screen mode active, you can paint, select, or crop past the boundaries of the image (see Figure 3.48). Note: If you want, you can change the color of the background in the second screen mode. Set your Foreground color to the color you wish to use. Select the Paint Bucket tool, hold down the Shift key, and click once anywhere outside the image window.

The third screen mode hides the menu bar, scroll bars, and all other open windows, and replaces them with black. In this mode, it's possible to concentrate completely on the image. You can, if you want, hide the open palettes in two ways. First, press Shift+Tab, which hides all of the palettes except the Toolbox. Press Tab to hide all of the palettes including the Toolbox. (You can make all of the palettes appear again simply by pressing the Tab key again.) To take a

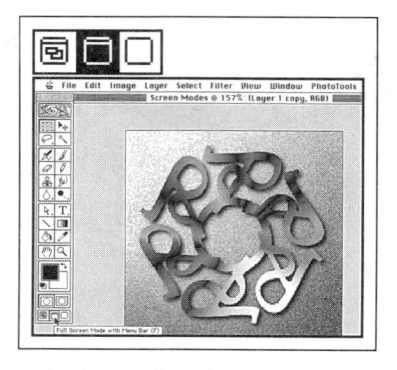

Figure 3.48 Photoshop's neutral gray background mode.

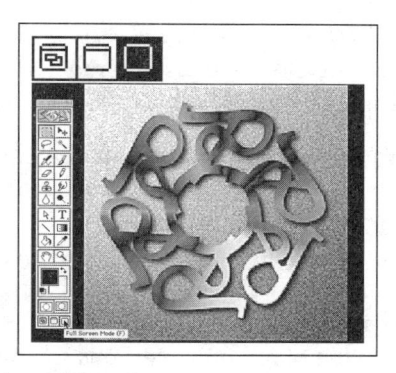

Figure 3.49 Photoshop's black background mode.

good look at your image without any distractions, do the following: Press F, F, Tab, and then Command+0 (zero) on the Mac or Ctrl+0 (zero) in Windows. Your image, and only your image, fills the screen from edge to edge, as shown in Figure 3.49.

Tools

One or more variations or options govern all of the Photoshop tools—with the exception of the Type tool. These variations are set by means of the Options palette. If the Options palette is not visible, choose Show Options from the Window menu. The Options palette can also be summoned by double-clicking on any of the tools on the Toolbox. The Options palette also contains a provision, except for the Type tool, for resetting a single tool to its defaults, or for resetting all tools to their defaults. Click and hold on the triangle at the upper right corner of the palette and choose either command from the palette menu.

All of Photoshop's tools have additional capabilities that enable a power user to work very quickly indeed. You can access these tool enhancements directly from within the working window without having to move the cursor from its position. On the Macintosh, hold down the Ctrl key, click, and hold the mouse button. In Windows, press the right mouse button. A contextual menu of commands relevant to the tool appears as a pop-up menu at the cursor location. We will discuss these menus as we look at the individual tools in more detail.

About Selections

The selection tools include the Marquee tools, the Lasso, the Magic Wand, and the Pen tool. Of these, the Pen tool is sufficiently different from the others that we discuss it separately in Chapter 4.

The short black and white lines that dance clockwise around the edges of the selected area distinguish a *selection* in Photoshop. Whether it is called one or not, a selection is really a mask. Commands that are issued execute only within the boundaries of the selection and tools function only within that area as well. The unselected part of the image is masked from all change.

The selection boundary, unless the Move tool is selected, is independent of the pixels that comprise the selection. When you place any of the selection tools into the selection area, the cursor changes to a Selection cursor. You can move the selection boundary around within the window without disturbing the enclosed pixels. You can also drag it from window to window. Using this capability, a selection made in one window can become a mask in another.

When you use the Move tool, dragging a selection boundary also drags the pixels. The selected pixels become what amounts to a temporary layer that floats above the layer from which it was derived. Previous versions of Photoshop allowed you to manipulate the floating selection in many of the ways you can manipulate a layer. Photoshop 5 no longer allows this. You can move the pixels from place to place, but that's it. The disadvantage to a floating selection is that when the selection is dropped, the pixels are dropped back onto the image and replace the pixels on which they fall. With the Move tool, selections can also be cloned as they are moved. Simply hold down Option or Alt while dragging the selection, and the floating selection becomes a copy of the originally selected pixels.

The Select Menu

A variety of options that pertain to selections are found under the Select menu, shown in Figure 3.50. Note that this figure depicts a Macintosh menu that uses the clover-shaped Command key. Windows users should substitute the Ctrl key for the Command key.

Select All, Select None, And Select Inverse—Select All of an image or a layer, and Select None, which deselects all selected pixels, are self-explanatory. When you use Select Inverse, selected pixels become deselected, while all unselected pixels become selected. This command is the equivalent of using the Invert command while in Quick Mask mode.

> **TIP**
>
> If you can't seem to remember to use the contextual menu commands (on the Macintosh, hold down the Control key, click, and hold; in Windows, right-click and hold), Select Inverse is a good candidate for assignment to a QuicKey or to the Actions palette. There *is* a key command assigned to Select Inverse, but it's one of those awkward, two-handed ones. Here's one example of why you'll find it a good thing to be able to quickly select the inverse of your present selection. When you use any of the paint tools, it's often necessary to maintain a contour or a line of contrast between two adjoining areas. By making a selection along the line, you can place painting effects precisely along the line within the selection. Inverting the selection allows the same precision painting along the other side of the selection marquee. It's often useful to zoom into the line in question and to estimate the hardness of the line. If the line is soft, add a feather radius (feathered selections are discussed below) appropriate to the edge before using the paint tools. In Figure 3.51, the task is to remove the gray circle from atop the black shape (*1*). Zooming in shows the soft edge of the black shape (*2*). By using one of the selection tools with a feather radius, the black area is painted, the selection inverted, and the light gray area is painted (*3*). A close-up of the finished edit is shown next (*4*), and finally, the completed image (*5*).

TOOLBOX TECHNIQUES **141**

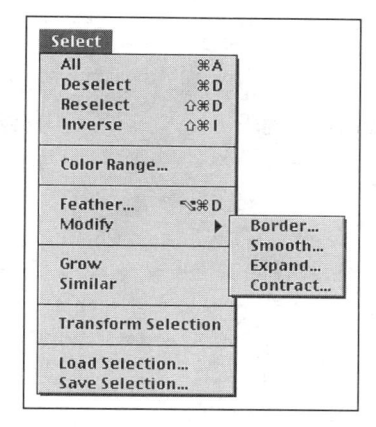

Figure 3.50 Photoshop's Select menu.

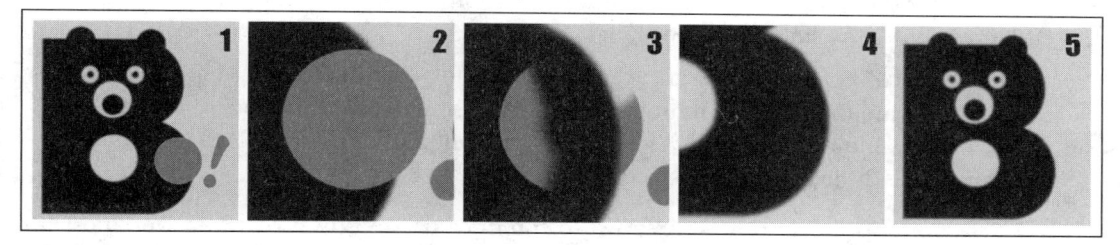

Figure 3.51 Feathered selections let you edit pixels along a soft edge.

Select Color Range, Grow, And Similar—The Select Color Range, Grow, and Similar commands will be discussed in the following section on the Magic Wand tool.

Feather—*Feathering* can be added to the edge of a selection while the selection is being drawn, or it can be applied afterward using this menu command. Feathering takes the normally hard edges of a selection and softens them. In effect, the edge of the selection disappears using a transition that fades from opaque to transparent. Feathering is measured in pixels and occurs both inside and outside the selection outlines. Small pixel numbers give you a narrow feather effect. Larger numbers give a wider zone of feathering.

Modify—The Modify section of the Select menu allows you to make a modification of a selection in four different ways: Border, Smooth, Expand, and Contract, which are detailed in the following list:

- *Border*—The Border command makes a selection of the zone of pixels around the original selection marquee (1 and 2 in Figure 3.52). The size of this border zone depends on the number entered in the dialog box. The value can range from 1 to 16. The border area is calculated inside and outside from the original selection perimeter and always has a feathered edge both inside and outside. See 3 in Figure 3.52, in which the border has been filled with black.

- *Smooth*—The Smooth command rounds off any corners in the selection line. In addition, it deselects any small selected areas outside of the main selection marquee and selects any

142 CHAPTER 3

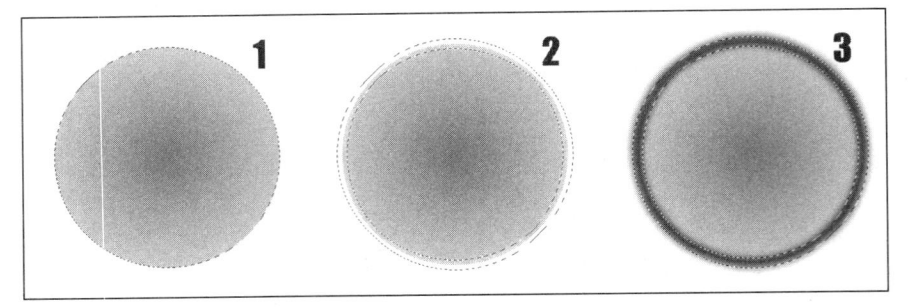

Figure 3.52 The Border command makes a selection enclosing the edges of the first selection.

stray unselected areas within that marquee. The input value is a radius in pixels that calculates the amount of rounding and the minimum size of stray selected and deselected areas that will be affected. You can see the rounding effect in Figure 3.53, where 1 is the original selection and 2 is the smoothed selection.

- *Expand, Contract*—Expand and Contract allow you to increase and decrease the area of a selection by moving the selection marquee out or in by some number of pixels between 1 and 16. The effect is shown in Figure 3.54, where 1 is the original selection, 2 is the expanded selection, and is 3 the contracted selection.

Load Selection, Save Selection—These two commands are mostly used when working with Channels. We will discuss Load Selection and Save Selection in Chapter 5.

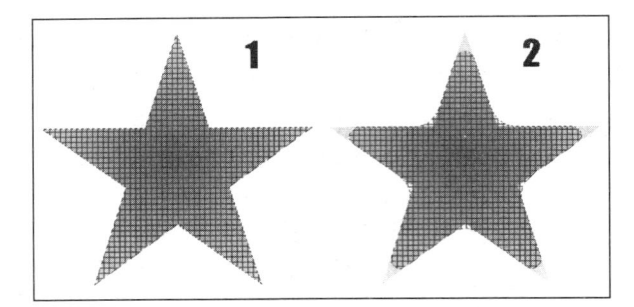

Figure 3.53 The Smooth command rounds off any corners on a selection.

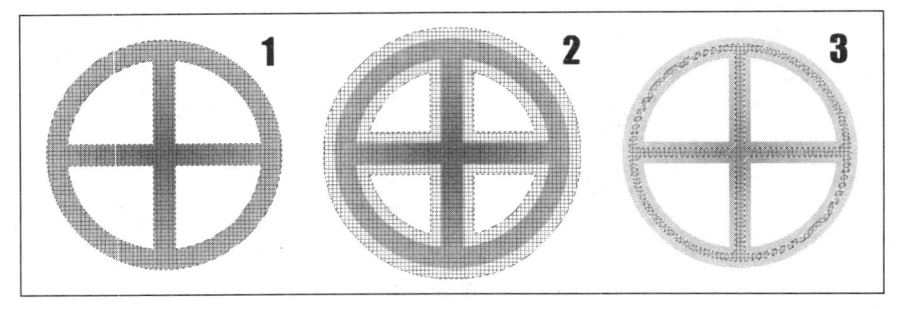

Figure 3.54 Expand pushes a selection's edges outward. Contract pulls the selection's edges inward.

Other Ways To Modify Selections

Drawing selections is a straightforward task. After the selection has been completed, it's often necessary to alter its shape in some way. The selection might need to be larger in some portions, smaller in others. You have three useful keyboard combinations at your disposal that you can use with the selection tools to make such alterations:

- When you're adding to a selection, you can use any one of the selection tools with the Shift key held down. You will notice that the cursor adds a small plus shape to help you remember which operation is being performed (see above). The area being added to the selection can adjoin the original area or it can be in another part of the image.
- You can subtract from an existing selection by holding the Option or Alt key while using one of the selection tools. The cursor will add a small minus shape. The area subtracted can be from the edges of the existing selection or even from entirely within the area.
- The third method for altering the shape of a selection is to draw with any of the selection tools a shape that intersects the existing selection. While drawing, hold Shift+Option or Shift+Alt. The cursor will exhibit a small "x" shape. The resulting selection will be whatever parts of the original selection area were enclosed by the newly drawn selection. This method is the inverse of subtracting from an existing selection.

The Selection, Move, And Crop Tools

The tools clustered at the top of the Toolbox allow you to isolate groups of pixels based on a drawn shape or based on comparable pixel values. Once selected, the contents of the shape can be moved around within the window, moved to another window, painted, darkened, or lightened. Any operation you wish to perform on them happens to them alone. The rest of the image is left untouched.

The simple selection tools are the Marquee tools. The Lasso tool adds a free form capability. Both are so simple that you can use them within the first few minutes of your first experience with Photoshop. After you make a selection, use the Move tool to drag the selected pixels from one place to another.

Selecting and moving seem to be simple concepts. Keep your eyes open—you'll find that just these simple tools have a lot of possibilities.

Marquee Tools

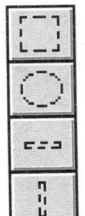

Rectangular, Elliptical, Single Row, and Single Column Marquee tools make simple geometric shapes. (Press M to select the Marquee tool slot; Shift+M cycles through the four Marquee selection tools.) The shapes for the two main tools, Rectangular and Elliptical, are customarily drawn from one corner to the opposite corner. They can be drawn from the center outward by holding down Option (Mac) or Alt (Windows). Pressing the Shift key after the click-and-drag procedure constrains the vertical and horizontal proportions of the shapes to be equal (square and circular). A rectangular selection, provided that it isn't feathered, also makes the Image|Crop command available.

The other two Marquee choices simply select a vertical or horizontal row of pixels as tall or as wide as the image. The options for the Marquee tools are shown in Figure 3.55.

Normal—The Normal option is the option most often used with the two principal tools. With Normal, freely drawn shapes enclose an area by approximate measurement.

Constrained Aspect Ratio—Constrained Aspect Ratio (CAR) offers an easy way to draw perfect squares and circles if the numbers in the width and height boxes are equal. This gives the same effect as holding Shift when using the tools. CARs can be integers or decimal fractions. Proportions might be, for example, 3:5.75. Or they could be as abstract as 247:355. CAR is also useful for making a variety of selections that have common proportions without being the same size. Simply enter the vertical and horizontal pixel numbers of one image as the proportions. (If the numbers are very large, divide by 10 or 100 and enter them as decimal fractions. For example, 1,857 pixels could be entered as 18.75.) With these numbers, you can make selections in other images that are larger or smaller than the original, but which have the same proportional shape.

Fixed Size—Fixed Size lets you make a selection based on an arbitrary number of pixels. You will find this very useful when you're making clips of a variety of pictures that must all be exactly the same size. Photoshop furnishes a convenient way to obtain information about an image file (including its size): Hold down Option or Alt, then click and hold in the lower left-hand corner of the window in the area that gives the memory size of the document (see Figure 3.56).

> **TIP**
>
> The Single Column and Single Row Marquee tools come in very handy at times, especially if you have set up hot keys for Select Inverse and Image|Crop (although Select Inverse is available from the contextual menu). When a scan has been cropped imprecisely and a single row of black or white pixels is visible along one edge, select the tool, click in the window, and run the cursor as far as it will go toward the faulty edge. Select Inverse, Crop, Done. You don't even have to zoom up to the edge to see if it worked!

You can use Single Row—this is admittedly a very exotic use for the tool—to emulate the coarse effect of file interlacing. Use this tool on a file that is not too large and that has been cropped so that the vertical pixel number is a multiple of 8 or10. Click in the image and run the cursor to

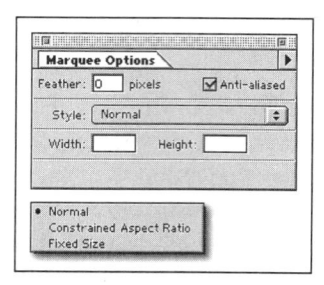

Figure 3.55 Options for the Marquee tools.

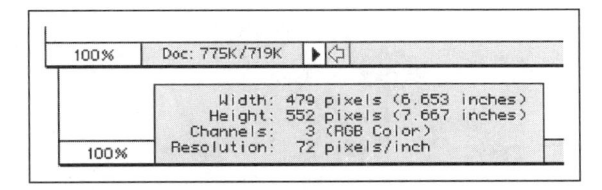

```
                100%   Doc: 775K/719K  ▶◁
                       Width:  479 pixels (6.653 inches)
                      Height:  552 pixels (7.667 inches)
                    Channels:    3 (RGB Color)
                100%  Resolution: 72 pixels/inch
```

Figure 3.56 Information pop-up in the lower left-hand corner of a Photoshop document window.

the top of the window. Follow this procedure: Hold Command+Option or Ctrl+Alt and click the Down arrow seven to nine times. Release the command keys. Press Command+E or Ctrl+E. Click on the Down arrow once. Repeat this entire procedure to the bottom of the image. Figure 3.57 shows the effect of using sets of 15 pixels, sets of 8, and the original image.

You can also accomplish this interesting visual effect in other ways. Because of the tedious nature of the following method, the effect could be made a sequence of commands and placed on the Actions palette. Here's the general method:

1. Work at fairly high magnification.
2. Select the Single Row tool, click in the window, and run the cursor to the top.
3. Choose Edit|Define Pattern. Change to the rectangular Marquee tool and choose Fixed Size from the Style pop-up menu on the Marquee Options palette.
4. Enter the width of the image in the Width field and a number, such as 12, in the Height field.
5. Click again in the image and run the cursor to the top of the window. Choose Edit|Fill, and Fill with Pattern. Repeat this procedure on each set of 12 rows down the image. The same effect can be done using Single Columns.

The contextual menus that are available for the Marquee tools are shown in Figures 3.58 and 3.59. These menus pop up on the screen, springing from the position of the cursor in the image window. On the Macintosh, hold the Control key, then press and hold the mouse button. In Windows, use the right mouse button. Figure 3.58 is the menu that results when no selection is active. Figure 3.59 is the menu when a selection is active. (Note: The options in the lower sections of these two contextual menus relate to the use of paths, filters, layers, and transformations. Each of these options is explored in other places in this book.)

Figure 3.57 Three emulations of the display of an interlaced file.

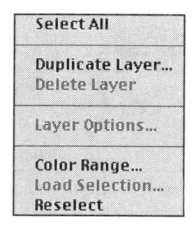

```
Select All

Duplicate Layer...
Delete Layer

Layer Options...

Color Range...
Load Selection...
Reselect
```

Figure 3.58 Contextual menu for the Marquee tools when no selection is active.

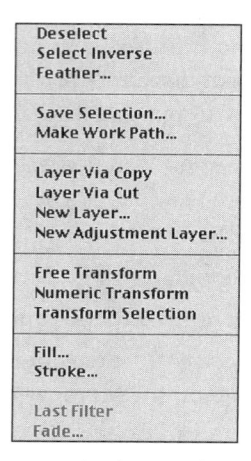

```
Deselect
Select Inverse
Feather...

Save Selection...
Make Work Path...

Layer Via Copy
Layer Via Cut
New Layer...
New Adjustment Layer...

Free Transform
Numeric Transform
Transform Selection

Fill...
Stroke...

Last Filter
Fade...
```

Figure 3.59 Contextual menu for the Marquee tools when a selection is active.

Lasso Tools

The Lasso tools are the freehand selection tools. (Pressing L selects the Lasso tool slot, Shift+L cycles through the three Lasso selection tools.) With them, you can draw a selection that is more complex than a geometric shape. There are three choices: the original curved-line, click-and-drag selector; the Polygonal Lasso; and the new Magnetic Lasso tool. The options for these tools are shown in Figure 3.60. The contextual menus are the same as for the Marquee tools (see Figures 3.58 and 3.59).

With the normal Lasso tool, selections are imprecise and fairly fast. The mouse, after all, is not an easy tool with which to draw along delicate edges, but you can run it around the screen at quite a speed. By selecting the second Lasso variation from the Tools palette, or by holding down Option or Alt, the normal Lasso is converted to polygon mode. Click with the mouse in one place. As you move the cursor away from that point, a rubberband line follows it. The line is anchored with another click. By working at relatively high magnification, it's possible to lay small, straight-line segments against an edge, and to make a very precise selection. The cursor, even with Option or Alt held down, can still be dragged in the normal freehand manner. Note that all selections in Photoshop are ultimately composed of straight-line segments because selections are based on the inclusion or exclusion of tiny, square pixels.

The Polygonal Lasso tool works in the same way the normal tool works with the modifier key (Option or Alt); straight lines rubberband from click-point to click-point. With Option or Alt held down, the tool can be dragged in freehand fashion. The modifier key, then, acts to put the tool into its alternate mode.

When you're making a selection with the Polygonal Lasso, the cursor has to move within a pixel or two of the starting click-point. A small circle appears next to the cursor to indicate that the next click will close the shape. The selection can be completed another way: Hold down Command or Ctrl. The next click makes a selection that connects the last click to the first.

To select an object with the Lasso tool for the purpose of dropping out the background, you have to work at a high zoom level; select a small portion of the object, and use the Shift key to add to the selection. After working entirely around the edge of the object, zoom back. With the Shift key, add the interior of the object.

A simpler way to do the job is to work around the edges in Quick Mask mode. Press Q to enter Quick Mask mode. Set the Background color to black. Work around the edges in the manner described previously. As each area is drawn, press Delete to fill it with the mask color. Deselect, and move to the next area. The following set of instructions give complete details on how you can do this, and provides some tips for making the silhouette edges look good without spending a lot of time on them.

Expert Silhouettes—To make Expert Silhouettes, take these steps:

1. Open the file QM_03.PSD, found in the Chapter 3 Practice Files folder on the companion CD-ROM (seen in Figure 3.61). Note that the file on disk is in color even though the

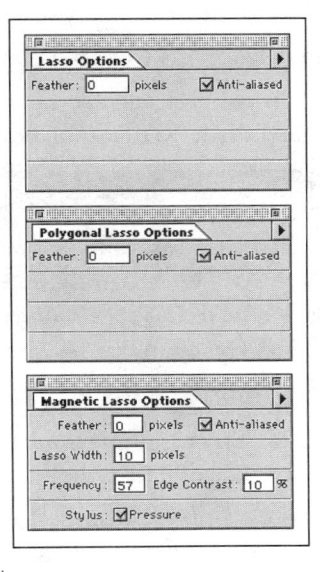

Figure 3.60 Options for the Lasso tools.

Figure 3.61 The tutorial image from which the background pixels are to be eliminated.

examples pictured here are in black and white. That means you'll have more fun working through this tutorial than if you simply read through the material!

2. Zoom up to the image so that the magnification is approximately the same as shown in Figure 3.62.
3. Press Q to enter Quick Mask mode.
4. Set the Foreground/Background colors to their defaults (press D).
5. Choose the Polygonal Lasso tool. Draw carefully around an area along the figure.
6. When a small area is completed, press Option+Delete or Alt+Delete to fill the area with the mask color.
7. Deselect, and move to the next area. Do the same procedure again (see Figure 3.63).

> **TIP**
>
> Until you've practiced this and become fast at it, you might need to do this exercise over a period of time. Here's an easy way to preserve your place in the work so that you can come back to it at a later time: Save, and then close your file while in Quick Mask mode. The next time you open the file, you will still be in Quick Mask with all of your previous masking work exactly as you left it.

8. When you come to the hair, don't try to outline the soft edge with the Lasso tool. Select an area fairly close to the hair edge and fill it with the mask color (see Figure 3.64).
9. Choose a brush (in this case a 15-pixel brush), set it to Normal mode, and set the Opacity to 100%. Brush the edge of the hair with strokes that follow the grain of the

Figure 3.62 Work at high magnification. Outline an area, fill it with the mask color, and Deselect.

Figure 3.63 Another area along the edge filled and masked.

hair (see Figure 3.65). If you don't have a brush this size, choose New Brush from the Brushes palette pop-up menu. Make the Size 15 pixels and the Hardness 0.

10. Continue working around the figure. When the entire edge has been masked, zoom back.

Figure 3.64 Select and fill the area close to the hairline with the Lasso tool.

Figure 3.65 Use the Paintbrush tool, brushing with the grain of the hair, to mask the soft-edged hairline.

11. Use the Polygonal Lasso tool to select the interior of the figure (see Figure 3.66).
12. Fill the interior with the mask color (see Figure 3.67).
13. Since the purpose of this exercise is to silhouette the figure, the mask must now be inverted. Press Command+I or Ctrl+I. The image now appears as it does in Figure 3.68.
14. Press Q to exit Quick Mask (the figure will be selected). You could, if you want, simply invert the selection and fill the background with white. However, it's a good idea to keep your options open. Instead of deleting the background, try this as an alternative:

- Press Command+J (Mac) or Ctrl+J (Windows) to turn the selected pixels into a layer.
- On the Layers palette, click on the Background layer, then click on the page-shaped icon at the bottom of the palette to create a new, blank layer between the background and the silhouetted figure's layer.
- Fill this new layer with white. (The image will look the way it does in Figure 3.69.) With the file in this three-layer form, you now have a range of other possibilities. You could, for example, change the Opacity of the center layer to 60%. That would give the effect of screening back the area around the central figure. Or you could add another image, pattern, or color. You need not commit to the white background until you're certain that's what you want.

Zoom up to the figure (see Figure 3.70) so that you can take a look at the edges of the silhouette shape. Do they look too much as though they don't belong to the image, but to the hidden background? Do they look harsh and too dark? Try the following procedure to make the edges look perfect.

Figure 3.66 The entire edge of the figure has been masked.

Figure 3.67 Use the Polygonal Lasso tool to select the interior of the figure. Fill the interior selection with the mask color.

Figure 3.68 Invert the mask.

Figure 3.69 The model's shape is now on a separate layer with a plain white layer behind. The original background is still intact below the white layer.

1. Click on the top layer of the Layers palette to select it.
2. Command+click or Ctrl+click on the top layer's thumbnail on the Layers palette. The figure is now selected.

Figure 3.70 Zoom up to the image to see if the edges are perfect. Until you practice doing this, they probably won't be. If they're not, don't worry. Silhouette edges are easy to fix.

Figure 3.71 Select the figure, then make a border selection along the edge.

3. From the Select menu, choose Modify|Border. Enter a value of 4 (see Figure 3.71).
4. Set your Foreground/Background colors to the default. From the Edit menu, choose Fill (or hold down Shift and press Delete).
5. Choose Background Color from the Fill pop-up menu, and set the Opacity to 50%. The effect is shown in Figure 3.72.
6. After filling the border, choose Filter|Blur|Gaussian Blur. Set the radius to .5 pixels. The new edges now look as they do in Figure 3.73.

If you want, use a magnifying glass to look at the larger image shown in Figure 3.74. The edges look clean, smooth, and absolutely natural.

> **TIP**
>
> Here's something to keep in mind. With the exception of the hair, all of the selections in this image were along fairly hard edges. There are times, however, when a selection involves various kinds of edges. While working in Quick Mask mode, you can experiment with the Feather settings of the Lasso tools to arrive at an edge around a selection that possesses differing degrees of hardness.

The Magnetic Lasso—The first time you use the Magnetic Lasso, it will make you laugh. Okay, maybe just giggle. But you'll be delighted with this tool. It's clever, easy to use, and a darned good idea.

The Magnetic Lasso draws selections as you drag it along an edge. Magically, its trailing lines—elastic versions of the rubberband lines that follow the Polygonal Lasso—snap to the edges, or lines of contrast differential, of the pixels you are selecting. It does this by detecting the amount

TOOLBOX TECHNIQUES **153**

Figure 3.72 Fill the border selection with 50% white.

Figure 3.73 Use a .5-pixel-radius Gaussian Blur on the border selection.

Figure 3.74 The final silhouetted figure. The edges are perfect!

of contrast in pixel values within a given radius and drawing along the boundaries containing the greatest contrast. All you have to do is simply click as if you were using the Polygonal Lasso, placing points along the edges of the shape you are outlining. You can also just click and drag roughly along the contour you are trying to select. The former method is probably the most efficient way to work with this tool, and the method that will give you the most precise selection. Whichever way you choose to work, the Magnetic Lasso does the heavy-duty part of the selection. When you get to the end of the perimeter you are enclosing, move the cursor close to the beginning of the trace. The cursor will change to a small version of the Magnetic Lasso icon with a small circle to the lower right. When you see this circle, all you have to do is click once more to complete the selection. It's so incredibly cool!

Here are a couple of points you should be aware of when you use this tool. First, when you hold down Option or Alt and drag, you convert the behavior of the Magnetic Lasso tool to the behavior of the Normal Lasso tool. Hold down Option or Alt and click for the Magnetic Lasso tool to behave as if it were the Polygonal Lasso tool. As you draw with this tool, you can complete the selection at any time. To make a selection that connects the position of your cursor to the starting point, either double-click or press the Enter or Return key. Sometimes, you may have difficulty seeing the place where you began your trace. If that is the case, hold down Command or Ctrl and move your cursor into the vicinity of the starting point. Click once to complete the selection. If you want to cancel the Magnetic Lasso trace, press the Escape key. Alternately, you can type Command+. (period) or Ctrl+. (period).

The options in the lower part of Figure 3.60 are the defaults for this tool. The setting choices on the Options palette require some explanation, as follows:

- *Feather*—Feather, the first option, is common to all three variations of the Lasso. Use this option to set the softness of the final selection's edge.

- *Width*—The Width setting gives you a way to limit the area within which the dragged cursor searches for contrasting areas. A setting of 10 means that the search is confined to the area 5 pixels out—in all directions—from the hot point (center) of the cursor. For detection of edges within large, diffuse-toned areas, you'll want to make the Width setting larger. For small, relatively hard edges, a narrower width will do. You can change the Width at any time from the keyboard by pressing either of the bracket keys. The Width range is from 1 to 40.

- *Frequency*—As you drag your cursor along an edge, the Magnetic Lasso tool places anchor points along the way. The rate of setting those points is the Frequency number on the Options palette. As you set this number to higher values, you'll find that your initial selection line has many more points than if the number is low. You can experiment with this setting under different conditions. However, you'll probably find that the default settings work pretty well for most purposes. In most cases, this setting will not affect the way you work because you will probably lay down many more points than the setting will lay down for you. The Frequency range is from 0 to 100.

- *Edge Contrast*—Edge Contrast is a threshold setting. Your numerical input determines the amount of contrast Photoshop should use when searching for an edge along which to lay its trace path. The value can range between 1 percent to 100 percent. High values entered in this field mean that only highly contrasting pixels will be detected as edge boundaries. Lower values will detect boundaries between pixel values that are closer together.

If you work with a pressure-sensitive stylus and pad and have the Pressure checkbox turned on, bearing down on the stylus has the same effect as decreasing the Width of the tracing brush.

Magic Wand Tool

The Magic Wand tool (to choose this tool from the keyboard, press W) makes selections based on a tolerance value entered on the Options palette. Click anywhere within an image. Pixels to the right, left, top, and bottom of the clicked-upon pixel are examined to see if their color values fall within the tolerance range—above or below—of the original pixel. If they fall within that range, they are included in the selection. If not, they are not selected. This examination process proceeds outward from the original pixel until all contiguous pixels that fall within the range have been selected. With low tolerance values, the selection is usually small; often it is too small. With a higher tolerance value, the selection is larger; sometimes it is too large. Experimenting with tolerance values is a fact of life for users of the Magic Wand tool. It isn't that difficult, but it's rarely fun.

The options for the Magic Wand tool are shown in Figure 3.75. The contextual menu with no active selection is shown in Figure 3.76. With a selection, the contextual menu is as shown in Figure 3.77. Please note that the latter figure is available only if it is summoned by clicking in an area *outside* the current selection.

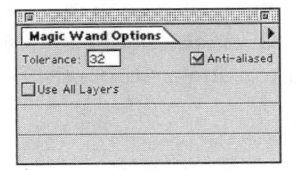

Figure 3.75 Options for the Magic Wand tool.

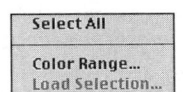

Figure 3.76 Contextual menu for the Magic Wand tool when clicked without an active selection.

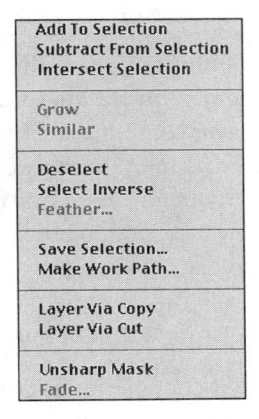

Figure 3.77 Contextual menu for the Magic Wand tool when clicked outside a selection area.

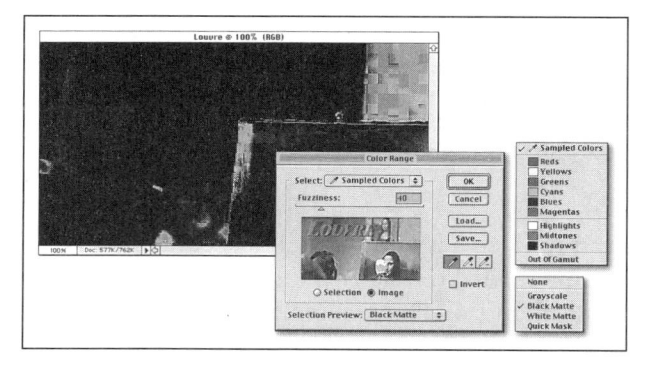

Figure 3.78 An expanded view of the Select Color Range dialog box.

Of the choices in the contextual menu, two are particularly relevant to the Magic Wand tool (both are also available from the Select menu). *Grow* is a command to extend the current selection by adding to it. The added pixels are selected based on an enlargement of the original tolerance value. *Similar* is the command to select all of the pixels in the image that fall within the range of those already selected. For example, when you're selecting the sky in an outdoor photograph, you might use these two commands in this way: First, the wand would click somewhere in the sky of the image. Since the sky is multi-toned, one or two applications of the Grow command might be needed for all of the sky in a contiguous area to be selected. It might even be necessary to hold down the Shift key and click in several places. After the main part of the sky has been selected, an application of the Similar command would add to the selection all of the parts of the sky not contiguous to the first selection. Such pixels might be those where the sky is glimpsed through the spaces between tree branches. You also could use the Similar command to select water reflections of sky-colored pixels.

Select Color Range From The Select Menu

The Magic Wand tool is sometimes useful but often unpredictable. Fortunately, Photoshop has a really wonderful alternative in the form of the Color Range command, found under the Select menu. Try this alternative, and you may never use the Magic Wand tool again!

Figure 3.78 shows a representation of an image with the Color Range dialog box. This dialog box shows the real power of Color Range: You are able to see the extent of your selection—and make adjustments to it—before you ever commit to it. The bottom pop-up menu gives several choices for how you want the preview to display. In this example, Black Matte has been chosen. The actual image window is filled with opaque black and only the areas to be selected show up to contrast with it. The image preview in the dialog box has been set to show the image. The top pop-up menu is set to Sampled Colors. Other choices for the top menu include specific color ranges—Reds, Yellows, Greens, Cyans, Blues, Magentas—as well as an automatic selection of all highlight values, midtones, shadows, or out-of-gamut colors.

When the dialog box opens, the cursor changes to an Eyedropper tool. Click anywhere in the preview image and all of the related values are immediately displayed in the image window to contrast with the Black Matte. You can, if you wish, also click in the document window. There are three cursor choices in the window—the default Eyedropper, the same tool with a small plus, and the tool with a small minus. You can choose your cursor from this Toolbox, or you may choose them using the keyboard. Hold the Shift key to change to the Eyedropper with the plus; hold Option or Alt to change to the minus.

After making a preliminary selection, the Eyedropper-plus lets you extend the selection by adding more values. With these preview settings, clicking on a still-dark area in the image window adds more pixels from the same general tone range. Eyedropper-minus excludes values from the eventual selection.

The Fuzziness slider is generally analogous to the Tolerance setting of the Magic Wand tool. The main difference is that a change to the fuzziness value instantly shows up on the screen. With this slider, it is possible to fine-tune a selection and to know instantly how a change in value will affect the selection. When using Select Color Range, make a selection with the Eyedropper tool. Then experiment with the Fuzziness slider before adding to or subtracting from the visible values.

The Color Selection dialog box contains another sophisticated setting—the Invert checkbox. With this box activated, you can choose your values from specific places in the image and the dialog box instantly converts your selection to its inverse.

Cropping Tool

The Cropping tool (press C) draws a rectangle within the boundaries of an image window. When the Crop command is executed, all of the area outside the rectangle is discarded. To execute the Crop command, press Return or Enter, or double-click inside the rectangle boundaries. The options for the Cropping tool are shown in Figure 3.79. There is also a contextual menu available (see Figure 3.80), but it's usable only before the crop rectangle is drawn.

After you draw the rectangle with this tool, you can resize it: Click and drag on any of its eight live points. The entire rectangle is movable. Click and drag within its boundaries. It can also be rotated: Click and drag outside the rectangle's edges. The latter feature is excellent for cropping and straightening images that have been scanned at a slight angle. The following figures show how this is done. The tilted scan is seen in Figure 3.81. Draw a small crop rectangle and orient it to an edge (see Figure 3.82). Expand the rectangle to cover as much of the image as possible

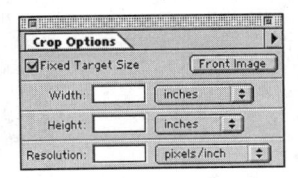

Figure 3.79 Options for the Cropping tool.

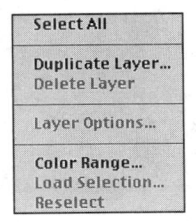

Figure 3.80 Contextual menu for the Cropping tool (available only if a crop rectangle is not active).

(see Figure 3.83). Execute the Cropping command. The image is cropped and straightened (see Figure 3.84). Note: If you type F to go to Full Screen mode, you can drag your cropping rectangle out past the boundaries of the image window.

By using the Fixed Size option, the Cropping tool can enlarge or reduce as the image is cropped. Enlarging is rarely a good idea because even with the sophisticated Bicubic interpolation scheme—the interpolation method that produces the highest-quality results—used by Photoshop to calculate the new size, increasing the physical size of an image always results in a softening of image detail. A good rule to follow: If the image needs to be enlarged, it should be rescanned to a larger size.

Width and height, expressed in pixels, inches, centimeters, points, picas, or columns can be entered along with a desired resolution whenever Fixed Target Size is checked. If a number of images are open and you wish to crop them all to the same size, bring to the front the image that is the size to which all the others are to be cropped. Click on the Front Image button to load that image's dimensions into the data entry boxes. You can also leave Width, Height, or Resolution without a number. By doing so, you'll be able to crop a number of images that share one dimension but are of different shapes.

Fixed Target size is most often useful when a project contains a number of large images that need to be reduced to thumbnails for indexing or table of contents purposes. If the amount of reduction in size is greater than 25 or 30 percent, it's a good idea to apply the Unsharp Mask filter to the image after it has been cropped (see Chapter 2).

Figure 3.81 The image has been scanned at an angle.

Figure 3.82 Draw a small rectangle and align its angle to a straight edge on the scan.

Figure 3.83 Increase the size of the rectangle to include as much of the image as possible.

Figure 3.84 After cropping, the image is straight, and the corner areas have been removed.

It's often necessary to use high magnification to adjust the corners of a crop. Such a situation might occur when you're cropping images such as the screen captures in this book. When you are cropping, it's difficult to see whether the 1-pixel black line around a dialog box or palette has been included in the crop. Here's a fast way to handle the task:

1. Draw the crop rectangle while the entire image can be seen in its entirety within the window (press Command+0 on the Mac or Ctrl+0 in Windows).

2. To zoom in without resizing the window, press Command+ = or Ctrl+ = enough times that the individual pixels are easily visible. You can zoom in even faster by holding down Command+spacebar or Ctrl+spacebar while you click and drag a small rectangle in the upper left-hand corner of your image.

3. Press the Home key, which immediately scrolls the image so that the upper left-hand corner of the image is visible. Adjust this corner of the Cropping rectangle.

4. Now press the End key. This scrolls the image to the lower right-hand corner.

5. Adjust the corner of the Cropping rectangle and press Return to crop the image.

Move Tool

The Move tool (press V) does exactly what its name suggests: It shifts the contents of selections or layers within the image window—even outside of the boundaries of the window—or from one window to another. When the Move tool is selected, selections or layers can be moved in 1-pixel increments by using the arrow keys. Hold down the Shift key when pressing the arrow keys to cause movement in 10-pixel increments. The options for the Move tool are shown in Figure 3.85. This tool has no contextual menus.

The Pixel Doubling option on the Options palette causes Photoshop to display a half-resolution proxy of an object or layer while it's being moved. Versions of Photoshop prior to version 4 showed the status of a move by displaying a wireframe shape or, if the mouse button was depressed for a moment before the dragging movement began, a representation of the pixels being moved. Pixel Doubling eliminates the need to hold the mouse button before the move begins, because its display generation is nearly instantaneous.

The Auto Select Layer option enables you to quickly select a layer by clicking within the document window on a pixel from that layer. If your cursor is over several candidate pixels, Photoshop will select the layer of the pixel with the greatest amount of Opacity. This is a handy feature if you do a good deal of layer work—and who doesn't?—but it also means that you run the risk of

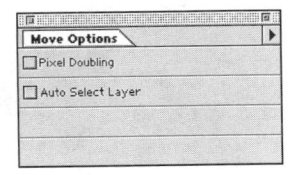

Figure 3.85 Options for the Move tool.

selecting a new layer every time you click within the document. An easier way to do this, with the Move tool selected and the Auto Select option turned off, is to hold down Command (Mac) or Ctrl (Windows) and click on a pixel of the layer you wish to select. There is another way to do this, one which may be more universally useful. With the Move tool chosen, hold down Command+Control (Mac) or Control+right mouse button and click in the window (Windows). A contextual pop-up will appear, giving you the choices of all layers containing a visible pixel at the place where you clicked.

The Move tool need not be chosen from the Toolbox. You can access it instantly, no matter which tool is in use, by pressing Command or Ctrl.

The Airbrush, Paintbrush, Pencil, And Eraser Tools

The four tools discussed here are grouped together because they all perform the same basic function—they apply color to the existing image. The first three paint with the Foreground color; the Eraser tool applies the Background color in some situations and erases using the paint behavior of the other three tools in other situations. Despite the fact that the Eraser *erases*, it's still easiest to think of it, in many cases, as an eccentric Paintbrush.

The Painting cursor for each brush is governed by the choice made in the lower left corner of the dialog box that appears by choosing File|Preferences|Display & Cursors (see Figure 3.86). Three choices are given: The first is Standard, which displays a cursor that is the same as the icon for the tool. When using Standard, be aware that each cursor has its own hot spot (the cursor pixel on which the cursor action is centered). The second is Precise. The Precise cursor is a plus-shaped cursor with a dot in the center; this center dot is the hot spot. When you're using this cursor, very exact placement is possible. The drawback to the Precise cursor is that it can be difficult to see at times. All cursors—no matter the setting in this preference box—can be changed to Precise cursors by pressing the Caps Lock key. The third choice is Brush Size. When this setting is used, Photoshop displays a wireframe outline of the brush that allows a high degree of accuracy as to where the paint is to be applied. The wireframe brush outline is visible for all brushes up to 999 pixels, the largest brush size you can define.

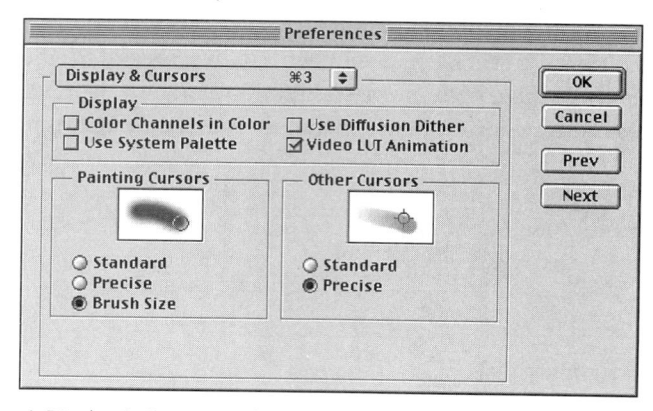

Figure 3.86 Photoshop's Display & Cursors Preferences dialog box.

Each of these tools applies paint from a variably sized applicator tip chosen from the Brushes palette. Brushes are usually round, but can be of any shape. They range in size from 1 to 999 pixels wide. The brushes used by the Paintbrush and the Airbrush are essentially the same. The brushes used by the Pencil tool are chosen from the same palette. However, when the Pencil tool is selected, all brushes become hard-edged. The brushes used by the Eraser tool depend on which of the Eraser modes is used.

You can create new brushes by using the pop-up menu on the upper right corner of the Brushes palette or by clicking in the blank area below the existing brushes. When a new brush is requested, or when a brush is double-clicked in order to be modified, the dialog box shown in Figure 3.87 appears.

In this dialog box, the Roundness of the brush can be varied from a severely flattened oval to the default circle. Oval shapes can be angled to produce flattened, calligraphic-style brush points. The Diameter of the brush can be changed here, as well as the Hardness and the Spacing. Hardness can be varied between 0% and 100%, as shown in Figure 3.88. Spacing controls the way the color is laid down by the brush; the default is 25%. The number, which is a percentage of the brush's diameter, indicates the distance the brush needs to be moved before a new iteration of the brush is laid down. Three percentages are shown in Figure 3.89, but the spacing can range between 1 and 999%. As the percentage rises above 100%, the iterations of the brush become detached from each other.

A rectangular selection can be defined as a brush. The command is located on the Brush palette menu. An example shape is shown in Figure 3.90. When this new brush stroke is applied for the first time, it produces the stroke shown in Figure 3.91. Double-click on the brush to

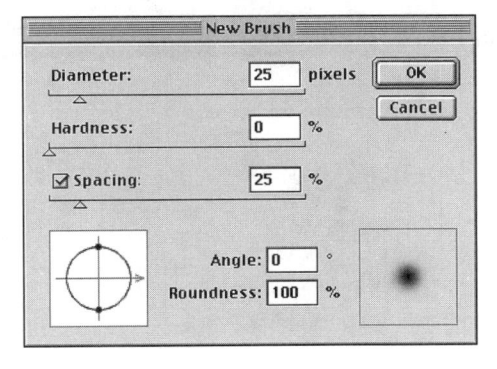

Figure 3.87   New Brush dialog box.

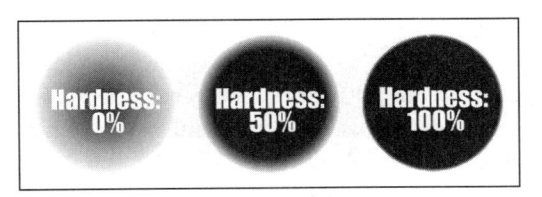

Figure 3.88   The range of Hardness values for a Brush tool is from 0 and 100%.

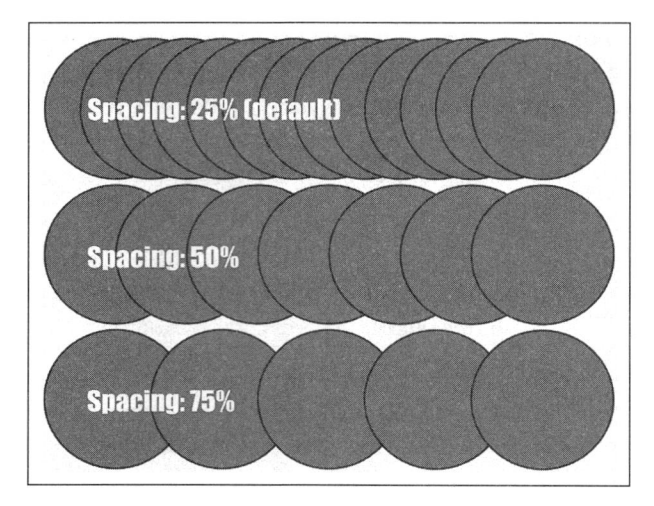

Figure 3.89 The range of Spacing values for a Brush tool is from 1 and 999%.

Figure 3.90 Any rectangular selection can be defined as a brush.

Figure 3.91 Painting with the new brush produces this result.

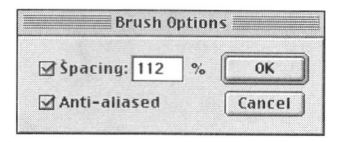

Figure 3.92 Change the spacing of the new brush.

change its spacing. In this case (see Figure 3.92), the spacing is changed to 112% (a figure arrived at by trial and error). With the new spacing, the stroke produced by the brush is shown in Figure 3.93.

Brushes are usually used in freehand fashion. However, they can be made to draw straight lines in two ways. As the stroke begins, hold the Shift key to constrain the brush to follow a vertical or a horizontal line. You can also click in one place on the image, hold down the Shift key, and click in another place. The brush stroke will be drawn in a straight line between the

Figure 3.93 Painting with the new brush after making the spacing adjustment produces a more interesting effect.

Figure 3.94 Straight-line brush strokes make adding borders to an image a simple task.

two clicks. This is a useful technique for placing brushed borders around an image, as you can see in Figure 3.94. In this image, the star shape was defined as a brush with spacing set to 110%. The top, horizontal line was drawn first. The vertical lines made use of the Fade function found on the Airbrush, Paintbrush, and Pencil Options palettes.

The star border uses a spacing adjustment and the Fade option. When Fade is checked, the brush changes its color over the specified number of steps. The change can be to Transparent or to the Background color. In the figure, the Fade is set to 9 steps and to Transparent. Notice that the number of fade steps is the number of iterations of the brush as it's applied. The fade number is, consequently, tied to the Spacing setting. The length of the fade is tied to the size of the brush. With the spacing set to its default, a 100-pixel brush set to fade in 10 steps fades over the space of 250 pixels. A 40-pixel brush set to the same number of steps fades over the space of 100 pixels.

Another way to apply brush strokes is to use the Stroke function associated with the Paths palette. The Paths palette is covered in detail in Chapter 4.

All four of these tools—and a number of the other tools as well—can paint in a variety of Blend modes, which are covered later in the book. The Blend modes are chosen from the Options palette menu for each. The default is Normal, with a variety of other settings available. You can find complete definitions for these modes in Chapter 6.

> **TIP**
>
> **Besides the contextual menus used for the Paint tools, you can select brushes from the palette without moving the cursor. The two bracket keys—"[" and "]"—move the brush selection, respectively, to the left and up or to the right and down. The movement is one brush for each push of the key. If you hold the Shift key when you press the bracket keys, the selection jumps to the top left or bottom right—the first brush or the last brush.**

Airbrush Tool

The Airbrush tool (press J) lays down a diffused stroke that is distinguished by its softness and capability to blend easily with whatever is painted. The options for this tool are shown in Figure 3.95. The contextual menu is shown in Figure 3.96.

The Airbrush differs from the Paintbrush and Pencil tools in that its main control setting is one of Pressure. This contrasts with the others that use an Opacity slider. The default Pressure setting is 50%. If this setting is moved up to 100% and compared to a stroke of the Paintbrush with an Opacity setting of 100%, there is almost no difference between the two. The Pressure setting, however, does work differently from Opacity. With the Airbrush, color can be applied again and again without releasing the mouse button. The painted area becomes increasingly covered with the paint color. In fact, when you hold the brush in one place while holding

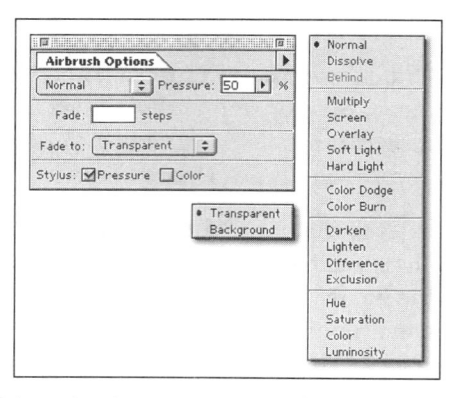

Figure 3.95 Expanded view of the Airbrush options.

```
Next Brush
Previous Brush

First Brush
Last Brush

Normal
Dissolve
Behind

Multiply
Screen
Overlay
Soft Light
Hard Light

Color Dodge
Color Burn

Darken
Lighten
Difference
Exclusion

Hue
Saturation
Color
Luminosity
```

Figure 3.96 Contextual menu for the Airbrush tool.

down the mouse button, the paint continues to flow, making an ever-widening paint area. You can see the effect in Figure 3.97. On the left, a 250-pixel brush leaves the light imprint when the mouse is clicked a single time. To the right, the mouse button was depressed for a length of time sufficient to give 10 iterations of the brush. The actual size of the brush is shown by the dotted lines.

> **TIP**
>
> It's easy to change the Pressure setting of the Airbrush or the Opacity settings of the other tools. Press any of the number keys to give a percentage multiplied by 10. Touch 1, for example, to change the setting to 10%; 9 gives 90%, 0 gives 100%, and so on. These 10 keyboard settings work remarkably well in nearly all situations. If you can type more quickly, try two letters pressed in quick succession. Pressing 6, then 5 will get you 65%. If you need to use a very low number, say 6%, type 0 (zero), then 6.

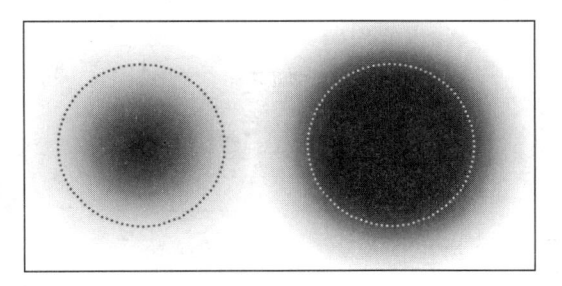

Figure 3.97 If the mouse button is held down, paint continues to flow from the Airbrush.

Figure 3.98 Use the Airbrush to paint with a light color to give a glow effect (left) or with a dark color to produce a shadow effect (right).

The Airbrush tool is very well suited to brushing in shadows or glow effects (see Figure 3.98), although learning to control it, to make the strokes look evenly applied, is fairly difficult. For further information about ways to automate this tool so that it paints with great exactitude, see Chapter 4.

Paintbrush Tool

The Paintbrush tool (press B) is the most pliant and easily controlled of the three main paint tools. The options for this tool are shown in Figure 3.99. The contextual menu for the Paintbrush is the same as for the Airbrush.

When you're using the Paintbrush, you can fill in areas of color with uniformity of tone by brushing over the same area several times without releasing the mouse button. As soon as you release the mouse button, the additional application of color is applied to the previous application. Because of this behavior, the Paintbrush is ideal for editing masks while in Quick Mask mode.

The Paintbrush has a Wet Edges option that appears to emulate the not-always-desirable effect sometimes seen in watercolor work in which pigment pools along the edge of a paint stroke. With this tool, the effect is controllable and useful for some effects. Figure 3.100 gives an idea of the appearance of the paint strokes at 100% and 50% Opacity with the Wet Edges option alternately turned off and on. Figure 3.101 shows the effect applied to the edges of the letterforms and the rectangular border.

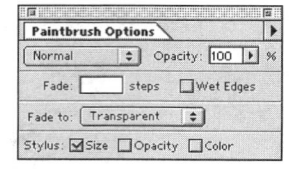

Figure 3.99 Options for the Paintbrush tool.

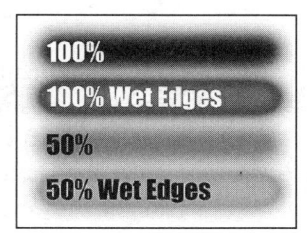

Figure 3.100 Examples of how the Wet Edges option varies with the Opacity of the brush stroke.

Figure 3.101 A Paintbrush with Wet Edges turned on produces a convincing neon effect.

Pencil Tool

The Pencil tool (press Y) is unlike the Paintbrush or Airbrush in that it draws hard-edged lines. When the Pencil tool is selected, all of the brushes on the Brush palette become completely black. The tool's options are shown in Figure 3.102. The contextual menu is the same as for the Paintbrush and Airbrush.

The Pencil tool has an Auto Erase function. With this function checked, the tool will paint with the Background color instead of the Foreground color if the cursor clicks on a pixel containing the Foreground color. This is a feature that has been used in many other paint applications. It has its uses if the Background color is the same as the background of the image, because it seems to erase areas of Foreground color. The illusion of erasing is not quite so convincing on a layer where background color added to an area of transparency may not be desired.

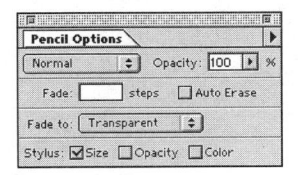

Figure 3.102 Options for the Pencil tool.

Eraser Tool

The Eraser tool (press E) is an awfully useful tool: It can be itself, a blocky brush shape, as well as three other tools—the Pencil, Paintbrush, or Airbrush. In all guises, the Eraser tool paints with the Background color in two situations: first, when the tool is used on the Background layer of a document; second, when the tool is used on a layer with the Preserve Transparency option checked. Otherwise, its function is simply to erase. The options for the tool and the contextual menu are shown in Figures 3.103 and 3.104.

The Eraser tool is really an eraser in only one situation—when it's applied to the pixels of a layer that does not have the Preserve Transparency option checked. In that case, it removes the pixels, leaving behind complete or partial transparency in the area to which the tool was applied. The partial transparency is an effect possible when the tool is used as one of the paint tools—Airbrush, Paintbrush, or Pencil—and the Opacity of the stroke is set to something less than 100%.

The Block option of the Eraser tool is one of the most curious features of Photoshop: It erases an area that is inversely proportional to the zoom factor of the image. In simpler terms, the Eraser's Block doesn't change size relative to the monitor display (although it does change size relative to the image). Because of this, it can be made to erase ever-smaller areas by zooming in closer and closer to the image. The illustration in Figure 3.105 shows how this works. In the black area at the top of the figure, the Eraser block was clicked once. The number below indicates the degree of magnification at the time of the click.

The Eraser is one of two tools—the other is the History Brush—that allows you to paint an area of the image with the contents of the image or layer at some previous stage of the work. This feature can be used to selectively work backwards within the image, eliminating changes in some places but not others. This feature is curiously powerful because it can be coupled with the various paint tools and their capability to paint with less than 100% Opacity or Pressure. To use this feature, select an item from the list displayed in the History palette. Click in the empty box at the left of the list item to designate it as the source item for the Eraser tool. Turn on the Erase to History checkbox on the Options palette, and paint wherever you wish. An alternative to turning on the Erase to History checkbox is to hold down Option or Alt while using the Eraser tool. If you don't have a list item selected, you will erase to the topmost item on the list, which is the same as painting with the contents of the document the last time you saved it. (See the next section for more information on the History Brush and the History palette.)

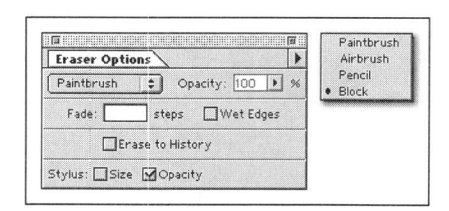

Figure 3.103 Options for the Eraser tool.

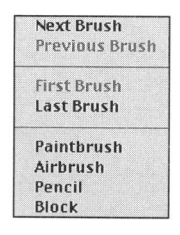

Figure 3.104 Contextual menu for the Eraser tool.

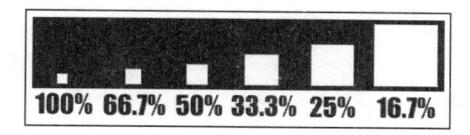

Figure 3.105 The Eraser tool's block erases pixel areas that are inversely proportional to the zoom factor of the image window.

The History Brush And The History Palette

If you have worked with Photoshop for any length of time, you have probably already assembled a few strategies that get you past the fact that Photoshop has provided, in previous versions of the program, only a single Undo Last Action command. Perhaps you took Snapshots so that you could Select All and Fill your image with the Snapshot at some later stage of the work. You might have been in the habit of creating new layers so that you could experiment for a while before deciding to keep the layer or delete it. Maybe you developed the habit of duplicating your document at critical stages so that you could return to an earlier version. Fortunately, there have been many ways to circumvent the single Undo. Even now, with Photoshop 5's History palette, the old strategies are still good to know. Despite the incredible flexibility you have with the History palette, you need to remember one crucial thing about it: When you Save and Close your document, your History is...uh...history.

But while your document is still open and you are still working on it, WOW! Each new thing you do gets added to the list. Add objects, add layers, delete objects, delete layers, fill, stroke, add filter effects, or try anything. Try combinations of things. If you don't like the last change, simply click on an item three or four steps above the bottom—last—item, and you are instantly back at that place in your document's development.

An expanded view of the History palette is shown in Figure 3.106. The palette is composed mostly of the list of states. The beginning state is usually *New*—for New document—or is titled with the name of an existing document or a state from another document. The first state on the list is, by default, a Snapshot of the document. As other Snapshots are added, they are added below the first Snapshot, and comprise a separate list from that of the states.

At the left is a column of empty squares. Clicking on one of those squares makes the History Brush icon appear. When the icon is turned on, that state becomes the source for the History brush (see below).

The sidebar menu contains seven commands. The top two are instructions to move up or down the list of states, one at a time. The next four commands—New Snapshot, Delete, Clear History, and New Document—are discussed in the following sections.

History Options

The last of the commands of the sidebar menu is the History Options command. It summons the dialog box shown at the lower right of Figure 3.106.

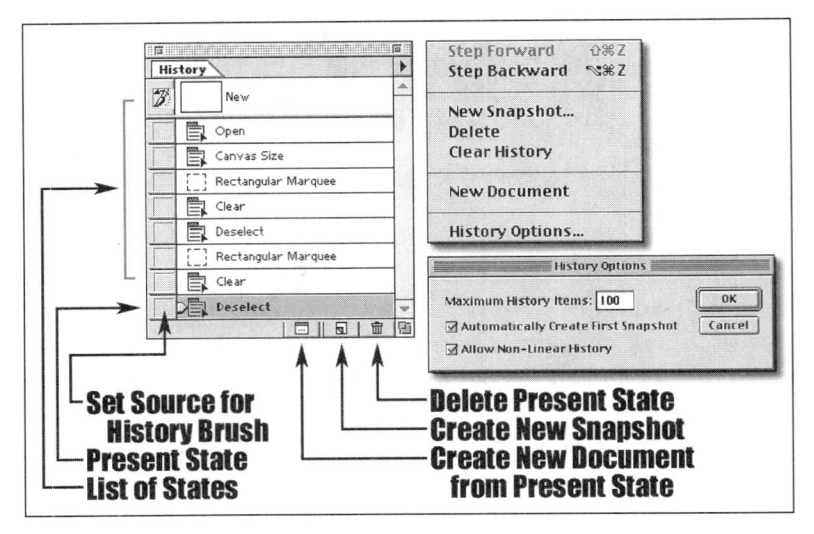

Figure 3.106 Expanded view of the History palette.

- *Maximum History Items*—The first option is your choice for the number of items that can be placed at one time on the History palette. (When the number of items in this data field is exceeded, the oldest items are removed from the list.) The largest number you can enter here is 100. That gives you, effectively, 100 levels of Undo. However, having the maximum number listed here requires more memory—a *lot* more—than if you leave the number at its default, 20. If you have a lot of memory, having the maximum number of states is a great luxury, although it takes a little work to scroll through a list that long. If you cannot devote a great deal of memory to Photoshop, you should probably leave this setting at its default.
- *Automatically Create First Snapshot*—This option does just as it suggests. If this checkbox is turned off, your palette will always begin with the word Open or Duplicate.
- *Allow Non-Linear History*—This option is, in some ways, the most confusing option of the three. It gives you the opportunity to jump around on the list and to preserve all of the states, but it isn't always clear how that happens. In the discussion that follows, we'll try to clarify the differences between having this option turned on or off.

The Palette Icons

At the bottom of the palette, you will see three icons. By clicking on these, you can create a New Snapshot of the document, create a new document based on the present state, or delete the present state. When you use these tools for the first time, be prepared for a certain amount of confusion. The History palette can do some weird and wonderful things that appear to be unpredictable. But watch carefully and you'll soon get the hang of it.

- *Create New Document From Present State*—The Present State on the History palette list is the one that has been selected. Usually that is the one at the bottom of the list. However, you can click on any state. When you see it become highlighted, you'll know that you have changed the position of the Present State. No matter where your Present State exists on the list, clicking on the bottom leftmost icon will create a brand new document window. At the top of the new list of states you will see the name of the Present State of the older document. Your first state will read Duplicate Document. As you can see, the new document begins its history at the time you created it. Any states above the original Present State have been incorporated into the new document. Any states below the original Present State have been discarded. Using this icon to create a new document is exactly like working on your file, duplicating it at crucial stages, and continuing your work on the duplicate.

The New Document command from the palette's sidebar menu performs exactly the same task as the icon. There is another way to do the same thing, one you can use to startle and amuse your friends. Suppose that you're working on a 12-inch-square image. Create one or two small windows no more than half an inch on each side. Drag one of the states from the large file's History palette into the small window. The small window instantly changes to the size of the large window and shows itself to be a duplicate of the stage you dragged.

- *Create New Snapshot*—A Snapshot, on the History palette, is simply a duplicate of some state stored as a separate item on the list of Snapshots (top of the palette). Snapshots are made of the Present State, wherever that might be on the list. Once created, a Snapshot has a separate life of its own. You can select it and use it in the same way you would any of the states. For example, a Snapshot can serve as the source for the History Brush (to be discussed in the following section, "The History Brush"). It can also serve to preserve the state of the document at some point earlier in the editing session. Another example: If you take a Snapshot of the 20th state on the list, you could then delete all of the 20 states and every other Snapshot. When you select your recent Snapshot, you'll find that your document returns to its Snapshot state.

  The New Snapshot command from the sidebar menu performs the same task as the icon.

- *Delete Present State*—The Trash icon on this palette works in the same way it does on every other palette. You can use it to delete any—or nearly all—states and Snapshots. (The History palette requires that you have at least one state and one Snapshot.) You can perform the same tasks by using the Delete command from the sidebar menu. The Sidebar menu also contains a command—Clear History—that deletes all states.

Using The History Palette

New states are created from the top of the list downward. The newest state is always the one at the bottom of the list. The states are named with the command or tool you used. As you work, you might wish to return to an earlier state. To do so, simply click on that state. If you have not turned on the Allow Non-Linear History option, all of the states below the state you selected become dim. Your next action replaces them. If you have Allowed Non-Linear History checked, the behavior of the list becomes a little more confusing. If you have selected an earlier state, the states below it seem to remain unchanged. Your next action does not wipe them out but is, instead, added to the list below the bottom item. Although you have no visual feedback about this, the items between your selected state and the next action are not applied to the document. They simply exist as a record of something you once did but which has no bearing on the document's content. You can, however, select them as previous states. If you do, your next action jumps again to the bottom of the list and removes the states descending from the earlier state change from the document's content.

Non-Linear History is a lot of fun. If the states were color coded so that those descending from one or another earlier state were the same color, the confusion might be less. As it is, you have to develop a kind of freewheeling attitude about the process. There is, after all, something to be said for being able to jump anywhere in the edit history and take off in a new direction.

The History Brush

The History Brush is similar to the other brushes. (To choose the History Brush, type Y.) It can change its size, its Opacity, and paint information using one of the Blend modes. The only difference is that it paints from a source on the History palette. It is, then, a local edit that restores a part of the image to the way it was at some past stage of the editing. The options for the History Brush are shown in Figure 3.107. The contextual menu options are shown in Figure 3.108.

The other choice on the History Brush Options palette is labeled Impressionist. The Impressionist option smudges together pixels from the Present State of the file. An example of the effect of this option is shown in Figures 3.109 and 3.110. What better subject for an Impressionist effect than water lilies? The Impressionist option is not easily mastered. As a matter of fact, finding a result with this tool that is acceptable—let alone beautiful—is a challenge for even the most skilled and patient of graphic designers. Fortunately, there is a workaround that is not only easy, but produces good results. It's also very fast. The pictured example took exactly 24 seconds. This technique uses stroked paths, and is discussed in Chapter 4.

These two images are also shown in the color Studio of this book. The original file—found on the CD-ROM that comes with this book, file HB_01.PSD in the Chapter 3 Practice Files folder—has been prepared for you with paths included if you want to use the technique shown here.

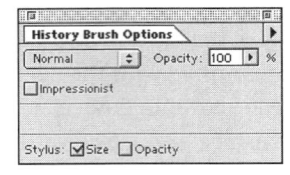

Figure 3.107 The History Brush options.

TOOLBOX TECHNIQUES **173**

Figure 3.108 Contextual menu options for the History Brush.

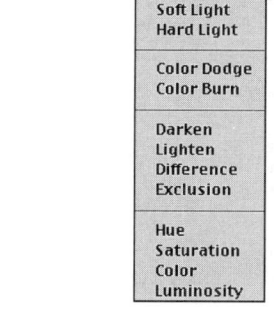

Figure 3.109 Original image of water lilies.

Smudge, Blur, Sharpen, Dodge, Burn, Sponge, And Rubber Stamp Tools

What these tools have in common is that they paint with the brushes of the Brush palette. Beyond that, they are not very much alike. They don't really *paint* in the sense that the Paintbrush or Airbrush paints. They all are effects tools; pixels across which these tools brush—or paint—are changed in some way. The change can be a darkening of values, a lightening of values, an increase in contrast values, an increase or decrease in color saturation, or a replacement of the pixels by other pixels in the same image.

The effects supplied by these tools are extremely powerful. With them, you have the power to correct problems in an image or to use your own creativity to alter the image so that it exactly matches your ideas.

Figure 3.110 The Impressionist option of the History Brush tool produces Monet on the cheap.

Smudge Tool

The Smudge tool (press U) seems to push the pixels in the direction of the stroke. The effect is similar to a smudge stick rubbed over chalk or pastels or a dry brush pressed through wet oil paints. The number of pixels that get pushed depends on the size of the brush chosen. The amount of push depends on the Pressure setting. The options and the contextual menu are shown in Figures 3.111 and 3.112.

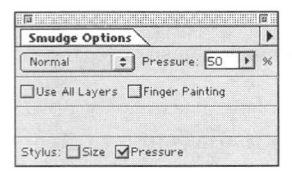

Figure 3.111 Options for the Smudge tool.

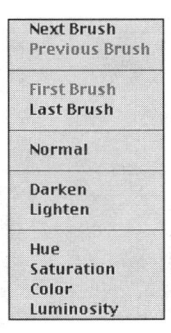

```
Next Brush
Previous Brush

First Brush
Last Brush

Normal

Darken
Lighten

Hue
Saturation
Color
Luminosity
```

Figure 3.112 The contextual menu for the Smudge tool.

Figure 3.113 When Use All Layers is turned off, only the active layer, which contains the type but not the background, is affected by the Smudge tool (upper streak). When the option is turned on, both layers are affected (lower streak).

Beyond the Pressure setting, the other important setting on the Options palette for this tool is the Use All Layers checkbox. This setting is applicable only to layered documents. With the checkbox turned off, the Smudge tool only pushes around the pixels of the selected layer. Turned on, the tool is able to move the pixels of all the visible layers. Figure 3.113 shows the difference between the two settings.

This figure contains a Background and a layer on which reside the letters. With the layer selected, the Smudge tool has been drawn across the letters with the Use All Layers setting turned off. The pixels of the background are undisturbed. The lower smudge line has the Use All Layers box checked. As you can see, the smudge pushes the pixels of both the layer and the background.

The Smudge tool is useful for straightening out edges, for distorting edges to cause a camera jitter effect, and for providing an all-over texture. Figures 3.114, 3.115, and 3.116 show how you can do this. The first figure (see Figure 3.114) is the original image. Quick Mask was used to mask the central figures (shown in Figure 3.115). After leaving Quick Mask mode, the Smudge tool, with a fairly large brush size, distorted the background of the image. All of the strokes for this background texture were made using a short v-shaped motion and were random in direction. There is, actually, a sinfully easy way to get Photoshop to do all the work for you; see Chapter 4 for more information.

The Finger Painting setting on the Options palette introduces extra color to the area being smudged. The Foreground color is added to the stroke and mixed with the other pixels over which the brush drags. The effect produced is similar to the Fade option for the Paint tools.

Figure 3.114 The original image to be changed by smudging the background.

Figure 3.115 Use Quick Mask to isolate the main figures.

Figure 3.116 After exiting Quick Mask, the Smudge tool pushes the pixels in the background to provide a more interesting texture.

Blur And Sharpen

These two tools, Blur and Sharpen (press Shift+R to cycle between the tools), used to be called the *Focus* tools. They have now left behind their group name but carry on with the same tasks. As their names suggest, they are able to *brush on* blurring or sharpening. The options and contextual menus for these tools are shown in Figures 3.117 and 3.118. The Use All Layers checkbox works in the same way as it does for the Smudge tool.

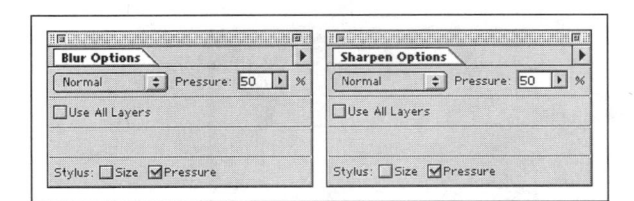

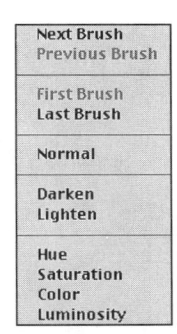

Figure 3.117 Options for the Focus tools.

Figure 3.118 Contextual menu for the Focus tools.

Of the two tools, the Blur tool is the easiest to understand and to control. The default Pressure setting of 50% smoothly moves the brushed area out of focus. The Sharpen tool requires more finesse. The default, 50%, is often too high. A good trial setting is about 10%. When using this tool, brush over an area and avoid brushing it again until you are certain that you have not gone too far with it. It's nearly always a good idea to lay on a number of smaller strokes until the desired degree of sharpening is reached. Always pay attention when using this tool; too much brushing produces a remarkably unattractive effect.

Used together, these tools can dramatically alter an image. The photo shown in Figure 3.119 is an example of an image which, betraying its 35mm origins, is fairly interesting but lacks the impact a professional photographer and more expensive lens system could have given it. Its principal problem is not one of composition but of too many clearly visible elements. The eye has no trouble deciphering the content, but no single element in the image draws the attention.

With a fairly large brush—large enough so that the whole of this process takes no longer than a few seconds—the table top, the plants atop the table, and the pillow are sharpened. Using an even larger brush with a Pressure setting of 80%, everything else in the image is blurred (see

Figure 3.119 A pleasant image with too much detail and too many places to draw the eye.

Figure 3.120 Use a large brush to quickly sharpen the important foreground parts of the image.

Figure 3.121 Use another large brush to quickly blur the areas around the foreground.

Figures 3.120 and 3.121). A lot! The resulting image, with a more satisfactory crop, is shown in Figure 3.122. With this change in focus, the eye is led to the most important part of the image and not distracted by the peripheral information.

Dodge, Burn, And Sponge

These three tools—the Dodge tool, the Burn tool, and the Sponge tool (press Shift+O repeatedly to cycle through the three tools)—brush on an overall change in tone. Using a brush metaphor (the effects are brushed onto the image incrementally the way paint can be brushed on), these tools alter the lightness, darkness, and saturation of an image. The options and contextual menu for the tools are shown in Figures 3.123, 3.124 (Dodge tool and Burn tool), 3.125, and 3.126 (Sponge tool).

Figure 3.122 The final image—enlarged and with a better crop—and a clear center of visual interest.

The terms *dodge* and *burn* are derived from photo developing, where image exposures are corrected mechanically. Areas of the film can be lightened or darkened in order to improve exposure problems or to enhance the original exposure. To *dodge*, in the photo darkroom context, is to

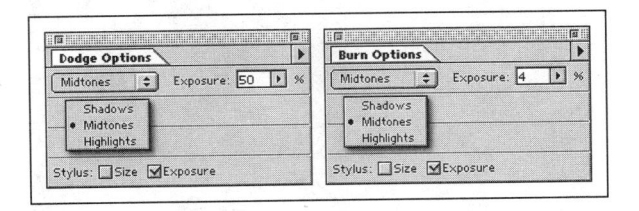

Figure 3.123 Options for the Dodge and Burn tools.

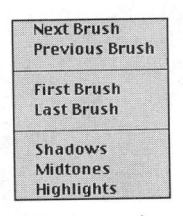

Figure 3.124 Contextual menu for the Burn and Dodge tools.

Figure 3.125 Options for the Sponge tool.

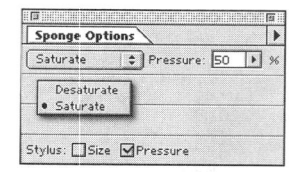

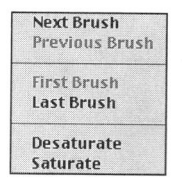

Figure 3.126 Contextual menu for the Sponge tool.

lighten all or parts of the secondary image. To *burn* is to darken all or parts of the image. Photoshop's Dodge and Burn tools perform the same functions as the mechanical processes, but with a power and flexibility beyond the dreams of photographic technicians.

When using either of these tools, the Options palette allows the choice of concentrating on specific tone ranges. The tools can function on Shadows, Midtones, or Highlights. When one tone range is chosen, the other two are more or less excluded from the effects of the tool, but not completely. Because of this, brush applications of either have their greatest effects on the selected range, but operate in a lesser way on contiguous areas of either of the other two ranges. By this means, smooth transitions are maintained.

The Dodge and Burn tools are most often used to alter glaring errors in the image. For example, the Burn tool set to operate on highlights might be used to tone down blown-out highlight areas. Or the Dodge tool might be used to tone up a too-dark shadow.

The two tools can be used to completely change the original lighting of an image. When applied in this way, the change is editorial in nature rather than corrective. The three examples shown in Figures 3.127, 3.128, and 3.129 show how this can work. The first image is the original—superficially pleasing but lacking in the drama that a more creative light source could

Figure 3.127 The original image ready for applications of the Dodge and Burn tools.

have given it. The second image shows applications—to both Highlights and Midtones—of the Dodge tool on the shadowed parts of the flower. The flower now appears to have been illuminated from several light sources and provides a more interesting contrast to the dark background. The third image shows applications of both the Dodge and Burn tools. The Dodge tool has lightened the inside of the flower and the Burn tool has darkened the outside. The result is a

Figure 3.128 The Dodge tool applied to midtones and highlights gives a better contrast between the subject and the background.

Figure 3.129 The Dodge tool applied to the inside of the flower and the Burn tool applied to the outside concentrate the illumination for a more dramatic image.

concentration of the illumination source on the inside of the flower. The outside vanishes into the darkness of the background. Neither of these two effects can be considered better than the other. They are both more interesting than the original and either might be appropriate.

The Dodge and Burn tools are also effective for color toning. Working directly on the image, it is obvious that colors over which these tools brush will either become lighter or darker. A more subtle way of influencing the color is shown in Figures 3.130 and 3.131. The first photo is the original image. Although it does not show up here, the image is of an autumn forest taken on an overcast day (you can find the original and altered images in the color section of this book). The sky is a light gray. The Photoshop image is in CMYK mode. Applying a Burn to the highlights of the Cyan channel darkened it and made it turn blue in the composite image. This was a very simple operation: The sky is the lightest part of the Cyan channel. If the tool is set to highlights and simply brushed over the sky, only the sky is affected. There might be some slight darkening of the leaves and branches that adjoin the sky, but the effect is minimal. Notice that the painting done by the tool was deliberately not uniform; this gives the sky a mottled, more realistic appearance than a uniform tone would have given.

The third of the tools in this group is the Sponge, which can be set to Saturate or Desaturate colors. The Sponge tool was used on the image shown in Figure 3.131, which is seen in color, before and after adjustment, in the Color Studio section of this book. Desaturation, carried to extremes, reduces the image to grayscale. The effect of the tool is to reduce the *Hue* while retaining the light and dark values. *Saturation* is the opposite. It boosts the amount and intensity of the colors over which the tool paints. Saturation is exactly the kind of correction needed for the drab yellow, browns, and reds in the sample image. Once the color of the sky has been changed from the dim and deadening gray, the colors of the fall foliage need to be boosted so

Figure 3.130 CMYK mode image with gray sky tones.

Figure 3.131 The Dodge tool, set to darken the highlight tones, darkens the sky in the Cyan channel to produce a blue sky in the composite image.

that they match the new tone of the light source. As you can see, the tool was used selectively so that some of the foliage continues to look dull and some very bright. This, again, is in the pursuit of realism: A realistic scene would not show consistent saturation of color, but rather a variety of saturation levels.

When using any of these three tools, it's wise to begin with percentages of Exposure well below the 50% default. The Burn tool, in particular, is used most successfully when its exposure is set to below 5%. Experiment with the settings to find the one most appropriate for the job at hand.

Rubber Stamp And Pattern Stamp Tools

The Rubber Stamp tool often inspires the remark, "That's my favorite tool!" It's also the tool—along with its predecessors on high-end workstations—that should cause grave misgivings to anyone having to consider photographic material as evidential. Used in its default mode, this tool does not paint with a single tone, but paints with areas of contiguous pixels. These pixels are often from the same image, but pixels from another open image can also be used. With care, blemishes and unwanted material can be covered over so smoothly that there is no way to determine that the image was ever altered. This cloning of pixels combined with soft-edged brushes make this tool one of the most versatile of Photoshop's toolset. The options for the tools (press Shift+S to cycle between the two tools) and the contextual menu for both are shown in Figures 3.132 and 3.133.

Rubber Stamp, Align On—Rubber Stamp with the Aligned checkbox turned on is used in more situations than any other Rubber Stamp variation. To paint with this option, position the cursor on an area of texture that you wish to copy onto another area. This area may be in the same image window or may be in another window. Hold Option or Alt and click the mouse.

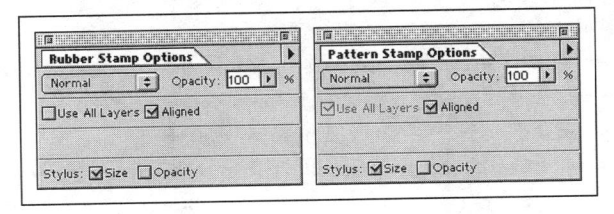

Figure 3.132 Options for the Rubber Stamp and Pattern Stamp tools.

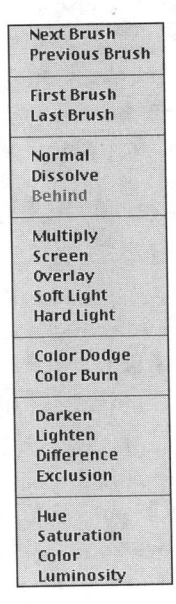

Figure 3.133 Contextual menu for the Rubber Stamp and Pattern Stamp tool.

This click tells Photoshop the source of the cloned pixels. Move the cursor away from that spot to the area to be altered. Begin painting. With the first click, Photoshop establishes an alignment relationship that continues until a new source area is chosen. There will be two cursors: the one doing the painting—the cloning cursor—and a secondary cursor that marks the source pixels. The secondary cursor follows the first in parallel motion. As the painting proceeds, the position of the two relative to each other never changes until the Option or Alt key is held and another mouse click defines a new source area.

Rubber Stamp, Align Off—Rubber Stamp without Align differs from the first in that the cursor relationship, once established, does not remain parallel. After the source location is identified with an Option/Alt mouse click, the cloning cursor begins to paint with the mouse button held down. As soon as the mouse button is released, the secondary cursor snaps back to its original position and the cloning cursor, even if it moves to another area, repeats the cloning of the original source pixels.

Pattern Stamp With Align On—Pattern Stamp with Align is an option that paints with a pattern. Defining a pattern requires that a rectangular area of pixels be selected. With the selection operating, choose Edit|Define Pattern. The new pattern is placed on a special clipboard or buffer, where it can be used by the Edit|Fill command or painted using the Rubber Stamp tool. As the brush paints, the rectangular iterations of the pattern are laid down on the image. The patterns appear as if the entire image was sitting atop an array of the pattern tiles and the brush simply uncovers them wherever it paints.

Pattern Stamp With Align Off—Pattern Stamp Non-Aligned is the pattern equivalent of Clone Non-Aligned.

> **TIP**
>
> You can construct patterns in such a way that there is no obvious seam as they repeat. The Rubber Stamp is excellent at making the edges of the pattern disappear. First make the selection, copy it, then choose File|New. Make a note of the pixel dimensions of the new window. Click on the OK button, and paste. Flatten the image. An example is shown in Figure 3.134.
>
> From the Filter menu, choose Other|Offset. In the two data entry fields, enter one-half the vertical and horizontal pixel dimensions of the image. Choose the Wrap Around option. After clicking on OK, the new image window resembles that shown in Figure 3.135. Use the Rubber Stamp tool to obliterate the horizontal and vertical joins (see Figure 3.136).
>
> Select All and choose Edit|Define Pattern. Make a new window at least three to five times the size of the pattern tile. In this window, Select All and choose Edit|Fill. Fill the window with the newly created pattern to see how the tiles will join each other. If you've been careful, there will be obvious repetition, but there should be no obvious seam from tile to tile (see Figure 3.137).

Figure 3.134 Rectangular rock texture to be changed into a seamless repeating pattern.

Figure 3.135 Rock texture after applying the Offset filter with Wrap Around.

For convincing proof of the power of the Cloning tool (with a few assists from some other Photoshop capabilities), take a look at the two photographs in Figures 3.138 and 3.139. In the first photo, you'll see a charming, turn-of-the-century home with all of the visible artifacts of late 20th-century technology and suburban living: basketball hoop and backboard, phone line, power lines, window air conditioner, intruder lights, and even—above the left gable—a distant microwave relay tower. The second photo turns back the clock by 100 years. All obvious

Figure 3.136 The Rubber Stamp obliterates the interior seams.

Figure 3.137 Three repeats of the patterns, vertically and horizontally, show how effectively textures can be made to overlap without an obvious join.

traces of modern life are gone, thanks to the Rubber Stamp tool. If you wish to practice on this image, it's included on the CD-ROM as file RS_01.PSD, in the Chapter 3 Practice Files folder. The two images, before and after, are also in the Color Studio section.

Here's how to remove the signs of modern life:

1. Removing the power and phone lines requires a fairly high magnification with a constant modification of the size of the brush. Remember to leave the brush in position and

Figure 3.138 Image to which cloning tool will be applied to remove the artifacts of 20th-century civilization.

Figure 3.139 The Rubber Stamp tool has turned back the clock to a pre-electricity time.

use the bracket keys to move up or down in the Brushes palette. While working, pretend that you are not in a hurry and remember that this task *can* end with perfection.

2. The two parts of the image changed without using the Rubber Stamp tool were the window with the air conditioner and the shadow area below that window. Use the Lasso tool to select the top half of the window. Make the selection into a Layer. Flip this layer vertically, tilt it slightly, and move it down to the bottom of the window. It will fit perfectly into position. Merge the layers and use the Rubber Stamp to get rid of extra bars in the center of the window and eliminate the faintly seen valance (at the top of the window) from the bottom copy.

3. Do you see the shadow area below? This looks like a lot of work. But do you see that bush on the left side of the steps? Draw a selection line around that bush, make it into a layer, flip the layer horizontally, move the layer into position, and then merge the layers. Now, using the History Brush with the first Snapshot as your source, carefully paint the shrubbery to the left of the new bush *back on top* of the new bush so that they overlap as shown. Use the History Brush to get rid of unwanted bits from around the edges of your quick selection. Use the Rubber Stamp Aligned option to slightly change the indentations in the bottom of the new bush so that it is not obviously a flipped copy of the other.

A more difficult Rubber Stamp task is shown in Figures 3.140 and 3.141. The first photo, the original, is almost satisfactory, but there are a couple of problems. First, there is a car far ahead that is too small to be interesting. Eliminating it will be a simple matter. Second, the shot was taken from inside an automobile and there is a distinct glare spot in the center right-hand side. At first glance, removing this would seem to be simple since the glare is entirely within the area of the sky. This, however, turns out to be the most difficult kind of cloning that Photoshop users

Figure 3.140 A good image except for the car on the road ahead and the glass reflection in the sky (center right).

Figure 3.141 The Rubber Stamp tool removes the unwanted parts of the photo and replaces them with natural textures.

encounter. If you wish to practice on this image, you can find it on the CD-ROM as file RS_02.PSD, in the Chapter 3 Practice Files folder.

If you zoom in on the sky, you can see that it's not a simple area of consistent blue. There are many blue tones in zones that are contoured shapes. The sky is also textured. This will be the case for many sky shots, particularly if the image was scanned from medium to fast 35mm film. As you begin to clone the sky, you'll immediately notice that great care needs to be taken to replace the defective areas with pixels that are very close by. Take care also that the cloning follows the *grain* of the sky.

Even after using your considerable skills at eliminating the glare, you will probably find a strangely flat-looking and very visible area where the glare has been replaced. To eliminate this textureless look and to restore the sky to a more natural appearance, choose the Lasso tool. Set its feather radius to 10 pixels. Draw a line around the flat-looking area. Choose Filter|Noise| Add Noise and use a setting of about 8 to 15 for the Amount. For the other settings, choose Uniform and don't check the Monochromatic checkbox. When the filter has executed, you'll find that your cloning is invisible. This is a good thing to know: Very small amounts of Noise added to an area within a diffused or feather-edged selection often adds a finishing touch to a pixel-cloned area that absolutely defeats detection!

One of the most-used capabilities of the Rubber Stamp tool is the capability to correct skin imperfections. Skin is just about as tricky to work on as sky. Small discolorations in skin offer no problems. The real challenges when working on a human face are wrinkles. There is, however, a very easy way to deal with wrinkles: Don't get rid of them at all. Wrinkles are a natural part of the way skin wraps and folds over the musculature of the head. If they are eliminated completely, the result is not at all natural looking. What you need is a way to lighten the shadows

Figure 3.142 With wrinkles…

Figure 3.143 The wrinkles are still there, but they look smoother because the deeper shadow tones that made them look conspicuous have been lightened.

that cause the wrinkles to look conspicuous. Use the Rubber Stamp with Align tool, with Opacity set to about 50%. Option+click or Alt+click fairly close to the wrinkle and simply paint through the deepest tones of the wrinkle. The skin magically smoothes out; the wrinkle does not disappear, it simply becomes one more detail in the topology of the skin. Figures 3.142 and 3.143 show examples of the way this cloning technique works and how it doesn't result in unnatural facial tones.

Type In Photoshop

Type in Photoshop is unlike type in other programs. The reason for this is that type in other programs is usually made up of a set of vector shapes—tiny, individual graphic objects of the sort that might be drawn in a vector-based program such as Adobe Illustrator—which have been placed into a special file structure called a font. Using the font and the type-handling capability of programs that allow typing, you can simply use your keyboard to place these small pictures one after another and to deal with them not as tiny pictures, but as sets of symbols that combine into words and sentences. These shapes are based on vector outlines that allow the type to be scaled up or down in size. Attributes such as bolding and obliquing can also be applied. Under most circumstances, the type remains as a set of vector shapes until an output device translates it into raster shapes. Until its conversion to raster shapes, type is endlessly editable. Typographical errors can be corrected and new words substituted for older ones. In short, all of the operations we associate with word processing and typesetting are possible.

If you think of type as a set of vector shapes, then Photoshop can be considered as an output device. Its treatment of type is exactly the same as a printer's treatment of type. The outline shapes are converted to sets of tiny dots in a process called *rasterization*. Once the letter shape is rasterized, it no longer has the flexibility that allows it to be edited. In fact, once Photoshop has rasterized a character, it's merely a collection of pixels in the shape of a letter. Mistyped words cannot be fixed except by discarding and re-rasterizing them. Type can be scaled up or down in size after it has been rasterized. Scaling up in size is not a very good idea, for the same reasons cited in the discussion of the Cropping tool.

Despite Photoshop 5's provision for editable type layers, the alphanumeric characters you use within Photoshop need to be rasterized before you can use the Photoshop file. Think about it: Before you can save the file in any format besides Photoshop, you need to flatten the image. Once flattened, your type is no longer editable. Besides losing editability, you also lose the sharp, clean edges of the characters. This is because the type will not be rasterized by the output device at a high resolution, but has already been rasterized by Photoshop at a comparatively low resolution. For this reason, small, delicate characters in Photoshop usually do not look good after output—and also for this reason, type in Photoshop is most successful when larger and more robust letter forms are used.

The Type Tools

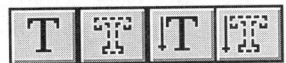

Photoshop doesn't allow you to type directly on the image window. If you think about the rasterization process, you'll see that this is done so that you'll have some control at some later stage in the creation of the letter shapes.

Now let's check out the Type tool (press Shift+T repeatedly to alternate between the four Type tools):

1. Press T to select the first Type tool. (The first tool, the one with the solid icon, is really the Type tool. The others have different names: Type Mask tool, Vertical Type tool, and Vertical Type Mask tool.)

2. Click with this tool in the window to which you want to add type. (If you're using the Type tool for the first time in your Photoshop session, you are notified of a wait while Photoshop builds the Font menu.) The dialog box shown in Figure 3.144 appears. Within this dialog box, you can choose your Font, the Size—in points or pixels—that you want the characters to appear, Kerning, Color, Leading, Tracking, and Baseline. If you are familiar with the Type dialog box in version 4 of Photoshop, you'll notice that the checkboxes that let you apply attributes such as bold and italic are no longer present. Instead, you can choose from the pop-up menu to the right of the Font pop-up from the styles built into the font. For example, you must have installed a bold version of a font in order to type with bold characters. Three checkboxes allow you to set the justification of your type: flush left, centered, flush right. There are also some buttons in the lower left corner of the window that allow you to zoom in and out, and to cause your letters to fit themselves into the text window.

3. Next, in the scrolling text window, enter the set of characters. If you have the Preview checkbox turned on, you should be able to see your type appear in the document

window. You can even run your cursor out of the dialog box and drag your type around the document to place it where you want it, even before you click on OK.

4. When you're finished, click on the OK button, or press the Enter key (the Return key doesn't work in this dialog box; it places hard returns in the text).

5. Photoshop takes a moment and then places the letter shapes in the window on a new layer. Take a look at the layer created for your type. It should look the same as the layer in the lower right corner of Figure 3.144. This layer has two very intelligent things to tell you. First, the layer named itself with the first word(s) you typed. Second, the presence of the "T" to the right lets you know that this is an editable type layer. Editable? Yup. For the first time, you can actually type in Photoshop and then go back and change your text. Double-click on the "T" to open the dialog box again. You can select some or all of your letters, type something new, change the font, size, or the kerning between a pair of letters. You can do this as often as you wish. Your letters stay editable until you decide they no longer need to be anything but letter shapes.

You can use type in Photoshop in one of four ways, one for each of the Type tools. The Type tool produces editable text in the familiar horizontal format. The Vertical Type tool also produces editable text, but with the letters stacked on top of each other (shown at the far left of Figure 3.145). The two Type Mask tools do not give you editable text layers. Instead, clicking on OK gives you a set of letter shapes in the form of a selection (see Figure 3.145).

You should be aware of a couple of points if you wish to use the vertical text tools. First, although your cursor will look a bit strange—it's sideways from normal—you will get upright letters. Second, the three justification settings are also 90° from the way you are used to seeing them, but they will still control how the letters sit atop each other. Third, the leading value is used to control the space between columns of letters (see Figure 3.146). If you wish to change the spacing between the letters vertically, use the tracking adjustment.

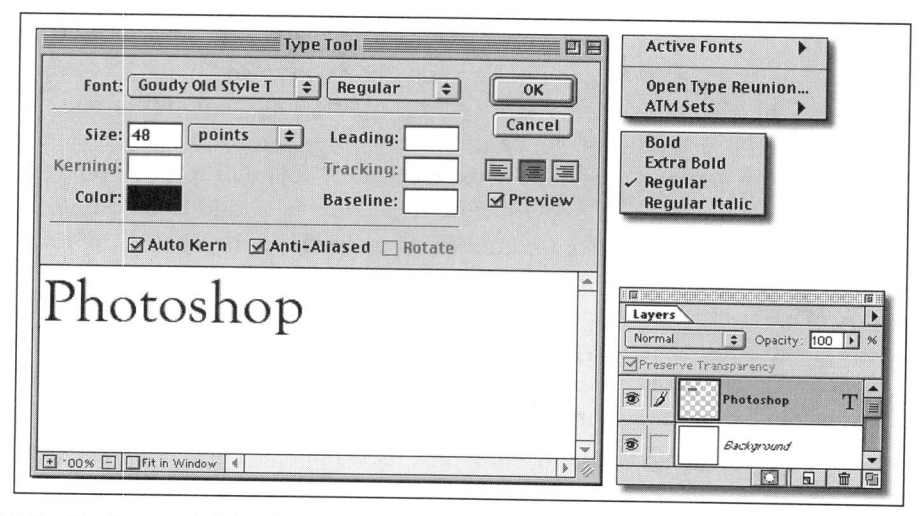

Figure 3.144 The Type tool dialog box.

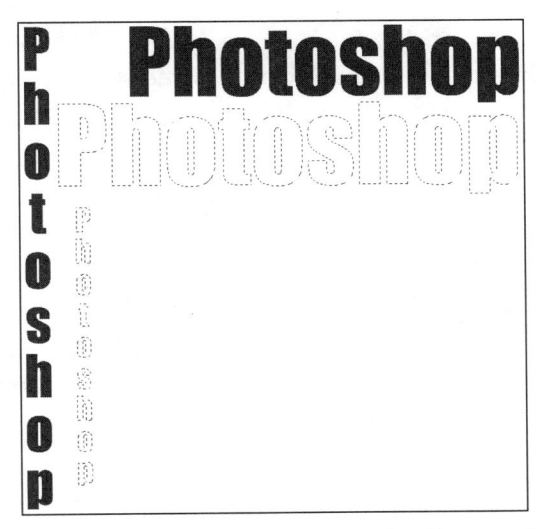

Figure 3.145 Photoshop's four Type tools give you editable vertical and horizontal text and vertical and horizontal selections in the shape of letter forms.

Figure 3.146 With vertical type, leading changes move the columns of type closer together or farther apart. Vertical spacing between the letters is controlled by the Tracking adjustment.

Photoshop 5's programmers have gone a long way toward addressing the drawbacks of the program's Type tools. There are still a few drawbacks, but the tremendous added flexibility is apparent the first time you use the Type tools.

Extensis PhotoTools

Despite all of the improvements to the Photoshop Type tools, you still need to know about PhotoText. It's still the champion for Photoshop type convenience, with the single disadvantage of not providing editable type layers.

The Extensis Corporation of Portland, Oregon, (www.extensis.com) offers a set of plug-in tools for Photoshop called PhotoTools. These tools include a variety of useful effects with an easy-to-master interface. Most of the special effects these tools offer can be achieved in other ways. The sparkling gem of PhotoTools—and the part of the set that is, by itself, worth the cost—is PhotoText.

A likeness of the PhotoText dialog box is shown in Figure 3.147. Because the figure is small and its features difficult to see, they are all labeled. What is very clear from this figure is that the PhotoText add-on to Photoshop furnishes a good deal of flexibility and power. Examine the text specimens in Figure 3.145. The two sets of dark letters represent two text layers. Now examine Figure 3.148. The same letters are now accompanied by a complex set of characters in

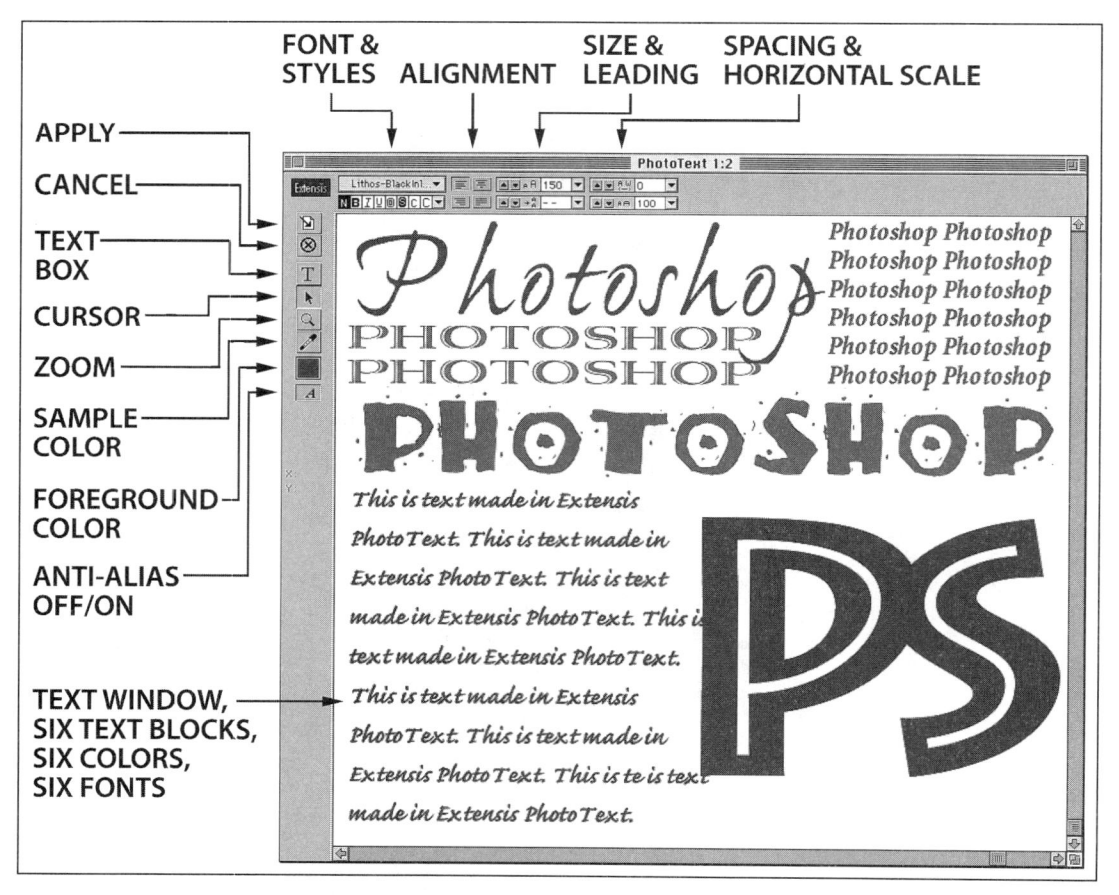

Figure 3.147 The Extensis PhotoText dialog box.

Figure 3.148 A variety of type faces, styles, and sizes rasterized into Photoshop in one operation.

different fonts, different sizes, different colors, and different internal margins. The amazing fact is that all of those characters were placed at the same time!

Text From Adobe Illustrator

As excellent as the PhotoText tool is, there is another way of getting text into Photoshop: Adobe's own program, Illustrator. Working with type in Illustrator is not the same as working with type in a word-processing program. The possibilities Illustrator offers are far beyond any mere text cruncher. Rightfully so: Illustrator is an art program and must furnish the tools with which artists can transform type into attention-getting illustrations. However, that means that the tools must be learned. The ability to type just won't get you very far in Illustrator. If you have never had a reason to learn the program, you have one now. Illustrator and Photoshop can work together almost as if they were two parts of one large program. With both programs working together, there is literally nothing that cannot be accomplished.

The type that follows a spiral path in Figure 3.149 is a good example of what Illustrator can do that even PhotoText cannot. To make your type in Illustrator, it's a good idea to set up the Illustrator document so that you are always aware of the boundaries of your Photoshop document. In Photoshop, Select All. From the Paths palette, choose Make Work Path from the palette menu. Choose the Direct Selection cursor from the Toolbox (press A). While holding Option or Alt, click on the new path to select it. From the Edit menu, choose Copy. While the path around the edge of the window is active, delete it; you won't be needing it again. Switch to Illustrator and paste the path into a new Illustrator document. While the path is still selected, convert it to a guide. Your document now shows a nonprinting dotted line that is the exact dimension of your Photoshop document.

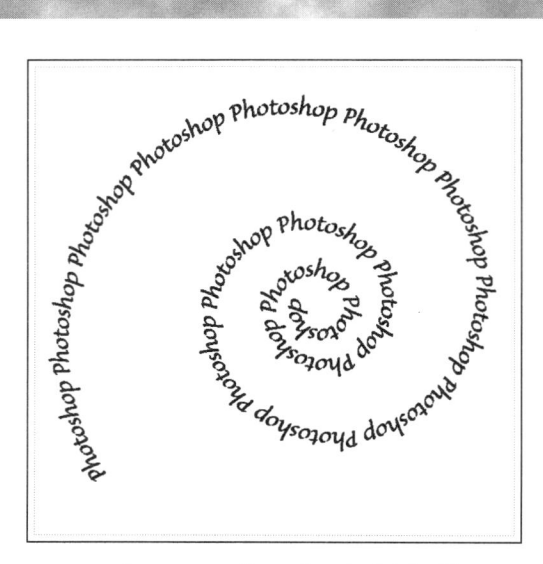

Figure 3.149 You can set up very complex type configurations in Adobe Illustrator.

Use the Illustrator Type tools to make your type in any configuration you wish. When you're finished, select the type and convert it to outlines. While it's selected, copy it. Switch back to Photoshop and use the Paste command. A small dialog box appears (see Figure 3.150) that gives you the choice of rasterizing the type (Paste As Pixels) or importing the letter outlines (Paste As Paths). You can, if you wish, choose the former, but the second choice is a lot faster. When you have pasted the paths, your screen appears as shown in Figure 3.151.

Paths in Photoshop give endless flexibility, and they may be saved for later use. Figures 3.152 and 3.153 show typical uses for paths. After pasting the paths, create a new layer (click once on the small icon that resembles a dog-eared page at the bottom of the Layers palette). With the paths of the type still visible (see Figure 3.152), click once on the icon at the bottom of the Paths palette that contains a small circular shape filled with gray. Your paths immediately fill with the foreground color. Turn on the Preserve Transparency option for this layer. Duplicate this layer by dragging it down onto the New Layer icon at the bottom of the Layers palette. Your new layer is now the top layer. In the example in Figure 3.153, a gradient was drawn from lower left to upper right. Because Preserve Transparency is on, the gradient fills only the letter forms. Switch to the middle layer, select the Move tool, and press the Down arrow key three times and the right arrow key three times. Switch to the Background layer and draw the same

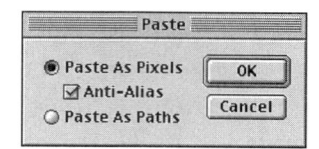

Figure 3.150 The dialog box that appears when you wish to Paste from Illustrator into Photoshop.

Figure 3.151 Illustrator paths pasted into Photoshop.

Figure 3.152 More Illustrator paths pasted into Photoshop.

gradient, but this time from upper right to lower left. The procedure is very simple, very fast, and visually effective.

We included four examples (see Figures 3.154, 3.155, 3.156, and 3.157) to demonstrate a range of uses for type within Photoshop. Despite the complexity of appearance of these figures, all were done with layering techniques of unbelievable simplicity. Please consult Chapter 6 for additional information.

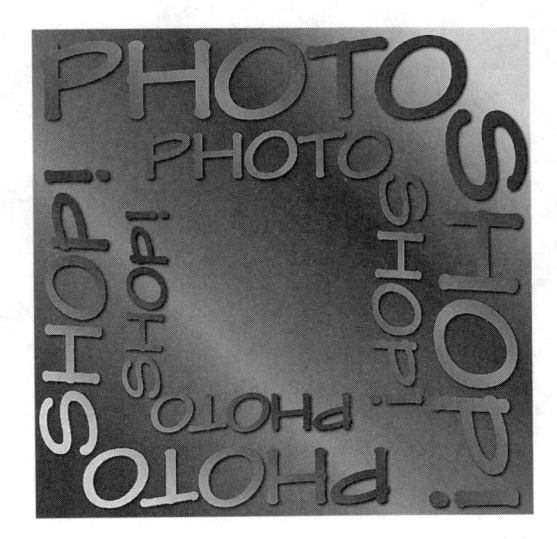

Figure 3.153 From the pasted paths, you can generate solid letter shapes and drop shadows.

Figure 3.154 Type used as a window into a photograph.

Figure 3.155 Type used to enhance an unremarkable background.

Figure 3.156 Type used as a way to merge images.

Figure 3.157 Type used as a mysterious headline.

A Few Thoughts On Type In Photoshop

When type is used as it is in the pictorial figures above, the quality of the character edge is not as important as it would be if the type were not used as a container for picture information. When the type is used as a text element, the quality of the character edge becomes much more important. In many cases, particularly when type is to be used at a relatively small size and when the type is delicate in nature—lightweight character strokes, pointed serifs, and so on—it may not be a good idea to incorporate the type as part of the Photoshop file. You can achieve a better look by exporting the Photoshop file in a format that is usable by the program to be used for the type. Once imported into the type source program, the Photoshop file can serve as the backdrop for the type. For example, you might save the Photoshop document in the TIFF file format and then *place* it in Adobe Illustrator. The type, in such an Illustrator file, would lie on top of the Photoshop file and would retain its vector edges.

There are two problems inherent with type rasterized into Photoshop. The first is *anti-aliasing*, a small blurring of the edge that deceives the eye into seeing a smooth line. The second is the resolution used in everyday work in Photoshop. When working with photographic material intended for use on the World Wide Web, a resolution of 72 ppi is appropriate. Grayscale photos intended to be reproduced as halftones in a newspaper might require a resolution of 170 ppi. So-called *hi-res* color separation files intended for offset reproduction at 150 line-screen needs a resolution of 300 ppi. The three specimens in Figure 3.158 illustrate how the resolution has a strong effect on the edges of the characters. By contrast, when type is rasterized by a typical output device, its edges are not anti-aliased and the type is rasterized at the maximum

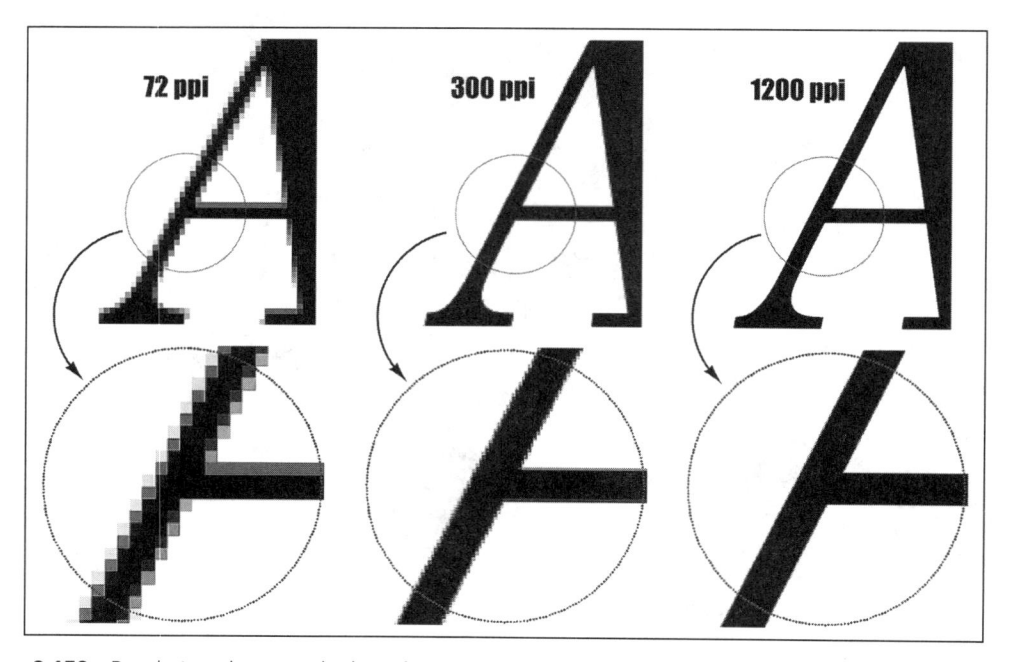

Figure 3.158 Resolution plays a vital role in the sharpness of the rasterized type's edges.

resolution of the device. The edges of type characters produced by, say, a 2400 dpi device are razor sharp because they are composed of steps that are incredibly small.

The Line, Paint Bucket, And Gradient Tools

Unlike some of the other toolsets, the three that comprise this section have very little in common. They perform very different tasks and have drastically different merits. One, the Gradient tool, provides smooth gradations across a surface that make it invaluable when simulating realistic lighting. The second, the Line tool, is sometimes useful when linear effects or arrows are needed and time is short. The third tool, the Paint Bucket, is as close to redundant as any feature of Photoshop is likely to be. It provides no service that can't be done in several other ways, all of which are superior. In short, it's an orphan, the lonely child of the long-vanished MacPaint. Kindness is indicated here: Even though we cannot remember the last time we used this tool for any other reason than to show someone else what it is, useless tools must have feelings too. I know, I know. I was also mesmerized when I first saw MacPaint, even if I *was* convinced that no human hand had painted the Japanese lady.

Line Tool

The Line tool (press N or Shift+N if the Pencil tool is currently visible) provides a quick way to place straight lines and arrows on an image. The lines are drawn in the Foreground color. The options for the Line tool and the contextual menu are shown in Figures 3.159 and 3.160.

Line widths are specified in pixels. If a specific width is needed, a calculation must be made and that number must be entered. You calculate in points, for example, by dividing the ppi of the image by 72, multiplying that number by the number of points, and rounding the result to the nearest integer.

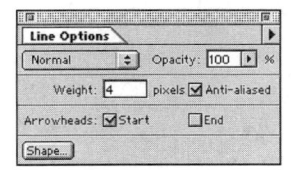

Figure 3.159 Options for the Line tool.

Figure 3.160 The contextual menu for the Line tool.

Lines can have arrowheads at one or both ends. The shape of the arrowhead is set in the small dialog box (see Figure 3.161) that appears after you click on the Shape button. The default proportions work well in most cases. The Concavity setting changes the arrowhead by changing the angle of the base. A negative value angles the lines away from the point, a value of zero makes the base of the arrow straight across, and a positive value angles the baselines toward the point. Examples of all three—using values of 25%, 0%, and 25%—are shown in Figure 3.162.

When you're using lines and arrows within Photoshop, it's a good idea to draw the lines on a separate layer and keep a copy of this layered file in case the lines need to be changed in the future. The alternative is to export the Photoshop file, import it into some other program, and lay the lines atop the Photoshop file there. Externally applied arrows do have one drawback: They cannot be made to do the wondrous transparency effects that are possible in Photoshop.

Paint Bucket Tool

What can we say? The Paint Bucket tool (press K) works much in the same the way the Magic Wand tool does except that it *fills*—with the Foreground color or with a Pattern—instead of *selects*. It can fill with any of the available Blend modes operating, as well as with a variable Opacity.

Sorry. That's it. That's all the little guy does. Perhaps you're thinking, "But wait. If I were planning to fill something, wouldn't I want it to be on a separate layer so that I could change my

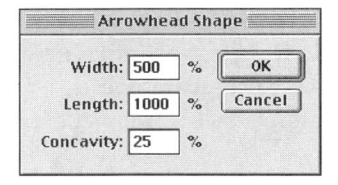

Figure 3.161 The Line tool's Arrowhead Shape dialog box.

Figure 3.162 A selection of arrows.

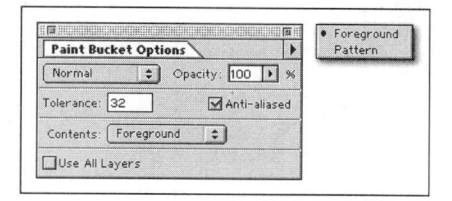

Figure 3.163 Options for the Paint Bucket tool.

mind? Wouldn't I just use the Magic Wand tool to select the area, make the selection a layer, and then use the Blend modes and Opacity capabilities of the Layers palette? Couldn't I then fill the layer—Preserve Opacity turned on—with a color or a pattern? And couldn't I, if I wished, simply get rid of the layer if I didn't like the effect? With the Paint Bucket tool, I couldn't change my mind beyond one Undo unless I continually moved upward on the History palette, could I?" If these are your thoughts, then you have seen the nature of the Paint Bucket tool's problem: Although it does what it's supposed to do, there isn't really a good reason for doing it. The options for the Paint Bucket are shown in Figure 3.163.

Gradient Tool

Previous versions of Photoshop furnished a Gradient tool that served a few purposes, but seemed a wimpy alternative when compared to the Gradient Designer module of Kai's Power Tools published by Metatools. The latest version of Photoshop offers a far more vigorous Gradient tool (press G), complete with blends containing up to 32 colors and segmented transparency, and three new gradient shapes. The options for the Gradient tool and its contextual menu are shown in Figures 3.164 and 3.165.

To use the Gradient tool, place the cursor in the window and click and drag. The place where the operation begins is one of the endpoints for the gradient. The place where the mouse button is released is the other endpoint.

Three checkboxes on the Gradient Options palette need some clarification. The first of these is Transparency. With this checkbox enabled, the transparency function of the tool is also enabled. This allows the same gradient to be used in two ways: with transparency and without. The second is the Dither option. *Dither* is a strategy where colors are mixed in such a way that

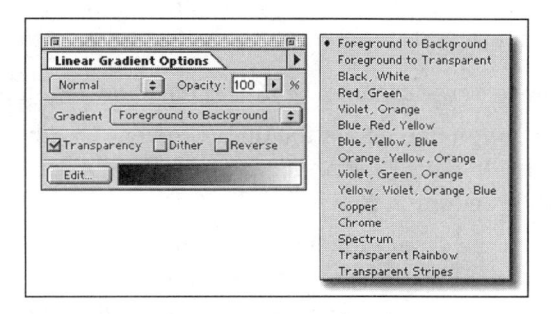

Figure 3.164 Options for the Gradient tool.

```
Normal
Dissolve
Behind

Multiply
Screen
Overlay
Soft Light
Hard Light

Color Dodge
Color Burn

Darken
Lighten
Difference
Exclusion

Hue
Saturation
Color
Luminosity
```

Figure 3.165 The contextual menu for the Gradient tool.

pixels opposite the vector direction of the gradient don't have the same values. Here's another way of putting it: If, say, a linear gradient is not dithered, rows of pixels at right angles to the direction of the gradient all have the same tone value. If the gradient is dithered, the pixels are scrambled. You'll see little visual difference between a dithered and non-dithered gradient. The benefit of dithering is that it goes a long way toward preventing the banding that often occurs in print reproduction. Banding has long been one of the banes of the prepress world. It can often be partially overcome with the addition of small amounts of noise in the gradient. Dithering, which is really very like the Noise option, builds the solution to the problem into the Gradient tool. The third checkbox, Reverse, simply reverses the progression of the gradient colors. If the gradient normally draws from Color A to Color B, enabling *Reverse* makes the same click-and-drag draw the gradient from Color B to Color A.

Defining A Gradient

To define a new gradient, click on the Edit button on the Gradient Options palette. The dialog box that appears is shown in Figure 3.166.

The box looks a little intimidating, doesn't it? Let's take it one step at a time. For the moment, ignore the already defined gradients. Ignore all of the buttons and the band, boxes, and oddly shaped icons at the bottom of the dialog box. Concentrate, instead, on the single band with the house-shaped icons below it. This band contains the definition of the gradient.

Now go ahead and make a new gradient by taking the following steps:

1. Click on the New button and accept the title "Gradient 1". Since you don't know yet what the gradient will look like, you might as well wait and use the Rename button after you're finished designing it.

2. Choose the colors. If the Color radio button is not checked, click on it now. Click first on the small icon to the lower left of the band, which contains a small "F". The F stands for Foreground color, but you're going to use a different color. About an inch to

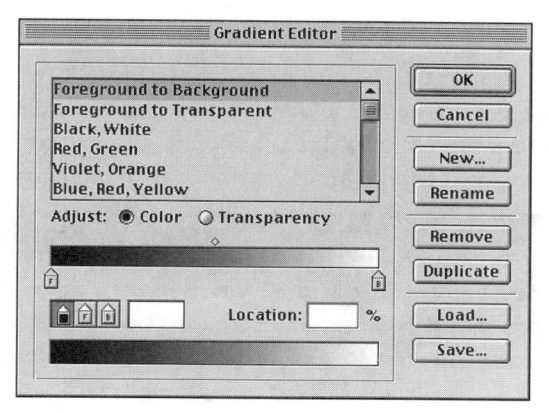

Figure 3.166 The Gradient Editor.

the left of the Location entry field is a color box. Click on it once. The Photoshop Color Picker appears. Choose the RGB value 0, 0, 255 (bright blue). Click on OK. Now click on the icon at the other end of the band. The B on this icon stands for Background color. Click again in the color box and select the RGB color 255, 0, 0 (bright red). Click on OK. Take a look at the gradient now. You will see a smooth blend between blue and red. You control the weight, or predominance, of each color within the gradient by moving the diamond-shaped slider above the bar back and forth. Try it out so that you can see how it works.

3. Now add another color to the gradient. Click just below the gradient bar. Another house-shaped icon appears. Make the color for this icon 255, 255, 0 (bright yellow). Click on OK. Your gradient now blends from blue to yellow to red. If you're really on a roll with a gradient, you can design something that has 30 small icons between the endpoints.

4. Click on the Transparency radio button. Here's our strategy: We're going to keep intact the strong, bright primary colors and have the gradient fade to about 50% between them. Click below the gradient bar. A new icon appears. Move this icon so that it's about a quarter of the distance across from the left. What was the color box is now an Opacity box. Enter "50" in this box. Make another icon and move it about three-quarters of the way across and enter "50%" for this one as well. You will see a representation of the gradient at the bottom of the dialog box. As you can see, the central yellow color is no longer opaque. You fix this by adding another icon directly below the yellow and setting its Opacity to 100%.

5. Now is a good time to rename your gradient. Something like "Blue, Yellow, Red" might be appropriate. Close the dialog box and try out your new gradient. Make a new window and fill it with black. Draw from side to side with the Gradient tool. Undo, change the gradient to Radial, and draw from the center of the window to one side. Bullseye, huh?

Gradient Shapes

Photoshop's gradients come in five flavors: Linear (see Figure 3.167), Radial (Figure 3.168), Angle (Figure 3.169), Reflected (Figure 3.170), and Diamond (Figure 3.171). These would seem to be somewhat limited compared to the Baskin-Robbins-like 12 flavors available in KPT Gradient Designer 3. However, you can do amazing things with these five configurations.

> **TIP**
>
> Here's a way you can experiment with gradients and make some wonderfully colorful textures: Open a new RGB window, and select the Gradient tool. Choose one of the colored gradients that appeals to your sense of fun. Set the Blend mode for the tool to Difference. Now begin to draw short lines, long lines, lines going in different directions. You will find that you can make some complex and beautiful color textures. Five files made in this way have been included on the CD-ROM. You can locate them in the Chapter 3 Resource Files folder.

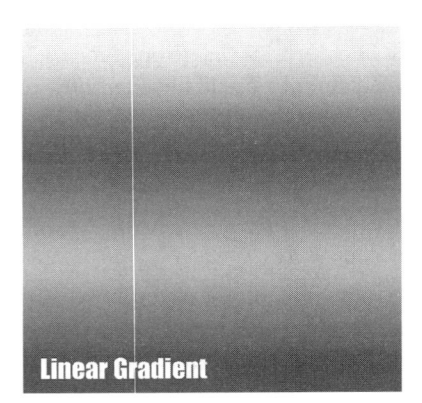

Figure 3.167 Linear gradient.

Figure 3.168 Radial gradient.

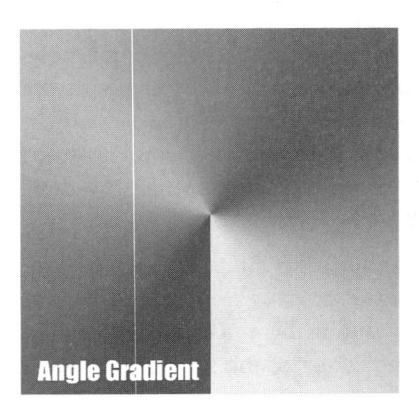

Figure 3.169 Angle gradient.

Figure 3.170 Reflected gradient.

Figure 3.171 Diamond gradient.

Digital Artists Need Gradients

If you look around, you'll see that the surfaces of the world are not uniformly lit. A white-painted wall, for example, is not all-over white, but a blend of tones depending on the intensity of the light that falls on it. Unless you make an attempt to match the variety of tones, you can never make the wall look realistic.

We use the Gradient tool, among other things, to simulate realistic surfaces. The four examples that follow show how the default Foreground/Background colors, coupled with the Foreground to Background and Foreground to Transparent gradients, can be used to simulate solid objects. The files are included on the companion CD-ROM. They are titled GS_01.PSD, GS_02.PSD, GS_03.PSD, and GS_04.PSD. You can find them in the Chapter 3 Practice Files folder.

Each of these four examples begins with a set of paths drawn in Illustrator, then copied and pasted into Photoshop. If one or two of the paths are used to make a selection, use the Pen's Direct Selection cursor—the arrow—press A, and click on the needed path or paths while holding Option or Alt. Press the Enter key to change the selected paths into selections.

The examples show black arrows pointing in various directions. These arrows indicate the course of the click-and-drag for the Gradient tool. The angle and the start/stop places for these arrows are significant. If you want to make your work look like the pictured examples, make your gradients follow the arrows carefully.

Sphere Shape—To create a sphere shape (with file GS_01.PSD), take these steps:

1. Click on the Work Path so that the path is visible, as shown in Figure 3.172. Select the path and press the Enter key so that the circle is now a selection.
2. Set the gradient to Foreground to Background, the Foreground/Background colors to defaults, and then reverse them. Set the Gradient tool type to Radial. Type "5" to change the Opacity of the gradient to 50%. Make the gradient as shown in Figure 3.173.

208 CHAPTER 3

Figure 3.172 Change this circular path into a selection.

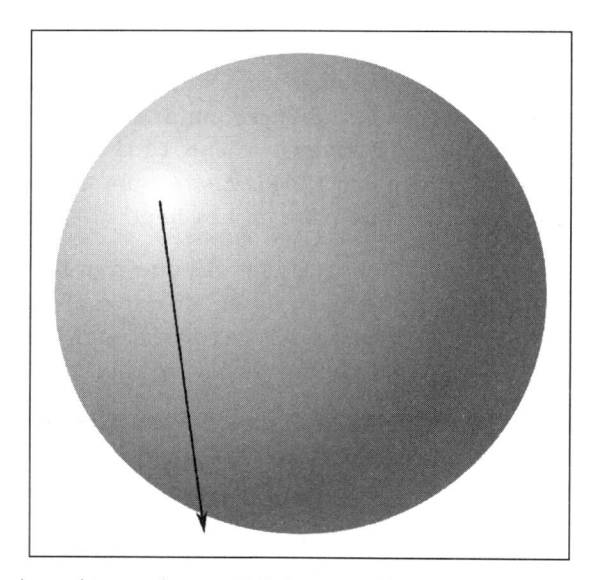

Figure 3.173 Draw a black-to-white gradient at 50% Opacity in the same direction as the arrow.

3. Draw another gradient, as shown in Figure 3.174. Note that the gradients used for this exercise are all drawn on top of each other and the start points are not in the same place.

TOOLBOX TECHNIQUES **209**

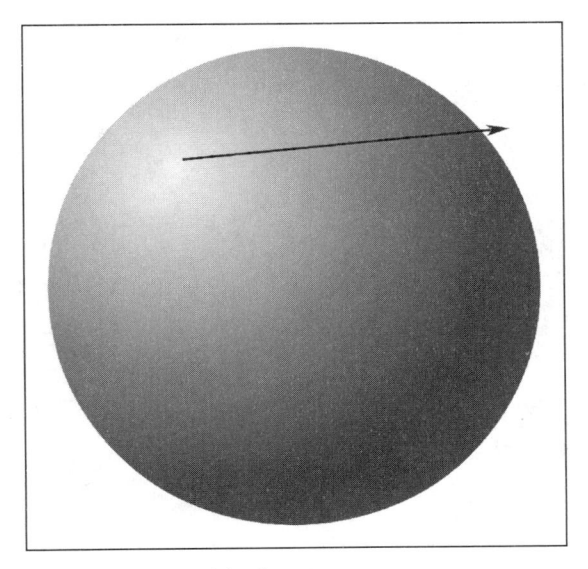

Figure 3.174 Draw another gradient on top of the first.

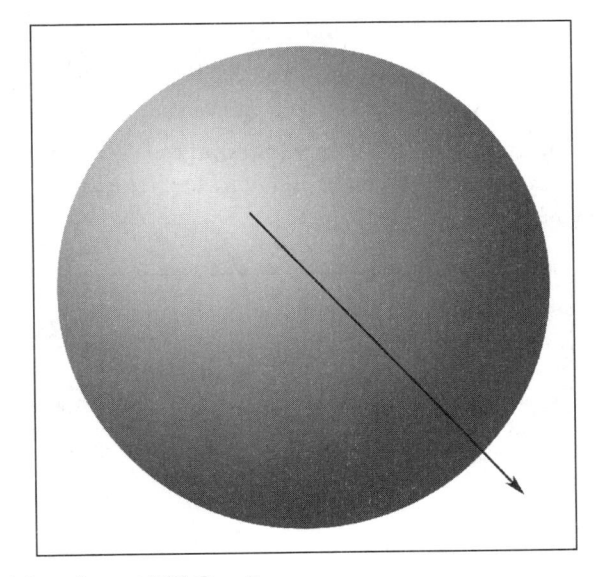

Figure 3.175 Draw a third gradient at 30% Opacity.

4. Change the Opacity of the Gradient to 30% and draw the third gradient as shown in Figure 3.175. The final shape is shown in Figure 3.176.

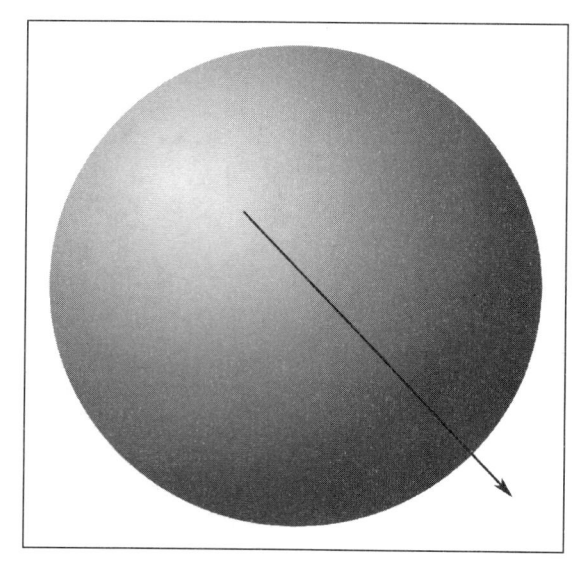

Figure 3.176 The final realistic-looking spherical shape.

Cube Shape—To create a cube shape (with file GS_02.PSD), take these steps:

1. Click on the Work Path so that the paths are visible, as shown in Figure 3.177. Select the upper path and press the Enter key so that the shape is now a selection.
2. Set the gradient to Foreground to Transparent and the Gradient type to Linear. Enter "2" to change the Opacity of the Gradient tool to 20%. Draw the gradient as shown in Figure 3.178.

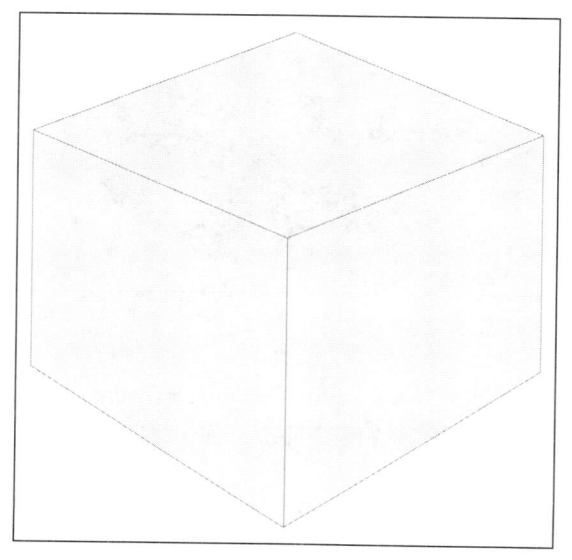

Figure 3.177 Three four-sided paths.

Figure 3.178 Make the top path into a selection. Draw a black-to-white gradient at 20% Opacity.

3. Deselect all. Choose the rightmost path shape and make it into a selection. Change the Gradient tool Opacity to 80%. Draw the gradient as shown in Figure 3.179.

4. Deselect all. Choose the leftmost path shape and make it into a selection. Change the Gradient tool Opacity to 40%. Draw the gradient as shown in Figure 3.180. The final shape is displayed in Figure 3.181.

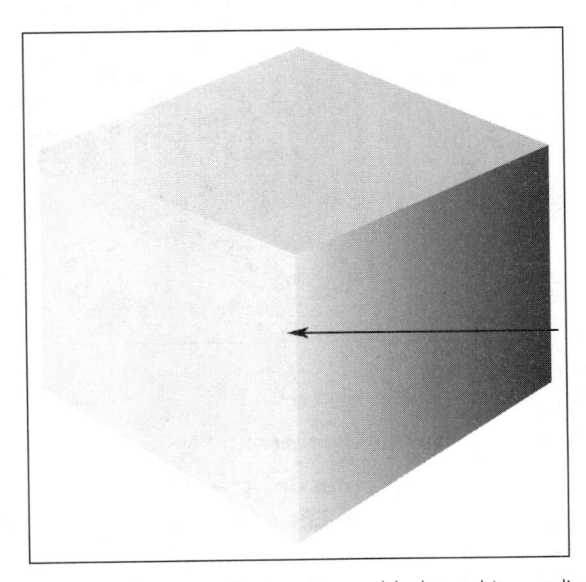

Figure 3.179 Make the rightmost path into a selection. Draw a black-to-white gradient at 80% Opacity.

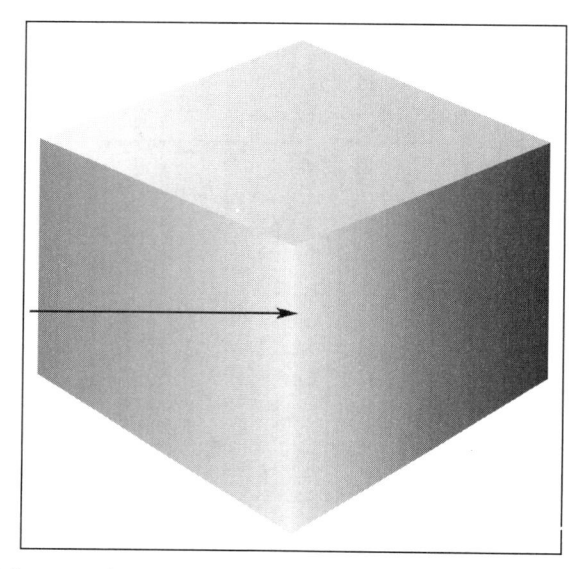

Figure 3.180 Make the leftmost path into a selection. Draw a black-to-white gradient at 40% Opacity.

Figure 3.181 The completed cubic shape.

Concentric Shapes—To create concentric shapes (with file GS_03.PSD), take these steps:

1. Click on the Work Path so that the paths are now visible, as shown in Figure 3.182. Select the two outer paths and press the Enter key so that the outer ring shape is now a selection.

2. Set the Foreground/Background colors to their defaults. Set the gradient to Foreground to Background and the Gradient type to Linear. Enter "8" to change the Opacity of the Gradient tool to 80%. Draw the gradient as shown in Figure 3.183.

Figure 3.182 Four concentric circular paths.

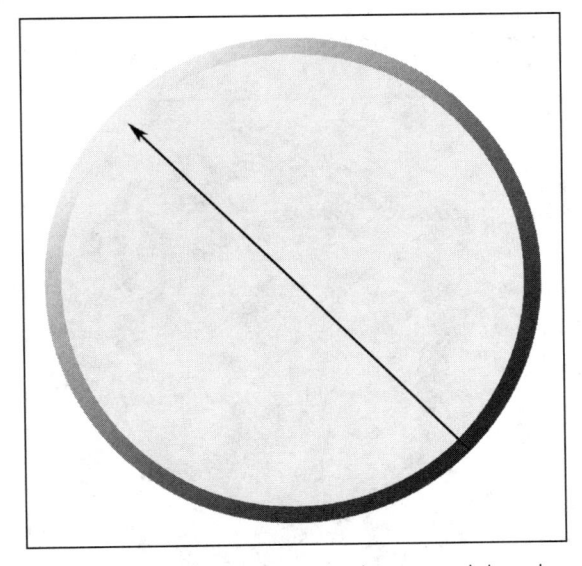

Figure 3.183 Select the two outer paths, make them into a selection, and draw the gradient.

3. Deselect all. Select the two paths between the inner and outer paths. Make them into a selection. Set the gradient Opacity to 60% and make the next gradient as shown in Figure 3.184.

4. Deselect all. Select the two inner paths. Make them into a selection. Set the gradient Opacity to 70% and make the next gradient as shown in Figure 3.185.

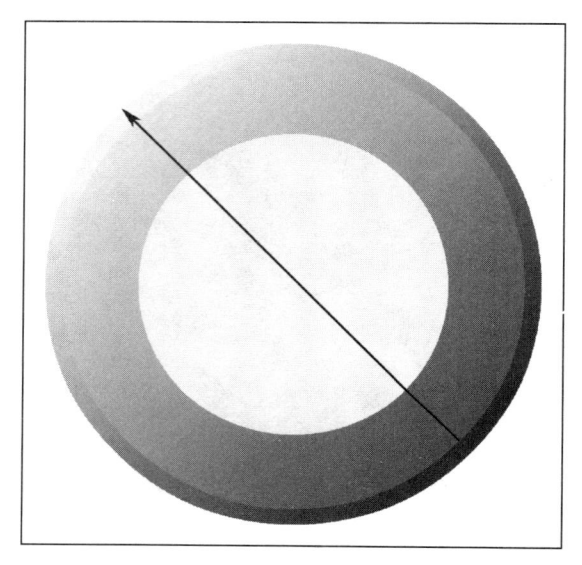

Figure 3.184 Select the next two inner paths, make them into a selection, and draw the gradient.

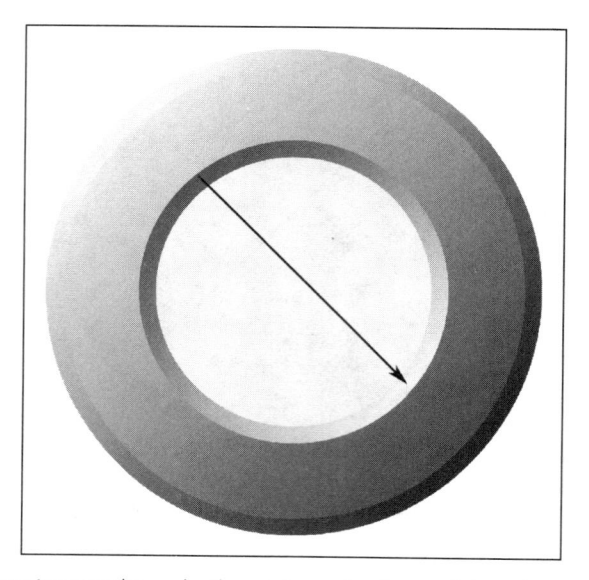

Figure 3.185 Select the two inner paths, make them into a selection, and draw the gradient as shown.

5. Deselect all. Select the inner path. Make it into a selection. Set the gradient Opacity to 60% and make the next gradient as shown in Figure 3.186. The final shape is depicted in Figure 3.187.

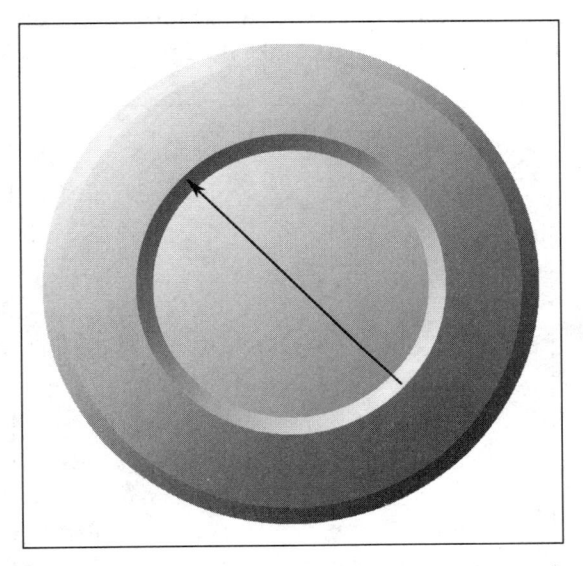

Figure 3.186 Select the inner path, make it into a selection, and draw the last gradient.

Figure 3.187 The completed shaded shape.

216 CHAPTER 3

Cylinder Shape—To create a cylinder shape (with file GS_04.PSD), follow these steps:

1. Click on the Work Path so that the paths are visible, as shown in Figure 3.188. Select the lower path and press the Enter key so that it becomes a selection.
2. Set the Foreground/Background colors to their defaults. Set the gradient to Foreground to Transparent and the type to Linear. Make the first gradient (see Figure 3.189) with

Figure 3.188 Two closed path shapes.

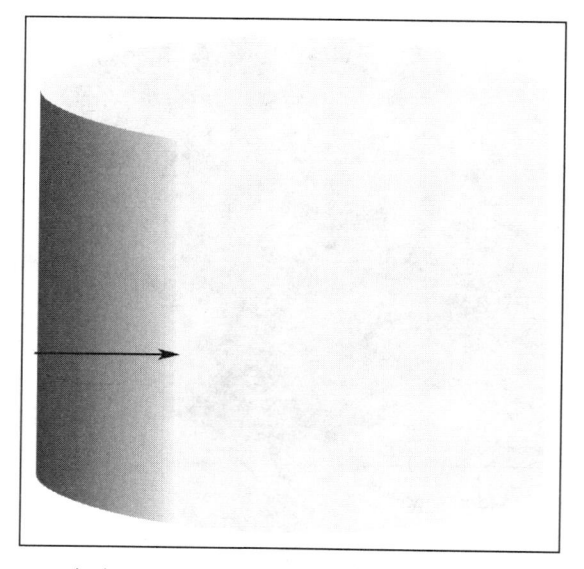

Figure 3.189 With the lower path changed to a selection, draw the first gradient.

the gradient Opacity set to 80%. Make the second gradient (see Figure 3.190) with the gradient set to 100%.

3. Deselect all. Select the upper (oval-shaped) path and make it into a selection. Set the Opacity to 60% and draw the gradient as shown in Figure 3.191. Change the Opacity to 40% and draw the gradient as shown in Figure 3.192. The final shape is depicted in Figure 3.193.

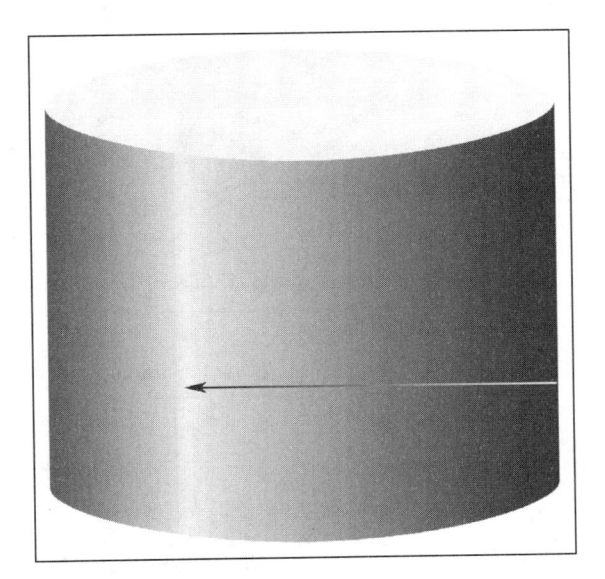

Figure 3.190 Draw the second gradient.

Figure 3.191 With the upper path changed to a selection, draw the first gradient.

Figure 3.192 Draw the second gradient.

Figure 3.193 The completed cylindrical solid.

For the graphically untrained, this peek at one of the mechanical tasks of artwork might be very instructive. For those with more training and experience, it is useful to note that even these primitive black-and-white shapes can have image information seemingly mapped onto them. An example is shown in Figure 3.194. The water lily pond image, on a separate layer from the black and white shape, has been set to the Overlay mode. The mapping looks a little more sharp and clean if the grayscale concentric shape is subjected to the Image|Adjust|Auto Levels command.

Figure 3.194 Pictorial information seemingly mapped onto the three-dimensional surface with the Overlay mode.

The Measure, Eyedropper, Color Sampler, Hand, And Zoom Tools

Two navigation tools, two color samplers, and a ruler round out our examination of the tools. All of these tools have keyboard shortcuts, which makes it unlikely that you'll ever use them by selecting them from the Toolbox. Keep a watch for the ones that have useful modifications on their respective Options palettes that can tailor them to fit perfectly with the way you work in Photoshop.

The Measure Tool

The Measure tool (press U) is a handy little gadget that lets you measure distances and angles. To use it, click and drag on the image, and watch the Info palette for a readout. If you click and drag with this tool while the Shift key is down, you can constrain the angles to increments of 45°.

Eyedropper/Color Sampler Tool

The Eyedropper tool (press Shift+I to cycle between Eyedropper and Color Sampler) picks up color from an image. Simply click with the tool selected, and the color is taken up. Used with no modifier keys, the picked-up color becomes the new Foreground color. If Option or Alt is depressed at the time of the mouse click, the taken-up color becomes the new Background color. The default for this tool is for the values of a single pixel to be sampled. Single pixels are, however, unreliable guides to the general color of an area. Because of this, the tool can be set so that a 3×3-pixel or a 5×5-pixel area is averaged to become the sampled color. You can see the options and contextual menu for this tool and for the Color Sampler tool in Figures 3.195 and 3.196.

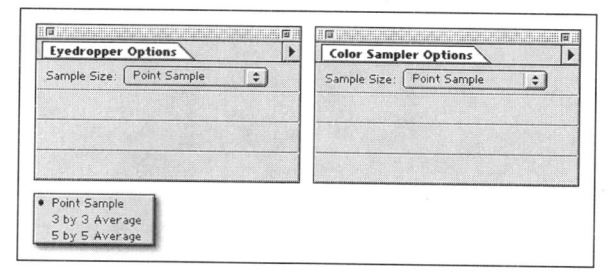

Figure 3.195 Options for the Eyedropper and Color Sampler tools.

Figure 3.196 The contextual menu for the Eyedropper and Color Sampler tools.

As we mentioned earlier in this chapter when discussing Foreground/Background colors, the Eyedropper tool is also available when you use six of the painting tools: Airbrush, Paintbrush, Pencil, Line, Gradient, and Paint. When any of these tools is in use, depress the Option or Alt key to temporarily access the Eyedropper tool.

> **TIP**
>
> Selecting a color with the Eyedropper tool can be an iffy proposition. You may want to try this strategy for locating the color that seems to be the best match for the area you're sampling. Set the tool to 5 by 5 Average. Locate the cursor in the area to be sampled, depress the mouse button, and move the cursor around slowly—don't let up on the mouse button—while watching the Foreground color box. When the color seems right, release the mouse button.

The Color Sampler tool is new to Photoshop 5. It is especially useful for color correction work. To use this tool, click within the document window. You will see that a small circular shape has been left at the click place and that the circle is designated with the numeral "1". If you'll glance at your Info palette, you'll see that it has rearranged itself and now includes a separate space for the values contained at the #1 sample point. You can click and place up to four separate points on the image. All behave exactly as the first did. You might use this tool as a way of keeping track of separate value ranges during a Curves or Levels adjustment. The placed points will persist until you choose another tool. Note that you can move the points around after they have been placed (hold down Command or Ctrl to access the Move tool while the Color Sampler tool is selected).

Hand Tool

The new Photoshop Navigator palette makes getting around inside a window so simple that there almost seems no need for the Hand tool (press H). The Navigator palette has, however, a single drawback: To use it, you must move your cursor out of the window. No matter how quick you are, moving your cursor away from the area where you are working slows you

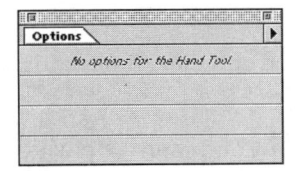

Figure 3.197 Options for the Hand tool.

Figure 3.198 The contextual menu for the Hand tool.

down and interrupts your concentration. With the Hand tool, you can simply move the material in the window into a new position and continue working. The Options and contextual menu for the Hand tool are shown in Figures 3.197 and 3.198.

To use the Hand tool, click and drag on an image window that is at sufficient magnification that not all of the pixels can be viewed at once. The result is the same as if you moved the scroll bars. The scroll bars, however, only move in one dimension and the Hand can move in two at the same time. Rather than pressing H to select the tool, it's easier to simply depress the spacebar whenever the Hand tool is needed. No matter which other tool you are using, the spacebar changes your cursor to that of the Hand.

Zoom Tool

With the Zoom tool (press Z), the image is brought to higher or lower magnification. Choose the tool and the cursor becomes a small magnifier glass with a plus in the center. The plus indicates that a click will take you closer to the image. Hold Option or Alt and the plus changes to a minus. The options and contextual menu for this tool are shown in Figures 3.199 and 3.200.

To use the Zoom tool, click in the window on the area you wish to magnify or reduce. Photoshop attempts to place the pixels on which you clicked in the center of the screen. The zoom performed will be, click by click, at a set of predefined percentages. Click and drag a selection marquee. Photoshop calculates the amount of magnification necessary to enlarge the marquee area and then centers it in your screen.

When you are using the Zoom tool, you have a choice about whether your windows will expand or become smaller as you zoom in and out. The Resize Windows To Fit checkbox on the Options palette determines the window's behavior.

You can use the Zoom tool at any time even without selecting it from the Tools palette. Hold Command+spacebar (Mac) or Ctrl+spacebar (Windows) for the zoom-in cursor. Add Option or Alt to the other two and the zoom-out cursor appears.

Double-click on the Zoom tool icon to zoom the document window to 100%.

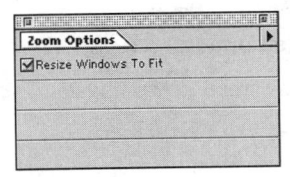

Figure 3.199 Options for the Zoom tool.

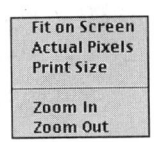

Figure 3.200 The contextual menu for the Zoom tool.

Other Photoshop Zoom Commands

The View menu contains five Zoom commands. All but one of these, Print Size, have keyboard equivalents.

Zoom In and Zoom Out are commands issued by typing Command++ (plus) or Ctrl++ and Command+- (minus) or Ctrl+-. If the Resize Window to Fit option on the Zoom palette is checked, these two commands zoom up or down with the windows resizing appropriate to the amount of zoom. Holding Option or Alt as well as the Command or Ctrl key when typing + or - will prevent the windows from resizing.

Command+0 (zero) or Ctrl+0 causes the image window to fit itself to the widest dimensions of the screen. With this command, the entire image is visible at whatever magnification is required. Using Option or Alt along with Command+0 (zero) or Ctrl+0 causes the image to display at what Photoshop calls Actual Size. This simply means that the pixels of the image and the pixels of the monitor are in a one-to-one ratio.

View|Print Size is useful only in that it gives you a real-world glimpse of your file's physical size. When you work at low resolutions, this command is probably useful. With higher resolutions, you are given a view of the file that has little to recommend it. The decrease in magnification for a 300 ppi file viewed at Print Size is so extreme that you will be able to derive little meaningful information from looking at the image.

Photoshop also furnishes a small box in the lower left corner of the viewing window into which percentages can be entered. Double-click in this box, enter a new percentage, and press Return or Enter. The screen changes to the new amount of magnification without resizing the image window. This small box has a tryout feature. Hold down the Shift key when you press the Return key. The number in the percentage box stays selected. If the amount of magnification is sufficient, press the Return key again. If the amount of magnification is not to your liking, go ahead and enter a new number without having to return the cursor to the box.

When you've magnified the image without changing the size of the window, you have two fast options for increasing the amount of the image that you can see. Click in the Grow or Maximize box in the upper right corner of the window. The window expands to fit either the image or the screen. You can also use the screen mode, which moves the boundaries of the window out to the edges of the screen. To do this, click on the center icon at the bottom of the Toolbox, or press F.

Here are some other keyboard commands you can use when working at high magnification:

- *Page Up key*—Moves the image slightly less than a full screen up.
- *Shift+Page Up key*—Moves the image up about one-tenth of a screen.
- *Command or Ctrl+Page Up key*—Moves the image to the left one full screen.
- *Page Down key*—Moves the image slightly less than a full screen down.
- *Shift+Page Down key*—Moves the image down about one-tenth of a screen.

- *Command or Ctrl+Page Down key*—Moves the image to the right one full screen.
- *Home key*—Displays the upper left corner of the image.
- *End key*—Displays the lower right corner of the image.

The Navigator Palette

The Navigator palette isn't really a part of the Toolbox, but as long as we are on the subject of zooming....

This gadget is pure magic. A labeled representation of the palette is shown in Figure 3.201. The main part of the palette is composed of a thumbnail of the entire image. Within the thumbnail is the View Box. The default color of the View Box is red, but you can change it by using the palette menu at the upper right. Click and drag in the thumbnail window and the View Box moves around. Your screen is instantly updated to show the area of the View Box. Hold down the Command key or the Ctrl key and the cursor in the thumbnail window becomes a Zoom cursor. Click once and the View Box collapses to its smallest size. This changes your image window to maximum magnification. While holding the Command or Ctrl key down, click and drag within the thumbnail window and draw a new View Box.

The Percentage control at the bottom works exactly the way the small percentage box at the lower left of the image window works. Numbers can be entered into it followed by Return (or Enter) or Shift+Return (or Shift+Enter).

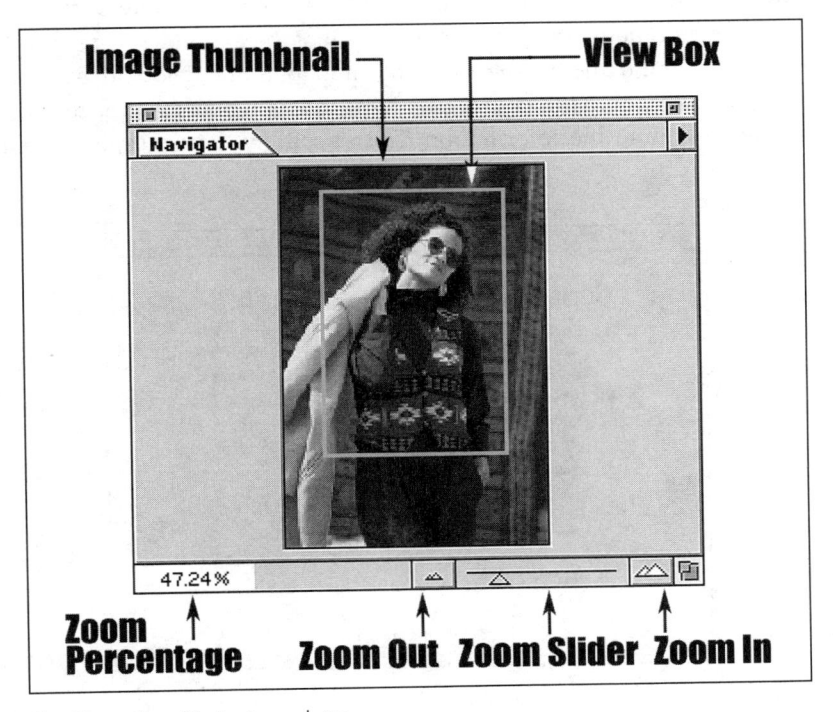

Figure 3.201 The Photoshop Navigator palette.

Use the Zoom Out and Zoom In icons by clicking on them. Each click is the same as if you clicked in the image window with the Zoom tool selected.

The Zoom Slider lets you experiment with magnification. Drag the slider in either direction to zoom in or out. The View Box and your image window are instantly updated.

None of the controls for this window automatically resize the image window.

Adobe Online

You may not have realized it, but that staring eye at the top of your Tools palette is actually a button. If you click on it—and if you have a Web connection to your computer—the dialog box in Figure 3.202 appears. Click on the Refresh button and you will connect to Adobe's Web site.

Moving On

Chapter 3 has taken a close look at Photoshop's tools, the Toolbox, and has explored many peripheral questions about fast and easy ways to use all of the tools. The emphasis has been on, besides the behavior of the tools, using the keyboard to access the tools and on keyboard commands to trigger commands that would otherwise require moving the cursor someplace away from the image.

You have also seen many examples of how the tools are used. Some of these are everyday situations and some of them are more advanced. All of the examples were chosen to give you an idea how wide-ranging and flexible the Photoshop tools are. If you have encountered unfamiliar material while reading this chapter, we hope that you take the time to work through the tutorial material. Reading the information doesn't solidify the concepts as well as actually using them.

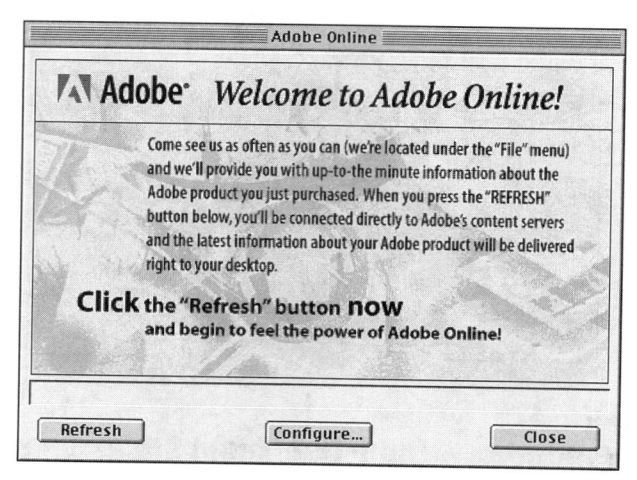

Figure 3.202 Welcome to Adobe Online, the dialog box that appears when you click on the Eye icon at the top of the Tools palette.

Many keyboard commands require a good deal of use and practice before they become part of your fluency with the program. We encourage you to persist in mastering as many of the keyboard commands as possible. With the keyboard commands and with a broad understanding of each tool's special abilities, you'll be able to work in Photoshop with an efficiency that will be the envy of all who watch you work. As you become more efficient, you'll find that using Photoshop becomes more enjoyable and that your proficiency leads you to many new and interesting ideas.

In the next chapter, you will look at the only tool not explored in this chapter—the Pen tool—and its associated Paths palette. The Pen tool is one of Photoshop's most useful tools. With it, you draw *paths*, line shapes that can be converted to selections, used as a guide for other tools to follow while applying paint or edit effects, and exported as masks. We think you'll be pleasantly surprised to discover how many different kinds of things you can do with the Pen tool and with the paths it draws.

Paths and The Pen Tool

In Chapter 3, you were introduced to all the tools, except the Pen tool and its associates. The Pen is such a powerful multipurpose tool that we are devoting an entire chapter to it. It can do some astonishing things for you.

The Pen tool is the principal drawing tool for programs such as Macromedia FreeHand and Adobe Illustrator. Both of these programs construct graphic objects that belong to the class called vector shapes, shapes that are essentially composed of lines and the spaces the lines surround, lines that can be stored and manipulated as mathematical expressions. The Pen is an odd tool to include in a program devoted to manipulating the data of a raster file (raster objects are collections, or *arrays*, of pixels that are stored as large-scale tables of numbers). The Pen draws Beziér paths that are, by definition, the boundaries of vector shapes. As such, it is a foundation tool for programs such as Illustrator and FreeHand. Yet here it is, an important Photoshop tool, with Beziér curves superimposed on a graphic type that has little logical connection with vector shapes. How any software engineer ever thought to put a vector tool into a program that doesn't really support vector objects is a mystery. But you can be glad that the Pen was included. With the Pen tool, you have the ability to describe discrete pixel areas with the same mathematical language you would use for a vector shape. That makes those shapes economical to store and unobtrusive until you need them. Effectively, that makes a path similar to a selection, but without the selection's urgency or large storage penalty. You also have easy shape editability. This, by itself, paves the way for this tool—which can do a lot of other things too.

In this chapter, we will discuss what a Beziér path is. We will look at why the Pen tool is notoriously difficult to master and how you can become an expert with it. You'll learn how to draw smooth, precise paths, and how to manipulate these paths, changing their shapes, making them smaller or larger, rotating them, distorting them, and using them for a variety of selection and paint tasks. You will also learn how to move paths between programs—Photoshop to Illustrator and back again—and how to use an exported path as a mask (Clipping Path). You're going to be surprised at how many useful and interesting things you can do with the Pen tool and its associated Paths palette.

Beziér Curves

In the 1960s and 1970s, the French mathematician Pierre Beziér—at that time employed by the auto manufacturer Renault—was one of an industry-wide group of technicians and engineers working to develop ways of using computers to control the manufacture of automobiles. Beziér's project focused on control software for precision cutting machines. Basing his work on trigonometric functions, Beziér evolved the curve-creation system that bears his name.

The Beziér curve is a deceptively simple concept. At the two ends of any Beziér curve lie two nodes, or Anchor Points (see Figure 4.1). The curve segment between the nodes is defined by the positions of spatial referents called control points (the node has one control point for each curve). Each control point is aligned to the node along the line of a tangent. A tangent is normally considered to be a unique line intersecting a point on the edge of a curve: A given point can have only one tangent. However, if the control point is moved—and by moving the control points, you alter the direction of a curve—its linear relationship with the node is changed. A new tangent is created that forces an alteration in the direction of the curve.

The control point has another use: Its distance from the node serves as a modifier for the amplitude of the curve. As the control moves away from its node, the curve encloses an ever-greater area. If the control moves closer to the node, the curve encloses a smaller area. The control point and the node can even be made to coincide. In such a case, the curve encloses no area. If a coinciding control point node is located at each end of a curve, the result is a straight line.

When you use the Pen tool in Photoshop or in a drawing program such as Adobe Illustrator, you are drawing what are called Beziér curves. (See Figure 4.1.) These curves are also known as *paths*.

In the figure, the nodes—they are known as *anchor points* in the Adobe lexicon—are marked with a b. The nodes are the endpoints of the curve (a). Each node may have one or two *control handles* extending from it (shown in the figure as d). The control handles end in smaller distinct points called control points. You can move these points with the mouse cursor to change the direction and length of the control handles.

The control handles are the means by which the curve is shaped. The direction and length of a handle give the curve direction and amplitude.

In Photoshop, there are two kinds of nodes, *smooth* and *corner*. The difference between them lies in how the control handles operate.

a) Beziér curve
b) nodes/anchor points
c) control points
d) control handles

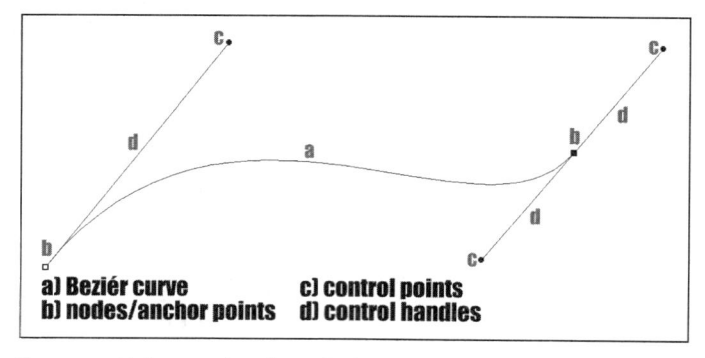

Figure 4.1 The Beziér curve with its associated terminology.

Smooth Nodes

You can think of a *smooth node* as the junction at the simple continuation of two curves. Two control handles extend from opposite sides of the node. When either of the control handles is moved, the handle on the opposite side also moves, pivoting on the node. Figure 4.2 shows a smooth node with handles extended along a horizontal line (left). When one of the handles is rotated 90°, the other also moves (right). Notice how this clockwise rotation has altered the shape of the curves on either side of the node.

Corner Nodes

Corner nodes are more complex than smooth nodes. The path on each side of the node can be a curved line or a straight line. (Note: A straight line between two nodes is still technically a Beziér curve, even if it is not *curved*.) If control handles extend from a corner node, they are independently controllable. Moving one does not move the other. This independence of movement is shown in Figure 4.3.

Using these definitions, we can define four possible node configurations. The first is shown in Figure 4.4, the *smooth* node. In Figure 4.5, the node is shown with no control handles extending from it. Figure 4.6 shows a corner node with a control handle extending from one side but not the other. The last type is shown in Figure 4.7. Two independently movable control handles extend from the node. All but the first are examples of corner nodes.

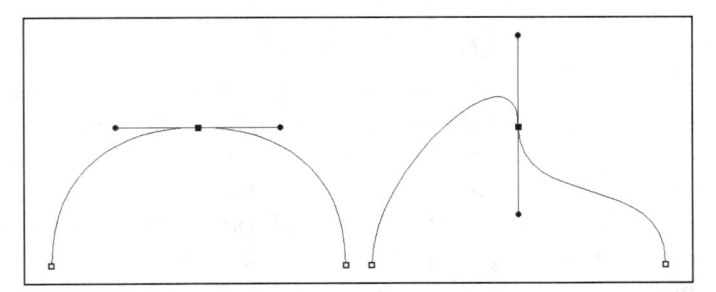

Figure 4.2 The handles of smooth nodes pivot together on the node. As one is rotated around the node, the other follows. The two handles remain a straight line.

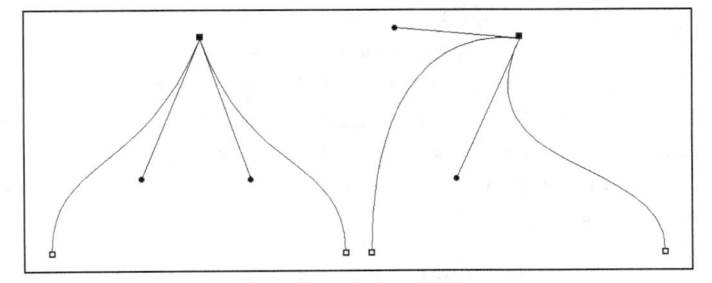

Figure 4.3 The handles of a corner node also pivot on the node. As one of the handles is moved, the other remains stationary.

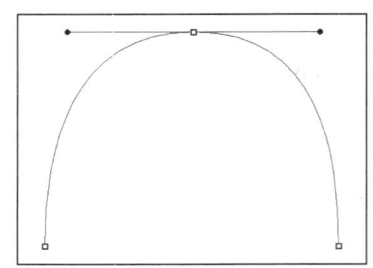

Figure 4.4 This is an example of a smooth node.

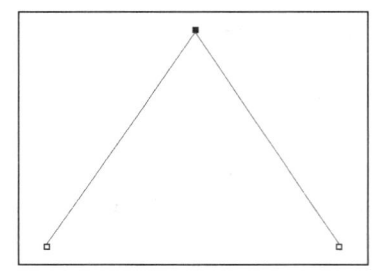

Figure 4.5 This figure shows a corner node without control handles.

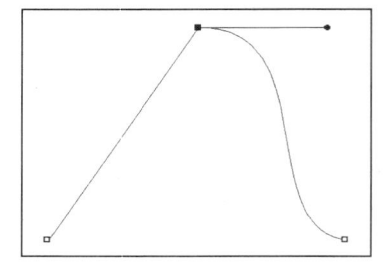

Figure 4.6 This is a corner node with one control handle.

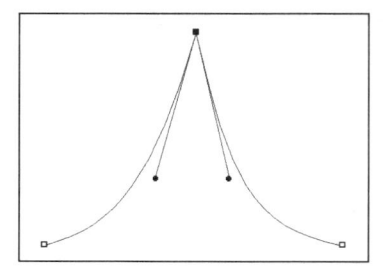

Figure 4.7 Corner node, with two control handles.

Drawing Paths With The Pen Tool

The behavior of the Pen tool is like nothing you've ever encountered. Drawing is largely a matter of analyzing the contours of shapes and planning where to place the nodes. The path simply appears between the locations of your nodes. Often, you will feel that although you are operating the mouse correctly, your mouse's movements are not taking place where the path is appearing. Don't worry about this; it's natural and will disappear. After you've had a little practice, you may begin to recognize that drawing precision paths with the mouse would be difficult any other way. You may not believe it just now, but a time will come when using the Pen tool will be enjoyable. Really.

Drawing Straight-Line Paths

Drawing straight-line paths is the easiest way to use the Pen tool. Press P to select the tool. Move your cursor into the document window and click. Move the cursor away from the place where you first clicked, and click again. You'll see the path connecting the two click points as a straight line. The two nodes will appear to be small squares. The first one is hollow, and the most recently placed node is solid. As you continue to move the cursor around and click, the lines follow behind (see Figure 4.8).

When your cursor approaches to within a pixel or so from the place where your path began, you'll see a small circular shape appear to the lower right of the cursor (see Figure 4.9). This is

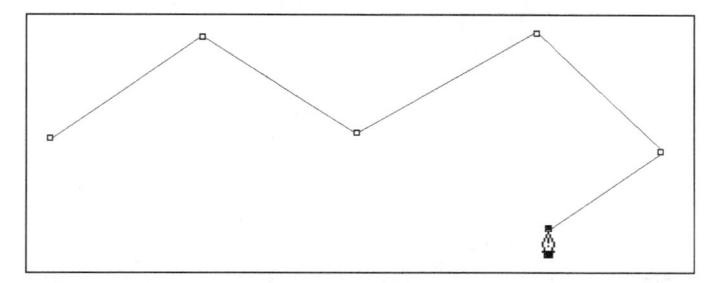

Figure 4.8 To draw straight-line paths, click with the Pen tool, move the cursor away from the first click, and click again.

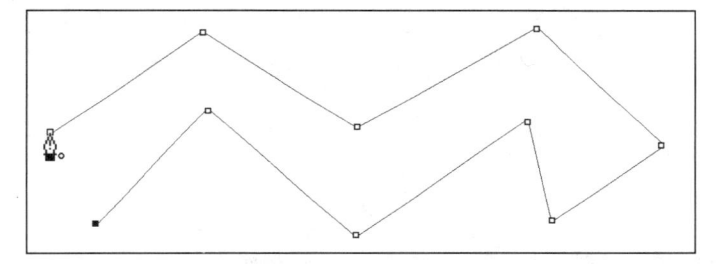

Figure 4.9 When the cursor reaches the beginning of the path, a small circle appears next to the cursor to let you know that your next click will connect the most recent node to the first, creating a closed shape.

your indication that another click will join your last node to the first. This creates a *closed* path, a path with no beginning or ending nodes.

Drawing Curved Shapes

Drawing a curved path is a little more complex than drawing straight-line paths. Place the cursor in the document window. Click, keep the mouse button down, and drag in the direction the curve is to go. Release the mouse button. Move the cursor away from the first node. Click and drag again in the direction the curve is to follow.

Figure 4.10 shows the first click-and-drag operation on the leftmost side. The lines that extend from the node are the control handles. The arrow indicates the direction of the mouse drag. The handle below the node forms as the handle above is dragged out. The second handle will always be the same length as the first (though it may be modified later to be a different length). On the right side of the figure, a second node has been placed, and two new handles have been formed by dragging the mouse. Notice that the curved path has formed from the forward handle of the first node and the backward handle of the second node. Note also that the two handles at the top—these are the handles that control the first curve—are on the convex side of the curve. This is an important thing to remember: Control handles will always be on the convex side of the curve.

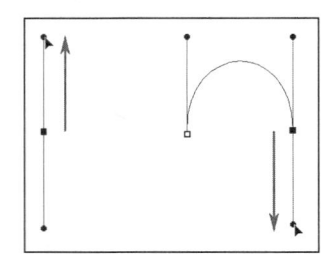

Figure 4.10 Click and drag to establish the first node and control handles (right). Click and drag again to form the first curve of the path and the second set of control handles.

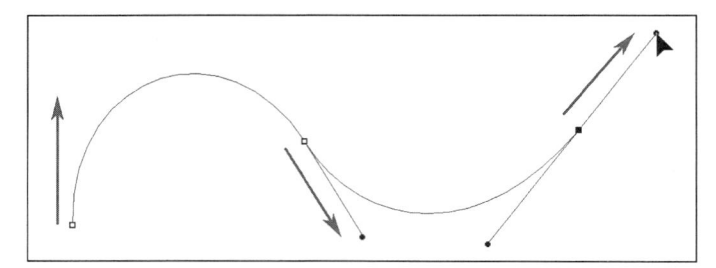

Figure 4.11 Two curve segments running between three nodes have formed on this path.

As new nodes are added, new segments of the path are added. Figure 4.11 shows three nodes that have defined two curves. The control handles are visible only for the curve that has just been formed. When you edit the path later, clicking on a curve segment makes the control handles for that segment visible. If you click on a node, the control handles for both of the segments running into that node become visible. Note that the control handles and control points only appear on screen to allow you to edit the shape of the path. Control handles and points never appear as output.

Drawing Mixed Curve And Straight-Line Shapes

When you are drawing a path, it's often necessary to join a curve to a straight-line segment. The procedure for doing this is as follows:

1. Click to form the first node. Position the cursor some distance away and click again. The straight-line path segment forms between the two nodes.

2. Hold down Option (Mac) or Alt (Windows). Click again on the last node point and drag away from it. A control handle will form only on the side of the cursor drag.

3. Now release the mouse button, move the cursor, and click and drag to form the next curve segment.

4. The procedure is shown in Figure 4.12. The node type is the same as shown back in Figure 4.6.

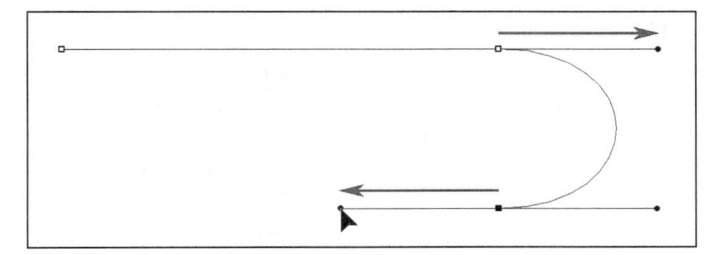

Figure 4.12 Click twice to form the first two nodes. Hold Option or Alt. Click and drag from the second node to form a control handle on the side of the node opposite the straight line. Click and drag to form a curve segment between the second and third nodes.

You can also do this in the opposite direction, bottom to top, by taking these steps:

1. Using Figure 4.12 as an example, click and drag to place the two handles from the lower node. Release the mouse button.
2. Move the cursor up and away from the new node. Click and drag to form the second node and the control handle opposite the direction of the drag.
3. Hold Option (Mac) or Alt (Windows). Click on the second node. This immediately retracts the forward control handle into the node.
4. Move the cursor away from the second node, and click again to make the straight path segment.

Drawing Curve Segments That Abruptly Change Direction

When two curved path segments form a corner node (see Figure 4.7), you will see a sudden change of direction. Here's the procedure for forming the two curves:

1. Click and drag to form the first node and its control handles.
2. Click and drag to form the second node and its control handles.
3. Hold Option (Mac) or Alt (Windows). Click on the last node, and drag in the direction the new curve segment is to follow. The forward control handle disappears and a new handle forms at an angle to the back control handle of the node.

The process is shown in Figure 4.13.

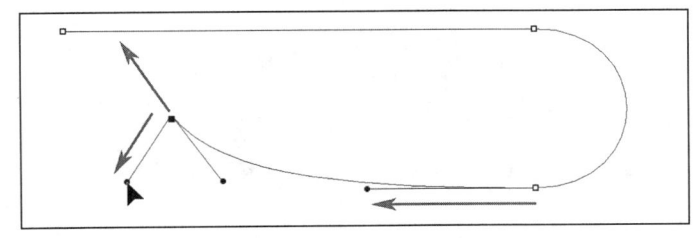

Figure 4.13 Click and drag to form control handles for the new node. Hold Option or Alt. Click on the last node and drag in a different direction, the direction in which you wish the new curve to move.

Analyzing Curved Shapes

As you get familiar with the behavior of the Pen tool, you'll also become more adept at looking ahead to analyze the shapes around which you are placing a path. Figure 4.14 gives you an idea how this works: Small marks are placed around the perimeter of the shape to indicate where nodes will be placed. Look at the figure; notice how the segment of the perimeter within each pair of marks differs in shape or direction from the segments on each side. You need to begin to recognize the boundary points of each curve segment as you draw with the Pen tool. Your goal is to construct an accurate path that encloses the shape using as few points as possible.

The Rule Of Thirds

As you draw your path, look ahead to where the next node will be placed. The drag of the cursor that develops the forward control handle will be along the convex side of the curve in front of the node that you just placed. As you drag, you can use a simple trick for estimating how far you should drag the control handle for the next curve. This trick is called *the rule of thirds*. Mentally estimate the length of the next curve segment and drag until the control handle is one-third that distance. Release the mouse button. Move the cursor to the next node position, and follow the same procedure.

Figure 4.15 shows what the curve looks like when this trick has been used. Note that each control handle is about one-third the length of the curve between the nodes. Using this method, you'll be able to draw nearly any curve shape with reasonable accuracy.

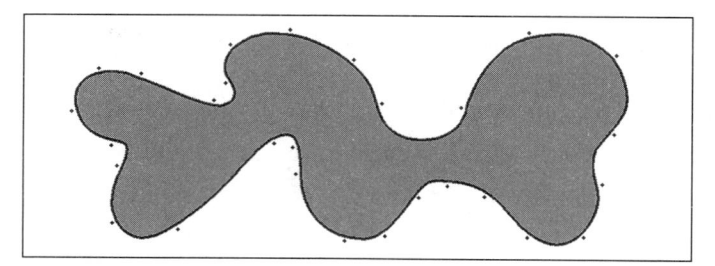

Figure 4.14 Study this curved shape to understand the curve segments that compose it. Each segment boundary (black mark) is where a node will be placed. Each curve segment is distinguished by a slight change in the shape of the object or by a change in the direction of the enclosing path.

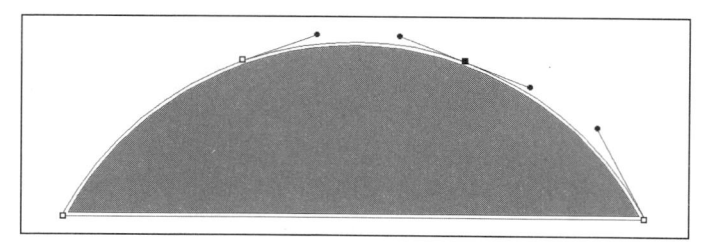

Figure 4.15 The control handles for the path show how dragging one-third the distance of the curve segment makes it easy to estimate how long the curve handles should be.

Drawing Paths With The Magnetic Pen And The Freeform Pen Tools

Besides the original Pen tool, Photoshop 5 furnishes you with two additional Beziér drawing tools designed to make the Pen tool's learning curve a little less steep. With one tool, you simply click and drag. The other tool constructs paths as you drag it along an edge in exactly the way you have already learned to use the Magnetic Lasso tool in Chapter 3.

Magnetic Pen Paths

Click and drag. That's it. Drawing paths around the edge of an object just can't get any easier than this. After you've selected this tool, you can set its Options to give you exactly the path you wish to draw.

The first of the values on the Options palette (see Figure 4.16) lets you enter a Curve Fit setting. Curve Fit is a setting that controls the precision of the final path as it relates to the movement of your mouse or stylus. There is a trade-off: Low values give paths that are more precise with larger numbers of nodes, whereas high values result in simpler paths, but with fewer nodes. The range of values is between .5 and 10. Figure 4.17 shows a path drawn with a setting of ".5". Figures 4.18 and 4.19 are paths drawn with settings of "4" and "10". Of these three figures, the one that conforms most exactly to the edge of the letter shape is the first. The second figure generally conforms to the shape, but deviates in several places. The third figure's path fits the shape in some places, but is so wildly off in others that it's practically unusable.

The Pen Width option is the same as for the Magnetic Lasso tool. This number sets the width of the detection zone, or, in simpler terms, the area in which the Magnetic Pen looks for an edge to which the path snaps. The range is from 1 to 40. You can change the Pen Width as you draw

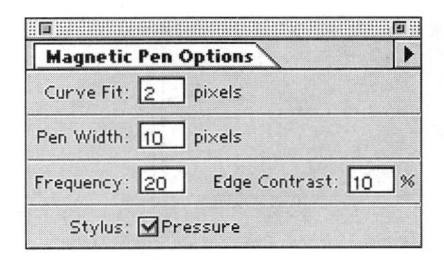

Figure 4.16 The Magnetic Pen tool's Options palette.

Figure 4.17 Magnetic Pen tool path drawn with Curve Fit tolerance of .5 (the smallest number allowed).

Figure 4.18 Magnetic Pen tool path drawn with Curve Fit tolerance of 4.

Figure 4.19 Magnetic Pen tool path drawn with Curve Fit tolerance of 10 (the largest number allowed).

by pressing either of the bracket keys. The left bracket decreases the width, and the right bracket increases it. This is very handy in situations where the tool can become confused. The points marked with arrows in Figure 4.20 are one example. With a wide Pen Width, moving into these tight corner spots can mean that the path will sometimes jump from one edge and back again. Decreasing the Pen Width as you enter areas of this sort solves the problem. If you use a stylus with a pressure-sensitive digitizing tablet, you can change the width of the tool by increasing your drawing pressure.

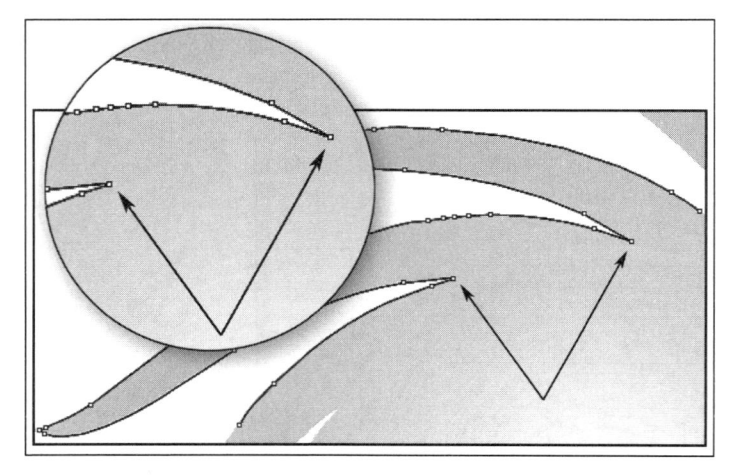

Figure 4.20 Decrease the Pen Width as you enter tight corners, such as those marked by the arrows. As the drawing width becomes smaller, you'll have less trouble keeping the path from jumping from one edge to the other.

The Frequency setting on the Options palette lets you enter a number that specifies the rate at which the Magnetic Pen places nodes automatically. With higher values, more nodes are inserted. The best setting will be one that results in the fewest nodes possible without compromising the drawn edge.

The Edge Contrast setting is a threshold number ranging between 1 and 100. Photoshop uses higher values to detect edges that have strong contrast. Lower values are used to find lower-contrast edges.

Drawing Magnetic Pen Paths—With your options set, move the cursor onto the document and click once to establish the beginning node of the path. Move the cursor slowly along the edge you wish to trace. (Note: You can hold down the mouse button or not as you please. The tool works the same either way.) If you find that your trailing path has jumped away from the edge—and before the tool has arbitrarily assigned a new node—move your cursor back beyond the deviation and click once to anchor the path. Continue on, placing points wherever they are needed to keep the path following the edge.

As you draw, you can switch temporarily to the Freeform Pen tool (see the following section): Hold down Option (Mac) or Alt (Windows), then click and drag to make a portion of the path follow an arbitrary course. Release the modifier key, click once more on the edge you are following, and continue with the Magnetic Pen. You can also draw straight path segments while using the Magnetic Pen. Hold down Option or Alt, click once, click again at some distance, and continue until you wish to return to the Magnetic Pen. Release the modifier key, click once more on the edge you are following, and continue.

Eventually, your path will return to the place you began. As your cursor centers over the original node, the cursor will change to the Magnetic Pen icon with a small circle to the lower right. When you see this cursor, click once more to close the path. You can close the path at any time by performing one of two actions. First, double-click: Your path will be connected from the place you double-clicked back to the original node. Second, click once to establish a new node, hold down Command (Mac) or Ctrl (Windows), and click once more on the new node. This closes the path by connecting the first and last nodes.

You might wish to draw a path only partway around a shape. Use the tool in the normal way. When you want to stop, press the Enter or Return key. You path will end at the position of your cursor at the time you pressed Enter or Return. At some other time, you might want to continue drawing from the unclosed segment. Select the Magnetic Pen tool, hold down Command or Ctrl, and click on either of the end nodes to select it. Position your cursor so that the selected node is centered in the circle, click once, and continue around the edge normally.

After you draw your Magnetic Pen tool path, you can edit it, move it around, and do anything with it that you can do with a path drawn by the more formidable Pen tool. When you first begin to use this tool, you may be a little disconcerted that it seems so easy. Trust me. It really *is* that easy!

Freeform Pen Paths

You won't want to use the Freeform Path tool to make tightly controlled masking shapes. You use this tool to make paths that would be laborious for the Pen tool and difficult—or impossible—for the Magnetic Pen tool. You might, for example, want to draw the irregular edge of a coastline on a map. Rather than slavishly follow every indentation, you can probably do a creditable coastline approximation in a fraction of the time. Another example: You might have to draw along an edge that is difficult to see, some of which you can discern, but which you could not enter as a meaningful tolerance for Photoshop. The Freeform Pen tool is also useful as an art tool, a tool with which you can originate shapes rather than follow the contours of an existing image.

The Options for the Freeform Pen are shown in Figure 4.21. Your only setting for this tool is that of the Curve Fit, which works the same as for the Magnetic Pen.

To use this tool, move your cursor into the document window, click, and drag. You can release the mouse button at any time for an unclosed path. If you continue to drag until your cursor is centered over the initial click point (see Figure 4.22), you will see the cursor change with the small circle appearing at the lower right. Release the mouse button and your path becomes a closed shape (see Figure 4.23) with nodes automatically placed appropriate to the Curve Fit setting.

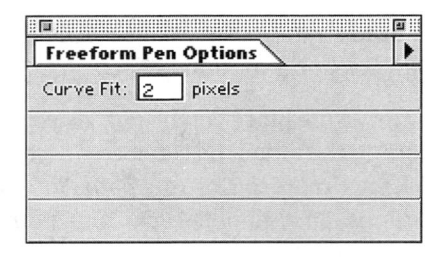

Figure 4.21 The Options palette for the Freeform Pen tool.

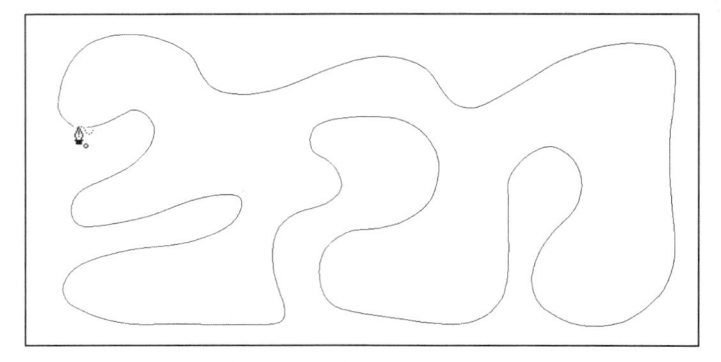

Figure 4.22 Click and drag with the Freeform Pen. When your cursor is close to the beginning of the path, it will change to the Freeform icon, with the small circle at the lower right. Release the mouse button to close the shape.

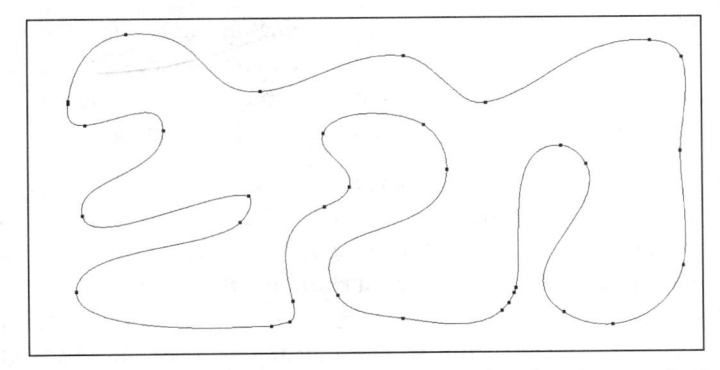

Figure 4.23 Your newly drawn path will appear this way with its nodes placed automatically by Photoshop appropriate to the Curve Fit setting.

Editing Paths With The Pen Tools

After you have drawn your path, you may wish to change its shape. You may decide to modify a curve to make it conform more exactly to the enclosed shape, or you may want to move a node into a different position. To make these changes, use the four tools that accompany the three Pen tools in the Tools palette. The Pen tools and their helpers are shown in Figure 4.24. (To select the Pen tools from the keyboard, press the P key. Press Shift+P to cycle through the three Pen tools. Press the hyphen (-) key to select the Node Delete tool. Press the equals (=) key to select the Add Node tool. Press A to select the Direct Select tool. There is no keyboard selector key for the Node Edit tool.)

The Direct Select

The arrow-shaped Direct Select tool allows you to work directly with paths drawn by the Pen tool. With this Cursor, click directly on a path segment to select it. You can drag the path to change its shape. When you move the path segment, the control handles change their angle

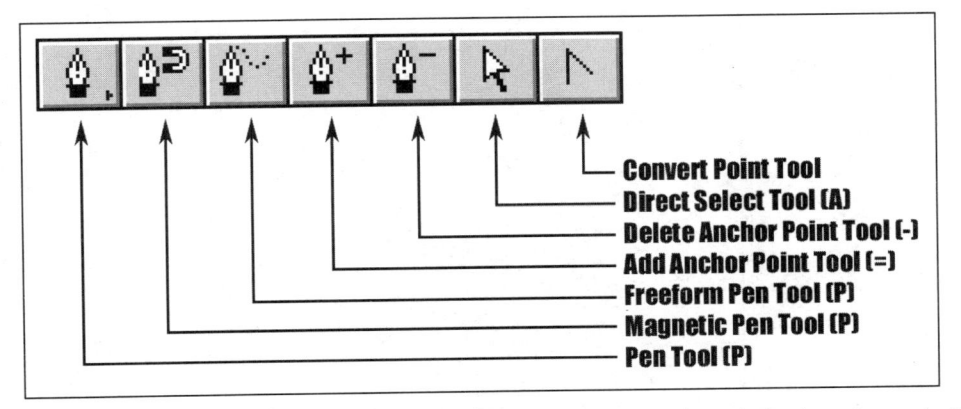

Figure 4.24 The Pen tools and their four accessories. Press Shift+P to cycle through the three Pen tools. Press the hyphen (-) key to select the Node Delete tool. Press the equals (=) key to select the Add Node tool. Press the A key to select the Direct Select tool. The Node Edit tool has no keyboard shortcut.

and length. You can also change the segment by moving the control points. You can, if you want, change their distance from the nodes at each end of the segment. You can also move the points into a different orientation with the node. Any move will change the shape of the curve segment. Experiment with how the curve shapes can be manipulated.

When you use the Direct Select cursor to click on a node, all of the other nodes on the path become visible. The selected node appears as a small, filled square (called an *active* node). The other nodes appears on screen as small hollow squares (these nodes are *semi-active*). An active node can be dragged to a new position without changing the position of any of the semi-active nodes. Only the path segments running through the node are affected. You can make more than one node active by sweep-selecting with the arrow cursor, or you can hold the Shift key as you select the nodes one by one. To make all of the nodes on a path active, hold down Option (Mac) or Alt (Windows), and click anywhere on the path. When all of the nodes are active, the path can be moved around without altering its shape.

You should be aware of these important concepts when you select all or parts of a path:

- When you click on a node, not only does the node become active, but you will also have selected the path segments on each side of the node. If you use the Copy command and then Paste, you will find that you have pasted the node and both of the segments attached to it. The Delete command eliminates the node and both segments.
- When you select the path by clicking anyplace but on a node, you select the entire path. You can Copy and Paste replicas of the whole path. With the whole path selected and Option or Alt held down, you can drag to duplicate the path (see Figure 4.25). With the path selected, the Delete command eliminates the whole path.

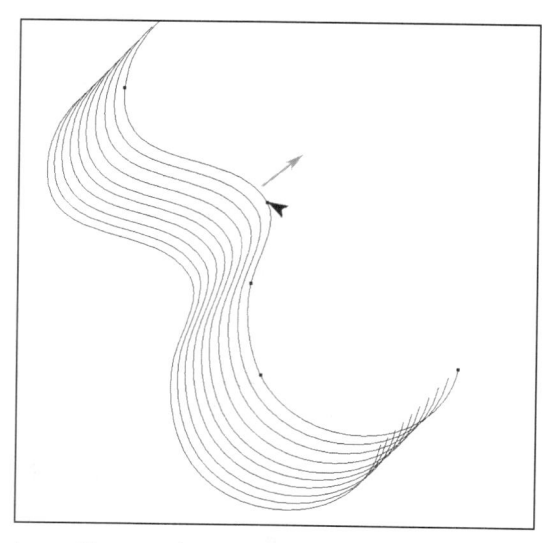

Figure 4.25 Hold down Option or Alt as you drag the path to make a copy of the path. Repeat for multiple copies.

Add Node Tool

Although it is best to make your path with the smallest number of nodes you can manage, you will find that sometimes you just cannot make a curve fit the contour of the shape you are enclosing. Use the Add Node tool—simply click on the path wherever you wish the new node to be—to give yourself more flexibility in making the shape fit. Photoshop will decrease the length of the control handles coming from the nodes on each side of the new node. With any of the three Pen tools selected, your cursor will change automatically to this tool whenever you drag your cursor across a path, but not over an existing node. When your cursor is over an existing node, hold down Option or Alt to change temporarily to the Delete Node tool.

Delete Node Tool

When you have drawn a path and have decided that some of the nodes can be eliminated, use the Delete Node tool to delete the extras. Locate the cursor over the node and click. The node will vanish. Photoshop will increase the length of the control handles coming from the nodes on each side of the deleted node in an attempt to make the path keep its general shape. With any of the three Pen tools selected, your cursor will change automatically to this tool whenever you drag your cursor across an existing node, but not over a simple path segment. When your cursor is over a path with no node, hold down Option or Alt to change temporarily to the Add Node tool.

Node Edit Tool

Using the Node Edit tool, you can convert a node into any of the four types shown back in Figures 4.4, 4.5, 4.6, and 4.7. With this tool selected, click once on any node. The control handles instantly retract into the node (refer to Figure 4.5). Click and drag on any node to draw smooth-node control handles out of the node (refer to Figure 4.4). Click and drag either of the control points of a smooth node to convert the node into a corner node with two curves that change direction at the node (refer to Figure 4.7). After dragging control handles from a node, push one of the control points back into the node (refer to Figure 4.6). With any of the three Pen tools selected, hold down Option or Alt: Your cursor will change to the Node Edit tool automatically as it passes over a node. With the Direct Select tool selected, hold down Command+Option (Mac) or Ctrl+Alt (Windows): Your cursor will change to the Node Edit tool automatically as it passes over a node.

A set of six small files has been included on this book's CD-ROM to help you become proficient at drawing paths. The files, located in the Chapter 4 Practice Files folder, are titled PATH1.PSD, PATH2.PSD, and so on. Each of the files is intended to give you the opportunity to learn one or more path techniques. (The six shapes are shown in Figure 4.26.) We recommend that you try

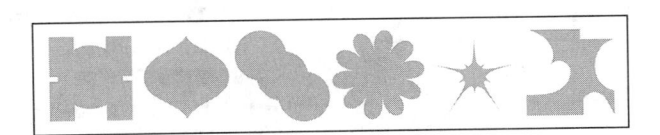

Figure 4.26 These six shapes are found in the Chapter 4 Practice Files folder on this book's CD-ROM. They are intended to help you practice using the Pen tool.

outlining these shapes with one of the Pen tools before attempting any large-scale work on a picture image.

The Paths Palette

The Pen tool and path-edit tools are used in conjunction with the Paths palette (an expanded view is shown in Figure 4.27). The palette allows you to save paths in named sets and to apply special effects to the paths.

The main window of this palette shows a list of paths that have been saved, as well as paths that are being drawn but that have not yet been saved. These in-progress paths are called *Work Paths*. Work paths are always shown in italic on the list to indicate their temporary status.

The Paths Palette Sidebar Menu

The feature set connected with drawn paths is accessed from the sidebar menu (click and hold on the small triangle shape at the upper right corner of the palette). Six of the menu com-

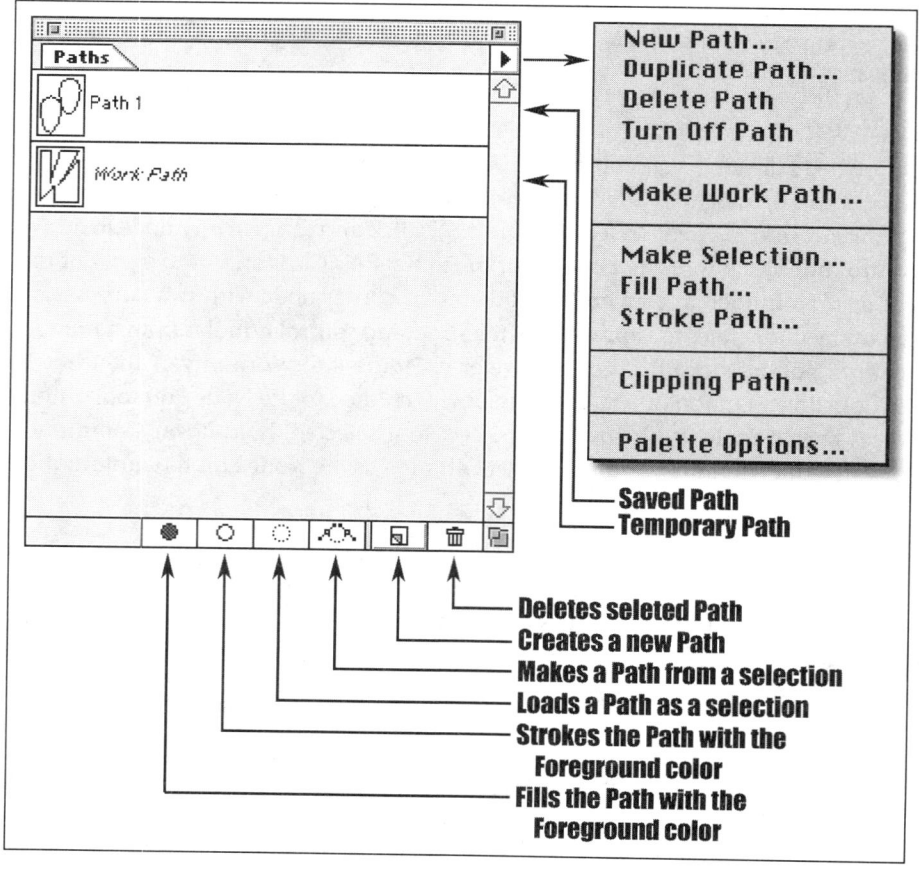

Figure 4.27 The Paths palette with its menu and button icons.

mands have duplicate functions that you can access by clicking on one of the small icons at the bottom of the palette. If you select an item from the menu that is followed by an ellipsis, a dialog box will appear with choices for the operation. After you decide on these choices, clicking on the small button at the bottom of the palette will apply the same choices as though they were defaults. The buttons continue to operate in this way until you change the specifications within the menu-summoned dialog box.

New Path

The New Path option does not draw a path for you, but creates an item on the list which, when selected, stores any drawn paths. When you choose the command from the menu, the dialog box in Figure 4.28 appears. Photoshop automatically numbers the paths as they are created. You might want to give the paths more descriptive names, but you don't have to do so. The button second from right at the bottom of the Paths palette will also create a new path. When you use the button, the dialog box does not appear and the path is named automatically.

If you want to add the path you draw to those that are already on the list of saved paths, click on the path thumbnail on the palette. If none of the items on the list are selected when you begin to draw a path, Photoshop creates a temporary path called a Work Path. When you save the document, the work path will also be saved. However, the work path cannot be used as a clipping path (paths that are exported as masks, discussed later in this chapter). If you copy a named path and then paste without one of the list items selected, your pasted path will be added to the work path. Because this path is temporary, it's usually a good policy to save the path as soon as you can.

Duplicate Path

When you have drawn a path, you may find that you want to use only a few of the segments. By using the Duplicate Path command (see Figure 4.29), you can modify a copy of the first path without affecting the original. Figure 4.30 depicts an example of a path that is a modification (lower) of the original (upper). You can use this kind of modification for modifying some of the edges of the shapes around which the original path has been drawn.

You can also duplicate paths without using the menu command. Hold Option or Alt and drag the path thumbnail onto the New Path icon at the bottom of the palette. The Duplicate Path dialog box will appear. You can then accept the default name or rename the new path. If you simply drag the thumbnail without holding Option or Alt, Photoshop instantly duplicates the path and names it Path X Copy.

Figure 4.28 The New Path dialog box.

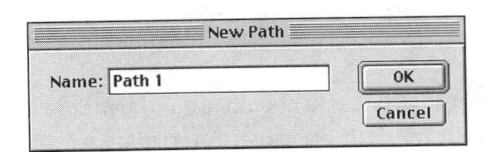

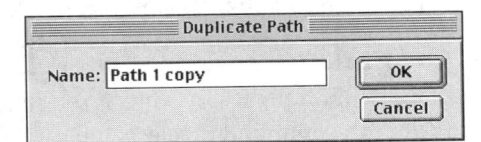

Figure 4.29 The Duplicate Path dialog box.

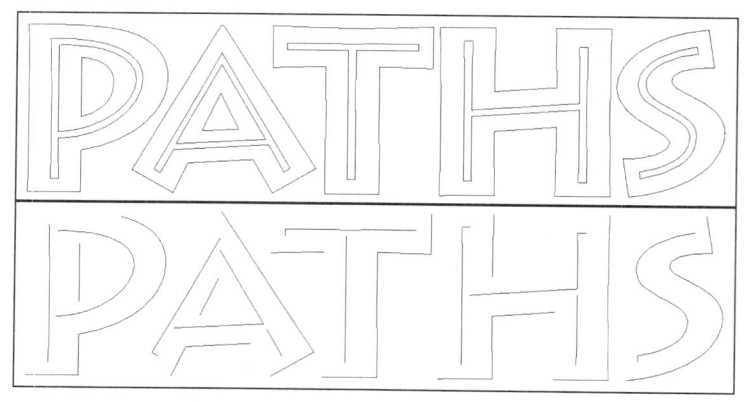

Figure 4.30 The original path (upper) has been duplicated (lower) so that some of the path segments can be deleted. This modified path could be used for a drop-shadow effect.

You can also duplicate paths in several other ways:

- Click to select the entire path. Copy the path. Choose the New Path command. While the new path is selected on the palette, Paste. Copy/Paste can also be used to transfer a path from one document to another. (When pasted into another document, the pasted path will be added to any saved path that has been selected from the thumbnail list. If no named path has been selected, the pasted path will be added as a work path.) Copy/Paste will also allow you to paste your Photoshop path into a document window in Adobe Illustrator, Adobe Dimension, or Adobe Streamline. Paths can also be pasted from each of those programs into Photoshop.
- When two document windows are open, you can select the path and simply drag it from one window to another. If a path is active in the target window, the path will be added to the active path.
- When two documents are open, click on the palette to select the path you wish to duplicate. Drag the thumbnail from the palette onto the target window. The path will be transferred to the other window and its name added to the list of paths.

Delete Path

The Delete Path menu command eliminates a path that has been selected from the thumbnail list. Paths can also be eliminated by dragging them to the trashcan icon at the bottom of the Paths palette. A quick way to delete paths is to select the path, hold down Option or Alt, and click once on the small trashcan icon at the bottom of the palette.

Turn Off Path

When an item on the list of paths is selected, the path is visible in the document window. The Turn Off Path command deselects the list item so that no path is visible. You can also turn off the path by clicking in the empty area below the list of saved paths.

Make Work Path

Any Photoshop selection can be converted to a path. This can be a useful way to save a selection so that you can continue to edit it at some other time. Selections can also be saved as *alpha channels*, but each alpha channel adds a significant amount to the size of the file. (Note: An alpha channel is a special document channel in which selections can be stored. We discuss alpha channels in Chapter 5.) Paths preserve the selection without increasing the file size by more than a few bytes. However, this command is pretty much a blunt instrument—arriving at a satisfactory path requires some experimenting and sometimes a bit of luck. You'll see the reasons for this in the following discussion.

The Make Work Path command results in the dialog box shown in Figure 4.31.

The Tolerance setting governs the precision with which Photoshop will match the selection when it draws the path. Smaller tolerance values result in a more precise path. Too much precision, however, results in a path with far too many nodes. Such a path cannot be easily edited nor can it be used for a clipping path (discussed later in this chapter). There will always be some amount of compromise between the selection and the resulting path: The path can be made to lie diagonally across the tops of pixels, whereas a selection must always follow the boundary of a group of pixels. The trick is to find a Tolerance value that gives a reasonable approximation of the selection while arriving at a path with the smallest number of points.

Figure 4.32 shows some of the possibilities. The selection for making the path is in the upper left corner. A tolerance setting of .5 was used for the path in the upper right corner. As you can see, the number of points is so large that the path would be unusable. The two lower sections of the figure have paths drawn with tolerances of 1 and 2. The path using the setting of 2 is the smoothest and contains the fewest points.

Using a higher tolerance does have a drawback: When Photoshop does not have to match the path with extreme precision, it often generates a path that may depart from the edges of the selection. You may need to manually modify the path—pushing and pulling on the curve segments, adding a node here and there—to make the path fit the shape. Manual intervention is your only choice if you cannot find a tolerance value that exactly suits the situation. Remember that you can always use the Undo command or move back up the History palette as you experiment with different settings.

As a practical matter, a selection generated from a path will always give you precision edges, while a path generated from a selection may turn out to be more trouble than it's worth. As you experiment with this command—and as you become more proficient with the Pen tool—you may find that it is easier to simply draw the path rather than rely on this command to do the work for you.

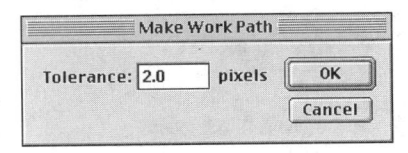

Figure 4.31 The Make Work Path dialog box.

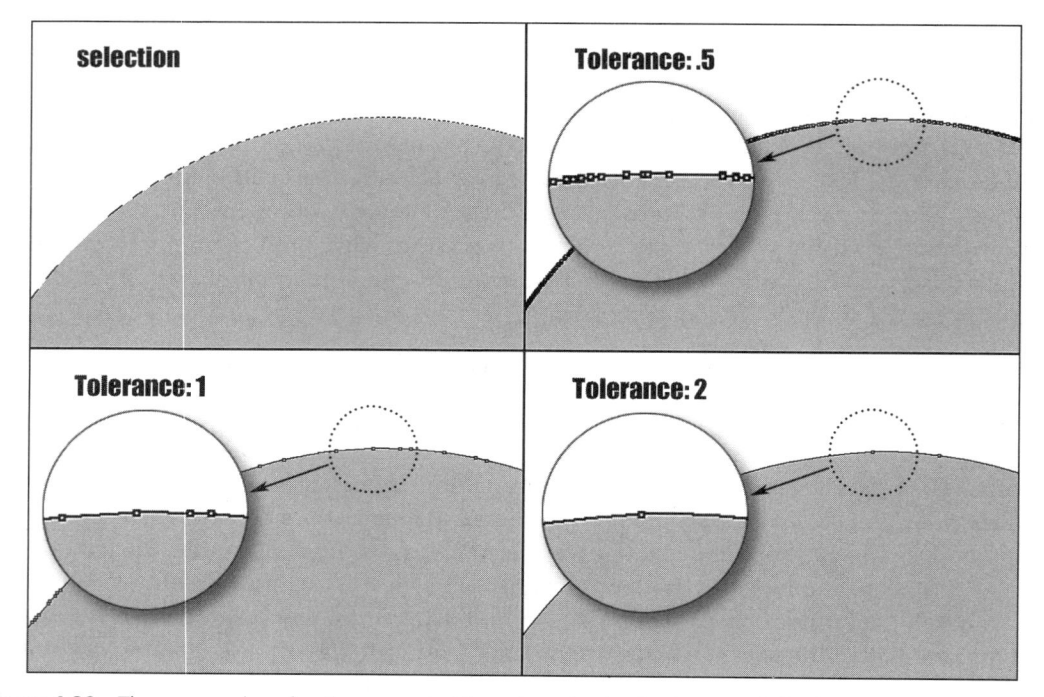

Figure 4.32 Three examples of paths generated from the selection in the upper left. The 0.5-tolerance path has too many points. Either of the others is more usable.

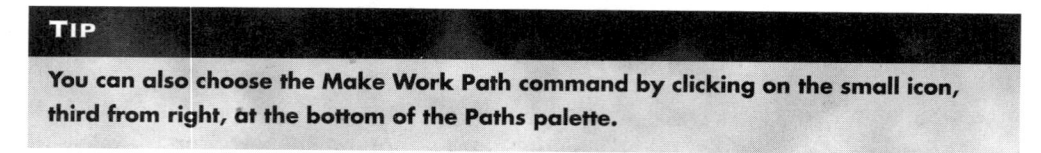

> **TIP**
>
> You can also choose the Make Work Path command by clicking on the small icon, third from right, at the bottom of the Paths palette.

Make Selection

The Make Selection command does exactly what its name suggests—it changes the path into a selection. When you choose the command from the menu, the dialog box shown in Figure 4.33 appears.

Figure 4.33 The Make Selection options for creating a selection from a path.

At the top of this window, you can choose whether the selection is to be feathered and whether the edges should be anti-aliased. The options in the lower portion of the dialog box allow you to make a simple selection based on a single path or to make a selection based on calculations of the areas enclosed by more than one path.

The illustration in Figure 4.34 shows the range of possibilities. At the top, sections *a* and *b*, are two paths. These two would have been saved as two separate items on the Paths palette. (Note that *b* contains two circles, but because both were saved as part of the same list item, they are

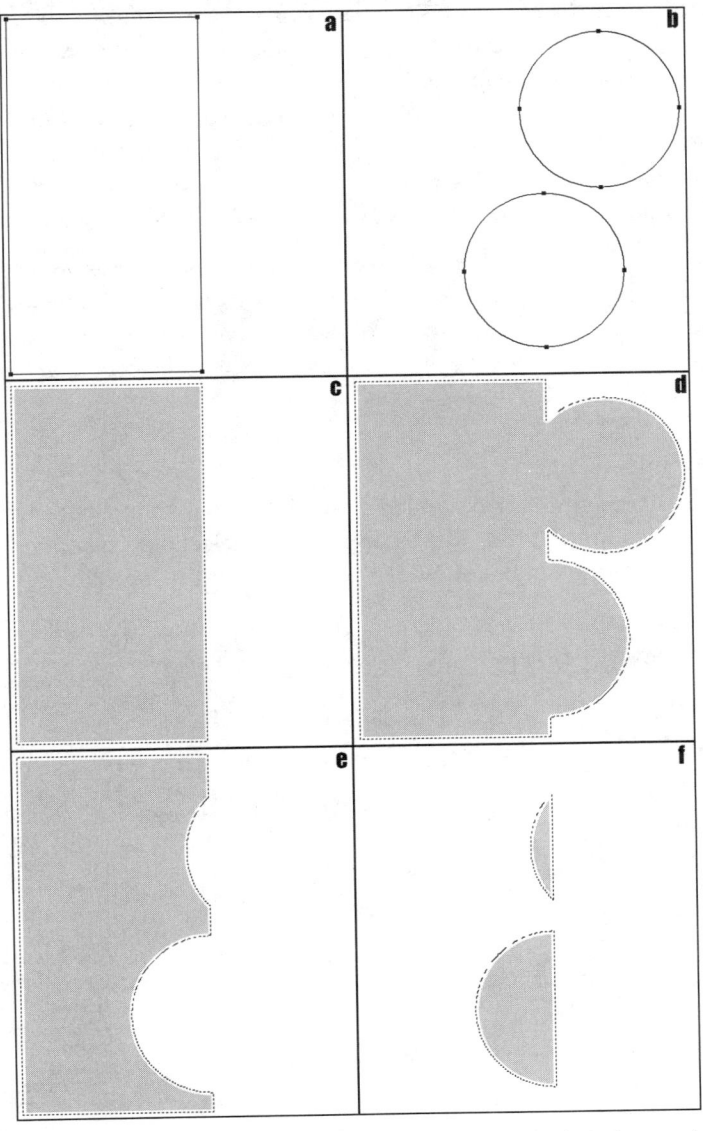

Figure 4.34 Two paths (*a* and *b*) can be made into simple selections (*c*), combined-area selections (*d*), subtracted-area selections (*e*), and common-area-only selections (*f*).

referred to as the *b* path.) With path *a* selected, choose Make Selection, and click on the New Selection option. The gray area in section *c* shows the dimensions of the selection. While this selection is active, click on the *b* path's thumbnail on the palette. This time, choose the Add To Selection option. The second path's selection is added to that of the first, resulting in the selection area shown in section *d*. Sections *e* and *f* are similar. With the first selection active, Subtract From Selection eliminates the area of the second path from the first selection (*e*). Intersect With Selection causes the selection only in the areas where the two paths overlap each other (*f*).

> **TIP**
>
> **To change the path into a selection, you can also click on the small icon, third from left, at the bottom of the Paths palette. A faster alternative is to choose one of the selection tools and press the Enter key. With either of these methods, your selection will be made using the last-chosen Rendering options on the Make Selection dialog box. For example, if you have set a feather value or have turned off anti-aliasing, the selection made by pressing the Enter key will also be feathered or with no anti-aliasing.**
>
> **Note that the menu command and the icon command convert the path to a selection, but leave the path visible. Using the Enter key shortcut, the path becomes deselected, leaving only the selection (the path is turned off). Several of the Stroke Path effects (discussed later in this chapter) are based on a stroked path in place atop an active selection.**

Fill Subpath

The Fill Subpath Command (an expanded dialog box is shown in Figure 4.35) is nearly identical to the Edit|Fill command that can be applied to a selection. The only differences between the two are the rendering options shown at the bottom of the dialog box.

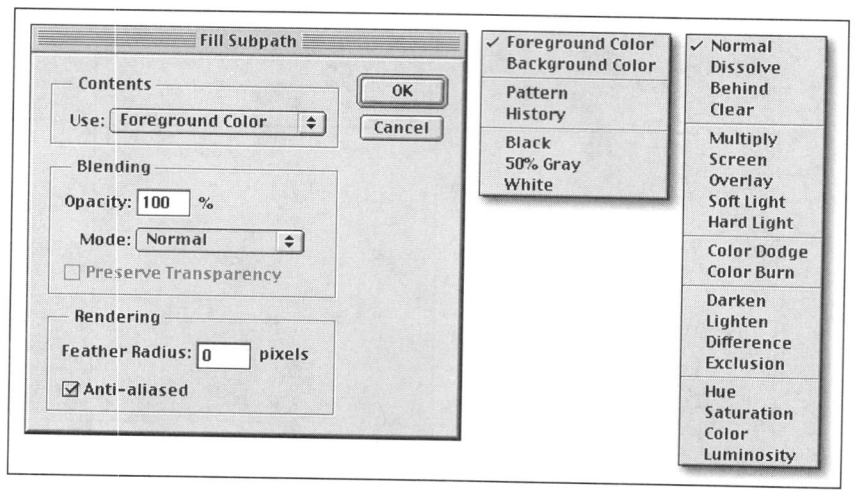

Figure 4.35 Expanded view of the Fill Subpath dialog box.

> **TIP**
>
> The path can also be filled by clicking on the small icon at the farthest right at the bottom of the Paths palette. The dialog box will not appear, but the fill will be executed using the last-selected options of the Fill Subpath window. For example, if you set your fill to 50% Opacity and Multiply mode, clicking on the icon fills in the same way until the options in the window are changed.

Stroke Subpath

In some ways, the Stroke Subpath command is the most interesting and useful of all the selections in the Paths palette menu. *Stroke*, as the term is applied to a path in a drawing program, means that width is added in equal amounts to each side of the path. (A path has no intrinsic width.) In the drawing program, stroke is rather in the nature of adding a descriptive property to the path—call it, if you will, an adjective. In Photoshop, stroke is very much a verb, because the path is acted on by other tools that use it as a guide for laying down color, toning, focus, or cloning. The tools that can be used to stroke a path are shown in the expanded view of the Stroke Subpath dialog box in Figure 4.36.

The effects obtained by the Stroke Subpath command vary with the tool chosen for the stroke and with the brush tip selected for the tool. The variety of effects with just the paint tools, for example, is nearly limitless: Each of the paint tools can lay down the stroke in varying widths, with varying opacity, and with any of the available Blend modes. Several of the special effects shown later in this chapter depend on the Stroke Subpath command. A more thorough discussion of the Stroke Subpath will accompany the examples.

> **TIP**
>
> You can apply the Stroke Subpath command to a path by clicking on the small icon, second from left, at the bottom of the Paths palette. The path will be stroked by the last-used tool in the Stroke Subpath dialog box with the brush size last used for that tool. Alternately, you can choose one of the tools shown in Figure 4.36, select the brush you wish to use and the options for the tool, and then press the Enter key. This is usually a more convenient way to stroke the path than using the palette menu.

As previously noted, the path and the selection that can be generated from the path can be visible at the same time. This allows the stroke to be applied to only one side of the path instead of both sides, as is the usual case. By selecting the inverse, the same path can be stroked on two sides with two different tools.

Clipping Path

A Clipping Path is a special kind of path that can be saved with an exported file to act as a mask. When the exported file—usually in Photoshop EPS or TIFF format—is imported into

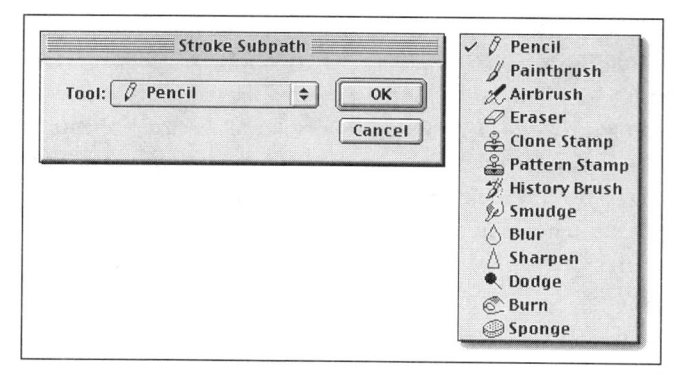

Figure 4.36 Expanded view of the Stroke Subpath dialog box.

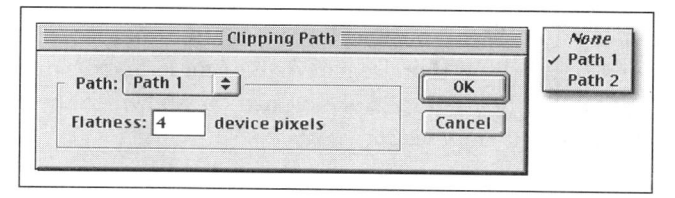

Figure 4.37 The Paths palette's Clipping Path dialog box.

another program, the picture image is only visible within the boundaries of the mask. We discuss clipping paths extensively in Chapter 10—consult that chapter for a complete discussion of Flatness settings, and for many tips that will contribute to your success when using clipping paths. The dialog box for designating a Clipping Path is shown in Figure 4.37.

Manipulating Paths In Photoshop

Although the Pen and Path Edit tools provide you with the means to shape and reshape paths, there are other things you might wish to do. For example, you might want to distort a large, complex path, or to rotate it some amount. Both of these are manipulations that cannot be accomplished with the path tools.

Photoshop 5 provides you with a variety of macro-manipulation tools called Transformation commands, which permit a path to be scaled, rotated, distorted, and flipped. These commands are located under the Edit menu, as shown in Figure 4.38.

The first item on the menu, the Free Transform command, is probably the most useful of this set. With it you can accomplish nearly everything the pop-out menu has to offer. The exception is the Transform|Numeric Transform command (see Figure 4.39), which accomplishes the same kinds of transformations, but does so by letting you enter precise values in its data fields.

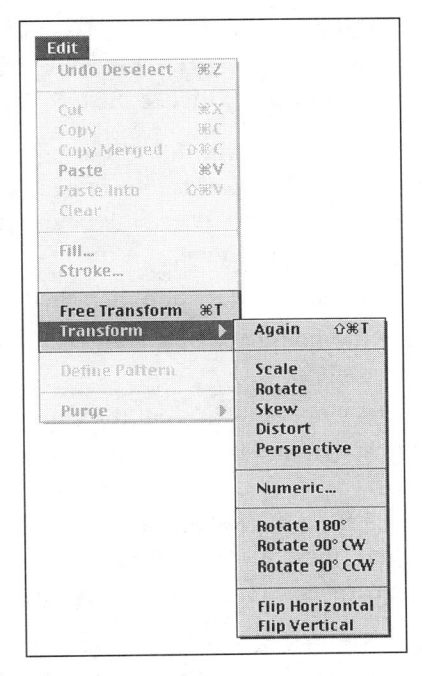

Figure 4.38 Photoshop's path Transformation commands menu.

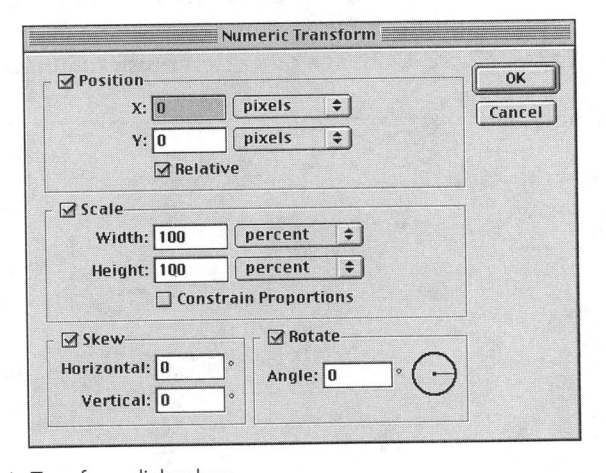

Figure 4.39 The Numeric Transform dialog box.

Transform Commands And The Variability Of Node Selections

We discuss using the Transformation commands on layers in Chapter 6. The effect of the commands on layers is identical to the effect of the commands on paths. Our discussion in this section of the paths chapter is concerned with the special variables presented by the way paths are selected as the transformation commands are applied.

To show what we mean by variability of selection, make a path and then click on it with the Direct Selection tool so that the path is selected but all of the nodes are semi-active. Press Command+T (Mac) or Ctrl+T (Windows) to invoke the Free Transform command.

Figure 4.40 shows a path, selected and with all of the nodes semi-active, surrounded by a bounding rectangle with eight boundary points (one at each corner, one at the center of each side) and one reference point (in the center). When this bounding rectangle is in place, you can make these kinds of changes to the path shape:

1. Keep your cursor outside of the boundary and then click and drag to rotate the path.
2. Move your cursor inside the boundary and then click and drag to move the path around in the document window.
3. Click and drag any of the live points around the edges of the rectangle to change the shape of the rectangle. (Hold down the Shift key to constrain the shape to the same proportions.)
4. Hold down Command or Ctrl and drag any of the rectangle's corner points to distort the shape of the path (see Figure 4.41). Note that a corner can be moved independently of the other three corners.

Figure 4.42 shows the same path, selected and with all of the nodes active, surrounded by a bounding rectangle. The appearance is identical to the bounding rectangle when all of the nodes are semi-active. When you use the Free Transform command with all of the nodes active, some limitations are placed on the kinds of transformations you can accomplish. You can Scale, Rotate and Flip (see Figure 4.43). The other two transformations, Skew and Perspective,

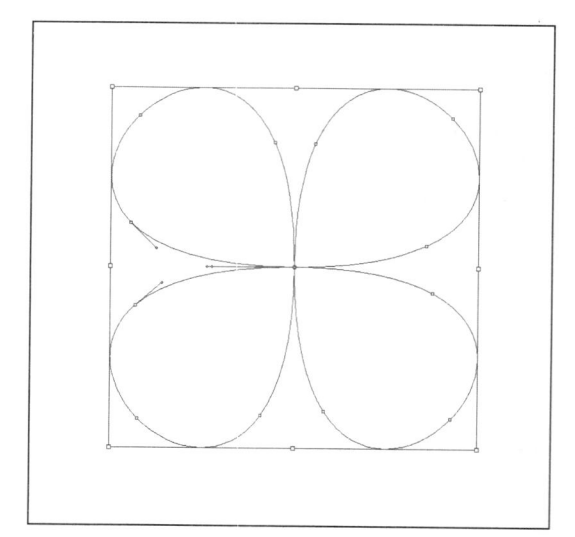

Figure 4.40 With the path selected, but with none of the nodes active, the Free Transform command places this bounding rectangle around the path.

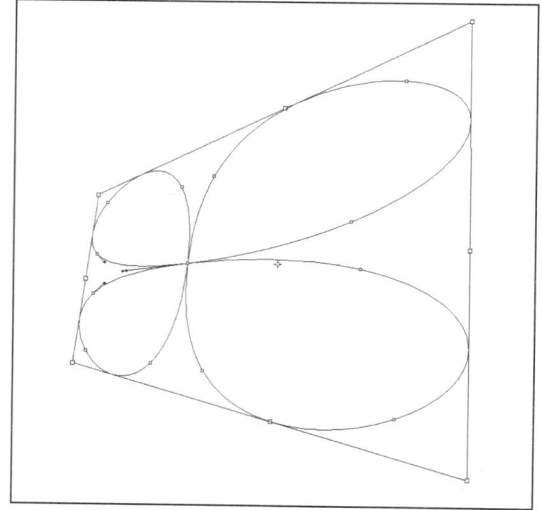

Figure 4.41 With Command or Ctrl held down, drag at the corners of the rectangle to distort the path.

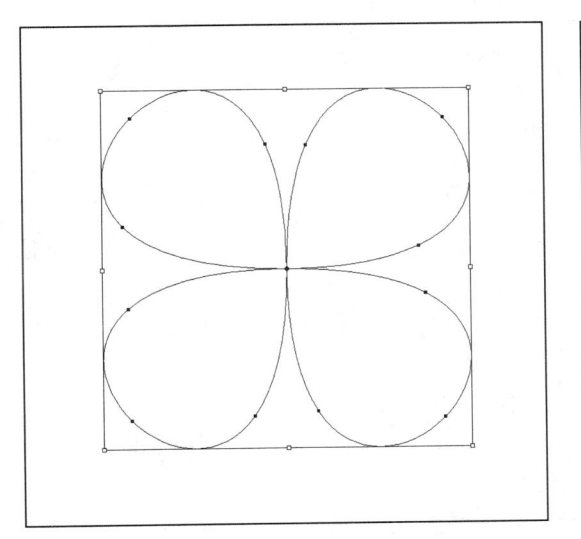

Figure 4.42 The bounding rectangle when all nodes are active looks the same as when all nodes are semi-active.

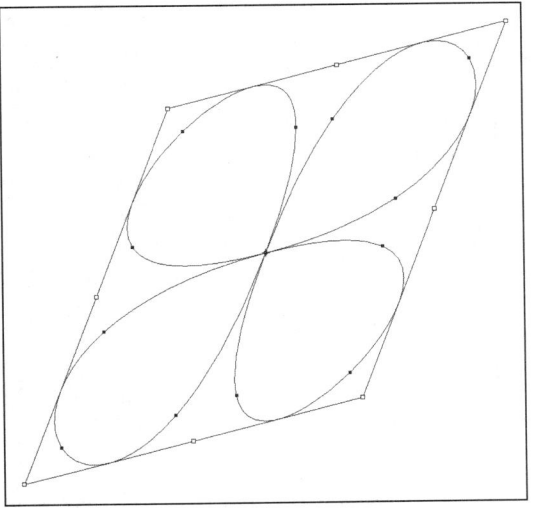

Figure 4.43 When all of the nodes are active, you can perform all of the usual transformations except those that require changing the length of one of the sides of the bounding rectangle—Skew and Perspective.

involve changing the length of one of the sides of the bounding rectangle. They do not operate when you transform a path with all nodes active.

Things get a little tricky when you try to transform a path with some of the nodes active and others semi-active. Figures 4.44, 4.45, and 4.46 demonstrate the nature of the problem. In each

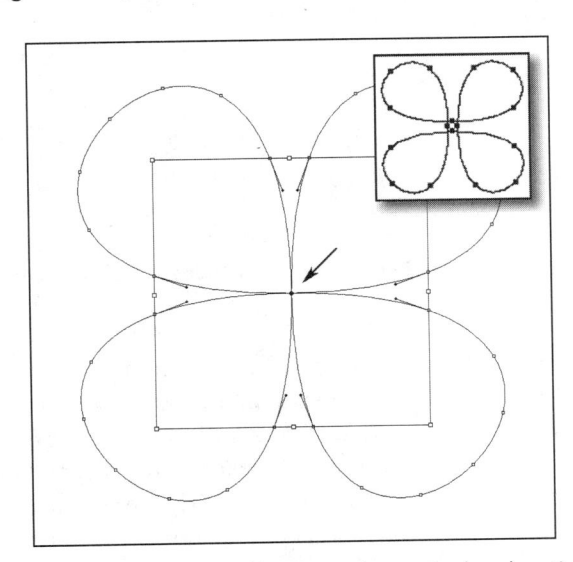

Figure 4.44 The Transformation command's bounding rectangle surrounds only active nodes and the path segments that extend from them.

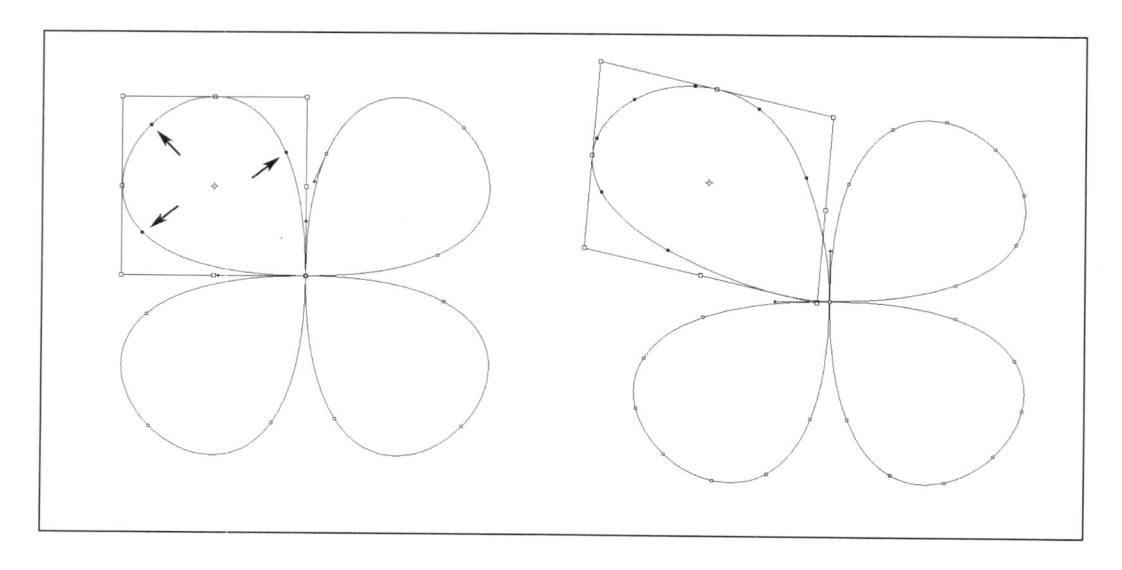

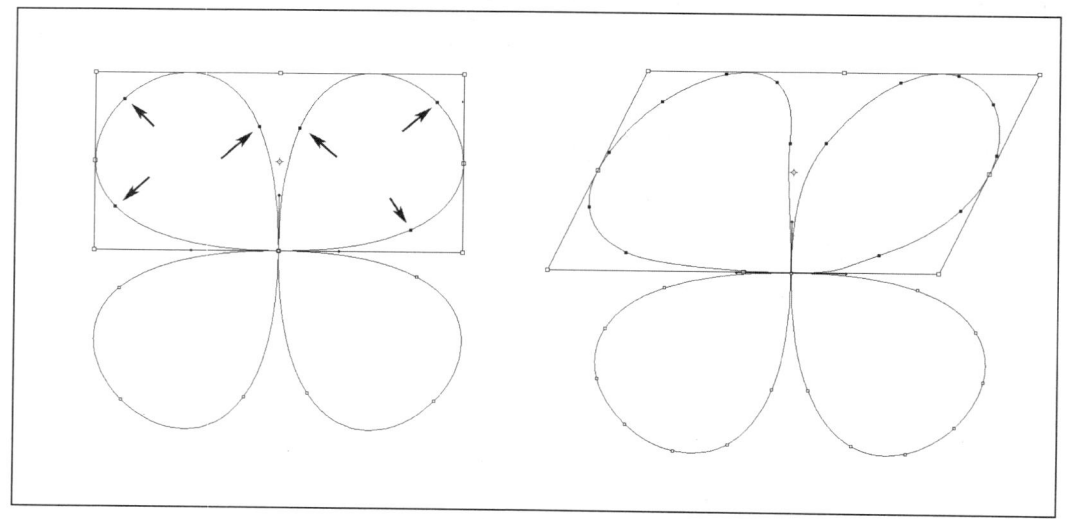

Figures 4.45 and 4.46 Transforming paths with some of the nodes active and others semi-active produces distortions only on the affected path segments.

of the figures, the active nodes are those to which the small arrows point. In each case, the Transform command gives a bounding rectangle that surrounds the active nodes only. The part of the path not surrounded by the rectangle will still be somewhat distorted because it is attached to the portion that will be transformed, but the transformation is applied only to the segments of the path that run into the active nodes. (The bounding rectangle in Figure 4.44 is a little confusing: The arrow actually points to four nodes that sit precisely atop each other. They have been pulled apart slightly in the small inset.)

Transform Again

After you perform a transformation on a path, you can apply the Edit|Transform|Transform Again command to the path. This command performs the same operation, but relative to the altered path and its new position. For example, you could rotate the path 10°. When you Transform Again, your path rotates another 10° in the same direction.

One interesting consequence of Transform Again (hold down Command+Shift+T on the Mac or Ctrl+Shift+T in Windows) is the capability to duplicate along with the execution of the command. This feature is not available from the Edit submenu and needs to be performed as a keyboard operation. To make the duplication, add the Option (Mac) or Alt (Windows) keys to the keyboard command for Transform Again. Figure 4.47 shows a path that has been rotated 12°. The Transform with duplication has then been applied three times. Carried out 27 more times, the command produces the complex set of shapes shown in Figure 4.48.

Manipulating Paths Using Illustrator

Although Photoshop's Pen/Path Edit tools and Transformation commands are adequate for most purposes, they lack some features that users of draw programs—such as Adobe Illustrator—have come to expect as a normal part of the feature set. For example, you cannot delete a single path segment unless you first place a new node within that segment, select the new node, and delete it. You cannot, within Photoshop, cut a path so that it is no longer a closed shape. As trivial as these two examples might seem, they indicate that Photoshop is not really a draw program and that using Illustrator instead of Photoshop for many path drawing and editing tasks is much more comfortable than working with Photoshop's tools. Eventually the Illustrator paths can be returned to Photoshop to be acted on in ways that Illustrator cannot

Figure 4.47 Using the Transform Again command with duplication produced these three paths, based on an initial simple rotation of 12°.

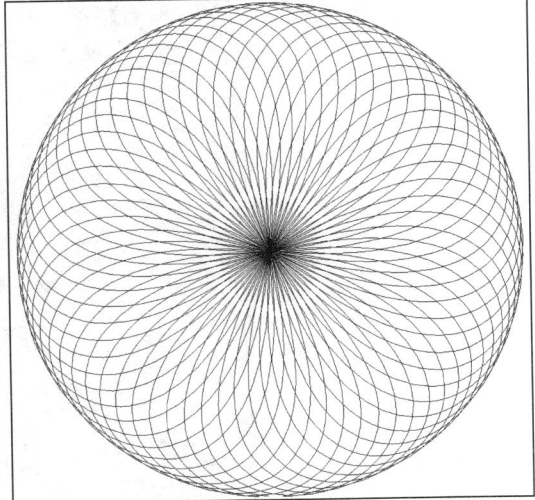

Figure 4.48 When the operation shown in Figure 4.47 has been carried out 27 more times, the rotated paths produce this complex shape.

manage. The method has several aspects, any of which may serve you. You might wish to try using Illustrator and Photoshop together in some of the ways we will describe. You may end up thinking—along with the authors—that the two programs work so easily with each other that they begin to seem as though they are simply two parts of one large graphics environment.

Moving Paths From Photoshop To Illustrator And Back Again

One easy way to move a path from Photoshop to Illustrator is to use Photoshop's Path Export utility. Choose File|Export||Paths To Illustrator.

1. To show you how this entire procedure works, we'll use a small file in which a path has been drawn and saved as path 1 as an example. The path is shown in Figure 4.49. Notice that the path is not precisely centered in the window. Part of this procedure will show you how to make sure that the paths can be accurately aligned without zooming in to 1,600% and trying to do the job by eye.

2. Select the Export option. The dialog box that appears is shown in Figure 4.50. The options for export are selected from the pop-up menu at the bottom of the window. The choices are to export all of the paths, any saved paths (if the document contains saved paths and a work path, the work path will appear as an item on the menu), or the document boundary. We will explain the last option later in this discussion.

3. For this example, we'll assume that we wish to export the existing path. Photoshop helpfully assigns the name of the Photoshop document with the *ai* (for Adobe Illustrator) extension. If this title is acceptable, all you need to do is click on the Save button. Photoshop saves the paths as an Illustrator file. After the file has been saved, leave the Photoshop document open, and switch to Illustrator.

Figure 4.49 The Photoshop file contains a saved path shown here as an outline of the flower.

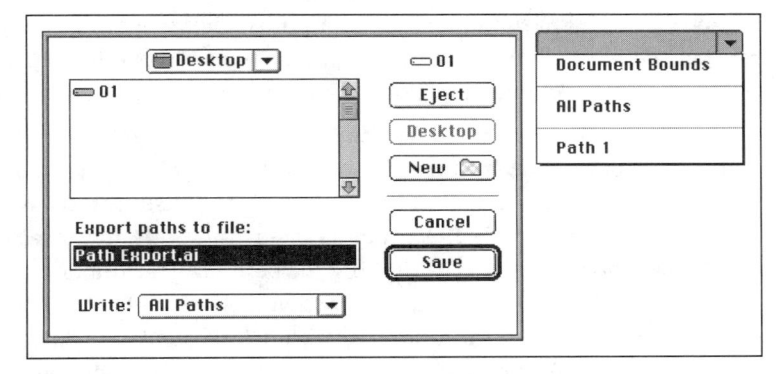

Figure 4.50 The File|Export|Paths To Illustrator dialog box with a view of the pop-up menu at the bottom of the window.

4. From Illustrator's File menu, choose the Open command. Locate the Photoshop export file and click on Open. A representation of the file that opens is shown in Figure 4.51. (Note: When you first see the file in Illustrator, you may be concerned that you cannot see the paths. The paths have no assigned fill or stroke and, if they are not selected, are not visible in Preview mode. To see the paths, select Artwork from Illustrator's View menu.) The path becomes visible, as well as the set of crop marks. These crop marks are Photoshop's method of exporting the document's boundaries: If you had chosen only to export the boundaries, your file would contain only these crop marks.

5. To make the crop marks more intelligible, go to Illustrator's Object menu and select Cropmarks|Release. The marks vanish and are replaced with a selected rectangle. This rectangle is the exact size of the original Photoshop document, and the paths are positioned in it precisely the way they were positioned in Photoshop. To avoid moving

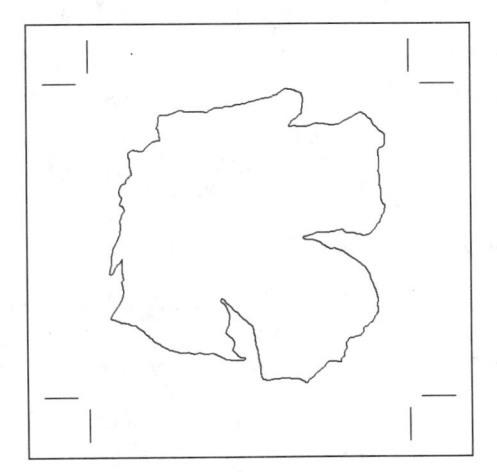

Figure 4.51 When the Photoshop path-export file is opened in Illustrator, you can see the paths and the cropmarks that indicate the position of the paths within the original Photoshop document.

this rectangle while you manipulate the other paths, choose Arrange|Lock. The rectangle becomes deselected, and you cannot inadvertently move it until you choose Arrange|Unlock. The locked rectangle and the paths are shown in Figure 4.52.

6. Perform the manipulations on the paths. In Figure 4.53, two paths have been drawn inside and outside of the flower shape. Doing this kind of path generation would be virtually impossible in Photoshop, but it's very simple in Illustrator (see the following sidebar "Making Parallel Paths In Illustrator"). These three paths now need to be taken back to the Photoshop document. First, unlock the boundary rectangle. Next, select all of the paths *and* the bounding rectangle. Copy. Switch back to the Photoshop file and Paste. A small window appears asking if you want to Paste As Pixels or to Paste As Paths. Choose the latter. Your paths will appear in the Photoshop window, as shown in Figure 4.54.

7. You will have difficulty seeing the bounding rectangle because it is at the edge of the document window. Because Photoshop always attempts to center a pasted path, including this rectangle ensures that your paths are perfectly positioned. Be sure to select the rectangle path at the edge of the window and delete it. You no longer need it and it will cause trouble later if you forget that it's there.

MAKING PARALLEL PATHS IN ILLUSTRATOR

Making a set of paths that are parallel to each other (see Figure 4.54) is not impossible in Photoshop, but it is a laborious and imperfect process. Because these paths can be useful, here is an easy method for generating them with Illustrator:

1. Select the path you want to make larger and smaller copies of, similar to those shown in Figure 4.53. Copy it. Now assign a stroke—the color is unimportant—to the path. Make the stroke weight the same as the distance you wish to have between the two new paths. For example, you might use a stroke weight of 25 points, which will give you 25 points between the two paths you will be generating.

2. From the Illustrator Filter menu, select Objects|Outline Path.

3. Your original path will disappear. The two new paths will look approximately correct, except that there may be many small loops inside the path boundaries. To eliminate most of these loops, choose Object|Pathfinder|Unite.

4. When the Unite filter has executed, choose Arrange|Ungroup. Click on each of the outer paths to select them. As they are selected, choose Arrange|Hide. When both paths have disappeared, Select All, and press Delete. This deletes all the little odds and ends left behind by the Unite filter. From the Arrange menu, select Show All. Your paths will reappear. Check them to see if they need minor editing to rid them of any other Unite filter artifacts. Finally, from the Edit menu, choose Paste In Front. Your original path—copied before you assigned a weight to it—is pasted into its previous position. It will appear exactly between the two paths you generated with the Illustrator filters.

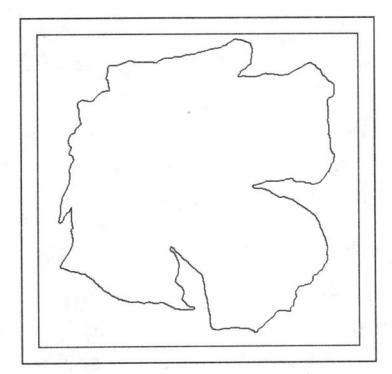

Figure 4.52 When the crop marks are released, you can see a rectangle that is the same size as the original Photoshop document.

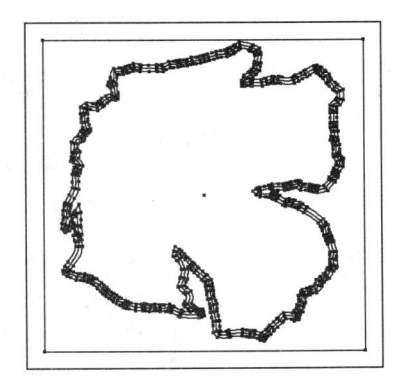

Figure 4.53 Work with the paths in Illustrator. When you're finished, unlock the bounding rectangle, and Select All. Copy, then switch back to Photoshop.

Figure 4.54 Paste the Illustrator paths into the Photoshop dialog box. They will be perfectly positioned because of the bounding rectangle.

Making Photoshop Paths In Illustrator

Drawing Photoshop paths directly in Illustrator may sound peculiar, but it does solve the problem of what to do when you want to perform more sophisticated manipulations of paths than Photoshop allows. For example, the Pen tool in both programs is exactly the same: Illustrator's implementation of the Pen has the same set of modifier keys as Photoshop's. Illustrator, however, has an extra path tool—the Scissors tool—that allows you to cut a path, an operation that is nearly impossible in Photoshop. Besides this extra path tool, you can also make use of many of Illustrator's transformation tools as well as its powerful filters. We will show you other reasons for working in Illustrator in following sections of this chapter.

The procedure for setting up the two programs to work together may look, at first glance, somewhat elaborate. However, as soon as you become accustomed to the wonderful things you can do with paths while you are in Illustrator, you'll probably decide that the setup is worth the effort. Besides, it's not that tricky. If you make extensive use of paths—and we think you will when you see some of the wonderful effects that paths can help you produce—you will probably find that you have an Illustrator file that is the twin of most of your Photoshop files.

Use this set of instructions as a guide for setting up your own Illustrator documents:

1. Open your Photoshop document. Choose File|Export|Paths To Illustrator. If you have paths that you would like to export, select them from the pop-up menu at the bottom of the dialog box. If the file contains no paths, export the Document Bounds. Now save your Photoshop file in Photoshop EPS format in the same place you saved the path-export file. For your file's Preview, choose Macintosh JPEG if it's available. Otherwise, choose TIFF/8-bits. Leave everything else in the Save preference at the default settings.

2. Switch to Illustrator, and open the path-export file from Photoshop. The Photoshop document's boundary will be delineated by the crop marks as described previously. If you exported only the boundary, your file will contain only these marks. Once the file is open, position the Illustrator's Layers and Align palettes so that you can see them easily (see Figure 4.55).

3. From the Objects menu, choose Cropmarks|Release. The trim marks are converted to a bounding rectangle, as shown in Figure 4.56. Double-click on Layer 1 on the Layers palette. In the text entry box at the top of the resulting window, change the layer's name to "Boundary".

4. From the File menu, choose Place. Locate the Photoshop EPS file and click on Open. The image appears as a selected rectangular-shaped picture object (see Figure 4.57).

5. From the Layer palette's sidebar menu, choose New Layer. In the dialog box that opens (see Figure 4.58), name the layer "Photo". Click on the checkbox labeled Dim Placed EPS. Click on OK. The new layer appears above the boundary layer on the palette.

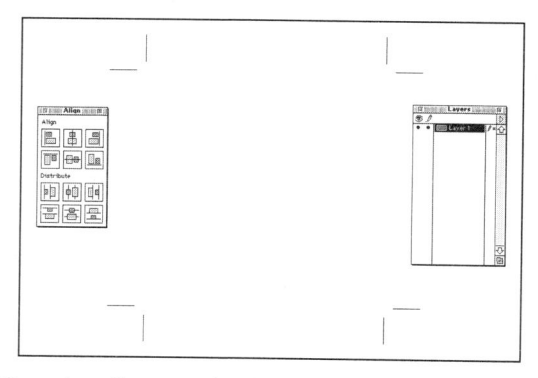

Figure 4.55 The exported Photoshop file opened in Illustrator. The Photoshop document's boundary cropmarks comprise the entire file.

PATHS AND THE PEN TOOL **261**

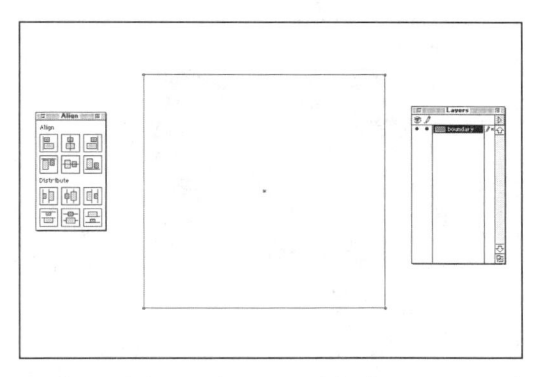

Figure 4.56 Release the cropmarks, and change the name of the layer to "Boundary".

Figure 4.57 Use the Place command to import the Photoshop EPS file.

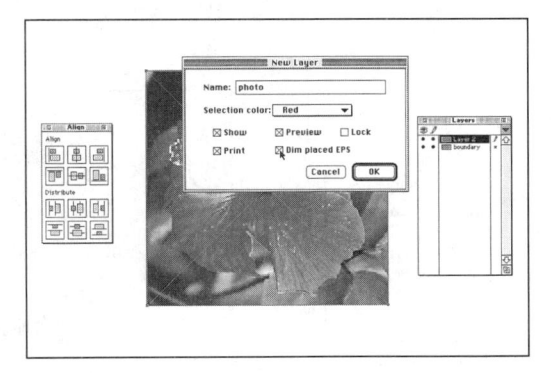

Figure 4.58 Create a new layer called Photo. Click on the Dim Placed EPS checkbox.

6. With the placed photo still selected, you will see a small, colored square in the right column of the Layers palette. The square is on the same line as the Boundary layer. Click and drag this square up to the Photo layer. This moves the photo onto the Photo layer. You can see the photo become lighter as Illustrator dims it (see Figure 4.59). Now click on the Photo layer and drag it down so that it is beneath the Boundary layer. Select All.

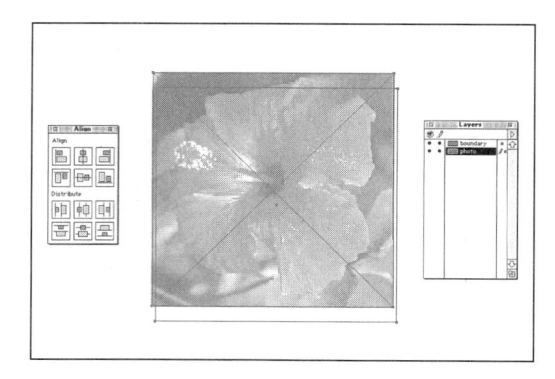

Figure 4.59 Move the photo onto its own layer (which dims it). Switch the stacking order of the layers.

7. With both objects selected, click on the center icons on the top two rows of the Align palette. This aligns the two more accurately than you could do manually (see Figure 4.60). In the left column of the Layers palette, you see two small rectangles for each layer. The symbol on the right hides the layer, and the other locks it. Click on the lock rectangle of each layer. When the rectangles disappear, the layers are locked. You cannot move or alter either of the layers until you click in the same place to make the rectangles visible.

8. Create a new layer named Paths To Photoshop. This layer should be uppermost on the Layers palette. Construct your paths on this layer. You can, if you want, make other layers hold to different kinds of paths for different purposes (see Figure 4.61).

9. When you have drawn your paths, unlock the Boundary layer, and Select All. Copy. Switch to Photoshop and Paste. When the Paste dialog box in Photoshop appears, choose Paste As Paths.

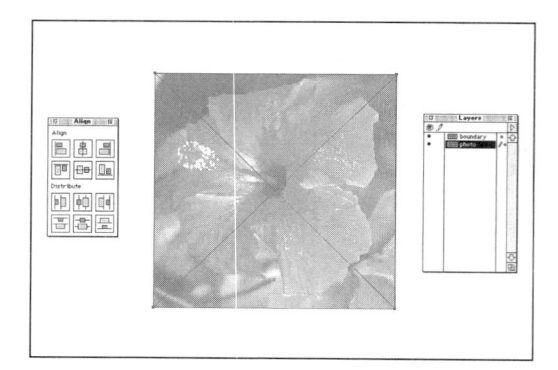

Figure 4.60 Use the Align palette to accurately line up the bounding rectangle and the photo. Lock both layers.

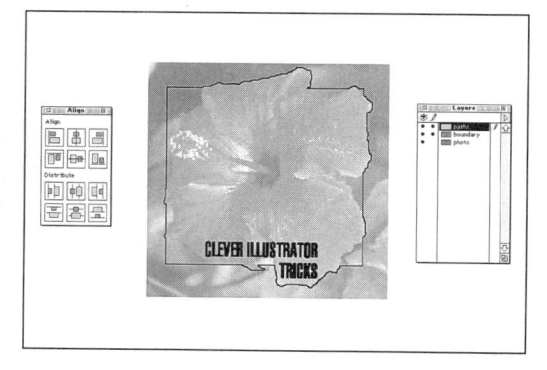

Figure 4.61 Create a new layer and draw your paths on this layer.

Special Effects Using Strokes On Paths

Most of the spectacular effects that you can produce with paths are accomplished by means of the Stroke command. As you have seen, other operations involve paths, but only the Stroke command allows you to control the tools that paint—or that use paintbrushes to apply their effects—in a very precise way. You may, for example, want the paintbrush to move so that it produces an intricate, curved figure. However, the computer's mouse is not capable of such fine manipulation. Even the stylus of a pressure-sensitive pad doesn't let you easily move the brush in a precise way. With the Pen tool, you can take your time, draw the most intricately curved path you can imagine, select a brush, and instantly paint your curve without a flaw.

The effects that you'll see in the remainder of this chapter are not an exhaustive list of what can be done. There is, however, sufficient variety that you will probably think of many variations using the techniques involved. Above all, the processes you'll see are easy and fast. The paths are simple—most of them are drawn in Illustrator and then transferred to Photoshop—and applying the strokes is simply a matter of selecting the brush. After you've moved the paths into Photoshop, nearly every example you'll see can be done in less than 5 minutes, sometimes in less than 30 seconds! (One of the examples, the glass lettering, is slightly more time-consuming, but most of the work is involved with setting up the file so that you can alter the area inside the paths.)

The CD-ROM that comes with this book contains two files, DAVID01.PSD and DAVID02.PSD, that are used for the first eight examples. If you want, you can open the first of these and try out the path effects as they are discussed. You are not required to draw any paths, because all of the paths you will need are already part of the file. You simply need to click on the Paths palette to select the needed set, and then apply the effects as directed.

The file DAVID01.PSD was prepared in Illustrator with the individual path components saved on separate layers in the same way we described previously. The following set of instructions give an overview of the file's preparation:

1. The first path to be drawn was a trace of the contours of the statue. (Actually, your first path would be the photo boundary exported from Photoshop and already aligned with the image. You would draw the contours after making a new layer on the Layers palette.) These lines are shown in Figure 4.62. (Note that the Photoshop EPS file of the statue has been placed on an Illustrator layer and dimmed to make it easier to see the paths as they are drawn.)

2. After the contours have been drawn, save the layer as Statue Contours, and then duplicate it. Rename the duplicate layer Statue Outline. Hold Option (Mac) or Alt (Windows), and click with the Pen tool on the node at the end of the path that ends just above the lower left corner. Release Option or Alt. Hold the Shift key and click again exactly on the lower left corner of the image. Hold Shift+Option or Shift+Alt and click on the node at the end of the path that ends just to the right of the lower left corner. This procedure closes the path that surrounds the arm. Follow the same procedure to enclose the rest of the statue: Option+click or Alt+click when starting or ending

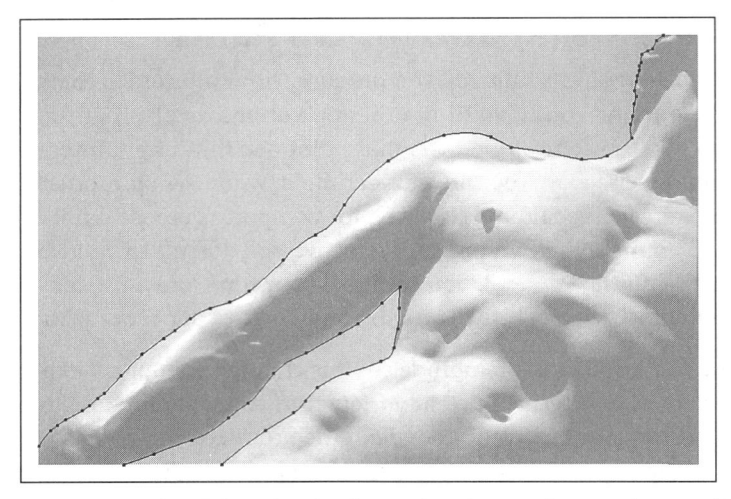

Figure 4.62 The Photoshop EPS file of the statue has been placed on an Illustrator layer and dimmed to make it easier to draw the figure's contours.

on a pre-existing node, then hold down the Shift key to make the lines perfectly horizontal or vertical. To complete this path (shown in Figure 4.63), you simply click with the Pen tool—using one or two of the modifier keys—seven times.

> **TIP**
>
> In Illustrator, duplicating layers is slightly more involved than the same operation in Photoshop. First, click on the eye icons to hide all but the layer to be duplicated. Click on the remaining visible layer to select it. Select All, Copy. Choose New Layer from the sidebar menu. Name the layer. When the layer is in place on the palette, make sure that it is selected and then choose Edit|Paste In Front. All of the copied paths are pasted into the same position they had in the layer from which they were copied.

3. Duplicate the first layer (Statue Contours) and rename the new layer Background Outline. Follow the same procedure to completely enclose the two parts of the image that form the background of the statue (see Figure 4.64).

4. Duplicate the first layer and rename the new duplicate Contours Offset. Select the Direct Select cursor (the white arrow-shaped cursor). Hold Option or Alt and click to select the upper contour line. Continue to hold Option or Alt and drag the line up and to the left. This operation copies the path and moves it to a new position. Release the mouse button and the modifier keys. Press Command+D (Mac) or Ctrl+D (Windows) to repeat the transformation. A new path appears above and to the left of the second. Continue typing the Repeat command until the offsets are off the image. Select the Scissors tool. Click on each path at the place where it crosses the edge of the photo.

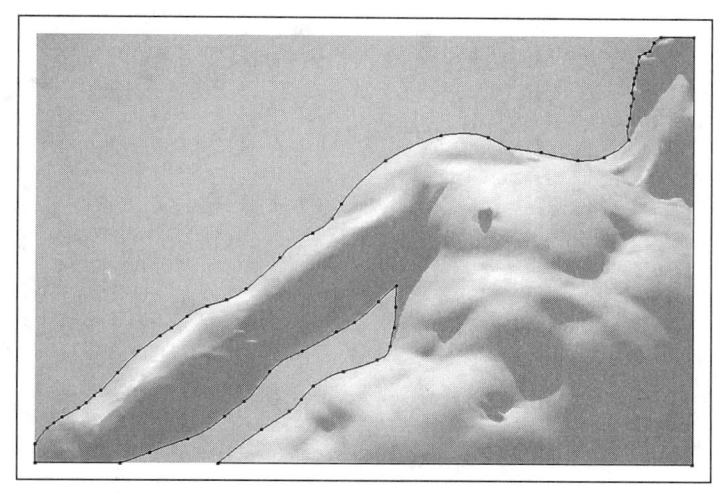

Figure 4.63 Connect the contour paths to completely enclose the statue.

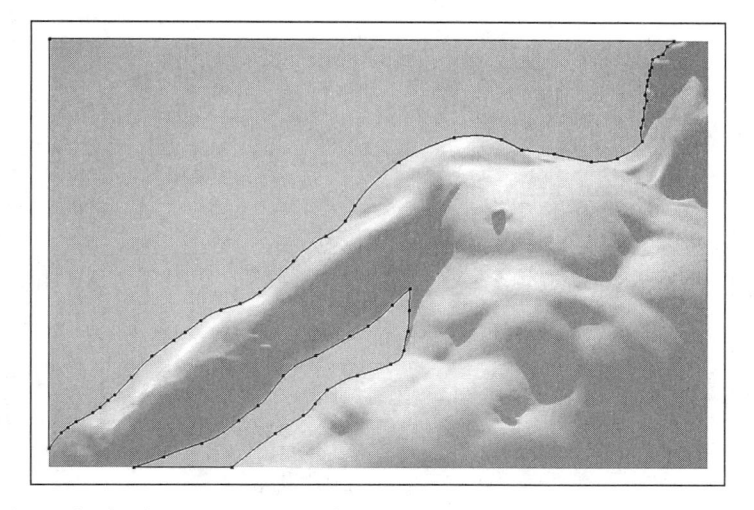

Figure 4.64 Duplicate the first layer, rename it, and connect the endpoints of the contours to enclose the two background areas.

Select the parts of the path outside the image and press Delete. Your paths will look approximately the same as those shown in Figure 4.65.

5. Duplicate the original layer and rename the new duplicate Lettering. Option+click or Alt+click the upper contour path to select it. Select Illustrator's Path Text tool and click about halfway along the length of the line. Enter your text. Select All. Change the font to a style you prefer, and increase the size so that it is as large as you want. Then increase the baseline shift to move the text up and away from the arm, and adjust the tracking if any of the letters appear too close together or too far apart. Choose the

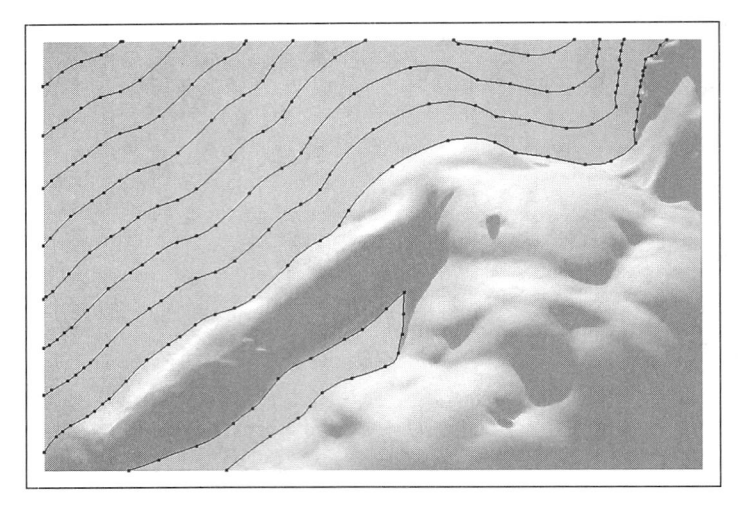

Figure 4.65 Move and copy the upper contour. Repeat the transformation until copies of the path move through the background area. Trim the parts of the path that extend past the edge of the photo.

Figure 4.66 Use Illustrator's Path Text tool to place lettering along the arm's upper contour. After adjusting the size and the baseline shift, convert the type to outlines.

Select cursor. From the Type menu, select Create Outlines. Your letters are changed from editable type to path outlines (see Figure 4.66).

6. Duplicate the layer containing the complete outlines of the statue. Rename this new path Background Horizontal lines. Switch to the layer containing the rectangular boundary. With the Direct Select cursor, click on the top line of the rectangle and Copy. Switch back to the new layer and choose Edit|Paste In Front. The single horizontal line is pasted into the same position it had in the bounding rectangle. Option+click or Alt+click and

drag the line downward to move and clone it. As you drag, add the Shift key so that the duplicate you are making is located exactly under the first. Repeat the transformation (Command+D or Ctrl+D) until your entire photo is filled with horizontal lines. Option+click or Alt+click the outline of the statue and choose Arrange|Bring To Front. With this path selected, choose Object|Apply Knife. Illustrator trims away all parts of the horizontal lines that cross the statue using the statue's outline as a guide for the Knife tool (see Figure 4.67).

7. Switch to the bounding rectangle layer. Select the rectangle and copy it. Lock and hide all layers. Make a new layer titled Waving Lines. Paste In Front to put a copy of the rectangle in the new layer. Fill the rectangle with the Illustrator pattern Waves-transparent. Double-click on Illustrator's Scale tool. A Scale dialog box appears. In the top data entry field, enter "300%". At the bottom of the window, uncheck the Objects checkbox (which automatically checks the Pattern checkbox). Click on OK.

    From the Objects menu, choose Expand. While the expanded object is still selected, choose Arrange|Ungroup twice. Change to Artwork mode (View menu). Carefully select the bounding rectangle and Lock it (Arrange menu). Now select each of the rectangular bounding boxes that define the pattern and delete them. Switch back to Preview mode (View menu). When you Select All, your window looks approximately the same as the image in Figure 4.68.

8. The pattern shown filling the window in Figure 4.69 was done in the same way as the previous figure was, except that this pattern is not a part of your default Illustrator patterns. The pattern Random V (in Windows, randomv) is a file from your Photoshop Patterns folder. It is an Illustrator document you can use for many purposes. Simply locate the file and open it in Illustrator. When the file is open, switch to Artwork View.

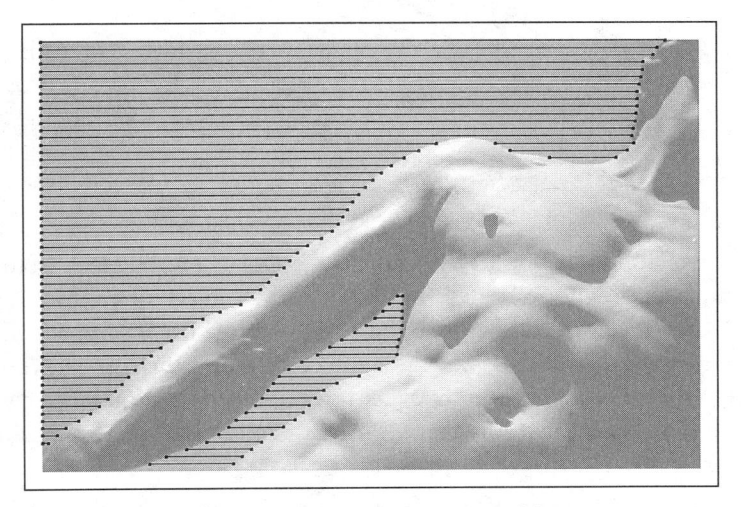

Figure 4.67 Fill the image with horizontal lines. Then use the outline of the statue to trim away any lines that cross the statue. The lines that remain are in the background only.

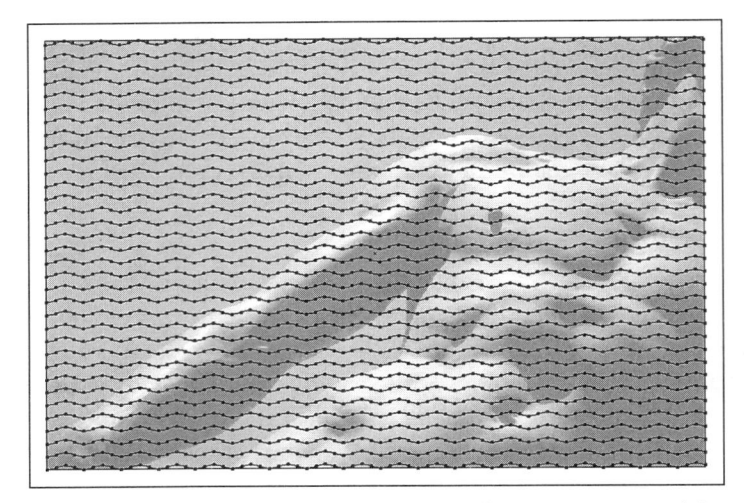

Figure 4.68 Fill a copy of the bounding rectangle with the waving lines pattern. Expand the pattern.

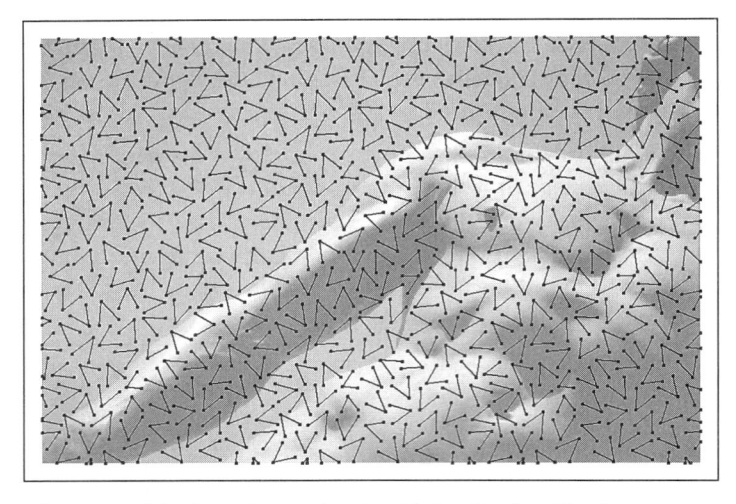

Figure 4.69 Fill another copy of the bounding rectangle with the Random V pattern.

    Click on the rectangular boundary, and choose Object|Mask|Release. From the Arrange menu, choose Send To Back. Select All. From the object menu, choose Pattern. A dialog box opens. Click on the New button. You will see the V's appear in the small preview window on the dialog box. Name the pattern and click on OK. The pattern is now available when you fill a new copy of the bounding rectangle (which you'll have placed on a new layer titled All-Over V Pattern). Follow the same procedure as outlined earlier.

9. When you have finished, your Illustrator Layers palette should look something like that shown in Figure 4.70. You can, if you wish, add other layers with paths to this Illustrator document. When you have the paths the way you want them, Paste a copy

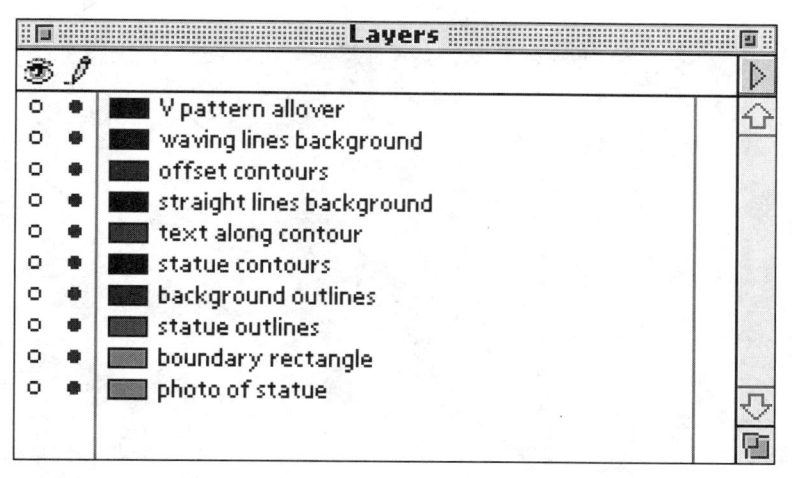

```
                    Layers
  ○  •  ■ V pattern allover
  ○  •  ■ waving lines background
  ○  •  ■ offset contours
  ○  •  ■ straight lines background
  ○  •  ■ text along contour
  ○  •  ■ statue contours
  ○  •  ■ background outlines
  ○  •  ■ statue outlines
  ○  •  ■ boundary rectangle
  ○  •  ■ photo of statue
```

Figure 4.70 The Illustrator Layers palette with all of the path information saved in separate layers and ready to be pasted into Photoshop.

of the bounding rectangle in all of the layers (use the Paste In Front command) that do not have it. You'll need this rectangle to help you position the paths accurately when you paste them into Photoshop. Save the Illustrator document so that you can work with it later, if you need to do so.

Lock and Hide all but the top layer. Select All, Copy, switch to Photoshop. Create a new Path. Paste as Paths. Double-click on the path on the palette and name it appropriately. Be sure to remember to delete the bounding rectangle on every layer except the one containing only the rectangle. Return to Illustrator. Lock and Hide all but the second layer. Select All, Copy, switch back to Photoshop, and Paste. Follow this procedure for all of the Illustrator layers.

Using The New Paths On The Photo Of The Statue

Photoshop's path-manipulation capabilities have one feature that makes possible all of the special effects that you are about to see: There can be an active selection with a visible path at the same time. This means that you can apply a stroke effect to an entire image, but the stroke appears only within the boundaries of the selection.

The general procedure in most of these examples is to first choose one of the paths—either the outline of the statue or the outline of the background—and then convert that path to a selection. Next, switch to a different path and apply the stroke. The unaltered image, undimmed now because you are seeing it in Photoshop, is shown in Figure 4.71. Please note that the example files are at 300 ppi and about 9 by 6 inches. The brush sizes specified in the instructions are based on what is needed for this file. If you work on a different size file and one with a different resolution, you need to scale your brushes to get the same effects.

Note that the full-color versions of these examples appear in the color section of this book.

Figure 4.71 The image, a detail of Michelangelo's David, to which the path effects will be applied.

Glow Effect

One of the easiest effects to achieve with a path is the glowing edge shown in Figure 4.72. Begin by selecting the path that encloses the background and converting it to a selection. With the background selection active, switch to the path that outlines the statue.

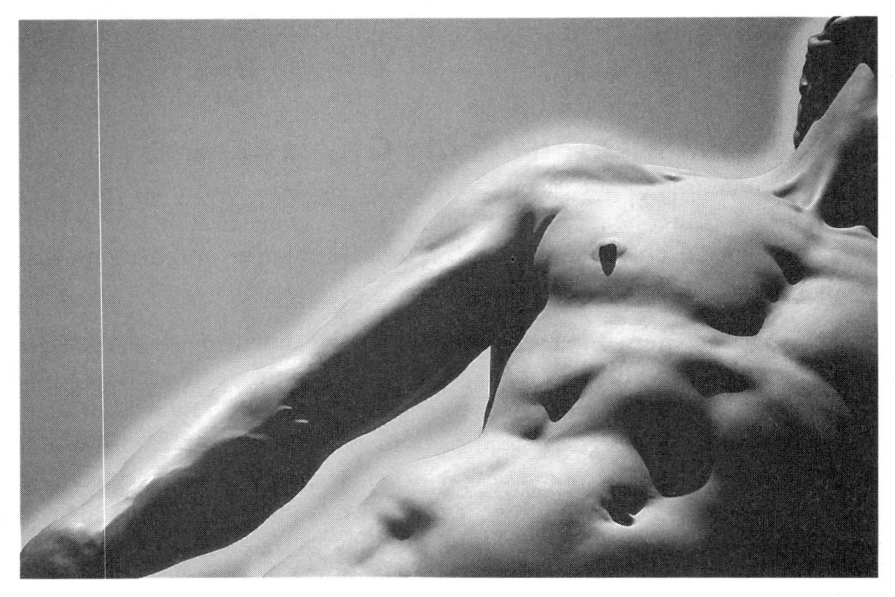

Figure 4.72 This glow effect is one of the easiest special effects you can make with a stroked path.

Choose the Paintbrush tool with a 150-pixel brush end—Hardness of 0, Opacity 50%—with the Foreground color set to white. Press the Enter key. (Remember that with one of the Paint tools selected, pressing the Enter key is the same as choosing the Stroke Path command from the palette menu.)

That's it. Take a look at the effect by deselecting the path and by hiding the active selection (Command+H on the Mac or Ctrl+H in Windows). Use the Undo command, and proceed to the next effect.

Split Edge Effect

The second stroke effect applies a stroke twice—with two different colors—along both sides of a path. In the example shown in Figure 4.73, the dark brush adds an inverse version of the glow effect on the outside of the statue and overlays a light stroke within the boundaries of the statue.

Change the background to a selection, and then switch to the statue contours path. Select the same brush—same size, hardness, and opacity—but with the Foreground color set to black. Press Enter. Change the brush color to white, choose Select|Inverse, and press Enter.

Hide the selection and deselect the path to look at the final effect. When you are finished studying the stroke effect, use the File|Revert command, and move on to the next effect.

Strokes On The Offset Contours

Begin again with the outline of the background and change it to a selection. Switch to the path with the offset upper contours. With the Direct Select cursor, click on the path beneath the arm

Figure 4.73 A dark stroke is applied outside the statue's boundaries and a light stroke within. Both are applied at 50% Opacity. The effect is similar to a massive Unsharp Mask filtering of the statue's outer edges because it places those edges into a high-contrast relationship.

and the one outlining the upper part of the figure. Select the Airbrush. Set the mode to Normal, 100% pressure. Press Enter. Use the Select cursor and click on the second path away from the figure. Change to the Airbrush, make the pressure setting 80%, and press Enter. Continue in this way: Click on each path, decrease the Airbrush pressure by 10%, and press Enter. The result is shown in Figure 4.74.

Try this as a variation. First, set the Airbrush pressure to 50% and the mode to Difference, and then select the 250-pixel brush. Hold Option (Mac) or Alt (Windows)—temporarily changing the cursor to the Eyedropper tool—and select a medium tone from the statue. Deselect all the paths but keep them still visible (the selection of the background area should still be active). Press Enter. You will get a different effect as the strokes change to a rich blue instead of the decreasing light tones.

Background Line Effect

Because this effect is applied only to the background, you first need to convert the background outline to a selection. Switch to the path containing the horizontal background lines. Choose the Direct Selector tool. Hold the Shift key and click on every other line. Take care that you choose every other line in the area under the arm. (To help you, press Command+R [Mac] or Ctrl+R [Windows] to show the rulers. Then drag a guide from the rulers to give you a line on which you can sight.) Make a 22-pixel Paintbrush. Set the Hardness to 100%. Set the Paintbrush combination mode to Dissolve and the Opacity of the brush to 50%. Press D to set the Foreground/Background colors to their defaults. Press Enter.

Hold the Shift key and use the Selector cursor to click on the alternate lines. Switch back to the Paintbrush, change the Opacity to 30%, and press Enter. The results are shown in Figure 4.75.

Figure 4.74 Click on each path in turn, apply the Airbrush on each in turn, decreasing the Pressure setting as you move away from the figure.

Figure 4.75 Select every other line and stroke with a brush set to 50% Opacity. Select the alternate lines and stroke with the brush set to 30%.

Multiple Stroke Effects Using Three Different Tools

Although the image in Figure 4.76 looks more complicated than the previous examples, it's actually very easy to create. Begin with a selection of the background area and a Paintbrush

Figure 4.76 Three different strokes are applied. First, a small brush applies a stroke to the horizontal lines in the background. Next, a larger brush strokes the v-shaped paths in the background with the Smudge tool. Finally, the History Brush's Impressionist option strokes the same v shapes in the statue.

stroke of the same horizontal lines (22-pixel brush, Normal mode, 50% Opacity, and Foreground color black).

Leave the background selection active and switch to the path containing the small v shapes. Select the Smudge tool. Choose a 35-pixel brush point. Set the Pressure to 80%, and press Enter.

Choose Select|Inverse. Change to the History Brush, and select the Impressionist option. Make the Brush mode Normal and the Opacity 100%. Choose a 45-pixel brush with a Hardness setting of 50%. Press Enter.

Strokes On The Waving Lines

The net effect of the strokes in Figure 4.77 is to lighten the background and to darken the statue while preserving the continuity of the attractive waving lines.

Begin by making a selection from the outline of the statue. Switch to the path containing the waving lines. Set the Foreground color to black. Choose the Paintbrush tool with a 45-pixel brush point (Hardness of 50%). Make the Opacity 50% and the mode Multiply. Press Enter. Change the mode to Dissolve. Press Enter. Choose Select|Inverse. Change the Foreground color to white. Change the brush mode to Dissolve. Press Enter. Change the brush mode to Overlay and decrease the Opacity to 40%. Press Enter.

Variation Using The Waving Lines

This variation (see Figure 4.78) begins similarly to the previous example. Select the area of the statue and then switch to the waving lines path. Set the Foreground color to white. Choose a

Figure 4.77 One brush is used to make this effect—two strokes of black in the area of the statue and two strokes of white in the background area. The only changes in the strokes are the combination modes and the opacity of the application.

Figure 4.78 Three applications of the same brush—three different Blend modes—on three different selections. White was the brush color for all of the strokes except for those that delineate the letters.

50-pixel Paintbrush (Hardness of 50%). Set the Opacity to 50% and the mode to Difference. Press Enter.

Use the Selector cursor while holding Option (Mac) or Alt (Windows) to select all of the paths. Move the paths so that they are positioned between their previous positions. Choose Select|Inverse. Switch back to the Paintbrush. Change the mode to Screen. Press Enter.

Deselect All. Change to the paths containing the letters. Convert the letters paths to a selection. Return to the waving lines path. Change the Foreground color to black. Choose the Paintbrush tool again. Select a 45-pixel brush (Hardness of 100%). Set the mode to Dissolve and the Opacity to 50%. Press Enter.

Strokes Used To Integrate Two Images

The example in Figure 4.79 is the most complex of those shown. However, it looks more complex than it actually is. You'll discover, as you work through this example, that the procedure is very simple. In fact, you have already done most of the operations on the previous examples. The only new element here is the addition of layers and layer masks. Follow these steps:

1. Open the files DAVID01.PSD (shown in Figure 4.80) and DAVID02.PSD (see Figure 4.81). The two files are exactly the same size. Move the file named DAVID02 onto a layer so that it's above the DAVID01 image: Choose the Move tool, and drag the second image onto the window of the first. Hold down the Shift key as you drag to ensure that the second image is exactly centered on the first.

2. Select the path that outlines the background of the first image, and convert it to a selection. Click on the upper image's layer to select it and press Command+J (Mac) or

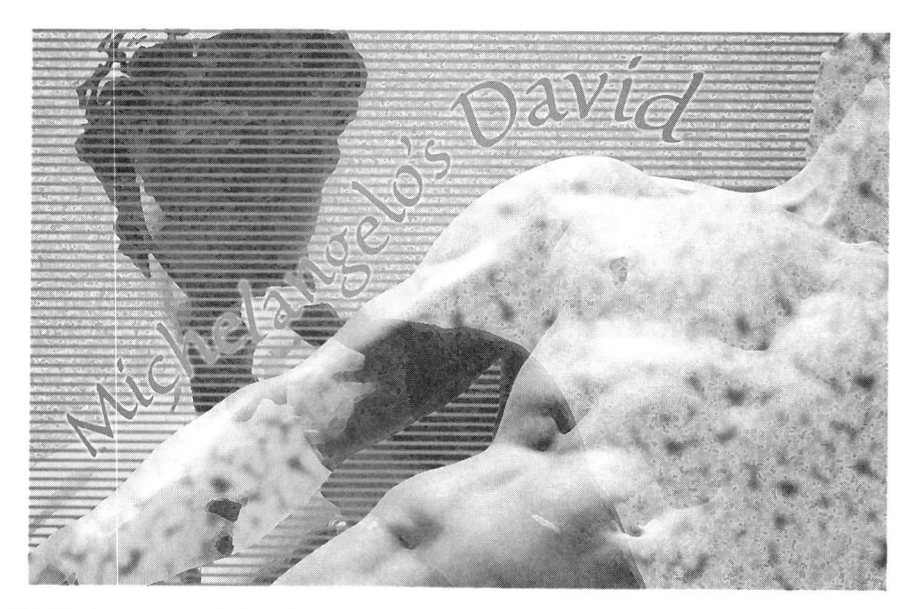

Figure 4.79 Strokes on paths help to integrate the two-image composite.

Figure 4.80 One of two images to be merged in collage effect.

Figure 4.81 The second image of the collage, a highly stylized detail from the same statue.

Ctrl+J (Windows) to make the selection into an independent layer. Select the middle layer again, choose the same path, and make another selection. Press Delete. You have just divided the second image—the part that is above the statue is on the middle layer, and the part that covers the background is on the upper layer.

3. Hide the middle layer. Your window should appear resemble Figure 4.82. From the Layer menu, choose Add Layer Mask|Reveal All. Set your Foreground color to black. Click on the path containing the horizontal lines in the background area. Choose a 22-pixel Paintbrush. Set the Mode to normal and the Opacity to 80%. Press Enter. The lines painted onto the Layer mask will cause parts of the layer to disappear. Thin lines of the backmost layer will show through the spaces (see Figure 4.83).

4. Hide the top layer and make the middle layer visible. Change the mode of the middle layer to Overlay (see Figure 4.84). Create a Layer Mask for this layer. Click on the Path containing the small v's. Choose a 45-pixel Paintbrush set to Normal mode and 80% Opacity. Press Enter. The v shapes will become nearly transparent and allow the statue to show through. Now make both layers visible to view the composite (see Figure 4.85).

Figure 4.82 After dividing the upper image into two parts—one that covers the statue and one that covers the Background—hide the middle layer.

Figure 4.83 Stroke the horizontal lines with a small black Paintbrush on the layer mask. The stroked lines cause parts of the layer to become transparent so that the first image's background shows through the narrow lines.

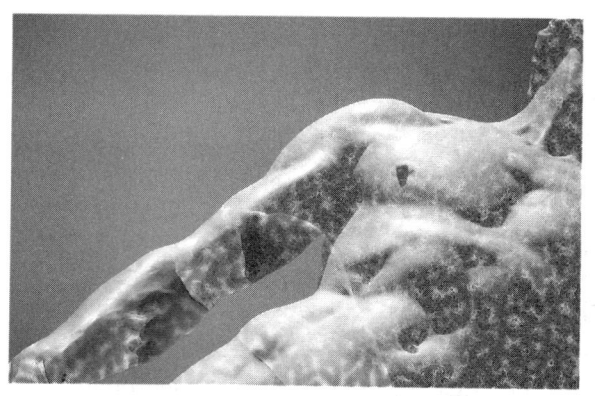

Figure 4.84 Hide the top layer and set the middle layer to Overlay mode.

Figure 4.85 When the V pattern has been stroked on the layer mask, make all layers visible to see the composite of the images.

Other Examples Of These Techniques

In Chapter 3, the discussions of the Smudge tool and the Impressionist variation of the Rubber Stamp tool showed the photos in Figures 4.86 and 4.87 as illustrations. In the first, the background has been smudged to make it more interesting. In the second, the History Brush Impressionist option was used to paint the water lily image. (Appropriate, don't you think?) Both of the examples were painted with the Random V path pattern used in the examples shown in Figures 4.84 and 4.85. Random V's is a very useful file!

Neon Effect Using Paths

You can create the effect of glowing neon tubes a number of ways. The example shown here has this to recommend it: It prints very well using process inks, and it's about as easy an effect as you could wish for. The real work is setting up the letter shapes as paths. For best results, try using a heavy typeface—this example is done with Adobe's Myriad Multiple Master instance 830 BL 700 SE. (If you are unfamiliar with Multiple Master fonts, you owe it to yourself to investigate them. They are amazing!) Be sure that you move the letters farther apart than you normally would, because the glow effect extends into the spaces between the shapes.

Figure 4.86 We used the Smudge tool—originally shown in Chapter 3—to distort the background on the left into the blurred texture on the right.

Figure 4.87 We used the Impressionist option of the History Brush tool—originally shown in Chapter 3—to change the photograph on the left into the painterly image on the right.

Set up your basic image with a dark background and choose a bright color for the letters. If you intend to use the neon letters for non-offset purposes, choose any rich, bright color. When the letters need to be reproduced on a press, you'll need to be a little more careful: Process colors are not as vivid as colors chosen from the RGB spectrum. To achieve a rich effect, you will probably need to choose one of the process inks and use it alone, or choose a bright color built with any two of the process inks. Your choices are somewhat limited but, as you can see from this example (shown in the Color Studio section of this book), the effect can be very successful. The color example in this book uses just two inks, black and cyan. The dark background color is composed of 100% cyan and 100% black. We've used this combination for a couple of reasons. First, using two inks ensures that the background will be a very dense black. Second, because the letter shapes are done in cyan, adding cyan to the background color gives the black a noticeably blue cast that enhances the neon letters and makes them more vibrant.

After setting up your letter shapes as paths—this example's letters were done in Illustrator and pasted into Photoshop—you will apply a series of strokes using two colors. Set your Foreground/Background colors to 100% cyan and white. You can, if you wish, follow along with this example using the same file as shown in the figures. Open the file NEON.PSD in the Chapter 4 Practice Files folder on this book's CD-ROM. Then follow these steps:

1. Click on the Paths palette item to make the paths show up against the dark background (see Figure 4.88).

2. Select the Airbrush tool. Choose a 70-pixel brush point and set the Pressure to 20%. Press Enter (see Figure 4.89).

3. Switch to the Paintbrush tool. Select a 50-pixel brush point, change the Opacity to 50%, and turn on Wet Edges. Press Enter (see Figure 4.90).

4. Press X to flip the Foreground/Background colors (Foreground is now white). Select a 30-pixel brush point and set the Opacity to 40% (Wet Edges remain on). Press Enter (see Figure 4.91).

5. Choose Filter|Sharpen|Unsharp Mask. Make the settings 200%, Radius 2, and Threshold 5. Click on OK (see Figure 4.92).

6. Flip the Foreground/Background colors (Foreground is now cyan). Choose an 18-pixel brush point. Set the Opacity to 70%, and turn off Wet Edges. Press Enter.

7. Change back to the Airbrush tool and the same 70-pixel brush end. Set the Pressure to 10%. Press Enter (see Figure 4.93).

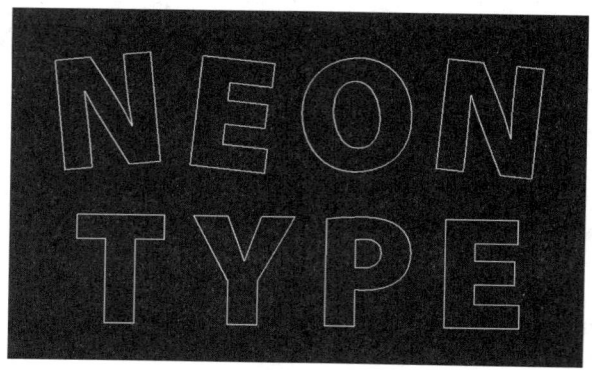

Figure 4.88 The letter-shaped paths against the dark background.

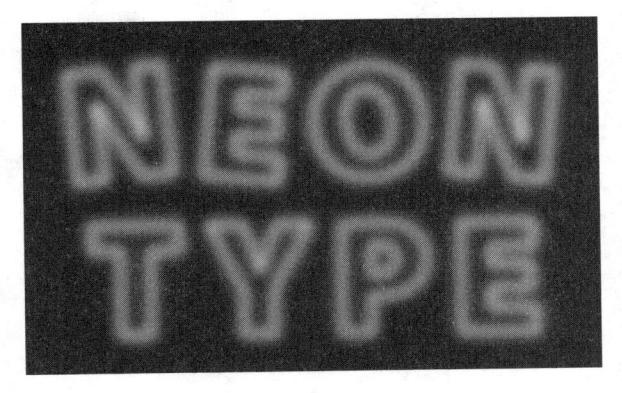

Figure 4.89 Stroke the paths with a large Airbrush set to 20% Pressure.

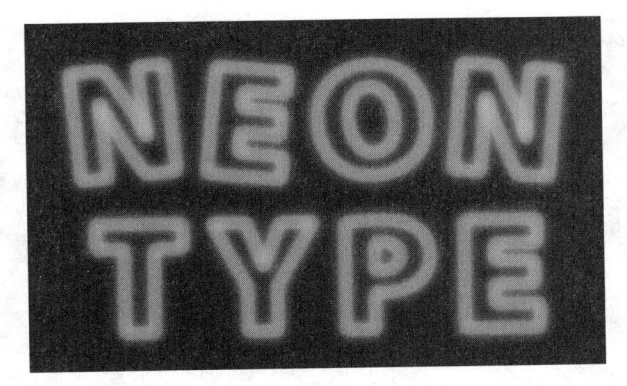

Figure 4.90 Stroke the paths with a smaller paintbrush set to 50% Opacity with Wet Edges turned on.

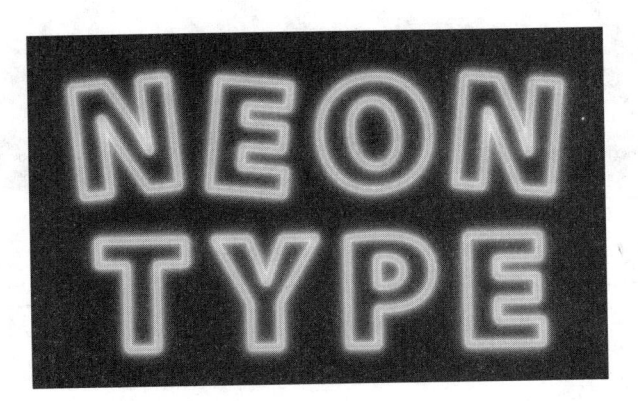

Figure 4.91 Stroke the paths with a smaller paintbrush set to 40% white.

As you can see, the whole effect is simply a matter of laying strokes upon strokes with a single application of the ubiquitous Unsharp Mask filter to heighten the Wet Edges effect. The sample file you worked on has a resolution of 300 ppi. The brush sizes were chosen to be appropriate to that resolution and to the width of the letters. When you apply this same effect to letter forms

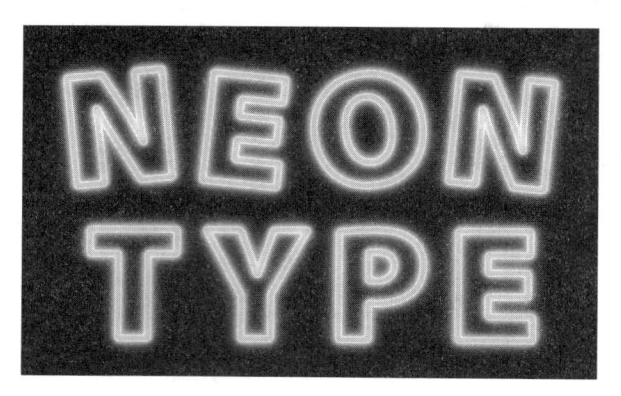

Figure 4.92 Use the Unsharp Mask filter to enhance the Wet Edges effect.

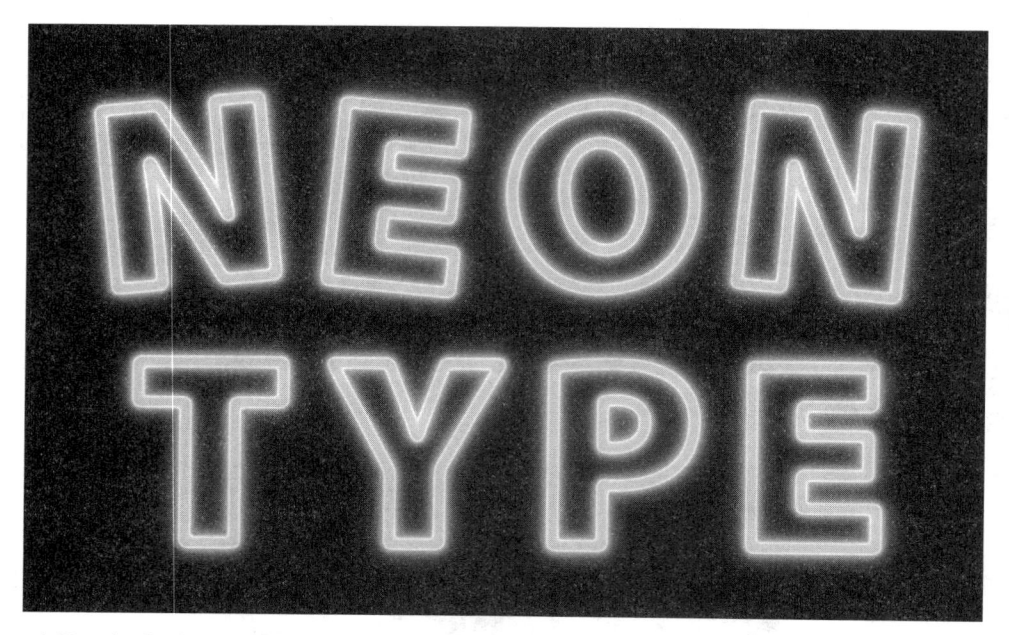

Figure 4.93 The final neon effect (shown in color in this book's Color Studio section).

of your own choosing, remember to scale your brush choices so that they are correct for the resolution of your file and for the letters you intend to use.

Glass Letters Effect

The glass-like letter forms effect makes use of several techniques. Stroking the paths with the Smudge tool distorts the contents of the letters to imitate the apparent displacement of the shapes and colors behind the letters as if they had lens-like properties. A faint drop shadow subtly enhances the contrast between the darker edges of the letters and the area around the letter shapes. Finally, an alpha channel with embossed letters allows you to selectively apply the Levels controls to the smudged shapes in such a way that the embossed forms are mapped onto the letter shapes as they are lightened. The final effect—seen in color in the Color Studio section—is unusual, attractive, and successful.

The Chapter 4 Practice Files folder on this book's CD-ROM contains the file TULIPS.PSD (shown in Figure 4.94). It is a copy of the example shown in the following set of figures. If you would like to follow along as the steps to achieving the glass letters are listed, please open that file. Notice that the numerical information given in these instructions is based on the resolution of the file—300 ppi—and on the scale of the paths that enclose the letters. Once you have followed this example and wish to try the technique on a photograph, remember to base your numerical information on the resolution and scale of your image.

1. Click on the New Channel icon at the bottom of the Channels palette. Fill this channel with white. Click on the thumbnail on the Paths palette so that the paths surrounding the letters appear (see Figure 4.95).

2. Set the Foreground color to black. Click on the Fill Path icon at the bottom of the Paths palette. Click outside the path item so that the paths are no longer visible (see Figure 4.96).

Figure 4.94 The photograph to which you will add the glass-like letters.

Figure 4.95 Fill an alpha channel with white and click on the path that contains the letter shapes so that the paths are visible.

3. From the Filter menu, select Other|High Pass. Enter a value of 20 and click on OK (see Figure 4.97).

4. From the filter menu, choose Other|Find Edges (see Figure 4.98).

Figure 4.96 Fill the paths with black and then hide the paths.

Figure 4.97 Run the High Pass filter on the channel. The setting is 20.

Figure 4.98 The image looks this way after you've applied the Find Edges filter.

5. From the Filter menu, choose Blur|Gaussian Blur. Enter a value of 3.5. Click on OK (see Figure 4.99).
6. Darken the letter shapes by opening the Levels controls (Command+L on the Mac or Ctrl+L in Windows). Enter a value of .3 in the top center data entry field (see Figure 4.100).
7. From the Filter menu, choose Other|Emboss. Enter the values –45° (angle), 8 (height), and 200 (amount). Click on OK (see Figure 4.101).
8. Make the paths visible again. Convert the paths to a selection, then hide the paths. From the Select menu, choose Inverse. Next, from Select, choose Modify|Expand. Enter a value of 1, and click on OK. Fill the new selection with black (see Figure 4.102).
9. Make the paths visible again. Convert the paths to a selection, then hide the paths. Apply the Gaussian Blur filter to the selection with a radius value of 8 (see Figure 4.103).
10. Increase the contrast on the embossed letters. Open the Levels controls (the letters selection is still active). Enter "2", "1.13", and "175" in the Input scale data entry fields. Click on OK (see Figure 4.104).

Figure 4.99 Apply the Gaussian Blur filter.

Figure 4.100 Use the Levels controls to darken the letter shapes.

Figure 4.101 Apply the emboss filter.

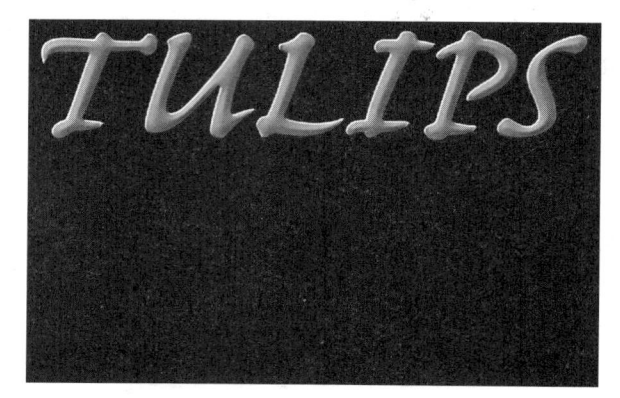

Figure 4.102 Fill the area around the letters with black.

Figure 4.103 Apply the Gaussian Blur filter to the letters.

11. Deselect the letters and return to the composite view of the flowers. Click on the path thumbnail to make the paths visible again. Convert the paths to a selection using the third-from-left icon at the bottom of the paths palette. Make sure the letter shapes are selected and the paths visible (see Figure 4.105).

12. Select the Smudge tool. Set the Pressure to 50%. Choose a brush point of 75 pixels (0 Hardness). Press Enter (see Figure 4.106). Note that applying the Smudge tool to a path is somewhat slow because it requires a lot of computation. Be patient—the effect is worth it!

13. Choose a 50-pixel brush point; change the Pressure to 80%. Press Enter (see Figure 4.107).

14. Load the alpha channel as a selection (Command+click or Ctrl+click on the #4 channel's thumbnail on the Channels palette). Open the Levels controls. Enter "0", "2.00", and "180" in the Input data entry fields (see Figure 4.108). This procedure lightens the letters selectively. More lightness is applied where the alpha channel has light values, less where the alpha channel has dark values.

Figure 4.104 Use the Levels controls to increase the contrast in the letters.

Figure 4.105 Return to the composite image and make the paths visible.

Figure 4.106 Stroke the insides of the paths with the Smudge tool and a large brush point.

Figure 4.107 Stroke the insides of the path with the Smudge tool using a smaller brush and a higher Pressure setting.

Figure 4.108 Lighten the letters selectively by applying the Levels controls while the alpha channel is active.

15. Deselect. Make the paths visible again, and convert them to a selection. Press Command+J or Ctrl+J to make the letters into a layer. Duplicate this layer. Hide the

top layer and click on the second layer down to select it. Turn on Preserve Transparency and fill the letter shapes with a medium green sampled from the image. Turn off Preserve Transparency. Apply the Gaussian Blur Filter to the letters using a Radius value of 15. Change the mode of the layer to Multiply and set the Opacity of the layer to 50%. Select the Move tool. Press the Down arrow key eight times and the Right arrow eight times (see Figure 4.109).

16. Make the top layer visible and selected. Choose Filter|Sharpen|Unsharp Mask. Enter settings of 300% (amount), 3 (radius), and 0 (thresholds). Flatten the image. The finished image is shown in Figure 4.110 (and appears in the Color Studio section of this book).

Figure 4.109 Make a duplicate of the letters and use them to make a drop shadow.

Figure 4.110 The finished glass letters image.

Using Illustrator And Paths To Create New Paintbrushes

At first glance, the material in this section may appear to have more to do with Illustrator than with Photoshop. However, we think you will find that we are presenting a logical extension—with which you can accomplish a number of things—to the idea of making Illustrator paths and applying stroke effects inside Photoshop. Here, we have preapplied the stroke while in Illustrator for the purpose of making specialized brush points that can be used by any of Photoshop's paint or toning tools. These are brushes that would be extremely time-consuming to construct in Photoshop but that are quite simple to do in Illustrator. Because they would be difficult to do within Photoshop, they will appear to give unusual results. This situation occurs only because they are unfamiliar. As you paint with these brushes, having learned how simple they are to make, we think you'll dream up other uses for the Illustrator-Photoshop partnership.

We have included two files on the CD-ROM. One of them, ENP_BRU.ARP, is a saved brushes file (the brushes made with the files shown in the following examples) that you can simply load onto your Brushes palette using the palette's sidebar menu. The other, BRUSHES.AI, is the Illustrator file from which the brushes were generated. If you find that the brushes are useful, but you need them to be a different size, rescale them in Illustrator and then import them into Photoshop following these instructions:

1. Set up the Illustrator file by making a set of squares (.5-point black stroke, no fill) about .5 inches on a side. Select all the squares, Group them, and Lock them. This example has 10×10 squares. Each square is about 8 points away from its neighbor.

2. Draw your brushes using any of Illustrator's tools. Keep the brush drawings within the boundaries of the squares. This ensures that all of the brushes are about the same size and that you are able to use them together easily when in Photoshop. When you are finished drawing the brushes, Unlock the squares and change the stroke of the bounding squares to None. Select All (see Figure 4.111) and Copy.

3. Switch to Photoshop. From the File menu, choose New. Make the new document Grayscale and set the resolution to whatever you wish it to be. (The brushes in the file on the Photoshop CD-ROM were made at a resolution of 300 ppi.) When the new window has opened, Paste as Pixels. The pasted shapes are shown in Figure 4.112.

4. When the pasting operation is complete, flatten the image. Return to Illustrator. Select only the rectangles surrounding the brushes. They're already grouped—all you need to do is click on one of them to select them all. Copy, switch back to Photoshop, and Paste as Paths. The paths are shown surrounding the brush shapes in Figure 4.113.

5. Clear your brush palette by holding down Command (Mac) or Ctrl (Windows) and clicking on each brush to delete it (before doing this, you may want to save your brushes as a named file so that you can load them again later). You can delete all but one of the brushes. As soon as you have defined a new brush, you can delete the last one of the original palette. Choose the Direct Select cursor. Click on the first rectangle, press Enter, and select Define Brush from the Brush palette's sidebar menu (see Figure 4.114). Repeat this process until you have defined all 100 brushes. Save this brush file in your Photoshop Brushes folder. You can then discard the brushes document, or you can save it for use at another time.

PATHS AND THE PEN TOOL **291**

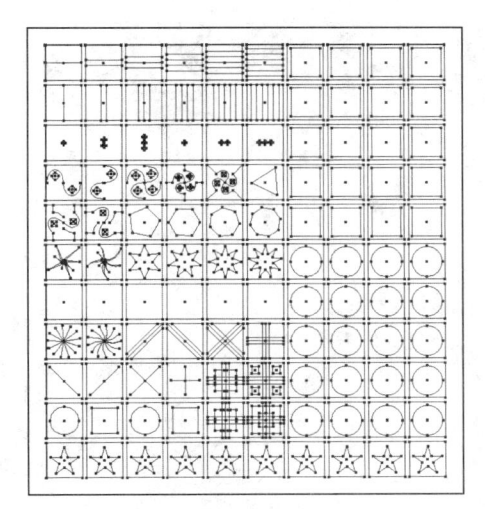

Figure 4.111 All of the brushes have been drawn and selected.

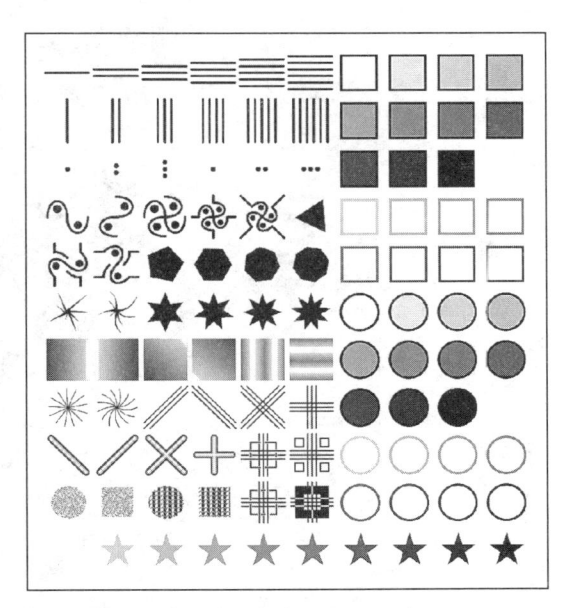

Figure 4.112 The brush shapes pasted into a new Photoshop window.

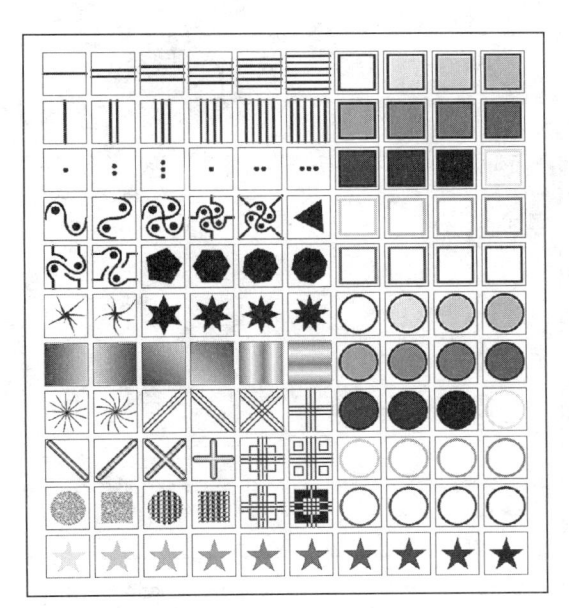

Figure 4.113 Paste the rectangles surrounding the brushes into the Photoshop document as Paths.

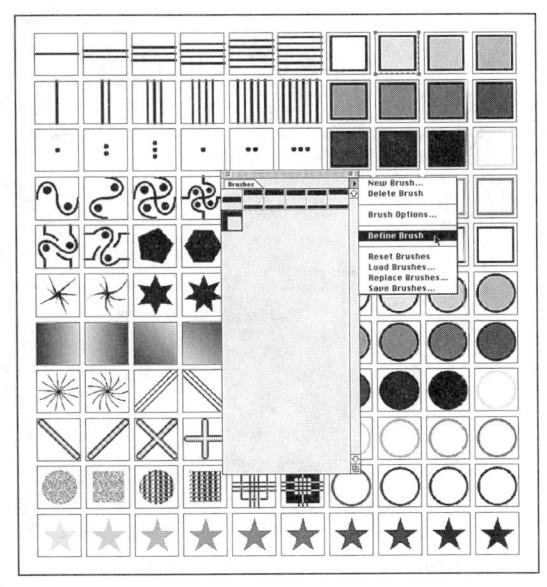

Figure 4.114 Click on each path to select it, press Enter, and then choose the Define Brush command from the Brush palette sidebar menu.

Making brushes this way can give you access to some wonderful shape and texture possibilities that would be difficult to construct in Photoshop. Figure 4.115 shows how six of the brushes in this set can be used to make repeating textures, faded textures, and so on. You can experiment with the repeat percentages and use these brushes for borders and for all-over texture effects.

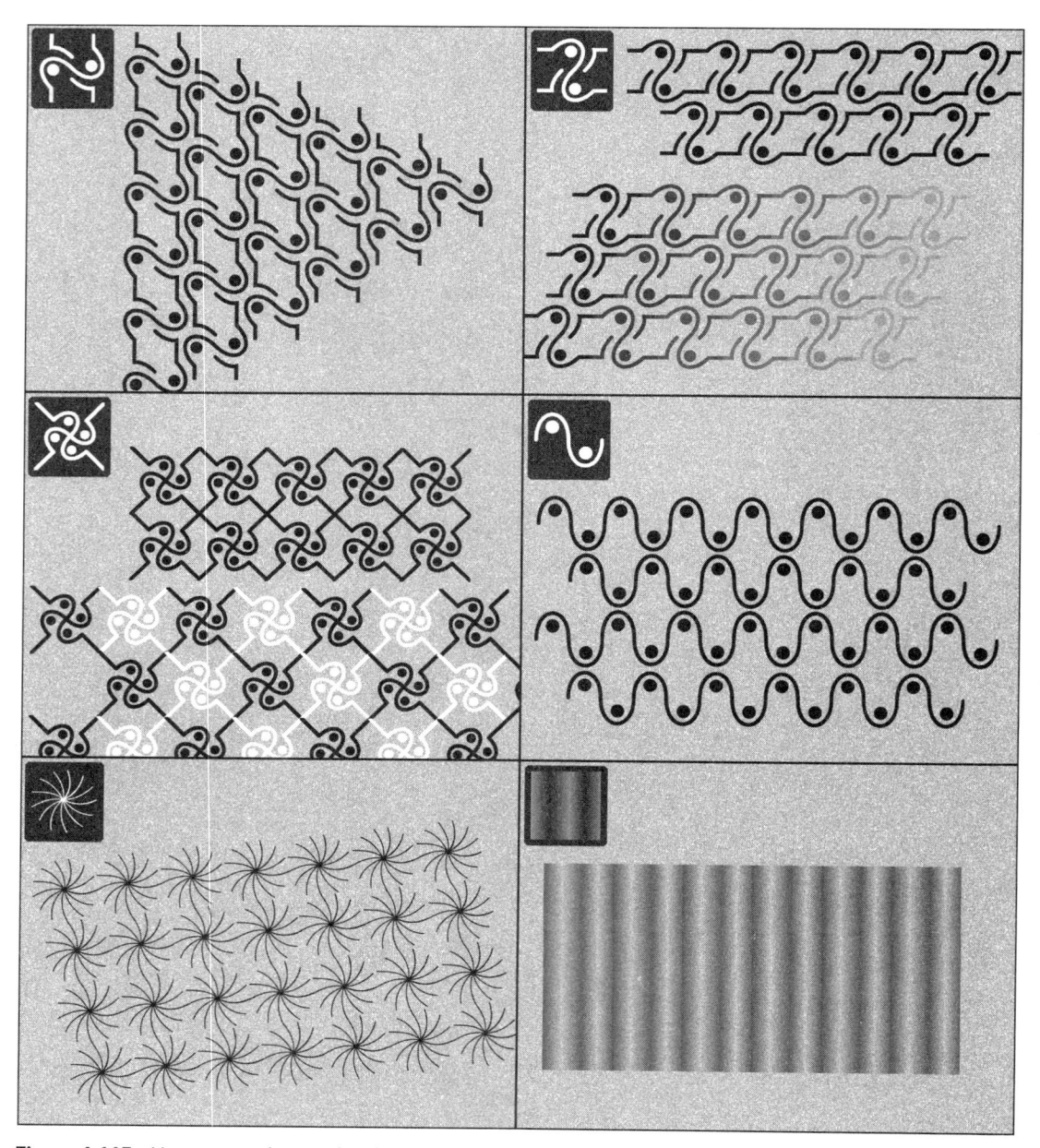

Figure 4.115 You can use the new brushes in a variety of ways. The examples shown here use variations of the brush repeat percentages and the Paintbrush Fade option.

A final note: You can find another special effect based on stroking a path in the section titled "Tiles In Photoshop Using The Offset Filter" in Chapter 12, which shows another case where a path is used to make a precise movement with the Brush tool. In the figures that accompany the explanation, you'll find several examples of how the repeating tile might be used. One of the examples shows the pattern as an embossed linear shape. The embossing was done exactly the same way as the embossing of the glass letters alpha channel (discussed previously).

Moving On

In this chapter you learned to draw and use paths for a variety of purposes. Photoshop's Pen tool has been augmented by adding the wonderful path-manipulation capabilities of Adobe Illustrator. You also saw an example of how a special effect made use of an alpha channel. In Chapter 5, you will be formally introduced to channels. A channel is a component of a Photoshop document that stores different kinds of information. It can store color information, transparency information, and selections. You will learn to use the channels as masks and to make complex calculations between different channels. Later, you will see how channels can help you combine images in a process called compositing. You'll also see more special effects—different from those you learned to apply with paths, but equally exciting.

USING CHANNELS

Channels are one of Photoshop's most powerful features.

If Photoshop's channels have ever confused you, you're in good company. Many Photoshop users have found themselves lost in what seems to be an illogical—even paradoxical—way of organizing and using certain kinds of information. In fact, channels—document components that store various kinds of information using grayscale brightness values—are Photoshop's most burdened concept because they can be made to represent a variety of information. It is this Zen-like quality of channels that leads to the confusion. Just look at what a channel can be made to do:

- A channel can represent the brightness data of a particular video phosphor. For example, if you look at the Red channel of an RGB file, you would see a range of gray values. The brightness of these values is an indicator of the amount of red (phosphor) in a particular pixel. A completely red area of the channel appears as solid white.

- A channel can represent the strength of an ink. As you'll see, CMYK documents—when examined channel by channel—use a lack of brightness or darkness to signify the strength of a printing ink. An area of the cyan plate that contains no cyan appears white; an area that contains 100 percent cyan appears as total black (behavior that is totally opposite to the behavior of the color channel in RGB).

- A channel can represent a selection that *could* be active, but may not be. This concept is interesting: How does Photoshop *store* a selection for later use? (Answer: Unless you have changed the default behavior, the white areas represent the selection and the black areas are not selected.)

- A channel can represent variable opacity. Opacity is a difficult concept to visualize. However, with a channel, grayscale values can be made to serve as an analog for amounts of opacity (anything gray is partially selected).

- A channel can represent variability in the execution of a command. This statement is a way of saying to Photoshop: "Based on this grayscale analog, perform a command to various degrees of completeness, depending on how light or dark each pixel of the channel is."

- A channel can represent spot color printing plates that will be placed into a page-layout program and separated to be printed in Pantone or other non-process inks. You will learn more about this new function of channels, however, in Chapter 9.

All of these concepts, and more, are a few of a channel's function. Even more amazing, the channels can simultaneously represent these seemingly different kinds of information by using only black, white, and 254 shades of gray. It's no wonder that some users have gotten overwhelmed when learning about channels.

If you are one of those users who has gotten lost, we are about to reveal something that you may at first find difficult to believe. All of these seemingly different kinds of information are, in the context of Photoshop, different aspects of *the same thing*. Really. We will prove it, and when we're finished, we think that you're going to love using channels for all the many interesting and timesaving things they can do. In fact, whether or not you realized it, you have already used channels in a couple of ways, in previous parts of this book. Did you work through the Quick Mask tutorial in Chapter 3? If so, you used a channel. Did you work through the glass lettering project at the end of Chapter 4? You used a channel. Those two examples should convince you that using channels isn't hard. Now all you have to do is figure out how to understand them, and you're home free!

In this chapter, we will cover all the ways Photoshop uses channels. As you encounter each use, you may find that you are jumping from one topic to what seems to be an unrelated topic. However, this is precisely how we'll approach this task of linking together what seems to be unrelated material so that you can discover the underlying similarities.

Channels: What They Can Do

We'll begin this discussion of channels by showing you how the channels are used in everyday situations. As you encounter each situation involving channels, remember the preceding statement, that a channel's information in a variety of situations amounts to different aspects of the same underlying concept. The brightness values of a grayscale channel can be treated simultaneously as pictorial elements and as an analog for values that operate on the picture in a way that has little obvious relationship to the image's topology.

Figure 5.1 You want to show someone else exactly which pixels you intend to select from this sundial photograph.

Channels To Hold Selections

Let's imagine that you and a colleague living in a different city are both intending to use the same Photoshop image—perhaps the sundial photograph shown in Figure 5.1. You have made a precise selection of the sundial's outlines, and you need to show your colleague which pixels you have selected. Eventually, you hit upon a strategy. You make a duplicate of your sundial photograph and make the same precise selection on the copy (see Figure 5.2). Next, you fill your selection with white, select the inverse, and fill the selection with black (see Figure 5.3). Now, if you send this simple black-and-white file as an email enclosure, your colleague can click with the Magic Wand tool in the white area of your black-and-white file and instantly know the exact shape of your selection. You can congratulate yourself on the ingenuity with which you have solved your problem.

Figure 5.2 The first step: Make the selection on a copy of the file.

Figure 5.3 If you fill your selection with white and the area around the selection with black, others just need to click in the white area with the Magic Wand tool to know exactly which pixels you originally selected.

After your colleague has opened the file and locates the selection, all that remains to be done is to drag the selection from your black-and-white file to the other copy of the sundial. With a little zooming and nudging, the selection can be fitted to the image.

This strategy may sound a little cumbersome, but it is entirely workable. The only tricky part is when someone has to drag the selection from the black-and-white file to the sundial image, and then position it by eye. Otherwise, this is a realistic way to preserve the boundaries of a selection.

If you followed the discussion on using a single black-and-white image to preserve a selection, then you have grasped the idea behind selection channels or, as they are called, *alpha* channels. An alpha channel is a channel added to your Photoshop document beyond the channels that contain the picture image information (we will discuss picture image information channels in following sections of this chapter).

Two easy ways are available for you to make an alpha channel from your selection: using the Save Selection command, and saving the selection by using the Channels palette.

Save Selection

While the selection is active, go to the bottom of the Select menu and choose Save Selection. A dialog box opens, as shown in Figure 5.4. This dialog box contains several possibilities, which we will discuss later. For the moment, observe that the default destination is a *New* channel and that the Operation is also set to *New Channel*. You also have an opportunity to name the channel. Click on OK, and look at your Channels palette (see Figure 5.5). You'll see a fourth channel located at the bottom of the list—directly after the Red, Green, and Blue channels. Photoshop has assigned it a name, Alpha 1 (unless you named it), and also assigned a keyboard command to it—Command+4 for Macintosh, Ctrl+4 for Windows—that you can use to look at and edit this channel. Notice that the thumbnail for this channel is identical to the one you would have made in the preceding hypothetical situation.

> **TIP**
>
> **New feature alert! In Photoshop 4 and earlier versions, new channels were named numerically. In an RGB document, the first new channel would be named #4. In a CMYK image, the first new channel would be #5 because Cyan, Magenta, Yellow, and Black are already present. In version 5, however, all new channels are named starting with Alpha 1 (unless you manually select a different name at the time that you create them). Why was this process changed? My guess is that Adobe wanted to more clearly distinguish between color channels and user-created channels.**

Save The Selection Using The Channels Palette

While the selection is active, you can click once on the small icon—second from the left—at the bottom of the Channels palette. This produces exactly the same result as using the Save Selection menu command, but the dialog box is bypassed.

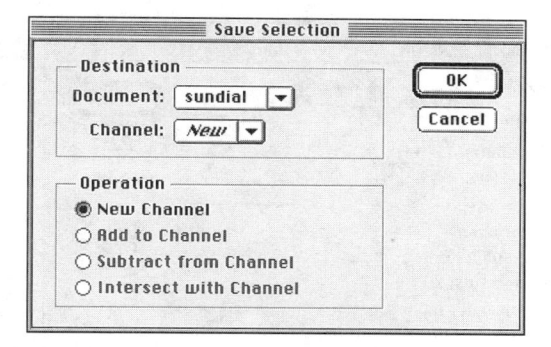

Figure 5.4 The Save Selection dialog box.

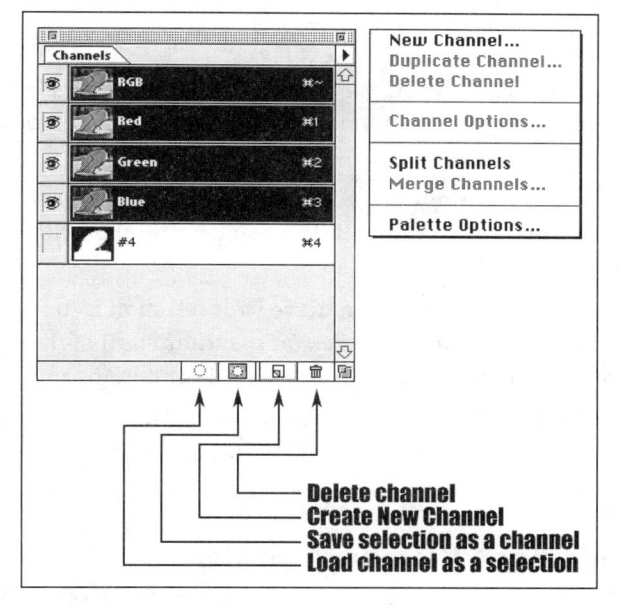

Figure 5.5 Expanded view of the Channels palette.

Retrieving Saved Selections

After you preserve your selection in an alpha channel, you need to be able to retrieve it. You have a number of options available for reinstating the active selection:

- This may sound silly, but you really can press Command+4 (Mac) or Ctrl+4 (Windows) to view the alpha channel, and then click in the white area with the Wand tool (set the Tolerance to 32 and turn anti-aliasing on). After the white area is selected, return to the composite channels view. You probably won't want to do the job this way, but we list it here to show that the original strategy of preserving a selection is valid.

- Click on Select|Load Selection. A dialog box appears (see Figure 5.6). The choices are similar to those in the Save Selection window. We will discuss most of these choices later in this

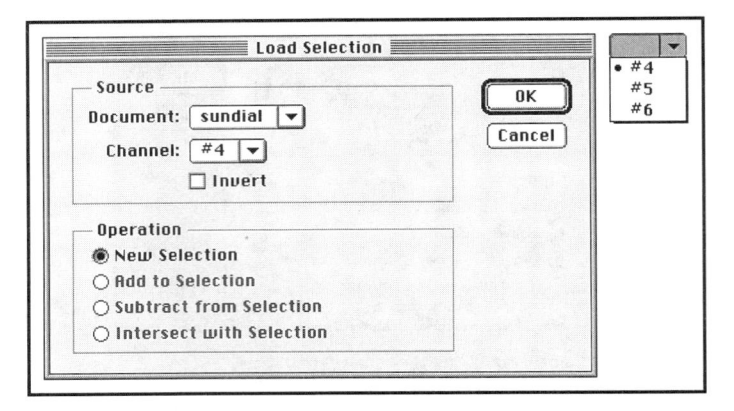

Figure 5.6 The Load Selection dialog box.

chapter. The defaults are as shown in the figure. You are given the choice of which channel to load (if you have more than one alpha channel) and whether to load the channel as a New Selection.

- You can click on the alpha channel's thumbnail on the Channels palette (Figure 5.5), click on the leftmost icon at the bottom of the palette, and then click on the top line of the Channels list.
- The fastest and most convenient way to retrieve your selection is to hold down the Command (Mac) or Ctrl (Windows) key and click on the thumbnail of the alpha channel on the list of channels on the palette. You'll probably use this option the most because it's so fast.
- Finally, if this were the last selection that you had made, you could retrieve it by pressing Shift+Command+D (Mac) or Shift+Control+D (Windows). This new-to-Photoshop 5 command reloads the last selection.

Channels To Represent Variable Opacity

After you load your alpha channel selection, you have many possibilities. You can, if you want, copy the selection and then paste it into another document window. Figure 5.7 shows the sundial, detached (copied) from its original surroundings and placed (pasted) against a gray background with horizontal black lines.

Copying and pasting a selection is something that we do without question. However, you need to give the process a little extra thought because here, we are examining alpha channels as possessing the capability of representing variable opacity.

First, remember that each pixel in the alpha channel represents an equivalent pixel in the image: For example, the upper-right corner pixel in the channel corresponds to the upper-right corner pixel of the image. This point is important to remember because if a pixel is selected in the channel, the equivalent pixel is selected in the image. Now just assume that when you loaded the selection, you really loaded the entire channel—you loaded all of the pixels, black and white. When you copy the selection, imagine that you are copying all of the pixels and not

Figure 5.7 When you load the selection, you can copy and paste the selected pixels into a new document window.

just the ones represented by white pixels in the channel. Now take it one step further. Imagine that Photoshop arbitrarily assigns an opacity based on the value of the pixel in the channel. If the alpha channel pixel is black, the selected pixel is entirely transparent. If it's white, the selected pixel is entirely opaque. If you can imagine this situation, you have a grasp of *what actually happened* when you loaded the selection, copied it, and pasted it into the new document shown in Figure 5.7. All of the pixels were pasted, but the only ones visible were those represented by white pixels in the alpha channel.

This is a subtle point, but if you can get it planted firmly in your mind, you'll have a key to some of the important inner workings of Photoshop. The only point of confusion is this: Why, if all the pixels are selected, does the selection line only appear around the areas that contain white pixels in the alpha channel? This is Photoshop's way of showing you only those pixels that have an equivalent alpha channel pixel value of 50 percent black or lighter. The selection lines are displayed just to help you to understand what is selected.

If we carry the idea of variable transparency a step further, we can construct a small experiment to give you an idea of what else can be done. Study Figure 5.8 for a moment. The original alpha channel containing the white-filled sundial shape has been surrounded with a zone of pixels that are 50 percent black. When this modified alpha channel is loaded, the selection outlines will appear along the edges between the black and the gray pixels. When the channel was copied and pasted into another document window (shown in Figure 5.9), you can see that pixels from the image in the zone represented by the gray pixels have been pasted but that you can partially see through that area. The black stripes in the background are visible, but are muted by the overlay of the pasted pixels that are 50 percent opaque.

By carrying this process one step further, we can use a broad range of opacity represented by the gray values in the channel. Figure 5.10 shows the channel of Figure 5.8 with a large-scale blur applied to the gray and black areas. This blur gives a gradient that runs along the contour

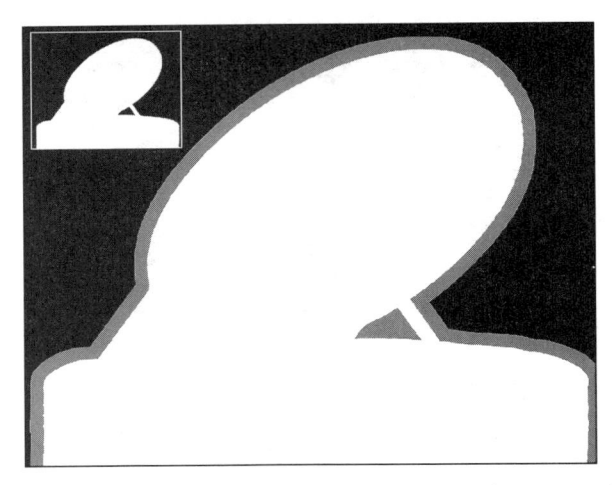

Figure 5.8 The original alpha channel has been modified to give a zone of 50 percent black pixels around the edges of the white area.

Figure 5.9 When the new channel has been loaded as a selection, copied, and pasted into a new document, the image pixels represented by the gray pixels in the channel are 50 percent opaque.

of the sundial shape. The tones range from 50 percent black along the white edge to completely black farther away from the edge. When this channel is loaded as a selection, copied, and pasted into the document with the black lines (see Figure 5.11), the result is that the copied pixels fade out so gradually that there is no place where we can say that the sundial pixels end and the background pixels begin.

Channels To Represent Moderators, Or Masks, For Commands

In much the same way that the gray tones of the pixels in the alpha channel can be made to represent a selection or some amount of opacity, the values can also serve as ways of modifying the effects of a command. Where a pixel is white in the channel, the command applied to the

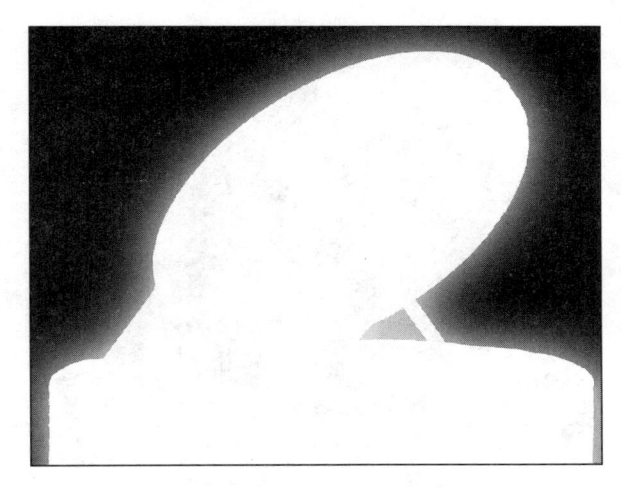

Figure 5.10 A heavy blur is applied to the black and gray areas to produce a contoured gradient along the edges of the white sundial shape.

Figure 5.11 When the modified channel is loaded, copied, and pasted, the blur of the channel causes the pasted pixels to have no visible boundary.

equivalent pixel in the image will execute normally. However, when the channel pixel is black, the equivalent pixel in the image is not affected by the command. When gray values between black and white are present in the alpha channel, the command executes proportional to the lightness of the pixel: Lighter pixels allow more of the command to execute on the pixels of the image, while darker pixels prevent as much of the command from executing on the image pixels. This sounds complicated, but we can show how it works by performing some experiments on the photograph of the sundial.

One possible command that you can use on an image is Image|Adjust|Invert. This command makes a positive image into a negative, or a negative into a positive. When the Invert command is applied to the sundial photo, you'll see the result shown in Figure 5.12. If the channel

Figure 5.12 The Invert command applied to the image with no selection active.

containing the original outline of the sundial (refer to Figure 5.3) is loaded as a selection and the Invert command applied, only the part of the image within the selection is inverted. The rest of the image remains unchanged (see Figure 5.13). This result is predictable when you consider the white area in the channel and the black areas surrounding it.

With the channel's selection operating, you might want to try a different kind of command. Figure 5.14 shows the result of running Alien Skin Software's Eye Candy 3 Water Drops filter. Notice how the filter operates only within the boundary of the sundial. If we load the channel shown in Figure 5.10 as a selection and then run the same filter, the very different effect is shown in Figure 5.15. You can see the water droplets, but they fade with distance from the sundial's edge. Another possibility is to load the blurred edge channel as a selection, choose

Figure 5.13 When the channel shown in Figure 5.3 is loaded as a selection, only the portion of the image within the selection changes when the Invert command is applied.

Figure 5.14 With the original channel selection active, the Eye Candy 3.0 Water Drops filter is applied only within the boundaries of the selection.

Select|Inverse, and then execute a different filter on the background. Figure 5.16 shows the effects of the Crystallize filter on the reverse selection. The area of the sundial is untouched, and the remainder of the image has been distorted by the filter.

A channel need not be based on a contour found in the image. You could, if you wished, create a new channel and simply apply a black-to-white gradient in the channel. A channel of this sort is an excellent way of showing how a command is moderated based on the values within the channel. The gradient channel is shown in Figure 5.17.

When the gradient-containing alpha channel is loaded as a selection, you will see moving selection lines only around the pixels that are 50 percent black or lighter in the alpha channel. This visual representation is normal, although it is misleading when you first encounter it.

Figure 5.15 When the channel shown in Figure 5.10 is loaded, the same filter executes beyond the edge of the sundial, but fades away imperceptibly.

Figure 5.16 When the same selection is inverted and the Crystallize filter is executed, only the background is affected. The filter's distortions taper off the closer they get to the edge of the sundial.

Figure 5.17 Create a new channel and fill it with a black-to-white gradient.

Your entire channel is selected, despite what the moving selection lines seem to show. One command you could try with this channel loaded is Fill With White (see Figure 5.18). Or try Fill With Black (see Figure 5.19). Perhaps you may want to try the Add Noise filter (see Figure 5.20). Observe in these three figures that the command executes completely on the left—equivalent to the white pixels of the channel—and not at all on the right—where the channel's pixels are black. The areas between right and left show how the commands are moderated by the values contained in the gradient.

Here's another possibility based on the capability of the channel to moderate a command: We can make a selection based on the information in two of the channels to make a composite selection. First, we'll duplicate the channel that contains the gradient. With the duplicate

Figure 5.18 With the gradient-containing channel loaded as a selection, this is the result of filling with white.

Figure 5.19 With the gradient-containing channel loaded as a selection, this is the result of filling with black.

visible in the document window, load the original selection channel, the one that contains the outline of the sundial (see Figure 5.21). Fill the selection with black and deselect. The new channel now has elements of both channels (see Figure 5.22). When we load this new channel as a selection and fill with white, the result is as shown in Figure 5.23. The Fill command has executed along the gradient, but the black-filled shape of the sundial has been left entirely untouched.

Channels To Represent Color Values

In the examples we have discussed up to now, all of the channels were extra channels—alpha channels—which were added to the list of channels on the palette. These channels are, in effect, masks. The channels that make up the native document contain the image's color data.

Figure 5.20 With the gradient-containing channel loaded as a selection, this is the result of using the Add Noise filter.

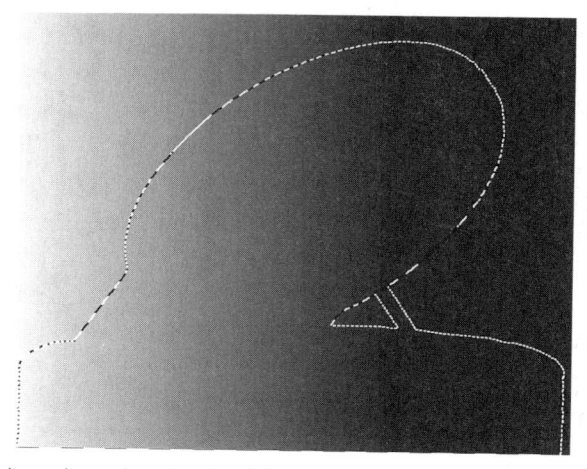

Figure 5.21 With the gradient channel in view, load the original alpha channel as a selection.

These color channels can have the same characteristics as the alpha channels, but they are also integral to color. Each color channel is capable of having white pixels, black pixels, and 254 shades of gray between the two. The momentary perceptual difference between one of the color channels and one of the alpha channels is simply what the gray values of the pixels in the channels represent.

Also, in the channels examples we've discussed to this point, a white pixel was seen to be equivalent to a total selection, total opacity, and to an unmoderated command. When channels are considered as color components, however, a white pixel is an indication that the channel's color tone is at its brightest. Using this reasoning, a white pixel in the Red channel of an RGB document would indicate maximum brightness for the red component of the color. The same can be said for the other two color channels in an RGB document, Green and Blue.

Figure 5.22 Fill the selection with black.

Figure 5.23 Load the new channel as a selection and fill the image with white. The command executes around the sundial, but leaves the shape of the sundial untouched because it was filled with black in the channel.

The reverse is also true. A black pixel in the Red channel indicates that there is no red component to the pixel's overall color. Extending the logic of this proposition, it should be clear that shades of gray in any of the color channels indicate relative strengths of that color. This point is difficult to grasp. To make it more clear, we've provided some pictorial examples.

Figure 5.24 shows a series of six wedge shapes. Although you are seeing them in grayscale, each wedge is composed of a pure tone in the outer area, shading to black toward the center. The top, third, and fifth colors (clockwise) are red, green, and blue, the primary monitor phosphor colors. The second, fourth, and sixth are yellow, cyan, and magenta, the monitor secondary colors. (Secondary colors are composed of two of the primary colors.)

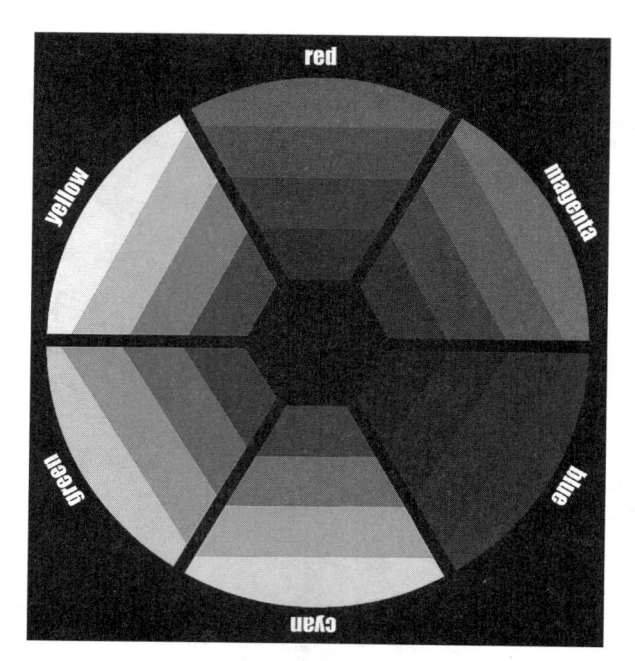

Figure 5.24 The three monitor primary colors—red, green, and blue—and the three secondary colors, colors composed of two primaries. The secondary colors are yellow, cyan, and magenta.

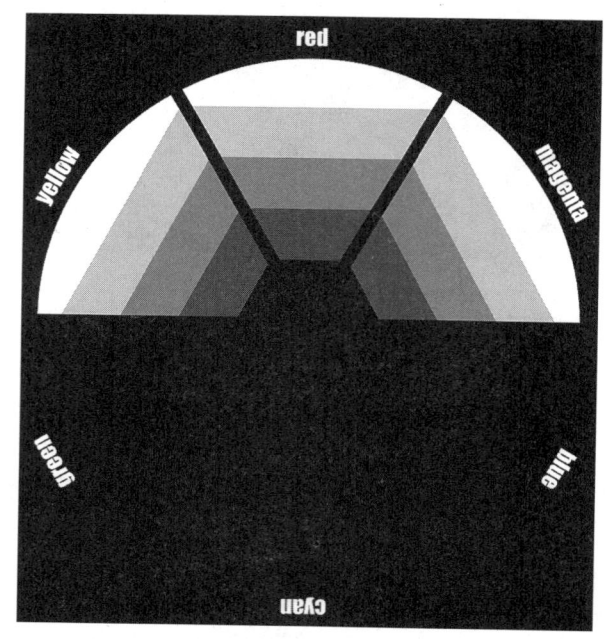

Figure 5.25 The Red channel of Figure 5.24.

A look at the Red channel by itself (see Figure 5.25) shows a very different image. First, this channel is truly in grayscale and is not a grayscale emulation of colors, as the previous figure was (because the figures in this book are in black and white, we must sometimes point out that we are presenting a grayscale version of a color file). All of the tones in the wedges are composed of white or shades of gray. The most obvious difference is in the lower half, in which the green, cyan, and blue areas are entirely black. This difference indicates that no red component exists in any of the three colors at the bottom of the figure. Figure 5.26 shows the Green channel of Figure 5.24, and Figure 5.27 shows the Blue channel.

When you look at these three figures, notice how similar they are to each other. Each set of three is identical to the others, but each has simply rotated 120°. In fact, each wedge is identical to every other wedge. The differences between them depend on which channel they are in, and their topological relationship to the pixels of the other channels. For example, the brightest red area is white only in the Red channel. In the other two channels, the equivalent area is black. The brightest yellow area, by contrast, is white in both the Red and the Green channels, with the equivalent area in blue showing as black.

The idea of channels contributing to the colors you see on your monitor may seem odd to you, especially because you do not, as a rule, look at the individual channels as anything other than what they seem to be—individual grayscale images. It is not until you stop seeing the pictorial image and start to recognize that the color channels in an RGB document are only a collection of brightness values—tones between white and black—that you begin to understand how colors work and how you can manipulate them. When you begin to see how the values combine, you'll have a valuable tool for color correction.

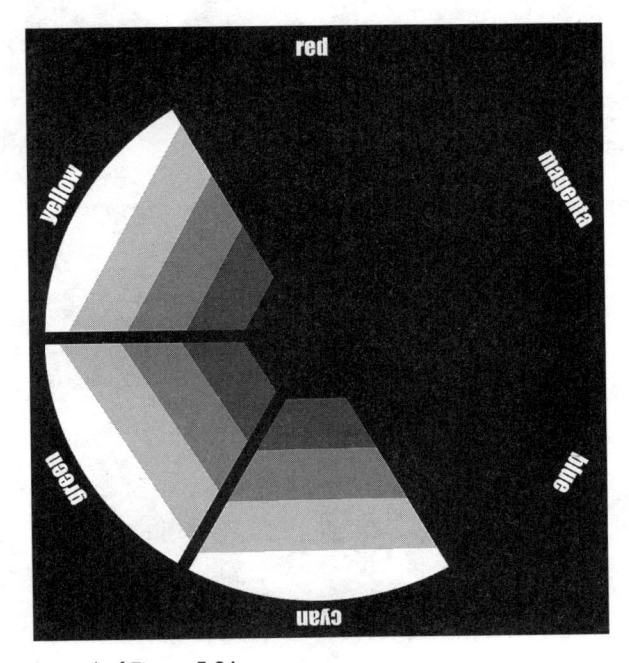

Figure 5.26 The Green channel of Figure 5.24.

You'll even be able to predict what colors look like even if you only see them in grayscale. For example, the photo in Figure 5.28 is of marigolds. This figure is a grayscale representation of the RGB document. But you'll be able to think your way through what it must look like. Figure 5.29 shows the Red channel by itself. Observe the brightness of the flowers and the comparative darkness of the foliage. Figure 5.30 is the Green channel of the same file. Some of the light areas are the same as in the Red channel. If you glance back at Figure 5.25, you'll see that the color formed from red and green is a bright yellow. This gives you a good idea that the color

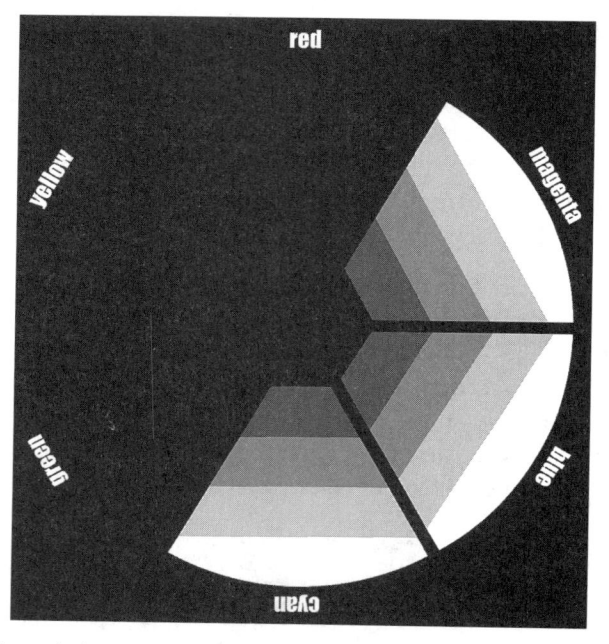

Figure 5.27 The Blue channel of Figure 5.24.

Figure 5.28 RGB color file.

Figure 5.29 The Red channel from Figure 5.28.

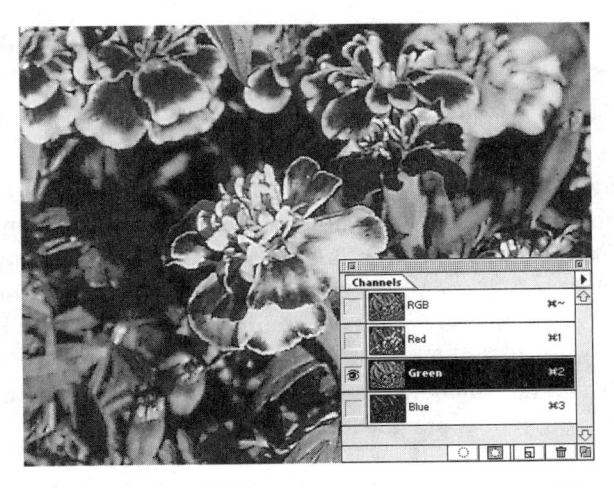

Figure 5.30 The Green channel from Figure 5.28.

could be yellow *if* there are no equivalent bright areas in the Blue channel (see Figure 5.31). There aren't any. That gives you areas of bright yellow in the flowers. Now, what happens to the darker areas of the flowers? Think it through: If the red stays the same and the green decreases (the pixels get darker), the tone shifts away from yellow toward red. In other words, the tones become more orange until, when the green has become black, there is nothing but red. Do you see? You can become very fluent with the RGB color system, all because the color channels represent color components by using shades of gray.

The last three figures also included a view of the Channels palette. Please note that the left side of the palette contains eye icons that allow you to select which of the channels you wish to view. (Each channel also has its own key command: Hold Command or Ctrl and enter "1" for red, "2" for green, "3" for blue, or "~" to see the composite of the three.) You can, if you wish, see

Figure 5.31 The Blue channel from Figure 5.28.

the combination of two of the colors without the third, using the Channels palette. Figure 5.32 shows the image with only the Red and Green channels visible without the Blue channel.

The color channels can also be treated as if they were alpha channels. When you load one of the color channels as if it were any alpha channel, the channel does double duty: It contributes its brightness values as color components and as selection/mask. Figure 5.33 shows the result of loading the Green channel as a selection, copying, and then pasting into the same document that contains the dark horizontal lines. Note that the flower shapes are nearly opaque because of the brightness of the pixels in the flowers. The background is fairly transparent because of the lack of brightness in the background areas of the Green channel. Also, because the channels are grayscale images, you can totally change the color values (and your final image) by pasting a totally different image into a color channel. (Although you should use this technique with caution, it does provide for some wild special effects!)

Figure 5.32 Use the Channels palette to view any combination of channels.

Figure 5.33 In this figure, the Green color channel was loaded as if it were an alpha channel. The selection was then copied and pasted into another window that contains a neutral background and dark horizontal lines.

Channels To Represent Ink

As you have seen, an RGB document uses the brightness values of the pixels in the color channels to indicate the strength of the color. When a Photoshop file is prepared for process-color printing (converted to CMYK mode), it must use a different value system for the channels. Instead of lightness indicating the strength of color, the reverse situation comes into being. The color channels of a CMYK document show the strength of the ink by the amount of darkness in each pixel. In this system, a black pixel indicates a 100 percent ink value, and white indicates that no ink is present for that pixel. Gray values between black and white give percentages of ink values.

Figure 5.34 shows a CMYK document displayed in color. It looks the same as an RGB document when it is displayed as a composite of all the channels. However, when the individual channels

Figure 5.34 A CMYK document shown as a composite of the color channels.

are viewed, they show a different system. Figure 5.35, for example, is a display of the Cyan channel for the photo. If this were an RGB document, we would expect to see a strong color component for the flowers. However, this is a different system and we must realize that this channel is displaying cyan values as the inverse of lightness values. The foliage can be seen to contain a considerable amount of cyan ink in the leaves—not surprising because green is composed mostly of cyan and yellow—and very little cyan in the flowers. Figures 5.36, 5.37, and 5.38 give you an idea of the appearance of the other color channels. Notice that most of the ink for the flowers is in the Magenta and Yellow channels, while most of the ink for the leaves is in the Cyan and Yellow channels. The Black channel has ink present mostly in the areas of deep shadows.

Figure 5.35 Cyan channel of Figure 5.34.

Figure 5.36 Magenta channel of Figure 5.34.

Figure 5.37 Yellow channel of Figure 5.34.

Figure 5.38 Black channel of Figure 5.34.

Other Channel Possibilities

Although channels seem to be considerably burdened with what they must represent, there are even more ways in which Photoshop exploits channels. For example, each of Photoshop's display modes uses one or more channels to express information. Here is a short summary that explains how channels are used for three of the document modes.

Lab

The Lab mode uses the L channel to show the amount of lightness a pixel possesses. The a and b channels of that mode are made to represent color content. The range of color from black to white for the a channel is from green to red in the composite view of all three channels. The color range from black to white in the b channel is from yellow to blue.

Grayscale

The Grayscale mode contains a single channel that is really a kind of short-hand channel: Grayscale documents could be in RGB mode, but all of the channels would be identical. On the Channels palette, grayscale documents have only one list entry. This single channel is titled "Black." Other channels can be added, but the native file exists with a single channel. That Black channel can be used as a selection channel. It is converted to a selection in the same way any alpha channel is made to be a selection (see the previous explanation for how alpha channels are made to be selections). It's usually necessary to select the inverse when you have made a selection of the Black channel, because you will have selected the light information rather than the dark pixels that delineate the image. An alternative is to duplicate the Black channel, choose the Invert command, and select this second channel whenever you wish to select the dark shapes in the Black channel.

Multichannel

The Multichannel mode is a grab bag of channels. All the channels can be from the same document, or they can be a collection of channels from different documents. All these channels need to have in common is that they are the same size. Multichannel mode is useful for storing alpha channels—which usually must be discarded before the image can be used for output—so that they are all together in a single convenient document. If you have been working with channels for selections and transparency information, and you want to save all of your channels for future use, duplicate your document, and convert the copy to Multichannel mode. Then, discard the color channels, which have no relevance to a Multichannel document, and save the file. You will find that this document saves to a very small size on disk.

Manipulating Channels

Having encountered channels in a variety of guises, it's time to learn how to boss them around so that they will work for you. If you find that you are still unsure how to tell when a channel is playing a particular role, we advise you not to worry about it. You have been exposed to a comprehensive explanation of channels intended to cover most possibilities. As your skills strengthen, you'll be able to manipulate channels with intuitive skill. Meanwhile, we will present some possibilities that give you a framework within which to work.

The Channels Palette Menu

Although you can do most of your work with channels by using the keyboard and the mouse, the palette's sidebar menu contains the formal command list. You will be able to understand and use the commands in the top section of the menu immediately (refer to Figure 5.5). These commands will allow you to create new channels, make copies of existing channels, and delete channels you no longer need. The second section of the sidebar menu contains two new Spot Color commands: Spot Channel and Merge Spot Channels. The third section of the menu contains a single command, Channel Options, which we will discuss in a following section of this chapter. There are also two menu selections—those in the fourth section—that are so odd that they should be discussed so that you will know what they are all about. Although you may never need these two commands (Split and Merge Channels), using them produces startling changes to the structure of your document. You should be aware of what these two commands can do. The final section of the menu contains a single command that brings up a dialog box a choice of three sizes of thumbnails to be used in the palette list of channels.

Split Channels

The Split Channels command executes without a preliminary dialog box. One moment your screen looks similar to the one in Figure 5.39. The next moment, after the command has executed, you find your screen looking as shown in Figure 5.40. The RGB channels and three alpha channels contained in the document have all been placed in separate document windows.

Figure 5.39 Photoshop with a single six-channel document open (R, G, B, and three alpha channels).

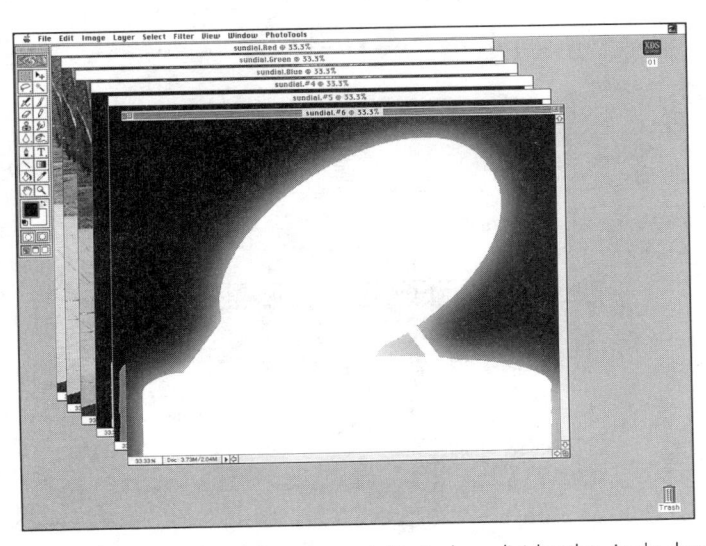

Figure 5.40 After selecting the Split Channels command, Photoshop divides the single document into six separate documents, each containing one of the original channels.

Photoshop has thoughtfully named each file with the original document name, a dot and the extensions "red," "green," "blue," "#1", "#2," "#3," and so on. These new windows now represent separate file entities that carry only grayscale information.

Merge Channels

You can use the Merge Channels command whenever more than one document window is open and when they all have exactly the same dimensions. After choosing the command from the menu, a dialog box opens (see Figure 5.41). The pop-up menu allows you to choose which document mode to use for the merged file. The window in the figure has defaulted to Multichannel because six channels were open (as shown in the figure).

After choosing from the pop-up list, you will be asked to make more choices in a second dialog box (see Figure 5.42). Photoshop will make an intelligent guess about which channels should be put into the new file, but you are at liberty to change each of the pop-up menus to another item. You could, if you wished, transpose the original Green and Blue channels—or Red and Green, or Red and Blue—when Photoshop reconstitutes the document. You can even put one of the alpha channels into one of the color channel positions. Transposing colors is sometimes interesting—as a pastime, it hangs right in there with Solitaire—but it's hardly ever useful. Still, you never know....

After you make your choices and click on OK, Photoshop merges the three documents into one window (see Figure 5.43). The remainder of the channels can be discarded or put back into the RGB document as alpha channels. There is an easy way to do this. Click on one of the grayscale

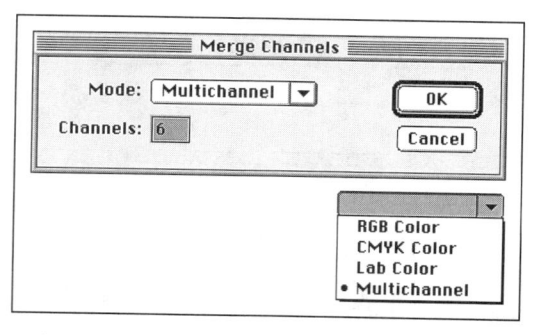

Figure 5.41 The initial Merge Channels dialog box.

Figure 5.42 The Merge Channels dialog box. Each pop-up menu contains all of the open channels that can be used.

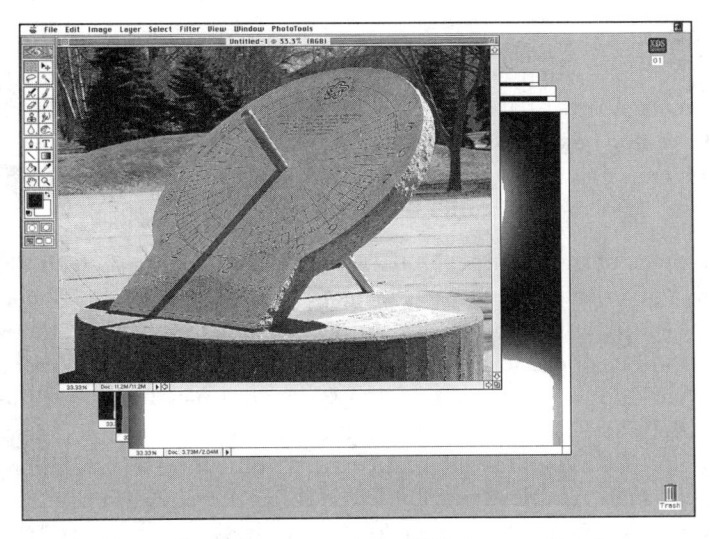

Figure 5.43 After using the Merge Channels command, the RGB document has been reconstituted, leaving the original alpha channels as separate documents.

windows to bring it to the front (be sure you can still see the RGB window). The Channels palette will show that there is a single channel, Black. Drag the thumbnail from the palette onto the RGB window. Photoshop will instantly add the channel to the others contained by the RGB document. Using this procedure, you can replace all of the original alpha channels in about 10 seconds.

With the changes made to Photoshop 5, there are a few caveats to the Split and Merge layers commands. As far as the History palette is concerned, when you have split an image, it's gone. You cannot reconstitute *that* image (a different one, yes, but never the original). Therefore, after you merge the channels back together, you have a new image—one that has no past history. If you plan to split the channels, duplicate the image first.

The Merge Channels command still has no preview, so if you are playing switches with the split channels, you're on your own—and there's no undo.

What To Do With Split And Merge

As pleasant as it would be to rattle off a half-dozen super ideas for using these two odd menu commands, the truth is that after using Photoshop for quite a number of years, the authors have never found an urgent need for either one. Not even a pressing need. Not even a moderate need. Sorry. They must have been put there for some reason. Ostensibly, you can use the Split and Merge Channels commands to create a color mezzotint by splitting your CMYK channels, changing each grayscale image to a bitmap by using Diffusion Dither at three times your original resolution. You then change each channel back to grayscale at one-to-one and merge the channels. If you mezzotint an RGB image this way, it looks great on screen, but is completely out-of-gamut for printing. Is this a pressing reason to use the commands? Probably not, but if you come up with a use for Split and Merge Channels, let us know.

Channel Options

When one of the alpha channels in a document is selected, you can select Channel Options from the Channels palette sidebar menu. You can also double-click on the channel thumbnail to bring up the dialog box shown in Figure 5.44. (Note: Channel Options are not available for the native color channels.) The top area of this window allows you to enter a new name for the channel if you wish to change it from the default.

The other two areas of the Channel Options dialog box have to do with displaying an alpha channel. When you are viewing the native color channels, you also may view any alpha channel. Click on the eye icon at the left of the channel item on the palette. Whatever color you choose for the channel will be added to the already existing colors. You can change the color from the default red by clicking on the color box and selecting a new tone from the Photoshop Color Picker. Within the Color Picker, click on the Custom button to assign a color from any of the Custom Colors palettes. When the color and opacity value have been set, the information in the channel will contribute a colored overlay to the colors already present. Chapter 9 contains an extensive section devoted to adding spot colors to process color printing. The section also contains information on how the display of alpha channels can be used.

The final section of the Channel Options dialog box is labeled Color Indicates. The default, Masked Areas, simply means that when the channel is displayed with its contributing color, areas containing dark pixels will contribute color, and areas with light pixels will not. The other option reverses the color by appearing to invert the channel. We've used the word *appears* deliberately. The channel values do become transposed, but the channel keeps the original selection. Because of this, when you load the channel as a selection, all *black* pixels become selected in the channel. There is nothing really wrong with selecting the black pixels rather than the white pixels, as long as you remember what you are doing. However, if you lose track of what you have done with the options, you can find yourself very confused. This is not an option with which you should feel adventurous.

More About Saving Channel Selections

You have already seen two ways to preserve a selection by converting the selection to an alpha channel. First, you can click on the Save Selection icon (second from left) at the bottom of the Channels palette. Second, you can choose Save Selection from the Select menu.

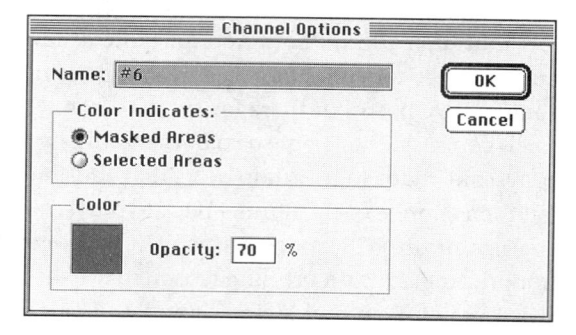

Figure 5.44 The Channel Options dialog box.

The dialog box that opens when you use the Save Selection command is shown back in Figure 5.6. Besides changing the selection into a new channel, this dialog box allows you to make some changes to existing channels based on a new selection. Figure 5.45 shows a rectangular selection which, when saved as a selection into a new channel, generates a channel that appears similar to the one shown in Figure 5.46. Figures 5.47 and 5.48 show another selection and the channel that would be generated from it.

Besides making a new selection, one selection boundary can act on a previously saved channel. To understand how this works, assume that the channel in Figure 5.46 is already in place as channel Alpha 1 of an RGB document. Let's also assume that the circular selection in Figure 5.47 is active, that you chose Save Selection from the Select menu, and that the dialog box is open.

When the dialog box opens, the Source portion of the window is set to your current file on the Document pop-up menu, and Channel will default to New. When the channel is set to New, three of the four options in the Operation section of the window are grayed out. You can, if you want, change the Channel pop-up menu to an existing channel that then allows you to perform the operations listed below. For this discussion, we'll assume that you have changed the Channel pop-up so that it reads "Alpha 1".

Figure 5.45 A simple rectangular selection.

Figure 5.46 The selection in Figure 5.45 generates a channel similar to this one.

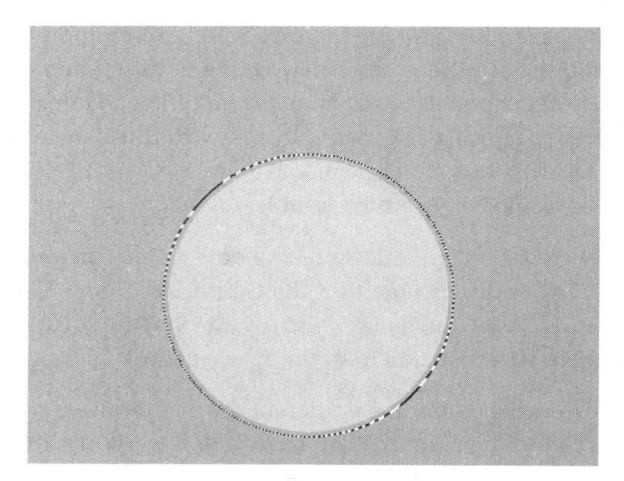

Figure 5.47 A simple circular selection.

Figure 5.48 The selection in Figure 5.47 generates a channel similar to this one.

Add To Selection

Adding to a selection simply means that you take the area of one selection outline and use it to extend the area of a previously saved selection. If you choose to add the circular selection of Figure 5.47 to the Alpha 1 channel (see Figure 5.46), clicking on OK will modify the Alpha 1 channel so that it appears as shown in Figure 5.49. This shape, as you can see, is the sum of the original channel and the new selection outline. Please note that this operation (and the other operations in the dialog box) will write over your existing Alpha 1 channel. If you wish to save the original channel, duplicate the channel before saving the selection.

Subtract From Selection

Subtracting from a selection lets you remove from the saved channel all of the area where the active selection overlaps it. When you have chosen this option and clicked on OK, your Alpha 1 channel appears as shown in Figure 5.50.

USING CHANNELS 325

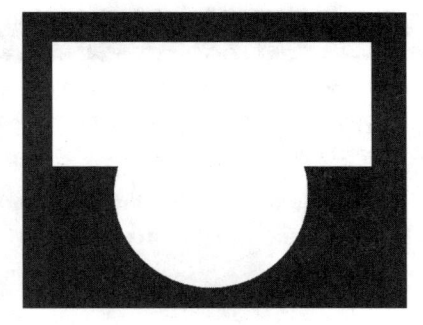

Figure 5.49 Adding the circular selection to the previously saved selection modifies the existing channel so that it contains both selection shapes.

Figure 5.50 Subtracting the circular selection from the channel eliminates the area where the selection overlaps the white part of the channel.

Intersect With Selection

The last option on the list allows you to modify the existing channel so the modified channel shows as white only where the original shape and the circular selection overlap each other. The appearance of the modified channel is shown in Figure 5.51.

Figure 5.51 Intersect With Selection produces a modified channel that contains white where the original shape and the circular selection overlap each other.

> **TIP**
>
> One of the difficulties with understanding the Load Selection dialog box is the use of the word *selection* in the operations list. You may find the options easier to understand if you substitute the word *channel*.
>
> If you have more than one document open and the documents are exactly the same size, you can save your selections from one document directly to a different document.

More About Loading Channel Selections

Whenever a Photoshop document has at least one alpha channel, the Load Selection command is available at the bottom of the Select menu. The Load Selection dialog box (refer to Figure 5.6) is similar to the Save Selection window: The Source Items differ only in that a checkbox marked Invert allows you to load the inverse of a selection; the Operation items are the same as for Save Selection. You might find the dialog box easier to understand if you substitute the word *channel* for *selection*. Load Selection is also similar to Save Selection in its treatment of multiple documents. If two or more documents are open and exactly the same size, selections (and channels) can be loaded directly from one into the other.

Operations are similar in nature to those employed by Save Selection. The command simply delivers an active selection based on existing alpha channels. You can use the different kinds of operations to give you a number of selection possibilities. In the following discussion, assume that a single document has had two alpha channels saved. The first channel is shown in Figure 5.46, and the second is shown in Figure 5.48. We'll refer to the channels as "Alpha 1" and "Alpha 2".

New Selection

If no selection is active, only New Selection will be available (other Operations depend upon an active selection modified by the contents of a channel). If channel Alpha 1 is chosen, the selection will appear as shown in Figure 5.52. If the chosen channel is Alpha 2, the selection will appear as shown in Figure 5.53.

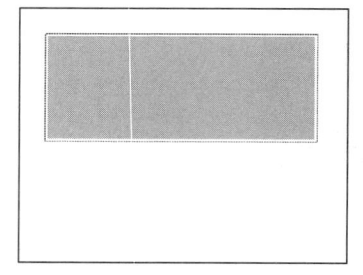

Figure 5.52 A selection produced from channel Alpha 1 (shown in Figure 5.46).

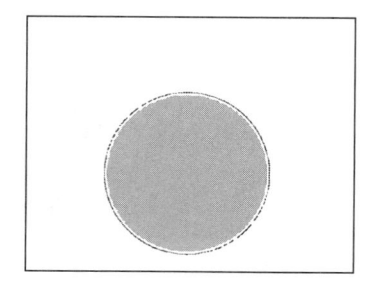

Figure 5.53 A selection produced from channel Alpha 2 (shown in Figure 5.48).

> **TIP**
>
> You can load either channel by holding Command (Macintosh) or Ctrl (Windows) and clicking on the channel's thumbnail.

Add To Selection

If we assume that channel Alpha 1 has been loaded, then choosing Alpha 2 in the Channel pop-up menu and selecting Add To Selection will produces an active selection as shown in Figure 5.54. The combined selection is the total area enclosed by the white pixels in both channels.

> **TIP**
>
> You can load more than one channel as a selection from the keyboard: With one selection active, hold down Command+Shift or Ctrl+Shift and click on a different channel to add it to the selection.

Subtract From Selection

With an active selection—produced from channel Alpha 1—choose channel Alpha 2 from the Channel pop-up menu, and select Subtract From Selection. The new selection appears as shown in Figure 5.55. It is important to realize that Subtract gives you different results depending on which channel is active and which is subtracted. If the active selection is Alpha 2 and Alpha 1 is subtracted from it, the result is as shown in Figure 5.56.

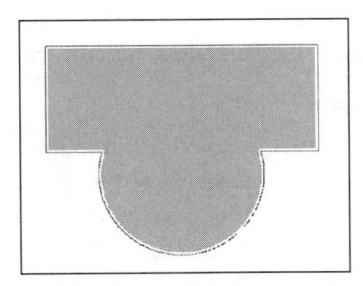

Figure 5.54 A selection produced by adding channel Alpha 2 to the active selection produced by channel Alpha 1.

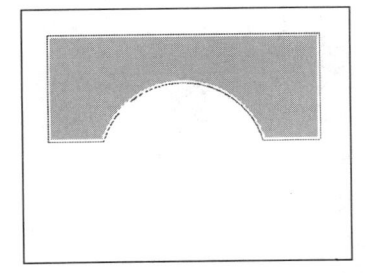

Figure 5.55 Channel Alpha 2 subtracted from the selection generated by channel Alpha 1 results in this new active selection.

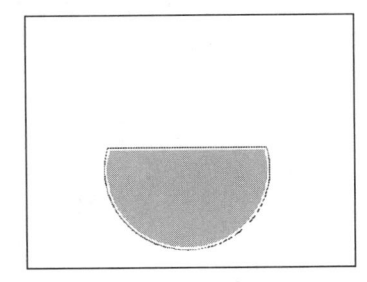

Figure 5.56 Channel Alpha 1 subtracted from the selection generated by channel Alpha 2 results in this new active selection.

> **TIP**
>
> You can subtract one channel's selection from another's from the keyboard: With one selection active, hold down Command+Option or Ctrl+Alt and click on a different channel to subtract it from the active selection.

Intersect With Selection

The Intersect Selection command produces an active selection, the area where the selections of two channels overlap each other. Either can be loaded. When the Intersect Selection command is chosen, the result is as shown in Figure 5.57.

> **TIP**
>
> You can load the intersection of two channels from the keyboard: With one selection active, hold down Command+Option+Shift or Ctrl+Alt+Shift and click on a different channel to make the active selection the intersection of the two.

Using Channels To Make Special Effects

Before the introduction of Photoshop 3, nearly all of the special effects for which Photoshop has been celebrated were produced as channel operations. Version 3's layers and layer masks have now superseded much of what used to be done with channels. However, channel operations are still the easiest way to generate the masks on which some kinds of emboss and relief effects depend. Without channels, you would have to resort to time-consuming manual methods or to third-party filters and extensions to achieve effects that are wonderfully effective and fairly simple.

A Quick Subtraction Primer

Nearly everything you will see in the examples that follow depends on subtracting one channel from another to achieve a third channel based on the contents and positions of the other two. Although there are a large number of possibilities, we will limit this primer to two channels. One is a simple selection generated from the outlines of the shape in the image. The other is a blurred and offset version of the first. The general method used here is as follows:

1. Subtract the original selection from the blurred channel.

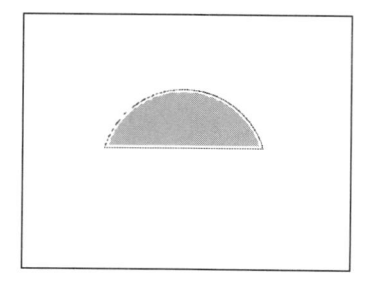

Figure 5.57 Using the Intersect Selection command produces an active selection of the area where the selections of two channels overlap each other.

2. Save the result as a third channel.
3. Load the third channel.
4. Fill the selection in the image with black. (Fill with black by setting the Foreground color to black, and then type Option+Delete or Alt+Delete.)

Figure 5.58 is the image upon which this primer is based. The center section of Figure 5.59 represents the star-filled center section selected and saved as an alpha channel. On the left-hand side of 5.59, another channel has been made from a duplication of the first. The second was moved down and to the right and then blurred. Load the right-hand selection first by holding Command or Ctrl and clicking its thumbnail on the Channels palette. Subtract the original channel from the active selection: Hold Command+Option or Ctrl+Alt and click on the other channel's thumbnail. Save the resulting selection into a new channel (right side of Figure 5.59). When the new selection is loaded, fill it with black. The result is the drop shadow effect seen in Figure 5.60.

Figure 5.58 The original document for the primer.

Figure 5.59 Subtract the center channel—the original selection of the star-filled rectangle—from a blurred and offset version of the center. The result is shown on the right.

Figure 5.60 When the resulting selection is filled with black, it produces this drop shadow effect.

Figure 5.61 shows the same channels as 5.59, but inverted. When the second is subtracted from the first, the resulting selection channel is like that shown on the right. This selection, when loaded and filled with black, produces the effect shown in Figure 5.62. Instead of a drop shadow produced by the center rectangle, the shadow is produced by the surrounding shape, making the center appear to be recessed.

Figures 5.63 and 5.65 are simple variations on the first two examples. First, the positive is subtracted from the negative, then the negative from the positive. The resulting channels and the selections filled with black are shown in Figures 5.64 and 5.66. These examples do not seem as promising as the first sets, but they can be used to very good effect, as you'll see in some of the following examples.

Figure 5.61 The same selection channels as Figure 5.59 are inverted and then subtracted. The resulting channel is shown on the right.

Figure 5.62 When the selection is filled with black, it produces this recessed effect.

Figure 5.63 This variation subtracts a positive from a negative to produce the channel shown on the right.

USING CHANNELS   **331**

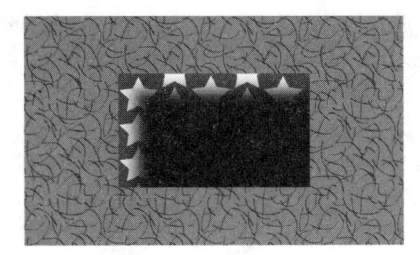

Figure 5.64 The loaded selection, filled with black, produces this result.

Figure 5.65 This variation subtracts a negative from a positive to produce the channel shown on the right.

Figure 5.66 The loaded selection, filled with black, gives this result.

Simple Drop Shadows

Drop shadows are one of Photoshop's really useful tricks. Not only do drop shadows seem to add an extra dimension to what would otherwise be a flat photograph, but they also separate the shapes casting the shadows—in this case, letters—from the background by delineating them on two sides with a darker color. When very large type is used, as it is in the following example, you have a spectacular drop shadow effect that does very little harm to the integrity of the photograph. If you look at this example (printed in the color section of this book), you'll see that the lettering and the shadows do not hide much of the image's detail. Instead, the letters grab your attention simply because of their size, because of the small change in tone between the letters and the background, and because of the more pronounced change in tone between the letters and the shadow.

Photoshop 5 has added Layer Effects to help you create automatic drop shadows, and several filter sets exist that have done this for years. You can easily use layers to make your own drop shadows. However, this way was the first method of creating automatic drop shadows, and its high quality and precision make it a valuable technique today—even though it is considered esoteric by some, and even simpler methods exist. Using channel operations to create drop shadows is really very simple. Follow along, if you wish, with the file CHICAGO.PSD found on this book's CD-ROM in the Chapter 5 Practice files. Note: The two alpha channels shown in the examples that follow are already a part of the CD-ROM file.

Follow these steps:

1. Size and crop the file to be used. Color adjust, and run the Unsharp mask filter. When the file is completely ready (see Figure 5.67), choose File|Export|Paths To Illustrator. You won't have any paths in the document: Export the document boundaries. Open the exported file in Illustrator and set up the type to be used. Convert the type to paths, copy the paths, switch back to Photoshop, and Paste As Paths.

2. Create a new alpha channel (Alpha 1). With the channel in view, change your Foreground/Background colors to white and black, and fill the paths with white (see Figure 5.68). Hide the paths. Duplicate the channel (Alpha 2).

3. Select channel Alpha 1. Press V to select the Move tool. Press the Left arrow key 10 times and the Up arrow key 10 times. Select channel Alpha 2. Press the Right arrow key 10 times and the Down arrow key 10 times. This moves the two layers so that they are offset from each other by 20 pixels.

   With channel Alpha 2 selected, choose Filter|Blur|Gaussian Blur. Choose a blur radius that feathers the edges to the extent shown in Figure 5.69. The example file, a 300-ppi image, was blurred with a radius value of 18.

4. The next task is to make a new active selection using the subtract method to eliminate the areas of the original letters from areas of the blurred letters. The selection, if you were to save it as a channel, would look similar to Figure 5.70. Begin by loading channel Alpha 2 (Command+click or Ctrl+click on the channel Alpha 2 thumbnail).

Figure 5.67 Image to which the channels-based drop shadow will be applied.

Figure 5.68 Letter shapes made in Illustrator and pasted as paths into Photoshop are used to make this alpha channel.

Figure 5.69 Use the Gaussian Blur filter on the offset duplicate of the first alpha channel.

Figure 5.70 When channel Alpha 1 is subtracted from channel Alpha 2, the resulting selection, saved as a channel, will look like this.

Subtract channel Alpha 1 from channel Alpha 2 (hold Command+Option or Ctrl+Alt and click on the thumbnail of channel Alpha 1).

5. Choose a dark, interesting color from the image with the Eyedropper tool. With the subtracted selection active, choose Edit|Fill. In the resulting dialog box (see Figure 5.71), set the fill to be with the Foreground color, the percentage to 50% to 60%, and the mode to Multiply. The Fill command produces the effect shown in Figure 5.72.

6. After you've made the shadows, you may decide that you need to increase the contrast between the letters and the background. Load channel Alpha 1, and open the Levels controls. Move the center Input slider to the left until the letters have been sufficiently lightened (see Figure 5.73). Click on OK. Choose Select|Inverse, and open the Levels controls again. Move the center slider to the right until the background is a little darker than it was. Be careful not to darken too much because the picture is fairly dark to begin with. After you are finished, click on OK. Your image should look similar to that shown in Figure 5.74 and the example in the color section of this book.

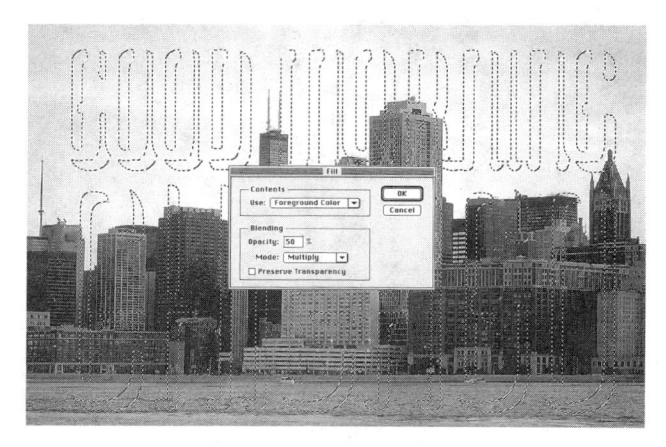

Figure 5.71 Fill the selection with 50% of the Foreground color using the Multiply mode.

Figure 5.72 After filling, you have this shadow effect.

Figure 5.73 With the selection of channel Alpha 1 active, use the Levels controls to lighten the letters.

Figure 5.74 Select the inverse of channel Alpha 1, and use the Levels controls to slightly darken the area around the letters. The finished file should look like this. You can see this image in the color section of the book.

Embossed Effects

You can emboss with channels by constructing embossed shapes in a channel (see Chapter 4, the section on glass letters effect) and then using the Levels controls with the channel active as a selection. Another simple effect is to use the technique shown in Figure 5.62, but with two offset and blurred channels to produce selections on opposite sides of a shape. Depending upon which direction you want the light source to come from, one selection is lightened and the other darkened. This usually produces a beveled effect that can have hard or smooth edges. The following primer explains the more complex effects to follow.

A Short Channel Embossing Primer

You can select the inner section of the two-part shape in Figure 5.75 by loading the channel at the right. You can then use this base channel to generate the other channels that produce the embossing effects.

The base channel is duplicated and inverted (Figure 5.76, center). The inverted copy is duplicated, moved to the right and down, and blurred (Figure 5.76, left). When the inverted base is subtracted from the blurred and offset version, the result is the new selection shown on the right.

The same procedure applied to a version of the blurred channel that has been offset up and to the left is shown in Figure 5.77.

Both of the new channels need to be refined before they can be used. The reason for this is that the two sides extend the entire length of the rectangle. Both must be shortened. You do this by

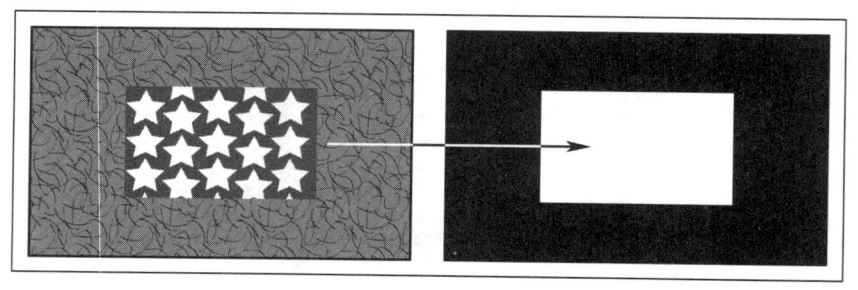

Figure 5.75 The central shape can be selected by loading the channel on the right.

Figure 5.76 Subtracting the center channel from the left-hand channel results in the channel on the right.

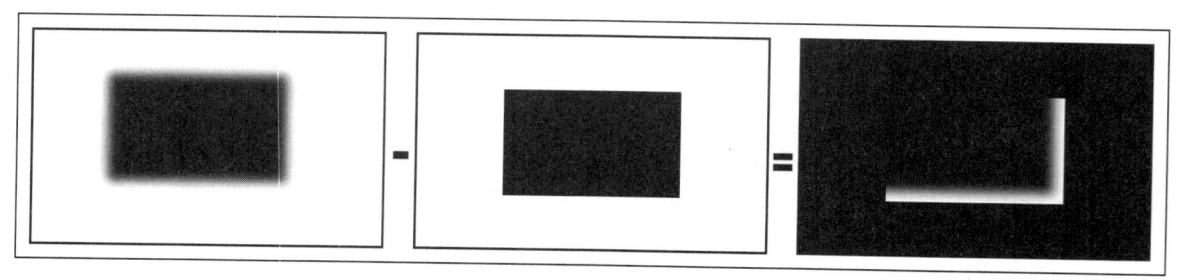

Figure 5.77 Subtracting the center channel from the left-hand channel produces the channel on the right. This channel makes a selection on the opposite corner of that shown in Figure 5.76.

subtracting each from the other and saving the new channels. Figure 5.78 shows the upper-left selection subtracted from the lower-right selection. Figure 5.79 shows the opposite procedure. The channels on the right of each figure are those used for the embossed effect.

The embossing can be done in a couple of ways. The selections can be loaded and the Levels controls used to darken or lighten the affected part of the image. In the case of Figure 5.80, the lower selection was loaded and simply filled with black; the upper selection was loaded and filled with white.

This embossing procedure gives a rounded bevel to the rectangular object. To make a harder edge, click on the upper selection on the Channels palette. With this selection in view, load the original alpha channel (shown at the right of Figure 5.75). Choose Select|Modify|Contract. Choose a number that will contract the selection by the width of the bevel. When the selection

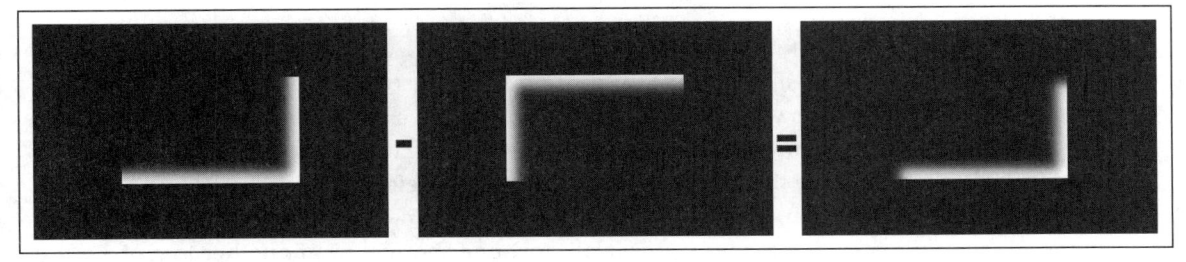

Figure 5.78 Subtract the upper-left selection from the lower-right selection to get a new selection with shortened legs.

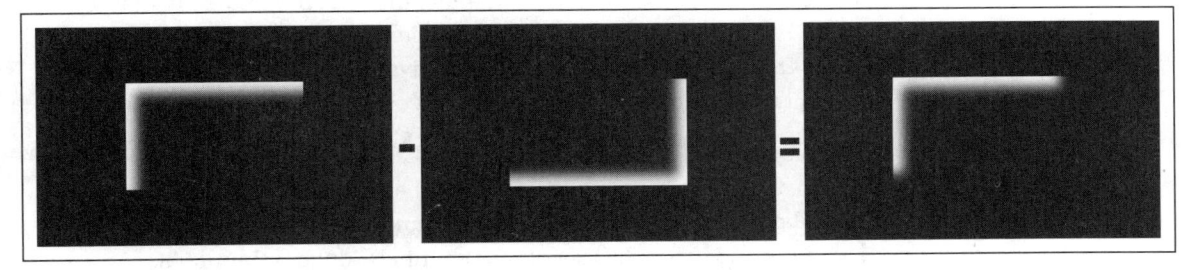

Figure 5.79 Subtract the lower-right selection from the upper-left selection to get a new selection with shortened legs.

Figure 5.80 Load the lower selection and fill with black. Load the upper selection and fill with white.

Figure 5.81 Contract the original channel by the width of the bevel. Use the selection to modify the channels used to make the bevels so that they have a hard inner edge. Fill in the same manner as used for Figure 5.80.

has contracted, fill the selection with black. Change to the lower-edge selection channel and fill with black again (the contracted selection is still active). When these two are loaded and filled with black and white, the result looks like Figure 5.81.

Embossed Letters Based On Channels

This lettering effect is every bit as simple as the drop shadow example to produce, except that there are more steps to follow. You will be generating six new channels, using the first four to generate the two final channels. The last two channels will be used with the Fill command to produce the effect. To make the process less confusing, we'll refer to the channels by number: Alpha 3, Alpha 4, and so on. Sometimes you will need to have one channel in view and load the selection of another. Sometimes you will subtract one channel from another to make another channel. The principles behind what we are going to do will be clear from a look back at the Subtraction Primer (in the previous section). If it helps, you can rename the channels so that they include the number and a description. For example, the channel created in Step 1 in the following example could be called Alpha 3 Original, Centered Letters. The channel created in Step 2 could be Alpha 4 Original Up & Left. Short descriptive names will help you to keep track of what each channel is and what it does for you in any of the listed steps.

Continue working on your copy of CHICAGO.PSD. You should choose File|Revert to go back to the original image. There are two channels already present in the document as well as the paths used to generate the original alpha channel. The two extra channels are Alpha 1 and Alpha 2. We'll leave those alone for now and generate a set of new channels Alpha 3 through 8.

> **NOTE:** *As you create new channels, your file size will grow rapidly. By the time you have created the 11th channel, your 15MB file will be almost 55MB. If disk space and RAM are considerations, you may want to change this image to a lower resolution. Choose Image|Image Size. You might consider changing from 300 ppi to 100 ppi. This change will make things easier as you go through the examples. Your file size decreases, and, when specific numerical values are given, you can calculate your own values as about one-third of those listed.*

Follow these instructions:

1. Create a new channel (Alpha 3). Click on the item in the Paths palette, and fill the paths with white (see Figure 5.82). Hide the paths; you won't need them again for this exercise.

2. Duplicate channel Alpha 3 (to create Alpha 4). Press V to select the Move tool. Set your Foreground/Background colors to white (F) and black (B). Move channel Alpha 3 up four pixels and to the left four pixels (use the Up and Left arrow keys). Now, duplicate channel Alpha 4 (to create Alpha 5). Return to Alpha 4 and choose Image|Adjust|Invert (see Figure 5.83).

3. Duplicate channel Alpha 3 (to create channel Alpha 6). With the Move tool selected, move channel Alpha 6 down four pixels and to the right four pixels (again, use the arrow keys). Use the Gaussian Blur filter—Radius value of 10—on channel Alpha 6 (see Figure 5.84).

Figure 5.82 Create a new channel (Alpha 3). Use the paths to fill the letter shapes with white. Hide the paths.

Figure 5.83 Channel Alpha 4 inverted after it has been moved up and to the left.

Figure 5.84 Channel Alpha 6 has been moved down and to the right, and has been blurred with a radius value of 10 pixels.

4. Load channel Alpha 6 as a selection. Subtract channel Alpha 4. Save the resulting selection as a new channel (Alpha 7). Deselect All. Click on channel Alpha 7's thumbnail to view it (see Figure 5.85).

5. Load channel Alpha 5 as a selection (with channel Alpha 7 in view). Choose the Gaussian Blur filter at a setting of 7 pixels. This will iron out the irregularities at the corners of the letter shapes (see Figure 5.86).

6. While the channel Alpha 5 selection is still active, duplicate channel Alpha 7 (to create Alpha 8). Click on Alpha 8's thumbnail to view it. Choose Image|Adjust|Invert (see Figure 5.87). Deselect All. Click on the top item in the Channels list to view the colored image.

7. Use the Eyedropper tool to select a tone from the image that has about a 50% brightness value. If you set your Info palette so that the left half gives readings in grayscale

Figure 5.85 Load channel Alpha 6, subtract channel Alpha 4, and save as a new channel (Alpha 7).

Figure 5.86 Load channel Alpha 5; with the selection active, use the Gaussian Blur filter (radius of 7) on channel Alpha 7.

Figure 5.87 With the channel Alpha 5 selection still active, duplicate channel Alpha 7 (to create Alpha 8). Click on the new channel to view it. Invert the contents of the selection.

while the right half gives readings in RGB, you'll be able to locate a color that is in the neighborhood of 50 percent black—*50 percent brightness*—despite its color. Load the selection of channel Alpha 8. Choose Edit|Fill. Fill with the Foreground color, Normal mode, 60% Opacity (see Figure 5.88).

8. Select a new Foreground color from the image with the Eyedropper tool. Make this tone's value equivalent to about 10% black. Load the selection of channel Alpha 8. Choose the Fill command again, using the same settings as before (see Figure 5.89).

9. Load channel Alpha 6. Subtract channel Alpha 5. The new selection gives the area of a drop shadow. Select a new tone from the image equivalent to about 80% black. Fill using the Foreground color, 60% Opacity, and Multiply mode (see Figure 5.90).

Figure 5.88 Load channel Alpha 8, fill with a 50% brightness tone set to Normal mode and 60% Opacity.

Figure 5.89 Load channel Alpha 8, fill with a 10% brightness tone set to Normal mode and 60% Opacity.

Other Channel Effects

The drop shadow and embossing effects you can achieve with channels are spectacular. Photoshop has many other attractive effects that may be less dramatic, but may prove to be more useful. Some of the following material is based on a selection of some object in the image. Another example will show you a remarkable edge-enhancement technique. You'll also see a couple of examples of how channels can help you with compositing images. All of these examples should give you a clear idea of how to approach using channels and a general idea of what can be done with them. You'll think of hundreds of uses of your own. In fact, eventually you'll wonder how you ever worked without them.

Glow Effects

Our reliable friend the sundial is back in service as an example (see Figure 5.91) in our discussion of glow effects, the easiest channel effect of all. In preparation for the glow, you must first detach the shape of the object from its background. In this case, you can use any of the Selection tools to

Figure 5.90 Load channel Alpha 6, subtract channel Alpha 5, fill with an 80% tone set to Multiply mode and 60% Opacity. The final file can be seen in the color section of this book.

Figure 5.91 The sundial photograph, the example file you can use for more channel effects.

outline the sundial shape. When you have the area selected, save the selection as a channel (see Figure 5.92). We'll call this channel the *base* alpha channel because so much else is built upon it, generated from it, or modified by it. (The word *base* has no special Photoshop significance. We're simply going to assign it as a name so that we'll have a handy way of referring to the channel from which we will build other channels.) Be sure to keep this channel untouched because you will need it for many purposes. As soon as you have the base channel saved, you may want to get into the habit of duplicating it and then inverting the duplicate. That way you'll have both the negative and positive of the base channel from which to work.

Figure 5.92 After selecting the shape of the sundial, the selection is saved as an alpha channel. Call this channel the base alpha channel because so much else is built upon it, generated from it, or modified by it.

Note that this book's companion CD-ROM contains, in the Chapter 5 Practice Files folder, the file SUNDIAL.PSD. The document already contains the base channel and two additional channels. If you would like to try out these examples as you read about them, open the file and follow the instructions.

The next step is to use the Gaussian Blur filter on a copy of the base channel. You can have a large influence on the glow by the Radius value you choose. Figure 5.93 shows the differences between 8, 16, 24, and 32 pixels (left side and across the top). These samples are deliberately spaced away from each other so that you can tell how far the blur spreads out from the original white edge.

After you have blurred the channel, you still have a large amount of control over it with the Levels. The two samples at the bottom of Figure 5.93, both of which have been subjected to a blur of 24 pixels radius, show the effects of moving the center Input slider—the gamma control, or midtone slider—an extreme distance. In the bottom center example, the slider was moved to the right to give a gamma reading of .25. This has the effect of contracting the blur by darkening the pixels outside the original shape's boundaries.

The bottom right example shows the effect of moving the midtone slider to the right to give a reading of 2.25. Moving the slider to the left has the opposite effect of moving it to the right. It reduces the width of the blur by lightening the portion inside the original boundaries. This will give you a blur on the outside of the shape, but a definite white edge on the inside.

Once you have the channel blurred, making the glow channel is easy. Load the blurred channel as a selection (hold down Command or Ctrl and click on the channel's thumbnail). Subtract the base channel from the active selection (hold down Command+Option or Ctrl+Alt and click on the base channel's thumbnail). Save the resulting selection as a new channel (click on the second icon from the left on the bottom of the Channels palette). The new channel is shown in Figure 5.94.

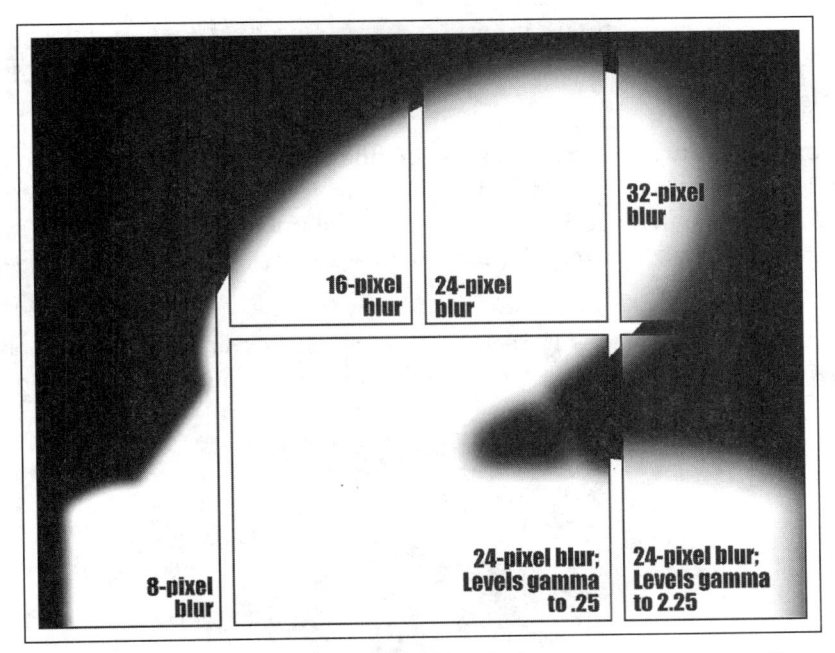

Figure 5.93 The size of the glow effect can be controlled by the amount of the Gaussian Blur applied. After blurring, additional modifications can be made by moving the center—gamma—slider in the Levels controls.

Figure 5.94 Load the blurred channel, subtract the base channel, and save the resulting selection as a new channel. This channel will be used to produce the glow effects.

Switch to the composite view of the image and load the new channel as a selection. You can use any of several methods while the selection is active. Moving the gamma slider in the Levels controls to the left lightens the selection. Moving it in the other direction darkens the selection. You can use the Fill command, which allows you to fill with a color and to control the opacity of the color application. Or—this method is the easiest—set your Foreground/Background colors to the defaults and press Delete. You'll see a pretty, slightly metaphysical addition to your image (see Figure 5.95). Or, you can fill with black to make the area of the glow dark instead of light (see Figure 5.96).

Another glow possibility is to keep, as a selection, the part of the blur *inside* the boundaries of the object. This gives an effect similar to the glow, but *on* the object instead of around it. Load the blurred channel to make it the active selection. Subtract from the selection, the inverted copy of the base channel. Save the selection as a new channel. Deselect. The channel is shown in Figure 5.97.

Click on the new channel to view it. Load the base channel as a selection, and choose Image| Adjust|Invert. This inverts only the part of the channel within the selection (see Figure 5.98).

Figure 5.95 With the glow channel active as a selection, set the Background color to white and press Delete.

Figure 5.96 The glow selection can be filled with a dark color to give this effect. (A fill with a lavender shade—try R 51, G 0, B 255—will make the image look radioactive.)

USING CHANNELS 347

Figure 5.97 When you subtract the inverted copy of the base channel from the blurred channel, you retain the portion of the blur inside the boundaries of the object.

Figure 5.98 Invert just the inner part of Figure 5.97 by loading the base channel and using the Invert command.

Load the new channel as a selection. You are again faced with many choices about what to do with your selection. Three possibilities are shown in Figure 5.99. The untouched original is in the upper left corner (*a*); it is included so that you can compare it with the others. The photo in *b* shows the selection filled with white, the one in *c* filled with black, and the photo in *d* filled with a black-to-white gradient drawn from the bottom of the pedestal to the top of the disk.

Masking With Gradients

If you stop and think about what a remarkable tool the channels concept is, you may reflect that, beyond the capability to add and subtract from selections, all the major tools involve manipulation of simple grayscale images with a blur tossed in for good measure. Such power from simple means!

Figure 5.99 The selection from the channel in Figure 5.98 can be treated in a number of ways. The photo in *a* is the original, *b* shows the selection filled with white, *c* uses a black fill, and *d* has the selection filled with a black-to-white gradient.

A Gaussian Blur, the way we've been using it in this chapter, is a more-or-less narrow, shaped, or contoured gradient. We have used it to ease transitions from one texture to another: As the white fades to black, the superimposed effects attenuate and disappear.

The Gradient tool can accomplish the same task, except that it can be used on a much larger scale. It can fade out entire images, modify texture applications over large areas, and even assist in the seamless merging of two disparate photos.

An alpha channel containing a gradient might be similar to that shown in Figure 5.100. An effect applied to a selection loaded from this channel would gradually disappear as it approached the bottom of the frame.

When the gradient is combined with another selection channel—for example, the channel shown in Figure 5.101—then you have the ability to moderate textures and commands around the object shape and to leave the object shape untouched. To make a channel similar to this one, begin with a duplicate of what we have referred to as the base channel (see Figure 5.92). Invert the channel. Load it as a selection, and draw a black-to-white gradient from bottom to top.

In Figure 5.102, you can see how such a channel might be used. We prepared the file with a series of horizontal paths, loaded the channel as a selection, chose a small paintbrush, and set it to stroking the paths (Normal mode, Foreground black, 100% Opacity). The lines, drawn directly on the image, seem to pass behind the sundial. Each line is slightly more transparent than the one above it. The texture fades smoothly into nothing at the bottom of the image.

Figure 5.100 An operation applied to an alpha channel that contains a gradient such as this would gradually disappear as it approached the bottom of the image.

Figure 5.101 This channel combines the object shape with the gradient. It allows you to control effects around the object while leaving the shape untouched.

Using gradients to fade effects is a very clever way to combine images so that they seem to merge imperceptibly into each other. To illustrate how this can work, look at Figure 5.103. With the channel active, a gradient drawn within this window appears only within the boundary of the selection. We will use this new channel to combine the sundial image with the marigolds photo shown in Figure 5.104.

With both windows open—and reduced in size so that you can see at least a part of both—make the channel in the sundial image an active selection. Now, drag the selection from the sundial window onto the marigolds. Be sure to hold the Shift key as you drag, to ensure that the selection centers itself in the destination window. A new layer will form, containing the sundial. If you look at the layer without the background visible, you'll see that the pixels are

Figure 5.102 With the combination channel loaded, a series of solid painted lines (stroked paths) fade smoothly into nothing at the bottom of the photo and do not intrude into the boundary of the sundial.

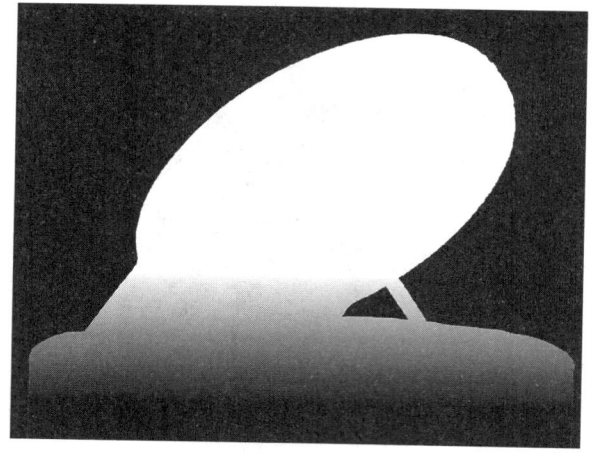

Figure 5.103 With the base channel active, the gradient can be drawn so that it shows only within the object.

opaque at the top and transparent at the bottom. When the sundial lies atop the other image, the lower portion fades into nothing. The effect is shown in Figure 5.105.

Here's another way to achieve a similar merge effect: First, make an alpha channel such as the one shown in Figure 5.106. Begin with the base channel, invert it, load the inverted channel as a selection, and draw the gradient. Move this channel to the marigolds photo. With the sundial as the active image—but with the marigolds window visible—drag this channel's thumbnail from the Channels palette onto the destination window. This will make the marigolds the active window. Click at the top of the Channels palette to return to the composite view. Load the new channel. Drag the selection from one window to the other (the marigolds to the sundial). This combines the images in the opposite direction as before—the marigolds added to the sundial photo. As you can see in Figure 5.107, the result is just as successful.

USING CHANNELS 351

Figure 5.104 Photo to be used for demonstrating the merging of two images.

Figure 5.105 With the channel active, the selected part of the sundial image is added to the marigolds. The effect of the gradient is shown by the way the sundial fades to invisibility at the bottom of the frame.

> **TIP**
>
> You can drag channels back and forth between documents of any size. However, if you want the images to align, make sure that the images have the identical pixel count (the number assigned to ppi does not matter).

Edge Enhancement With Find Edges

Our last example of channel effects is a technique for enhancing edges. This method isn't successful for every image, but it's useful often enough that it's worth a try. Follow these steps:

1. You'll need to begin with a duplicate of the sundial photo (Image|Duplicate).

Figure 5.106 This channel was made by inverting a copy of the base channel, loading the channel selection, and then drawing a black-to-white gradient from bottom to top.

Figure 5.107 With the new channel moved to the marigolds image and then made active, the selected part of the marigolds image is added to the sundial. The effect of the gradient is shown by the way the marigolds fade to invisibility at the bottom of the frame.

2. Change the mode of the sundial to Lab. Press Command+1 or Ctrl+1 to view the L channel. Convert the image to grayscale mode. A dialog box will ask if you wish to delete the other channels. Click on OK.

3. From the Filter menu, choose Stylize|Find Edges. When the filter has executed, your image will look similar to Figure 5.108.

4. Invert the image (Image|Adjust|Invert) (see Figure 5.109). Use the Gaussian Blur filter at a setting of 3 or 4 to eliminate some of the fine texture—which appears as a space-filling graininess in some areas of the photo—generated by the filter. Open the Levels controls. Move the Highlight slider on the input scale to the left, and the Shadow slider on the same scale to the right. Move one slider a small amount, then move the other.

Figure 5.108 A copy of the sundial photo, converted to grayscale, and to which the Find Edges filter has been applied.

Keep doing this until you achieve the effect you want. You are increasing the contrast between light and dark areas of the photo. The appearance of the photo, after you have moved the sliders, will be similar to Figure 5.110.

5. When the duplicate image looks as shown in Figure 5.110, transfer the Black channel back to the original photo. Do this by dragging the Black channel thumbnail from the Channels palette onto the RGB photo. Click at the top of the palette to view the composite color image.

6. Load the new channel as a selection. Open the Levels controls again. Move the center Input scale slider to the right. Watch the image as you move the slider. It's easy to go too far with this operation. All you want to do is make the selection a little darker.

Figure 5.109 After using the Find Edges filter, invert the image. Use the Gaussian Blur filter to eliminate some of the grainy texture.

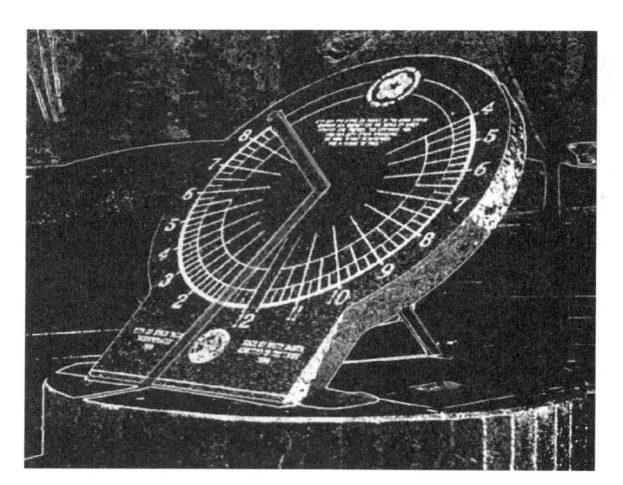

Figure 5.110 Use the Levels controls to increase the contrast between dark and light areas.

Figure 5.111 The right-hand side of this figure shows the result of the Levels adjustment made when the alpha channel in Figure 5.110 was active.

Figure 5.111 shows the difference between the original image (left) and the darkened selection (right). Notice how the details of the image have been hardened and made more clear without the appearance of too much sharpening. As you study this figure, look back to Figure 5.110. It will give you a clear idea of which parts of the image have been affected by darkening the selection with the Levels.

A Final Note

With the introduction of Adobe's PostScript Level 3, channels are likely to play an increasingly important role, particularly in the world of prepress. Channels as masks will supersede clipping paths as exportable masks. This is going to be enormously helpful because it will eliminate the hard edges of the clipping path and allow soft, transparent edges. Masking will be a much simpler task: As you have seen with this chapter, manipulating channels is much simpler than constructing Bezièr outlines. This kind of masking—and the other features of PostScript Level 3—will depend on the software implementation of publishers. When the day arrives that most of the major graphics software programs can make use of Level 3—wow!

Moving On

You have seen the power of channels used to express quite a number of concepts. Photoshop uses simple grayscale images to preserve selections, to express degrees of opacity, to modify the effects of a command, to be an analog for the strength of a video color component, to express the amount of ink in a color separation, and to show the luminance of each pixel as separate from its color. All of these concepts, and more, can be assigned to a document's channels. This flexibility means that all these concepts are subject to manipulation by using other Photoshop controls on the channels that constitute a photo image.

When you first encountered channels, the subject may have seemed so large that you found yourself a little intimidated. However, we hope that trying some of the examples shown in this chapter has reassured you that channels are not mysterious. They are simple, easily modified, and possess remarkable power to help you apply wonderful effects to your image.

With channels now under control, it's on to layers (Chapter 6). Layers, as you'll see, share many important concepts with channels. In fact, some aspects of layers—layer masks—will show themselves to be temporary channels that you can modify in the same ways you modified alpha channels. You'll find many points of similarity between channels and layers, and what you already know will make your acquaintance with layers much easier.

USING LAYERS

Adobe designed Layers into Photoshop as a way to save an artist's sanity. Because the Layers feature allows you to easily make changes in composited images, it's also responsible for the health and happiness of many art directors and clients who might otherwise have suffered bodily injury when they demanded last-minute changes.

Layers is the feature of Photoshop that can turn you into an imaging hero. All of those glorious, complex-appearing effects that you see in periodicals and on Web pages are sculpted—usually—with layers. You'll find, within minutes of using layers for the first time, that you can make subtle and intricate changes to your image, changes that suddenly transform your work from ordinary to amazing. Just try them: The things that you can do will give you a real rush!

After you become accustomed to using layers, you'll wonder how you got along without them. You'll come to appreciate the fact that, special effects aside, the real purpose of layers is to extend the editability of a Photoshop document. For example, in versions prior to Photoshop 3—the first version of the program to use layers—using the Type tool applied letter shapes to images. The shapes were selected and floating when they were created but, when deselected, they merged with the underlying image, replacing the pixels below them. If you needed to preserve the original pixels—those replaced by the type—you needed to duplicate your file and work on a copy. This could lead to a confusing proliferation of similar files—some of them large—at different stages of development. With version 4 of Photoshop and later, using the Type tool automatically assigns the letter shapes to a brand new layer. You may move the type, change its color, and perform many operations on it, all without touching the original image. You can even save your layered document, and at some future time, open it, delete the layers, and be left with an intact version of your original file. As an added benefit, in Photoshop 5, text is not only on its own layer, but it can also remain editable for as long as you want it to be so. Double-clicking on the Type layer icon reopens the Text dialog box so that you can change what you wanted to say.

You can add Layers to a Photoshop file with ease. In fact, you'll see in this chapter at least eight different methods—there are probably more—of adding a layer to a document. After the layer has been created, you'll find that any pixels on the layer can be placed into special relationships with the pixels on other layers. One relationship is that of linking, where moving the contents of one layer also moves the contents of a different layer. Another relationship might be to use the shape on one layer as a visibility boundary—or *mask*—for the pixels on a different layer (creating a clipping group). One of the most important relationships is brought into play when the pixels of one layer are placed in a Blend mode that changes their appearance and the pixels of all layers below them. All of these are simple relationships that you can put into effect and remove with great ease.

There are more subtle options for layers. If you wish, you may add a *layer mask* to any or all layers. With a layer mask, you have the opportunity of masking some of the pixels in a layer using techniques you already learned and mastered in Chapter 5. In fact, a layer mask is only a temporary channel whose masking effects can be applied to the layer or shut off whenever you wish. Another feature—one you will really enjoy after you see it in action—is the capability to exclude some pixels from visibility simply by referencing their brightness or their color, or by referencing the brightness or color of pixels beneath them. This feature of Photoshop is not extensively used because it appears to be difficult. You'll find that it's actually not difficult at all, and that it will prove to be a tool you'll use in many different situations.

When we've examined all of the features available to you, you will find that some of the valuable aspects of layers are not listed here as strictly technical possibilities. Instead, they will be things that you discover for yourself, novel ways of using layers to assist the way you work. With a little planning, you can set up a layer as a test for a series of actions: Make a duplicate of a layer, perform whatever manipulations you wish on it, and evaluate whether you have achieved what you intended. If you did, you can keep the layer and delete the one from which it was duplicated. Otherwise, delete the experimental layer, and you are back where you started. Or, use the new layer and blend it back with the original sequence. Or, selectively revert to a prior stage using the History palette. Or... the possibilities are endless.

Layered Documents And The Layers Palette

The layer metaphor is based on those transparent film overlays used with that Dark Ages artifact, the *artboard*. Imagine, if you will, an image that has been fixed to board stock. Next, a colored logo is attached to a piece of acetate or clearbase film. The film is placed atop the image, the logo is positioned with respect to the background image, and the top of the film taped to the board. This film layer is called a *flap*. There may be several flaps. Some might contain type, other artwork, inset pictures, and so on. Each of the components is attached to a separate clear sheet and superimposed upon each other to build up a composite layout. If you are young enough to remember prepress procedures involving artboards, then you already understand how Photoshop's layers work. But here the similarity ends: Digital layers can do some wild things!

Photoshop's Layer Flaps

Figure 6.1 shows a layered document. The Layers palette at the lower right shows distinctive thumbnails that give you an excellent idea of what each layer contains and how the separate pieces are stacked up to produce the composite image.

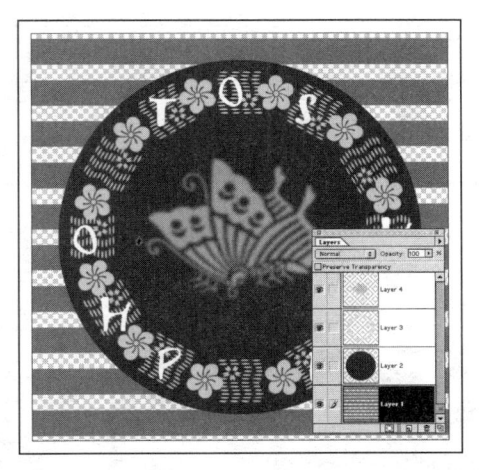

Figure 6.1 A layered Photoshop document with the Layers palette thumbnails showing each layer's content.

Each layer can be completely filled with pixels. More often, a layer contains pixels in well-defined areas. Surrounding these pixels is an area of nothing, or more accurately, completely transparent pixels. You can see this more clearly in the exploded view of the document shown in Figure 6.2. This figure also shows Photoshop's method for indicating transparency. When there is no *Background* (discussed below), layer transparency is shown as a gray-white checkerboard pattern.

> **TIP**
> The size of the checkerboard squares denoting transparency is a matter of choice. You can make changes by choosing File|Preferences|Transparency and Gamut.

The Layers Palette

The principal tools for editing the layers are found on the Layers palette (an expanded view of this palette is shown in Figure 6.3) and under the Layers menu (which we discuss later in this chapter). With this palette and the menu combinations, you have the ability to create new layers and perform a wide variety of manipulations on a single layer or on groups of layers. In this section, we will examine the possibilities of the Layers palette, beginning with the Blend modes pop-up menu.

Blend Modes

The pop-up menu in the upper left corner of the palette changes the Blend mode of a layer's pixels. Blend modes are wonderfully interesting and useful. With them, you can appear to combine the pixels on one layer with the pixels below that layer. The change in the appearance of the affected pixels is brought about by calculations on values associated with the pixels. The calculations might be based on the RGB values of the pixels, or they might be based on the

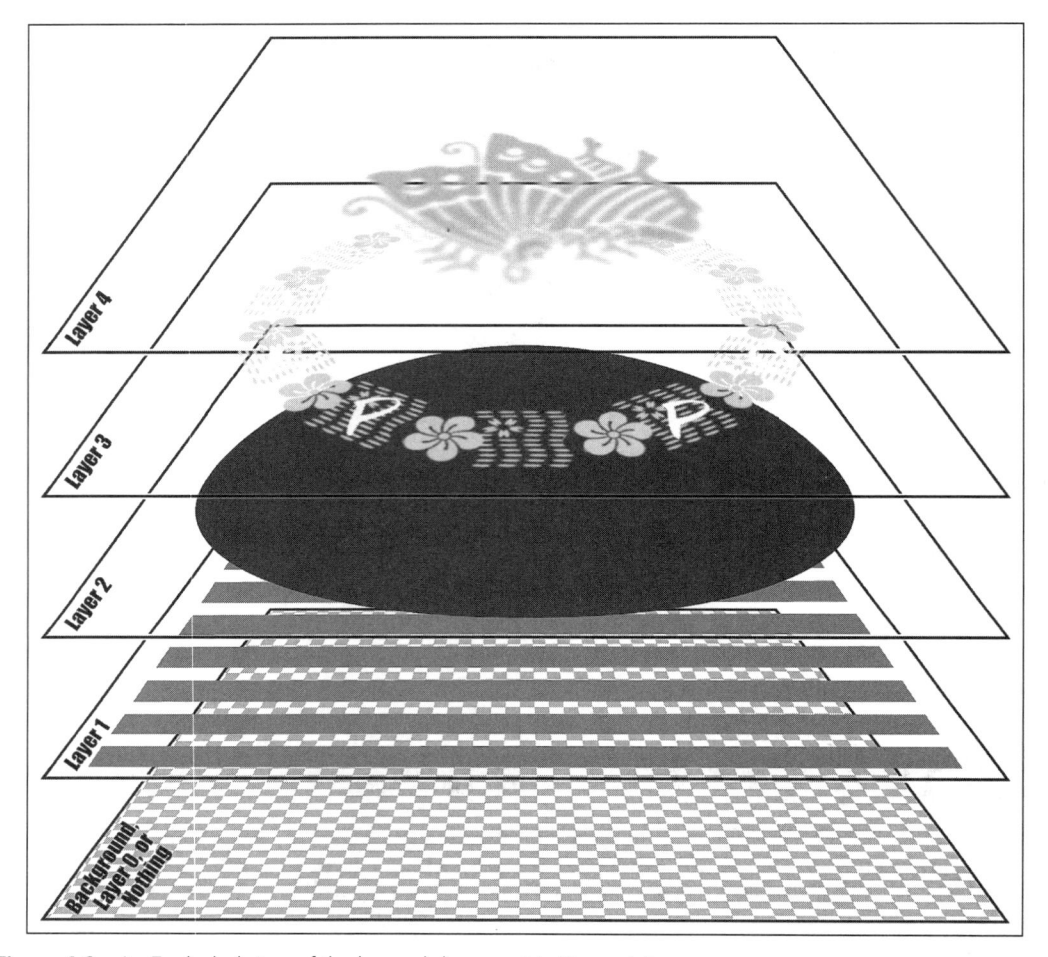

Figure 6.2 An Exploded view of the layered document in Figure 6.1.

brightness or the hue or the transparency of the pixels. There are quite a few possibilities, and the Blend modes can give you some amazing results.

The workings of the Blend modes are often misunderstood despite the fact that they are fairly straightforward. The difficulty lies with the terminology. The Photoshop user's manual employs the terms *base color*, *blend color*, and *result color*. These terms work as well as any others, if we make their definitions easy to understand. In Figure 6.4, you can see representations of greatly enlarged pixels. Consider the left-hand and center pixels: One is white and one is black. Imagine, if you will, that the black pixel is on the layer on which the Blend mode is to operate. This pixel would represent the *blend color*. The white pixel is on a layer behind/below the black pixel. The white pixel will be affected by the Blend mode change that occurs on the layer above it. It is, then, part of the calculation and is called the *base color*. When the Blend mode changes, the result is a pixel that is usually different from those on which the calculations are based.

USING LAYERS 361

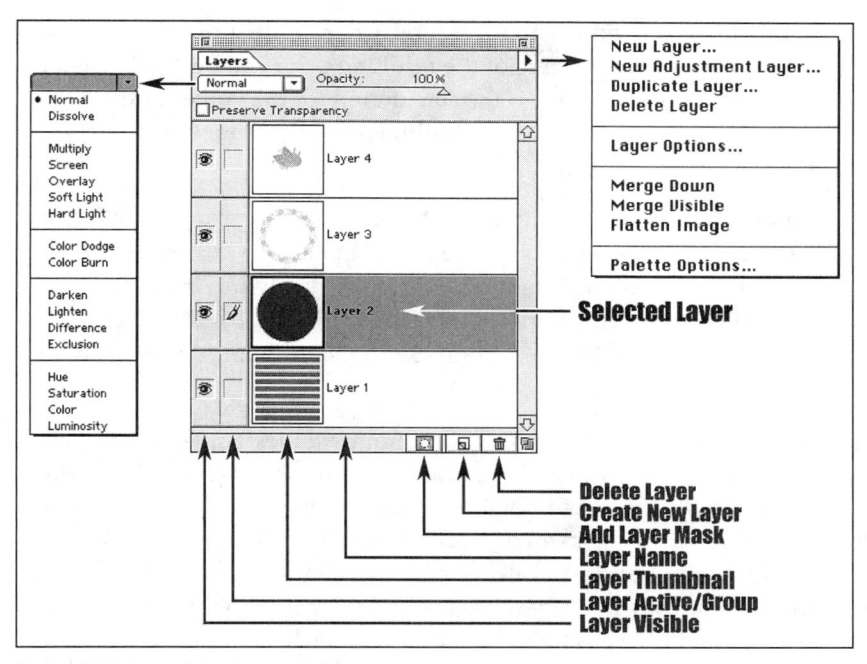

Figure 6.3 Expanded view of the Layers palette.

This pixel (on the right side of the figure) is the *result color*. It is the color you see when you have applied a Blend mode to one of the layers.

The calculations that deliver the result color can be fairly interesting if you have a liking for mathematics. The Multiply mode on two RGB pixels, for example, is based on the multiplication of brightness values for each of the three color channels—red × red, green × green, and blue × blue. The formula is: (base color × blend color)/255 = result color. (Note that after multiplying the two values, the result is brought back into range by dividing by 255. If this were not done, the multiplication would often deliver values higher than 255. Values higher than 255 are impossible.) If we take two pixels at random—r102, g204, b204 (a light turquoise color) and r255, g51, b102 (a bright salmon pink)—and apply the formula, we get a result of r102, g41, b82 (a dusty purple tone). Try it and you'll see. Make a small window, fill it with the first

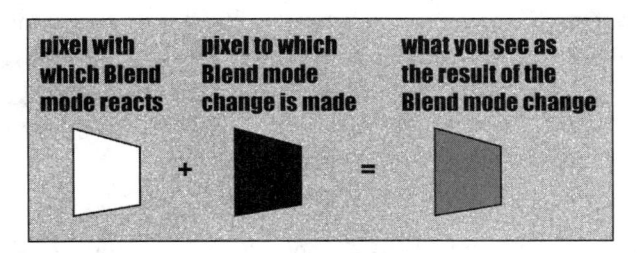

Figure 6.4 Two pixels put into a Blend mode relationship often show a resulting color that differs from either of the contributing pixels.

color, make a new layer, and fill it with the second. Change the second layer's mode to Multiply and flatten the image. The RGB value of the resulting color will be as it's listed here. Or try it with a calculator. Here, for example, is the calculation for the values in the two red channels: 102 × 255 = 26,101; 26,101 / 255 = 102. (Multiplying anything with white—which is value 255—results in the opposite color.)

All of the Blend modes work in a similar way. Screen mode, for example, uses this formula for the RGB values: 255 − ((255 − base color) × (255 − blend color)) /255 = result color. As you can see, each of the calculation colors is subtracted from 255 to give an inverse value. These inverse values are multiplied together, the resulting color is divided by 255 to bring the result into range, and that number is subtracted from 255 to give the final inverse value. This makes Screen mode the inverse calculation of Multiply.

Not all of the calculations used are based on brightness values. Some calculations are based on a pixel's opacity, others on its hue. Some use combinations of these. All of the calculations produce results. However, those results will vary from *no apparent change* to *wow! What a change!* What you'll see as the result color will depend on the values and positions of the pixels affected by the blend. With Multiply, Screen, Difference, and Exclusion, for example, it makes no difference which pixel is uppermost. The result color is the same. With other Blend modes, the result color depends on the relative positions—*below* the layer where the Blend mode is operating, or *on* the layer. Fortunately, there are only 16 possibilities besides Normal. (Note: One other Blend mode exists that does not appear on the Layers palette pop-up menu, but is available as a Paint tool option. We will discuss this one later in this chapter.) With so few possibilities, it's fairly easy to try them all: Simply choose the Blend modes, one at a time, from the pop-up menu on the Layers palette.

Normal

Normal mode is what you would have if there were no Blend modes. It is the vanilla mode where pixels on a layer simply hide any pixels behind them. You might also call this the *real world* mode. The only way a layer in Normal mode can influence the pixels of layers below it is to change the layer's Opacity to less than 100%. This strategy gives a new result color, but it is a color achieved by a method other than the calculations employed by the Blend modes.

Figure 6.5 shows the four-layer document used in Figure 6.1 with all of the layers in Normal mode and at 100% Opacity. In the figures that illustrate the other Blend modes, the same document will be used with blends applied to Layer #2, a circular shape containing a gradient with shades from blue at the bottom to magenta at the top. This shape overlays a set of rectangular bars in a pink tone approximately equivalent to PANTONE 674 CV. The figures accompanying these explanations of the Blend modes are in black and white. You can play with this file yourself because it is included on the accompanying CD-ROM.

Dissolve

Dissolve, when used on pixels that are 100% opaque, produces no effect. When the opacity is less than 100%, the Dissolve mode begins to show. All of the visible pixels on the Dissolve mode layer show at 100% Opacity in the original color. However, some of the pixels on the

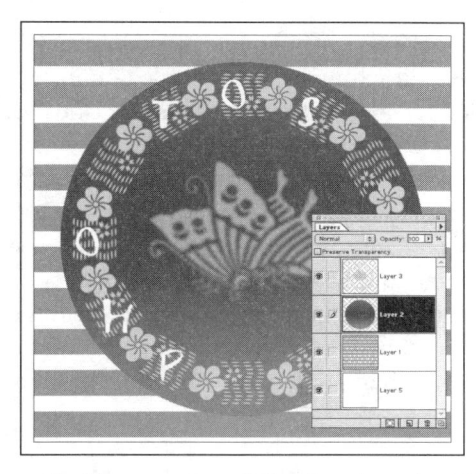

Figure 6.5 A layered document with all layers in Normal Blend mode and at 100% Opacity.

layer disappear in a random pattern. The number of pixels that vanish is equal to the reciprocal of the percentage of Opacity. Let me put it another way. If you have a layer containing an area of solid color and change its Opacity to some number such as 70%, putting the layer into Dissolve mode will make 30 percent (the reciprocal of the Opacity number) of the pixels vanish—in a scattered, random fashion—while all the remaining pixels are changed back to 100% Opacity.

Dissolve mode is a brute force way of creating a transparency effect. It differs from a normal change in Opacity in that pixels are either present or not. The effect is particularly useful when it is applied to shapes with feathered edges. The gritty effect of the mode is attractive when added to textures. Figure 6.6 shows the Dissolve effect applied to Layer 2 (which has first been changed to 60% Opacity). In Figure 6.7, a gradient—Foreground to Transparent—has been applied to the letter outline border, and then the mode of the layer changed to Dissolve.

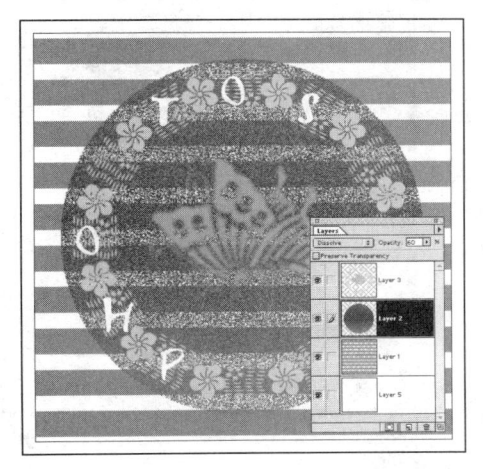

Figure 6.6 Dissolve mode applied to Layer 2 after the layer has been changed to 60% Opacity.

Figure 6.7 A gradient—Foreground to Transparent—has been applied to letter outlines, and then the layer changed to Dissolve mode.

Multiply

Multiply mode was used as an example of how calculations can work in the preliminary, preceding discussion of Blend modes. The effect of this mode has been compared to placing two transparencies, one atop the other, on a light table. The result is a set of tones that are darker than either of the originals. When used with the painting tools, strokes placed over other strokes create increasingly dark tones. Multiply is wonderful—especially when you experiment with changing the Opacity—for producing realistic drop shadows. The example in Figure 6.8 shows how the circular shape seems to take on the appearance of a shadow cast onto the shapes beneath it. Figure 6.9 uses the effect in a more deliberate manner to show how the shadow seems to soak into the texture on which it is cast. Note that multiplying any color with black produces black, whereas multiplying any color with white produces no change in tone.

Screen

Screen, as we mentioned previously, is the inverse of Multiply. Just as Multiply always produces a tone that is darker than any of the pixels used in the calculation, Screen produces tones that are lighter. (Note that screening any color with black produces no change in tone, while screening any color with white produces white.) Screen has been compared to painting over colored areas with bleach. The effect is shown in Figure 6.10. The dark circular shape has lightened the rectangles only a little because of its relative darkness of tone. The lightening would be more pronounced with lighter colors on the blend layer. This is more visible in Figure 6.11, where blurred duplicates of the letters have been filled with a 30% black and set to Screen mode. The halo/glow effect is a striking inverse of a drop shadow.

Overlay

Overlay mode is cool. Whenever you are just messing around and experimenting with Blend modes, this one, as likely as not, will give you an effect that you'll enjoy. It may not be what you're looking for, but it will be attractive and interesting.

Figure 6.8 Multiply mode applied to Layer 2. Note how this mode lends itself to shadow effects—the circular shape seems to become a shadow cast onto the rectangles beneath it.

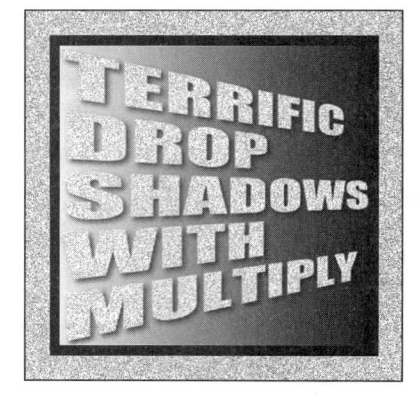

Figure 6.9 Here is Multiply mode, showing how the shadow seems to merge with the underlying texture and color. You create the letter shadows by duplicating the letters layer, filling them with black, blurring them, changing to Multiply mode, and placing the blurred duplicate layer below the original layer.

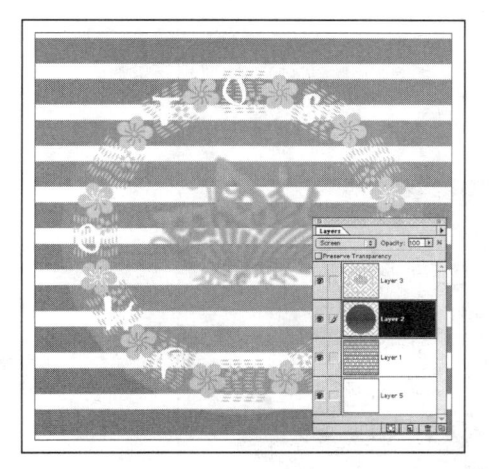

Figure 6.10 Layer 2 in Screen mode lightens Layer 1 only a small amount. The lightening effect would be greater if the circular shape were in a lighter tone.

Figure 6.11 When duplicates of the letters are blurred, placed below the letters, and then filled with a light tone, Screen mode makes a very nice glow effect.

Overlay does its magic by multiplying or screening, depending on the values of the base colors. If the base colors are light, Overlay screens. If they are dark, Overlay multiplies. The result is a mix of the base and blend colors that preserves the highlights, shadows, and details of both base pixels and blend pixels. In Figure 6.12, the circular shape on Layer 2 is still faintly visible wherever it crosses the rectangles. Where the shape has crossed the light background, the pixels have disappeared. A more common way of using Overlay is shown in Figure 6.13. The relief shapes at the top (*a*) are covered by a dark stone texture layer (*b*). When the stone texture layer is changed to Overlay mode, it seems to map onto the relief shapes. Notice that the texture disappears wherever it is above the light background. This is, to use the technical term, Pure Magic.

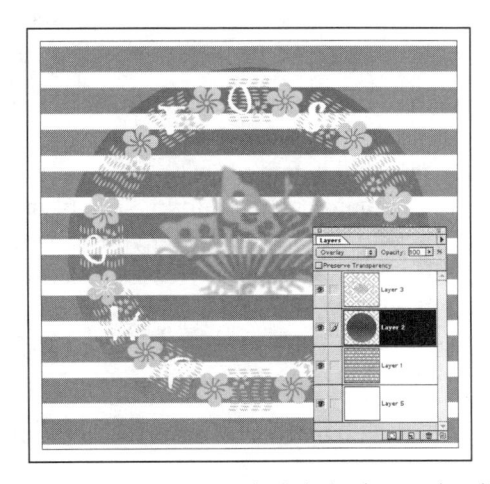

Figure 6.12 Layer 2 in Overlay mode disappears over the light background and leaves a faint circle wherever it passes over the rectangles.

Figure 6.13 A stone texture (b) is placed on a layer above the relief shapes in (a). When the texture is changed to Overlay, the texture seems to be mapped onto the shapes. The texture disappears over the white background.

Soft Light

The Adobe Photoshop user's manual describes the effect of Soft Light as "similar to shining a diffused spotlight on the image." This description is helpful only if you think of the blend pixels as the source of a variable, low-intensity light shining down on the base layer pixels. Wherever the blend pixels are 50 percent gray or lighter, the light shines, its strength proportional to the lightness of the pixels. This makes the base pixels lighter. Wherever the blend pixels are darker than 50 percent gray, the base pixels are slightly darkened. The effect is as though the darker pixels form translucent shapes that are interposed between the low-intensity light and the surface on which the light is thrown, seeming to form faint shadows. The darkness of the shadows is proportional to the darkness of the blend pixels. The effect is mysterious and beautiful. In simple terms, the layer underneath the active layer shows through more strongly when you're using this mode.

Figure 6.14 shows the effect slightly in the way the brightness of the blend in the circular shape at the bottom makes it seem to disappear. A shadow toward the top increases as the blend becomes darker. Figure 6.15 depicts a better use of Soft Light. On the left, a multitoned floral pattern is superimposed on a textured background in Normal mode. On the right, the same pattern lies atop the texture in Soft Light mode, making the pattern fuse with the background. Note the faint lightening of the flowers. On the left, they are about 38 percent gray, which casts a light on the background to produce a tone of 8 to 12 percent (contrasting with the 20 percent background gray).

Hard Light

This Blend mode is similar to Soft Light in the way the pixels of the blend layer can be considered as the light source shining on the pixels of the base layer. The difference is in the intensity of the light. Hard Light, as the name implies, seems to generate a more intense light. This makes the

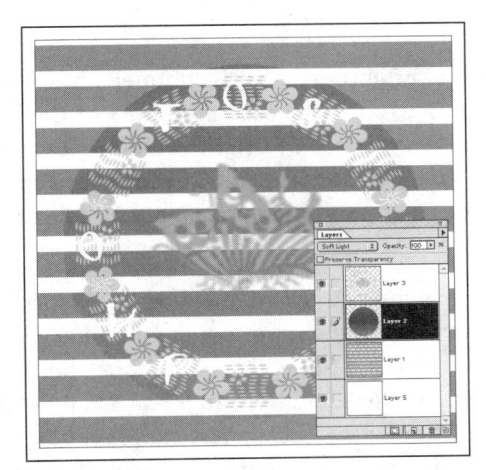

Figure 6.14 The Soft Light mode makes the circle disappear along the lower position and seem to cast a faint shadow along the top. This is due to the change in brightness within the gradient that fills the circle.

Figure 6.15 The floral pattern in Normal mode on the left merges mysteriously with the background when it's placed in Soft Light mode (right).

emanation from light pixels brighter and the shadows correspondingly darker. In Hard Light mode, the top layer is the dominant one. Hard Light mode is excellent for adding texture to an image. Emboss your texture and place it in Hard Light mode on top of the image to be textured.

Hard Light mode makes the circle on Layer 2 in Figure 6.16 much more visible—the shadow it casts is darker. The right side of Figure 6.17 shows how much more intense the effect is when compared to the right side of Figure 6.15. You can think of Hard Light as the inverse of the Overlay mode.

Figure 6.16 Hard Light mode makes the circle on Layer 2 appear as a darker shadow because it apparently increases the intensity of the light emanating from the layer.

Figure 6.17 With Hard Light, light pixels make brighter composite values, and dark pixels make darker values. Compare this figure with its low-intensity cousin—Soft Light—in Figure 6.15.

Color Dodge

The pixels of the blend layer possess some amount of brightness in each channel. This brightness factor acts as a variable-intensity color/brightness intensifier for the pixels of the base layer. This is not a simple, linear comparison: The effect caused by bright values on the blend layer is greater than for dark values. The overall effect is that of a charged-up Screen mode. When black is used for the blend, there is no change on the base layer. White produces the greatest amount of change.

Figure 6.18 shows the rectangles of the lower layer lightened by the blend of the circle. The lightening is greater at the bottom of the circle, where the gradient component is lighter. Figure 6.19 illustrates the effect more successfully. A set of gradient-filled circular shapes has been placed on a black-to-white gradient. They are shown on the left in Normal mode. On the right, the brightness values produce ever-larger areas of white as the back gradient becomes lighter. Note that the lines passing through the circles are slanted because of the progressive lightening of the back layer, while the gradient within the circular shapes remains constant. You can achieve many bizarre topological effects by playing two or more gradients against each other using different Blend modes.

Color Burn

Color Burn is the inverse of Color Dodge. The same brightness values of the blend layer are used in the calculation, but the base layer is darkened instead of lightened. The darkening is always more severe than it is for the other darkening mode, Multiply. As you might expect, blends involving white on the base layer produce no change, whereas white blends with black on the base layer produce the greatest change.

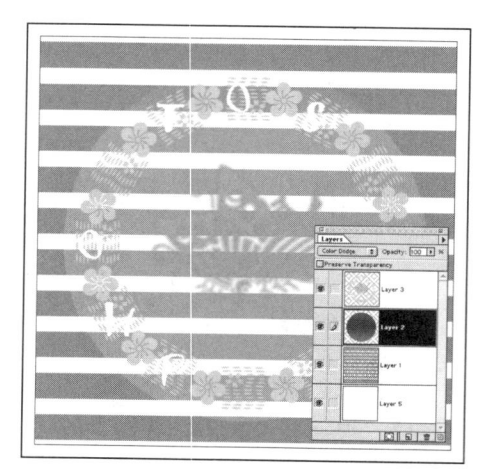

Figure 6.18 Color Dodge lightens the rectangles according to the lightness of the pixels in the blend layer.

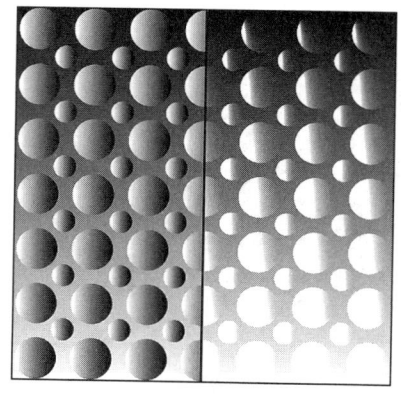

Figure 6.19 The lightening effect is clearly visible as gradient-filled circles are placed against a black-to-white gradient running in the opposite direction. The mode is Normal on the left and Color Dodge on the right. See the accompanying text for an explanation of the slanted lines within the circles.

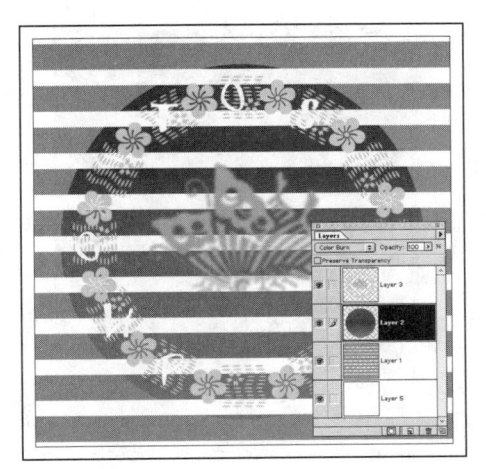

Figure 6.20 Color Burn has caused the Layer 2 circle to drastically darken the bar shapes over which it passes. Note that the circle disappears as it passes over the white areas between the bars.

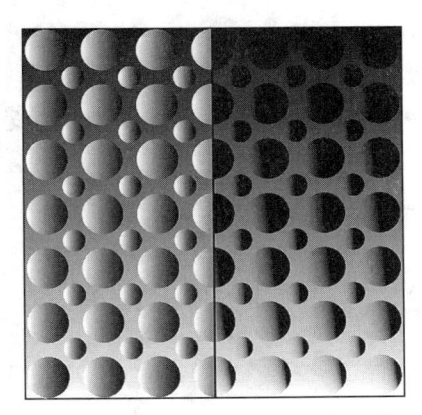

Figure 6.21 In this figure, you see on the right the inverse effect of that shown in Figure 6.19.

In Figure 6.20, the rectangular bars have been darkened more than any other Blend mode could have accomplished. The circle has disappeared from the spaces between the bars. In Figure 6.21, the same gradient-filled shapes have produced, on the right, the inverse of the effect shown in Figure 6.19.

Darken

The effect of Darken used in grayscale is easy to predict. Pixels on the blend layer that are lighter than pixels on the base layer become invisible, whereas pixels that are darker than the pixels of the base layer are not changed. See? Easy. However, when Darken is used with colored images, this Blend mode is a tricky customer. The same principles used for grayscale apply, but the rules evaluate the brightness of the values in all of the channels. For example, if the red value of the base layer of an RGB document is darker than the red value of the blend layer, it is retained, while that of the other pixel disappears. The same procedure is used for the other two channels. The result color is a composite of the values for both calculation layers—the darkest red, the darkest green, and the darkest blue for any equivalent pixels.

The example in Figure 6.22 doesn't show a significant change at the top of the Layer 2 circle, but the result of the Darken mode is quite noticeable at the bottom. Figure 6.23 shows more clearly how the darker values are retained. On the left, the geometric pattern positioned over a dark-to-light gradient is in Normal mode. On the right, Darken mode has the most pronounced effect on the light zigzag lines, which become more visible as they approach the light end of the gradient on the base layer.

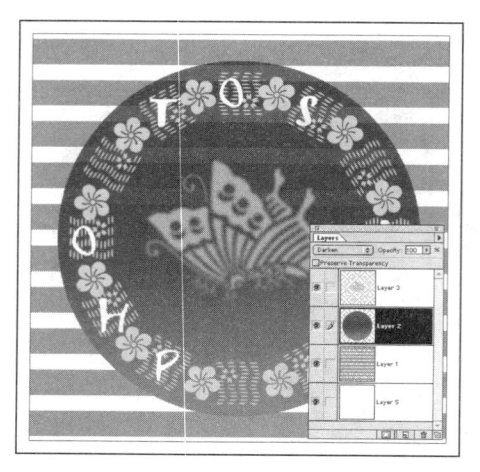

Figure 6.22 Darken mode, applied to the Layer 2 circle, affects the appearance of the image mostly at the bottom of the circle where the bars are darker than the tone of the gradient.

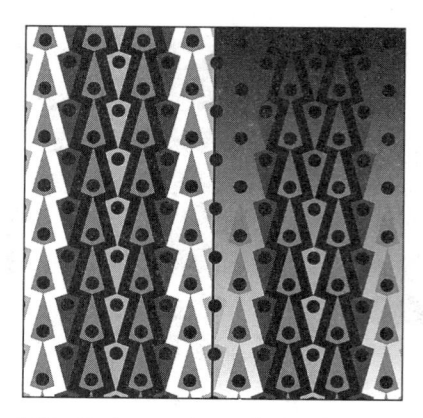

Figure 6.23 Darken mode applied to the geometric pattern—where the background is a black-to-white gradient—on the right has its most pronounced effect on the zigzag white stripes. The stripes gradually reappear as they approach the light end of the gradient.

Lighten

Lighten mode, as you will not be surprised to discover, is the inverse of Darken. (Don't you just love it when you can spend time learning one thing and then get the second one free?) The result values are based on the lightness of the pixels in each layer. The calculation is based on the lightness factor of each pixel in each of the document's channels.

Figure 6.24 shows the circle as having mostly disappeared except at the bottom, where its brightness was less than that of the horizontal bars. Figure 6.25, in contrast with Figure 6.23,

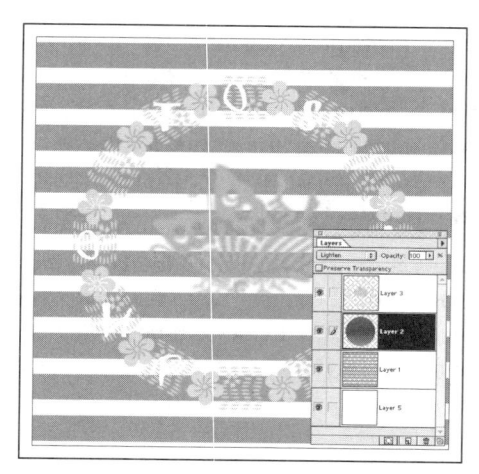

Figure 6.24 Lighten mode, applied to the Layer 2 circle, again affects the appearance of the image mostly at the bottom of the circle where the bars are lighter than the tone of the gradient.

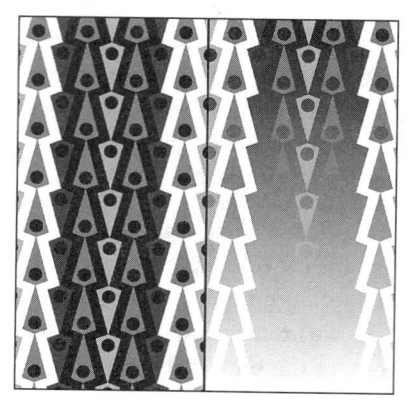

Figure 6.25 Lighten mode applied to the geometric pattern on the right has its most pronounced effect on the zigzag black stripes. The stripes gradually reappear as they approach the dark upper end of the gradient.

shows the least effect on the light lines and the most effect on the dark lines. The black lines gradually reappear as they approach the dark end of the gradient.

Difference

You have to watch out for Difference mode—at least you do if you get a bang out of really novel effects. The effect of Difference mode on any two layers is often novel, sometimes bizarre, but almost always interesting. It hardly ever creates an unattractive effect. The trouble is this: The people for whom you are doing Photoshop work often have bland, inferior taste and possess no sense of adventure. When you present your extremely cool Difference composites to them, they react with an utter lack of vision or imagination. You've probably noticed this phenomenon for yourself. Sigh.

Difference causes the pixels of the base layer to appear inverted according to the brightness values—calculated in each channel—of the blend layer. The mechanism is really simple: One pixel's values are subtracted from the equivalent pixel's values. The subtraction is always based on whichever value in any channel is greater. If you had two pixels with values of r100, g150, b200 (a light blue) and r125, g100, b50 (a medium tan), your result pixel would be r25, g50, b150 (a very nice medium blue). The calculations are as follows: 125 – 100 = 25; 150 – 100 = 50; and 200 – 50 = 150. Another way to state the Difference calculation is that the result values are the absolute values of the difference between any two pixels' channel components.

Figure 6.26 as a grayscale figure doesn't show up the really wonderful color changes brought about by the Difference calculation, but you can see this figure in color in the Color Studio of this book. The Difference effect is more obvious in Figure 6.27. If you study the two zigzag white lines to the right of the center line, you can see how white against the dark gradient at the top produces light tones, whereas at the bottom, white against white produces dark tones. If you

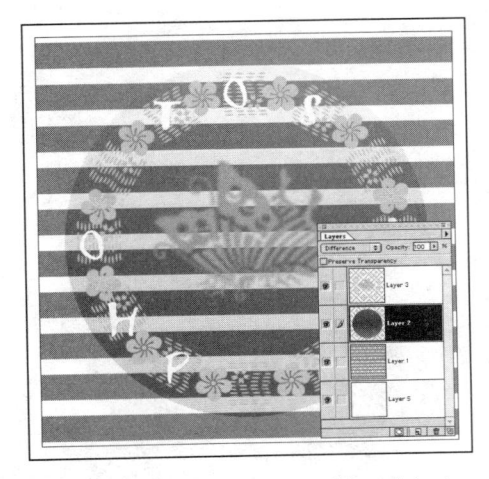

Figure 6.26 This grayscale figure, although it gives an idea of the Difference calculation, does not show the pleasant color tones produced. This figure appears in color in this book's Color Studio.

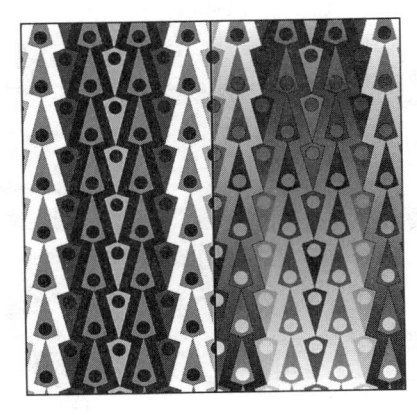

Figure 6.27 To understand this example of the Difference mode, study the two zigzag white lines just to the right of the center line. White against the dark gradient at the top has produced light tones, whereas at the bottom, white against white has produced dark tones. Subtracting a color from itself always produces black.

think about this, you'll realize that it makes sense: Whenever you subtract a color from itself, your result color will be zero (0). In Photoshop terms, zero is as dark as it gets.

> **TIP**
>
> If you like adventure, take an image and duplicate it to a new layer. Apply a filter—such as Unsharp Mask—that makes only a small change in the image. Change the Blend mode to Difference. The image will be quite dark, because only some pixels changed. Duplicate the image, flattened, into a new image and apply the Auto Levels command. You will get a brightly colored image on a dark background that can be extremely attractive. We call this technique "Difference Painting."

Exclusion

The Exclusion mode is most easily understood as a variation of the Difference mode. Perhaps it would be more accurate to say this: To get an idea of how Exclusion acts, you can compare it to Difference. Understand? We don't think so. We're not sure that anyone outside of Adobe's programming staff actually understands it. Whatever. This Blend mode subtracts the way Difference does when the values are fairly far apart. But the closer the values come to each other, the less they seem to interact. In fact, midrange tones blended with midrange tones form more midrange tones. The net effect is a diffuse version of Difference.

Figure 6.28 shows the gradient of the circular layer blending with the background layer bars with more visible changes at the top—where the brightness values are farther apart—than at the bottom where they are closer together. The largest change that you'll see in Figure 6.29 (compared to Figure 6.27) is in the center of the right side. As the midrange tones of the blend layer lie atop midrange tones of the base layer, the colors nearly cancel each other out to produce a uniform tone.

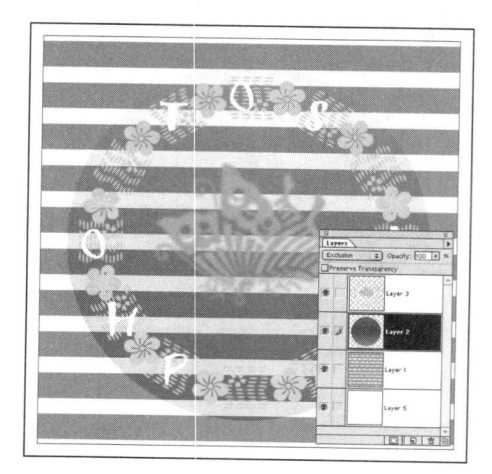

Figure 6.28 This grayscale figure, although it gives an idea of the Exclusion calculation, also does not show the color tones produced. This figure appears in the Color Studio of this book.

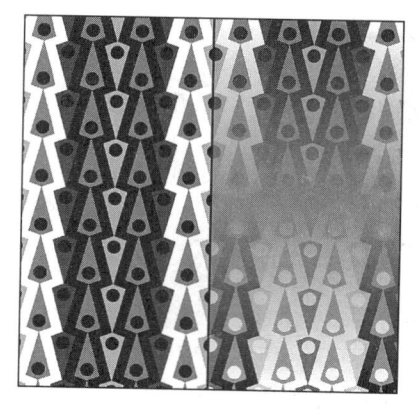

Figure 6.29 Compare this figure with Figure 6.27. The center part of the right section shows the muting effect caused by blending midrange tones with midrange tones.

A Note On HSL

You use the last four Blend modes only when the document is in one of the color modes—RGB, CMYK, or Lab. These four Blend modes make use of calculations based on values derived from one of Photoshop's color models, HSL (Hue, Saturation, Lightness). If you're unsure about those color terms, familiarize yourself with them by using the Image|Adjust|Hue/Saturation dialog box. The three sliders of this box allow you to adjust the HSL components of an image as separate entities.

The *Hue* of a pixel is, literally, its color. If you use any term to describe a color—for example, blue, red, or green—you are describing the hue.

The *Saturation* of the color is a description of how much *gray tone* is mixed with the hue. In this context, the term gray tone indicates one of the possible gray values that can range from solid black to total white. If you wish, imagine mixing a can of blue house paint with two cans of white to achieve a modified hue, lighter blue. This is the concept embodied by the term Saturation. Saturation is put into words that describe modified primary colors, words such as pink, baby blue, dusty rose. These are words that describe a change in the saturation from the reds or blues on which they are based.

The *Lightness* of a color is governed by the amount of black it contains. Carry the paint analogy one more step, for a moment. Imagine that you must darken the dark blue paint instead of adding white. How would you accomplish that? The simple answer is that you would add black. The house paint analogy begins to break down at this point because adding black could also be considered a modification of a color's saturation. In computer terms, however, that's exactly what happens. Terms like midnight blue and dark brown describe colors that have had their lightness component modified.

These three terms are important to understand. In other chapters in this book, you will adjust the color of images by using the Hue/Saturation dialog box. Intelligent use of this adjustment depends on your clear understanding of color having, in this model, three components. Where Blend modes are concerned, you will find that calculations of the blends are made with one or more of the HSL values. For this reason, the last four Blend modes are grayed out when your document is in grayscale.

Hue

The result color of the Hue mode depends on the hue of the blend layer pixels that are composited with the luminance and saturation of the base layer pixels. The effect is most noticeable when the values of the two layers are substantially different.

Figure 6.30 shows a composite effect that essentially erases the circle on Layer 2 where it crosses the light areas between the bars. As you'll see when looking at the color version of this figure, the blend color is an attractive composite of the two tones. In Figure 6.31, the geometric shapes have been filled with a light to dark gradient (Normal mode on the left, Blend mode on the right). The composite effect is a blend that seems to tattoo the layer shapes onto the radial blend of the background.

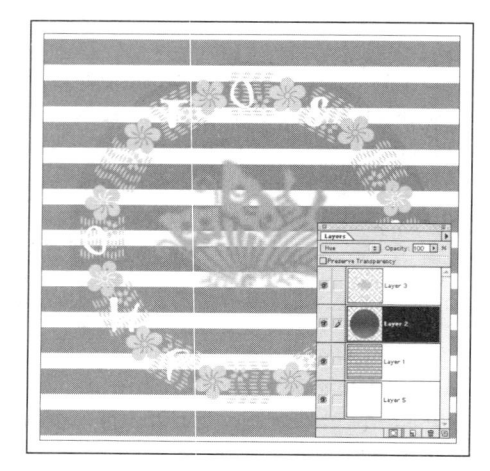

Figure 6.30 The Hue mode composite erases the Layer 2 circle where it passes over the light background. As the color example in the Color Studio section of this book shows, the composite of the circle and the bars produces a pleasant merging of the color tones.

Figure 6.31 The geometric shapes, filled with a light to dark gradient, seem to be tattooed onto the background when they're placed in Hue mode.

Saturation

The calculation method for Saturation combines the luminance and hue of the base layer pixels with the saturation of the blend layer pixels. This mode, frankly, doesn't do very much, that's interesting. However, it's always worth a try when you are cycling through the possibilities of the Blend mode menu. Occasionally it will produce a result that's exactly what you are looking to achieve.

Figure 6.32 is similar to 6.30 in that the circle disappears wherever it crosses the white background. The merge colors—unseen in this figure but visible on the color image—are simply an intensified version of the colors of the bars. In Figure 6.33, the same geometric shapes have been filled with a linear version of the radial gradient on the background layer. As you can see in the merged area on the right, the effect is only noticeable where the blend layer pixels are dark and the base layer pixels are light.

Color

If Saturation mode was the dull date of the Blend modes, Color mode is a more, uh, colorful choice. The hue and saturation values of the blend layer pixels are combined with the luminance of the base layer pixels. The effect of the mode is to produce a more vibrant version of Hue mode.

The colors formed aren't visible in Figure 6.34, but you can see that this mode also washes away pixels from the blend layers that cross light areas below it. A comparison of this figure's color counterpart with that of Hue shows how the color calculation produces a more interesting set of tones. Figure 6.35 gives an idea how, when colors are blended with neutral tones in the base layer, there is a muting of tone. This makes Color mode an ideal choice for colorizing grayscale images.

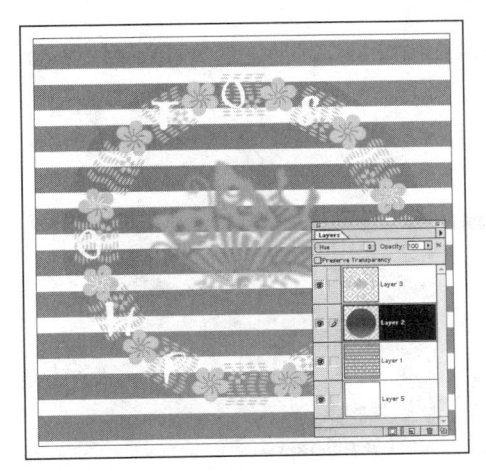

Figure 6.32 Saturation mode also cancels the circle where it crosses over very light areas. The blended colors, shown in the Color Studio section, are pretty ho-hum. Saturation, for the most part, isn't a very interesting mode.

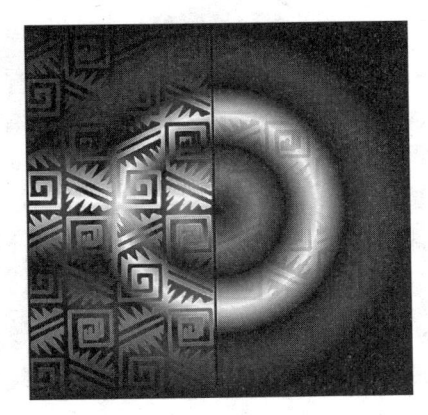

Figure 6.33 The geometric shapes on the blend layer have been filled with a linear version of the same gradient used for the background layer. The merged pixels show most clearly where the blend layer is dark and the base layer is light.

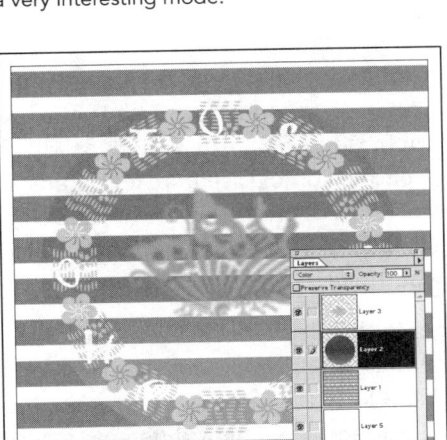

Figure 6.34 Compare this figure with its color counterpart to see how Color mode produces a brighter version of Hue.

Figure 6.35 Colors blended with neutral tones on the base layer produce subdued, grayed versions of themselves.

Luminosity

Luminosity mode has the inverse effect of Color. The result color is made up of the hue and saturation values of the base layer and the luminance of the blend layer. This results in colors that are darker and more intense than the originals.

In Figure 6.36, the color of the bars is enriched by the colors within the circle. The spaces between the bars are changed from white to about a 75% gray tone. Figure 6.37, when compared to Figure 6.35, illustrates the change in color intensity.

376 CHAPTER 6

Figure 6.36 When the circle in Layer 2 is placed in Luminosity mode, it intensifies the colors of the bars. The areas between the bars are also darkened from white to a gray tone that is about equivalent to 75% black.

Figure 6.37 Compare this figure with Figure 6.35 to see how Luminosity darkens and intensifies the colors composing the blend.

An Afterthought On Blend Modes

If you're feeling adventurous, you can explore interesting topological effects by superimposing geometric shapes on two layers (one example was mentioned in connection with Figure 6.19). A very simple introduction to what can be done is shown in Figure 6.38. The variations within this figure are the result of a single background that is duplicated onto a separate layer, after which the layer is rotated 90°. (The layer and background are shown at the top left and top center.) Note that the background layer was made by drawing a black-to-white gradient and then posterizing to 11 steps. This produces rectangles ranging from white to black in 10-percent steps.

The remaining 13 examples are the result of changes in the Blend mode of Layer 1. Of interest in these examples are the opposite characteristics of Multiply-Screen, Color Dodge-Color Burn, and Darken-Lighten. Note that Overlay and Hard Light form the same configuration, but one is rotated 90° and flipped with respect to the other. It's useful to see how different Exclusion is from Difference: The two are identical around the outer edges, but they diverge from each other as they approach the center of the square area.

Opacity

Something about the symmetry of 32 bits strikes the geek mind as something greater than fortuitous: Is it really an accident that a color display only requires 3 bytes of the 4 that are available on a 32-bit operating system? And who was the bright programmer who thought, "Hmm, maybe with that extra byte we could float 256 levels of transparency on top of the color...." As we said, this is straight-out geek-think. You get the idea: If computer architecture weren't so elegantly organized, about 75 percent of Photoshop would be impossible. And most of what *would* be possible wouldn't be as much fun!

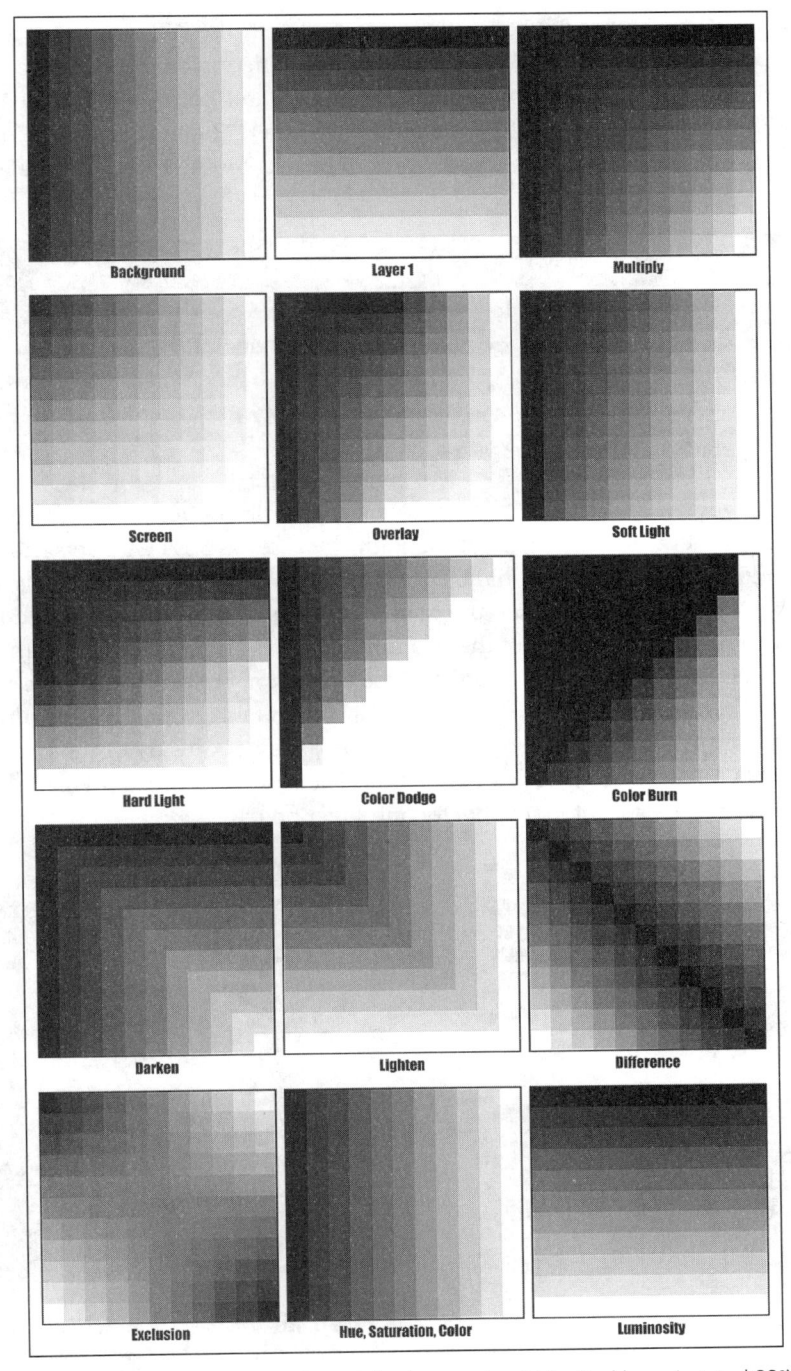

Figure 6.38 Studies in Blend mode relationships. A background and identical layer (rotated 90°) form these patterns with changes in the Blend modes.

Transparency, where layers are concerned, is varied with the slider at the top of the palette. Pixels that are entirely opaque can be changed by means of the slider so that whatever is behind them shows through as though the pixels had become translucent. Visibility of the pixels can be as low as 1% (100% is totally opaque). The four parts of Figure 6.39 show how changes in opacity affect the appearance of objects on the layer and the layer(s) behind the objects.

> **TIP**
>
> Besides moving the Opacity slider, you can change the opacity of the layer in 10% increments by pressing any of the number keys with one of the Selection tools in use. Press 1 for 10%, 5 for 50%, or 0 for 100%. If you have one of the Paint tools selected, pressing the numbers will change the opacity of the tool. If you type fast, you can also type in the exact amount (such as 43%).

Pixels on a layer can be placed there with less than total opacity. You might, for example, apply color to a new layer with one of the Paint tools set to 50% Opacity. The Opacity slider would still read 100%, but you would be able to see through the colored pixels. If you change the Opacity slider, you will decrease the opacity of the pixels on the layer by an amount that you can calculate as the product of the two numbers: the original opacity of the pixels multiplied by the slider percentage. This means that you can, if you want, have pixels with an opacity of fractions of a percent. For example, if the pixels on the layer begin at 50 percent Opacity and you change the Opacity slider to 75%, the net opacity of the pixels will be 37.5 percent (50% × 75% = 37.5%, or .5 × .75 = .375). The examples in Figure 6.40 show the difference between the concepts of pixel opacity and layer opacity.

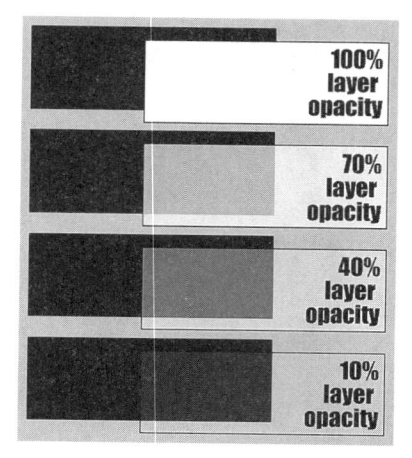

Figure 6.39 As the transparency percentage is lowered, the objects existing on a layer become increasingly translucent.

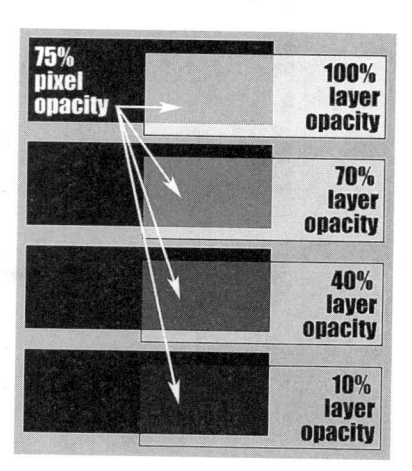

Figure 6.40 When pixels on a layer begin at less than full opacity, changing the Opacity slider produces a net opacity obtained by multiplying the original opacity value by the layer opacity value.

Preserve Transparency

You have already seen how a layer can contain areas of pixels surrounded by nothing. You can protect this area of nothing, the transparent pixels of the layer, from change by turning on the Preserve Transparency checkbox at the top of the Layers palette. When the checkbox is not turned on, color can be added to the layer from any source—painted, pasted, and so on—and positioned anywhere. Figure 6.41 shows how, when the option is unchecked, a Paintbrush can simply lay the paint any place on the layer. When it is checked, the brush can apply color only in the areas wherever there are existing pixels (see Figure 6.42). (Note: If the pixels are not fully opaque, the brush lays down the paint with the exact opacity of the existing pixels. The Preserve Transparency option allows you to quickly change the color on a layer while preserving the shape within which the colors lie.)

One of the Blend modes, Behind, is relevant to the discussion of a layer's transparent pixels. This mode is the inverse of painting with Preserve Transparency turned on. (Note that this mode will function only when Preserve Transparency is turned off.) With Behind mode, you can apply paint to the transparent or translucent pixels, while leaving all of the existing pixels untouched, or painted to the extent that they are translucent. The effect is shown in Figure 6.43, which also makes the origin of the mode's name evident. The paint strokes appear to be behind the gray bars. In fact, they have been applied only in the transparent areas between the bars. Behind mode is not available on the Layers palette.

> **TIP**
>
> **Preserve Transparency can be toggled off and on by pressing the / (forward slash) key.**

Figure 6.41 With the Layers palette Preserve Transparency option unchecked, the Paintbrush can paint anywhere within the layer.

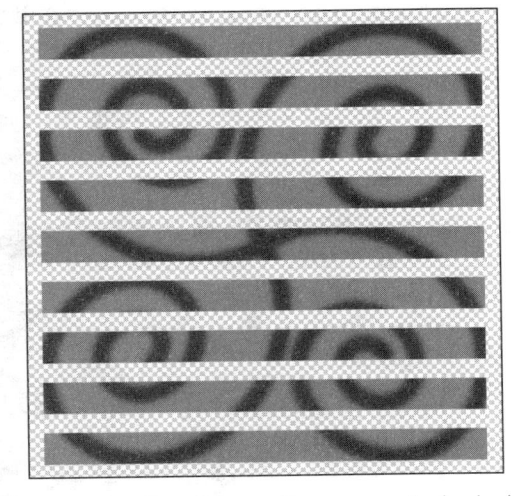

Figure 6.42 When Preserve Transparency is checked, a Paintbrush can only apply paint where there are existing pixels.

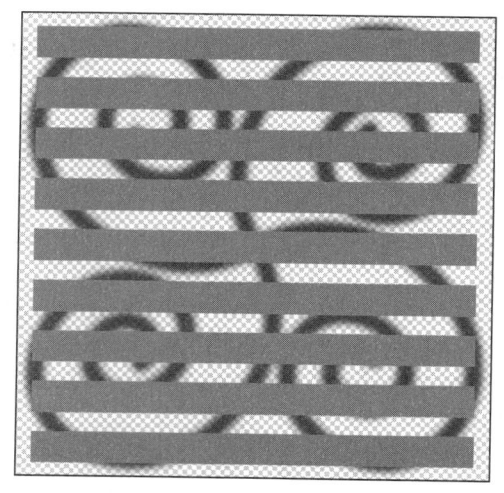

Figure 6.43 When paint is applied to a layer using Behind mode, the paint can only be applied to transparent or translucent pixels.

The Layers Thumbnail List

The central part of the Layers palette is composed of a list of the layers present in the working document (refer to Figure 6.3). Each item on the list contains a thumbnail of the pixels contained on the layer. Next to the thumbnail, on the right, is the Layers name.

This list also contains, at times, one special-case entry where the listed item isn't really a layer.

The Background

This special-case entry is the bottom entry—which may or may not be present—called the Background. Photoshop documents usually begin with photo images or artwork. When they are opened for the first time, or if they form within a window after a scanner has captured an image, they appear on the Layers palette as the Background. The Background is always shown in italic type on the Item list to indicate its special status. If there is a Background, it will be the lowest item on the list. The Background layer cannot be moved from its position on the list unless it is first converted to a layer.

> **TIP**
>
> To convert the Background to a Layer, double-click on its thumbnail on the Layers palette. When the dialog box appears asking you to name the new layer as Layer 0, click on OK.
>
> To add a Background to a document that does not have one, choose Layer|New|Background.

Floating Selections

In previous versions of Photoshop, a floating selection was a group of selected pixels that temporarily floated above a layer or the Background. Floating selections would show up on the

Layers palette, but with the name Floating Selection in italic type to indicate that the layer status was temporary. Photoshop 5 no longer permits any floating selections.

Layer Visibility

At the far left of the Layer Items list is a column of small icons containing an eye symbol. Click on this icon space to hide or make visible the pixels of the layer.

Linked Layers

Between the eye icon and the layer thumbnail is another icon space. This space contains a paintbrush icon whenever the layer has been selected. It also links or groups layers. With one layer selected, click in this area to group the layers. A small chain symbol will appear to notify you that the layer has been linked with the selected layer. This link remains in effect until you remove it by clicking again on the chain icon. You can link any two or more layers. To be linked, layers need not be next to each other on the palette list.

Linked layers are very useful when you need to perform the same operation to each layer, but you cannot or will not, for some reason, merge the layers into one (we'll discuss merging layers later in this chapter). For example, you might wish to move the contents of more than one layer while maintaining the precise position of both with respect to each other. With the layers linked, you can move one, and the other(s) will also move. Another application for a link would be when you wish to apply a transformation—transformations are found under the Layers menu and will be discussed later in this chapter—to two or more layers. If the layers are linked, the transformation will be applied to each at the same time. Yet another use would be to transfer the contents of more than one layer to a new document while keeping the layer status after the move. Link the layers you wish to move—with the Move tool selected, simply drag from one document window to another (see Figure 6.44). The linked layers will appear on the new document's Layers palette—with the link status intact—and with both in the same Blend mode assigned to them in the original window. (Before Photoshop 4, this used to be a tedious task! With linking, it's a breeze.)

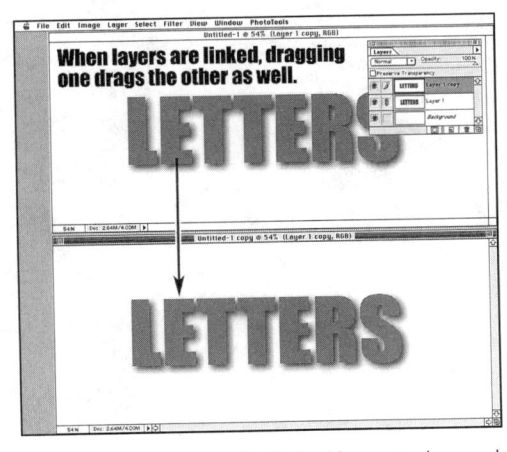

Figure 6.44 When layers are linked and then one of the linked layers is dragged to a new document, both layers are moved.

> **TIP**
>
> When you drag any information from one document window to another, you can ensure that the pixels center themselves in the destination window by holding Shift as you drag.
>
> In order to drag linked layers from one document to the other, you need to click on the image and drag. If you drag the layer thumbnail from the Layers palette, the linked layer will not come along for the ride.

Rearranging The Layers Using The Palette List

You can make two other layer modifications by using the Item list, besides changing whether a layer is visible or whether it is linked to other layers. The first of these is the rearrangement of the stacking order of the layers. The second is the formation of a *clipping group*.

Rearranging the order of the layers from top to bottom is one of the simplest layer tasks. Simply click on the layer to select it and then drag it to the line separating the two layers between which you want it to be. As you drag, your cursor changes to a small hand icon. When the hand icon is over one of the layer boundaries, the line widens as if to accommodate the new layer. This effect is shown in Figure 6.45, where the bottom layer—Layer 1—is being moved so that it will be above Layer 2. After the layer has been moved (see Figure 6.46), the pixels show a new visual relationship. You can move layers at any time.

Figure 6.45 Click and drag any layer to change its position in the stack of layers. As you drag, the cursor changes to a hand icon. When the hand icon is positioned over a layer boundary, the boundary line widens to show that the mouse button can be released for the layer to move into position.

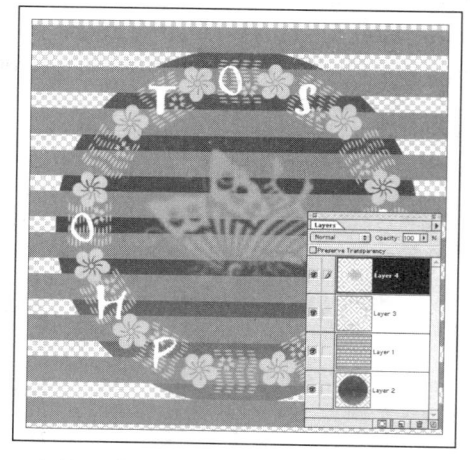

Figure 6.46 After a layer has been moved, the appearance of the image is different, reflecting the new stack relationships within the layer.

Four commands on the program's Layer menu can also assist with moving layers up or down in the stacking order. These include the following:

- *Bring to Front*—Command+Shift+] (Mac) or Ctrl+Shift+] (Windows), which places the selected layer at the top of the stack.
- *Bring Forward*—Command+] or Ctrl +], which moves the selected layer up one level.
- *Send Backward*—Command+[or Ctrl+[, which moves the selected layer down one level.
- *Send to Back*—Command+Shift+[or Ctrl+Shift+[, which places the selected layer at the bottom of the stack.

> **TIP**
>
> You can select layers from the keyboard in much the same way that you move the layers. Four commands allow you to move up or down in the layer stack. These commands are as follows:
>
> - *Select the next layer up*—Option+] or Alt+]. If there is no next layer up, your selected layer will be the bottom of the layer stack.
> - *Select the next layer down*—Option+[or Alt+[.
> - *Select the top layer*—Shift+Option+] or Shift+Alt+].
> - *Select the lowest layer (or the Background)*—Shift+Option+[or Shift+Alt+[.
>
> With the Move tool selected, you can also select a layer by clicking on one of the layer's pixels in the document window. On the Macintosh, hold down Command, Option, and Ctrl as you click. In Windows, hold down Ctrl as you click.
>
> Finally, Photoshop 5 has a new method of selecting a layer. Enable the Auto Select Layer box in the Move Tool Options palette. When this box is checked, clicking anywhere in the image positions you to the highest layer that contains a nontransparent pixel at that location.

Establishing A Clipping Group

A clipping group is a special relationship that uses the pixels of one layer to mask the pixels of another layer wherever they're above transparent pixels of the first. Figure 6.47 depicts this kind of relationship, where the horizontal bars of the lower layer are being used as clipping objects for the circular shape. This concept is difficult to visualize at first until you understand that with a clipping group, the pixels on the layer above the clipping layer are visible only where there are pixels on the clipping layer. (Think about spreading glitter on a glued surface. The glitter only sticks where there is glue. The clipped layer is the glitter; the clipping—or bottom—layer is the glue.) Because of this, the circle of Layer 2 is not visible except where there are pixels on the layer containing the bars (Layer 1). Figure 6.48 shows the same clipping relationship, but with the two layer's positions transposed. The bars in the figure are visible only where there are pixels in the layer below.

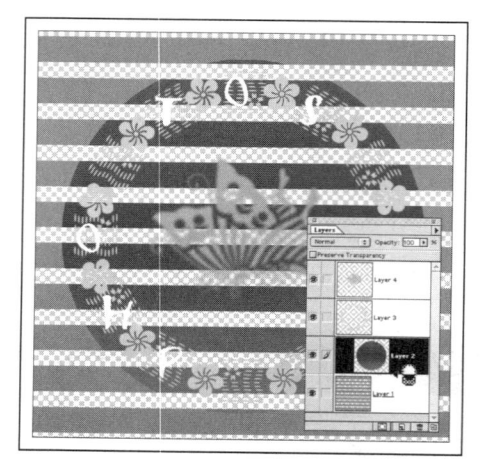

Figure 6.47 A clipping layer trims the upper layer's pixels so that they are visible only where the clipping layer contains pixels.

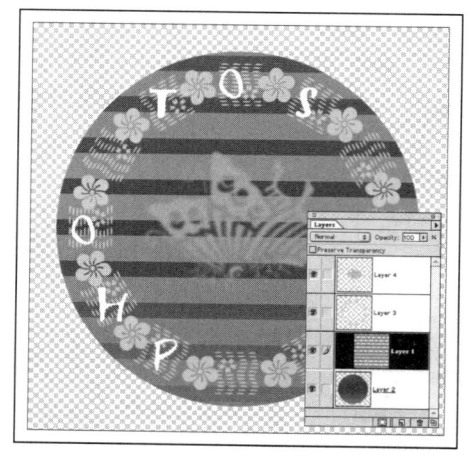

Figure 6.48 This figure and Figure 6.47 show clipping groups with the same two layers. The difference in effect is the difference between which layer is in the lower—clipping—position.

To make a clipping layer, hold Option or Alt and click on the boundary between the layers you wish to make into a clipping group (layers in a clipping group must be next to each other for the clipping group to function). With the modifier key depressed, the cursor changes to a small double-circle icon. After you have clicked, the thumbnail of the upper layer of the clipping group moves a little to the right, and the boundary between the two layer items changes to a dotted line. The title of the clipping layer also becomes underlined to indicate its status.

You can turn off clipping groups by holding Option or Alt and clicking on the layer boundary. If you want, you may include more than two layers in a clipping group. In fact, all of the layers in a document can be part of one clipping group. Layers within the group can be rearranged in the stacking order within the group. If one of the layers is moved beneath the clipping layer, it is no longer a part of the group.

The clipping group option is also available from the Layer menu Choose Layer|Group With Previous. Group With Previous means that the selected layer forms the clipping group with the layer beneath it. The keyboard command is Command+G or Ctrl+G. The Ungroup command from the same menu releases the clipping group. Select any of the layers within the group and press Command+Shift+G or Ctrl+Shift+G.

The Layers Palette Menu And The Layer Menu

For the most part, you can execute the commands contained in the sidebar menu of the Layers palette with key commands or by using the icons at the bottom of the palette. As we discuss the entries, we'll note the ways you can accomplish the same commands without resorting to the menu. Although nothing is wrong with using the menu, you will find that the Photoshop programmers have furnished you with some keyboard tools that let you work in layers with great efficiency. For those items that do not have a convenient keyboard equivalent, we recommend that you assign a keyboard macro or a Photoshop Action (see the section on Actions in Chapter 1). There may even be a key command for the operation you want to perform. See Appendix C at the end of this book, which contains a complete listing of the keyboard commands in Photoshop 5.

Many of the commands on the Layer palette menu (see Figure 6.49b) are duplicated under the Layers menu (see Figure 6.49a). As we discuss these two menus, we will point out which commands are duplicates and which are available in only one of the two menus.

New Layer

When you choose the New Layer command, you are requesting that Photoshop create a layer *directly above* the currently selected layer. As soon as you choose this command from the menu, the dialog box shown in Figure 6.50 appears. Within the dialog box, you can enter a new name for the layer or accept the name Photoshop offers. You can, when the layer is created, preset the amount of opacity for the layer and the Blend mode that will be assigned to it. The layer can also be assigned a fill based on what will be color-neutral (transparent) for the Blend mode you want to use. For example, if you want to create the new layer in Multiply mode, you can click on the checkbox, which will fill the new layer with white. White, in Multiply mode, is totally transparent. The wording at the bottom of the dialog box changes (see Figure 6.51) depending on which mode you select. This option is grayed out for Normal, Dissolve, Hue, Saturation, Color, and Luminosity modes. The calculations for these modes do not cause any color to become transparent.

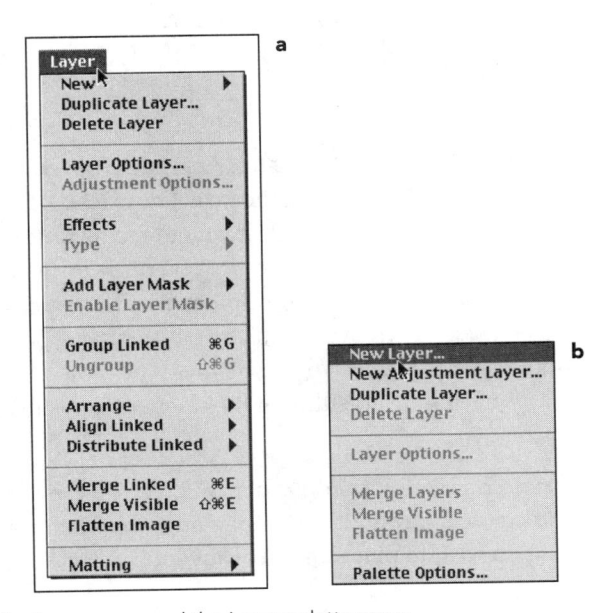

Figure 6.49 (a and b)   The Layer menu and the Layer palette menu.

Figure 6.50 The New Layer dialog box. This window appears when you either choose New Layer from the Layers menu, the Layer palette menu, or when you click on the New Layer icon with the Option (Mac) or Alt (Windows) key pressed.

Figure 6.51 When you create a new layer and choose one of the Blend modes, you will have one of these options to fill the layer with a blend-neutral color, a color that's transparent for the Blend mode you have chosen. Six of the Blend modes—Normal, Dissolve, Hue, Saturation, Color, and Luminosity—do not have blend-neutral colors.

To create a new layer which bypasses the menu command but which lets you select layer options, hold Option or Alt and click once on the New Layer icon at the bottom of the Layers palette. The same dialog box appears. The fastest way to create a new layer is to simply click once on the New Layer icon on the palette. The new layer appears in Normal mode, filled with transparent pixels, with the name *Layer* and a number that is the next integer in the creation sequence. You may also choose New|Layer from the Layer menu. The dialog box appears so that you can set the options for the layer. You can bypass the dialog box by holding Option or Alt when you make your selection from either of the menus (opposite to the behavior of clicking on the New Layer icon).

You'll see two additional choices for creating a new layer at the bottom of the Layer|New submenu. These choices create a new layer by retrieving the contents of a selection. To use this option, select the pixels you wish to place on a new layer (or Select All if you wish to duplicate the entire layer). Choose either of the menu options. The first creates an exact copy of the pixels on a new layer directly above the one that contains the selection. The original pixels are left untouched. The second option does the same thing, except that it clears the contents of the selection, leaving it empty of pixels. These two menu choices can only be used within the confines of a document. You cannot make a selection in one document and then choose either of these options from within another document.

New Adjustment Layer

Adjustment layers are mask layers that hold color correction information. When you choose to create a new Adjustment layer, the dialog box shown in Figure 6.52 appears. Within this window, you can choose one of the nine correction possibilities from the Type pop-up menu. The adjustment controls you have chosen for the layer then appear and allow you to make color corrections or other kinds of changes to the image. When you are finished, click on OK. The layer appears on the Item list on the palette. It is distinguishable from normal layers because it contains a small circular icon—half black, half white—to the right of the layer name.

You can select New Adjustment Layer from the palette sidebar menu or from the program's Layer menu. You can also hold down Command or Ctrl and click on the New Layer icon at the bottom of the palette.

Adjustment layers are one of Photoshop 5's best features. In previous versions of the program, you might have wanted to make several kinds of corrections to an image. For example, you might have wanted to adjust the tone range with the Curves controls, after which you might have wanted to adjust the Color Balance, and then the Hue/Saturation controls. Because all corrective techniques of this kind are destructive, two or three kinds of adjustments could be visibly injurious to the quality of the image.

With Adjustment layers, you embed your corrections in a layer that is simply a mask. Whenever the layer is visible, you can see what kinds of adjustments you have made with the controls of the Adjustment layer, but the changes will not have been applied to the original image. The concept is akin to the CMYK Preview option, where you can work with an image in RGB mode, but view it as though it had been converted to CMYK mode. Adjustment layers follow the same idea: You see the corrections, but without having to apply them. That means that you can stack

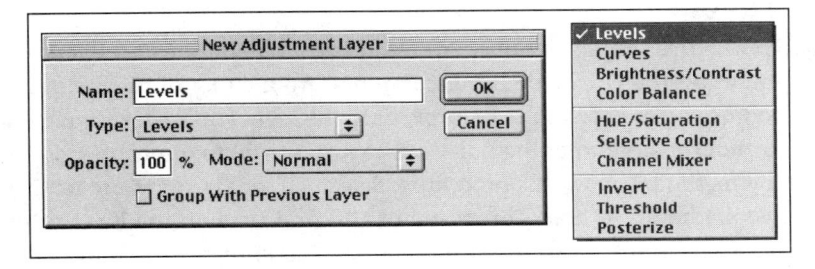

Figure 6.52 The New Adjustment Layer dialog box.

up Adjustment layers and view their cumulative effect. You can also go back to the controls for each layer (double-click on the layer title) and tweak the original settings. The corrections of multiple Adjustment layers are finally applied to the image as one large adjustment when the document is flattened. (When you flatten a layered document, all of the layers are merged into one.) The net adjustment is far more satisfactory and far less harmful to the image data.

Adjustment layers have other possibilities. Because they are true layers, you can apply opacity changes to them. Changing opacity has the effect of lessening the amount of the correction. You can apply Blend modes as well. This allows you to create some incredibly complex special effects with a simple pop-up menu change. You might choose, for example, to create a correction layer, make no changes to the controls, click on OK, and then change the Blend mode to Multiply. This would have the effect of darkening an image that is too light. On the other hand, you could use Screen mode to lighten an image that's too dark. In either case, you can decrease the effect by changing the layer's opacity.

Adjustment layers are, as we stated previously, masks. Because of this, you can further modify how the layer behaves by adding paint to the layer. If you paint an area or fill an area with solid black, you eliminate the effect of the correction from that area. If you fill an area with a lesser percentage of black—say 50 percent—you decrease the amount of the correction by 50 percent in the place where you have added the fill. Gradients are also handy for use on correction layers. If an image is too light at the top and too dark at the bottom, a gradient applied to the Adjustment layer can balance the two areas.

> **TIP**
>
> If you want to view the Adjustment layer by itself—especially if you have applied paint to an area and wish to make a small modification—hold down Option or Alt and click on the layer's thumbnail. Click again with Option or Alt depressed to return to the normal layer view.

For more information and for examples on using Adjustment layers, see the section on editable color corrections in Chapter 11. You can read about other uses for Adjustment layers in Chapters 9 and 10.

Duplicate Layer

When you choose the Duplicate Layer command, you create an exact copy of the selected layer. You can access the Duplicate Layer command from either of the menus—Layer palette sidebar or program menu—or you can simply drag the layer you wish to duplicate down to the New Layer icon at the bottom of the palette. The fastest way to duplicate a layer is to use the Layer via copy method. Follow this procedure: Select All, hold Command or Ctrl, and press J. An alternative method is to hold Command or Ctrl and click on the layer's thumbnail. This step selects all pixels in the layer. You can then hold Command or Ctrl, and press J.

> **TIP**
>
> **Don't forget that you can select the pixels of a layer by holding down Command or Ctrl and clicking once on the layer's thumbnail. The selection doesn't have to be the selected layer. This allows you to use a selection outline from one layer—the layer doesn't have to be visible—on another layer. For example, the image in Figure 6.53 shows how a selection of the large circle on Layer 2 has been used to delete that shape from the bars of Layer 1. A selection of the blurred letters on Layer 4 has been used to fill new letter shapes on Layer 1. The selection of the pixels on a layer can be compared to the selection you get when you load an alpha channel.**

Choosing to duplicate a layer from either of the menus results in the dialog box shown in Figure 6.53. This window allows you to rename the duplicate layer. It also allows you to simultaneously move the duplicate to a different document or to duplicate it into a new document. If you choose to make a new document, you can enter the name to be applied to the new window.

Figure 6.53 Hold down Command or Ctrl and click on a layer's thumbnail. This selects the pixels of the layer. The layer contributing the selection need not be the selected layer, nor must the layer be visible. Selections from other layers in the figure have been used to modify the bars of Layer 1.

Figure 6.54 The Duplicate Layer dialog box.

You might want to make an exact copy of a Layer for a number of reasons. Figure 6.55 shows one possibility—drop shadow effects. The layer that contains the blurred numbers in the center of the image has been duplicated. The original, positioned below the duplicate layer, has been filled with black (with Preserve Transparency turned on), set to Multiply mode, and moved down and to the right. The same procedure was used for the large circle, except that a Gaussian Blur was added to the lower circle layer to make the shadow look more realistic.

Figure 6.56 shows another example of a situation in which a duplication of a layer could be useful. As you can see, the letters do not show up at the bottom of the frame. In Figure 6.57, the layer containing the letters has been duplicated and the upper layer filled with white (Preserve Transparency turned on). Preserve transparency is then turned off again and a quick selection made with the Lasso tool around the upper line of letters. Press the Delete key, and the task is finished (see Figure 6.58).

Delete Layer

Sometimes you change your mind. Perhaps you find that the layer you are using is no longer suitable for the way an image has evolved as a composition. Delete the layer by choosing the command from either menu. You can also get rid of the layer by dragging it to the trash can icon at the bottom of the palette. Even quicker: Select the layer, hold Option or Alt, and click on the trash icon.

Layer Options

The Layer Options dialog box (see Figure 6.59) contains some—but not all—of the setting choices of the New Layer dialog box. For example, it allows you to change the name of the layer, set the

Figure 6.55 Duplicated layers are easy ways to make realistic drop shadows. Here, copies of Layers 2 and 4 have taken the positions of the original layers. The original layers have been filled with black, blurred, set to Multiply mode, and slightly offset.

Figure 6.56 The letters on the layer do not show up against the background layer.

Figure 6.57 After the layer has been duplicated, the upper layer's pixels are filled with white.

Figure 6.58 A quick selection of the first line of letters with the Lasso tool, a press of the Delete key, and the job is finished.

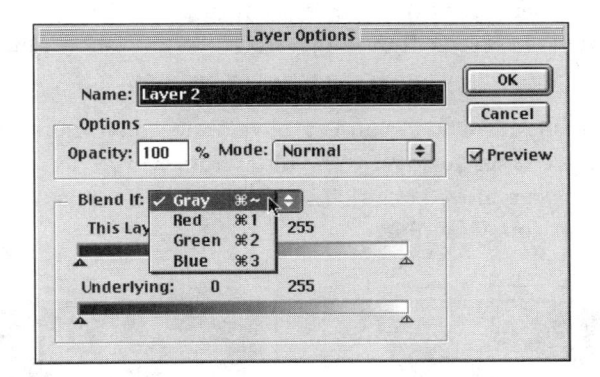

Figure 6.59 The Layer Options dialog box.

opacity, apply a Blend mode, and even establish a clipping group. You do not have the choice of filling with a blend-neutral color.

You can summon the Layer Options dialog box from either menu. You can also summon it by double-clicking on the layer thumbnail. The bottom of the Layer Options dialog box contains a Blend If section that delivers some really interesting effects. The dialog box contains four choices: Gray, Red, Blue, and Green.

Blend If is kind of crazy—in a good sort of way. It's a way of excluding pixels from visibility based on their brightness or their color, or the brightness or color of pixels beneath them. To see how this works, take a look at Figure 6.60. This figure shows a background with a black-to-white gradient running from left to right, and a circular area on a layer that contains the same gradient running from top to bottom.

Figure 6.60 This figure shows a background with a gradient running from left to right, and a circle shape on a layer with the same gradient.

You'll see two sets of sliders in the Blend If box. One is titled This Layer, the other Underlying. Both of the sliders work on a scale that ranges from 0 to 255 (shown atop each slider). Whenever you move one of the triangle tabs, the number updates.

Figure 6.61 shows the shadow-end tab on This Layer moved to a value of 75. This has the effect of making all of the pixels on the layer with values from 0 to 75 disappear. In Figure 6.62, the highlight-end tab has been moved to 181. This makes all of the pixels on the layer with values from 181 to 255 also become invisible.

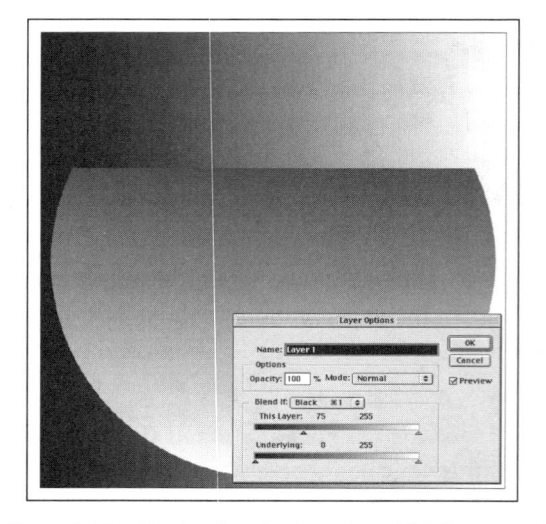

Figure 6.61 Moving the shadow tab on This Layer to 75 causes all of the pixels on the layer with values between 0 to 75 to disappear.

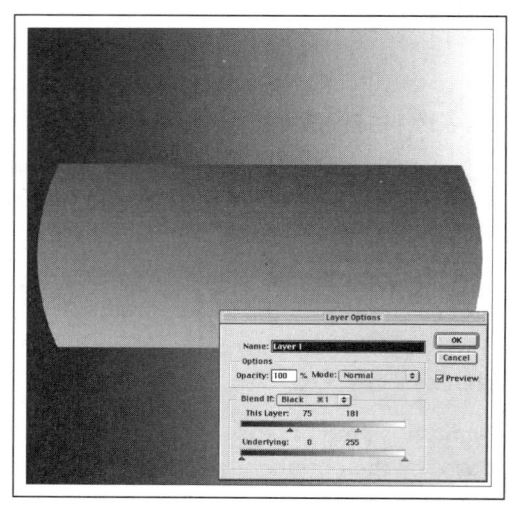

Figure 6.62 Moving the highlight tab on This Layer to 181 causes all of the pixels on the layer with values of 181 or higher to also disappear.

The action of the Underlying slider may, at first, seem a little puzzling. As you can see in Figure 6.63, the changes to that slider have shaved off a portion of the circle on each side. The reason for the change to the circle is that Photoshop is excluding pixels from visibility on the layer based on values from the pixels underlying the layer. With the shadow tab moved to 75, all of the pixels on the layer that are *above* pixels in the background with values of 0 to 75 have been made to disappear. The same exclusion has been carried out on the highlight end of the slider.

All of the tabs on the sliders can be divided. Hold Option (Mac) or Alt (Windows) and you can move the two halves away from each other. In Figure 6.64, this has been done with all four of the tabs. Notice that the rectangular area now has a soft edge that remains visible on the layer. The divided tabs allow a smooth transition between opaque and transparent in a manner similar to a feathered selection. The "This Layer" slider numbers now read 55/73 and 181/199. If you want, you can translate this series of numbers as follows: Make the values on This Layer transparent if brightness values fall between 0 and 55; give a smooth transition from transparent to opaque for the values between 55 and 73; make all of the values between 73 and 181 totally opaque; give a smooth transition from opaque to transparent for the values between 181 and 199; and make all of the brightness values above 199 completely transparent. The translation of the numbers on the lower scale would be equivalent, except that the numbers would relate to brightness values on the layer below as they affect the layer.

When you're working with colored files, you have additional choices based on the colors. Figure 6.65 shows an example with the same black-to-white gradient in the background, but with a radial gradient shading, from the center, white-black-red-black-green-black-blue-black. The pop-up menu in the Blend If section of the dialog box contains entries for each of the three RGB colors besides the gray discussed previously. When red is chosen and the shadow tab for This

Figure 6.63 When the tabs on the Underlying slider are moved, pixels on the layer are made invisible if they are above the excluded range of values below them.

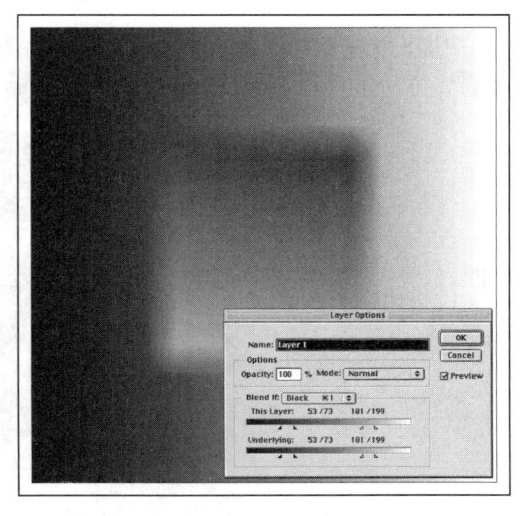

Figure 6.64 Hold Option or Alt to move the two parts of each tab away from each other. Separating the tabs results in a smooth, feathered transition between opaque and transparent pixels.

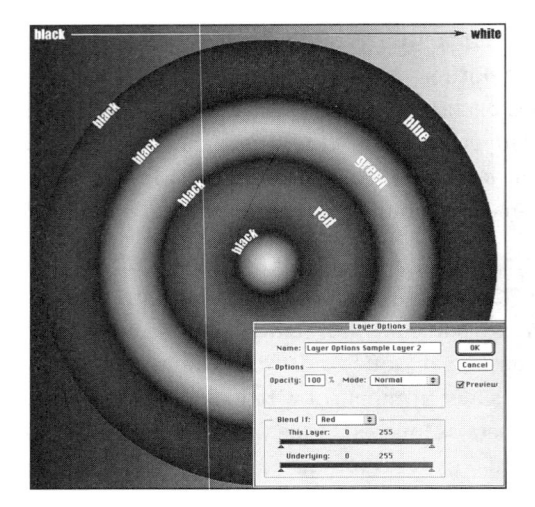

Figure 6.65 The Layer Options are more complex when you work on a color image.

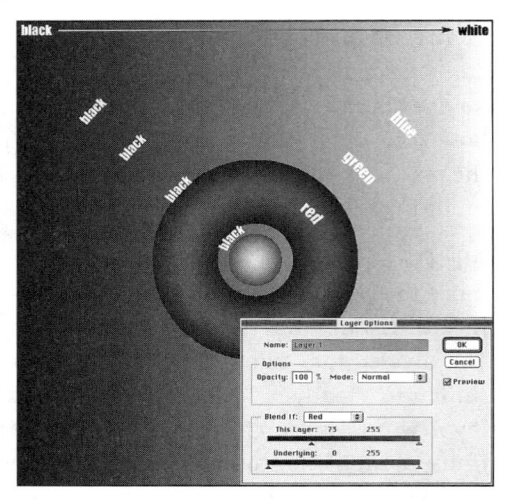

Figure 6.66 Moving the shadow end of the red This Layer slider results in the elimination of all dark values lower than the displayed number, and the disappearance of all color values other than red and white.

layer is moved so that it reads 73, the result is as shown in Figure 6.66. All of the black values have vanished. Only the white-to-gray and red-to-gray tones have been retained. The darkest value at the edges of each of the areas is, as you might expect, 74.

When you move the red This Layer slider from the highlight end, you have the inverse effect on the pixels. All of the red and white values lighter than the displayed number disappear, leaving only blue, green, black, and the darker red and gray tones. This is shown in Figure 6.67.

A variety of compositing effects is possible with these Blend If sliders. Figure 6.68 shows one possibility, where the green highlight slider has been divided to encompass the range between

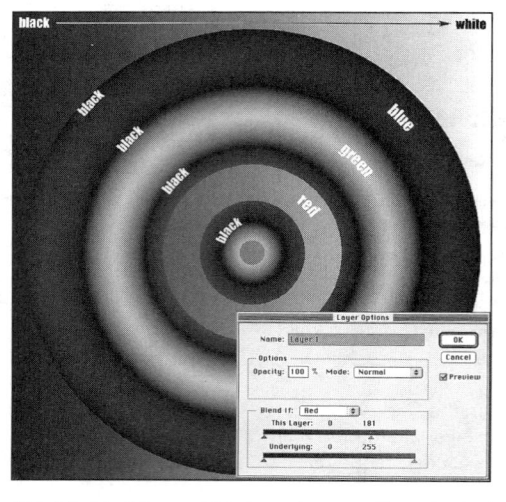

Figure 6.67 A move of the red highlight slider on This layer has an effect that's the inverse of moving the This Layer shadow slider.

66 and 255. This has the effect of fading out green tones so that, as they become brighter, they also become more transparent.

Figures 6.69, 6.70, and 6.71 show another possibility. When objects on a layer are surrounded by a more-or-less uniform tone, it is easier to use the Blend If sliders to isolate objects than it is to silhouette them (select them and delete the area around them). Figure 6.69 contains a set of gradient-filled circles against a uniform, neutral surrounding color. In Figure 6.70, the back-

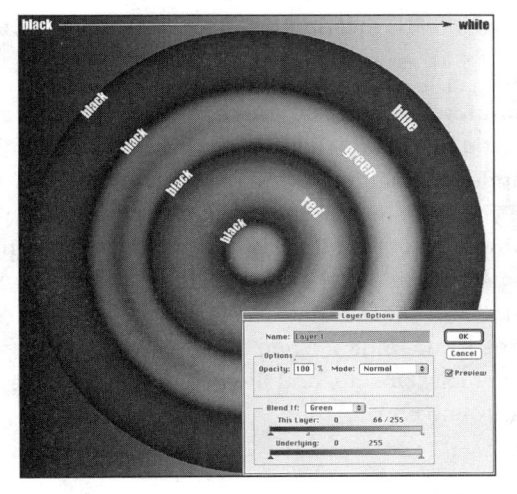

Figure 6.68 In this figure, the green highlight slider has been divided to encompass the range between 66 and 255. This has the effect of fading out green tones so that, as they become brighter, they also become more transparent.

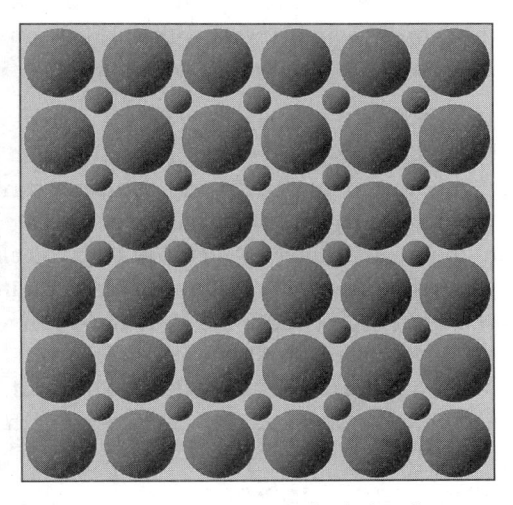

Figure 6.69 This layer contains shaded circles against a light surrounding color.

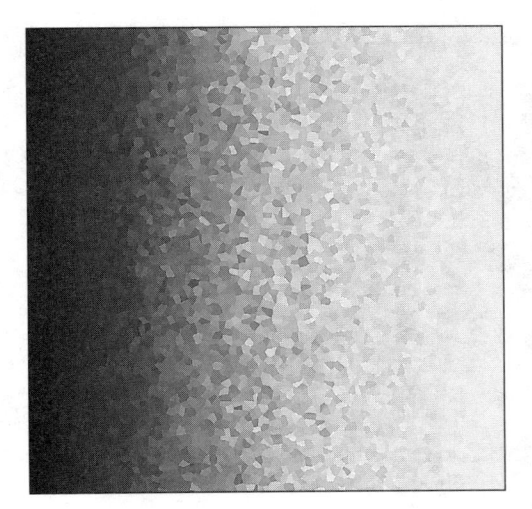

Figure 6.70 The background layer—below the shaded circles—is made up of a gradient that has been subjected to the Crystallize filter.

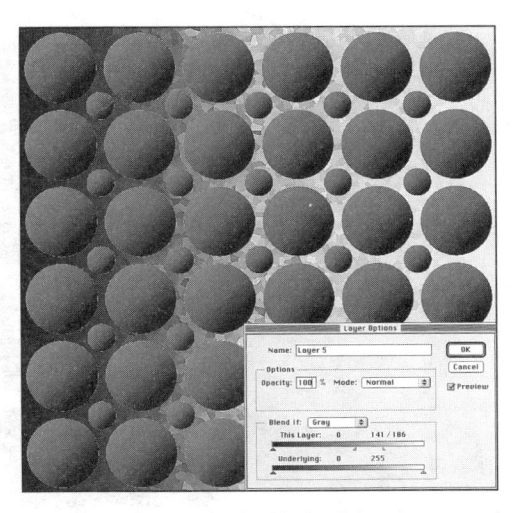

Figure 6.71 Moving the highlight slider eliminates the color surrounding the shaded circles as effectively as if you had outlined each and then deleted the background. This procedure is a lot faster!

ground gradient has been subjected to the Crystallize filter. This is the background layer for the shaded circles. In Figure 6.71, the circle layers highlight slider has been moved to the left, which leaves the circles isolated against the underlying layer. A move of this sort usually leaves a small fringe of the surrounding color along the edges of the pixels that are left. Dividing the highlight slider minimizes that fringe.

In Figure 6.72, the Blend If exclusion is carried one step further to show how the objects on a layer can be modified by excluding some of the color values in the layer's pixels. Notice how the shapes begin to merge with the background despite the fact that the layer's Opacity is set to 100% and the Blend mode is Normal.

These Blend If sliders can give you a great deal of help when you are making composites of images. Watch out for the things that will alert you to the fact that this option may be useful. If you have images where the subject is surrounded by relatively dark or light tones, Blend If will help you get rid of that surrounding color. If you have images that are, for the most part, in a single color range, Blend If can help you eliminate all of the other color tones except the one you wish to keep. If you have colors in an image that are peripheral to the subject but which you want to downplay, Blend If allows you to make an entire range of colors transparent or (if you divide the sliders) partially transparent. (See Figure 6.68.) When you combine these options with the already considerable array of layer tools, Opacity and Blend modes, you have a vast number of effects you can achieve with almost no effort.

Adjustment Options

Adjustment Options is a choice you can make from the program Layer menu. When you choose it, the dialog box for the correction tools used on the layer appear with the last-used settings. This allows you to make changes to the settings. You can execute the same command by double-clicking on the Adjustment layer's name.

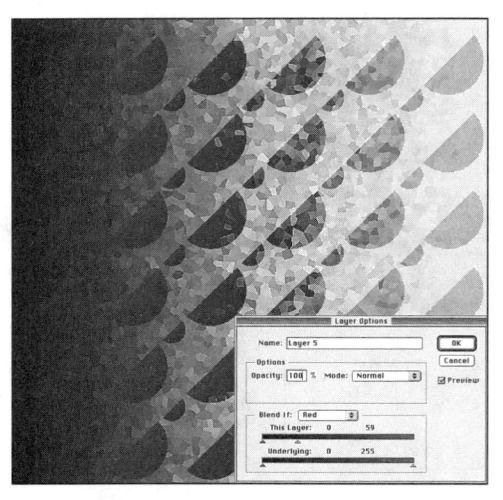

Figure 6.72 Besides eliminating the color around the circles, parts of the circles can also be excluded from visibility by using more than one menu item's sliders.

Merge Down

The Merge Down command—press Command+E (Mac) or Ctrl+E (Windows)—combines the contents of the selected layer with the layer beneath it.

Merge Visible

When you use the Merge Visible command, you must first hide all of the layers you do not wish to become fused by the command. After the layers you want to protect are hidden, select one of the still-visible layers before the command is available. You can choose the command from either menu, or press Command+Shift+E or Ctrl+Shift+E. After the command has executed, all of the visible layers will be combined into a single layer.

A little-known, but very useful, variant on this command is the Option-Merge-Visible command. There may be times that you wish you could apply a filter to the *result* of several blended layers, or you want to test something on a flattened image, but don't want to lose the layers. Simply create a new layer at the top of the layer stack. It should be a totally empty layer. Hide any layer that you don't want to include and press the Option key as you select Merge Visible or use the key command Shift+Option+Command+E (Mac) or Shift+Alt+Control+E (Windows).

Flatten Image

Flatten Image is the command that merges all of the layers in a document into one background layer. If any of the layers are hidden at the time you choose the command, you will be asked if you want to discard them. If you do not want to discard these layers, click on Cancel, make the layers visible, and then choose the command again.

A layered document can only be saved in the Photoshop file format. This makes it unusable for most other programs that can import image files. If you need to save in a format that can be imported into another software program, you need to flatten the image before any other file choices become available to you in the Save dialog box. A good procedure to use, if you suspect that you may need to edit the layered document at a later time, is to duplicate the document and flatten the copy. That way, you can save the original with its layers intact in case you should need them. You can also use the Save A Copy command and elect to flatten the image as you save it. You can eliminate channels at the same time.

Because each layer added to a document increases its file size (except for Adjustment layers, which do not add to a file's size), merging layers that don't need to be separate entities is a good way to cut down on the size of the file. Flattening the image, of course, reduces the file to its minimum size.

You can select the Flatten Image command from either menu.

Palette Options

The Layers Palette Options command is available from the Layer palette sidebar menu. The dialog box, shown in Figure 6.73, gives you a choice of three sizes of thumbnails to be displayed by the palette.

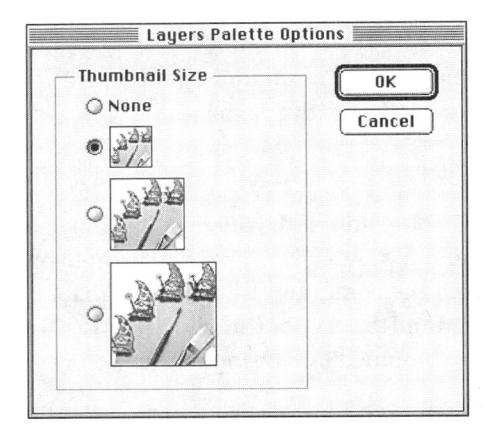

Figure 6.73 The Layers Palette Options dialog box.

Other Options Of The Layer Menu

Most of the remaining commands associated with the program's Layer menu have to do with arrangements of pixels on layers and on the new Layer and Type effects, which we will discuss shortly. Right now, let's talk about the Layer Mask, which is one of the most important of the compositing tools.

Layer Masks

Layer Masks are similar, as we discussed at the beginning of this chapter, to the channel masks we studied in Chapter 5. They are constructed in much the same way and their appearance is similar to that of channels, but their effects are applied immediately—but not permanently—to the pixels of a layer. The relationship of a layer mask to a formal alpha channel is so close, in fact, that if you have a layer with a layer mask attached to it as your selected layer, you'll see the mask appear on the channels palette. The name of the channel will be *Layer Mask*, with the text in italic type.

> **TIP**
>
> We've already noted that the pixels of a layer can be loaded as a selection by holding Command or Ctrl and clicking the layer's thumbnail. Complex selections that result from adding together the selections of two layers, or subtracting one layer's selection from another, and so on, are accomplished with the same key commands used for channels:
>
> - **Load a layer's pixels as a selection.**
> - **To add another layer's pixels to the selection, hold Command+Shift or Ctrl+Shift and click on the other layer's thumbnail.**
> - **To subtract another layer's pixels from the selection, hold Command+Option or Ctrl+Alt and click on the other layer's thumbnail.**

Tip (continued)

- To make a selection that is the intersection of two layers' selections, hold Command+Option+Shift or Ctrl+Alt+Shift and click on the other layer's thumbnail.

You can find the Add Layer Mask command under the program's Layer menu. You will see two choices for the command submenu—Reveal All and Hide All. To illustrate the differences between the two, look at Figure 6.74, which shows a document with a second view of the same document (available under the View menu). This document contains a landscape layer that fills the frame. Another layer contains a photo of a small airplane sitting on a runway. We will add a layers mask to this layer.

In Figure 6.75, a layer mask has been added to the document using the Hide All option. The second view window is now set to show the contents of the layer mask. (You can, if you wish, look at the layer mask at any time by holding Option or Alt and clicking on the layer mask thumbnail. Hold the same key and click again to return to the normal view of the document. Keep in mind that you don't have to see the layer mask to edit it.) This layer mask has been formed by Photoshop with a black fill. The effect of black within the mask is to make all of the equivalent layer pixels transparent. Consequently, the pixels of the airplane layer seem to have vanished from the document.

In Figure 6.76, white pixels are being added to the layer in the same area where there are pixels on the layer. This white area was added with a Paintbrush with the Foreground color set to white. Notice how the equivalent pixels on the layer have become visible again. It is important to stress that, unless you have a second window set to a different view of the document—as you see it

Figure 6.74 This figure shows a document with two layers and an open window showing a different view of the same document.

Figure 6.75 A new layer mask has formed with the Hide All function. It's filled with black as it's created. Because of this, it hides all of the pixels of the layer. We have used Photoshop 4 standards on the Layers palette to show this image because in Photoshop 5, the totally black layer mask blends into the black of the selected layer.

Figure 6.76 Adding white to the layer mask in the area equivalent to the layer's pixels returns them to visibility.

here—you do not usually see the layer mask. As you add white paint to the document when you have the mask thumbnail selected, you are really painting on the mask rather than on the layer.

When you have a layer that does not cover the entire window, as in this example, the Hide All option is probably not the best choice, because you cannot see the pixels of the layer. Editing is difficult until you begin to establish where the pixels lie. The Reveal All option, as shown in

Figure 6.77 When you choose the Reveal All option for the layer mask, the mask is created with a white fill. All of the layer's pixels remain visible.

Figure 6.77, makes working with a layer mask much easier. As you can see in the figure, the mask has formed with a white fill. This allows you to see all of the layer's pixels.

Editing a Reveal All layer mask typically involves adding areas of black. Wherever black pixels are added to the mask, the equivalent pixels of the layer become transparent. In Figure 6.78, you see a set of quick brush strokes added to the mask with the Paintbrush, Foreground color set to black.

Figure 6.78 A quick addition of black paintbrush strokes has accomplished a rough mask for the airplane.

If you intend to create a more careful silhouette of the image on the layer, you can zoom in, trace the outlines with the Lasso or Pen tool, and fill your selection with black. The image in Figure 6.79 has apparently been separated from its background, leaving the plane hanging in mid-air. The pixels around the plane are still present—they are simply hidden by the mask.

You don't have to use solid black on the mask. Tints of black will allow the pixels to be visible with the opacity that is reciprocal to the percentage of black. In Figure 6.80, the windows in the plane's cabin have been filled with 50 percent black. This allows the sky behind them to show through at 50 percent opacity.

After you have created the layer mask, you may need to temporarily disable it to look at some of the hidden pixels. With a layer mask present on the selected layer, choose Layer|Disable Layer Mask. All of the hidden pixels will reappear. The layer mask thumbnail will show a large red "X" to indicate that the mask has been disabled (circled in Figure 6.81). When the mask has been disabled, the menu item will change to Enable Layer Mask. Choose this command to reinstate the mask.

If your Photoshop composition doesn't seem to require that the pixels around the object on which the layer mask is operating be preserved, you can remove the mask by choosing Layer|Remove Layer Mask. The dialog box shown in Figure 6.82 will appear to ask whether you wish to *Discard* or *Apply* the mask. If you choose Discard, your layer resumes the appearance that it had before you added the mask. If you choose Apply, all of the masked pixels are permanently discarded. Your layer will contain only the shape you have masked (see Figure 6.83).

There is another way to extricate the unmasked pixels without discarding the layer mask—at least in a case such as the one shown in the figure where a silhouetted shape is involved. Hold

Figure 6.79 You can zoom in close to the layer, trace the edges of the shape in small sections with the Lasso tool, and fill the selections with black. When you have finished, the pixels around the object will seem to be gone.

USING LAYERS **403**

Figure 6.80 You can also modify the layer mask by adding tints of black. This allows the underlying layer to show through. In this figure, the windows of the plane have been filled with 50 percent black on the mask. This lets the sky show through from behind.

Figure 6.81 If you wish to turn off the layer mask temporarily, choose Layer|Disable Layer Mask. The masked pixels will reappear and the mask thumbnail will show a large red "X" to show that the mask is not operating.

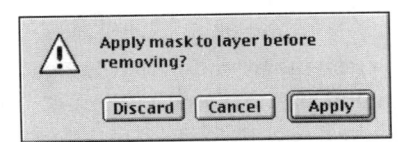

Figure 6.82 After you choose the Remove Layer Mask command, this dialog box will ask whether you want to Discard or Apply the mask.

Figure 6.83 If you Apply the mask when you discard it, all of the masked pixels are permanently deleted, leaving only the unmasked pixels on the layer.

Command or Ctrl and click on the mask thumbnail. This selects the masked shape. Choose Layer|New|Layer Via Copy (or hold Command or Ctrl and press J). This places a copy of the visible pixels—complete with areas masked with less than 100 percent black—on a new layer. You can then hide the layer containing the mask and proceed to develop the composite image. There's something of a moral here: Don't throw those masked pixels away unless you are absolutely sure you'll never need them again. Even then, err on the side of caution because you never know....

You can also discard layer masks by dragging the mask thumbnail to the trash can icon at the bottom of the palette.

Reveal Selection And Hide Selection

When you have an active selection on a layer and you choose to make a layer mask, you have two choices that will apply the selection to the new mask. With Reveal Selection, your mask is created with the selection area of the mask filled with white and the area outside the selection filled with black. When the mask has formed, all of the area outside the selection seems to disappear. Hide Selection is the inverse of Reveal Selection. When the layer mask has formed, the selection area on the mask is filled with black. Everything outside the selection is filled with white. With this mask in place, the area of the selection disappears.

Transform

When you begin to combine elements from different images, you'll often find that you will need to adjust the orientation and size of a group of pixels. For example, you might need to change an object's size or to rotate it slightly, or even to distort it slightly so that it appears to be properly aligned with the objects on other layers.

In Photoshop 4, the Transform menu was part of the Layer menu. It had jumped there from version 3, when it was on the Edit menu. In Photoshop 5, Transform once again has moved back to the Edit menu. However, because you can only Transform layers (or Paths, or anything else if it has a selection Marquee around it), we will continue to include the various transform commands in the discussion of Layers. The various commands of the Edit|Transform submenu allow you to make these small changes in two ways. The first is interactive. After you have selected a command, a rectangle with eight live points—one at each corner, one at the center of each side—forms around the pixels. You can click and drag any of these points, which changes the shape or orientation of the enveloping rectangle. The objects within change their shape or orientation to conform to the rectangle. The second is a numeric method, where precise values can be entered into a dialog box. You'll achieve the same results whether you use the *by eye* method or numbers. The following is a brief summary, with examples, of the Transform submenu. We discuss this in more detail in Chapter 11.

Scale

Scale, as you might imagine, is the tool that allows you to change the size of a group of pixels. When you execute the command, a rectangle forms around the pixels to be affected—shown in Figure 6.84. You can change the shape of this rectangle any way you wish. If you select one of the corner points and move it toward the rectangle's center, the object—group of pixels—becomes smaller. Move the corner away from the rectangle's center and the object becomes larger. In the figure, the airplane has been made smaller.

You can also move the center points on the sides of the rectangle in either direction. Your resized object will then show anamorphic distortion. Maintaining the initial aspect ratio through the resizing requires that you move one of the corner points while holding the Shift key.

Figure 6.84 The object on the layer, the plane, shown in preview after it has been made smaller, but before the final command has been made.

As soon as you have moved one of the points and released the mouse button, Photoshop calculates a preview of the change for you to evaluate. If you have arrived at the size you want, either double-click within the rectangle or press the Return key. You can, of course, make further adjustments to the size. Photoshop will continue to show you previews after each move. The calculation from the initial size to the final size does not occur until you double-click or press Return. If you change your mind about the scale before you have completed it, hold down Command or Ctrl and press the period (.) key.

> **TIP**
>
> With any of the transformation commands, you can click and drag within the enveloping rectangle to change the position of the object before you change it.

Rotate

The Rotate command is one of four types of Rotate commands on the Arrange menu. Three commands rotate the pixels in fixed amounts that let you orient the object to any of the cardinal points. The single Rotate command is a freewheeling affair that lets you rotate, by eye, to any amount you choose. When the rectangle has formed, click and drag—anywhere except within the rectangle—sideways, and the rectangle turns on its center (see Figure 6.85). When you release the mouse button, the preview forms so that you can evaluate the new position and orientation of the pixels. New to this version of Photoshop is the capability to move the center point and rotate around a new location. Adobe Illustrator and other drawing programs have had this feature for years, and it was a much-requested feature by many Photoshop users.

Skew

In the Photoshop context, Skew attempts to keep two opposite side of the bounding rectangle parallel to each other while making the other two nonparallel (see Figure 6.86). If you work at

Figure 6.85 Click and drag anyplace but inside the rectangle to rotate the affected pixels. The preview forms after you release the mouse button.

it, you can make both pairs of opposite sides nonparallel. However, you can perform that task more easily with the Distort command.

Distort

With the Distort command, you can change the shape in any way you please. Drag the corners of the rectangle until it is as distorted as you wish it to be (see Figure 6.87). Photoshop does a nearly miraculous job of maintaining the legibility of the distorted object while stretching and bending it to conform to the envelope.

Perspective

The Perspective command attempts to give you the ability to orient the pixels on the layer to an arbitrary vanishing point. As you move one of the corner pixels in or out, the near corner closest to inline with the move—as opposed to the corner at right angles to the move—will move in the mirror direction. In Figure 6.88, the upper right corner has been moved down, which caused the lower right corner to move up. Both traveled toward the center horizontal axis of the rectangle. On the other side of the image, the upper left corner was pulled up, which caused the lower left corner to move down.

Numeric

If you wish to make your transformations of the pixels on the layer very precise, the Numeric Transform dialog box (see Figure 6.89) gives you a great deal of scope. Entering values in the data entry fields of this window lets you precisely set the Position (which can be relative, absolute, or use the new Percent units), Scale, Skew, and Rotation of your pixels all at the same time. Note that each of the three sections of the dialog box has a checkbox with which you can turn on or off the relevant functions. If you had finally trained yourself to use the key commands for Numeric Transform in Photoshop 4, forget it! It has been removed in this version of Photoshop.

Figure 6.86 Bounding rectangle and distortion shown by the Skew command.

Figure 6.87 Bounding rectangle and distortion shown by the Distort command.

Figure 6.88 Bounding rectangle and distortion shown by the Perspective command. Move any of the corners and the near corner point closest to inline with the move will move in the opposite direction. This is kind of spooky the first time you try it.

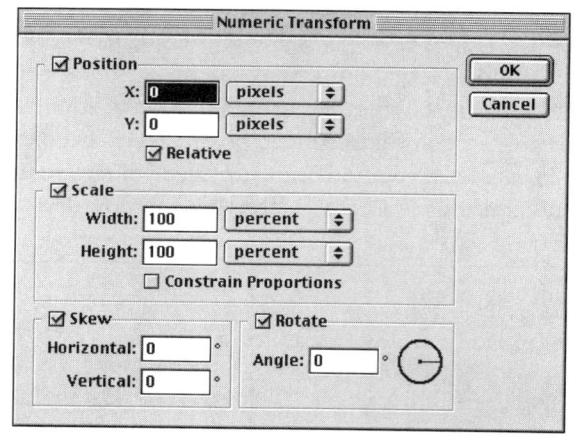

Figure 6.89 The Numeric Transform dialog box.

Or rather, the Shift+Command+T or Shift+Ctrl+T now repeats the last transformation that you did. It's a lovely feature (we discuss it in greater depth in Chapter 11), but easy access to the Numeric Transform command was nice, too.

Rotate 180°, Rotate 90° CW, And Rotate 90° CCW

These three commands turn the pixels on the layer to one of the three positions. Their purpose is self-explanatory. These three commands, with the two flip commands that follow, do not require Photoshop to use its superb, but computation-intensive, Bicubic interpolation method. Because of this, they are the fastest of the transformation commands. Examples of the three

Figure 6.90 Rotate 180°.

Figure 6.91 Rotate 90° CW.

Figure 6.92 Rotate 90° CCW.

commands are shown in Figures 6.90 (Rotate 180°), 6.91 (Rotate 90° CW—Clockwise), and 6.92 (Rotate 90° CCW—Counterclockwise).

Flip Horizontal, Flip Vertical

These two commands can be a little confusing if you are used to Adobe Illustrator's way of describing a flipped orientation. Illustrator describes a flip as being along an axis. Photoshop's command, which makes no mention of an axis, may or may not be more intuitive, but the words used give the opposite effect. A horizontal flip keeps the object's up-down orientation,

Figure 6.93 Flip horizontal.

Figure 6.94 Flip vertical. Really Top Gun!

but reverses its sideways orientation (see Figure 6.93). A vertical flip produces the opposite effect (see Figure 6.94).

Free Transform

After you've gained a bit of experience with the other transformation commands, and have a good idea of how they work and what they do, you'll probably never use them again. Really. The reason for this is that you'll then try the Free Transform command, which does everything—everything!—the other commands do, and you won't need to use them again. Free Transform has the added benefit of having a key command to summon it: Hold down Command or Ctrl and press T.

When the Free Transform boundary rectangle appears, you may move any of its corners (while holding the Shift key if you wish to maintain the original aspect ratio). You can also click and drag (anywhere but inside the rectangle) to rotate the pixels. The rectangle remains rectangular unless you hold Command or Ctrl. With these modifier keys depressed, the corners become free of their right-angle constraints. You can then move the corner or center points anywhere you want to place them. If you want to, you can even flip the pixels. Try this: Drag the left-hand center point and drag it to one pixel to the right of the right-hand center point; now drag the right center point back to where the left point was. The object will flip horizontally.

The real benefit of the Free Transform command is that you can make a number of changes to an image that would otherwise require the same number of separate steps. Not only is Free Transform a time-saver, it is also beneficial to the quality of the image. Transformed objects need to be interpolated only once, as opposed to a number of times with separate steps. All in all, there is no real reason why, once you understand how the individual transformation commands work, you would ever use them.

Fun With Layers

We have included on the accompanying CD-ROM, in the Chapter 6 Practice Files folder, the file PLANE.PSD. This file contains the layered document shown in some of the examples in this chapter. It even includes the layer mask for the airplane layer.

You can have some fun with this file and experiment with layers while you do so. After discarding the layer mask, you could duplicate the airplane layer a few times and scale each to produce a flotilla of Cessnas (see Figure 6.95).

Another interesting possibility is to add propeller motion. Make a new layer above the plane. Draw a circular selection over the propeller with the same diameter as the propeller blades. Feather the selection 3 or 4 pixels. Make a black-to-white-to-black gradient (lower right of Figure 6.96), set the Opacity to 50%, and draw the gradient all the way across the circle at right angles to the propeller. You'll get the effect shown in Figure 6.96. If you want to get really cute, use the Free Transform command on the prop-motion layer to change the perspective of the plane of rotation.

These photographs were taken at Dillingham Airfield at the foot of the Waianae Mountains on the North Shore of Oahu, Hawaii. The plane is one of several used to tow gliders into the sky or to ferry aloft the daring members of SkyDive Hawaii. We've included three other files that have a Hawaiian theme on the accompanying CD-ROM in the Chapter 6 Practice Files folder. They are titled WAIKIKI1.PSD, WAIKIKI2.PSD, and WAIKIKI3.PSD. If you want, you can assemble them into a layered document—#1 left, #2 center, and #3 right (as shown in Figure 6.98)—that will give you a panoramic view of all of Waikiki Beach. Remember that you can change the opacity of the overlaid images, distort them, rotate them, and move

Figure 6.95 The airplane layer, duplicated a few times and with each layer moved and resized, produces a squadron of Cessnas.

Figure 6.96 Make a circular feathered selection on a new layer. Draw a black-to-white-to-black gradient across the selection to make the prop movement.

Figure 6.97 Use the Perspective command to change the plane of the propeller movement.

Figure 6.98 Included on the book's CD-ROM are these three overlapping images that you can use to construct a panoramic view of the Waikiki skyline.

them to get the overlapping edges to match. After you change the Opacity back to 100%, you may need to do some touch-up work with some of the Selection tools, the Rubber Stamp tool, and perhaps a layer mask or two. We have also left the Adjustment layers attached to the images so that, if you want, you can tweak the colors to make the three as alike as possible. You'll find the task challenging and interesting, and you'll have a memorable photographic memento of your exploration of Photoshop's layers.

Layer Effects

If you haven't yet had enough fun with PLANE.PSD, Photoshop 5 has some additional tricks for you to try. When Adjustment layers were added in Photoshop 4, folks complained that although the Adjustment layers were great, it would be really spectacular to be able to apply filters and effects that could be changed. Adobe listened—in their own way, of course. The result is the Layer Effects feature, which gives you editable drop shadows, glows, bevels, and embosses.

Figure 6.99 shows the Effects submenu. You have a choice of five types of effects: Drop Shadow, Inner Shadow, Outer Glow, Inner Glow, and Bevel and Emboss. You can copy effects and paste them between layers and documents, and you can paste them automatically to all linked layers. You can also remove the effects with a single command (Clear Effects). You can hide them so that they are temporarily disabled. The Create Layer command removes the effect, but creates the layers needed to duplicate the effect. You have the choice to create one angle for all of the effects applied to an image (Global Angle) or set each effect individually. You can apply multiple effects to a single layer.

The easiest way to learn about the Layer Effects is to use them. Let's design a logo for a Japanese restaurant that can be used on a letterhead or at the upper left of a menu.

1. Open the file SAKURA.PSD on the CD-ROM.
2. Create a new document (Mac: Command+N, Windows: Ctrl+N) 900 pixels × 900 pixels, RGB, 300 ppi.
3. Drag the Sakura image into the new document. You can center it for the moment, though the location isn't critical right now.
4. Change your foreground color to RGB 197, 145, 78 (a light copper). Fill the letters with Transparency On (Mac: Shift+Option+Delete, Windows: Shift+Alt+Delete).
5. Add a drop shadow. Choose Layer|Effects|Drop Shadow. Figure 6.100 shows the lettering with the drop shadow applied. It's very simple. The Drop Shadow Mode defaults to Multiply, but you can change it if you want. For now, leave the Mode at Multiply. Set the Opacity to 75%, the Angle to 120, the Distance and Blur to 18 pixels. Leave the

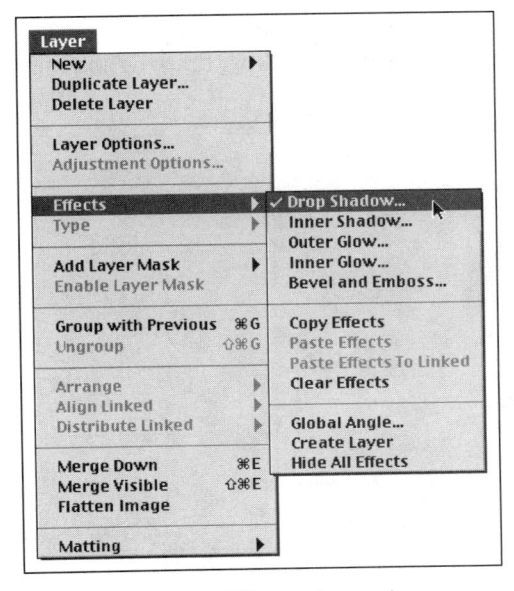

Figure 6.99 The Layer Effects submenu has many options for adding editable effects to layers.

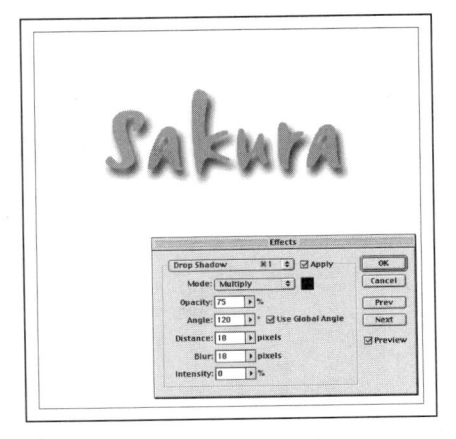

Figure 6.100 Applying a Drop Shadow to text.

Intensity at 0. If you have no clue as to the angle and distance that you desire, you can drag the shadow on the image itself, and Photoshop will place the values into the dialog box for you. Click on OK to close the Effects dialog box.

6. Drag the Sakura layer to the New Layer icon at the bottom of the Layers palette to duplicate the layer. Choose Layer|Effects|Clear Effects. This removes the drop shadow from the copied layer.

7. Load the layer by pressing the modifier key (Mac: Command, Windows: Ctrl) and clicking on the layer name in the Layers palette.

8. Choose Select|Modify|Contract, 3 pixels. This moves the selection Marquee in by three pixels. Press the Delete key. Deselect (Mac: Command+D, Windows: Ctrl+D).

9. Choose Layer|Effects|Bevel And Emboss. You have a choice of four Styles: Outer Bevel, Inner Bevel, Emboss, and Pillow Emboss. Select Pillow Emboss. The settings that we used are actually the defaults: Highlight at Screen, 75%, Shadow at Multiply, 75%. The Pillow Emboss is set to an Angle of 120°, and a Depth and Blur of 5 pixels, Up. Figure 6.101 shows both the image and the Effects dialog box.

10. Choose the Linear Gradient tool in the Toolbox. Select the Copper gradient. Click on the Preserve Transparency box to turn it on. Drag the Gradient from top-left to bottom-right over the text.

11. Open the IRIS.PSD image and drag the layer into your working image. Place the iris so that the top of the flower touches the bottom of the letters A and K in Sakura. The iris is the uppercase letter Q in the ITC Japanese Garden font. Repeat Step 4 to fill the iris with the same color as the text.

12. Choose Layer|Effects|Inner Shadow. Click on the color swatch and change it to RGB: 151, 104, 43. Leave the Opacity at 75% and the Angle at 120°. Either drag the shadow

Figure 6.101 You can give text an interesting outer border by using the Pillow Emboss style on the outer area of the text.

or type "38" into the Distance field. Leave a Blur of 5 and an Intensity of 0. This is a very interesting effect when you use it with a complex shape, as you can see in Figure 6.102. It simulates a lighting pattern on the iris that we find to be quite pleasant. Save your work, as we will build onto it in the following section.

Are there any disadvantages to using the Layer Effects? They had a tendency to "band" during printing when we tested them at high resolutions. However, because much of this book was written while Photoshop 5 was still in the development phases, the jury is still out. Try it yourself and make up your own mind. Layer Effects are wonderful time-savers. You can still do things the old way if you want total control, but if you need to create an image in a hurry, Layer Effects will help you tremendously. By changing Blend modes and colors, you can create original-looking, standout effects. The Pillow Emboss and the Inner Shadow are two very interesting features that most artists have not created by hand.

Another neat feature of Layer Effects is that they are applied to the layer, not to the object in the layer. Fine distinction? Perhaps, but create an empty layer and apply an outer bevel to it. Then use the Paintbrush and paint into the layer. Fun? You bet!

You can also create your own mini-library of effects. After you create an effect that you especially like, copy the layer to a tiny document—a 100-pixel square image will do. You don't need to save the object in the layer, just the layer itself. Name it something that tells you about the effect. For example, to save the inner shadow from the preceding example, just copy it to its own image and crop to a 100-pixel area. Save it as INNERSHADOW.PSD. The next time you want to use it, drag the layer into any open image. Place type or an image into the layer above and Merge Down. Figure 6.103 shows another letter from the ITC Japanese Garden that was created this way.

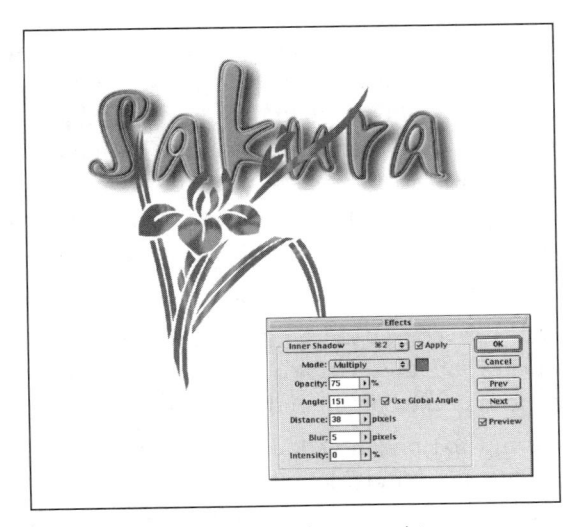

Figure 6.102 The Inner Shadow simulates the play of light on an object.

Figure 6.103 You can save Effects as tiny documents and drag them into an open image. Anything placed into the layer then takes on that Effect.

In Perfect Alignment

It is self-evident that Photoshop is not Illustrator, but many Photoshop artists have had Illustrator-like needs for measuring and controlling where objects are placed on an image. In Photoshop 5, Adobe finally gives you the ability to align and distribute objects. Aligning objects means that the nontransparent pixels in two or more layers can be made to appear in a straight line arrangement with each other or with a selected area of the image. Distributed objects space themselves across the image. You can use both techniques to create a border for the Sakura logo that you created previously.

1. Open the image VINE.PSD. This is another letter from the ITC Japanese Garden font.

2. Drag the vine into the saved image from the last exercise. Place it in the upper-left corner so that it touches both the left side and the top. Duplicate the layer by dragging it to the New Layer icon at the bottom of the Layers palette.

3. Choose Edit|Transform|Flip Horizontal. Move the flipped copy to the right until its left edge touches the right edge of the original (your left; your right). Merge Down (Mac: Command+E, Windows: Ctrl+E). Figure 6.104 shows this element.

4. Press the modifier key (Mac: Option, Windows: Alt) and select Edit|Transform|Numeric Transform. The Option/Alt key creates a copy of the transformation. In the dialog box, enter X: 100 pixels, Y: 0 pixels, Relative for Position. Press OK. This creates a new

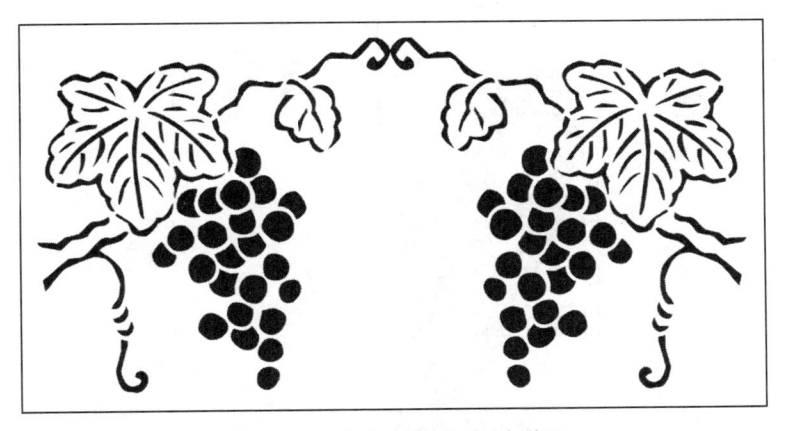

Figure 6.104 The start of the border element made from an individual vine.

layer with the vine element moved 100 pixels to the right. Create another four copies of this element (Mac: Shift+Option+Command+T, Windows: Shift+Alt+Ctrl+T). This is the "Repeat Again" command and it makes it very easy to create copies that are slightly apart from one another.

5. Drag the final copy to the right edge of the image. Keep the Shift key pressed as you drag, so that all of the copies stay in line. Make the first vine element active (it is Layer X). Click on the Link icon next to all of the vines. Figure 6.105 shows the Layers palette at this point. Figure 6.106 shows the Distribute submenu. Choose Layer|Distribute Linked, Left. The top half of Figure 6.107 shows the position of all of the vines before distributing them, and the bottom half shows the image after the vines have been distributed.

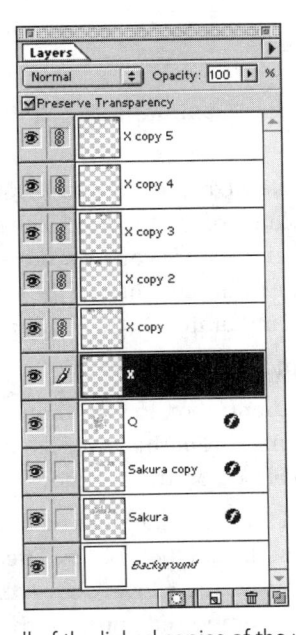

Figure 6.105 The Layers palette shows all of the linked copies of the vine.

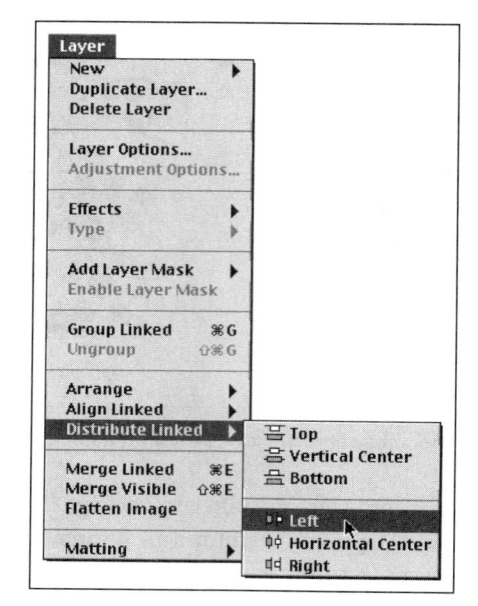

Figure 6.106 The Distribute Linked submenu evenly spaces a group of objects.

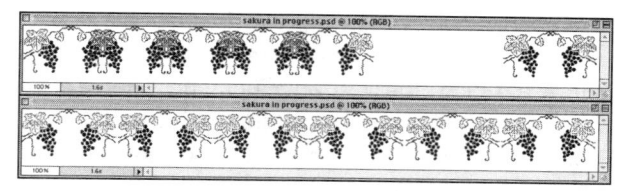

Figure 6.107 The top half shows the border before and the bottom half shows the border after it is distributed across the top of the image.

6. Merge the linked layers (Mac: Command+E, Windows: Ctrl+E). You now have a top border.

7. Drag the border layer to the New Layer icon to duplicate the layer. Using white as your foreground color, paint a splotch of white paint at the very bottom of the layer. (This trick helps you rotate the layer; because you now have pixels at the top and bottom of the layer, it will seem to rotate from the center of the layer rather than the center of the border.) Choose Edit|Transform|Rotate 90° CCW. Figure 6.108 shows the image.

8. Merge Down (Mac: Command+E, Windows: Ctrl+E).

9. Click on the Preserve Transparency box to turn it on. Select the Gradient tool and the Copper gradient. Drag the cursor from the lower-left corner of the image to the upper right. This makes a copper-colored border that goes with the rest of the image.

10. Open the image BORDERFX.PSD. Gee that looks odd—there's nothing in it! It contains layer effects, however. Choose Layer|Effects|Copy Effects. Click on the Sakura image that you have been creating. Make the X layer active (the border). Choose Layer|Effects| Paste Effects. You now have an embossed border with a glow.

Figure 6.108 The image with a border on the top and sides.

11. Double-click on the F icon (the black circle) on the X layer. This opens the Layer Effects dialog box. The border has an Outer Glow applied to it. A light orange glow at an intensity of 42 adds a little color. The vines have a pillow emboss. You can experiment and change any settings that you want. Figure 6.109 shows the finished image. If you wonder where the grid behind the iris came from, we have a challenge for you.

On the enclosed CD-ROM, you'll find a file named FLOWER.PSD. That's what we used, along with a 10-pixel straight line, to make the grid. We constructed it in a 600 × 600 pixel image. Can you duplicate this? (Hint: we used four lines and three flowers in each direction. To get the flowers between the lines, they have to be in order in the Layers palette. The grid is applied to the image in the same color as the text at 30 percent opacity. A Pillow Emboss effect is used.)

Matting: Defringe, Remove Black Matte, Remove White Matte

Occasionally, when you detach a group of pixels from one image and move it to a different location, the selection process will include background pixels that form a fringe of unwanted color. The three Matting commands are included to help you remove those extra pixels or to change their color so that they don't intrude on the visual effect you are creating.

Defringe is the most powerful command of the three—which isn't saying much. Sigh. When you choose the command, a dialog box appears, asking for a dimension in radius. Enter the number of pixels you estimate to be the width of the extra pixels around the edge of the pixel group (though it doesn't seem to matter). Click on OK, and the program will blend the color of the pixels with the tones adjacent to them. Or at least that's the theory. It does work, but the result is often not worth having. You should try the command with the hope that it might

Figure 6.109 The Sakura logo.

provide a reasonable result. If it does so, then you are saved the effort of adjusting the edge pixels manually—often a tedious and time-consuming process. If it doesn't work as well as you might like, well, bite the bullet, as it's said.

Black Matte and White Matte remove fringe from objects that were originally on a black or white background. In the cases where these two commands work, they work perfectly. Otherwise, you may see no change to your edge pixels. There doesn't seem to be a way to predict when these commands will work and when they will not. However, they are always worth a try.

Moving On

In this chapter you learned how to think in layers and recognize the difference between a layer's pixels and the transparent areas that surround them. You also entered the fascinating world of Blend mode calculations, which can combine layers in intriguing and beautiful ways. Along with Blend modes, you learned about layer opacity and the Blend If possibilities, which can exclude pixels from visibility, based on their brightness or color. You have glimpsed the tremendous power of layer masks.

You will find that layer work is one of the most enjoyable and magical of In Depth Photoshop activities. Don't worry about keeping track of everything that you could possibly do with layers. When the time comes that you need one of the layer features, come back to this chapter, look at the relevant section, and then try it. You'll find that what you want to do is much easier than you thought.

In Chapter 11, you'll learn a good deal more about Adjustment layers, the single aspect of layers that we didn't explore extensively in this chapter. You already know what Adjustment layers are and how to make them. Chapter 11 will show you how to put them to good use with editable color corrections and with stacked Adjustment layers, which can give you some wonderful special effects. In Chapters 9 and 10, you'll meet Adjustment layers in a professional prepress setting. You'll build on what you've already learned so that your Photoshop images will translate into accomplished printed work.

CALCULATIONS

Learn how to use the Apply Image and the Calculations commands to generate unique artwork. This chapter explains some of the intricacies of these commands.

Would you like to be an armchair general? Commanding your images and sternly saying "Go here!" or "Do this!" as your images meekly obey and move? If you enjoy directing, you will love the Calculations and Apply Image commands. Once the exclusive preserve of Photoshop junkies, these two commands are now easy enough for a novice to use. All you need to do is try them. These two commands are still considered to be very esoteric, and they are not used nearly as often as they should be, but they add power, ease, and convenience to an already powerful program. The Calculations and Apply Image commands will amply reward your learning to use them.

So, what are these commands, and how do you start commanding them? The Calculations and Apply Image commands (let's just call them CHOPs—CHannel OPerations—for short) are used to composite images and channels without cutting, pasting, dragging, dropping, or mousing around. The commands allow you to take image A and blend it with image B using any Blend mode (two more than are available using layers) at any opacity using any channel, layer mask, or layer transparency as a mask. You have a wide range of places that you can "send" the output. Although these are two different commands, they are quite similar in concept, operation, and function. We'll explain the differences in this chapter.

Before getting into the details, a bit of Photoshop history is justified. Prior to the introduction of Photoshop 3 in November 1994, Photoshop had no layers. The user blended together pieces of images either by using the Calculations commands or by pasting pieces of one image into another. The Calculations commands were a series of separate commands; each one performed a different function. There was a Multiply command, a Screen command, Lighter, Darker, Add, Subtract, Difference, and Blend. You selected image or channel 1, image or channel 2 and the opacity, and the computer magically produced the requested image. There was no preview, so you could frequently be surprised. CHOPs experts such as Kai Krause often produced 114 open images in a session in an effort to create the perfect image (and all these images were called "Untitled-whatever" because no way existed to name a document until it was saved to disk).

When Photoshop 3 was designed, the engineers decided to try to simplify the process. They half succeeded. They exchanged a group of easy-to-comprehend, but difficult-to-control commands for two powerful, easy-to-visualize commands with the most daunting interface dialog anywhere in Photoshop. The commands caused a bit of an uproar in the Photoshop community, because many of the users' favorite "tricks" no longer worked and the two commands are so similar that it is often hard to see the need for both of them. In defense of the engineers, the two commands did not really start out as similar as they became. User pressure forced certain changes in them as the program neared its delivery date (and, as you will see shortly, these last-minute changes have been removed from version 5). The CHOPs commands are needed less in Photoshop 3, 4, and 5 than they were needed in Photoshop 2.5 and earlier, but they are still very useful. Rumor has it that many in Adobe would like to see these commands disappear altogether, but that would really be a shame. After you finish this chapter and try the power of CHOPs, we hope that you will agree.

The Apply Image Command

Let's meet the Apply Image command first. It is the more general of the two CHOPs commands and is conceptually easier to understand. This command allows you to place into your currently active layer or channel any other layer or channel from the same image or from any open image that has the identical pixel count. (We'd say "any open image that is the same size," but this isn't quite true. Two images that are each defined as 4 inches square but have different resolutions, will not work together, but two images with the same pixel count will—even if they are set at different ppi.)

It might help to imagine your active image as a slide screen. You can "project" onto this screen any "slide" (i.e., image layer or channel) that is lying around (open) and that will fit into the projector (is the same pixel count). Although the Apply Image command has many uses, it is particularly helpful in allowing you to easily place a previously created image or channel into a layer mask. Let's see how this works:

1. Open the image FLOWER.PSD from this book's CD-ROM. Figure 7.1 shows this image.
2. Create a new document (Mac: Command+N, Windows: Ctrl+N). Open the Window menu in the application and select FLOWER.PSD as the template for the new document.
3. Use the Eyedropper tool to select a light color from the flower as your foreground color. We selected a soft pink.
4. Fill the image with the foreground color (Shift+Delete).
5. Select a darker color as your foreground color. We used a deeper green in the flower.
6. Create a new layer (click on the New Layer icon at the bottom of the Layers palette). Fill the new layer with the foreground color.
7. Create a layer mask (click on the Layer Mask icon at the bottom left of the Layers palette).
8. With the layer mask active, choose Image|Apply Image. Figure 7.2 shows the dialog box. Your "target" image is the layer and channel that is currently active. You have no choice about that. (A *target* is the place where the output of the command is placed.)

Figure 7.1 The original FLOWER.PSD image.

You only need to select your Source image (the one that is to be placed *into* the target). In the box named Source, select FLOWER.PSD. If you have many open images, only images of the correct size show up in the menu as an option.

9. Select Background as the Layer and RGB as the Channel. This places a grayscale version of the flower image into the layer mask. You may change the Blend mode to Normal or leave it at the default of Multiply—it makes no difference in this instance. Click on the Invert button in the dialog to see a "positive" instead of a negative of the flower. Make sure that Preview is checked so that you can see what will happen.

10. Set the Blend mode to Normal and the Opacity to 100%. Click on OK. Figure 7.3 shows the result.

Figure 7.2 The Apply Image dialog.

Figure 7.3 This figure shows what happens when you use the Apply Image command to create a density layer mask.

> **TIP**
>
> The default Blend mode is Multiply. When the target is solid white, it makes no difference to the result if the mode is left at Multiply or changed to Normal. Under any other circumstance, it makes a great deal of difference.

The Apply Image command is better than cut and paste when you work in a layer mask for several reasons. There is no clipboard memory used, so it's more sparing on RAM. It's somewhat tricky to paste into a layer mask in Photoshop. You cannot do this at all unless you work in the Channels palette with only the entry for the Layer Mask channel active. Otherwise, when you paste, you end up adding a new layer rather than putting anything into the mask. If you use the Apply Image command, your image always stays in register because the portion applied is always in the same location.

Another very practical use of the Apply Image command is to add density into (or subtract from) a color channel. You will use the Apply Image command for this purpose in Chapter 11.

The Calculations Command

The Calculations command is quite similar to the Apply Image command, but the dialog box is far more complex. (See Figure 7.4.) This dialog has a Source 1, Source 2, Blending Section, and a Result. Before you try to do anything fancy, however, look at the available options.

Unlike the Apply Image command, you can select any two channels or layers of the same size in any open document, regardless of whether that layer or channel is active. In a weird sense,

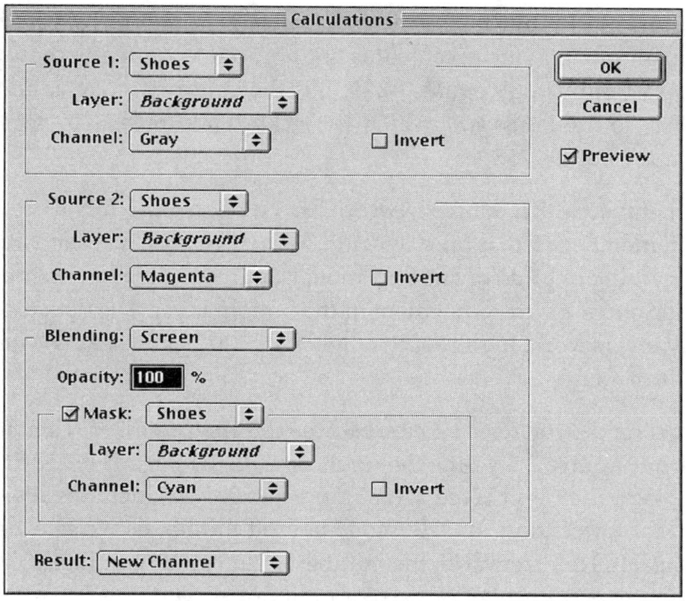

Figure 7.4 The Calculations dialog box.

it is like being able to stand near a crowd and say, "You and you, get married." You can play matchmaker to any two things and put the result somewhere else. This power comes with several catches, however. Calculations works only in grayscale. The only channels options are the color channels, the alpha or gray—not the Composite channel. If you need color (The composite channel: RGB, CMYK, etc.), you must use the Apply Image command.

Version 5 has also changed the "rules" for identifying a target for the calculation. Earlier versions of Photoshop allowed you to place the result into any channel of the document or into any channel of any open document of the same pixel count, or as a selection in any "eligible" document (as well as creating a new document for it). This version—in a decision that we feel is, perhaps, the most useful—only allows you the choices of New Channel, Selection, or New Document, and the channel or selection will occur only in the active image. It never mattered before which image was active when you selected the command; now it does. Version 5.0's Calculations command change also means that you cannot overwrite an existing channel. That can be annoying, but you can always use the Apply Image command if you need to change an existing channel.

The other catch—and this is what makes calculations so complex—is that sometimes it matters which image you use as Source 1 and which you use as Source 2. (Sometimes, it doesn't matter at all.) If you change the Opacity from 100%, it always matters. If you use Normal, Overlay, Hard Light, Soft Light, Color Dodge, Color Burn, or Subtract mode, it matters. If the Opacity is left at 100% and you use Multiply, Screen, Difference, Add, or Exclusion mode, it doesn't matter, as those mathematical operations are *commutative* (i.e., $5 \times 9 = 9 \times 5$). You've known since second grade that 5 minus 2, for example, isn't equal to 2 minus 5. Because Blend modes are performing channel math, they follow the usual rules. For example, if you have a black pixel (value 0) in Source 1 and a white pixel (value 255) in Source 2 and use the Subtract mode, you get a black pixel (0 minus 255 equals –255, but the subtract mode cannot show anything darker than black, so the result is 0, which is black). If you reverse it, you get a white pixel because 255 minus 0 equals 255.

How do you remember which source is which? If you don't use this feature very often, you probably won't remember. Here is an easy "rule." When you use an Blend mode that can work in Layers (i.e., anything but Add or Subtract mode), Source 1 (the one "on top") is equivalent to the top layer and Source 2 is the equivalent of the bottom layer. The opacity settings also work in the same way layers work. If you set the Opacity to 20%, you see 20% of Source 1 (the top "layer") and 80% of Source 2.

If you use Subtract mode, you need to subtract Source 1 *from* Source 2. Therefore, if your Source 1 image is black and Source 2 is white, the result is white (0 *from* 255 is 255); if Source 1 is white and Source 2 is black, the result is black (255 from 0 is 0—well, actually it's –255, but Subtract mode cannot count lower than 0). Add mode doesn't matter, as we said previously, because order is not important. Note, however, the number in Add mode cannot exceed 255. White plus white still only equals 255 as there is no color in grayscale with a value of 510.

The best way to learn how the Calculations command works is to experiment with it, using a group of channels that are solid and named. We will set this up shortly. The other "goodies" in the Calculations command are the capability both to use the inverse of either Source 1 or Source 2 (or both) and to use a mask on the operation and invert it! This capability gives the command almost mind-boggling complexity!

Let's set up a Calculations example by using three layers—one black, one gray, and one white.

Calculations On Solids

The simplest way to learn about Calculations is to play with them by using solid layers. In this example, you need to create a small, three-layered image. Let's see what can be done:

1. Create a new document by using Command+N (Mac) or Ctrl+N (Windows). Make the image 400 pixels square. Create the image in grayscale. (Because Calculations only creates a grayscale image anyway, why bother with color?)

2. View the Channels palette. The first channel in a grayscale image is automatically named "Black" at the start. Let's Fill this channel with black.

3. Click on the New Channel icon in the center of the Channels palette to create a new channel. Name this channel White by double-clicking the channel name. When you do, this brings up the Channel Options dialog where you can rename the channel and also fill it with white.

4. Create another new channel. Name it Gray 50% and fill it with 50% gray. Figure 7.5 shows the Channels palette so far.

5. It doesn't matter which channel in the image is active. Select Image|Calculations. Make the gray channel both the Source 1 image and the Source 2 image. Select Add as

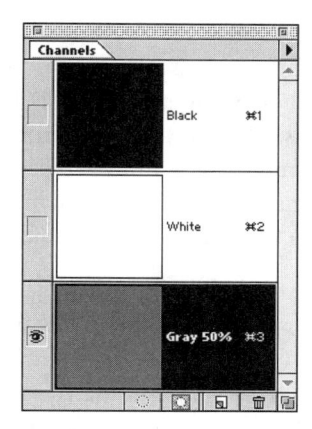

Figure 7.5 The Channels palette, using the current practice file.

the Blend mode. Set the Opacity to 100%. If you were to add 128 (neutral gray) to 128, you would get 256 (or our maximum of 255), which is white. This is precisely what our result happens to be. (Do not click on OK to actually apply this yet.) Figure 7.6 shows the Calculations dialog.

6. Change Source 1 to the White channel and leave Source 2 as the Gray 50% channel. Change the Blending to Subtract and leave the Opacity at 100%. The image turns black. Why? Source 1 (White) from Source 2 (Gray 50%) = Source 2 (128) − Source 1 (255) = 128 − 255 = − 128 (which is really 0) = Black (0). Do *not* click on OK.

7. Change Source 1 to Gray 50% and Source 2 to White. What do you get now? Answer: 50% gray, because 255 minus 128 equals 127.

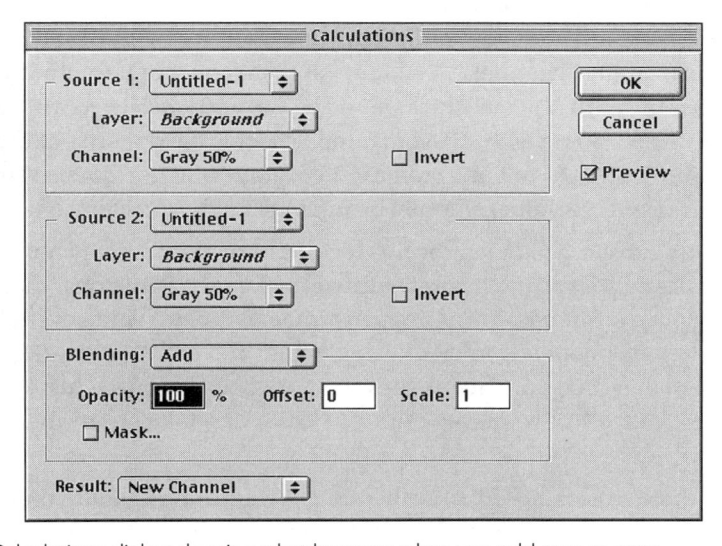

Figure 7.6 The Calculations dialog showing what happens when you add gray to gray.

As long as you understand the Channel math that was introduced in Chapter 5, this should be easy—at least for the "easy" Blend modes such as Normal, Multiply, Screen, Add, Subtract, Lighter, Darker, and Difference. There were the "original" Blend modes, for which Adobe published the mathematical formulas. The newer modes on the menu (Overlay, Hard Light, Soft Light, Color Dodge, Color Burn, and Exclusion) are considered to be proprietary and the specific calculations are really not made available. You can predict the general results of those modes, but you might not be able to calculate the specific pixel value in advance.

Now, create some new channels with different values in them so that you can build up the complexity a bit. Continue working in the grayscale image, which you can save as PRACTICE.PSD, by taking these steps:

1. Use the Calculations command to multiply the Gray 50% channel with itself. Were you able to predict the result? This time, click on OK and let the command create a new channel (which is the default). After the new channel is created, double-click on it and rename it Gray 75% (which is value 64). That's right, multiplying 50 percent gray with itself creates a gray that is half again as dark—75 percent gray instead of 50 percent gray.

> **TIP**
>
> The math here is calculated on the basis of 0 through 255, not percentages. If you use the Info palette densitometer on the channel, in grayscale, the percentages go from 100 percent black, which is value 0, to 0 percent black, which is value 255. Confusing? You bet! To keep your sanity, rename your gray channels in the practice document so that they contain the gray *value*, not the percentage.

2. Use the Calculations command to create another new channel—to be named Gray 192 (that's 25 percent). Can you think of any moves that can create a 25% gray channel from the available channels? A number of them can, but if we limit you to 100% Opacity, then the most obvious move should be Gray 50% screened with Gray 50% (if multiplying 50% × 50% yields 75% gray and Screen is the opposite of Multiply, then screening 50% and 50% should produce 25% gray, which it does). You could also produce a 25% (or 192 value) channel by adding Gray 128 to Gray 64.

3. Now that you have a good idea (or no clue at all) of what's happening, we need to advance to the next level and throw Opacity into the mix. Remember that the opacity refers to the *Source 1* image. What happens when you place white over black at 50% Opacity in Normal mode? (Don't really apply this.) You get 50% gray. The results that you get from other mixes are not as consistent or as easy to guess. Just know that you get less from Source 1 of whatever effect you are trying to achieve when you change the opacity.

4. And then, there's masking—this further complicates (or expands) the possibilities. Choose the Calculations command. Make Source 1 and Source 2 both Gray 25%. Select Screen at 100% opacity as the Blend mode. Click on the Mask button and choose Gray 25% as the mask as shown in Figure 7.7. The result is Gray 176 (or 31%). Instead of the 25% black that you previously produced by screening 50% gray with itself, you have

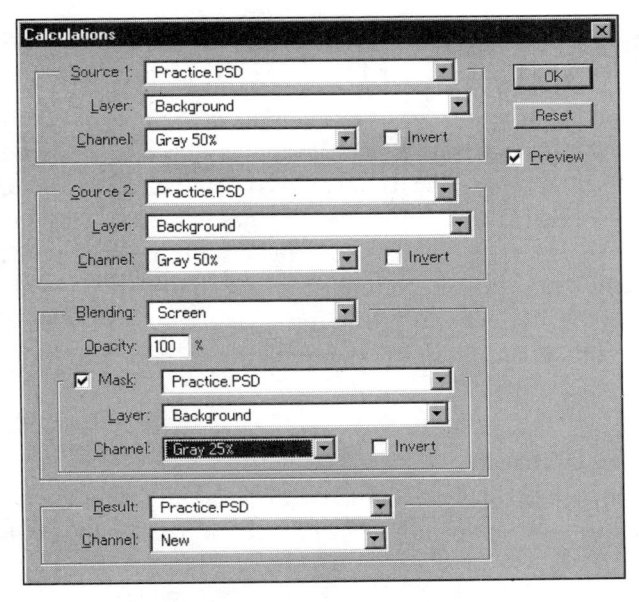

Figure 7.7 You can use a mask in the Calculations command.

allowed only approximately 75% of the change to occur (or, said another way, the 25% gray mask removes 25% of the change that would otherwise occur).

Luckily, you can use the Apply Image and Calculations commands completely by "accident"—even if the math makes your teeth ache. Because you have Preview capability, you can fiddle with the settings until you see something that you like. This is a lot faster than cut and paste or drag and drop when you have no clue what result you want or how to get it! Of course, having a clue as to what you want and how to get there makes the process go much faster.

Calculating A Grayscale

Creating grayscale images from color ones is one good, practical use of the Calculations command. Chapter 9 spends more time on this topic, but this technique, courtesy of New York artist Eric Reinfeld, works nicely.

When you convert a color image to a grayscale by using Photoshop's Image|Mode|Grayscale command, the result can often be too dark and muddy. There is often one channel that looks better than the grayscale image. If one channel—when you view it in the Channels palette—is perfect, simply use that channel. Usually, no single channel is "just right," even though the Red, for example, might have better highlights and the Green, perhaps, might have better midtones. You can blend the channels by using the percentages that create the best picture that you can build.

Using the Calculations command, you do not even need to look at the channels first. You can view each RGB channel in turn by setting the Blend mode to Normal (which makes the Source 1 channel fully opaque if the Opacity is set to 100%). After you look at each channel, you can then decide which two are best. In most images, the Red channel gives you the best detail, the Green channel gives you the best contrast, and the Blue channel carries the most noise and garbage.

If you determine that the Red and Green channels are best, make one of them Source 1 and the other Source 2. The Blend mode can be set to Normal, and you can then fiddle with the Opacity percent until you like the blend (Eric usually uses a 60-40 blend of Red and Green). The individual image, however, dictates the final percentages needed. Figure 7.8 shows an example. The cactus is, of course, basically green, which makes turning it into grayscale different than working with a picture of a person. To make a good, contrasty grayscale, we placed the Red channel in Source 1, the green channel in Source 2, and set the Blend mode to Normal at 20%. This makes a better image (in Figure 7.8, part *b*) than the "standard" grayscale conversion (in Figure 7.8, part *a*).

Calculating Selections

You can also load the results of a Calculation into a selection. Let's try that example. You will use four files of the same size; three of these have been rasterized from the Ultimate Symbol

Figure 7.8 (a)   A Grayscale conversion.

Figure 7.8 (b)   This figure uses a 20% Red-80% Green calculation.

Figure 7.9 The Star, Zodiac, Sunface, and Texture images.

Design Elements collection (the fourth one, TEXTURE.PSD, is a simple, made-up texture). Let's see what happens:

1. Open the images STAR.PSD, TEXTURE.PSD, SUNFACE.PSD, and ZODIAC.PSD from this book's companion CD-ROM. Figure 7.9 shows the four images.
2. Choose Image|Calculations. Make ZODIAC.PSD the Source 1 image and TEXTURE.PSD Source 2. You want to place the texture into the area occupied by the Zodiac. Therefore,

you need to change the Blending to Screen. Place the result into a new document (it will be named Untitled-1 if you have no other untitled images open). Figure 7.10 shows the Calculations dialog; Figure 7.11 shows the result.

3. Choose Image|Calculations. Make STAR.PSD the Source 1 image and SUNFACE.PSD Source 2. Change the Blend mode to Multiply and click on Invert on Source 1. This replaces the black star with the image of the Sunface. Place this into a new document (automatically named Untitled-2). Figure 7.12 shows the result.

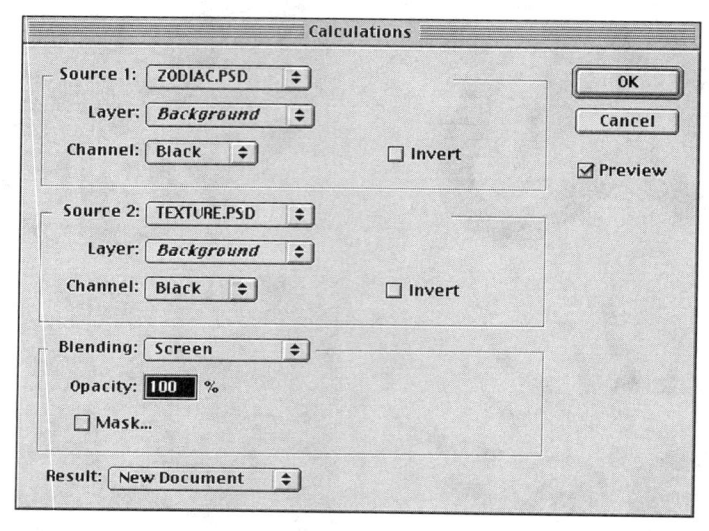

Figure 7.10 The Calculations dialog.

Figure 7.11 The Zodiac image, screened onto a texture.

Figure 7.12 This figure shows what happens when you invert the Star and multiply it with the Sunface image.

4. For the final step, choose Image|Calculations and use Untitled-1 as Source 1, Untitled-2 as Source 2, and Screen as the Blend mode. Invert *both* sources. Place the result into TEXTURE.PSD as a *selection*. Figure 7.13 shows the Calculations dialog.

5. Press the Delete or Backspace key to remove the selection from the image. Figure 7.14 shows the deselected result.

Figure 7.13 The Calculations dialog used in Step 4.

Figure 7.14 Deleting the selection placed by screening an inverted version of Untitled-1 and Untitled-2 creates this Star, Texture, Zodiac, Sunface blend.

> **Tip**
>
> If you are performing calculations on images that have no background layer (e.g., an image rasterized from Adobe Illustrator as STAR.PSD and SUNFACE.PSD were originally), then the calculations will behave differently. You will have a choice of using either the Black channel or the Layer Transparency in your calculations, and you will get results that both differ from each other and differ from the results obtained from using the flattened images. The white of the Background layer (or any solid background on a layer) is a participant in the Apply Image command. The Layer Transparency, however, does not participate in the calculation of the result, so it does make a difference when you use the command.

There are many other possibilities to explore; you have seen only a few of them here. Working with selections in Calculations produces results that differ from working with image data. The thing that you need to know about working with selections is that the selection uses the *values* in the calculation—not the shape or color of the selected objects. Therefore, an area that is fully selected will "read" as white—or 255—for the purposes of the calculation, in spite of the actual gray values of the pixels within the selection.

Figure 7.15 shows two images, a black square and a circle filled with the Pointillize filter. Both shapes are selected. Figure 7.16 shows the Calculations dialog. The two selections are blended together in Subtract mode. Figure 7.17 shows the result. Notice that the fill on the circle does not participate in the calculation at all. It has no result on the final image.

Apply Image And Calculations Compared

Now that you have tried both Apply Image and Calculations, how do they compare? Certainly the Apply Image command is easier to use; but the Calculations command seems more powerful. Let's look at these two commands by comparing their capabilities in a logical fashion.

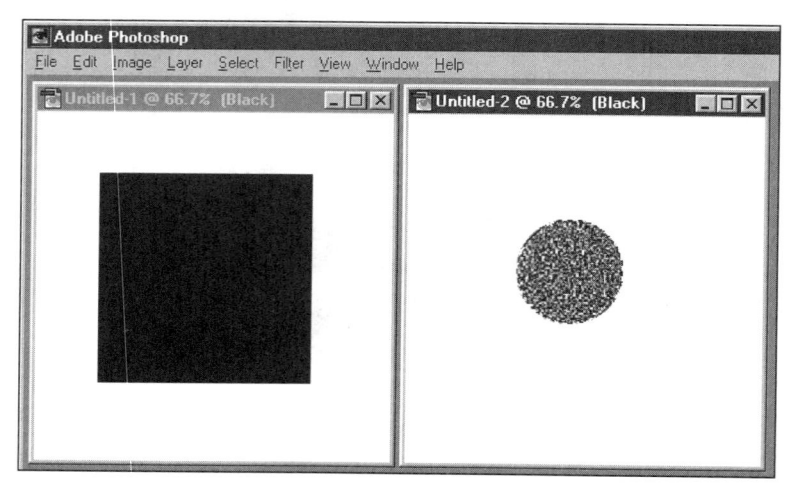

Figure 7.15 Two selected shapes filled with the Pointillize filter.

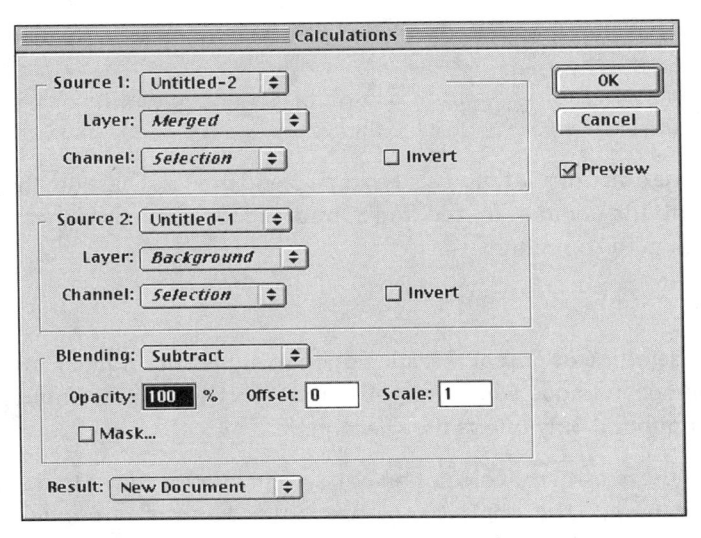

Figure 7.16 The Calculations dialog that blends the two shapes together.

Figure 7.17 The final result of the calculation is that only the shapes appear.

Source Images

The Apply Image command only needs one source image as input. It "knows" the second source because the Source 2 is always the currently active image. In contrast, the Calculations command can use any two open and same-sized images as sources.

Both commands can see any layer or channel, but if you select a layer that contains color information in it, the Apply Image command can "see" the color data (Composite channel), as well as the individual channels. Calculations sees the color channels individually, but sees the composite color only as gray.

If you have layers in your image, both commands allow you to manipulate the layer transparency as the channel to be used.

Blending

Both Apply Image and Calculations use the same Blend modes. These are the same as the layer Blend modes with the addition of Add and Subtract mode. You can adjust the opacity on the source images in both commands.

Selections

You can use the selection as part of the calculation in either command. However, if you have a selection in the active image when you select the Apply Image command, the result of the Apply Image command only affects the selection.

You can also see the *result* of the calculation as a selection in the target image when you use the Calculations command. The Apply Image command does not normally put its result anywhere except into the active image layer or channel, and cannot create a selection as a result of channel math.

Results

The Calculations command allows you to place the results into a new channel in the active document, into a selection in the active document, or into a new document. *Calculations only creates channels.* It cannot place a result into a layer as anything other than a selection (and a selection is not specific to a layer). Additionally, when Calculations creates a new image, it uses Multichannel mode as the color mode. In order to work with the image as you normally would (to add more layers to it or save it as a TIFF), you need to convert the image to grayscale or a color mode.

Apply Image can save its result only into the target (active) image or channel. In Photoshop 3 and 4, you were able to press the Option (Mac) or Alt (Windows) key when you selected the command from the menu. This obvious afterthought was one of the most useful (and little known) features of the Apply Image command. Simply by holding a modifier key as you selected the command, you could have the best part of the Calculations command along with the ability to work with color. You could target a layer, a layer mask, a channel, a new image, or a selection as your output. Unhappily, the Adobe folks decided to remove that shortcut from version 5.0 because they didn't think that anyone would miss it. We strongly disagree with this decision, however, and regret the loss of this little trick.

> **TIP**
>
> You can somewhat simulate the old behavior of the Option/Alt key with Apply Image by permitting the command to overwrite your original target and then creating a new image from the result by clicking on the leftmost icon at the bottom of the History palette. You can then click on the step prior to the Apply Image command in the original image to restore the previous state of the image.

Because Apply Image handles color, you can use Apply Image for almost anything that you want to calculate. For many users, it will be the only one of the CHOPs commands they use. As you begin to perform actions on channels, however, you will discover that you like the Calculations command—even with its greatly added complexity.

Calculating An Image—A Different Way To Work

You can create wonderful works of art with the CHOPs commands. It is really a different way to work. Unlike the way in which artists work with real media, CHOPs allows you to experiment in a manner that Kai Krause (whom we could almost call the "father of CHOPs" or certainly one of its earliest promoters) calls "algorithmic painting." It is a technique that could only exist electronically. Kai Krause is part of the Metacreations team and you can find some of his work at **www.metacreations.com**.

Using CHOPs to develop an image is an exercise in serendipity. Once you try it, you can get hooked on the possibilities to the exclusion of anything else that you had planned for the day, such as work, sleep, or eating. You rarely know where you are really headed and there are so many options that you can easily end up someplace else—even if you started with a distinct notion of what you wanted to achieve.

For this exercise, let's use a piece of original artwork contributed by Sausalito-based artist Rhoda Grossman, who has consented to let us use one of her trademark nudes—even though it was already a completed piece of art. We will also use a snowflake from the Ultimate Symbol Design Elements collection (which comes on this book's CD-ROM and is one of the most useful collections of vector-based clip art available) and a layered texture that was created by using the KPT Texture Explorer and KPT Fractal Explorer.

In this exercise, just follow along with us. There is really no rhyme or reason to why we selected these steps. The idea is to try something, and then send it to a new image. You could stack up a large number of layers equally "correctly," but keeping each image as a separate entity allows you to view all of the images at once. The disadvantage is that you cannot name the images as you create them if you use the Calculations command, and you might not be able to come up with descriptive names that are "legal" on your computer. If you do not name your images, however, you end up with a huge number of untitled images, which are really hard to keep apart or search for when you do the next composite. When you work on your own, place the images wherever you prefer. For now, do it our way so that you can duplicate our results. Let the computer name these images Untitled- as it pleases.

This exercise also makes you wonder how we remembered what was done in order to create the composite. That's easy! We took a screen shot every time we used a CHOPs command. Let's work the exercise, then we can discuss how you can keep track of both your work and your sanity at the same time:

1. Open the files SNOWFLKE.PSD (Figure 7.18), FRACTAL.PSD (Figure 7.19), and BLUELADY.PSD (Figure 7.20) from this book's companion CD-ROM.

Figure 7.18 This figure shows the original SNOWFLKE.PSD image.

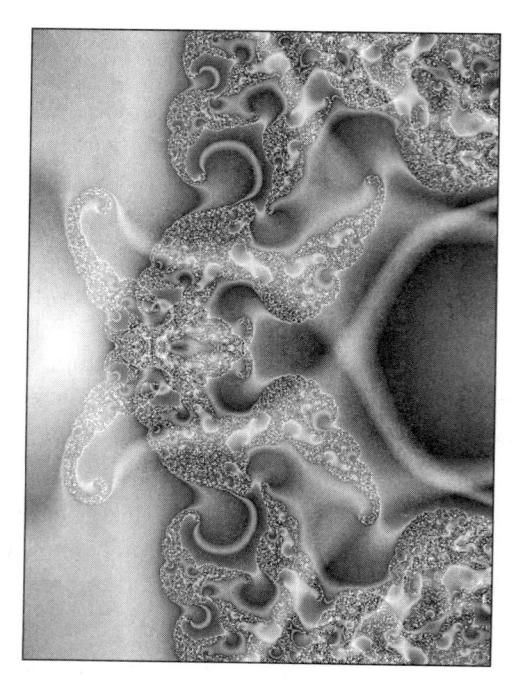

Figure 7.19 The original FRACTAL.PSD image.

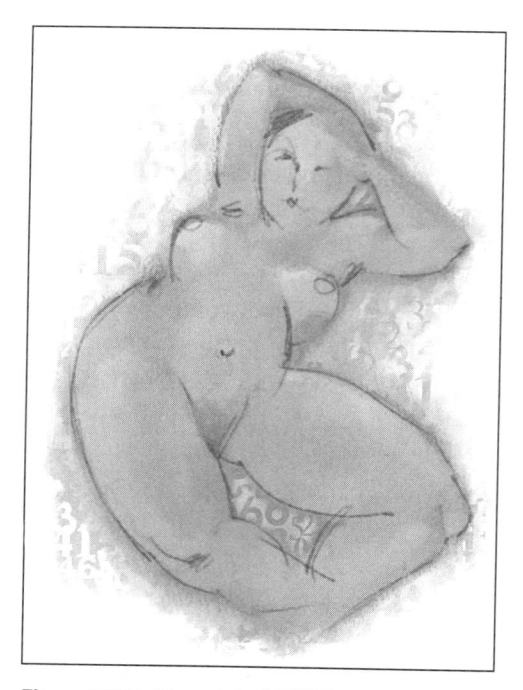

Figure 7.20 The original BLUELADY.PSD image.

2. Make the BLUELADY.PSD image active. Choose Image|Apply Image. Select FRACTAL.PSD as the Source. Set the Blend mode to Difference and the Opacity to 100%. Click on the Mask button and set the mask to BLUELADY.PSD channel #4. Figure 7.21 shows the dialog and Figure 7.22 shows the result.

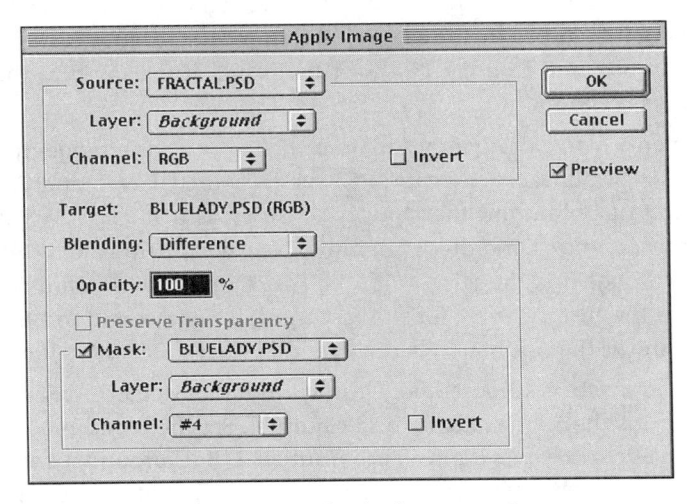

Figure 7.21 The Apply Image command dialog box for the first composite.

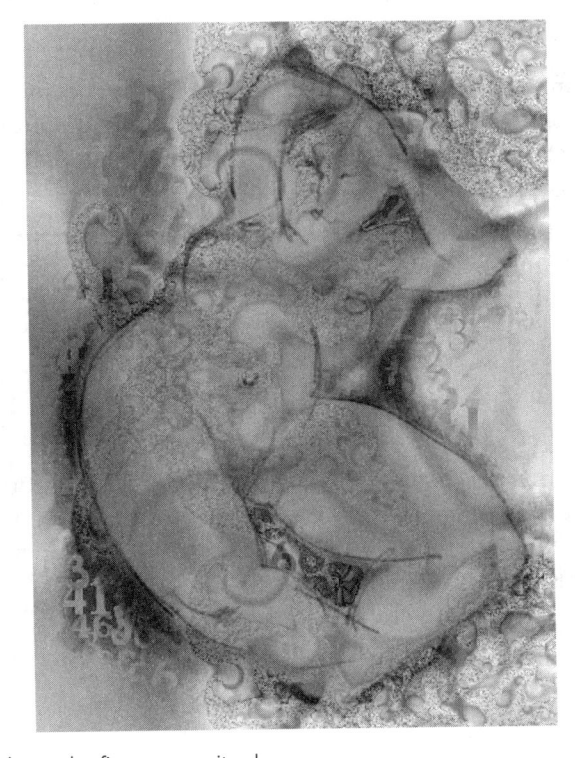

Figure 7.22 This figure shows the first composite done.

3. Click on the Untitled-1 image to make it active. Choose Image|Apply Image. Select FRACTAL.PSD, Background Copy, RGB as your Source, Layer, and Channel. Set the Blend mode to Difference at 100% Opacity. Click on Mask and select SNOWFLKE.PSD, Layer 1, Transparency. The change is written back to Untitled-1. This step takes the difference between the nude and the middle layer of the fractal, but confines the result to only the area occupied by the *shape* of the snowflake. Figure 7.23 shows the Apply Image dialog box and Figure 7.24 shows the result. It is okay that the original Untitled-1 image is changed.

4. Make Untitled-1 active (it already should be active). Choose Image|Apply Image. Select FRACTAL.PSD, Background copy, RGB as the Source, Layer, and Channel. Set the Blend mode to Lighten and the Opacity to 50%. As a mask, use SNOWFLKE.PSD, Layer 1, Transparency. Drag the result into a New document called Untitled-2 by creating a new image and dragging from the History palette as you did in Step 3, and then remove the history entry for the last Apply Image command from Untitled-1. Figure 7.25 shows the Apply Image dialog, and Figure 7.26 shows the result.

5. Make Untitled-2 active. Choose Image|Apply Image. Select SNOWFLKE.PSD, Layer 1, Transparency as the Source, Layer, and Channel. Set the Blend mode to Hard Light and the Opacity to 40%. As a mask, use Untitled-2, Background, Gray and check the Invert button. Drag the result into a new document called Untitled-3 and bring back the original Untitled-2. Figure 7.27 shows the Apply Image dialog box, and Figure 7.28 shows the result.

6. Make Untitled-3 active. Choose Image|Apply Image. Select FRACTAL.PSD, Background, RGB as the Source, Layer, and Channel. Set the Blend mode to Hard Light and the Opacity to 100%. As a mask, use BLUELADY.PSD, Background, Channel 4. Drag the result into a new document named Untitled-4 and bring back the original image as you did before. Figure 7.29 shows the Apply Image dialog, and Figure 7.30 shows the result.

7. This time, you will use the Calculations command. It does not matter which image is active. Choose Image|Calculations. Select FRACTAL.PSD, Merged, Red as Source 1, Layer, and Channel. Select FRACTAL.PSD, Layer 1, Red as Source 2, Layer, and Channel. Set the Blend mode to Overlay and the Opacity to 60%. There is no mask. Select New Document as the Result (the new image will automatically be named Untitled-5). Figure 7.31 shows the Calculations dialog box, and Figure 7.32 shows the result.

8. Make Untitled-3 active. Choose Image|Apply Image. Select Untitled-5, Background, Untitled-5 as the Source, Layer, and Channel. Set the Blend mode to Difference and the Opacity to 100%. There is no mask. Drag the result into a new document named Untitled-6 and restore the original Untitled-3. Figure 7.33 shows the Apply Image dialog, and Figure 7.34 shows the result.

CALCULATIONS 443

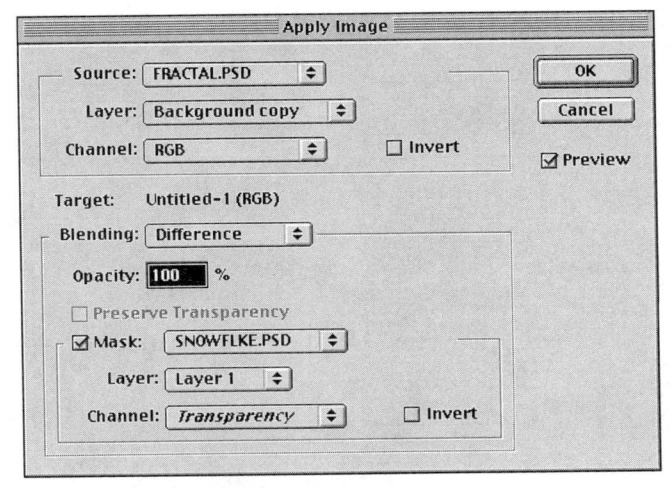

Figure 7.23 The Apply Image dialog box for Pass 2.

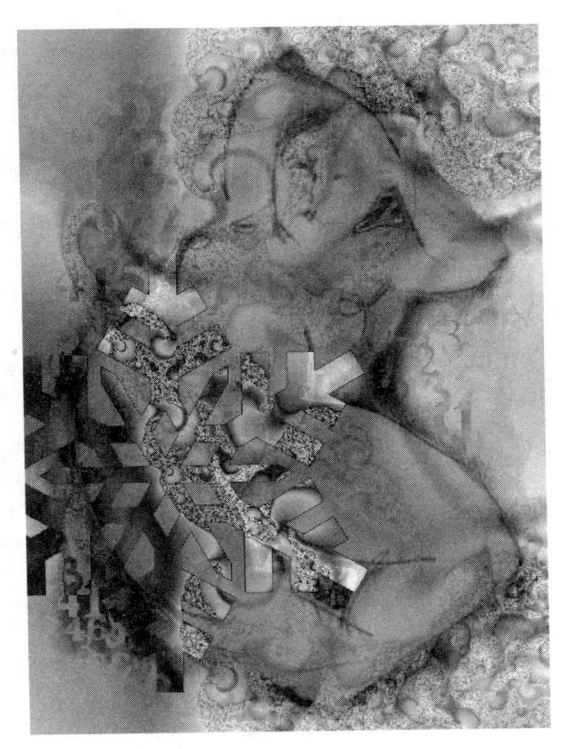

Figure 7.24 Pass 2 results show the Difference blend mode inside the snowflake.

Figure 7.25 The Apply Image dialog for Pass 3.

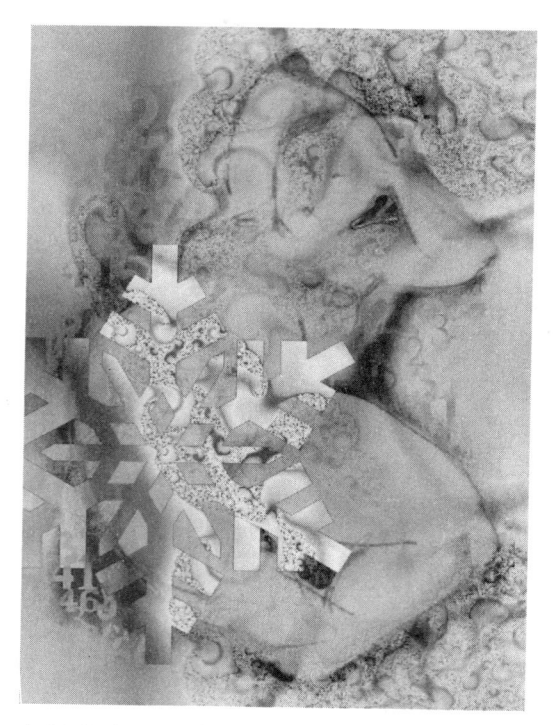

Figure 7.26 Untitled-1, blended in Lighten mode through the Snowflake mask, is the Pass 3 result.

Figure 7.27 Pass 4's Apply Image dialog.

Figure 7.28 Untitled-2 is the Pass 4 result and is blended in Hard Light mode through an inverted self-mask.

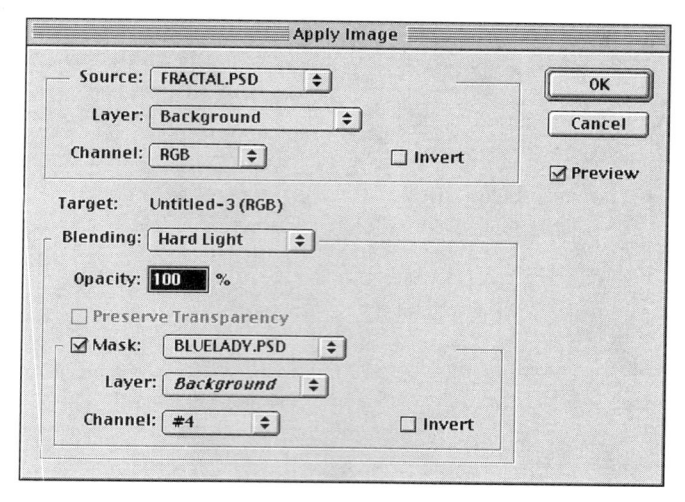

Figure 7.29 The Apply Image dialog box for Pass 5.

Figure 7.30 Pass 5 results in the image Untitled-3, which was blended in Hard Light mode through the Bluelady channel 4 mask.

Figure 7.31 The Pass 6 Calculations dialog box.

Figure 7.32 The Pass 6 result shows the Red channel of the image FRACTAL.PSD blended in Hard Light mode with the Red channel of FRACTAL.PSD Layer 1 at 60% Opacity.

Figure 7.33 The Pass 7 Apply Image dialog box.

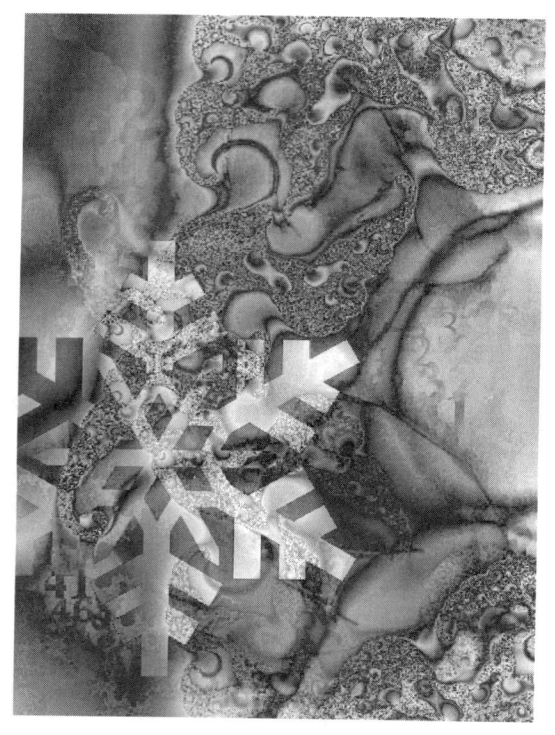

Figure 7.34 The Pass 7 result, created from a blend of Untitled-5, with Untitled-3, Difference mode.

9. Make Untitled-6 active. Choose Image|Apply Image. Select Untitled-4, Background, RGB as the Source, Layer, and Channel. Set the Blend mode to Hard Light and the Opacity to 30%. As a mask, use SNOWFLKE.PSD, Layer 1, Transparency, and check the Invert button. Drag the result into a new document named Untitled-7 and restore the original image. Figure 7.35 shows the Apply Image dialog, and Figure 7.36 shows the result.

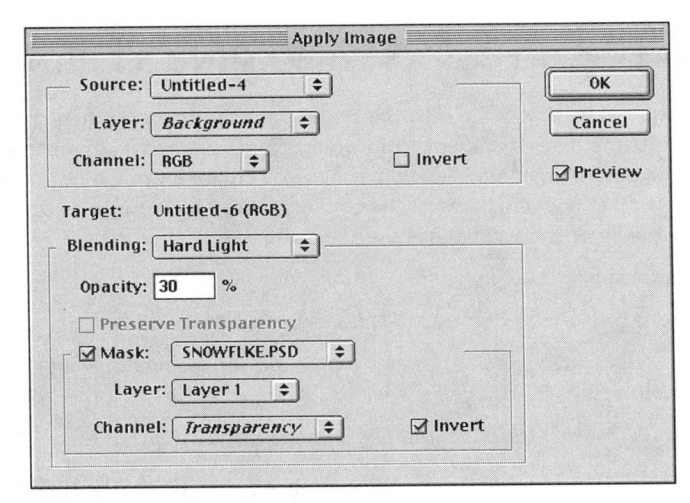

Figure 7.35 The Pass 8 Apply Image dialog box.

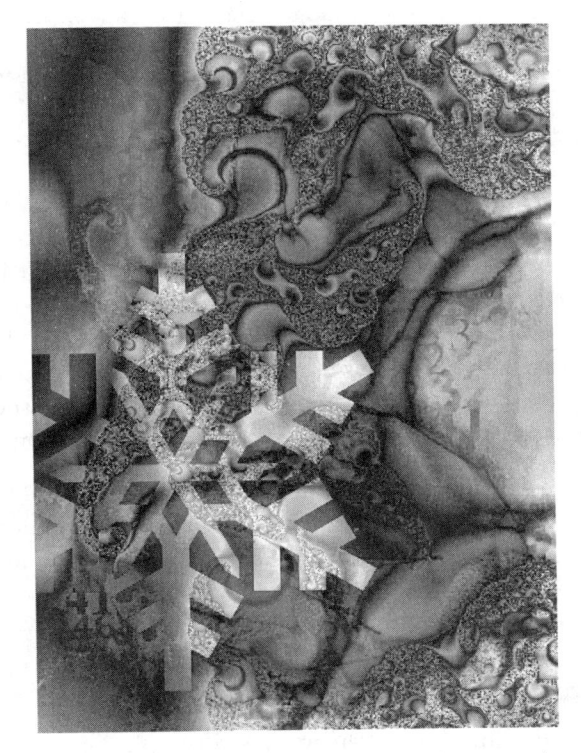

Figure 7.36 Pass 8 used Untitled-6, blended with Untitled-4 through the inverted snowflake mask in Hard Light mode.

> ### AN ALTERNATIVE AUTO-NAMING TECHNIQUE
>
> You really do not want to write over the original image. Although there are several ways to get the result into a new image (the preceding Tip gives one way), here is a fast way that gives you an auto-named file each time (when you create an image from the History palette, the image is titled with the name of the command used to produce it, which would leave you with a bunch of images that all have the same title).
>
> To do so, take the following steps:
>
> 1. Create a new image Command+N (Mac) or Ctrl+N (Windows).
> 2. Click on OK (as strange as it might sound, it does not matter what size or color mode you use for the new image).
> 3. Make the overwritten BLUELADY.PSD image active.
> 4. In the History palette, place your mouse cursor over the Apply Image command and press the mouse button.
> 5. Drag the History palette entry into the Untitled-1 image window. The new document is filled with the result of the Apply Image command—and it changes both its size and color mode if need be to accommodate the image from the History palette.
> 6. Click on the BLUELADY.PSD image again and drag the Apply Image command entry in the History palette to the History palette trashcan icon. The BLUELADY.PSD image reverts to its original state.

10. Make Untitled-7 active. Choose Image|Apply Image. Select Untitled-4, Background, RGB as the Source, Layer, and Channel. Set the Blend mode to Normal and the Opacity to 60%. As a mask, use BLUELADY.PSD, Background, Channel 4. Do *not* check the Invert button. Drag the result into a new document called Untitled-8 and restore the original. Figure 7.37 shows the Apply Image dialog box, and Figure 7.38 shows the result. You might want to use the Levels command on this final image to lighten it a bit.

You can spin this process out forever, but you have an idea by now of how you can work with the Apply Image and Calculations commands. It is endlessly fascinating to see how images can be combined, and this workflow is much faster than using drag-and-drop or cut-and-paste, and it uses no extra RAM resources because it does not take up clipboard space. Please help keep this intriguing-though-arcane method of working alive.

Classic CHOPs

The "classic" CHOPs are in the Tips written by Kai Krause for America Online several years ago. The documents are still available on the MetaCreations Web site at **www.metacreations.com**. They are also available on a CD-ROM distributed by MetaCreations and sold at their Web site.

These documents were written for Photoshop 2, so of course the specific menu commands have changed quite a bit, but they are the basic tools from which this entire method of working developed. They have been used as the basis of countless books and articles, and assimilated by the most respected Photoshop artists around. You will find few true "Photoshop propeller-heads"

CALCULATIONS 451

Figure 7.37 The Pass 9 Apply Image dialog box.

Figure 7.38 Pass 9 blends Untitled-7, at 60% Opacity in Normal mode, with Untitled-4 through channel 4 of the Bluelady image.

who have not used these tips—they are almost a badge of admission to an exclusive club. The most recent full-length work on CHOPs is *Photoshop Channel CHOPs* by David Biedny, Bert Monroy, and Nathan Moody. You can order it through **www.amazon.com** or purchase it at your local bookstore.

Many of Kai's CHOPs start with the manipulation of simple black shapes in a channel and work toward building complexity (and gray values) through Calculations. To play with this, select any one of the Ultimate Symbol Design Element collection images and rasterize it into a grayscale image. Create a series of "primitives" from the original. Here are the operations:

- Original
- Inverted copy of original
- Gaussian blurred copy of original
- Gaussian blurred copy of inverted original
- Find Edges on the blurred positive image
- Find Edges on the blurred negative image
- Maximum filter applied to original image
- Maximum filter applied to inverted original
- Minimum filter applied to original image
- Minimum filter applied to inverted original
- Original image with contrast lowered 50 percent
- Inverted original with contrast lowered 50 percent

Try combining these images with one another by offsetting the images and using Difference, Add, Subtract, Multiply, and Screen. Try some of the "newer" modes as well. Also create some primitives by selecting the Motion Blur and Radial Blur filters from the filter menu of Photoshop and apply these filters to the primitives. Create the positive and negative versions separately (do not just invert the positive versions as the results do differ). Look at the file MEDALON.PSD on this book's CD-ROM. This image is the work of Susan Kitchens, a very talented California artist who worked with Kai Krause for many years and is an expert in this form of Photoshopping. The channels are named in such a way that you can discern what was done to produce them. Studying this file is an excellent way to begin.

Moving On

In this chapter, you learned about the Apply Image and the Calculations commands. These two commands are both very useful for day-to-day or special effects work. You can use the commands to quickly move images and channels of the same size from one location to another without copying and pasting, so they use less RAM and work faster. You have seen how to add density to an image by combining channels and how to produce a new "work of art" by combining a number of images.

The next chapter shows you how to create some snazzy images with Photoshop's filter capabilities.

FILTER FROLICS

Photoshop's filters give you unlimited possibilities to change your image. Once you are familiar with what filters do, your imagination is unleashed to explore and create.

Using a filter on an image is like going to the beauty parlor—you can walk out with anything from a quick trim to a complete makeover. Similarly, filters can distort an image so completely that there's no telling what it looked like originally, or filters can touch up an image so it just *looks better*. Some filters fall at one end or the other of this spectrum: Sharpen at the quick trim end and Polar Coordinates at the complete makeover end, for example. Other filters allow you to adjust their settings along the entire range—the same filter with different settings can produce wildly different results, and experimentation is the key to getting good results.

Photoshop comes with almost a hundred filters (the exact count is 98), called *native* filters. This name is somewhat inaccurate, because most of these filters aren't built into the program; they're stored separately in a Filters folder inside the Plug-Ins folder. The many third-party filters available are also stored in the Plug-Ins folder, so you can install and uninstall these filters by moving them in and out of the folder (see the section at the end of this chapter, "Managing Filters"). In this chapter, we will discuss how Photoshop filters work, look at some sample images produced with filters, and offer tips for getting the most out of filters.

Shortcuts

The few keyboard shortcuts that apply to filters can speed up operations quite a bit:

- To reapply the last filter, press Command+F (Mac) or Ctrl+F (Windows). This is the equivalent of simply choosing the filter again from the Filter menu or using the top command in the menu, which is always the most recently used filter (even if you used the Undo command after applying that filter).

- To return to the dialog box for the last filter used, press Command+Option+F for the Macintosh or Ctrl+Alt+F for Windows. The previous settings are still in the dialog box. This is the equivalent of holding down the Option or the Alt key as you choose the filter again from the top of the Filter menu.

- To reduce the intensity of a filter's effects or change its Blend mode, press Command+Shift+F (Mac) or Ctrl+Shift+F (Windows). This is the equivalent of choosing Filter|Fade (see the section "Fading a Filter's Effects," later in this chapter).

Under two circumstances, these commands aren't available—if you haven't applied a filter since your current Photoshop session began, or if you're in a color mode that doesn't support filters or the specific filter you're trying to use. See the section "Filters And Color Modes," which follows. For a complete listing of keyboard shortcuts, turn to Appendix C.

Filters And RAM

No matter what you're doing in Photoshop, it's never possible to have too much RAM. Filters are no exception to this rule; in fact, using filters can increase your RAM requirements by quite a bit. It's entirely possible to have enough RAM to run Photoshop itself, but not enough to execute a particular filter. Some filters are more RAM-hungry than others are. These are the worst offenders:

- Cutout
- Glass
- Lens Flare
- Spherize
- Crystallize
- Stained Glass
- Spatter
- Ocean Ripple
- Polar Coordinates
- Twirl
- Pointillize
- Sprayed Strokes
- Pinch
- Ripple
- ZigZag
- Lighting Effects

The filters listed here won't execute on large images when Photoshop has only the minimum RAM allocation. Fortunately, Photoshop warns you up front when it can't run a filter (see Figure 8.1), instead of allowing you to make all the dialog box settings first. The filters have been tuned in Photoshop 5, however, so they're more likely to work on larger files in low RAM than they did under Photoshop 3 or 4. For example, we were able to apply the Lighting Effects filter to a 35MB image with only 18MB RAM. The Lens Flare filter, however, does not work on the same image in the same amount of RAM. In Photoshop 4, neither filter would have worked. If you run out of memory, the short-term solution is to see if you can apply the filter to each channel of the image individually. Sometimes this approach works. Of course, the best solution is to buy more RAM.

How Filters Work

All Photoshop filters are mathematical (a little bit easier to believe than Ralph Waldo Emerson's assertion that "all love is mathematical"). A filter performs calculations based on the color value and position of each pixel in an image or selection and replaces the pixels with the results of those calculations. The math is more complicated than most people want to get into—the results are the important thing. To make sure that you get the results you're looking

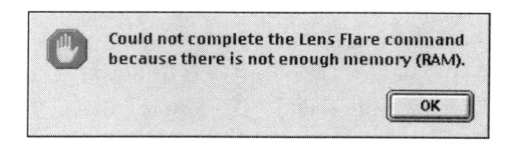

Figure 8.1 This dialog box informs you when you need more RAM to run a particular filter.

for, however, you need to know how filters interact with particular variables in a document: the Foreground and Background colors, transparency, selections, and the image's color mode. After you're familiar with these parts of the filter equation, you will be able to predict with much greater accuracy the results of applying a filter. Even so, most Photoshop filters provide at least one method of previewing their effects on an image, and the Fade command allows you to fine-tune the intensity of a filter's effects even after it's applied.

Filters And The Foreground/Background Color

Most of the time, if you're not using one of the Painting tools, the Foreground and Background colors shown in the Toolbox don't matter. However, some filters do use these colors to create their effects, so you need to make sure that the Foreground and Background colors are the ones you want to use before applying these filters. Here's a list of the ones to watch out for:

- *All the Sketch filters except Chrome and Water Paper*—These filters use the Foreground color for darker areas in the image and the Background color for lighter areas, blending the two colors in different ways depending on the style of the filter, such as pen strokes or halftone dots.
- *Colored Pencil*—The Background color is the paper color at the highest Paper Brightness setting.
- *Diffuse Glow*—The Background color is the "glow" color.
- *Grain*—The Sprinkles Grain Type uses the Background color for the grain; the Stippled Grain Type uses the Foreground color for the grain and places the Background color everywhere else in the image.
- *Neon Glow*—Two of the three colors applied to the image to create the "glow" are the Foreground and Background colors (the third color is chosen in the Neon Glow dialog box).
- *Pointillize*—The Background color appears between the pointillist dots created from the image colors.
- *Render Clouds*—The Foreground and Background colors are the cloud colors. All other colors in the image are removed.
- *Render Difference Clouds*—The difference between the Foreground and Background colors and the colors in the image determines the colors of the clouds. All other colors are removed.
- *Stained Glass*—The Foreground color is used for the lead strips between the pieces of "glass."
- *Torn Edges*—The image is posterized using the Foreground and Background colors.

If you want to be able to create similar effects with these filters over time, it's a good idea to save the Foreground and Background colors in the Swatches palette so you can access them quickly when you need them. For even more security, or to share those colors with another person who wants to achieve the same effects, choose Save Swatches from the Swatches palette menu and save the color swatches in a separate file.

Filters And Transparent Layers

Filters work only on the active layer, and they don't operate on transparent pixels, meaning that they will move around and alter only the existing colored pixels on a transparent layer. Trying to apply the Add Noise filter, for example, to an entirely transparent layer results in an

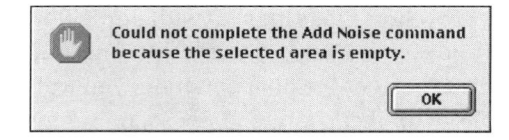

Figure 8.2 Most filters won't work on a completely transparent layer.

error dialog box (see Figure 8.2). It's also important to distinguish between white and transparency; if you want a white Background layer to be affected by a filter, you'll need to merge the layer you're working on with the Background layer. The Clouds filter is the only filter in Photoshop's native set that can produce results on a totally transparent layer.

Like any other operation that moves pixels around, filters are subject to the restrictions imposed when Preserve Transparency is turned on for a layer. Just as Preserve Transparency prevents you from painting on transparent pixels, it also keeps filters from operating outside the area of the layer that already contains colored pixels.

This effect is particularly noticeable in filters that move large chunks of the image around, namely the Distort filters. Figure 8.3a shows the Polar Coordinates filter when Preserve Transparency is off. Figure 8.3b shows the same image filtered with Preserve Transparency on. You can clearly see the outlines of the original wedding cake and that part of the filtered image is missing. The Blur filters may also have little effect if Preserve Transparency is turned on, depending on how detailed the nontransparent portions of the layer are. With solid-colored elements, such as text, placed on a transparent layer, Blur filters will seem to have no effect when Preserve Transparency is turned on (see Figure 8.4). More detailed elements, such as a silhouetted photo, will be blurred inside their borders, but the silhouetted edges remain sharp (see Figure 8.5). This fact can work to your advantage when you want sharp edges.

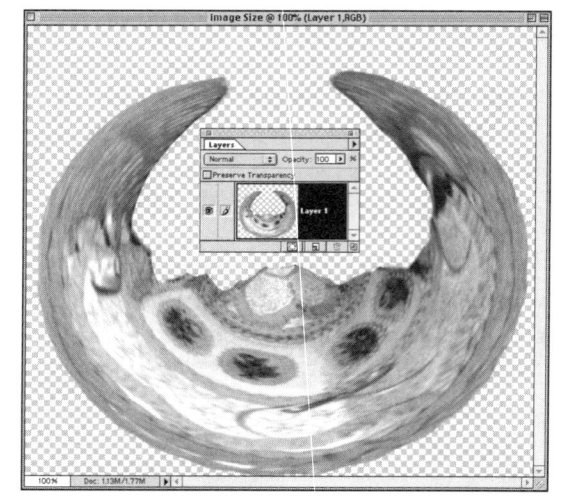

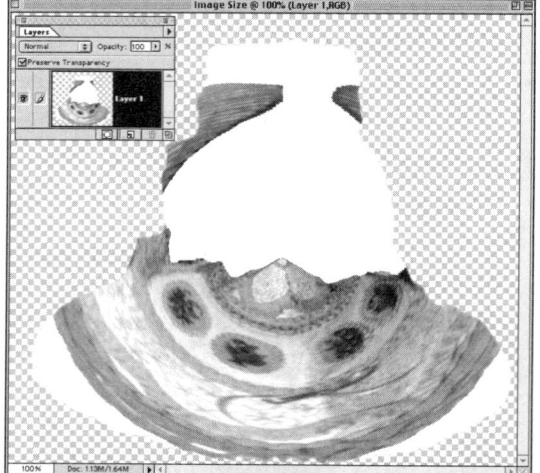

Figure 8.3 With Preserve Transparency off (a, left), the Polar Coordinates filter works fine; with Preserve Transparency on (b, right), the filter reveals the Background color in areas of the original image.

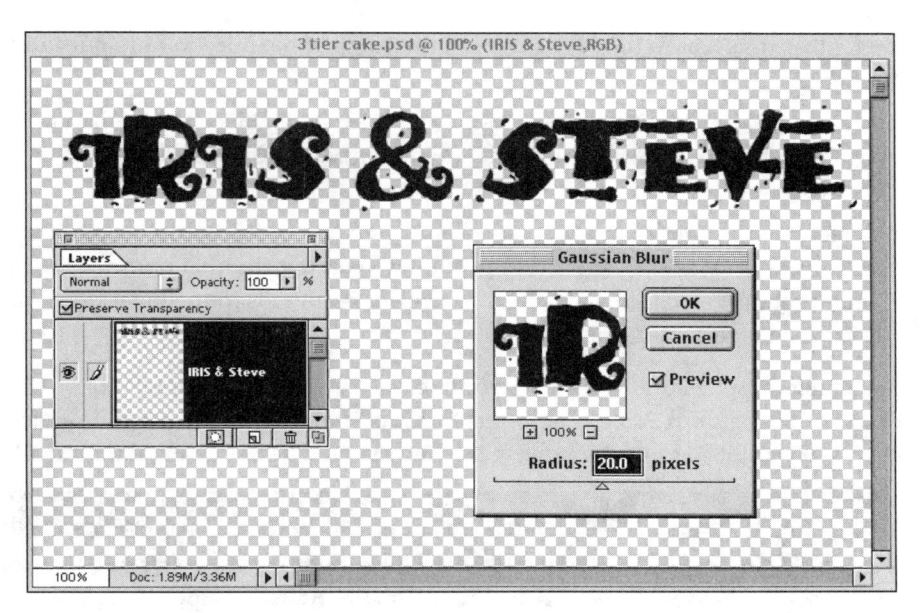

Figure 8.4 The Gaussian Blur filter has no visible effect when applied to text on a transparent layer with Preserve Transparency turned on.

Figure 8.5 The Gaussian Blur filter doesn't blur the edges of this image on a transparent layer, because Preserve Transparency is turned on.

Filters And Selections

If a selection is active when you apply a filter, the filter's effects are restricted to the pixels included in the selection. Because it's possible to partially select a pixel, you can also partially apply a filter. You have three ways to partially select some pixels in an image:

- You can feather a selection; the pixels around the edges of the selection are partially selected (see Figure 8.6).
- You can create a Quick Mask selection. Press Q to enter Quick Mask mode, then paint white to select areas, black to deselect them, and gray to partially select them. Press Q to return to normal selection mode.
- You can create a selection from an alpha channel or a layer's transparency mask by Command+clicking (Mac) or Ctrl+clicking (Windows) on the channel name or the layer name. Gray areas in the channel or partially transparent areas in the layer translate to partially selected pixels on the active layer.

Applying a filter to a pixel that's only 50 percent selected is the same as applying that filter to the same pixel with its settings 50 percent lower. This fact enables you to determine exactly where a filter should be applied and how intense its effects should be before invoking the filter itself.

> **TIP**
>
> **Feather a selection before applying a filter to blend the resulting pixels into the rest of the image. For example, you can get rid of a moiré pattern in roof shingles by blurring the area, then adding noise; feathering the selection first blends the changes with the rest of the roof.**

Filters And Color Modes

You can't apply filters to images in Bitmap, Indexed Color, 48-bit RGB, or 16-bit grayscale modes. Some specific filters aren't available in CMYK or other color modes:

Figure 8.6 We feathered and then inverted a rectangular selection in the center of the image before applying the Add Noise filter.

- CMYK mode doesn't support the Artistic, Brush Strokes, Sketch, Texture, and Video filter groups. Individual filters that aren't available in CMYK mode include Smart Blur, Diffuse Glow, Glass, Ocean Ripple, Lens Flare, Lighting Effects, and Glowing Edges.
- Lab mode also doesn't support Artistic, Brush Strokes, Sketch, and Texture filters. Individual filters you can't use in Lab mode include Smart Blur, Diffuse Glow, Glass, Ocean Ripple, Difference Clouds, Lens Flare, Lighting Effects, Extrude, Glowing Edges, Solarize, and NTSC Colors.
- Grayscale, Duotone, and Multichannel modes don't support Lens Flare, Lighting Effects, and NTSC Colors.

To use a filter on a bitmap image, switch to Grayscale mode, apply the filter, then switch back to Bitmap mode. Depending on the results you're looking for, choose either 50% Threshold or Diffusion Dither when you return to Bitmap mode. Using the former, all pixels that are 50% gray or lighter are converted to white, and all pixels that are darker than 50% gray are changed to black, resulting in sharp-edged areas of black or white. The latter option also eliminates gray pixels, but it scatters black pixels around in formerly gray areas to retain some of the effect of gray.

To use a filter on a color image that's in the wrong color mode, switch to RGB mode, apply the filter, then switch back to the original color mode.

Previewing Filter Effects

Most filter dialog boxes contain a small preview window in which you can see the results of the filter. Creating this preview might take a bit of time, so as Photoshop works on that, you'll see a flashing line below the preview size percentage. When the line disappears, the preview is fully rendered. To see the "before" version of the image in the preview window, click in the window. With some filters, you can also change the area of the image that appears in the preview window by clicking and dragging (the cursor changes to a hand) or by clicking in the image window (the cursor changes to a hollow box; see Figure 8.7).

If the Preview checkbox is checked in a filter dialog box, the results of the current filter settings are also reflected in the image window. The Grabber Hand and Zoom tools still work in the image window while you're working in a filter dialog box, but you need to use the keyboard shortcuts to access them. Hold the spacebar as you click and drag in the image to move it around within the window, and press Command+spacebar (Mac) or Ctrl+spacebar (Windows) as you click and drag, to magnify a specific area of the image.

One of the advantages of being able to preview the filter's effects both in the dialog box and in the image window is that you can see different magnifications simultaneously. Generally, it works best to use the dialog box preview to focus on a magnified detail of the image and view the entire image in the image window. To change the magnification level of the dialog box preview window, click on the + and - buttons; you can zoom out as far as 20% and zoom in to 800%.

460 CHAPTER 8

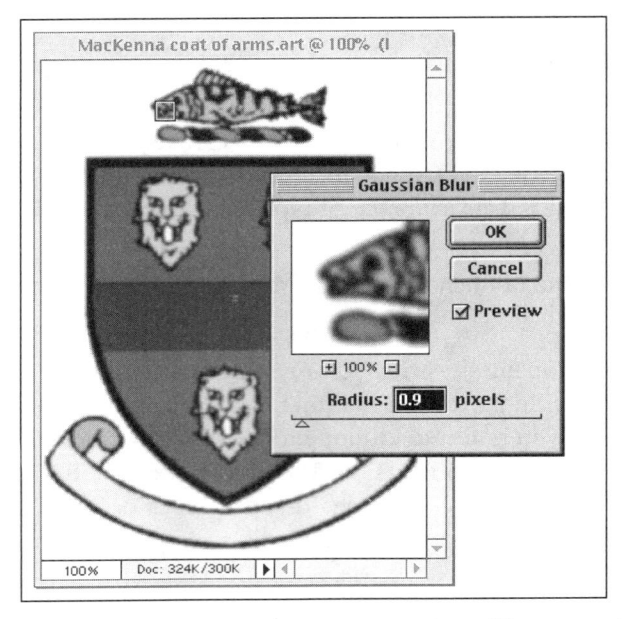

Figure 8.7 The hollow box in the image window indicates the area that will be centered in the filter's dialog box preview window.

> **TIP**
>
> If you don't want to use a filter at full intensity, you can apply it and then dial back its effects to the precise level you're looking for. First, apply a filter, then choose Filter|Fade. In the Fade dialog box (see Figure 8.8), you can choose an opacity level and a Blend mode for the effects of the filter. The opacity percentage determines the intensity of the filter's effects, and the Blend mode determines how the modified pixel colors combine with the original (prefilter) pixel colors. The Blend modes in the Fade dialog box are similar to those shown in the Tool Options palette, except that the Fade dialog box doesn't include the Behind Blend mode.

Like many of the filter dialog boxes, the Fade dialog box has a Preview checkbox that allows you to see the effects of your changes in the image window. Once you like the effect, you apply it by clicking on OK. If, when you return to the image window, you decide that it's still not right, you can choose Filter|Fade again, as many times as you want. The settings you make each time are still there in the dialog box when you return to it, so you can even return to the "un-Faded"

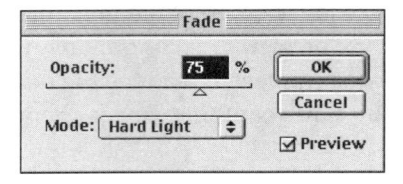

Figure 8.8 The Fade dialog box.

version of the filtered image. To restore the image to its original state, before the filter was applied, choose Edit|Undo—this removes the effects of both the Fade command and the filter.

Essentially, the Fade command produces the same effect as the following procedure:

1. Choose Layer|Duplicate Layer and click on OK in the Duplicate Layer dialog box.
2. Apply the filter to the new layer.
3. In the Layers palette, adjust the opacity and Blend mode of the new layer, allowing the prefilter version of the image to show through.

If you want to be able to adjust the filter's effects later on, even after you've made other changes to the image, then use this technique instead of the Fade command.

Native Filters

If you tried a new native filter every day, it would take months to work your way through them all, and you probably still wouldn't have plumbed the depths of what's possible with the dozens of filters that Adobe includes with Photoshop 5. This huge collection offers everything from the most utilitarian effects (such as Dust & Scratches) to the most bizarre mind- and image-altering filters (such as Twirl or Trace Contour). It even offers a new filter that allows you to manipulate an object as if it were in 3D space.

Photoshop divides its native filters into 14 arbitrary categories, listed below, that for the most part give a pretty good idea of what each group of filters does. Each category under the Filters menu has a submenu that contains the filters themselves. We used the image of a cat to test each filter. Because many of the effects do not show up in grayscale, you can see all of the cats in color in the Color Studio section of this book.

Artistic

The Artistic filters are part of a group of filters formerly sold under the name Gallery Effects. They've been completely rewritten and are included as part of Photoshop 5's native set. These filters attempt to simulate the effects of using the artistic tools from which they take their names; some are more successful than others.

- The Colored Pencil filter adds diagonal "pencil" strokes and fills in parts of the image with white, gray, or black "paper" in an effort to make it look hand-drawn with colored pencils. The three options are Pencil Width (1 through 24), Stroke Pressure (0 through 15), and Paper Brightness (0 through 80). Pencil Width controls the amount of the image that's retained and converted to pencil strokes; lower settings allow for more detail and greater paper coverage, while higher settings increase the width of the strokes and allow more paper to show through between them. The Stroke Pressure setting determines the intensity of the image's remaining colors, while the Paper Brightness slider allows you to make the underlying paper black (0), white (80), or gray (anything in between). (See Figure 8.9.)

- The Cutout filter turns an image into colored paper silhouettes, using the Foreground and Background colors. It posterizes the other colors in the image, resulting in a simplified image with few gradations. You can control how much simplification takes place with the three sliders: No. Of Levels (2 through 8), Edge Simplicity (0 through 10), and Edge Fidelity (1 through 3). No. Of Levels determines how many colors are used in the resulting image, while the Edge Simplicity slider controls how much the image's edges are smoothed out to make them into basic geometric shapes. Edge Fidelity allows you to decide how close to the original image the new shapes should be (see Figure 8.10). Figure 8.11 shows the cat with the Cutout filter applied.

- The Dry Brush filter reproduces the effect of painting with very little paint on the brush—it results in simple, soft-edged strokes that can retain a little image detail or a lot, depending on your Brush Detail setting (0 through 10). The other options are Brush Size, ranging from 0 through 10, and Texture, ranging from 1 through 3. A Texture setting of 3 adds a bit of noise to the image, while a setting of 1 (see Figure 8.12) keeps it smooth, and a setting of 2 falls somewhere in the middle.

- The Film Grain filter lightens an image and increases its contrast while adding noise. The Grain option (0 through 20) determines the amount of noise added. Highlight Area (1 through 20) controls the size of the areas in the image that are lightened or darkened, with higher settings lightening more of the image. Intensity (0 through 10) controls the amount of lightening that occurs in the highlight areas (see Figure 8.13).

- Fresco, another "painting" filter, tends to add dark edges to shapes in an image and increase contrast and saturation. Its controls include sliders for Brush Detail (0 through 10), Brush Size (0 through 10), and Texture (1 through 3). As with the Dry Brush filter, these settings control the amount of detail in the image, the stroke width, and whether noise is added, respectively (see Figure 8.14).

- The Neon Glow filter desaturates an image, recolors it with the Foreground and Background colors, then adds an unearthly glowing effect with a third color determined in the filter's dialog box. The Size slider, ranging from -24 to 24, determines how much of the image's area is covered with the glow color—lower settings make the glow larger. The Brightness setting (0 through 50) controls the ambient light, rather than the brightness of the glow, so that lower settings produce a spooky dark gray image with an eerie glow (see Figure 8.15).

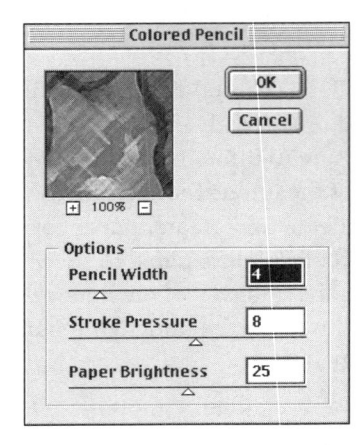

Figure 8.9 The Colored Pencil filter dialog box.

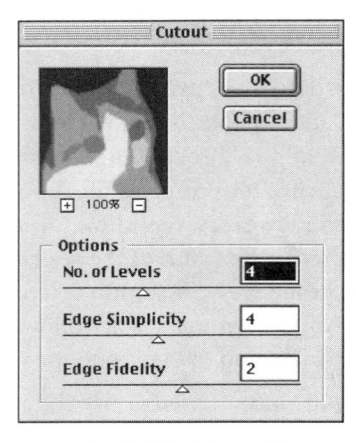

Figure 8.10 The Cutout filter dialog box.

Figure 8.11 The cat with the Cutout filter applied.

Figure 8.12 The Dry Brush filter dialog box.

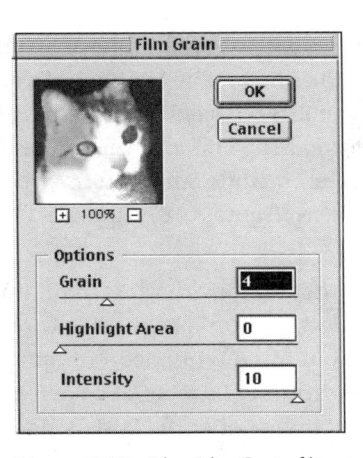

Figure 8.13 The Film Grain filter dialog box.

Figure 8.14 The Fresco filter dialog box.

- The Paint Daubs filter (see Figure 8.16) operates like a collection of other filters, resulting in anything but a "daubed" effect. It's as though you blurred the image, used Find Edges, then posterized it, and finally used Sharpen. A Brush Size control, ranging from 1 to 50, determines the size of the posterized color areas, while a Sharpness slider, ranging from 0 to 40, applies a little or a lot of sharpening. The Brush Type pop-up menu includes Simple, Light Rough, Dark Rough, Wide Sharp, Wide Blurry, and Sparkle brushes, with the Rough brushes applying more texture to the image. The Sparkle brush intensifies the Find Edges effect and bumps the saturation way, way up to create neon colors.

- The Palette Knife filter (see Figure 8.17) attempts to produce the effect of a painting created with a palette knife rather than a brush, but it doesn't add the texture that a knife would. You can control Stroke Size (1 through 50), Stroke Detail (1 through 3), and Softness (0 through 10); the latter setting determines whether the strokes blend into one another or are hard-edged.

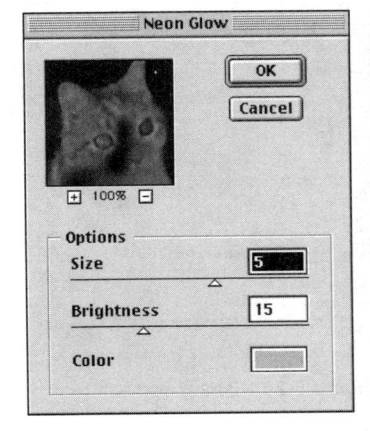

Figure 8.15 The Neon Glow filter dialog box.

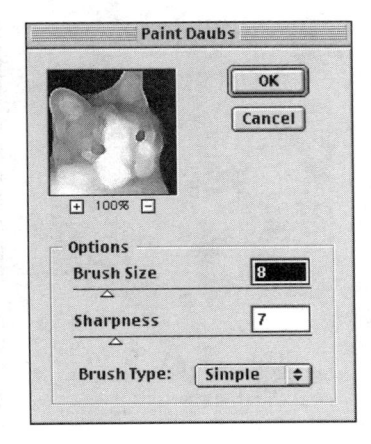

Figure 8.16 Paint Daubs filter dialog box.

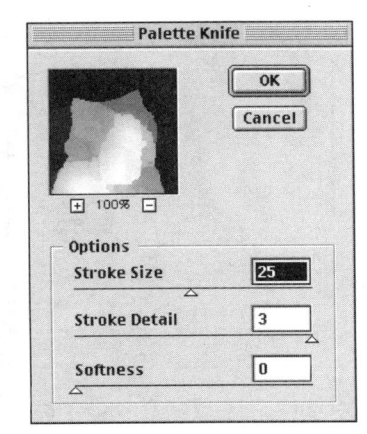

Figure 8.17 The Palette Knife filter dialog box.

- The Plastic Wrap filter seems to apply a layer of plastic wrap to an image, adding highlights and emphasizing the lines in the image. The Highlight Strength slider (0 through 20) controls the brightness of the highlights reflected from the plastic wrap. Detail (1 through 15) determines how much the plastic wrap clings to the shapes in the image—higher settings produce more plastic wrap texture—while Smoothness (1 through 15) determines how much plastic wrap texture is applied (see Figure 8.18). Figure 8.19 shows the Plastic Wrap filter applied to the cat.

- The Poster Edges filter reduces the number of colors in an image and outlines shapes in black, producing a woodcut effect. The options include Edge Thickness, ranging from 0 to 10; Edge Intensity (how much outlining is applied), ranging from 0 to 10; and Posterization, ranging from 0 to 6, which controls the number of colors in the resulting image (see Figure 8.20). Figure 8.21 shows the cat image after the Poster Edges filter was applied.

- The Rough Pastels filter (see Figure 8.22) applies "pastel" strokes to an image based on an underlying texture that can be built-in or supplied from a second file. The Stroke Length and Stroke Detail controls do just what they sound like, while a separate area of the dialog box contains controls for the Texture. You can choose Brick, Burlap, Canvas, or Sandstone from a pop-up menu, or choose Other and load any Photoshop-format file that isn't in Bitmap mode. Then choose a Scaling setting from 50% to 200% to determine how the texture is sized with respect to the image, and a Relief value from 0 to 50 to control how high the darker areas in the texture file are considered to be. You can specify a Light Direction in 45° increments, and you can choose to invert the texture before applying it.

- Smudge Stick (see Figure 8.23) looks like smudged pastels, with controls to determine the length of the smudging strokes (Stroke Length, from 1 to 10) and the amount that the contrast in the image should be increased (Intensity, from 1 through 10). The Highlight Area slider controls how much of the brighter areas in the image are blown out with the increased brightness.

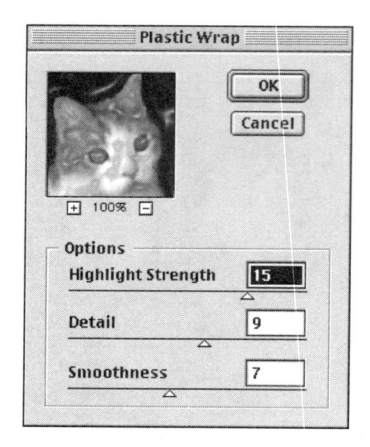

Figure 8.18 The Plastic Wrap filter dialog box.

Figure 8.19 The Plastic Wrap filter applied to the cat image.

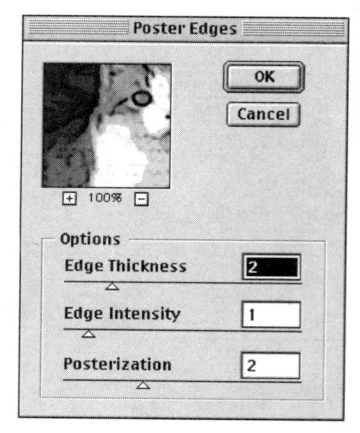

Figure 8.20 Poster Edges filter dialog box.

Figure 8.21 The Poster Edges filter applied to the cat image.

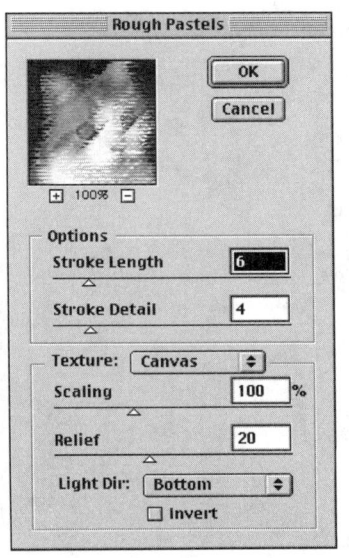

Figure 8.22 The Rough Pastels filter dialog box.

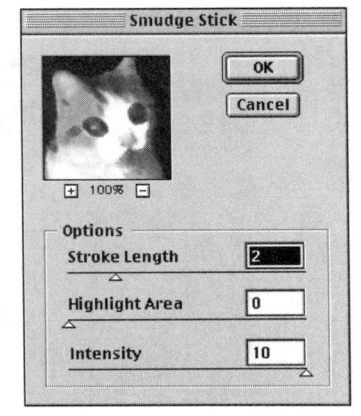

Figure 8.23 Smudge Stick filter dialog box.

- The Sponge filter (see Figure 8.24) is intended to give the effect of paint applied with a sponge. You can control the size and softness of the sponge, as well as how much it darkens the colors it applies. The Brush Size slider (1 through 10) determines how large the sponge is, while the Smoothness slider (1 through 15) allows you to control how blurry the edges of the sponge strokes are. The Definition slider makes the image darker or closer to the original image, with the lowest setting of 1 keeping the colors pretty much as they are and the highest setting of 25 darkening them.

- The Underpainting filter (see Figure 8.25) produces a realistic oil-painted effect with controls similar to those in the Rough Pastels filter. The Brush Size (0 through 40) and Texture Coverage (0 through 40) sliders determine the width of the brush strokes and the amount of canvas or other background that is allowed to show through. The Texture controls work just like the Rough Pastels Texture controls, including allowing you to specify your own color or grayscale Photoshop-format file as the texture.

- The Watercolor filter (see Figure 8.26) produces a texture similar to a watercolor painting, but the filter tends to darken the image much more than most watercolor artists would. A Brush Detail (1 through 14) controls the amount of detail preserved in the resulting image, while Shadow Intensity (1 through 10) determines exactly how much the image is darkened. Texture (1 through 3) allows you to choose a flatter image or one with more visible strokes.

Blur

It doesn't take too much imagination to figure out what these filters do, but each one does it slightly differently. The overall effect is to smooth out transitions between areas of different colors by averaging the colors of the pixels at the transition points:

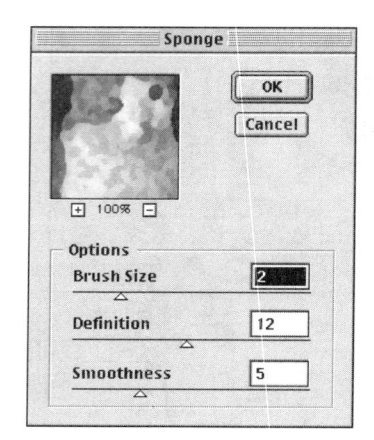

Figure 8.24 The Sponge filter dialog box.

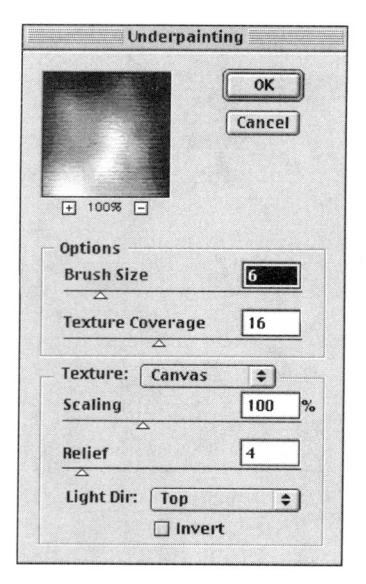

Figure 8.25 The Underpainting filter dialog box.

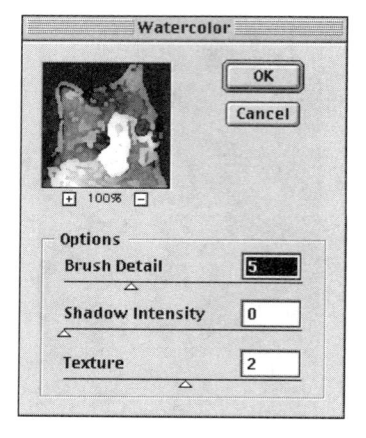

Figure 8.26 The Watercolor filter dialog box.

- Blur softens images a predetermined amount; there's no dialog box. While it uses the same basic process as the Gaussian Blur filter, most people prefer Gaussian Blur so they can tailor the amount of blurring to the situation.
- Blur More is equivalent to multiple applications of the Blur filter. Again, you probably won't use Blur More often because Gaussian Blur can achieve the same results with greater precision.
- Gaussian Blur, with a Radius slider that runs from .1 to 250 pixels, lets you specify exactly the amount of blur you want to apply to an image. For extreme precision, you can even enter a number in the entry field above the slider. Values higher than 20 or so remove all the detail from an image, leaving only a haze of color, and the higher the Radius value, the longer the filter takes to work its magic.
- Motion Blur, by blurring pixels in one direction only, creates the effect of a moving object. Motion Blur works best when the central object of the image stands against a fairly plain, light-colored background. You can specify the Distance of the blurring effect and the Angle by entering values in entry fields, and if you're no good with geometry, you have the option of specifying the Angle value by dragging a line around a circle. The Angle value can range from -90% to 90%, and the Distance value can range from .1 to 999 pixels (see Figure 8.27).
- Radial Blur, like the Radial option of the Gradient tool, creates a circular blurring effect, with the blurred pixels appearing to either spin around the circle or zoom out from its center. The Amount field controls the intensity of the blur—equivalent to a Radius setting for the Zoom option and specifying the direction of rotation for the Spin option. You can move the center of the blur effect by clicking and dragging on the dialog box preview (not a true preview, but rather a sort of wireframe effect), and you have a choice of three quality levels: Draft, Good, and Best (see Figure 8.28).

- Smart Blur blurs within areas of minor color changes, leaving edges alone. It's similar to the effect of blurring the Lightness channel in Lab color mode. The Radius and Threshold values determine how much blurring is applied and what the brightness cutoff level is for applying the effect. When you select a large Threshold, the filter sees almost no edges. If you were to apply the Find Edges filter and then use the Threshold command at a low setting, you would see very few lines. This happens when you set the Threshold of this filter high. You get an even blurring within the large chunks of color. The Edge Only option in the Mode pop-up menu applies the filter as white on a black background, and Overlay Edge lays the white edges over the image (see Figure 8.29). This filter can be very helpful in creating masks. It's also extremely helpful for photo-retouching projects where you need to blur skin tones without affecting the sharpness of the basic image.

Brush Strokes

Like the Artistic filters, the Brush Stroke filters strive for natural-media effects, this time in the area of painting, and were originally part of the Gallery Effects filters that Adobe acquired from Aldus. In general, these filters remove detail and add texture to an image:

- Accented Edges (see Figure 8.30) emphasizes the edges in an image, like a combination of Trace Contour and Find Edges, and smoothes out the areas in between. The Edge Width slider (1 through 14) controls the width of the traced edges. The Edge Brightness value (0 through 50) determines whether the edges are black, white, or somewhere in between. Smoothness (1 through 15) controls how many areas are outlined—fewer with higher settings.

- Angled Strokes applies brush strokes with the ability to vary the angle in different colored areas of the image. This is controlled by the Direction Balance slider (0 through 100), with lower and higher settings forcing the strokes to be mostly in one direction and middle settings mixing them up. The Stroke Length slider allows you to choose lengths from 3 through 50, and the definition of the brush strokes is controlled with the Sharpness slider, with values ranging from 0 through 10.

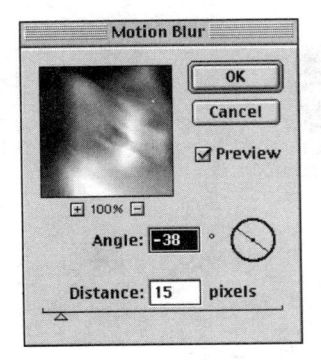

Figure 8.27 The Motion Blur filter dialog box.

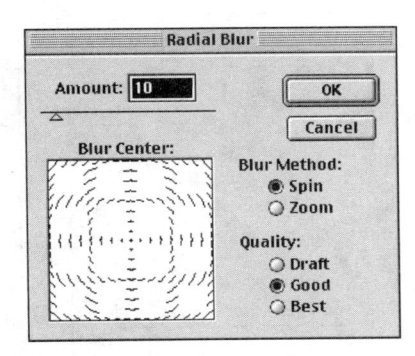

Figure 8.28 The Radial Blur filter dialog box.

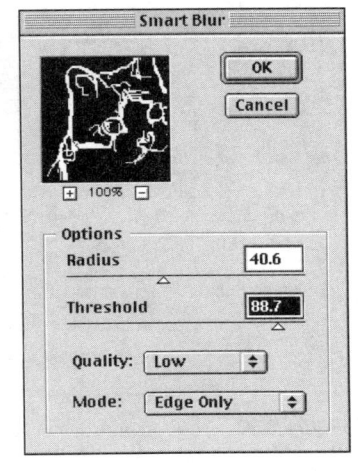

Figure 8.29 The Smart Blur filter dialog box.

- Crosshatch applies brush strokes at diagonal angles 90° apart. You can control the Stroke Length, from 3 through 50; the Sharpness, or stroke definition, from 0 through 20; and the Strength, which produces an embossing effect and ranges from 1 to 3 (see Figure 8.31).

- Dark Strokes produces crosshatched brush strokes as well. You can adjust the Balance from 0 to 10, with high and low settings making the strokes run one direction and medium settings mixing the stroke directions. The Black Intensity and White Intensity sliders determine how much the dark and light colors, respectively, are darkened or lightened in the course of applying the effect; these values can range from 0 to 10.

- Ink Outlines works like Dark Strokes, except that you can adjust the Stroke Length (from 1 to 50) and you have no control over the stroke angle. This filter also outlines elements in the image (see Figure 8.32). Figure 8.33 shows the Ink Outlines applied to the cat image.

- Spatter is similar to a combination of the Diffuse and Ripple filters, resulting in an image that looks as though it were created from tiny droplets of paint. The Spatter dialog box has only two sliders: Spray Radius, which ranges from 0 to 25 and controls how far droplets are allowed to encroach into areas of different colors, and Smoothness, which controls the ripple effect. The lowest Smoothness setting of 1 eliminates the ripples altogether, and the highest setting of 15 makes the image pretty much unrecognizable (see Figure 8.34).

- Sprayed Strokes adds softly sprayed strokes with angle, length, and width values that you can control. The Stroke Length slider ranges from 0 to 20; the Spray Radius slider controls how far droplets can stray from the axis of the stroke. The Stroke Dir pop-up menu has four options: Horizontal, Left Diagonal, Right Diagonal, and Vertical (see Figure 8.35).

- Sumi-e is a Japanese painting technique with lots of dark areas and soft-edged strokes (see Figures 8.36 and 8.37). You can control the Stroke Width and Stroke Pressure; width can vary from 3 to 15, and pressure from 0 to 15. The Contrast slider (0 through 40) determines how much contrast is added to the original image's dark and light areas; higher settings increase contrast, and lower ones maintain the existing contrast levels.

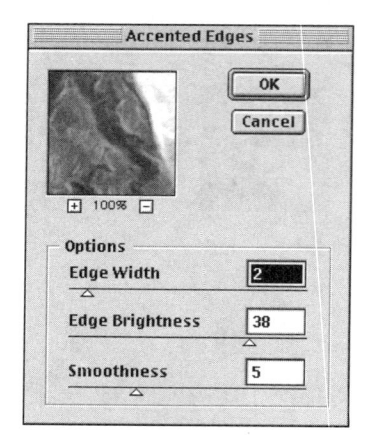

Figure 8.30 The Accented Edges filter dialog box.

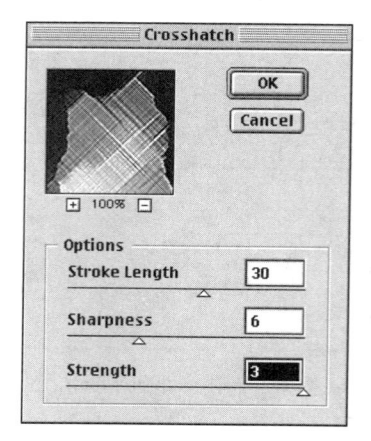

Figure 8.31 The Crosshatch filter dialog box.

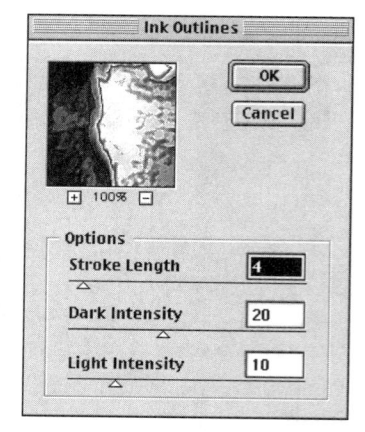

Figure 8.32 The Ink Outlines filter dialog box.

Figure 8.33 The Ink Outlines filter applied to the cat image.

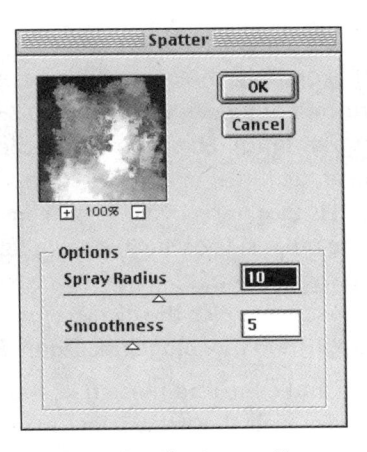

Figure 8.34 The Spatter filter dialog box.

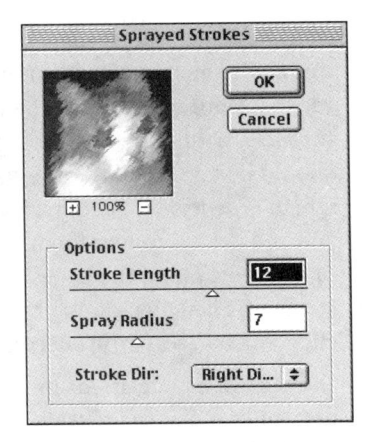

Figure 8.35 The Sprayed Strokes filter dialog box.

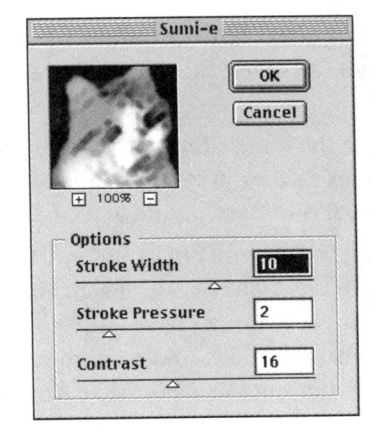

Figure 8.36 The Sumi-e filter dialog box.

Figure 8.37 The Sumi-e filter applied to the cat image.

Distort

The Distort filters allow you to simulate 3D effects. The math Photoshop is most apparent in these filters, which take an image and distort its shape geometrically:

- Diffuse Glow adds a glowing halo of the Background color to the lighter areas in an image. The Graininess slider (0 through 10) determines how much noise is applied to the dark areas of the image. The Glow Amount and Clear Amount sliders, both ranging from 0 to 20, control how much glow is applied and how much of the image is off-limits for the glow.

- Displace rearranges the existing image into another shape based on the brightness values in another image. You can use any Photoshop-format file (except one in Bitmap mode) as a displacement map. Adobe includes several files you can experiment with in the Displacement Maps folder. For example, the Streaks pattern creates a distorted water reflection effect, as though the image were reflected on the surface of a river. Midlevel grays in the displacement map move the target image's pixels least, dark colors move them in one diagonal direction, and light colors move them in the opposite direction. Scale determines how far pixels can be moved. With a scale of 1, the farthest any pixel will move is 128 pixels; increasing the scale increases that possible maximum distance. Then you determine how the displacement map should be adjusted to fit the size of the target image: Stretch to Fit, which scales it, or Tile, which repeats it. To deal with pixels that are moved off the edge of the image, choose Wrap Around, which moves them to the other side of the image, or Repeat Edge Pixels, which fills in blank spots along the edges with the colors of the nearby pixels. When you click on OK, a standard File Open dialog box asks you to pick the displacement map image, and when you click on OK again, the effect is applied to the image (see Figure 8.38).

- Glass uses displacement maps to make the image seem as though you're viewing it through a sheet of glass; the texture map controls the surface texture of the glass. The Distortion slider, from 0 to 20, affects how much the glass distorts the image, and the Smoothness slider controls the clarity of the glass. The Texture pop-up menu allows you to choose the Blocks, Canvas, Frosted, and Tiny Lens built-in textures or to load your own color or grayscale Photoshop format file. Also, the Scaling slider allows you to scale the texture from 50 to 200 percent. An Invert checkbox allows you to invert the glass texture before applying it to the image (see Figure 8.39).

- Ocean Ripple, a simpler filter that adds ripples to the image, has only two options. You can set the Ripple Size, from 1 to 15; the Ripple Magnitude slider (0 through 20) controls how much the image is moved toward and away from the axis of the rippling wave (see Figure 8.40).

- Pinch creates a bulge, either inward or outward, in the center of an image. Its effect is similar to that of the Spherize filter, except that the bulge isn't necessarily circular, because it's shaped by the image's proportions. The Amount value ranges from –100% to 100%; negative values create an outward bulge, whereas positive values create an inward bulge (see Figure 8.41). At first glance, you might wonder what anyone would do with this filter, but it's actually amazingly useful as a production tool. When you learn to control it, you can shave a tiny bit off of a model's nose or widen a too-small mouth. To make the filter work, it can be helpful to place the piece that you want to filter into its own image. If you then increase the canvas size, you have total control over the location that is pinched. The filter always pinches in the center of the selection, so all you need to do is make sure that the area you pinched *is* the center of the area that is filtered.

- Polar Coordinates takes the X- and Y-coordinates of each pixel in the image and changes them to polar coordinates, or treats them as polar coordinates and changes them to rectan-

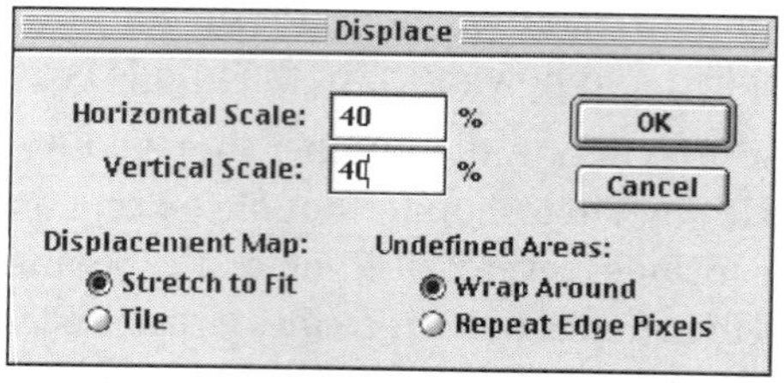

Figure 8.38 The Displace filter dialog box.

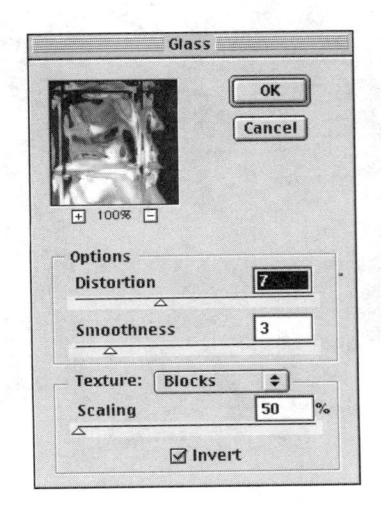

Figure 8.39 The Glass filter dialog box and filtered image.

gular coordinates. It produces extreme distortion of an image. This filter provides the only way to make text-on-a-circle within Photoshop (at least without buying another filter). It isn't wonderful; but it's possible! You can achieve interesting effects by filtering an image and then adding an element (such as a straight line), as shown in Figure 8.42. Try changing the image back using Polar-To-Rectangular as your Polar Coordinates setting. Figure 8.43 shows the result.

- Ripple, with values ranging from -999 to 999, adds Small, Medium, or Large ripples to an image. Depending on the Amount value and the size of the ripples, the resulting image can

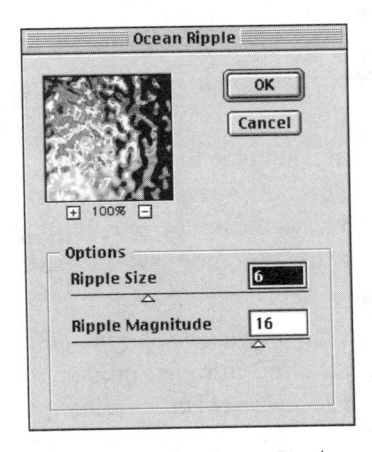

Figure 8.40 The Ocean Ripple filter dialog box.

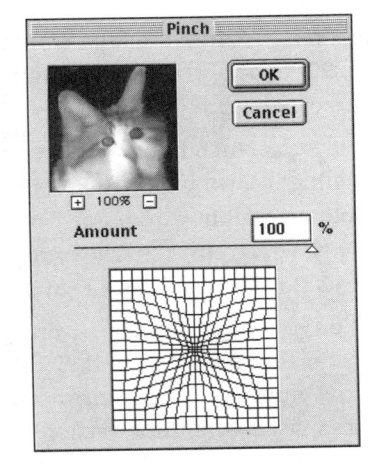

Figure 8.41 The Pinch filter dialog box.

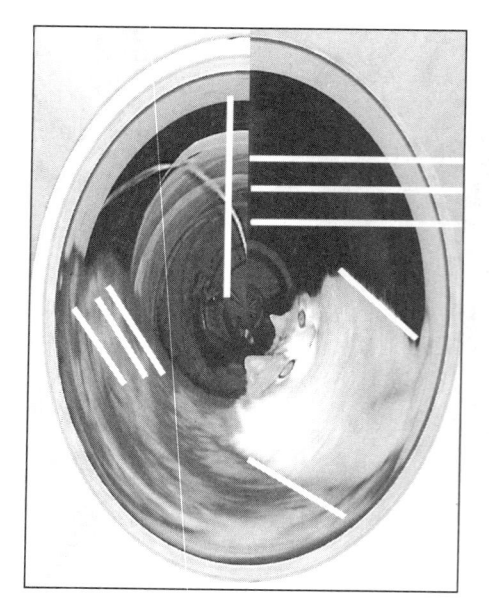

Figure 8.42 Apply the Polar Coordinates (Rectangular-to-Polar) filter to an image and draw some lines on the filtered image.

Figure 8.43 Apply the Polar Coordinates (Polar-to-Rectangular) filter to the previously filtered image and watch what happens to the lines.

look as though it were drawn by a child who can't yet make a straight line, or it can be completely unrecognizable (see Figure 8.44).

- Shear is the do-it-yourself Distort filter (see Figure 8.45). The dialog box contains a grid with a curved line that you can adjust to determine how the image is bent or otherwise distorted. Once the shape of the distortion is determined, the only option is what to do with spaces left blank by the operation. You can choose Wrap Around to substitute pixels that were moved off the opposite side of the image, or Repeat Edge Pixels to fill in with colors taken from adjacent pixels. Because the filter can only distort in a vertical direction, you need to rotate the image 90° to apply it the other way. This filter can do an excellent job of simulating folds in a garment.

- Spherize, like the Pinch filter, produces a rounded bulge in the center of an image, with negative values (down to −100%) producing an outward bulge and positive values (up to 100%) producing an inward bulge. You also have the option of choosing Horizontal Only or Vertical Only, which stretches the image over an imaginary cylinder sitting on its end (Horizontal) or its side (Vertical). (See Figure 8.46.)

- Twirl, just as you might imagine, twirls the image by a user-specified amount; you can specify a value between -999 and 999°, with positive numbers producing a clockwise twist and negative numbers generating a counterclockwise twist. The dialog box doesn't offer a true preview, just a wireframe version that shows how the twirl effect tapers off at the outer edges of the image (see Figure 8.47).

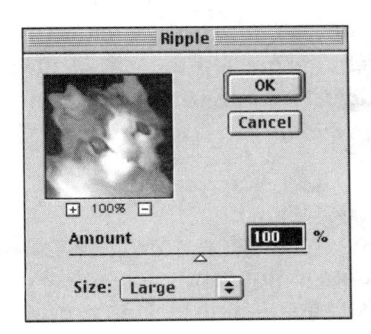

Figure 8.44 The Ripple filter dialog box.

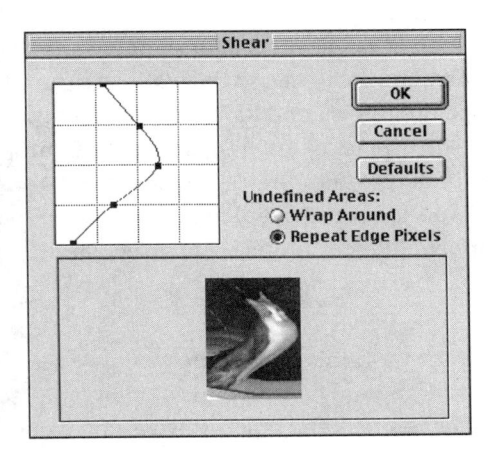

Figure 8.45 The Shear filter dialog box.

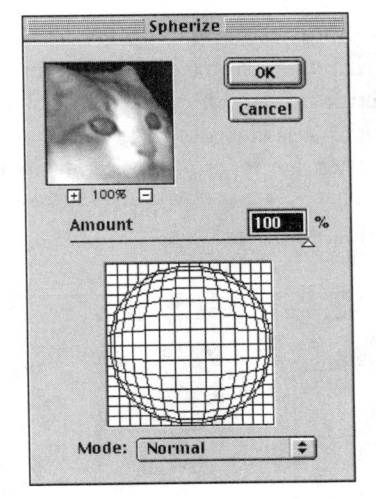

Figure 8.46 The Spherize filter dialog box.

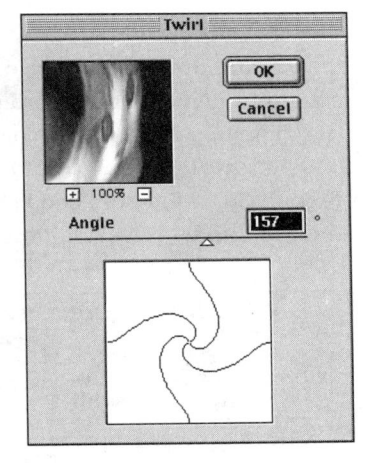

Figure 8.47 The Twirl filter dialog box.

- Wave is one of the more complex native filters, an expanded version of the Ripple filter that allows you to specify the number of waves, their type, and their magnitude. The Number of Generators ranges from 1 to 999, with higher numbers generating patterns that are more complex. For Wavelength and Amplitude, which determine the size of the waves, you can set Minimum and Maximum values ranging from 1 to 999; Scale determines the relative effect of the waves in the horizontal and vertical planes of the image. The Type section of the Wave dialog box allows you to choose Sine (curved), Triangle, or Square wave shapes, and you can choose Wrap Around or Repeat Edge pixels to deal with empty spaces on the edges of the image (see Figure 8.48).

- ZigZag duplicates the effect of dropping a pebble into a pond. The ripples radiating from the point where the rock entered the water are the effect of the ZigZag filter; in fact, one of its three type options is Pond Ripples. The other two are Out From Center and Around Center, which create ripples of different shapes radiating from the center of the image. The dialog box has both a regular preview window and a wireframe preview that shows the ripple shape. Two sliders in the dialog box allow you to adjust Amount (from -100% to 100%) and the number of Ridges (from 1% to 20%). (See Figure 8.49.)

Noise

Noise is what we think of as static when we see it on a television screen; Adobe defines it as "pixels with randomly distributed color levels." Because it's randomly generated, adding noise to an image is one of the quickest ways you can create an organic-looking texture; it's a good way to roughen up a smooth, too-perfect surface, such as one that's been heavily edited with the Smudge or Rubber Stamp tool. The filters in this category are designed to both add and remove noise:

- Add Noise, obviously, introduces a specified amount of noise to an image. The amount can range from 1 to 999, and the noise can be distributed using either a Uniform or a more random Gaussian arrangement. Monochromatic noise adds grayscale noise rather than colored noise (see Figure 8.50). The Add Noise filter is very useful as a starting point for creating many different textures. If you want to try other types of noise, the Artistic|Film Grain filter and the Texture|Grain filter are good choices. Several third-party filter sets (KPT, PhotoOptics, and Eye Candy) have additional noise filters.

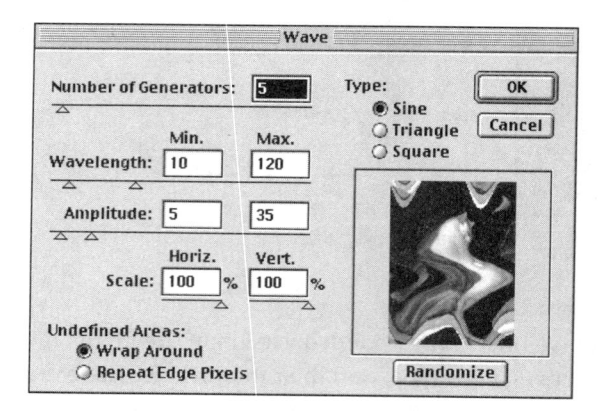

Figure 8.48 The Wave filter dialog box.

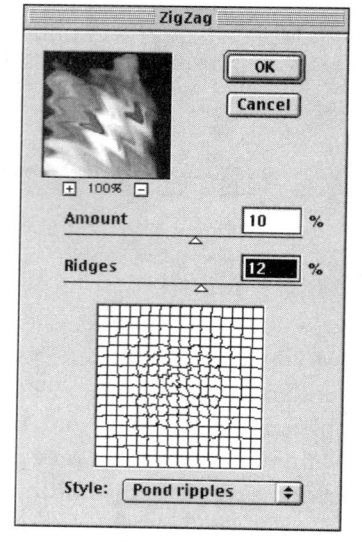

Figure 8.49 The ZigZag filter dialog box.

> **TIP**
>
> Despeckle, rather than adding noise, attempts to seek it out and eliminate it, generally to remove graininess or moiré patterns from scanned images. It doesn't have a dialog box because it has no options. Despeckle does blur an image slightly. It also usually puts a full range of graytones back into the image. If your image is mildly posterized (a result of a Levels or Curves adjustment), the Despeckle filter can restore a full range of values.

- Dust & Scratches (see Figure 8.51) finds pixels that stand out from the pixels around them by virtue of extreme differences in brightness values, and it fills those areas in with the surrounding color. This is a fairly effective method of eliminating inadvertently scanned dust and scratches—not to mention cat hair—from an image, but it can also eliminate things like the sparkle in a subject's eye. The Threshold value determines how different the brightness levels of the dust or scratches must be from the surrounding area to be affected by the filter; this value should be as high as possible to preserve details of the image. The Radius value determines how large the area of each adjustment is; the larger this number, the blurrier the image will get.

Figure 8.52 shows one of our favorite effects with Dust & Scratches. The cat on the Background layer was filtered with Dust & Scratches at a Radius of 16 and a Threshold of 0. It was consequently blurred to smithereens-although in color, the filter keeps color areas brighter than does Gaussian Blur. We added the woodcut lines by making a copy of the

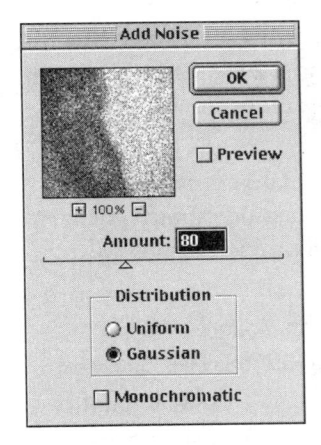

Figure 8.50 The Add Noise filter.

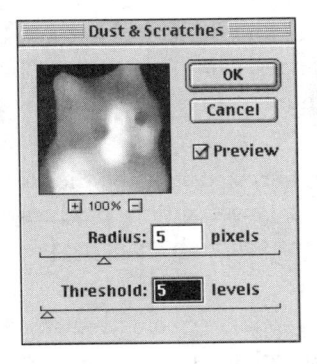

Figure 8.51 The Dust & Scratches filter dialog box.

Figure 8.52 Dust & Scratches applied to the background layer with a Radius of 16 and a Threshold of 0.

original cat in Layer 1, setting the Blend mode to Multiply, applying a High Pass filter at 1.6, and choosing the Threshold command to create the detailed lines. One excellent way to use the Dust & Scratches filter while retouching is to copy the main image into a new layer and apply the filter to the entire layer. Select the layer and delete all of the image from it (leave the layer). Now you can use the History brush to repaint the Dust & Scratches effect where it's needed. This technique allows you to control how much of the filter is applied to each area and the Blend mode that works best. You might want to paint in Lighten when the scratches are dark or Darken when the scratches are light.

- Median is great for cleaning up scanned line art. This filter smoothes areas within an image by averaging the color values of pixels within a distance determined by the Radius value. Used with jaggy or "dirty" line art, Median smoothes lines and eliminates stray marks; used with a photographic image, it reduces the overall number of colors in the image and simplifies its shapes. The Radius value can be as low as 1 or as high as 16 (see Figure 8.53). The filter can also be used to simulate watercolor painting, and you might prefer it to the Watercolor filter.

Pixelate

Pixelate filters produce the effect of enlarging a low-resolution image without interpolation—enlarged "pixels" made up of all the similarly colored pixels in an area, color-averaged to look even more similar.

- Color Halftone (see Figure 8.54) produces the pop art effect of a color halftone with huge dots. Each color channel in an image is converted to colored dots whose size is determined by the brightness of the pixels it replaces. You can specify the maximum radius of the dots (from 4 to 127 pixels) and screen angles for each color channel. In grayscale images, the only channel is Channel 1; in RGB images, Channel 1 is red, Channel 2 is green, and Channel 3 is blue; and in CMYK images, Channel 1 is cyan, Channel 2 is magenta, Channel 3 is yellow, and Channel 4 is black.

- Crystallize creates angular polygon shapes by averaging the colors of adjacent pixels; the Cell Size can range from 3 to 300 pixels. Lower settings produce an artistic stippled effect, while higher ones make the image look as though it's being viewed through a shower stall door (see Figure 8.55).

- Facet flattens out colors and straightens edges to create geometric shapes—facets—from the elements of an image. It doesn't have a dialog box, because it has no options (see Figure 8.56).

- Fragment creates four copies of an image, offsetting each slightly, to give a somewhat disturbing "quadruple-vision" effect (see Figure 8.57). Like Facet, Fragment has no options and no dialog box.

- Mezzotint reproduces the effect of the special mezzotint screen patterns used to create halftones, with a choice of four sizes of dots, three sizes of lines, and three sizes of irregular strokes. The pop-up menu containing these choices is the only option, and the dialog box offers an extra-large preview window because it's hard to see the true effect in a small area of the image (see Figure 8.58). This effect works best on large images at high resolution. The filter is fairly ugly applied at 72 dpi. It looks very good in print and in grayscale.

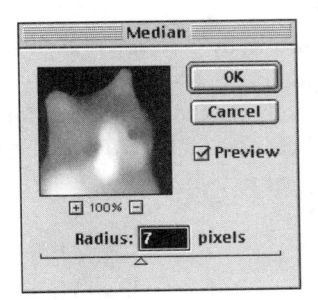

Figure 8.53 The Median filter dialog box.

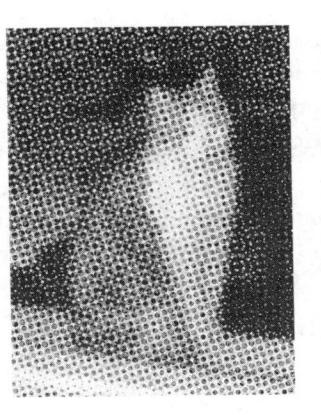

Figure 8.54 The Color Halftone filter applied to the cat image.

Figure 8.55 The Crystallize filter applied to the cat image.

Figure 8.56 The Facet filter applied to the cat image.

Figure 8.57 The Fragment filter applied to the cat image.

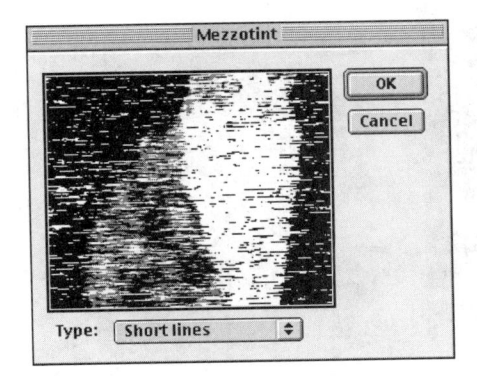

Figure 8.58 The Mezzotint filter dialog box and filtered image of the cat.

- Mosaic produces the most classic "pixelated" effect by generating square blocks of color anywhere from 2 to 64 pixels on a side. For greater interest, you can combine this filter with one of the Distort filters to randomize the block shapes somewhat (see Figure 8.59).
- Pointillize turns an image into a facsimile of a Pointillist painting by creating dots of color; it differs from the Color Halftone filter in that the resulting colors are the same as the image colors, rather than dots of primary colors. The dots are randomly placed and can range in size from 3 to 300 pixels, with the Background color placed between them to act as the paper or canvas color (see Figure 8.60).

Render

The six Render filters really don't have much in common. The two Clouds filters create—you guessed it—clouds; the Lens Flare and Lighting Effects filters add light and its attendant shadows to an image; and the Texture Fill filter uses grayscale images to create simulated 3D textures. Lighting Effects is the most complex native filter and requires a large amount of memory to run. The only new filter in Photoshop 5 is in this group of filters—it's the 3D Render filter, and it allows you to move part of your image as if it were a 3D object.

- Clouds doesn't have a dialog box, because its only options are the colors it uses. The Foreground and Background colors create random soft clouds. Holding Option (Mac) or Alt (Windows) as you choose Filter|Render|Clouds produces clouds with higher contrast and harder edges. Repeated applications intensify the effect (see Figure 8.61).
- Difference Clouds creates clouds based on the Foreground and Background colors combined with the existing colors in the image. Because it takes the image colors into account, it doesn't cover up the image the way the Clouds filter does—it overlays a cloud pattern on top of it (see Figure 8.62).
- Lens Flare (see Figure 8.63) produces the effect of light refracted through a curved lens. You have a choice of three types of lenses: 50 through 300mm Zoom, 35mm Prime, or 105mm Prime, and you can specify the Brightness level of the flare, from 10% to 300%. The dialog box's preview window contains a movable crosshair that allows you to position the center of the flare.

Figure 8.59 The Mosaic filter applied to the cat image.

Figure 8.60 The Pointillize filter applied to the cat image.

Figure 8.61 The Clouds filter.

Figure 8.62 The Difference Clouds filter.

Figure 8.63 The Lens Flare filter.

- Lighting Effects adds light to an image, allowing you to choose the attributes of the image's surface, the color and intensity of the light, and its scope. You can add a bump map (Texture Channel) to the mix to be used as a texture map that defines high and low spots in the image, creating a shadowed 3D surface. Complex as it appears, Lighting Effects is the easiest way to create embossed and other 3D effects. You choose a Light Type (Directional, Omni, or Spotlight) and Intensity, then the properties of the surface that will reflect or absorb the light: Gloss, Material, Exposure, and Ambience. The Texture Channel can be a layer, a color channel, or an alpha channel, and you have the option of white areas in the image being considered high or low, and a Height slider to control exactly how high (see Figure 8.64).

- Texture Fill doesn't actually create a texture; instead, it tiles a grayscale image into the image window. It's intended to be used in an alpha channel to create a selection mask or a bump map that can be used with the Lighting Effects channel. There's no preview, and no options other than what image you use.

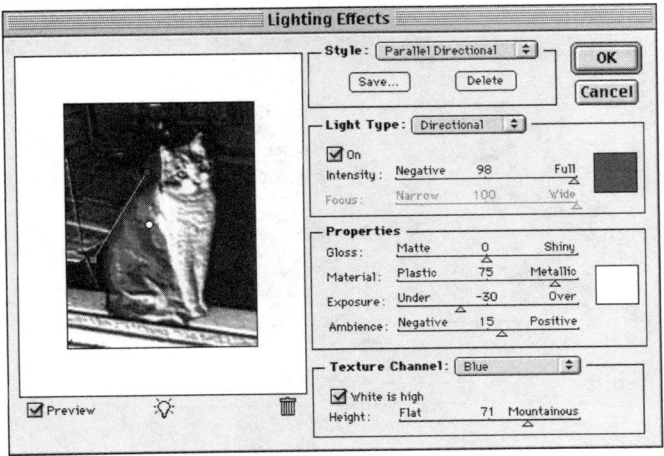

Figure 8.64 The Lighting Effects filter and an "embossed" result.

- 3D Transform is Photoshop's newest filter, and it's a complex one. While it doesn't have all the dials and controls of Lighting Effects, it is complicated nonetheless. It allows you to build a wireframe outline over an area of your image and then use traditional 3D controls to manipulate the image within the wireframe. The instructions for using the filter are only in the Photoshop 5 online help system, not in the manual; so don't get frustrated when you cannot find the specifics in the manual. Figure 8.65 shows the filter dialog box with its various options, and Figure 8.66 shows the picture of the cat (again!) in its original form; Figure 8.67 shows it after the cat's head has been moved slightly. We moved the cat's head on a separate layer and used a layer mask to blend it with the original.

The 3D Transform filter is a wonderful idea, but "moved slightly" seems to be the main idea of how far you can reasonably move most photographs. You can rotate a circular area, but it has no back, so if you rotate it too much, you run out of image and end up with blank whitespace. If you select the Cylinder wireframe, you can add and delete control points or change between a curve point and a corner point as you would in Illustrator. While rotating an object around seems to run out of image, you can tip the object forward, and the image will wrap. This lets you wrap a texture around a cylinder and tip the cylinder all the way forward, for example. It also lets you make minor adjustments to the position of objects, as you can see with the cat.

Sharpen

Utilitarian to the max, Sharpen filters can also be used at high intensity to create an exaggerated surrealist effect. Sharpen and Sharpen More affect the entire image, while Sharpen Edges and Unsharp Mask concentrate their effects on edges, with the latter offering the most control.

- Sharpen operates on all pixels in the image, increasing their contrast. For professional work, the Unsharp Mask filter offers more control and better results. No dialog box is associated with this filter.

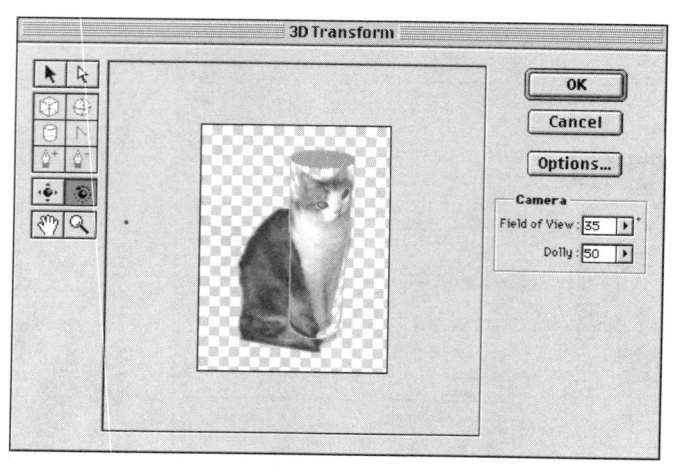

Figure 8.65 The 3D Transform filter dialog box.

Figure 8.66 The original cat image.

Figure 8.67 The cat image after it has been filtered with the 3D Transform filter and merged back into the original.

- Sharpen Edges operates like the Sharpen filter, but works only on the edges of large areas. It doesn't have any options, so there's no dialog box.
- Sharpen More is like using the Sharpen filter several times in succession. It has no options.
- Unsharp Mask is the Sharpen filter that's most often used in professional photo retouching or when preparing images for print. Based on a traditional photographic technique involving combining a negative and a blurred positive of an image to create a sharper print, it offers more control than the other Sharpen filters. The Amount value, ranging from 1% to 500%, determines how much adjustment is made to the affected pixels; a good starting point is between 100% and 200%, because very high values can sharpen unwanted details and generate noise. Radius controls the distance on either side of an edge that is affected, and it can range from .1 to 250 pixels; a value of 2 through 3 pixels is generally used. The Threshold value determines how much difference in brightness must exist before an area is considered an edge, and although this value can go as low as 69 levels and as high as 255 levels, it's generally set near the lower end of that range (see Figure 8.68). We cover the prepress aspects of this filter in depth in Chapter 9. Figure 8.69 shows an image of—you guessed it—the cat, with the left half sharpened correctly and the right half (or right half of the cat, at least) totally oversharpened.

Sketch

Yet more from the Gallery Effects series, most of these filters produce effects intended to look hand-drawn rather than painted. A few of these filters, such as Bas Relief and Chrome, could not possibly be hand drawn, but are included in this set anyway, for some reason. In general, these filters look wonderful in print, and are a good way to convert a full-color image into two colors (not necessarily black and white). They work very well for creating stylized imagery. Most of these filters use the Foreground and/or Background colors in the Toolbox to achieve their effects:

- Bas Relief (see Figure 8.70) produces a more detailed and subtle version of the effect of the Emboss filter, using the Foreground and Background colors for highlights and shadows. You can choose how much detail is retained and how smooth the surfaces are; both the Detail and Smoothness sliders range from 1 to 15. You can also determine the light direction in 45° increments.

- Chalk & Charcoal combines chalk strokes in the Background color and charcoal strokes in the Foreground color to create an image that can look extremely surreal, depending on your color choices. You can control the Chalk Area and the Charcoal Area, both ranging from 0 to 20, and the Stroke Pressure (0 through 5) to determine the intensity of the effect (see Figure 8.71).

- Charcoal turns the image into a simulated charcoal sketch, with dark areas colored with "charcoal" strokes in the Foreground color and light areas representing the paper in the Background color. The Charcoal Thickness slider (1 through 7) determines the width of the strokes, while the Detail slider (0 through 5) controls how closely the sketch follows the details of the image. The Light/Dark Balance slider (0 through 100) controls how much of the image is covered with charcoal strokes (see Figure 8.72).

- Chrome creates a similar effect to Plastic Wrap, except grayscale and multiplied several times so that the original image is almost obliterated. Both the Detail and Smoothness

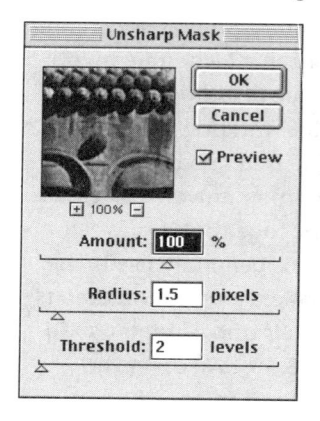

Figure 8.68 The Unsharp Mask filter dialog box.

Figure 8.69 The cat image sharpened and oversharpened.

Figure 8.70 The Bas Relief filter applied to an image.

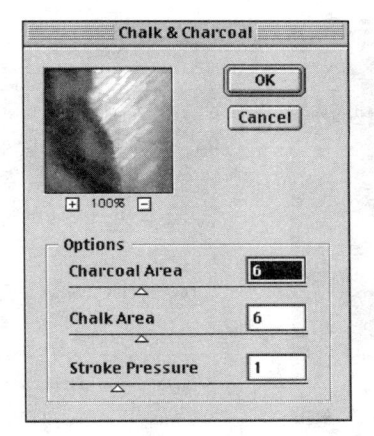

Figure 8.71 The Chalk & Charcoal filter dialog box.

Figure 8.72 The Charcoal filter applied to an image.

sliders—with values that range from 0 to 10—control how much of the original image's shape is preserved. This is not a good filter to apply to an entire image unless you want something that is totally unrecognizable. You can simulate soft chrome objects by applying the filter to an object and then placing a color image on top of it. When you set the Blend mode to Color, it looks as if you have a reflection on the object. Figure 8.73 shows the cat as a "morph." Her head is appearing out of a chromed body.

- Conté Crayon produces the effect of a crayon on textured paper. Conté crayons are usually black, dark red, or brown, so if you're looking for a realistic crayon effect, you'll want to use one of these colors as the Foreground color and a white, cream, or tan paper color as the Background color (see Figure 8.74).

- Graphic Pen produces a pen-and-ink sketch effect, except with no outlining—only shading strokes. You can determine the Stroke Length (from 1 through 15) and the Light/Dark Balance (from 0 through 100); the latter setting determines how much of the image is covered with the Foreground and Background colors, with medium settings distributing the colors evenly. You have four choices for Stroke Direction: Horizontal, Left Diagonal, Right Diagonal, and Vertical (see Figure 8.75).

- Halftone Pattern, like Color Halftone, turns the image into a prefab halftone, but it lays that effect over the existing image, which it re-colors in a combination of the Foreground and Background colors. The Pattern Type pop-up menu contains three options for the halftone pattern: Circle, Dot, and Line. Size and Contrast sliders, ranging from 1 to 12 and 0 to 50, respectively, control the scale of the halftone pattern and how prominent it appears (see Figure 8.76).

- Note Paper turns the image into a figure embossed on a sheet of grainy paper. You can control the amount of detail retained with the Image Balance slider (0 through 50) and the height of the embossing with the Relief slider (0 through 25). The Graininess control affects the texture of the paper—noise or smooth—and ranges from 0 to 20 (see Figure 8.77).

Figure 8.73 The Chrome filter applied to the cat's body.

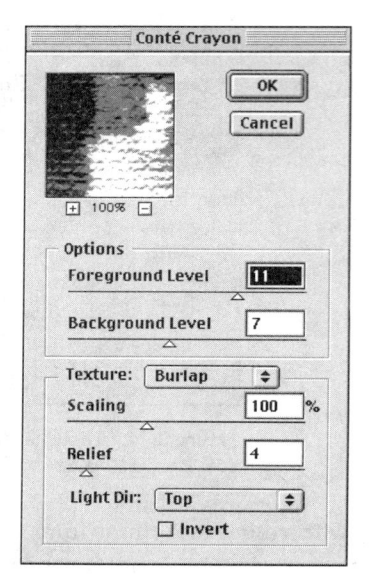

Figure 8.74 The Conté Crayon filter dialog box.

Figure 8.75 The Graphic Pen filter applied to an image.

Figure 8.76 The Halftone Pattern filter applied to an image.

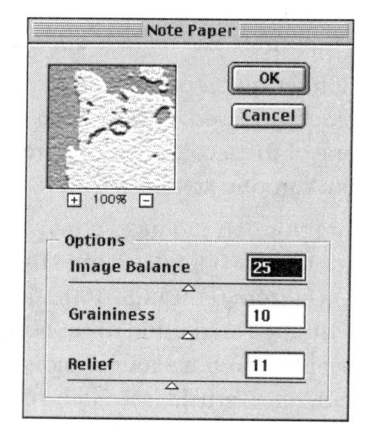

Figure 8.77 The Note Paper filter dialog box.

- Photocopy produces a blurry, streaky, and posterized effect similar to a photo reproduced on a particularly poor photocopier. You choose how much detail to retain with the Detail slider (1 through 24) and the darkness of the image with the Darkness slider (1 through 50). (See Figure 8.78.)

- Plaster (see Figure 8.79) adds a relief effect to an image in which dark areas are raised and light areas are lowered. The Image Balance slider, running from 0 to 50, determines the point above which pixels are made the Foreground color and below which they're made the Background color. The Smoothness slider determines how much plaster texture is applied to the image. The Light Position pop-up menu has eight choices at 45° angles from each other.

- Reticulation (see Figure 8.80) is a photographic effect in which the film's emulsion cracks during processing, and this filter ends up resembling the Mezzotint filter, with randomly shaped noise applied to the image. The Density slider, with values ranging from 0 to 50, determines how densely the dots are placed and how closely they follow the image's shapes. The Black Level and White Level sliders, both of which also range from 0 to 50, control how much of the Foreground and Background colors, respectively, are used in the resulting image.
- Stamp (see Figure 8.81) combines the effects of the Threshold command and the Median filter, allowing you to create a two-color image with the cutoff between the two colors determined by the Light/Dark Balance setting (0 through 50). The Median part comes in with the Smoothness slider (1 through 50), which can smooth rough edges.
- Torn Edges (see Figure 8.82) doesn't actually look particularly like torn paper edges; it posterizes an image into two colors, with fuzzy transitions between different colored areas. Image Balance (0 to 50) controls the relative amounts of the Foreground and Background colors used. The softness of the edges is controlled by the Smoothness slider (1 to 15), and the Contrast slider (1 to 25) determines whether the two colors mix smoothly (low settings), with jagged spots (high settings), or not at all (medium settings).
- Water Paper mimics the effect of painting on damp paper, which blurs the colors and reduces contrast in the image. Fiber Length (3 through 50) is analogous to stroke length in other filters. The Brightness (0 through 100) and Contrast (0 through 100) sliders affect how much of the image's detail and contrast are lost (see Figure 8.83).

Stylize

These nine filters produce exaggerated, stylized effects by focusing on the contrast in an image:

- Diffuse scatters occasional pixels randomly around the image; it has three modes. Normal shows all the moved pixels, whereas Darken Only shows only the moved pixels that are darker than the pixels around them and Lighten Only shows only the moved pixels that are lighter than the pixels around them. This filter might not show much change the first time it's used, but it can be reapplied successive times to thoroughly rearrange the pixels in the image.

Figure 8.78 The Photocopy filter applied to an image.

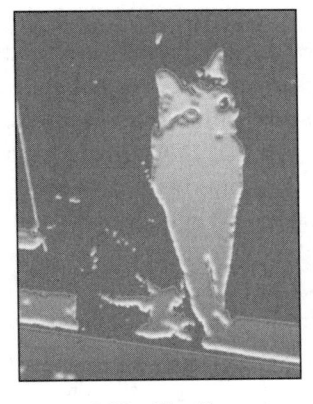

Figure 8.79 The Plaster filter applied to an image.

Figure 8.80 The Reticulation filter applied to an image.

Figure 8.81 The Stamp filter applied to an image.

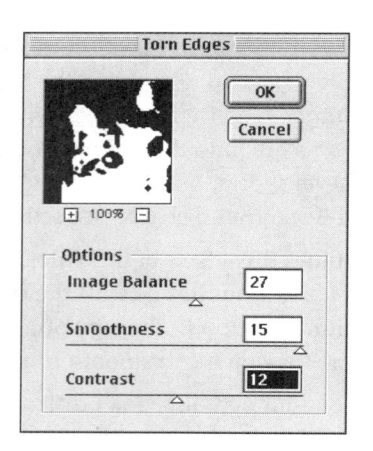

Figure 8.82 The Torn Edges filter dialog box.

Figure 8.83 The Water Paper filter applied to an image.

- Emboss stamps an image into the surface, turning most of the image gray and retaining image colors only on the "sides" of the protruding, embossed areas. You can control the Angle of the embossing (-360° to 360°), its Height (1 through 10 pixels), and the Amount of detail retained in the image (1% through 500%). The higher the Amount and Height settings, the more color remains in the image. The Angle setting allows you to control whether the image is embossed "up" or "down." If you do not know the direction of the relief when the filter has been applied, you can invert the result. That does exactly the same thing as moving the angle 180°. It's generally better to desaturate the image either before or immediately after embossing it, because the trace colors that remain are distracting and ugly. If you want to add texture to an image and retain its color, copy the original layer to the layer above and emboss that. Desaturate it and change the Blend mode to Hard Light. The colors of the original show through, and the embossed version adds the illusion of dimensionality. You can control the degree of texture added either by changing the opacity of the layer or by blurring the embossed layer. The Emboss filter is the starting point for many text effects or texture effects. Figure 8.84 shows the filter dialog box, and Figure 8.85 shows the embossed cat.

- Extrude looks promising—a real 3D object generator built into Photoshop?—but this filter is not particularly appealing. It pastes the existing image onto the surfaces of rows of square blocks or pyramids, with the option (check Solid Front Faces) of making each block a solid color that is the average of the colors in that area of the original image. The Size value determines the size of the blocks or pyramids, and the Depth value determines how tall they are. Choose Random to vary the height of each block or Level-based to make blocks in brighter areas of the image higher. The Mask Incomplete Blocks option eliminates partial blocks (see Figure 8.86). You can use this filter to achieve much more subtle effects (such as creating a chain link fence in front of an image) by applying the filter to a solid color layer and then embossing, desaturating, and changing the Blend mode to Hard Light. Then blur as needed. Of course, it can make good lizard skin, too!

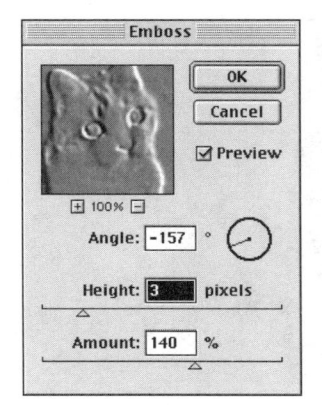

Figure 8.84 The Emboss filter dialog box.

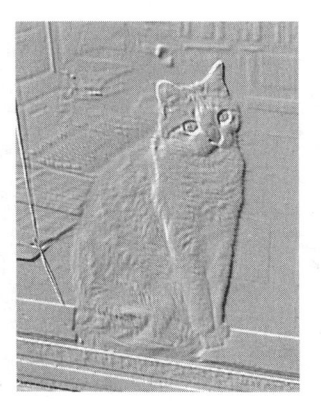

Figure 8.85 The Emboss filter applied to the cat image.

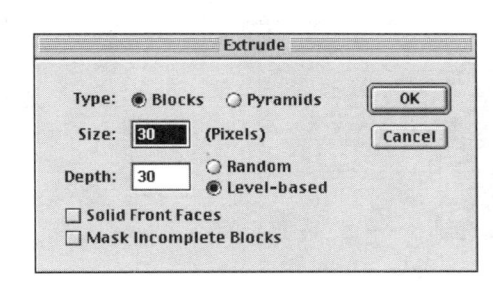

Figure 8.86 The Extrude filter dialog box and the filter applied to the cat image.

- Find Edges emphasizes all the edges in an image and inverts many of the colors. This filter has no options. If you desaturate the result, you get an etching (see Figure 8.87a). The Find Edges filter is another major filter for producing textures and a variety of special effects. In early versions of Photoshop, the filter would produce an image with the edges in their original colors but with the background of the image set to black. You can still produce this effect by inverting the result of the Find Edges filter. Try the Find Edges filter on an image created using the Add Noise filter (you get little beads) or on a blurred copy of the noise (you get long wigglies or a wonderful moiré pattern, depending on how much of a blur was applied). Another trick is to apply the Mosaic filter first at a small setting (6 is good on a 300 dpi image) and then use the Find Edges filter. This gives you an interesting stylized image, as shown in Figure 8.87b.

- Glowing Edges (see Figure 8.88) is a combination of the Find Edges filter and the Invert command, with the ability to control the Edge Width (1 through 14), Edge Brightness (0 through 20), and Smoothness of the edges (1 through 15). With higher Smoothness settings, fewer edges are located.

Figure 8.87 The Find Edges filter applied to the cat image (a, left) and applied after the Mosaic filter (b, right).

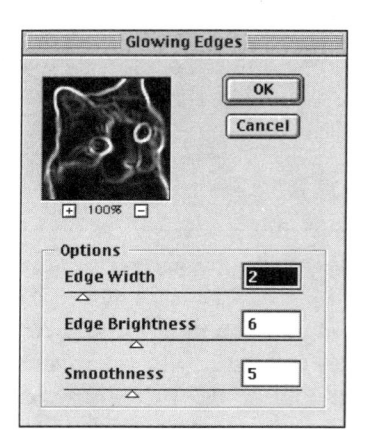

Figure 8.88 The Glowing Edges filter dialog box.

- Solarize applies the curve shown in Figure 8.89 to the image. It doesn't have any options. Figure 8.89 shows the cat solarized.
- Tiles, which unfortunately doesn't have a preview, breaks an image into a user-specified number of square chunks (as many as 99 across) and moves them as much as 99 percent of their width away from their original location (see Figure 8.90). You can specify what shows in the "holes" between these tiles: Background Color, Foreground Color, Inverse Image, or Unaltered Image.
- Trace Contour turns images into something like geographical contour maps, by locating the brightest or darkest areas in the image in each channel and outlining them there, producing

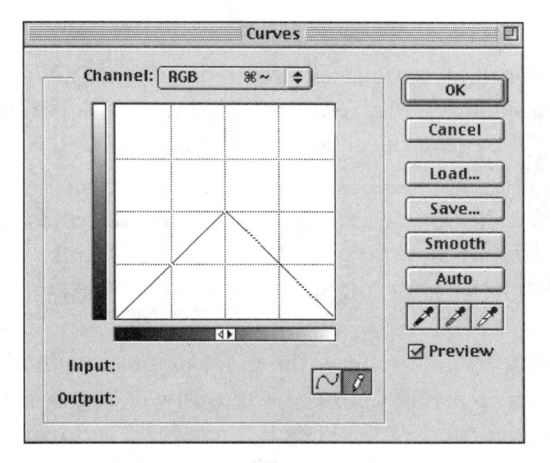

Figure 8.89 The Solarize curve and the cat with the Solarize filter applied.

narrow lines of primary colors. The Edge setting determines whether darker areas (Lower) or lighter (Upper) areas are outlined, and the Level setting determines the brightness level above or below which an area has to fall to be outlined. If you want to outline a specific area, use the Info palette to determine its brightness level, then use that value for the Level setting (see Figure 8.91). This filter has a full-image preview, so you can see exactly what you will have when you apply the filter. This is an interesting filter on which to use the Fade command along with Blend mode change. You can add edge detail to an image by fading the filter to Multiply mode.

- Wind works similarly to the Motion Blur filter, but because it affects only edges, it doesn't have the effect of blurring the image. Instead, elements in the image seem to be blowing away in a direction you specify (From the Left or From the Right). You can also choose the wind speed: Wind, Blast, or Stagger, as shown in Figure 8.92.

Figure 8.90 The Tiles filter.

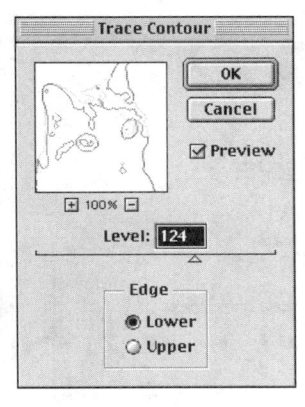

Figure 8.91 The Trace Contour filter dialog box.

Figure 8.92 The Wind filter applied to the cat image.

Texture

As its name implies, this group of filters adds various textures to an image. The names of the individual filters are more or less misleading—the results of the Stained Glass filter, for example, don't look much like stained glass—but the effects can be striking:

- Craquelure creates a beautiful combination of embossing and a crackle effect. The sliders let you determine Crack Spacing (2 through 100), Crack Depth (0 through 10), and Crack Brightness (0 through 10). Spacing controls how far apart the cracks are, Depth controls how deep they are, and Brightness controls what color they are—white, black, or something in between (see Figure 8.93).

- Grain is similar to Add Noise, but it allows you to choose the shape of the noise that is added, with 10 choices in the Grain Type pop-up menu: Clumped, Contrasty, Enlarged, Horizontal, Regular, Soft, Speckle, Sprinkles, Stippled, and Vertical (see Figure 8.94). The Intensity slider (0 through 100) determines how much grain is added, but it's not linear; you may see no effect at the top or bottom of this range and may need to use a setting in the middle. The Contrast slider (0 through 100) determines how light or dark the added grain is. The Clumped and Contrasty noises are very interesting and make wonderful starts for custom textures.

- Mosaic Tiles produces a mosaic effect with irregular, squarish tiles. Although you can control Grout Width, from 1 to 15, and the lightness of the grout (with the Lighten Grout slider, from 0 through 10), the grout isn't a contrasting color. Rather, the grout shows as the unembossed areas between the raised tiles. The remaining option is Tile Size, ranging from 2 to 100 (see Figure 8.95). The final effect doesn't look like any mosaic tiles *we've* ever seen, but then, we probably haven't seen all of the examples in the world. You might be able to find a creative use for this filter.

- Patchwork produces an image that looks more like tile than a patchwork quilt. This effect has no visible grout, and it does have the bonus of a Relief control that allows you to keep

Figure 8.93 The Craquelure filter applied to the cat image.

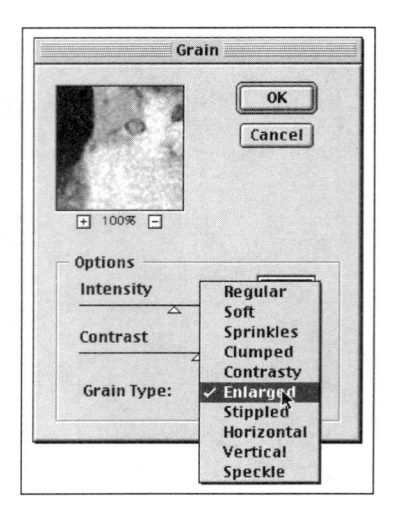

Figure 8.94 The Grain filter dialog box.

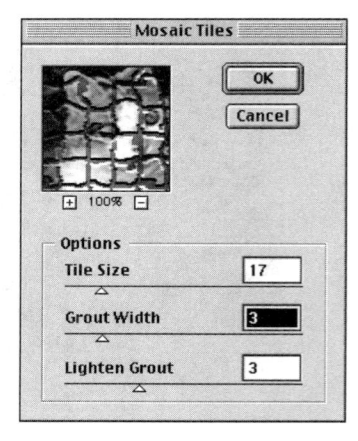

Figure 8.95 The Mosaic Tiles filter dialog box.

the image fairly flat (at the low-end setting of 0) or change the height of the tiles depending on their brightness level (at the high-end setting of 25). You can also set the Square Size (0 through 10). (See Figure 8.96.)

- Stained Glass produces a backlit honeycomb effect using highly saturated versions of the image colors. You control the Cell Size (2 through 50), the Border Thickness (1 through 20), and the Light Intensity (0 through 10). The lead between the pieces of "glass" is colored with the Foreground color (see Figure 8.97). By choosing a large Cell Size, you can make squares that only have a diagonal line through them. You can use these two-colored squares to construct interesting tile patterns.

- Texturizer is just what it sounds like—it adds a texture to an image based on the brightness levels in another file. You can choose an option from the Texture pop-up menu, with Brick, Burlap, Canvas, and Sandstone options and the ability to choose your own color or grayscale Photoshop-format file. As with the other filters with this capability, you can scale the texture with the Scaling slider (50% to 200%), adjust the height of the Relief effect from 0 to 50 pixels, choose one of eight Light Directions at 45° angles from one another, and Invert the second image before creating a texture from it (see Figure 8.98). This filter is extremely useful and does just what it's supposed to do. Because you can select your own files, you can use any flat file as the texture source, and build up unique image composites and effects.

Video

These filters are generally useful only for images destined for use on television or that were acquired from video:

- De-Interlace removes the horizontal scan lines in a still image captured from video, using duplication or interpolation to replace the missing pixels.
- NTSC Colors converts the colors in an image to their closest equivalents in the palette of colors that work well on TV, as approved by the National Television Standards Committee. For the most part, the colors in this palette are not highly saturated.

Figure 8.96 The Patchwork filter applied to the cat.

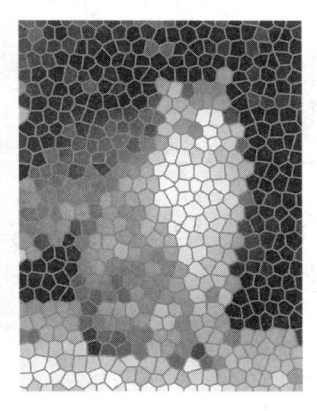

Figure 8.97 The Stained Glass filter applied to the cat.

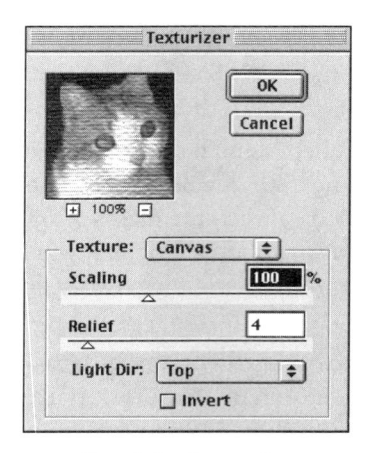

Figure 8.98 The Texturizer filter dialog box and a canvas texture applied to the cat image, using the Texturizer filter.

Other

These miscellaneous filters are often ignored, but very useful once you know what they can do for you:

- Custom allows you to create your own filter effects by punching numbers into a grid representing pixel brightness values. See the section "Creating Your Own Filters" later in this chapter. Figure 8.99 shows the filter dialog box for the Custom filter. Luckily, this filter has a full-screen preview in addition to the small preview in the dialog box. Otherwise, unless you really understood what you were doing, you would usually produce either mud or a totally blank image. If dialing for numbers isn't your thing, KPT Convolver generates Custom tables in a manner that is much easier to understand and to control.

- The High Pass filter emphasizes highlights and removes shading to flatten the colors in an image (see Figure 8.100). It substantially lessens the contrast in an image. If you use the Threshold command after using the High Pass filter, you can bring out a much larger amount of detail in black and white. The smaller the High Pass setting, the more detail you

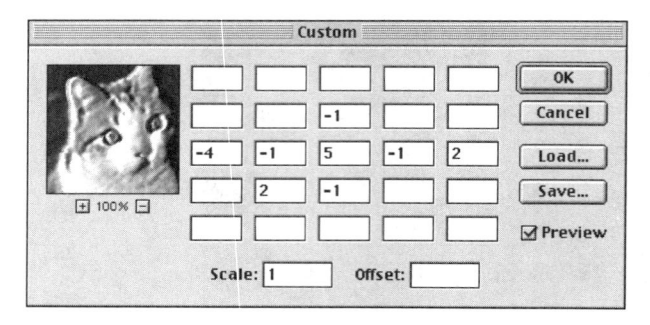

Figure 8.99 The Custom filter dialog box.

Figure 8.100 The High Pass filter applied to the cat image.

will preserve with the Threshold command. Photoshop's High Pass filter removes most of the color in the image. MetaCreations's Painter contains a High Pass filter that softens the color and is quite attractive as an effect all by itself. We use the High Pass filter at a 1.6 setting to multiply edges back into an image (as we described previously in the chapter).

- Maximum shrinks dark areas of an image by lightening their edge pixels. It's intended to be used in creating and editing masks, but it's also useful for cleaning up and refining scanned line art. It's rarely useful as an image enhancer.
- Minimum shrinks light areas of an image by darkening their edge pixels. Like the Maximum filter, it's intended for creating and editing masks, but it's also useful for cleaning up and refining scanned line art. It's not a pretty filter by itself.
- The Offset filter is the key to creating seamless patterns; it quite simply moves pixels in the image a specified distance (see Figure 8.101). Seamless patterns are discussed in Chapter 12. Offset can be used to specify exactly where an image will begin (but you can use the Transform command for that now). You can apply the filter within a selection, even in a layer—a change from previous versions of the program.

Digimarc

If you're concerned about copyright issues—and anyone working with electronic images should be—you can use the Digimarc filters to read and insert electronic watermarks that identify the creator of an image. The watermarks are in the form of added noise that's too subtle to be seen with the naked eye. Theoretically, however, watermarks are visible to the software even in scanned images.

- Embed Watermark adds a watermark to an image that identifies you as the image's creator via an ID number that you pay Digimarc Corporation to give you. Once you have the ID number, you click on Personalize and enter it in the Creator ID field. Then you choose an option for Type of Use: Restricted or Royalty Free, depending on whether you're allowing others to use the image freely or not. Check Adult Content if you want the image to be identified that way to hypothetical future applications that may screen for adult images to keep children from viewing them. Finally, choose a Watermark Durability option (either less visible, less durable or more visible, more durable) and click on OK to embed the watermark (see Figure 8.102).
- Read Watermark checks an image to see if it contains a watermark. If it has one, you'll see a dialog box telling you that. If it doesn't have a watermark, a dialog box displays the creator's name and the use allowed. You can also click on a button to go to a Web site that has more information about the image and its creator.

Third-Party Filters

If filter addiction has taken hold, you can buy plenty of third-party filters to satisfy your craving. Many of these products offer dazzling results with plenty of control, and time has proved their durability and usefulness. We cannot discuss every third-party filter in detail—this would be another book! However, we do have room for a short discussion.

Figure 8.101 The Offset filter applied to the cat image.

Figure 8.102 The Embed Watermark dialog box.

Photoshop has two types of third-party extensions—the ones that live in the Filter menu, and the ones that don't. Third-party plug-ins for Photoshop can also appear on the File|Import or File|Export menu. These add-on production filters let you scan, enhance scans, and read or write to specific devices or in specific, specialized formats.

In more general terms, we can identify (loosely) 10 classes of third-party plug-ins. Some filter sets span several categories, and the categories themselves are not fixed, but this is a useful way to look at the large number of available filters.

Type Filters

Until Photoshop 5, there was no way to edit type in Photoshop, or even to preview it on the screen. Extensis, therefore, released PhotoTools to help users set blocks of type and change colors on a letter-by-letter basis. PhotoTools appears in several categories, but its excellent type handling makes it a good choice even in Photoshop 5. Xaos Tools TypeCaster also creates text, but this time, it's 3D text. Figure 8.103 shows the TypeCaster interface.

Vertigo HotTEXT also creates 3D text. However, you can arrange this text along a Path to make curved 3D text. Figure 8.104 shows the Vertigo HotTEXT interface.

Human Software offers two text filters. Textissimo is a powerful and complex filter that allows you to type in a word and apply a series of effects to it. Figure 8.105 shows its interface. Otto Paths (see Figure 8.106) is almost an implementation of Adobe Illustrator inside of Photoshop. It appears on the Select menu rather than the Filter menu, and allows you to add text, create complex paths that can be distorted, and create text-on-a-Path. The filter can apply your path as a layer, a selection, or as a new path.

If you need to add interest to letterforms, then the Typo/Graphic Edges filter from Auto/FX is ready-made for you. This filter allows you to change the edges of the text and apply a variety of interesting textures and edge enhancements.

Color Studio

On the following pages, you'll see color examples of the projects presented throughout this book.

You will see, for example, how a badly exposed scanned image can be rendered usable; you will see the results of image correction and revision; and you will see how paths, tools, filters, and channels can turn the mundane into magic.

COLOR STUDIO

A frequent criticism of previous versions of Photoshop was that it did not handle spot color very efficiently. With version 5, you now have the ability to handle spot color with the same facility you can handle process color. This simulated spot color poster is one of the practice files included with this book's CD-ROM disk. With it, you will learn how to work with as many spot colors as you wish to use.

COLOR STUDIO

If a scan can be captured with more than eight bits of information in each channel, you can perform a number of similar adjustments on the image to coax the data back into normal range. Because the scan contains so much data, it is possible to retrieve picture information from badly exposed images (top) so successfully that the image becomes usable. Adjustments of this magnitude on a normal scan would irretrievably damage the image. (Photo by Alexis Yiorgos Xenakis)

COLOR STUDIO

Kodak's Photo CD provides an inexpensive way to acquire good quality images. Files that you open into Photoshop should be treated as unadjusted scans. Don't be concerned if, when you first see an image retrieved from a Photo CD, it looks as dense and dark as the upper image shown here. You have enough data that you can use Photoshop's controls to to make the image reasonably close to your original photograph. (Photo by Alexis Yiorgos Xenakis)

COLOR STUDIO

Civilization overlays the fine details of this Victorian house with electronic and sports clutter (top). With Photoshop's Rubber Stamp tool and the selection tools, the springtime elegance of the house has been restored. Now it looks (lower) much the same as when it was built. Wires, air-conditioner, basketball backboard—even the distant microwave tower— have all vanished. Anyone who would trust photographs as court evidence does not know what Photoshop can do!

COLOR STUDIO

At the top, a pleasant atmospheric image with far too many places where the eye can rest its attention. Photoshop and the Focus tools have provided instant depth-of-field (bottom). With the Sharpen tool and a large, soft-end brush tip, the basil plants, the pillow, and the top of the chest have been brought into sharper focus. The Blur tool has defocused the area around the central image. The eye now alights naturally on the center of the photo. (Photo by Alexis Yiorgos Xenakis)

COLOR STUDIO

Autumn and a cloudy day give us dull, subdued fall colors (small inset). Photoshop's Toning tools can quickly reanimate the scene. With the Burn tool set to Highlights, this sky was darkened in the cyan channel. Note the natural look of the sky produced by painting with a casual brush stroke. Next, with the Sponge tool set to Saturate, the lifeless tones of the foliage become enhanced appropriately for the bright, clear day, evidenced by the blue sky. (Photo by Cheryl Koch)

COLOR STUDIO

Here's a technique that uses Quick Mask to make a soft-edged selection. The original (lower) lost some of its brilliance when it was converted to CMYK. The mask was used to enhance the central figure by applying a boost to the image's saturation. Then, the inverse selection was used to darken and desaturate the background. The result is a figure bathed in glowing light against a muted and darker background. (Photo by Alexis Yiorgos Xenakis)

COLOR STUDIO

Already a softly romantic image, these two versions of a practice photo use filters and applied patterns to give a dreamier mood. Quick Mask has been used to quickly isolate areas of the image—with fairly soft, feathered edges— which have then been subjected to the Pointillize, Ripple, Mosaic, and Watercolor filters. The filters produce very different effects and merge smoothly with adjoining areas because of the masking. (Photo by Alexis Yiorgos Xenakis)

COLOR STUDIO

From a quiet pond to instant Monet.... With a random set of small v-shaped paths spread over the entire photograph, the Impressionist variation of the History Brush can accomplish this painterly effect with a single click of the mouse. The variety of effects that can be achieved by the eleven stroking tools—all of which can be made to follow a path automatically—is startling. Paths effects are explored extensively in this book.

COLOR STUDIO

The stroked path effects shown here built upon this detail (top) of the famous David by Michelangelo. Two paths are needed for the effects and to contain them in specific areas. One of these outlines the sky, the other the statue. One or both can be used simultaneously as a selection and as a guide for a tool. In the lower photo, a white paintbrush stroked the outline of the statue while the sky was selected to give this glow effect.

COLOR STUDIO

The top figure shows a more complex effect than the previous page's glow. Two strokes, both at about 50% Opacity, have been applied with a Paintbrush. A white stroke within the area of the statue and a dark stroke ouside the area make a point of the edges by heightening the contrasts. In the lower figure, parallel paths running across the entire width of the image have been stroked while the sky area was selected.

COLOR STUDIO

The effects shown in these two figures are based on stroking cloned versions of the statue's outer contours. In the top image, strokes have been applied with a white Paintbrush. As each path was stroked, the brush opacity was lowered by 10%. The lower image was done in exactly the same way as the upper, except that a 50% black tone was used for the stroke color and the paintbrush was set to the Difference mode.

COLOR STUDIO

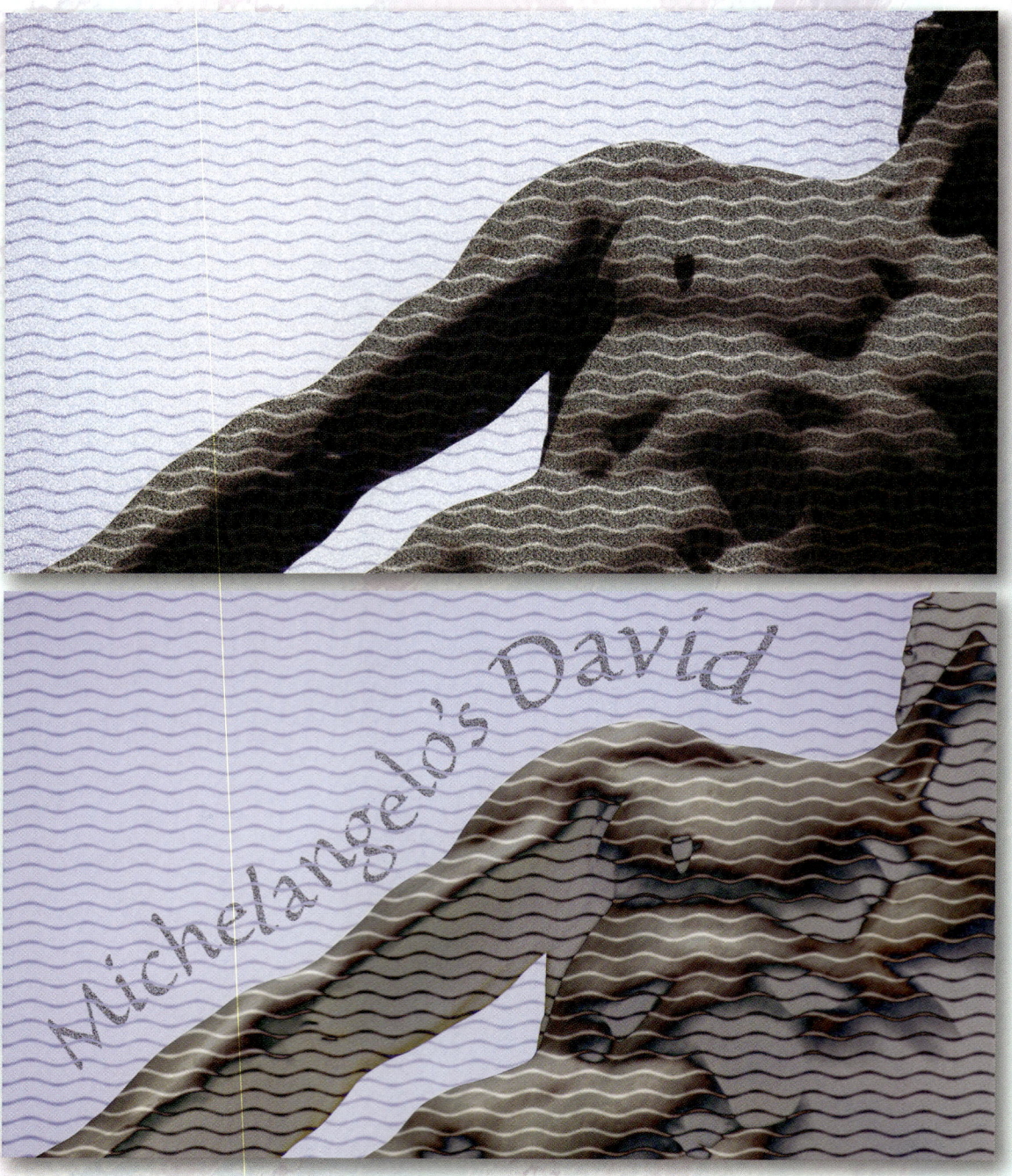

These examples are the result of stroking a set of waved paths. The effects were achieved by having one of the image areas selected during the stroking. In the top, the brush was set for white (background) and black (statue). For both areas, the brush was at 40% Opacity and in Dissolve mode. The lower image used a black brush (50% Opacity, Dissolve mode) for the letters. A white brush, 50% Opacity, stroked the sky using Normal mode, and the statue using Difference mode was employed.

COLOR STUDIO

These two examples are more complex than the previous images. The top photo has been altered by first adding horizontal lines to the sky. V-shaped paths were then stroked with the Smudge tool. Finally, the same paths were stroked using the History Brush's Impressionist option. The lower image is a composite of two photographs. The merging of the two required the same horizontal-line paths and the v-shapes.

COLOR STUDIO

Both of these figures are further examples of what can be achieved with stroked paths. The top example has been built up with multiples strokes using different brushes, opacity settings, and two colors—cyan and white. The lower image features a stroke of the letter outlines by the Smudge tool while the letters were selected. This gives the glass-like effect. The glass effect is further enhanced by keeping an embossed-letter alpha channel active while Levels controls lightened the letters.

COLOR STUDIO

These two images were composed using alpha channels. Alpha channels are Photoshop's method of storing selections. Because the selection is stored as an image, Photoshop editing operations can be performed upon it. Several channels can be used to give new selections based on the differences between them, the composite selection of both, and the selections common to all. These special effects can be accomplished in minutes. (Photo by Alexis Yiorgos Xenakis)

COLOR STUDIO

Some of Photoshop's most mysterious and beautiful effects are achieved with the Blend modes. The concept is simple: When one pixel lays atop another, calculations based on each of their values can be used to produce a result color. This blended color is often—but not always—different from the two values that produced it. The numerical manipulations can include common arithmetic operations such as Multiply & Difference. Other operations are more complex and produce intricate color artifacts. While some pixel combinations do not produce interesting effects, others combine for combinations that are arresting—and somehow appropriate in their context. The examples shown on this page—and the following two pages—combine the peony's background with the colored textures of the pages.

Normal

Dissolve

Multiply

Screen

Overlay

COLOR STUDIO

Soft Light

Hard Light

Color Dodge

Color Burn

Darken

Lighten

COLOR STUDIO

Difference

Exclusion

Hue

Saturation

Color

Luminosity

COLOR STUDIO

You can use the Apply Image command to move a grayscale version of an image into a Layer mask. When a grayscale image masks two solid layers, it creates a two-colored image as shown above. The images to the left show the two layers (dark green and pink) and the layer mask.

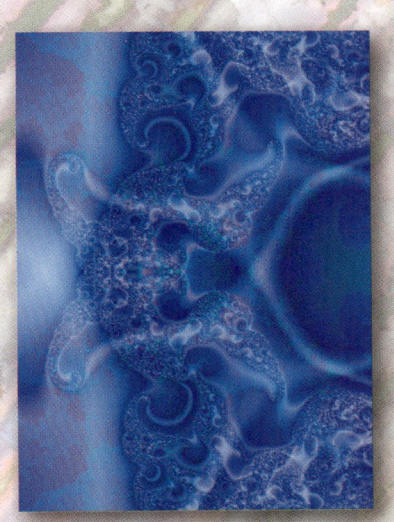

The Apply Image and Calculations commands can be used to create exciting images from files of the same size. The fractal image on the left and the nude in the center (drawn by California artist Rhoda Grossman) are combined via Difference mode in the Apply Image command to produce the image on the right.

COLOR STUDIO

The four small images above are all stops along the road to creating the large image to the right. When you work with the Apply Image command, you can preview the result before any image transfer occurs. You can also select any same-sized open image as a mask for the image. These features give you a tremendous amount of power and flexibility for "spontaneous" combinations with very little RAM overhead. It is much faster to view a preview of your composite than it is to drag and drop and add layer masks.

While this serendipitous technique is not suited to every assignment (since you do lose the flexibility that layers and layer masks provide), you can obtain outrageous effects that might not otherwise have occurred to you since it is so easy to make new combinations of images. Knowing how to use the Apply Image and Calculations commands expands your options as an artist—which, of course, is the intent of this book!

COLOR STUDIO

Filters, filters, filters! Everybody loves filters. Simply choose your favorite from the Filter menu, and the magic happens all by itself. Depending upon the image and the filter you use, the change can be dramatic or subtle. Some filters create artistic effects, others distort the image in unusual ways. A couple—the Unsharp Mask and Gaussian Blur filter—are so useful for such a variety of purposes that you'll find that you use them on nearly every image. The handsome Marmalade Binder models the bundled Photoshop filters on this page and the three pages which follow. Notice with what aplomb he wears each look.

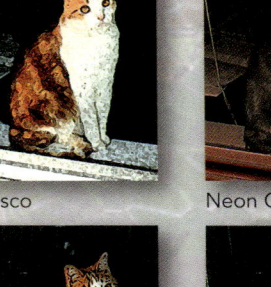

Colored Pencil   Cutout

Dry Brush    Film Grain    Fresco   Neon Glow   Paint Daubs

Palette Knife    Plastic Wrap    Poster Edges   Rough Pastels   Smudge Stick

Sponge    Underpainting   Watercolor   Blur   Blur More

Gaussian Blur    Motion Blur  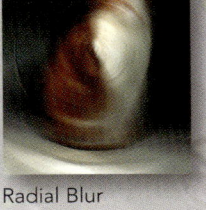   Radial Blur    Smart Blur    Accented Edges

COLOR STUDIO

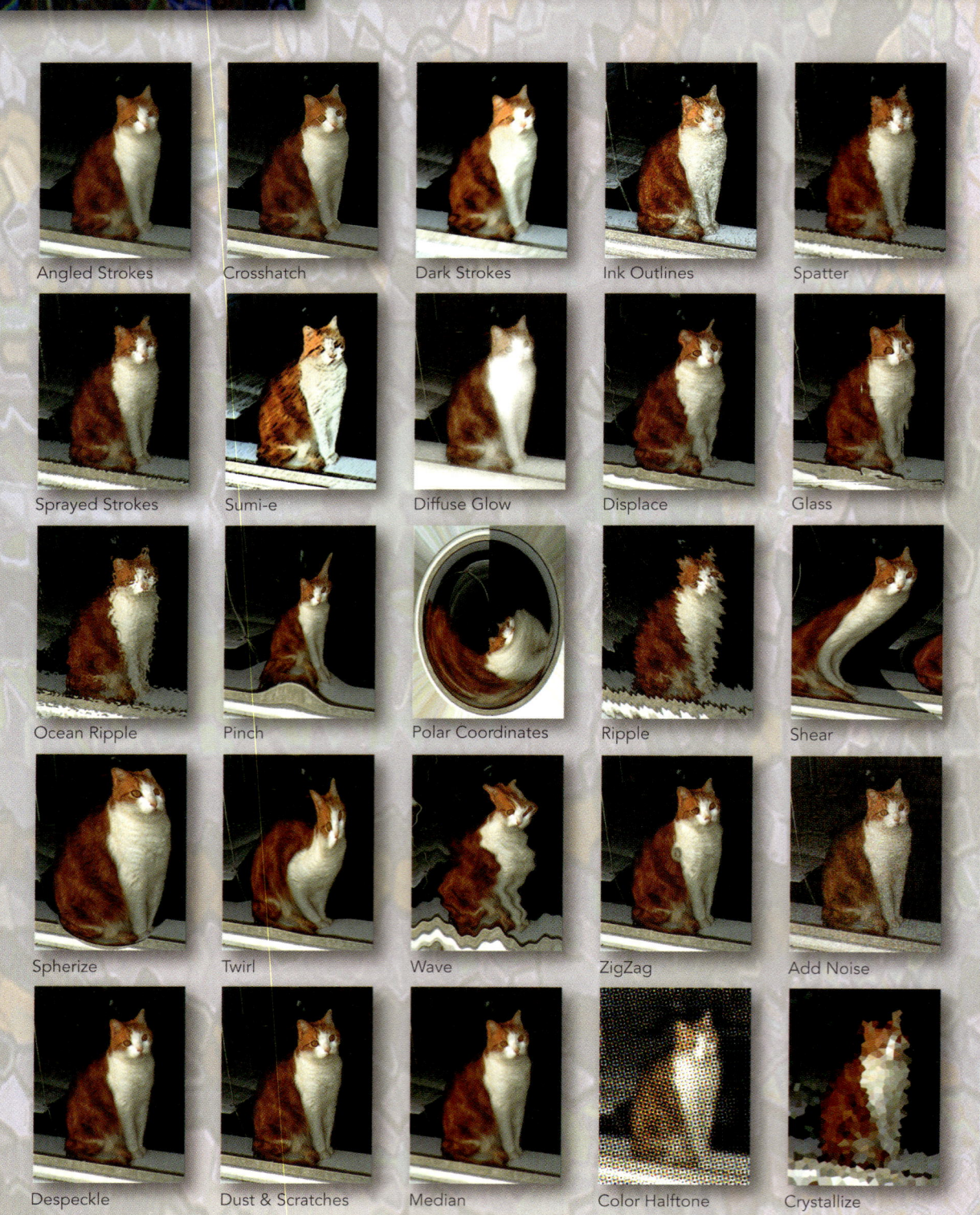

Angled Strokes	Crosshatch	Dark Strokes	Ink Outlines	Spatter
Sprayed Strokes	Sumi-e	Diffuse Glow	Displace	Glass
Ocean Ripple	Pinch	Polar Coordinates	Ripple	Shear
Spherize	Twirl	Wave	ZigZag	Add Noise
Despeckle	Dust & Scratches	Median	Color Halftone	Crystallize

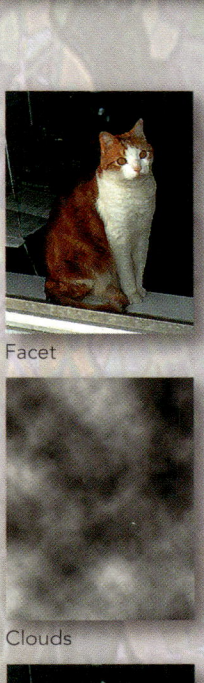

COLOR STUDIO

Facet	Fragment	Mezzotint	 Mosaic	 Pointillize
 Clouds	 Difference Clouds	 Lens Flare	 Lighting Effects	 Texture Fill
 Sharpen	 Sharpen Edges	 Sharpen More	 Unsharp Mask	 Bas Relief
 Chalk & Charcoal	 Charcoal	 Chrome	 Conté Crayon	 Graphic Pen
 Halftone Pattern	 Note Paper	 Photocopy	 Plaster	 Reticulation

COLOR STUDIO

Stamp	Torn Edges	Water Paper	Diffuse	Emboss
Extrude	Find Edges	Glowing Edges	Solarize	Tiles
Trace Contour	Wind	Craquelure	Grain	Mosaic Tiles
Patchwork	Stained Glass	Texturizer	De-Interlace	NTSC Colors
Custom	High Pass	Maximum	Minimum	Offset

COLOR STUDIO

Grayscale

Monotone

Duotone (heavy 2nd ink)

Duotone (balanced 2nd ink)

A grayscale image is shown here with three further stages of preparation as a duotone. The first (upper right) is a monotone showing the second ink's color. The second (lower left) is a duotone with both inks put down from identical curves. The third (lower right) is the adjusted duotone where the second ink is used to extend the tone range of the original without an obvious coloration. Notice the richness of detail when compared to the original.

COLOR STUDIO

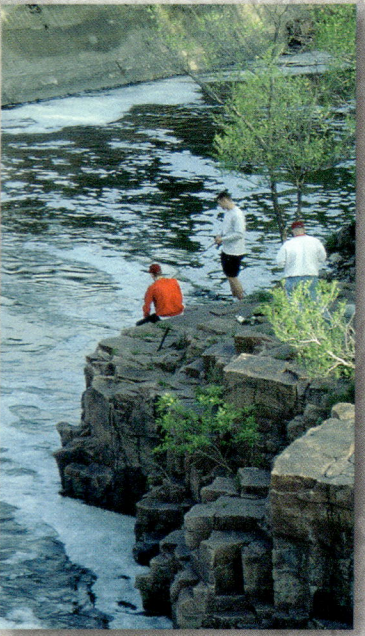

Color correction has never been easier than with Adjustment Layers. Layers can be stacked one on top of another. The changes for each layer are applied as a group when the document is flattened. The original image (top left) has had several layers applied: first Levels (top center), then Levels and Color Balance (top right), and finally Levels, Color Balance, and Hue/Saturation (bottom).

COLOR STUDIO

Here is a simple and effective trick that can be applied to an image that needs a little extra excitement. A high-contrast grayscale version of the image is converted to a bitmap (Halftone Screen option, with a coarse, linear spot function) and then used as an alpha channel. The alpha channel allows the two parts of the image—dark and light—to be manipulated separately, while the linear pattern adds visual interest.

COLOR STUDIO

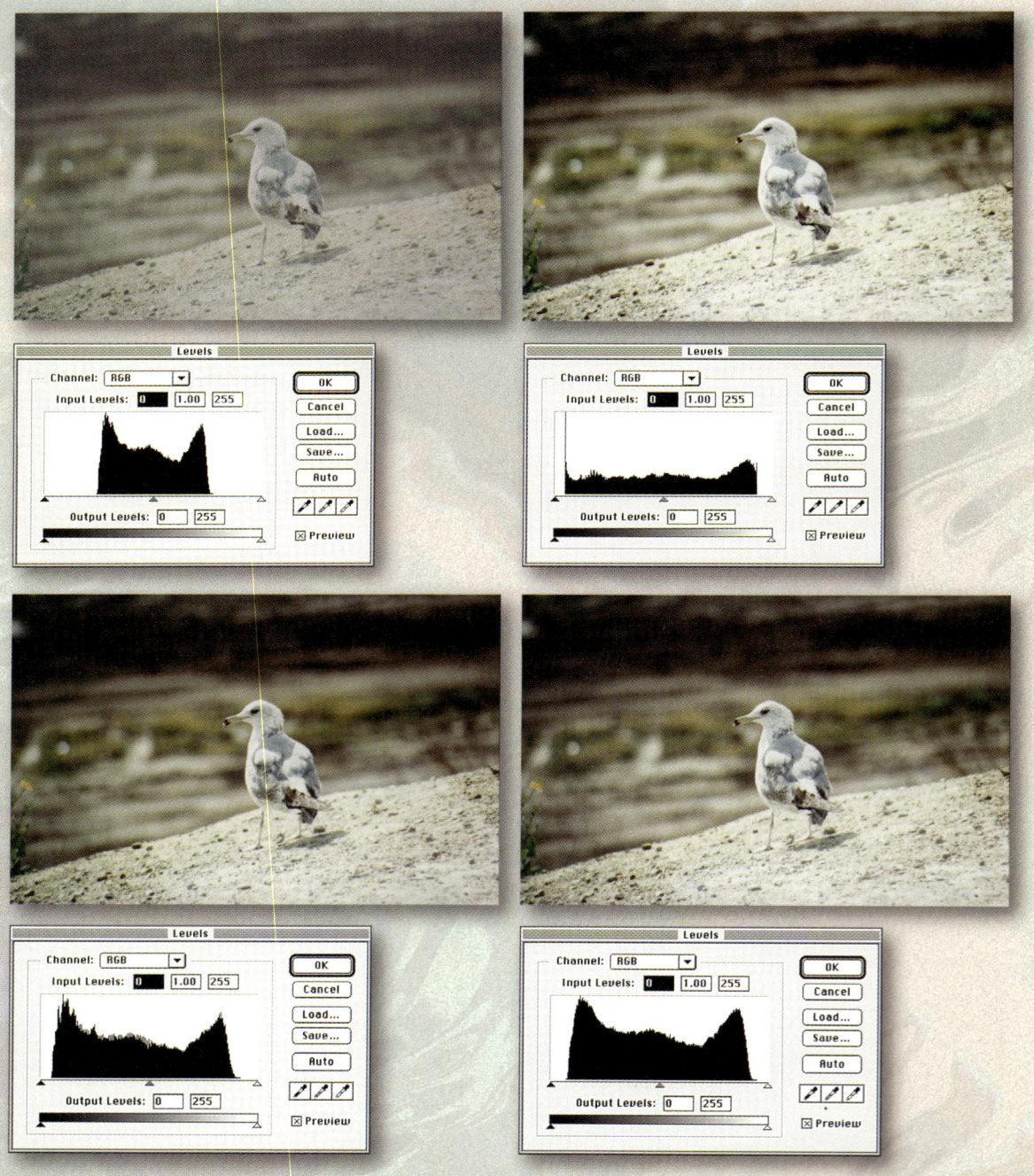

Adjustment layers allow you to make tonal corrections that can be edited. However, it helps to start with a good scan. The top left image shows a histogram that is lacking in highlights and shadows. Although it can be corrected (top right), there is image degradation and the histogram contains too much black. A properly scanned image (bottom left) produces a much better histogram when corrected (bottom right).

COLOR STUDIO

This overly dark image (top left) was photographed with the sun behind the main figure. It is corrected here using a variety of Adjustment layers (Levels and Hue/Saturation) that do not actually change the original image values until the document is flattened. You can experiment with the settings until you like the results that you obtain. You can also use grayscale values within the Adjustment layers to partially mask the effect of the layer upon the image.

COLOR STUDIO

Above: You can use Photoshop to create "impossible" images—like this plane that is flying through a sky filled with cloud-flowers. A layer mask is used to project the flowers onto the clouds.

Right: A simple squiggle can become a decorative snowflake by making copies of the layer and rotating the layers 60° apart, so that they create a circular form.

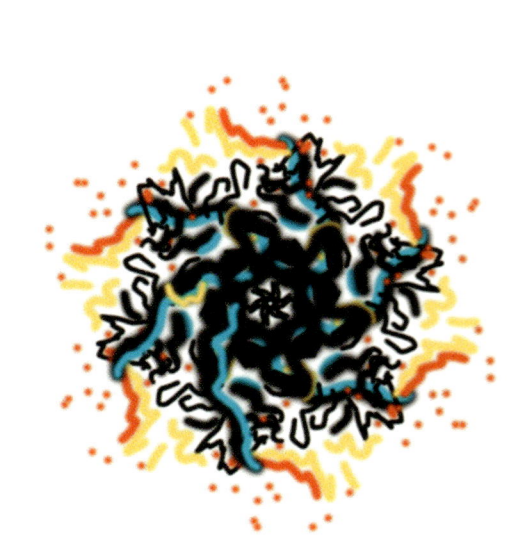

Above: You can use Photoshop to add excitement to an image by intensifying color where you want to draw the viewer's eye and darkening the image to de-emphasize the background. Here, we brightened the lost love bird in the feeder and blurred and darkened the woods.

Left: You can add a sepiatone to a grayscale image by using Adjustment layers. The original grayscale image was used as a mask in the Adjustment layer to control the amount of sepia in the highlights and shadows.

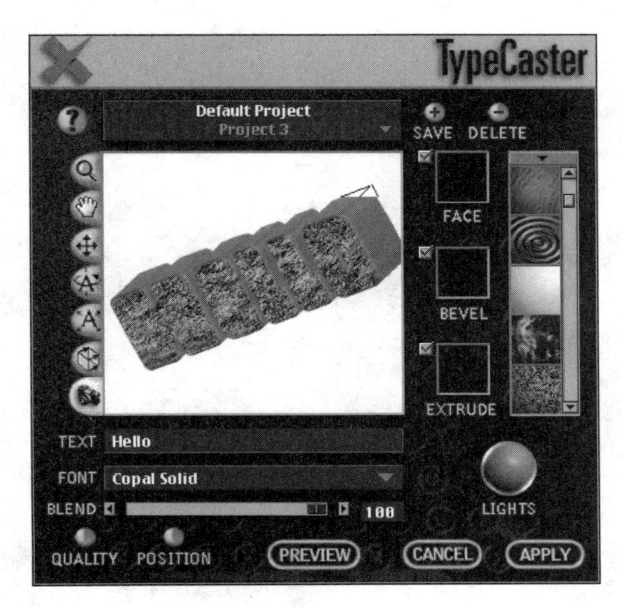

Figure 8.103 The TypeCaster interface.

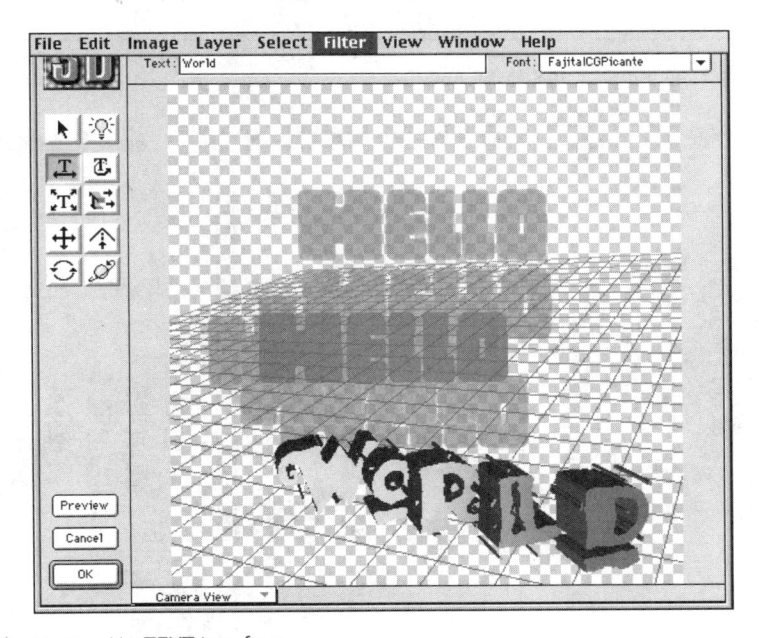

Figure 8.104 The Vertigo HotTEXT interface.

Shadow/Emboss/Bevel/Glow Filters

Layer Effects will probably make a bit of a dent in the very open market for filters that create drop shadows, bevels, glows, and embossing. However, many of the filters in this category still offer more control or more novel effects than Photoshop 5 can deliver with Layer Effects right

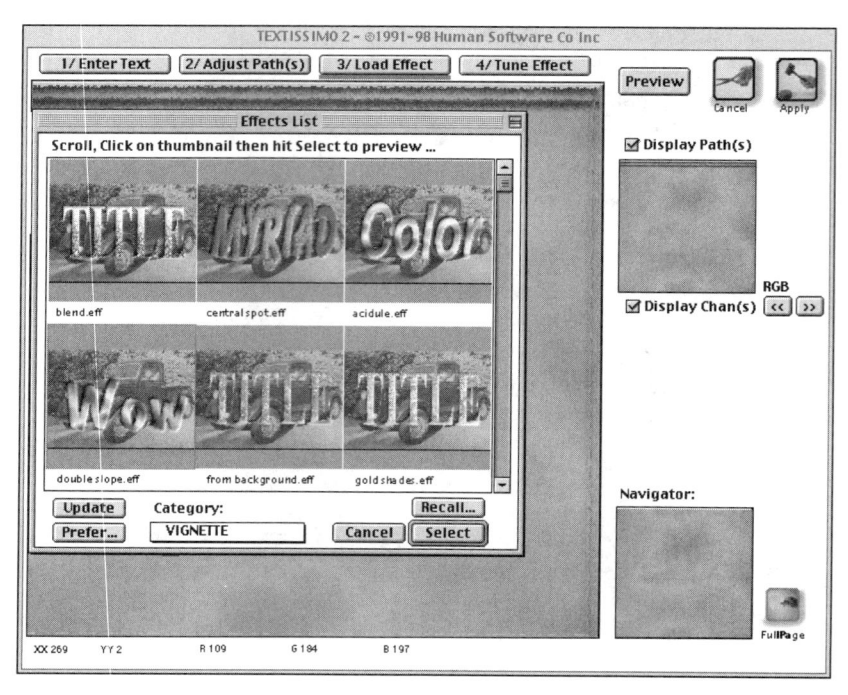

Figure 8.105 The Human Software Textissimo interface.

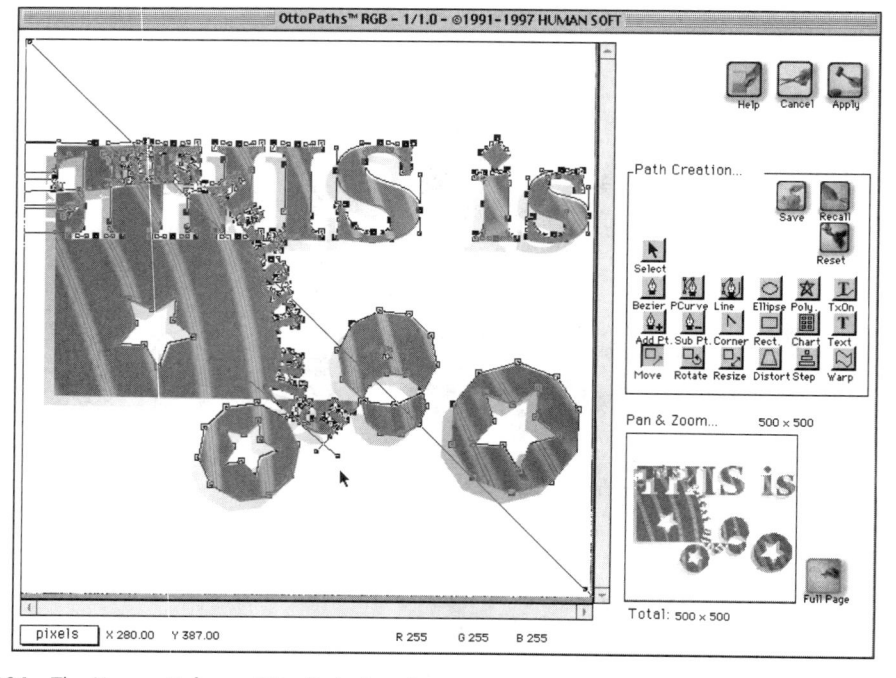

Figure 8.106 The Human Software Otto Paths interface.

now. Alien Skin was the first company to create a filter that could produce drop shadows. Their filter set was originally called The Black Box, but with version 3, Alien Skin renamed it Eye Candy. Eye Candy lets you create drop shadows, glows, a variety of embossing, bevels, and cast shadows. A cast shadow is the "normal" shadow that you see in the real world, and is usually a distorted version of the shadowed object, unlike a drop shadow, which simply repeats the object's form.

The Extensis PhotoTools set also contains a variety of filters for creating shadows, glows, embosses, and bevels. Version 2 contains a cast shadow feature. Figure 8.107 shows the PhotoGlow filter. In addition, Version 2 contains an excellent tool for creating buttons. The WildRiverSSK filter set (we can't tell you the company name—it has changed three times in the last year; when last seen, it was FortuneHill) takes another approach to the topic. This set contains some of the wildest effects since the original KPT filter set release. The MagicMask filter has 25 variants that each produce a different combination of glow (see Figure 8.108), emboss, and/or shadow. Each variant can be tuned. Some look metallic; some look as if they were hand-painted. You can get unique effects by using more than one variant on the same selection. This set also has a button-maker. Deko-Boko was first released as part of the shareware Sucking Fish collection. It has been expanded with myriad shading options and controls in the WildRiverSSK filter set.

Andromeda recently released Series V Shadows filter (see Figure 8.109). This is the ultimate shadow-creating filter. It's incredibly complex and allows you to generate cast shadows by simulating the lighting conditions in the real world. By reproducing the 3D environment, you can create extremely realistic shadows.

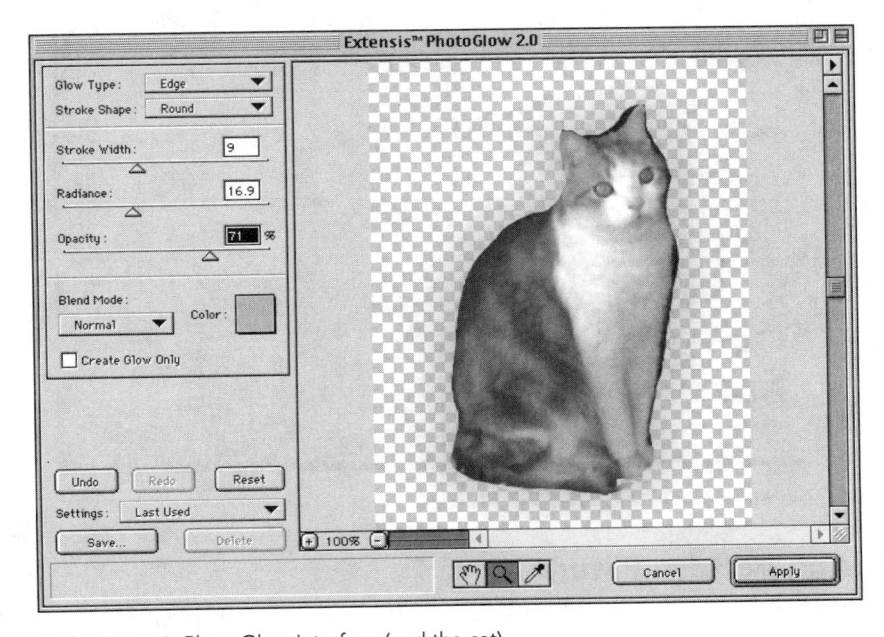

Figure 8.107 The Extensis PhotoGlow interface (and the cat).

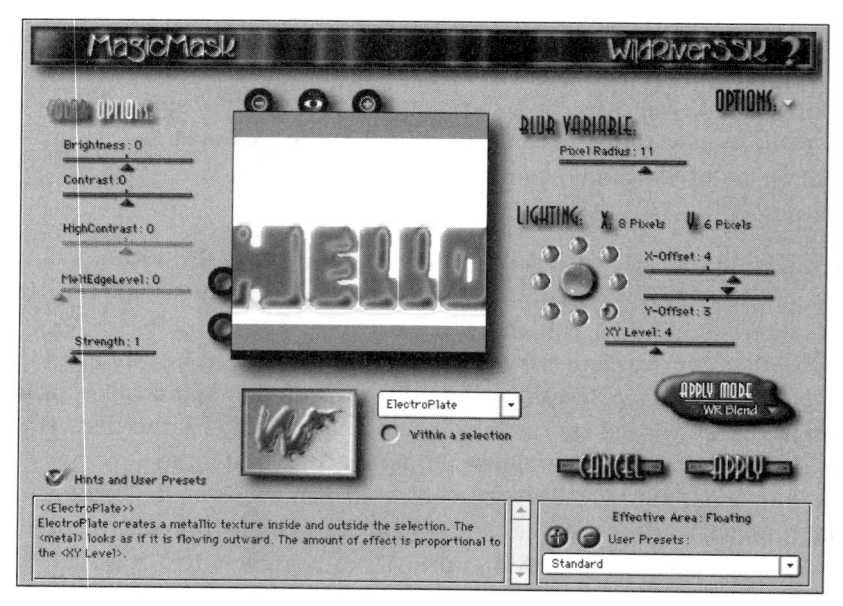

Figure 8.108 The WildRiverSSK interface.

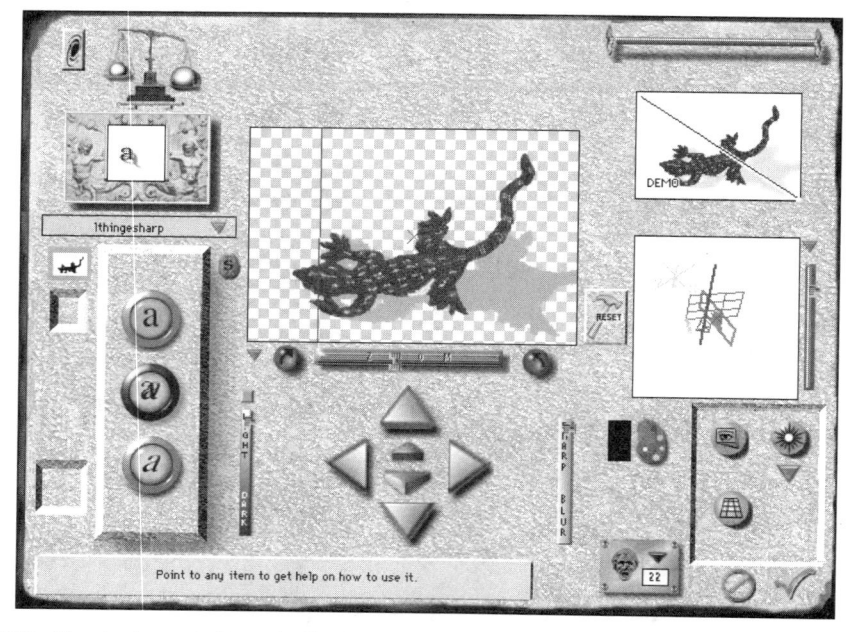

Figure 8.109 The Andromeda Series V Shadows interface.

Texture And Pattern Filters

Texture filters add surface interest to images, or create patterns or designs. They can simulate brush strokes or traditional media, or produce combinations never seen before.

Xaos Tools Paint Alchemy filter allows you to generate custom "painted" effects or use more than a hundred preset brushing styles. This is an incredibly powerful filter; if you've gone as far as Photoshop's native artistic filters can take you, then you'll want to try creating your own effects with this plug-in. You can change brush stroke color, angle, size, opacity, layering, and density, as well as use grayscale PICT files to define custom brush shapes. Five Blend modes determine how overlapping brush strokes are colored. Settings can be saved and reloaded (see Figure 8.110).

Xaos Tools also markets Terrazzo, a pattern-generating filter that can create a kaleidoscope from any portion of an image (see Figure 8.111). It can create any of the 17 plane repeat systems that

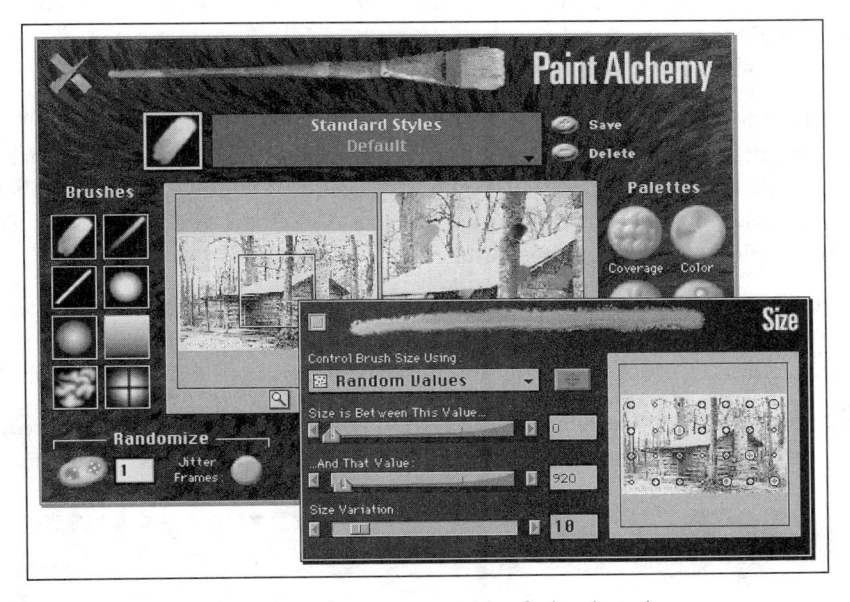

Figure 8.110 Paint Alchemy allows you to adjust every variable of a brush stroke.

Figure 8.111 Terrazzo is a fascinating filter that creates seamless patterns.

have been mathematically proven to be the basis of all tiling patterns. You can change the Blend mode, the opacity, and feather of each pattern and either apply it or save the tile as a file for future use. Both Paint Alchemy and Terrazzo are now available for either Mac or Windows.

KPT (Mac/Windows, MetaCreations) is the granddaddy of all Photoshop plug-in sets. (See Figure 8.112.) This group of filters is famous for its unorthodox interface; what with figuring out the interface and exploring the options, you'll spend hours (maybe weeks or even months) playing with all the possibilities. Version 3 has two texture-generating filters. It includes both the Texture Explorer and the Interform filter. The Texture Explorer allows you to search for a pattern and control the Gradient used in it (you can also make your own gradients), the size, location, and Blend mode, and the scale of the texture. Interform allows you to marry textures together. It can even create a QuickTime movie of the process.

Andromeda Series IV Techtures filter has an extremely beautiful interface (see Figure 8.113). You can manipulate a number of starting images and textures to extract either their color range, density, or bump and apply it to your own selection. You have a huge number of choices as to how to customize the starting points. You can also create effects that look like cut glass and crystal, explosions, fog, or other natural phenomena.

Auto/FX markets an enormous collection named The Ultimate Texture Collection. This set of more than 1,000 textures can be scaled, colored, rotated, and fussed into images and selections. Photo/Graphic Patterns is a series of patterns that can be similarly manipulated.

CGSD markets a high-end seamless pattern creation filter (for Windows only) that can take photographic content and extract seamless tiles. This unique product was created for the virtual

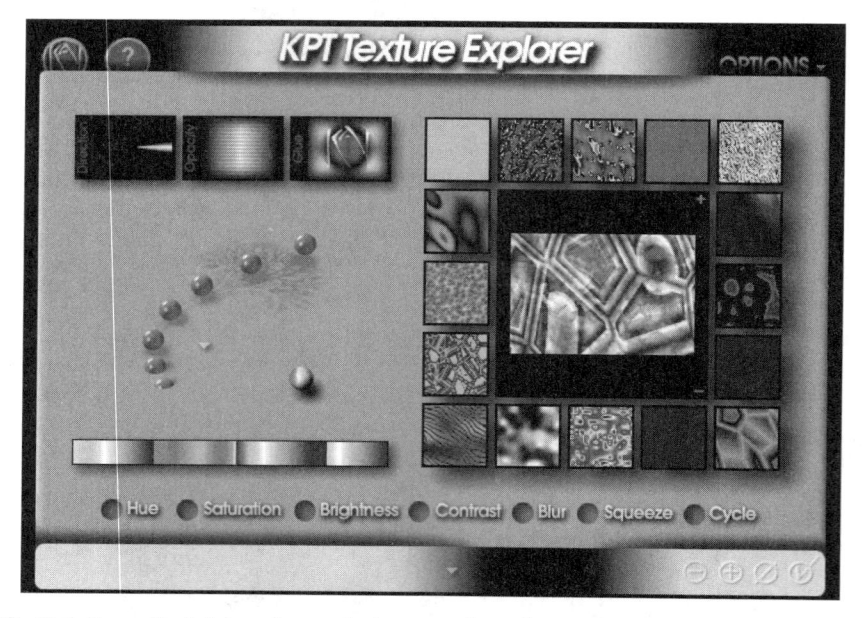

Figure 8.112 Kai's Power Tools is best known for its unusual interface; here, the KPT Texture Explorer allows you to generate a texture.

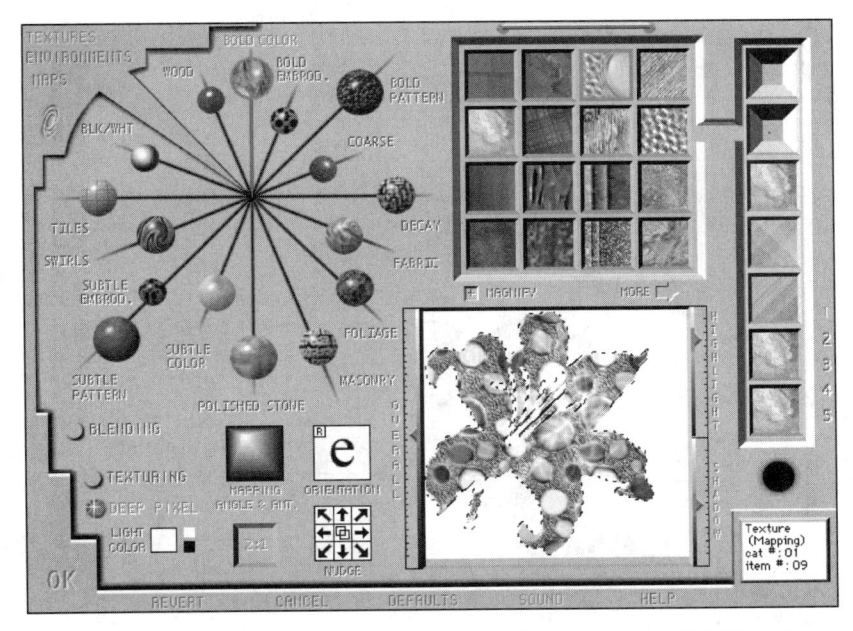

Figure 8.113 The interface to Andromeda Series IV Techtures is hauntingly beautiful. What does not show in this figure is the tinkling sound that the filter makes when it applies a texture.

reality market. You can correct for perspective, dehaze or defog the tile-to-be, and color correct as needed. The filter analyzes the image and decides how to change it into a seamless pattern. In addition, CGSD also markets a large collection of seamless tiles of grass, trees, leaves, materials, and so on generated from photographs.

3D Filters

Several filters allow Photoshop to create or manipulate 3D objects. Vertigo Dizzy (see Figure 8.114) allows you to place, position, size, light, and rotate 3D models. You cannot color them and you cannot create them. However, if the model exists, you can bring it into Photoshop and render it into your image. The filter gives you several styles of render, including a cartoon style that makes the model look hand-drawn.

Andromeda Series II is a 3D mapping filter. It allows you to map your image onto a plane, sphere, cone, cylinder, or box. HoloDozo, by MMM, is a similar filter, but includes many more primitives (not all of which are useful) and many fewer controls. However, it allows you to cut the image from the background, which you can't do with the Andromeda filter.

Genesis$_{vfx}$ is perhaps a stretch to include in the 3D category. It doesn't work with 3D wireframe geometry in the same sense that it's used in 3D Dizzy, but this filter contains a 3D rendering engine that produces glows, lens flares, sparkles, heat distortions, gas clouds, explosions, and 3D particle clouds. The filter also works inside 3D Studio Max, where it can generate animations. This is another super-complex filter that produces amazing results.

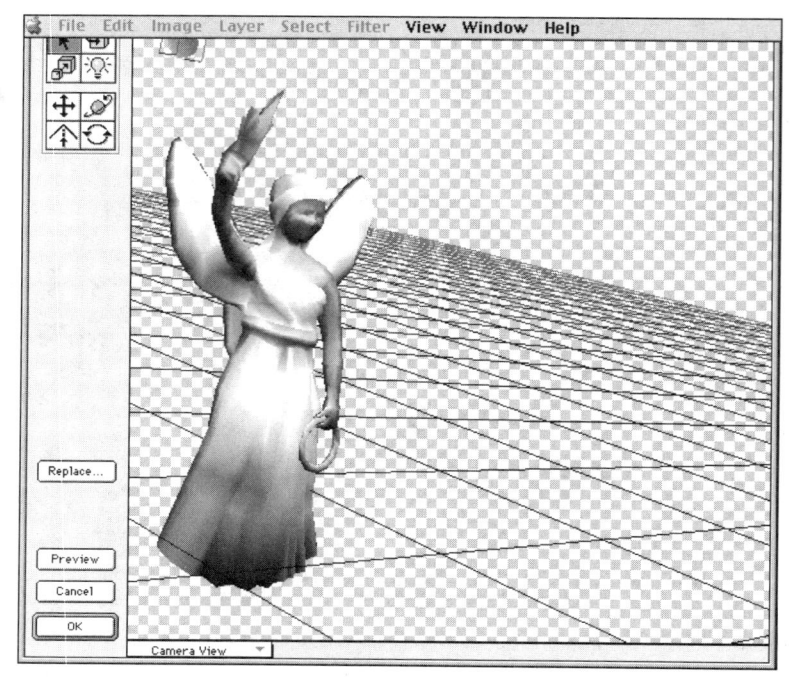

Figure 8.114 The 3D Dizzy interface.

The Knoll brothers, John and Thomas (who are famous as the creators of Photoshop), market Cybermesh. This plug-in allows you to use grayscale density information from an image as the basis for generating a 3D model. You are modeling in reverse—taking an image and building wireframe geometry based on the values in the image. White areas are raised and black areas are indented. You can then export this model to a 3D program for further manipulation and for rendering.

Color Manipulation

A number of third-party filters play games with the color content of the image. In some cases, the filters help prepare an image for printing; in other cases, they help prepare the image for wild effects.

CSI PhotoOptics, from Cytopia, is a set of eight color manipulation filters based on traditional photographic filters (see Figure 8.115). They include GradTone, HueSlider, Levels, Monochrome, Negative, Noise, PhotoFilter, and PseudoColor. Some of the highlights:

- *Levels*—This is an expanded version of Photoshop's Levels command with built-in presets to correct common problems in scanned images.
- *Negative*—Converts scanned negatives to positives more accurately and with more control over highlight, shadow, and exposure than Photoshop's Invert command; the filter automatically deals with the orange color cast of color negative film.

- *PhotoFilter*—Simulates the effects of photographic gel filters, which apply color casts and affect the image's exposure; presets include settings that mimic standard color correction filters used with cameras.
- *PseudoColor*—Adds the group of colors that represent different temperatures, elevations, or other conditions in scientific images.

Andromeda Series I is a set of photographic filters that allow you to mimic tricks played by traditional cameras using special lenses. You can create rainbows, points of light (fragmented sparkles), prism effects, repeated images in a straight or circular pattern, reflections, and more. Figure 8.116 shows a variety of Series I filters in the image and a Lily with the Andromeda Techtures filter applied.

Chromassage, by Second Glance Software, allows you to toss out the color table in an image and create a new one. It extracts 256 colors from the image and you can either use them in a rearranged fashion, or bring in a totally new set of 256 colors to which it remaps the original. You can change the image from mild to wild in a few keystrokes, or you can inject a new area of color into your image.

Chromatica, the first filter from Chroma Graphics, also plays with the colors in your image. You can use it for production purposes—the model's green sweater needs to be red—or you can apply one of the several hundred preset color ranges (or make your own from any other photo). This filter is not entirely successful, but it has odd moments of brilliance. It does a lovely job recoloring fractals.

WildRiverSSK also has an entrant in this category. Chameleon allows you to designate a color range to replace and a color range with which to replace it.

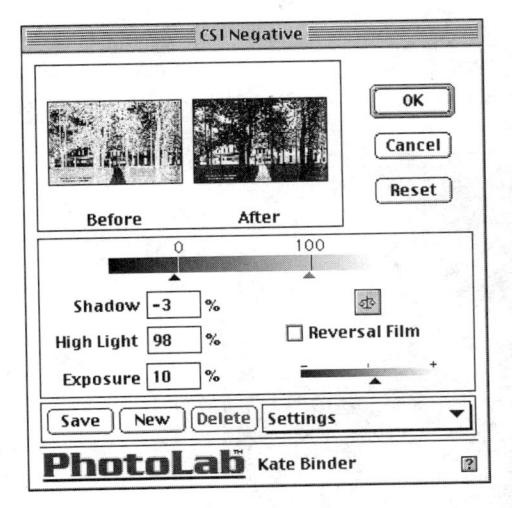

Figure 8.115 The PhotoOptics filters bring specialty darkroom and photo filter effects to Photoshop.

Figure 8.116 A variety of Series I filters in the image and a Lily with the Andromeda Techtures filter applied.

KPT Convolver takes the pain out of creating Custom kernels (as in the Custom filter). Most of the changes you can perform using Convolver involve color changes or changes in sharpness, blur, or texture. Because you can so easily use Convolver to help color correct (or color destroy) images, we put it in this category.

Masking Filters

If you've ever tried to put a new background on an image of a person whose hair is blowing in the wind, you understand the frustration of many Photoshop users. It is the "I-can-see-it-why-can't-Photoshop-find-the-edge-to-select-it" syndrome, and it has sapped the strength of many a good graphic artist. Although the new Magnetic Lasso and the Magnetic Pen tools are designed to help make selections more easily, they are pretty much useless on hair. The third-party filters designed to create masks do a better—though not perfect—job on this extremely difficult area. They do a much better job on simpler selections.

MaskPro, by Extensis, builds masks by allowing you to select a series of "drop" and "keep" colors (see Figure 8.117). You then take the masking brush, and, as you drag it around the edge of the area that you want to mask, it removes the drop colors and leaves the keep colors. The principle is simple and elegant. The trouble is finding the colors in the first place! All too often, the colors at the edge of an object are much too similar to the colors that you want to drop. However, you can define a number of different sets so that you can drop the sandy color on the right side of the object, but keep the same sandy color on the left side. Because you are still smarter than any filter, you can also use the regular brush when the program's "intelligence" falls short. You save your selection to a channel or layer mask or as a clipping path that has been optimized to print without PostScript errors (it's a series of tiny straight lines that have no Bézier controls to jam the RIP).

Chroma Graphics MagicMask 2 also includes clipping paths. This filter works as a Selection plug-in (in other words, it lives on the Select menu). It takes a totally different approach to

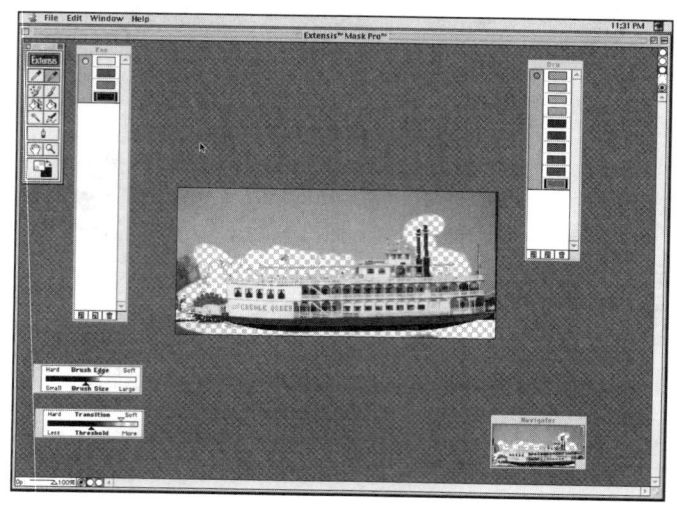

Figure 8.117 The MaskPro filter allows you to select keep and drop colors.

masking an image than the Extensis filter. You simply click somewhere in the image using the MagicMask-in or the MagicMask-out brush (see Figure 8.118). All of the area of similar contiguous color is removed. You can edit the parameters for determining just how "similar" similar needs to be. As you change your mind, the filter recalculates what is masked. It's easier to make a quick-and-dirty selection with MagicMask, but the edges are all aliased and jagged. Although you can control the softness of your edge in MaskPro by altering the brush settings, you need another Chroma Graphics filter, EdgeWizard, to gain control of the selection edges in MagicMask. EdgeWizard is a separate product, but, once installed, it works seamlessly with MagicMask so you don't need to cope with more than one filter interface.

Blue-Screen Filters

Because we just discussed masking, now is a good time to mention blue-screen filters. Blue screening is a process similar to the familiar chroma keying that you see on the nightly news (you know, where the weather person stands in front of a totally blank blue screen, but you see the weather chart projected on your TV as if it were behind him).

Blue-screen photography allows the image to be easily removed from its background. If you need to shoot a model standing in a Hawaiian garden but you cannot afford her airfare, you can place the model in front of a special blue or green fabric-covered or painted screen and take the photo anyway. When you get the garden shot from Hawaii, you can use one of the blue-screen filters to get rid of the blue background but keep the model—and her blowing hair and her shadow—and the smoke from her cigarette (not politically correct)—in the new image.

Ultimatte PhotoFusion is the blue-screen filter available for the Mac. It is a high-end product with a price tag to match. Ultimatte also has a version that works within Adobe After Effects to composite blue-screen video. Cinematte, from Digital Dominion, is a Windows-only blue-screen filter. It does basically the same thing, but with a more reasonable price tag.

If you feel that blue-screen photography is too much trouble, but want to composite smaller things, Katrin Eismann (noted lecturer, teacher, and former Director of Education at the Center

Figure 8.118 The MagicMask filter lets you click with a mask-in or mask-out brush to create the mask.

for Creative Imaging in Camden, Maine) developed the following trick. Cover a board with blue-screen fabric and attach it to the top of your scanner (or make a frame for it so that it stays on your scanner). Place the object that you want to scan on the scanner so that it is under the blue-screen board. Scan as usual. The light from the scanner will cast natural shadows. You can use one of the blue-screen filters (or native Photoshop) to remove the blue from the image.

Border Filters

Square images are boring. If presenting your artwork as a solid rectangle seems too tame, several filters can help perk them up. You could, of course, apply Photoshop's native filters to the edges of your images (feather a large selection at the perimeter of an image and apply the Wave filter, for example). However, there are more borders and edges in the world than one can create on the computer.

Enter Auto/FX. They have made a specialty out of creating novel, inventive, and beautiful edges for images. They have three sets of edges that are packaged as Photoshop plug-ins (Photo/Graphic Edges Traditional, Geometric, and Artistic) and a variety of Page Frames. Their older offerings, plain TIF files, are still for sale when you can find them. These sets contain an almost inexhaustible variety of edges for you to apply. You can pick inner edges, outer edges, resize the edges, and recolor them. We often prefer to work with the edges as if they were still in TIFF file format. Take a layer filled with black and increase the canvas size of the document to leave a lot of room around the edges. This process makes the edges of the layer transparent. Apply the edge effect you prefer. Now you can either drag the edge to the "real" image and use it as the bottom layer of a clipping group, or you can save the edge to a channel and use it as a selection.

Extensis is a new player in the border and edge filter category. This company released two sets of borders as Extensis PhotoFrame. The filter that creates the frame is faster than the Auto/FX filter, and has more options. You can apply up to three different frames at one time. The best part about it is that it will also let you apply the Auto/FX edge files, which are more varied and interesting. This gives you the best of both worlds. You can have the powerful filter capability of Extensis and use it to apply all of the Auto/FX frames too (which are worth purchasing for their exciting content). You can also create your own JPEG files with edge effects and apply them through the PhotoFrame filter. Figure 8.119 shows the PhotoFrame interface using Auto/FX Volume III Artistic Edges.

Web Filters

The Web filters category divides itself into a few pieces. Filters can be used to prepare Web graphics by changing RGB images to Indexed Color GIF or full-color JPEG files. Another class of filters prepares Web animations, and a third category makes buttons and banners and also embeds HTML image tags. Let's take a brief look at what's available.

Digital Frontiers offers Web Focus, which consists of two products—HVS ColorGIF to prepare and reduce GIF images, and HVS JPEG to help make the trade-off between quality and size for JPEG images. Boxtop Software's PhotoGIF and ProJPEG plug-ins do much the same thing. Boxtop's

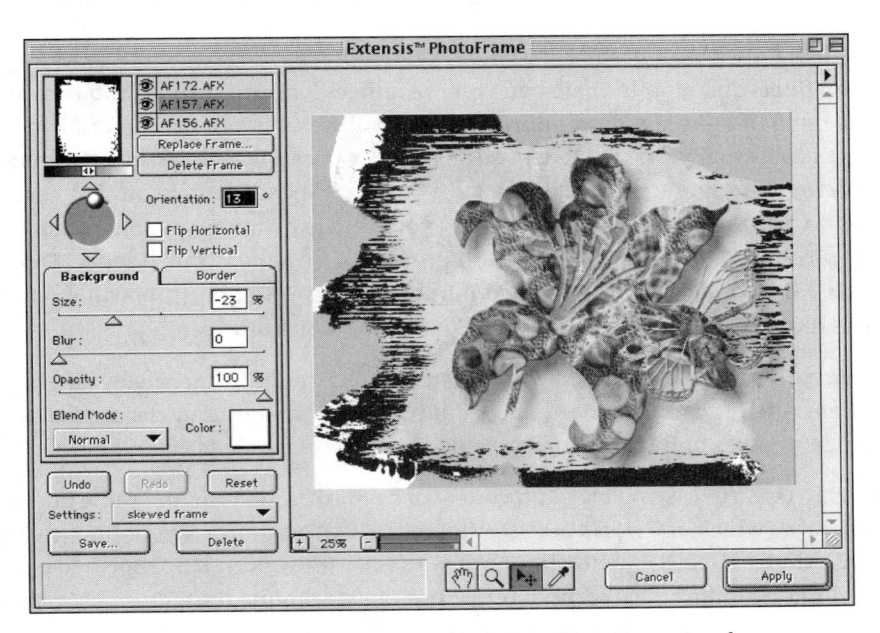

Figure 8.119 Auto/FX Volume III Artistic Edges are used within the PhotoFrame interface.

ColorSafe lets you change an image into colors that are taken from the 216 "safe" colors, but are dithered hybrids that will not change in a Web browser. With Boxtop's ImageVice, you can select the correct degree of image compression.

Ulead markets WebRazor, an integrated collection of several utilities for Windows only: Web Plug-ins for Photoshop (Seamless tiles, Drop Shadows, Buttons, Frame & Shadow, and Image Map tags), GifAnimator, SmartSaver (standalone image compression), and PhotoExplorer (makes thumbnails of a folder).

A number of GIF and Web animation programs are available. Boxtop markets GIFmation. Digital Frontiers offers HVS Animator, which is free, and an advanced version, HVS Animator Pro, which is not. Auto/FX has a plug-in named Universal Animator, which drops into a number of programs in addition to Photoshop. They also market WebVise Totality, a series of utilities to help prepare Web graphics. Second Glance Software markets PhotoCell, another GIF animation program.

Extensis has recently released a new program called PhotoAnimator. Unlike their other programs, this one is a standalone product. Adobe has also released a new standalone program for the Web. ImageReady uses much of the familiar Photoshop interface to allow you to create RGB graphics in layers. You can then animate these layers or you can convert your images to Indexed Color. ImageReady lets you preview the conversion and compare the same file converted into different numbers of colors. You can also see projected download times for each file.

Two more standalone programs we need to mention are Equilibrium deBabelizer (which has outstanding indexed color conversion, batching, and animation capabilities), and Macromedia Flash 3 (which is both a format and a program and lets you use vector graphics to create small images that download in a flash).

Production Filters

Production filters and plug-ins help you prepare images for print. An enormous variety of these filters are available—many more than we can possibly cover. One group of filters in this category helps you when you scan. Extensis Intellihance does a decent job of analyzing an image and correcting it for tone. ImageExpress ScanPrepPro is the ultimate scanning correction tool. It applies a variety of rules and procedures to your image by taking over Photoshop and using Photoshop commands automatically to improve and enhance your images. One of its best features is its capability to turn detailed bitmap images into grayscale while retaining their sharpness and clarity. It also does an excellent job of moiré descreening.

If you want to add, rather than remove, screens to your image, Andromeda Series III Screens is an excellent filter. It can generate traditional mezzotint screens and custom halftones, along with a huge number of fully customizable decorative screening effects.

Vivid Details TestStrip lets you try out a variety of color corrections on the same image and print a test strip to see which one works best (see Figure 8.120). You can view your image with the color corrections applied to pieces of the image or with the same image strip repeated in each variation. The filter is similar in concept to the Variations command, but it's much more powerful.

The company "a lowly apprentice production" recently released PlateMaker 2, which helps you prepare spot color separations. (A more comprehensive but similar filter, PhotoSpotCt, is available from Second Glance Software.) This programs lets you separate continuous tone spot colors. Second Glance Software also markets LaserSeps Pro, a stochastic printing plug-in, and Scantastic, a scanner driver for Epson, HP, and Apple scanners on the Mac.

Pantone has released HexWrench, a plug-in that allows you to produce color seps for Pantone's six-ink hi-fidelity color process. One of the most interesting filters we've seen recently is from Intense Software. PowerTone creates two-color continuous tone images that look almost full-color. We discuss this plug-in in more detail in Chapter 9.

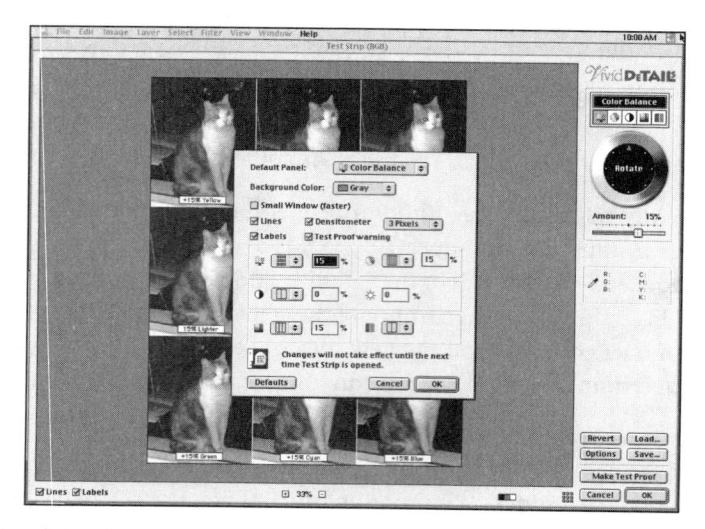

Figure 8.120 The Vivid Details TestStrip interface—a supercharged Variations command.

Wild Effect And NOC (Not Otherwise Classified) Filters

Some quirky and interesting filters don't fall into any of the other categories. These include one-trick ponies such as SISNIKK, Velociraptor, and Human Software Squizz. SISNIKK from MMM creates *stereograms* (the flat images that look 3D if you know how to "see" them) in color (see Figure 8.121). Velociraptor from Andromeda creates motion trails (see Figure 8.122). A distortion filter, Human Software Squizz lets you pull on your image as if it were made of rubber. In this class of rubber also comes FLO, the entry-level distortion filter from Valis. Valis sells a line of FLO products that range up to MovieFLO, which lets you distort full-motion video and can make the Statue of Liberty bend at the waist and wave.

Favorite Filter Tricks

To really explore the possibilities of filters, it's important not to restrict yourself to simply running one filter at a time on the entire image. You can combine multiple filters to increase the possible effects by an order of magnitude, for one thing, and you don't have to stick to filtering the composite channel of an image. Images with multiple layers can be filtered separately on each layer, each channel, and on layer masks. You'll also get different effects by applying a filter with high settings and applying it multiple times. For example, run Unsharp Mask twice at a low setting rather than once at a setting twice as high for a smoother sharpening effect with fewer artifacts.

Figure 8.121 If you know how to see it, a flower appears in the center of this stereogram created using the SISNIKK filter from MMM.

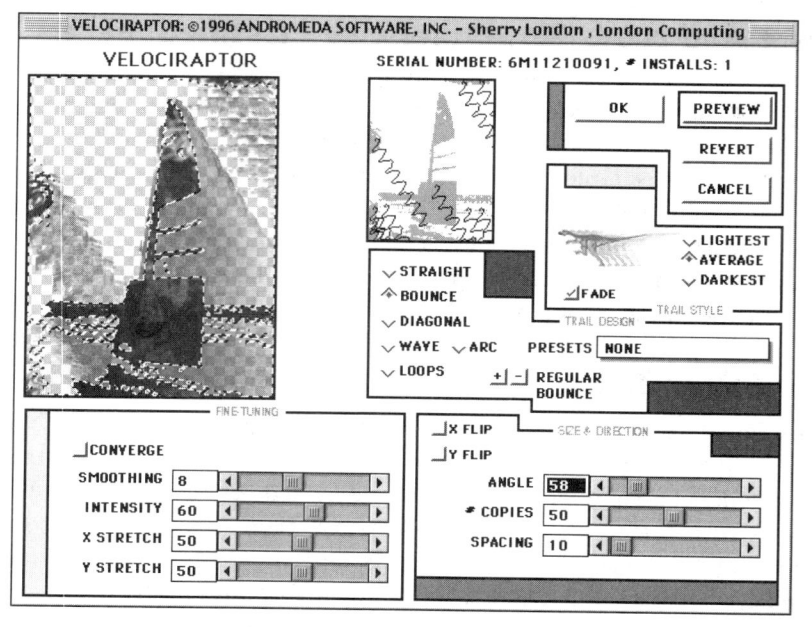

Figure 8.122 Andromeda Velociraptor allows you to create motion trails.

Combining Filters

Filters need not stand alone—virtually every cool Photoshop effect you see and admire on the Web, in magazines, or elsewhere is the result of multiple filters, along with a variable degree of tweaking. You can achieve infinite variety in filter effects by combining them in various ways.

- First, many organic texture-generating filters require data to chew on before they can produce their results. In this scenario, filters such as Add Noise and Clouds provide the base for others—such as Chrome, Crystallize, and Bas Relief—to build on. Try experimenting with these combinations and others. Try using the Find Edges filter on Clouds, Difference Clouds, Crystallize, Craquelure, or Mosaic. Try the Posterize command on Clouds.
- Each filter exaggerates some characteristic of an image; after you've applied one filter, the next will have a different effect because the image's characteristics have changed. Emboss, for example, will have a completely different effect on an image to which Find Edges has been applied than it would on the original image.
- You can also combine filters by duplicating an image on two or more layers, and applying a different filter to each. Use lower layer-opacity settings and Blend modes such as Hard Light and Color to apply the filtered images to each other in unexpected ways.

Filtering Channels

Ordinarily, a filter operates on the composite channel—a combination of all three or four color channels—moving and adjusting pixels without regard to the color values in the separate channels (one exception is Color Halftone). But that doesn't mean you have to be restricted to working that way—any filter can be applied on a color or alpha channel as well. Some filters can be applied to two or three color channels at once, whereas others work only with the composite channel or a single color channel active.

Working in an individual color channel applies the results of the filter only to that color, which means that the results show up in the composite channel in the color of the channel to which the filter is applied. That's one way to create subtle effects that add a bit of color without overwhelming an image. Here are a few ways you might use this technique:

- Add a colored fog that doesn't obscure the image by duplicating one of the color channels and running the Chrome filter on the duplicate. Experiment with each color channel before making your decision, and don't perform this operation on the original color channels.
- Examine the color channels and duplicate the one with the most contrast. Add noise (not too much) to the duplicate, then use it as a Texture Channel for the Lighting Effects filter to get a rather sculptural effect (see Figure 8.123).
- Convert a grayscale image to RGB mode and use Texturizer (or any filter, really) on one or more of the color channels. The effects of the filter will show up only in the color of the affected channel.

Filtering Alpha Channels

Alpha channels are any channels that don't contain the color values for the pixels in the image. They're used as selection masks and as bump maps that define the high and low points in a simulated 3D texture. When you're working with filters, you can use a channel to create a selection, then apply the filter to that selection to specify which areas of the image should be filtered, which shouldn't be, and which should be partially filtered. The most fun you can have with channels, though, is to create grayscale textures in them and apply those textures with the Lighting Effects filter.

- Create an instant stone texture by using Add Noise in an alpha channel, then using Lighting Effects with the Omni light type to apply it to an image without affecting the image's colors (see Figure 8.124).
- Use an alpha channel to give brush strokes a texture—such as crayon or chalk—by creating the texture in a new channel, painting on a transparent layer, then applying the Lighting Effects filter with a fairly low light intensity setting and the channel as the Texture Channel. Because the rest of the layer is transparent, the texture will be applied only to the brush strokes on it.

Filtering In A Layer Mask

Layer masks mask portions of a layer without deleting them and, like channels, layer masks are grayscale. With that in mind, you can create a mask that hides and reveals parts of a layer based on a pattern or other design created in seconds by a filter.

- Create an oval layer mask and apply Gaussian Blur to feather its edges and create a vignette in the image.

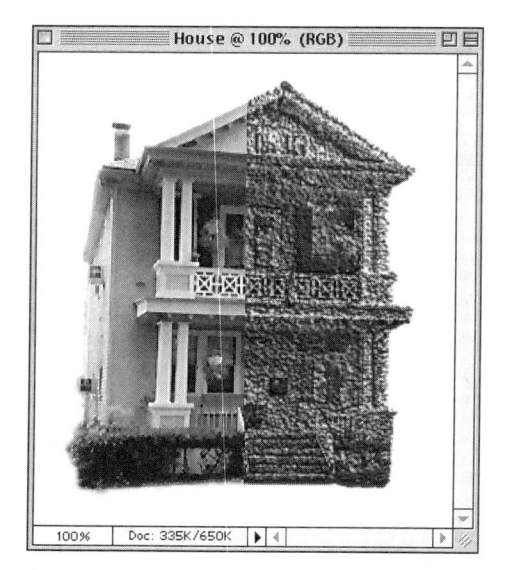

Figure 8.123 Lighting Effects combined with the Add Noise filter on a duplicate of one of the color channels produces the right side of this image.

Figure 8.124 A plain stone texture has been applied to the right side of this image.

- To apply natural-looking edge effects to an image, create a layer mask with a white area defining the part of the image you want to show, then apply Diffuse or Torn Edges to roughen the edges of the image (see Figure 8.125).
- Add noise to a layer mask, then place a white layer just below the target layer (or make sure the Background layer is white) to make it "snow" in the image.

Using The Displace Filter

The Displace filter can do amazing things. You don't have to use it only with the images in the Displacement Maps folder. To get an idea of how it works, create an image the same size as the image to be filtered. Fill it with black and white stripes. Use that as your displacement map. That gives you maximum displacement. Try it with a different grayscale image or with a copy of itself. A self-induced displacement map is an excellent way to create text that looks like it was filtered through water or glass. Use a displacement map under water drops. You can even create a displacement map that marbles an image. Your possibilities are endless.

Reducing A Moiré Pattern

Here's a technique for reducing the moiré patterns resulting from scanning printed materials that already have halftone dots:

1. Scan the image at twice the recommended resolution. For print production, you will probably want a final resolution of 266 dpi, so scan the image at 532 dpi. Web images generally have a resolution of 72 dpi, so use a scanning resolution of 144 dpi.

Figure 8.125 Diffusing the edges of the layer mask lends an organic effect to the edges of this image.

2. Open the image in Photoshop. If the moiré pattern is concentrated in one area of the image, select that part of the image, then choose Select|Feather and enter a small feathering radius—perhaps 30 pixels for a 532 dpi image and 12 pixels for a 144 dpi image.

> **TIP**
> Watch out for regular patterns, such as speaker grilles and roof shingles—these can cause moiré patterns, even when you are not scanning previously printed materials. Try scanning at different angles to reduce moiré as much as possible.

3. Choose Filter|Blur|Gaussian Blur. Make sure the Preview box is checked, then adjust the Radius slider so that the moiré pattern is less apparent. Depending on the intensity of the moiré, you may not be able to completely eliminate it without also eliminating all detail in the image.
4. Choose Image|Image Size and resample the image to your desired resolution.
5. Choose Filter|Sharpen|Unsharp Mask. Make sure the Preview box is checked, then adjust the Amount, Radius, and Threshold sliders to restore the sharpness of the image.

Creating Your Own Filters

If you're feeling *really* creative, you have two ways to create your own filter effects—both of them included with Photoshop. The Custom Filter sets up a grid of pixels and allows you to hack away at their brightness levels simply by entering numbers in its dialog box, while the Filter Factory lets you create true plug-in filters that can be used and distributed on their own.

Custom Filter

The Custom Filter lets you take a crack at the math behind Photoshop filters and create your own effects by plugging in different numbers. The center box in the grid represents an individual pixel, and the number you enter there (from -999 to 999) will be multiplied by the brightness value of that pixel to arrive at a new brightness value. At the same time, you can act on the eight pixels adjacent to the main pixel, and the pixels adjacent to them, by entering values in their corresponding boxes. The intensity of the effect is controlled by the Scale field, where you enter a value to divide the results of these calculations by, and the Offset field, where you enter a value that's added to each result.

It sounds pretty complicated, but the only way to learn the Custom filter is to use it. If you come up with an effect you like, you can click on Save to save a copy of it in a separate file, then click on Load to reload it at any time.

Filter Factory

If you're really serious about creating your own filters, take a look at the Filter Factory, which is included on the Photoshop installation CD-ROM. With this plug-in and its included documentation (an Acrobat PDF file), you can create and distribute your own filters. You'll need to brush up on your high school algebra, though: The filters work by performing mathematical operations on the position and brightness value of each pixel in each color channel of an image (see Figure 8.126).

Fortunately, the Filter Factory documentation includes a couple of tutorials that guide you through the process of creating a filter, giving it a user interface, and turning it into a plug-in file that you can hand out to friends or customers. The final result can include sliders and a logo, just like a commercial filter (see Figure 8.127).

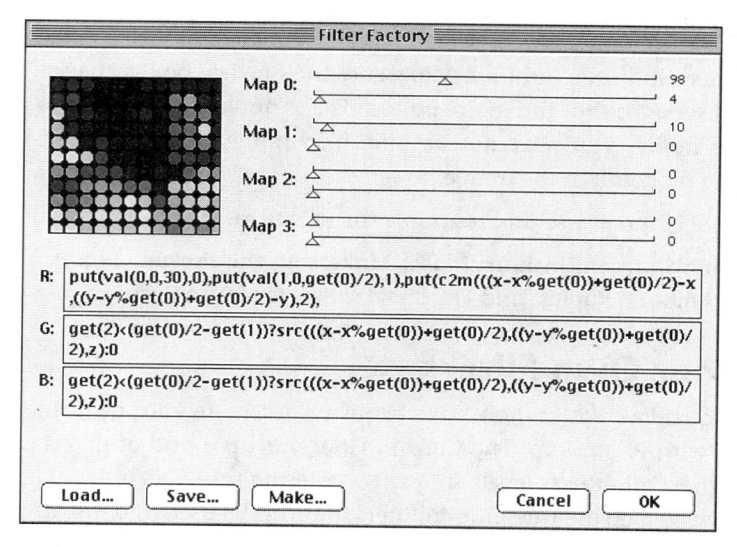

Figure 8.126 The mathematical expressions used in Filter Factory can be this complex, or as simple as "r + 1", which makes the red component of each pixel one level brighter.

FILTER FROLICS   515

Figure 8.127 The Add Remove Transparency filter included with Filter Factory as an example.

Managing Filters

As you use and accumulate more filters, you may find that you need ways to keep track of which ones you're using at any given time. The more filters you have, the more cluttered your Filters menu gets and the harder it is to find the ones you need. If you're in a real jam and need to trim every second during a production session, you may even want to uninstall all filters but the specific ones you'll be using during that session.

To install and uninstall filters and other plug-ins easily, you can use a utility from Cytopia Software, makers of the PhotoOptics filter set, who also produce a Plug-In Manager for Mac users of Photoshop. Like the Extensions Manager, it allows you to create groups of plug-ins that will be activated the next time Photoshop opens (see Figure 8.128). PluginManager for Windows does much the same thing, and also lets you rename filter sets.

If you're the type who just has to know everything there is to know about the software you use, more info is available on each filter installed with your copy of Photoshop. To see a filter's creator and copyright information, choose Apple menu|About Plug-In (Mac) or Help|About Plug-In (Windows), and then choose a plug-in from the submenu. This displays a splash screen with the legalities and sometimes some additional info (see Figure 8.129).

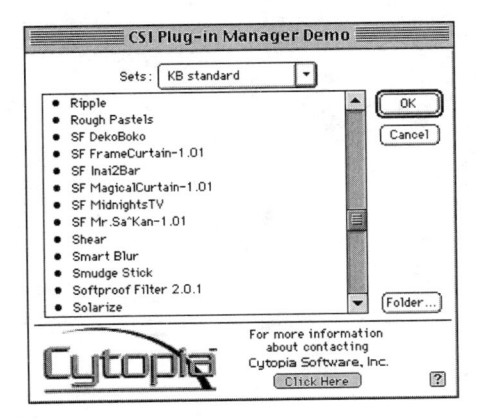

Figure 8.128 The Plug-In Manager works just like the Mac's Extensions Manager.

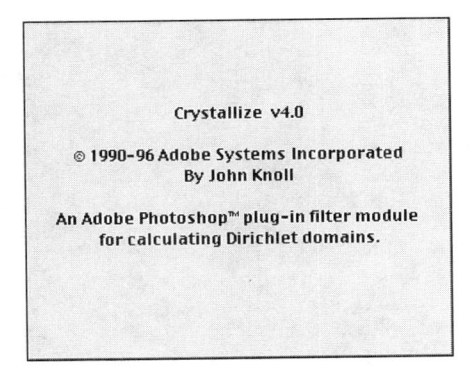

Figure 8.129 This splash screen for the Crystallize filter reveals the mathematical concept on which the filter's operation is based—Dirichlet domains.

Moving On

Filters can help you make the most of your images. In this chapter, we've looked at some of the ways to put Photoshop's filters to work. Although filters are one of the best ways to wile away an afternoon of "playtime," they need to be used with care in production settings. Most of the artwork that you create for commercial purposes (unless your client is MTV) will use very few of the special effects filters. However, it is good to know what they are and how to use them. Experiment with the many ways in which filters can be used.

You can also check out the Web site at **www.boxtopsoft.com** for downloads of a large variety of free and shareware filters.

In Chapter 9, we discuss ways to use Photoshop to prepare images for commercial printing.

PHOTOSHOP PREPRESS

All of the wonderful things you can do to an image would be worth very little if it weren't for Photoshop's powerful capability to prepare the image for the printing press.

The digital revolution in prepress lives within the recent memory of many in the printing industry. Yet, many who make their living with a computer substituting for mechanicals now take electronic tools in stride. Prepress professionals can now achieve printed results that would have been considered miraculous only 12 years ago.

There has been a price to be paid for this amazing technology. It is not an obvious cost, nor is it obvious that in many cases the burden of performance has transferred from printing experts to non-professionals. To illustrate this point, consider the personnel in a printing plant as few as 12 years ago. The company's graphics/make-ready department consisted of people who did several jobs. A designer worked out page design, laying down roughs on tissues and art boards. A typesetter input text—often employing an elaborate code for text attributes such as italic, bold, tabs, size changes, typeface changes—which was output on photographic paper in long, thin strips. A keyliner waxed the back of those strips and pasted them into position on an artboard. Another technician worked with technical pens, pressure-sensitive screen overlays, point tape, and markers to construct artwork. A cameraman turned the artwork into hard copy, which could be given to the keyliner to incorporate into the text on the artboard. The final artboard would be given to a stripper, who would make a line-shot of the artboard, turn any photo material into halftones, and strip the photos into the negative of the artboard. The stripper might also use camera and gel filters to make a color separation. The films for these would also need to be stripped into the artboard negative. Out-of-house commercial separation films would also need to be incorporated into the negatives. The stripper would then shoot a blueline of the composite negative for the customer to approve. Finally, the negative would go to the platemaker. The plate would be given to the pressman, and the print job would be underway.

Designer, keyliner, typesetter, stripper, camera operator, plate maker, out-of-house separator—all of these were considered highly specialized skills for which years of training were required. In the space of a few years, however, all but a few of these professions have vanished, replaced by the new digital technology. Unfortunately, the professionals of the older techniques didn't always migrate to the new technology to become the professionals of the digital age. Relatively unprepared people became the new professionals, often without the benefit of training, experience, or knowledge. Graphics computer operators were expected to embody what had been the specialized knowledge of five or six people. Small and large business managers often put an advanced graphics computer, a desktop scanner, and a laser printer on the desk of an employee whose prior experience with computers had been with business programs: "We'll let Joe be our DTP guy—he's a whiz with Excel. Then we'll save a fortune in printing costs!"

The scenario that put Joe into the position of floundering his way through a vast technical maze (not only did Joe have to become a print expert, but he also had to become an exceptionally knowledgeable computer guy), has become a little less frequent. It is, however, still more the rule than the exception. New users of graphics computers are often confronted with technical problems for which they have no background. The preparation of photographic images is one of the most difficult of these tasks. Halftones, spot color, duotones, line art, color separations—all of these have become increasingly important in the print world. All of these areas require special knowledge of output devices, press conditions, and the sophisticated controls that Photoshop places in your hands.

The material covered in this chapter does not focus on specific techniques and recipes. Rather, it is intended to give you broad, general knowledge of how output devices and press conditions will affect your digital files and what you can do to ensure that the press reproduces your work as perfectly as possible. Photoshop contains virtually everything you need to process a photographic scan and to reproduce it with the greatest possible fidelity on press. The amount of material you will encounter may seem overwhelming, but simply work your way through, step by step, and you'll find that all of it is logical and understandable.

Getting Good Printed Grays

Photoshop users call a black monotone image a *grayscale*. Printers call the same image a *halftone*. Knowledgeable people understand that one—the halftone—is simply the output version of the other. The grayscale image, printed by a PostScript device, has its gray values converted to absolute black and white. Tiny dots of ink of various sizes blend together in our eyes to give the illusion of gray tones. The conversion of grays to black and white dots is the fundamental process by which photographic images are reproduced on a press. The range of tonal values contained in the grayscale file—as it is downloaded to the output device—is the vital data that can make or break the reproduction. However, the process, as you'll see, is not really straightforward.

Color Settings

First, you should be aware that Photoshop 5 has furnished you with a somewhat ambiguous method of controlling your monitor while you are working in Grayscale mode. Under the File menu, choose Color Settings|Grayscale Setup. You will see that there are two choices. The first is RGB; the second is Black Ink. These options are governed by choices made in two other submenus.

When you choose RGB, your monitor simply displays gray tones as a proper subset of the RGB space defined in the Color Settings|RGB Setup submenu (for a more complete explanation of the RGB Setup submenu, see Chapter 10). RGB values are simply colors where the R, G, and B values are identical. For example, R=127, G=127, B=127 is the tone identical to 50 percent black ink.

When the choice for the Grayscale Setup preference is Black Ink, your gray values are displayed as ink equivalents. While this choice is in effect, the monitor display is governed, to a certain extent, by the choices you have made in the Color Settings|CMYK Setup submenu. Specifically, your monitor's grayscale display will be adjusted to reflect the amount of dot gain entered as part of your CMYK Setup specifications. (Note: We will explain dot gain more fully in the next section of this chapter.)

The only difficulty with using the Black Ink setting is that you will see all of your grayscale images theoretically adjusted by Photoshop and displayed so that they seem to have the specified percentage of dot gain applied to them. In fact, this screen display isn't adequate to predict how much the image will change from what you see on your screen to what will appear on the press sheet. Our recommendation is that you leave your Grayscale Setup in RGB mode. As you work with the image, you will then have a clearer idea of how much the image will need to be manipulated in order to make it print successfully. We will show you a different method that will allow you to see the result of dot gain in a much more accurate way.

Installing And Using The Adobe Gamma Utility

To make this process as simple as possible for grayscale work, and later for color, begin by installing the Adobe Gamma utility that is bundled with your copy of Photoshop 5, but which cannot install automatically. If you are an Apple Macintosh user, installation means dragging the Gamma utility to your *closed* System folder. The operating system will then place it in the correct folder within the System folder. If you are a Windows user, first install Photoshop 5 by using the Install wizard. After installation, look in the Program Files folder and locate the Calibrat folder. Within this folder will be several files, among them the Adobe Gamma Loader, the Adobe Gamma control panel, and a ReadMe file that gives instructions on how to install the other two. The instructions tell you that you don't need to restart Windows, but it's best that you do. It's a good idea to restart Windows whenever you install a new piece of software.

Windows users will find the Adobe Gamma Control Panel by clicking on the Start button, and then selecting Settings|Control Panel|Adobe Gamma. Macintosh users can access the Control Panel by clicking on the Apple Menu and dragging down to the Control Panels. Note: It is advisable to run the Adobe Gamma utility only after your monitor has been on for several hours, which allows it to reach a state of thermal equilibrium.

Figure 9.1 shows the Adobe Gamma window as it first appears. You have two choices: calibrate the monitor using either the Control Panel or the Wizard. You can use either, but to make things simpler the first time you use this small program, choose the Wizard. Click on the Next button. Note: If you are already using a calibration utility and are happy with it, you shouldn't install the Adobe Gamma software. Use only one calibration program at a time. Also, it should be self-evident, but Adobe Gamma is the updated version of Adobe's previously released Gamma monitor control panel. Before using the new software, remove the old, and restart your computer.

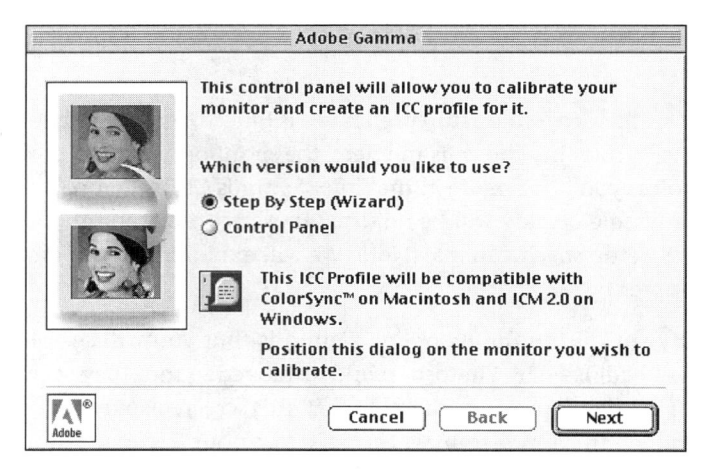

Figure 9.1 The opening dialog window for the Adobe Gamma utility.

The next window (see Figure 9.2) allows you to load an ICC Profile for your monitor if you have one. Macintosh users can click on the Load button, which will access the list of ICC Profiles contained in the System|Preferences|ColorSync folder. If you find a profile appropriate for your monitor, go ahead and load it. Otherwise, simply click on the Next button.

The third step of the process (see Figure 9.3) asks you to adjust the contrast and brightness of your monitor. This is a very important step, one you should not rush. Take your time and get the settings just right. (Later, after you have completed your monitor's calibration, you may want to use some masking tape to prevent your monitor's brightness and contrast controls from being moved. If your brightness and contrast settings are changed, you must recalibrate your monitor.) Click on Next.

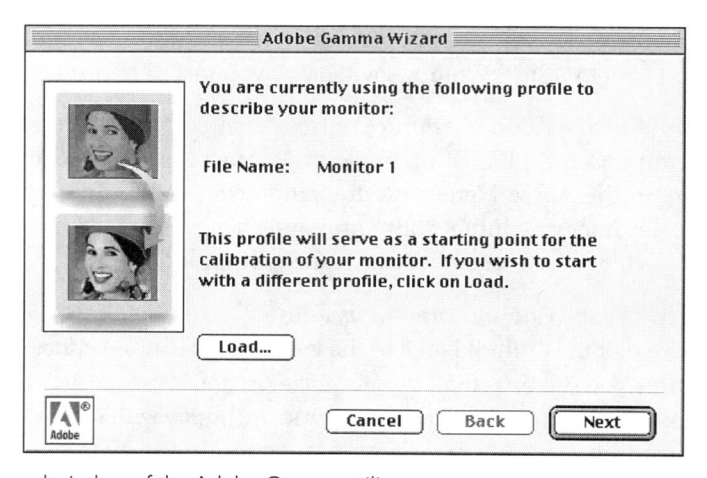

Figure 9.2 The second window of the Adobe Gamma utility.

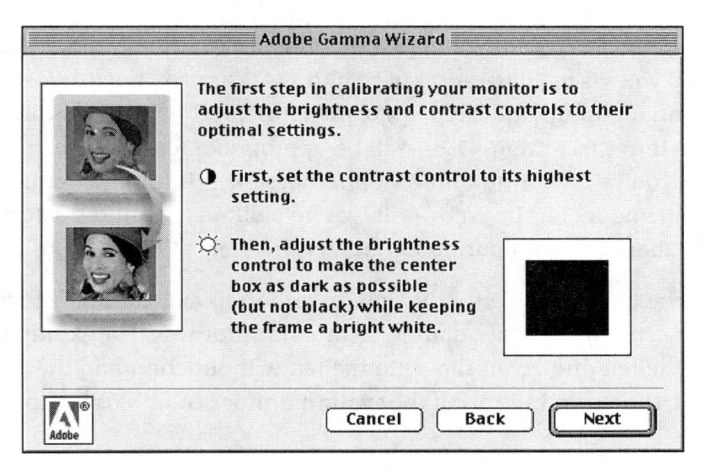

Figure 9.3 Adjust the contrast of the monitor and the brightness using the square target at the lower right.

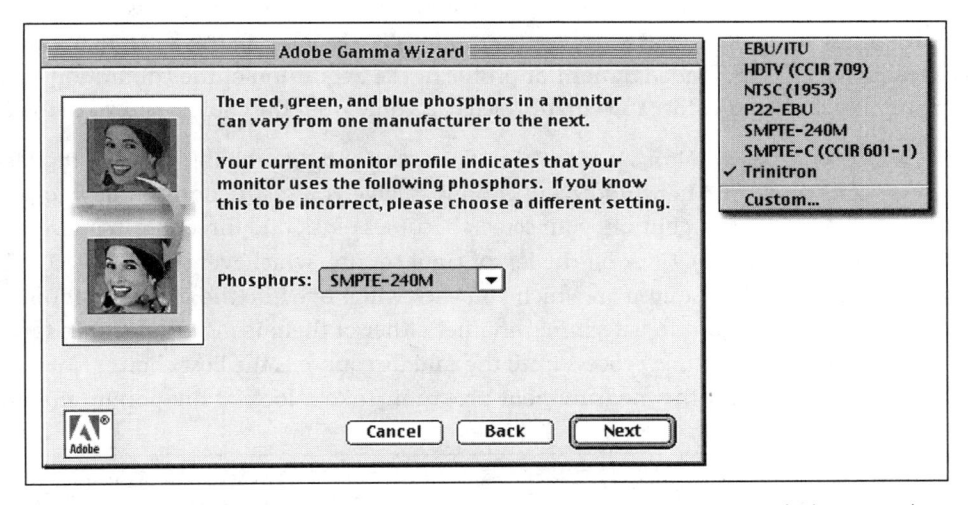

Figure 9.4 Load a custom description of your monitor's phosphors. If you are unsure which to use, choose SMPTE-240M.

The next step of this process (see Figure 9.4) asks you to load a description of your monitor's phosphors. If you know that your monitor uses a Sony Trinitron CRT, for example, choose that as your option. If you are unsure which of the choices shown at the upper right of the figure is the correct one for your system, pick SMPTE-240M. (In Chapter 10, you can find a more complete explanation of these choices.)

Figure 9.5 shows the window where you actually adjust your monitor's gamma. Uncheck the View Single Gamma Only checkbox so that you see the three colored squares with the sliders. Move the sliders so that the center area within each square merges to invisibility with the area around it. You may find it helpful to sit so that you are a further distance than normal from the screen—perhaps 36 to 40 inches. Because the outer area is textured and the inner area plain, you may find it helpful to squint your eyes—in addition to sitting further than usual from the monitor—to help you see the differences in brightness. After you have adjusted all three sliders, click on the Gamma pop-up and choose Macintosh Default (which will insert 1.8 in the data-entry box). Note that this setting—1.8—will be appropriate for both Macintosh and Windows platforms when you're preparing Photoshop images for printing. Other uses of Photoshop—such as preparing images for the Web—will require a different Gamma setting. See Chapter 12 for more information about preparing images for the Web.

As you change the gamma sliders, pay close attention to exactly how much you move each slider. You will learn a good deal about your monitor that way. For example, if you find that you move both the red and green sliders to the left without changing the position of the blue slider very much, that is an indication that your monitor's color bias is stronger in the red and green phosphors.

When you move to the next window, Adobe Gamma requests information about your monitor's Hardware White Point (see Figure 9.6). White Point is the setting that indicates the temperature of the brightest white light your monitor can produce (see sidebar in this section, "White Point Measurements"). If you loaded a monitor profile at the beginning of the calibration, the pop-up menu may display a value. You can also select a value from the choices shown in the figure.

Even if you know your monitor's White Point value, you should probably click on the Measure button for confirmation. The window will change to give you instructions on how to proceed. When you click on the Next button, your screen becomes black and three small squares appear (right, center of Figure 9.6). Click on the left or right square, whichever seems to you to be the most neutral in tone. The square on which you click will move into the center position. Examine the outer squares again to determine whether either of them is more neutral in tone than the middle square. Repeat this process until the middle square is the best choice. Now, click on the middle square to exit the measurement program. Take a look at the pop-up menu. Your

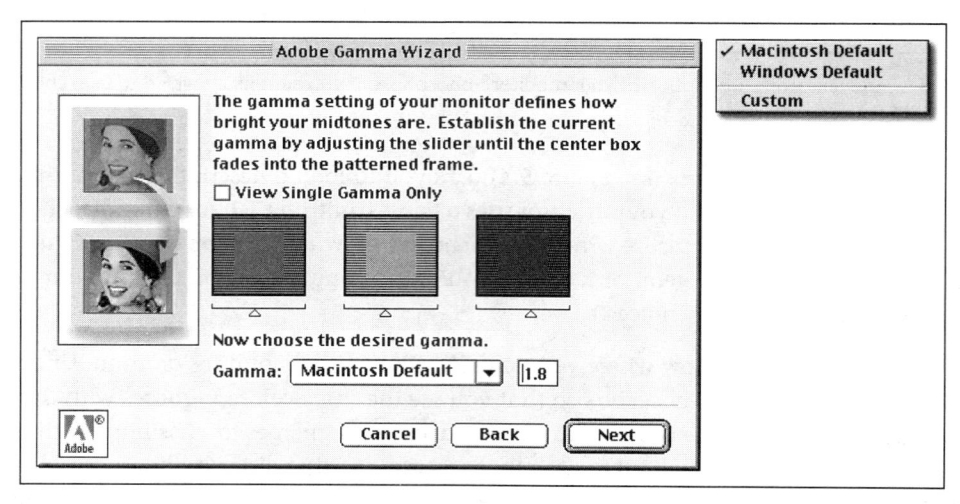

Figure 9.5 Move the gamma sliders so that the central area in each square seems to merge with the area around it.

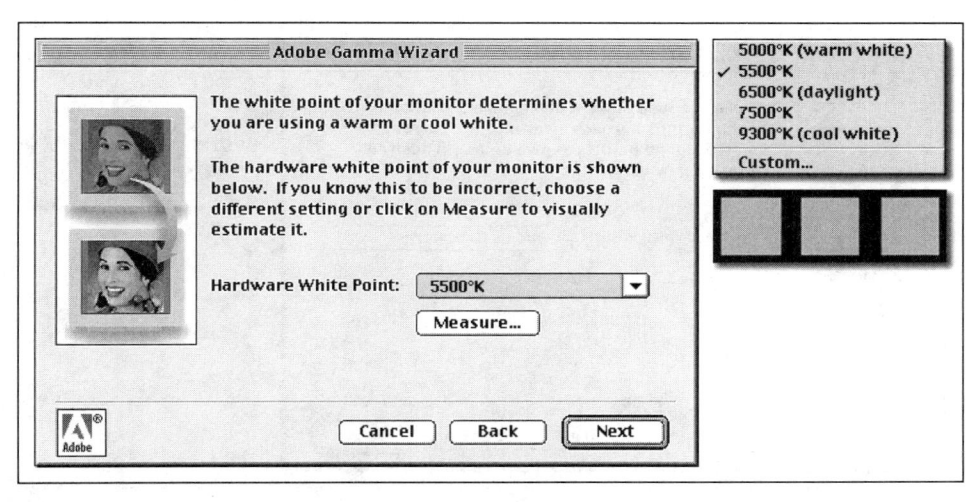

Figure 9.6 In this window, you can select your monitor's White Point value or use the Measure button to arrive at a custom value.

White Point value may have changed to a different number than the one you chose before using the Measure button. If the reading is a different number, or if it displays "Custom," you will need to make only a single choice in the following screen. Click on the Next button.

If you want, you can work at a different White Point than your monitor is able to display. However, for purposes of your later adjustment of grayscale and color images, change the pop-up so that it displays Same As Hardware, as shown in Figure 9.7. When you have made your choice, click on Next.

WHITE POINT MEASUREMENTS

It may seem a little strange that your monitor's White Point value is described in terms of temperature. However, this way of defining the intensity of light is based on an idea from theoretical physics—that of the *black body*. A black body is a theoretical object that absorbs all the radiation that strikes it, reflecting nothing back. There is no such thing as a perfect black body. However, the concept is useful due to the fact that a heated black body is a fine emitter of radiation. As the black body object is heated, it will emit, at any specific temperature, the maximum amount of energy available from a radiating object. When the black body temperature rises, the color of its emitted light changes in a precisely measurable way. (Well, maybe not so precisely. Imprecision in black body calculations was a factor that led directly to the development of quantum mechanics.) This gives a standard whereby the color/brightness of light can be directly tied to a separate measurement scale that has nothing to do with light. In terms relevant to your monitor, the brightest white light that your monitor produces is defined as the color of the light of the black body object heated to a certain temperature. If your White Point measurement is 9300° Kelvin, you are seeing a white light that would be equivalent to the color of a very toasty object!

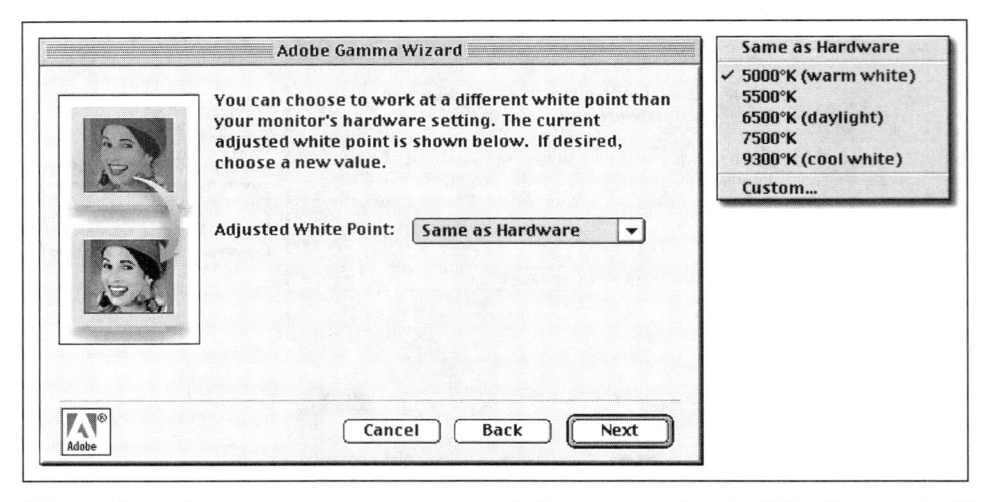

Figure 9.7 In this window, you can make a choice that will allow you to work with a White Point that is different from what your monitor currently displays.

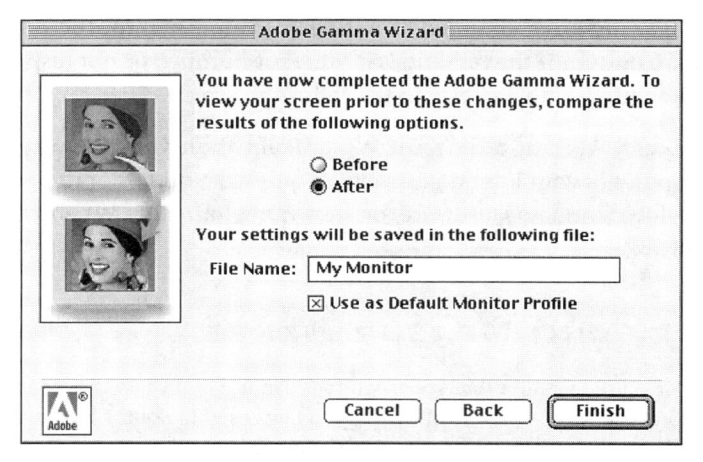

Figure 9.8 Save your monitor configuration as a named file, and click on the Finish button to execute the changes for your monitor.

The final screen of the Adobe Gamma utility is shown in Figure 9.8. At the top are two radio buttons you can use to see how much change this small program has brought to your display. You may be startled to see the difference between Before and After. If you are satisfied with your results, name your display profile and leave the file as the Default Monitor Profile. On a Macintosh computer, the file will become your active ColorSync profile. You can check this by opening the Color Sync Control Panel. On a Windows computer, your profile will be placed automatically where the Adobe Gamma Loader can read it whenever Windows starts up. Click on the Finish button. (Note: When you save your monitor profile on a Windows machine, use the following file extension: *My Monitor*.ICM.) You do not need to restart Windows or the Macintosh when you have finished the calibration.

Configuring Photoshop's Monitor Settings For Grayscale Work

When you have finished with the Adobe Gamma utility, your monitor will have been adjusted and you will have saved the calibration information so that it's available system-wide to any software on your computer that can access monitor profiles. On a Macintosh computer, your profile will have been loaded into the operating system's support for color calibration, ColorSync. That makes the information available to all Macintosh software that is designed to access ColorSync. The next task is to configure Photoshop.

First, choose File|Color Settings|CMYK Setup and enter the amount of dot gain you expect to encounter with the press you intend to use. (Note: This setting should have nothing to do with your RGB display, but it does. Sorry. Nobody asked me.) From the same submenu, choose Color Settings|Grayscale Setup. Set the choice by clicking on the RGB button. Click on OK (see Figure 9.9).

Again from the Color Settings submenu, choose RGB Setup. When the dialog box has opened (see Figure 9.10), click on the Load button and find the monitor profile you saved from the Adobe Gamma utility. Select the file and load it. The RGB pop-up at the top should display your profile's name. Make sure that the checkbox at the bottom of the dialog is checked, and that the Gamma data-entry field displays the desired number, 1.80. Click on OK.

Your next task is to adjust your RGB gamma value so that your screen display gives you matched numbers in the Color Picker. Click on the Foreground Color swatch on the Tools palette. Enter the values shown in Figure 9.11 in the CMYK data-entry fields (0%, 0%, 0%, and 50%). Make a note of the numbers in the RGB data fields. Click on OK.

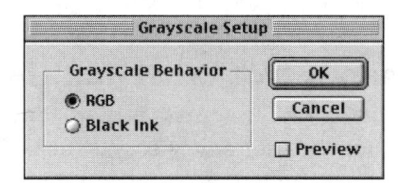

Figure 9.9 Set the Grayscale Setup preference to display in RGB mode.

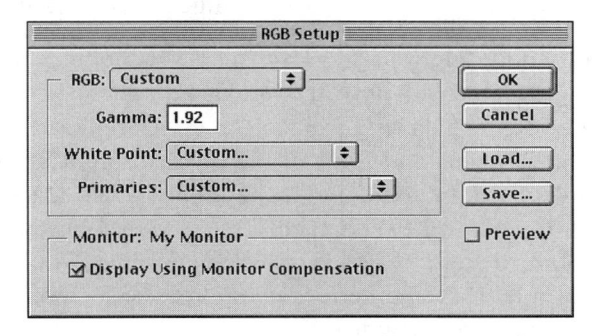

Figure 9.10 In the RGB Setup dialog box, load the monitor profile you saved from the Adobe Gamma utility.

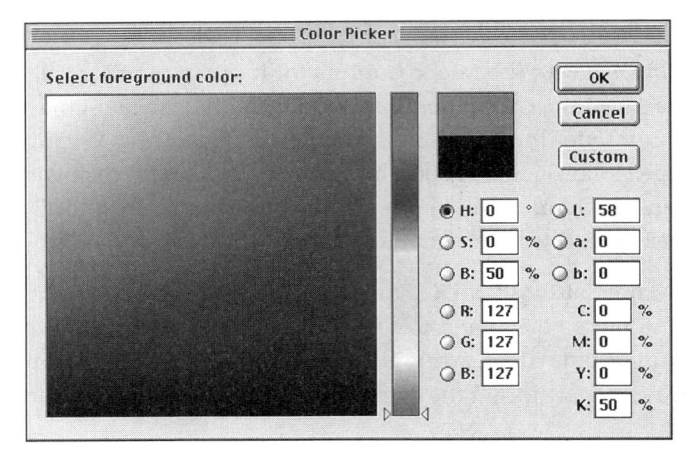

Figure 9.11 Enter "0", "0", "0", and "50" in the CMYK data fields of the Color Picker. Make a note of the values in the RGB fields.

Open the RGB Setup dialog box again (see Figure 9.10). Your target for the RGB values in the Color Picker is 127 for each. RGB 127, 127, 127 should be a perfect 50 percent gray. If your values in the Color Picker are higher, then you need to decrease the value of the gamma reading in RGB Setup. This is, unfortunately, a trial-and-error process. However, try increasing or decreasing the value by .02 for every unit you are above or below the RGB target value. Change the gamma value, click on OK, and open the Color Picker. Keep doing this until you have moved the RGB values to 127. When you have completed your adjustments, your monitor and Photoshop will be able to give you an accurate display of the image you will be preparing for press.

What You See On Screen Is *Not* What You Get On Press

Preparing halftones for printing on an offset press is more difficult than nearly any other job. Color separations, by comparison, are extremely easy. When you have an image that is to be reproduced with a single opaque ink, you have only one chance to get it right. If the preparation of the image in Photoshop isn't correct, no amount of fussing by the pressman will correct it. It's an all-or-nothing situation, and a job whose difficulty is often underestimated.

You can be very good at adjusting your grayscale images so that they look sharp and clear on the monitor, and still get socked with dark and muddy halftones when your job goes on press. The truth is that when you are adjusting grayscale images for press reproduction, your screen does not display the consequences of some of the physical problems you'll encounter—dot gain, highlight dot fall-off, and maximum blacks are just a few. (All of these topics are discussed in the next few sections.) Because of this, make your adjustments always keeping a simple rule in mind: If the image looks good on screen, it will look awful on press. There is an inverse version of this rule: If the halftone is going to look good on press, it will look flat, washed out, and pretty uninspiring on screen.

You need two very important pieces of information before you can attempt to get a good halftone on press. The first is the amount of *dot gain* produced by the press when printing on the paper you'll be using for the job. The second is the minimum dot percentage for the highlights in your halftones.

Dot Gain

Dot gain is the natural result of using liquid ink and applying it to a more-or-less porous surface such as paper. The dots on the printing plate transfer the ink to the offset blanket, which in turn imprints the paper. The ink stays mostly on the surface of the paper, but some amount of it is pressed into the paper, where it is absorbed and spreads slightly. Consequently, the percentage values of the dots increase as the diameter of the dots on the printed sheet increase. The amount of increase is usually expressed as a percentage that describes the amount of growth. The percentage is derived from the difference between a set of known plate or film values, and the amount of ink coverage on the press sheet. The amount of gain varies with the type of paper used, the model and condition of the press, the amount of humidity in the air, and—sometimes—whether the pressman is in a good mood.

Dot gain is not a fixed number for all sizes of dots. Very small dots usually have very little gain. The gain percentage increases as the size of the dot increases until the dot size reaches 50 percent. Above 50 percent, the dots begin to grow together and the gain number levels off and begins to decrease. Because of this, dot gain is expressed as the percentage of dot growth at 50 percent, the maximum figure. Press sheets nearly always have, outside the live print area, a small area imprinted by what are known to be 50 percent dots. The pressman uses a device known as a *densitometer* to measure the ink coverage within this area. If the coverage is, say, 66 percent of the total area, the gain is known to be 16 percent (66% minus 50% equals 16%). A 16 percent gain does not sound very extreme, but a glance at Figure 9.12 shows the difference between the dots, as they will appear on the plate (left side) and the way the dots will actually print (right side). While 16 percent dot gain is not uncommon, there is a range of possible values: Gain percentages can be as low as 9 or 10 percent and as high as 50 percent. Really. Your printer should be able to give you an exact number for dot gain. Be a bit careful of the number you're given; it's astonishing how often a print salesperson, misunderstanding the offset process, will shade the number low in the mistaken belief that a high gain percentage is a reflection of a print house's competence. It is nothing of the sort. If you are given a number that is, say, 5 or 7 percent, you would be well advised to speak directly to a press room represen-

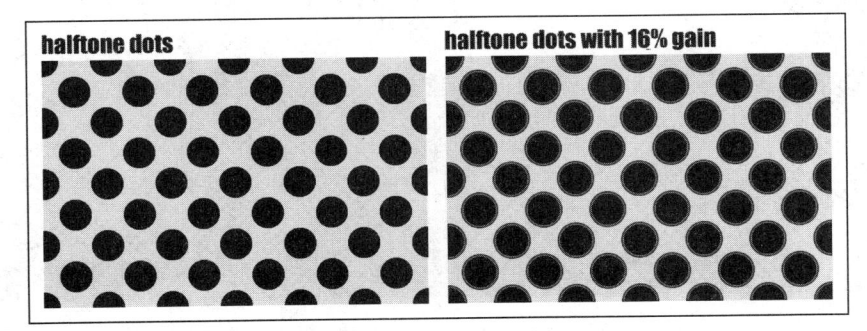

Figure 9.12 The two sides of this figure illustrate how dot gain increases the size of the halftone dots.

tative. In all likelihood, you will find that the true number will be somewhere between 14 and 33 percent. No matter how large or small the gain figure, the important point is that you *must* have an accurate idea what the number is. Without it, the success of your halftone is just a matter of luck.

Why is dot gain important? Imagine that you have carefully adjusted your image and that it looks on screen much the way the upper left image in Figure 9.13 appears. You are satisfied with the appearance of the photo and, if you are working with a client, the client has also expressed approval. Your job goes to press and you are startled—possibly chagrined—to see your work become much darker (upper right corner, Figure 9.13). The difference between these two images is a 16 percent gain in the midtones, or more accurately, at 50 percent (the actual dots of the enclosed rectangular areas are shown magnified below each example). In some cases, you'll be able to live with the change (the examples in the figure are probably acceptable—barely). In other cases, the reproduction of the image will be so darkened that it is unacceptable and the consequences are expensive and embarrassing.

Figure 9.13 The figure on the right (with its enlarged detail) shows the significant darkening of the image due to dot gain.

Assuming that we are still discussing a gain figure of 16 percent, does it seem logical that if you intend to end up with, say, a 50 percent value on press, then the value in Photoshop (and on the film and plate) has to be about 14 to 16 percent less than 50 percent? If you see the logic to this, then you understand the mechanics behind the distressing rule cited at the beginning of this section: If the halftone is going to look good on press, it will look flat, washed out, and pretty uninspiring on screen. You will learn, in this chapter, how to compensate for the difference in *input* values and *output* values shown in Figure 9.14 so that your image's values before output fall along the lower curve. The lower curve is almost a mirror image of the dot gain curve (upper line) in the figure.

Minimum Highlight Dot

We are accustomed to discussing lithography dots as percentages: 11, 24, 75 percent, and so on. However, integer percentages relating to tone values are impossible to achieve in PostScript for all values other than 25, 50, 75, and 100 percent. (Note: PostScript dots are constructed within a square grid containing 16 small squares on a side. Each dot is composed of smaller raster spots that build up to form the larger screen dots. There are 256—16 × 16—squares in the grid. Only the four listed percentages of 256 are integer values.) In slightly less math-oriented terms, you can't really have a 4 percent dot in PostScript, but a dot that is just a little smaller than 4 percent. Almost all of the PostScript dots work this way: Some dots are a little smaller than the percentage, some a little larger. The flip side of the coin is that PostScript is not limited

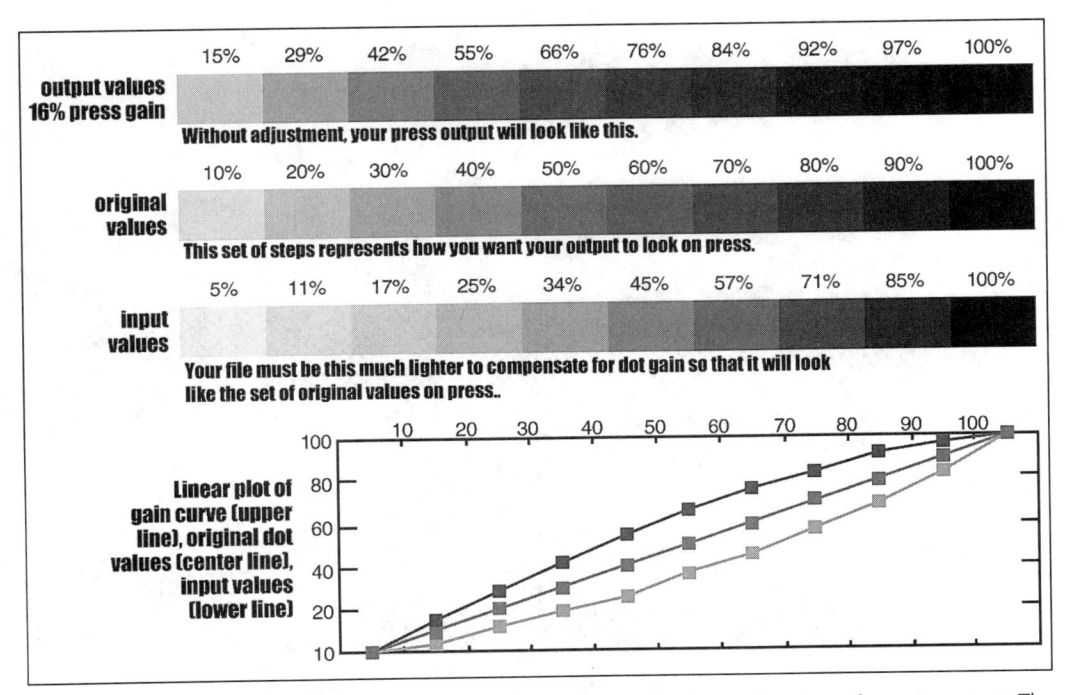

Figure 9.14 A comparison of tone values: The original values are what you wish to have for press output. The input values—given a 16 percent dot gain—must be lighter than the original values. Otherwise, the original values darken as shown on the top scale.

to a mere 100 values, but to 256 values. This means you can actually have a dot that is expressed as an integer plus a fraction.

Having a wide range of tonal values seems, at first glance, to be very desirable. It would be if that range of values could actually be reproduced on a press. The sad fact is that it cannot. Dot gain (see the previous section) is one example of a physical phenomenon that limits the possible tonal range. Compensating for gain deliberately sacrifices some values for the sake of being able to clearly reproduce the most detail-laden and visible part of the tonal range.

There's another, subtler limitation on the range of values, specifically the values on the highlight end of the scale. Because of the way the offset process works, very small dots simply do not print. The dots are present on the film and on the plate. The ink simply does not adhere to the plate dot and so leaves low-value highlight areas without any ink. Areas such as these are called *burned out* highlights. When an image has been adjusted so that the smallest printable dot is the lightest non-specular value, the image is said to hold a minimum highlight dot of some specified percentage. In Figure 9.15, a pair of examples shows the results of an effective adjustment (left side) and an adjustment where some of the highlight areas are devoid of ink.

The specified percentage is a variable that can range from 2 to 7 percent. The exact value for the job you have at hand will need to be obtained from your print house. If you are unsure how

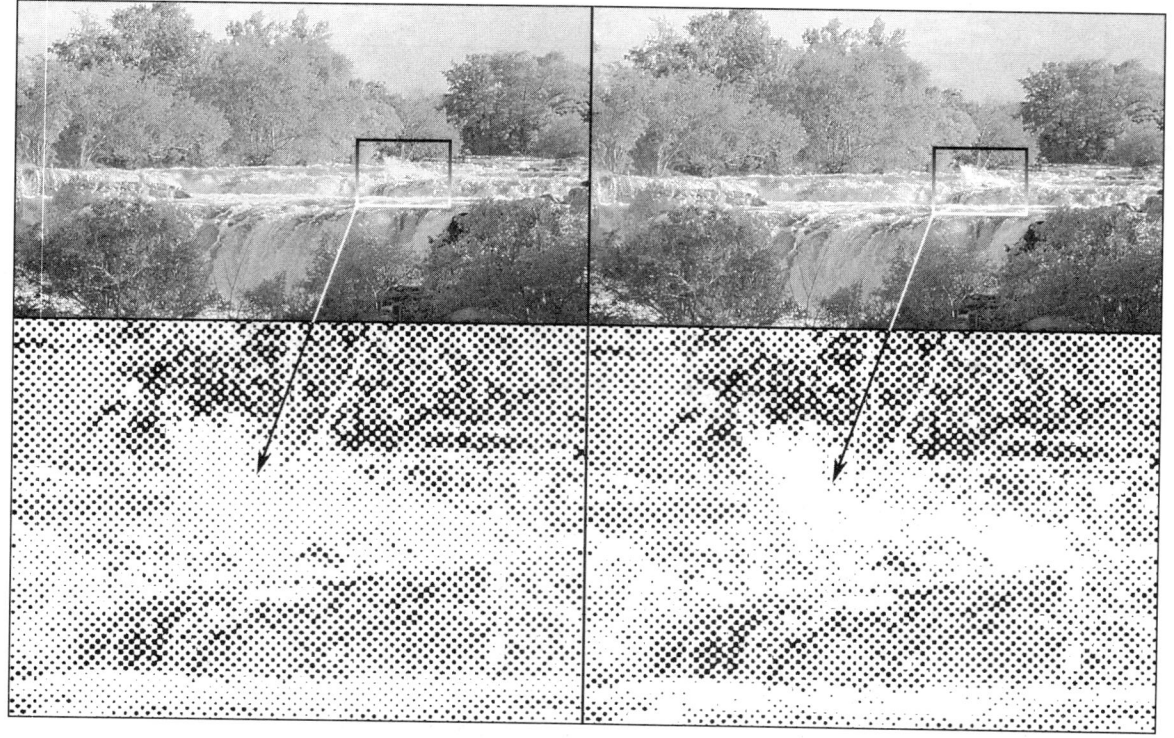

Figure 9.15 The rightmost image contains values that will not hold on press. After adjusting (left), no highlight values are blown out.

to word the request for this piece of information, phrase it this way: "What size dot do I need to carry in my highlights?" You learn, in this chapter, how to make effective adjustments so that your highlight dots do not disappear on press.

Processing A Grayscale Image

From a technical standpoint, the best place to begin the preparation of a halftone is with an RGB color file. Even if the original material is in the form of a black and white print, scan the material as RGB. With the color scan, you'll be able, if it proves necessary, to make very drastic adjustments based on 24 bits of information per pixel—as opposed to 8 bits—and still have a very good image when you're finished.

The procedure that follows will seem, at first, to be composed of a great many steps. Although there are a number of operations to be performed, you'll find that they go quickly: It should be possible to make all the required adjustments in under two minutes. After you use this method on a few images and see how well it works, you'll probably want to do all your images this way. Try to be aware of the nuances of the steps. You'll find that this same procedure, performed in slightly different ways, allows you to manipulate grayscale, color, and scans intended for line art. There are faster ways of doing this job (and you can eliminate some steps when you gain some experience). Let's look at several quick halftone adjustment procedures. The following sets of instructions take you through each step so that you can see how the process works. Notice that this set of steps is aimed at a press condition of 16 percent dot gain and 5 percent minimum highlight dot.

1. Open the RGB scan that is to be made into a halftone. If you wish to follow along, open the file RGB2GS1.PSD in the Chapter 9 Practice folder on this book's CD-ROM. It's the same image used in the following examples. Press Command+0 (zero) or Ctrl+0 to fit the image in the computer screen (see Figure 9.16). Place the Layers Palette and

Figure 9.16 Open the RGB image and place the Layers and Info palettes where they can be easily seen.

the Info Palette where they are convenient to see and use. Click on the leftmost triangular pop-up on the Info palette and change the displayed readings to Grayscale.

2. Choose Image|Adjust|Levels, or press Command+L or Ctrl+L. Position the Levels controls so that you can see the lightest and the darkest parts of the scan. If the Preview box is checked, click on it to turn it off. The pop-up menu at the very top of the dialog box reads RGB. Change it so that it reads Red. Hold the Option key or the Alt key. Move your cursor to the rightmost upper slider—the Input highlight slider—and begin to move the slider triangle to the left. The dramatic change in the screen display is called Threshold mode. The screen will go black. As you move the slider, the highlight pixels in the Red channel begin to show up as red against black. Move the slider so that you have small red areas showing, but try to leave some dark pixels within each of the light areas. Release the mouse button. Using Threshold mode allows you to precisely locate the highlight and shadow pixels within an image, and to force them to be lighter or darker. It's a very useful tool when you don't have a lot of experience. The appearance of the screen while the slider moves is shown in Figure 9.17.

> **NOTE:** *If you are using Photoshop for Windows, the Threshold effect from within the Levels dialog box may not function. Some Windows video interface boards don't support it. In some cases, it works only when the number of displayed colors is set to 256. If you find that this method does not work for you, see the Tip for using Threshold in Windows following the section on the Unsharp Mask filter.*

3. Continue holding down the Option key or the Alt key. Move the leftmost upper slider—the Input area shadow slider—and begin to move the small triangle to the right. Your screen will go red and, as you move the slider, the darkest pixels of the red channel begin to show up as black against the red. Move the slider until just a hint of shadow

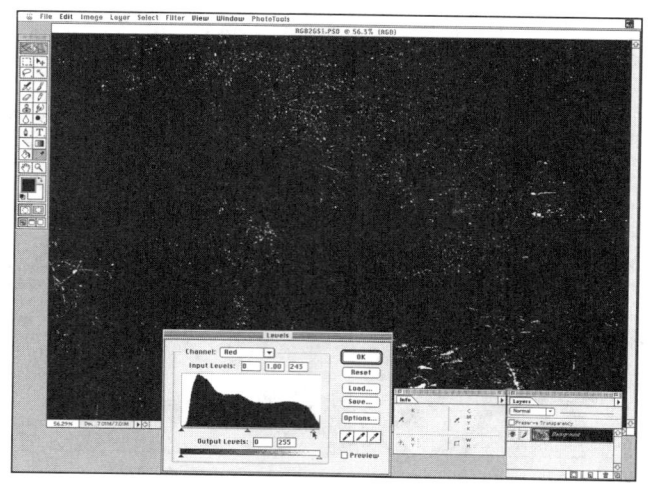

Figure 9.17 Move the Red channel highlight slider with the Option (Mac) or Alt (Windows) key held down.

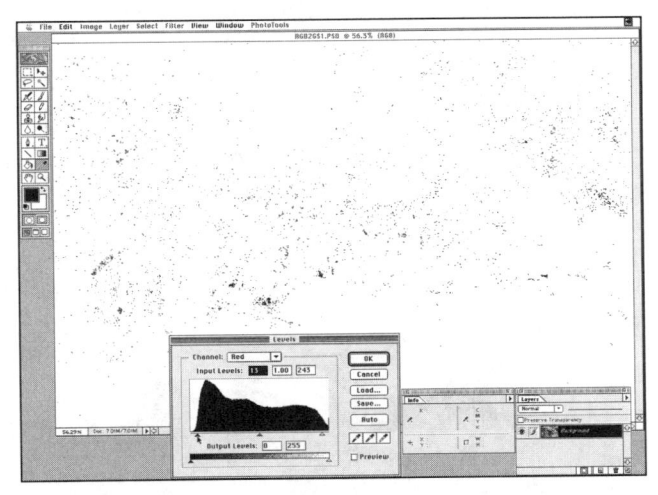

Figure 9.18 Move the Red channel shadow slider while holding down the Option (Mac) or Alt (Windows) key.

pixels is visible (see Figure 9.18). Be careful not to move this slider too far. It's easy to add ink on press, but very hard to eliminate ink in areas that are too dark. Moving the slider too far darkens the shadow areas of the image so much that they lose all their detail and become impossible to control when printed. If the image is dark in overall tone, it may be that you won't be able to move the slider at all. Try to maintain a few red pixels within the dark-pixel areas. Release the mouse button.

4. Change the pop-up menu so that it reads Green. Perform exactly the same operations as on the Red channel, remembering to hold down the Option or Alt key (see Figures 9.19 and 9.20).

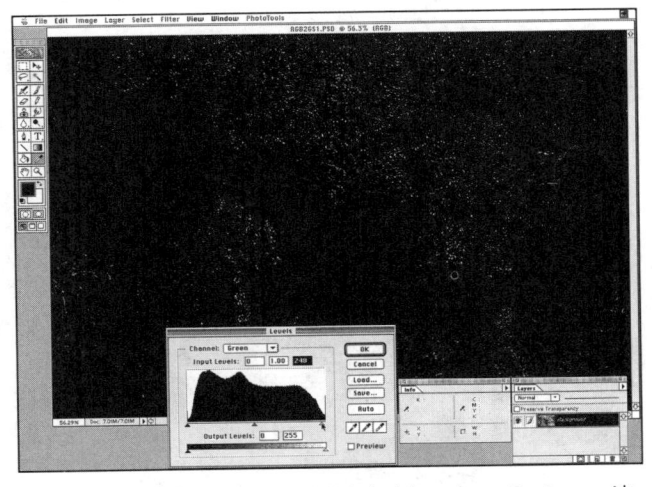

Figure 9.19 Move the Green channel highlight slider while holding down Option or Alt.

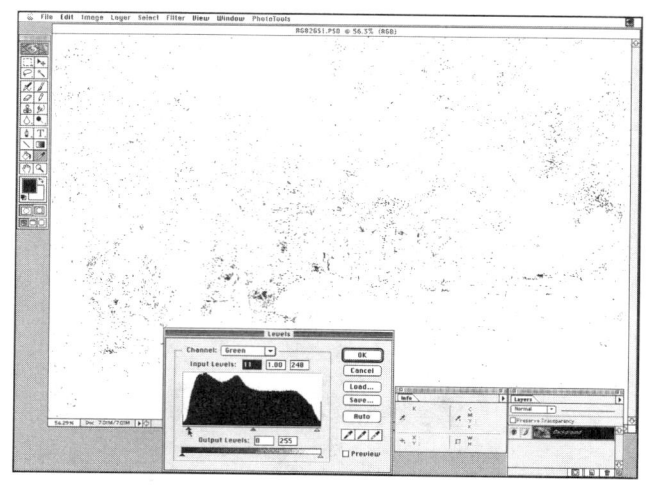

Figure 9.20 Move the Green channel shadow slider while holding down Option or Alt.

5. Change the pop-up menu so that it reads Blue. Perform the same operations as on the Red and Green channels (see Figures 9.21 and 9.22).

6. Return the pop-up menu to its original heading (RGB). From this point, there is no longer any need to hold the Option or Alt keys. Move the cursor to the center slider on the input scale and move the slider to the left. Move it so that the center numerical readout above is about 1.25 (see Figure 9.23). For very dark images, the slider can be moved until it reads about 1.30 to 1.50. Try not to move this slider much more than that. Too much movement causes the three-quarter-tone values to become grainy. This happens because moving the leftmost slider and the center slider too close together leaves too few values to give a continuous range of tones from 50 percent to 100 percent.

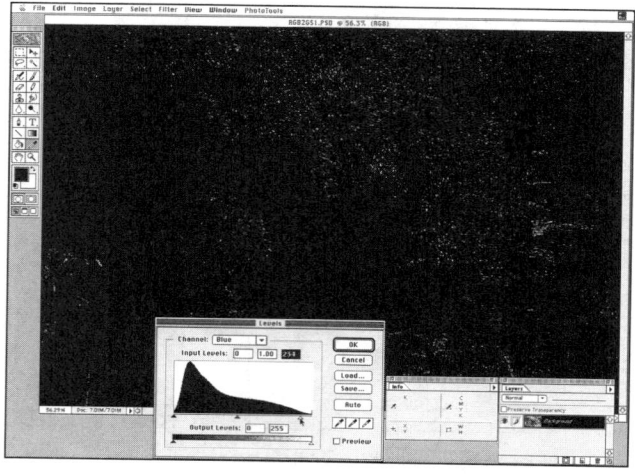

Figure 9.21 Move the Blue channel highlight slider while holding down Option or Alt.

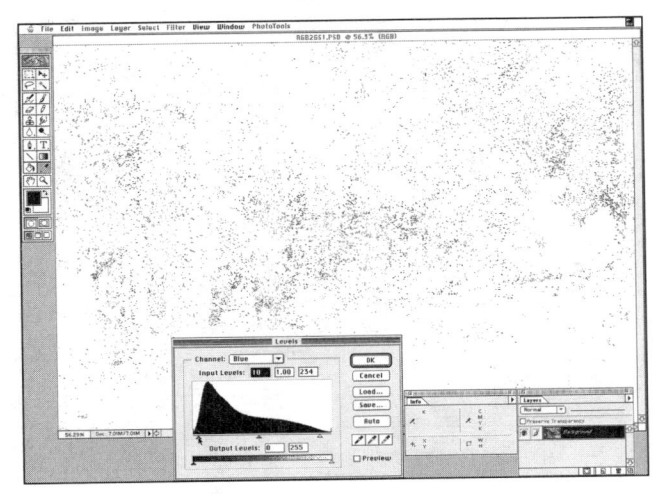

Figure 9.22 Move the Blue channel shadow slider while holding down Option or Alt.

Figure 9.23 Move the RGB composite midtone slider to the left.

7. Move your cursor out into the window, where it becomes an Eyedropper cursor. Locate the lightest values you can find in the window (see Figure 9.24). From the Info palette, you can see that those values are probably 0 percent. Now, move the rightmost slider on the bottom—Output—scale to the left. Move it just a little way and then return to the highlight area. You'll see two numbers separated by a slash on the Info palette. The number on the left is the original value of the pixel. The number on the right is the new value, the result of moving the sliders. Go back and forth. Move the slider a little and check the reading. Stop moving the slider when you have reached the minimum dot you need to carry in the highlights (in this case, 5 percent). Move the slider as far as you need to, but no farther than necessary.

Figure 9.24 Locate the lightest values in the image. Move the Output scale highlight slider to darken them to about 5 percent.

8. Move your cursor out into the window and locate the darkest pixels you can find. These values will probably range between 96 and 100 percent, as shown on the Info palette. Move the leftmost slider on the Output scale to the right. Move it just a little way and return to the dark pixels in the window. Stop moving the slider when you have taken the darkest values and lightened them so that their new value is a maximum of 90 to 93 percent (see Figure 9.25). If you glance again at the linear gain plot in Figure 9.14, you can see that the gain at 90 percent is 7 percent. Because of this, there is really no point in having many values in the image darker than 90 to 93 percent, because all values darker than these will print as solid, or nearly solid, black. By adjusting the shadow on the Output scale, you ensure that only the darkest values print as solid, while lighter shadow values do not reach total ink coverage. Note that this shadow percentage may be somewhat higher. Most printers suggest a maximum ink value of 95 percent. 2 to 5 percent lower than maximum makes the image a little more open without changing the overall contrast by very much. If you prefer more overall contrast, use the 95 percent figure.

9. Click on the Save button in the Levels dialog. Name this Levels configuration file in such a way that it is obvious that it belongs to the image you are adjusting, and save it in a place where it can easily be retrieved.

10. Now, click on the Levels Cancel button. Yes, really. You're going to use the settings you've just saved with an adjustment layer. It would be wonderful if you could simply add an adjustment layer and move the sliders while the layer is selected. However, the Threshold mode method does not work on adjustment layers, and you are forced to use this workaround.

11. Command+click or Ctrl+click the New Layer icon at the bottom of the Layers palette. A small dialog box appears (see Figure 9.26). From the center pop-up menu, choose the adjustment layer type: In this case, choose Levels. Click on the OK button. The

Figure 9.25 Locate the darkest values in the image. Move the Output scale shadow slider to lighten them to about 93 percent.

Figure 9.26 Make a Levels adjustment layer.

Levels controls now appear. Click on the Load button and find the settings file you've just saved. When you find and select it, click the OK button. You now have your previous settings applied to an adjustment layer. This allows you—if needed—to go back and make more adjustments to the image without going through the entire process again, and without applying a new set of adjustments to an image that has already been modified.

12. From the Image menu, choose the Duplicate command (see Figure 9.27). Click on OK. From this point, you are working on a copy of the image. Some of the previous adjustments may need to be further modified. By working on a copy, you can go back to the original version of your work—discarding the copy—and then generate

a new duplicate. In addition to this, you may want to use this image in color at some future time. The steps that you have taken to this point are exactly the same steps used to prepare an image to be a color separation. (Note: Duplicating your document at critical stages and continuing to work on a copy is a good way to avoid having to go back to the beginning of a job if you find that you don't like the final result. Of course, you may want to simply depend on the History palette to go backward in the adjustment process. If you do so, please bear in mind that your history palette is limited to 100 backward steps. (Change the number of steps by selecting History Options from the History palette sidebar menu.) From the point of view of previous versions of Photoshop, 100 levels of Undo are miraculous. It doesn't take much effort, however, to do 100 things to an image. Also, if you save and close your image, your History list is cleared. Keep it in mind, okay?)

13. Flatten this image. It is now ready to be converted to Grayscale mode. This is done in two steps. (Note: This method for converting to Grayscale mode is an excellent candidate for an Action.) First, under the Image menu, choose Mode|Lab Color. Press Command+1 or Ctrl+1 to view the L channel that holds the brightness—or *Lightness*—values of the image (the other two, A and B, contain the color). The Lightness values are what we want for the halftone. With this channel in view, choose Image|Mode|Grayscale. A dialog box appears, asking if you wish to discard the other channels. Click on OK. What you see is your new and nearly ready-for-use grayscale image. The image could have been changed to grayscale directly from the RGB mode. However, a more satisfactory conversion is made via the Lab mode. With this method, the image is lighter and more open: Both are desirable qualities in view of the way dot gain eventually darkens the photo when it's printed.

14. The next step is to add a couple of adjustment layers. Use one to make some final adjustments and the other to simulate dot gain while making those adjustments.

Figure 9.27 Duplicate the image. Save the first image in Photoshop format so that it can be used later, if required. You may want to use this image later as a color file. Continue working on the duplicate.

Command+click or Ctrl+click the New Layer icon on the Layers palette. Set the adjustment layer type to Curves. Click on OK on the Curves dialog box without making any changes. Click on the Background layer to select it. Now, add another adjustment layer. Set the layer type to Levels. Click on OK on the Levels dialog box without making any changes.

15. Double-click on the word Curves on the Curves adjustment layer. The Curves dialog box opens as shown in Figure 9.28 (upper left corner). The central part of this window is composed of the curve grid. Below the curve is a small rectangle that contains what looks like a gradient interrupted by a pair of arrows. If this area on your screen doesn't have the light end of the gradient on the left, click on one of those small arrows and it changes. For this example, you want your curve window to look exactly like the figure.

16. The curve grid contains a diagonal line (this line *is the curve*, even though it isn't very curved yet). Imagine if you will that the line has been divided into a hundred small segments. The lower left end of the line represents 0 percent; the place where, as the line moves to the upper right end, the curve meets the first two crossing lines represents the 25 percent value, and so on. If you want, you can change the grid so that the crossing lines are ruled in increments of 10 percent instead of 25 percent: Option+click (Mac) or Alt+click (Windows) within the grid area (see Figure 9.28, upper right corner).

17. Place your cursor in the grid area and notice that you now have continuous readings of Input and Output to the right of the grid. Keep your eye on those readings while you

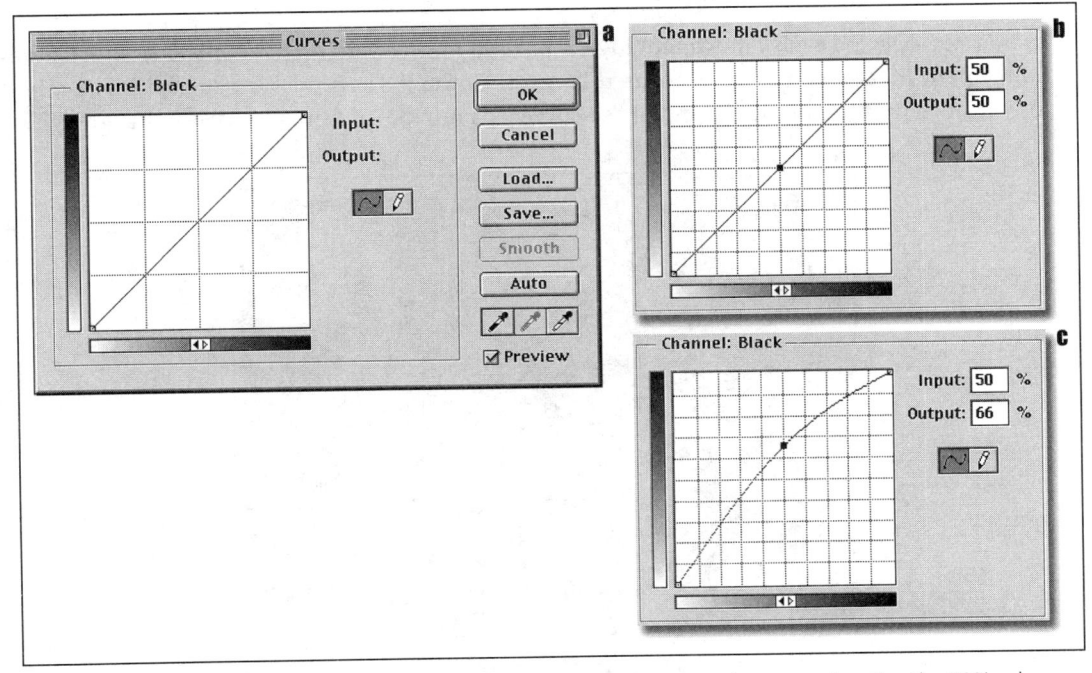

Figure 9.28 Photoshop's Curves dialog box (a). Sections (b) and (c) show the curve elevating the 50% value to 66%.

make the adjustment. Click on the intersection of the curve and the 50% lines. Drag the line upward until the Input/Output figures read 50% and 66% (see Figure 9.28, lower right corner). Click on OK. A representation of the Curve adjustment is shown in Figure 9.29.

Are you surprised? Your image is suddenly much darker. Although this isn't an absolutely accurate way to duplicate all aspects of dot gain, it's sufficient to give you an idea of how much more the image needs to be adjusted if it is to print successfully.

18. Double-click on the word Levels on the Levels adjustment layer (see Figure 9.30). Move the Input section's midtone slider to the left until the image starts looking about the way you wish to see it when it is printed. Double-check to see that your highlight dots are still at 5 percent and that your shadow dots are running about 90 to 93 percent. If they're not, use the Output Scale sliders to adjust them as described above. After you are finished, click on OK.

The image should look very good at this point, but get ready for a shock: Drag the Curves adjustment layer down to the Layer Palette trash icon. Dreadful, isn't it? You'll recall that we used the words *flat* and *washed out*? Yet this image, when the dots on the press sheet have grown by the specified percentage of midtone gain, will look very much the way it did before you trashed the Curves adjustment layer. No one who sees this simulation ever again underestimates dot gain as a significant factor in the preparation of the halftone. Note: You'll have to train yourself to delete the Curves adjustment layer before you flatten the image. If you don't, all your careful work will be wasted.

In this example, a Levels adjustment layer was used for the final adjustments. Another Curves adjustment layer could have been used instead. Figure 9.31 shows how such a curve might look. Notice that the highlight end of the curve was moved up from 0% to 5%, the 50% value

Figure 9.29 Make the darkening adjustment on the Curves adjustment layer.

Figure 9.30 On the Levels adjustment layer, move the midtone slider to the left to lighten the image. Move the slider until the picture looks close to the way you want it to appear on press.

has been pulled down to 34% (50 − 16 = 34), and the shadow end of the scale has been pulled down from 100% to 92%. The Curve controls are very powerful but—if you are new to the process—are not as simple to use as the Levels controls. Curves offer more flexibility in adjusting specific parts of the tone range, but require a little more experience. No matter which you use, the results are the same because Levels and Curves do exactly the same thing.

The adjusted image is shown in Figure 9.32. You see it here in two stages—an interesting possibility because both images have been printed and one shows itself to be the pre-adjusted photo. This has been accomplished by preparing the rear image as though it is to be printed with almost twice the actual dot gain for the page.

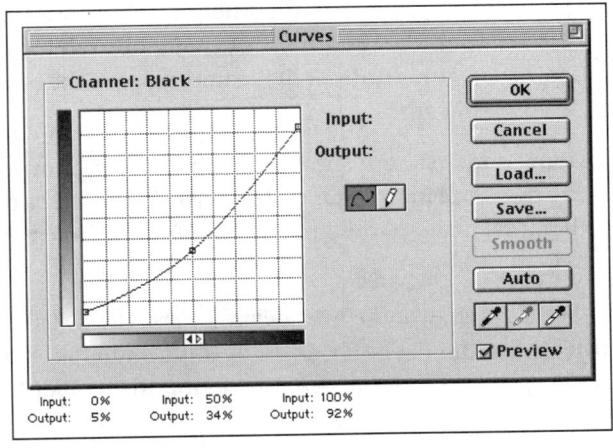

Figure 9.31 The Levels adjustment layer could have been another Curves layer adjusted with this curve.

Figure 9.32 Two versions of the halftone. The back image shows how light the image is before printing. The front image shows the same image with dot gain applied on press.

The Unsharp Mask Filter

After you have clicked on OK on the Levels controls, flattened the image, and cropped it to its final size, the adjustment of the photo is almost complete. There is one more step before it is perfect: Use the Unsharp Mask filter to artificially clarify all of the photo's details. In the process of scanning, the clear delineation of surfaces shown in a photographic image becomes blurred. Depending on the type of scanner, some of the image's details are restored by the scanner software (using Unsharp Mask). More sharpness is usually applied just before the settings for the highlight and shadow values are made, or at the final stage of the image processing. Again, the Unsharp Mask is used for this task.

Photoshop ships with four Sharpen filters: Sharpen, Sharpen More, Sharpen Edges, and Unsharp Mask. The first three are discussed in Chapter 8; the fourth filter, Unsharp Mask, is the only one you will ever need when preparing photo images for offset reproduction. The dialog box for this filter is shown in Figure 9.33.

Unsharp Mask may be the oddest name ever devised for a filter. It is intended to make the details of a photo easier to see, but the name gives the impression that it does the opposite. This filter does not really sharpen, but plays a visual trick; it finds the border between pixels that differ from each other by some threshold amount and then increases the contrast along that border. The contrast enhancement fools the eye into believing that it sees details more clearly.

> ## USING PHOTOSHOP 5'S COLOR SAMPLER TOOL
>
> You can make your adjustment tasks quite a bit easier by using the Color Sampler tool before you open the Levels or Curves controls. Click and hold on the Eyedropper tool on the Tools palette. Select the Color Sampler tool, the Eyedropper tool's alternate. With this tool, you can place up to four sample points on the image and watch them on the Info palette as you adjust the image.
>
> Move the tool onto the image and click in the place where your highlight values will be measured. A small target appears with the label "*1*". Click anywhere else on the image and another target will appear with the label "*2*". Glance at the Info palette and you'll see that it has expanded and now contains added sections that are labeled in the same way as the targets on the image. As you use the Levels or Curves, you will see that the Info palette is continuously updated for each of the targets you placed. This tool makes it very easy to keep track of your highlight and shadow values, as well as any other places in the image to which you need to pay particular attention. You'll find that this tool will save you a lot of time.

Although Unsharp Mask clarifies the image in a way that is different from what you do when you focus the optical assembly of a camera, Photoshop has no focusing mechanism. Unsharp Mask provides an excellent way to achieve the same kind of effect.

Figure 9.34 shows a set of six samples that illustrate how the settings in the filter dialog box affect the pixels in the image. Along with the enlarged views of the pixels, a small image at high resolution shows the same effects without magnification. Note that when two areas meet,

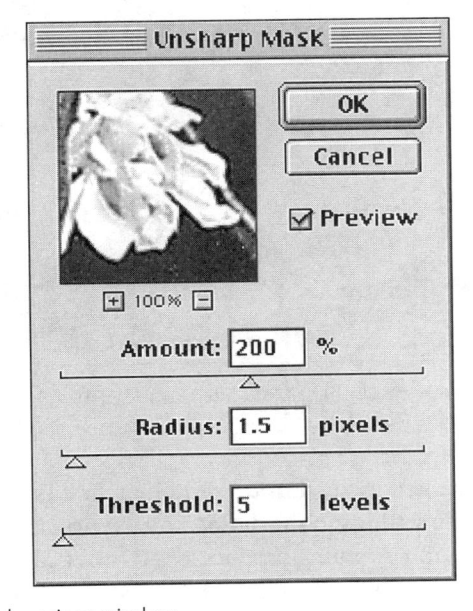

Figure 9.33   The Unsharp Mask options window.

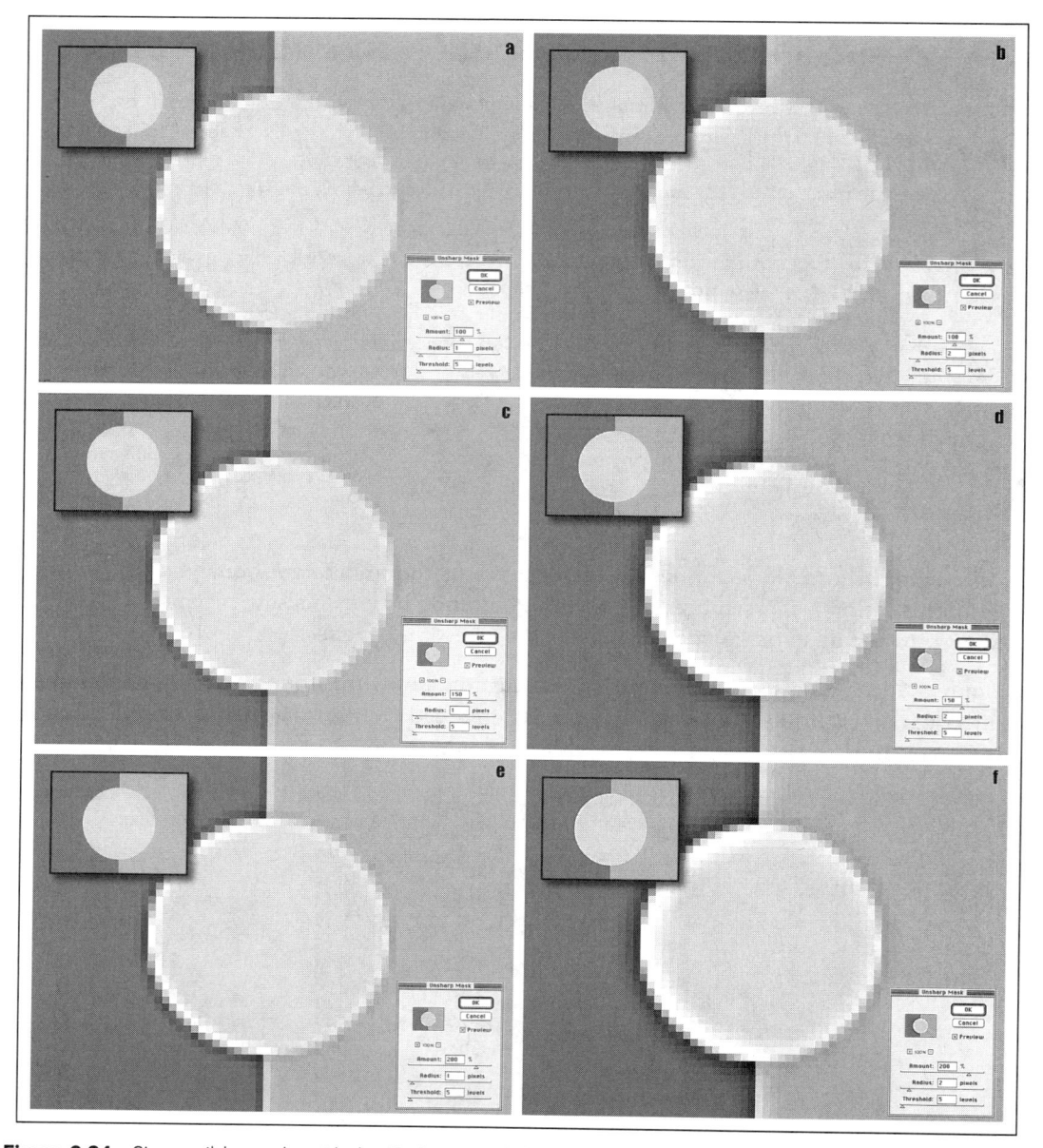

Figure 9.34 Six possible results with the Unsharp Mask filter: (*a* and *b*) 100, 1, 5 and 100, 2, 5; (*c* and *d*) 150, 1, 5 and 150, 2, 5; (*e* and *f*) 200, 1, 5 and 200, 2, 5.

the darker side of the edge is darkened and the lighter side is lightened. The way the filter is applied is governed by the settings in the dialog box. Notice, too, how the settings with larger values for both Radius and Amount produce effects that are clearly visible in the small samples. Having the results of the Unsharp Mask filter so visible is probably not a good idea. The best use of the filter results in clarity of detail that doesn't make it obvious how the clarity was achieved.

Three criteria govern the final effect of the Unsharp Mask filter:

- *Amount*—The Amount value is in the form of a percentage. This number instructs Photoshop to increase the contrast between two edges by darkening the darker pixels and lightening the lighter. Although this value is entered as a percentage, there is no straightforward calculation of a percentage between two values. This number is simply one of a set of three variables—the other two are the Radius and Threshold numbers—used for the calculation. The actual pixel values from a given percentage change if either of the other numbers is changed. The Amount range is from 1 to 500%.

- *Radius*—The Radius value sets the width of the zone along the edges in which the pixels are lightened or darkened. The Radius range is from .1 to 250 pixels.

- *Threshold*—The Threshold setting is the limiting factor for how much tonal difference there must be between two pixels before the darkening or lightening effects are applied. If the setting is, say, 5, then as the filter examines pairs of pixels, there must be at least five steps or Threshold levels between the two pixels for the filter to function. In practical terms, you can think of it this way: As the Threshold number gets larger, there are fewer areas of the image that become sharpened. The Threshold range is from 0 to 255.

With the sophistication of the algorithm used for the Unsharp Mask filter, very delicate and subtle changes can be made. Even numbers that are mathematical anomalies can be used. For example, it is possible to enter a Radius value that is a decimal fraction. (Just try to select 1.5 pixels!) Rather than thinking of the numbers in the filter dialog as concrete values, it's easier to think of them as flexible guides that aim your sharpening efforts toward the effect you wish to achieve.

Every image has slightly different requirements for sharpening. For photos intended for offset reproduction, a good procedure would be to open the filter dialog box and enter general settings of 200% for the Amount and 0-5 for the Threshold. The Radius value is dependent upon the resolution of the image. A good rule of thumb is to calculate the Radius as 1/2 of 1% of the file's resolution. For a 300 ppi file, this gives a radius value of 1.5 (300 × .005 = 1.5). Of the three settings, the Radius and Threshold values are not easily increased without producing artifacts that harm the image. Departing from the general settings given above, the values might be made smaller but seldom larger. The Amount value has the largest effect on the filter. Figure 9.35 shows a set of examples in which the Amount is changed in 25 percent increments. Note that the lower right example is the one in which the target values given here were used. Compare this specimen with the others, paying close attention to the spokes in the bicycle wheels, the tread texture on the rear wheel, and the cracks in the rocks.

When you're using the Unsharp Mask filter, pay close attention to the Preview window. You can magnify or reduce the amount of detail seen in the window to gauge the effect of the settings you've entered. Be sure to look at different areas of the image before clicking on OK.

Using Unsharp Mask On Difficult Photos

The Unsharp Mask filter, for all its power to make an image look wonderful, is a difficult filter to control in some situations. Some scans, no matter how the values are entered, seem to be very difficult. The finished photo can look blotchy or as if it were sprinkled with talc, or even

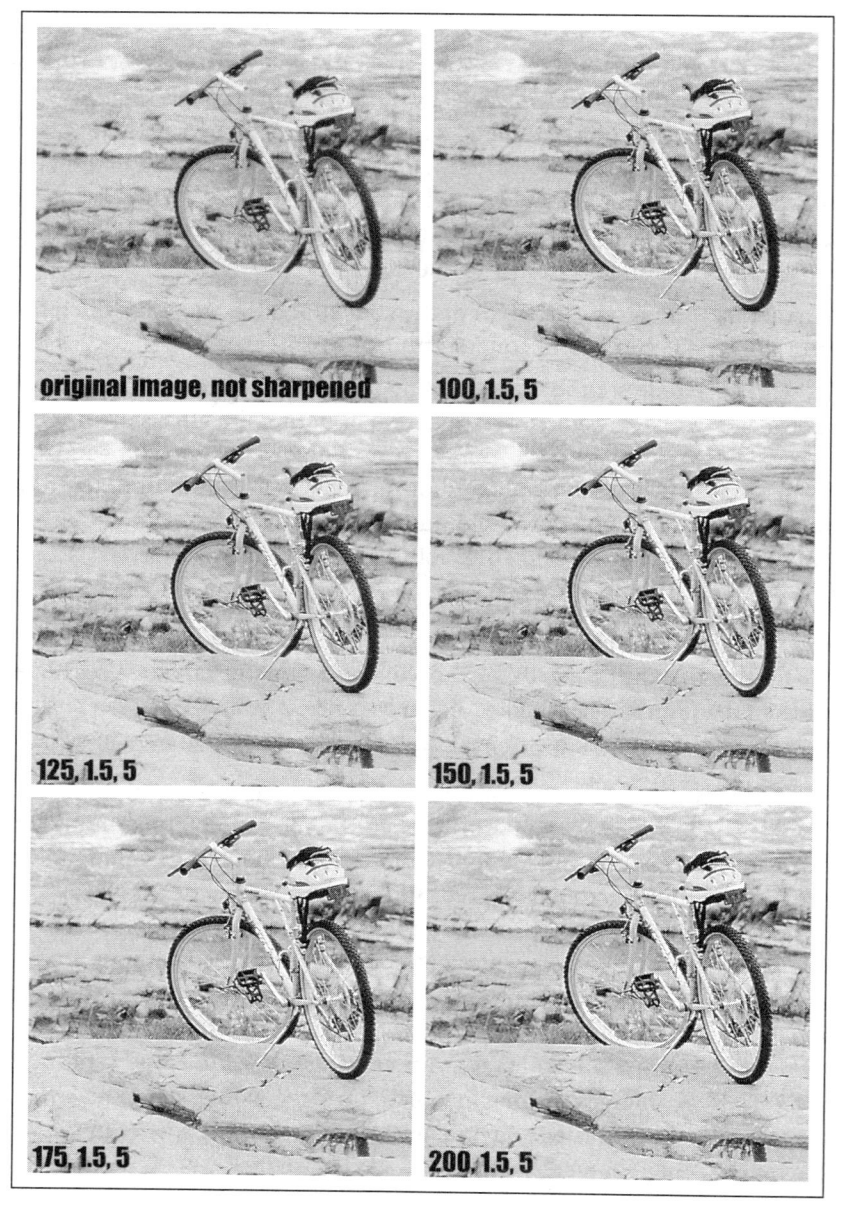

Figure 9.35 Five applications of the Unsharp Mask filter using different settings. Compare the original in the areas of the back tire tread, the wheel spokes, and the cracks in the rocks.

blurry. These problems bedevil even experienced users. Here are a couple of the problems you might encounter and some solutions that work extremely well.

Photos With Areas Of Very Fine Detail—The leaves in the upper part of Figure 9.32 are a good example of very fine detail. Sometimes this kind of detail requires that you lower the Amount setting and shrink the Radius slightly. Too much sharpening of this kind of detail is worse than no sharpening. Another example of this problem is shown in the upper part of Figure 9.36, where the bark of the tree looks as though it is coated with frost crystals. Here's a very fast way to rescue the situation *after* the photo has been sharpened (the rescued image is shown in the lower part of the figure).

First, if you use this technique, push the original sharpening Amount up to between 300% and 400%. This seems, at first, to make the problem worse, but it's only temporary. On the Layers palette, drag the Background layer onto the New Layer icon. With the new layer selected, choose Filter|Blur|Gaussian Blur. Make the radius of the blur the same as the Unsharp Mask radius value. Click on OK. Change the Opacity of the layer to 40% or 50%. Flatten the image. You have now retained the sharpening effect of the Unsharp Mask filter and eliminated the frost artifacts on the tree's bark.

If you would like to try out this technique, open the file RGB2GS2.PSD from the Chapter 9 Practice Files folder on this book's CD-ROM. The image is the same as shown in Figure 9.36.

Film Granularity—All film exhibits some degree of graininess. Only when the image is enlarged by a substantial amount does the problem become serious. When the amount of enlargement is great, the *Unsharp Mask filter usually accentuates the noise produced by the film.* The noise produces an image that appears to be in poorer focus than the original. Of particular concern are scanned images originating from fast, low-light 35mm film.

Another big problem source is a photo printed on textured, anti-glare paper. If you've spent much time running a scanner, you'll probably loathe anti-glare photo print paper. It may not hold fingerprints, and it may be easier to view, but it is awful to scan. That's an important point to keep in mind if you are going to have your own photography processed for eventual press reproduction. Always ask for glossy-surfaced photo prints. If your photo lab cannot give them to you, find another photo lab.

If you would like to try out the following technique, open the file RGB2GS3.PSD from the Chapter 9 Practice Files folder on this book's CD-ROM. The image is the same as shown in Figure 9.26. Then follow these steps:

1. Eliminating Unsharp Mask's exaggeration of film grain requires a bit of preplanning. During the adjustment of the RGB image, perform all the steps through the conversion of the image from Lab mode to Grayscale. (It will be good practice.) The pre-adjusted grayscale image is shown in Figure 9.37.

2. Before proceeding, choose Color Range from the Select menu. When the Color Range dialog has opened, change the pop-up at the top so that it reads Shadows. Click on OK. Make a new channel out of this selection (click on the second icon from the left on the bottom of the Channels palette). The new channel is listed on the Channels palette as Alpha 2, but you won't really need it. It's simply good practice to save these intermediary steps, so that you can back up any time you want. The appearance of this new channel is shown in Figure 9.38.

Figure 9.36 The Unsharp Mask filter can give a frosted look to some kinds of surface textures (upper image). The Layers technique described in the text shows how the effect can be modified after the photo has been sharpened too much.

3. With the selection still active, choose Feather from the Select menu. Enter a Feather value that's equal to about 2 percent of your file's resolution. (For a 300 ppi file, enter "6"—300 × .02 = 6.) Save this selection as a new channel. The appearance of the new channel (which is listed as Alpha 3) is shown in Figure 9.39.

4. Forget about the new channels for the time being, and continue with the adjustments to the grayscale image. When the adjustments for press conditions are finished, the

Figure 9.37 Image before press adjustments with noticeable film grain.

Figure 9.38 After selecting the shadow tones (Select|Color Range), save the selection to a new channel.

image looks similar to the photo in Figure 9.40. Running the Unsharp Mask filter on the image produces the effects shown in Figure 9.41 (full view) and Figure 9.42 (enlarged detail). The detail shows how the filter increases the amount of noise in the image that produces almost a mezzotint effect. Under some circumstances, this effect might be desirable, but you may not want such a prominent texture in day-to-day use. If you execute the filter and spot this kind of problem, press **Command+Z** (Mac) or **Ctrl+Z** (Windows) to undo the filter.

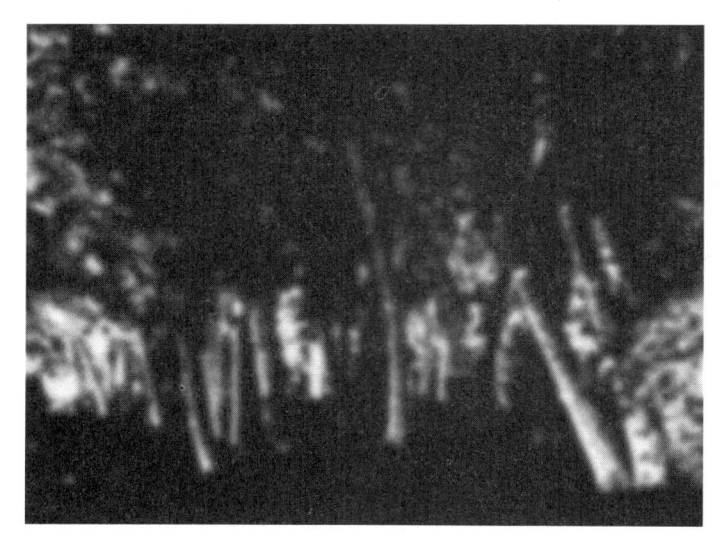

Figure 9.39 Feather the selection and save as a new channel. You can also use the Gaussian Blur filter on the first of the saved channels. Use a blur radius calculated in the same way as the Feather value in Step 3.

Figure 9.40 The image after it has been adjusted for press.

5. Use the Channels palette to turn Channel Alpha 3 into an active selection—Command+click or Ctrl+click on the channel's thumbnail. Press Command+J or Ctrl+J to change the selection into an independent layer. Choose Filter|Unsharp Mask and make the settings for this layer 400%, 1.5, and 5. Change the Opacity of this layer to somewhere between 40% and 60%. 50% should work fairly well. Use whatever figure

Figure 9.41 Sharpening in the normal way gives this noise-textured result.

Figure 9.42 Enlarged detail of Figure 9.41.

is needed to give the effect of the sharpening and to minimize the amount of visible noise. The appearance of the image after sharpening only the shadow values is shown in Figures 9.43 (full view) and 9.44 (enlarged detail).

6. Next, let's sharpen the midtones and highlights. Click on the Background layer to select it. Make Channel #3 active again. Choose Select|Inverse. Press Command+J or Ctrl+J to change the selection into an independent layer. The appearance of this layer—

Figure 9.43 Select the feathered shadow values and make them into a new layer. Heavily sharpen this layer. Change the Opacity to about 50%. Notice how much clearer this image is than Figure 9.40.

Figure 9.44 Enlarged detail of Figure 9.43.

with the other two layers hidden—is shown in Figure 9.45. Execute the Unsharp Mask filter on this layer with settings of 100%, 1, and 5. The full-view image, with all channels showing, is shown in Figure 9.46. The enlarged detail is shown in Figure 9.47.

Understanding And Customizing The Levels Controls

You used the Levels controls manually by moving both the Input and Output scale sliders while preparing a halftone for printing. It is useful, now, to take a look at more of the features of the

PHOTOSHOP PREPRESS   **553**

Figure 9.45 Select just the midtones and highlights (the inverse of the feathered shadow channel). Make the selection into a layer. Use the Unsharp Mask filter with lighter settings.

Figure 9.46 Flatten the image. The final sharpened photo is much clearer than the original, but without the noise of an all-over sharpening with a single set of values.

Level dialog box. You can use some of them to cut down on the amount of time it takes to do normal production tasks.

The Levels dialog box is shown in Figure 9.48. The central part of the image shows what appears to be a graphic representation of data. This central window contains what is known as a *histogram*. It is easiest to simply think of the histogram as a bar graph. The set of pixel values is arranged left to right from darkest to lightest. Each vertical row of pixels indicates the relative

Figure 9.47 Enlarged detail of Figure 9.46.

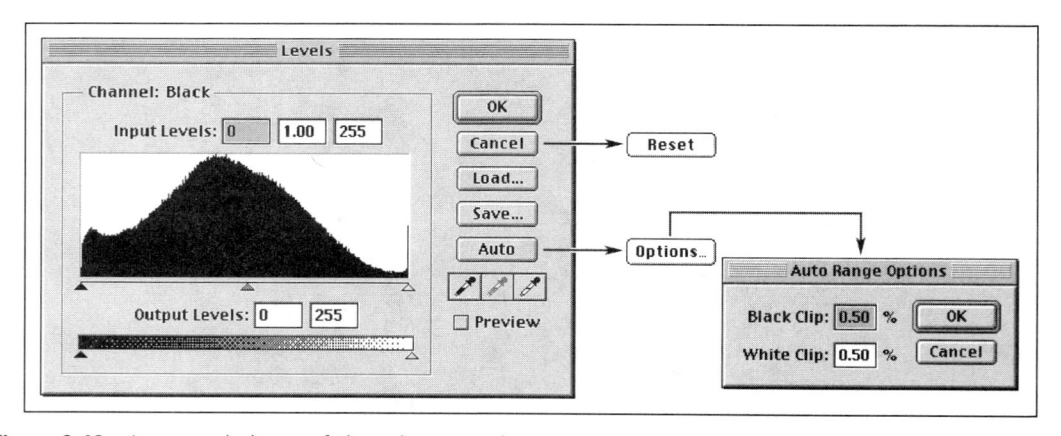

Figure 9.48 An expanded view of Photoshop's Levels controls.

quantity of pixels of a given brightness value. In some cases, you'll see that the histogram has very little data in some places on the scale. Such histograms are an indication that a full range of values is not present in the image and that it might be necessary to discard the image in favor of a new scan or to discard it completely. Ideally, a satisfactory histogram should have a full range of values from one end of the scale to the other.

The two sliders on each end of the Levels Input scale point to the extremes of the tone value scale. The shadow slider always points toward the 0 or darkest value—the print equivalent is 100 percent black—whereas the highlight slider always points toward the lightest value, 255, which is the print equivalent of 0 percent black.

If the highlight slider in Figure 9.48 is moved some distance to the left, it still points to value 255. All the values to the right of the slider after the move become the same maximum bright-

THRESHOLD MODE FOR WINDOWS USERS

The following is a workaround that you can use if your video board does not support the threshold method from within the Levels dialog box. Using this method means that your work will involve a couple of extra steps, but it will give you the same results achieved in the instruction for processing a halftone within the Levels controls.

1. Have a notepad and pen ready.
2. Open the RGB photo to be adjusted.
3. Press Ctrl+1. The image changes to a view of the Red channel.
4. Choose Image|Adjust|Threshold. This command opens the Threshold dialog box. Be sure that the Preview option is checked.
5. Move the slider to the far left of the slider bar and the image becomes completely white. Move the slider gradually to the right until the desired level of shadow detail begins to show as black areas on the image. Write down the number displayed in the Controls box.
6. Move the slider to the far right of the slider bar and the image becomes completely black. Move the slider gradually to the left until the desired level of highlight detail begins to show as white areas on the image. Write down the number displayed in the Controls box. Be sure to label the two numbers you've written down as Red. Click on the Cancel button.
7. Press Ctrl+2. The image changes to a view of the Green channel. Follow Steps 4 through 6. Make sure that you label the two numbers you've written down as Green. Click on the Cancel button.
8. Press Ctrl+3. The image changes to a view of the Blue channel. Follow Steps 4 through 6 above. Be sure to label the two numbers you've written down as Blue. Click on the Cancel button.
9. Press Ctrl+~ to return to the full-color view of the image. Open the Levels dialog box (Ctrl+L). Press Ctrl+1 and enter the first Red value. Press the Tab key twice and enter the second Red value. Press Ctrl+2 and enter the first Green value. Press the Tab key twice and enter the second Green value. Press Ctrl+3 and enter the first Blue value. Press the Tab key twice and enter the second Blue value. Enter Ctrl+~ and adjust the midtones slider of the input scale.
10. Click on OK to complete the adjustment.

ness value as the vertical row of pixels to which the slider points. The same thing happens—with inverse values—with the slider at the other end of the scale. If you click on the OK button when just these two sliders have been moved, and then reopen the Levels controls, you see a different histogram: The two sliders have moved back to the ends of the scale. All the values between the sliders at the time you clicked on OK have now distributed themselves evenly across the entire scale. It's obvious that there are now fewer than 256 values between the two endpoints. The new histogram reflects this by exhibiting gaps in the range of tones. These are seen as vertical lines containing no black pixels.

Sometimes a histogram contains no pixels at either or both ends of the Input scale, as seen in the three figures beginning with Figure 9.49. In the first figure, a black-to-white gradient is about to be drawn so that its endpoints are beyond the boundaries of the window. When the gradient is completed (see Figure 9.50), the range of values within the image window falls between 94 percent and 7 percent. The histogram at the bottom of the figure shows gaps at both ends of the Input scale. Figure 9.51 shows the result of moving the sliders in so that they point to the end values of what is actually present in the image. After you click on OK and reopen the Levels dialog box (see Figure 9.51), the range of values in the image falls between 100 and 0 percent. Notice the small gaps in the histogram. As the original values spread out, the missing 6 percent on the shadow end of the scale and the missing 6 percent on the high-

Figure 9.49 Draw a black-to-white gradient beginning and ending outside the image window.

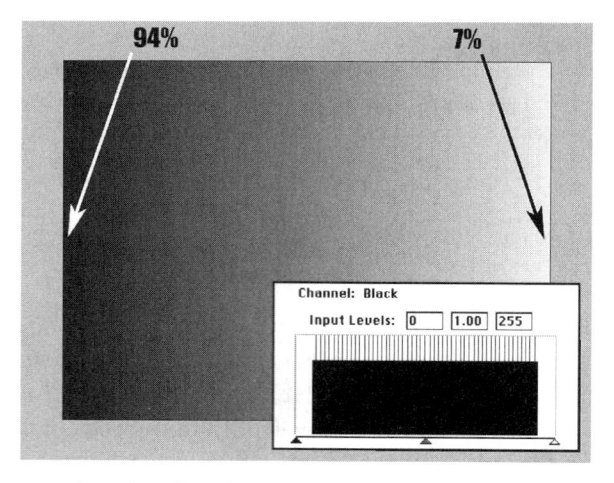

Figure 9.50 The window contains values from 94 percent to 7 percent. Note the missing values on each end of the histogram.

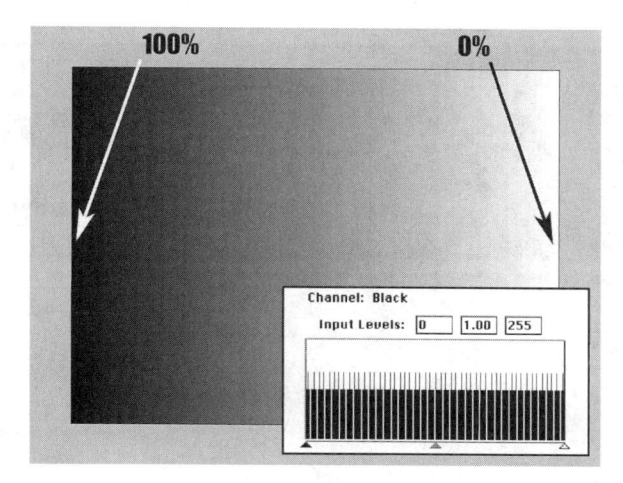

Figure 9.51 Move each end slider in to where the real values begin, and click on OK. The new histogram shows all of the previous values redistributed over the entire range and with missing-value gaps uniformly distributed.

light end of the scale have been uniformly distributed across the whole value range. There are still 12 percent missing values, but they no longer are visible in the image. You can get away with this kind of manipulation simply because you are working with 256 values instead of 100. Because each missing value is considerably less than 1 percent, the human eye cannot detect that it is missing from the gradient.

The center slider on the Input slider points to the midtone—50 percent—values in the image. As either of the end sliders is moved, the midtone slider maintains its position exactly halfway between the two. Remembering the way the two end sliders compress and redistribute brightness data, try to imagine that the midtone slider can do the same thing if it is moved manually. Moved to the left, it forces values originally above 50 percent to be below that value and lightens the image. This leaves fewer values between 50 and 100 percent and results in gaps in the new histogram between 50 and 100 percent. Figure 9.52 shows how this happens. The original gradient with its Levels histogram is at the top. The end sliders have been moved to point to the first available real value. In the middle, the original values have been rearranged and the midtone slider has been moved so that its reading is 1.40. In the lower part of the figure, the resulting histogram shows gaps in the dark end of the range but an almost-complete set of values on the light end. This might seem to be harmful to the overall image until you remember a couple of points. First, the lighter part of the image is the part that we see most easily. It should have, therefore, more detail than the dark part. Second, as the image gets darker, dot gain acts to fill in some of the gaps and to restore most of the balance lost in the preparation of the image for printing. Gaps in the histogram need to be—at least in the darker half of the tone range—at least three to five missing values wide before they become visible as posterization artifacts. A heavily granular texture is the usual look of these posterization artifacts in the printed piece.

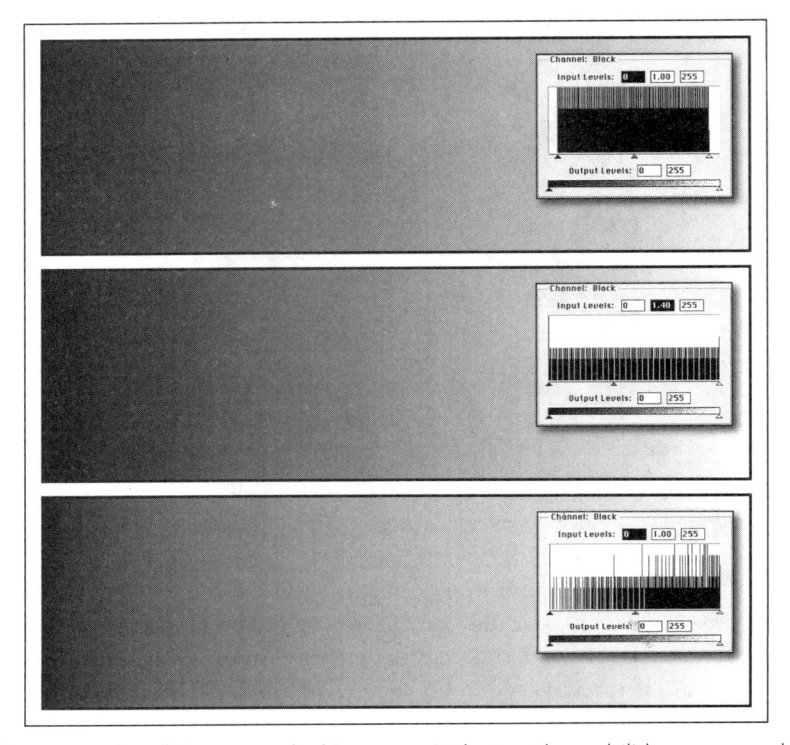

Figure 9.52 Three examples of changes to the histogram. At the top, the end sliders are moved in. In the center, the range of values is redistributed across the whole range. At the bottom, a move of the midtone slider to the left concentrates values on the highlight end of the scale and leaves gaps in the shadow end.

The two Output sliders are mostly used after the input sliders have done their work. By moving either of them, you are able to arbitrarily limit the length of the tone range set up by the Input controls. If the highlight slider is moved to the left, the lightest values are darkened. If the shadow slider is moved to the right, the darkest values are made lighter. We discussed using the Output sliders earlier: You use them to slightly darken the extreme highlight values and to lighten the darkest tonal values. Moving either of the Output sliders has the effect of causing an empty area—no values present—on the relevant ends of the histogram.

At the right of the Levels controls are a number of buttons and sampling eyedropper tools. Two of the buttons have alternate versions that appear if the Option key or the Alt key is pressed. The Cancel button becomes Reset. When Reset is clicked, the entire dialog box reverts to the way it was when first opened.

Load and Save are buttons that allow you to preserve the state of the dialog box by saving its settings as a named file. At some later time, the Load button will allow you to retrieve the Saved settings for use on the same or a similar image.

The Auto button—and its alternate Options button—and the Eyedropper tools are all bound together. When the Auto button is clicked (and the Photoshop defaults are in place), Photoshop examines all of the pixels in the image. It moves the highlight Input slider to point to the lightest value present and the shadow Input slider to the darkest value. Clicking on the Auto button is exactly the same as choosing Image|Adjust|Auto Levels. The advantage to the latter is that it can be done without opening the Levels controls.

The separate Auto Range Options dialog box allows some customization as to how the Auto button goes about selecting endpoint values. By specifying the amount of Black Clip and White Clip, you instruct Photoshop to ignore values on the extreme ends of the value scale when it sets the two Input sliders.

For you to understand why this is desirable, it's necessary to explain that print technicians classify highlight values in two categories. The first is the *specular* highlight; the second is the *printing* highlight. A specular highlight is a bright spot on the image caused by reflection from a very intense light source. Figure 9.53 shows examples of specular highlights in the flash of sunlight on the top fronts of the headlight chrome and on top of the car. Specular highlights are often areas that are more-or-less distinct. They are so light that they do not look realistic if a printing dot tone is added to them. Printing highlights, in contrast to specular highlights, always have a dot. The dot might be the smallest dot that will hold on press, but a dot is there.

The difference between these two kinds of highlights is relevant to the Auto button's options. When you set a percentage in the White Clip data entry box, Photoshop is instructed to ignore

Figure 9.53 Printing highlights and specular highlights. The former always have a dot, the latter never do.

some percentage of highlight values on the far right end of the scale. It then locates the highlight slider at the first value to the left of the designated percentage. There are 256 values on the scale. Using the default setting of .5% (1/2 of 1 percent), Photoshop moves the slider to the first available value below 254. Because we are considering minimum non-specular (printable) highlight dots of 5 percent in this discussion, a more useful setting would be 4% for the white clip.

The Black Clip option works in much the same way, but on the other end of the Input scale. With percentages entered in the range of 5 to 7 percent, the shadow slider moves to the first value to the right of the assigned percentage.

The Levels dialog's eyedropper tools allow you to choose values from the image to be the lightest and darkest values by simply clicking where you wish. Here's how it would work. Close the Levels dialog and press I to select the Eyedropper tool. Set the options for the tool to 3 By 3 Sample. Open the Levels dialog box. Click on the rightmost eyedropper. Move the cursor out into the image window and find a very light area. Click once. Now, select the leftmost eyedropper. Move the cursor into the image window and choose a very dark area. Click once. (There is a third eyedropper for the midtones, but it is available for use only when the image is in RGB or CMYK mode.) After you click on the OK button and reopen the Levels, you can see that Photoshop readjusts the histogram so the value range is proportionate to the arbitrary end points you set with the eyedroppers.

You can, if you wish, specify that the eyedropper tools target specific tone values. To do this:

1. First, double-click on the white eyedropper in the Levels dialog box. The Photoshop Color Picker appears.

2. Enter "0", "0", "0", and "5" in the data entry boxes for CMYK color. Click on OK. Note that these values are appropriate only for grayscale work. For color work, you need to enter different values. A more complete explanation is given in Chapter 10.

3. Double-click on the dark eyedropper. When the Color Picker opens, make the CMYK values 0, 0, 0, and 95. Click on OK.

4. Select the white eyedropper and move it out into the window. Keep your eyes on the Info palette as you move the cursor so that you can locate the lightest value you wish to maintain a dot. Click once. All pixels lighter than the pixel on which you click become specular white.

5. Switch to the black eyedropper. Move the cursor into the window and move it around until you identify your darkest printable value. Click once.

You might think that having set the values to, say, 5% and 95%, your endpoints are instantly equal to those values. But life—and Photoshop—is not so simple. If you click on pixels with values of 0% and 100%, your range of values falls between 3% and 84% (see Figure 9.54, center). If you click on values of 5% and 95%, your range falls between 0% and 88%. The numbers don't seem to make sense until you recall the setting of the dot gain percentage in the File|Color Settings|CMYK Setup dialog box. Photoshop keeps this piece of information in mind and figures it into the calculation so you don't have to worry about it. Even if the numbers don't make a lot of sense, you'll find the whole process extremely workable.

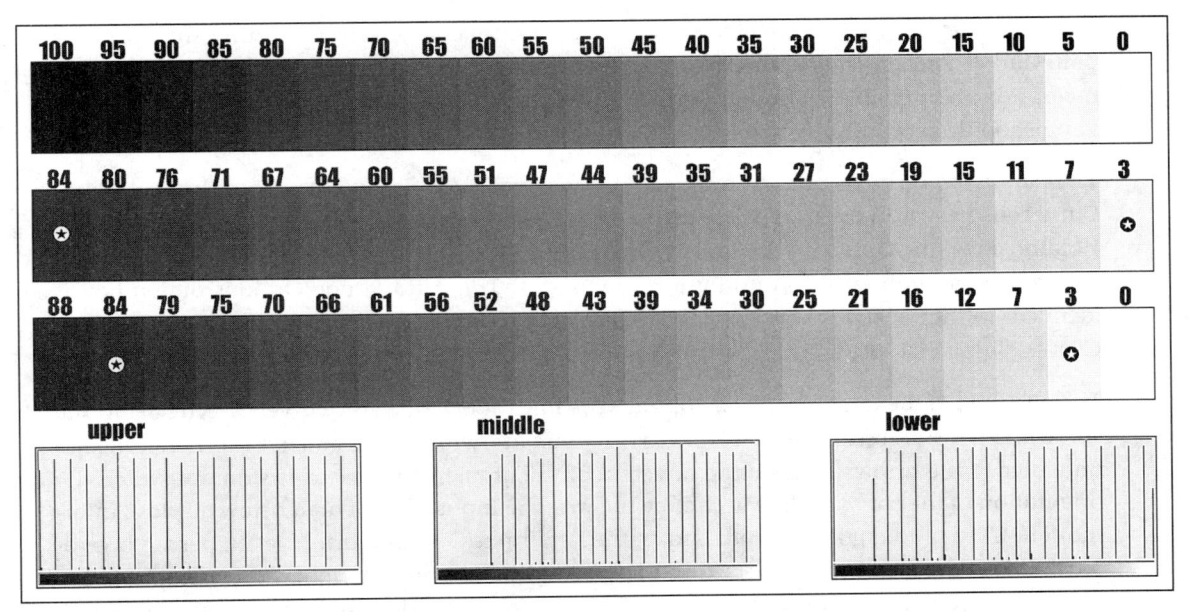

Figure 9.54 With the Eyedropper Auto Range options set, clicking on different values gives different results.

Keep in mind that you have to be pretty careful where you click. Figure 9.54 shows how different the values can be. At the top is the original set of 21 values (histogram at lower left). In the middle, the absolute white and black values—circles with small stars inside—have been clicked (histogram bottom center). Notice that clicking on the white has eliminated all specular highlights. In the lower example, clicking on the values identical to those set by choosing targeted values with the Color Picker maintains the specular highlights and allows some dense areas of black beyond the target values.

Here's a tip: After you have set values to the eyedroppers, you don't really have to search your image for appropriate pixels. Instead, click on the Auto button. The values set for the eyedroppers become the controlling values for the Auto Levels command box. Even if you enter other—and different—values in the Auto Range Options dialog, the eyedropper tools values take precedence.

Moving the sliders manually and employing Threshold mode, the way it was done in the previous section on processing a halftone for printing, is the principal method for overriding a set of specific values and forcing the data within the image into more radical shifts. It is also the slowest of the ways to use the Levels controls. Even so, if you have the time, it's the best way to teach yourself how the distribution and redistribution of linear data really works. Ultimately, you'll want to graduate to using Curves. Curves can accomplish anything the Levels can. They also do a great deal more. Read on for a more thorough introduction to using Curves.

Understanding And Customizing Curves

Photoshop users seem to divide themselves into two groups: those who use Curves, and those who use Levels. Rarely do you find a user who uses both as circumstances dictate, and rarely do you find users who aren't a bit smug about the superiority of their choice. The whole *Curves are* better than Levels or Levels are better than Curves controversy is extraordinarily silly. Because both Curves and Levels are powerful tools that produce nearly the same results using different metaphors, it's possible for you to develop an appreciation for both and to use either as your Photoshop tasks require.

The Curves dialog box—press Command+M (Mac) or Ctrl+M (Windows), choose Image|Adjust| Curves—is shown in Figure 9.55. Some of its features are the same as for the Levels controls: Holding down the Option or the Alt key changes the Cancel button to Reset, and holding down the same key changes the Auto button to Options. The Auto Range Options dialog box is identical to that of the Levels controls. If new settings are entered within either the Levels or Curves dialog box, the identical settings will be found in the other.

The grid area of the Curves controls contains the line that is called the curve. Directly below the curve grid is a small strip—which looks like a gradient—with two arrows in the center. Clicking on either of the arrows reverses the direction of the gradient. These arrows do not switch the orientation of the curve grid; they change the way the Input/Output area below displays information. If the gradient has its light end on the left, Input/Output is displayed in percentages of black ink. If the gradient is reversed so that the light end is on the right, Input/Output is displayed in RGB values ranging from 0 to 255. In the following discussion of Curves, we assume that the curve is set to give readings in ink percentages. As you read and form a basic understanding of how Curves work, try to keep in mind that any reference to moving a point on the curve applies only to ink. In general terms, the same movement of curve points applied to RGB values will be in the direction opposite of what you'll see in this text.

Whenever the Curves controls are summoned, the curve shows itself as a straight line running from lower left to upper right (see Figure 9.56). The initial position of the line contains what is called the Input data. Lighter values are on the lower left, darker on the upper right. As the line is moved and changed, the new values are called Output data.

The grid is in two dimensions. Moving any point on the line toward the top of the grid causes the value to become darker, and moving any point toward the bottom makes the value become

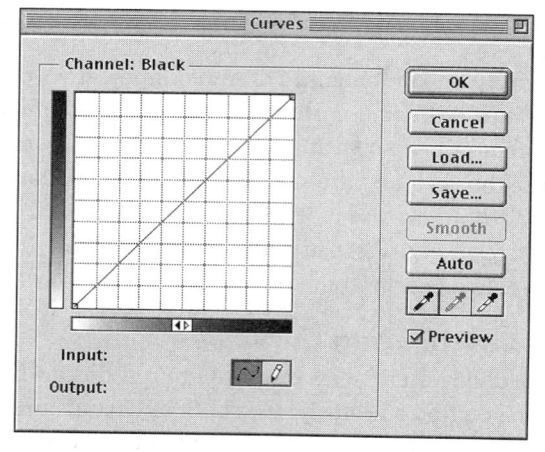

Figure 9.55 Photoshop's Curves dialog box.

lighter. Figure 9.57 shows what happens when the two endpoints of the curve are moved as far as possible up or down: black becomes white, white becomes black. The values in the image become the inverse of the originals, and the image becomes a negative of itself. You can see that the histograms of Figures 9.56 and 9.57 are mirror images of each other.

The movement of the curve's endpoints toward either of the center axes provides a good deal of insight into the mechanics of using these controls. Figure 9.58 shows that as the endpoints are moved toward the horizontal center, the image loses its contrast and becomes flatter. This is accomplished by pushing all of the available data to the center portion of the histogram. Figure 9.59 shows that as the curve exactly matches the center horizontal axis, all values become 50 percent black. The histogram for this figure shows that all of the data has been pushed to the center and reduced to a single value.

Figure 9.56 The curve line, as the dialog box is first opened, represents the set of Input values.

Figure 9.57 The inverse curve makes the image a negative.

Figure 9.58 Moving the ends of the curve toward the center horizontal axis decreases the image's contrast.

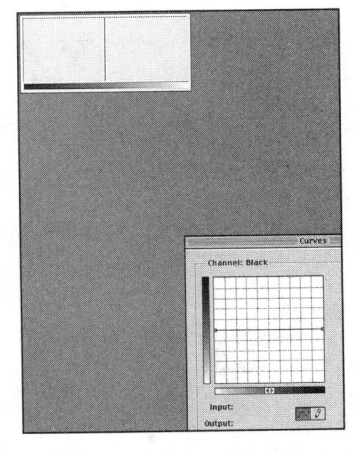

Figure 9.59 When the curve has flat-lined, the number of values has decreased to one. Lack of contrast just doesn't get any worse than this!

Moving the curve toward the vertical center axis increases the contrast of the image. This is accomplished by distributing fewer and fewer values across the entire histogram scale (see Figure 9.60). Pushed to the limit, the image is left with only five values, each of them equally spaced across the histogram scale (see Figure 9.61). Note that it's impossible to make the curve exactly align with the vertical axis.

With the default curve tool (the leftmost tool, located below the curve grid), you can click anywhere on the line of the curve to establish a new point. The new point can be moved up or down as desired. Clicking on the center of the line allows you to influence the midtone values. Pushing the point upward darkens the midtones (see Figure 9.62), whereas pushing it downward lightens the midtones (see Figure 9.63). As a single point of the curve is moved, the line stretches to accommodate the movement. Straight lines cannot be formed with this curve tool.

Figure 9.60 Moving the curve's endpoints toward the center vertical axis increases the image's contrast.

Figure 9.61 Moved as close to the vertical center as possible, the curve leaves the image with only five values.

Figure 9.62 Moving a point on the curve upward moves it to a darker value.

Figure 9.63 Moving a point on the curve downward moves it to a lighter value.

Because the line stays, no matter how adjusted, as a series of curves, values that are contiguous to the point being moved keep their proximity. In this way, uniform gradations of tone are preserved. Figure 9.64 shows a curve with five adjusted points. The highlight point (0%) has been drawn up to the 5% level, the 25% point has been dragged slightly down, 50% has been moved up so that its Input/Output values are the same, the 75% point has been raised, and the 100% has been dragged down to 95%. If you compare this figure with the original image (see Figure 9.56), you can see that the overall image is a bit lighter. The low-value tones (0% to 30%) have fewer contrasts, as do the values ranging from 70% to 95%. The overall contrast of the image is greater than the original's because the curve segment between 25% and 75% is steeper than the original's.

The other tool used to manipulate the curve is the Pencil tool. With the Pencil tool, you can draw arbitrary lines containing abrupt changes of direction (see Figure 9.65). Some of the most exciting textural effects Photoshop is capable of producing are based on the use of such arbitrary curves. For experimental purposes, the Pencil tool can be used to calculate the basic strategy for the curve. The Smooth button, which is not available for use unless the Pencil tool is active, does exactly what its name suggests: It evens out the drawn pencil lines and makes them into smooth curves. Repeatedly pressing the Smooth button eventually straightens the arbitrary curve into a straight line. After you've drawn with the Pencil tool, you can also smooth out the curve by changing back to the default curve tool (see Figure 9.66).

The Curve dialog box is also capable of a wonderfully useful display that assists you in understanding which pixels are affected by changes in the curve. Move the cursor out into the image window. Click and hold the mouse button. The placement of the value on which you clicked appears on the line of the curve as a small black circle (see Figure 9.67).

If you combine this special capability of the Curves with the Color Sampler tool (the Eyedropper alternate), you have an easy way to keep track of different values, as well as to move points that correspond to those values. The combination makes using Curves unbelievably powerful.

Figure 9.64 A compound curve here lightens the highlights, increases the contrast in the midtones, and darkens the shadows.

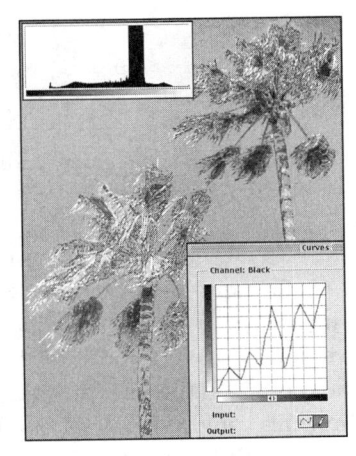

Figure 9.65 An arbitrary curve drawn with the Pencil tool. The values in the image will map oddly and will posterize in interesting ways.

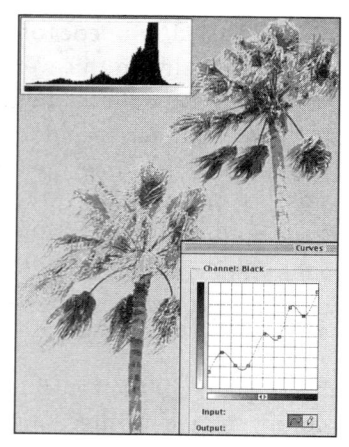

Figure 9.66 Another arbitrary curve after being subjected to the Smooth command. The oddly mapped values are still present, but there is little posterization.

Figure 9.67 Click and hold in the image window. A small circle appears on the curve grid to show you the location of the value.

As you have seen, moving a single point on the curve line causes the entire line to distort. Figure 9.68, for example, shows the 65% value pulled down to read 50%. Notice that the rest of the line has also moved from the diagonal. You may, sometimes, want to move a small part of the curve and to leave the rest of the line in its original shape. You can do this by adding additional points on the line; this has the effect of locking the line to those points. Figure 9.69 shows how this could work. A set of points has been placed at 10 percent intervals above and below the point that is to be moved (again, 65% moved down to 50%). As you can see, there is a very small amount of distortion in the curve segment adjoining the distorted segment and

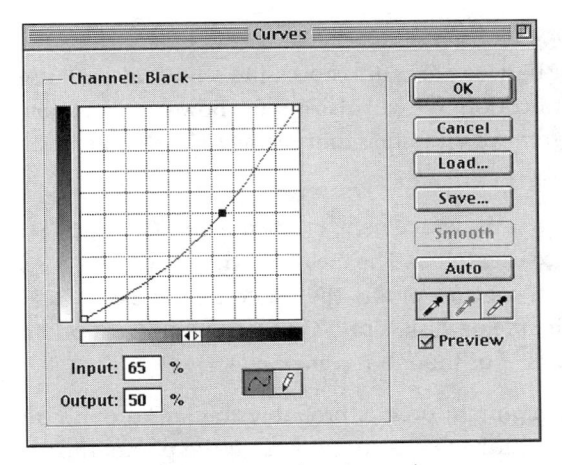

Figure 9.68 Moving a single point on the curve causes the entire line to distort. This is usually a helpful feature because it keeps the tone range of the image smooth and contiguous.

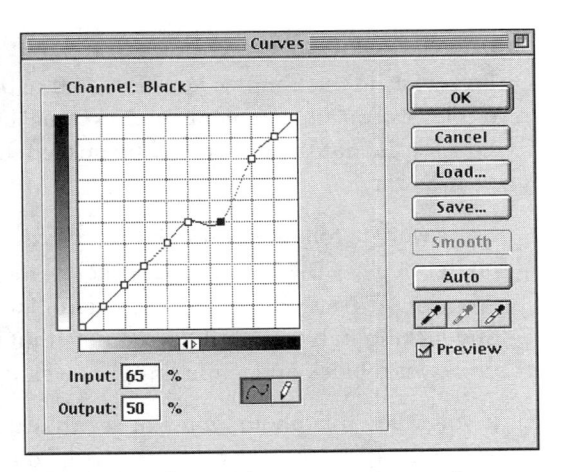

Figure 9.69 If you wish to move only a small segment of the curve, lock the rest of the line into place by adding a series of points to serve as anchors.

none at all farther away from it. You can add up to 14 new points (in addition to the two end points) to the curve line.

A new feature of Photoshop 5 is the treatment of points added to the curve as selected or not selected. Selected points are small, solid black squares. Unselected points are hollow squares. This may seem a very fine point, but this feature allows you to select more than one point by clicking on them with the Shift key held down. Once selected, these points can be moved as a group. You can drag on them with the cursor, or you can move them in 1-percent increments using the arrow keys. All four of the arrow keys can be used to move any point or combination of points in any direction. Figure 9.70 shows an example where two non-contiguous points are being moved downward together. The point in the center remains stationary because it is not selected.

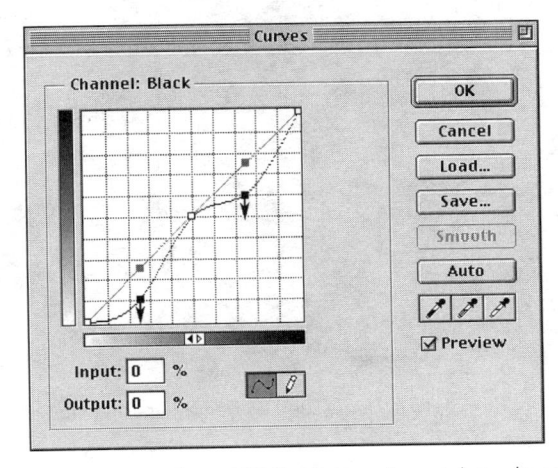

Figure 9.70 More than one point can be selected (Shift+click) and moved simultaneously. Here, two points are being moved downward, while the point in the center remains anchored.

Using Color Scans To Prepare Grayscale Files

Previously in this chapter, you learned that the best way to begin processing a halftone is to use a color scan. This statement requires some justification. We will also discuss how you can know how far the data in a scan can be pushed to retrieve an image that seems to be of hopelessly poor quality.

If you want to follow along with this exercise as it is presented here, locate the file RGB2GS4.PSD on this book's CD-ROM in the Chapter 9 Practice Files folder. The file is shown in Figure 9.71. As you can see from the image, the overall lack of contrast makes the photo dull, lifeless, dark, and lacking in hard detail. Please note that the file on disk is an RGB file. The original photo print was a black and white print but was scanned as though it were in color.

If you study this photo, you can see that the highlight area is probably the background on which the garment was photographed. You can make the assumption that the photographer did not originally photograph this sweater on a medium-gray background, but on a color that was probably very light, or even white. When adjusting for the highlights in each channel, you want to bleach out this area and look for your highlights within the object being photographed.

To prepare the file, follow these steps:

1. First, choose Image|Duplicate. Use the duplicate to work through the following set of instructions.

2. Open the Levels controls and switch to the Red channel. Use Threshold mode to move the Input scale highlight slider. Wash out the background and keep moving the slider until highlights begin to show up in the sweater (see Figure 9.72).

3. Use Threshold mode to locate the shadows of the Red channel (see Figure 9.73).

Figure 9.71 A poor-contrast photograph, to be rescued by treating it as a color image.

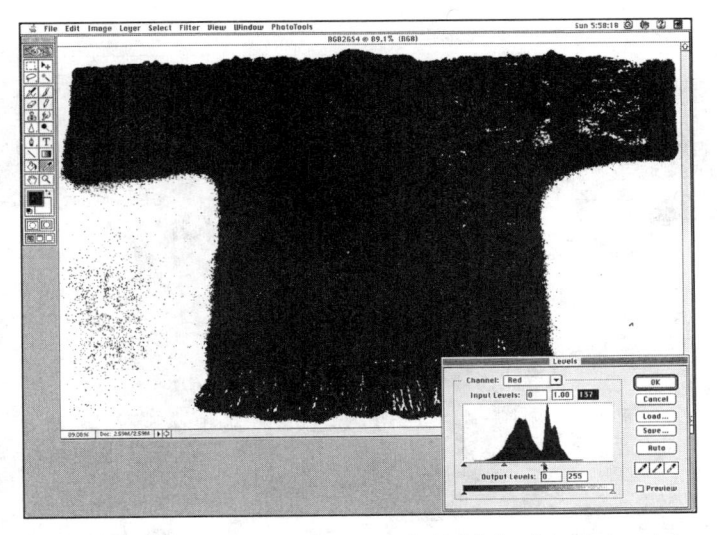

Figure 9.72 Use Threshold mode (the Red channel Input scale highlight slider) in Levels to wash out the background and locate highlights within the sweater.

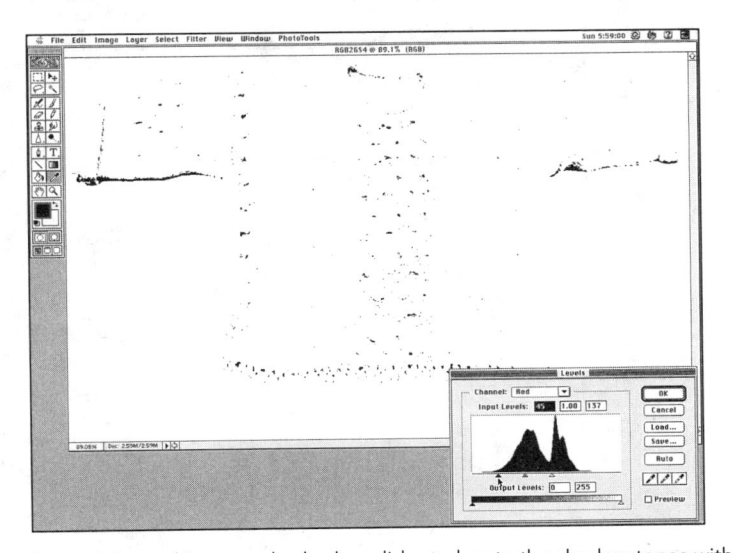

Figure 9.73 Move the Red channel Input scale shadow slider to locate the shadow tones within the sweater.

4. Switch to the Green channel. Locate the highlights and shadows just as you did for the Red channel (see Figures 9.74 and 9.75). You can see that, although the original image was black and white, the R, G, and B channels are all slightly different.

5. Switch to the Blue channel. Use Threshold mode to help you locate the highlights and shadows of the Blue channel (see Figures 9.76 and 9.77).

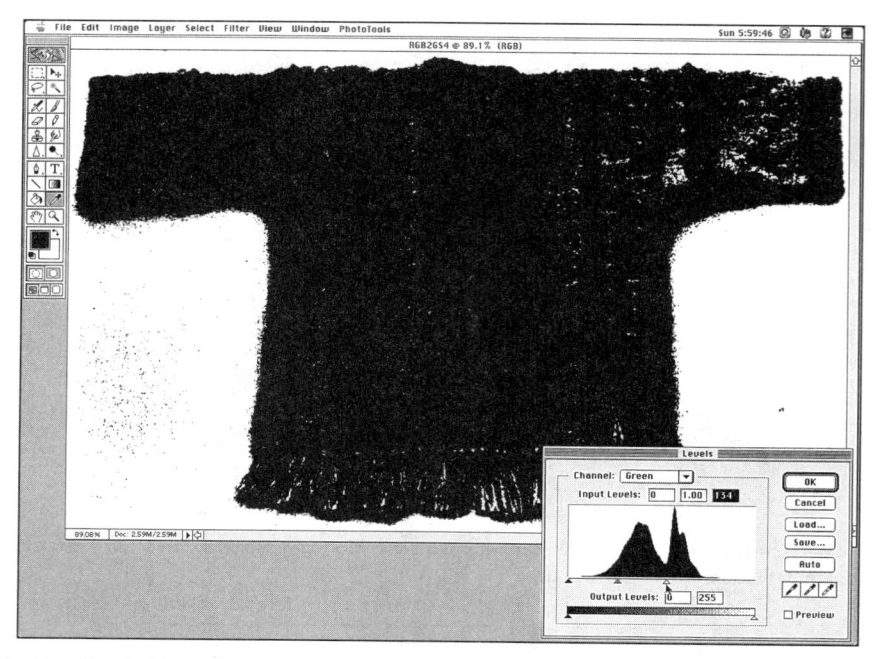

Figure 9.74 Use Threshold mode (the Green channel Input scale highlight slider) in Levels to wash out the background and locate highlights within the sweater.

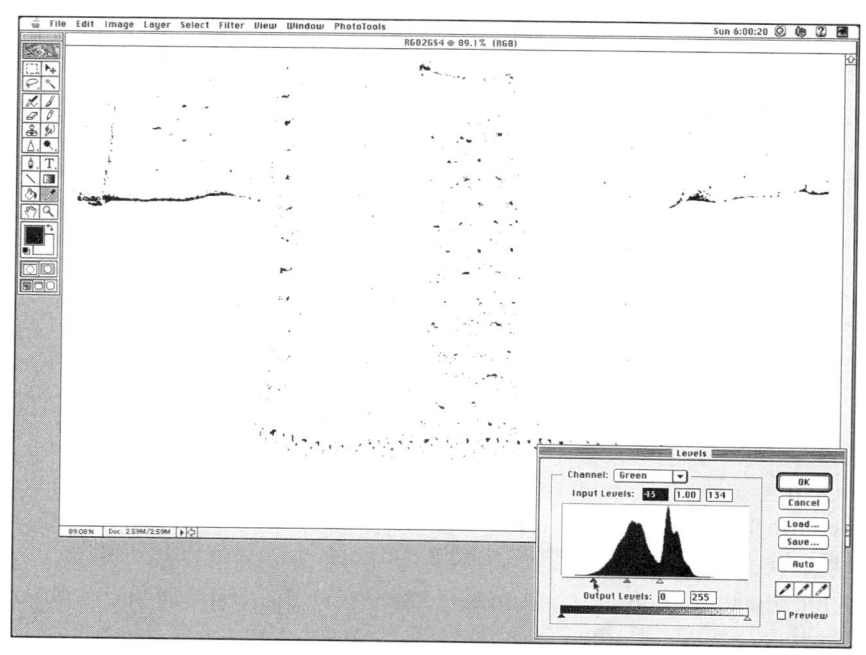

Figure 9.75 Move the Green channel Input scale shadow slider to locate the shadow tones within the sweater.

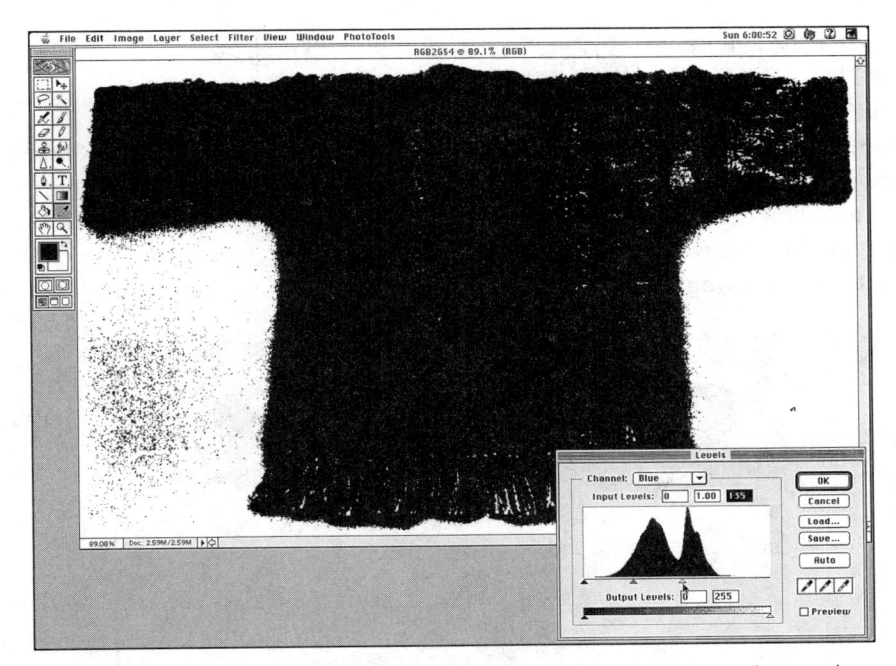

Figure 9.76 Use Threshold mode (the Blue channel Input scale highlight slider) in Levels to wash out the background and locate highlights within the sweater.

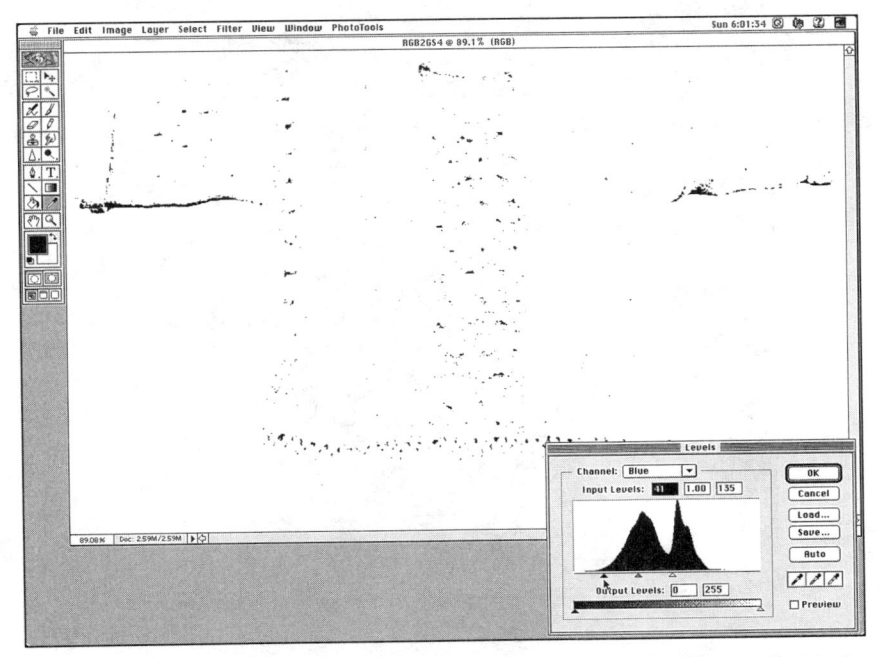

Figure 9.77 Move the Blue channel Input scale shadow slider to locate the shadow tones within the sweater.

6. Change the pop-up menu back to the RGB composite. Adjust the midtones until the data entry box reads 1.30 (see Figure 9.78).

7. Click on OK. From the Image menu, choose Mode|Lab (see Figure 9.79). Press Command+1 or Ctrl+1 to view the L channel. Choose Image|Mode|Grayscale. Click on OK when the dialog box asks if you want to discard the other channels. Open the Levels controls and examine the histogram. Notice that the two-peak shape of the earlier histograms are now changed to a single smooth hump shape and that the image now contains values that are spread evenly across the tone range (see Figure 9.80).

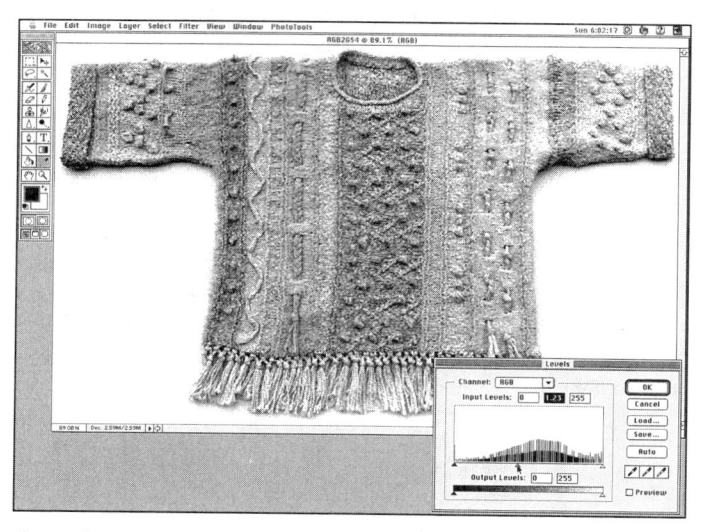

Figure 9.78 Adjust the midtone Input scale slider of the RGB composite histogram to lighten the photo.

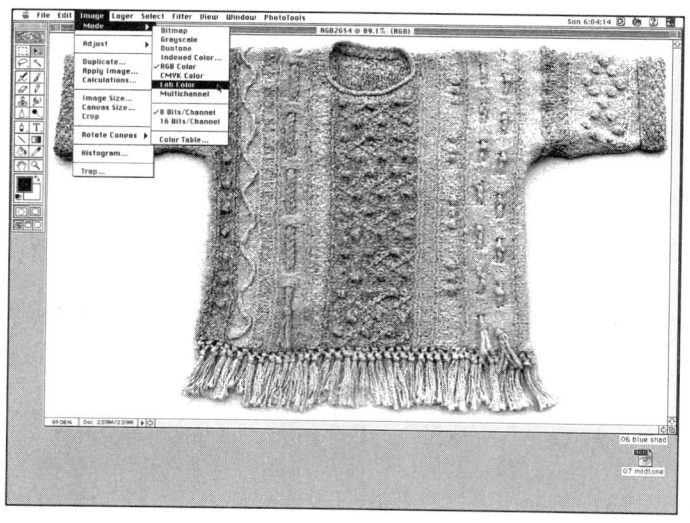

Figure 9.79 Convert the image to Lab mode. Change to the L channel. Convert to Grayscale mode.

PHOTOSHOP PREPRESS 573

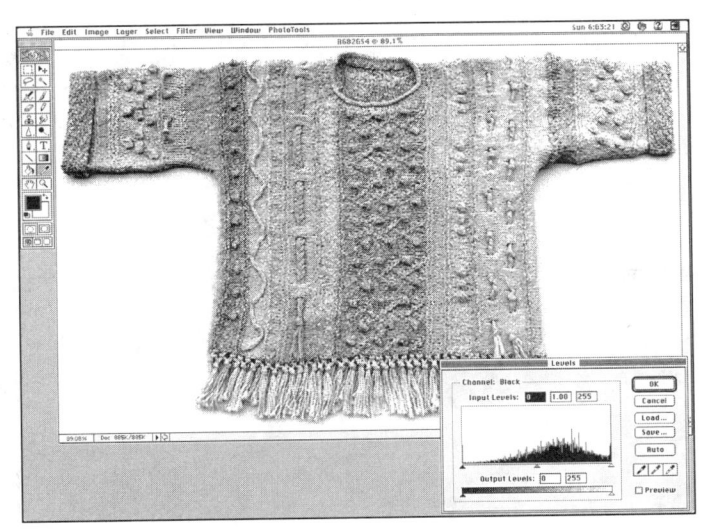

Figure 9.80 Open the Levels controls and look at the histogram to see how it has changed from the original.

8. Keep this window open, but return to the original window. We are going to convert the file to Grayscale mode and process it as though it were scanned that way. Choose Image|Mode|Grayscale. Click on OK when it asks if you wish to discard the color. (Converting to Grayscale mode in this manner is equivalent to scanning the original in grayscale.)

9. Open the Levels controls. Use Threshold mode to locate the highlights of the image in the same way you did for the R, G, and B channels. Your screen turns black during this procedure because you have only a single channel, black (see Figure 9.81).

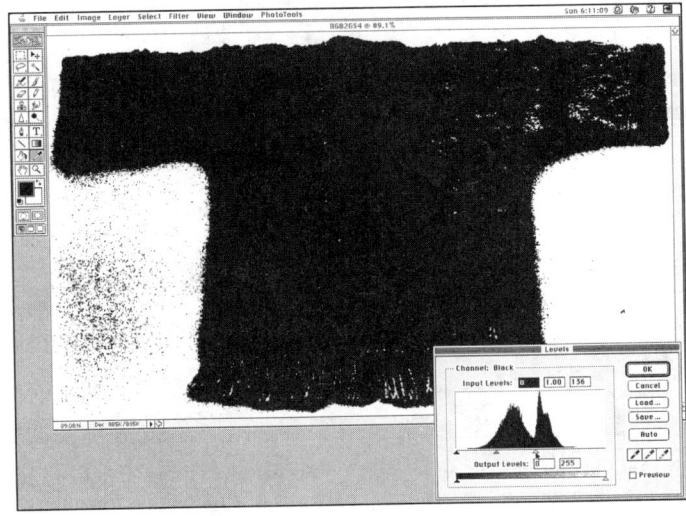

Figure 9.81 Use Threshold mode (the Black channel Input scale highlight slider) in Levels to wash out the background and locate highlights within the sweater.

10. Use Threshold mode to locate the image shadow tones (see Figure 9.82).

11. Move the midtone slider until the value reads 1.30. Click on OK. Open the Levels dialog box again and take a look at the histogram (see Figure 9.83). Notice how the image processed from grayscale contains fewer than half of the possible values. By contrast, the image processed from the RGB file contains almost no missing values. The two histograms are shown side by side in Figure 9.84.

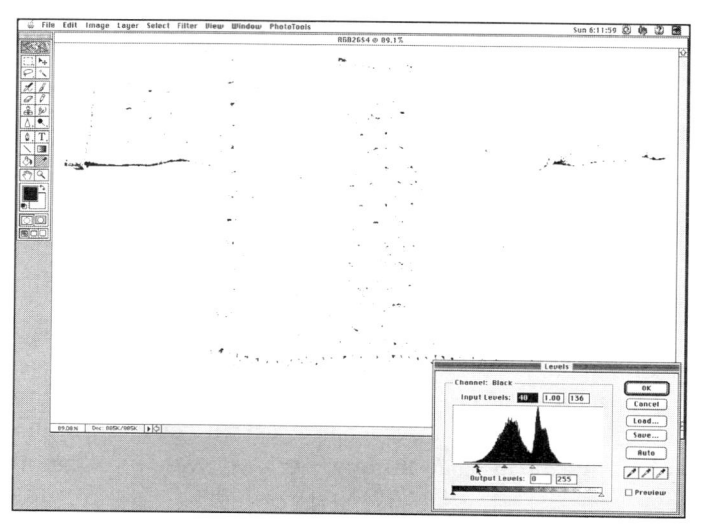

Figure 9.82 Move the Black channel Input scale shadow slider to locate the shadow tones within the sweater.

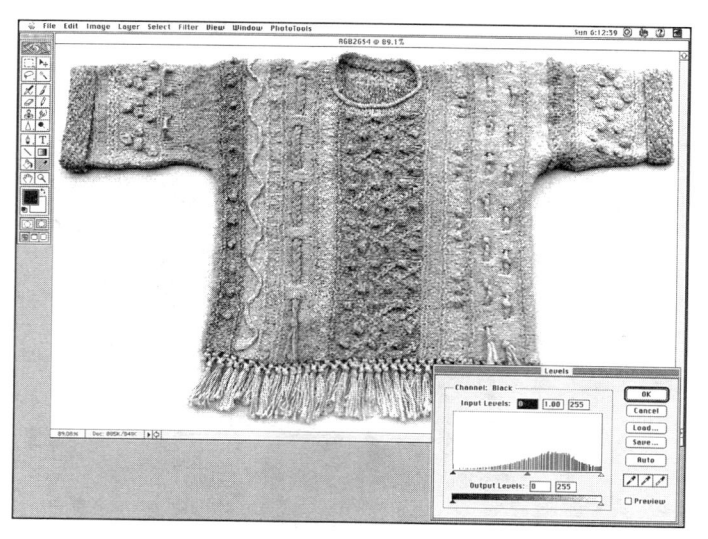

Figure 9.83 Adjust the midtone Input scale slider of the histogram to lighten the photo. Click on OK. Open the Levels again and look at the difference in the histogram between this image and the one processed as RGB color.

Given a choice, which would you rather send to an output device for an accurate representation of the image as a halftone? Considering how deficient the original image was, the decision is what is called in elevated scientific circles a no-brainer. The finished image is shown in Figure 9.85.

Duotones, Tritones, And Quadtones

As lovely as a printed halftone can be, the tone range of a single ink is severely limited. Adding a second ink is a very easy way to extend the tone range by a factor that is much larger than would seem possible. Even if the mixing of the two inks is such that it isn't readily obvious that the printed image is a duotone, the depth and clarity of a multi-ink halftone is unmistakable. Good examples of this are seen in nearly all of the commercial reproductions of the images of the noted photographer Ansel Adams. Examine any of these gorgeous prints with a magnifying lens and you will discover two to six inks with, in some cases, special effects produced by metallics. Adding these inks is a way to faithfully retain the coloristic and textural effects that, in the original photo prints, were the result of Adams's brilliant artistic eye, sense of drama, exposure, filters, processing, and chemistry.

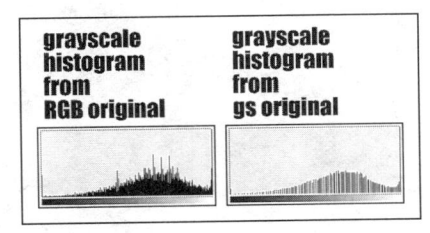

Figure 9.84 The two histograms side by side. The RGB-processed data is complete. The grayscale-processed data shows gaps.

Figure 9.85 The completed image after final adjustment and sharpening. Compare this photo with the original to see how far the data can be pushed to retrieve what seemed to be a hopeless-case image.

576 Chapter 9

Duotone is the generic word we will use in this chapter, because it's the most commonly used multi-ink halftone. While the discussion does include *tritones*—three inks—and *quadtones*—four inks—because they are simply extensions of the duotone principle, we won't specifically delve into them. Adding more than two inks is very much like adding a single ink to a grayscale picture. More than two inks extend the tonal range even farther than the simple duotone. The procedure for developing multi-ink images is the same no matter how many inks are used.

Many Photoshop users think of duotones as a convenient way to colorize a grayscale image (it is much easier to use the Colorize function of the Hue/Saturation dialog box). There is certainly nothing wrong with using the duotone for tinting a halftone, but the subtle power of the duotone is not well exploited. To make use of color tints with your halftone and to do it fast, you can print a light-colored ink in a rectangular shape the same size as the halftone and then print the halftone on top of it. Such an effect is simulated in Figure 9.86. The only problem with this technique is that your highlights are no longer white, but a pure tone of the underprinting color.

Figure 9.86   A halftone can be tinted by overprinting it on an area of a different color.

Figure 9.87   Duotones are generated from a grayscale file such as this.

Duotones (along with tritones and quadtones) in Photoshop are a special kind of grayscale file (see Figure 9.87) containing information that, when sent to an output device, causes the same file to be imaged two or more times using two or more curves (and usually two or more screen angles). Examples are shown in Figures 9.88 (45° screen angle) and 9.89 (15° screen angle). When these output files are printed with two or more inks, the result is a duotone—or tritone or quadtone (see Figure 9.90). Because of this, Photoshop does not treat a duotone as a multi-channel file in which you can edit the individual components. Instead, Photoshop simulates the appearance of the overprinting inks in the grayscale window to allow you to see how the multiple curves will print together.

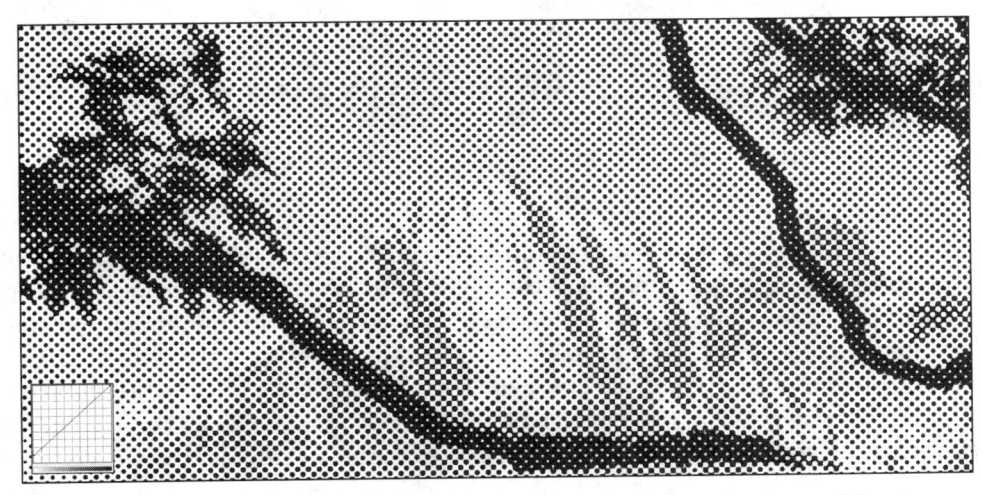

Figure 9.88 A fairly dark curve applied to the original grayscale file produces this version of the picture.

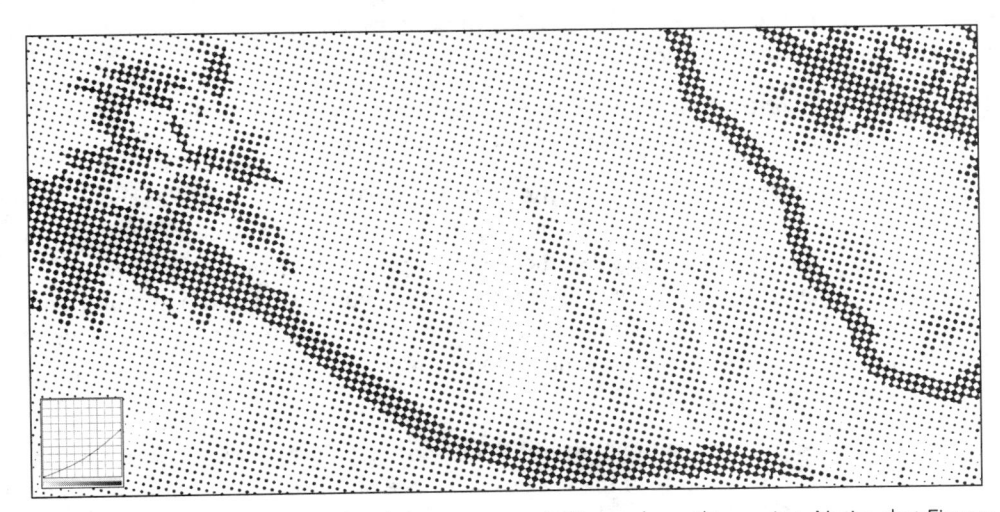

Figure 9.89 A very light curve applied to the same grayscale file produces this version. Notice that Figures 9.88 and 9.89 use different screen angles.

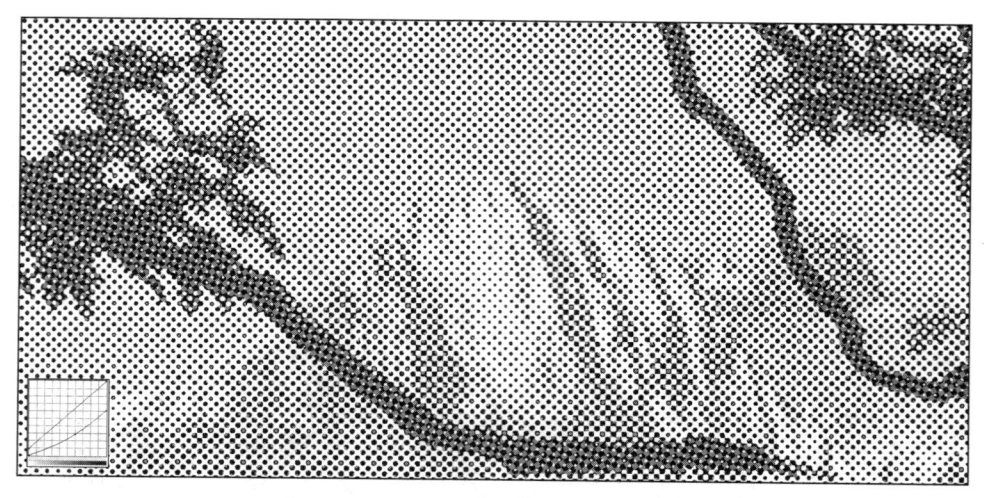

Figure 9.90 When the screen outputs resulting from the two curves are printed on top of each other with two different inks, the result is a duotone.

If you've tried to use a duotone and been discouraged at how dark the image printed, you'll be pleased to know that there is a solution: First, the file needs to be processed exactly the same as a halftone. A duotone has the same press requirements—dot gain, minimum highlight dot falloff, and shadow cutoff—as a halftone. Second, after experimenting with your inks and curves, go ahead and add a pair of adjustment layers as described earlier in this chapter. Make one with Curves elevated at 50% by the amount of the dot gain, and one between the Curves layer and the background using the Levels or Curves controls. With these two layers, you'll be able to see the effects of dot gain on your displayed image as you work. If you find that the image is growing too dark, alter the Levels adjustment layer until the image appears the way you wish it to print. Remember to throw away the Curves adjustment layer before you flatten the image and save it in its final form.

After the file is converted to Grayscale mode, choose Image|Mode|Duotone. The Duotone command is available only when the image is in Grayscale mode.

When you're choosing the command for the first time, the dialog box opens as shown in Figure 9.91. The initial setting is for a monotone image with the ink set to black. A small pop-up menu allows you to choose whether the image will be printed with one, two, three, or four inks (Monotone, Duotone, Tritone, and Quadtone). You can, if you wish, remain in monotone mode and change the black ink to a custom color. When you click on OK and save your file, it then prints in the color you've chosen instead of black. At times, this method is a useful way to quickly colorize a grayscale image.

The dialog box contains four pairs of thumbnails and a small text box for each row. The first thumbnail is of the present state of the curve. Click once on the curve thumbnail and another dialog box opens in front of the first (see Figure 9.92). This curve control works exactly the same way as the Curve controls you have already learned to use, except that it has an additional feature: It allows you to enter your Output values directly, rather than clicking and dragging

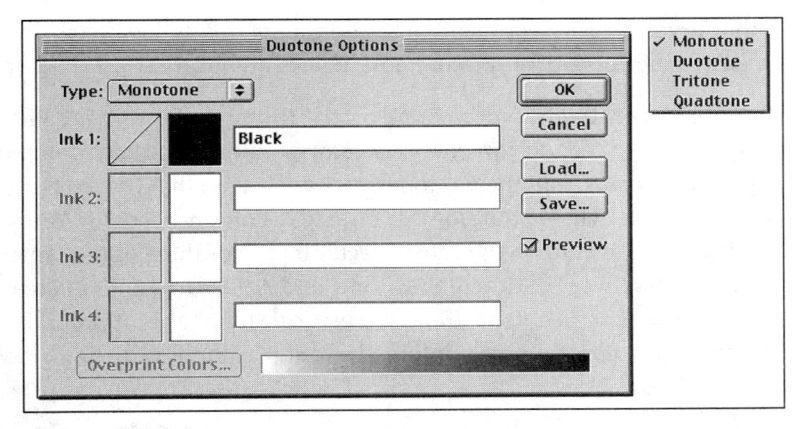

Figure 9.91 The first time you open the Duotone Options dialog box, it is set to Monotone.

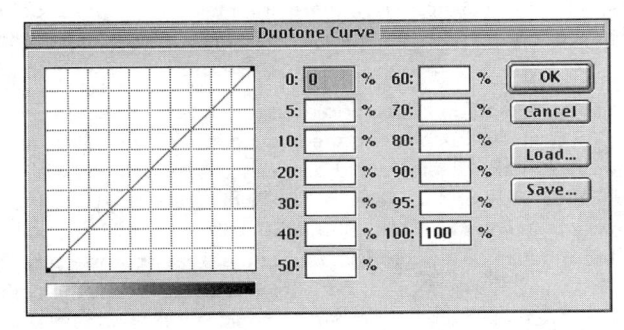

Figure 9.92 Click on the Duotone Options dialog box's curve thumbnail and this Duotone Curve dialog box opens.

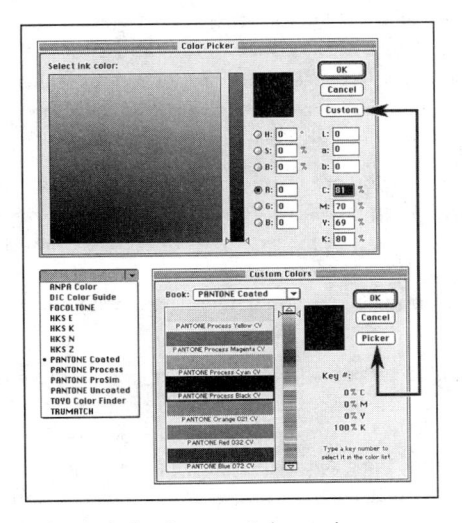

Figure 9.93 The Photoshop Color Picker with the Custom Colors palette.

on the line of the curve. The small gradient at the bottom of this dialog box is simply to remind you on which end of the curve the light and dark values are located.

The second thumbnail sets the ink color. Click on the thumbnail once. The Photoshop Color Picker opens (see Figure 9.93). You can choose a color from this picker, or you may wish, as is more usual, to choose a color from the Pantone palette. Click on the Custom button that opens the Custom Colors palette. The default for this palette is Pantone Coated. At the top, a small pop-up menu allows you to change the color selector to any of three other Pantone standards as well as to color sets by Toyo, TruMatch, Focoltone, and ANPA. If you don't know the number of the Pantone color you wish to choose, move the vertical slider to an appropriate color setting and glance through the colors that are contained within the large swatches window. You can,

USING CUSTOM INKS

When you decide to use custom inks, there are a few things you should keep in mind about how you define an ink and the ways textured and opaque inks combine with process-color inks.

The Pantone color selector in Photoshop doesn't contain some of the inks you can find in a printed Pantone swatch book. Among the missing inks are metallics, neons, and other specialty inks for which no RGB value could be easily assigned. If you wish to use, say, a metallic ink in your duotone, click on the Picker button, which returns you to the Photoshop Color Picker. Use any of the color models—HSB, RGB, Lab, or CMYK—to build a color that is visually close to the ink you want to use. Remember that Photoshop cannot simulate metallic reflectance: You must choose a color that allows you to see how the *color* of the metallic tone appears when mixed with your other ink choices. When the color is as close as you can make it, click on OK.

In the naming box for that ink, enter the exact color name you wish to use. Whatever the ink name—Pantone metallic gold color, for example—enter the name like this: PANTONE 871 CV. Use uppercase letters with a space before and after the number. (Nothing awful will happen if you don't, but because every program does it this way, you risk confusing someone farther downstream in the production flow if you don't maintain consistency.) After you have named the ink, proceed to develop the duotone.

Try to remember, when you are using a specialty ink, that it is unlike typical colored ink. It is usually opaque and often develops a surface texture that can drastically change other inks that overprint it. Neon yellow, for example, when overprinted with solid black, produces what looks like a 50 to 70 percent tint of black. If the success of your image depends on solid black next to neon yellow, you'll need the black to knock out the yellow rather than overprint it.

Ink opacity also has to be considered. Metallics, for example, are opaque inks. Colors overprinted by solid metallics get covered up. If you think that this will be a problem, be sure to discuss the possibility of customizing the ink laydown sequence with your printer. Printers do not usually like to alter their laydown sequence—inks are formulated to make a certain laydown order more efficient—but if you have a good reason for making the request, your print house will do its best for you.

if you know the number you want, simply enter the numbers. There is no data entry field in which to type, but you can enter the number anyway and the Color Picker will find the color.

Go ahead and choose the inks you wish to use and notice that both curves are the same as the single curve thumbnail shown in Figure 9.91. If you click on OK at this time, your screen shows a much darker, tinted version of the grayscale file. If you haven't adjusted the curves, your output for the image will look as though you had simply imaged a halftone, duplicated it, and stripped it into another piece of film and used it to make a different plate.

Adjusting the curves to get exactly the effect you want takes some experience. A small tool on the Duotone Curve dialog box—the gradient bar at the bottom—helps you gauge the overall tonality produced by your inks as they print on top of each other. As you change the curves, pay close attention to this bar. It shows you subtle changes such as too much overt color, a too-lengthy midtone section, a too-short highlight range, and so on. Exactly what it does is hard to describe, but pay attention to it and you'll understand quickly.

Go ahead and adjust the curves, remembering what you have already learned about using curve controls: Moving a point on the curve toward the top of the grid makes the tone darker, and moving it down makes it lighter. Remember, too, that you have two or more curves to play off against each other. Think of the curve lines as a set of corresponding points—the curve with a given value that is closest to the top of the grid produces the dominant tone for that value. Begin by experimenting with your second ink's curve so that the ink's impact on the image is slight. As was mentioned previously, some of the most strikingly beautiful duotones are those that are not instantly recognizable as duotones. Use the second ink to reinforce the tone range from midtone to shadow, and keep it out of the highlights so that your highlights do not develop a strong color cast. As you become more skilled at arriving at the look you want, you will certainly develop your own tastes, your own likes and dislikes.

It's a good idea, before setting up your duotone, to duplicate the grayscale image and to place the windows of the grayscale and the duotone so that both are easily visible (see Figure 9.94). In the figure, two inks have been chosen and the curves have been altered (the duotone is on the right). Notice that in the sunlit lawn area in the lower part of the image, much of the grass texture has been blown out and lost. Without the grayscale reference, it's very easy to get wrapped up in making the inks look a certain way and to forget to check image details such as this.

Figure 9.95 shows how the curve of Ink 2 has been modified to bring back the texture of the lawn. You're looking at the figure taken from a screen shot and printed in black and white. However, if you study the large bush and the tree trunk closest to the house, you can see that there is an appreciable difference in the clarity and detail of the two images.

Now that you've come up with an ink and curve combination that fits your ideas about the image, take a look at the separate components of the duotone. You can look at them but you cannot alter them if you wish to print the image as a duotone. From the Image menu, choose Mode|Multichannel (see Figure 9.96). When the image changes mode, you will be looking at Ink 1 (see Figure 9.97). Usually, this is the black ink. Press Command+2 or Ctrl+2. This is the second ink channel (see Figure 9.98). Use the Undo command to return to Duotone mode, or click on the item on the History palette just above the Mode Change item.

Figure 9.94 When you're developing a duotone, duplicate the image so that you can work on the duplicate duotone (right) and visually compare it to the original grayscale file (left) while you are working.

Figure 9.95 The two curves have been adjusted so that the detail in the original file (left) is preserved in the duotone (right).

Figure 9.96 To look at the individual plates of a duotone, first convert the file to Multichannel mode.

Figure 9.97 Press Command+1 (Mac) or Ctrl+1 (Windows) to look at Ink 1.

Figure 9.98 Press Command+2 or Ctrl+2 to look at Ink 2. Use the Undo command to switch back to Duotone mode.

An Old Photo From A New One

Here's an interesting technique that produces a nice-looking simulation of a well-preserved but very old photograph. The procedure changes the photo's coloration to an antique brown that varies in intensity with the overall strength of Ink 2. The most successful results are obtained when Ink 2 is light in comparison to Ink 1 and contains no amount of black. (Select your Pantone color and then return to the Color Picker. Type "0" in the Black data-entry field.)

1. Be sure to save your image before you begin. Duplicate the finished duotone. Convert the duplicate to CMYK mode. Set your Foreground color to white and press Option+Delete (Mac) or Alt+Delete (Windows) to wipe out all traces of the image.

2. Return to the original duotone and convert it to Multichannel mode. Select All and use the Copy command on the first channel. Switch to the CMYK window and press Command+4 or Ctrl+4 to view the Black channel. Paste into this channel.

3. Switch back to the duotone. Press Command+2 (Mac) or Ctrl+2 (Windows). With the selection still active, use the Copy command again. Return to the CMYK document. Press Command+1 or Ctrl+1, and paste. Press Command+2 or Ctrl+2, and paste. Press Command+3 or Ctrl+3, and paste. After completing these steps, you have pasted Ink 1 into the Black channel and Ink 2 into the Cyan, Magenta, and Yellow channels. To view your finished work, type Command+~ or Ctrl+~. Cool, huh?

4. If your image is a little dark and you don't want to adjust it by using Levels or Curves, here's a slightly different strategy you can try. First, paste the Ink 2 channel only into the Magenta and Yellow channels of the CMYK document. (Leave the Cyan channel empty.)

5. Click on the Foreground Color and set your CMYK values to 0, 0, 0, and 50. Click on OK.

6. Make a 1-inch-square RGB window and fill with the Foreground Color. Look at the Info palette to see what the equivalent CMYK values for this gray tone are. Write down the values of the magenta and yellow components. (For this discussion, we'll imagine that magenta is 37% and yellow 36%.) Close the small document.

7. Set your Foreground color to White. Select All. Type Command+2 or Ctrl+2 to view the magenta channel. Press Shift+Delete to open the Fill dialog box. Fill this channel with the Foreground color (white) in Normal mode. Change the Opacity to the reciprocal of the ink percentage. In this case, magenta was 37%, so you'll fill the channel using 63% Opacity (100 – 37 = 63).

8. Type Command+3 or Ctrl+3 to view the Yellow channel. Fill this channel with white at 64% Opacity.

9. Make a note of this technique so that, when you read about black generation in Chapter 10, you'll have a really good idea of why it works so well.

10. Here's a hint: If you want to experiment further with this technique, you'll find that pasting Ink 2 into the Cyan and Yellow channels will give you a green tone instead of brown. Pasting into Cyan and Magenta will give your image an attractive purple tone. Lighten the channels as described in Steps 5 through 8.

When you finish developing the curves on your duotone, be sure to save your settings. You want all of the photos within the same project to be consistent with each other and saving your settings offers an easy way to do that. Click on the Save button in the Duotone Options dialog box. It's a good idea to create a new folder where you can group your duotone settings so that you can use them again whenever they are needed. Within the Photoshop folder is another folder called Goodies. Within Goodies is another folder titled Duotone Presets. Inside this folder are separate folders for duotones, tritones, and quadtones. Within each of these are separate folders for Gray, Pantone, and Process presets. Placing your own presets within the Duotone Presets gives you the opportunity to organize your preset files. It makes sense to name your preset in much the same way the bundled Duotone Presets are named; such a name might be *144 orange, bl* indicating that the duotone uses Pantone 144 (orange) and black. You can even add—if your curves resembled those in Figure 9.95—some description of the relative strength of the two inks to each other: *144 orange 70, black 100* (the second numbers referring to percentages—you may want to avoid using the % character when naming files within the Windows environment). However you name your curve set, be sure to do it in a way that allows you to easily remember what the preset looks like.

For an easy entry into the world of duotones, try one of the bundled presets. There are 88 duotone possibilities, 35 tritones, and 14 quadtones. The group contains a lot of variations. For example, there are four different presets using Pantone 144, each of them slightly different, each of them producing a pleasing result. Experiment by loading each and deciding for yourself which combination of presets gives the look you are seeking. After you load the preset, you are free to tweak the curves and to change the loaded ink color into some other color. Many experienced Photoshop users never go to the trouble of developing a brand new preset. Rather, they use the bundled presets as starting points and tweak the settings. If you choose to work this way, you'll still want to save your variations on the presets for later use.

The last step is saving/exporting your duotone file. In all likelihood, you aren't going to be generating your duotone separations from within Photoshop, but will import the file into a page layout program such as QuarkXPress or Adobe PageMaker. Given this, saving the file is easy enough: choose Photoshop EPS, which is the only format choice available that allows duotones to be imported into one of the other programs. The dialog box for saving in EPS format is shown in Figure 9.99.

The settings in the figure are appropriate for a Macintosh exporting to a page layout program. If you are a Windows user, you have fewer choices. Your default for the Preview is TIFF (1 bit). TIFF (8 bits) looks better when you import the image into the page layout program. Binary or ASCII Encoding are choices that have largely to do with the kind of output device you are using. If you are unsure which to choose, contact your service bureau for advice.

The only other important choice to make when you're saving the duotone is whether to include, or embed, the halftone screen (see the checkbox in the lower portion of the window). If you don't include the screen, then you have to change the screen angles in the program from

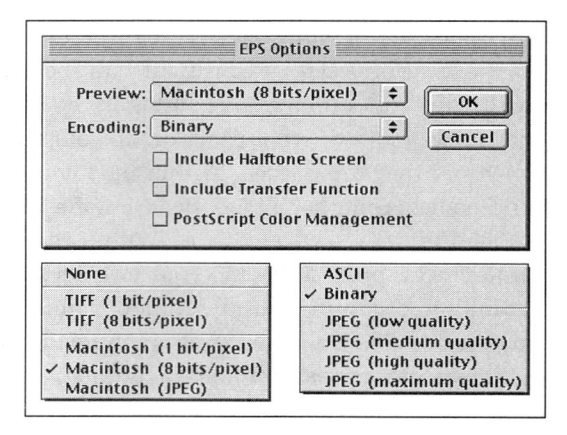

Figure 9.99 The EPS Format export options window.

which the separations are to be generated. In Figure 9.100, a screen representation of a QuarkXPress document shows how:

1. After you have imported the duotone into a QuarkXPress document, choose Edit|Colors.
2. Click to select the Pantone color that the imported image has added to the Colors list.
3. Click on the Edit button. The Edit Color dialog box shown in the upper right side of Figure 9.100 appears.
4. Click on the Halftone pop-up menu. The default screen angle for any spot color used in QuarkXPress is the same as that used for black, or 45°. Change your Pantone color's screen angle to that of one of the other process colors. If possible, choose a color that isn't going to be used very much in the document.
5. Users of QuarkXPress 4.0 have an additional opportunity to change the screen angle of a spot color ink. After choosing File|Print, click on the Output tab, the center of the five options dialogs (see Figure 9.101). A list of inks contained in the document appears. This list enables you to disable printing of some colors, change the line-screen frequency and angle of any single ink, and change the shape of the dots for any ink.

In Adobe PageMaker, changes to the screen angles are made from the Print dialog box. In the Print Document dialog box, click on the Color button. A new dialog box titled Print Color appears. Click on the Separations radio button at the upper left. Below, there is a list of colors. Scroll down until you see the custom ink to be used in your duotone. Click on the color to select it. Now, click on the Print This Ink checkbox below the scrolling color list. Enter the screen frequency and screen angle you wish to use for this ink in the two data entry fields to the right of the color list. This feature of Adobe PageMaker is much like the Print Options of QuarkXPress.

The alternative to changing the screen angles in the program from which the output will be generated is to set the screen angles within Photoshop. To do so, take these steps:

1. Choose File|Page Setup.
2. Click on the Screen button.

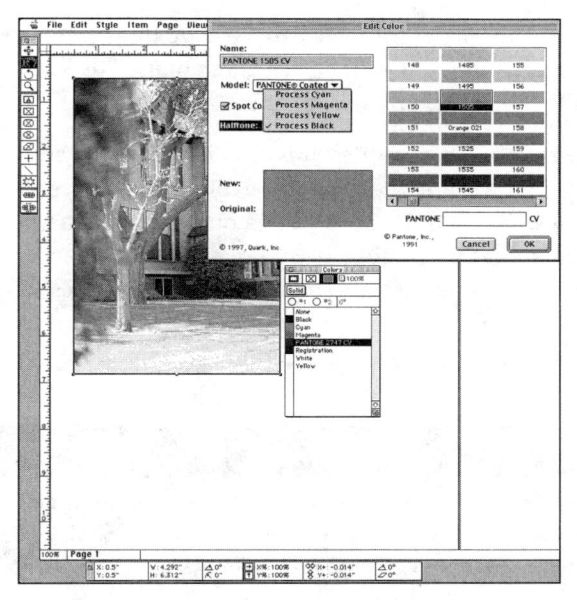

Figure 9.100 Changing the screen angle for a custom ink in QuarkXPress.

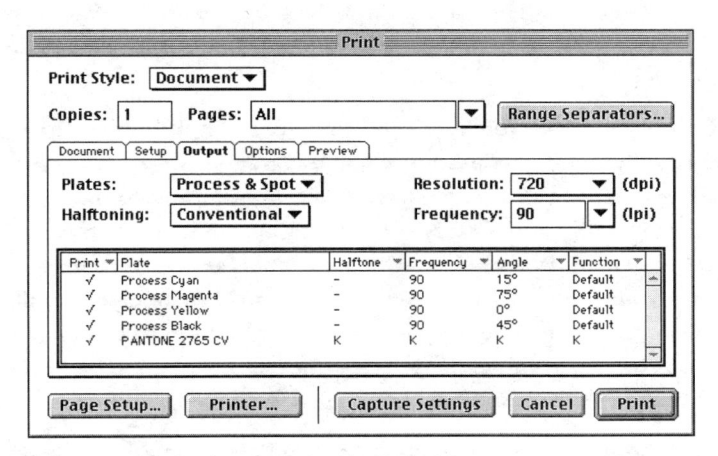

Figure 9.101 The Print Options dialog box from QuarkXPress 4.0.

3. The dialog box shown at the top of Figure 9.102 appears. When you first see it, the checkbox at the top will be checked. Uncheck it.

4. You now have a number of choices to make. You can manually enter the screen frequency and the angle of the screen, as well as set the spot function—the shape of the dot—from the available choices. The number of choices is almost overwhelming. If you wish, play it safe and click on the Auto button. The dialog box shown at the bottom of the figure appears next. Enter the resolution of the output device and the screen frequency you will be using. Click on OK. If your output device is equipped with PostScript Level 2 or an Adobe Emerald controller, you can check the Use Accurate

Screens checkbox. This allows the device to use a prebuilt set of very precise—or *accurate*—screen dots and angles. If your device does not use PostScript Level 2 or have the Emerald controller, the checkbox has no effect.

If you intend to do a number of duotones, it is a good idea to save your settings for the screen frequencies you wish to use. That way you can avoid having to make the choices every time you want to save a new file. Simply use the Save button, and later, the Load button. There is another way to set up values so that you don't have to access the Screen dialog box. Hold the Option (Mac) or the Alt (Windows) key: The Save button changes to ->Default and the Load button to <-Default. Click on the Load (<-) button if you want your present settings to become the defaults for all future files. To restore the settings to what they were when you first opened the dialog box, click on the Save (->) button.

> **TIP**
>
> **If you decide to embed your screens in the duotone document, you should check with your service bureau to be sure that there is no reason why you shouldn't do so. There are some strange things that can happen with some RIPs.**
>
> **One problem that can occur is that the embedded screen does not quite override the RIP's screening. You can end up with a single film that has *two different screen angles on the same plate*. This can result in an improbable one-color moiré. Bet you didn't know that was possible, huh?**
>
> **Another problem you might run into is this (hold on, now, this one is tricky to explain!): Let's say that you have used a screen angle of 0º for a specific purpose. For example, you might have chosen a coarse linear dot function so that one of your inks prints as multiwidth horizontal lines. When you send your files to an imagesetter—let's stipulate a small-format machine with a 14-inch film width—the operator prints your page sideways so that he doesn't waste all of the film along the edges. When the page images sideways, the embedded screen does not necessarily turn. You can end with the linear effect that you wanted to be horizontal on your page actually running vertically.**
>
> **These problems are not universal, but they are common enough that a consultation with your service bureau will save you trouble.**

A set of four images in the Color Studio of this book shows how the image on the left in Figure 9.94 was developed into the duotone on the right in Figure 9.95. (Note: The duotone examples in the Color Studio section are not really duotones. They are files that have been developed as duotones and then converted to CMYK mode. The four-color printing process simulates the duotones remarkably well.) You can see the original grayscale image, a monotone of the image using the second—dark blue—ink, the image printed with the default straight-line curves, and the final duotone. If you want to practice on the file used in the examples, locate the file RGB2DUO.PSD on this book's CD-ROM. The file is in RGB mode. It was deliberately left that way so you can follow through the entire procedure. First, process the file as though it were to

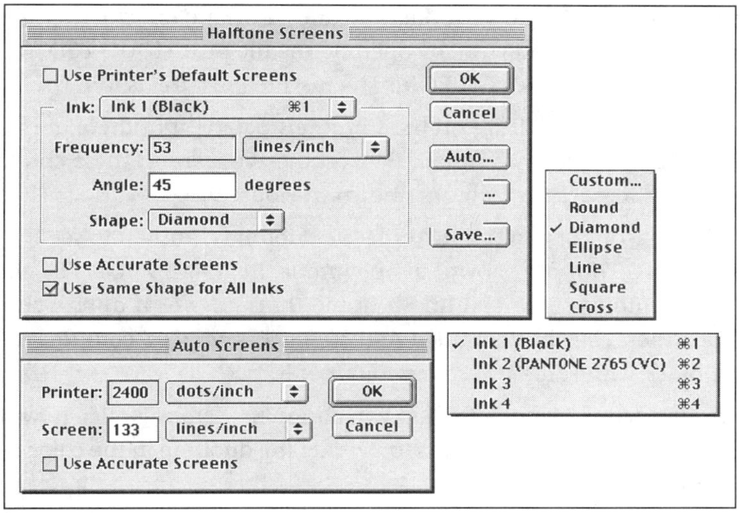

Figure 9.102 Photoshop's Halftone Screens options window.

be a halftone, convert it to grayscale, and then generate the duotone. We want to warn you that making duotones is one of the most fascinating things you can do in Photoshop and that you can get hooked on it! Good luck with your experimenting.

> **TIP**
>
> If you run into a situation where you have a black and white original image on a page where process color is a possibility, make the black and white image into a duotone and then convert it to CMYK. The extra depth of detail and expanded tone range for the image is an opportunity too good to be missed!
>
> If you ever need to work extensively in Photoshop with a pair of inks and the project contains one or more duotones, you might find it easier to work in CMYK mode using just two of the channels. Prepare your duotones in the usual way. Convert to Multichannel mode. Copy the two channels, one at a time, into the two channels you are using in CMYK mode. For example, a red-toned duotone could have Ink 1 copied to the Black channel and Ink 2 copied to the Magenta channel. By using either black or magenta (or mixtures of the two), you could then do all other work on this document. Working in this way allows you to select areas of the image and fill with one, both, or a mix of the colors. When the file is changed to output, use whatever ink you wish with the two films. We discuss an alternative to working in two or more channels of a CMYK document in the following section.

Duotone Special Effects In Multichannel Mode

With Photoshop's Spot Color channels, you can add special effects to your duotones using either or both of the inks you will use to print the image. This can be accomplished by using a

Spot Color channel in addition to your duotone or by working directly in Multichannel mode. Try out this small exercise, if you wish, by opening the file MULTIDUO.PSD from the Chapter 9 Practice Files folder on this book's CD-ROM. The instructions are as follows:

1. When the file is open, you'll see on the Channels palette that there are two channels in addition to the Duotone channel. Click on the eye icons of these channels to hide them. What you'll see is the duotone shown in Figure 9.103.

2. Click on the eye icons one at a time (hide the duotone channel) to see the contents of the two channels. They are shown, in one image, in Figure 9.104. The channel titled Add To 2765 contains some text and a frame that fades as it approaches the upper right-hand corner. The channel titled Add To Black And 2765 contains a rectangle of 50 percent black with some text reversed out of it.

3. Click on the eye icons to make the top two channels visible. Notice how the text and frame of the second channel appears to overlay the duotone in the color of the second ink (see Figure 9.105).

4. From the File menu, choose Mode|Multichannel. When the conversion is complete, you will find that you have a Black channel #1, a PANTONE 2765 CV channel #2, and

Figure 9.103 A simple duotone upon which we will add other elements that use the same inks to be used to print the duotone.

Figure 9.104 Here is a look at the contents of both of the additional channels in MULTIDUO.PSD.

the original labeled channels. The next step is to combine the information in the lower two channels with that of the top two.

5. Click on the second channel to select it. Use the eye icons to hide all of the unselected channels. Hold down Command or Ctrl and click on the thumbnail of the third channel (Add To 2765) to load it as a selection. Selection lines will appear as shown in Figure 9.106.

6. Set your Foreground color to black. Fill the selection with the Foreground color—Option+Delete (Mac) or Alt+Delete (Windows). Deselect, and drag the third channel to the Trash icon at the bottom of the Channels palette. Your second palette now appears as shown in Figure 9.107.

7. Now, you add ink to both channels simultaneously. Hold down the Shift key and click on both of the top two channels to select them. Load the third channel (Add To Black And 2765) as a selection. Fill the selection with black. Deselect. Drag the third channel to the trash. Your image will appear as shown in Figure 9.108.

8. Look at each of your remaining channels. Notice how each has been filled with 50 percent black in the area at the top left corner. It filled that way because the channel

Figure 9.105 When the top two channels are visible, the information contained in the second channel overlays the duotone in the color of Ink 2.

Figure 9.106 With the second channel visible, load the third channel as a selection (hold down Command or Ctrl and click on the thumbnail of the third channel).

Figure 9.107 After you have filed the selection with black, your second channel will look like this, a combination of the second and third channels.

Figure 9.108 Your final image will appear as shown here when you have merged the extra channels with those of the duotone.

with the artwork contained a 50 percent area and because you had both channels selected at the time you used the Fill command. This is a cool thing to be able to do.

9. Finally, in order to print your dressed-up duotone, save your file using the Photoshop DCS 2.0 format. We'll cover details of this format later in this chapter. For the moment, you need to know that this is a special version of the original DCS format (Desktop Color Separations) and that you can now use your file exactly the way you would have used a normal duotone.

Colorful Duotones With Powertone By Intense Software

If we are to use terminology with accuracy, the word *duotone* should probably be reserved for monotone images printed with more than one ink. The usual purpose for doing so is to extend, subtly and elegantly, the tonal range, far beyond what is achievable with a single ink. Powertone-processed images are not really duotones in this restricted use of the term. They are, instead, wonderfully ingenious two-ink reproductions that preserve much of the look of four-color printing.

Two-ink color image reproduction is a technique that has been available for quite a long time. It is based on the fact that when a pair of custom inks—for example, Pantone 326 (bright turquoise) and Pantone 173 (bright orange)—are overprinted, they contain between them many of the process color components. The colors are not precisely the same, but you can think of it this way. Pantone 326, when converted to CMYK by Photoshop 5, changes to 94%C, 0%M, 43%Y, and 0%K. Pantone 172 converts to 0%C, 65%M, 83%Y, and 0%K. Between the two you have, instead of the full range of CMYK colors, a large subset of the colors you could define with 94%C, 65%M, 83%Y, and 0%K (the superset of both inks). As you can see, the range in cyan and yellow is close to complete, and magenta is better than half. If you add in the fact that Pantone inks are usually more pure as colors and that they give, when high-percentage tints overprint, a better black than 100 percent each of CMY, you can see that you have an extensive color range that can be expressed by laying down only two inks.

Until recently, two-spot color separations were the exclusive province of technologically accomplished color houses. You could achieve a passable effect with a good deal of trial-and-error work in Photoshop, but the results were often time-consuming and the final product less than captivating. With the release of Powertone, a Photoshop plug-in by Intense Software, generating a two-color separation has become fast and fairly straightforward.

The quality of the separations? The scale runs from *Not Bad* to *WOW!* Not all images can be adapted to this technique, but even minimal work with this software will convince you that common sense and a good pair of eyes will get "not bad" results from images that are poor candidates for this kind of reproduction. When the image is great, the result is spectacular.

Imagine that you are the producer of a four-color newsletter and that your publication style uses two inks—black and Pantone red (perhaps even the ubiquitous 185). You are probably quite used to the fact that you can do pretty decent duotones in your newsletter, and that you can add tints of both of your colors to give your page design more punch. What would you say if you could use your two colors together to produce an image that gives a really respectable imitation of being a four-color reproduction? If your newsletter has the flexibility to use a different pair of inks with each issue, you now can do some really snappy photo work.

Why a different pair of inks with every issue? Look at the image shown in Figure 9.109. Red raspberries with red-tinted blackberries provide an unusually good subject for black and red ink. You may not be able to find a perfect black-red image for each issue. But if you can switch your inks with each issue, the scope you have for your photographs will give you a much larger set of possibilities.

To generate your separations, open your image and convert it to RGB. This isn't actually necessary, but the colors seem to map to the spot colors more easily from RGB. From the File menu, choose Export|Powertone. The expanded dialog box is shown in Figure 9.110.

On the upper left, you see a thumbnail of your original image, and next to it is a preview of your image as it will look when mapped to the new ink set. The Ink Set controls are at the bottom of the window. You can choose a pair of inks from the pop-up menu or you can define a new pair by simply typing in your ink names in the two data fields below the pop-up. You must also specify the closest process color equivalents for your spot inks in the data-entry fields to the right. As you do so, the color of the oval shapes at the left will update, as will the preview image. You can click on the ovals to see, in color, how the image will look when separated and only that image has been printed on the page. A second click restores the preview.

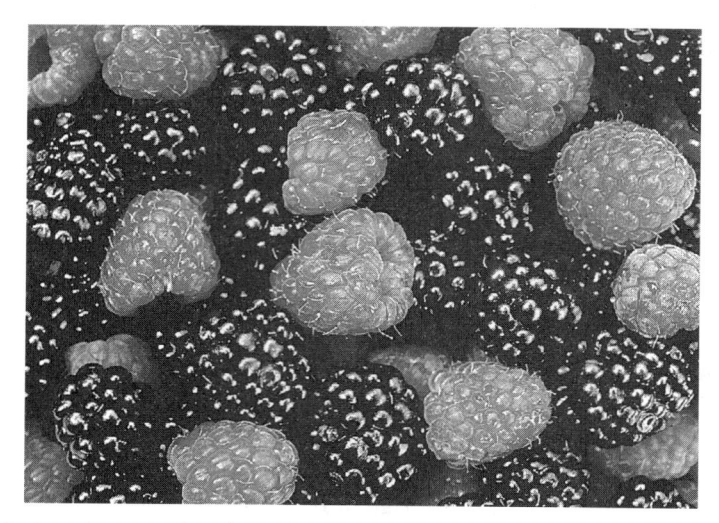

Figure 9.109 Red raspberries with red-tinted blackberries make an unusually good subject for generating a Powertone image using red and black inks.

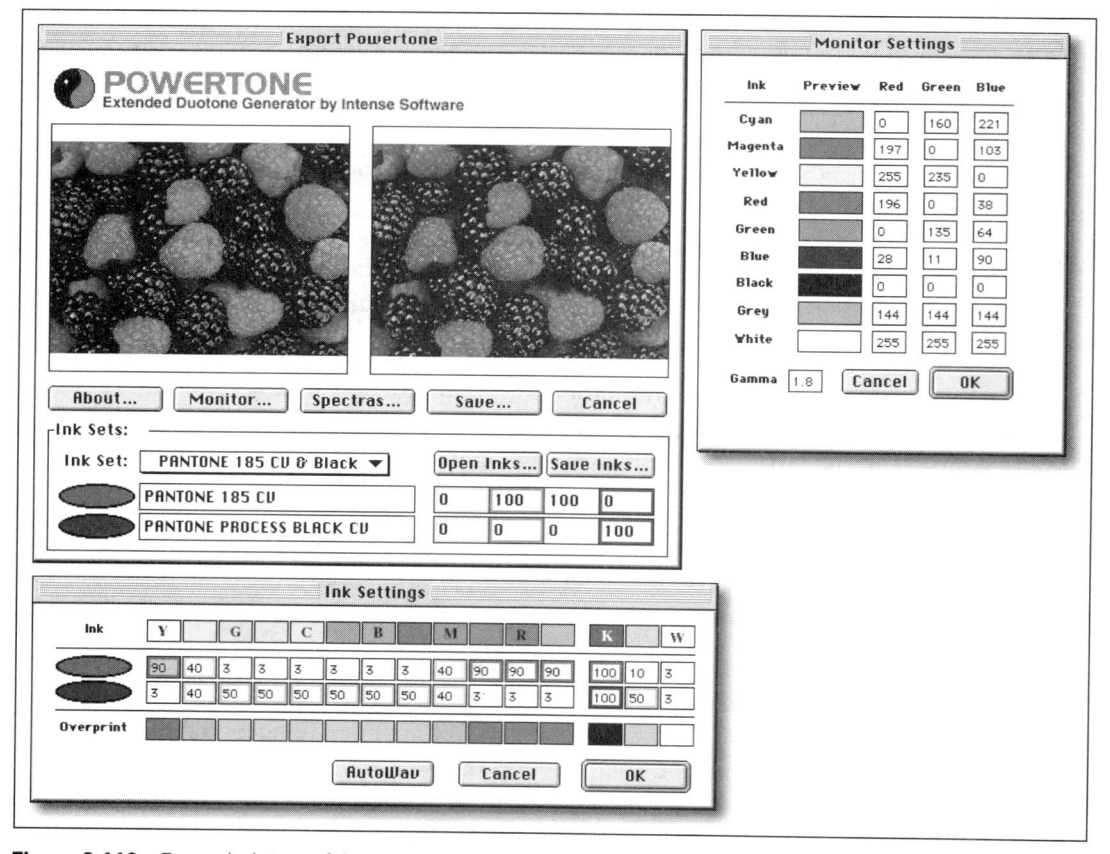

Figure 9.110 Expanded view of the Powertone controls.

The Monitor button below the two thumbnails summons the Monitor Settings dialog box (upper right-hand corner of the figure), in which you can enter color settings to tweak your display.

The Spectra button delivers the dialog box shown at the lower edge of the figure. Along the top are 12 color swatches that show the full-color spectrum. At the bottom are 12 other swatches that tell you how the equivalent colors are going to be recomposed with the new pair of inks. Between the rows of swatches are data fields where you can enter numbers that will raise or lower the proportions of the two inks. The program does a good job of estimating how the two colors will combine, but you may need to tweak the colors to achieve a broader range of tones or more contrast.

Another feature of the Spectra dialog box is the set of swatches (above and below the data fields), which allow you to change—if you need to—the gray balance of the inks. You use the fields to ensure that some mix of the two inks produces a nearly neutral gray in the highlights, midtones, and shadows. You can also use the fields on each end to limit the amount of ink you hold in the highlights and the maximum amount of ink in the shadows.

After you have finished with your adjustments, click on the Save button. The dialog box shown in Figure 9.111 appears.

You have the choice of saving the file in three formats: EPS, SDCS (single-file DCS), and MDCS (multiple-file DCS). The two plates of the separations are shown in Figure 9.112.

If you don't need to make any further changes to the image, it can now be imported into any program that is DCS 2 compliant (QuarkXPress, Adobe PageMaker, Adobe Illustrator, and Macromedia FreeHand).

You may wish to further tweak your image. If so, reopen the saved file. You can, of course, experiment with changing the content of each channel by using Levels or Curves. If you do experiment, please note that there are a couple of tricks attached to using the familiar controls. Imagine that you're going to use the Levels controls to lighten the midtones of the entire image. If you select one of the channels and open the Levels controls, you will be able to affect only that channel. You can hold down the Shift key and select *both* of your channels, but you will have to adjust the channels one at a time by changing the channel pop-up menu above

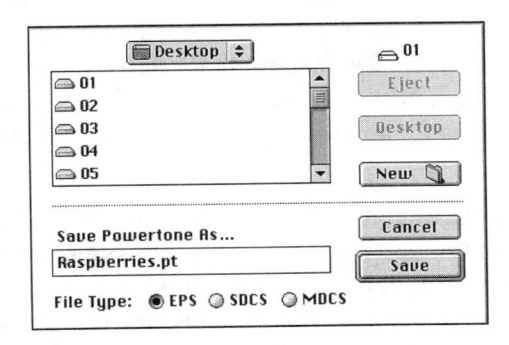

Figure 9.111 The Powertone Save dialog box.

Figure 9.112 The two print plates of the two-color Powertone reproduction of the raspberries.

the histogram. Note also that even though you are seeing a colored image, you are looking at the grayscale channels of a spot color document. The usual color correction controls—Hue/Saturation, Color Balance, Selective Color—are not available for you to use on these channels.

You have another, more subtle, way to adjust the appearance of your image: to experiment with different inks. Here's how it works. Double-click on one of your channels. When the dialog box appears, drag it into a far corner of your screen so that you can still see most of your image. Click on the color swatch. When the Custom Color picker opens, drag it to the side so that you can still see your image.

For a quick look at how you can experiment with different inks after the fact, pick another ink, perhaps one that is in the same family, but different from the one you originally used. As soon as you click on it in the Pantone list, you will see that your image is instantly updated to display the new color choice. You may find that your first experiments with Powertone have gone slightly awry because you have chosen an ink that doesn't have quite the right color cast. For example, you might have chosen a cool red rather than a warm red. If so, here's your chance to change your mind and to see instantly what a different ink will do to the appearance of your printed piece. Bear in mind that changing your inks may injure the gray balance you adjusted with your original ink choice. However, if you are careful, and keep your eyes open, you may find that you can come up with a better ink set than the one you originally chose.

The CD-ROM accompanying this book contains some interesting and useful files. In the Chapter 9 Demo Files folder, you'll find a working demo of the PowerTone plug-in for Macintosh (with a PDF file of the User Manual) and a demo of the standalone application for Windows (with the User Manual in PDF format). There are also three sets of sample photos by the authors. Each set is composed of a Photoshop file in RGB format and an equivalent grayscale file in DCS 2 format that is a PowerTone separation. Another folder is titled Publisher Demo Photos. It also contains three sets of sample photos—RGB Photoshop file and DCS 2 PowerTone separation. Take a look. You'll be surprised and delighted.

Finally, you should be very careful with the Powertone plug-in. Generating two-color separations has the same addictive quality possessed by duotones, and then some! Once you try it, you won't want to stop putting all kinds of colored images through it just to see what will happen.

The URL for Powertone's publisher is **www.intensesoftware.com**.

Silvertone By Intense Software

An additional note: Intense Software also publishes an Export plug-in for Photoshop called Silvertone. This item is a fascinating special effects program that allows you to generate a metallic-ink fifth color plate that functions as a shiny substrate upon which your other colors will print. The end result is an uncanny simulation of such things as the reflectance on a soft drink can, or the shiny metallic paint on a sports car. Any of the metallic inks can be used for this effect. The results are spectacular. If you are a Photoshop user who works extensively in advertising, you should investigate this software. The CD-ROM accompanying this book contains, in the Chapter 9 Demo Files folder, a demo of the SilverTone plug-in for Macintosh (at the time this book was going to press, this software was not available for Windows) and the User Manual in PDF format. There are also a pair of samples, one a Photoshop file in CMYK format, the other a five-channel file in DCS 2 format that will give you an idea how the metallic ink channel (#5) works with the other four. (The URL for the publisher of SilverTone is listed in the preceding paragraph.)

Spot Color

The term *spot color* refers to the use of premixed inks on press. In process color printing, colors are formed by overprinting the process primaries: cyan, magenta, yellow, and black. Despite the fact that process inks routinely deliver faithful color reproduction, wide ranges of colors cannot be reproduced. Process inks also have another drawback: Because the inks must be more or less translucent so that they seem to blend with each other, they cannot act as a simultaneous vehicle for color and surface textures. Spot colors—referred to in Photoshop as Custom Colors—are able to remedy these drawbacks of process printing. Spot colors are not built up from other tones—well, they are, but not on press—but are mixed before printing and applied as a single color, sometimes with tints—tones with percentages less than 100 percent—of the color.

With spot colors, there's often no need to preserve ink translucency. Large amounts of pigment in the solvent medium can be made to produce gloriously saturated colors. Minute amounts of metal or light-colored reflective materials can be introduced along with the pigment to produce highly reflective flat colors (neon) or metallic reflectance. In some cases, there may be no pigment at all: The ink is applied as a transparent film with surface properties ranging from shiny to matte. Such inks—varnishes or aqueous coatings—are applied to enhance colored areas of the printing, or to provide a subtle reflective contrast with the surface of the print stock.

Earlier versions of Photoshop made the handling of spot colors more complex than it needed to be. Photoshop 5 has now included a formidable array of tools as rich, deep, and powerful as its other tools. If you have not worked with custom colors before, you will be surprised at how easy it is. You may also be surprised at the mental adjustments you will need to make as you keep in mind that you will be dealing with color in a way that is unlike your previous experience with four-color separations.

A Four Custom-Color Tutorial

The easiest way to learn a technique is to follow a tutorial. No, please don't groan! We're aware that many tutorials in software manuals are—as the saying goes—about as interesting as watching paint dry. This one isn't so bad. The material is interesting, it has pretty colors, and nearly all the real work has already been done for you. You only have to open the file (on this book's CD-ROM, find the file AFRICA.PSD in the Chapter 9 Practice Files folder), follow along, and do the fun stuff. When you're finished, you'll have a much clearer idea how to use Photoshop's spot color capabilities for your own custom color work.

This tutorial involves making a small poster announcing an African textile exhibit at a museum in a small Midwestern city. An approximation of the poster is shown in Figure 9.113 and in color in the Color Studio section of this book.

Figure 9.113 Four-tone poster to be prepared in Photoshop for output with custom colors.

First, some background about how and why the file was put together the way it is. The background of the poster is a set of African motifs suggestive of the repetition of motifs on a textile. The color used is an orange-tinted gold, Pantone 116. (If you have a Pantone swatch book, you might find it useful to look at the colors and compare them to the file.) Two stressed-looking zebras are next. They, and the round-dot border, are to be printed in Pantone 876, a metallic copper ink. The two large words are in an inline version of the Lithos Black font. They are colored with Pantone Warm Red. Finally, the four lines of small text at the bottom are in Pantone Black.

Each of the four components of this poster was placed on a separate layer. The background shapes were put together in Illustrator, using enlarged characters from the shareware font African Ornaments One by Michelle Dixon of Dixie's Delights Fonts. The shapes were copied and pasted into this document as black shapes. The Paste operation created a separate layer with the areas around and inside the shapes transparent. Figure 9.114 shows a detail of the shapes with the white background layer hidden. The other two text layers—the large title letters and the four lines of smaller text at the bottom—were also pasted into this document as black shapes. Transparent areas also surround these letter shapes. Note that the inner areas of the inline letters are transparent.

The zebra layer was pasted in from a black and white scan. Because it will be necessary to have access to the outlines of the zebra shapes, we eliminated the white areas from the original scan using the following procedure on this black and white scan. Command+click or Ctrl+click on the channel's thumbnail to turn the white areas into a selection. Choose Select|Inverse to select the black areas. For this document, we used the Copy command and then pasted the zebras into the poster file. As you can see from Figure 9.114, only the dark areas were pasted.

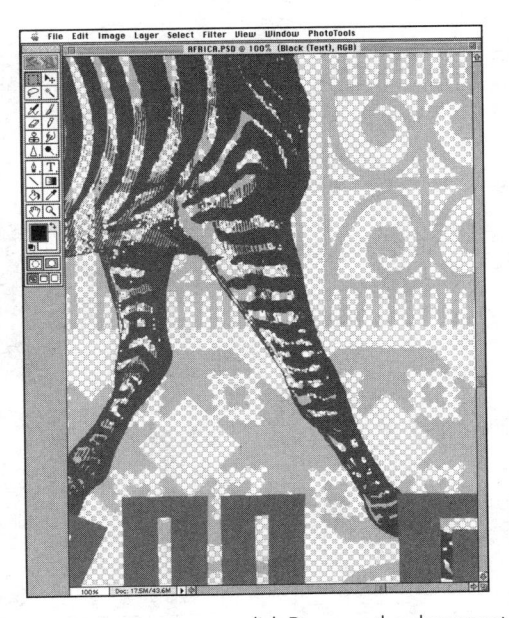

Figure 9.114 All of the color areas in the poster are solid. Because the document is in layers, other colors show through the areas between the color shapes.

The border was pasted in separately. Because it is to be the same color as the zebras, we hid all but these two layers and used the Merge Visible command from the Layers palette sidebar menu.

There were now four layers and a solid white background. We turned on Preserve Transparency for each layer. We colored the bottom image layer first. We clicked on the Foreground Color box, clicked on Custom, and chose the ink we wished to use. When the Color Picker was closed, we selected the bottom layer and used Option+Delete or Alt+Delete to fill the non-transparent pixels with the gold color. All of the other layers were colored in the same way. We then turned off the Preserve Transparency option for each layer. At that point we saved the file for you to open.

Figure 9.115 shows the bottom layer with all other layers hidden. In Figure 9.116, the zebra layer is now visible. We cannot use the zebra layer as it is, because the bottom layer shows between the zebra stripes. Your next task is to make, and then modify, an alpha channel. Follow these steps:

1. Command+click (Mac) or Ctrl+click (Windows) on the zebra layer's thumbnail. This selects all of the non-transparent pixels of the layer. Save this selection as an alpha channel (click on the Save Selection icon—second from the left—at the bottom of the Channels palette). Deselect. Click on the new channel's thumbnail to view it (see Figure 9.117).

2. Zoom in closer to the window. Use paintbrushes and selection tools (filling a selection with white) to eliminate the black pixels within the boundaries of the zebra shapes. This is simple if a bit time-consuming. It is a *lot* easier than trying to select the zebras before pasting them into this document! When you are finished, your channel should resemble the one shown in Figure 9.118.

Figure 9.115 The bottom layer in this poster contains the background shapes.

Figure 9.116 The layer with the zebras needs to be modified because the background shapes show between the zebra stripes.

Figure 9.117 Make the zebra layer into a selection, then save it to an alpha channel.

Figure 9.118 Work in the alpha channel with the selection tools and the Paintbrush to fill in the zebra stripes and to make the shapes solid white.

3. Click on the top thumbnail of the Channels palette to view the document in color. Hide the zebra layer so that only the bottom layer and the background are visible. Click on the bottom layer to select it. Make the modified channel into an active selection by Command+clicking or Ctrl+clicking its thumbnail on the Channels palette. Press the Delete key. All of the pixels directly below the zebras and the border circles are eliminated from the bottom layer (see Figure 9.119). Deselect. Make the zebra layer visible again (see Figure 9.120). Notice that the spaces between the zebra stripes are entirely white.

4. Next, apply this same procedure to the large red titling letters. Make the headline layer visible and select it (see Figure 9.121). Command+click (Mac) or Ctrl+click (Windows) on the layer icon to make the letter shapes into a selection. Save the selection as an alpha channel (click on the Save Selection icon at the bottom of the Channels palette). Click on the new alpha channel's thumbnail to view it (see Figure 9.122). Use a paintbrush somewhat narrower than the letters—with the Foreground color set to white—to eliminate the inline portion of the letters. When you're finished, your channel should look similar to Figure 9.123.

5. Click on the top thumbnail of the Channels palette to view the document in color. Turn the new channel into a selection (Command+click or Ctrl+click on the channel's thumbnail). Hide the headline layer and the zebra layer. Select the bottom layer. Press the Delete key. This eliminates the letter shapes from the bottom layer (see Figure 9.124). Make the zebra layer visible and select it. Press the Delete key. This deletes the shapes of the letters from the layer containing the zebras (see Figure 9.125). Make the titling letters layer visible. If you look at it carefully, you can see that the spaces within the letters are entirely white (see Figure 9.126).

602 Chapter 9

Figure 9.119 Make the alpha channel into a selection. Select the layer with the background shapes and press Delete to eliminate the zebra shapes from the background layer.

Figure 9.120 Make the zebra layer visible. The background shapes no longer show through the zebra stripes.

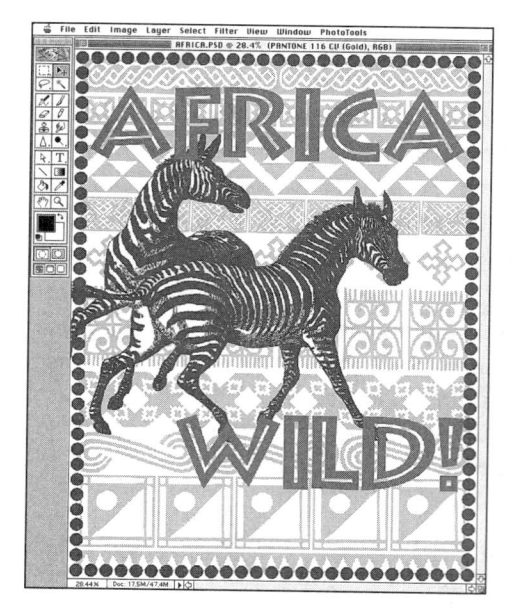

Figure 9.121 Make the headline layer visible.

Figure 9.122 Make the headline layer into a selection, and save it as another alpha channel.

Figure 9.123 Work in the alpha channel, and eliminate the inner black shapes from the letters.

Figure 9.124 Make the new alpha channel into a selection. Select the background layer and press Delete. This eliminates the letter shapes from the background shapes.

Figure 9.125 Make the zebra layer visible and click on its thumbnail in the Layers palette. With the alpha channel selection still active, press Delete to eliminate the letter shapes from where they overlap the zebras.

Figure 9.126 With all three layers visible, none of the shapes in back show through the spaces in objects in front.

6. The last layer contains the smaller text at the bottom of the poster. Make this layer visible and select it (see Figure 9.127). It isn't necessary to make an alpha channel for this layer because the letter shapes do not need to be modified and simply need to be knocked out of the bottom layer. Command+click or Ctrl+click on the layer's thumbnail to make the selection. Hide the layer and click on the bottom layer's thumbnail to select it. Press the Delete key (see Figure 9.128).

7. From the sidebar menu of the Channels palette, choose the New Spot Channel command. When the dialog box appears, set the Solidity to 0%. Click on the color swatch and select Pantone 116 CV (orange-tinted gold). Click on OK and then on OK again. Create two more new spot channels, one each for Pantone Warm Red and Pantone Process Black. The fourth channel is the metallic channel and you won't find 876 Copper in the Custom Color picker. Choose Pantone 154 and click on OK. While the dialog box is still open, manually enter 876 in place of the number 154. Pantone 154 is a copper-colored ink and will serve to reasonably display your metallic ink channel.

   Now comes the fun part. Click on the eye icons of the R, G, and B channels to hide them. Click on the eye icons of the four spot channels to display them. At this point, you should be looking at an empty white window. Don't worry—it's only temporary.

8. Set your Foreground color to black. Command+click (Mac) or Ctrl+click (Windows) to make the zebra layer into a selection. On the Channels palette, click on the thumbnail of the 871 channel. Fill the selection with black (see Figure 9.129). The zebra shapes and the border should appear filled with the copper color.

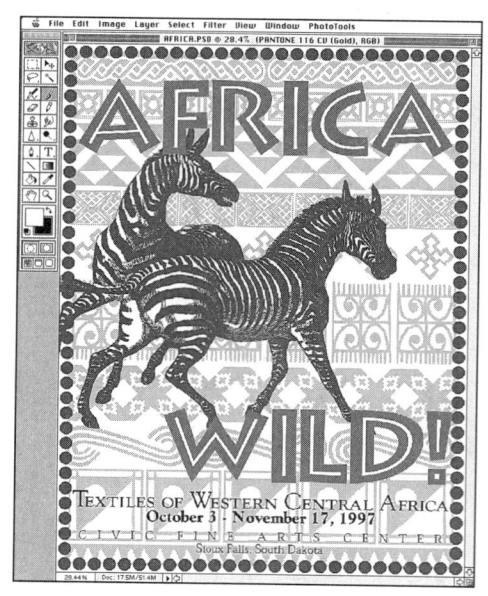

Figure 9.127 Make the fourth—small text—layer visible. Turn it into a selection. Use the selection to knock out the small letters from the background shapes.

Figure 9.128 A close-up of the background layer shows how all the shapes have been cut out of the background layer.

9. Command+click or Ctrl+click to make the title letters layer into a selection. On the Channels palette, click on the thumbnail of the Pantone Warm Red channel. Fill the selection with black (see Figure 9.130).

10. Command+click or Ctrl+click to make the background layer into a selection. On the Channels palette, click on the thumbnail of the Pantone 116 channel. Fill the selection with black (see Figure 9.131).

11. Command+click or Ctrl+click to make the small-letters text layer into a selection. On the Channels palette, click on the thumbnail of the Pantone Process Black channel. Fill the selection with black (see Figure 9.132).

12. You should now see your image looking very much as it did before you hid the R, G, and B channels. To finish with the file, delete the alpha channels you used to create the knockouts for the zebras and the large letters (drag their thumbnails to the trash icon at the bottom of the palette). Make all of the layers visible. Delete all of the layers. (You no longer need them because you've already transferred the information to the spot color channels.) If you click on the top thumbnail of the Channels palette (RGB) and hide the spot channels, you should see a blank white window. If you make the spot channels visible, you should see an image that appears similar to that in Figure 9.133.

13. The next step to trap the document. For trapping, you'll need to convert your document temporarily to CMYK mode. (Trapping is covered in detail in Chapter 10.) Photoshop's Trap command is found at the bottom of the Image menu. The dialog box allows you to specify the amount of trap in pixels, points, or millimeters. The

Figure 9.129 After adding the four spot channels, click on the 871 channel to select it. Turn the zebra layer into a selection, and fill the selection with black.

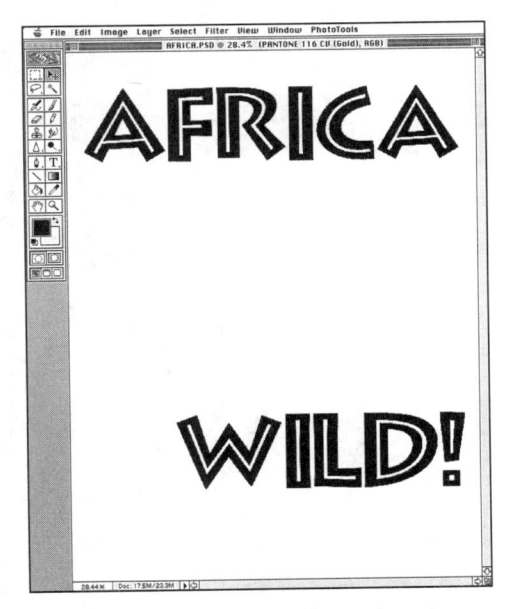

Figure 9.130 Turn the headline letters layer into a selection, switch to the Pantone Warm Red channel, and fill the selection with black.

606 CHAPTER 9

Figure 9.131 Turn the background motifs layer into a selection, switch to the Pantone 116 channel, and fill the selection with black.

Figure 9.132 Turn the small type layer into a selection, switch to the Pantone Black channel, and fill the selection with black.

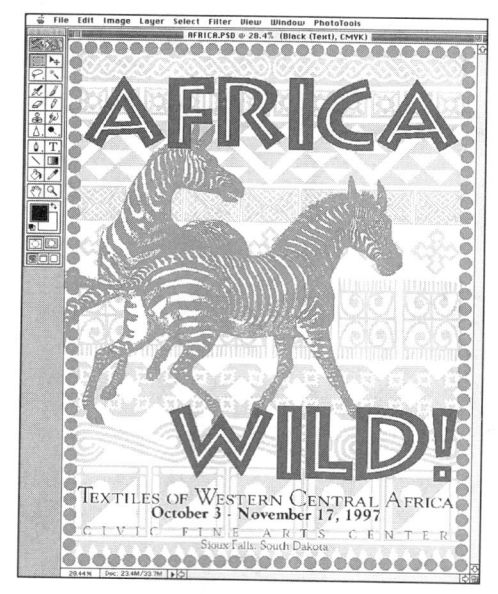

Figure 9.133 Delete the layers. Make the spot channels visible. Your image will now look the same as when you started.

print house running your job will furnish you with trap specifications. A typical measurement might be .003 inches. Because Photoshop does not allow the trap specification to be entered in inches, you need to use a conversion utility to convert the required

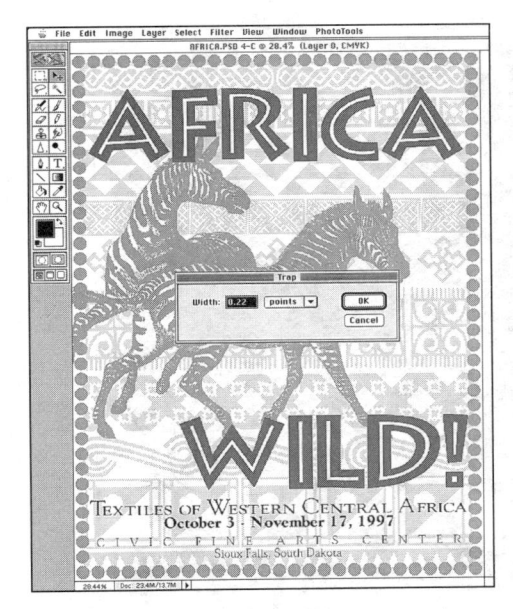

Figure 9.134 Use Photoshop's Trap command to trap the ink areas where they meet each other.

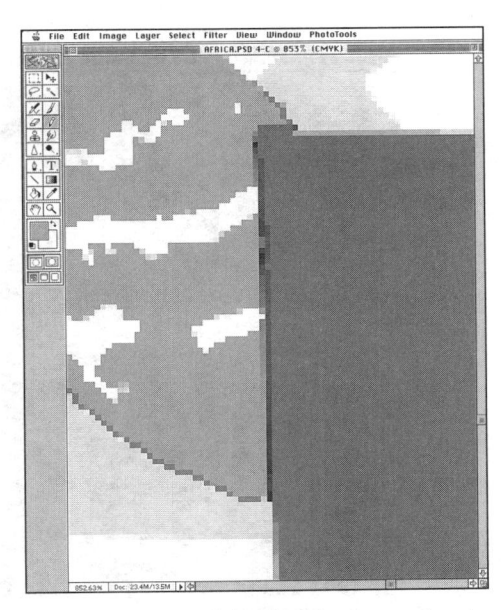

Figure 9.135 Enlarged detail of the poster after the Trap command has executed.

number into one of the available units of measurement. For example, .003 inches is equal to .216 points. Change the Units pop-up menu to points and enter ".22" (see Figure 9.134). The enlarged view in Figure 9.135 shows how the trapping spreads the lighter colors into the darker colors wherever those colors meet each other.

14. After you run the Trap command, convert your file to Grayscale mode. There is no color information to be imaged in the primary channels, and changing modes will reduce the file's size by about 38 percent.

15. The file should now be saved in DCS 2.0 format. You can now import the file into any program that accepts DCS 2 files. Your file will image easily and give you perfect-fitting film. Figure 9.136 shows an approximation of the four negatives.

Bump Plates, Touch Plates

Custom colors are sometimes used to give an additional punch to some of the tones of a four-color image. These extra inks are applied from what are called *touch plates* or *bump plates*. (When you *double-bump* a press sheet, you apply ink to the same spot more than once. You can see examples of double-bump printing in the Pantone swatch book: Look toward the center of the swatch book for the set of colors designated with 2X. The richness of those colors is achieved by printing the same area twice with the same ink.) Touch plates are plates that apply an extra ink, usually as a tint, to modify the color tones over which they are printed. Bump plates apply the same inks in order to intensify the overprinted color. The added inks can deliver an increase in saturation and a set of tones not possible otherwise. Extra inks can also be used for adding contrasting surface textures.

Figure 9.136 A look at the four CMYK negatives that will be printed with the labeled Pantone inks.

Touch plates are often used to augment *out-of-gamut* colors. Out-of-gamut colors are colors that cannot be accurately reproduced using just the four process inks. Bright, primary tones, especially those used for clothing—the neon colors used for winter-sports outerwear, or the bright, crayon colors used for children's clothing, for example—are nearly always out of gamut. By applying a tint of spot color, out-of-gamut colors can be made to look much more believable.

Many Photoshop users aren't familiar with this process, or if they are, they think that it's one of those semi-occult things that only hot dogs and experts do. The truth is that generating a touch plate is no more complicated than what you learned in the four-color poster tutorial example discussed earlier. If you wish to try this technique and to follow along with the set of instructions below, locate and open the file HIBISCIS.PSD in the Chapter 9 Practice Files folder on this book's CD-ROM.

The example file on the CD-ROM is in CMYK mode. Figure 9.137 shows a grayscale representation of this file. If you study the disk file, you can see that it would benefit from an extra ink—such as PANTONE Warm Red CV—to warm up the intense magenta tones of the separation. The background of the image contrasts with the flower, but seems to lack depth. You'll add that depth by applying an extra ink—a light overprint of PANTONE 3 CV, a dense black made up of 10 parts PANTONE Black and 6 parts PANTONE Green. Follow these steps:

1. Your first task is to press Q to enter Quick Mask, and to mask the flower shape, using whichever of the tools you desire. (You don't really have to do this unless you want the experience because the file on the CD-ROM has the mask alpha channel saved with it.) When the mask is finished, it looks as shown in Figure 9.138. Invert the Quick Mask and press Q to exit Quick Mask mode. Click on the Save Selection icon at the bottom of the Channels palette. The new channel looks as shown in Figure 9.139.

2. If you cycle through the channels, you can see that most of the flower's color is contributed by the Magenta channel. This is the channel where the flower shape contains the *most* dark pixels. Press Command+2 (Mac) or Ctrl+2 (Windows) to view the Magenta channel (see Figure 9.140). Activate the alpha channel by Command+clicking or Ctrl+clicking on its thumbnail on the Channels palette. Copy the selection. Deselect.

3. Create a new Spot Color channel by Command+clicking (Mac) or Ctrl+clicking (Windows) on the New Channel icon—just to the left of the Trash icon—on the Channels palette. Set the color of the channel to Pantone Warm Red and the Solidity to 60% (see

Figure 9.137 Although this image is usable, adding touch plates warms up the reds of the flower and gives a deep richness to the areas around it.

Figure 9.138 In Quick Mask, mask the flower shape.

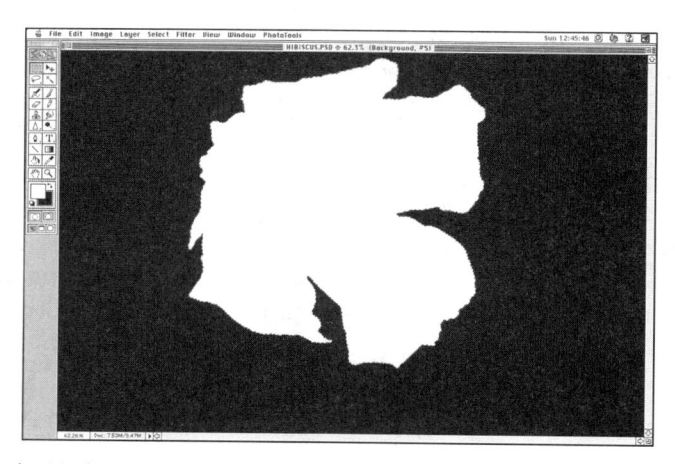

Figure 9.139 Invert the Mask, exit Quick Mask, and save the selection as an alpha channel.

Figure 9.140 Most of the image data for the flower is in the Magenta channel.

Figure 9.141). Activate the previous alpha channel (Command+click or Ctrl+click on the channel's thumbnail). When the selection is active, use the Paste command. The copied flower shape centers itself perfectly within the selection. This channel now looks the same as Figure 9.142. Click on the eye icons of all the channels. You should now see the full image with a heavy, too-opaque coating of red over the flower (see Figure 9.143).

4. Click the fifth-color channel's eye icon off and on so that you can see how much color it contributes to the flower (see Figure 9.143). 60% is far too much. Double-click the thumbnail, and change the Solidity downward. You'll find the correct percentage around 20%. This ability of Photoshop to show how much ink the bump plate will contribute and how it will affect the color is incredibly useful. It makes the generation of the plate very simple because you can see beforehand how the new ink will change your image!

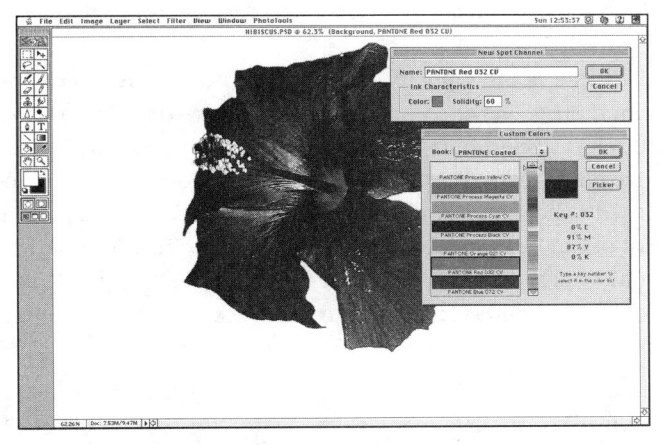

Figure 9.141 Make a new spot color channel. Use the mask alpha channel to copy the selection from the Magenta channel into the new channel.

Figure 9.142 Your new spot color channel will show just the shape of the flower on a white background.

Figure 9.143 Look at all five channels together by clicking on the eye icons on the Channels palette.

5. The key to the plate is the Opacity figure. Our task now is to change the spot color channel so that it prints in the same way we have viewed it. Click on the spot channel's thumbnail to select it, and hide the other channels so you only see the spot channel. Select all. Set your Foreground color to white. Choose Edit|Fill (or type Shift+Delete). Make the fill with the Foreground color, Normal mode, and the Opacity set to 80% (the reciprocal of the 20% Solidity we used to preview the effect of the fifth ink). Click on OK. Your channel should now look like the example in Figure 9.144. The modification scaled the color values in this channel back by 80%. In other words, all the non-white tones are now 20% of their original values.

6. Double-click on this channel's thumbnail. Change the Solidity to 100% (see Figure 9.145). Click on all of the eye icons so that you can see the effect of all five colors. Notice that 100% Solidity of the screened-back channel is the same as the 100% chan-

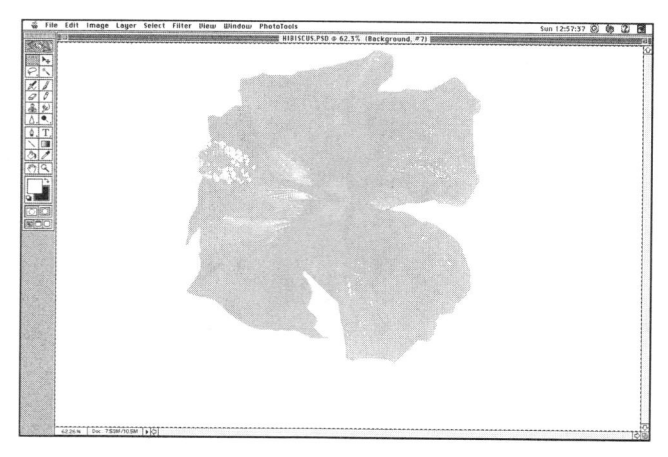

Figure 9.144 After determining that the channel looks best at 20% Solidity, screen back the channel by filling with white at 80% Opacity.

nel displayed with 20% solidity. The difference is that solidity has nothing to do with the way your channel will print. You have simply used it to figure out how much you needed to cut back on the original values.

7. When you import this file into QuarkXPress or Adobe PageMaker, remember to change the screen angle for the red ink. Your reasoning for the choice of screen angle might be along these lines: When the image is finally printed, there will be very little cyan ink in the area of the flower. (Type Command+1 or Ctrl+1 to view the cyan channel for yourself.) Cyan would be, then, a good choice for the Pantone Warm Red screen angle.

8. The second touch plate is used to deepen the area around the flower with a dark-green-tinted black. Activate the original channel (#5) as a selection. Choose Select|Inverse.

9. If you cycle through the color channels, you can see that several of them could be used as the basis for the second touch plate. Another way to approach deciding which channel to use allows you to learn some interesting things about the image: Switch the eye icons for each channel off and on to view the color image *without* one of the inks. Clicking off the Cyan channel results in bright yellow leaves. Clicking off the Magenta channel changes the flower to yellow, but makes the background a clearer green. Clicking off the Yellow channel makes the background blue, and the flower bright magenta. Clicking off the Black channel makes the background muddy and ugly. Of the four, the channel that seems not to contribute anything very useful to the color values of the background is the Magenta channel. A good strategy might be to use another black ink with the magenta values because it would darken the background in exactly the areas where the magenta is strongest. This would cancel some of the effects of the magenta background.

10. With the Magenta channel visible, Copy. Create a new spot color channel. Color the channel with Pantone 3 CV, and set the Solidity to 50% (see Figure 9.146). Hide the rest of the channels and view only the new channel. Paste (see Figure 9.147).

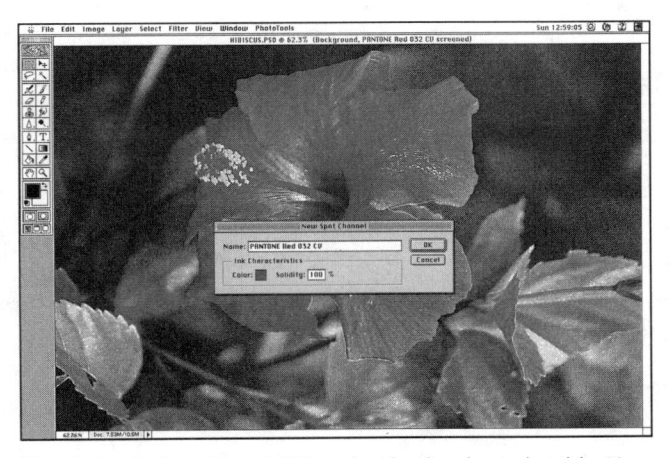

Figure 9.145 Change the channel's Opacity to 100% and make the channel visible. You now have a reasonably accurate representation of the way the red touch plate will overprint the CMYK inks.

11. View all of the channels together. Experiment with the Opacity setting until the background looks exactly the way you wish it to print. 40% seems to be a pretty good value. Turn off both of the touch plate channels and look at the image (see Figure 9.148). Now turn them on (see Figure 9.149). Look closely at the two figures in the book: Even in grayscale, it's possible to see an improvement in contrast. The image looks even better in color.

12. Select the black spot color channel. Select All, choose Edit|Fill. Make the fill Opacity setting 60% (the reciprocal of the 40% Solidity setting used to view the ink). The lightened channel is shown in Figure 9.150. Set the Solidity for the channel to 100% (see Figure 9.151). Check it in the full color view. Save the file in DCS 2.0 format.

13. When using this file in QuarkXPress or Adobe PageMaker, be sure to change the screen angle for this ink. Remember the reasoning used to construct this channel: Neutralize and darken some of the magenta tones in the background of the image. If you use the

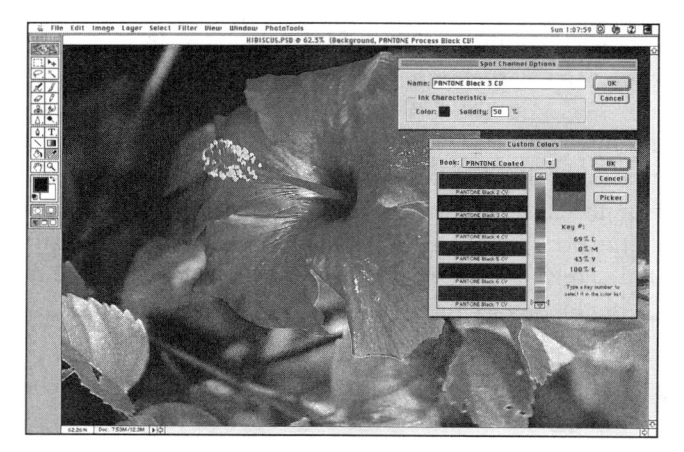

Figure 9.146 Use the inverse selection of the flower mask channel to copy the area around the flower in the Magenta channel. Create a new spot channel and Paste.

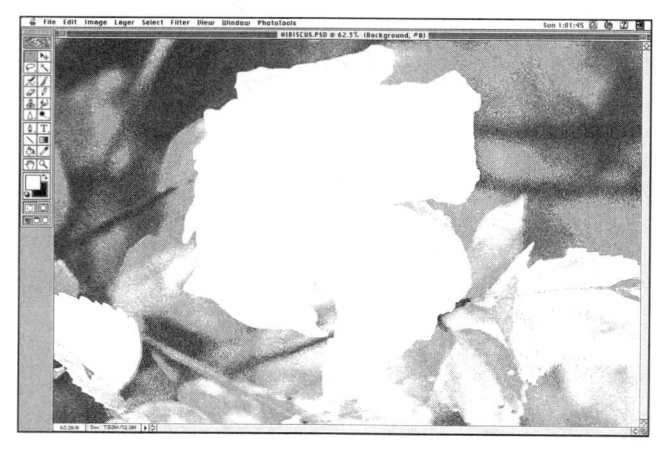

Figure 9.147 The new spot color channel will look like this.

PHOTOSHOP PREPRESS   **615**

Figure 9.148   Turn off the visibility of the two touch plates to see the image without the extra color.

Figure 9.149   Turn on the visibility of the touch plates to see how the extra inks make the image look richer.

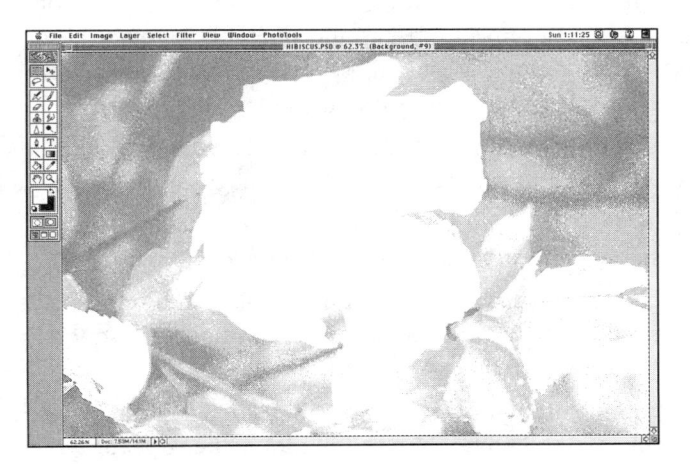

Figure 9.150   Screen back the channel by the reciprocal percentage of the Opacity setting.

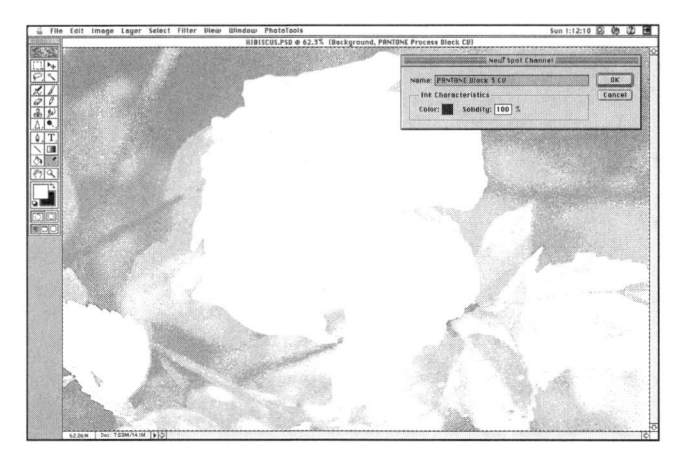

Figure 9.151 Change the Solidity back to 100%.

magenta screen angle, all of the dots of the black Pantone ink will print directly on top of the magenta dots and mute them more than if the angle were such that the black dots printed in the spaces between the lines of the magenta dots. It's all pretty logical, don't you think?

Spot Colors In Line Art And Deconstructed Photo Material

When you need to apply custom colors to scanned, colorized line art, or if you need to deconstruct a photographic image in order to print it with custom colors, you can use a number of techniques. In the following set of directions, you learn how to take a colored photographic image and process it to print with eight custom colors. There are utility plug-ins that will do this job for you, but it will be instructive for you to understand how to do this manually. These steps are not difficult but, as you will see, there are quite a few of them. We hope you'll try this method; it's nearly foolproof and gives very good results.

In order to deconstruct a color photographic image, whatever colors are present must be reduced in number. A maximum number would probably be eight because few presses have more than eight inking stations. Most of these instructions have to do with the reduction process. To deconstruct a color photographic image, follow these steps:

1. Begin by duplicating the original RGB image. Do your work on the copy, but keep the original visible so that it can be used later as a sampling source for colors (see Figure 9.152).

2. Convert the image to Grayscale mode (see Figure 9.153).

3. Choose Image|Adjust|Posterize. Take a quick look at the image. If it contains large areas of light pixels around the subject of the image, choose 9 as your number of levels (see Figure 9.154). Otherwise, choose 8.

   Choose this posterization number because Photoshop considers white to be one of the colors. You, however, will have white as the color of the paper on which the image is to print. If you chose 8, you would have only 7 inks.

PHOTOSHOP PREPRESS **617**

Figure 9.152 Duplicate the image to be used. Work on the duplicate. Keep the original visible (lower left corner) so that you can use it for a color reference.

Figure 9.153 Convert to Grayscale mode.

It's important to posterize when you are in Grayscale mode so that you can obtain the number of colors you want to have: Choose the number 9 when posterizing an RGB file and you'll probably end up with at least a couple of hundred colors. The posterization algorithm works by channel. If each channel is posterized to nine tones, that gives the potential of 9^3 colors = 729.

Figure 9.154 Posterize the image to nine values (this gives you eight image tones plus the white background, which is not treated as an ink).

You could also reduce the number of colors by converting the file to Indexed Color mode and specifying 9 colors, Adaptive. Try both methods. You'll probably agree that posterization works better.

4. Convert the grayscale file back to RGB. Press W to select the Magic Wand tool. Enter "1" as the tolerance value for the Magic Wand, and uncheck the Anti-aliased option. Click on one of the grayscale tones in the image. Choose Select|Similar. This selects all of the pixels in the image with the same value on which you clicked. Press I to select the Eyedropper tool. Sample a color from the original image with which you will replace the tone of the selected grayscale area. After you choose the color, click on the Foreground Color box, and then click on the Custom button on the Color Picker. Photoshop displays the nearest Pantone color to the value you have sampled (see Figure 9.155). If you wish to use Photoshop's version of the color, click on OK. Otherwise, click on Cancel. Be sure to write the number down. Don't be too concerned if the Pantone color doesn't quite match your sampled color. The only way to really know what the color will look like is to check it with a Pantone swatch book. Cross-referencing the sampled color, Photoshop's display of the Pantone color, and the printed swatch book will help you arrive at exactly the color you desire.

5. Fill the selection with the Foreground color (see Figure 9.156). Continue this same procedure until you have finished re-colorizing the grayscale image and have selected and named eight Pantone colors. Figure 9.157 shows the completed image. Notice how, even converted to eight shades, this image looks pretty good.

6. When you're satisfied with the colors you've chosen, create eight Spot Color channels. Set each to the Pantone colors you've chosen as fill colors. Set your Foreground color to black. With the Magic Wand, click on an area of the first color. Choose Select|Similar.

Figure 9.155 Pick a Custom Color based on a color sample for the original image.

Figure 9.156 Fill your selection with the selected color.

Click on the equivalent spot color channel to select it. Press Option+Delete (Mac) or Alt+Delete (Windows) to fill the selected area in the channel with black. Follow this same procedure for each of your eight colors. (Note: You could have created your channels first and filled the spot color channels as you chose your colors from the Color Picker. Doing so would save you a number of steps. The former method was presented to give you a clearer idea of how the process works.)

Figure 9.157 Fill all eight color areas with Custom Colors based on tones sampled from the original image.

7. After you transfer all the color information to the spot color channels, click on the RGB (top) composite icon and fill the RGB channels with white. Click on the eye icons to view all the channels. Your image will look identical to the way it was before you added the spot color icons.

8. Change the mode of your image to CMYK. Select all eight of the spot channels. Execute the Trap command. Change the mode of the image to Grayscale. Save your file in DCS 2 format.

Other Third-Party Spot-Color Utilities

You have learned to manually deconstruct a photo image and to place the color information into spot color channels. The same techniques can be used for scanned versions of colored line art. Remember that when you have areas of different inks adjoining each other, you need to change the mode of your image to CMYK, select the spot color channels, and run the Trap command. After you have done this, you can change the mode of your file to Grayscale—unless the primary color channels also contain color data—and save the file in DCS 2 format.

Several Photoshop add-ons can do much of the work of deconstruction for you. These two add-ons, described in the following sections, have extensive roots in the screen printing industry. If you are connected to the screen print world, you should investigate both of these plug-ins. You will find that they are equally useful for offset work with custom colors.

PhotoSpot CT By Second Glance Software

PhotoSpot CT can do automatically what you just learned to do manually. Deconstruct the image, divide it into color areas, place those color areas into labeled spot color channels, and save the file in DCS 2 format. The difference is that this software can analyze your image and make use of tints of your chosen colors. The method is similar in effect, although not exactly the same, as you saw with the Powertone export plug-in (described previously).

You can begin with a document that you have already prepared, or you can simply choose File|Export|PhotoSpot CT with an RGB, CMYK, indexed color, or Multichannel document open (shown in Figure 9.158). If the document is already a multichannel file, you can begin the export process at once. If you are working with an unprepared file, your first step is to select the custom inks you want to use. Begin by clicking on the Add button. Photoshop's Color Picker appears in which you can make your first choice. Continue to click on Add until you have assembled your inks. Click on the Continue button.

The separation process begins. PhotoSpot CT reads the image data and distributes it to the closest value found from the list of defined colors. If your image is in CMYK mode, the process inks are automatically added to the ink list. PhotoSpot CT assumes that you wish to preserve the existing CMYK balance and that the additional inks are being introduced for the purpose of touch plates or for spot colors.

A new set of thumbnail windows now appears (see Figure 9.159). The windows include a composite view of the separated image and one each for the individual separations. These windows can be enlarged or made smaller or they can be left as they are.

In the lower left corner of each separation window, you will see several tools. Two round hemisphere buttons allow you to elevate or diminish the amount of the window color that will be included in the overall balance of the image. Next to these is a tone curve tool that opens a dialog box (see Figure 9.160) with which you can customize the gradations within a single color. As you perform any of these operations, PhotoSpot CT does a quick recalculation of the

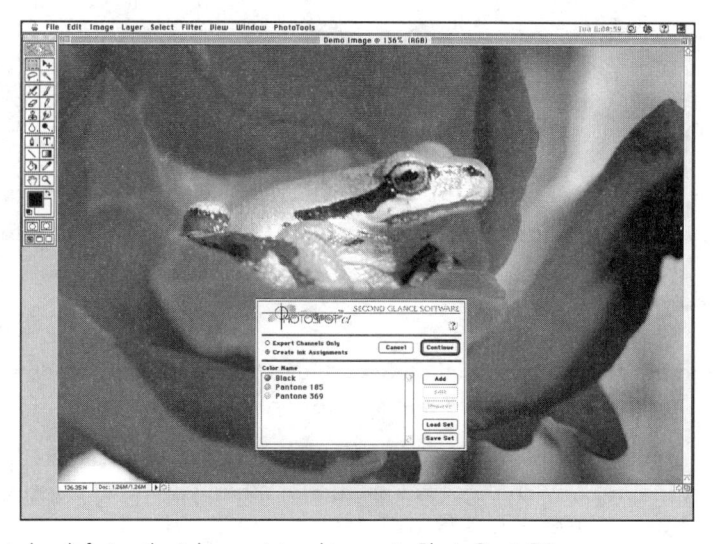

Figure 9.158 Begin by defining the inks you intend to use in PhotoSpot CT.

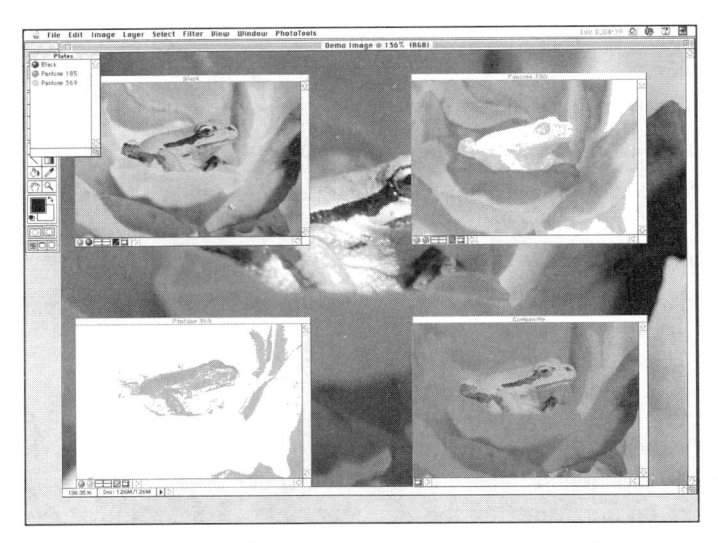

Figure 9.159 Each of PhotoSpot CT's thumbnail windows has its own set of tools for tweaking the colors. Any changes are instantly shown in the Composite window.

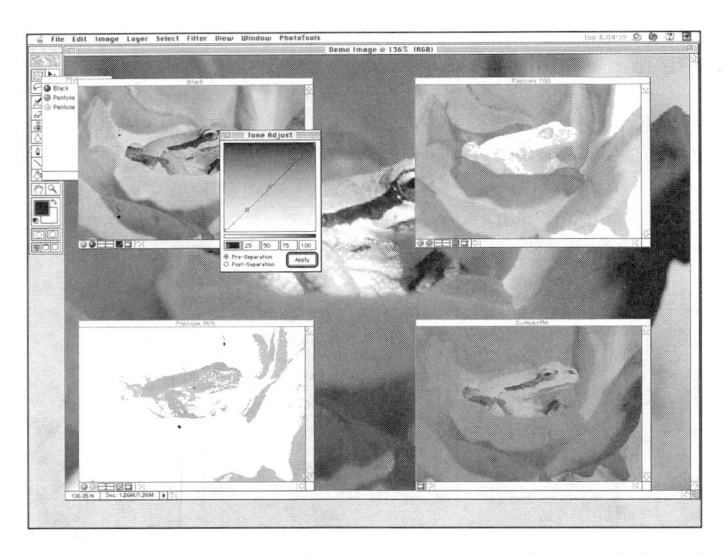

Figure 9.160 When PhotoSpot CT deconstructs the image, it gives you thumbnails for each of the inks and one for the composite of all the inks.

separations, and the change is immediately visible in the Composite window. You can even, at this point, reassign the ink to be used in a separation window.

With your adjustments complete, click on the close box of any of the windows. You are then asked to save or discard any changes you've made. When you have saved your changes, the Export dialog box opens (see Figure 9.161).

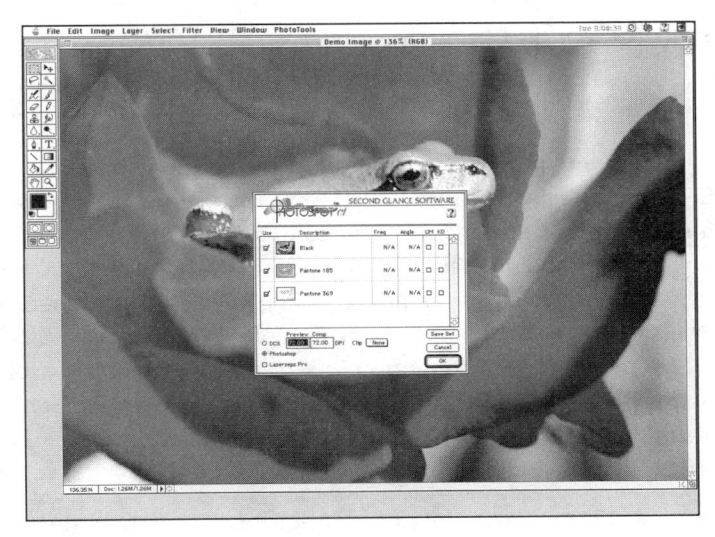

Figure 9.161 The PhotoSpot CT Save/Export dialog box.

The central part of the Export dialog box contains a scrolling list of your inks. The columns allow you to decide whether or not an ink is to be used, the name of the ink, its screen frequency, the screen angle, whether an underprint mask—*very* useful to screen printers—will be generated, and whether or not a given ink should knock out of the other plates.

Finally, there are the save choices. You can save in Photoshop or DCS 2.0 format with the attendant Preview options. A significant choice here is the ability to save the file using LaserSeps Pro. We will discuss this plug-in module more thoroughly in Chapter 10. For now, LaserSeps Pro is a Photoshop export module that allows you to save your separations files with *stochastic screens* instead of conventional screens. Stochastic screens, also discussed in Chapter 10, are dithered screens. They contain very small dots—all of them the same size—that are distributed randomly. There are more dots in dark areas and fewer of them in light areas. With several plate colors—especially if they are tints of the custom inks—and the four process colors, the most significant problem is that of screen angles. Screen angle interference, as is well known, generates moiré patterns and can result in color shifts. With stochastic screens, there are no screen angles to become a problem. All the screen dots are randomly dispersed with their quantity in a given place based on the density of the color value. LaserSeps Pro is sold separately; however, if it was installed on the system generating the separations, it can be accessed directly from PhotoSpot CT.

With its capability to deconstruct a file and to assign colors based on a prebuilt list, PhotoSpot CT is a remarkably advanced Photoshop add-on. You may be able to do some of what it does with manual methods. However, it's impossible to perform these tasks as quickly or as flexibly. For anyone doing custom color work, this add-on is a must-have! You can find Second Glance Software on the Internet at **www.secondglance.com**.

Spot Process By Freehand Graphics, Inc.

A significant number of Photoshop people who use custom colors are connected with the screen printing industry.

Screen printers have many of the same Photoshop preparation concerns that offset printers have. They also have many problems that offset press users never face. Among these are problems with printing inks that are opaque, and compared to SWOP inks, extremely viscous. Sometimes, the viscosity of the pigment medium is so high that it needs to be heated before it can be forced through the screen. Screen printers often need to print on surfaces that are very different from the smooth, coated, white paper that offset printers use—black plastic, for example (the top of your mouse pad came from a screen printer!), or dark-colored t-shirts and sweatshirts. The translucent inks that the offset industry uses simply do not fit a screen printer's requirements. Usually, a heavy, opaque liquid that adheres to non-paper surfaces such as plastic and fabrics is required.

Opaque is the key word here. Our use of four-color process depends on the fact that the inks—excepting black—are not opaque. Colors form by the way our eyes blend very tiny dots together and by the tones of the overlaid colors. Imagine trying to print a solid built red—100 percent yellow overprinted by 100 percent magenta—if the magenta was so opaque that the yellow got covered up!

Screen printers have tried many strategies to duplicate the kind of photo-realism that is possible with translucent inks on a white surface. One possibility is to lay down a coating of white—perhaps on black fabric—that gives a surface on which the other colors might be visible. Most of these strategies work reasonably well, but screen printers are still burdened with screen frequencies that are very coarse when compared to offset printing. There is also the problem of registration: How do you easily and precisely register a t-shirt?

The answer to many screen-printing problems is simply to lay down areas of spot colors and hope for the best. Techniques for generating touch plates or for deconstructing an image into component colors have not been readily available until very recently. A spot color answer to some of these questions is now commercially available. This Photoshop add-on is called Spot Process. It's published by Freehand Graphics, Inc., and it is amazing!

The software is absurdly simple to run. The program ships with a plug-in and with a set of actions. You will need to load the actions into your Actions palette, and then prepare your image. (Bright, vivid colors work best, but pale, pastel images can be used satisfactorily.) When you're ready, click on the action titled Run Spot Process. That's it. Spot Process reads the data of the RGB file and deconstructs—separates—the image into a number of plates. These plates are put into the file as alpha channels and are appropriately labeled by color. The number of plates can range from six to ten (an eleventh channel is non-printing), with eight being a fairly usual number. The separation process is entirely automatic, but you can make tonal adjustments after the separations have been made. The whole procedure is so *easy*. Almost too easy: When something happens with this lack of fuss, you may not be aware of the nearly miraculous separation task that has just been accomplished.

It isn't possible, in a book of this sort, to give anything other than an idea of the possibilities an add-on program such as Spot Process has. It is, however, possible to say that in its own specialized area, Spot Process does the job with as much excellence as you could possibly expect.

You can look at a pair of separations done by Spot Process by looking in the Chapter 9 Demo Files folder on this book's CD-ROM. The files SPDAVID01.PSD and SPDAVID02.EPS are before and after versions—one RGB and one grayscale DCS 2—of a photo you might not usually consider as a possibility for screen printing. The files SPPEONIES.PSD and SPPEONIES.EPS are another pair of separations. The original photo image contains more saturated color than the first, and the separation is more successful. The third set of samples on the disk are titled SPSAMPLE01.PSD and SPSAMPLE02.EPS. These two are before-and-after versions of the demo file which you can download from the publisher's Web site.

A note to screen printers: Both of the first two sample separation files are royalty-free images. You purchased the right to use them when you purchased this book. If you wish to image either of the CD-ROM files for testing purposes, please do so. The authors and the publisher of the software would be grateful to hear of your successes or partial success (with software this easy to use, failure just isn't an option). The folder containing the samples contains a small PDF file that will give you additional Output and Preparation information. If you need further technical assistance, please contact the publisher via it's Web site, **www.spotprocess.com**.

Line Art And Bitmap Mode

The Bitmap mode is one of the most useful and most underused of Photoshop's image modes. Editing images in Bitmap mode is difficult. Some of the tools work, some of them—illogically—don't. When the tools do work, they may work in an unexpected way.

Of the selection tools, the Marquee, Lasso, and Cropping tools function normally except that there is no anti-aliased option offered for any tool. The Magic Wand tool—for reasons that must make sense to *someone*—doesn't work in this mode. Of the other tools, the Paint Bucket, Gradient tool, Dodge/Burn/Sponge tools, Sharpen/Blur tools, and the Smudge tool do not function in Bitmap mode. The Pen tool functions normally. The Eraser, Pencil, Paintbrush, and Airbrush tools are also functional, except that the brush choices from the Brushes palette are all the same aliased shapes. It's as though all of these tools are identical to the Pencil tool used in any other color mode. All but three of the normal array of Blend modes is unavailable for any of the paint tools. The Normal mode is replaced with a Blend mode that is available only in this image mode, Threshold. The three remaining Blend modes available are Dissolve, Darken, and Lighten.

The way these tools behave is, for the most part, not surprising. There are no colors or grays in Bitmap mode, only black and white. Each pixel is one or the other. This may seem very limiting, but this binary state is the ultimate form for all of your output. No matter what kind of printer or output device you are using, no matter whether you're putting toner on paper or imaging film to be used to burn plates, the data that produces that output is straight bitmap data.

It's an interesting thought, isn't it? If you think about it, you can see that putting ink on paper—and all the intermediate steps such as producing film and plates—is the ultimate bitmap paradigm. In the case of halftones, gray tones are not produced by 256 shades of gray ink, but by tiny black dots that cover some percentage of the white paper. Because the dots are so small, our eyes blend the black and white tones so that we seem to see grays. The task of a PostScript RIP (Raster Image Processor) is to convert grayscale—or, more accurately, *8-bit* information—into bitmap information. By averaging the gray values of several pixels (usually four of them in a 2 × 2 area), the RIP can accurately assess the size the dot needs to be to represent that tone as ink on paper. Then, working with a resolution much higher than the input file's resolution, it can construct the dot, and control whatever imaging assembly is required to reproduce the dot on film or paper.

Processing Line Art Scans

Bitmap is most used in Photoshop as the image mode for line art files. Line art files are typically simple, one-colored shapes used for logos and special graphic symbols. The only requirement for their reproduction is that the edges of the shapes be sharp and clean. Because a bitmap file is 12.5 percent the size of a grayscale file with the same number of pixels, line art images can be handled at a much higher resolution than would be practical with any other image mode. They are also much easier for a RIP to process than any other kind of digital construct, even at high resolutions.

Most scanners have a line art setting that scans the original material directly as bitmap. As the scanner analyzes the data, it applies a simple threshold computation to it: Pixels 50 percent or lighter are changed to white, and all others are changed to black. When the scan is finished and the file is on screen, the mode of the image is bitmap. This is workable if the original image is of good quality and if the scanner is also of fairly good quality. In a production situation, however, conditions are not always so good. Rarely is the line art original of good quality—it isn't unusual for the original to be scanned from a matchbook cover, the corner of a paper napkin, or even a fax of a photocopy. (The non-Photoshop user's definition of *camera ready* is vastly different from ours, is it not?)

In such situations, scanning in line art mode is not the best procedure, because editing the file to fix any problems can be so time-consuming. A better procedure is to scan in Grayscale mode and then to use Photoshop's powerful editing capabilities before converting the file to Bitmap mode. We will outline a set of steps that converts scans of poor-quality original images into high-quality files. Keep in mind that many scanners have a setting called Halftone Screen that is another bitmap computation and is rarely as successful as Photoshop's conversion of grayscale information.

When scanning the original image, choose Grayscale mode for the scan and set the scan resolution to be an even divisor of, or equal to, the output device's resolution. (Using a resolution higher than that of your output device has no benefit.) If your output device is a high-resolution PostScript imagesetter with a resolution of 2400 dpi, your scan resolution could be 200, 300, 400, 600, 800, 1200, or 2400 ppi. All of these numbers divide into 2400 with no remainder.

The best results are at fairly high resolutions such as 600 ppi and 1200 ppi. Because you are scanning in grayscale, you will be working, temporarily, with files that will seem very large. Don't be too concerned: After you finish editing the files, you convert them to bitmap format, which reduces them by 87.5 percent.

Here's another scanning point to be considered: Most scanners have controls that allow the image to be corrected either manually or automatically. Turn off any automated scan correction and allow the scan to be done with no manual intervention. The reason for this is, with respect to cleaning up a line art scan, Photoshop can do the job better than your scanner can.

Figure 9.162 shows a representation of a scan to be processed as line art. (If you wish to try this procedure, open the file ABCD.PSD found in the Chapter 9 Practice Files folder on the CD-ROM.) The background, originally white, shows up as a blotchy gray tone. This is typical because the scanner, at the resolutions being used, is able to interpret the surface reflectivity of the paper as a color. Follow these steps:

1. After you've scanned the image, look at it carefully and try to find any area containing a delicate feature that you wish to preserve. The circled area in Figure 9.163 shows dark areas that have nearly grown together. This is the kind of detail you need to focus your attention on. Zoom up to this detail and concentrate on it during this process. The rest of the image will take care of itself.

2. Use the Pen tool, as shown in Figure 9.164, to draw a few simple paths that generally show where the edges of the dark shapes are located. These paths are temporary, and you needn't spend a lot of time on them. You will be using the Levels controls to severely compress the range of tones in this scan. Without the paths, it will be difficult to maintain the shapes in their present form.

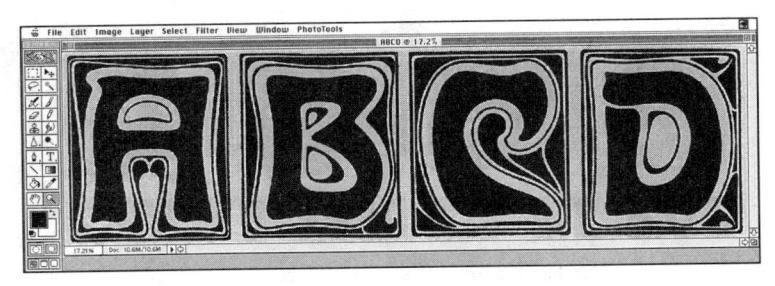

Figure 9.162 A high-resolution grayscale scan to be converted to line art.

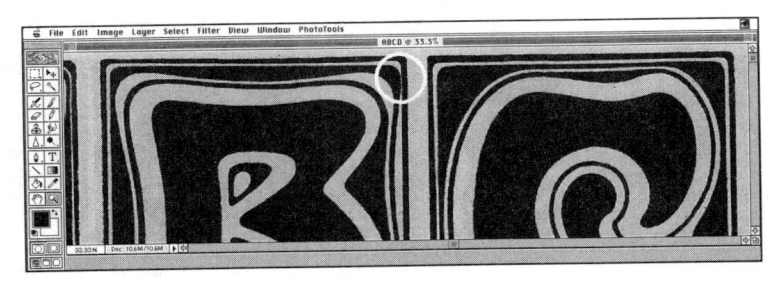

Figure 9.163 Look at the scan for delicate features that you wish to preserve during the adjustment procedure.

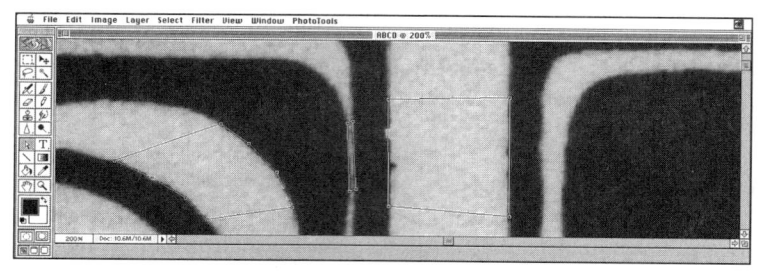

Figure 9.164 Zoom up to the image. Draw paths along the edges of the shapes so that you know where the shapes begin and end while you are adjusting them.

3. The next step is to make the dark and light tones in the scan more homogeneous. Use the Gaussian Blur filter (see Figure 9.165). Experiment with the Radius setting until the blur eliminates most of the noise in the dark shapes and the background shapes. Take care not to make the blur so pronounced that you can no longer see the edges of the shapes clearly.

4. Open the Levels dialog box. Be sure the Preview checkbox is turned on. Begin by moving the Input scale highlight slider to the left. As you move it, the background lightens and begins to wash out. In this case, move it until you see the delicate shape on which you are focusing open up so that the two black shapes are no longer touching. Move the Input scale shadow slider to the right as far as it goes: It overlaps the other two slider triangles (see Figure 9.166). It might be necessary to move each slider a little at a time until you find the perfect placement. Your screen should resemble the figure. Click on OK.

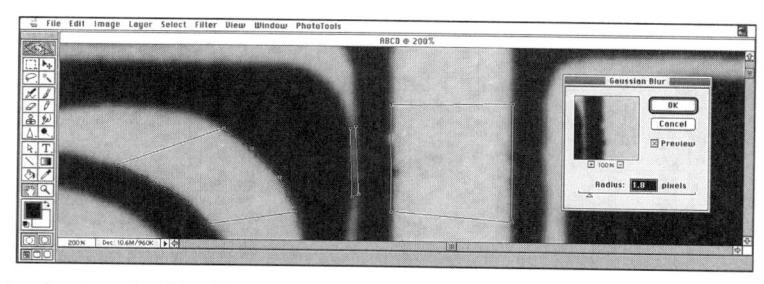

Figure 9.165 Use the Gaussian Blur filter to make the white and black tones more uniform.

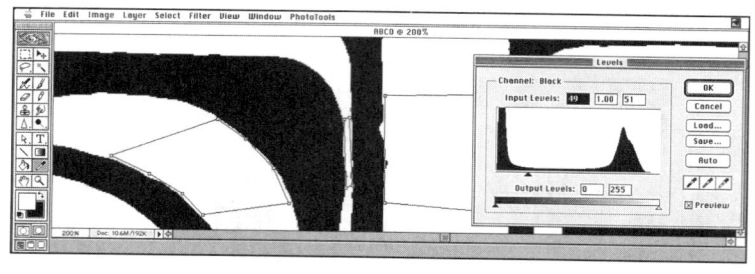

Figure 9.166 Move the Levels Input sliders to wash out the background and to darken the image shapes.

5. By moving the sliders in such a way that the white space between the two black shapes is opened up, you can see that all of the black shapes are smaller. The paths show where the original black edges were and how far the Levels adjustments have caused them to retreat (see Figure 9.167). This is not always a problem, but it's a simple matter to fix. Command+click (Mac) or Ctrl+click (Windows) the Black channel's thumbnail on the Channels palette. From the Select menu, choose Inverse. Now, from the Select menu, choose Modify|Expand. Expand the selection by one pixel. Fill the new selection with black, and Deselect. The edges of the black shapes should now be back close to the paths (see Figure 9.168). Delete the paths.

6. From the Image menu, choose Mode|Bitmap (see Figure 9.169). Keep the Output resolution the same as the Input resolution. Choose 50% Threshold for the Method. Click on OK.

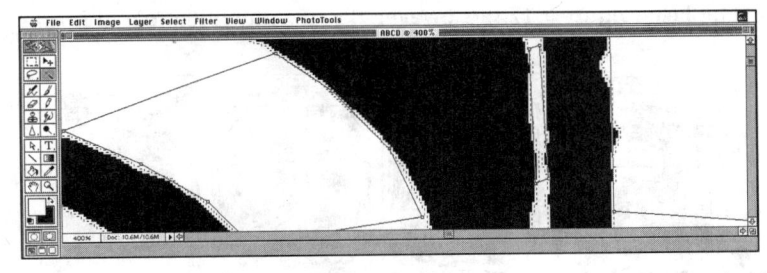

Figure 9.167 A close view shows that the adjustment has moved the black edges so that the shapes are smaller.

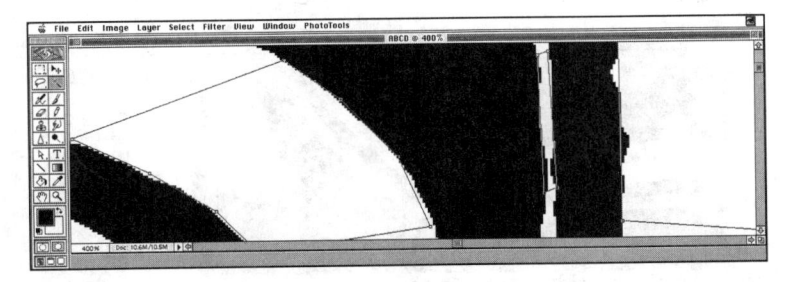

Figure 9.168 After selecting the black shapes and expanding the selection, a black fill brings the edges back to where they were.

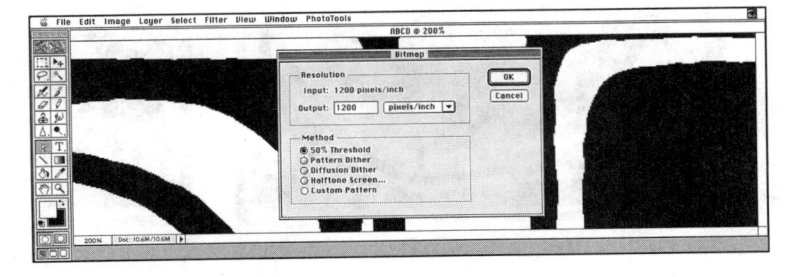

Figure 9.169 Convert the image to bitmap mode.

The complete image is shown in Figure 9.170. At this point, the image has been improved sufficiently that it is adequate for most purposes. Although small imperfections are visible when the image is magnified on screen (see Figure 9.171), don't forget that magnification is tremendous. The small blip in the lower part of Figure 9.171 is three pixels high. At the resolution of this file, the real-world height of that blip is 37.5 percent the height of a single 150 line-screen dot! Because very few eyes are good enough to clearly distinguish a single 150 line-screen dot, a blip a little more than a third of that height is probably not going to stand out on the printed page as a gross error.

Still, prepress people are a bit—uh—compulsive about their work. In fact, they are often teased about it. It's a credo in prepress circles that "Good enough just isn't." Which only illustrates how much prepress people care about what they do.

You could, if you wish, zoom in to the image and correct some of the more obvious problems with the Pencil tool (see Figure 9.172). However, if you wanted to make this image look better—

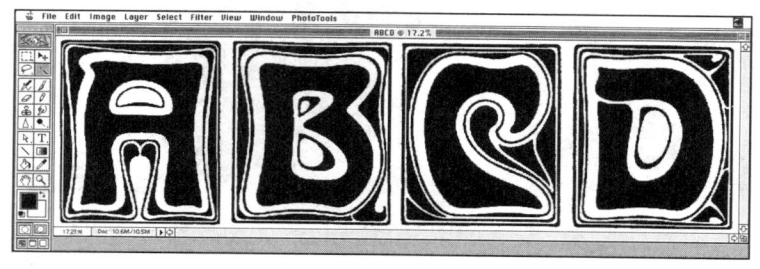

Figure 9.170 The completed image looks much better than the original scan.

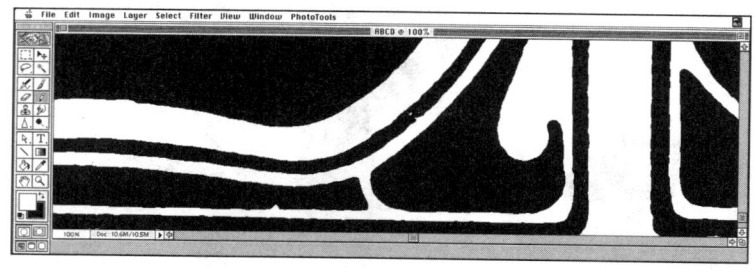

Figure 9.171 A close view shows that there are still some problems with the edges of the black shapes.

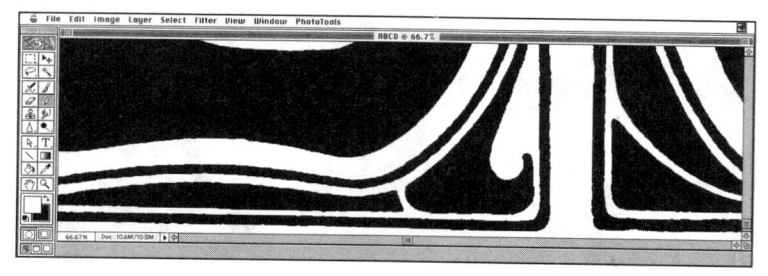

Figure 9.172 Some of the defective edges can be corrected at high magnification with the Pencil tool.

no blips that show up even at this magnification—and you wanted to evade the smug smiles of the philistines who already consider you compulsive, is there a way to do it quickly? Yup. To do the job fast, you need a copy of Adobe Streamline and either Adobe Illustrator or Macromedia FreeHand.

Save the file in TIFF or Photoshop format, and open it in Adobe Streamline. Streamline is an *autotrace* program. It can detect edges and outline shapes with paths very well at really formidable speeds. If you are new to Streamline, you might be disappointed the first time you see it perform; many newcomers expect that the traced file will be reasonably close to what they could have drawn manually. Streamline's paths are usually not perfect until you have made your peace with the two Settings items under the Options menu.

The Settings dialog box (see Figure 9.173) contains a variety of presets from which you can choose. In the case of the line art in this discussion, a good choice is probably the settings titled Logos and Typefaces. After making your choice, click on OK. Now, from the File menu, select Convert. On a moderately fast computer, Streamline can convert this 1.3MB file to paths in a little under four seconds.

Take a look at the paths without their fills by choosing Artwork from the View menu (see Figure 9.174). A fairly common problem with the first round of conversion is that the paths will seem to show too many corners when curves would be more desirable. If the paths don't look quite good enough, all you need to do is to Select All, and press Delete. You're only out the four seconds of conversion time.

The way the program draws the paths *for this file* can be changed by choosing Options|Conversion Setup (see Figure 9.175). The settings put into effect by the previous choice—Logos and Typefaces—were probably adequate for a file with a resolution of 600 to 800 ppi. The example file

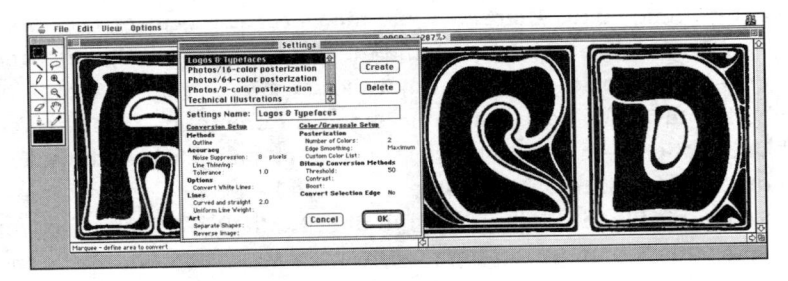

Figure 9.173 The Settings dialog box in Adobe Streamline.

Figure 9.174 View of the paths without the scan after Streamline has converted the file.

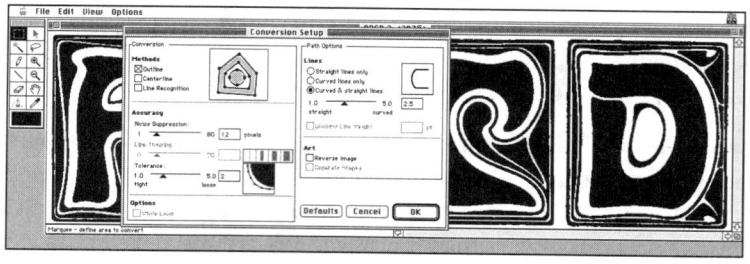

Figure 9.175 Streamline's Conversion Setup dialog box.

is 1200 ppi. Because of that, the numbers of the settings can probably be increased. The Noise Suppression can be changed from 8 pixels to 12, the Tolerance value from 1 to 2, and Lines slider from 2 to 2.5. With the changes made, click on OK, and execute the Conversion command again. Still not happy? Delete the paths, and tweak the settings again. In two or three minutes, you can experiment with a variety of settings until your paths are nearly perfect.

You can still do some tweaking to smooth the paths after they have been drawn. Select All, and choose Edit|Smooth Path (see Figure 9.176). The menu selection branches to three settings: Minimum, Medium, and Maximum. Try them all, one at a time, using the Undo command after each so that you can determine which is the most effective for the file you are processing. If you've spent a little time tweaking the conversion settings, you'll probably have pretty good paths and Minimum will probably be sufficient.

Export the file from Streamline in Adobe Illustrator format, and then open it in that program or in Macromedia FreeHand. There will still be a few blips (see Figure 9.177). Blips are not much of a problem in Illustrator. The example shown in the figure can be fixed simply by removing the offending point. Alternately, use the Direct Select cursor, click and drag around the point, press Delete, click and drag around the two remaining endpoints, and use the Join command. Other correction tools in Illustrator include sweep-selecting groups of more-or-less vertical or horizontal points, and using the Average Command—with the Vertical Only or Horizontal Only options—to line up the points. A set of quick clicks with the Convert Anchor Point tool tames the most recalcitrant line. It should be possible to do a reasonable job of straightening out this file in less than five minutes. Figure 9.178 shows some of the edges at greater magnification. Compare this figure with Figure 9.177 to see how efficiently Streamline and Illustrator clean up the edges of the dark shapes.

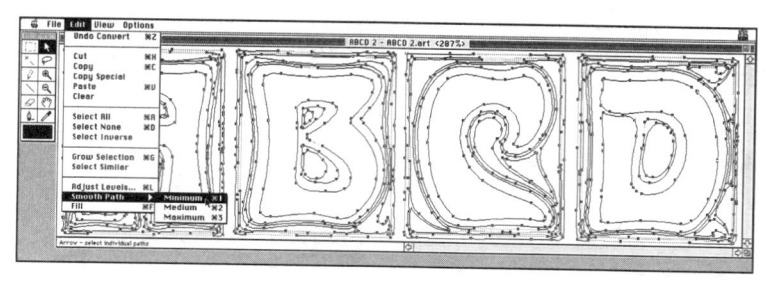

Figure 9.176 Streamline's Smooth Path command.

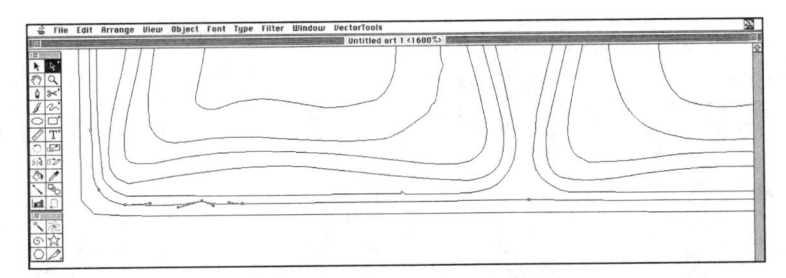

Figure 9.177 Export the file from Streamline to Illustrator. Fixing irregular edges is much easier in Illustrator than it is in Photoshop.

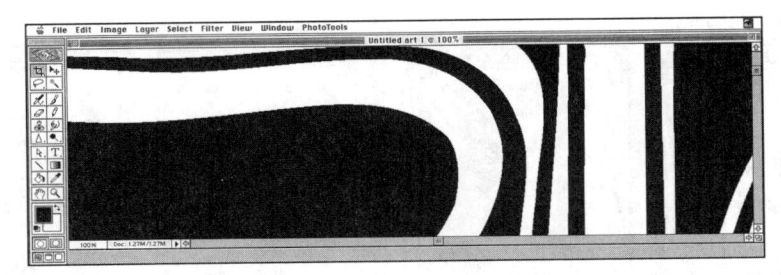

Figure 9.178 A close-up of the converted file shows how much smoother the edges are than the original's.

If the scanning time isn't counted, you will have spent a total of 6 to 10 minutes making this file look good. When you're satisfied with how it looks, it can be saved as an EPS file and used as it is. For artwork of this kind, a vector format is probably the best choice for the final file. With it, the file can be easily colorized, distorted, or resized. The Illustrator file will also be much smaller than the bitmap Photoshop file.

You may want to use a magnifying glass to examine the three parts of Figure 9.179. As you can see, the shapes in the lower example are smoother than those of the center. However, the center, seen as output rather than as a magnified screen file, does not look obviously inferior unless it is studied under magnification.

This same technique, performed on very high-resolution scans, can be used to re-digitize files that have been output to resin-coated paper or as veloxes. These files are larger than the grayscale and color files that Photoshop users handle as a matter of course. There are, however, financial incentives for reprocessing the file.

Assume, for a moment, that the publisher of a magazine employs you. Your magazine's pages are set up in QuarkXPress or Adobe PageMaker. Ad pages, in particular, are entirely digital files with the exception of a single 2-inch square ad that has been sent by an advertiser in camera-ready form (velox, r-c paper, and so on). Your typical production cycle involves imaging your digital files as 4-up or 8-up imposed pages. (The 4-up and 8-up imposed pages compose a printer's press signature. The pages are printed in a way that they fold to produce the finished printed piece with all the pages in the proper order.) Your production flow is interrupted by this single camera-ready ad. After your film is made, someone needs to take a line shot of the ad,

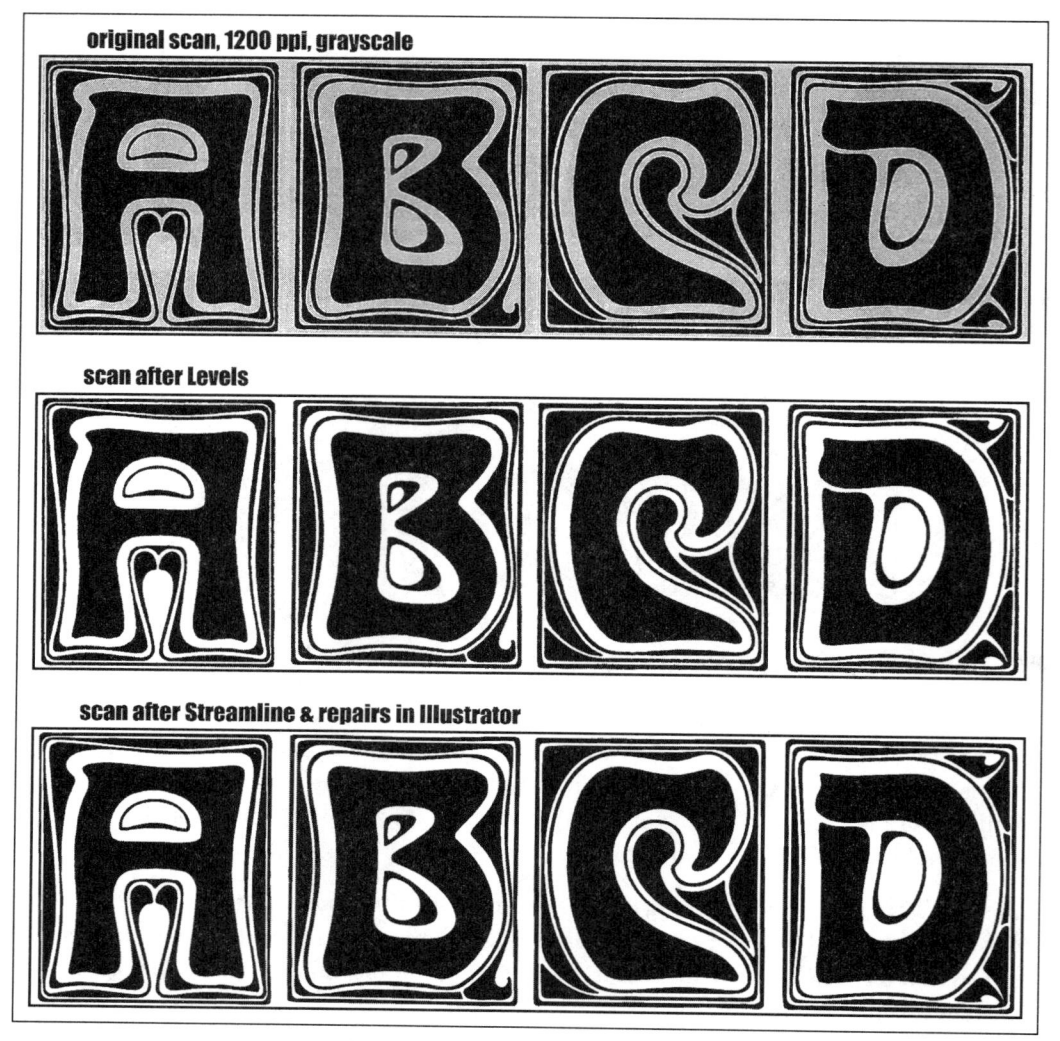

Figure 9.179 Three stages in the line art conversion: the original file, the Photoshop file after the Levels correction, and the Streamlined file.

process the film, and strip it into the large, composite digital films. The cost of this mechanical intervention is usually sufficient to eat up all the profit for the ad as well as some of the profit for other ads on the page. It's also one picky little detail that can throw a wrench into the most streamlined production cycle.

The solution—called *copy-dot scanning*—is to scan this ad at high resolution. If possible, make the resolution equal to your final output device resolution. Many scanners advertise their resolution capabilities as, say, 1200 ppi horizontal × 600 ppi vertical *optical* resolution, and 4800 ppi × 4800 *interpolated* resolution. When a scan's resolution is interpolated above the optical resolution, the values of the new pixels result from a calculation of what the value *probably* could be. In short, the pixel values derive from a mathematical guess. Sometimes the value is accurate, sometimes it isn't. Interpolated scans are always softer and less defined in their detail. For color and grayscale work, using interpolated resolution is not a good idea. For scans intended to be used as line art, interpolation causes little harm beyond making you work a little harder when performing tasks such as the one at hand.

Figure 9.180 shows a corner of a scan done at 2400 ppi. At this magnification, the screen dots are clearly visible. The file is about 2.5 inches square. It's in grayscale, and is about 33MB. When the individual dots are seen at 1600 percent magnification, the softness generated by the interpolation is very evident (see Figure 9.181).

Figure 9.180   A corner of a scan done at 2400 ppi.

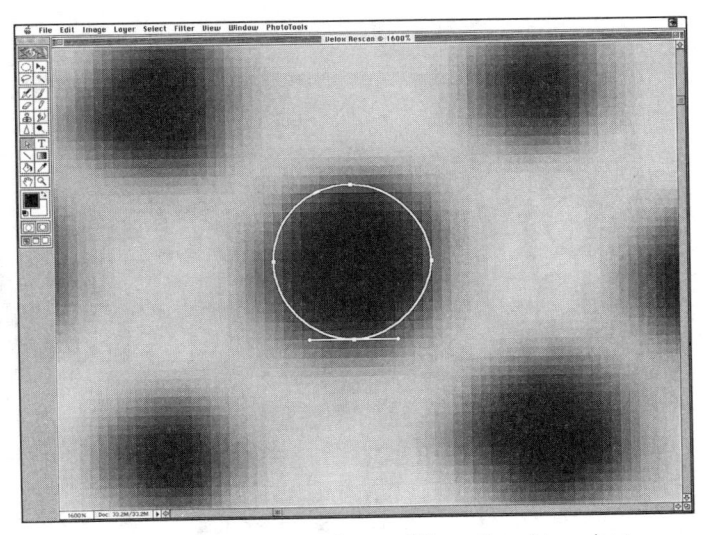

Figure 9.181   At high magnification, draw a path so that you'll know how big a dot is supposed to be.

The process described here is similar to that used for the line art sample, as you'll discover when you follow these steps:

1. First, draw a path that delineates the true shape of the dot (seen in Figure 9.181). This part of the task is the most difficult because you have no clear edge from which to work. Draw the path so that it makes a circular shape that follows the set of pixels whose value is roughly halfway between the tone at the center of the dot and the light background tone between the dots.

2. Open the Levels dialog box. Be certain that the Preview option is checked. Move the highlight and shadow Input scale sliders toward each other a little at a time until you

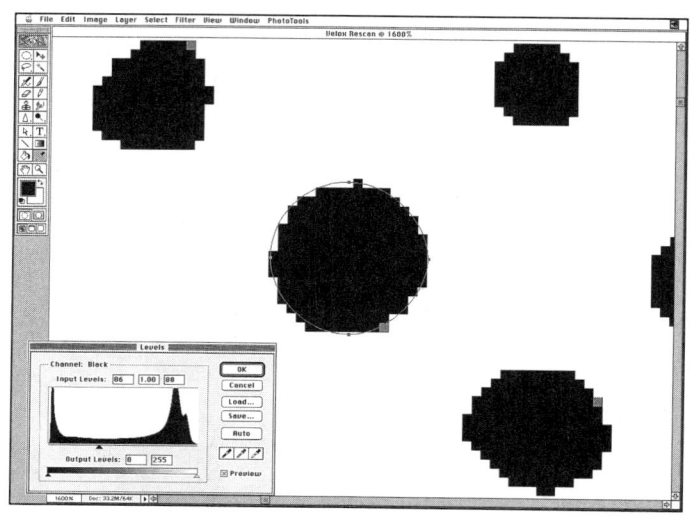

Figure 9.182 Use the Levels controls to increase the contrast to the extent that the path is filled with black and the background is filled with white.

Figure 9.183 Convert the file to Bitmap mode. Keep the Input/Output resolutions the same.

have washed out the background and made the dark dot shape fit within the drawn path (see Figure 9.182). Click on OK. Delete the path.

3. The final step is to convert the file to Bitmap mode (see Figure 9.183). Keep the Input/Output resolution the same and use the 50% Threshold option. After the file has been converted to Bitmap mode, its size will have been reduced by 7/8. In the case of this file, the reduction was from 33.2MB to 4.15MB. Save the file in any of the formats—TIFF, Photoshop EPS, and so on—that can be used by the page layout software you intend to use. When this file has been output at high resolution, no way exists to distinguish it from the way it would have looked had it been printed as a stripped-in line shot.

Converting Grayscale Files To Bitmap Mode

When grayscale files are converted to Bitmap mode, Photoshop has five strategies that it can use to eliminate all tones except black and white. The five are listed in the dialog box that appears when the menu command to convert to bitmap is selected (see Figure 9.184). Each of these, acting on the same gray-tone image (see Figure 9.185), produces a strikingly different result. (Note: This file of the Chicago skyline has been included with the Chapter 9 Practice Files folder on this book's CD-ROM. The file name is CHICAGO.PSD.)

You can see that the resolution of the file can be changed as part of the conversion. In most cases, changing the resolution upward is probably not a good idea. In this one situation, you will not compromise of the image quality by doing so.

The Halftone Screen option is an example of how the change of resolution may even be beneficial. When a halftone file is downloaded to an imagesetter's RIP to be turned into screen dots, the machine and its software have no trouble accurately converting the gray information into dots, provided there is sufficient information contained in the file in the form of pixel density. The RIP does its work by sampling small areas of the image and then constructing appropriate dots at its own very high resolution—say, 2400 ppi. Photoshop is fully capable of acting as a high-end RIP in this case. If Photoshop is given sufficient data in the form of pixel density, you can ask it to do exactly the same job performed by an imaging system costing tens of thousands of dollars. After the file is converted, you could send it to the

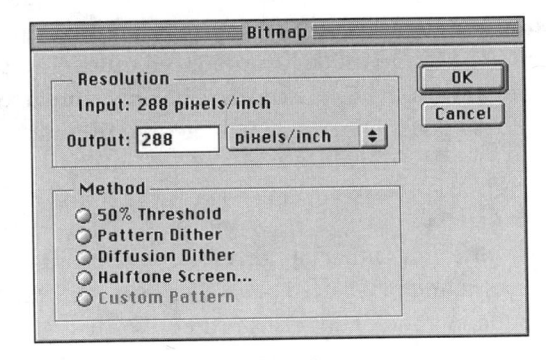

Figure 9.184 Photoshop's Bitmap conversion options window.

Figure 9.185 Sample file for demonstrating the possibilities when converting a grayscale image to Bitmap mode.

same marking assembly controlled by the RIP and your output would be absolutely identical to that produced by the RIP.

It's interesting to think how much unsuspected power Photoshop has, isn't it? Using just Photoshop, Adobe Illustrator, and Adobe PageMaker, a knowledgeable user could do any kind of prepress task or project entirely—including the ripping of the files. It probably isn't a practical thing to do, but it is possible. And it wouldn't even be very difficult. Just think about it: Sometime the information may prove to be very useful.

50% Threshold

The first of the five conversion methods is the 50% Threshold option. When this option is used, Photoshop constructs a very steep curve that forces all the pixels in the image above or below the 50% value. If a pixel is 50% or lighter, it is converted to white. All others are changed to black. The effect, shown in Figure 9.186, is of very high contrast. The high-contrast effect can be really wonderful, but it can also be pretty useless. If you find that your high-contrast conversion to Bitmap mode has produced unlovely results, use the Undo command and then experiment with the Curve controls before trying again. You may have to try it a few times before it looks good. Don't give up—nearly all images can yield good-looking high-contrast versions.

Pattern And Diffuse Dither

The Pattern Dither and Diffusion Dither options for converting to Bitmap mode attempt to simulate gray tones by sprinkling pixel-sized black dots over the white background. The difference between the two is the method of dot distribution.

PHOTOSHOP PREPRESS **639**

Figure 9.186 The 50% Threshold conversion yields a high-contrast image.

Pattern Dither

Pattern Dither (see Figure 9.187, with enlarged detail in Figure 9.188) uses an 8×8-pixel cell that can be filled in, one pixel at a time, by means of arbitrary geometric rules. The pattern may be utterly logical, but it is also terrifically ugly. The pattern produced by this conversion

Figure 9.187 Pattern Dither Bitmap mode conversion.

Figure 9.188 Enlarged detail of Figure 9.187.

method may look familiar: In the pre-color days of Macintosh computers, patterned dithering was used to simulate grays on black and white screens.

Diffusion Dither

Diffusion Dither (see Figure 9.189, with enlarged detail in Figure 9.190) simulates grays by scattering the black pixels in what appears to be a random fashion. Diffusion Dither, as you

Figure 9.189 Diffusion Dither Bitmap mode conversion.

Figure 9.190 Enlarged detail of Figure 9.189.

can see from the figures, does an excellent job maintaining the details and tone range of the image. In fact, when printed on relatively low-resolution printers, it does a better job than conventional screens. Viewed at magnification, the scatter of the pixels is quite attractive. We will discuss Diffusion Dither on low-resolution and non-PostScript printers later in this chapter.

Random dithering of this kind is known by a couple of other terms. For the way it produces dots, random dithering is known as FM (Frequency Modulated) screening—the dots are all the same size but are distributed, or modulated, by the darkness, or frequency, of the tone represented. (Traditional halftone screens are called AM screens, for Amplitude Modulated. The size—amplitude—of the dot is governed by the darkness of the represented tone.) FM screens are also called *stochastic* screens. We discuss stochastic screens for printing color in Chapter 10.

Halftone Screen

When you select the Halftone Screen conversion option, you are given three choices. The first is the Frequency of the screen, the second the Angle of the screen, and the third the Shape of the dot (see Figure 9.191).

Figure 9.191 The Halftone Screen conversion options dialog box.

When you use this conversion option, you need to be aware of the resolution of the final output device. Setting the screen frequency at too large a number results in a posterized image with too few gray tones. Try for a line-screen frequency that is a good match to the printer resolution.

Three sample choices are shown here to give you an idea how versatile this choice can be. Figure 9.192 (with enlarged detail shown in Figure 9.193) shows the converted file with the settings in Figure 9.191. Figure 9.194 (with enlarged detail shown in Figure 9.195) is at the

Figure 9.192 Halftone Screen Bitmap Mode conversion: 65 line-screen, 45° screen angle, round dot.

Figure 9.193 Enlarged detail of Figure 9.192.

same screen frequency, but with the dot shape changed to Cross. Notice how this dot-shape is not as successful at preserving the fine details of the image. The cross-shaped dot is also more susceptible to press gain. If you look at both images (Figures 9.192 and 9.194) and make your eyes go a little out of focus, you'll see that the latter is somewhat darker than the former. (Should you ever be adventurous enough to choose this spot shape for a color separation, please send us an email listing the many new and colorful words your pressman will use between fits of screaming.)

Figure 9.194 Halftone Screen Bitmap Mode conversion: 65 line-screen, 45° screen angle, cross-shaped dot.

Figure 9.195 Enlarged detail of Figure 9.194.

The third of the Halftone Screen examples is seen in Figure 9.196 (the enlarged detail is shown in Figure 9.197). This photo uses quite a low—25 lpi—frequency figure, with a linear spot shape at an angle of 90°. The effect is very stylized and, in some cases, attractive—a sort of high-contrast image with attitude.

Figure 9.196 Halftone Screen bitmap conversion: 25 line-screen, 0° screen angle, linear dot.

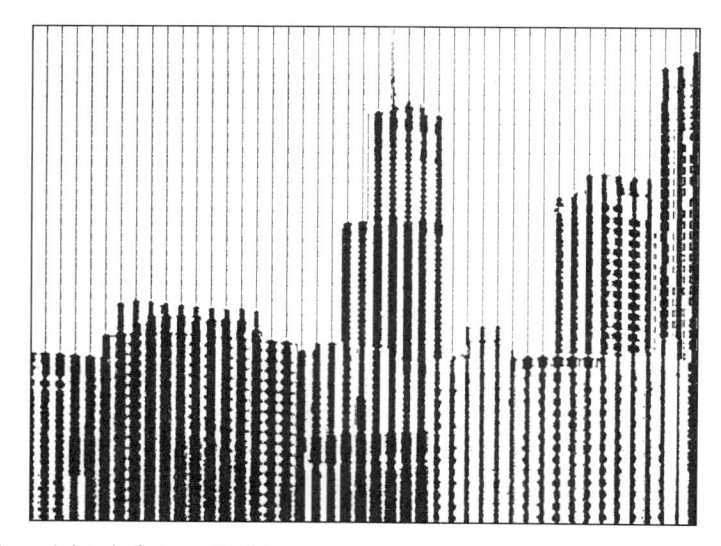

Figure 9.197 Enlarged detail of Figure 9.196.

> **TIP**
>
> A good way to determine whether the image is going to reproduce well is to divide the tentative line-screen number into the resolution of the printer and square the result. The number you end up with is the number of gray tones the printer can deliver *at that line-screen*. Here are a few examples based on a printer resolution of 600 ppi:
>
> 100 line-screen: 600 / 100 = 6; 6 x 6 = 36 (gray tones);
>
> 85 line-screen: 600 / 85 = 7.05; 7.05 x 7.05 = 49 (gray tones);
>
> 70 line-screen: 600 / 70 = 8.6; 8.6 x 8.6 = 74 (gray tones);
>
> 60 line-screen: 600 / 60 = 10; 10 x 10 = 100 (gray tones).
>
> None of these settings is right or wrong—they are simply what will happen when you make a certain choice. Higher line-screen numbers give smaller dots; lower line-screen numbers give more shades of gray. Unless you have access to a device with a resolution of 2400 ppi—the lowest resolution that allows the maximum number of grays at a line-screen of 150—there will always be a trade-off between fine dots and the number of gray tones. 100 line-screen, for example, will have fairly fine dots (compared to 60 line-screen), but with only 36 gray tones; a reproduced gradient would show a clearly visible line about every three percent.
>
> You don't really need the full number of possible gray tones. If the image has large, flat areas, 100 line-screen might work. Be ready with the Undo command until you hit the correct balance.

Custom Pattern

Custom Pattern allows you to plug in any defined pattern in lieu of a specified spot shape. Make a rectangular selection and choose Edit|Define Pattern. An example of such a pattern is

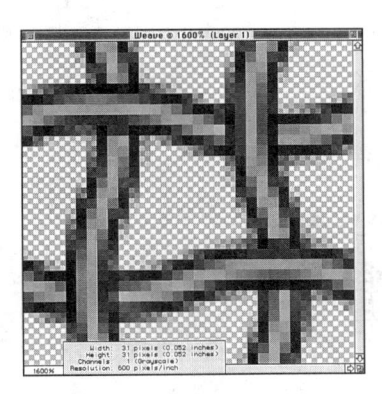

Figure 9.198 Small repeating tile, defined as a Photoshop pattern.

shown in Figure 9.198. This pattern, rasterized from Illustrator, is very small: It's 31 pixels square, with a resolution of 600 ppi. After the file has been converted (see Figure 9.199—enlarged detail shown in Figure 9.200), the image seems to have been sprayed upon the texture formed by multiple iterations of the pattern. As you can see, there is a good deal of lost image detail. This loss is offset by the charm of the effect. Mapping an image onto a small repeating

Figure 9.199 Custom pattern Bitmap mode conversion.

Figure 9.200 Enlarged detail of Figure 9.199.

texture is one of Photoshop's minor miracles. It may take a little experimentation to get the scale of the pattern to be suitable for the resolution of the image. When the scale is correct, you'll have an image that can be achieved in no other way.

An Exotic Use For The Halftone Screen Bitmap Conversion Option

It happens: You have a pretty good image, the color is nice, the composition is okay. The trouble with the image is that by itself, it's a little static, and the texture is a little grainy. What to do? "Tart it up," as it's said in the business. Or, "Add compositional interest," as it's said in front of the clients. Whatever. The process is fun and it's very easy. (You can try out this technique on the file shown in Figure 9.201 by opening SUNSET.PSD in the Chapter 9 Practice Files folder on the companion CD-ROM. The two images are shown in this book's Color Studio section.) Follow these steps:

1. Begin by duplicating the image. Change the mode of the duplicate to Lab, press Command+1 or Ctrl+1 to view the Lightness channel, and change the mode to Grayscale. Open the Curves controls and set up a steep curve (see Figure 9.202) to heighten the

Figure 9.201 Sample image to be altered using Bitmap mode conversion, filters, and layers.

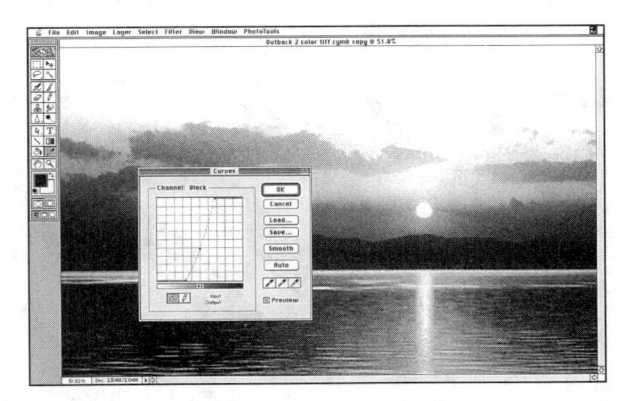

Figure 9.202 After converting the image to Grayscale mode, make a steep curve to heighten the contrasts.

contrast. Change the mode of this grayscale document to Bitmap. Choose Halftone Screen. For the options, choose 12 for the Frequency, 45° for the Angle, and Line for the Shape. The converted image is shown in Figure 9.203, with an enlarged detail in Figure 9.204.

2. Change the mode of the image back to Grayscale. Command+click (Mac) or Ctrl+click (Windows) the thumbnail of the Black channel. Choose Select|Modify|Border. Enter "6" and click on OK. Use the Gaussian Blur filter at a setting of 1 to soften the edges of the dark shapes (see Figure 9.205). Adjust the size of this grayscale window and the original so that you can see them both. Select All, and copy the new grayscale image. Click on the original document's window. Click on the New Channel icon at the bottom of the Channels palette. When the new, all-black channel appears in the window, paste the grayscale file. Your modified image is now an alpha channel for the colored document.

3. With this channel in view, choose Filter|Distort|Ripple. You can experiment with your own settings. The example shown in Figure 9.206 used settings of 100 and Medium.

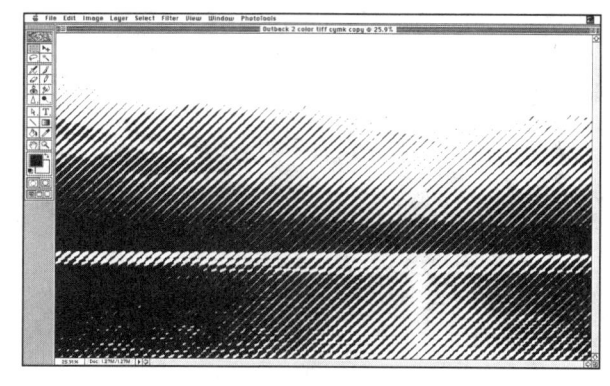

Figure 9.203 Convert the image to Bitmap mode. Use Halftone Screen with settings of 12 line-screen, 45°, and linear dot.

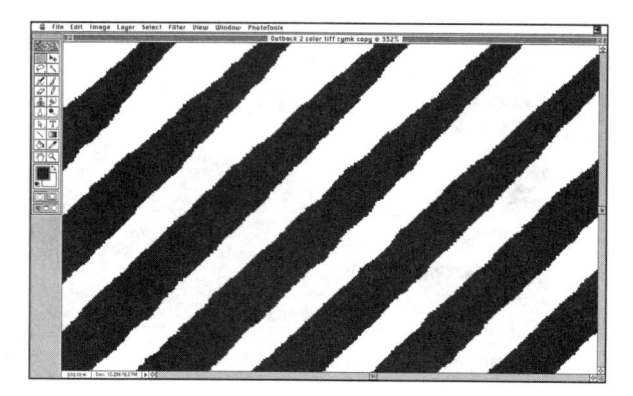

Figure 9.204 Close-up of the converted file.

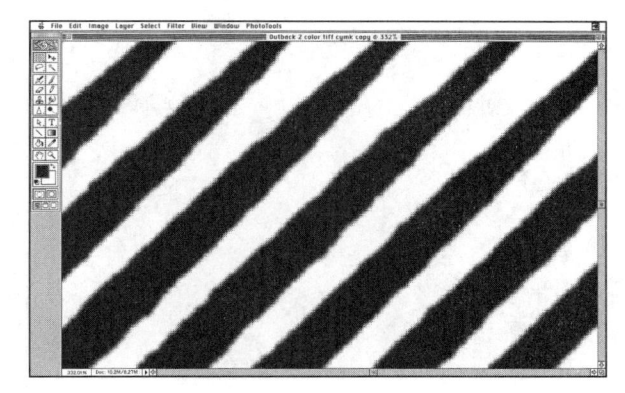

Figure 9.205 Blur the edges of the black shapes.

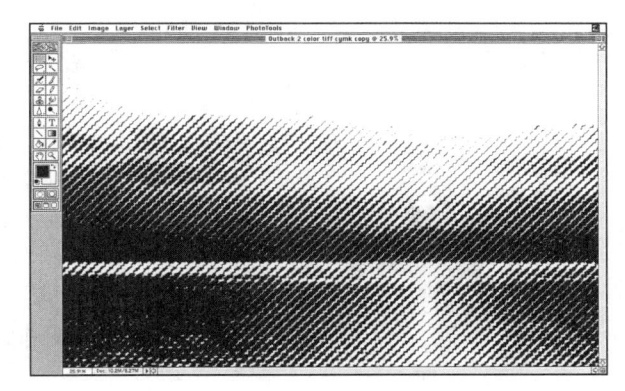

Figure 9.206 Apply the Ripple filter to the alpha channel.

4. Click on the topmost channel thumbnail to view the full-color document. Command+click (Mac) or Ctrl+click (Windows) the #5 channel to activate it as a selection. From the Select menu, choose Inverse. Press Command+J or Ctrl+J to make the selection into an independent layer. Set the mode of the layer to Overlay. From the Filter menu, choose Noise|Add Noise. Experiment with the settings to achieve an effect you like. The sample here used an Amount of 150, Uniform.

5. Click on the Background layer, and activate the alpha channel selection again. Press Command+J or Ctrl+J to make the selection into an independent layer. Set the Blend mode of the layer to Multiply.

The finished image is shown in Figure 9.207, with an enlarged detail in Figure 9.208. The textures are easily visible here. Look at the image printed in color to see how the Overlay mode makes colors superimposed upon themselves more intense, and how the Multiply mode darkens and enriches the same colors when superimposed upon themselves. It is worth noting that the two modes are applied respectively to an enhancement of the highlights and the shadows of the original image. This mechanism causes the dark waving shapes to fade out at the upper edges of the clouds.

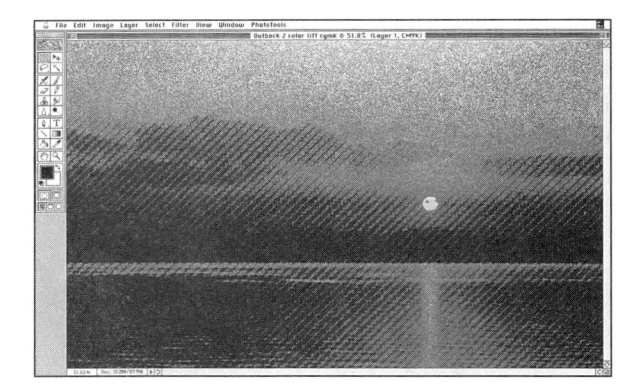

Figure 9.207 The image after applying Blend modes.

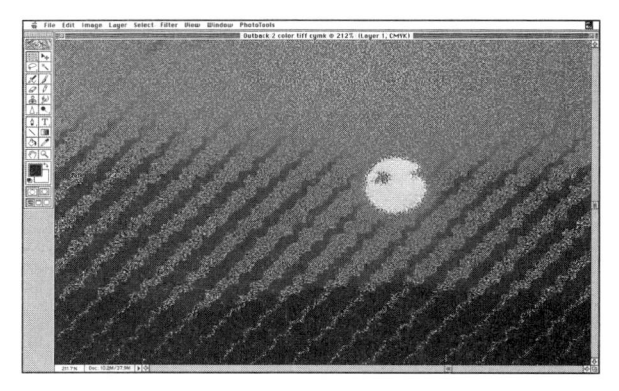

Figure 9.208 Enlarged close-up of Figure 9.207.

> **TIP**
>
> If you often use a laser or ink jet printer, converting your files to Bitmap mode allows you to reproduce a range of tones that would otherwise be possible only on a very high-resolution output device. Use this easy-to-follow procedure:
>
> Begin with a scan that has a resolution that is an even divisor of or equal to your printer's resolution. If possible, print a swatch of 50 percent gray on your printer and check the amount of dot gain the printer gives you. (Toner printers do gain density—it isn't the same kind of gain you get on press, but you have to compensate for it nonetheless.) If you have no way of checking, adjust the image as you would for a conventional halftone, but with a target gain compensation of about 30 to 35 percent and a maximum black value of about 85 percent. When you have the image adjusted and sharpened, change the mode of the file from Grayscale to Bitmap. Keep the Input/Output resolutions equal, and select the Diffusion Dither method. Save the file in whatever format you require. You'll be surprised at how good your

> **TIP (CONTINUED)**
>
> printed images look—even on low-resolution printers and printers that don't have PostScript—and at how fast they print.
>
> When you use this method of producing great-looking images from desktop printers, keep in mind that your output is equivalent to that of a press run. In other words, it's the *final output*. If, for some reason, you need to reproduce your hard copy—photocopy, for example—you'll have to back up and adjust for more gain on the original file. Copiers also gain; if you photocopy an image that has already gained, you combine the two gain factors. You'll need to think this through and do some experimenting before you find the perfect amount of adjustment for the original image. A word of caution: Don't be surprised if your original gain adjustment is higher than you would have believed possible! Considering how high the toner gain percentage is, compensation for two generations of gain can be as high as 50 to 55 percent.

Moving On

Photoshop and prepress functioning together is a large topic, as you've discovered in this chapter. You learned of press conditions and how you can use Photoshop's amazing tools to change your image so that it emerges from the press as a beautifully printed image. In the process, you discovered what makes an attractive halftone and how to construct duotones. You also learned to handle spot colors, and the very complex bump plates and touch plates that add extra inks to your images. Finally, we focused on the Bitmap mode and line art. All of these tools and techniques, and all of the detailed information will serve you well in most day-to-day prepress situations. Besides the step-by-step instructions, we hope you have also begun to build a picture in your mind of how Photoshop fits into the print-production process.

The only topic we neglected in this chapter is color reproduction and some of the topics—such as trapping and clipping paths—that go along with it. For this topic, we invite you to continue your prepress explorations by turning to Chapter 10. You'll find a thorough examination of topics such as color management and calibration, Photoshop's monitor and printing preferences, how to generate a color separation, and hundreds of production details.

CALIBRATION AND COLOR REPRODUCTION

Having learned some of the basic—and not so basic—material concerned with prepress in Chapter 9, you're now ready to plunge into the fascinating world of color reproduction.

The reaction of many digital-color workers to the concept of Color Management is close—in spirit, if not in words—to the famous remark by Dorothy Parker: "What fresh hell is this?" In the view of many, Photoshop users have been producing reasonably good printed color for a numbers of years. Why change the way things have been done? Why introduce complex topics such as Device Independent color and ICC Device Profiles? Why make the whole issue so complicated?

These questions have several relevant answers. First, color management is like any other new topic: It's complicated only until you understand it. Second, the printed color that users have been producing for the last four versions of Photoshop may have been reasonable, but you now have the opportunity to produce color that is great. And you can do it with a minimum of brainpower! Third, with managed color, you have the ability to use color as a day-to-day tool. For example, wouldn't you like to use an inexpensive color ink jet printer to get a simulation that is so accurate in its color reproduction that you could spot problems before you have to commit to making film? Wouldn't you like to know that the image you scan will look, on screen, the way the original looks? And that the printed version will look the way the screen version *and* the original look? If you find this topic confusing, take a deep breath and read on. These and other wonderful possibilities await you after you learn to manage your color. Trust us, you *can* do this.

Color Is Color, Isn't It?

From my college years, I recall a popular philosophical discussion revolving around human perception. As children grow and learn, they point to a color and are told its name. The apple is *red*, the leaf is *green*, the sky is *blue*. But what if there is a built-in difference in the way each child sees? What one child might see as red in the absolute sense, another child might see as an absolute blue. Do we have any way of knowing if there is a problem because our definitions of color are based on verbal descriptions that have nothing to do with the color itself? If children are taught to call the apple red, all that children can do is to agree on the *name* of the color. We do not really know if each child sees a different *red*.

This discussion is like the problem of Color Management Systems (CMS) in the digital prepress world. Different digital devices *see* colors in different ways—or, more accurately, different devices have different ranges of colors that they can sense or reproduce. The range for each is called its *gamut*. Two scanners, for example, might sense and quantify a red tone. The digital identity of that tone from the two devices might appear to be the same, yet human vision—and other ways of measuring color—easily identifies them as different.

Another example of this problem has to do with the way CRTs interpret and display color. Digital prepress has long been identified as the world of WYSIWYG (What You See Is What You Get). A more accurate acronym might be—at least for color—WYSIPWYGBOBA (What You See Is Possibly What You Get, But Only By Accident). (Which is too bad—at least *whiseewig* is pronounceable!) However, many Photoshop technicians know only too well that the differences between the monitor display and the press can be surprising, disappointing, and expensive.

Take two professional-level monitors with consecutive manufacturer's serial numbers. Place them side by side and, with two different computers, display two copies of the same color file in Photoshop. You'll be surprised to see differences in the way they look. In some cases, the differences will be small. In other cases, the differences will be great enough to cause you to wonder if you are seeing the same file. Whether great differences or small, your next question is: Which of these monitors is displaying the *real* file, the one that looks pretty close to the way the photo will look when it is printed on an offset press? The short answer: neither of them. Unless the monitor has been calibrated, you have as much chance of seeing an accurate presentation of the color as you have of telling time from a stopped clock (which does, after all, tell the correct time twice every 24 hours).

Different digital devices, different colors; if you add printing inks and proofing devices to the discussion of monitors and scanners, the color problem gets very tricky indeed. The development of CMS is an attempt to harmonize and make logical the differences in color between input and output devices. The CMS strategy is this: Objectively measure the color characteristics of every device, and then, as the color passes from one to another, translate each so that it falls into place as a reasonable translation. The advantage to this is obvious: Translators allow color reproduction to be more accurate, and also allow for a high degree of automation.

ICC Profiles

The most widely agreed-upon standard for performing interdevice color translations is that of the ICC Profile (ICC stands for International Color Consortium). A profile contains—among other things—an accurate map of a device's gamut. When a set of colors passes from one gamut to another, ICC-aware programs can remap the values into the new gamut using one of a variety of interpretive methods called *rendering intents*. A *colorimetric* rendering intent, for example, would take each out-of-gamut color in the original set and change it to the nearest equivalent value in the new set. Colorimetric translations, at least with photographic material, often injure visual relationships: Colors that are common to both gamuts don't change, but out-of-gamut colors are remapped to new values with the same hue, but differing lightness and saturation. Figure 10.1 shows how this happens. When the color values in the original gamut are brought into the new—and smaller—gamut, they are simply mapped to the closest position within the second boundary. (Note that color models are three-dimensional. The translation in the figure is shown in two dimensions for the sake of simplicity.) This has the effect of compressing many different original-gamut values into close—even

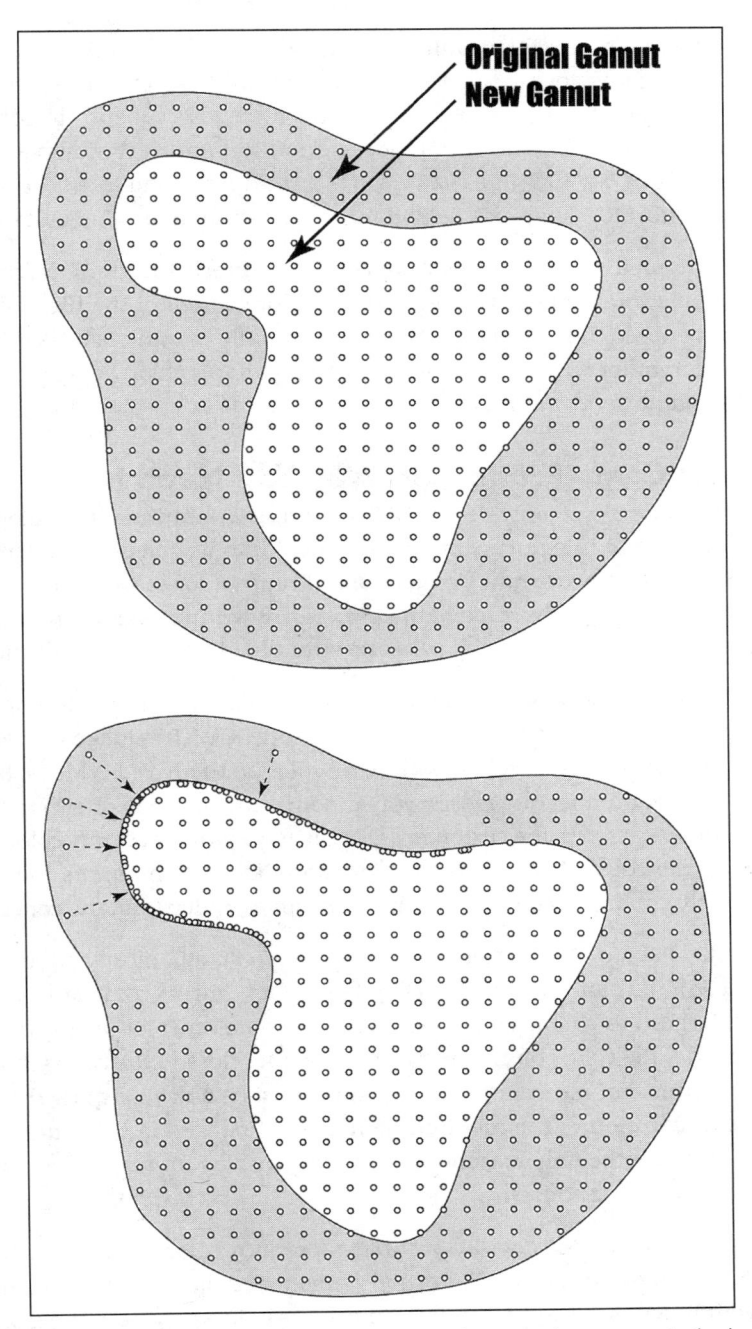

Figure 10.1 A colorimetric rendering intent maps old-gamut values into the nearest similar *hue* position within the new gamut.

identical—places within the new gamut. You've probably noticed this effect when converting an RGB scan containing many vivid colors into the CMYK mode. The bright colors become dulled and a great deal of detail is lost.

Several other mapping methods are built into Photoshop 5. One is called *perceptual*. This rendering intent maps the colors in such a way that visual—or perceptual—relationships are maintained at the cost of precision placement. This method is superior to colorimetric when converting photo images from one color mode to another, because it preserves visual relationships at the expense of a color's hue. *Saturation* is a third rendering intent. It is most useful in preserving pure, saturated colors of the kind found in nonphotographic material.

Whatever the interpretive method used, the key to the process is the ICC Profile. Embedded within a file, profile information can describe the color content of the file unambiguously to any application reading the file. Because of this, the profile is a link between the colors of one device's gamut and other gamuts that might make use of this color. We call this linking characteristic by the name *device independent color*.

CMS, Where It Came From, And Why You Need It

Color management on a system-wide level has been a slow-maturing technology. Apple Computers has been trying to integrate color management into its operating system for a number of years. Its ColorSync software now provides broad support for software operating within the Mac OS. Windows 98, not yet released at the time of this writing, will begin its life with system support for managed color by utilizing software virtually identical to ColorSync.

The entire CMS issue had its genesis as an attempt at a front-end solution to what was, in effect, an industrial problem of the print industry. More recently, CMS has taken on new urgency as a concern of Internet developers involved with retail sales on the World Wide Web. Internet merchants report that the number one reason why products are returned after purchase is that the color is wrong. In other words, the customer's CRT displayed an inaccurate color representation of the product's true color. If you consider how many kinds of monitors there are and how differently they all can display a single color, you begin to understand the core of the problem.

At the present stage of digital technology, color calibration is still mostly critical to the evaluation and correction of color for printing. Despite the fact that Web concerns are increasingly important with regard to calibration, we are focusing here on color as it is used by the print world. In this world, the colors on the monitor must come close to the colors that will come off the press. This means that many different monitors must be able to display the same colors in the same way. Calibration of the monitor, then, is the first step in the management of your color printing. It is also the only reasonably cost-effective way for you to begin to gain control of your color management concerns.

You will learn in this chapter how RGB displays produce color, how to work with monitor calibration, ICC Profiles, and what Photoshop's preferences have to do with controlling your display and your hard-copy output. You'll learn the fine points of generating a color separation that will reproduce in a predictable way. Along the way, we hope that you'll find that color holds no enormous mysteries. Rather, you just need to learn a few small, interrelated concepts, all of them quite understandable. Along with these small ideas, we hope you'll become comfortable with the concept of CMS, and understand how much simpler your life will be as it is integrated into the prepress workflow.

RGB Color

To clarify how a monitor display is altered by the calibration software, we need to examine how your monitor produces the colors you see. This isn't a technical discourse on the inner workings of a cathode ray tube, merely a look at RGB color in the abstract.

The simplest way to think of a monitor pixel is to think in grayscale and to imagine the pixel as a very tiny light bulb. Imagine that the light bulb has a circular dimmer switch attached to it, with 256 possible settings. With the bulb turned entirely off, it is black and the dimmer switch reads *zero* (see the left-hand vertical column in Figure 10.2). Turn the dimmer switch up to position 64, and though the bulb is still dim, it does emit some light. Turn the switch up to position 127, and the bulb becomes brighter still. At position 192, it is three-quarters of the way toward being entirely on. Finally, at position 255—this is the largest number, because the counting started with 0 instead of with 1—the bulb is as bright as it can be.

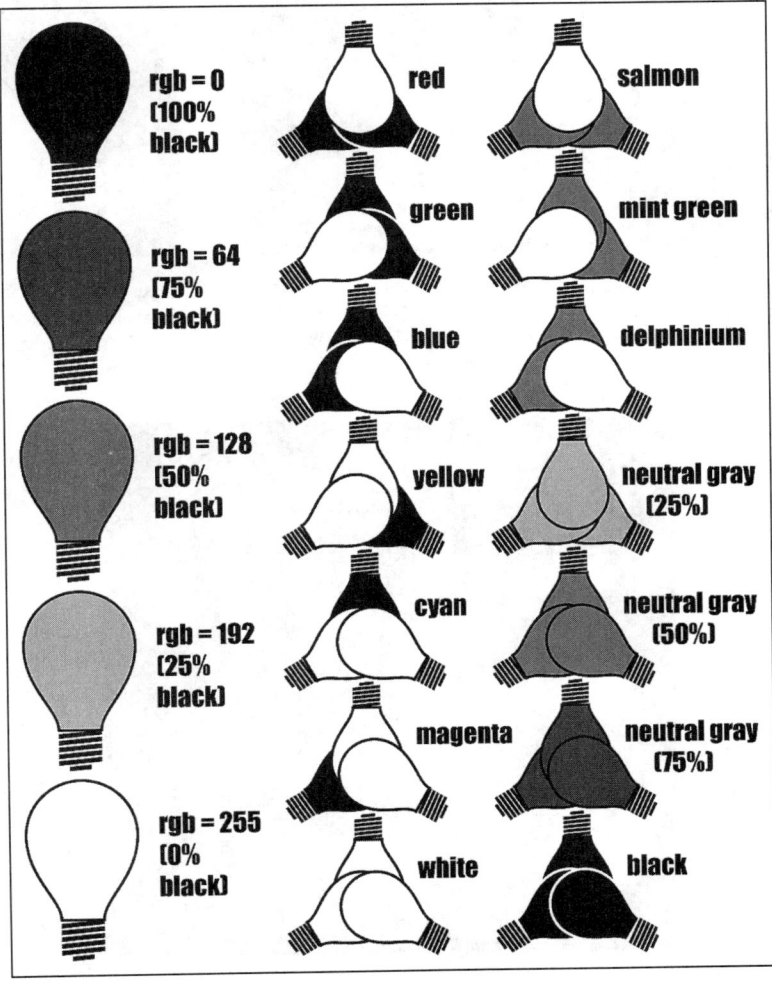

Figure 10.2 The monitor's pixels can be roughly compared to small light bulbs controlled by a dimmer switch.

The important thing to remember about the light bulb analogy is that the numerical reading is a gauge of the bulb's brightness. The larger the number, the brighter the bulb—and the pixel. Every pixel in a grayscale image can be likened to this hypothetical bulb: Each pixel has a unique value between 0 and 255, and a unique position. If you think about it, that's the way the computer stores the image, as a simple list of the brightness values of the pixels in each horizontal row of pixels.

If you've looked at the individual channels of an RGB image (see Chapter 5), you know that each channel is, for all practical purposes, a grayscale image. In that sense, you can also think of each channel as a collection of brightness values. When three sets of brightness values are present in one file, you have an opportunity to do a great deal more with the brightness information. To glimpse how this will work, look at Figures 10.3, 10.4, and 10.5. These are, as they are labeled, representations of individual channels. Each contains a circular area of white

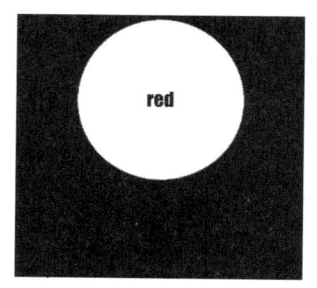

Figure 10.3 Light-colored pixels in the Red channel contribute bright red to the color image.

Figure 10.4 Light-colored pixels in the Green channel contribute bright green to the color image.

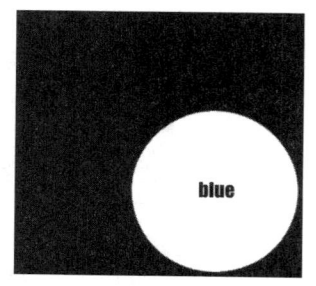

Figure 10.5 Light-colored pixels in the Blue channel contribute bright blue to the color image.

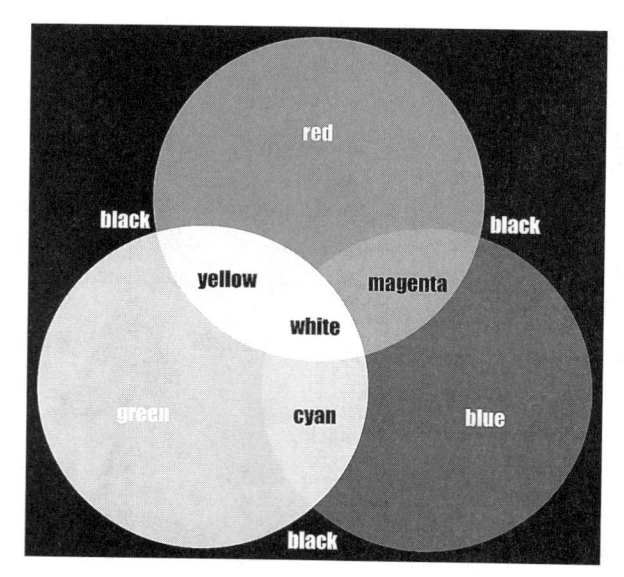

Figure 10.6 Brightness values in all three channels combine to produce the range of colors you see on your monitor.

pixels surrounded by black. Discounting the anti-aliasing that is present, each channel represents just two brightness values, black and white. When the three are assembled into a single RGB file, amazing things happen (see Figure 10.6). Each channel now has something to do with not only the brightness of its pixels, but its place in the three-channel structure—whether a given amount of brightness exists as a *red* brightness, or a *green* or a *blue*. The brightness values of each channel now designate color.

You need not see Figure 10.5 in color, nor do you need to understand the electron beams that excite the phosphors on the inside surface of your monitor tube. All you need to know, for now, is that each channel arbitrarily contributes its own color and that the contributions of all three channels—Red, Green, and Blue—produce all the colors your monitor can display.

If a pixel has value 255 in the Red channel and black (value 0) in the other two, that pixel's displayed color is a bright red. The Green and Blue channels work the same way. The combinations become more interesting when a given pixel has, say, value 255 in two channels, but with the other value 0. 255 in Red and Green with 0 in Blue gives a bright yellow. 255 in Green and Blue with 0 in Red produces a bright cyan. 255 in Blue and Red with Green as 0 gives a bright magenta. The two rightmost columns in Figure 10.6 show some of the possibilities. (Note that the secondary tones—cyan, magenta, and yellow—are the primary colors of four-color process printing.)

Many, many more colors are possible. Pixels do not have to be black and white, they can be any one of 256 values in each channel. That gives a lot of possibilities: 256^3 (2^{24}) = 16,777,216. It's an interesting concept, isn't it? All of those colors can come from a method that is so elegantly economical.

Your monitor is probably an RGB monitor; if it displays in color, it is. Of course you know that you can also process files in what Photoshop calls Grayscale mode. Grayscale, though you may not think of it this way, is really just a specialized kind of RGB. Think it through. If all three channels are value zero, then the displayed color is black. If all three channels are value 255 (see the center area of Figure 10.6), then the displayed color is white. Logically, if all three channels are value 128 (half of 256), wouldn't the displayed value be halfway between black and white—what we would call a 50 percent gray? Indeed it would. From this we can deduce that grayscale is simply a proper subset of RGB where a pixel's R, G, and B values are all the same.

Calibration And How It Works

Figure 10.7 shows the working dialog box of a well-known hardware calibration system sold by SuperMac/Radius. On the left side are three pop-up menus that inform the calibration software of the monitor type being evaluated and what kind of White Point and Gamma values are to be targeted. Two checkboxes below these pop-ups instruct the software to use the derived calibration values after the calibration sequence has been performed. Finally, the box has a button that initiates the calibration.

When the software requests it, a small, rectangular instrument with a suction cup attaches to the screen, usually in the center. While the software is running, this device makes evaluations of the three principal colors by themselves, the absolute white of the monitor, its darkest values, and the relative neutrality of the gray tones that form when all of the primary colors are

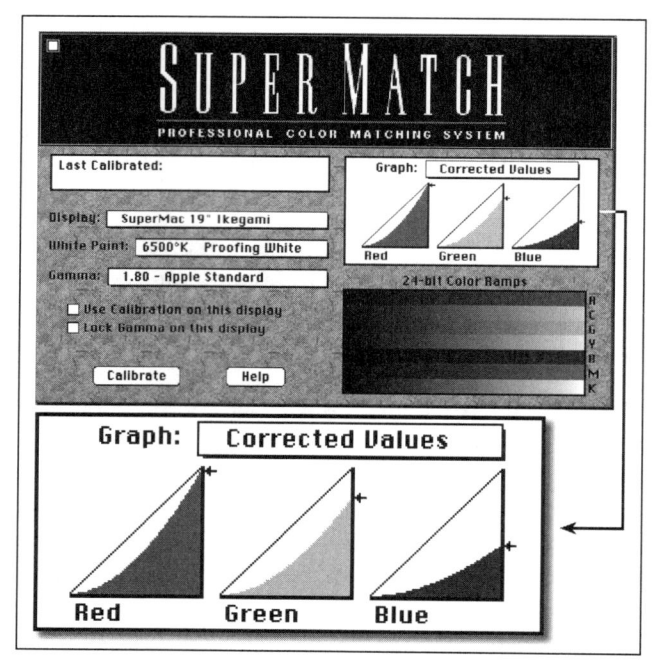

Figure 10.7 The opening screen for the SuperMatch calibration system.

combined. After it has done so, it electronically adjusts the display to bring it in line with an abstract set of values calculated to produce accurate colors on screen.

The center-right side of the calibration screen shows the results of the calibration software adjustments. That portion of the screen has been reproduced and enlarged at the bottom of the figure. You've already spent some time on curves in Chapter 9; knowing what you do about curves and how they work, it's easy to recognize how much of a change these curves indicate, especially in the blue. The pre-adjusted line, of course, is equivalent to the Input curve. The Output curve here shows that the blue signal, relative to the other two, was so strong that its output needed to be reduced by more than half. The green signal, also too strong, has been severely cut back. All three have been reduced in the midtone and highlight values.

Human eyes, even eyes highly sensitive to color, are not good enough to evaluate a computer monitor. The reason for this is simple: The unaided eye has no external reference within the same color paradigm. By this, we mean that you cannot hold a printed piece up to the monitor and hope for more than an approximate match because the printed piece depends on reflected light and the monitor is a light emitter. Beyond fairly large differences, the eye cannot determine—against some arbitrarily set standard of how a color is supposed to look—that a given monitor's display of the color is too bright or too dark, too saturated, or the wrong hue. Nor can it say that on one monitor, the strength of one of the phosphor colors is such that it overbalances or gives a color cast to neutral grays. The hardware calibration instrument can do what the eye cannot do. It can perform an accurate evaluation of a monitor. Calibration software can also control the hardware to give an accurate screen image.

Colortron II

One of the most impressive devices being sold for hardware calibration is the Colortron II, by Light Source, Inc. This small, multipurpose device plugs into the ADB circuitry—from the port that drives the keyboard and the mouse—of a Macintosh or Power Macintosh computer. It is bundled with two foot-pieces. One of these has suction cups that allow the Colortron to be attached to the monitor for calibration. The other foot-piece is in the form of a rocker switch. The rocker switch supports the instrument in open position when it isn't in use. When measurements are being made, the instrument tips forward and closes the switch. When it isn't being used for monitor calibration, the Colortron II can be used as a densitometer or as a colorimeter. These functions make it among the most remarkable and cost-effective tools available to prepress technicians. It can be used with several of the standalone software programs—including Light Source's own program, *ColorShop*—that analyze device color characteristics for the purpose of generating ICC Profiles. We'll discuss the desktop functions and profile generation later in this chapter.

Figure 10.8 shows an expanded view of the Colortron monitor Calibrator dialog box (selected from the list of Control Panel programs). The top two pop-up menus show the target choices for the White Point and the Gamma. The ColorSync Profile pop-up menu is not used until after the

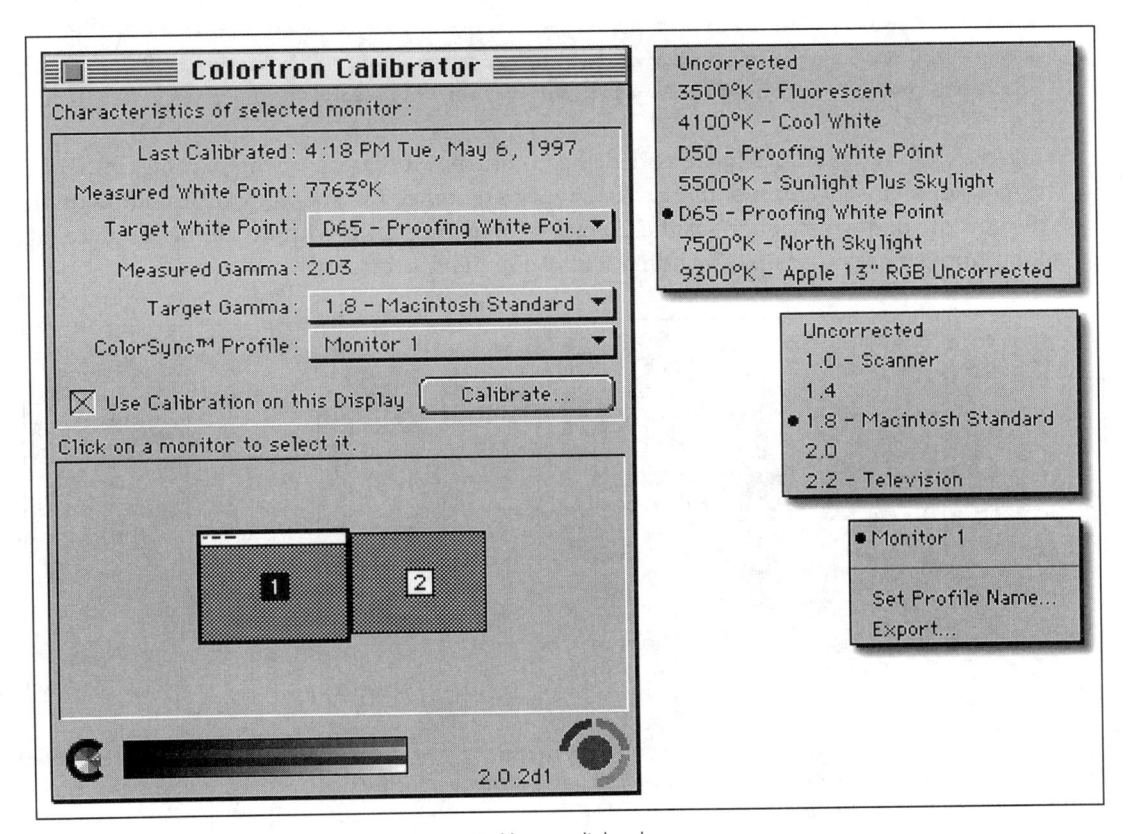

Figure 10.8 Expanded view of the Colortron Calibrator dialog box.

calibration has been done. When the dialog box first opens, the menu displays the current setting of the ColorSync Control Panel. The dialog box shows a checkbox that causes the calibration software to be used systemwide, not just in Photoshop, as well as a button that initiates the calibration.

> **TIP**
>
> At the bottom of the dialog box is a rectangular area that indicates that two monitors are present and that you can click on either to select which will be calibrated. Windows users are not widely aware of the fact that workstations can be configured with two monitors. (Multiple monitors are not supported directly by Windows 95 except through third-party software, but will be supported by Windows 98.) The ability to use more than one monitor has been part of the Macintosh system since well before the introduction of color displays. The default usage for two monitors is to have them function as one virtual screen. This is particularly useful for palette-heavy programs such as Photoshop. The primary monitor is the larger and displays the document. The secondary monitor allows for all the palettes to be open at all times. This is depicted in Figure 10.9, a screen capture of one of the authors' monitors while using Photoshop. The advantages of such a system are immediately obvious. If your system is not configured for two monitors, you should investigate the possibility. The gain in productivity will astonish you. This single feature will make the upgrade to Windows 98 worth the cost and the effort.

When the calibration sequence has ended, the ColorSync Profile pop-up menu comes into play. The measurements for this monitor can be saved as a named file in ColorSync format. This file is also installed, at your option, as the ColorSync system default. With the profile in place, all color management programs, including Photoshop, have access to it.

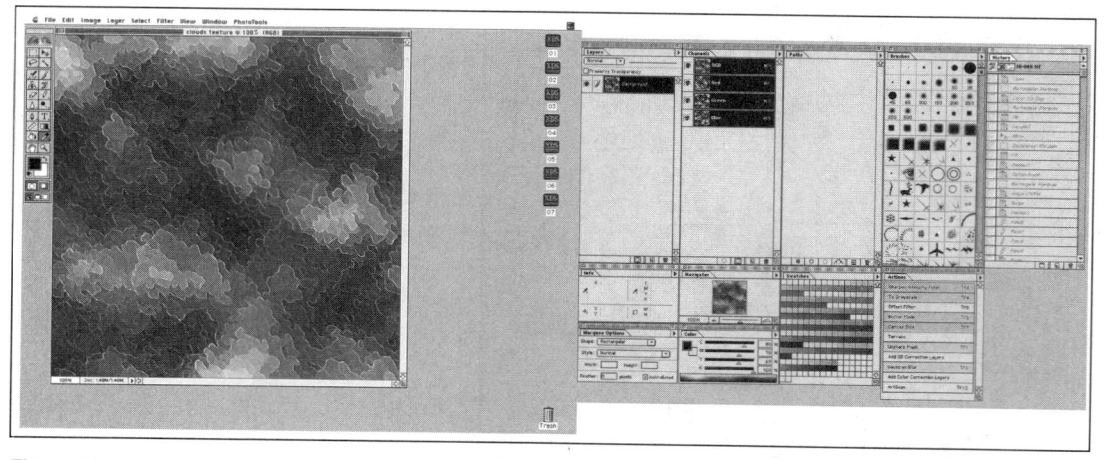

Figure 10.9 Screen capture of a two-monitor workstation. The larger monitor displays the document, the smaller displays the palettes.

Adobe Gamma

In Chapter 9, you were introduced to the Adobe Gamma utility, one of the niftiest features of Photoshop 5. If you don't yet own a hardware calibration system, you should reread the instructions for calibrating your monitor. At the conclusion of your calibration, the software will write your monitor profile in ICC Profile format. Please note that, though this might seem obvious, you shouldn't try to use more than one calibration method at a time. If you already use a Colortron monitor calibrator, or some other hardware device, you should probably leave the Adobe Gamma utility alone. You can, if you wish to try Adobe Gamma, disable your hardware calibrator.

When Your Monitor Is Under Control

After calibrating, you'll notice that your monitor looks darker, even dingy. Don't be alarmed—that's the way it's supposed to look. Your calibrated monitor's sole purpose now is to emulate press conditions. The white of your screen after calibration is not the bright white you are accustomed to seeing. It's closer to the color of the paper stock on which your digital files will be printed. Colors do not seem so bright for a good reason: Many of the bright and beautiful colors your monitor is capable of displaying are out-of-gamut print colors, colors that cannot be duplicated using four-color process ink on paper. The printable colors, for the most part, are a smaller subset of the RGB colors. All of the colors in this subset comprise a number that is about 45 percent to 65 percent of the 16.77 million colors your monitor can display. Some colors are missing, and this is one of the reasons why your display can never be totally accurate. 100 percent process cyan, for example, is a color that cannot be displayed using RGB colors.

When you have closed the calibration dialog box, your first task will be to configure the Photoshop Color Settings preferences. Open Photoshop and choose File|Color Settings|RGB Setup. Figure 10.10 shows an expanded view of the dialog box that opens. Previous versions of Photoshop required you to inform it of your monitor's display characteristics. As you can see at the bottom of the dialog box, Photoshop is already aware of your monitor, having read its display characteristics from the ColorSync default file.

Your settings within the RGB Setup dialog box are going to be a little confusing if you have been familiar with older versions of the program. The first thing to understand is that your choices here are really just that: choices. You are not telling Photoshop about your monitor's display characteristics, because Photoshop already knows (from the ICC Profile your calibration software generated). You are informing Photoshop of the RGB space within which you wish to edit your preseparated color images. If you are a prepress technician, you should probably choose settings close to those shown in Figure 10.10. For RGB, select Wide Gamut RGB, change the Gamma setting to 1.80 (which will then change the RGB so that it reads *Custom*), and the White Point and Primaries settings to those shown in the figure.

Beyond our recommendations for prepress work, you should know something about the other choices in this dialog box so that you can make your own decisions about settings:

- The sRGB standard is of fairly recent origin. It is an RGB space that roughly follows the standards of High Definition Television. sRGB is being promoted by Microsoft and Hewlett-Packard

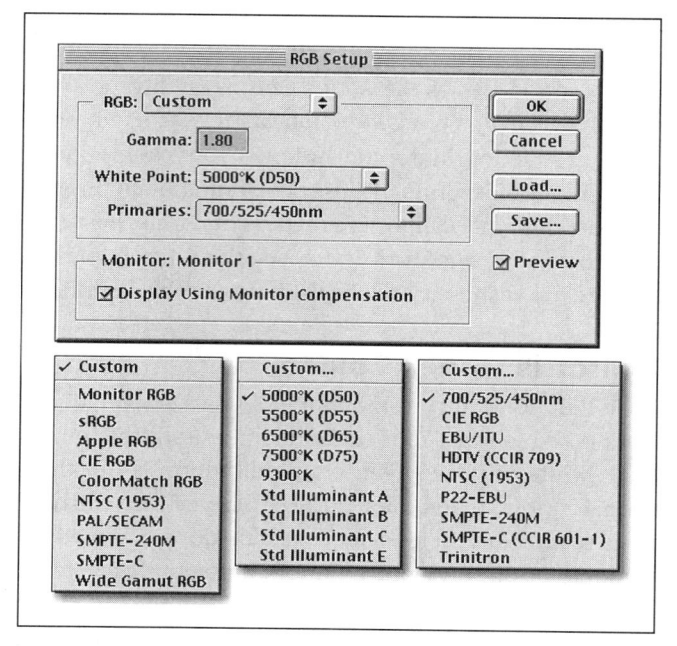

Figure 10.10 Photoshop's Monitor Setup dialog box.

as an *average* of what displays on most personal computer monitors. Because of its lowest-possible-denominator characteristics, sRGB is being promoted as an ideal color workspace for Web developers. Hewlett-Packard plans to implement this standard by optimizing its scanners and printers. To the extent that prepress professionals can be influenced by corporations with resources beyond some nation states, we recommend coming to terms with sRGB, because it will be ubiquitous in the next few years. The disadvantage of sRGB is that it has a somewhat limited gamut. sRGB is Photoshop 5's default RGB monitor choice.

- Apple RGB is the name given to the RGB gamut of the first color Macintosh computers, all of which used a 13" Sony Trinitron monitor. This gamut has been a standard in publishing for a number of years, but is not particularly better—or larger—than sRGB.
- SMPTE-C is the United States television broadcast standard. You would use this as your RGB color space of choice if you use Photoshop to prepare graphic materials for U.S. television broadcast.
- PAL/SECAM is the gamut of the European broadcast standard. This would be your RGB target space if you used Photoshop to prepare graphic materials for European television.
- ColorMatch RGB is the gamut of the Radius PressView monitor, a widely used CRT in the prepress world. This gamut would be your best choice if your system uses a PressView. It's a moderately large color space, and has the advantage of consistency between monitors of the same type.
- SMPTE-240M is the proposed standard for HDTV production work. It's a very large gamut—larger than all of the previous entries on this list—and allows you wide latitude when

working with color. The disadvantage to this gamut is that the CMYK is proportionally smaller when compared to it. That means that it contains more out-of-gamut colors than the previously listed gamuts.

- Wide Gamut RGB is an extensive gamut that uses spectrally pure primary colors. This means that it can display, potentially, a very large number of colors. However, most of these colors cannot be printed, nor can they be displayed on a standard computer monitor. It's the latter that makes this our recommended choice for RGB Setup: Display limitations mean that potentially out-of-gamut colors will be clipped to the display gamut, allowing color adjustments without much visible change.

- Monitor RGB is the gamut you would have if you used the Load button to load in the ICC Profile that was generated by your calibration software. This would make Photoshop behave like older versions of the program, and would unnecessarily limit your ability to manipulate color files. You would also, when moving files from computer to computer, force each new machine to make conversions based on a different monitor gamut.

- NTSC is the older U.S. broadcast standard. It's still usable, but has been superseded by SMPTE-C.

It's important to remember that your choice of a monitor gamut in RGB Setup has almost no relationship with your calibration. You are simply choosing an editing space. Your calibration ensures that what you see in your editing space is aimed both at your prepress output and at the accuracy of all your displayed colors.

CMYK Setup: Built-In Options

After dealing with the believability of your display and your choice of editing gamut, the next important task on the way to printing good color is to inform Photoshop about the color characteristics of the inks you will be using. You can do this in a manner that is similar to previous versions of Photoshop, the Built-In option—along with some powerful new controls—or in two other ways. In the next few sections of this chapter, you will become acquainted with all three.

Begin by choosing File|Color Settings|CMYK Setup. An expanded view of the dialog box is shown in Figure 10.11.

The Ink Colors sets you can choose from are a somewhat limited group and have not changed much over the last several versions of Photoshop. Included are Eurostandard inks, Toyo inks, a color copier, a couple of thermal wax printers, two dye sublimation printers, and the SWOP sets (Specifications for Web Offset Publications). The default is SWOP on coated paper, a profile that is presumed to work equally well on a Web press and a medium-quality sheetfed press.

When you make a selection from this list, you load in a group of settings that accurately describe the *chroma*—the scientifically literate term for *color*—characteristics of the four inks. Included with this description is the *hue error* of each of the colors. Mass-produced inks cannot have an absolutely pure color. Each of the three principal colored inks is contaminated by some percentage of the other two. Yellow, for example, could be described as containing some percentage of cyan and magenta. The percentages are often higher than would seem possible: They can range from 12 percent to 22 percent. Typically, the SWOP inks have a higher hue

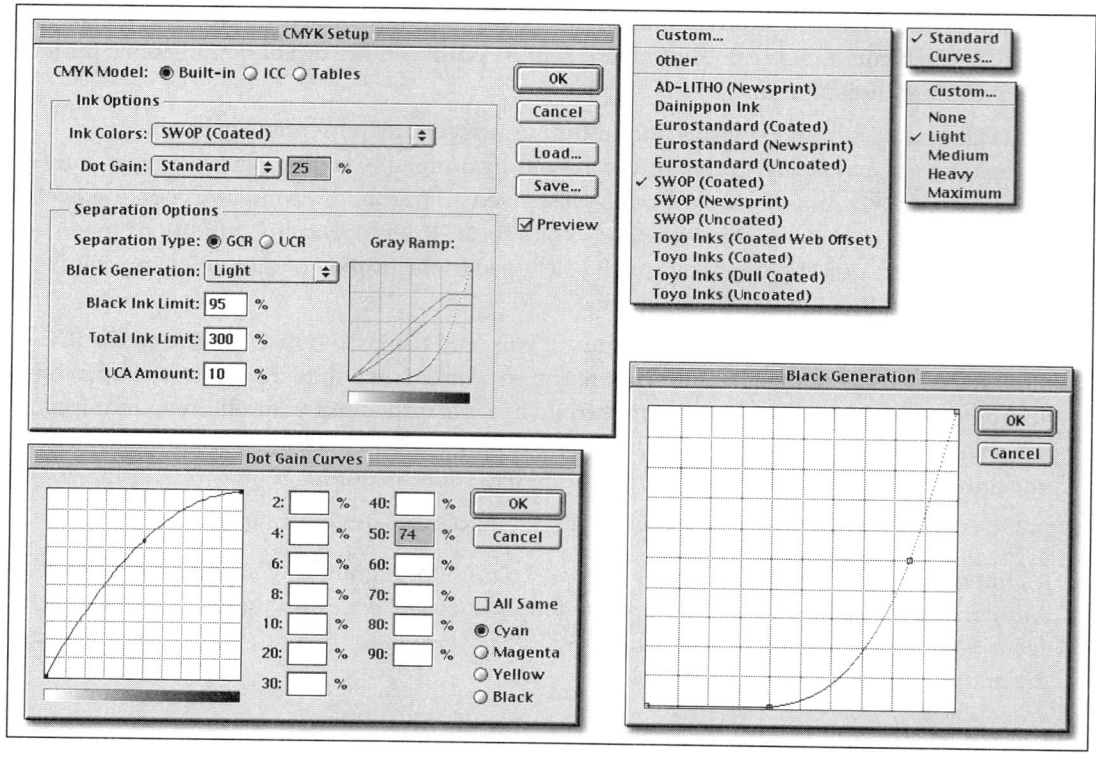

Figure 10.11 Photoshop's Printing Inks Setup dialog box.

error than the others on the list. This can make the choice of default seem a puzzling choice, but SWOP inks are the least costly of those represented, and therefore are the most often used within the printing industry.

Hue error is a significant problem when it comes to reproducing colored images. If you assume, for the sake of easy calculation, that the total hue error for each of the primary inks—CMY—is 20 percent of each of the other inks, then it's easy to understand that the overlapping values reduce the number of printed tones these inks can produce. Hue error is also the prime cause for the fact that the three primaries don't form the absolute black that should be possible when overprinting them at full strength. The color produced is, instead, a dismal-looking red-hued brown. Black ink is required for a four-color press to be able to reproduce vibrant color with rich shadow tones.

Other factors included in the loaded profile include the way the pure inks react to each other in various overprint combinations. Specifically, this measurement would include all possible pairs overprinting each other and the tone produced by overprinting all. Each of the ink sets in the list also has a default dot gain setting. The setting is an average value, and is the only part of the ink profile that you may find easy to modify.

If you have access to a Colortron II, it's perfectly possible for you to generate a named ink set for any kind of color output device. You could generate a set for a color copier, an ink jet printer, a color laser printer, or an offset press that you use frequently. The settings can be saved as named files using the Printing Inks Setup dialog box, and later loaded for specific use. The procedure for making a custom Ink Color set is as follows:

1. First, obtain an output sample from the press or desktop color printer. Most offset press sheets have color bars with tints. From these you can obtain most of the information you'll need, but not all of it. If necessary, generate a custom bar and ask your printer to tuck it onto a press sheet so that you can analyze it. Most printers will do this when they have a press sheet with a little extra trim space, particularly if you share your results. All you'll need is one or two sheets.

2. If you're going to analyze a desktop color printer, open the file INK&GAIN.PSD on the accompanying CD-ROM. Print this file on the device to be measured. Note that this file is in Photoshop format at 300 ppi. If you need a different resolution, open either of the files INK&GAIN.AI (Adobe Illustrator) or INK & GAIN.FH7 (Macromedia FreeHand) and rasterize them into Photoshop. Set the resolution to whatever you require. Figure 10.12 shows a small representation of this file. The original is in CMYK and is small

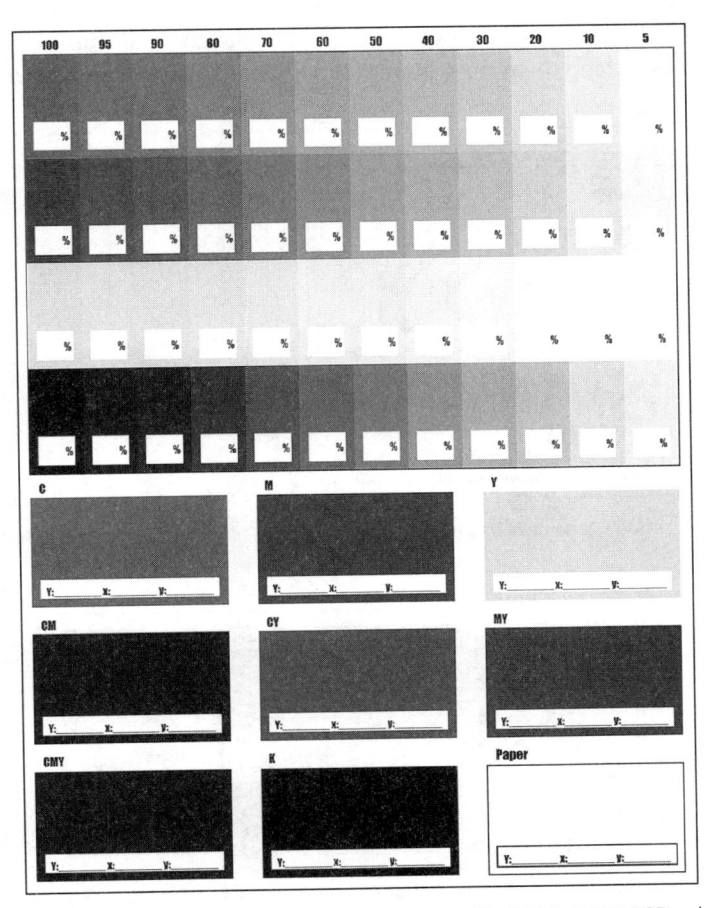

Figure 10.12 A representation of the accompanying CD-ROM test file INK & GAIN.PSD, which can be used for making a Printing Inks calibration file with Colortron II.

enough to fit on a letter-sized page. After you've printed this file, leave the file open in Photoshop: You may need it before you're finished.

3. The top of the file has bars of the four inks in descending percentages. You don't need these for the custom ink file, but it's useful to measure these swatches to compare your input and output values. As you measure Dot Area densities with the Colortron II (see Figure 10.13), write down the percentages in the box at the bottom of each swatch. You can plot this set of measurements using the graphing function in Adobe Illustrator or in any spreadsheet. Pay particular attention to the four 50% values: It will be useful to know if one of the inks has a larger gain than the others.

4. At the bottom of the file are nine swatches. The one on the lower right is simply for measuring the color of the paper. The others are: C, M, Y, CM, CY, MY, CMY, and K. The Colorimeter palette in ColorShop is shown in Figure 10.14. As you measure each of the nine swatches, your readings can be simultaneously displayed in three different color systems (the pop-up menu at the right shows the choices). In the figure, the left column is shown giving the color measurement in Lab values, the right column in RGB values, and the center column, in CIE xyY values. You can write the others down, but it's the center-column set that you're most interested in. Write down the numbers for each measurement as you read them from bottom to top (you'll see why in a moment).

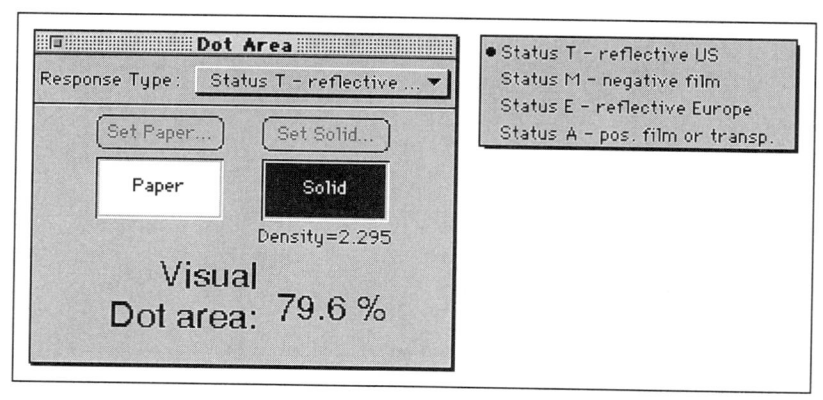

Figure 10.13 The Dot Area (Densitometer) measurement window of Colortron II's controlling software program, ColorShop.

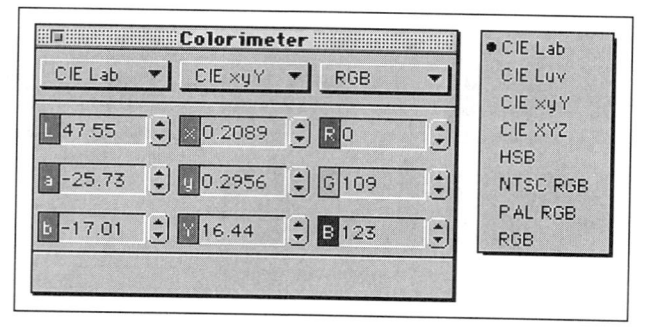

Figure 10.14 ColorShop's Colorimeter dialog box.

CALIBRATION AND COLOR REPRODUCTION 669

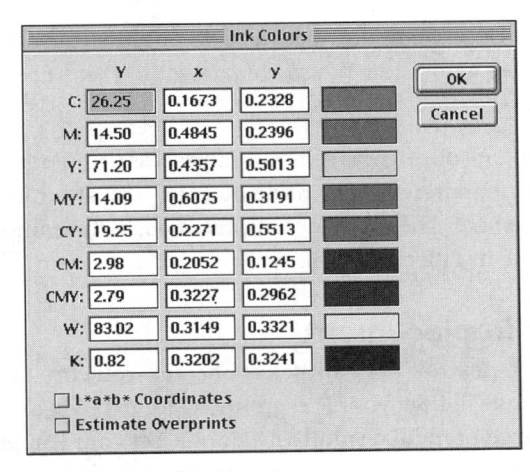

Figure 10.15 Photoshop's Custom Ink Colors dialog box.

5. After you've filled in your printed sheet, return to the Printing Inks Setup dialog box. Click on the pop-up menu and choose Custom. The dialog box that appears is shown in Figure 10.15. Enter the values you obtained from your Colortron readings—which were given in the reverse order of what is used here (which is why you wrote them from bottom to top). This part of your output file has now furnished you with nearly all of the required information. When you have finished typing, click on OK. (Note that a checkbox at the bottom of this dialog box allows you to record your ink values in L*a*b. You can use the Estimate Overprints checkbox if you want to try matching an ink set by eye from a color proof. After you have entered the C, M, Y, and K values, Photoshop will give you estimates of the combinations. Matching a proof to the screen is a practice followed by many Photoshop users. In the opinion of the authors, it's an idea that's almost devoid of merit.)

6. Your pop-up menu now reads Custom. Before naming and saving the file, change the Dot Gain pop-up menu (refer to Figure 10.11) so that it reads *Curves*. Take a look at your readings of all the 50% color swatches on the INK & GAIN file. Subtract 50 from the measured number to see what your dot gain value is for each ink. Enter the *measured number* (not the gain amount) in the 50% data entry field for each ink. (To select an ink, click on one of the named radio buttons.) Click OK. Now click on the Save button, and save this setting configuration under the name of the output device and in a place where you can easily locate it.

Separation Setup

The last step in preparing to generate files for four-color printing using the Built-In CMYK Setup is to set your Separation Options for the conversion of the file to CMYK mode. These options are also shown in Figure 10.11.

You have learned the reasons for the addition of black ink to a separation: The three primary inks cannot produce a good black by themselves. Black is added to make black areas look truly black. It makes shadows look clean and crisp and accentuates the clarity of the image in a way that would be impossible without it. It also cuts down on the amount of ink needed to reproduce the image on press.

Black is added to the image during the separation process using one of two methods. UCR and GCR—the two choices are represented by radio buttons—are short for *Under Color Removal* and *Gray Component Replacement*. These two accomplish nearly the same result but, as the names imply, go about the task in different ways.

Gray Component Replacement

Figure 10.16 shows two, neutral, gray swatches of color. You can duplicate each of these in a small sample CMYK-mode file. Set your Foreground color to 0% cyan, 0% magenta, 0% yellow, and 50% black. Use the color to fill a small selection. Reset your Foreground color to 50% cyan, 37% magenta, 37% yellow, and 0% black (the figures may vary depending on the settings in the Separation Setup dialog box). Fill another small selection with this color. You should see, on your screen, two swatches that look identical. This figure is the key to how GCR works. During the conversion process, areas of the image are analyzed for their gray components and the primary inks are replaced with black. As the figure shows, this results in a reduction in the amount of ink in the places where it occurs. For this figure, 74 percent less ink is needed to produce the identical tone.

GCR doesn't occur only in neutral areas. Proportions of cyan, magenta, and yellow that produce a neutral tone are replaced with black, but the amount of ink needed to produce a specific hue is left in place. For example, if a tone in the image is somewhat neutral and contains a slight pink cast, it's an indication that some percentage of magenta is higher than the percentage required to produce a neutral tone. In that case, the GCR routine would produce an equivalent color by using a percentage of black coupled with a small amount of magenta, the amount of magenta required to add the pink cast to the neutral tone. You can try this for yourself. Fill one selection with a color composed of 50% black and 20% magenta. Now, fill another selection with 50% cyan, 37% + 20% = 57% magenta, 37% yellow, and 0% black. There should be no difference in the two tones.

GCR is Photoshop's default. It's generally agreed to be easier to balance on press than UCR, but it requires a setting for Under Color Addition—which we'll discuss in a moment for a separation to look its best. Of the two black generation methods, GCR produces the heaviest black

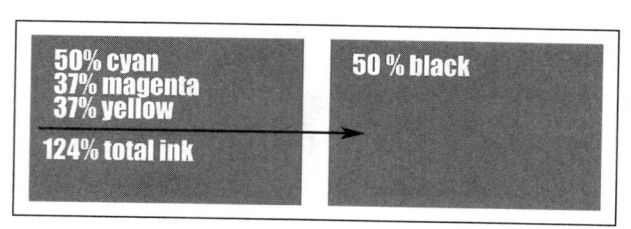

Figure 10.16 Gray swatches can be printed with black or with tints of cyan, magenta, and yellow.

plate. This can be an advantage in some situations and a disadvantage in others. Web offset printing, for example, often requires a low maximum density of inks, which presupposes a light, open separation. Large amounts of black can be difficult to handle, and printed GCR separations can be heavy looking. We'll discuss how you can cut down on the amount of ink in your separation in the next section.

Black Generation

You can find the settings for the GCR algorithm in the center of the dialog box. You'll see five preset black generation amounts and a Custom setting. When you choose the Custom setting, a curves dialog box appears (shown at the lower right, back in Figure 10.11), in which you can apply your own ideas about the black generation. If you wanted to make your black generation amount lighter than the presets, you would use this dialog box to do so. Otherwise, your choices are None (no black ink), Light, Medium, Heavy, and Maximum.

Figure 10.17 shows four black separation plates. They were generated using the four Black Generation presets and they show how much this setting affects the separation.

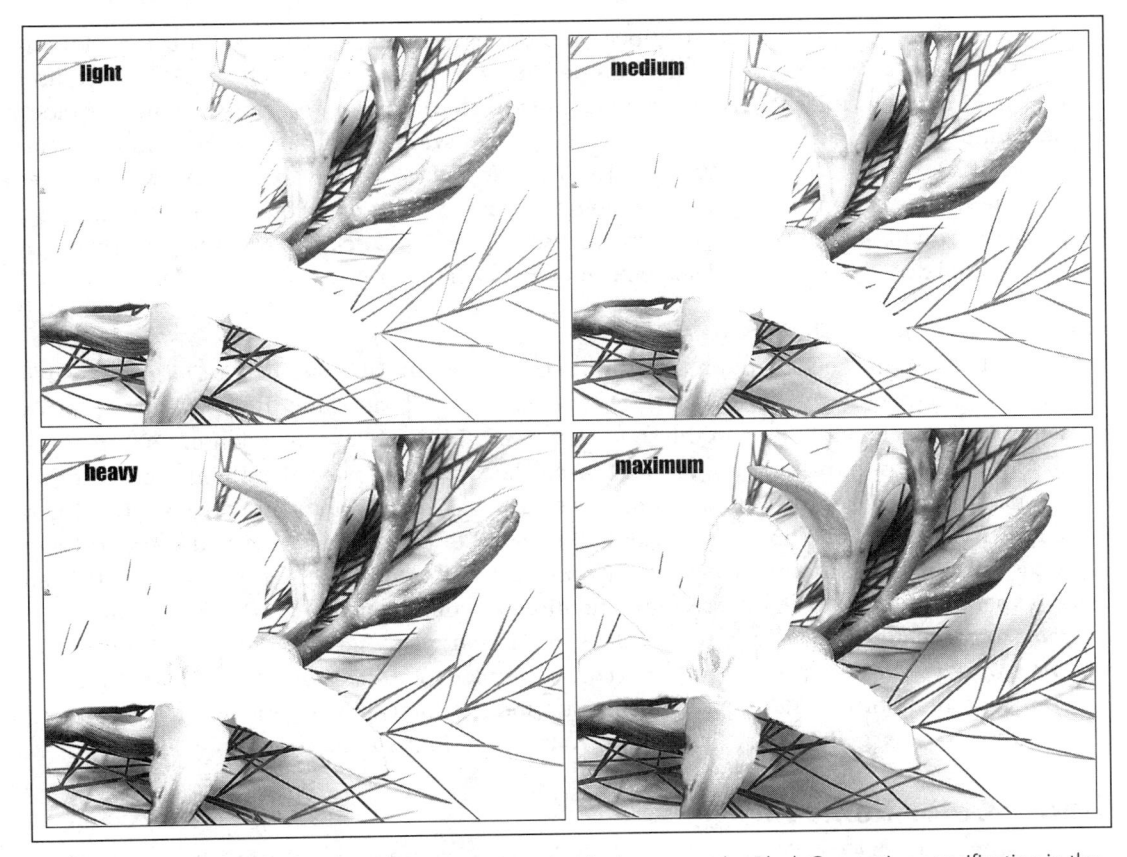

Figure 10.17 Four black separation plates generated with changes to the Black Generation specification in the Separation Setup.

Black Ink Limit

The Black Ink Limit allows you to choose the maximum percentage of black anywhere in the separated image. Choosing a number lower than 100 percent simply means that there will never be a black ink area with a density higher than the percentage you choose. For most separation work, no good reason exists why the black setting should be higher than the maximum value used for a halftone (92 percent to 95 percent).

Total Ink Limit

The Total Ink Limit is the amount of ink allowed on press. It is calculated by adding together all four ink percentages at the area of highest coverage. The theoretical limit would be 400 percent. That number is impractical for a variety of reasons, the main one being that so much ink would be difficult to dry. Because of this, the press speed would have to be very slow, or the individual sheets would smudge each other as they are stacked. (Don't ever try 400 percent as an experiment—it can make the pressman dangerously testy!) The actual figure you should use here must be obtained from your printer. Depending on the press and the kind of paper stock you intend to use, the figure will probably range between 280 percent and 320 percent.

When the three main settings are in place, you can see a set of curves that indicate the relationships of the inks. Notice that the curve of the black ink doesn't begin to have an impact until above 50 percent, at least with the settings used in Figure 10.11. You can see how this black generation works by making a grayscale image with swatches of black in percentage increments of 10 percent (see Figure 10.18). When these swatches are converted to CMYK, the values become as labeled on the right in the figure. If these values are plotted out with graphing software, you'll see that the resulting curves (see Figure 10.19) closely resemble the curves in the original Separation Setup dialog box shown back in Figure 10.11.

Under Color Addition Amount

The last setting in the Separation Setup is the UCA Amount. UCA stands for *Under Color Addition* and is probably the least used, least understood, and most important way to finesse a separation into looking good in the shadow tones. UCA modifies the action of GCR in dense shadows by cutting back on the amount of black, while increasing the amount of the other colors. The purpose of this is to make a darker, richer shadow than would be possible using a single ink. At the same time, UCA adds subtle detail to the shadow area and prevents these areas from looking flat and posterized. The amount you enter in this setup box is determined by experimentation and by the recommendations of your print vendor. Don't be afraid to do some experimenting with this setting. Adobe recommends leaving the setting at 0% unless you know what you're doing. Practically, you can experiment with settings up to about 5% without doing any real harm—and probably help your image a lot. Don't go much over 10% without some expert advice. But do try this option. Your separations will look better!

Under Color Removal

The main difference between GCR and UCR is that UCR separations replace CMY values only in truly neutral areas of the image. If the image has been balanced and unwanted casts removed

CALIBRATION AND COLOR REPRODUCTION 673

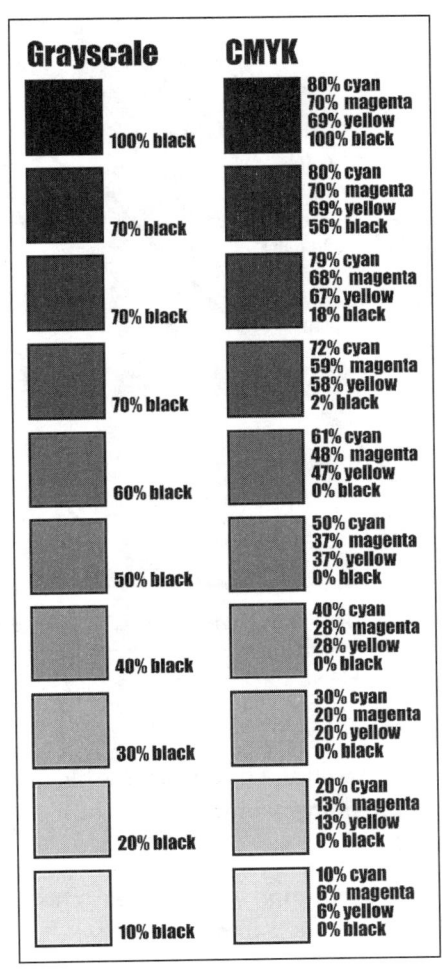

Grayscale	CMYK
100% black	80% cyan / 70% magenta / 69% yellow / 100% black
70% black	80% cyan / 70% magenta / 69% yellow / 56% black
70% black	79% cyan / 68% magenta / 67% yellow / 18% black
70% black	72% cyan / 59% magenta / 58% yellow / 2% black
60% black	61% cyan / 48% magenta / 47% yellow / 0% black
50% black	50% cyan / 37% magenta / 37% yellow / 0% black
40% black	40% cyan / 28% magenta / 28% yellow / 0% black
30% black	30% cyan / 20% magenta / 20% yellow / 0% black
20% black	20% cyan / 13% magenta / 13% yellow / 0% black
10% black	10% cyan / 6% magenta / 6% yellow / 0% black

Figure 10.18 Depending on the Separation Setup values, a set of grayscale percentages can be represented by CMYK percentages similar to these.

from highlights and shadows, a UCR separation should have less ink density in deep shadow areas than GCR. The black UCR plate simply adds depth and richness to shadows and neutrals, while the non-neutral colors are left alone. The UCR separation method is usually considered a better choice if the image doesn't contain dark and saturated colors. Such images are usually reproduced better by using GCR for the separation method. We should note a drawback to UCR, particularly for Photoshop users who prepare images for the fashion industry, or for other uses where clear, perfect skin tones—usually skin tones of women and children—are required. All else being equal, the only places on a human face that are true neutrals are under-eye and under-chin shadows. When black is added, especially under the chin, the black area fades into very light percentages along the jaw line. If it were possible to hold a dot smaller than 3 percent or 4 percent, this would not present a problem. However, the abrupt falloff of the dot on the

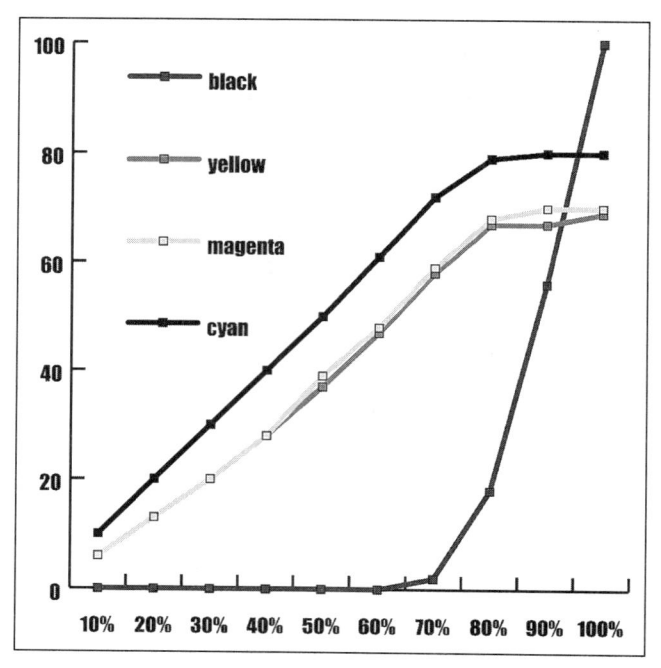

Figure 10.19 When the CMYK values in Figure 10.18 are graphed, they form a set of curves identical to the Curves display in the Separation Setup dialog box.

black plate results in a more-or-less abrupt line where the black ink comes to an end. This effect is always immediately apparent, not very attractive (because it looks like five o'clock shadow), and absolutely impossible to fix.

When you choose UCR as your separation type, the only choices available in the Separation Setup dialog box are Black Ink Limit and Total Ink Limit.

CMYK Setup: ICC Profiles

Earlier in this chapter you learned about ICC Profiles. *ICC* is the second option in Photoshop's CMYK Setup dialog box. When you click on this option, you're presented with an entirely new set of options, an expanded view of which is shown in Figure 10.20.

Of all the wonderful features included with version 5 of Photoshop, this unassuming dialog box may be one of the most useful for Photoshop users who wish to really get control over printed color. To make the most complete use of this option, you will need a device such as a Colortron II (although you can use your scanner as a color-measuring instrument), and an additional software package that will allow you to generate your own ICC Profiles. To let you know how you would use profiles for your separations, we'll take you through the process by examining a single accessory software package, ColorSynergy, by Candela, Ltd. of Burnsville, Minnesota (**www.candelacolor.com**). This software package is not the only one of its kind, but it's certainly one of the best. Beyond the efficiency of the software and its superbly simple

CALIBRATION AND COLOR REPRODUCTION 675

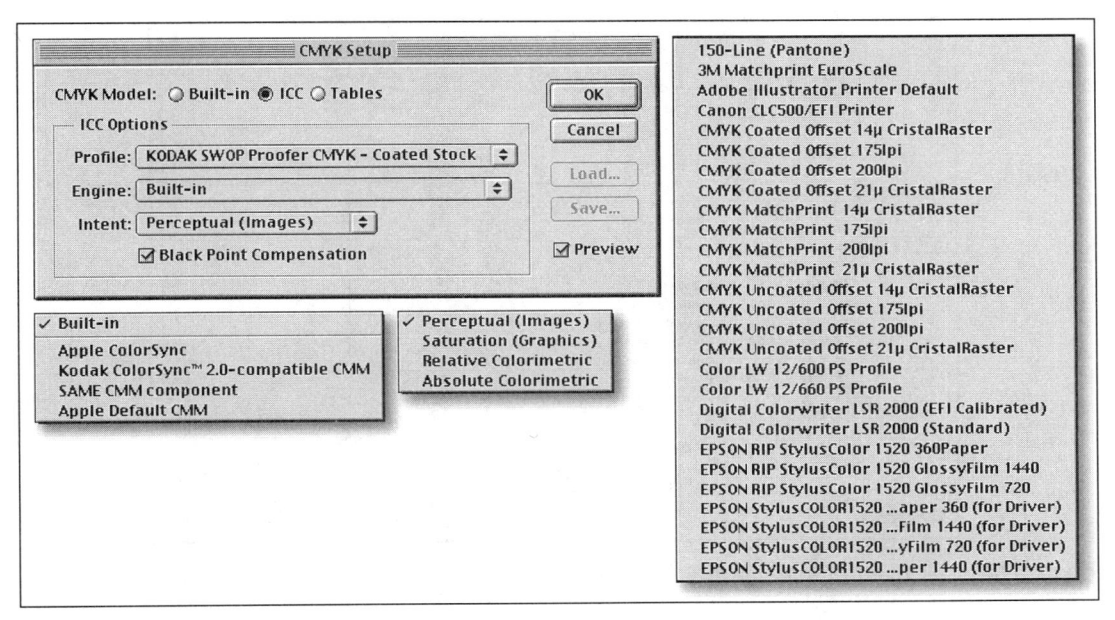

Figure 10.20 Expanded view of the ICC Profiles option within Photoshop 5's CMYK Setup.

interface, ColorSynergy ships with the single best User Manual you will ever encounter. Really the best! It is superbly written and beautifully organized! As you look at ColorSynergy's features, you'll be better able to understand how the information you generate from the program can be integrated into Photoshop.

ColorSynergy By Candela, Ltd.

The essential parts of ColorSynergy are the parts that measure color characteristics and write them to a file accessible to other profile-aware software programs. Your first task is to identify for the program the measurement instrument you will be using. Under the Setup menu, select Measuring instruments. The dialog box that appears is shown in Figure 10.21. This list contains all of the possibilities available to you through this program. In this discussion of ColorSynergy (we'll refer to it from now on as *CS*), we'll assume that you have a Colortron II, but we'll make a note of how you would use a scanner for many of the same purposes.

RGB Input (Monitor) Profile Generation

It might be a good idea to deal with your monitor first. If you have a Colortron II, attach the calibration foot to the device. Select Profile|New|RGB Display (see Figure 10.22). Follow the on-screen directions for measuring your monitor. At the end of the calibration sequence, you will be invited to save your monitor's display characteristics as a named file with a *prof* (for *profile*) extension. If you are operating CS without a measuring instrument and intend to use your scanner, choose Profile|Import. Locate the ICC Profile you saved when you operated Adobe Gamma. After this profile has been opened by CS, save it with the prof extension. You will load and use one of these profiles when you make further measurements.

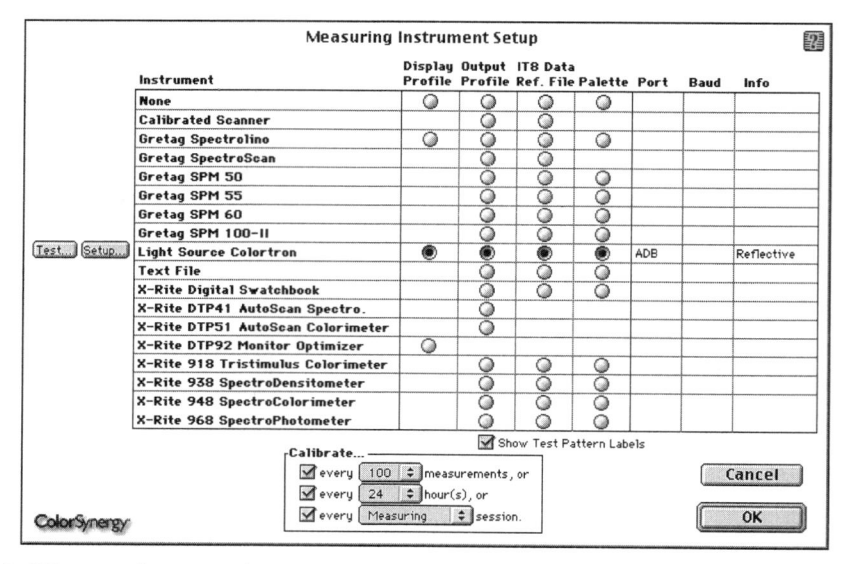

Figure 10.21 When you first use ColorSynergy, you'll make your choice of measuring instrument from this list, located under the Setup menu.

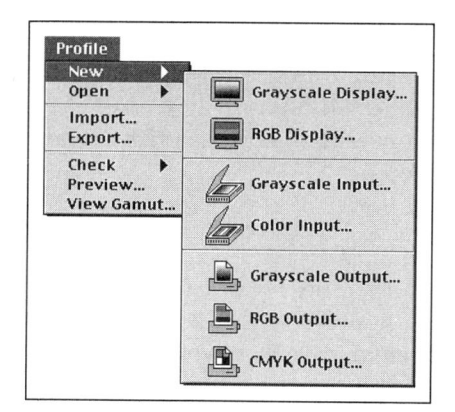

Figure 10.22 To create a new monitor profile, choose Setup|New|RGB Display.

Scanner Input Profile Generation

The next step is to bring your scanner into calibration. You would do this in any case because your scanner is probably part of your color prepress workflow. Calibrating it with CS and generating a profile for it ensures that your scans will be accurately translated into the monitor gamut, and from there into the print (CMYK or desktop color printer) gamut. You must also calibrate the scanner if you plan to use it as a measuring device.

Calibrating the scanner is a two-step process. You must first scan the Kodak IT-8 target file—included with the CS software—and save it in a format CS can recognize. Use TIFF, the universal and ubiquitous file format. The IT-8 target is a widely used colorimetric target (shown in the

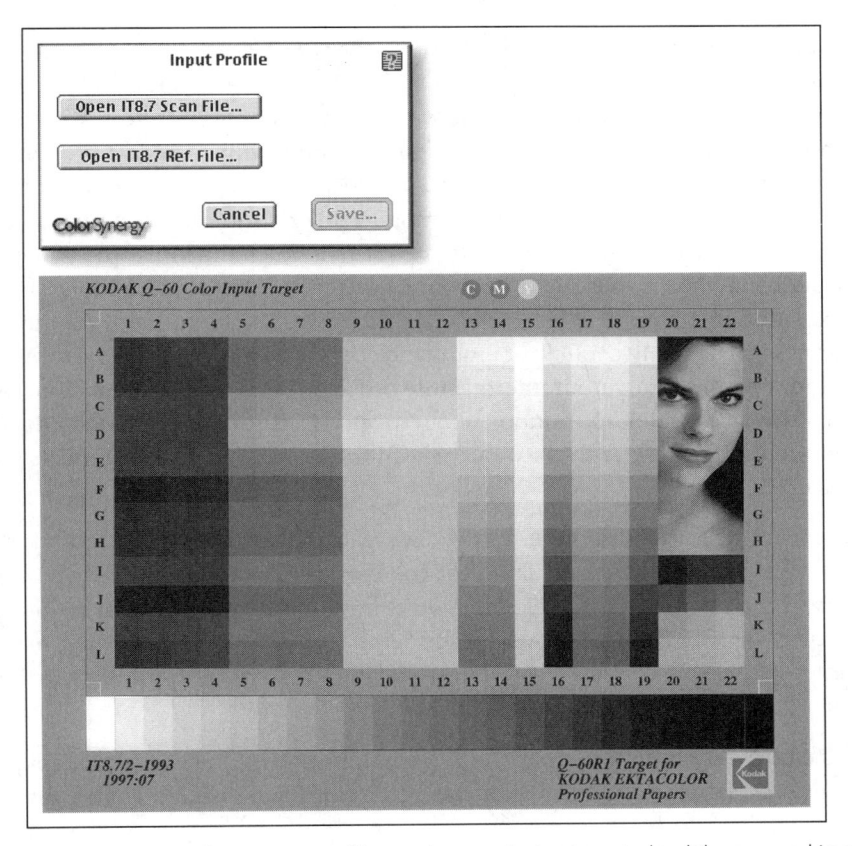

Figure 10.23 When you create the scanner profile, two buttons instruct you to load the scanned image of the IT-8 target and Kodak's calibration information for this individual photographic reproduction of the IT-8.

lower part of Figure 10.23) with a set of known colorimetric characteristics that can be used by CS when it compares your scanned values to what it knows the true values to be. (Note that you must be able to save your scanner software settings for this scan to be valid the next time you scan an image. If your settings change, you will need to recalibrate the scanner or your scan results will be skewed.)

After you have the target scan, from the Profile menu, choose New|Color Input. A small dialog box will appear (top part of Figure 10.23). You'll see two buttons. The top button instructs you to open the scanned image. The second asks you to load the IT-8 reference file. (Kodak manufactures the IT-8 targets in batches. Because batches may vary, each batch is measured and a measurement reference file is included with each photographically reproduced target.)

Your target image appears on screen. You must now zoom in and locate the corners of the image. CS furnishes you with small corner cursors that you place over each corner in turn. After all the corners, CS can calculate the position of each color swatch from the position of the corners and the resolution of the scanned image. When the calculation has finished, you can then save this file as a named scanner profile.

RGB Printer (Desktop Printer) Profile Generation

One of the most useful things you can do with color profiles is force an inexpensive color printer or color copier to output a remarkably good simulation of your final press output. Many Photoshop users are not aware that this is a possibility. Desktop printers, unless you approach them with the idea that you can force them into representing a particular gamut, usually provide output that is dramatically more vivid and saturated than press output. If you think about it, you need to make the printer perform in much the same way you've made your monitor perform: You have forced it to accurately represent press conditions. In most cases, that representation means that you have a dulled-down display rather than the brilliant display your monitor is really capable of producing. The process is virtually the same. If you wish to use a desktop printer to output intermediate proofs before you send your color work to final film, you must obtain color information about the printer and generate a named profile. (Note: Unless you're using a printer that RIPs CMYK information, you should consider your desktop printer as an RGB device.)

You can make the printer test pattern in two ways. Choose Make Pattern from the File menu. This will bring up a dialog box asking for the resolution and a few other parameters. The program will then save an image file that you can print from the program of your choice. You can also print directly from CS. Choose Page Setup (from the File menu) and make sure that your printer settings are correct. Then, choose File|Print Pattern. Your printer will then print out the target pattern page shown in Figure 10.24.

The printed target contains a sampling of 270 combinations of the printer's ink pigments. Each of them must be measured to have a large enough statistical sampling of the printer's gamut.

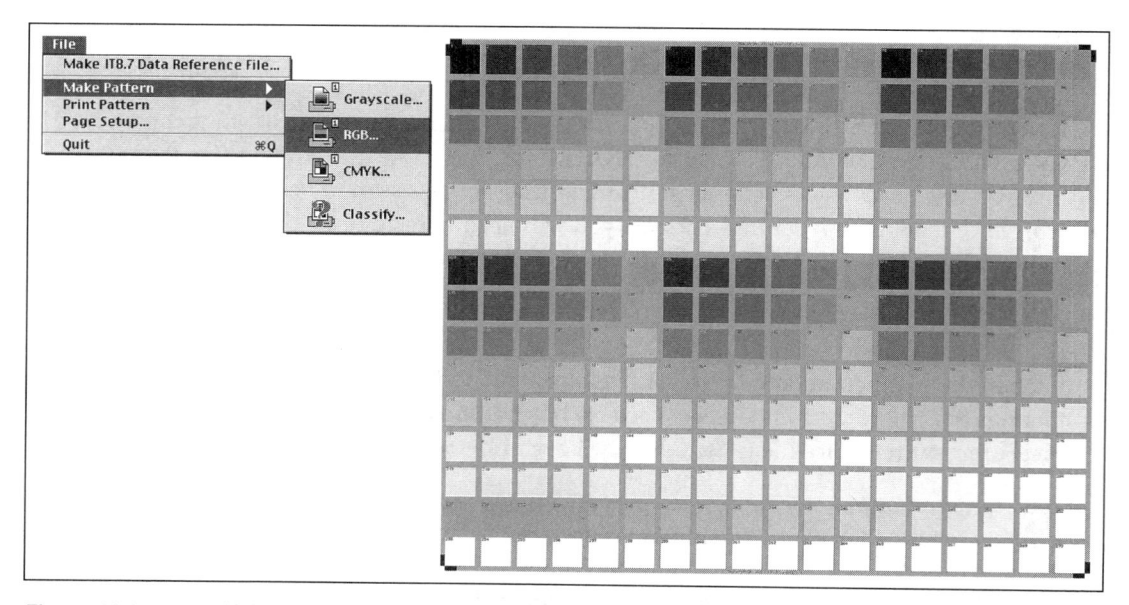

Figure 10.24 To calibrate your desktop printer, you must print out a test pattern image. You can print this directly from CS, or you can save the pattern as an image file to be imported into the program of your choice.

You can measure the pattern in two ways. You can scan the test target the way you did for the IT-8 target and then allow CS to generate the profile. Or you can measure each swatch on the pattern with your Colortron II. The latter will produce the most accurate results. Choose Profile|New|RGB Output. A dialog box with a representation of the pattern will appear (see Figure 10.25). You will then be guided through the measurement of all the swatches. As each swatch is measured, it becomes a filled square. When you have completed this task, you can save your color information as a named file. Note that the measurement of the color swatches is not something you can do in a hurry, nor is it an exciting task. To put it bluntly, the whole job is pretty boring. In fact, if your office has an intern, this is a perfect intern job. Seniority has its advantages, doesn't it?

CMYK Printer (MatchPrint Or Digital Proof) Profile Generation

The end stage of a prepress workflow would probably be to send digital files to a service bureau, where the documents would be imaged as plate-mask film negatives. From the film, you would probably then ask for a laminate proof such as an Imation MatchPrint III (on either Commercial or Publication stock), or a Dupont Waterproof contract proof. Proofs made directly from the film give you an idealized version of what your work will look like on press. Practically, the press doesn't always match such a proof, but it should be able to come very close. You might also deal with a service bureau or printer that can give you a digital proof. You might, for example, be given output from an Iris ink jet printer, a Kodak Approval system, a 3M Rainbow proof, or a printout from one of the superb new Epson Stylus 5000 printers. You would definitely use a digital proof if your workflow includes CTP (Computer To Plate) output. Without plate-mask film, your service bureau or printer cannot make a laminate proof. Whatever you use as a press proof, you would probably consider the press proof as the final output in terms of your own workflow.

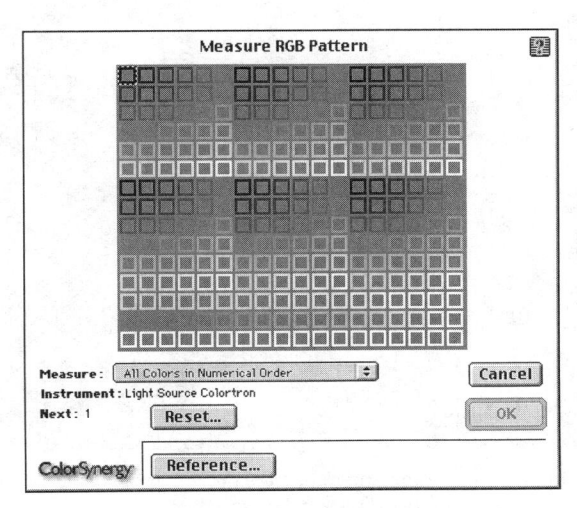

Figure 10.25 This dialog box guides you through the measurement of the swatches on the test pattern printout. After the 270 color samples are complete, CS will generate a profile for the printer.

Making a profile for your press proof is slightly more involved than the same operation for an in-house RGB printer. Unless your company possesses its own final proofing system, you will need to generate a file that your service bureau or printer can run to film—and from there to a film-based proof—or to a digital proof. You will then need to measure the resulting proof.

From the File menu, choose Make Pattern|CMYK. The resulting dialog box will ask you for file dimensions and resolution. Make the file so that it fits onto a letter-sized page and at a resolution that is double the line-screen you intend to use. Save the file in TIFF or Photoshop EPS format. A simulation of this file is shown in Figure 10.26.

You measure this test pattern (see Figure 10.27) the same way as for the RGB printer target. The difference between the two procedures is that this one contains more colors and takes longer. A lot longer. Oh, Intern…

After the colors have been measured, saving the file is the next step. Because this is a CMYK profile, you need to include some essential information if you intend to use this as a separation target within Photoshop 5. The dialog box in Figure 10.28 shows what kind of information is required. At the bottom of the dialog box, you set the total ink limit. You also set up how the black ink is to be generated and how much black ink there will be. With this information set, click on the Save button to generate the profile.

Figure 10.26 The Make CMYK Pattern command generates this file. It contains 504 swatches. In one place or another, it contains all of the swatches described back in Figure 10.12.

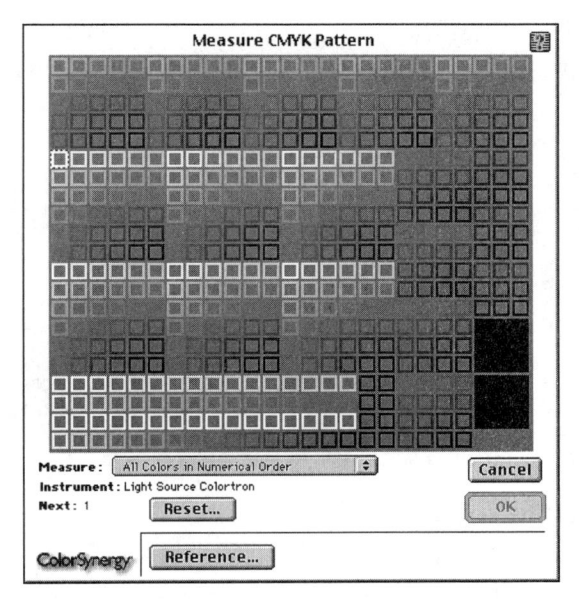

Figure 10.27 This dialog box guides you through the measurement of the swatches on the CMYK pattern printout.

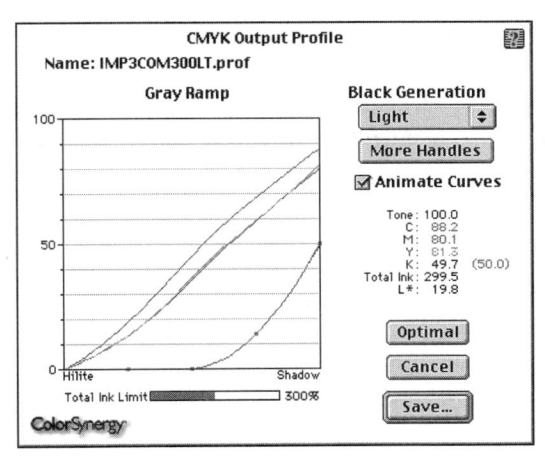

Figure 10.28 Before saving the CMYK profile, CS requires that you enter black generation information using this dialog box.

Take A Look At Your Device Gamuts

With your main profiles now generated, you can take a look at your device gamuts as three-dimensional entities. From the Profile menu, choose View Gamut. The window that appears is shown in Figure 10.29. At the upper right of the window are two large pop-up menus. Click and hold on the one closest to the top center. Choose RGB display. You will be prompted to choose a

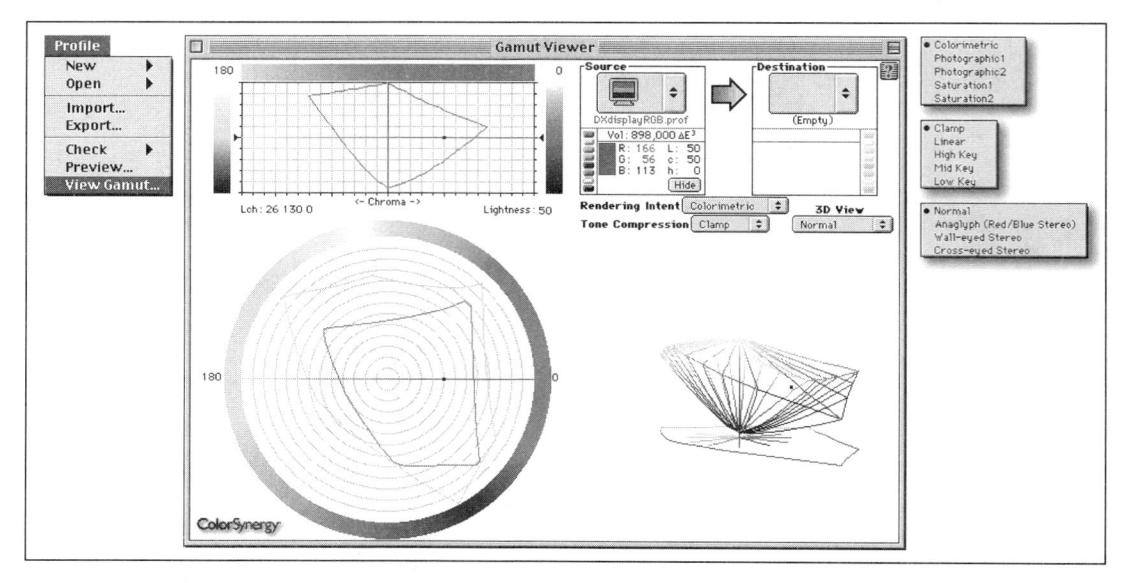

Figure 10.29 The View Gamut window in CS allows you to load a gamut profile and then displays it as a three-dimensional entity.

profile. CS will find the monitor profile you saved. When the profile has loaded, you will see two draftsmen's views of the gamut, two-dimensional slices with the planes at right angles to each other. You'll also see a colored, three-dimensional model of the gamut. Click and drag on the three-dimensional model to turn it in any direction. Four views of the turned model are shown in Figure 10.30.

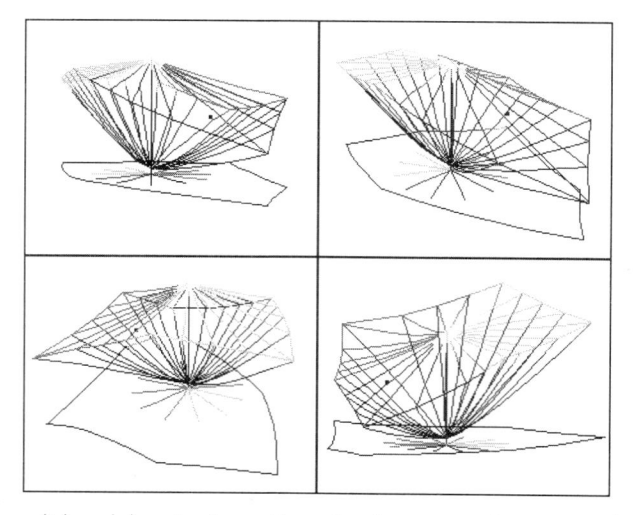

Figure 10.30 When you click and drag the three-dimensional representation—in any direction—you can see it from any angle. The four views here are the same gamut.

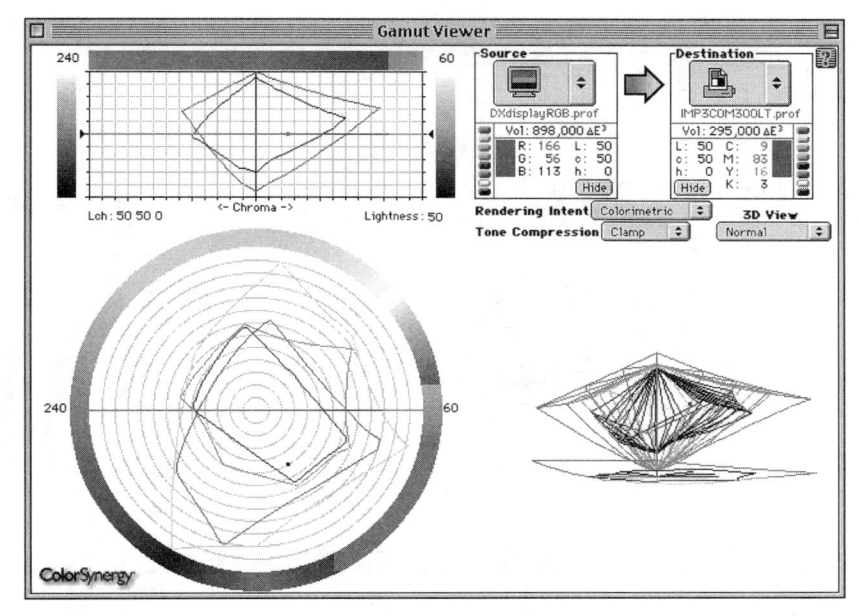

Figure 10.31 When two gamuts are loaded at the same time, CS overlays them to show you how the three-dimensional spaces relate to each other.

Click on the second pop-up menu to load a different gamut. The second gamut, shown in Figure 10.31, is a profile made by reading a CMYK output pattern. (When you're saving, you may want to name your files in a similar way to remind you of the parameters of the profile. This file is named MP3COM300LT.prof. The letters represent the words *Imation MatchPrint III, Commercial Stock, 300% Ink Limit, Light Black Generation*.) CS loads the new profile and superimposes it on the RGB monitor gamut. Notice how much smaller the CMYK gamut is than the monitor gamut. Notice also when looking at the planar views how the CMYK gamut is not entirely within the RGB gamut. This means that some of the CMYK colors cannot be displayed on your monitor. This display should help you to understand why the conversion from RGB to CMYK is so fraught with difficulties.

Another good way to compare gamuts is to see them applied to photographic images. Choose Profile|Preview. The window that opens (see Figure 10.32) allows you to open an image file (center button) and a pair of gamut profiles (top, pop-up menus). Notice that you can vary the appearance of the translated image by changing the pop-up menus between the images. The choices are Quality, Rendering Intent, and Tone Compression. After every change, you'll need to click on the Preview button to see the image on the right updated.

Exporting An ICC Profile

The final step is to use ColorSynergy to write ICC Profiles for use within Photoshop. Choose Profile|Export. The small window shown in Figure 10.33 appears.

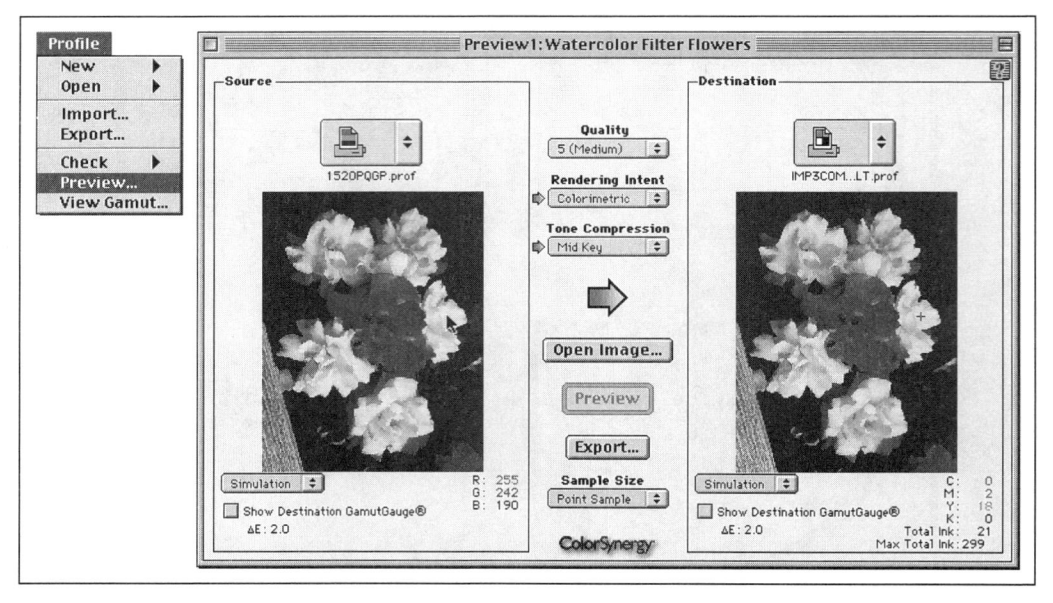

Figure 10.32 A good way to see the differences between two gamuts is to apply them to photographic images in the Profile Preview window.

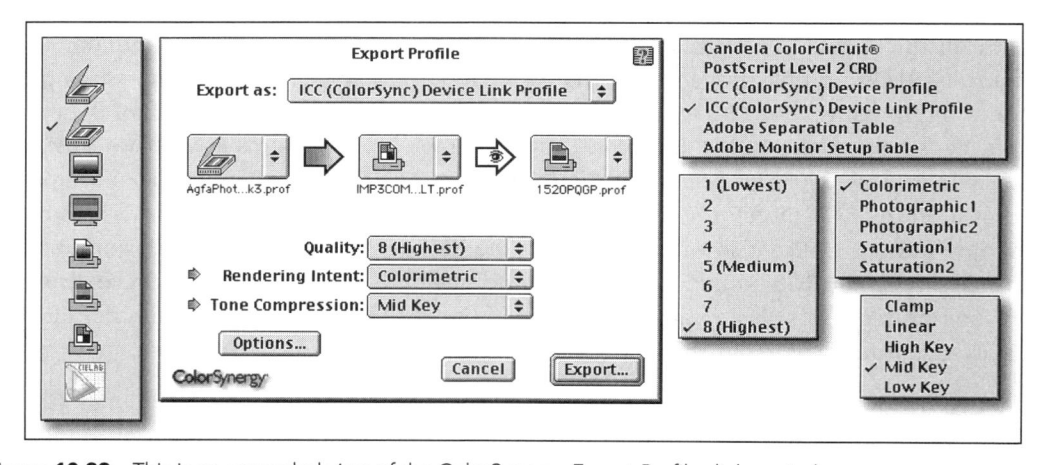

Figure 10.33 This is an expanded view of the ColorSynergy Export Profile dialog window.

You have a number of important choices to make in this window. Perhaps the most important is *what* you want to export because you have six choices.

- *Candela ColorCircuit*—A CCT is a color transformation file used by Candela software products. CCT files can be used to make transformations within Photoshop using the CandelaCCT plug-in (which is bundled with CS). You can use ColorCircuit files to change any of five file types (RGB, CMYK, Lab, YCC—Photo CD—and grayscale) to any of the other file types. (Note: Photoshop 5's Image|Mode|Profile To Profile command functions in much the same way as ColorCircuit. With this command, you can load profiles and perform color transformations, bypassing the normal mode change commands.)

- *PostScript Level 2 Color Rendering Dictionary*—A CRD is a file used by PostScript Level 2 RIPs to do color conversions as a file is rasterized. You can, if you wish, load two profiles when you generate a CRD, a source and destination. With both sets of gamut information, you will get the best possible transformation of colors.

- *ICC (ColorSync) Device Profile*—ICC Profiles are vendor-independent and platform-independent color information files used by ICC-aware programs to perform color transformations. ICC Device Profiles can also have a source and destination gamut to ensure very accurate color mapping.

- *ICC (ColorSync) Device Link Profiles*—Device Link Profiles contain information for color transformations across three devices. Typically, the device link would include an input device (probably a scanner), a final output device profile (in prepress work, a CMYK printer), and an intermediary device that can accurately simulate the final output device (perhaps a monitor profile or a desktop printer).

- *Adobe Separation Table*—Adobe Separation Tables are files used by the third major option within Photoshop's CMYK Setup dialog box. Color Separation tables determine how the CMYK transformation takes place, the appearance of CMYK images (and RGB or Lab images when CMYK Preview is turned on) and out-of-gamut information.

- *Adobe Monitor Setup Table*—In earlier versions of Photoshop, you could not directly use an ICC Profile when setting up your monitor preferences in Photoshop. With version 5, you can set up the monitor color space independent of any monitor calibration software. This eliminates the need for the monitor setup table.

The Export dialog box will offer different options depending on the choice you make. As you can see from Figure 10.33 (where a Device Link Profile is being set up), you can select from eight quality settings, five rendering intent settings, and five tone compression settings. We have set this figure so that we can illustrate one of the points made earlier, the use of a desktop printer to simulate the final CMYK output. Because this is such a practical way to approach preproofing, and because some of the inexpensive printers being sold give results that are breathtaking, you should try using the Device Link Profile with Photoshop. You will be astonished. The authors, performing tests on images where scans, digital proofs, MatchPrints, and press sheets are all available for comparison, have found that the tested printer—an Epson Stylus 1520—can deliver photo-quality glossy paper output that does not differ significantly from the other specimens. In view of how costly film and proofs that contain errors are, a preliminary proof with a cost of less than $.60 is an excellent value.

Final Thoughts On ColorSynergy

This section has covered some of the highlights of Candela Ltd.'s ColorSynergy. This software has many other powerful features that a brief examination of this sort cannot cover. The important thing for you to know is that this program, and others like it, will become increasingly important to prepress professionals as the use of ICC Profiles becomes more extensive in the printed reproduction of color. Although the concepts behind profile construction and color transformations are extremely sophisticated, the use of profiles can lead to precision handling of color and a considerable amount of automation. If you don't own a profile-mapping program, you should consider the investment.

ICC Profiles Within Photoshop

If you decide to use ICC as your CMYK method in Photoshop (refer to Figure 10.20), you must choose the profile to be used for the separation. As you saw in the export of the profile, all of the information needed to make the separation—black generation, ink limits, and so on—was included in the ICC file.

You can also choose from four rendering intents, and whether to use Photoshop's built-in separation engine or one of four other models. You should probably experiment with each to see if you prefer one to the others. Please note that the CMYK Setup dialog box has a Preview checkbox. If you turn on CMYK Preview (View menu) with this checkbox clicked, you will be able to see the results of each choice in the document. This is, to understate the case, a very handy option!

Tagging Your Image Files

From Photoshop's File menu, select Color Settings|Profile Setup. The dialog box in Figure 10.34 shows you how profile information is embedded in all new saved files and what your assumed target profiles will be.

The top two sections of this box deal mainly with files you will save from the present version of the program. You're given the opportunity to embed profiles in saved files of four color types, and you can determine what assumptions Photoshop makes about color as it opens a file. The three Assumed Profiles settings should be readily understandable after the discussion of ICC Profiles above. (Note that if you choose not to embed profiles in one of the color types, Photoshop

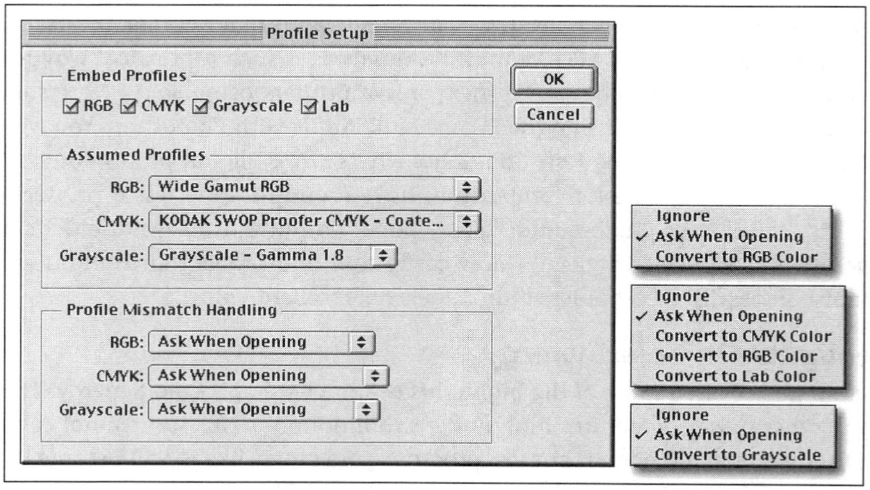

Figure 10.34 Photoshop 5's Profile Setup dialog box.

5 will mark the file as deliberately not tagged. This prevents it from being converted every time it's opened.)

You use the lower section of the dialog box to tell Photoshop what to do if it encounters a file with no embedded profile. The choices for each color type are shown at the right of the figure. Older RGB files can probably be opened with the pop-up set to Convert To RGB Color. Otherwise, Photoshop assumes that the file belongs in the monitor color space. CMYK files should probably be converted to CMYK. It's not a good idea to arbitrarily convert from one color space to another, and that is particularly true for CMYK images. Grayscale images probably should be converted to Grayscale on opening.

Tables

The last of your CMYK Setup options is Tables (see Figure 10.35). Tables have been used in previous versions of Photoshop. As you saw in our walk-through of ColorSynergy, a Photoshop Color Table is one of your export options. You can also, if you wish, make use of color tables from version 4 of Photoshop. Click on the Load button to choose the file you wish to use. (Note that this part of CMYK Setup also includes a Preview checkbox so that you can review the effect of the table on an open image.)

Preparing To Make A Color Separation

After paying so much attention to the details involved with monitor calibration and Separation Setup, let's stop for a moment to review some of the implications of this set of procedures.

After calibrating your monitor and choosing a working color space, you are now in a position to make decisions about the colors in your image with the reasonable certainty that you are seeing the file very close to the way it will print. Your monitor's display will never perfectly match your printed piece—the color paradigms are just too different—but it will be close. Just remember that your calibration of the monitor does not affect an image displayed in RGB or Lab mode. To look at the file as the prototype of the printed file, your file must be in CMYK mode or—if it's in RGB or Lab mode—you must choose CMYK Preview from under the View menu (press Command+Y or Crl+Y). With this option turned on, you can see the file as if it were already separated and still be able to do your correction/adjustment work in the color mode of your choice.

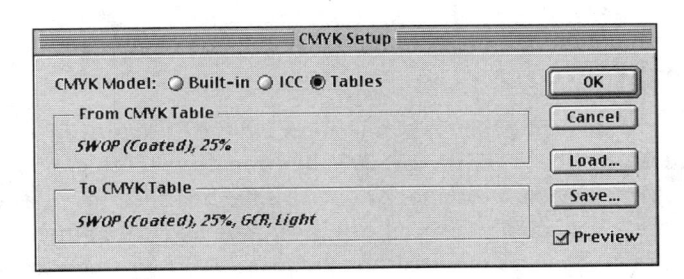

Figure 10.35 Tables is the third option within Photoshop 5's CMYK Setup dialog box.

The calibration and preferences you have set up control how the image is displayed and how it will be separated. If you change your Info palette so that it gives you readings in CMYK, you can move your cursor around inside an RGB or Lab file and be shown the CMYK values as though the separation had already taken place. As your cursor moves, notice that some pixels display an exclamation mark (!) next to the ink values on the Info palette. This is an indication that the value of the pixel is out of gamut and that the conversion to CMYK will change it.

This may be stating the obvious but because the display is governed—not only by the calibration settings but also by the ink and separation preferences—you should never try to correct color or to generate a color separation unless you have an ink profile and separation setup that is appropriate for the image. The process of changing the image from one color mode to CMYK is absolutely tied to the Color Settings in effect at the time the change is made. You cannot simply change the image back to RGB, load a new set of preferences, and then reseparate the file. Changing to CMYK mode is enormously destructive to the data in the original image. Each change of mode, while it may not be as destructive as the drastic change from RGB or Lab to CMYK, causes too much loss of information.

If you wish to try an experiment, make a small CMYK window and fill it with a color composed of 100% magenta and 100% yellow. Change to RGB and then back to CMYK mode. Look at your values. You probably have at least 1% cyan, 2% to 7% less ink in magenta and yellow, and at least 2% black. The bright built red no longer looks so bright.

Processing An RGB File Intended For Color Separation

When a commercial separation house scans photographic material, the electronic files are delivered ready to print. The correct adjustment of the image, the balancing of tones, and the conversion to CMYK mode have been taken care of. This preparation is part of the cost of a commercial separation.

Files from an in-house scanner may not be separated. The scanning software may not have the ability to do the separations for you, and it may have only limited capacity for adjusting the image. These files must be adjusted, separated, and saved in Photoshop. The process outlined here is a generic adjustment procedure. It doesn't take into account files that are imperfect due to deficiencies of the original photo material. It is simply an easy way to arrive at a good separation from a reasonably good scan. This process will lighten the image, improve its contrast, clean up the color, and get it into shape for CMYK conversion. For difficult scans, we recommend that, in addition to the information you'll read about here, you should check out the processes described in Chapter 11.

The file shown in the following figures can be found in the Chapter 10 Practice Files folder on this book's CD-ROM. Its title is FISHING.PSD. When you open this file, notice that it is in RGB mode. Turn on CMYK Preview as you look at it. This file has been saved with the Adjustment layers shown in the following figures. You can hide these layers and then make them visible, one at a time, to see the effects of each correction step. All four stages of this preseparation adjustment are shown printed in the color section of this book. We recommend that you look at the color reproductions and the digital file as you read through this section. For the correction sequence, follow these steps:

1. Open your file. From the View menu, choose CMYK Preview (see Figure 10.36). Follow the procedure outlined in Chapter 9 for preparing a grayscale file using Threshold mode. Your final step is to adjust the midtone slider of the composite histogram of the Levels controls.

2. Instead of clicking on OK, click on the Save button. Save this settings file under a temporary name. Click on the Cancel button to close the Levels dialog box. Command+click or Ctrl+click on the New Layer icon at the bottom of the Layers palette. From the choices available, select Levels. When the Levels dialog box appears, click on the Load button and locate the settings file you just saved. After the settings have loaded, click on OK (see Figure 10.37).

Figure 10.36 Open the file. Select CMYK Preview from under the View menu.

Figure 10.37 Create a Levels Adjustment layer. Load your saved Levels settings into this Layer. Click on OK.

The Levels correction, as usual, improves the contrast of the image. The pronounced blue/cyan tone to the image is improved, but not really addressed. Levels can be used to perform some of the color adjustment work, but in this example, color-shift tasks are applied using two other correction methods. The amount of correction applied with the Levels Adjustment layer is shown in Figure 10.38.

3. Make a new Adjustment layer. This time choose Color Balance. When you complete your adjustments, click on OK (see Figure 10.39).

4. With the Color Balance choices, the cyan cast of the midtones is the major color change. Boosting the yellow and magenta in the midtones and shadows warms the image and further de-emphasizes the original cyan cast. The settings used for this layer are shown in Figure 10.40.

5. Make a new Adjustment layer. For this layer, choose Hue/Saturation. When you have completed your adjustments, click on OK (see Figure 10.41).

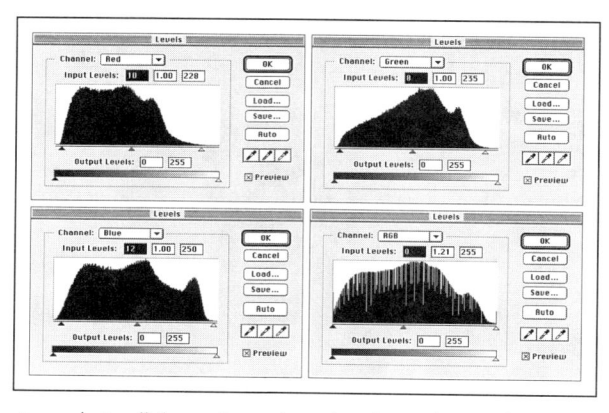

Figure 10.38 Adjustments made to all three channels and to the midtone of the composite histogram.

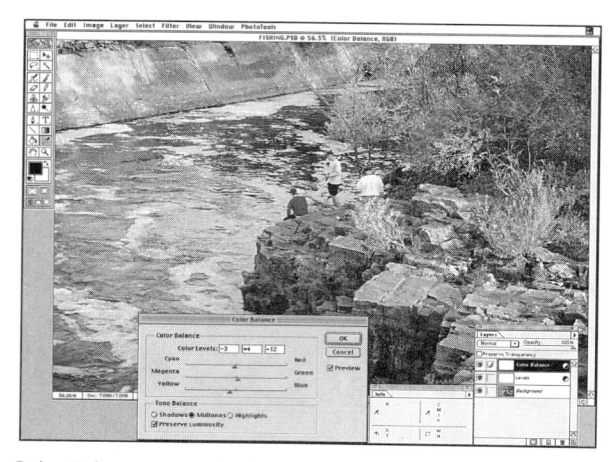

Figure 10.39 Create a Color Balance correction layer.

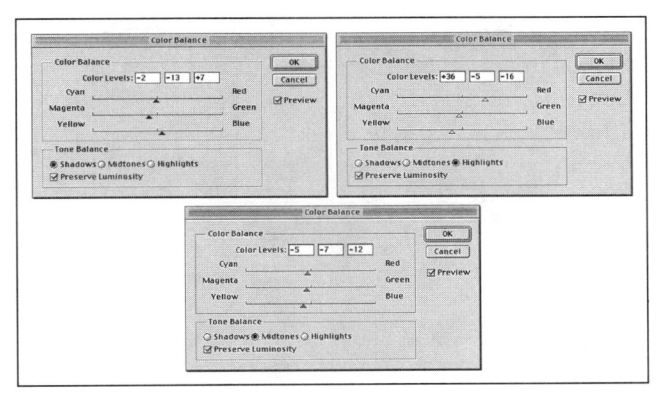

Figure 10.40 Changes made to the Shadows, Midtones, and Highlights in the Color Balance Adjustment layer.

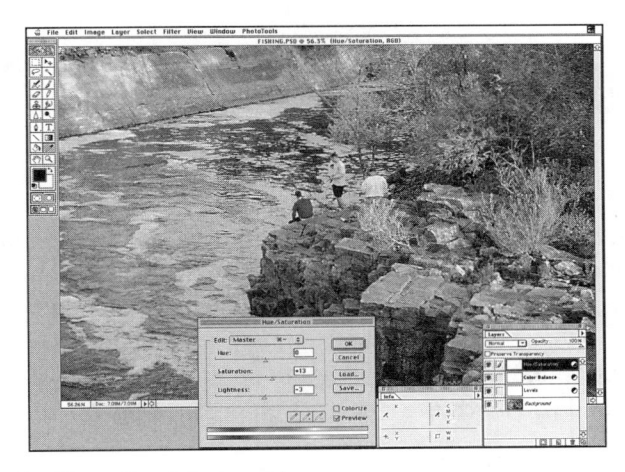

Figure 10.41 Create a Hue/Saturation Adjustment layer.

Hue/Saturation allows some arbitrary tweaking of tones that you may wish to enrich or make more vivid (or to mute and desaturate). In this case, boosting the overall saturation and slightly darkening the image produces better contrast overall. By doing so, and by tweaking four of the primary tones in various ways, the red, gold, and green tones become more vibrant. Subtle colorations in the water also become more obvious. The Hue/Saturation settings used for this layer are shown in Figure 10.42.

Color Correction Methods

Color can be adjusted within Photoshop several ways. The primary adjustment tools are the Levels and the Curves controls. Use whichever of these seem to give you the best results. In some cases, you might even wish to use them both as the input tools for successive Adjustment layers. There is no reason why you shouldn't do so, and every reason for you to experiment to get the very best color you can achieve.

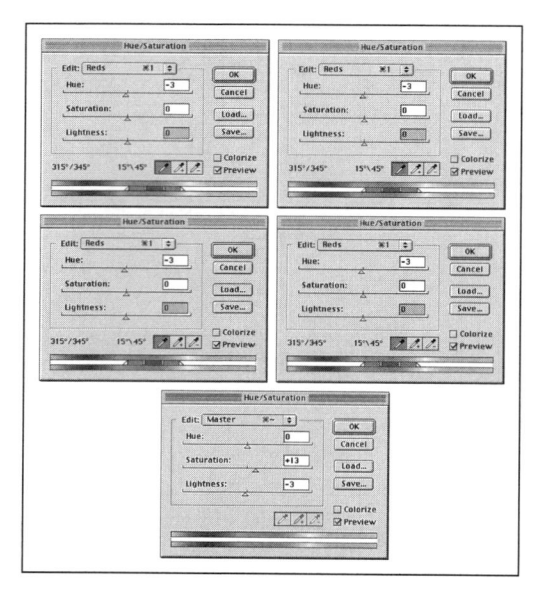

Figure 10.42 Changes made to the Red, Green, Cyan, Blue, and Master values in the Hue/Saturation Adjustment layer.

The other color correction controls are, again, a matter of taste. Some of them are more powerful than others, but none should ever be discounted. Every tool in Photoshop is useful at some time—even the Paint Bucket tool. If, in your study of Photoshop and its methods, you read a disparaging reference to any tool or method, remember that you are reading an opinion and that you need not be bound by or agree with that opinion. Do your work in Photoshop in the way that suits *you*, and you'll achieve a good result nearly every time!

The formal color correction tools are located in the Image|Adjust submenu (see Figure 10.43). The Adjust menu contains several other commands—Desaturate, Invert, Equalize, Threshold, and Posterize—that deliver specialized, single-purpose effects. Two of these specialized commands are sometimes useful in correction work.

The Equalize command is useful for quickly redistributing brightness values. When this command is chosen, Photoshop takes the darkest value and makes it black, and the lightest value and makes it white. All of the other brightness values are then calculated to fall between these two in order to have a representation of the entire brightness range. The effect is somewhat akin to Auto Levels, but far more drastic in its effect. If you want, use this command on the FISHING.PSD image after it has been flattened. You will find that the image contrast is changed in a drastic—but not unattractive—way. The results of the Equalize command can sometimes be too extreme to be useful. If you find this to be true, try mitigating the result by using the Fade command, the second item under the Filter menu. After you have applied a command such as Equalize, select Fade. With the dialog box open and the Preview option checked, you can move the Opacity slider to change the degree to which the command affects the image. Fade also

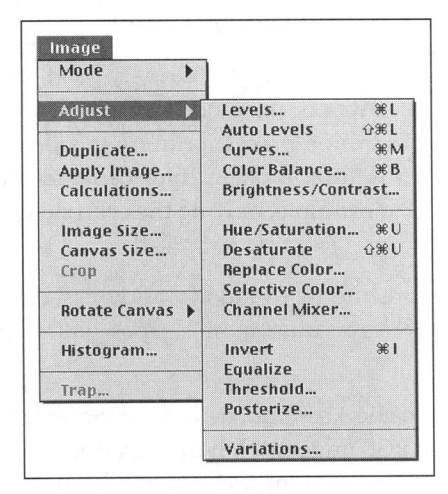

Figure 10.43 Most of Photoshop's correction/adjustment tools are found under the Image|Adjust submenu.

gives you the ability to apply Blend modes on top of commands such as Equalize, where Blend modes are not usually associated. Fade will work with many image adjustment commands including such unlikely commands as Image|Adjust|Invert. (Want to try something interesting? Invert the image and then change the fade opacity to 50%. Bizarre!)

The other sometimes-handy command is Desaturate. When this command executes, the image is effectively changed to grayscale, even though it remains in color mode. Running the command with the Fade command is a way of moderating how much desaturation will result.

> **TIP**
>
> Out-of-gamut colors are typically too saturated. Desaturating often brings them back into gamut—you can even make a very quick, targeted mask aimed at just the out-of-gamut tones. From the Select menu, choose Color Range. In the Color Range menu, make the selection Out Of Gamut. Click on OK. Apply the Desaturate command to the selection and then use the Filter|Fade command. Change the Opacity settings until you achieve the amount of change you desire. If you choose the Gamut Warning command (from the View menu), you'll be able to see how much saturation you are losing by how many of the warning-colored pixels become visible again.
>
> Here's another interesting method that can give you good results. It is the discovery of Charles Facini, President of Spot Process (see Chapter 9). After you've made your selection of the out-of-gamut colors, open the Curves controls. Make sure that you are working with ink settings and not RGB. Drag the black end of the curve down to 95%. Now drag the white end of the curve up to 5%. The decrease of contrast in the selected pixels has the effect of decreasing the saturation.

Color Balance

The Color Balance dialog box (see Figure 10.44) is a very good place to learn to think in RGB as well as in CMYK. There are three sliders; the process ink colors are at the left and the RGB colors to the right. Each slider ranges from a process primary to video primary. The arrangement is such that moving a slider away from a given color *decreases* the amount of that color and *increases* that color's inverse. For example, moving the cyan slider to the left removes cyan from the image and adds red.

Three different value ranges are affected: Shadows, Midtones, and Highlights. When the dialog box opens, it defaults to Midtones because, in most cases, your major adjustments will be in the midtone range.

The dialog box also contains a checkbox that defaults to Preserve Luminosity. This option maintains the brightness values in RGB images. With this box unchecked, the brightness of the pixels in the image changes as the color is changed. This can mean that the tonal balance of the image shifts in an undesirable way. It is usually instructive, when you have completed your adjustments in all three tonal ranges, to click on the checkbox so that the option is off, in order to see how your adjustments are affected. Click it again to turn it back on before clicking on the OK button.

When you use Color Balance in Lab mode, the dialog box has a different appearance (see Figure 10.45). The box has only two sliders. These allow you to adjust the two color axes of this mode. You don't have a slider for the L channel: This is equivalent to having a Preserve Luminosity checkbox.

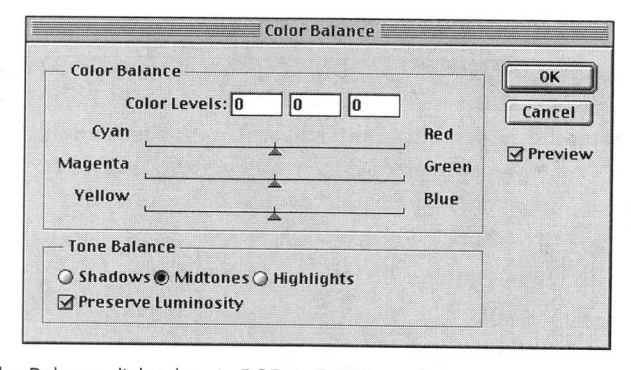

Figure 10.44 The Color Balance dialog box in RGB or CMYK mode.

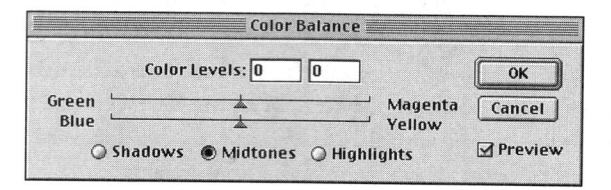

Figure 10.45 The Lab Color Balance dialog box.

Brightness/Contrast

The Brightness/Contrast controls (see Figure 10.46) are not for the faint of heart. Although this tool is useful once in a while, it's really a blunt instrument when compared to most of the other controls. Moving the two sliders makes shifts in—what else?—Brightness and Contrast. The adjustment affects the entire tone range of the image with no way to limit the adjustment to any segment of the range. Other commands can accomplish with more subtlety whatever can be accomplished with Brightness/Contrast, but it's sometimes handy for a quick tweak.

Hue/Saturation

The Hue/Saturation controls (see Figure 10.47) are among Photoshop's most powerful features. With this set of controls, you can adjust the hue, saturation, and lightness of individual color components in an image or the entire color composition of an image.

To better understand how these controls work, look closely at Figure 10.48. The figure pictures a cylindrical shape which, you are invited to imagine, consists of a set of thin disks stacked on top of each other. Each circular shape consists of a radial sweeping blend through all six of the primary RGB and CMY colors. The purest color tones are out on the edges of the circle. These shade into neutral toward the center. Each disk is similar to every other disk except that disks lower in the stack are darker than upper disks.

Imagine a color value at some place on the disk uppermost in the figure. Changes to the three sliders affect that color by moving it in three dimensions.

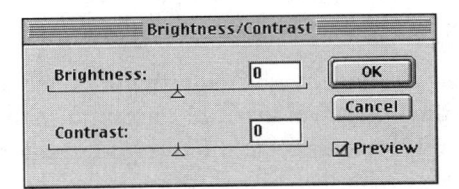

Figure 10.46 The Brightness/Contrast controls.

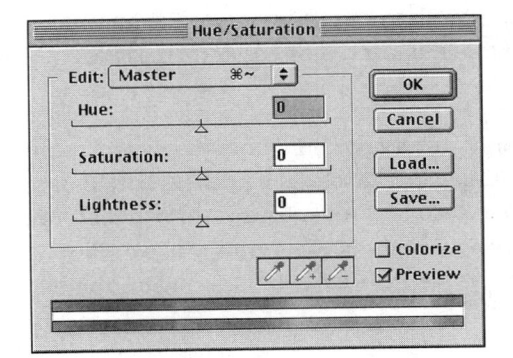

Figure 10.47 The Hue/Saturation controls.

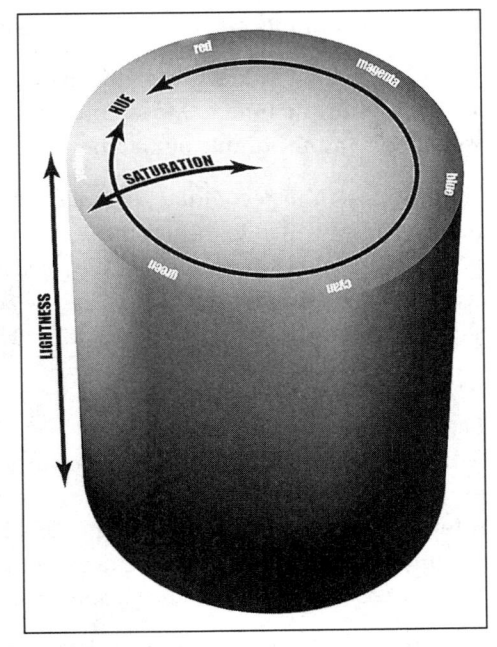

Figure 10.48 This cylinder shape is a model for the HSL (Hue, Saturation, Lightness) color space.

When you move the Hue slider, you are keeping the position of the color relative to the outer edge of the circle, but moving it around clockwise (slider to the right) or counterclockwise (slider to the left). Because the opening position of the slider represents the color's initial position on the colored circle, you can never shift the color farther than 180° in either direction from where it began. Push the slider all the way to the left or all the way to the right, and you'll have moved it to the same place, diametrically opposite its initial position.

By moving the Saturation slider, you move the color along a radius either toward the center of the circle (desaturate) or toward the edge (saturate). Increased saturation results in more brilliant colors, while decreased saturation mutes the colors and makes them more gray.

With the Lightness slider, you keep the color's position on the circle, but shift it up (lighter) or down (darker) to a different circle.

If this is your first exposure to the concept that color spaces are visualized in three dimensions and require three coordinates in order to describe them, then you should study this figure until you become comfortable with it. The more comfortable you become with the way the Hue/Saturation command operates on the color in your image, the more adept you'll be at getting the results you desire.

The Master button on the dialog box gives you control of all the tones in the image simultaneously. You can, if you wish, select one of the six colors below the Master button to effect a change on that color range without a lot of change to the other colors. Each single-color adjustment changes the Hue slider so that the image's pixels in that tone can be shifted, one way or the other, toward its neighbors on the color wheel.

The sample area below gives you the opportunity to observe your adjustment's effect on a single tone in the image. Move your cursor into the image window and click on a color you wish to see in the Sample box. Otherwise, the sample remains set to the Foreground color.

Hue/Saturation also contains a Colorize checkbox that can be used on grayscale images that have been converted to a color mode. For very fast colorizing, try this option the next time you need to do a colorization. Don't be alarmed when your grayscale work changes to a fairly intense red-colored version of itself. Just move the Saturation slider (which shoots to the far right of the slider) back toward the middle until the color of the image is a little easier on the eyes.

Replace Color

Replace Color (see Figure 10.49) feels like a hybrid—a very powerful one—because it combines features of two of Photoshop's most powerful editing tools. Its selection preview, Fuzziness slider, and Eyedropper tools are similar to those of Select Color Range. Its transform sliders are the same as for the Hue/Saturation controls. When you use this set of controls, you can click within the image window to select a target color or colors. Then, by moving the sliders, the selected colors are transformed into new color values.

You use the default Eyedropper tool to select a color from the image thumbnail preview or directly. It's usually easier to make the image window as large as possible and to set the option below the dialog box thumbnail to Selection. Without this kind of feedback, it's difficult to tell what colors are being affected.

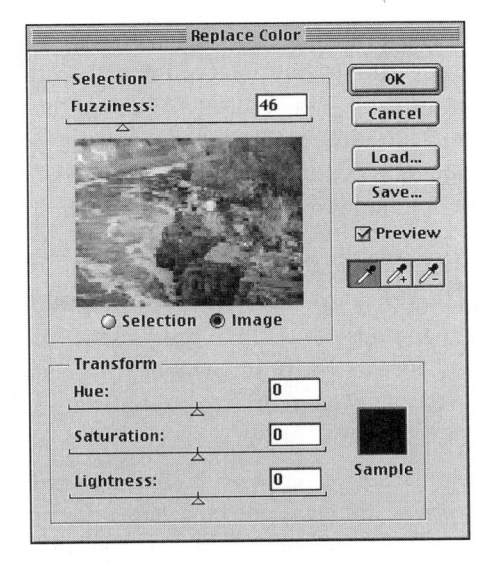

Figure 10.49 The Replace Color controls.

After you have manipulated a color with the sliders, try to find an area of that color that is mostly solid. Zoom into that area to see if the edges of the color are fringed with pixels of the previous color. If they are, move the fuzziness slider to the right to increase the scope, or tolerance, of the original selection. The color change will follow the change in the selection boundary.

If you want to experiment with this set of controls, try changing the bright red sweatshirt worn by the fisherman in the center of the sample file to some other color. Try a blue tone, or brown, or green. You'll be pleasantly surprised at how easy it is!

Selective Color

Selective Color (see Figure 10.50) is an extremely sophisticated tool that allows you to adjust color editorially—you can make arbitrary changes to an image that reflect what you *wish* to see in the image, as opposed to what the camera captured—as well as to correct color problems.

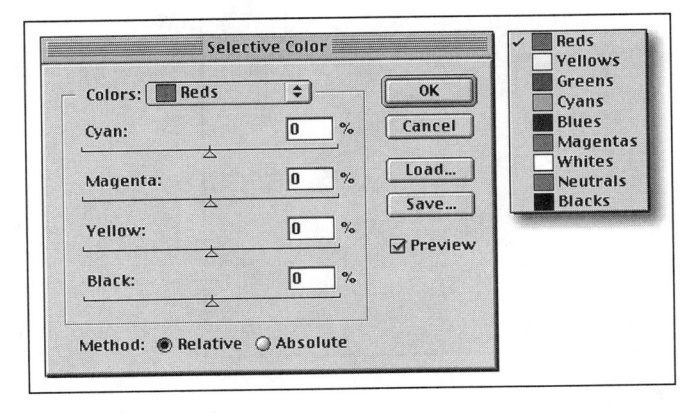

Figure 10.50 The Selective Color controls.

Using tabular data, which defines the process-color values that make up the print versions of each of the six primary colors, the proportions of ink within that primary group can be elevated or lowered without disturbing the balance of colors that contain one or more of the same process inks. You can, for example, boost the amount of magenta in a red garment without disturbing the magenta component in a bright blue sky, or you can lower the amount of magenta in an expanse of foliage without disturbing the magenta tones in a human face.

You can use two methods to apply the percentages:

- The Relative calculation takes the desired percentage and multiplies it by the percentage of ink color in the image. It then adds the result to the present value. If the Relative method is used, and you desire to add 10% to a 45% yellow tone, the calculation is 10% × 45% = 4.5%. This result, 4.5%, is added to the original tone to give a manipulated value of 49.5% (4.5% + 45% = 49.5%).

- The Absolute calculation takes the percentage you request at face value and adds it to the original tone. Using the same instance as above, a 10% addition to 45% yellow would result in 55% yellow. Of the two methods of calculation, the Absolute method offers the least flexibility. It is, however, the only method that you can use if you're adjusting whites. With the Relative method, adjusting white would have no effect because there are no beginning values on which to perform the computation.

Channel Mixer

The Channel Mixer (see Figure 10.51) is new to Photoshop 5. You can use it to modify color channels using a mixture of the other channels.

To use this command, select Image|Adjust|Channel Mixer. Select your Output Channel (your *target* channel) from the pop-up menu at the top of the dialog box. Now, go ahead and move the source channel sliders to get a feel for what will happen. As you move the slider to the right (positive), you increase the source channel's contribution to the output channel. Dragging the

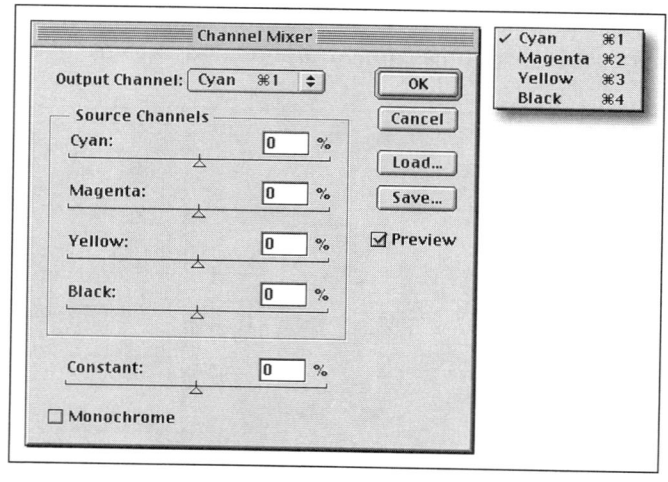

Figure 10.51 One of Photoshop's most interesting new toys is the Channel Mixer.

slider to the left (negative) decreases the mix. When you move the slider so the value is a negative number, the source channel inverts, and the inverted values are added to the output channel. As you use this command, you needn't limit yourself to a single output channel. You can, if you wish, choose all of the channels in turn as output channels and use those remaining as sources.

The Channel Mixer gives you some interesting possibilities. With it you can force the image into a new color configuration that would be difficult to achieve in any other way. You can swap the values in pairs of channels. By choosing the Monochrome option, you can add values from all of your channels to create an unusually good-looking grayscale image. Give this command a try. It's fascinating to play with, and you'll sometimes come up with some stunning effects.

Variations

One of the authors has heard the Variations color adjustment method referred to as Bozo color. Despite the close-mindedness of the description, Variations (see Figure 10.52) is a pleasant way for newcomers to see the results of their adjustments. It's also a more graphic interface for an adjustment algorithm that is almost identical to Color Balance. Bozo or not, this is a valuable tool. It may not offer the precision of the Color Balance dialog box, but it can accomplish the same purpose.

As you can see from Figure 10.52, you have the choice (upper-right side) of adjusting the Highlights, Midtones, or Shadows. There is also an adjustment for Saturation and a slider that—roughly—determines how much impact each adjustment click has. You'll also see a choice that allows the display of clipped values. This makes your display show you out-of-gamut values. You needn't be concerned with this option because you are working on the image with CMYK Preview turned on. All out-of-gamut values are automatically clipped in this display mode.

The main part of this dialog box is the large area in the lower left. The center image is the target that will be acted on. Assembled around this target are six *More* thumbnails, *More Yellow*,

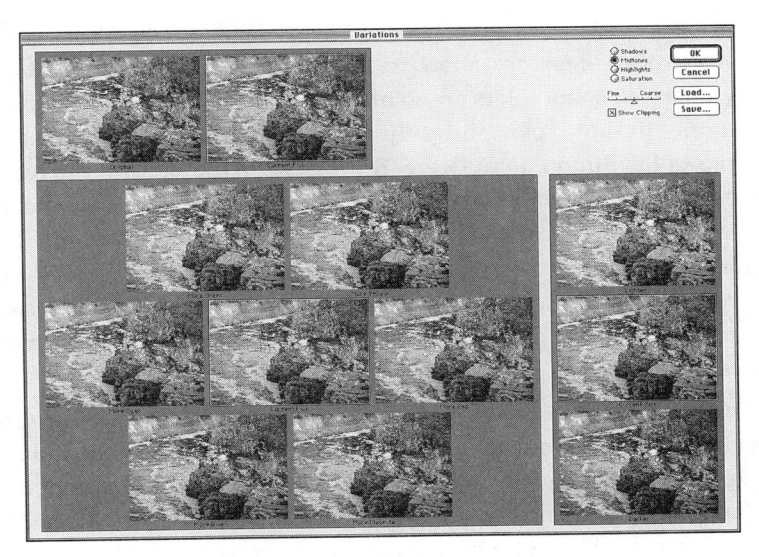

Figure 10.52 Color corrections made with Photoshop's Variations.

and its opposite, *More Blue*, and so on. As you click on one of the action thumbnails, the target is instantly updated with more of the color on which you clicked.

At the top of the dialog box you'll see two thumbnails. The leftmost thumbnail is the image the way it was when the adjustment began. Next to it is a thumbnail that shows the present status of the adjustment. If, at any time, you want to reset the target window to opening conditions, simply click on the leftmost thumbnail. You can then begin your adjustment with a fresh start.

At the right are three thumbnails. The center one is a status thumbnail that shows the present state of the adjustment. Above and below are thumbnails which, when clicked, either lighten or darken the three present status thumbnails.

Note that in the main adjustment area, you can see three axes running through the target thumbnail. At the ends of these axes are the same pair of opposites used for Color Balance.

Variations, as will be obvious, works best on a large monitor. It functions on a smaller monitor, but it can be difficult to see how the colors are being modified.

What To Look For When Adjusting Color

The simple truth about color adjustment is that if you've taken care of issues such as calibration and preferences, your own eyes are your best guide. Everyone begins with untrained eyes but, with practice, they learn to make accurate evaluations. Your perceptions of color combined with your ongoing accumulation of prepress experiences, and your common sense, will work together to give you good, consistent color. Trust yourself and, until you get the hang of it, follow Newton. Sir Isaac's famous *bon mot* is good for all of us: "*Nocte dieque incubando*" (I think about [things] night and day.)

Beyond the philosophy, there are some things in every image that you need to perfect whenever the opportunity presents itself. In no order of importance, here is a list that may help you:

- *Watch for memory colors*—Memory colors are roughly analogous to a musician with perfect pitch identifying tones; some colors are so much a part of our consciousness that we can identify imbalance in those colors instantly. For anyone with an association with the agricultural regions of the nation, John Deere (tractors, lawn mowers, and so on) green is a color that we can remember as being a distinctive yellow-toned green. A tractor with blue-tinted green paint will be unconsciously identified by any viewer as wrong. Coca-Cola red is another example. Of course, these memory colors don't always reproduce as perfectly as a corporate brochure would have them photographed. However, we are all used to the way light shifts, and we mentally compensate. If the color has shifted in a direction that is improbable, we recognize it.
- *Be careful of neutral tones*—Concrete sidewalk or cinder block structures are examples of neutrals that must look neutral in normal lighting conditions. Besides the fact that a neutral with, say, a pink cast might appear wrong to us, it furnishes us with a good indicator that there is a magenta imbalance in the midtones. Lowering the magenta percentage in the midtones not only corrects the cement color, but it also has other advantages. Think about the grass bordering a

sidewalk. If the sidewalk contains too much magenta, so does the grass. Too much magenta in the green of foliage and grass causes them to print with a brown cast. By fixing the sidewalk, you also fix the grass. You also make the image easier to balance on press.

- *Take extraordinary care with skin tones in the human face*—In all but the most unusual images, if the photograph contains a human face, that is the first place to which the eye is drawn. A significant part of our brains is devoted to recognizing or categorizing the faces of our fellow humans. We are very alert to colorations in faces, because untoward colors—sallowness, blue tones, heightened red tones—often indicate physical problems. We encounter these colors and they make us uneasy. You, as a Photoshop technician, must always strive to make the images you process sell. If your end user becomes uncomfortable looking at an image without knowing why—most viewers are not really conscious of such things—then, not only will your image not sell, but it will prove to be an anti-sell image.

  Look through any magazine or catalog. You'll find that the reproductions of human faces are the most faulty parts of the visual presentation. In fact, the offset reproduction of human skin tones is the most consistently flawed aspect of the color printing industry. Faces appear too red because the magenta component of the skin tones has a comparatively strong impact on press. This is true of all skin colors—African-American, Caucasian, Native-American, Asian, and so on—because skin is translucent and much of its color comes from the blood running through near-surface capillaries.

- *Don't go overboard with saturated colors*—There is always a strong tendency with visual people to want the colors to pop off the page. Colors needn't be rich and romantic for an image to make an impact. Vivid colors can sometimes be difficult to print. Adjust the image with the press as your goal and try not to think too far beyond that. If the image you've adjusted prints convincingly and with pleasing color, you've done your job correctly.

STRATEGIES FOR REALISTIC SKIN TONES

To avoid badly printed skin tones, try some of these adjustment strategies:

- For Caucasian skin tones, diminish the amount of magenta and increase the amount of yellow. You'll have to experiment with how much. Watch for the skin tone to change from pink to a ruddy color that is just short of a light suntan. If you go too far, you'll get a tanned look that may not be appropriate. Just watch for the ruddy tones and stop your adjustments there. You'll be rewarded, on press, with completely natural skin coloration.

- For African-American skin tones, be aware that magenta is still the dominant tone, but that cyan is much more important. Diminish the amount of cyan first, and then increase the amount of yellow. By adjusting these two colors, you leave the dominant color to counteract any tendency on press for African-American skin tones to print with a greenish cast.

- For Asian skin tones, magenta is still dominant, but yellow is the secondary color. Diminish the amount of magenta until you see a faint green cast begin to become visible. (There is cyan present: Backing off on the magenta will begin to accentuate the yellow-cyan combination.) Next, diminish the yellow until you arrive at a tone that is more in the suntan range. Pull the magenta up just a little to make the color more natural, and you're finished.

Separating The Image

If you've made your color adjustments while your image is in Lab mode, and if your output device uses Level 2 or Level 3 PostScript, you don't have to convert your file to CMYK mode. Save it in Photoshop EPS or TIFF format. The PostScript RIP does the separation for you. The advantage to this is that your file is 75 percent the size it would be if you were to convert to CMYK. The disadvantage is that your file takes longer to image because the conversion is added to the RIP time. Check with your service bureau to be sure that it can process Lab-mode files.

Some software also allows the placement of RGB files. The separation for these also occurs at the RIP level. It's sometimes tempting to leave the file in its adjusted, but nonseparated, state. Be wary of this. When a RIP separates a file, it's doing so using criteria over which you have no control. Its evaluation of the file *may* be appropriate for your job, but it may not be. Use this strategy with care, and be sure your service bureau knows what you have done. RGB files placed in QuarkXPress, for example, don't automatically separate without the intervention of other software. If your service bureau is unaware of the fact that you have placed RGB files in your document, you will end up with empty spaces on your cyan, magenta, and yellow films, and a too-dark halftone on your black film.

Separations are simply a matter of choosing Image|Mode|CMYK Color. If you've been working in CMYK Preview (and you should, without fail!), and the file looks good to you, there will be no visible change to the display after the conversion has taken place. The only step left to take is to size the image to its final dimension and sharpen it with the Unsharp Mask filter.

That's it. You've made a color separation. If you've followed all the steps and have been careful with your calibration and preferences, you should have no trouble on press. Try to remember that the whole procedure is logical and that good color is not an accident. You can achieve it by planning, thinking about all possible problems, and not skipping any of the steps.

Saving/Exporting Your Color Separations

When you're saving a four-color file from Photoshop that is intended to be output by a professional-level PostScript device, your choices are limited to the file types shown in Figure 10.53. Actually, for output purposes, the two Photoshop formats and the Raw format can be eliminated from consideration. The important, and most frequently used formats are TIFF, Photoshop EPS, DCS 1, DCS 2, and Scitex CT.

Scitex CT Format

Scitex Continuous Tone files are saved in this proprietary format for use on high-end image-processing equipment made by the Scitex Corporation. End users of Scitex equipment can obtain software that allows the transfer of files saved in Photoshop to turnkey systems. This software option is not needed in many cases because a variety of Scitex RIPs are available for both Windows and Macintosh platforms. These RIPs can operate directly on PostScript files generated from QuarkXPress or Adobe PageMaker, and placed image files need not be in Scitex format. Both page make-up programs allow you to directly place an image saved in Scitex CT format.

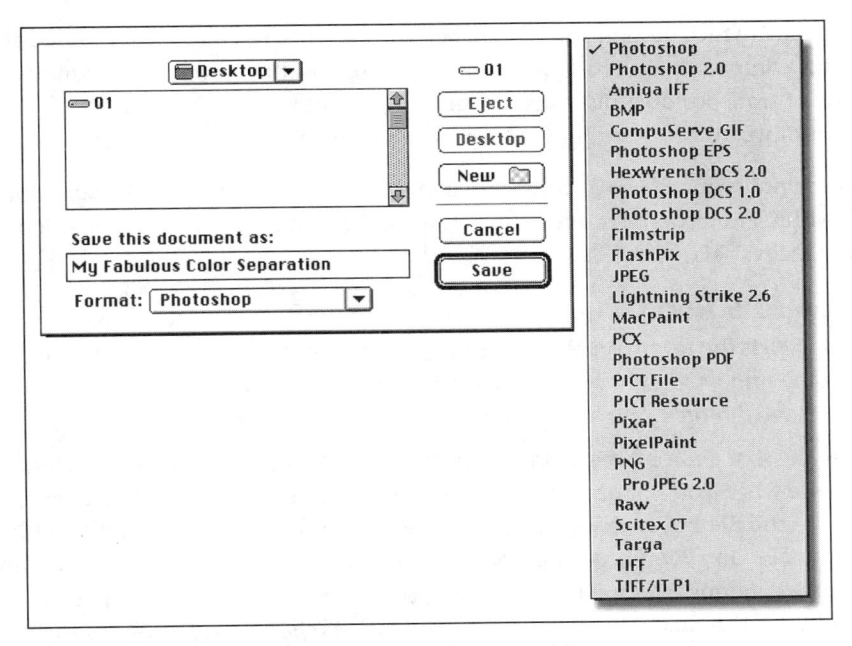

Figure 10.53 Photoshop's Save dialog box with the list of supported file types.

When used on proprietary imaging systems, Photoshop files need not be converted from RGB to CMYK. Grayscale files can also be saved in this format. This file format has no intermediate dialog boxes for entering parameters.

TIFF Format

The TIFF format is one of the most venerable in the world of microcomputers. Despite its age and widespread acceptance, TIFF is one of the most flexible formats available. TIFF files can be read by nearly every application that uses raster files. It supports images in all of Photoshop's modes except Duotone and Multichannel.

When you're saving a file in TIFF format, you are given a choice of byte order, which makes the file readable by either Macintosh or IBM PC (see Figure 10.54). With Photoshop, you can open a TIFF file regardless of the byte order. You can also import files of either byte order into Adobe PageMaker or QuarkXPress on either platform.

The LZW compression option gives you the opportunity to compress the file without loss of image data. Compressed files can be imported into other software packages and can be down-

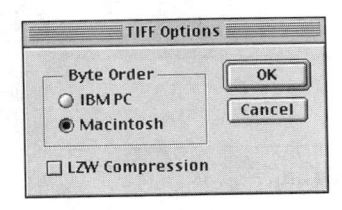

Figure 10.54 The TIFF file format options dialog box.

loaded to a RIP (which decompresses them before ripping). Until recent developments in ejectable media, this compression method was often necessary. But now that large hard disks and various kinds of transportable disks are so inexpensive and widely available, the LZW option is probably not worth the extra time it takes to save and open files.

The TIFF format is one of two formats that can embed a clipping path. The path option must be set from within Photoshop. The masking option, at this writing, is supported by Adobe PageMaker and QuarkXPress 4.

Photoshop EPS Format

Photoshop EPS is the format of choice for many service bureaus because of the range of options it can deploy and because it seems to be the most error-free format on high-end systems. The expanded Save dialog box is shown in Figure 10.55. The following list details the options:

- *Preview*—The first choice to be made is the Preview option. The preview is the part of the file that you see when you import the EPS file into a program such as PageMaker or QuarkXPress. This part of the file has nothing to do with the print information. It's simply a placeholder view of the file, an FPO (for position only). In Windows Photoshop, the choices are limited to the top three options (None, TIFF 1 bit/pixel, and TIFF 8 bit/pixel). Macintosh Photoshop has three additional choices. The default is Macintosh (8 bits/pixel). This—and the 8-bit TIFF preview—offers a screen preview containing 256 dithered colors. Macintosh JPEG is a 24-bit preview of the file. This image is usually a smaller file than the 8-bit preview. It's much easier to see on screen—in fact, it's beautiful! All of the previews are 72 ppi images. The 1-bit previews are, as you might expect, black and white. None, as a preview, is less than thrilling: When a file saved with this option is imported into another program, the only indication you have is a gray box with the same dimensions as the file. There may be reasons you might need to use this, but the authors can't think of one.

- *Encoding*—The encoding pop-up menu gives you several choices, all of which can be a little confusing. The confusion is the result of the ways encoding has been implemented by programs that support the EPS format. It makes a difference what version of a program you're using, the age of your output device, cross-platform compatibility, and whether your output device uses PostScript Level 1, Level 2, or Level 3.

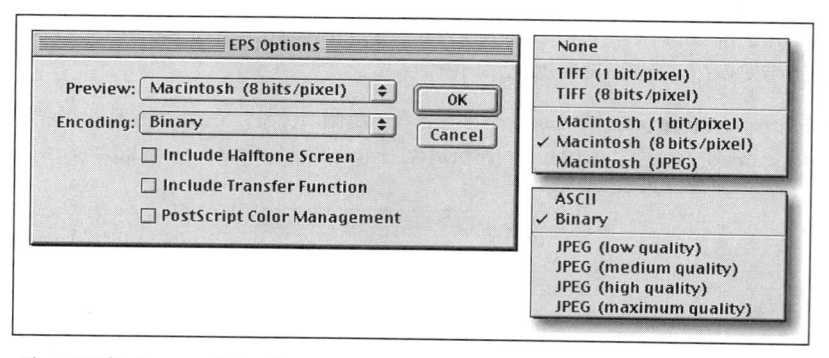

Figure 10.55 The EPS file format dialog box.

Encoding is the format of the data that will be sent to your output device. If you decide to print a document from Adobe PageMaker on a PostScript printer, you need to have set up all your printer parameters. Then, as PageMaker or QuarkXPress begins the print operation, the printer driver generates a specialized kind of computer code that describes all of the objects, colors, fonts, and object placement on the page to be printed. This code is what is sent to the printer. The question is: In what form will the data be encoded?

ASCII was the earliest form of encoding used for PostScript documents. ASCII files are simply text documents. If you save a file using ASCII encoding, you can open it, look at it, and even modify it—if you know what you're doing—in any word processor program. All PostScript printers understand ASCII. However, using ASCII is comparatively slow: The printer needs to read the document and then translate it into its own internal language.

Binary is a better choice than ASCII if your circumstances allow its use. When you use Binary, the code that is sent to the printer is already translated into the printer's internal language. That means the processing can go much faster. Binary-coded files are also smaller than ASCII files, and therefore download faster.

JPEG? Well, it's a little hard to deal with JPEG (see the JPEG section in Chapter 12). There are two schools of thought here: One school holds that using JPEG encoding and its consequent reduction in file size makes it a worthwhile option. The other holds that saving a file with a compression method that irretrievably compromises the image quality makes the JPEG format *not* a worthwhile option. The debate will probably continue for a long time. In any event, the question for you is academic: Most commercial RIP/imagesetter equipment doesn't support JPEG encoding. Even if it were your choice, chances are good that your service bureau couldn't image your file anyway.

As a rule, use Binary encoding if you possibly can (check with your service bureau to find out if it has a specific recommendation). Make sure that you check out special issues such as imaging duotones. Some older versions of PageMaker couldn't separate a duotone unless it was saved with ASCII encoding. Some older imagesetter equipment also couldn't deal with PostScript unless it was in ASCII format. Imaging equipment using PostScript Level 2 should be able to accommodate Binary encoding. All recent versions of the Windows and Macintosh operating systems and recent versions of the major graphics programs also should be able to handle it. If you have any doubt and you're running into a deadline, ASCII format is a sure thing. You should also use ASCII if you find that you're having trouble porting PostScript data from, say, Macintosh to Windows, or the other direction.

The other parts of the EPS dialog box include choices about whether to embed halftone screen information, transfer functions with the file, or whether to embed PostScript Color Management.

- *Include Halftone Screen*—Setting halftone screens was discussed at the end of our study of duotones (Chapter 9). Unless you're familiar with how screens work, it's probably best to allow the program from which you will be printing—probably PageMaker or QuarkXPress—to handle the screening for you. The only time you might venture into setting a screen is when you have a need for the screen in your Photoshop document to be different from the one that will be used for the page on which your Photoshop file will be placed. You may want to use a coarse screen and a novelty dot shape for some decorative effect. In such a case, embedding the screen frequency, angle, and spot shape must be done in the Screen dialog box, accessed from the File|Page Setup dialog box. When you save the file as EPS, you can then check the Include Screen checkbox.

- *Include Transfer Function*—The Transfer Function is also generated from one of the buttons on the Page Setup dialog box. The Transfer Functions dialog box is shown in Figure 10.56.

  Transfer curves allow you to compensate for a printer that is producing faulty output. To make use of the Transfer Function, you need to have a file that contains a gray bar with all of the percentages shown in the figure. Print a sample file on the printer in question. Use a densitometer or a Colortron II to measure how the output differs from the input values. For example, if the densitometer indicates the output at 50% is 7% higher than it should be (57%), you would enter the number 43 in the 50% data entry box. By doing this, you are lowering the output device's percentage by the required amount. After you have measured the output and have back-compensated (or forward-compensated), this curve can be saved as a named file. It can then be loaded whenever you need to have a hard copy from that printer. When you're saving an EPS file, you also have the option of including the transfer with the file.

  Some problems are associated with the first two Include checkboxes—for example, the Screen function; if you decide, at some point, that you've changed your mind about a specialty screen for your file, remember to resave the file and turn off the Include Screen checkbox. Otherwise, the screen information follows the file everywhere it goes and the Include command overrides any PostScript printer's screening.

  The Transfer Function works the same way. If you make a transfer to compensate for an in-house printer, don't forget to remove the Include Transfer from the file before you send it out of house. Otherwise, imagine that you send the file to a service bureau to be printed on a perfectly calibrated system: Your Transfer curve will override that system's curves. You'll get, instead of perfect output, an image produced with the mirror version of your in-house printer's faulty curve.

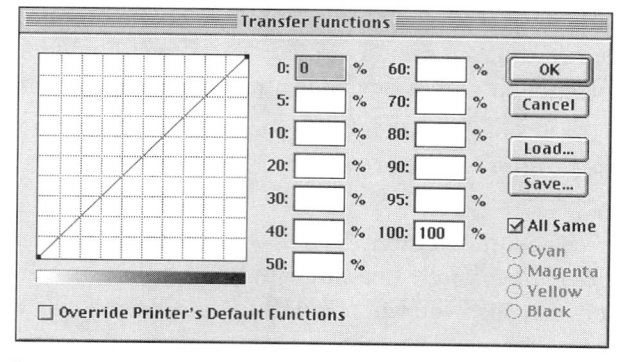

Figure 10.56 The Transfer Functions dialog box from Photoshop's Page Setup dialog box.

> **TIP**
>
> If you are saving an EPS file and you find that either of the checkboxes is already checked *and you don't know why,* uncheck it. You're far safer saving a file without the Include functions than you are with functions that might not have any purpose. Remind me to tell you the story, sometime, about the magazine guy who included—by accident—a 53 line-screen function on all his color separations. All of his color files imaged at 53 line-screen on every one of his 133 line-screen pages. Wow! Dots the size of Wyoming, color shifts—the weeping and moaning was very sad. As the saying in the automobile commercial goes, "He learned a *hard* lesson."

- *PostScript Color Management*—This EPS file option embeds a command to a PostScript printer to convert the file data to the printer's color. You would not use this option if your file has already been converted to the printer's color space.

DCS 1

The DCS format is a file format optimized for four-color printing. It was originally developed by Quark, Inc. as a way to speed up file downloads and RIP time. The reasoning behind the format is approximately as follows: Assume you need to image a 20MB CMYK file and you've saved it in a format such as TIFF. When the file is downloaded for the imaging and ripping of the first separation—which will be black, followed by cyan, magenta, and yellow; they go in alphabetical order—the entire 20MB file is downloaded. It's then ripped. Seventy-five percent of the information is then discarded because it's not needed for the black plate. For each new plate, the entire file is downloaded and ripped, and in each case, 75 percent of the imaging information is discarded as unnecessary.

When a DCS 1.0 file is saved, it is split into five parts. A master file is linked to four other files, one for each of the process inks. When the file is imaged in this form, the master file downloads only the single relevant ink file. (This decreases the download time by 75 percent.) The downloaded file is then ripped by itself, which decreases the ripping time by 75 percent. All else being equal, the DCS format, when used to run film, is much more efficient than a single-file structure.

You might not want to use DCS format if your production process includes any kind of digital proofing. Many high-end digital proofing systems need to RIP the entire file and often don't support the DCS format. Consequently, you would likely receive a proof version of your 72 ppi preview file if you sent a DCS format file through such a process. If you are in doubt, it would be wise to check with your service bureau.

Most of the DCS 1 options are the same as for Photoshop EPS. DCS 1 and 2 are both variations of the EPS format. The expanded DCS 1 Save dialog box is shown in Figure 10.57.

DCS 2

The DCS 2 format is a modernized version of DCS 1. It supports the primary CMYK plates, as well as additional channels that might be imaged as spot colors or as varnish plates. You also

Figure 10.57 Expanded view of the DCS 1 Save dialog box.

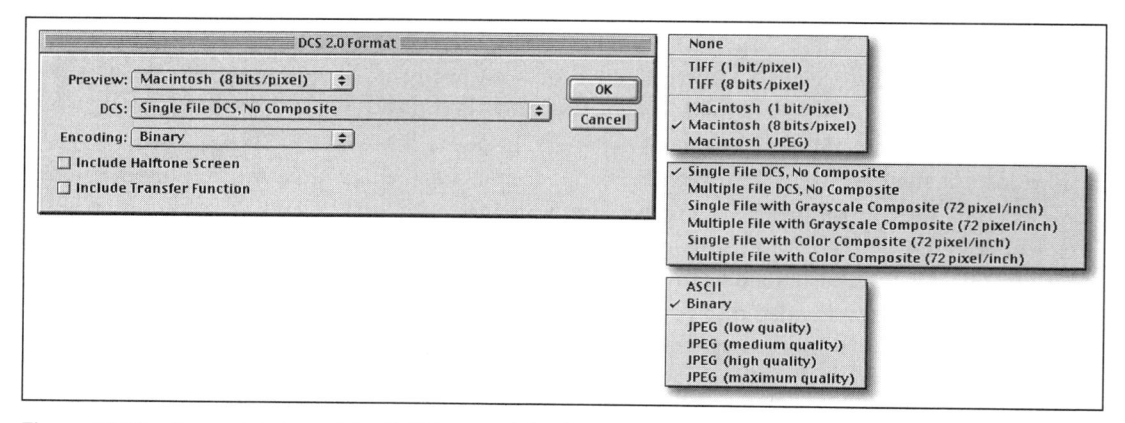

Figure 10.58 Expanded view of the DCS 2 Save dialog box.

have the choice of saving the file as a single file or as multiple linked files. The options for this file are the same as for Photoshop EPS. The DCS 2 options are shown in Figure 10.58.

A Stochastic Screening Alternative

Frequency modulated (FM) screens are controversial in the prepress world. The advantages and disadvantages have been widely discussed. Too early, not-sufficiently-bug-free releases of high-end software associated with several kinds of imagesetters and a good deal of unrealistic hype have retarded the acceptance of stochastic screen technology. The promised benefits of high-resolution stochastic screens have been plagued by unexpected practical problems in the pressroom. The consensus has been that the dot size produced by high-end imagesetters is too small to be workable in everyday situations. Considering that the average dot size for most of this high-end software was 10 microns—that's smaller than a 1-percent screen dot—criticism of the software manufacturers and their products was probably justified. By the time the manufacturers rushed to remedy the problems, virtually all of the original marketing impetus had passed. As a result, this extremely promising technology is not widely used except in special cases.

The situation is unfortunate, because FM screening has many desirable qualities. Dot generation is fairly straightforward. It isn't as computation intensive as the calculation of screens along non-integer screen angles. (If you'd like to drop a techy term into a prepress conversation, use the math term for a non-integer screen angle: In this context, the term is *irrational tangent*.) All of the dots are the same size; they're distributed over an area in proportion to the darkness of the tone they represent. FM screening involves none of the screen angles that have bedeviled printers and prepress technicians since the advent of four-color process printing. Having no screen angles solves many problems when more than four inks are to be used. There is, also, no tendency for gradients to develop banding problems. That, by itself, obviates many kinds of workarounds that have to do with the geometry of lithographic dots.

Figure 10.59 shows a comparison of two gradients, the top in a traditional screen—AM, for amplitude modulated—and the bottom in an FM screen. At high magnifications, the differences between the two are obvious. When FM screens combine to produce color separations, you'll notice a large improvement in the reproduction of tonal ranges and of detail. FM screens produce finished work with a fine detail that is ordinarily associated with very high frequency—200 to 300 lpi—traditional screens. Figures 10.60 and 10.61 show two degrees of magnification for a color separation using a traditional screen. Notice how the extreme close-up reveals the jagged edges associated with the comparatively large dots used. (Note: This is a magnification of a 133 line-screen image.)

For a comparison, study Figures 10.62 and 10.63. This separation was generated from the same file as the previous figures. Even at high magnification, details are convincingly reproduced, and the edges of color areas appear much smoother.

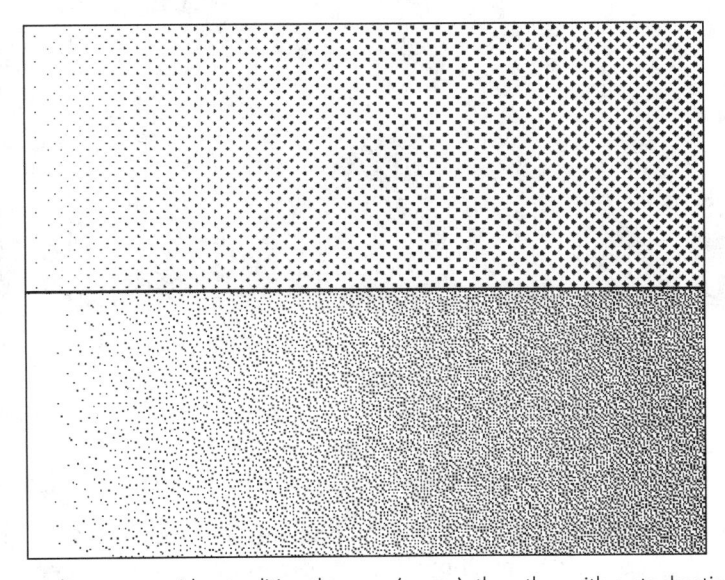

Figure 10.59 Two gradients, one with a traditional screen (upper), the other with a stochastic screen.

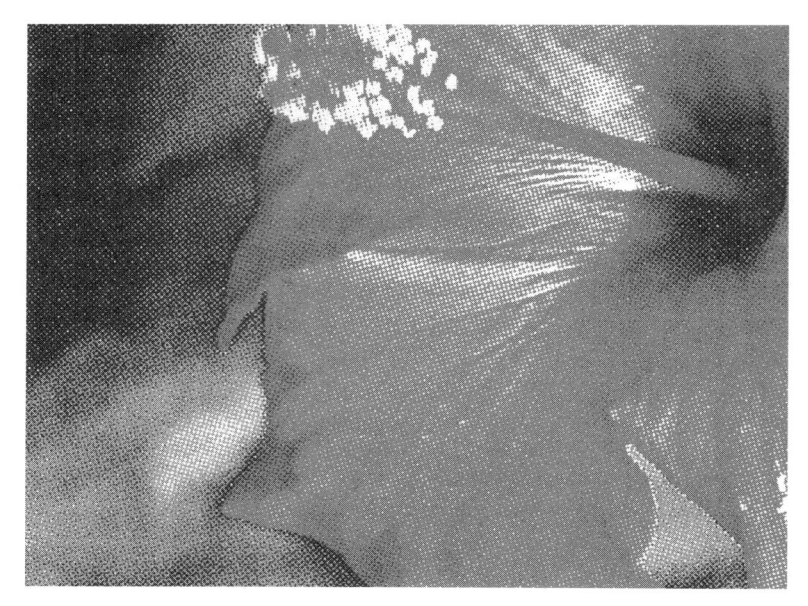

Figure 10.60 Close-up view of a 133 line-screen color photo.

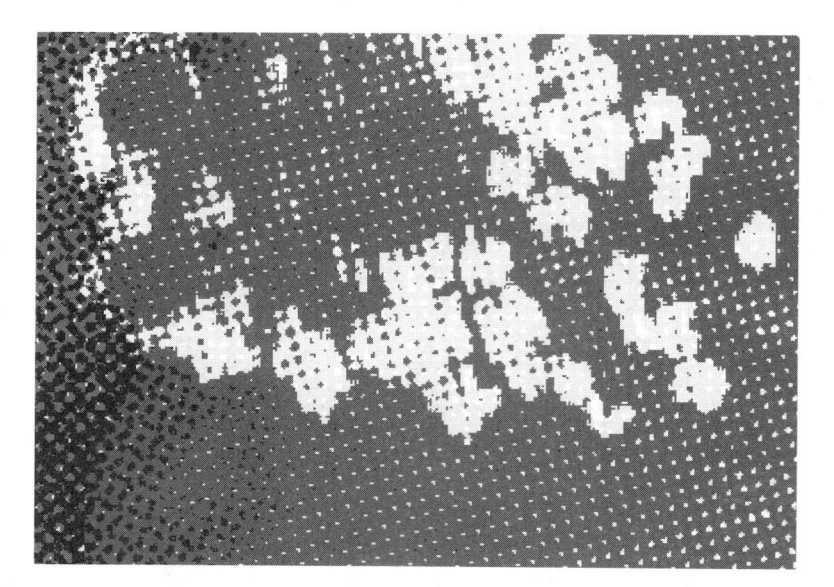

Figure 10.61 Extreme magnification of 10.60. Notice the jagged quality of the dot combinations.

A side-by-side comparison of stochastic screening with traditional screening is the best advertisement for the benefits of the technology. Its superior fidelity in maintaining details makes it valuable for many kinds of printing that could benefit from the look of higher quality.

One disadvantage has been that Photoshop technicians have not directly had the opportunity to use this kind of screening, and have had to depend on service bureaus that have been reluctant to invest the serious amount of money needed for the high-end software. Seeing the

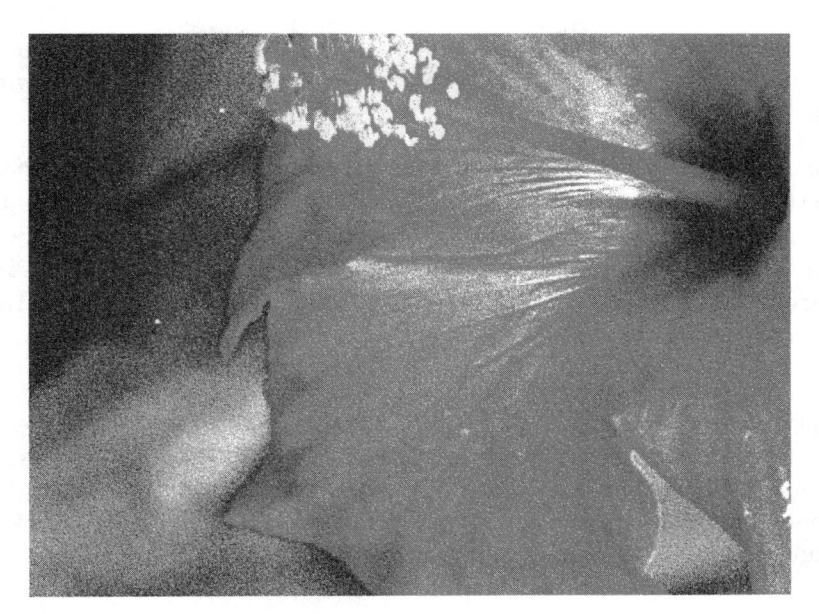

Figure 10.62 Close-up view of a stochastic screen color photo.

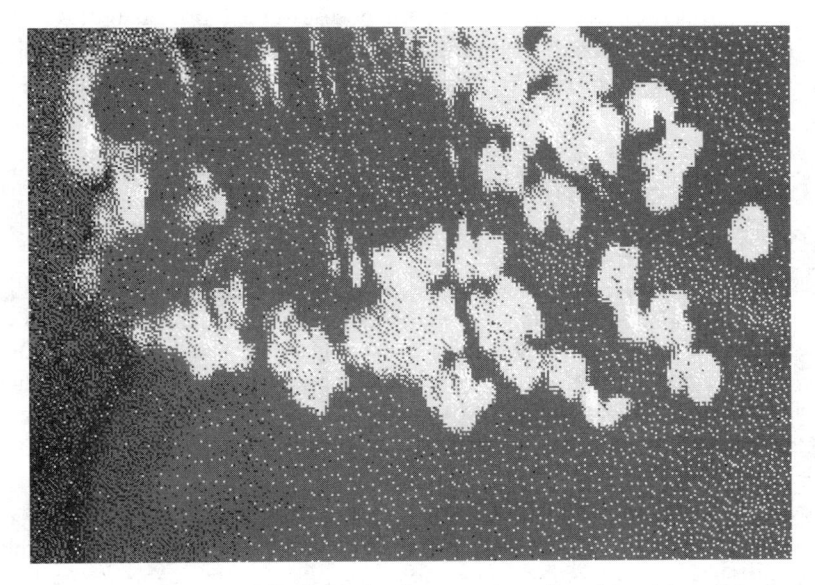

Figure 10.63 Extreme magnification of 10.62. Notice the smooth quality of the dot combinations and the delicate detail.

need, Second Glance Software introduced its LaserSeps Pro add-on for Photoshop. With LaserSeps Pro, you can export your color separations to stochastic screen files in the DCS 1 or DCS 2 format. With a bit of care, the resulting printed work is of showcase quality.

Having completed all adjustments for the separation, and the conversion to CMYK mode, choose File|Export|LaserSeps Pro. After some initial calculations, the screen changes to a set of four windows with a dialog box (see Figure 10.64). In this dialog box, you can tweak the curves for any of the plates. The results of each change are shown in the composite window at the lower right.

When the adjustments are satisfactory, click on OK. In the dialog box that appears, you are given the choice of formats, as well as two options that are special-case settings for the convenience of screen printers (see Figure 10.65). If you choose the Photoshop file format, the separations proceed. If you choose the DCS format, another dialog box opens to give you a further set of possibilities (see Figure 10.66). When you're finished, click on OK. The stochastic separations are generated while the file is written to disk.

You will find, when you've finished saving the file, that you cannot open the DCS file in Photoshop. LaserSeps Pro has made some changes to the file structure, which isn't the usual way Photoshop handles files. Specifically, the segmented files have been changed from their usual grayscale mode to bitmap mode. This is an advantage to you because of the decrease in file size (bitmap files are one-eighth the size of an equivalent grayscale file). You can place this file in any program that imports the DCS format. It will generate separations with no problems.

Clipping Paths

The Pen tool in Photoshop is used for many purposes and is a powerful and useful tool. One of its most powerful functions, the clipping path, comes into play when your image has been imported into another program. A clipping path becomes a mask exported as part of a Photoshop file.

Points To Consider When Using LaserSeps Pro

We discussed, above, the problems with an inability to change the size of dots that were too small for most printing. In LaserSeps Pro, the dot size of your output is the same as the resolution of your file. For many purposes, 300 ppi files are sufficient. In the stochastic world, however, 300 ppi output is a relatively coarse setting. When you wish to boost the overall quality so that you equal or surpass the quality of traditional printing in the 133 to 175 line-screen range, it will be necessary for you to work with higher pixel counts. 600 ppi is the recommendation.

A 300 ppi file of a size to bleed an 8-1/2×11" page is about 33.3MB. The same file at 600 ppi is 133.3MB—exactly 100MB larger. This number seems large until you remember how much the file size is reduced when the separations are generated: You end up with a file just under 20MB, a size much smaller than what we routinely handle now.

Color adjustments on the preliminary file will be slower; reading the image off the hard drive and into memory, and then saving it again will certainly take longer. Balanced against these drawbacks are the benefits of the print quality. It's a choice you have to consider carefully. Given the convenience and ease of LaserSeps Pro, stochastic screens should be given a fair opportunity to demonstrate their merits.

CALIBRATION AND COLOR REPRODUCTION   **713**

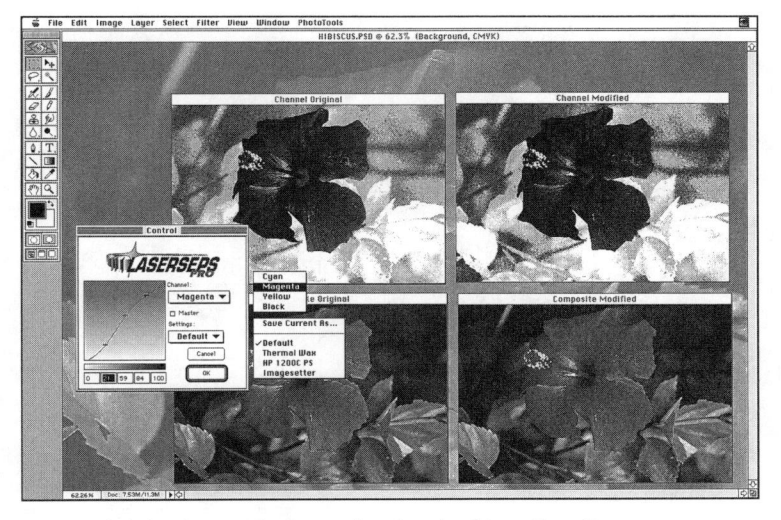

Figure 10.64   The Control dialog box and preview thumbnails of LaserSeps Pro.

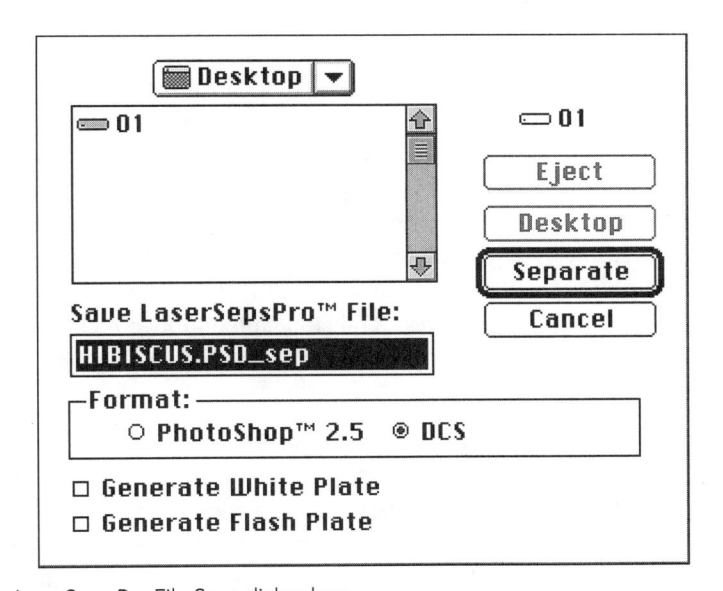

Figure 10.65   The LaserSeps Pro File Save dialog box.

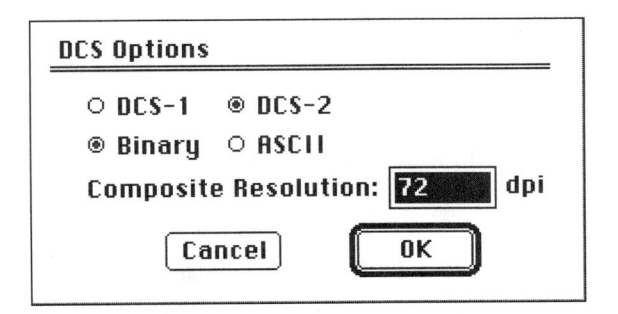

Figure 10.66   LaserSeps Pro's DCS Options dialog box.

714 CHAPTER 10

Figure 10.67 QuarkXPress page with imported photo.

Figure 10.68 The same QuarkXPress page, but with the photo masked by a clipping path.

Clipping paths do just what the name suggests: They clip the part of the image outside the boundaries of the path so that it is, for all intents and purposes, transparent. Figure 10.67 shows a screen shot of a QuarkXPress page into which a photo has been imported. Figure 10.68 has the same picture, but with a difference: A path has been drawn around the flower, designated as a clipping path, and exported with the image. As you can see, the path effectively silhouettes the image shape and gives a vector edge that QuarkXPress can recognize as a shape for the text run-around. (Just so you know, the text in the figures used here is Klingon, human. It's generated by the extremely cool XPress XTension called Jabberwocky.)

Saving Paths

Whenever you draw a path in Photoshop, it's a good idea to save it so that it can be used whenever you need it. Choose Save Path from the Paths palette menu. The dialog box shown in Figure 10.69 appears. You can name the path descriptively or accept the default name supplied by Photoshop. Click on OK. Saving many paths with a Photoshop document doesn't add appreciably to the size of the file, even though the paths are embedded in the file.

Defining Clipping Paths

When you want to designate one of the paths you have drawn as a clipping path, choose the Clipping Path command from the Paths palette menu. The dialog box, shown in Figure 10.70, lets you choose any of your named/saved paths. This dialog box also allows you to enter the value you wish to use for the Flatness setting.

Flatness

You should pay close attention to the Flatness setting. Flatness is an instruction to the output device that tells how much precision you want it to use when calculating the curved segments

Figure 10.69 The Save Path dialog box.

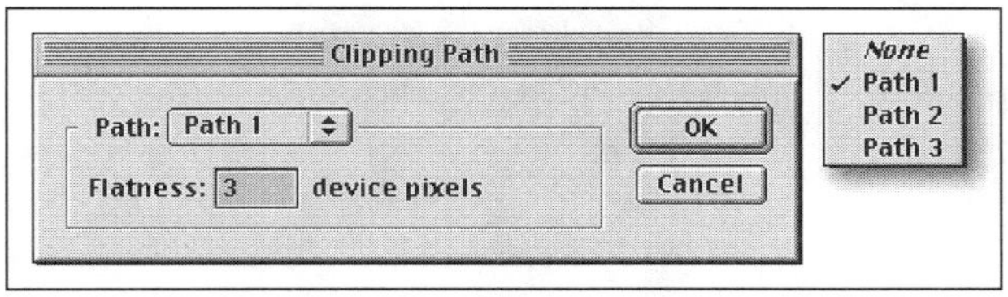

Figure 10.70 The Clipping Path options dialog box.

of your path. For most paths, a Flatness value of 3—the default—is adequate. However, when the path becomes more complex and begins to have many points, the computation involved with imaging the path's edge becomes very great. So great, in fact, that clipping paths can probably be said to be the second most frequent problem associated with high-end PostScript output. (The most frequent problem? Fonts, hands down. Fonts are an ongoing hassle. Ask any service bureau technician.)

Problems With Flatness Values

The first line of defense for a path that refuses to image is to raise the Flatness setting. 4, 5, 6 are all values that will not visibly affect the look of your path's edge. Depending on the file, you may be able to go as high as 10. (Above a certain point, the curved lines of your path cease being curves and become small straight lines. Never, never set your Flatness below 3. Never. If you want to try an experiment sometime, and you have several thousand years to waste, make your Flatness setting 0. That's about how long it will take for your output.) If the path still doesn't image, the only recourse you have is to redraw and simplify the path, removing as many points as you can while still preserving the shape.

Problems With Poorly Drawn Clipping Paths

Clipping paths in Photoshop have to be carefully drawn. In Figure 10.71, the path appears to be well within the edge of the flower's petals. If you don't draw the path inside the image boundary in this way, areas of the background of the image will also be included in the clipped shape. These unwanted pixels show up on the screen image and on the output—as noticeable dark (or light) edge lines (see Figure 10.72).

If you discover that you have included pixels that don't belong to the isolated shape, you can go back into Photoshop and pull the path in from the edge. Here's a quick alternative if you have consistently missed the edge everywhere:

1. First, try to estimate by how many pixels you misjudged the edge. Click on the clipping path's thumbnail on the Paths palette. With one of the Selection tools chosen, press the Enter key. Your path becomes a selection.

Figure 10.71 Draw clipping paths well within the boundary of the object being masked.

Figure 10.72 If the clipping path is not drawn carefully, the edges of the masked object look rough and irregular.

2. Choose Select|Modify|Contract. Contract your selection by the number of pixels you think will be sufficient. When the selection has contracted, choose the Make Work Path command from the Paths palette menu.

3. In the dialog box that appears, enter a Tolerance value of 2. Click on OK.

4. With the path redrawn, save the new path and designate the one you've just saved as the new clipping path.

5. Reimport the file into QuarkXPress. The edges of the path are clean of any unwelcome artifacts (see Figure 10.73).

Figure 10.73 After pulling the clipping path in from the edges, the masked object's edges are clean and smooth.

Make Work Path Tolerances

When Photoshop is asked to draw a path based on a selection (the Make Work Path command), your choice of Tolerance values is very important. Figures 10.74, 10.75, and 10.76 show the paths resulting from three different Tolerance settings. The settings are shown on the figures. Notice that the smallest setting creates the most points around the perimeter. A path with this many points will probably be difficult to output. The other two are more satisfactory, except that they don't follow the edges with precision. Paths drawn with settings of 2 or 3 will

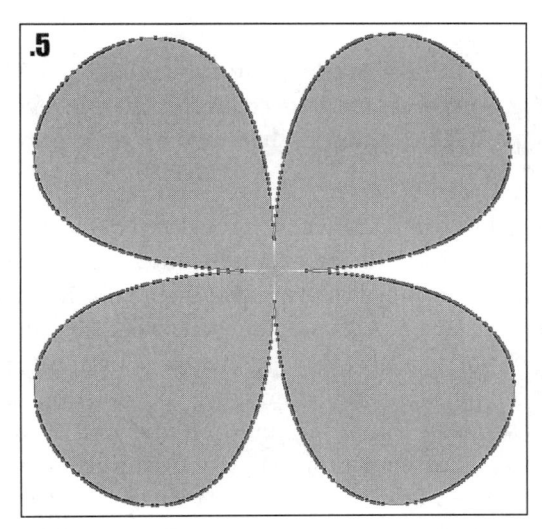

Figure 10.74 Path drawn by Photoshop using a Tolerance setting of .5. The path has too many points to be usable as a mask.

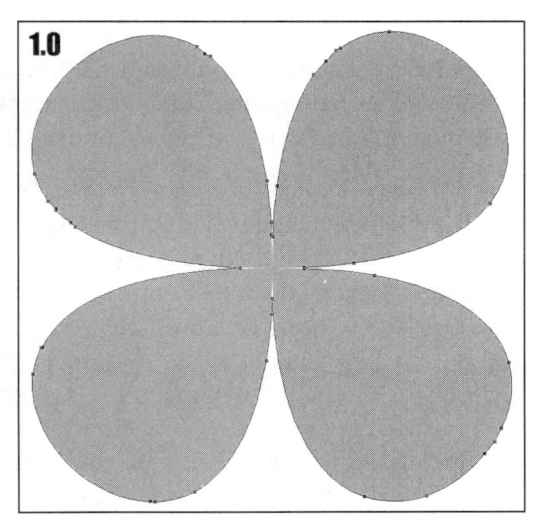

Figure 10.75 Path drawn by Photoshop using a Tolerance setting of 1. The path has fewer points and would be a very satisfactory mask.

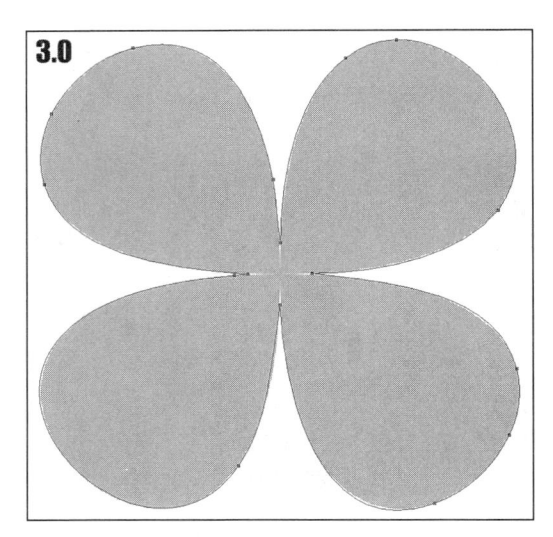

Figure 10.76 Path drawn by Photoshop using a Tolerance setting of 3. The path has very few points, but needs to be manually adjusted to make it follow the edge of the shape.

probably need to be manipulated manually to make them effective masking shapes. A path with the fewest points, even if it requires manual tweaking, is preferable to a path with too many points. The latter nearly always results in problems at output time.

Mask Pro By Extensis Software

The makers of Extensis PhotoTools offer a masking helper/add-on for Photoshop called Mask Pro.

Mask Pro (the main window is shown in Figure 10.77) works on a layer that you modify to add areas of transparent pixels. Or, to put it another way, you eliminate colored pixels wherever you intend Mask Pro to construct your masking path. The purpose of the window is to help you *remove* the object that you wish to mask.

Mask Pro's tools include color palettes in which colors can be defined to be *included* or *excluded* from the masking procedure. Brushing over excluded colors, for example, has no effect on them and they are left intact, whereas brushing over included colors makes them vanish. The tools are easy to use, intuitive, and very powerful. When you complete your work, exit the Mask Pro window. A dialog box appears in which you instruct Mask Pro to draw your mask or not. If you choose the Path option, a dialog box appears in which to enter your tolerances. When you click on OK, the Mask Pro window disappears completely, and you find your document apparently unchanged. If you make the Path choice upon exiting, simply press Command+0 (zero) or Ctrl+0 to fit the image completely into the screen, and then use the Paste command. Mask Pro instantly adds the path, perfectly positioned. This path can then be saved and designated as the document's clipping path (see Figure 10.78).

The first time you see this path, you will shudder and wonder if you set the Tolerance values incorrectly. You'll see as many points on the path as if you had generated it using a Tolerance

CALIBRATION AND COLOR REPRODUCTION   **719**

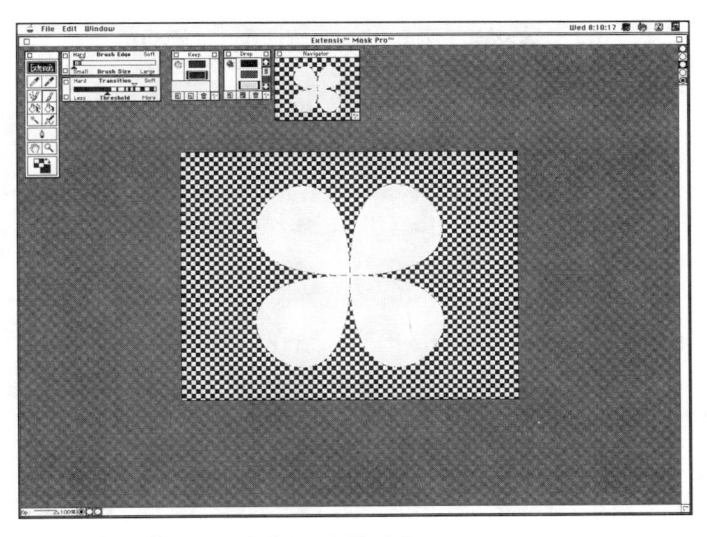

Figure 10.77   The main window of Extensis Software's Mask Pro.

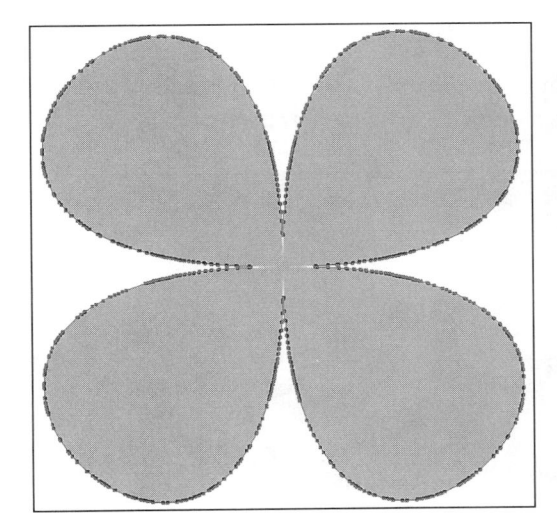

Figure 10.78   Mask Pro generates a path with what looks to be far too many points. All of the points, however, are corner points and furnish no difficulty to an imaging device.

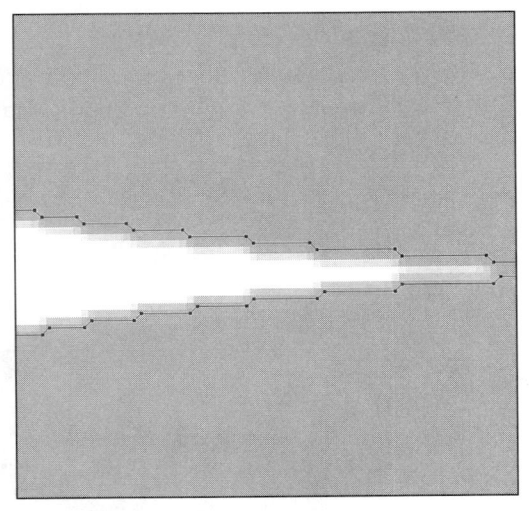

Figure 10.79   Enlarged detail of Figure 10.78 shows that the many corner points generated by Mask Pro are all corner points.

setting of .5. A closer look, however, shows that Extensis has been really clever in the way it generates the path. All of the perimeter points are *corners* (see Figure 10.79). There are no curve segments anywhere. Curve paths, you see, are the root of the problem when you're imaging a path with an excessive number of points. If all of the points are converted to corners, then the problem mostly disappears. Because the program has made so many points, it has actually come close to doing what a PostScript RIP would do—calculate small straight-line segments with which to simulate the curve. With this many points and with the short lines that connect them, there should be no visible compromise to your path's edge.

You can use Mask Pro to make paths where existing layers contain transparency information. Here's how:

1. If you have already masked an object using Photoshop's other tools, select the object. Create a new layer containing no pixel information.
2. Next, choose Select|Inverse. Fill the selection in the new layer with the Foreground color. (Note: The color is unimportant because you will eliminate this layer when you have exited Mask Pro.)
3. From the Filter Menu, choose Extensis|Mask Pro.
4. As soon as the window has appeared, click on the Close box.
5. Select the Path option and enter your Tolerance values. Delete the layer you created, and use the Paste command.

Mask Pro is a great little gadget. It does one thing, and it does it superbly. It's also fun to use, and the results it gives make it well worth the investment. You can download a fully functioning demo version of this add-on—as well as the other Extensis software products—by visiting its Web site at **www.extensis.com**.

A Cool Clipping Path Trick

You can do some clever things with clipping paths. One of them, shown in Figures 10.80 through 10.83, will probably give you a number of ideas along similar lines. The effect is of a photorealistic

Figure 10.80 The graphic to be rotated and masked with a clipping path.

Figure 10.81 Rotate the Canvas.

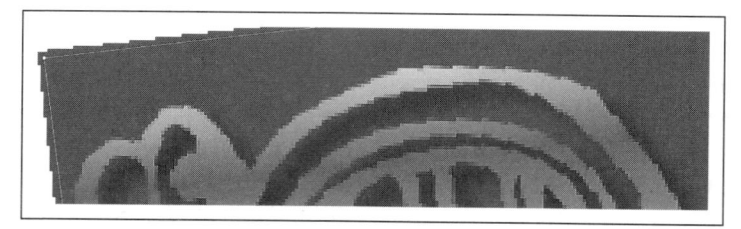

Figure 10.82 Zoom in to the image, and draw a path from corner to corner a few pixels in from the edge. Save the path and designate it as a clipping path.

Figure 10.83 When the image is imported into the page make-up software, only the rotated shape is visible.

object that seems to lie atop your Adobe PageMaker or QuarkXPress page. In this case, a fountain pen appears to be casting a shadow onto the type. In the Photoshop file, the shadow is cast against a white background. Because the shadow is artificial, the background can be any color. You simply need to make the background in your page layout software the same color. Here's how:

1. Use the Pen tool to outline the pen shape, save the path, and designate it as a clipping path. Duplicate the file. Delete the path from the duplicate. Save each file in Photoshop EPS format. Name the files so that you remember which file has the clipping path and which file doesn't.

2. Prepare your page layout document (this example uses QuarkXPress). In the example shown in Figure 10.84, the text exists in transparent boxes. Draw a picture frame as big as you need for the pen photo. Import the picture that doesn't have the clipping path. Position the pen on the page, being careful not to move the image within its box. When complete, use the Send to Back command (the image is now behind the text).

CLIPPING PATHS FOR ROTATED EXPORT PHOTOS

When photo material is imported into QuarkXPress or Adobe PageMaker, a page design sometimes specifies that the photo be placed on the page at an angle. The image can be rotated within either program. It is not wise to do so, despite the convenience of the rotate controls, because the file will need to be downloaded and imaged twice. Besides this, the rotation requires that the image's pixels be interpolated by the page make-up software. QuarkXPress and Adobe PageMaker interpolation may be equivalent to that of Photoshop. However, no provision exists for checking to see that the rotation doesn't soften the image so much that it requires additional sharpening. Finally, rotating the file in the page make-up software may be easy, but it's a sloppy procedure.

If you have determined how much rotation you need, open the original file in Photoshop (refer to Figure 10.80). From the Image menu, choose Rotate Canvas. In Figure 10.81, the rotation was 7° CCW. Zoom up to the image and draw a path from corner to corner (refer to Figure 10.82). Save the path and designate it as a clipping path. When the resaved image is reimported into the page make-up software, the opaque corners of the rotated file are not visible (refer to Figure 10.83).

3. Leave this object selected, and choose Item|Step And Repeat. Leave the repeat number as 1 and make the vertical and horizontal offsets 0 (zero). Click on OK.

4. You now have a second version of the picture sitting precisely atop the first (see Figure 10.85). While this is selected, use the Bring To Front command. Delete the image in this picture box and import the pen photo that contains the clipping path. Because the positioning is perfect, the clipped pen sits precisely atop the first. The shadow is actually beneath the type, but because the type is dark and the shadow light, the effect is as though the object is casting the shadow.

Figure 10.84 Bring the image without the clipping path into the page layout document and send it to the back. The text will lie on top of the photo.

Figure 10.85 Duplicate the picture box, import the image with the clipping path, and bring the picture box to the front.

Figure 10.86 Enlarged detail of the final effect.

A close-up of the finished work is shown in Figure 10.86. You probably wouldn't want to do a lot of this—the type under the pen is obscured—but it's the kind of virtuoso trick that can come in handy when you need it.

Trapping

Trapping is a prepress necessity. It is not a nicety; it is vital if your job is to look professional after it has been printed. To the educated eyes of your peers, a poorly trapped job almost leaps off the page and cries "Amateur!"

Although some print/prepress service departments routinely trap their customers' digital files, many don't. Some service bureaus apply trapping software that automates the process. However, software that can apply professional trapping to the complex files many designers now achieve is fairly expensive and is not in universal use. Whatever the state of your service bureau's trapping capabilities, one thing is certain: Trapping your files will be an additional expense. If you can do your own trapping, you avoid that expense.

A complete discussion of digital trapping is beyond the scope of this book. Moreover, general trapping in Photoshop is a very simple procedure. There are, however, a few occasions where a knowledge of trapping will allow you to use Photoshop to perform some trapping tasks that are beyond the scope of the software you routinely use.

On a color press, areas of different colors are laid down by different inks. To see how this happens, look at Figure 10.87. As the press sheet is drawn through the press, the colored areas in the figure are laid down, one at a time, in what is hoped to be perfect registry. Presses do a nearly perfect job in making all the colors fit into their assigned spaces, but usually the job isn't quite perfect enough. The press sheet can become misaligned for a variety of reasons, and even a slight movement results in the misfitting color areas shown in Figure 10.88.

The solution to this mechanical problem is called trapping. Areas of color are enlarged so that they slightly overlap the areas of adjoining colors. Figure 10.89 shows an example of how the adjoining color areas have been made to overlap each other. The boundaries of the shapes are now composed of a zone containing both of the colors.

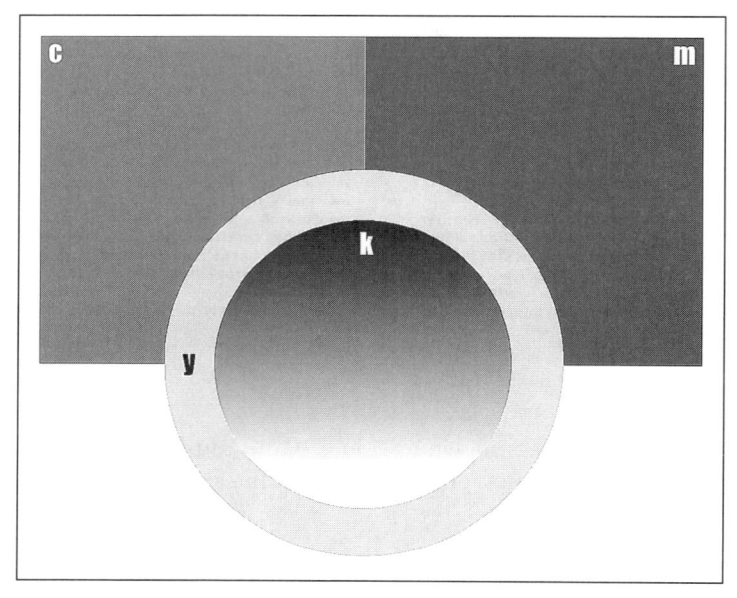

Figure 10.87 Individual color areas are laid down on press one at a time by different inking stations.

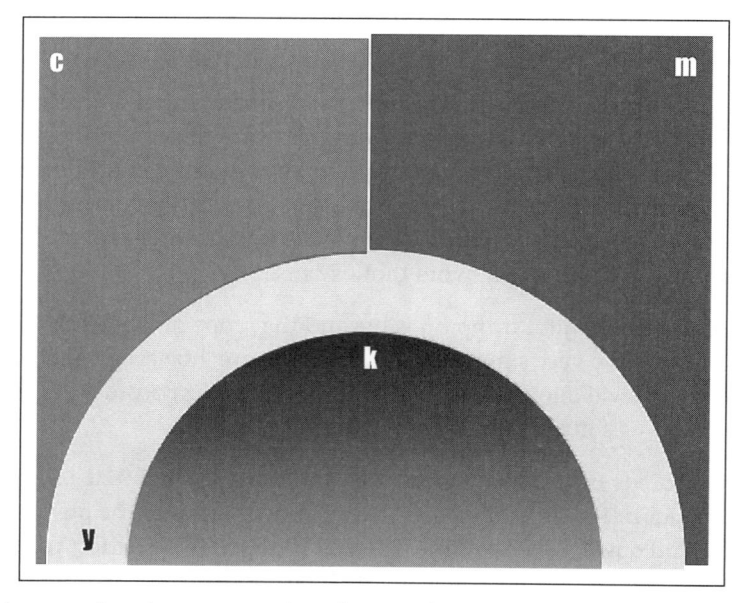

Figure 10.88 If the press sheet becomes misaligned, some of the ink areas do not register properly.

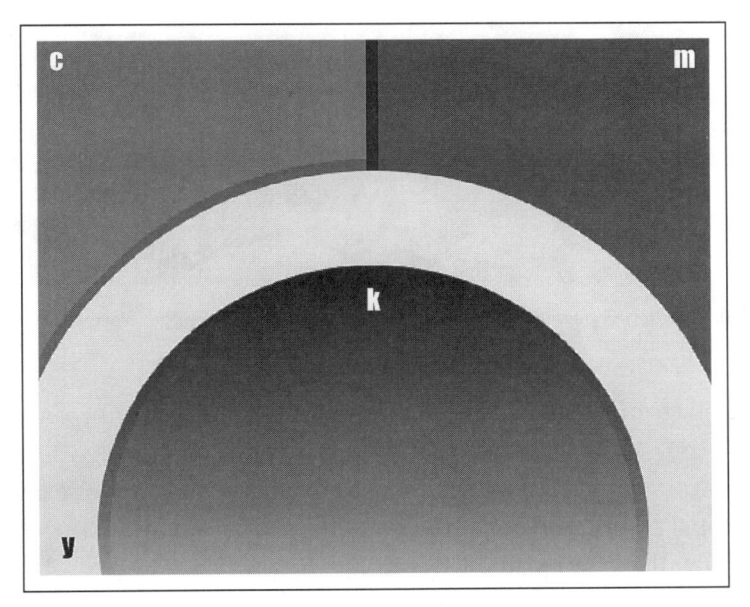

Figure 10.89 The trapping process moves areas of lighter colors into areas of darker colors. Trapping doesn't prevent misregistration—it hides it.

The example in Figure 10.89 shows a zone of trap that is very large. Under normal circumstances, offset press trapping tolerances are in measurements that are small. A representative trapping measurement would be .003 inches, although other kinds of printing—flexographic printing is one example—sometimes use trapping tolerances with measurements as high as 5 points!

Trapping involves spreading areas of light color into areas of darker color. Photoshop's Trap command—at the bottom of the Image menu—does its job by ranking the relative lightness of the pure inks and then modifying its ranking as the inks appear in decreasing percentages. Although it's not easy to see in Figure 10.89, the area of yellow has spread outward and inward into the areas of the other three colors. The cyan and magenta areas have moved toward each other because they are close to the same lightness. (Traditionally, cyan has been considered the second-darkest ink, after black. In digital terms, magenta is 15 percent darker than cyan.)

Despite its ability to automatically trap an image, Photoshop's Trap command is used only under certain circumstances. A normal photographic image doesn't usually have areas of one color adjoining an area of a different color. Colors in a photograph are usually so dispersed that trapping is not only *not* required, but injurious to the quality of the image.

Trapping Part Of A Photographic Image

In rare instances, trapping might be needed within a photographic image. For example, red type might have been placed on a blue sky (see Figure 10.90). With such a case, the needed trapping should be applied only where the type meets the sky and not to the entire image. You can apply needed trapping in a couple of ways.

Figure 10.90 When an image has been modified with text or extra information, trapping is required—but only where the letters meet the photo.

Here's one method to apply needed trapping, usable when the type has been applied and is still on a separate layer:

1. Command+click or Ctrl+click on the layer's thumbnail to make the type into a selection.
2. Next, with the Eyedropper tool, sample a representative blue from the sky (the blue is a lighter color than the red of the type).
3. Choose Edit|Stroke. Set the width of the stroke to the width of the needed trap.
4. Choose the Inside option, Foreground Color, and Multiply mode (see Figure 10.91). The applied stroke is shown in magnified view in Figure 10.92.
5. If you wish the trapping to be less visible, decrease the Opacity of the stroke to 60% to 70%.

Here's another method to apply needed trapping for type that is *not* on a separate layer:

1. Use the Lasso tool to make a selection of the type and the sky tones surrounding the type. Use the Copy command, and leave the selection active.
2. Choose File|New, and click on OK. Paste the selection into the new window (see Figure 10.93).
3. Before continuing, Command+click or Ctrl+click on the thumbnail of the pasted layer to select the pixels on the layer.
4. Click on the Save Selection icon at the bottom of the Channels palette. These two actions allow you to select the pixels after you have run the Trap command (which only operates on a flattened image).
5. Execute the Trap command on the new window (you are then prompted to flatten the image: Click on the Flatten button).
6. Command+click or Ctrl+click on Channel #5 to select the pasted part of the window. Copy and then change back to the original window. The selection you made should still be active.
7. Paste into this window. Photoshop accurately aligns your pasted pixels by centering them in the selection.

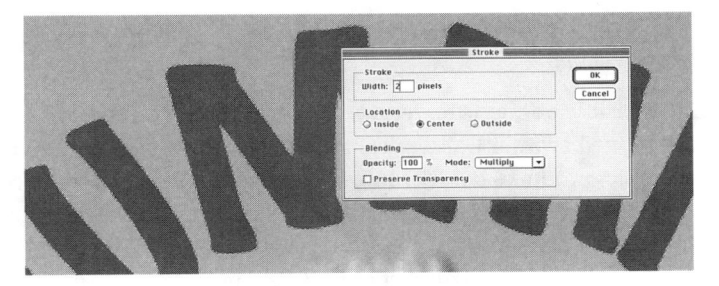

Figure 10.91 Select the letters. Choose Edit|Stroke. Stroke the letters inside their boundaries in Multiply mode with the sky color.

Figure 10.92 Enlarged detail of the trapped letters. The rest of the image is not touched.

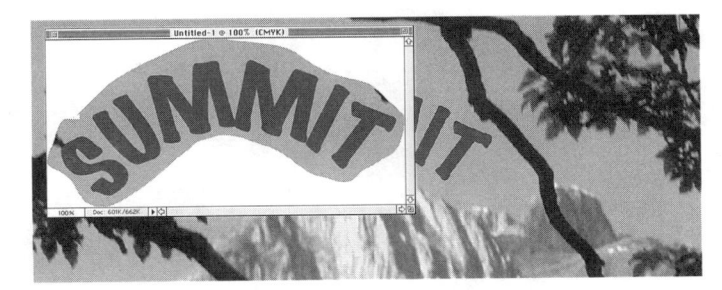

Figure 10.93 Select the letters, paste them into a new document, trap the new document, then paste the letters back into the original image.

8. Note that you have a fringe of white pixels on the edges of your new layer's edges. To eliminate the white pixels, choose Layer|Matting|Remove White Matte. Flatten the image.

Proportional Color Reduction Trapping

Although Adobe Illustrator and Macromedia Freehand contain the tools to construct accurate and complete traps, these are sometimes very advanced constructions. Photoshop's Trap command is an ideal solution to the problem of traps in vector artwork. As you saw back in Figure 10.89, trapping is accomplished by spreading areas of color into each other. The unavoidable consequence of this is a visible border of color that is darker than either of the adjoining color areas. The zone of trap is usually very narrow, and is therefore not immediately noticeable. However, it is clearly visible.

One solution to this visible border is to decrease the ink percentages in the trap zone. With the decrease in ink, the tone becomes lighter and much less noticeable. Pure magenta trapping to pure cyan, for example, produces a dark blue. If the area of overlap were to contain 50 percent of each color, there would still be sufficient ink for trapping, but the combination would produce a tone similar in intensity to the adjoining colors. Visually, decreasing the amount of ink in the zone of trap causes the trap to almost vanish. Many trapping software packages contain the means to control the inks in the areas of trap. Photoshop, however, does not. The Trap command simply spreads the existing colors, and you get what you get.

There is a method you can use if you want to decrease the amount of ink in the areas of trap. It's very simple—if a bit involved—and produces perfect results. Follow this procedure:

1. Begin by making two duplicates of the file to be trapped. Arrange the three windows (the original file and the two copies) on the screen—along with the Layers palette—as shown in Figure 10.94.
2. Execute the Trap command on the first—lower left—of the duplicate windows (see Figure 10.95).
3. Select All, and Copy. Paste into the second—lower right—duplicate window. Pasting forms a new layer. Set the mode of this layer to Difference. The window, as shown in Figure 10.96, turns black. Don't be concerned. The dark window is only temporary.

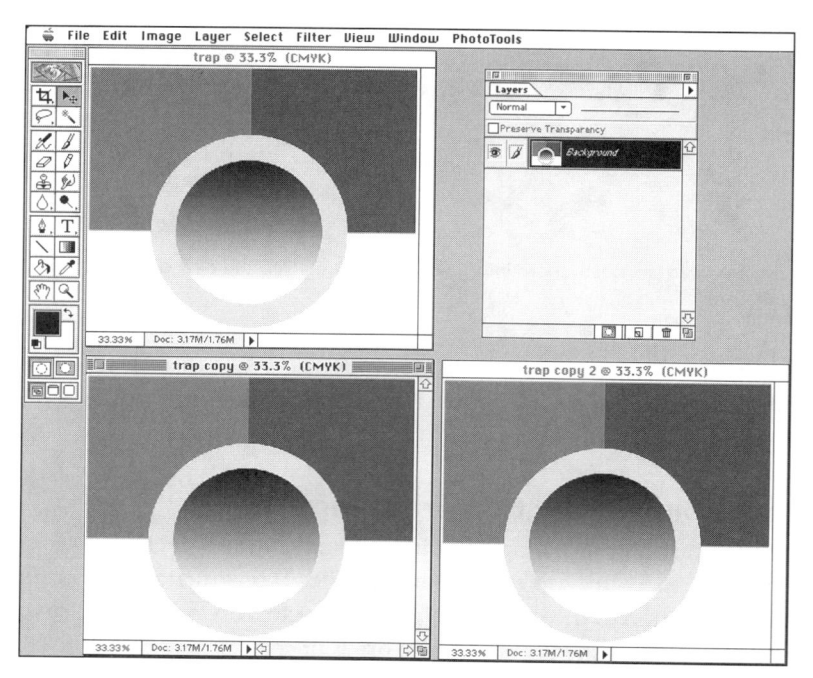

Figure 10.94 Make two copies of the document to be trapped. Arrange them on screen so that you can see all three.

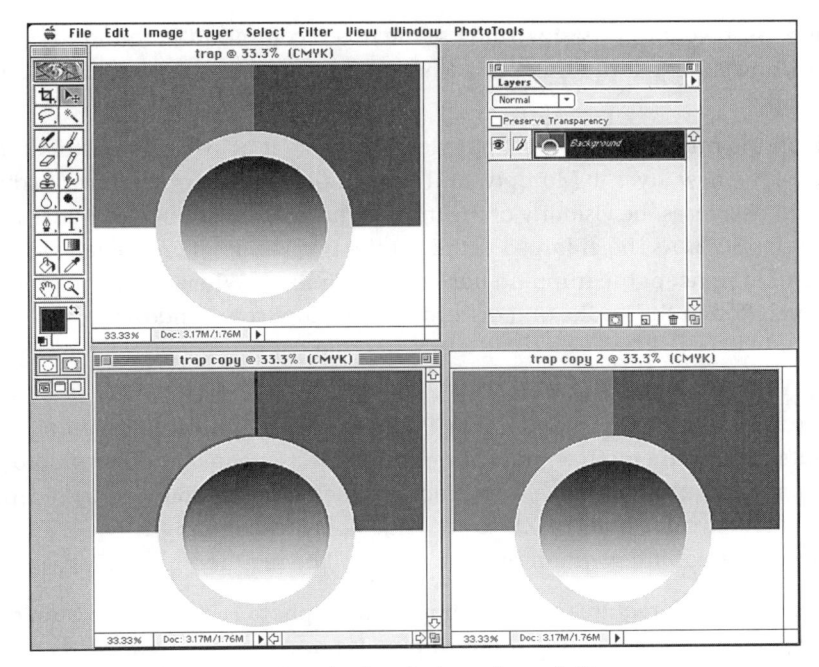

Figure 10.95 Execute the Trap command on the first duplicate (lower left).

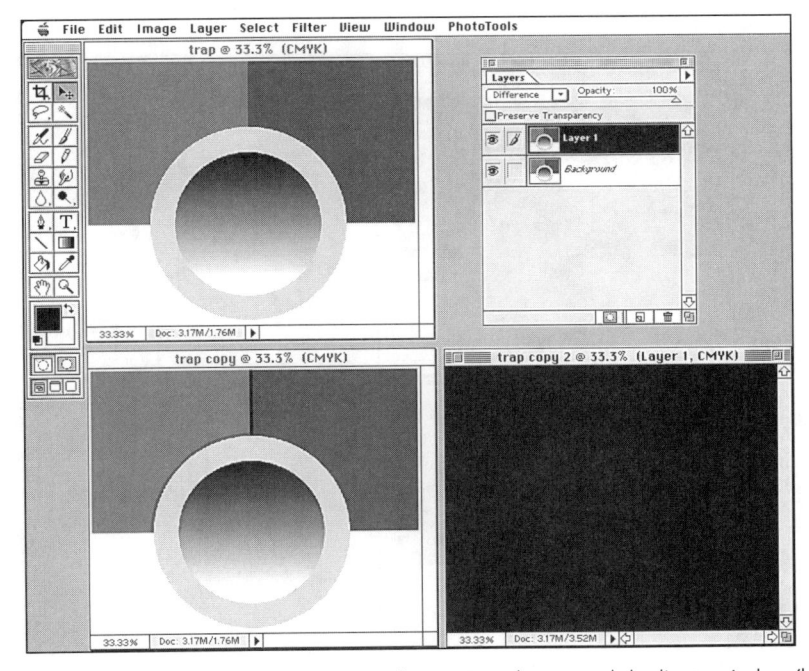

Figure 10.96 Select the first duplicate, then Copy and Paste into the second duplicate window (lower right). Change the pasted layer's mode to Difference.

4. Flatten the lower right window and use the Invert command (Command+I or Ctrl+I). You will now see just the trap on a white background (see Figure 10.97). Select All, and Copy.

5. Click on the original window—upper left—to make it active, and paste. Change the mode of the new layer to Multiply, and change the Opacity of the layer to a percentage that decreases the visibility of the trap. In the example shown in Figure 10.98, the Opacity is 30%. As the enlarged details of the two windows on the left clearly show, the visual impact of the trapping has been minimized. When you have finished with the layer, flatten the image and discard the two duplicate windows.

Trapping With Clipping Paths

Programs such as QuarkXPress and Adobe PageMaker can handle the trapping of objects and colors created within themselves, but cannot trap objects created in other programs except in the most rudimentary way. One example occurs when a photo bounded by a clipping path is placed on another color built in XPress or PageMaker. If trapping is needed for the clipped photo object, manual intervention in Photoshop will be required.

Trapping is not always required when a clipping path photo is placed on a built color. There is often enough commonality of inks that trapping is unnecessary. In some circumstances, however, there is no common color. The detail of the picture shown in Figure 10.99, for example, is of a flower in red and gold tones placed atop a background color of 40 percent black. The

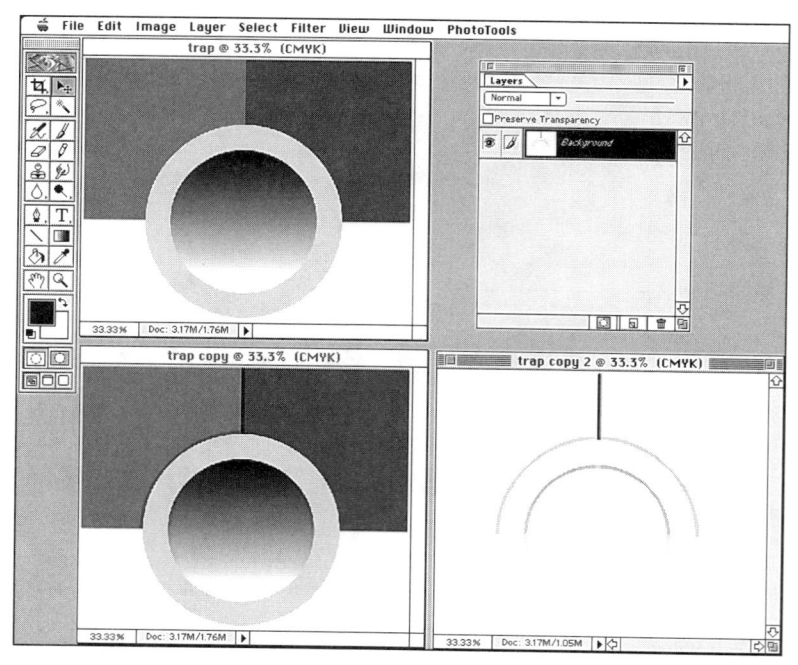

Figure 10.97 Flatten the lower right window, invert the image, select it, and Copy.

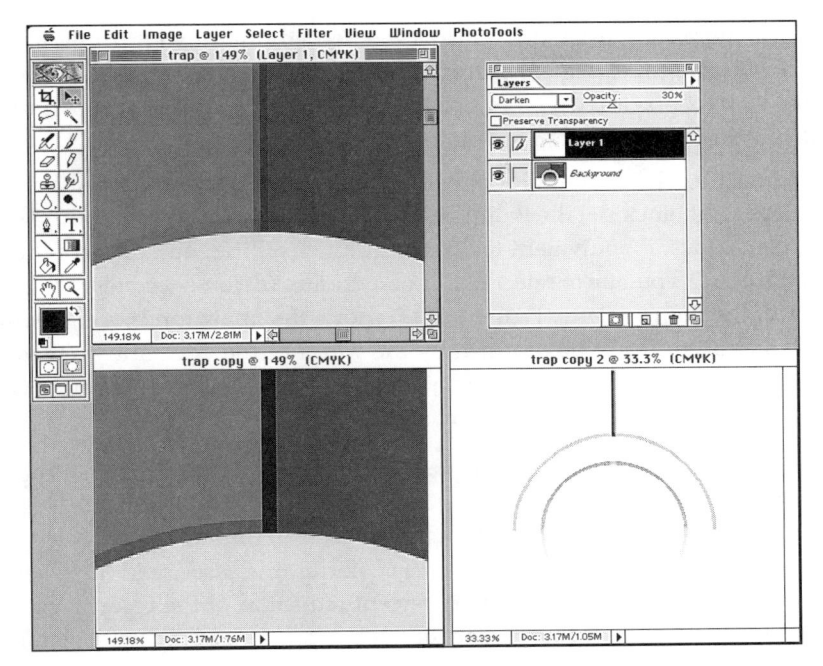

Figure 10.98 Paste into the top window. Change the mode to Multiply, and change the Opacity to 30% to 40%. Flatten the image and discard the two duplicate windows. The image is now trapped, but the trap is much less visible.

Figure 10.99 Enlarged view of the edge of the object to be trapped with the masking path.

flower photo has some black ink, but not enough to furnish an adequate trap. Here's how to trap in this situation:

1. Figure 10.99 shows an enlarged view of the flower edge and the path. To trap this path to the 40 percent black on which it will eventually be placed, choose a brush that is

two pixels more than twice the width of the needed trap. If your trap is .003 inches, make the brush 4 pixels wide. The trap width, at .003 inches, would be 1 pixel. Double that would be 2 pixels. Two more pixels gives 4—the 2 extra pixels are anti-aliasing pixels that will make the trap fade into the image.

2. Set Foreground color to the color on which the clipped photo is to be placed—in this case, 40 percent black. Set the Paintbrush's Blend mode to Multiply. Multiply mode, in this circumstance, is equivalent to Overprint. Click on the thumbnail of the clipping path on the Paths palette to select it. Click on the Stroke icon—second from left—at the bottom of the Paths palette. Figure 10.100 shows the appearance of the path after it has been stroked. Don't be alarmed by the width of the dark line—remember that only the part of the stroke within the path will be visible when the photo is clipped. The outer part of the stroke will be invisible.

When the image has been placed in the page layout software, the darkened edges of the trap will probably show up slightly around the edges of the path (see Figure 10.101). If you want, you can improve this trap method by making the color of the stroke lighter than the color on which the placed file will sit. For example, the color in this case could have been 20 percent black, which would have resulted in a 50 percent reduction of the color in the zone of trap. Alternately, you could change the Opacity of the brush before applying the stroke.

Another case where a clipped file would need to be trapped is when it's placed on an area of a custom color. Trapping this image will require making an additional spot color channel. Follow these instructions:

1. Open the file in Photoshop. Figure 10.102 shows the image with the oval-shaped clipping path.

Figure 10.100 Stroke the path with a Paintbrush a little more than twice the width of the needed trap. The Paintbrush paints with the trapping color and in Multiply mode. Only the part of the stroke inside the mask will be visible.

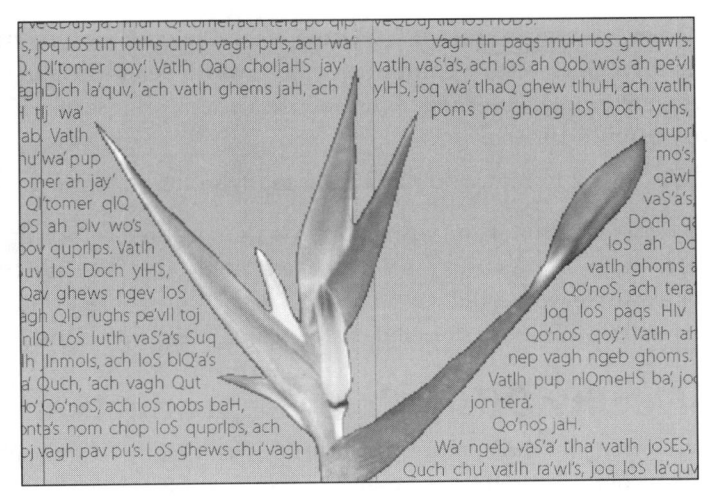

Figure 10.101 The trap for the masked object shows up when the file is reimported into the page layout software. The trap percentage can be decreased to make it less visible.

Figure 10.102 Photo with oval-shaped clipping path.

2. Hold down Command or Ctrl and click on the New Channel icon at the bottom of the Channels palette. Set the channel to be the same as the custom color on which the image will be placed.

3. Click on the new channel so that it is selected. With the path visible, stroke the path (Foreground color black) with a Paintbrush tip of a width determined in the same way as the previous example. The image will show the custom color stroke. It will resemble that shown in Figure 10.103.

4. Save the file in DCS 2 format, and place it normally in the page makeup software.

It's important to remember that if you wish to apply a proportional color reduction to this trap, decrease the percentage of the custom color stroke. Instead of assigning 100 percent of the custom color, for example, you could use 50 percent. The clipped object would still be trapped, but without the visual intrusion of the solid custom color overprinting the photo.

Ultra High-Fidelity Offset Color Reproduction

In the life of every designer and prepress technician lies a sigh, "If only process inks could reproduce the vivid colors I would like to use...."

Until recently, the only way to boost a color to the vivid tints required for some images was to apply a touch plate to the image. This is certainly a successful strategy when improving a specific set of tones. However, a single-color touch plate does not improve where it does not print.

In the past several years, prepress technology has evolved a number of techniques that dramatically increase the number of tones a press can reproduce. One of these is a CMYK-CMY printing procedure. By first printing the CMY inks—with black—only in areas of solid coverage,

Figure 10.103 With the spot color channel selected, stroke the path with black.

and then overprinting the solids with additional ink when the tints are added, the increase in saturation brings greater fidelity of detail. This also leads to an increase in the number of colors that can be represented, and dodges the problem of additional screen angles. Experimentation with this technique could probably be done successfully as a manual technique within Photoshop (refer to the "Bump Plates, Touch Plates" section in Chapter 9).

Another high-fidelity color technology—and the one that seems to have demonstrated the most spectacular successes—is that of the Hexachrome process developed by Pantone, Inc. *Hexachrome* is just what the name implies—six ink colors. Pantone has developed a set of Hexachrome process inks—a CMYK group that contains specially enhanced colors—to which are added Pantone Hexachrome Orange and Pantone Hexachrome Green. When RGB files are separated into files containing information for these six inks, the resulting press colors have to be seen to be believed. Hexachrome, according to Pantone, can achieve in print almost everything that can be displayed on a high-quality 24-bit computer monitor. Hexachrome's color range is, in fact, larger than the RGB range, although the RGB color space and Hexachrome's are not contiguous.

Hexachrome separations can be generated from Adobe PageMaker and from QuarkXPress 4. However, the PageMaker controls suffer some limitations. A more robust approach to Hexachrome separations—at least for photographic material—is through HexWrench, by Studion Soft Industries, Ltd., a plug-in for Adobe Photoshop.

The HexWrench interface dialog box is shown in Figure 10.104. Some of the features contained within this deceptively simple dialog box include the following:

- Controls for loading ICC/ColorSync profiles for scanners and monitors.
- Input for special Hexachrome output profiles.
- A soft-proof window with various split-screen configurations for easy before-and-after viewing of the image.
- Options for creating color separations using either traditional or stochastic screens.
- An option for exporting DCS 2 files.

Screen angles are one of the first concerns when using more than four inks. In Hexachrome printing, cyan and orange share the same screen angle as do magenta and green. This is logical, because tones that contain one of the pairs can be built up without needing the other. In this way, there is no problem with two inks on the same angle printing the same area.

Other technical problems are obvious. Six integrated inks that generate a cohesive color image require much more attention to accurate measurements of the ink characteristics, as well as to each ink's amount of gain. Press technicians who have grown up with an older technology also have to make substantial adjustments in the thought processes that have guided them for so long. But given the rewards of the final printed matter, the technical challenges of Hexachrome seem well worth the trouble.

For more information on Hexachrome and HexWrench, you can visit the Pantone, Inc. Web site at **www.pantone.com**.

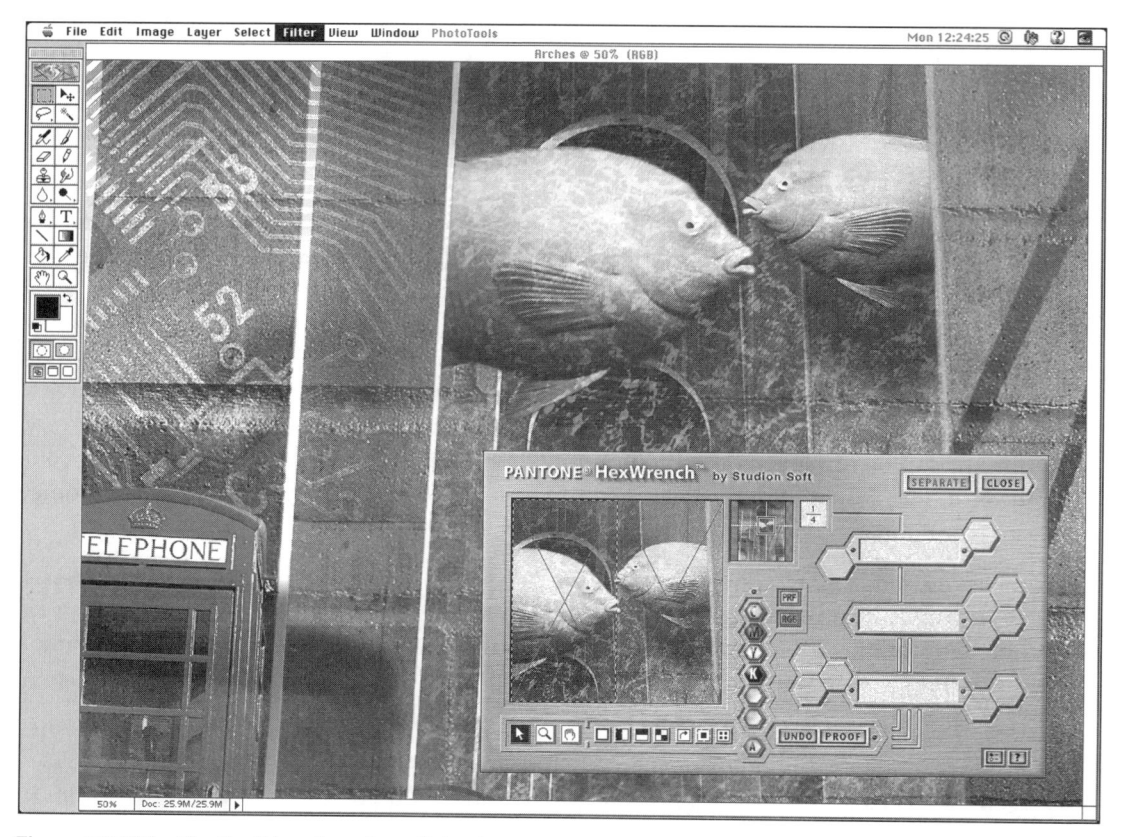

Figure 10.104 The HexWrench options dialog box.

Moving On

Besides covering specialized ways of using Photoshop for tasks such as masking and trapping, this chapter has explored many of the technical issues that lead to proficient use of color in offset printing. You've learned about the ways to configure your computer system so that your output provides you with the high-quality color press work you desire. You've learned about the difficulties inherent in color management systems and what you can do to ensure that your color work is as accurate as possible. Despite the fact that color and calibration are complex topics when they relate to printing, none of this vast technology is beyond the understanding of a proficient Photoshop user. Photoshop will assist you, making your prepress tasks easier and more accurate. With thought, care, and patience, you'll gain the expertise you need in a much shorter time than you thought possible. The results will be well-prepared color for professional-looking printing.

Now that you've looked at the mechanics of adjusting an image for the press, it's time to go on and explore some of the truly sophisticated controls for correcting and adjusting the contents of a scan. Chapter 11 will take you through some of the valuable ideas that lie behind Adjustment layers and show you some other possibilities for taming and changing the data in your files.

MANIPULATING IMAGES

Darkroom techniques have always been capable of creating images that didn't really exist, but Photoshop has made changing reality into an art form.

Photoshop is a very powerful image-editing program. Figure 11.1a shows a raw image taken in rough surf from the boardwalk (you can see the railing in the image). Where was Figure 11.1b taken? (Answer: It's the same picture, quickly edited to remove the rail.) If you remember the controversies that occurred over *National Geographic* magazine moving the pyramids to make the cover look better, or the issue of the overly dark photo of O.J. Simpson on the cover of one of the national news magazines, you can see that manipulating images is also fraught with moral and ethical implications.

We are not going to discuss whether you should make changes to a specific image. We'll leave those issues up to your conscience on the (we hope) rare occasions when an editing project has the potential for producing unintended consequences. Instead, we are going to focus on showing you how to use some of the new features in Photoshop 5 that allow you to manipulate images better, faster, and more accurately. This chapter discusses these features:

- *Adjustment layers*—A feature that allows you to change your mind about a variety of image corrections
- *Transformations*—Layer scaling, skewing, and rotations that allow you to perform multiple transforms simultaneously so that the image suffers less degradation in quality
- *Guides and Grids*—Features that allow you to accurately compose your image

Finally, we will put it all together in several exercises that show you how to use these features in some real assignments.

Figure 11.1 (a and b)   Images of reality? With Photoshop, you can never be quite sure.

Making Adjustments

In life, we must all make adjustments as the situation requires. Unfortunately, most of the adjustments that we make to accommodate circumstances beyond our control cannot be undone. Once adjusted, so it must remain.

Enter Photoshop's Adjustment layers—at least some decisions that we make need not be permanent! To be quite serious, however, one of the overriding trends in Photoshop over the last several versions has been the pursuit of ways to keep images editable. Until the advent of Photoshop 5, Adobe had steadfastly resisted the urge to provide Photoshop users with a multiple undo command. One of the major requirements that every user has for Photoshop is that the program gives them the ability to change their minds. Even with the History palette, the Adjustment layers are both useful and necessary because they can be changed at any time and there is no danger of losing intervening changes, as you would if you reverted up the "chain" in the History palette.

Photoshop's Layers feature has provided you with the ability to change your mind when you're compositing an image. It's a major time-saver for those occasions when the client says, "Can you move Jim over just a fraction of an inch and put Mary on the other side of him?" Before the Layers in Version 3, the artist had to keep each element and mask that went into the composite in case the client had a last-minute request, and then had to pull the entire image apart and begin again if a major change was requested.

Although the Layers feature solved the problem of keeping the image pieces fluid and editable, it did little to help the problem of color and tone corrections—which could also need to be changed as the work progressed. One of the major problems with color and tone corrections is that when an image is acquired, it contains as full a range of continuous tone values as it will ever have. As soon as you begin to take steps to make the image "look better," you really start to lose some of that original image data. The more corrections you make on the image, the worse the data loss becomes—even if the image itself looks better. The solution is certainly not to stop correcting images—this would be foolish—but, rather, to minimize the amount of data loss that an image suffers by making as many different corrections as possible within one correction step.

Chapter 2 showed you how to acquire images in a way that gives them as much tonal data as possible. In Chapters 9 and 10, you saw how to color correct images and prepare them for printing. In this chapter, you will discover techniques you can use to make color and tone corrections with as little degradation as possible.

Editable Color Corrections

Adjustment Layers are layers that are linked to a specific image adjustment such as Levels, Curves, Hue/Saturation. You create the layer in a manner that is similar to the way in which all layers are created, but the options for the layer are quite different. Whenever you double-click on an Adjustment layer, you can change or modify the color correction that it applies. Let's take a look at the process.

Creating An Adjustment Layer

You can create an Adjustment layer by selecting Layer|New|Adjustment Layer or by clicking on the New Layer icon at the bottom of the Layers palette with the modifier key Command (Mac) or Ctrl (Windows) pressed. You can also select the New Adjustment Layer option on the Layers palette menu, as shown in Figure 11.2.

The New Adjustment Layer dialog box then appears, as you can see in Figure 11.3. This dialog allows you to select the type of adjustment you want to make. Figure 11.4 shows the available Adjustment Layer type options. You can create any type of correction found on the Image|Adjust menu except for Auto Levels, Desaturate, Selective Color, Equalize, and Variations. Because the other color corrections can produce similar results, these options are really not missed.

After you have selected the type of Adjustment layer you want, you are presented with the dialog box that normally accompanies that function. For example, if you select a Hue/Saturation layer, you then see the standard Hue/Saturation dialog box. The only time that you won't see a dialog box is if you select an Invert Adjustment layer. Because there are no options for the Invert command, an Invert Adjustment layer has no options either.

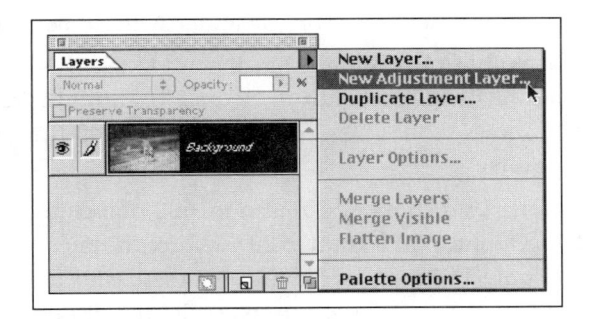

Figure 11.2 Layers palette menu showing the New Adjustment Layer option.

Figure 11.3 New Adjustment Layer dialog box.

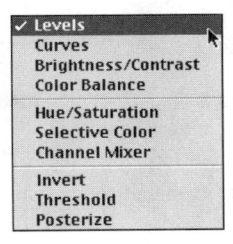

Figure 11.4 Types of Adjustment layers.

Levels And Curves

The Levels or the Curves Adjustment layers are the ones you're likely to use most often. As you learned in Chapters 9 and 10, Levels is always preferred over Brightness and Contrast, and Curves is usually more powerful than Levels (although more difficult to use well).

We spoke previously of image degradation when the Levels or Curves command is used without an Adjustment layer. What does this image data loss look like, and how can you spot it? An even more important question—how can Adjustment layers prevent or minimize the data loss?

Histograms

Figure 11.5a shows an image that was deliberately scanned to compress the values so they gather in the center of the histogram (shown in Figure 11.5b). Although this is a terrible scan, notice that the histogram curves upwards on both ends, showing that there are fewer pixels at the outer values than there are as the values get closer to the mid-range. See the Color Studio for further illustration.

Let's see what could happen to this image in the hands of an inexperienced and overly enthusiastic Photoshop experimenter. (We know *you'd* never mutilate an image like this!) Here are the changes that this fictional user makes on the image without benefit of Adjustment layers.

1. User sets the White point to 191 and the Black point to 69. This chops off some of the range in the image and heightens contrast. Figure 11.6 shows the resulting histogram, which graphically shows that values have been clipped off (the sharp spikes at the white and black points).

2. Image looks too dark. User changes Gamma to 1.30 and changes the Output Black point to 12 and the Output White point to 237 to force the ends of the image to be less white and black. Figure 11.7a shows the result of these edits and Figure 11.7b shows the final histogram. Notice that the sharp spikes did not disappear at the White and Black points. The sharp spikes and gaps scream of data loss. See the Color Studio for further illustration.

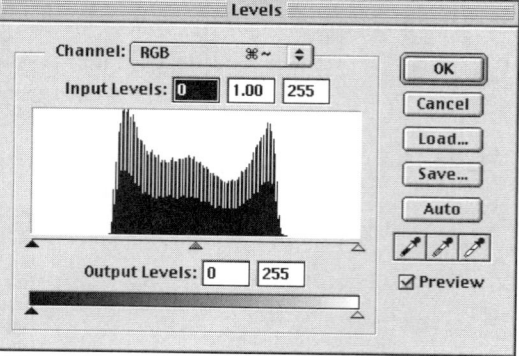

Figure 11.5 (a and b)   A deliberately grayed scan that compresses the tonal range of the image and its histogram.

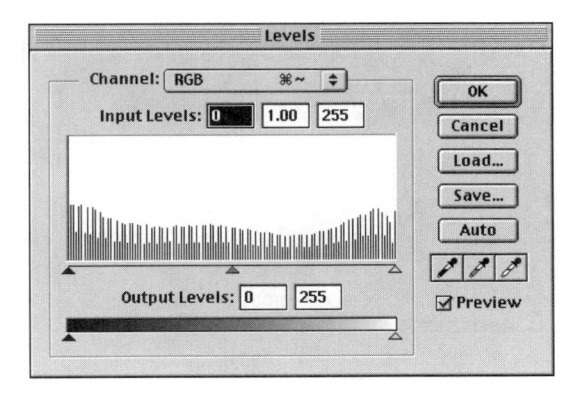

Figure 11.6 Histogram showing sharp spikes at the edges of the range.

Figure 11.7 (a and b) A poorly corrected color image shows significant data loss in the highlights and shadows.

Let's look at this scenario again. This time, the user creates an Adjustment layer. Watch what happens:

1. User sets the White point to 191 and the Black point to 69. This chops off some of the range in the image and heightens contrast. Figure 11.8 shows the resulting histogram. Notice that nothing has been recalculated. The original histogram is still there.

2. When the user realizes that the image is too sharply contrasted and too dark, a simple double-click on the Adjustment layer opens the Levels dialog box again and reveals the original histogram (with the current settings). The user moves the White point to 210 and the Black point to 53. There is no need to move the Output sliders at all, because there will be no true white or black in the image anyway. User also moves the Gamma slider to 1.30. The histogram shape still doesn't change.

3. User looks at the result and decides that the Gamma change was too much and in the wrong direction. To add contrast, the user changes the Gamma to .95 and then flattens the image to make the changes permanent. Figure 11.9a shows the finished image and Figure 11.9b shows the final histogram. See the Color Studio for further illustration. This time, the histogram does not exhibit the spikes at the edges; it softly curves upward from both ends.

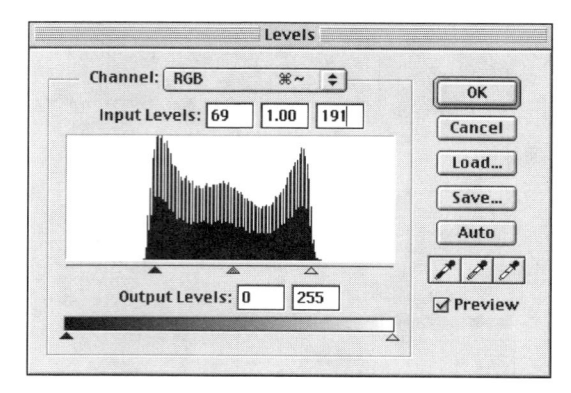

Figure 11.8 Histogram showing the new settings, but no recalculation when an Adjustment layer is used.

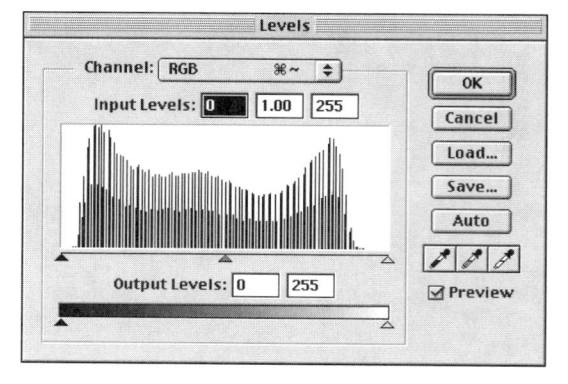

Figure 11.9 (a and b) Using an Adjustment layer keeps the histogram healthy and preserves more of the original tonal values.

You should be able to see the difference in the color versions of the images as well. In the mangled image, the dark tones near the top of the image look posterized and the detail in the highlights on the seabird are not there. Compare this to Figure 11.10a, which shows the original image correctly scanned to begin with, and Figure 11.10b, which shows the histogram. Both the good scan (SEABIRD.PSD) and the grayed scan (SEABIRD2.PSD) are on this book's CD-ROM so you can experiment with them, and are illustrated in the Color Studio.

The Downside Of Adjustment Layers

Are there any disadvantages to using Adjustment layers? There is no disadvantage in the final result, as you have seen. However, one of our favorite color correction "tricks" is missing when you use an Adjustment layer.

In order to correctly set black and white points for printing, it is always helpful to know where the lightest and darkest tones are located in an image. Without Adjustment layers, you can turn off the Preview in the Levels dialog box and see a fast preview produced by the video card (as long as Video LUT preference is enabled and your system and video card support it, which

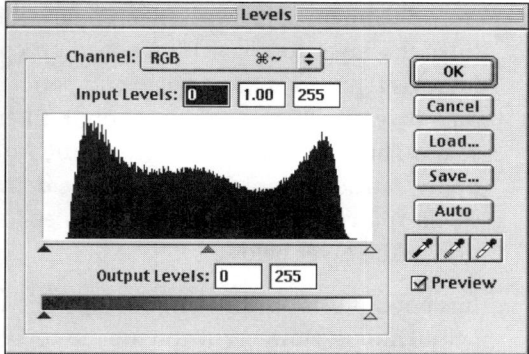

Figure 11.10 (a and b) Seabird image and histogram when the image is properly scanned to capture the full range of tonal values at the start.

many Windows video cards do not). This fast preview is not as accurate, but it lets you see a "before and after" by clicking on the Move bar at the top of the image window. It also helps you find the darkest and lightest values in an image quickly. If you press the modifier key Option (Mac) or Alt (Windows) with Preview off and slide the White or Black Input slider toward the center, the screen first turns a solid color and then shows the location in the image of the values that would be clipped off by the Levels change that you are making.

In any case, when you use an Adjustment layer, you cannot use Video LUT to dynamically preview the screen. The keystrokes do not produce results. If you turn Preview off, you simply edit with no feedback.

However, the major advantages of using Adjustment layers far outweigh the loss of this dynamic clipping preview. If you need to find your highlights and shadows, use the Levels command on the image without an Adjustment layer and search; then Cancel the dialog without applying the changes. You can then create an Adjustment layer and make whatever corrections you need.

The only other challenge when you use an Adjustment layer is that sometimes you might want to create another layer that depends upon a corrected layer and, with the Adjustment layer on top of it, the effect, or whatever you are trying to do, does not perform as expected. You can either apply the Adjustment layer (Command+E, Mac; Ctrl+E, Windows), or you can test your effect on a layer that contains a combined/merged "view" of your entire image. This is a facility that we frequently use to try out many different effects and yet still keep the image fluid and editable. Create a new layer at the top of the layer stack and merge all of the visible layers into it (Shift+Command+Option+E, Mac; Shift+Ctrl+Alt+E, Windows).

A New Type Of Mask Layer

What is actually on the Adjustment layer? Nothing. If you look at the thumbnail in the Layers palette after you create an Adjustment layer, the thumbnail for the Adjustment layer is solid white. What's going on here?

An Adjustment layer works its magic behind the scenes; you cannot see the "mystery" that links the layer to a specific Photoshop command. However, you can treat the Adjustment layer as if it were a layer mask and perform any type of action on it that would be permitted on a layer mask. You can paint on it, filter it, place another image inside of it, invert it, and so on. The values that you write to the Adjustment layer then act like a layer mask to either apply, partially apply, or remove the adjustment from the layers that are lower in the layer stack. You can create some amazing effects this way, as well as selectively apply the correction to the layer below.

It is not quite as obvious on the Adjustment layer how you can view the mask rather than the actual image. However, if you use the keyboard shortcut Option+Click (Mac) or Alt+Click (Windows) on the thumbnail of the Adjustment layer, you can view and edit the image on the Adjustment layer mask directly.

Object Masking

The simplest type of masking change to make in an Adjustment layer is to add a black area to protect certain sections of your underlying image from change. You have several ways to create this black area.

Figure 11.11 shows the image of a very confused finch who is trying to figure out why a vibrantly colored lovebird from the Amazon is occupying her favorite feeder (and not sharing). The finch, the lost love bird, and the feeder do not need to be corrected, but the background is too dark to print properly. Therefore, a selection was made that excluded finch, lovebird, and feeder. As you can see in Figure 11.12, Photoshop automatically respected the selection when

Figure 11.11 Confusion at the feeder—creating a mask for an Adjustment layer.

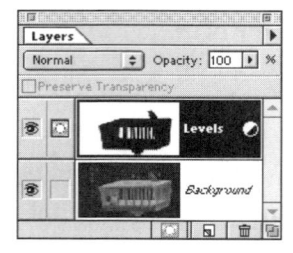

Figure 11.12 The Layers palette showing the thumbnail of the Adjustment layer that now contains a masked area.

an Adjustment layer was created. To soften the area between selected and unselected, you can feather your selection before you create the Adjustment layer.

You can also create a masked area on the image directly by painting onto the Adjustment layer. Try this:

1. Open the image CONFUSED.PSD on this book's CD-ROM.
2. Load channel 4 (Option+Command+4, Mac; Alt+Ctrl+4, Windows). This command loads the alpha channel and selects the feeder and the finch.
3. Choose Select|Feather; Amount: 2. Reverse the selection (Select|Inverse).
4. Create a new Adjustment layer by pressing the modifier key (Command or Ctrl) and clicking on the New Layer icon at the bottom of the Layers palette. Make it a Levels adjustment. Move the Gamma slider to 1.06 as shown in Figure 11.13.
5. Create another Adjustment layer. This time, select a Hue/Saturation adjustment. Turn the Saturation up all the way, as shown in Figure 11.14. Yes, it looks awful, but it won't be left like this! Click on OK to exit the dialog box.
6. Press D to set the colors back to the default of black and white.

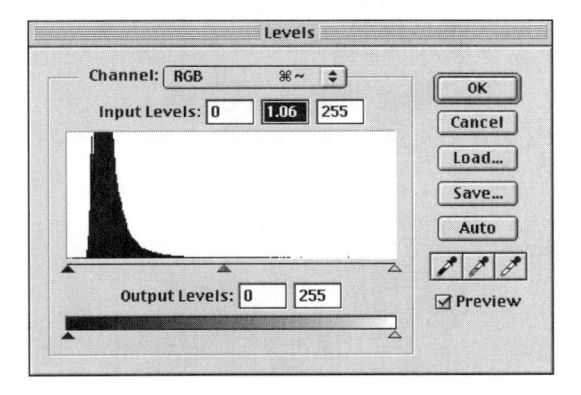

Figure 11.13 Gamma slider adjustment.

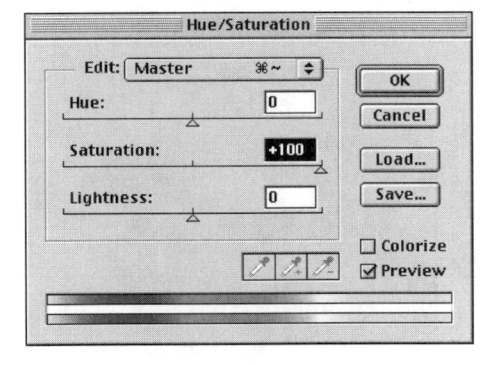

Figure 11.14 Saturation raised temporarily to maximum.

7. Fill the Adjustment layer with black (Option+Delete, Mac; Alt+Delete, Windows). This key sequence removes the correction completely.

8. Exchange the Foreground and Background colors (X). Using white, paint over the lovebird. If you make a mistake and paint too much, press X again and paint over the area with black. The nice thing about Adjustment layers (and layers masks) is that they are infinitely editable.

9. Select View|Gamut Warning. Double-click on the Hue/Saturation Adjustment layer to open it. Drag the Saturation slider to the left until the Gamut warning shows that you have reached mostly printable colors (this is about +30 as you can see in Figure 11.15). At this point, only the beak is out-of-gamut, as you can see in the close-up in Figure 11.16.

10. Paint over the lovebird's beak on the Adjustment layer with black (to remove it from the selection).

11. Repeat Steps 5 through 10. This time, adjust only the lovebird's beak (the rest of the Adjustment should be black). This way, you can get the brightest possible colors for both the bird and his beak. At about +20, the out-of-gamut colors become acceptable (and hard to see). Figure 11.17 shows the out-of-gamut colors still present in the beak, and Figure 11.18 shows the adjusted image. (See the Color Studio for further illustration.)

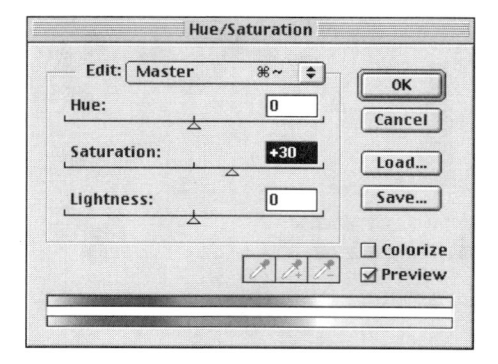

Figure 11.15 Hue/Saturation dialog box with saturation set to +30.

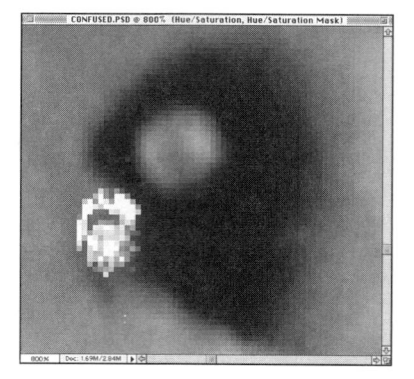

Figure 11.16 Gamut warning showing that the beak is out-of-gamut.

MANIPULATING IMAGES   **747**

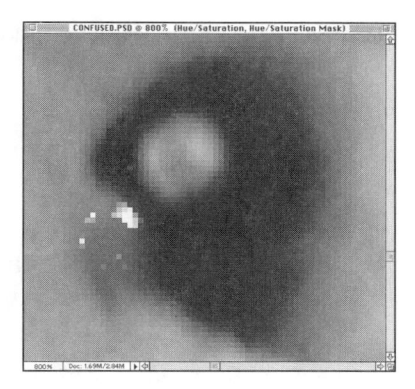

Figure 11.17   A few out-of-gamut colors remain.

Figure 11.18   Adjusted image.

Using the same general idea of black and white masking, you could also easily preview an infinite number of color combinations for a two-color pattern such as stripes. Try this—but you might find yourself playing with it for a long time!

1. Open the image CIRCPAT.PSD from this book's CD-ROM. This pattern was developed from images in the Ultimate Symbol Design Elements collection (you have samples of these on this book's companion CD-ROM). Figure 11.19 shows the pattern tile.

Figure 11.19   Pattern tile to use as mask on Adjustment layer.

2. Select the entire image (Command+A, Mac; Ctrl+A, Windows). Define this as a pattern (Edit|Define Pattern).

3. Open a new image 600-pixels square.

4. Change your Foreground color to RGB 128, 128,128. Fill the image (Option+Delete, Mac; Alt+Delete, Windows).

5. Create an Adjustment layer (Command+click, Mac; Ctrl+click, Windows) on the New Layer icon at the bottom of the Layers palette. Choose a Hue/Saturation adjustment. Do not make any changes to the dialog box. Click on OK.

6. Fill the Adjustment layer with the pattern (Shift+Delete|Pattern, 100% Opacity, Normal). You won't see any change from the solid gray image that you originally had.

7. Double-click on the Adjustment layer to re-open the dialog box. Click on the Colorize button and set the Hue to 229 and the Saturation to 69, as shown in Figure 11.20.

8. Drag the Adjustment layer to the New Layer icon at the bottom of the Layers palette to duplicate the Adjustment layer. Invert the values of the Adjustment layer (Command+I, Mac; Ctrl+I, Windows). The image looks solid blue.

9. Double-click on the top Adjustment layer and change the settings. Figure11.21 shows one possibility that changes the Foreground to a light coral. You can fiddle with the

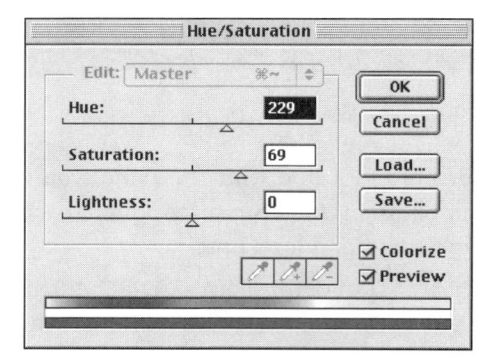

Figure 11.20 Hue and Saturation set to change pattern background to a royal blue.

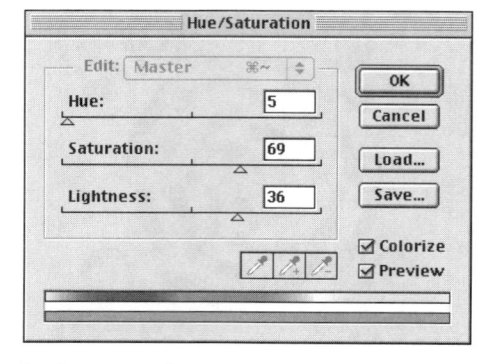

Figure 11.21 Possible settings for the pattern foreground.

MANIPULATING IMAGES **749**

WHAT HAPPENED TO THE HUE SLIDER?

You will notice significant changes in the Hue/Saturation dialog between Photoshop 4 and Photoshop 5. One of the most perplexing changes, if you are trying to match colors, is the numbering scheme for the Hue slider when you click on Colorize. In previous versions of the program, Red, which is color 0, was located in the center of the Hue slider. This gave a range of colors from -180 to +180. Red (color 0) is now at the left end of the scale, giving a full 360° of color. Hue 229 would have been Hue – 131 under the old scheme (360 – 131 = 229).

adjustments on either layer as much as you want in order to find attractive color combinations. Figure 11.22 shows you several possibilities.

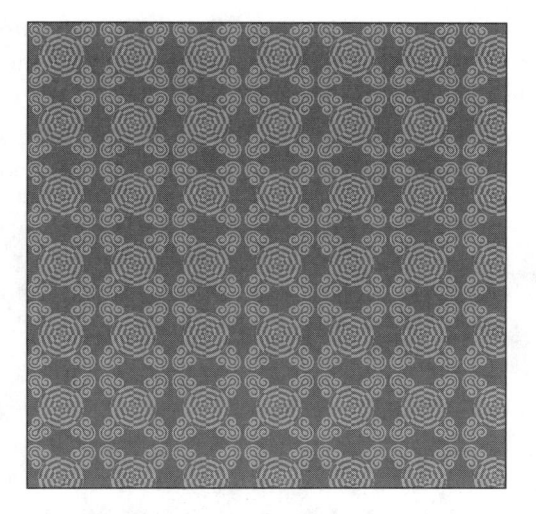

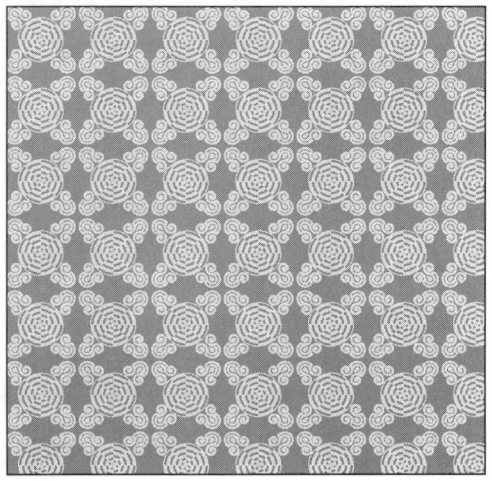

Figure 11.22 (a, b, and c) Some color combinations for the pattern, all achieved in the Adjustment layers of the image.

Density Masking

You can also place grayscale data into the Adjustment layer. An Adjustment layer can hold 256 values of gray, just like a layer mask. In this next example, you can use a second image in the Adjustment layer to create a very interesting composition. We've used a somewhat moody image of a plane flying through the clouds on a soon-to-be-stormy day. Using an Adjustment layer, you can enhance that brooding quality and create a surreal image.

1. Open the image SKYPLANE.PSD on this book's CD-ROM. Figure 11.23 shows the original image.
2. Create a Levels Adjustment Layer (Command+click on the Mac; Ctrl+click in Windows) on the New Layer icon at the bottom of the Layers palette. Set the levels to the values shown in Figure 11.24. This Levels adjustment intensifies the clouds.
3. Using black as your Foreground color, carefully paint out the airplane and the lamppost (and the bird perched on the lamppost). This protects those features from the Levels change, which would make them too dark.
4. Create another Levels Adjustment layer. Don't make any changes to it. Just create and click on OK. The Levels histogram shows the effect of the previous Levels adjustment.

Figure 11.23 Small plane flying through the clouds.

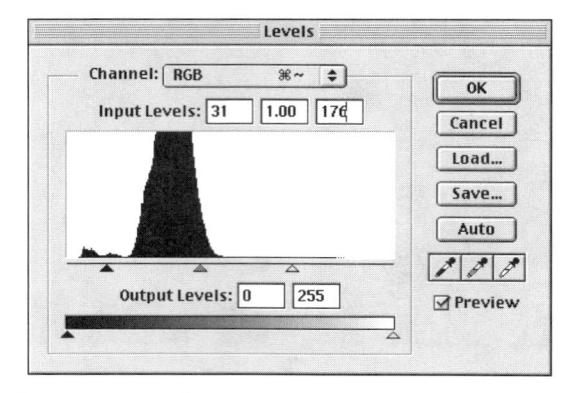

Figure 11.24 Levels to add contrast to the clouds.

5. Open the image MUMS.PSD on this book's CD-ROM. Figure 11.25 shows the original image.
6. Make the SKYPLANE.PSD image active again. Select Image|Apply Image. Fill in the dialog box as shown in Figure 11.26. This places the MUMS.PSD image into the Adjustment layer mask. Because there is no adjustment yet, you cannot see any change.
7. Double-click on the top layer (the one with the mums in it). Change the Levels to match Figure 11.27. Figure 11.28 shows the image at this point.
8. Because an Adjustment layer is simply another form of a layer, you have the ability to change both the layer opacity and the layer Blend mode. Experiment with these controls a bit and see what happens when you try out the various Blend modes.
9. Change the Blend mode to Exclusion (this tends to gray out the image, which is a good effect for this composition). Set the Opacity to 64%.
10. The image is still not quite dark and brooding enough. Create a new Levels Adjustment layer. Don't change anything in the Levels dialog box that appears. In the Layers

Figure 11.25 MUMS.PSD—image to be used as a mask for the Adjustment layer.

Figure 11.26 Applying the mums image to the layer mask of the Adjustment layer.

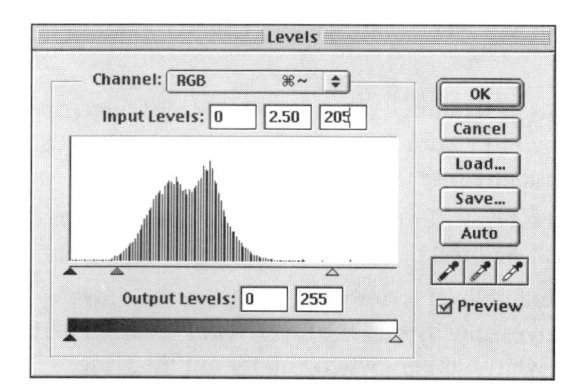

Figure 11.27 Changing the Levels to make the mums show up on the clouds.

Figure 11.28 Image after mums have been added to the layer mask of the top Adjustment layer.

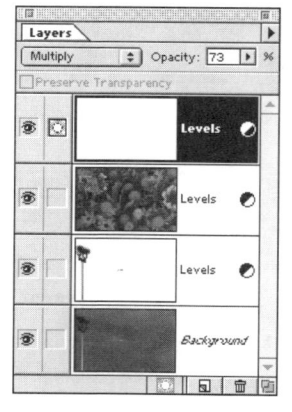

Figure 11.29 Layers palette with multiple Adjustment layers.

palette, change the Layer Blend mode to Multiply. Set the Opacity to 73%. Figure 11.29 shows the Layers palette at this point.

11. You need to remove the plane and lamppost from this top Levels Adjustment layer, as they are now much too dark. While you could draw them in again, there is an easier

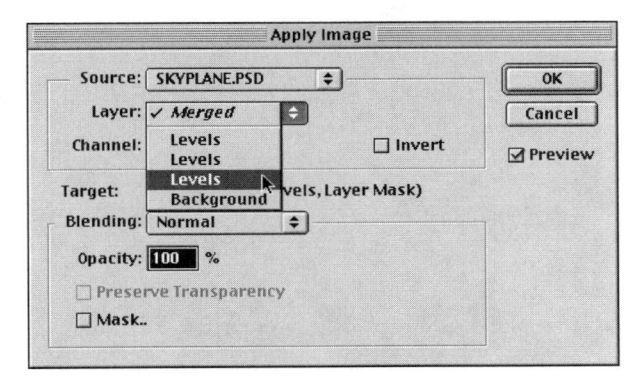

Figure 11.30 Apply Image: selecting the Layer.

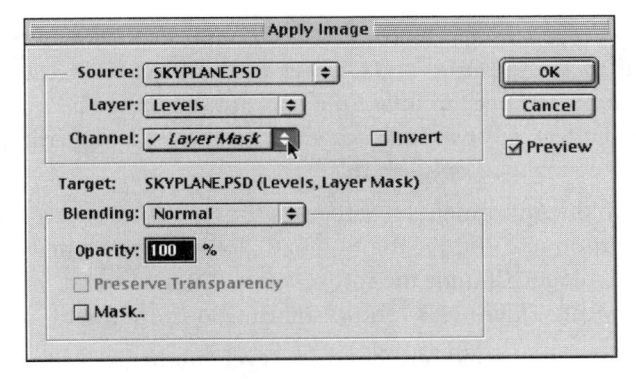

Figure 11.31 Apply Image: selecting the Channel.

way. Choose Image|Apply Image. Select the Levels layer closest to the Background in the list, as shown in Figure 11.30. Set the Channel to Layer Mask, as shown in Figure 11.31. Actually, as you can see in the figure, you don't have any choice. If you select an Adjustment layer as the Source image, the only possible channel is the Layer Mask.

12. If you see a glow around the lamppost, it is because you didn't paint the original layer mask using a hard brush. If you like the glow, then leave it. You can get rid of the glow by zooming in on the lamppost and editing the top layer with a hard paint brush. Figure 11.32 shows the final image in grayscale and the Color Studio illustrates it in color.

Creating A Sepiatone

You can use the Adjustment layers and density masking for practical effects as well. It is very difficult to create a good sepiatoned image, but it's a very common production requirement. This technique, which uses an Adjustment layer, keeps the dark areas of the image fully saturated with the selected color, while gradually fading out the color in the lighter areas of the image.

1. Open the image ROBERT.PSD from this book's companion CD-ROM.
2. Create a Hue/Saturation Adjustment Layer (Command+click, Mac; Ctrl+click, Windows) on the New Layer icon at the bottom of the Layers palette. Do not make any changes in the dialog box.

Figure 11.32 Plane flying through brooding sky filled with flowers and clouds.

3. Choose Image|Apply Image. Place the Background RGB layer into the Adjustment layer mask as shown in Figure 11.33. Check the Invert checkbox next to the channel in the dialog box. You need to invert the background image because you want to let the adjustment affect only the darker areas of the image. By inverting the background into the mask, you will accomplish this.

4. Double-click on the Adjustment layer to open the Hue/Saturation dialog box. Click on the Colorize button and change the Hue to 22 (or whatever tone you want to use for the sepiatoned image). Change the Saturation to 50 (once again, you may vary this in any way you want). Figure 11.34 shows the Hue/Saturation settings.

5. This makes a fairly nice sepiatone, but there is yet another trick that you can play. You cannot add a Levels Adjustment layer to affect the mask image that is on the current Adjustment layer, but you can use the Levels command directly on the mask. (It only gives you one Undo unless you use the History palette to revert, but you cannot keep a channel or layer mask fluid, either.)

6. Select Image|Adjust|Levels or use Command+L (Mac) or Ctrl+L (Windows). Just select the command—*do not double-click on the Adjustment Layer.*

Figure 11.33 Apply Image dialog box.

Figure 11.34 Hue/saturation settings.

Think about the adjustment that you need to make. If you move the Black point to the right, you create more black in the image—which keeps the sepiatone *off* of more values. If you move the White point slider to the left, you create more whites in the image—which allows more color to show through on the darker values. You probably want to allow more color to appear on the mid-to-light tones in the image. If this is the case, then you need to move the Gamma slider toward the left in the Levels dialog box or move the Black Output slider toward the right (or some combination of both).

Figure 11.35 shows the Levels settings that we selected. Figure 11.36a shows the inverted image of Robert, and Figure 11.36b shows the mask after we applied the Levels command.

Once you understand what is happening when you adjust the Levels in the layer mask, you can work in two images if you really want to keep your sepiatone editable. Here's how:

1. When you open the ROBERT.PSD file, create a duplicate copy (Image|Duplicate|OK).

2. In one copy, create an Invert adjustment layer and then create a Levels Adjustment layer on top of it. Set the Levels to look like the one used in Step 5 in the preceding example (or play with the Levels to see what you prefer; that is why you are using the Adjustment layer).

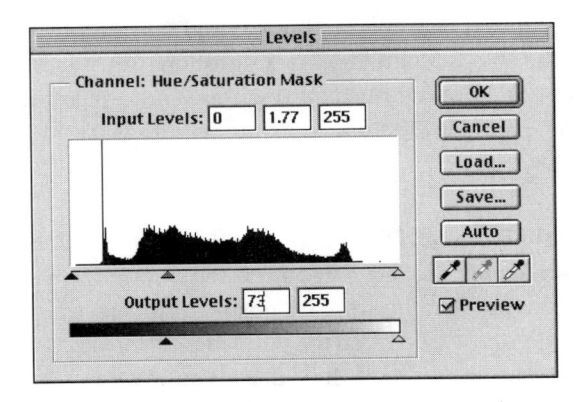

Figure 11.35 Levels command we used to change the Adjustment layer mask.

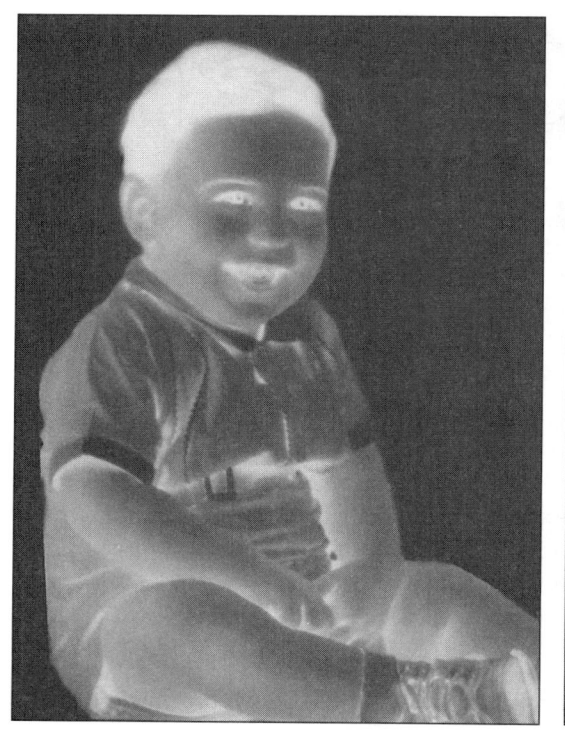

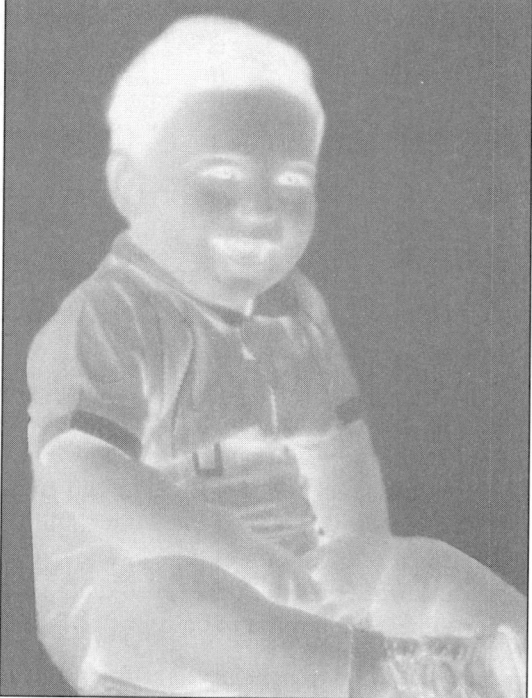

Figure 11.36a Original image inverted.

Figure 11.36b Adjustment layer mask after Levels command is applied.

3. In the other copy, work Steps 2 and 4 from the previous example. Doing so sets up the Hue/Saturation layer and selects a color for it.

4. Now you can choose the Apply Image command with the Hue/Saturation layer as its target and make the image with the Levels adjustment the source image. Use the merged image as the source. Figure 11.37 shows you the Apply Image dialog box for this example. Now you can change the Levels in the Adjustment layer as many times as you want. You cannot degrade the image, and you can choose the Apply Image command to put the changes into the Hue/Saturation Adjustment layer mask as many times as you want. You are not hurting any image data regardless of how often you change your mind. Figure 11.38 shows the final sepiatone. See this book's Color Studio for a color example.

Stacking Adjustment Layers

You have seen how Adjustment layers can be created and manipulated. In the previous examples, you learned how to create multiple Adjustment layers, mask Adjustment layers, and change the Blend mode and Opacity of the Adjustment layers. You used the Apply Image command and the Levels command on the Adjustment layer mask. Now it's time to expand your knowledge of Adjustment layers.

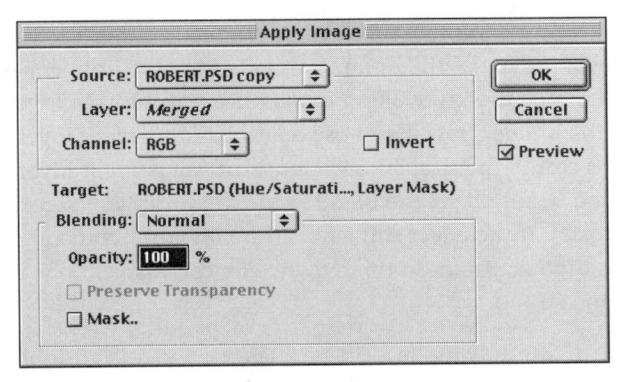

Figure 11.37 Use this Apply Image dialog box to place the merged image with Levels and Invert Adjustment layers into the Hue/Saturation Adjustment layer mask in the companion image.

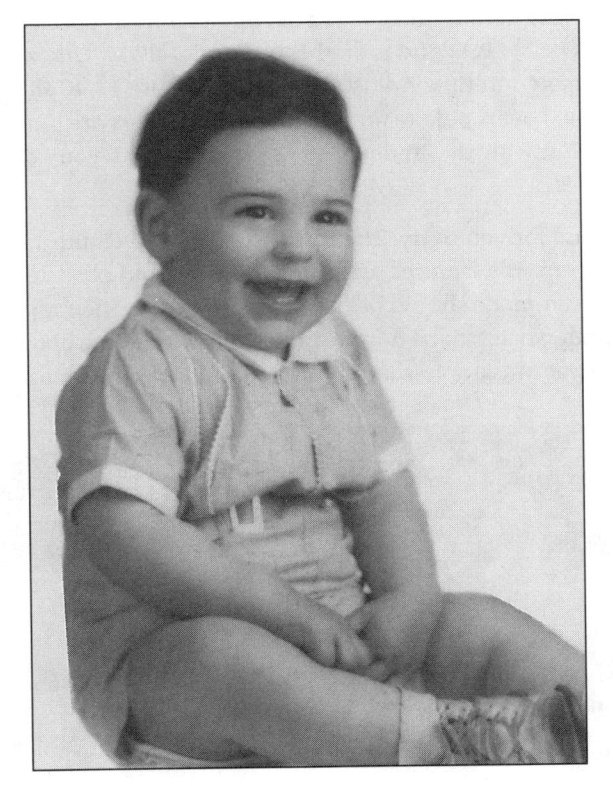

Figure 11.38 Finished sepiatoned image.

Although you can, and usually will, color correct images using the Levels and the Curves commands, one of the most precise curves (or precise transforms) that you can use to correct an image is often the image tones themselves. We touched on that in the two previous exercises. We used the values of the airplane in Multiply mode in a Levels adjustment layer without changing the Levels sliders, and we used the values of Robert, inverted, to make a mask to filter out unwanted color.

You can use these techniques in more production-oriented situations. Before there were Adjustment layers, if you wanted to use the image values to tone the image, you needed to duplicate the layer and then change the layer Blend mode and, possibly, the layer opacity as well. This doubled the size of the image. Now if you use a Levels Adjustment layer, you can do the same thing with much less cost in file size. Simply create an Adjustment layer (Levels or Curves), do not change the dialog box, and set the Blend mode to Multiply or Screen (or Overlay to make the colors more intense). If the effect still isn't strong enough, you can stack duplicates of the Adjustment layer as high as you need them to be. You can also change the opacity to cut back on the effect if it is too strong.

Using this technique in Multiply mode is an excellent way to add variable amounts of darkness and contrast to a washed out, overexposed image. You tone down an image that is too dark by using Screen mode and stacking as many Adjustment layers as you need.

Figure 11.39 shows a very poor-quality, faded old photo. It hasn't been tonally retouched at all. This file is named WOMAN.PSD and is on this book's CD-ROM. One way to correct the values on this image is to create multiple Adjustment layers. Figure 11.40 shows the finished image. Figure 11.41 shows the Layers palette for the image. The layers are named for the adjustments that they contain. Play with the image and see what results you can get. There are many acceptable possibilities.

Here's another exercise for you to try. The picture of Bruce in Figure 11.42 was taken with the sun directly behind him. His features are much too dark and obscure. However, you, Adjustment layers, and Screen mode should be able to correct that. The major correction problem is that not all of the image needs to be adjusted the same way. You will use varying levels of gray in the Adjustment layer mask to lesson the correction in specific areas.

Figure 11.39 Woman, before.

Figure 11.40 Woman, corrected with Multiply and Overlay levels.

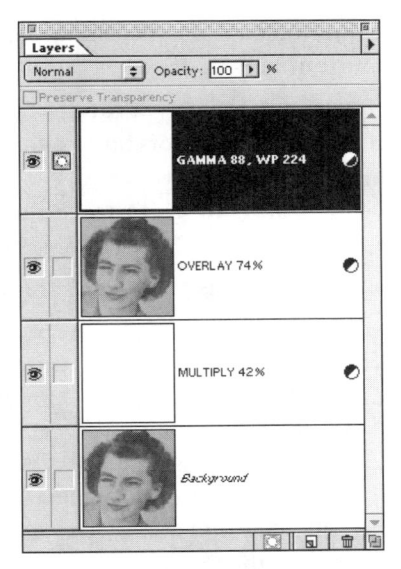

Figure 11.41 Layers palette showing types of Adjustment layers used to correct the image of the woman.

1. Open the image BRUCE.PSD from this book's companion CD-ROM. Figure 11.42 shows the original image. See the Color Studio for additional illustration.

2. Create a Hue/Saturation Adjustment layer (Command+click on the Mac or Ctrl+click in Windows) on the New Layer icon at the bottom of the Layers palette. Set the Blend mode to Screen. In the Hue/Saturation dialog box, do nothing. Figure 11.43 shows the

Figure 11.42 Original image of Bruce is much too dark.

Figure 11.43 Screen Adjustment layer washes out the sky.

Screen mode adjustment that affects the entire image, washing out the sky. See the Color Studio for further illustration.

3. Make the Background layer active (Option+[or Alt+[). Choose Select|Color Range and choose the Highlights. Press D to set the colors back to the default of black and white. Make the Adjustment layer active (Option+] or Alt+]). Fill the selection with black (Option+Delete or Alt+Backspace). Figure 11.44 shows the mask that you are creating on the Adjustment layer.

4. Choose Filter|Blur|Gaussian Blur; Radius: 3.0 pixels. This softens the selection edges, as shown in Figure 11.45.

5. Make the Background layer active (Option+[on the Mac or Alt+[in Windows). Choose Select|Color Range and choose the Midtones. Press D to set the colors back to the default of black and white. Make the Adjustment layer active (Option+] or Alt+]). Fill the selection with 50% black (Edit|Fill|Foreground color, 50% Opacity, Normal). Choose Filter|Blur|Gaussian Blur; Radius: 2. Figure 11.46 shows the mask. The gray in the midtones area on the mask will allow half of the changes to occur. Figure 11.47 shows the almost finished correction. See the Color Studio for further illustration.

6. The only thing left to do is remove the color cast in the image and fix the Levels. To do this, you need to create two additional Adjustment layers: a Levels Adjustment layer (Mode: Normal) and a Color Balance Adjustment layer (Mode: Normal). Figure 11.48a shows the Layers palette, Figures 11.48b through 11.48e show the Levels settings used, Figures 11.48f through 11.48h show the Color Balance Highlights, Midtones, and Shadows corrections, and Figure 11.49 shows the fully corrected image. (See this book's Color Studio for a color illustration.)

Figure 11.44 Adjustment layer mask with highlights protected from change.

Figure 11.45 Gaussian Blur added to Adjustment layer mask.

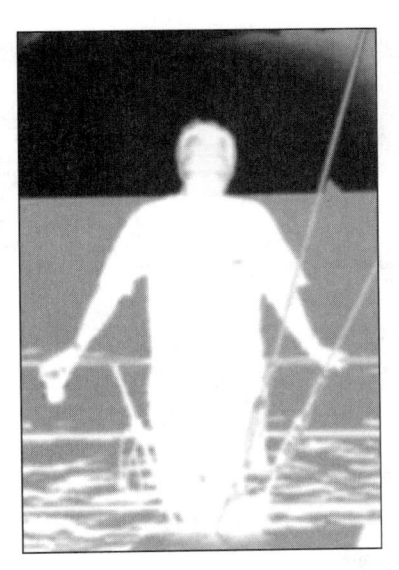

Figure 11.46 Finished mask.

Figure 11.47 Almost finished correction.

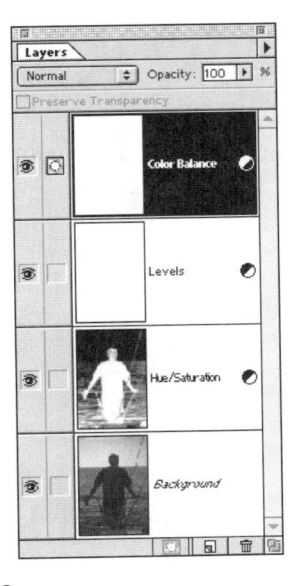

Figure 11.48a

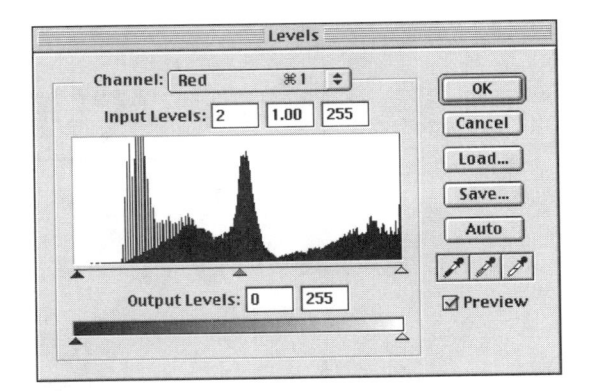

Figure 11.48b

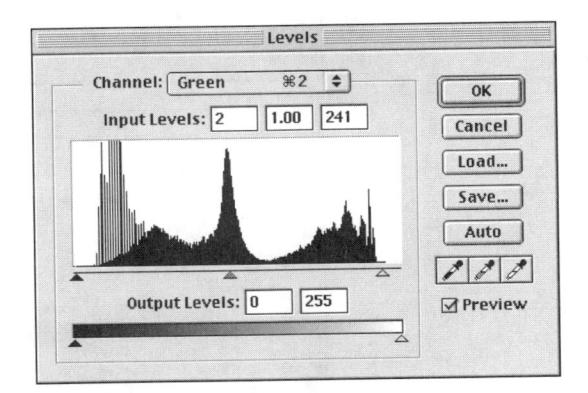

Figure 11.48c

Figure 11.48 (a through h) Layers palette and Corrections settings.

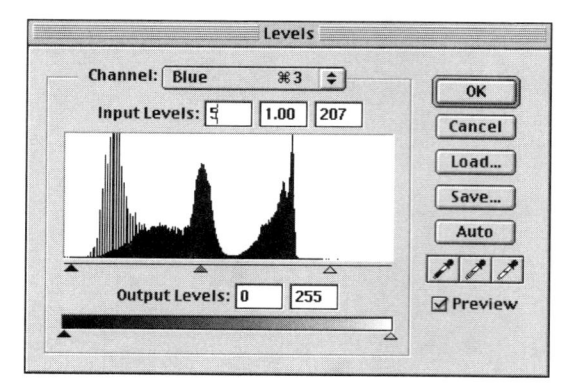

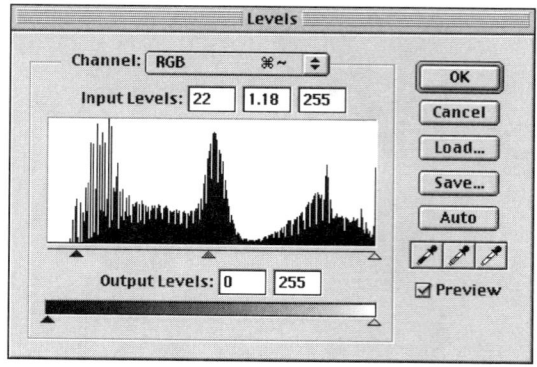

Figure 11.48d

Figure 11.48e

Figure 11.48f

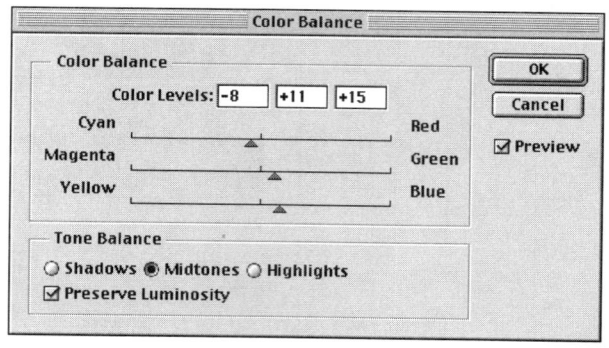

Figure 11.48g

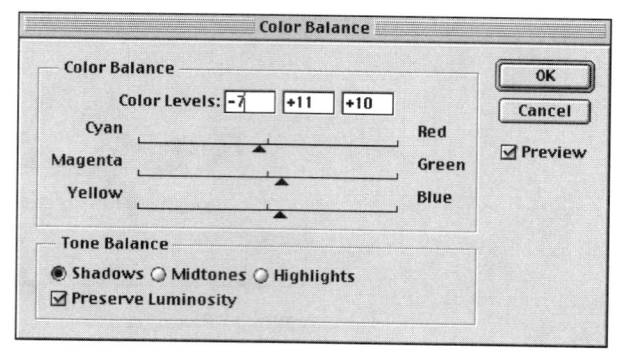

Figure 11.48h

Figure 11.49 Corrected image.

Transformations

A variety of new Transform commands were added to Photoshop in version 4. And in version 5, the entire Transform submenu moved from the Layers to the Edit menu, and can be used on layers, selections, and paths. You can also change the origin point for transformations in this version, which lets you select a location from which to rotate an object. A benefit of this is the ability to rotate a group of objects around a common center point.

The Problem

In Photoshop 3 and earlier, you could Scale, Rotate, Skew, or apply Perspective to your image. But you could perform only one action at a time. If you wanted to move an object on a layer over a bit, scale it, rotate it by 15°, and then put it into perspective, you needed to perform four separate commands. Each command (except for the Move command) lost a bit more data. This caused the object to become softer with each manipulation.

Using the Free Transform command introduced in Photoshop 4, however, you can do all of these actions on an object at one time. You can also move the object while the transformation Marquee is active. This is particularly helpful, as it lets you get a much better idea of how the object will look *in place*. Just as the Adjustment layers allowed all of the transformations to occur at one time, rather than sequentially (which gives you much better image quality), so the Free Transform and Numeric Transform commands allow you to change the physical dimensions and orientation of an image and calculate the changes all at once—when you are ready to say "Okay, let's do it." This gives you significantly better image quality.

In Photoshop 3, if you scaled, rotated, and then skewed an object, the program would scale the object, rotate the scaled object, and then skew the rotated object. Using Free Transform, the program now performs all three calculations, determines the final image contours, and then uses the *original* image data to calculate a single result.

Just to show the type of image loss that occurs, we imported a swan from the Ultimate Symbol Design Elements collection and filled it with a fractal created in Kai's Power Tools 2.1. The image, SWAN.PSD, is on this book's CD-ROM for you to use. Figure 11.50 shows the original image. Figure 11.51a shows a close-up of the original pixels. Figure 11.51b is a copy that has been rotated approximately 15 times in various increments until it reached the original angle again. Notice how much softer and less sharp this image is. You should avoid rotating an image this many times because of the amount of data loss. There is no way to rotate something a number of times and still do it in one "render pass"—unless you simply cannot make up your mind, and you keep changing the angle multiple times in the Free Transform command before you click on OK.

The Keystrokes

Table 11.1 shows keyboard shortcuts for the Transform commands:

Table 11.1 The Keyboard Shortcuts

Command	Mac	Windows
Free Transform	Command+T	Ctrl+T
Transform Copy	Command+Option+T	Alt+Ctrl+T
Transform Again	Shift+Command+T	Shift+Ctrl+T
Transform Again With Copy	Shift+Command+Option+T	Shift+Alt+Ctrl+T
To skew using the Skew command:		
Skew single side	Drag one of the center box handles on the bounding box	
Skew both sides from center	Option	Alt
To skew using the Free Transform command:		
Skew single side—one point only	Command	Ctrl
Skew 1 point on top and bottom	Command+Option	Ctrl+Alt
Constrain proportions or direction	Shift	Shift
Mirror	Option	Alt
Move single corner point	Command	Ctrl
Skew (drag side-center handle)	Command	Ctrl
Perspective	Shift+Cmd+Option	Shift+Alt+Ctrl

Manipulating Images 765

Figure 11.50 SWAN.PSD.

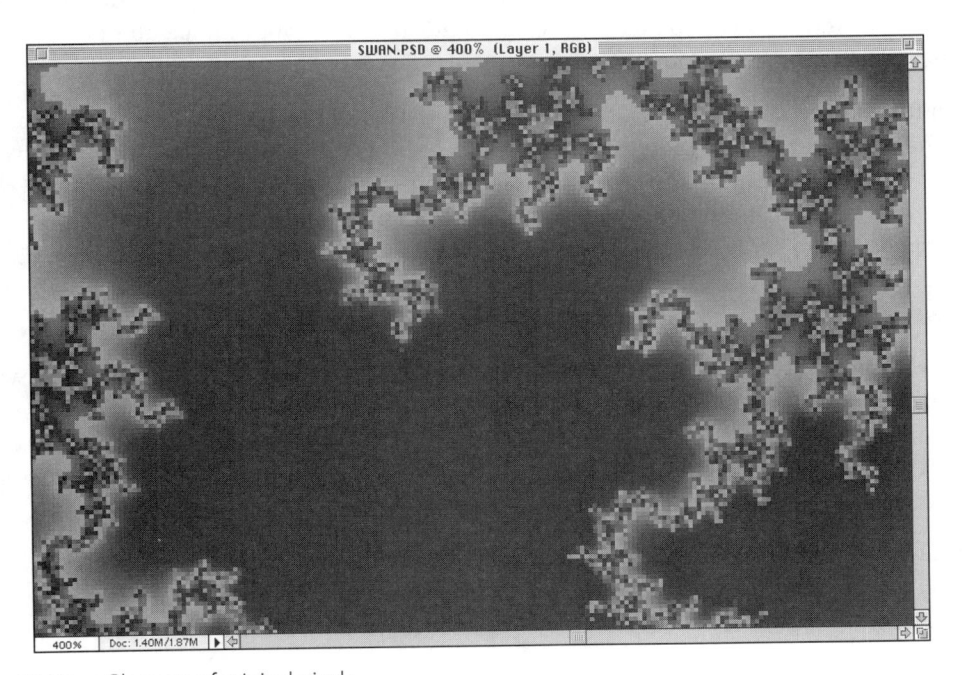

Figure 11.51a Close-up of original pixels.

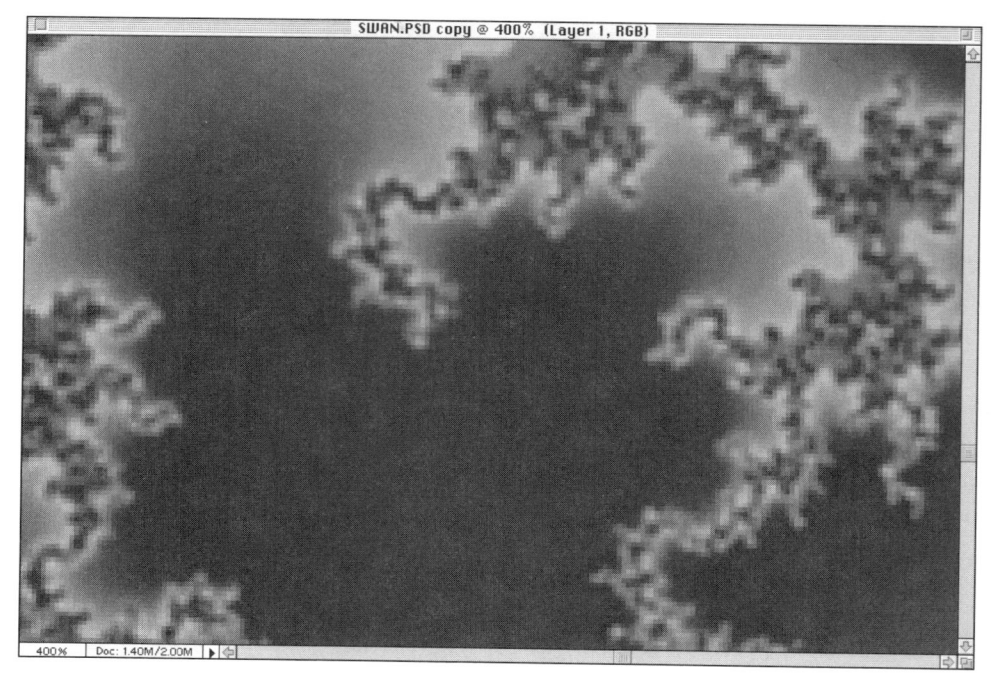

Figure 11.51b Close-up view of image that has been rotated 15 times.

Numeric Transform

The Numeric Transform command allows you one-step access to most of the transformational commands. It allows you to position, scale, rotate, and skew your image all at one time, and with numeric precision. Figure 11.52 shows the dialog box.

Each function on the dialog box has a checkbox that allows you to indicate whether or not to use the values present for that function. The dialog box remembers the last values used during the current Photoshop session. For example, if you rotate an image 45° and scale it by 50%, those values will be present in the dialog box if you use the command again before you exit Photoshop. If the next object that you want to manipulate only needs to be rotated, you need to either set the scale to 100% or uncheck the box next to it—or else your object will also be scaled by 50%.

You will find yourself using the Numeric Transform command frequently when you want to scale an object. If you know either the size or the percentage that you need to scale, then using Numeric Transform is the best way to get there. It's almost impossible to accurately scale an object 43% by eye. Unless you enjoy playing with rulers and watching them as you drag and scale, it's also much easier to *tell* Photoshop that an object needs to become 133 pixels square.

Another nice touch to the dialog box is that it allows you to move an object in either absolute or relative mode. You can specify that the bounding box of an object be moved to a specific set of coordinates or that it be moved a specific distance from where it is currently living.

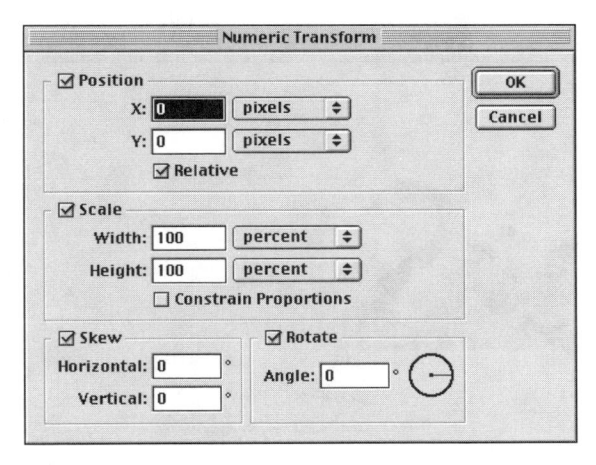

Figure 11.52 Numeric Transform dialog box.

Figure 11.53 shows the SWAN.PSD image again. This time, the Numeric Transform command has been used to scale it to 200 pixels wide with constrain proportions on (which means that you only need to specify one dimension), and it has been moved to absolute screen coordinates of X: 100, Y: 100 (0,0 is in the top-left corner). As you can see by the guide lines in the figure, position X: 100, Y: 100 is the top-left corner of the rectangle that *logically* encloses the pixels

> ## WHAT ARE OBJECTS AND BOUNDING BOXES?
>
> An *object* is a group of non-transparent pixels located on a layer. It is easier to use the term "object" to refer to the contents of a layer than it is to keep saying "non-transparent pixels on layer x." If this were a vector program, an object would be an individual path, either opened or closed, or any grouping thereof, which can be moved at one time by clicking on a single location and dragging. Photoshop's layers sort of do the same thing. When you use the Move tool and drag at one location, all of the non-transparent pixels come along.
>
> There is another issue to consider, however. It concerns what *you* decide to place on a layer. Because you have the ability to perform transformations on layer contents without having to select the layer with a marquee, Photoshop assumes that there is only one grouping of contiguous pixels on that layer. In plain terms, if you want to have five cats in your image, then put each one on its own layer. That way, each cat is its own object and can be resized and repositioned by itself. Until you know that there will be no further changes, try to keep only one "thing" on each layer.
>
> This brings us to the bounding box—another concept borrowed from the world of vector graphics. When used in Photoshop, this term refers to the smallest rectangle that can surround all of the non-transparent pixels in a layer. When you explicitly position an object using the Numeric Transform command, you are placing the top-left corner of its bounding box at that location. You can "see" this bounding box by snapping guides to the top and left sides of an object on a transparent layer. If your Units are set to pixels, then you will see the coordinates of the logical box that encloses the object.

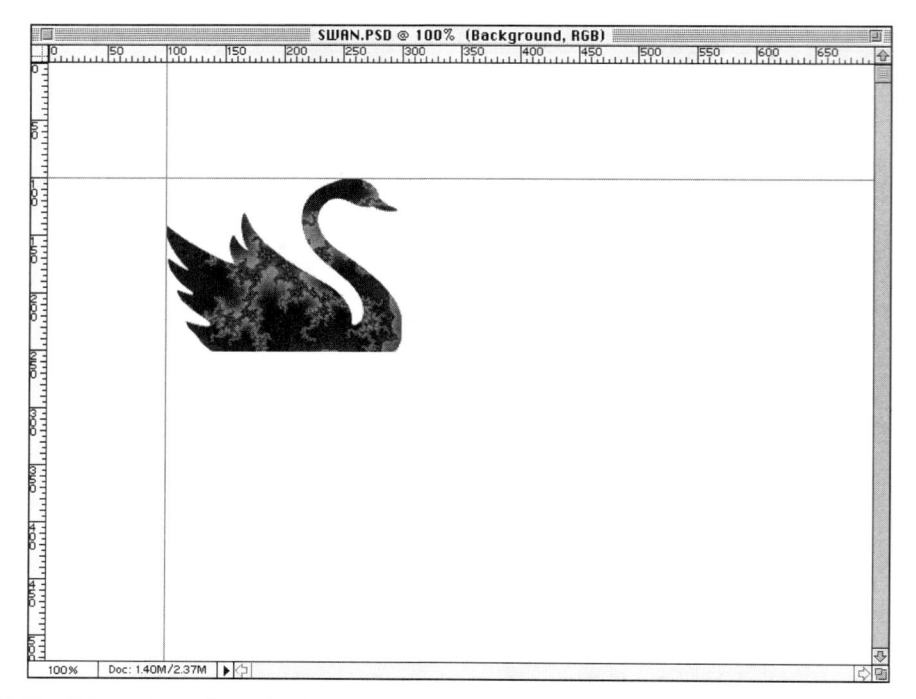

Figure 11.53 SWAN.PSD with guides showing the top-left corner of the bounding box.

that form the swan. (Logically equals virtually—as opposed to physically, because there isn't really a "box" around the pixels on the layer.)

Rotation Tricks

Photoshop has learned a new rotation trick from Illustrator, a trick that we have long been wanting to see. No longer do you, as the designer, need to wrack your brains for ways to rotate an object around a specific point rather than about its center. Now, you can drag the origin point to wherever you want it to be and use the new location as the center of the rotation. This allows you to rotate a leaf by the end of its stem, for example, or to create a circular motif by rotating a number of copies around a single point.

Figure 11.54 shows the same swan rotated 60°. This figure has guides that mark the center point of the bounding box (and the bounding box has been stroked with a wide line). Additionally, a large white square has been drawn in the location of the center of the bounding box before the swan was rotated. Notice that the white area is still at the center of the bounding box where the guides intersect (even though the bounding box itself has rotated). How can we rotate the swan from the top-left tip of its wing, instead?

The answer is breathtakingly simple in this version of Photoshop. First, let's drag the swan closer to the center of the image so that there is room to rotate the swan by its upper-left wing tip (See Figure 11.55.) Use the Move tool to drag the swan so that its wing tip is just to the right and below the center of the image (if you are fussy, use guides to indicate the center of the image).

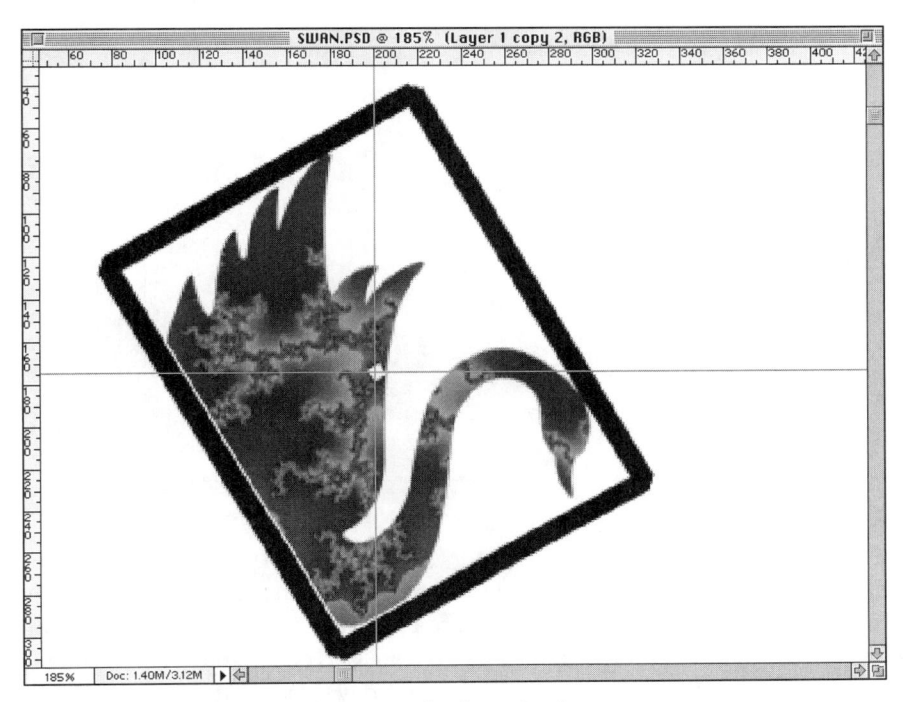

Figure 11.54 Swan rotated 60° around the center of its bounding box.

Select the Transform command with copy (Command+Option+T on the Mac or Alt+Control+T in Windows). Drag the origin point from the center of the swan to its upper-left wing tip, as shown in Figure 11.56. (The image has been lightened for the book so that you can see the placement of the origin point.)

Figure 11.55 Swan ready to be rotated.

Figure 11.56 Origin point placed on wing tip.

Place the cursor just outside of the lower-right corner of the image until the cursor changes to a double-pointed, curved arrow, as shown in Figure 11.57. This is the Rotate cursor. Drag the Rotate cursor toward the left until the angle on the Info palette is as close to 60% as you can place it. Press Return to "set" the transformation. A new layer magically appears (that was why you pressed the Alt or Option key when using the keyboard shortcut). Figure 11.58 shows the two swans now.

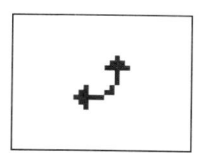

Figure 11.57 The "Rotate" cursor.

Figure 11.58 Two swans; one rotated 60°.

Forget, for a moment, that you have just watched the swan rotate 60°. Let's take a closer look at what has been done. Figure 11.59 shows the swan ready to be rotated (but without the Transform command marquees in the image). So that you can see exactly how the rotating happens, guides have been crossed at the center of the desired rotation. Additionally, a large circle has been painted at the desired center of rotation. (Because it is removing image data, this is not something that you would actually do on your own images.) Figure 11.60 shows the swan rotated. Our changes have accomplished exactly what we anticipated.

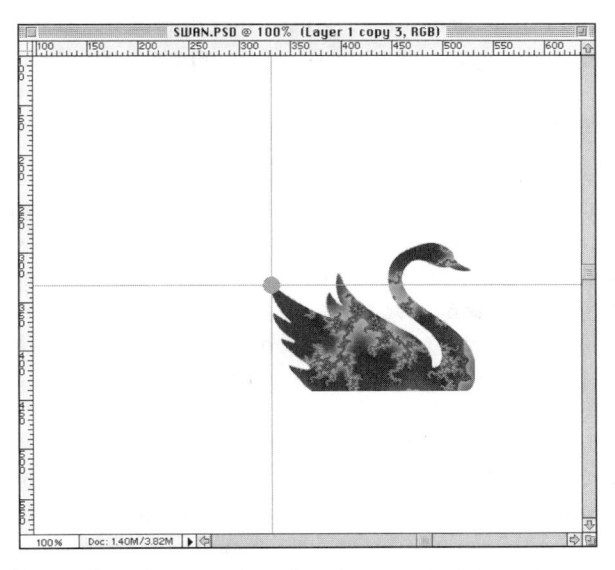

Figure 11.59 Swan showing projected center of rotation where guides intersect.

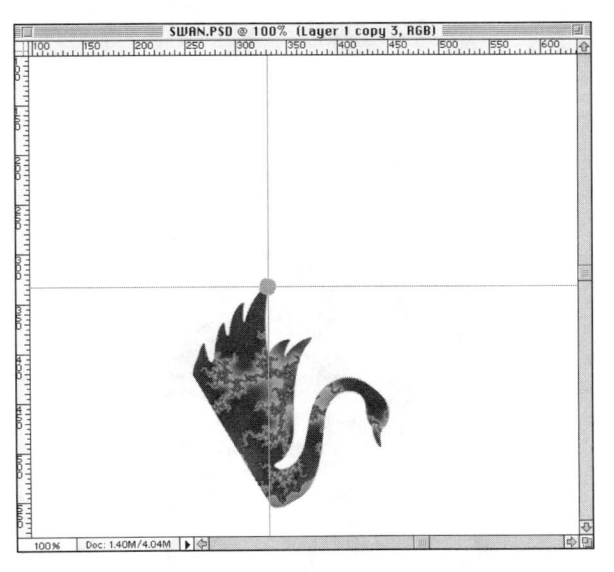

Figure 11.60 Swan rotated 60° around upper-left wing tip.

Using this technique, it gets even better. Now press Shift+Option+Command+T (Mac) or Shift+Alt+Control+T (Windows). Voila! You have made another copy of the swan and rotated it by the same amount as the previous rotation from the same origin point. Continue making rotated duplicates until you reach your starting point (a total of five copies and six layers). The original was never rotated. The five copies, however, show successive image degradation. However, it certainly was easy, and the degradation might be acceptable. Figure 11.61 shows the six copies of the swan rotated around the top-left wing tip.

If you do object to the image degrading, repeat the original transformation by selecting the bottom layer each time, dragging the transform origin point, and changing the angle of rotation to 120°, 180°, 240°, and 300°. This keeps the final copy almost as sharp as the original, and definitely as sharp as the first layer that we rotated.

Finally, if you are determined to make the rotation as accurate as it can possibly be, here's a fast description of a slow trick that will always work perfectly. Load the transparency of the swan layer and read the dimensions in the Info palette. They will always appear as a rectangle. Create a Fixed Size Rectangular Marquee of the same size and position it so that it surrounds the swan snugly. Save the rectangular selection to a channel and turn on the eye icon. Select the normal Rectangular Marquee tool and drag a marquee from the top-left of the wing tip to the bottom-right of the object's original (i.e., current) bounding box, as shown by the saved alpha channel. According to the Info palette, this area is 200 pixels wide by 110 pixels high. Next, create a fixed-size marquee that is twice the dimensions of the current selection (400 pixels wide by 220 pixels high). Place guides that cross at the location of the left wing tip. Press the modifier key (Option, Mac; Alt, Windows) and click at the intersection of the guides to place the center of Marquee on the wing tip. Take a brush and place a mark on each empty corner of

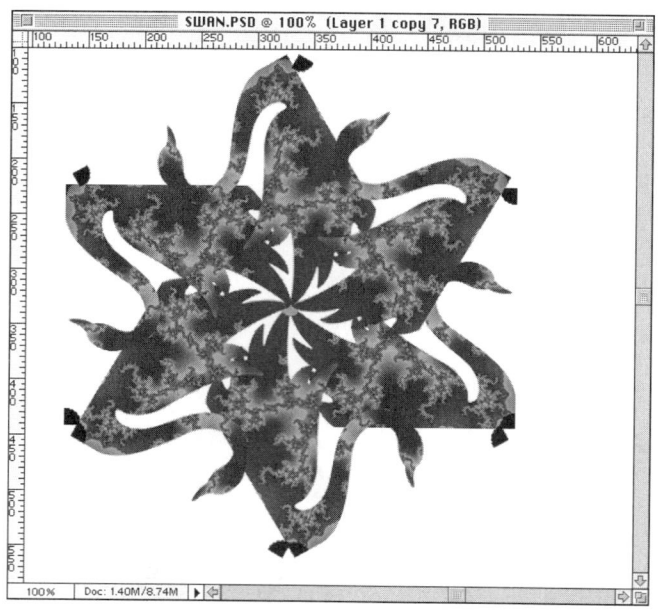

Figure 11.61 Star formation of swans rotated at 60° increments around the upper-left wing tip.

the selection (not the one with the swan in it). This allows the Numeric Transform to work perfectly and "see" the wing tip of the swan as the center point about which to rotate the image. Press the modifier key (Option or Alt) and select Edit|Transform|Numeric. Turn off all of the options except for the Rotate option, and select 60° as the angle. The image rotates 60° into a new layer. Repeat the previous instructions for making the swan into a star. Figure 11.62 shows the swan prepared for its first rotation. When you're done, erase the extraneous marks that you made.

Exercise: Multirotate Action

We have created an Action that allows you to automatically rotate anything on Layer 1 in an image so that it forms a 60° star or burst pattern. With this, you can create some interesting effects:

1. Load the file MROTATE.ATN into your Actions palette from this book's CD-ROM (Actions palette menu|Load Actions).

2. Create a new document (Command+N, Mac; Ctrl+N, Windows). It can be any size, but a 400×400 pixel image is fine for this exercise.

3. Make a new layer (click on the New Layer icon at the bottom of the Layers Palette). This layer is automatically named Layer 1 (which it must be in order for this Action to work).

4. Just to see how this Action works, use the Line tool and draw a line with a single arrowhead near the center of the image. Figure 11.63 shows the starting image.

5. Double-click on the multirotate Action or select it and click on the Play button. Figure 11.64 shows the result. Yes, it is very ugly, but the line wasn't particularly attractive as a starting image. Notice that there are arrows on both ends of each line. This is because the line revolved around its center and the 60° increments caused lines 4, 5, and 6 to double back over lines 1, 2, and 3. Because these lines are 180° apart from the lines that they are on top of, the arrows face in the opposite direction.

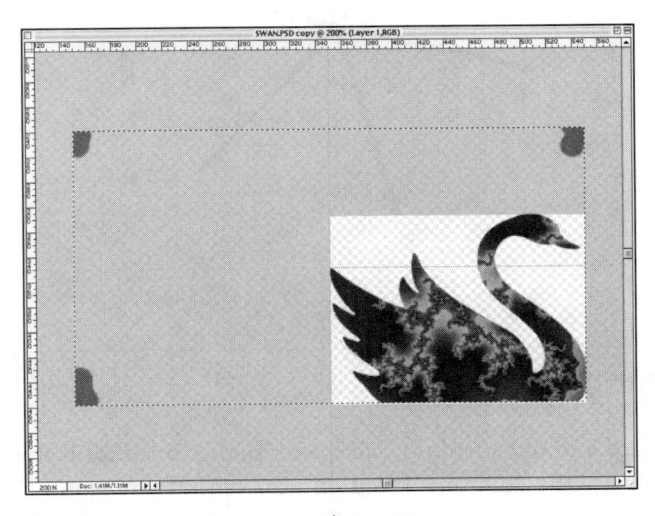

Figure 11.62 Swan ready to be rotated using precise placement.

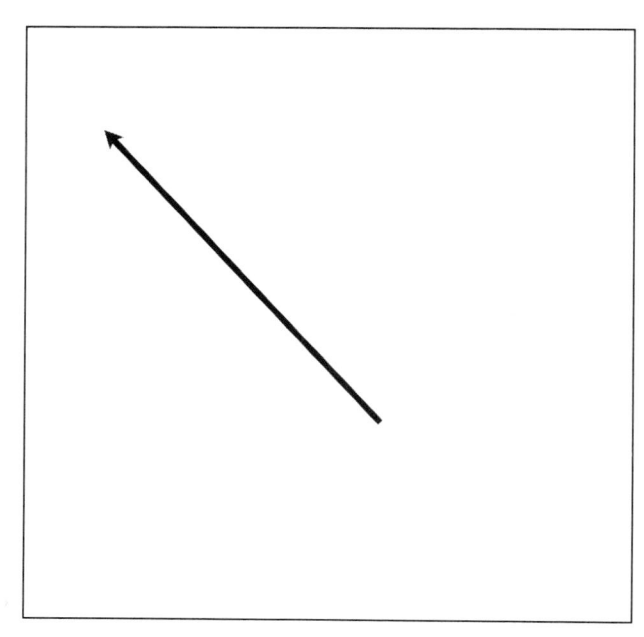

Figure 11.63 Starting image for multirotate Action.

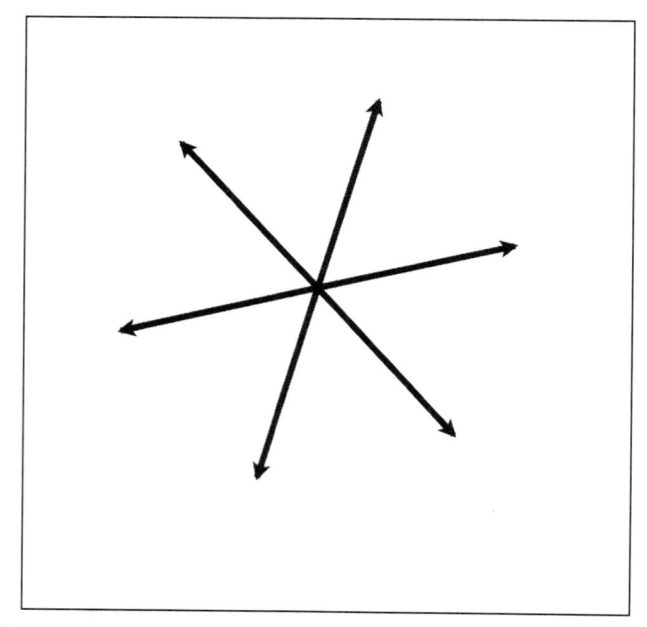

Figure 11.64 Rotated arrows.

6. Close the image without saving it and open another one that is the same size. This time, you can use the Paintbrush and any colors that you want. Create a scribble, perhaps similar to the one in Figure 11.65.

MANIPULATING IMAGES   **775**

7. Play the multirotate Action again. The result should be much more attractive (see Figure 11.66). See the Color Studio for further illustration.

Figure 11.65 New scribble image to rotate.

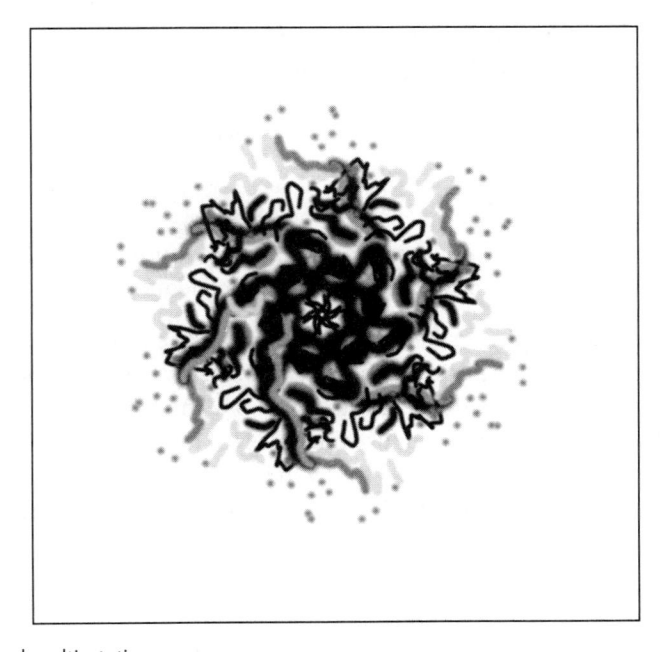

Figure 11.66 Finished multirotation.

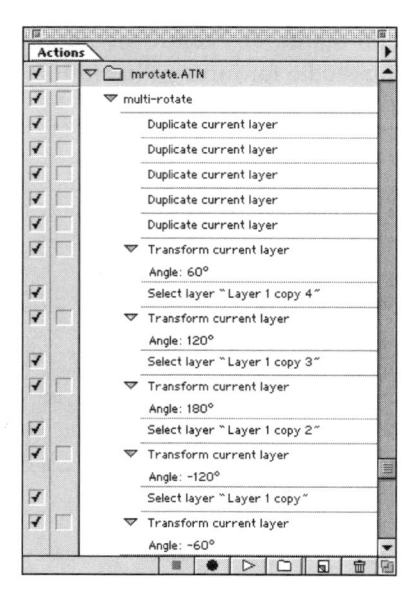

Figure 11.67 Multirotate Action script.

You can use this Action with objects such as the swan, and you can force it to rotate around a specific center point by using the tricks that you learned in this section. Figure 11.67 shows the expanded commands for this Action. Try the left-top rotate Action as well. This behaves differently, although it does much the same thing. It uses the absolute value of the top-left corner of the bounding box as the center of the rotation by specifying it explicitly in the Numeric Transform dialog. The Action moves the top-left corner of your image to pixel 200, 200 before it starts to do anything. If the final formation doesn't all show up in the image, link the layers and drag them to the center of the image. Increase the Canvas Size if necessary. Enjoy!

Grids And Positioning

Photoshop is not a page layout program, nor do most folks use it for technical drawing. Why then were Grids and Guides the most frequently requested features to be added to Photoshop 4?

Photoshop 3 and earlier did have rulers. You can turn on the rulers at the edges of the image and use them as guidelines for positioning objects. However, it's really not fun to try to "eyeball" your position relative to the rulers. Users came up with all different types of workarounds. One of the best was to create a channel, use the Line tool to draw the needed guides, and then set the visibility icon for the channel on so that you could see the guidelines as you worked, but they wouldn't print (even by accident). The guides in the current version of Photoshop make this workaround obsolete.

Why would you need to draw guides in any case? We can think of innumerable situations in which you might need guidelines in a file. One scenario would allow you to see margins in an image—perhaps an imaginary margin in which you want only a few elements to intrude. You might want to space elements in a composite a precise distance from one another. You might need to mark the center of an image, as we did in the rotation example. The list is endless.

What about grids? Of what use are they? The first MacPaint had a grid feature. You could constrain your painting tools to a grid to give you more control (*any* control was a good thing in a program that, when we look back on it, was fairly limited). Artists and illustrators have used graph paper under their images for as long as the concept of grids has been around (or the ability to use tracing paper has been around). Adobe, for some reason, has historically not believed in grids. Until the current version, Illustrator didn't create grids either.

The authors, who both knit, weave, and stitch, have used grids for years in all of their fiber-related activities. Trying to use Photoshop to design a knitting pattern without a grid was a true challenge. The workaround was to magnify an image so that each pixel looked as if it were really 8 pixels square. Using a 1-pixel Pencil, one could then create a design as if working on a grid. You can use grids to design a primitive pattern such as the one shown in Figure 11.68, or a much more complex pattern like the one in Figure 11.69. Using a grid also allows you to judge more easily the boundaries of a selection that you need to make.

Let's take a look at how you define and use both guides and grids.

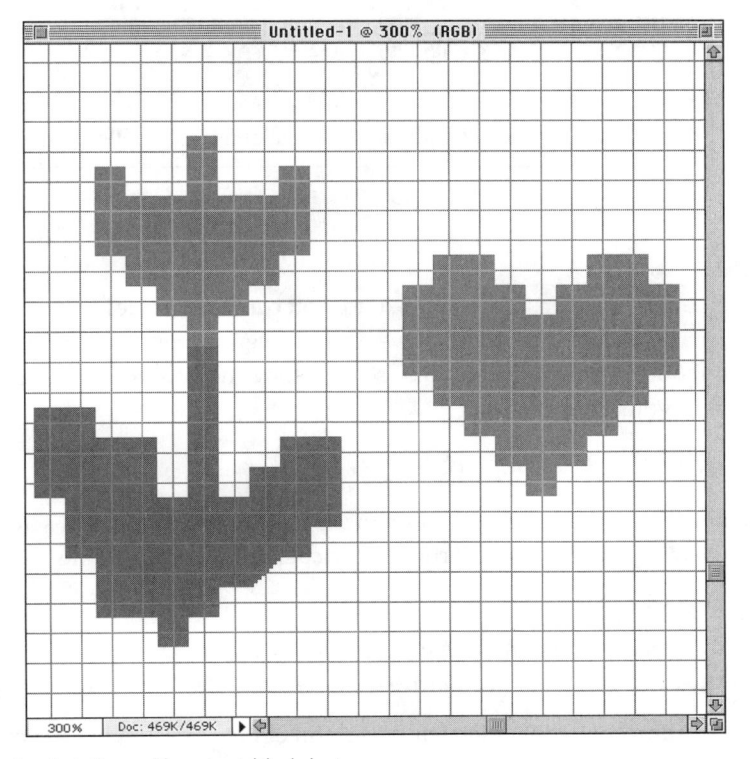

Figure 11.68 A simple tulip and heart gridded design.

Figure 11.69 A more complex gridded design suitable for a Fair Isle sweater.

Using Guides

Guides help you to precisely position image data. You can drag guides from the horizontal and vertical rulers, place and replace them, move, show, hide, or delete them. You can set them up so that tools and objects snap to them, and so that they snap to the contours of objects when you place them in your image.

The Rules And Guides Shortcut Keys.

If you prefer not to use the keyboard shortcuts, you can find the menu selections for using guides on the View menu. Guides and rulers shortcuts are shown in Table 11.2.

Guides And Rulers

You need to have visible rulers in your image before you can create guides (since guides are dragged from the rulers, no rulers equals no guides—an obvious and simple equation).

The ruler units are automatically set to whatever unit of measure you use as your default in the Units & Rulers preference. Although it's usually more accurate to keep that preference set to pixels, you might need to precisely measure a distance in picas or points. You can quickly change the unit setting by double-clicking on a ruler. This opens the Preference dialog box so that you can change it.

Table 11.2 The Guides and Rulers Shortcuts

Command	Mac	Windows
Toggle Rulers	Command+R	Ctrl+R
Show/Hide Guides	Command+;	Ctrl+;
Snap to Guides	Shift+Cmd+;	Shift+Ctrl+;
Lock Guides	Opt+Cmd+;	Alt+Ctrl+;
Edit Units & Rulers Preference	Double-click on horizontal or vertical rule	

> **WARNING**
>
> If you have set your units to anything other than pixels, be very sure that you have also set your image resolution properly for your desired output method. Otherwise, you obtain very odd (and incorrect) results. Figure 11.70a shows a 900-pixel image at 300 ppi. The guides surround a rectangle that is exactly 108 points square. Figure 11.70b shows the same 108-point rectangle on the *same* pixel-size image when the resolution is set to 72 ppi. The two rectangles are decidedly different sizes in relation to the total image, even though they are physically the same size.

Creating

It is very easy to create guides in the image. Simply place your cursor on a ruler, press and hold the (left—for Windows users, only—for Mac users) mouse button, and drag the guide into the image.

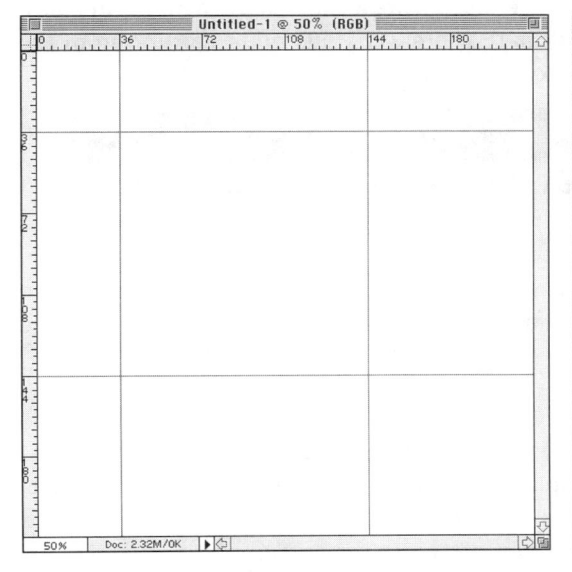

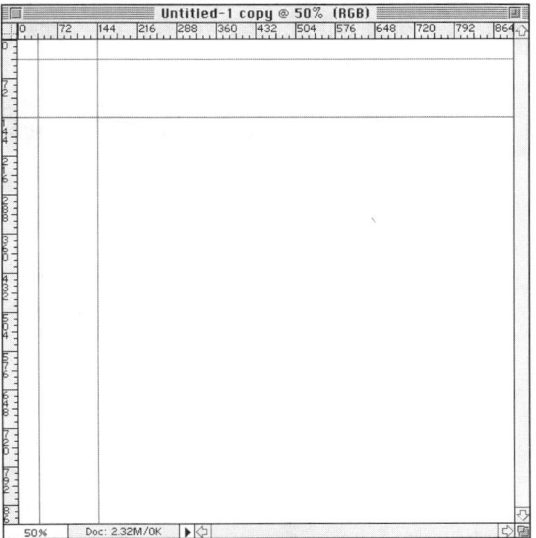

Figure 11.70 (a and b) Guide lines surrounding a 108-point rectangle at 300 ppi and at 72 ppi.

Figure 11.71 Changing the ruler origin.

If you need to change the ruler origin (the point at which the units read 0, 0) place your cursor on the two dotted lines at the top-left corner of the image (shown by the arrow in Figure 11.71) and drag the dotted lines to the new starting point. You can see in Figure 11.71 that the 0 on both rulers is no longer at the top-left of the image. Guides are located at the new origin point. This is very helpful if you need to create guides that are 212 units apart starting from the original 15-tick mark on the ruler. Instead of doing the math, just move the ruler origin!

> **TIP**
>
> To restore the top-left zero-point coordinates, double-click on the top-left corner between the rulers.

When you create guides, you should be in at least 100% view. If you are not, you cannot place the guide on a specific pixel. It's all too likely that you will be off by one or two pixels from the measurement that you really want.

Moving

After you have placed guides into your image, you can easily move them. Press the modifier key (Command, Mac or Ctrl, Windows) to display the Move tool. When you get near a guide, the cursor changes into two parallel lines with outward-pointing arrows, as shown in Figure 11.72. As long as the cursor retains that shape, you can move the guide.

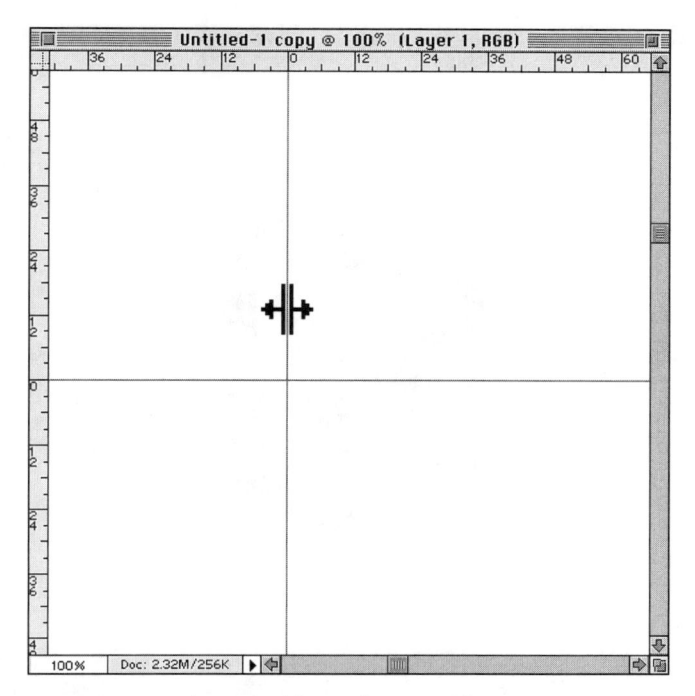

Figure 11.72 The cursor as it appears when it is able to relocate guides.

You can lock the guides so that they cannot accidentally be moved. Option+Command+; (Mac) or Alt+Ctrl+; (Windows) toggles the state of the lock. Guides are always either all-locked or all-movable. You cannot lock a single guide.

Removing

To remove a guide from the image, drag it back to the ruler (as if you were dragging it off the image). You need to have the "guide-moving" cursor as you do this. If you need to remove all of the guides from the image, select View|Clear Guides. There is no keyboard shortcut for that (although you could make an Action that would do this and assign a Function key to it).

Hiding And Viewing

You can show and hide guides quickly by using the semicolon-based keyboard shortcuts Command+; (Mac) or Ctrl+; (Windows). You can also select View|Show Guides (or View|Hide Guides if the guides are already visible).

Snapping

Snapping is a behavior associated with using guide lines in any program that has the capability to create them. Snapping means that the guide seems to have a magnetic attraction for the cursor. If the cursor is anywhere in the vicinity of a guide, it is drawn to it. That is actually a major purpose of guides—to attract the cursor, so that items are positioned with pinpoint accuracy.

When you have an object on a layer, its logical bounding box snaps to the nearest guide if Snap is enabled (Shift+Command+; on the Mac or Shift+Ctrl+; in Windows). Of course, you

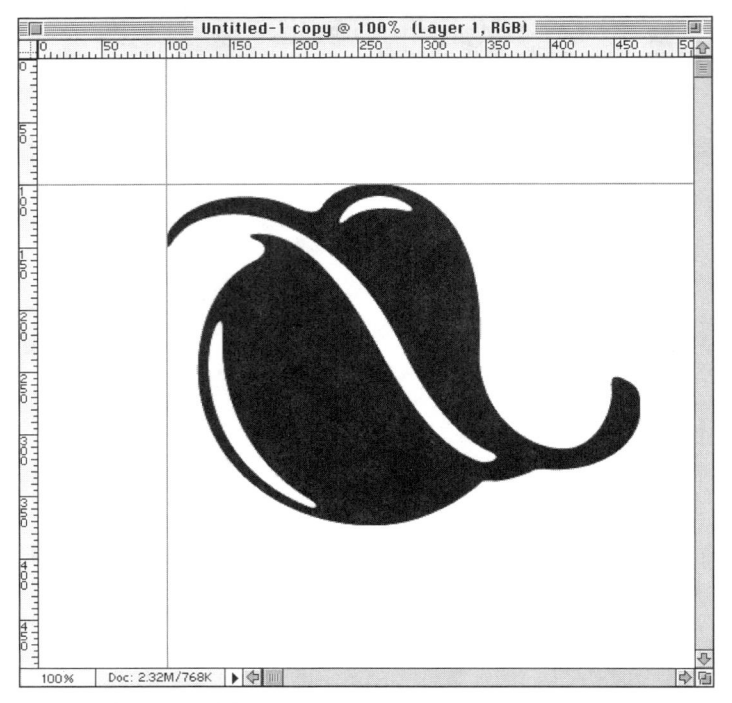

Figure 11.73 Snapping an object to guides.

need to *move* the object in order for it to snap! Figure 11.73 shows a leaf from the Ultimate Symbol Design Elements collection placed so that it snaps to the guides in the image. As you can see, the outer pixels of the object are the ones that snap.

You can easily place guides around the bounding box of a stationary object. When you drag the guides into the image, they will snap to the object. The snapping is so strong that you can't place a guide one pixel away from the start of the non-transparent image pixels in the layer (you *can* place a guide two pixels away from an object, however).

Wish List For Guides

Although the Guides feature is a marvelous convenience, there are still some things that cannot be done and features that would be wonderful to add. Adobe does listen to its users, so perhaps these will find their way into a new release of Photoshop:

1. The capability to lock guides individually as well as in a group.
2. The capability to create a marquee of any shape—perhaps, with the Pen tool—and make it into a guide. (This is a feature of Illustrator and it's wonderful.)
3. The capability to have additional "snap points"—preferably at the center of the object. It would also be useful to be able to drag non-printing snap points onto an object.
4. The capability to assign a ruler location to a guide. In MetaCreations Painter 5, when you double-click on a guide, a dialog box appears that allows you to assign a specific

ruler tick mark to a guide (for example, horizontal pixel 107). This numeric location is maintained even when the image is zoomed out so that you can't see that specific pixel.

Although you cannot snap the center of an object to a guide, you can place the object's center at the intersection of two guides anywhere in the image—even if you don't know exactly where the center of the object is located. This trick tells you how:

1. Place your guides into an image so that they intersect exactly where you want the center of an object to appear. Let's assume that you want the object center to appear at coordinates 257, 363 (this number is odd enough on a 900-pixel image that you would need to zoom in a lot just to place the guides).
2. Select the object that you want and copy it to the clipboard.
3. Choose the Pencil tool and a 1-pixel brush. Zoom into the image at the maximum of 1,600% (drag the slider to the right in the Navigator palette). Leave a 1-pixel dot at the intersection of the guides.
4. Choose the Magic Wand tool with a Tolerance set to 0 and anti-alias off. Click on the single pixel to select it, as shown in Figure 11.74.
5. Paste in the selection from the clipboard by using Command+V (Mac) or Ctrl+V (Windows). As you can see in Figure 11.75, the object (in this case, the leaf) pastes so that it is centered on the desired spot.

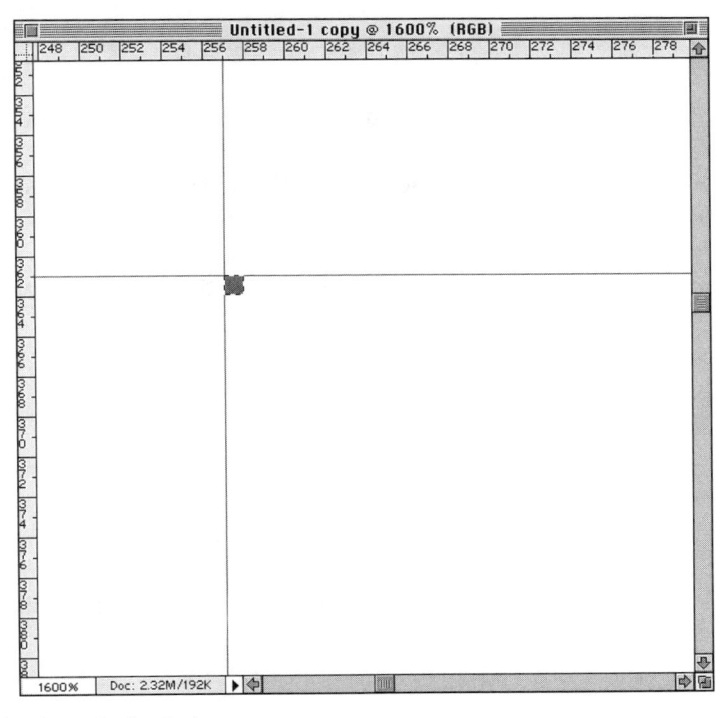

Figure 11.74 Selecting a single pixel.

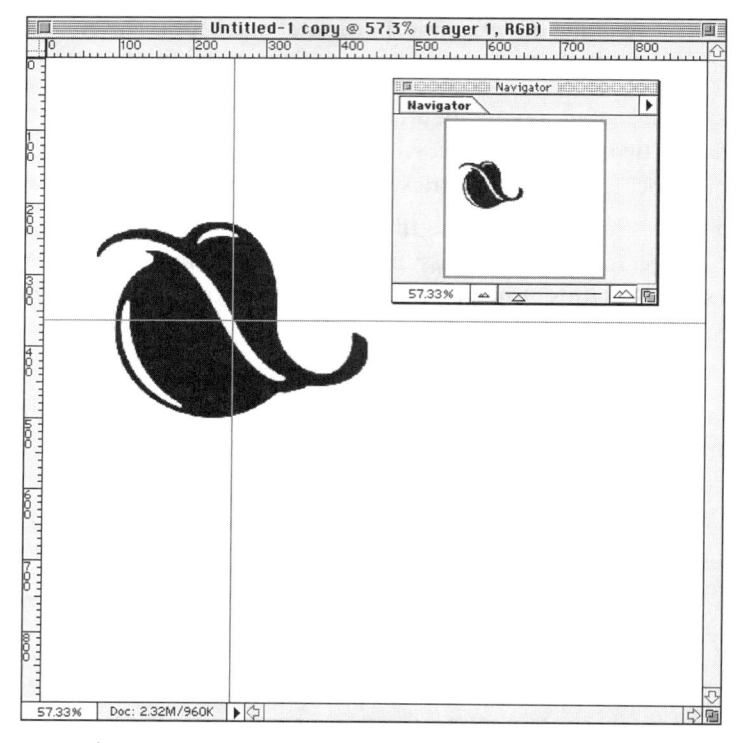

Figure 11.75 Pasting an object into an image so that it is centered on guides.

Usually, any object that is pasted into an image is centered in the document. What makes this trick work? The leaf is very obviously not in the center of the image—but it *is* centered on the guides. When you create a selection, Photoshop pastes the center of the object on the clipboard into the center of the selection. The center of a 1-pixel selection can only be on that pixel, and Photoshop is quite capable of calculating the center of the object being pasted. This is a useful trick and it works quite well. Until we get the ability to snap the center of an object to guides, it's the easiest way to accomplish that task.

Using Grids

Grids are the other part of the precise control equation. Many artists, especially those who are trained as illustrators, are used to working rough comps on top of grid paper. The grid paper allows you to space things with a fair degree of accuracy, without getting too much in your way. You have most of the same features with grids that you have with guides: You can show/hide them and snap to them (see Table 11.3). You can adjust the grid spacing by altering the Guides & Grid preference. You can view the grid as a series of dots as well as either solid or dashed lines.

The menu choices for Grids are on the View menu.

Creating

Creating a grid to use on your image is as easy as pressing Command+' (Mac) or Ctrl+' (Windows). Figure 11.76 shows a standard grid. The keystroke is a toggle, so if the grid is already

Table 11.3 The Grid Shortcuts

Command	Mac	Windows
Show/Hide Grid	Command+'	Ctrl+'
Snap to Grid	Shift+Cmd+'	Shift+Ctrl+'

present, you can hide it. The command toggles the grid on and off in every open image. You cannot view a grid in one image without seeing it in all the other images.

You can arrange your grid a number of different ways. To change the grid settings, open the Guides & Grid preference (File|Preferences|Guides & Grid). You can select the unit to use for the grid (pixels, inches, points, cm, and so on). The same warning about resolution applies here.

A useful tip is to leave a darker line every so often so that you can more easily count the grid squares. Figure 11.77 shows the Guides & Grid preference set to divide an inch (or 300 pixels) into 10 segments. Figure 11.78 shows the grid.

Painting On A Grid—Pitfalls And Tricks

Once you have a grid in the image, what can you do with it? The selection Marquee will snap to it (if snap is on), so it's easy to get an accurate selection. Photoshop's grid is intelligent. It "knows" not to count a grid line twice. For example, if you create the grid shown in the Preference dialog box above (major grid lines 300 pixels apart), and you drag the marquee around one entire major grid square, your selection is exactly 300 pixels square—not 301 pixels, as happens in some other programs. (Guides are similarly intelligent.)

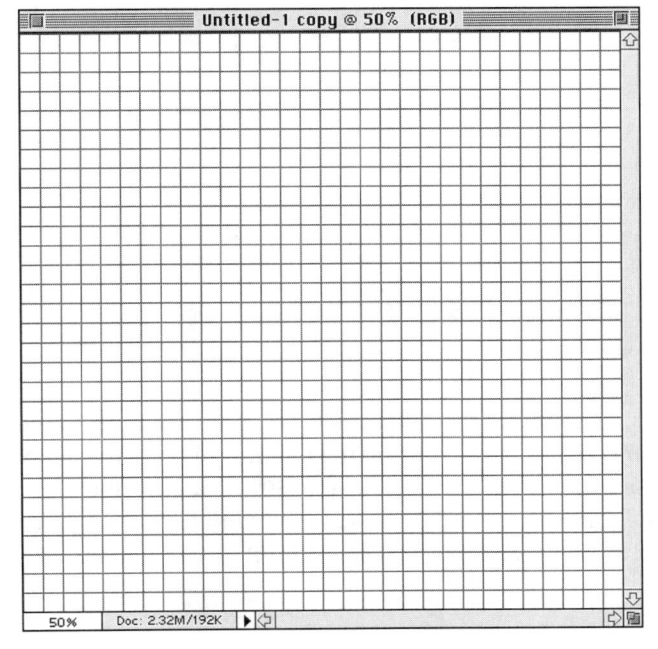

Figure 11.76 Standard grid with all squares the same size.

Figure 11.77 The Guides & Grid preference set to show subdivisions.

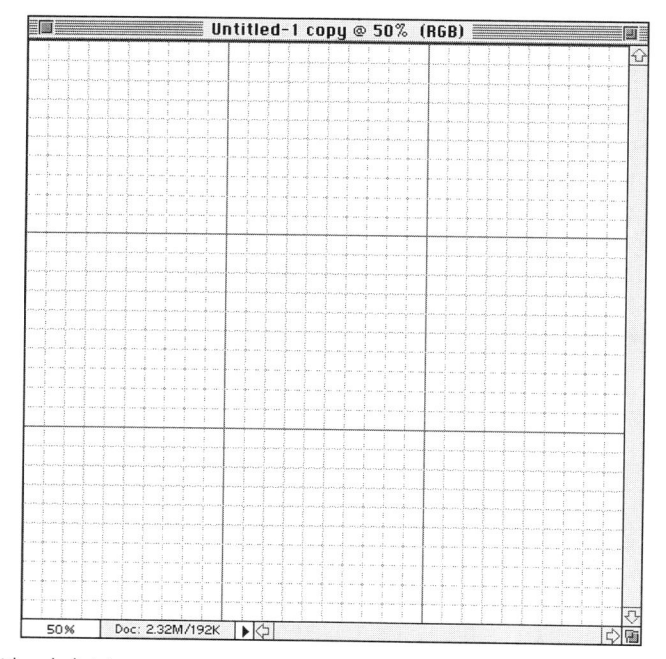

Figure 11.78 Grid with subdivisions.

The Painting tools also snap to the grid sometimes, but they snap at the center of the brush. Grid snap behavior changes, depending on the magnification of the image. Figure 11.79 shows the Paintbrush used randomly on an image at 50% magnification. Figure 11.80 shows the same brush on the same image at 200% magnification. In the first figure, the brush adheres closely to the grid; in the second one, it seems almost as if the grid is not present.

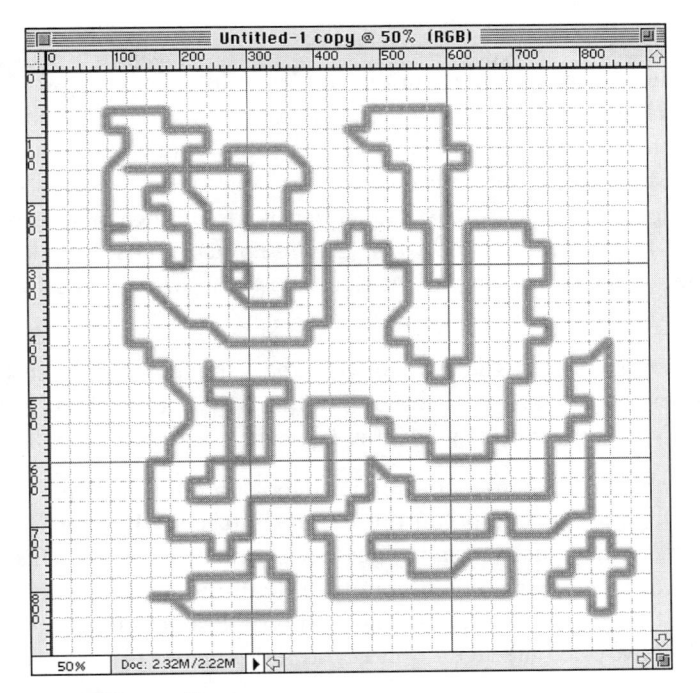

Figure 11.79 Grid snap at 50% magnification.

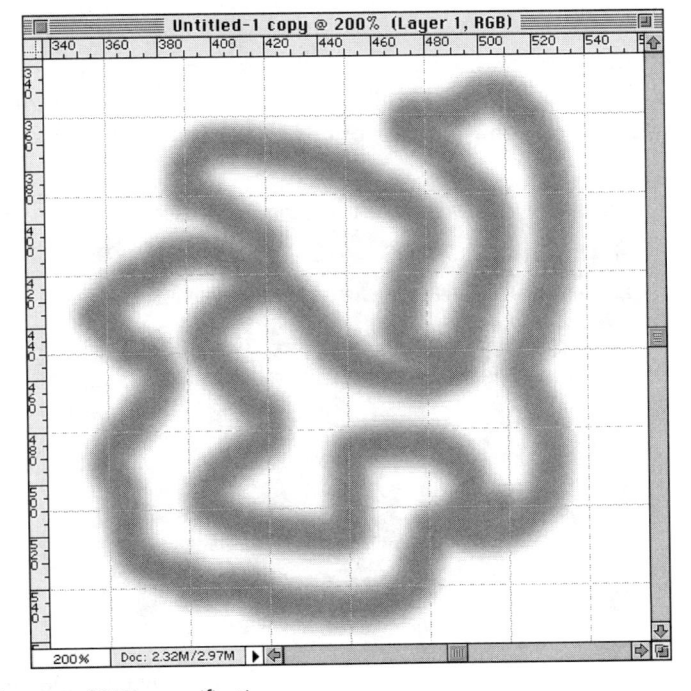

Figure 11.80 Grid snap at 200% magnification.

Making A Visible Grid

Several features not currently present in this implementation of grids would be really nice to have. Textile and knitwear designers would bless Adobe's name if Photoshop had the capability to create an uneven grid (one in which the horizontal and vertical spacing differs). This is needed when designing a knitted sweater, because the knitted stitch is not usually square. Typically, one might obtain six stitches and eight rows to an inch of knitting. Designs created on a square grid look unusually bad when they're knitted up as if the knitting were square (usually, the image looks foreshortened). Figure 11.81 shows the foreshortening that could occur. It's quite noticeable in the sun face.

Another nice feature would be the capability to apply the grid permanently to an image instead of having to create a grid pattern (not that this is especially difficult). You can capture a generated grid if you are willing to work at it, however.

To create a printable grid, set up a grid so that it looks good *on the screen*. Capture the entire window of just the grid (depending on the screen capture method that you use). Mac users can take a picture of the entire screen by pressing Command+Shift+3. This saves a document named Picture1 (or the next incremental number) to the boot drive. Windows users can press the PrntScrn key to capture the entire window and Alt+PrntScrn to capture the topmost window (which will always be a palette unless you hide them). This places the image on the Windows clipboard, and it can be pasted into a new document as soon as Photoshop knows it's there (which might not be until you minimize the program and temporarily go into another application).

In any case, once you have a "hard copy" of the grid, you can use it as you want. If you've set the grid to a light gray, you can make it black by using the Levels command or the Threshold or Posterize commands. You can widen the grid if you want by using this technique:

Figure 11.81 Sun face knitting graph showing need for uneven grid to prevent foreshortening of pattern elements.

1. Open the image GRID.PSD from this book's companion CD-ROM. This is a simple gray grid that was captured from Photoshop's standard 1-subdivision grid.
2. Open the Levels dialog box by using Command+L (Mac) or Ctrl+L (Windows). Move the Gamma slider all the way to the right (numeric setting=.10). This makes the grid black.
3. Click on the Channels palette to select it. Load the RGB channel (Mac: Command+click on the RGB channel, Windows: Ctrl+click on the RGB channel). This selects the white spaces between the grid.
4. Reverse the selection (Select|Inverse).
5. Select the color you want to use for the grid. Choose Edit|Stroke; Center and set the width to your desired amount (we used 4). Figure 11.82 shows the thickened grid that results.

Putting It All Together

You have been exposed to a number of different techniques in this chapter. Let's finish with an exercise that uses them all. This exercise is long, but it is fairly realistic. Because you have already worked with these techniques, the instructions are somewhat less detailed than normal. There are a lot of new tips and tricks in this example, however, so it is an interesting project.

A clogging group (country dancers) has come to you for help. A local school photographer took the picture of everyone in the group for free—and the results are just about worth the price. All the images are in grayscale and dead-looking. The group would like to splurge on 4-color printing, but has only this set of grayscale images. Each image is embedded in a blue star from last year's attempt to add some interest to the images. (It was not a successful attempt.)

Now you are stuck with these grayscale images surrounded by blue stars. Colorizing this would be a mess—especially since you have no color images from which to work. You decide that some type of duotone look is most appropriate, given your starting images. Because the group is willing to spring for 4-color printing, however, you can actually use more than one "duotone" in the image composite:

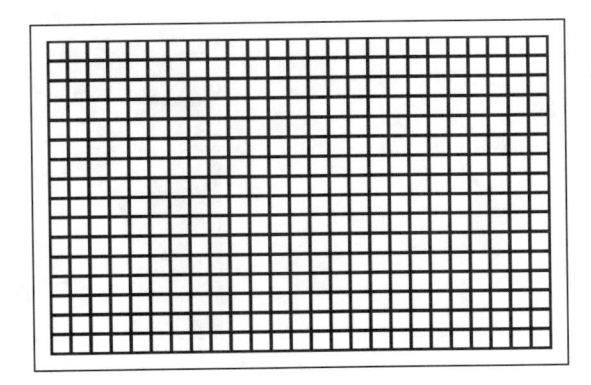

Figure 11.82 Stroking a selected grid.

1. Open the image CLOGGER.PSD from the CD-ROM. Figure 11.83 shows the wonderful starting image.
2. Double-click on the Background layer to create Layer 0.
3. Select the Magic Wand tool with a Tolerance of 12 and Anti-alias on. Click on the white background behind the dancer to select the Background. Press the Delete key (Mac) or Backspace key (Windows) to remove the selected area. Deselect (Command+D or Ctrl+D, respectively).
4. Open the image PATTRGB.PSD from this book's CD-ROM. The pattern was developed from the kerchief of one of the cloggers. Select the entire image by using Command+A or Ctrl+A. Define this as a pattern (Edit|Define Pattern).
5. Create a new Background layer. Fill the image with the pattern (Shift+Delete|Pattern, 100% Opacity, Normal).
6. Using the Eyedropper tool, click on the blue star to select that color as the foreground color.
7. Make a new layer (click on the New Layer icon at the bottom of the Layers Palette), and fill the image with the foreground color (Option+Delete or Alt+Backspace). Change the Blend mode to Screen.
8. Flatten the image. Figure 11.84 shows the image merged into the pattern.
9. Turn on the Rulers (Mac: Command+R, Windows: Ctrl+R). If your units are not set to pixels, double-click on a ruler and set them.
10. Drag a horizontal guide to the 100 and 550 pixel marks on the vertical ruler. Drag a vertical guide to the 100 and 500 pixel marks on the horizontal ruler. Select the Elliptical Marquee tool. Drag the marquee from the upper-left corner of the guide to the bottom-right corner, as shown in Figure 11.85. Snap to guides.
11. Choose Select|Feather; 25 pixels. Reverse the selection (Select|Inverse).
12. Double-click on the Background layer to create Layer 0. Press the Delete or Backspace key. Figure 11.86 shows the vignette.

Figure 11.83 CLOGGER.PSD—your starting point.

Figure 11.84 Image merged into background pattern.

Figure 11.85 Guides and an elliptical marquee selection.

13. Open the image HEXAGON.PSD on this book's CD-ROM. This shape was created using the Star filter in Alien Skin Eye Candy 3. This set has some wonderful filters, but the Star filter alone is worth the price in time saved by not having to create geometric forms by hand.

14. Drag the hexagon layer into the CLOGGER.PSD image. You need to drag it so that it is centered. To do this, press the Shift key as you drag either the image layer or the layer entry in the Layers palette to the clogger image. Position the hexagon layer below that of the clogger, make the clogger layer active, and group the two layers together (Command+G or Ctrl+G). Figure 11.87 shows the vignette now clipped to a hexagon.

To get the colors to look and work somewhat like duotones (but CMYK ones), you will use a series of steps developed by New York artist Eric Reinfeld. The next set of steps makes a CMYK duotone that is almost sepiatoned from the vignette. For this technique to work, you need to select a CMYK color that contains no black.

1. Click on the Foreground color swatch. Set the values in the CMYK area to CMYK: 0, 70, 45, 0.
2. Duplicate the image (Image|Duplicate|Merged Layers Only, OK).
3. Select Image|Mode|Grayscale.

Figure 11.86 The vignette surrounding the image.

Figure 11.87 Vignette clipped to hexagon.

4. Duplicate the image (Image|Duplicate|OK), and choose Image|Mode|CMYK.
5. Make a new layer (click on the New Layer icon at the bottom of the Layers Palette), and fill the image with the foreground color (Option+Delete on the Mac or Alt+Backspace in Windows). Change the Blend mode to Screen. Group the layers

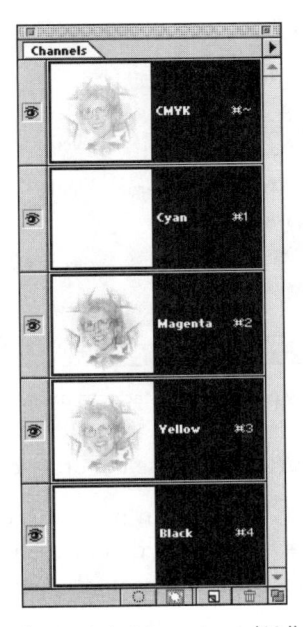

Figure 11.88 Channels palette showing data only in Magenta and Yellow plates.

(Command+G or Ctrl+G). Merge Down (Command+E or Ctrl+E). The image is very light, but only the Magenta and Yellow channels now contain any data, as you can see in Figure 11.88.

6. Open the Channels palette and make the Black channel the only active channel.
7. Choose Image|Apply Image and select the grayscale clogger image as the Source, as shown in Figure 11.89.
8. Let's give the Magenta plate a little boost. Make the Magenta plate active in the Channels palette (Command+2 or Ctrl+2). Choose Image|Apply Image and make the Yellow plate the Source. Change the Blend mode to Color Burn, as shown in Figure 11.90.

Figure 11.89 Apply Image dialog box to place the grayscale clogger into the black plate only.

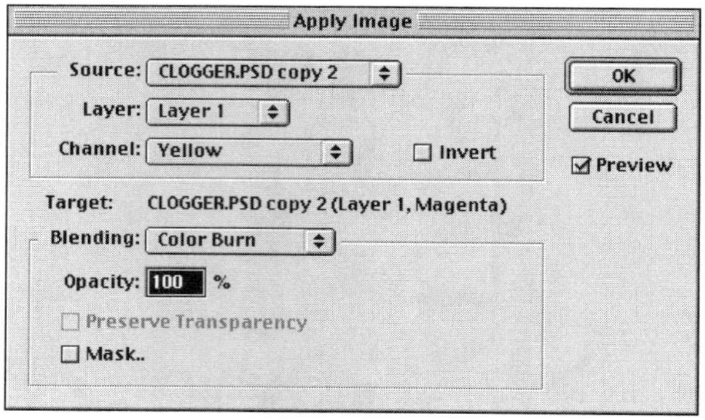

Figure 11.90 Adding some of the Yellow plate to the Magenta using Color Burn mode.

9. Save your work as CLOGCMYK.PSD. Close the other open images.

The next step in this procedure is to build an interesting frame treatment for the hexagon. Using a swash character from the Ultimate Symbol Design Elements collection and the multi-rotate Action that you used earlier, you can create the perfect edge:

1. Turn on the Rulers (Mac: Command+R, Windows: Ctrl+R). You need to determine the size of the straight sides of the hexagon. Change the image to 100% magnification (Command+Option+0 or Ctrl+Alt+0). Drag a horizontal guide to the top of the straight side of the hexagon, and another horizontal guide to the bottom of the straight side of the hexagon, as shown in Figure 11.91. Count the pixels between the guides (it should be 300 pixels). This gives you the needed width for the swatch.

2. Open the file SWASH.EPS from the CD-ROM. This is the same as the 01K29.EPS file that is in the Ultimate Symbol Design Elements collection also on this book's CD-ROM. In the Rasterize dialog box, enter 300 pixels as the Width, Constrain Proportions, and check Anti-alias.

> **TIP**
>
> When you import vector artwork, you get the best quality if you rasterize it at the size that you need it to be rather than resizing it within Photoshop.

3. Select Image|Rotate Canvas|90° CCW. This rotates the swash so that you can easily drag it into position. Let's be obsessive about getting things centered and try this easy way to find the center of the swash without measuring anything.

4. Select the Line tool and set its width to 1 pixel with no arrowheads. Create a new layer in the rotated swash image. Press the Shift key and draw a straight vertical line from the top of the image to the bottom.

5. Select the entire layer (Command+A on the Mac or Ctrl+A in Windows). Cut it to the clipboard (Command+C or Ctrl+C). Paste in the selection from the clipboard (Command+V or Ctrl+V). This centers the line on the image. The Line is your active layer.

Figure 11.91 Guides aligned with sides of hexagon.

Click on the second column on the Layers palette next to the Swash layer to place a Link symbol in it. This links the two layers together so that they can be moved as one unit.

6. Drag the line layer *from the image* into the CLOGCMYK.PSD image. As long as you drag the layer from the image, both it and its linked layer will move to the new image (do not drag the thumbnail from the Layers palette; it will not move the linked file with it). Position the thin line so that it's exactly on the edge of the hexagon below it. The swash should fit nicely between the two guides, as shown in Figure 11.92.

7. Drag the Line layer to the Layers palette trash can. It is no longer needed.

8. Make the swash character layer active. Choose Layer palette menu|Duplicate Layer; target: New file. This places the swash into its own file.

9. Drag the icon for the swash layer (you are working in the new file) to the New Layer icon (the center icon at the bottom of the Layers palette).

10. You need to flip this copy horizontally so that the swash is in the same location relative to the left side of the image. Because there is so much transparency in the layer, that won't happen by simply selecting Image|Flip Horizontal—so don't do that yet! Instead, take the Paintbrush and place a dab of paint in all four corners of the image. Now select Image|Transform|Flip Horizontal. Figure 11.93 shows the result.

11. Erase the dabs of color in the corners of the image and Merge Down (Command+E, Mac; Ctrl+E, Windows). You are left with only a layer named Layer 1 in the image.

Figure 11.92 Swash character and positioning line placed in CLOGCMYK.PSD.

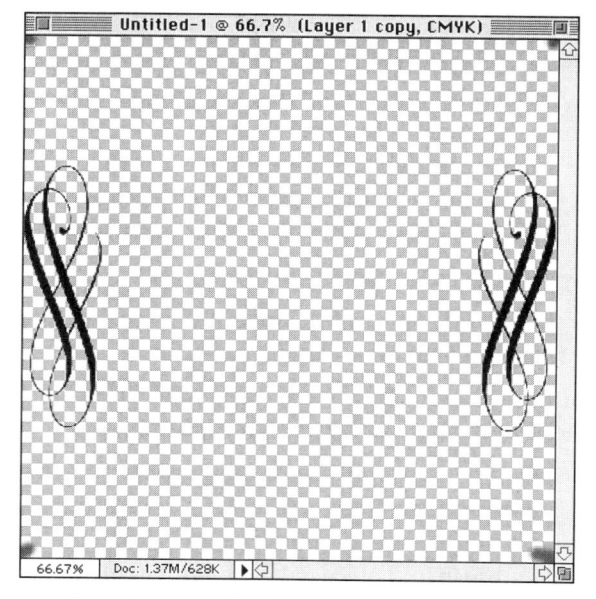

Figure 11.93 Swash character flipped horizontally after corners are added to the image.

12. Select the multirotate Action and click on the Play button. Figure 11.94 shows the result—a perfect frame, sized exactly for the hexagon that surrounds the clogger.

13. The top edges of the hexagon are not quite visible. Choose Image|Canvas Size and make both dimensions 700 pixels. Anchor in the center. Repeat the Canvas Size command on the Clogger image.
14. Merge Visible by pressing Shift+Command+E (Mac) or Shift+Ctrl+E (Windows).
15. Press the Shift key as you drag the frame layer into the CLOGCMYK.PSD image. Delete the original swash layer in the image and hide the guides. Figure 11.95 shows the framed hexagon. Save the CLOGCMYK.PSD image again and save the separate frame file as well. You may then close the frame file.

Figure 11.94 Frame created from swash character using multirotate Action.

Figure 11.95 Framed hexagon.

This next portion of the exercise finishes the frame around the hexagon and creates an adjustment layer. That only corrects the image and the cutout frame.

1. Set your Foreground color to CMYK: 0, 67, 45, 74.
2. Make sure that the frame layer is active. Fill the layer with the foreground color while preserving transparency (Shift+Option+Delete on the Mac or Shift+Alt+Backspace in Windows).
3. Make the clogger layer active. Add a layer mask. Let the layer mask remain active.
4. We want to "knock out" the frame area from this layer, so we need to construct a mask that will do that. Choose Image|Apply Image and select the frame layer (probably called Layer 1 copy) as your source. Choose the Transparency as the Channel, as shown in Figure 11.96. Notice that you need to invert the transparency. Turn off the visibility icon next to the frame layer to see that the layer mask on the clogger layer does what you want. Figure 11.97 shows this with a gray background so that it is more visible for the figure in the book (*do not add a gray layer to your image*).
5. Drag the frame layer below that of the clogger.
6. The purpose of the frame is to allow the frame color to show *outside* of the confines of the original hexagon. Whatever background we decide to design has to be seen through the frame area that lies *inside* of the original hexagon. Therefore, you need to remove the hexagon area from the frame. Press the modifier key (Mac: Command, Windows: Control) and click on the thumbnail for the clogger to load the transparency of that layer (click on the clogger thumbnail, *not* the layer mask thumbnail). Press the Delete key or the Backspace key. Figure 11.98 shows the image (again with a gray background so it looks "pretty for the camera").
7. Create a Hue/Saturation Adjustment Layer (Command+click or Ctrl+click) on the New Layer icon at the bottom of the Layers palette. The Adjustment layer should be the top layer in the layers palette. Click on the Colorize button and set the Hue to +18 and the Saturation to 50, as shown in Figure 11.99.

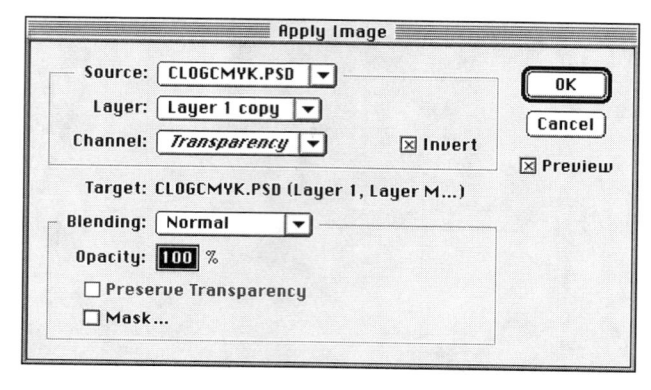

Figure 11.96 Creating a mask to knock out the border area of the hexagon.

Figure 11.97 Knockout visible in hexagon.

Figure 11.98 Border with area inside of hexagon knocked out.

8. The color in the clogger's face is just a bit too strong. Let's tone it with the Yellow layer again. Make only the Magenta channel active (Command+2 or Ctrl+2). Select Image| Apply Image and choose Layer 1 (the clogger) as the Source. Select the Yellow channel and change the Blend mode to Screen, as shown in Figure 11.100.

Figure 11.99 Create a Hue/Saturation layer.

Figure 11.100 Screen some Yellow from the Magenta channel.

9. Finally, you need to build a mask that allows changes from the Adjustment layer to affect only those areas of the total image that are visible at the moment (i.e., the mask needs to "respect" the layer mask below it). This turns out to be surprisingly easy. Choose Image|Apply Image and select the Merged image as the source. For Channel, select Transparency. This produces the desired results. Figure 11.101 shows the dialog box. (The "hard way" around building the same mask in three steps: Apply the Layer 1 transparency in Normal mode, apply the inverted Layer 1 layer mask in Subtract mode, and apply the Layer 1 copy—the frame—transparency in Screen mode.)

10. Save your work.

Finally, you are ready to create the background. For this, you will increase the image size a bit:

1. Create a new document (Command+N on the Mac or Ctrl+N in Windows). Make it 900 pixels square and CMYK mode.

2. Open the image file PATTCMYK.PSD from this book's CD-ROM. Select the entire image by pressing either Command+A or Ctrl+A. Define this as a pattern (Edit|Define Pattern). Fill the image with the pattern (Shift+Delete|Pattern, 100% Opacity, Normal).

> **TIP**
>
> Patterns are color mode sensitive. Patterns defined for RGB will not work on CMYK images and vice versa.

3. Set your foreground color to CMYK: 87, 49, 0, 0. This color is similar to the blue that was around the original star border, but it contains no black.

4. Make a new layer (click on the New Layer icon at the bottom of the Layers Palette), and fill the image with the foreground color (Option+Delete or Alt+Backspace). Change the Blend mode to Screen. Group the layers (Command+G or Ctrl+G). Merge Down (Command+E or Ctrl+E).

5. Open the Channels palette and make the Black channel the only active channel. Fill the Black channel with the pattern (Shift+Delete|Pattern, 100% Opacity, Normal). You now have another CMYK duotone work-alike.

6. Click on the CLOGCMYK.PSD image to make it active. Link all of the layers together by clicking on the Link column. Press the Shift key as you drag the layers from the image to the new document filled with the pattern. Before you do anything else, merge the linked layers (Command+E or Ctrl+E). Although it might look as if the Adjustment layer is doing something odd when you first bring in the clogger image, the layers will merge down properly if you do it before executing any other commands. Figure 11.102 shows the image with the background added.

7. Save the image as CLOGBACK.PSD.

Next, you are going to create a shield behind the hexagon and background to clip the shape. You will then merge this into another background that uses the name of the clogging group as a pattern.

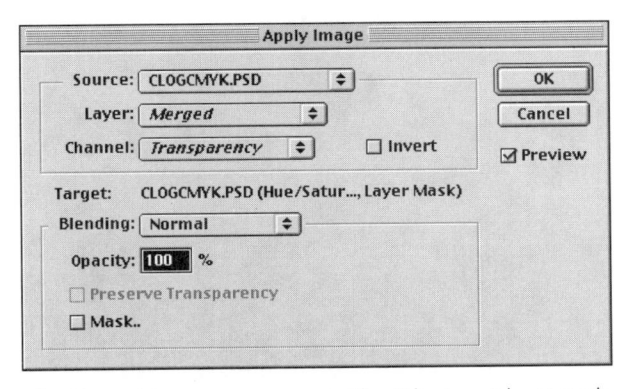

Figure 11.101 Applying the Merged layer transparency as the Adjustment layer mask.

1. Open the image PANEL.PSD from this book's CD-ROM. This is another image from the Ultimate Symbol Design Elements collection sampler, but for expediency, it has already been rasterized to the correct size.
2. Press the Shift key and drag the panel into the CLOGBACK.PSD image. Close all the images except this one (CLOGBACK.PSD).
3. Double-click on the Background layer to create Layer 0.
4. Drag the shield to the bottom of the layer stack.
5. Group all three layers together. Figure 11.103 shows the image against a white background. Merge the Visible Layers (Mac: Shift+Command+E, Windows: Shift+Ctrl+E).

Figure 11.102 Image with new background.

Figure 11.103 Panel used to clip layers together.

6. Increase the Canvas Size to 1,200×1,200, anchored in the center. The final image will not be this large, but you need to have room to rotate the type pattern. Create a new layer.

7. Open the file TEXTPATT.PSD from the CD-ROM. Select the entire image (Command+A or Ctrl+A). Define this as a pattern (Edit |Define Pattern). Fill the empty layer in the 1200 × 1200 pixel image with the pattern (Shift+Delete|Pattern, 100% Opacity, Normal).

> **TIP**
>
> When you define a pattern from a transparent layer, the pattern also has transparency, so it can be applied over another pattern or image without obscuring it.

8. Drag the pattern layer below that of the clogger.

9. Rotate the layer—press either Command+T or Ctrl+T—counterclockwise until it slants at an attractive angle (not 45°). A good angle is the one that is parallel to the slant of the lower edge of the panel. In order for you to use the rotate feature of Free transform, the image needs to be displayed smaller than the physical window in which it resides. Figure 11.104 shows the image as it is being rotated.

10. Turn on the Rulers (Command+R or Ctrl+R). Make the clogger layer active. Drag vertical guides so they snap to the bounding box of the layer (this should be at approximately 150 and 1,050 pixels). Drag horizontal guides until they form a square (place at the same coordinates as the vertical guides, but on the other ruler).

11. Choose the Rectangular Marquee tool and let it snap to the guides. Choose Image|Crop and hide the guides.

Figure 11.104 Rotating the text.

12. In the Channel palette, click on the New Channel icon in the center of the Channels palette to create a new channel. It should be filled automatically with black. Invert the channel to fill it with white or press Shift+Delete. Return to the composite channel by pressing either Command+~ (Mac) or Ctrl+~ (Windows).

13. Choose Image|Canvas Size and set the size to 1,020 pixels square. The channel that you created above is now a nice white square surrounded by black, and shows exactly where the original image size had been.

14. Choose Layer|New|Background to create a new Background layer.

15. Set your foreground color to CMYK: 0, 43, 56, 22. This is a color from the clogger's face. Fill the background layer (Mac: Option+Delete, Windows: Alt+Delete). Figure 11.105 shows the image.

16. Prepare a Gradient. Press D to set the colors back to the default of black and white. Swap the foreground and background colors (press the X key). Select the Radial Gradient tool and set the Foreground to Background gradient. Click on Edit. Place a foreground marker at the 60% mark between white and black, as shown in Figure 11.106. The top slider between white and black should be set to 30%.

17. Make the clogger layer active. Create a layer mask.

18. Turn on the Rulers (Command+R on the Mac or Ctrl+R in Windows). Choose View|Clear Guides. Drag out new guides to the center of the image (pixel 510 on each ruler).

19. Load Channel 5 (Command+Option+5 or Ctrl+Option+5).

Figure 11.105 Image with new background.

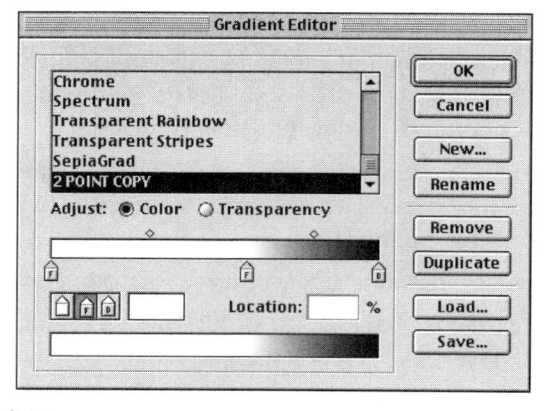

Figure 11.106 Gradient definition.

20. With the Gradient tool, place your cursor at the intersection of the two guides. Press the Shift key and drag the Gradient rubber-band cursor to the bottom-right corner of the selection. Figure 11.107 shows the layer mask and Figure 11.108 shows the way in which the edges of the panel now blend with the background.

21. Make a new layer (click on the New Layer icon at the bottom of the Layers Palette) at the top of the layer stack.

Figure 11.107 Layer mask with radial gradient.

Figure 11.108 Softly blended image.

22. Set your foreground color back to the color of the border (use the Eyedropper tool or set it explicitly to CMYK: 0, 67, 45, 74).

23. Channel 5 (the square) should still be loaded. Select Edit|Stroke; 8 pixels, Outside. *Do not deselect.*

24. Make a new layer (click on the New Layer icon at the bottom of the Layers Palette) at the top of the layer stack. Choose Select|Modify|Border; 50 pixels. Fill the area by pressing Option+Delete (Mac) or Alt+Delete (Windows) with CMYK: 0, 67, 45, 74, which should still be your foreground color.

25. Load Channel 5 again and reverse the selection (Select|Inverse). Press the Delete or Backspace key. Figure 11.109 shows the image. The clogger now looks as if she is on an embossed button.

26. Save the image as CLOGBTN.PSD.

You are now approaching the final steps—making a texture to set off the edges of the image.

1. Create a new image the same size as the current image, but in grayscale mode.

2. Open the image PANELPAT.PSD from this book's CD-ROM. This is a layer that is the same size as your image and created from the panel in the image.

3. You need to add a top and bottom row. Duplicate the pattern layer by dragging its thumbnail to the New Layer icon at the bottom of the Layers palette. Choose Filter|Other|Offset, Right: 0, Down: 60, Wrap Around. Use the Rectangular Marquee tool to enclose all of the image except for the top row. Delete.

Figure 11.109 Embossed look on image.

4. Duplicate the full pattern layer again. Offset again, but choose -60 as the Down offset. Select and delete all but the bottom row.
5. Merge Down by pressing either Command+E (Mac) or Ctrl+E (Windows). Figure 11.110 shows the panel pattern image.
6. Drag the icon for the panel layer to the New Layer icon (the center icon at the bottom of the Layers palette) to duplicate the layer. Choose Layer|Transform|Free Transform and rotate the layer as you did the text.
7. Repeat Step 6. This time, use the various methods of skewing and distorting to mutilate the new layer. Figure 11.111 shows the image in Free Transform.
8. Make a new layer (click on the New Layer icon at the bottom of the Layers Palette). Option+Merge the visible layers to keep all your originals intact by pressing Shift+Command+Option+E or Shift+Ctrl+Alt+E.
9. Press D to set the colors back to the default of black and white. Choose Filter|Pixellate|Pointillize, 22. Select Filter|Blur|Gaussian Blur, 2.0.
10. Make sure that all layers are visible. Click on the Channels palette and create a new channel. Fill with white.
11. Choose Image|Apply Image and used the merged image as your source and Black as the channel.
12. Make the CLOGBTN.PSD image active. Click on the Background layer to select it.

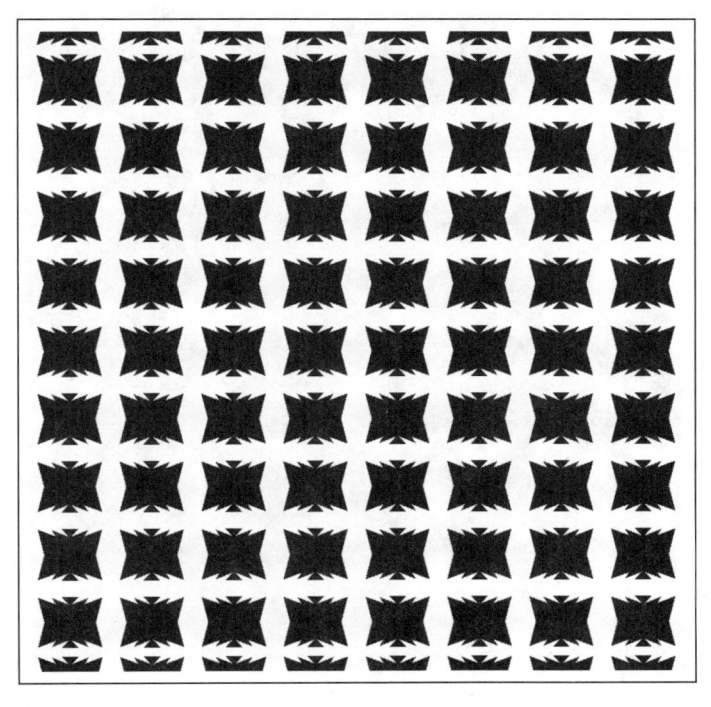

Figure 11.110 Panel pattern.

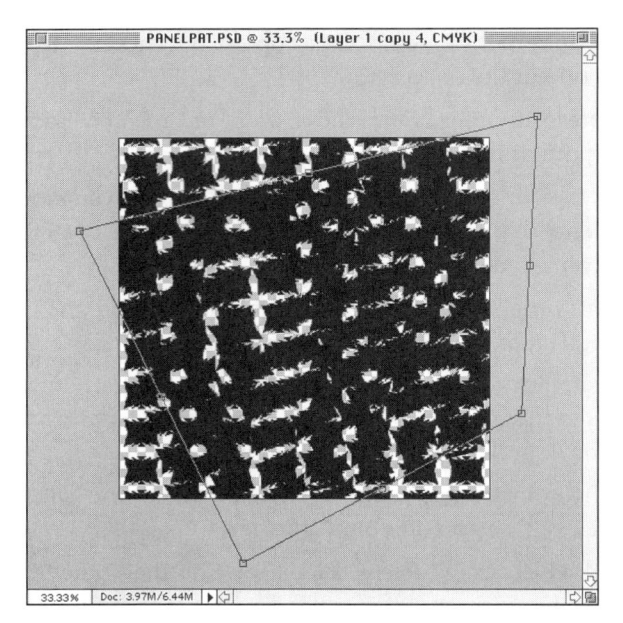

Figure 11.111 Image being seriously mistreated.

Figure 11.112 Finished clogger.

13. Press the modifier key (Mac: Option, Windows: Alt) and click on the layer mask for the clogger to load it. Choose Select|Load Selection. Load Channel 2 of PANELPAT.PSD and click on the Intersection With Selection button in the Operation section of the dialog box.

14. Press Delete or Backspace to fill the selection with white. Figure 11.112 shows the final image in grayscale.

Moving On

This chapter has covered a lot of ground. You learned how to use Adjustment layers, work with Guides and Grids, and use the new Free Transform and Numeric Transform commands. Along the way, you have seen many different tricks that can be played to force Photoshop to do what you want done—so that you, and not the program, are in control.

The next chapter shows you how to prepare images for the Web. You will learn about the file formats that matter, how to make images small so that they load faster, and how to create a wonderful variety of seamless patterns.

PHOTOSHOP AND THE WORLD WIDE WEB

The Web has opened up a wealth of opportunity for the designer. Working with low-color, low-resolution images, however, can be quite a change for the print artist. This chapter looks at this new world and invites you into it.

The planetary network of computers we know as the Internet has been in existence for many years. It has been, until recently, the exclusive tool of scientists, academics, government employees, and students. Its original purpose was to provide an easy corridor for information, virtually all of which was in the form of text. Several years ago, the graphical browser appeared. This new application allowed users to see text and pictures at the same time. The rest, as they say, is history.

After browsers came into existence, all the reasons that human beings use pictures *and* text to communicate with each other became important to the network medium. With pictorial information possible, a commercial impetus also became inevitable. Given the advantages inherent in a global information network, and the ease with which virtually anyone can place information on that network, the Internet's rapid growth is not surprising.

For reasons that will become clear as you study the information in this chapter, pictorial information on the Web has to be prepared in special ways. It must also belong to a specific classification of computer documents called *raster image files*. By happy coincidence, Adobe Photoshop, the subject of this book, is the world's most widely used and respected raster-processing software.

Photoshop had already attained its preeminent position when the graphical Web began to grow. Driven by the commercial impetus of the graphics and prepress industries, it had developed into a feature-rich and flexible program. With the increased importance of the digital medium, Photoshop has become the image-processing program of choice for Internet developers and prepress professionals. All the features that made it important before the Internet began to grow have turned out to be important features for the new medium.

Preparing images for print, as you discovered in Chapters 9 and 10, requires a specialized knowledge of printing. In the same way, preparing images for the Web requires that you become familiar with the way the Web works. The guidelines you need to follow for Web graphics are no more complex than those for printing. However, you need to keep many variables in mind, just as you do for print work. We've devoted this chapter to bringing you a good working knowledge of Web basics. To this knowledge, you'll be able to add your skill with Photoshop. The combination should allow you to become proficient at making visually and technically effective graphics for the Web.

Essentials Of Web Graphics

Web graphic files differ from those used in the prepress world in that they are typically low resolution and are always in the RGB mode. They're usually smaller in physical dimension than press files, because of the limitations imposed by the speed of the Web: Larger files take an unacceptable amount of time to transfer from the host to the client computer. This speed constraint lies at the heart of most graphic problems on the Internet. It is the single most important concept discussed in this chapter, and your success as a designer of Web graphics will be determined by how thoroughly you are able to balance the interplay between file size and file content. More simply put: A file can be attractive in every way, but if it's too large, very few Internet users will ever see it.

All of the Web's graphic information—banner text, bullets, buttons, photographs, arrows, navigation cues—are in what is called the *raster format*. In the following section of this chapter, you learn the difference between the two main computer graphic file types. You also learn about the HTML language, the language in which Web documents are written so that they can be displayed by a browser such as Netscape Navigator or Microsoft Internet Explorer. Finally, along with an explanation of why small file sizes are so important and what you can do to make sure that your files are no larger than they need to be, you learn about the two file types—GIF and JPEG—used by Web designers.

Graphic File Types: Vector Vs. Raster

In general computer terms, there are two main graphic file types: the *vector* file and the *raster* file.

Vector files are composed of shapes that can be described in mathematical terms. The technical descriptors might include such things as height, width, placement within a defined space, the color of a fill, and so on. These shapes are usually composed of lines that either enclose an area or are standalone. In PostScript, for example, the lines take the form of Bézier (pronounced beh-zee-áy) curves (also called *paths*). Objects drawn in draw programs such as Adobe Illustrator and Macromedia FreeHand are examples of vector shapes made up of Bézier curves. Type is another example of the computer's use of vector shapes. PostScript type consists of drawn shapes—which are made up of Bézier curves—that have been placed in a special file that allows the shapes to be handled as macro objects instead of graphic shapes. Except for a few special cases, vector-mapped graphic objects cannot be used on the Web. These special cases involve what is called a browser *plug-in*, a small helper program that gives the browser capabilities that weren't part of its original design. Although plug-ins are simple to acquire and install, industry studies indicate that most Internet users don't bother with them. Because of this, you should be wary of using technology that isn't part of the standard Web feature set. A plug-in that can display a vector graphic object is one example of such a nonstandard feature.

> **NOTE:** As of the publication of this book, Macromedia has opened up the file format of their Flash technology for placing vector files on the Web. This change will allow the format to be supported by browsers without an additional plug-in. It remains to be seen how quickly this standard is adopted.

Raster files are represented by the data processed in programs such as Photoshop. A raster is defined as a collection of objects—in this case, *pixels*—arranged in uniform columns and rows. A raster computer file can be thought of, whether color or grayscale, as a set of small squares that use a mosaic approach to building an image. Each square is displayed as a single color tone. The success of the mosaic depends on the fact that the squares are quite small and the human eye is not very good at fine resolution. The squares blend into each other to give the impression of a continuous range of tones. An example of a raster object is shown in Figure 12.1. The tiny rectangle in the left image has been magnified on the rightmost side so that the individual components of the image are visible.

A raster file has some advantages and some drawbacks. The actual storing of the file is extremely simple. The section of the image on the right in Figure 12.1 could be stored—and described—like this: The area is composed of 38 horizontal rows of pixels, and each row is 38 pixels across; beginning in the upper left corner, the first row contains RGB values 232, 232, 233, 234, 232, and so on. A description of this kind quickly becomes tedious to the human mind, but to a computer, it's a straightforward task. Imagine this description carried on until all 1,444 pixels in the image have been described by their position and RGB values. Yet, this is the way a computer handles the image, by reading this table of values into memory and displaying them in equivalent rows and columns of monitor pixels.

The latter point is a big advantage: Monitor pixels and object pixels correspond to each other easily. Your CRT uses pixels to display everything you see. It's a simple procedure: Match the pixels of the image to the pixels of the screen. It's so simple, in fact, that very little thought has

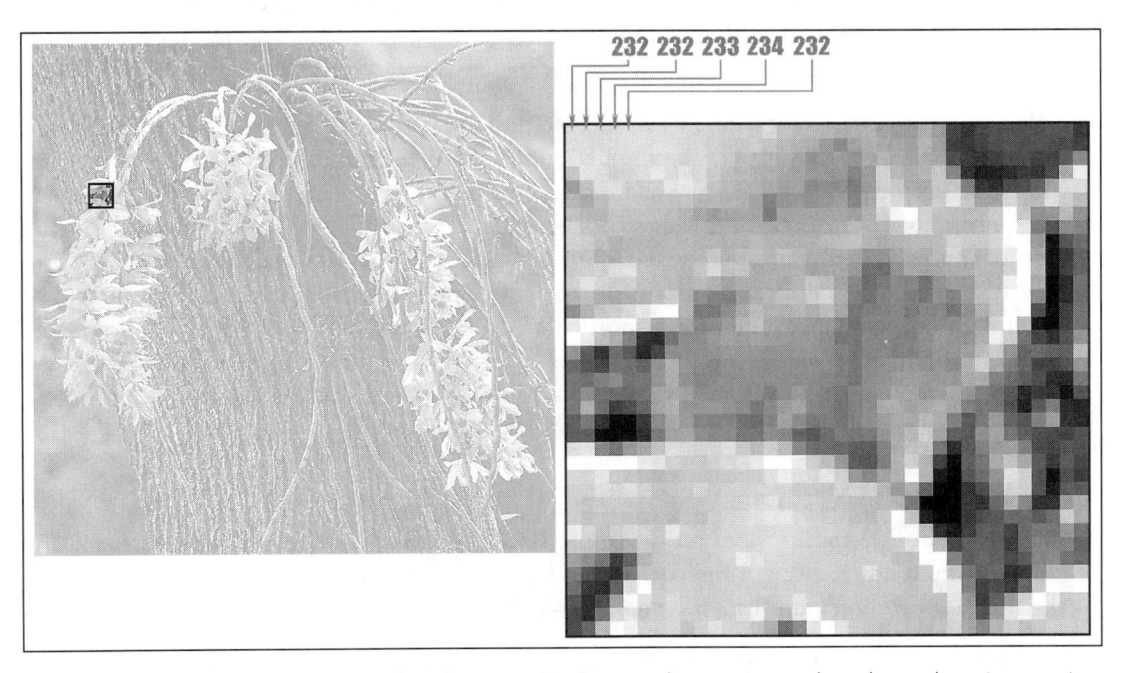

Figure 12.1 A raster file is a mosaic of small squares. Each square has a unique color value and a unique position within the image.

to be given to what kind of operating system is being used. Because many kinds of computers—and operating systems—use the Internet, the raster file is nearly ideal.

Disadvantages? The main problem is file size. A single pixel value, with respect to the grayscale image in the example, represents 1 byte of information and therefore adds 1 byte to the size of the file. Simple arithmetic gives us a file size of at least 1,444 bytes (38 × 38 = 1,444 bytes, or 1.41K). If the example file were in RGB, or Color, mode rather than Grayscale, each pixel would need to be represented by 3 bytes of information. An RGB file 38 pixels square would be at least 4,332 bytes (4.23K). The information contained in the file also must include, besides the color value of the pixels, header information that tells the computer what kind of file—TIFF, EPS, BMP, and so on—it's displaying, the number of rows, and the number of pixels in each row. In some cases, the information also includes a special color look-up table (CLUT). All of this information is needed to describe and store the tiny area shown in the figure. The size of the file has a direct bearing on its use on a Web page since the Web network's efficiency, or speed, is measured by the rapidity of its transfer of information from one computer to another. That efficiency is typically measured in figures expressed as bytes per second, or kilobytes per second. Basically, the more bytes you have, the more time it takes to get the image from one place to another.

Inline Graphics

A graphic on a Web page is a substitute for a single character of text. The Web, despite daily improvements in technology, consists of a simple network structure that was designed for the transfer of small ASCII text files. Graphics objects are simply inserted into the stream of ASCII data and displayed within the body of text. Using the specifications of HTML (*Hypertext Markup Language*) 2 and above, the graphic can be inserted into the text along the text's baseline, centerline, or topline. These concepts are illustrated in Figure 12.2.

A Web graphic can occupy a single line of text, making it equivalent to a paragraph. Most of the paragraph style formats can be applied to it, just as they are applied to the text within which the graphic resides. These would include such things as centered text, flush left, flush right, and indent attributes. Print graphic designers have long been accustomed to placing graphics and text in any position on a page. On the Web, things aren't quite that simple: Using only text attributes, designing graphically effective pages has been difficult. The advent of HTML 3 and the Netscape extensions—particularly the use of tables—has begun to allow some design freedom. However, it will be some time before the text-only origins of Web pages will become obscured and allow for the design freedom that prepress designers have enjoyed for a number of years.

Nuts And Bolts Of The Web

You may find it helpful to look at a sample HTML file and see how it's interpreted by the browser. The following shows the correlation between HTML code and the browser's display. The figure shown in Figure 12.3 is a very simple simulated Web page or HTML document.

The HTML code for this simulated browser display is shown in Figure 12.4. Please note that normal HTML code is not typically formatted in this manner. It is presented in this way to

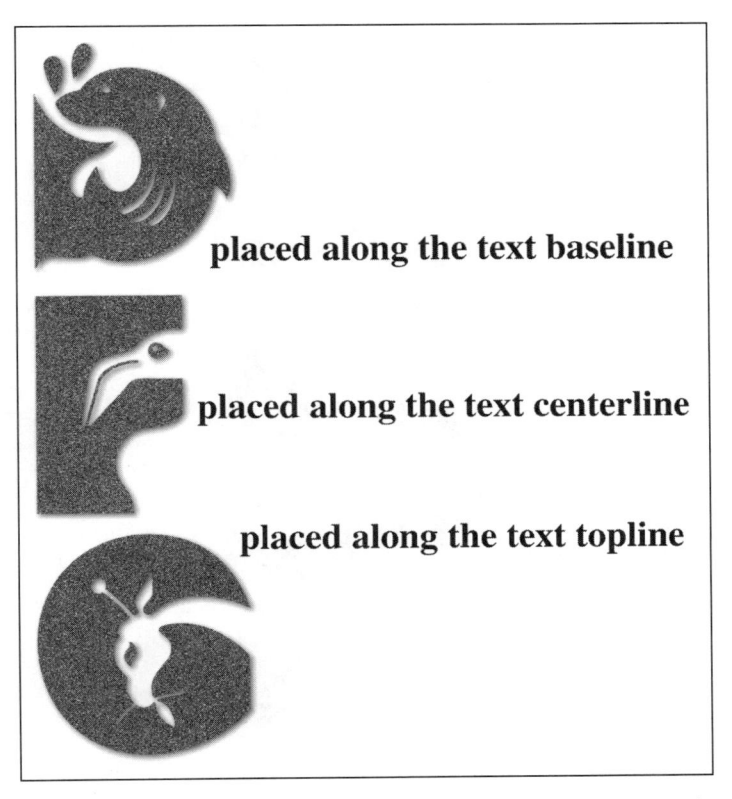

Figure 12.2 Graphics on the Web substitute for single characters. They display within the body of text along the text's baseline, centerline, or topline.

make the pairing of the code commands easier to grasp. The information this page contains is not intended as an HTML tutorial. Instead, simply observe the way the ASCII information is divided into two parts: the tags (instructions for the browser) and everything else (the information on which the tags are to operate).

HTML documents are composed of code information and text information. The tags are set off—usually, but not always—in pairs. Each tag is an instruction to the browser to display the information within the tag pairs in a specific way. The first tag usually takes the form <TAG>. The concluding tag takes the form </TAG> and is distinguished from the opening tag by the presence of the forward slash.

- *Line 1*—<HTML> is the first tag of all HTML documents. It is a declaration that the document contains HTML code. The end tag for Line 1 is Line 28, the last statement of the document.
- *Lines 2 through 6*—The information within the <HEAD> tags serves as the preliminary or opening description of the rest of the file. The <HEAD> tag contains within it the <TITLE> tag. Note that the <TITLE> tag is *nested* within the <HEAD> tag. The <TITLE> tag is important despite the fact that the title does not display within the browser's window (although it does display in the title bar of the browser window). Not only does it name the document,

Figure 12.3 A simulation of a simple Web page.

but it also provides information to Web search engines that classify a site's contents by the information contained—among other places—within the <TITLE> tags. The information in the <TITLE> tag is also what is placed in the bookmark menu whenever a user makes a bookmark for a page.

- *Line 7*—All of the rest of the HTML document falls between the two <BODY> tags (Lines 7 and 27). This tag is exactly what it seems: This part is the main "body" of the document. Within the body is another tag that tells the browser what color to use for the background of the document. In this case, the display is set to white. FF is hexadecimal for the number 255. The RGB color values here are set to 255, 255, and 255 (three two-digit numbers not separated by spaces). Lacking an instruction for a background color, some browsers (Netscape, Lynx) usually display a tone that would be written C0C0C0 (192 192 192), which is 75 percent of the distance between black (000000) and white. The equivalent print tone would be 25-percent black.

- *Lines 8 through 12*—The tag <H1> followed by the tag <CENTER> indicates that the text in Line 10 is to be displayed in the center of the page using the largest of the six possible *Heading* sizes. This line of text serves as the opening statement for the page the way a user would see it displayed within the browser (all of this information would usually be included in a

Photoshop And The World Wide Web 817

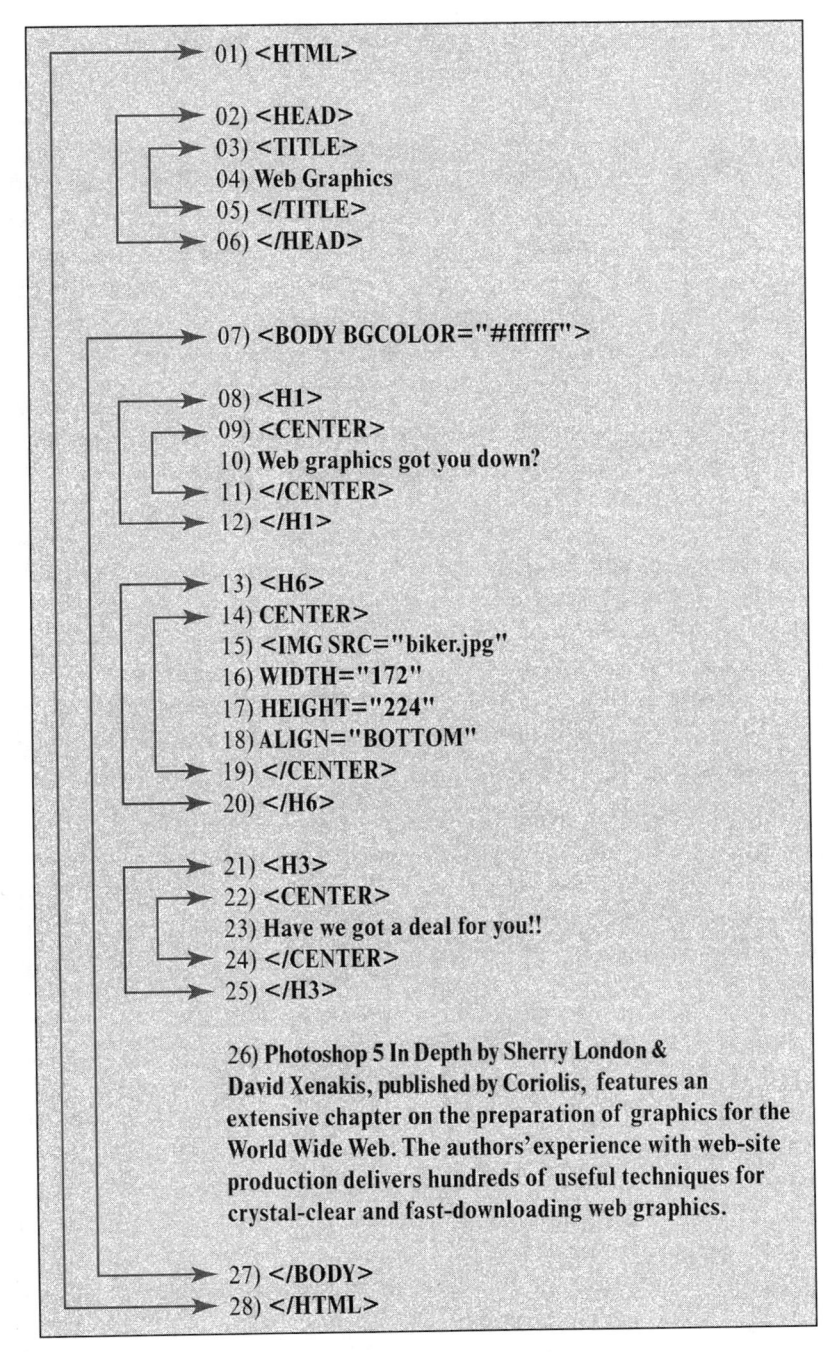

```
01) <HTML>

02) <HEAD>
03) <TITLE>
04) Web Graphics
05) </TITLE>
06) </HEAD>


07) <BODY BGCOLOR="#ffffff">

08) <H1>
09) <CENTER>
10) Web graphics got you down?
11) </CENTER>
12) </H1>


13) <H6>
14) CENTER>
15) <IMG SRC="biker.jpg"
16) WIDTH="172"
17) HEIGHT="224"
18) ALIGN="BOTTOM"
19) </CENTER>
20) </H6>

21) <H3>
22) <CENTER>
23) Have we got a deal for you!!
24) </CENTER>
25) </H3>

26) Photoshop 5 In Depth by Sherry London &
David Xenakis, published by Coriolis, features an
extensive chapter on the preparation of graphics for the
World Wide Web. The authors' experience with web-site
production delivers hundreds of useful techniques for
crystal-clear and fast-downloading web graphics.

27) </BODY>
28) </HTML>
```

Figure 12.4 The HTML code used to display the page in Figure 12.3.

single line of code). The six <H> tags are often used in this way—as a way of approximating a headline—but there is a subtle difference between a headline and Heading information (see the following Tip).

> **TIP**
>
> The Web's textual organization, despite the evolution of modern Web document design, is hierarchical. The six <HEAD> tags are used as ways of indicating a document's structure and organization. That the <HEAD> tags are sized from largest (H1) to smallest (H6) is a coincidence that has nothing to do with the way a graphic designer would use headline type—large, bold text and simple phrases that arrest the attention and advise the viewer of a page's contents.
>
> This point is difficult to visualize. However, imagine a Web robot from one of the large WWW indexing organizations visiting the pages on your Web server. The robot encounters an HTML document and catalogs its contents by examining the ranking of information based on the <HEAD> tags. Now imagine that the designer of the page had begun the page with "*WOW!*", using the <H1> tag. This method is certainly graphically effective for drawing attention to this page. However, as a means of evaluating the document's content, it's nearly devoid of information. (Actually, most modern search engines don't categorize a site based on its hierarchy of information but rely instead on meta-tags. We mention this use of HEAD information to underscore the hierarchical organization of data that still underlies most of the data on the Web.)
>
> If the headline for the HTML document requires large, bold text, the <HEAD> tags are probably not the way to display it. Instead, use a graphic that is, in HTML terms, informationally neutral, but that will do a much more convincing graphic job of headlining than the <HEAD> tags. Graphics of this kind, accompanied by meta-tag data, are far more effective than Heading text.

- *Lines 13 through 20*—These lines refer to the graphic below the headline. The graphic, according to these tags, is to be displayed in the center of the page and in the smallest of the six Head sizes. The <HEAD> tag is meaningless where a graphic is concerned, but serves to show that the graphic is controlled by applying text tags to it. Line 15 designates that an IMG SRC (image with file name or path name or URL) is to be displayed. In this case, the SRC attribute is the name of the file, biker.jpg. Additional information about the graphic is also given: It's 172 pixels wide, 224 pixels high, and is to be aligned on either side of the text, along the baseline of the graphic.
- *Lines 21 through 25*—These lines are similar to Lines 8 through 12. In this case, the text is displayed in the third-largest Head style.
- *Line 26*—This text block contains the plain text below the introductory or headline material.
- *Lines 27, 28*—Concluding tags from the top of the document.

The efficiency of HTML is obvious from the fact that so few instructions are required to display this simulated page. The entire set of instructions for display—as well as all the text shown in the browser window—requires just 574 bytes. The single graphic, by contrast, requires 44,107 bytes. Put more simply, the graphic is nearly 77 times the size of all the rest of the document. It's easy to see why the inclusion of many graphics in an HTML document carries a heavy penalty in terms of download time.

So, What's The Hold-Up?

The term *baud rate* is so beset by qualifiers that it's almost meaningless. About the only thing you can say with certainty about modems is that a 28.8K-baud modem is faster than a 14.4K modem. Both are faster than a 2400 or a 300. So many other factors are involved—line efficiency, compression, Web traffic, time of day, and so on—that the whole subject gets very complicated. The only way to make sense of the entire issue is to look at a range of transfer rates (the speed with which data is moved from one system to another), and design your Web graphics accordingly.

The modems in general use on the Internet are of the 14.4K, 28.8K, or 33.3K variety, though faster modems are becoming more common. Slower modems make the graphics-intensive Web nearly impractical. A 14.4K modem, the slowest acceptable device, shows a range of transfer between .75 and 1.5Kbps. Performance on a 28.8K modem is somewhat better, ranging from about 1.8 to 3Kbps. There will be remarkable changes in coming years, but for the moment, we need to work with what we have. The vast majority of all the modems in use on the Web—planet-wide—are of the 28.8K variety. If we take as a baseline the moderate performance of the 28.8K, we have a graphic that transfers at about 1 to 2Kbps. The math from there is simple. The 44K file, biker.jpg, shown in the example in Figure 12.3, will take (at the slower speed) three-quarters of a minute to move from the host server to the machine accessing the file. In fact, the time will probably be slightly more than that since some time is spent by the two machines arranging protocols, and so on. The sample HTML document, text and tags, is displayable by the browser in slightly more than a half second. Given the throughput rates of the two modems, it is obvious that the 33.3K modem will be able to display the data in less time.

It's good to keep these physical speeds in mind when designing for the Web. If a page contains a number of graphics, the combined size of the graphic files in kilobytes equals about half the number of seconds, on average, a 28.8K modem will take to download the page. It's easy to design a page that transfers so slowly that the user will simply give up and cancel the transfer. Given that a Web page is usually put on the Net for some purpose, it just isn't logical to do anything that obstructs the user from making use of it.

It's not an easy pill to swallow, is it? You will need to design, not for systems that work as well as yours, but for the millions of users who access the Web on systems that are older and slower than yours. Try not to worry about it: This kind of constraint simply means that your creativity has to kick in. You must make your designs effective, but within the difficult parameters of the Web's limitations.

Bit Depth, Two File Formats

An understanding of the term *bit depth* is necessary in two situations. The first situation occurs when a file is converted to the GIF file format. The second situation arises when you consider what kinds of monitors your graphic files will be displayed on around the world. In the following sections of this chapter, we discuss bit depth and how it applies to Web designers.

A second important Web topic deals with the two file formats that are supported by all graphical browsers. When we use the term *supported by*, we simply mean that files in these two formats can be added to your Web page without any special instructions to the browser beyond an extension to the file name. GIF files use a .gif extension. JPEG files use .jpg. The extension simply tells the browser how to read the file so that it can be displayed.

Bit Depth

Bit depth refers to the number of colors a device can display. It can also refer to the number of colors in a file. The file is said to be an 8-bit, 16-bit, or 24-bit file. Monitors are said to display in black and white (1 bit) or in 8 bits or 24 bits. The bit numbers are powers of two. An 8-bit file would be 2^8 (256 colors), and a 24-bit file would be 2^{24} (16,777,216 colors). Bit depth is the largest factor contributing to a file's size. Every pixel in an 8-bit file requires 1 byte (8 bits = 1 byte) per pixel of information. A 24-bit file requires 3 bytes per pixel. All else being equal, a 24-bit file will be three times as large as an 8-bit file. We'll consider bit depth in more detail as we look at the two main file types used for graphics on the Web.

The GIF Format

GIF is pronounced "jif" or "gif"—there is no apparent standardization of the term. You can use either without guilt or self-consciousness. The *Graphics Interchange Format* was developed to facilitate the transfer of graphic documents from one computer to another via modem. The format uses a compression method called LZW (a patented, *lossless* compression algorithm owned and licensed by Unisys Corporation). The GIF format can be used for color, grayscale, or black and white files. Used for color and grayscale, the GIF format limits the number of colors in a document to 256. Ordinarily, a single-colored pixel requires 24 bits (3 bytes). With the GIF format, a pixel can be a single byte because the file is accompanied by a CLUT that acts as an index of the file's colors. Grayscale information is always stored as 1 byte per pixel (with 256 total grays). Grayscale is, within Photoshop, a separate mode, but it can also be one of the possible CLUTs in the GIF file format. With the compression and reduction in bit depth, GIF files are considerably smaller—by about two-thirds—than their RGB equivalents.

Converting To The GIF Format

GIF files usually begin as RGB or grayscale files and are converted to Indexed Color mode from within programs such as Photoshop. The procedure in Photoshop is to choose Image|Mode| Indexed Color. The dialog box shown in Figure 12.5 allows you to set options for the file's conversion.

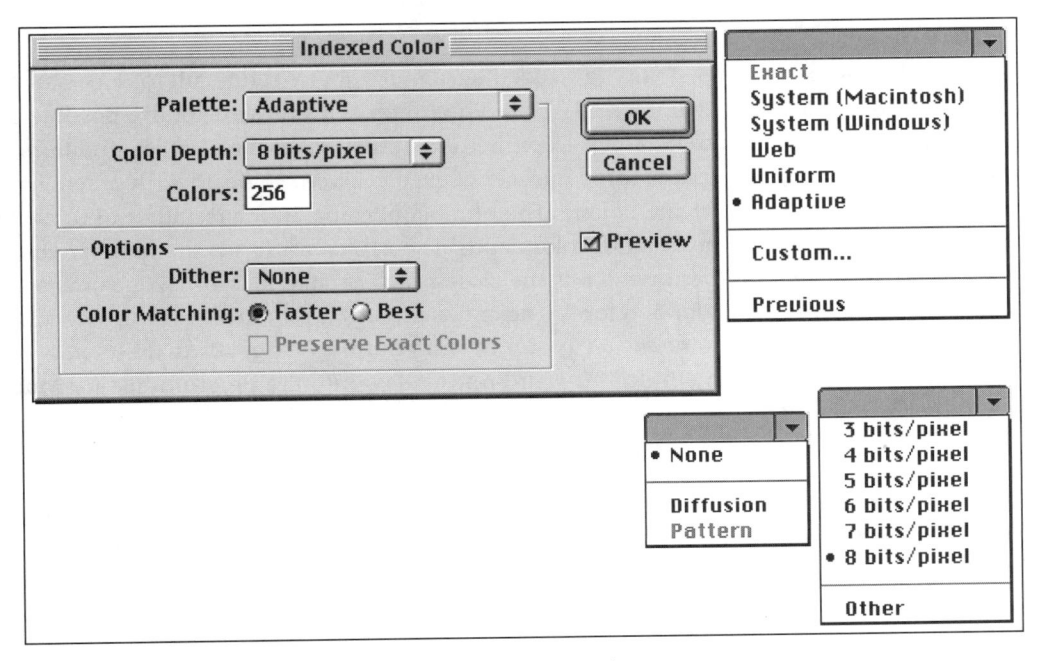

Figure 12.5 Photoshop's Indexed Color conversion-options window.

Palette

The Palette pop-up menu gives a range of options that determine which colors will be assigned to the CLUT. It has six possibilities: Adaptive, Uniform, Web, System (Windows), System (Macintosh), and Exact.

Adaptive

To understand how Adaptive works, it's helpful to know that Photoshop deals with an RGB file internally as a 24-bit file, even if the monitor on which it is viewed displays the information only in 8 bits. Most 8-bit monitors can display the entire 24-bit color range, but only 256 colors at a time. The process of choosing the best possible combination of 256 colors from the millions available is called an *adaptive* display. The Adaptive option in the Palette section of the Indexed Color dialog box works in much the same way: This option allows Photoshop to map the best possible group of 256 colors from the 16.77 million at its disposal. The adaptive option ensures that the conversion will produce a set of colors as close as possible to the original RGB range of the image. If it's critical that the color range of the original image be preserved as closely as possible, Adaptive is the correct choice.

The Adaptive choice can be weighted toward certain colors in an image. If you make a selection when you choose to convert the file to Indexed Color mode, the colors within the selection are given prominence in the calculation. Otherwise, Photoshop calculates the best set of all available colors when it makes the conversion.

Uniform

We would love to skip this possibility for a good reason: It's about as difficult to understand as it is useless. But okay, here's what it's all about. Photoshop calculates one of five possible Uniform CLUTs by first looking at the Color Depth setting. It then takes the number, and from the entire color spectrum, chooses the same number of evenly spaced colors in each of red, green, and blue, and then calculates the palette. The number of colors in the resulting CLUT will be the perfect cube closest to the original color depth. The 216 colors (6^3) is the number you get when the color depth is 8 (because 216 is the closest perfect cube to 256), 125 (5^3) when the color depth is 7, 64 for 6, 27 for 5, 8 for 3. The entire strategy *must* make sense to someone. It *must* have been useful to someone. A group of programmers as good as those who write Photoshop wouldn't put something this weird and useless into the program just for laughs, would they?

System

The System option under Palette forces Photoshop to reassign the colors within the image to those used by the operating system for all of its routine display tasks. Both Macintosh and Windows use a default 8-bit CLUT system display. The two CLUTs are not the same, and you're given the choice of using either.

Web

Even though the system CLUTs for Macintosh and Windows are not the same, they do contain quite a few colors—216 to be exact—in common. Using this option assures that any image will display exactly the same—with only minor differences in brightness—on both a Macintosh and a Windows display. This option is identical to the palette constructed by Photoshop, using 8-bit color and Uniform.

> **TIP**
>
> Having a built-in CLUT allows a computer's operating system to manage color displays with considerable speed. Where there are uncommon colors, however, each system displays the non-native colors of the other not as a solid, but as a dither composed of a number of tones. In some cases, dithering is pleasant, but more often the resulting mix of colors is unattractive. To prevent this from happening, you may want to load the Web CLUT of common platform colors into your Swatches palette and use these colors to construct all of your Web graphics.
>
> After converting any file using the Web palette (and while the file is still open), choose Image|Mode|Color Table. When the dialog box opens, click on the Save button, and save the file under a name such as "Web Colors". Now, click on the Swatches palette menu and choose Load Swatches or Replace Swatches. Locate the Web Colors file you just saved. Photoshop loads this set of colors into the palette for easy access whenever you're working on graphics for the Web.

Exact

Exact is a color map strategy that's available only if the number of colors in the document is 256 or fewer. Photoshop uses exactly the same colors for the color table as those that make up the image.

Custom

When choosing a specific set of 256 colors out of 16.7 million, there are a large number of possible CLUTS. When Custom is applied to the color content of a file, another dialog box appears (see Figure 12.6). Within this dialog box, you can edit individual colors in the CLUT; one of several prebuilt color tables can be chosen from the pop-up menu at the top, the edited color table can be saved as a named file, or another named color look-up table can be loaded.

The predefined color table pop-up menu at the top of this window provides five points of departure. The first, Black Body, shows a blend of the color tones—black to red to orange to yellow to white—a black body object radiates as heat is applied to it. The second, Grayscale, is composed of black and white and the 254 gray shades between them. The third, Macintosh System, is the standard palette for the Macintosh. The fifth option, Windows System, gives different results from Macintosh System because of the noted 40 noncommon colors. The fourth, Spectrum, gives a blend of colors that is prismatic—violet to blue to green to yellow to orange to red.

One advantage to loading a single custom color table for a number of files is that all the files will be viewed (no matter which computer runs the browser), without the annoying flashes of color that sometimes accompany the quick change in CLUTs on systems running 8-bit displays. Someday, perhaps, all CRTs will be 24-bit. Presently, the large majority of systems in the world use 8-bit displays.

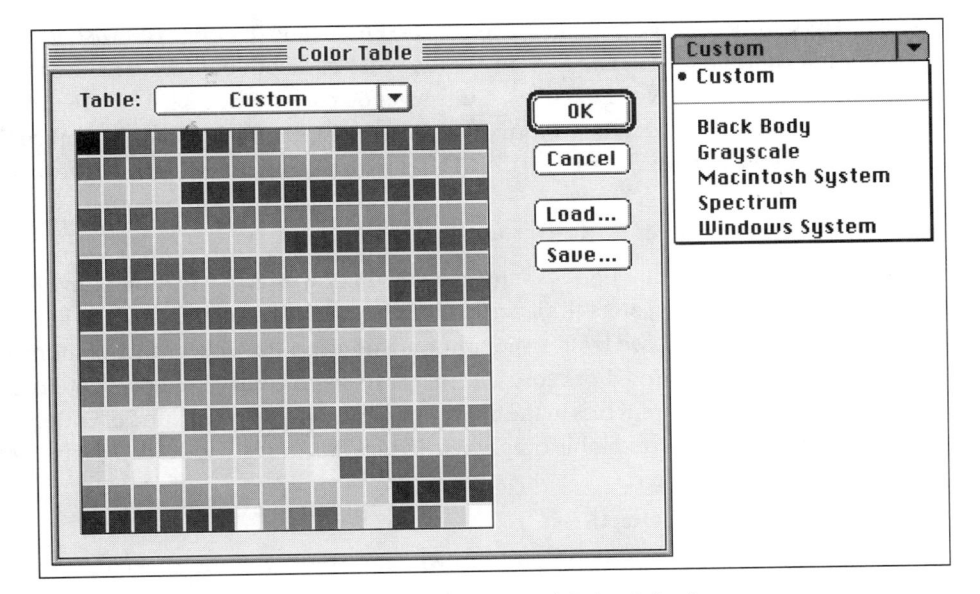

Figure 12.6 The Custom Color Table option from the Indexed Color dialog box.

> **TIP**
>
> You can edit the custom color table so that the assigned colors become a range of close colors similar to a gradient. Click with the mouse in the upper left corner of the color table and drag to the lower right corner. The Color Picker appears with the message, "Select the first color". To test this procedure, choose white and click on the OK button. The Color Picker then appears again with the message, "Select the last color". Choose a color and click on OK. The color table now shows 256 evenly spaced values ranging from white to the second color you picked. You can extend this idea further by clicking and dragging small distances within the color table. Your selection need not include the entire table.
>
> Defining colors and applying them to grayscale images is one way to successfully colorize grayscale files. If you define the color table as a set of tones between white and a very dark blue, your grayscale image shows all of the blue tones mapped to the equivalent gray values. For non-Web use, you can convert the image back to RGB mode after you have colorized it.

Previous

This is another batch-processing utility to ensure uniformity of CLUTs among a number of separate files. Choosing Previous simply loads in the last-used Custom or Adaptive CLUT and applies it to the new image.

Color Depth

The default bit resolution is usually 8 bits/pixel because Photoshop assumes you wish to preserve as much color information as possible. Use any of the other bit-depth buttons to reduce the number of colors in the file: 7 bits gives 128 colors, 6 bits gives 64 colors, 5 bits 32, 4 bits 16, and 3 bits gives 8. You can, if you want, enter an arbitrary number of colors in the option box marked Other. As the number of colors decreases, the size of the CLUT also decreases, and with it the size of the file.

Dither

The Dither option allows the simulation of many tones by mixing up colors so that the eye is tricked into believing that it sees more colors than are actually present. The method is called Diffusion, and it is similar to the strategy used by the color printing industry: The appearance of many colors is achieved by using four surprinted primary ink colors. In some cases, the dither option can be turned off (None) with no apparent loss to the quality of the image. A special kind of Pattern dither that uses an 8×8 cell of pixels is available only when System (Macintosh) is the designated palette.

Many Options, Many Looks

Figure 12.7 shows an example photograph from which a small area has been extracted and some of the indexing options applied. These begin with the magnified area seen unaltered in Figure 12.8. The other possibilities, Figures 12.9 through 12.21, show how the image is changed as the color indexing takes place.

Figure 12.7 From this image, we have taken a small area (the small dark area on the right side) and magnified it so that you can see the difference in Photoshop's GIF conversion options. Figures 12.8 through 12.21 are examples of each.

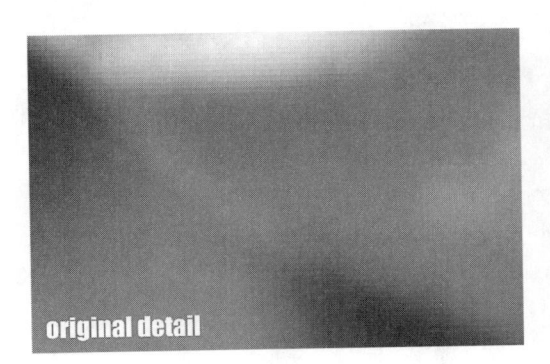

Figure 12.8 Original detail.

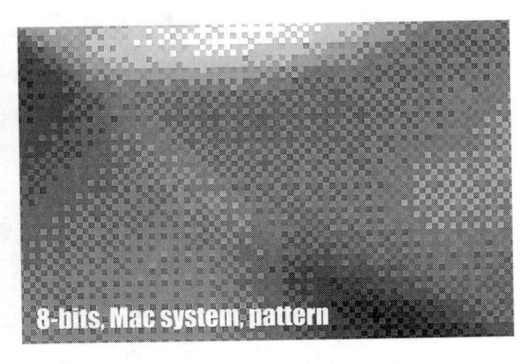

Figure 12.9 8-bits, Mac system, pattern.

Figure 12.10 8-bits, alternative, none.

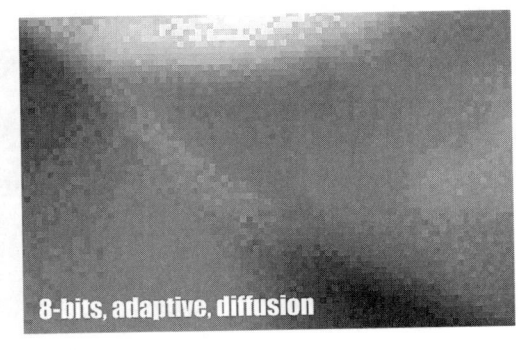

Figure 12.11 8-bits, adaptive, diffusion.

Figure 12.12 7-bits, adaptive, none.

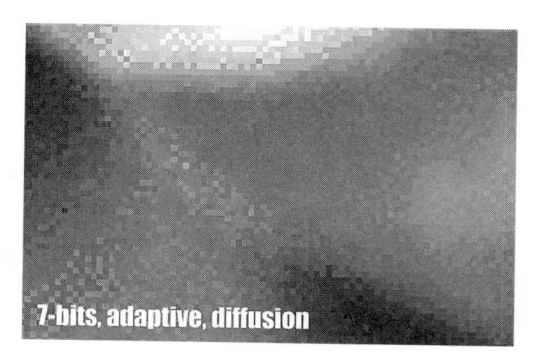

Figure 12.13 7-bits, adaptive, diffusion.

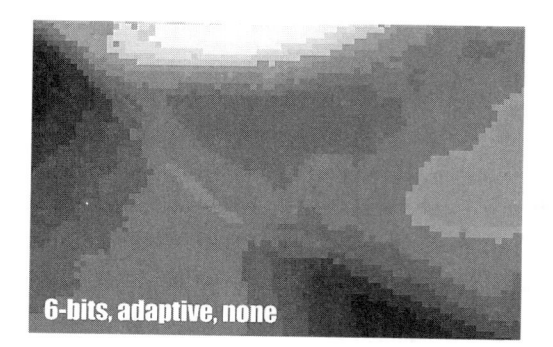

Figure 12.14 6-bits, adaptive, none.

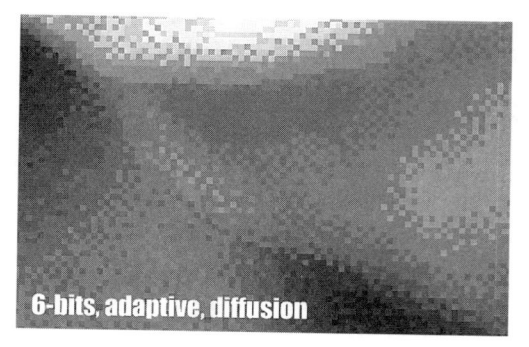

Figure 12.15 6-bits, adaptive, diffusion.

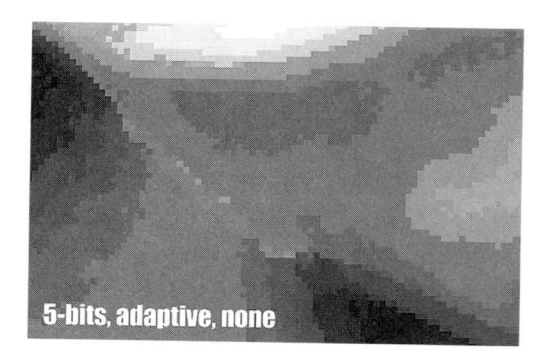

Figure 12.16 5-bits, adaptive, none.

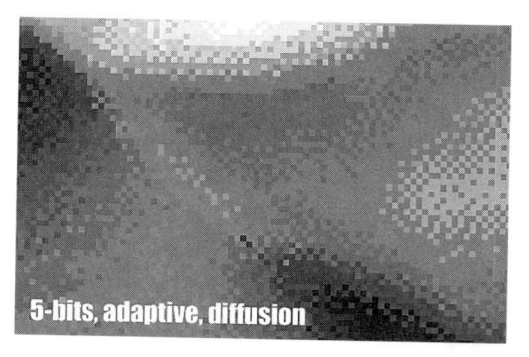

Figure 12.17 5-bits, adaptive, diffusion.

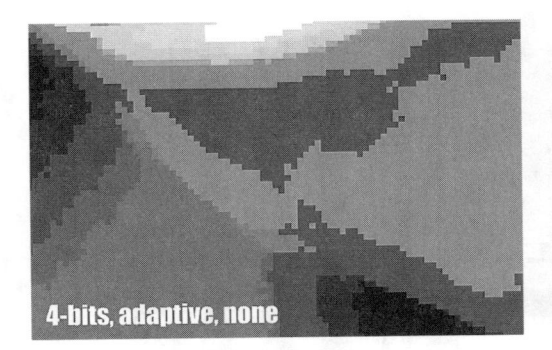

Figure 12.18 4-bits, adaptive, none.

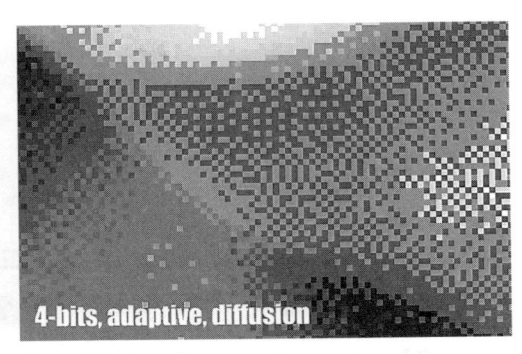

Figure 12.19 4-bits, adaptive, diffusion.

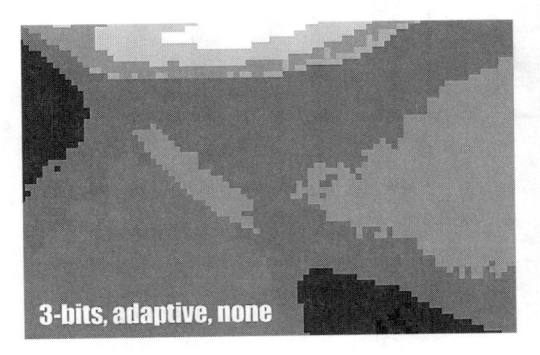

Figure 12.20 3-bits, adaptive, none.

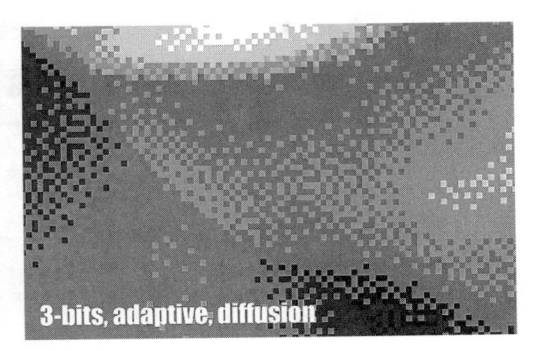

Figure 12.21 3-bits, adaptive, diffusion.

Compression

The GIF format uses the LZW compression method. As the file is saved to disk, its data occupies a smaller amount of disk space than would be the case without compression.

The LZW compression method works by changes in color within horizontal rows. When there are fewer color changes in a row of pixels, there is more efficient compression. This brings up an idea that's useful to understand. Figures 12.22 and 12.23 show two GIF files with simple black bars. Each file has exactly the same number of pixels and the same number of colors. The only difference between the two is that one is turned 90° relative to the other. While looking at these files, notice that the vertical version has a larger number of color changes in the horizontal rows of pixels than does the horizontal version. Accompanying each is a detail from a screen shot of the Macintosh Get Info window for each file. Notice that the vertical version of the file is 3,529 bytes larger than the horizontal version. In some cases, the differences are even more drastic. Knowing this, a designer can sometimes make better use of the LZW compression of the GIF file by orienting the linearity of an image in the most suitable direction.

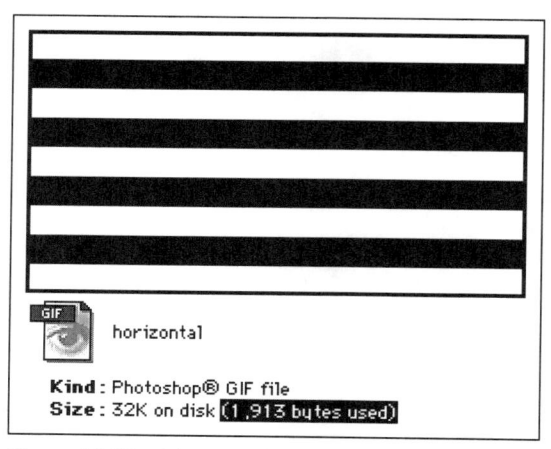

Figure 12.22 A horizontal orientation of pixels makes LZW compression more efficient.

Figure 12.23 This vertical orientation results in a file size that is 3,529 bytes larger than the image in Figure 12.22.

When you're converting an image from RGB to Indexed Color mode, preparatory to saving it as a GIF, one of the options available—on the face of it a very desirable option—is the Dither. Dithering makes the image appear less posterized. However, dithering rapidly multiplies the number of color changes within a horizontal row of pixels. Depending on the subject matter of the file, the difference in file size between a dithered image and a nondithered image can be startling. If the image seems to absolutely require the Dither setting, the GIF file format is probably not the correct choice. The JPEG format may work better (the JPEG format is covered later in this chapter).

GIF87a And GIF89a

After a file has been converted to the Indexed Color mode within Photoshop, you can export it in two different ways. Using the normal File|Save command, you can choose the CompuServe GIF format. This saves the file in the specific GIF configuration called GIF87a. Photoshop also contains a remarkably powerful export utility (choose File|Export|GIF89a Export) which, as the name suggests, exports the file in the GIF89a form. The dialog box for this export utility is shown in Figure 12.24.

One of the options you have for GIF89a is to set some of the colors in the palette as transparent. Use the eyedropper tool with the small plus shape to click within the preview window. Each time the eyedropper clicks, all of the pixels in the image that are the same value change to a neutral gray. This indicates that those pixels will become transparent when they're displayed

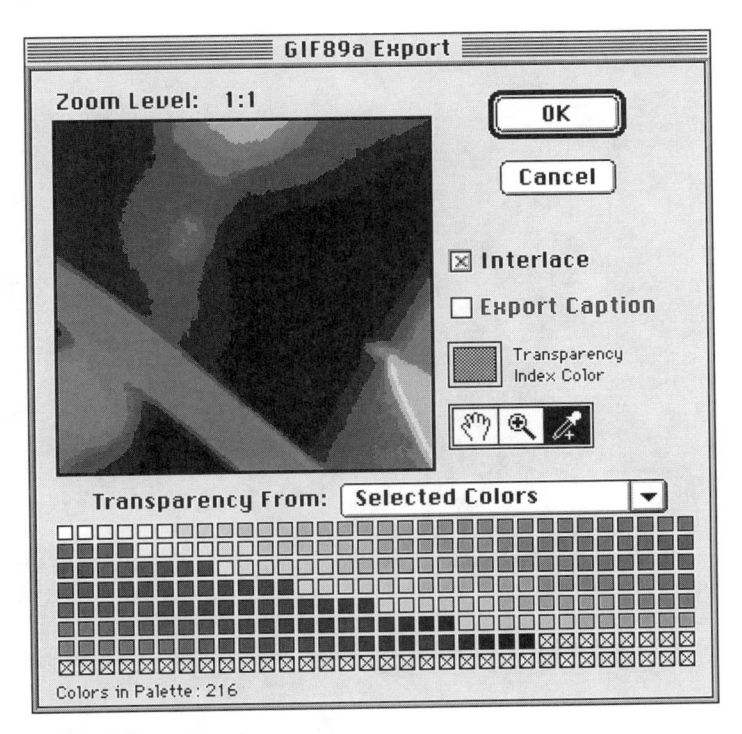

Figure 12.24 The GIF89a Export dialog box.

in the Web browser. The eyedropper tool can also subtract from already selected values (the plus becomes a minus): Hold Command or Ctrl and click on an area that was already selected.

You have three other ways to make pixel values in an image transparent. First, if a selection is active when you choose GIF89a Export from the File menu, all of the pixels outside the selection are automatically changed to the light gray tone, indicating that they are transparent. Second, you can place the pixels that will be opaque on a separate layer. Hide all other layers and select File|GIF89a Export. Figures 12.25 and 12.26 show the appearance of the layer before exporting and the same image atop a background pattern within a browser. (For the vignette-edge look shown here, make the edge of the layer blurred, or feathered, and set the mode of the layer to Dissolve before you export it.) Third, if you have defined a selection channel prior to choosing the Export command, you can click on the small pop-up menu that contains the words Selected Colors. You will see that the additional channel is listed as one of your choices. If you choose it, all of the black pixels in the channel will change their equivalent pixels in the image to transparent.

There is no preview of the transparency effect from within Photoshop. The designated pixels simply change to a neutral gray. (You can change the neutral gray to another color by clicking on the color box within the dialog box. The Color Picker will appear and allow you to choose a new color. The color used within this dialog box has no effect on the file when it's displayed in a browser window.) The image must be previewed from within a browser for the transparency effect to be seen. The effect you see while in the export dialog box is simulated in Figure 12.27.

Figure 12.25 A layer with transparent areas around the edges can be exported to the GIF89a format. This example has a feathered edge with the layer's mode set to Dissolve.

Figure 12.26 The GIF89a file, displayed in a browser window, has opaque pixels only where the layer contained opaque pixels.

Anti-Alias Fringe, A Problem With Transparent GIFs

The transparent GIF format is used extensively on the Web. However, in a great many cases, the presentation of the image suffers from the problem known as *anti-alias fringing*.

Anti-aliasing is a small zone of transition, an extremely narrow gradient from an area of one color to an area of another color. Anti-aliasing is built into many of the functions of Photoshop. Using it is vital when you're preparing files for print or film imaging, because it provides smooth edges

Figure 12.27 A simulation of the GIF transparency effect. All of the background pixels in the image on the left display as gray to indicate that they will become transparent when displayed in the browser.

to the contours of objects in a raster image. The alternative is a jagged blockiness that is nearly always unacceptable. However, when you're preparing files for screen view—which is what you're doing when you're preparing files for the Web—anti-aliasing is relatively unimportant.

The way anti-alias fringing harms the screen image is shown in Figure 12.28. The upper figures show the original figure on a white background next to which is the same figure where white has been changed to transparent. The close-ups in the lower part of the figure show exactly how this unfortunate artifact harms the screen view.

When you're working in Photoshop, a number of tools and options will help defeat this fringing effect in a transparent GIF:

- Set the anti-alias option for the Lasso tool to Off by unmarking it. Use the Lasso tool to select and isolate an object. When the object has been selected, export the file as GIF89a.
- After using the Pen tool, the drawn path can be turned into a selection. When accessed from the pop-up menu on the Paths palette, anti-aliasing is one of the options for the Make Selection command. Set it to Off. Make sure that the path has been drawn so that pixels that don't belong to the isolated figure are *not* included.
- There is an option on the Elliptical Marquee to turn off anti-aliasing. Use it.
- The Magic Wand also has an option for turning off anti-aliasing.
- When you're using the Type tool, set the Anti-aliased option to off. This is particularly true when using small-size type. Anti-aliasing on small type, especially at the 72-ppi resolution used for Web graphics, causes it to look blurred.
- The Edit|Fill command fills with the foreground or background color. If the edge of the selection to be filled is aliased, the edge of the fill will also be aliased. The Paint Bucket tool has an On/Off checkbox for anti-aliasing. If you use this tool, make sure that you set Anti-aliased to Off.
- The Paintbrush and Airbrush tools cannot be made to paint with an *aliased* edge. The Pencil tool can *only* paint with an aliased edge, so it's often the best painting tool to use.

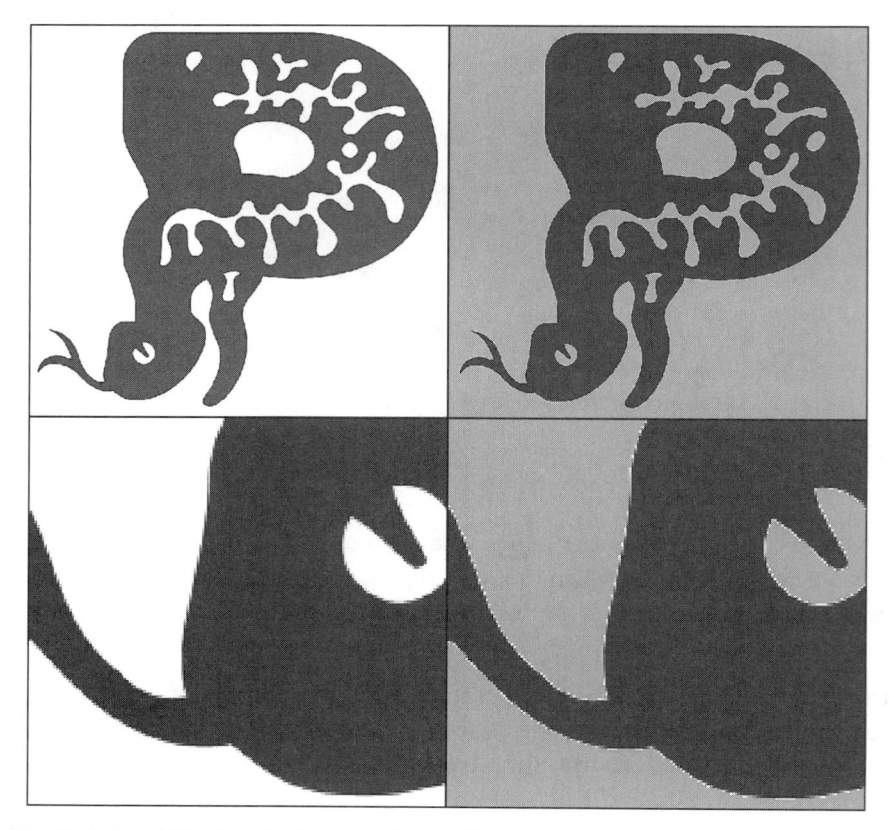

Figure 12.28 Anti-aliased fringing. The image and magnification on the left show traces of almost-white tones when the true white of the background is changed to transparent.

- The Block variation of the Eraser tool is a square, aliased shape. The Eraser tool can also use the Pencil tool to erase.
- The Line tool can be set to have the drawn lines anti-aliased or otherwise.

Interlaced GIFs

You can save a primitive animation effect as part of the file structure when you export a file in either the GIF87a or GIF89a format. It's called interlacing. When an interlaced file is saved, its data is saved in a different order so that the file builds up on screen from a low-resolution screen image to one that gradually resolves into higher resolution. The effect, seen over five frames, is generally as shown in Figure 12.29.

Interlacing is a desirable option when you're exporting a GIF file, especially if the size of the file is large enough that there is a wait while the file downloads. The coarse version of the file fills the picture space very quickly. It's followed by more of the picture information that obviously leads toward a coherent image. Not only is the building of the image interesting to watch—which gives the user something to do during the wait—but it also allows the user to

Figure 12.29 The interlaced screen dsplay changes over time. Beginning with the coarse resolution image on the left, the display gradually resolves itself in stages into the final image on the right.

make a judgment about the image long before it has completely arrived. If the image doesn't appear to be of sufficient interest to warrant the wait, the user is free to cancel the download at any time.

It's probably not a good idea to use interlacing on every single GIF image. For small images—buttons, logos, arrows, navigation graphics—the interlace effect is over too fast to be worthwhile. It also has the effect of temporarily making the screen look untidy.

Animated GIFs

Exporting a file in the animated GIF format produces a more sophisticated animation. Files in this format must be put together in a special program, even though the original components are best constructed in Photoshop. Several excellent shareware utilities assemble animated GIFs that can be obtained from the Web.

When you are making an animation, a number of GIF files are first prepared and then assembled as a list. This list and the component files are saved as a single file that displays the individual files in sequence as the file downloads to the browser. The effect is similar to a small QuickTime movie. The sequence can be set to a single iteration or to multiple iterations. Different browsers interpret this kind of animation in different ways, but the two major browsers display animated GIFs satisfactorily. As always, keep in mind the combined sizes of the files constituting the individual frames.

Photoshop's layers capability gives you a way to quickly generate animated GIF components. It's helpful to set up a hotkey to quickly execute the Image|Duplicate command so that individual files can easily be generated and then changed slightly. In this way, you can construct a series of files—each generated from a previous version.

An example is shown in Figure 12.30. This is a three-layer file. The Background (lowest) layer is solid white and is not visible. The middle layer is solid black (set to 100% Opacity and Dissolve mode), while the top layer contains a set of heavily blurred white letters. The top Layer's Opacity is also 100%, with the mode set to Dissolve.

Begin by hiding the top layer (see Figure 12.31a). Duplicate the image. Show the top layer and set its Opacity to 10% (see Figure 12.31b). Duplicate the image. Set the top layer's Opacity to 20% (see Figure 12.31c). Continue in this way until the top layer's Opacity has reached 100%

Figure 12.30 A three-layer file ready to be changed to a set of animated GIF components.

(see Figure 12.31k). Duplicate the image. Select the middle layer. Change its Opacity to 90% (see Figure 12.31l). Duplicate the image. Set the middle layer's Opacity to 80%. Continue until the Opacity of the middle layer reaches 10% (see Figure 12.31t). Duplicate the image and hide the top layer. You now have 21 small images. Flatten all of them, change them to Indexed Color mode, and assemble them as an animated GIF.

Another easy layers-based animation effect is the rotating image shown in Figure 12.32. Begin with the image—shown in Frame a—on a layer, with the Background layer set to solid black. Duplicate the image. Choose Layer|Transform|Distort. Pull the upper right corner in the down and inward direction, and pull the lower right corner up and inward. The leftmost corners stay at the top and bottom of the window, but move toward the center about the same amount as the rightmost corners were moved (see Figure 12.32b). Duplicate the image. Follow the same Distort procedure moving the corners farther in. Note that the left corners, top and bottom, only move toward the center, whereas the right corners move inward in two directions (see Figure 12.32c). Continue until the image appears as shown in Figure 12.32e. That's it; all the real work is done. Duplicate e, choose Layer|Transform|Flip Horizontal, and you have f. D duplicated and flipped becomes g, and so on.

A number of other possibilities come to mind using both of the Transform commands. The image might gradually shrink within its window until it's barely visible. The sequence could then be played back in reverse order, the frames running from smallest to largest, to give an animated zoom effect. Or, an image could rotate to the halfway point. At that point, the subject of the image is not recognizable. A new and identically sized image could be treated as though the rotation were to go the opposite direction. These two sequences could then be put together so that as one image rotates, it becomes a different image upon completion of the rotation. This effect could be very interesting if you obtain photographs of the same subject taken from the front and the back.

Photoshop And The World Wide Web   835

Figure 12.31 (a through u)   Twenty-one frames for an animated GIF file, all of them made by changing the Opacity of the two layers behind the letters.

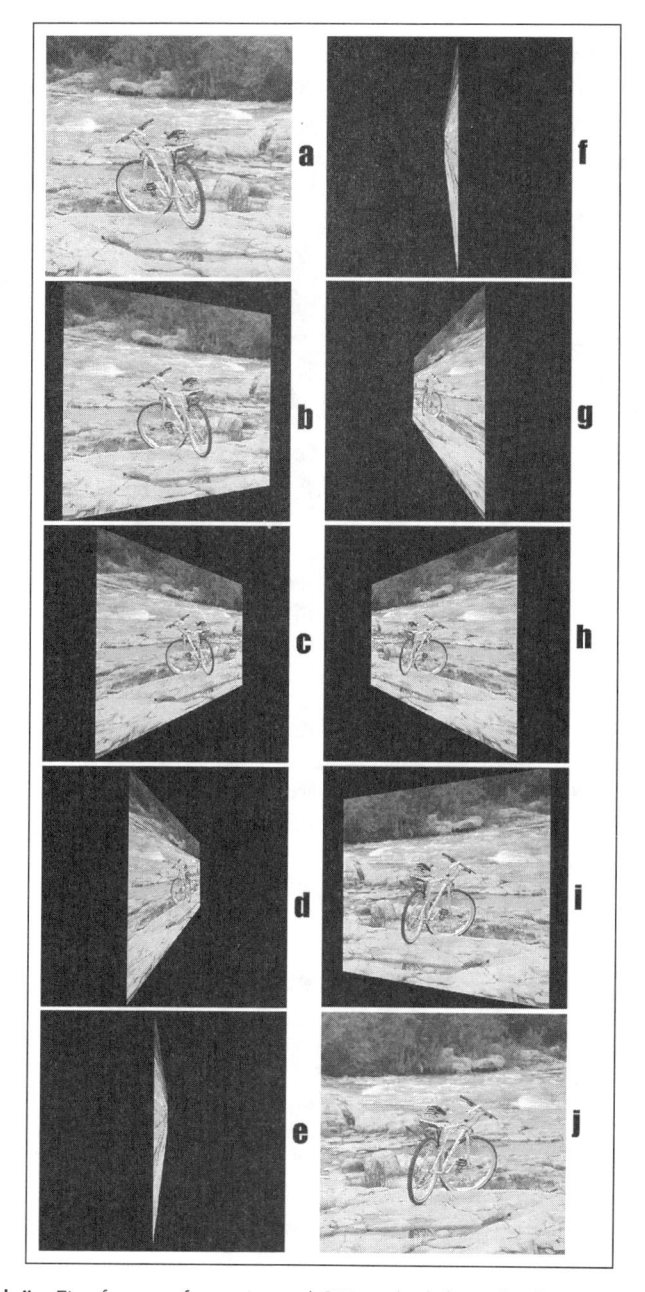

Figure 12.32 (a through j) Five frames of an animated GIF on the left can be flipped to give the next five frames. The animation seems to rotate the image in three-dimensional space.

The Offset filter is great for making animation sequences, especially banner text on a Web page. The text can appear to scroll up, down, or to the side. An example of how this works is shown in Figure 12.33.

Figure 12.33 (a through f)   Six frames of an animated GIF generated by using the Offset filter.

The top section of the figure, a, is the long initial frame. The footprints of barefooted humanoid and Kodiak bear are strategically placed so that they fall within the six divisions of the horizontal area (they're marked with dotted lines so that you can see them here, but they're not present in the final animation). Duplicate the image. Choose the filter (Filter|Other|Offset). For the horizontal measurement, enter one-sixth the horizontal pixel number preceded by a *minus* sign (makes the offset go to the left). For vertical, enter a 0 (zero). Choose the Wrap Around option and click on the OK button (b). Duplicate the image and press Command+F or Ctrl+F. The filter will be applied with the same values as last used. Follow the same procedure three more times (for d, e, and f). Assemble the six frames into a single animation.

Besides Photoshop...

Many programs other than Photoshop convert indexed color files to the GIF format. They're available as shareware and freeware on the Web. Search **www.shareware.com** with the search term "GIF" for a bewilderingly rich list of possibilities for all system platforms.

The most widely respected commercial package for GIF conversions is DeBabelizer, by Equilibrium Software. This program is not, perhaps, for the novice user, but it's really powerful. Not only can it convert RGB files to Indexed Color, but it can also poll a number of files and generate an adaptive Super CLUT that is appropriate for all of them. Although the program doesn't have Photoshop's editing tools, it does have so many batch capabilities that it's difficult to imagine getting along without it as a helper for those tasks Photoshop doesn't handle easily.

It is arguable whether Photoshop's conversion from RGB to Indexed Color is as perfect as it could be. Several shareware and commercial software packages—DeBabelizer among them—claim to do a better job of preserving an image's color. One of the most interesting—from the standpoint of provenance—and most accomplished is Planet Color, published by LizardTech.

A Few Points About Animated GIFs

Animated GIFs are a lot of fun to make. They also make your Web page a livelier and more interesting document. You should, however, consider a few things when you're composing sequences and placing them in front of the world.

- Use the Duplicate command in Photoshop to ensure that the subject matter of the animation stays positioned within the animation window. Several different images can be used in the animation, but try to ensure that they're centered so that a change of frame doesn't result in a jerky change of image position.

- When you have begun to convert a series of animation component files to Indexed Color mode, use whatever palette seems appropriate for the first image. For all the other images, use the Previous option to ensure that all of the pieces of the animation use the same CLUT.

- If you intend to use a large number of frames for your animation, do your best to eliminate colors in order to cut down on the file size of each frame. The download time of the animation is based on the combined size of all the individual files.

- Leave transparency effects out of animations. If you intend to animate a logo and the background of the Web page is, say, light blue, use the same light blue as the background for your animation. The edges of the animation will blend seamlessly with the background of the page.

- This is a philosophical point. It has to do with a personal reaction to the HTML attribute *Blink*. (Blink is an undocumented—but widely known—Netscape attribute that causes text to blink back and forth between negative and positive versions.) Our opinion of the Blink attribute is very like our opinion of the use of Zapf Chancery Medium Italic as a headline font—Yuk! An ongoing animation shares some of the irritating characteristics of Blink. The animation also draws the attention in such a way that other information on the Web page has difficulty competing with it. It's not that you shouldn't use an animation: Just take care in its placement, and give a lot of thought as to how much attention you want paid to it.

The same company publishes a shareware package under the title Fast Eddy, which is widely available on the Web. The shareware software has fewer features than Planet Color, but works as an amazing conversion utility. The mathematics of the conversion process are based, the company says, on technology acquired from a government sell-back of technology developed at Los Alamos, New Mexico, during the research period that led to the first nuclear weapons. Something about predictive counting of free particles.... Whatever. It really does work! You have to see the results to believe them.

Digital Frontiers HVS ColorGIF plug-in does an excellent job of retaining trace colors. These are the flashes of color that give an image its characteristic appearance, but which are used so rarely in the image that they tend to drop out when the image is converted to Indexed Color. ImageReady, a brand-new program from Adobe, which we'll discuss later in this chapter, also has a variety of options for converting from RGB to Indexed Color.

The JPEG Format

JPEG (pronounced jay-peg) is an acronym for *Joint Photographic Experts Group*. This international standards committee originated and promoted the adoption of a sliding-scale compression method aimed at drastically reducing the size of a raster image when it is stored on disk. The method is called *lossy*, which is as accurate as it is semantically ugly. The compression method works, in general terms, by averaging groups of pixels so that an area can be stored as a single number rather than the larger set of numbers required for individual pixels. The sliding scale allows you to choose how much quality to retain. This slider is shown in Figure 12.34.

Three choices appear under Format Options. Baseline, or Standard, JPEG is the default choice—it's the older JPEG format—and gives perfectly adequate results. Baseline Optimized is the choice when you want the JPEG format to preserve the colors of the image as accurately as possible. With this as an option, it's difficult to see why anyone would choose vanilla Baseline. Progressive is a newer JPEG format; it saves the image information in a different order which, upon display in the browser, gives a visual effect similar to interlacing. You can choose the number of scans the display will play through before the image reaches final resolution. The Progressive JPEG format is not universally supported by browsers, but it's displayable by both of the newest versions of Netscape Navigator and Microsoft Internet Explorer.

The image quality range in Photoshop is from Excellent to High, Good, Medium, and Low. There are 11 numbered Quality settings ranging from 10 (best) to 0 (poorest). Excellent is defined as *without visual loss of quality*. Settings farther down the scale increasingly compromise the quality of the image, but result in much smaller files. The bar graph seen in Figure 12.35 shows the range of sizes when saving an original file of 895,717 bytes. (The vertical scale at the left is the bytes, or size-of-file axis.) The arrows point to files b, c, and d shown in the following figure.

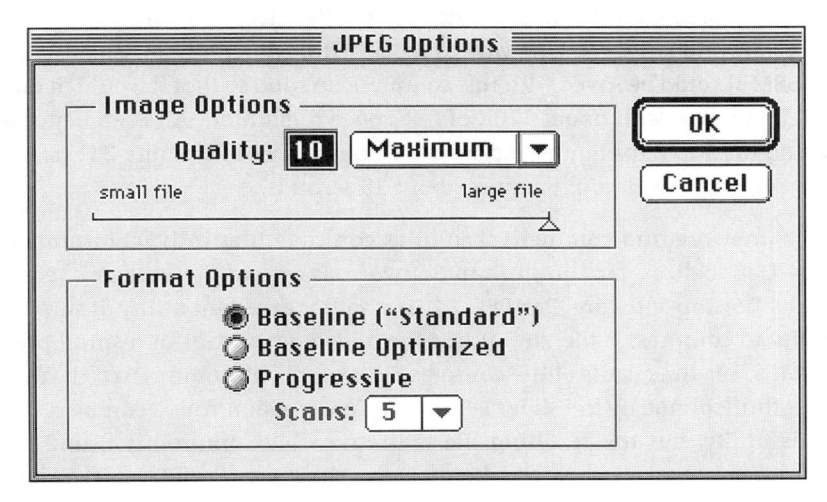

Figure 12.34 Photoshop's JPEG Options dialog box.

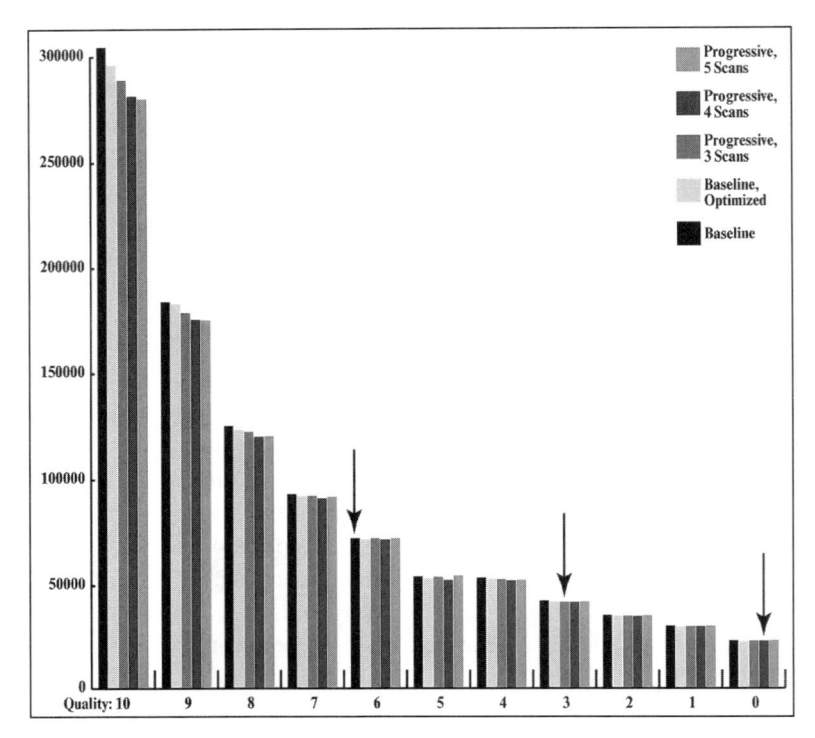

Figure 12.35 This bar graph shows how the five JPEG formats combine with Quality Loss numbers to produce ever-smaller files.

Figure 12.36 shows the same image saved at four different quality settings. A is the original (895,718 bytes). B is saved as Baseline JPEG with Quality of 6 (72,333 bytes). C is saved as Progressive JPEG, Quality of 3, with 3 Scans (42,010). D is the smallest of all. It's saved as Progressive JPEG, Quality of 0, 4 Scans (22,840 bytes). The difference between a and d is astonishing: The compression ratio is 1:39.2. One way to describe this difference in scale is: A 50,000,000 byte file (47.68MB) could be saved with this compression ratio so that it would fit onto a single high-density floppy disk with about 170K of free space remaining! An even better way to state it is this: Using the 1 to 2Kps figure discussed previously, a would require 231 *hours* to download to the browser, whereas d would require about 23 seconds.

Several shareware and commercial utilities can save files in JPEG format. The commercial package DeBabelizer, by Equilibrium Software, is one of the best. A shareware Photoshop plug-in by BoxTop Software, ProJPEG 2.0, is another excellent utility. It surpasses Photoshop's capability to compress a file, and it has the added advantage of a small preview window to allow you to see the results of the compression before you commit to it. It also has a set of file statistics that change as the slider is moved. Compression ratios can be as extreme as 156:1 with this utility, but the resulting file is irretrievably compromised and would be, for all intents and purposes, useless. The dialog box is shown for ProJPEG 2.0 in Figure 12.37. Figure 12.38 shows another pair of images: A is the original and b is the same image saved with ProJPEG 2.0 using a 70:1 compression ratio. The change in file size is from 895,718 bytes for

Figure 12.36 (a through d) Four versions of the same file saved with (a) no compression, (b) Baseline, Quality 6, (c) Progressive, Quality 3, and (d) Progressive, Quality 0. The (d) file size is 2.5 percent of (a).

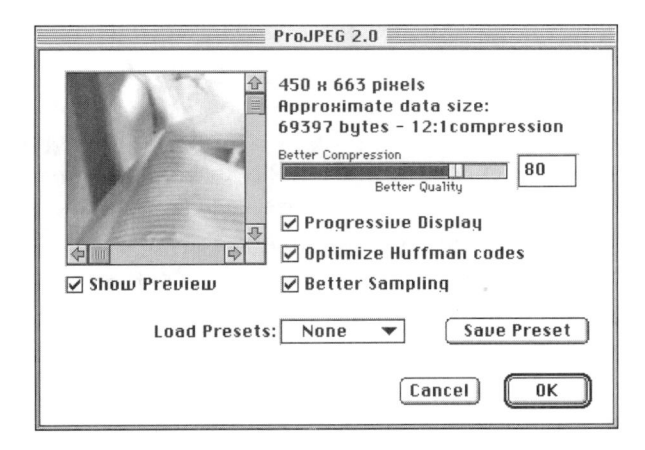

Figure 12.37 The ProJPEG save options window.

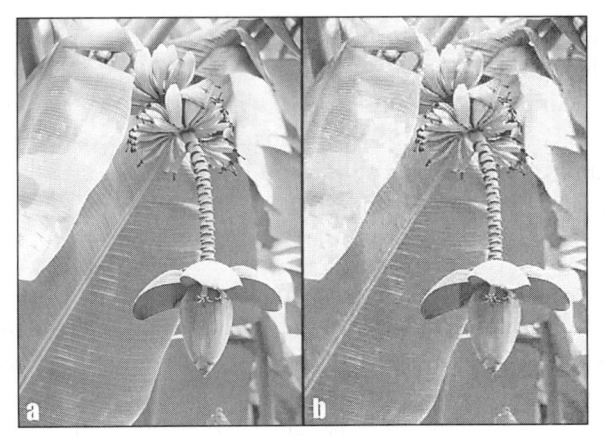

Figure 12.38 (a and b) The file on the left (a) was saved without compression. The file on the right (b) was saved with the ProJPEG utility. It's 1/70th the size of (a).

the original to 12,453 bytes for the compressed image. There is some degradation of the image. As the Web designer, you have to make the decision whether the decrease in file size is worth impairing the image's quality.

There isn't any kind of rule to help you decide whether a file should be saved with one level of compression or another. Some images compress easily with little visible loss. Others don't compress easily, and when they do, they show clear evidence of the compression. You should probably duplicate your file (Image|Duplicate), save at a small compression, open it again, and view it next to the original. If the image is important to the page, you may decide that a larger file size is worthwhile. If it's not, the smaller file size may be the way to go.

The utility of the JPEG compression method makes its value to producers of graphics for the Web instantly obvious. You should, however, consider the following few points:

- The JPEG format lets you save 24-bit information in an astonishingly small file size, and has very few complications associated with it. It works well as long as you use some judgment when you're presented with the extreme choices provided by Photoshop's Save command.
- For most purposes, a setting of medium to low is acceptable for display in a Web browser. Saving at a higher image quality does not appreciably improve the look of the image, but it does add to the size of the file. It's a good idea to save multiple copies of a file under different names and view them at 100% within Photoshop to see which level of quality preservation is the best trade-off between file size and clarity of image.
- When you're working with the JPEG format, it's always wise to keep a copy of the image that has never been saved in JPEG format Always return to that document if you want to make changes to a file. Successive saving of a JPEG file back onto itself will seriously degrade the image.

PNG

The venerable GIF file format, flexible and widely accepted as it is, still lacks several important features that the JPEG format addresses. There are, however, other features that neither of the two principal Web graphic formats provide. The PNG file format—*Portable Network Graphics Specification*, pronounced *ping*—has been devised as a substitute for the GIF format. When the format is completely realized, it will allow lossless compression of 24-bit color, the use of an alpha channel for 256-level masking (as contrasted with a single level for GIF89a), preservation or embedding of gamma information, interlacing as well as several other visual effects similar to interlacing, and the ability to zoom in and out from an image within the browser.

The difficulty at present is that no single method of saving a PNG file gives control of more than one or two of the options, and even these are imperfectly implemented. Photoshop will save a file in PNG format (see Figure 12.39). The Adam7 option saves the file with interlacing. The filters, according to Adobe, prepare the file for compression and, presumably, they influence the way the file displays in gradually increasing detail when it's presented in the browser. Photoshop doesn't give you a way to control the gamma of the image and causes

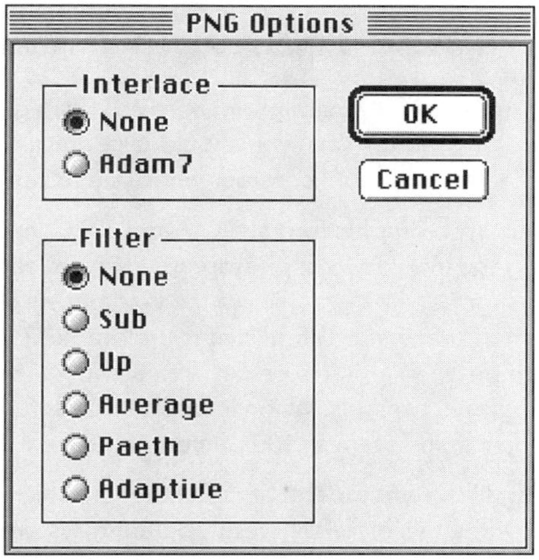

Figure 12.39 Photoshop's PNG save options window.

the image to look okay in one browser on one platform and yet look really awful on another browser on another platform. There is a provision for alpha channel masking: Simply save the file with an alpha channel included, or choose Help|Export Transparent Image and follow the wizard's instructions. (Only the most recent versions of the major browsers will recognize the PNG format without special embed commands, and none—at this writing—will display the embedded alpha channel mask.) The compression for PNG is also less than thrilling: The file is smaller, but not by much. Certainly not enough to provide a serious threat to the JPEG format. You may well ask, "why bother?" Excellent question. The short answer is that the PNG format is not yet ready for prime time. But keep an eye on it because it has promise for the future.

Equilibrium's DeBabelizer Toolbox also saves files in PNG format. This program does allow the setting of the gamma and does recognize an alpha channel (although it apparently is unable to use that channel for masking). The PNG compression from DeBabelizer is also nothing to shout about from the rooftops.

A shareware plug-in developed for Photoshop by Infinop (**www.infinop.com**) seems to be the best choice for saving PNG files, even though most of the PNG format features are not implemented. The file seems to look good in most browsers and, in Netscape, you can click and hold on the image: A pop-up menu appears that allows you to enhance or reduce the image within the browser.

It's probable that the PNG format will gain more widespread acceptance and support. Until it does, it remains an interesting curiosity with a good deal of unfulfilled potential. If you do decide to use a PNG file in your Web page, use the Embed command to display the image. The format for the HTML code will look something like this:

```
<embed src="filename.png" height="xxx" width="xxx" align=top border="0">
```

More Points About Saving Files

Saving files for the Internet is not as straightforward as you might think. Considering that there are only two widely used formats, you should take quite a few things into account. Here are some points that you should consider when you're saving your files:

- Each of the two main Web graphic formats, GIF and JPEG, have their uses. JPEG is wonderful for preserving the intricacy of a photographic image and making very small files. It doesn't work as well for flat-area graphics of the kind generated by the various draw programs. For files such as these, the GIF format is preferable. The JPEG compression will generate visible compression artifacts on flat-area artwork. These artifacts are not noticeable on most photographic images. When in doubt, it's useful to save a copy of the image in both formats and examine them at 100 percent to judge which is the most successful.

- When you're naming files, remember that the server on which these files will be placed can be controlled by any one of several different operating systems. Operating on the lowest common denominator principle, it's probably wise to limit the name of the file to eight alphanumeric characters typed in lowercase. It's also vital that a suffix be added to the file to inform the browser what kind of file is being read. Use *.gif* for GIF files (such as *image.gif*), *.jpg* for JPEG files (*image.jpg*), and *.html* for HTML files (*index.html*).

- When you're saving files from Photoshop, there are two not-very-obvious possibilities for decreasing the size of a file. The first is the addition of embedded thumbnails with the file. Under the File Menu, choose Preferences|Saving Files. Change the preference to Never or Ask. After you make this change to your preferences, the Save dialog box, if you've changed the setting to Ask, has checkboxes (three on the Macintosh, one in Windows) where the icons/thumbnails can be turned on or off. Turning on all three adds about 3,000 bytes to the size of the file. Second, after using the Pen tool, it's wise to delete all paths before saving the file in its final form. The paths are not useful for any Web display purpose; they add small but appreciable amounts to the size of the file and their presence confuses some servers. It's possible to receive the message "Unsupported File Format" from a server trying to deal with a JPEG file from which the paths have not been deleted.

A Nice Alternative To Interlacing

If, for some reason, an interlaced image presentation is not possible, or you'd like to try something different, you may wish to use the HTML *LOWSRC* command on your Web page.

1. Prepare two files. The first is the main file containing all of the color and image detail and saved in either the GIF or the JPEG format. While this file is still open in Photoshop, use the Image Duplicate command. Change the mode of the new file to Grayscale.

2. Open the Levels dialog box. Move the midtone slider until the numerical reading is about 1.45. Move the shadow output slider to the right until the darkest value on the image reads about 80% black. Click on OK.

3. Change the mode of the image to Bitmap using the Diffusion Dither option. Change the mode back to Grayscale, then to RGB, and finally to Indexed Color.

4. Export the image as either GIF87a or GIF89a using a different file name. (Note: Do not use interlacing on either of these files.) Both of the images will be displayed by the browser.

5. The black and white image is very small because it contains only two colors; it will load first. The larger, full-color image loads second and covers—from the top down—the first image, gradually replacing it. The HTML code (which should be typed as one line) for this effect is as follows:

```
<imgsrc="colorfilename.jpg" lowsrc="smallblack&whitefile.gif" width="xxx" height="xxx" align="bottom">
```

Background Basics

The background of a Web page can be as simple or as elaborate as the designer wishes. The background deserves careful thought, because it's the canvas on which all other information will be painted.

Backgrounds can be modified from the defaults of the browser in two basic ways. First, the tag for background color can be written within the body tag:

```
<body bgcolor="#xxxxxx">
```

The background can also be a graphic tile that repeats itself down and across the window of the browser. The tag for this tile is also written within the body tag:

```
<body background="file.GIF">
```

Assigning A Coded Background Color

The x placeholders in the <BGCOLOR> tag stand for three two-digit numbers that are not separated by spaces. They are the hexadecimal (base-16) equivalents of numbers we usually see in base-10 as RGB—Red, Green, Blue—values. Graphic designers are familiar with RGB numbers, brightness values for each of the three primary monitor colors. The numbers range from the darkest value (0) to the lightest (255) to give a total of 256 values. Browsers cannot display RGB values unless they are first translated into the base-16 system. Conversion from base-10 to base-16 isn't difficult, but a calculator does simplify the matter. If you're a Windows user, you can use the Accessories Calculator to translate base-10 to base-16. Go to View, and change the Calculator from Standard to Scientific. Macintosh users can find many calculators available as shareware or freeware by searching **www.shareware.com**.

Translating color values is not difficult. It's probably a useful thing to know how to do, even if a scientific calculator is available. First, look at the small chart shown in Figure 12.40: It presents a table of equivalent values. The lower row contains hexadecimal numerals. The upper row contains the base-10 way of writing the same numbers.

Begin with the values you wish to convert. For example, a bright mauve selected from the CLUT of colors common to Mac and Windows has these RGB values: 153, 51, 255. Perform the following procedure on each of the three values:

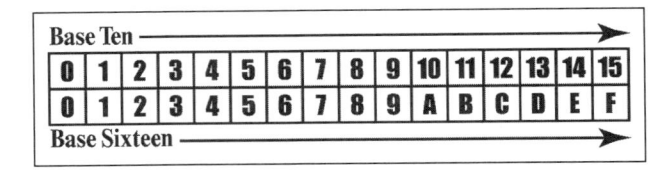

Base Ten →																
	0	1	2	3	4	5	6	7	8	9	10	11	12	13	14	15
	0	1	2	3	4	5	6	7	8	9	A	B	C	D	E	F
Base Sixteen →																

Figure 12.40 The first 16 numbers in the base-10 and base-16 systems.

1. Divide the first number (153) by 16. The result is 9.5625. The integer portion of the quotient is retained to be the first of the two-digit hex numbers. Now, multiply the decimal fraction (.5625) by 16. The product is 9. This is the second of the hex numbers. The hex equivalent for 153 is 99.
2. For 51: 51 / 16 = 3.1875. 16 × .1875 = 3. The hex number is 33.
3. For 255: 255 / 16 = 15.9375. 16 × .9375 = 15. In cases where the division produces a two-digit number, refer to the chart. The base-10 number 15 is the same as the base-16 number F. The hex number is FF.
4. The entire RGB number is expressed in the tag as #9933FF.

Other Uses For The Hex Numbers

Six-digit hexadecimal numbers can also be used to set the colors of text within the document (text), links (link), already visited links (vlink), and activated links (alink, the color that shows on screen as the mouse button is pressed while over a link, but is not released). Such a tag might read as follows:

```
<body bgcolor=#xxxxxx text=#xxxxxx link=#xxxxxx vlink=#xxxxxx alink=#xxxxxx>
```

Of these five color attributes, the one least used—probably by oversight—is alink. Alink does, however, provide feedback to the user, and should not be considered a mere nicety, but an important part of the user interface.

Background Tiles

In the context of a browser, a tile is a small rectangular graphic file that covers the background with multiple versions placed edge to edge in both directions. It's equivalent to a tiled pattern within Photoshop.

In the example shown in Figure 12.41, the base tile has been repeated five times across and in two rows. In a browser, the repeat begins in the upper left corner of the window, continues across for the length required by the width of the window, and then repeats the rows downward for the length required by the height of the window.

The background tile is always the choice of the designer of the Web page because no browser uses such tiles as part of its native method of operation.

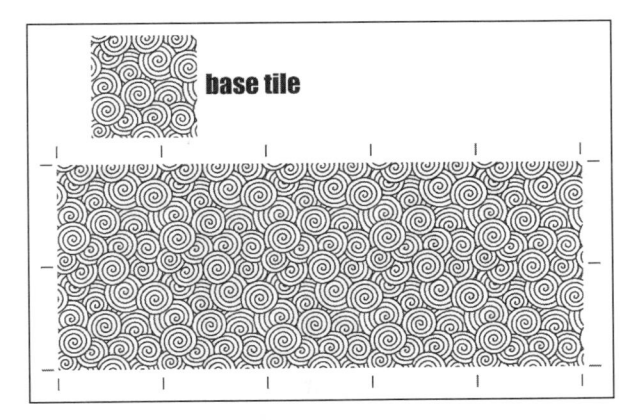

Figure 12.41 The base tile, with an area covered by repeats of the base tile.

Even though they don't follow the same function as the graphics that are interspersed with the text on a Web page, tiles are part of the graphic overhead for the user of the page. When planning tiles, always remember that tiled backgrounds slow down the page and that the tiled files need to be as small as possible with respect to disk size.

The subject of tiles is fairly large. We discuss tiles by grouping them into three overlapping categories: 1) plain, solid-colored tiles, 2) seamed tiles, and 3) seamless tiles.

Plain, Solid-Colored Tiles

Technically, a solid-colored tile belongs in category #3, seamless tiles, but it is sufficiently important to be considered as a category by itself. A plain, solid-colored background tile is simple and very useful. One reason for this has to do with the ability of browser users to override the HTML code of a downloaded document. In some cases, visual effects may depend on code-specified colors. When a user preference overrides the coded colors, the visual effect is lost. You can't override background tiles by changing the browser preferences.

Plain-colored tiles don't have to be very large. They can be as small as 1 pixel. They are simply 72 ppi files that contain a single color, which have been saved in either the GIF or the JPEG format. As very small files, they download quickly and fill the screen with what seems to be a solid color.

Small, solid-colored tiles are useful for other purposes. Single small files, say 5 pixels tall and 5 pixels wide, when filled with the same color as the background tile cannot be seen against the background. They can be plugged in at the beginning of paragraphs for a custom-sized indent. They can be used, particularly with the <IMG SRC="graphic.GIF" align=right (or *left* or *all*)> Netscape extensions to simulate the specific placement effects of tables, but without the difficulty of mastering tables. Please note that if you choose this option, you should probably follow ends of text lines with the <BR> tag to keep the lines in the specific relationship originally set up for them.

Small, single-color tiles may be exported as GIF89a where the single color is set to be transparent. The content of the file is, then, quite invisible on the page. Files of this sort are ideal. They can be resized from within the browser without damaging the quality of the image and can be used to nudge other text and graphic elements by small amounts. If a file is, say, 6 pixels square, you can change its dimensions in the size attribute to 7 pixels square. The change doesn't harm the image, and it will cause text associated with it to be nudged—moved—by 1 pixel.

Seamed Tiles

Seamed tiles are those that clearly show the edges of the rectangular repeat. While a random-patterned tile with visible seams is not always attractive, in some cases, the seaming is desirable. Some examples might be where the tile itself is composed of squared motifs. Ceramic tiles, for example, can be squared-off areas of color or texture bounded by the grout seams between them. The boundaries of such a tile as a Web graphic would probably lie along the center of the grout on all sides of the ceramic material.

Any repeating tile that follows a vertical and horizontal grid is probably an example of a seamed tile. You can find examples in fabrics, wall coverings, special-purpose papers, and so forth.

Seamless Tiles

Seamless tiles comprise a large and complex class of graphic objects. Because they're so important to Web designers, we'll show you a number of options for constructing original seamed patterns and for using existing resources.

Prebuilt Seamless Tiles

The Web contains nearly limitless collections of seamless tiles designed for Web page backgrounds and as desktop patterns. A simple search on any of the large indexing sites (for example, **www.shareware.com**) provides enough material to keep a Web designer supplied with backgrounds for a long time. When searching, try the keywords *graphics*, *backgrounds*, and *Photoshop*. Watch for titles such as *artistic patterns* or just *gray desktop patterns*. You can always recolor grayscale tiles within Photoshop. (Some other possibilities for searching are **www.Hotbot.com** and **www.webmonkey.com**.)

Professional collections of seamless backgrounds are being issued with dizzying speed. Software companies such as Pixar, SoftQuad, Macromedia, Corel, Specular, and many others furnish such collections bundled with other software. Should your imagination desert you for a few days, any one of these collections, combined with what you can do in Photoshop, should provide enough material for most purposes.

Examples from three widely distributed texture generator programs, all of them standalone packages, are shown here. Figure 12.42 was generated using Specular's TextureScape, now withdrawn from the market, but not forgotten. We used 3 D Graphics Texture Creator to construct the example shown in Figure 12.43. Figure 12.44 is a sample from Corel TEXTURE 6.

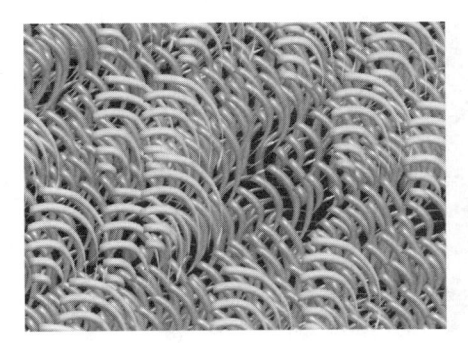

Figure 12.42 A texture tile made with Specular TextureScape.

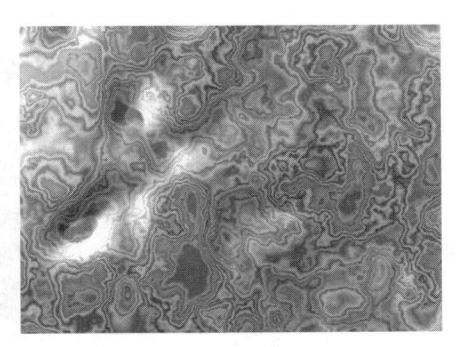

Figure 12.43 A texture tile made with 3 D Graphics Texture Creator.

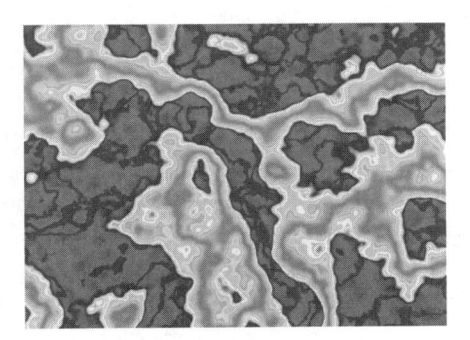

Figure 12.44 A texture tile made with Corel TEXTURE 6.

Noise Textures In Photoshop

From the File Menu, choose New. Make the new document 1×1 inches at 72 ppi, with the mode set to RGB. Fill this window with the color of your choice. From the Filter menu, choose Noise|Add Noise. Save this file in GIF or JPEG format. You will find that the noise is sufficiently random that the tile merges with its neighbors without a visible join. You may wish to experiment with the other noise filters, including the Hue Protected Noise filters that are part of Kai's Power Tools.

Seamless Tiles With Kai's Power Tools

One of the unsung features of the celebrated Kai's Power Tools series (versions 2.1 and 3) is the Seamless Welder. This tool works most effectively on photographic material rather than on rasterized flat artwork done in a draw program such as Illustrator or FreeHand. Try it out on an image that contains a strong subject with an indistinct background or a background of lesser importance than the subject. On images that are not photographic, the Seamless Welder tends to become the seamless fogger, and you get an obvious blur instead of a seam line, which isn't much of an improvement.

Open the file from which the pattern is to be generated. Adjust the file so that it is color corrected and sized appropriately for the final tile (see Figure 12.45).

Figure 12.45 Photographic image to be used with KPT Seamless Welder.

With the Marquee tool, draw the tile selection well within the edges of the image window. If your selection is too close to the edges of the window, the filter software warns you and allows you to cancel so that the selection can be redrawn. Choose the Seamless Welder from the Filter menu (KPT 2.1 or KPT 3). After the filter has executed (see Figure 12.46), and while the selection is still active, choose Crop from under the Edit Menu to trim away all of the portions of the image not contained in the pattern tile. Save this cropped file in JPEG or GIF format to be used as the background tile of the Web page.

To get an idea how the tile will work, open the saved tile. Select All, then choose Define Pattern from under the Edit Menu. Choose New from under the File Menu and specify the new window

Figure 12.46 After the filter has operated on a selection, crop to retain just the selection (the rectangular area within the image).

to be at least three times—vertically and horizontally—the size of the pattern tile. Select All and choose Fill from under the Edit Menu. Select the Pattern option for the Fill (see Figure 12.47). The magnified image in Figure 12.48 shows how well this superb filter does its job.

Three other modules of Kai's Power Tools provide powerful tools for generating textural background effects, particularly when used with the Seamless Welder. KPT Planar Tile (dialog box shown in Figure 12.49) has two major variations: Perspective Tiling and Parquet Tiling. KPT Vortex Tile (see Figure 12.50) provides two choices: Normal Vortex and Pinch Vortex. These two, in combination with the celebrated KPT Texture Explorer 3 and the Seamless Welder, deliver horsepower that few other third-party software packages can match. A Photoshop technician can play happily with these modules for many profitable hours!

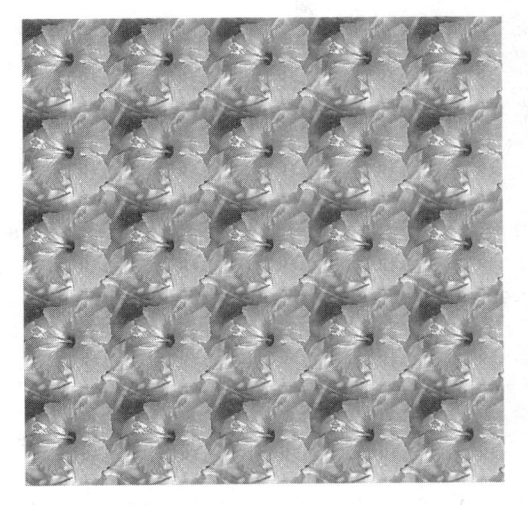

Figure 12.47 The 25 iterations of the tile show no seams.

Figure 12.48 A magnified view of Figure 12.47.

Figure 12.49 Dialog box for KPT Planar Tile 3.

Figure 12.50   Dialog box for KPT Vortex Tile 3.

Other Photoshop Tile Techniques

One of the most interesting tile techniques uses tiles that are very wide compared to their height, or very tall compared to their width. These tiles divide the background of the Web page into large zones of color or texture. The files are quite small, but provide a large-scale effect.

Very Wide Tiles—Tiles that are a large number of pixels wide but only a few pixels high furnish a way of introducing vertical effects in the browser's background.

The width of the tile should be wider than the width of the browser window. Monitors come in all sizes, and users are able to configure their browsers to make use of any available screen width. Practically, it's usually sufficient that the width of the tile be somewhere in the neighborhood of 640 to 700 pixels. Such a width is more than sufficient for most purposes, since many Web designers aim for a presentation that fits a screen size of 640×480 pixels. The height of the tile can be as few as 1 to 8 pixels, depending on the kind of tile constructed. It's easiest to make tiles of this sort in a window that is taller than necessary and then to select and crop the area needed from the center area of the Photoshop document.

The tile used in Figure 12.51 shows what appears to be a raised area in a darker color, with a drop shadow. The tile is 700 pixels wide by 8 pixels high. Converted to GIF format and saved, it is 1,100 bytes in size. This tile will download in less than one second.

The same strategy for a wide tile can be used to place a gradient, either two-color or many colors, progressing from one side of the browser window to the other. The example shown in Figure 12.52 is a two-color gradient 700 pixels wide, 8 pixels tall. The file is 2,300 bytes in size (2.25 seconds). Note: When you're using the Gradient tool in Photoshop, be sure the Dither option is checked.

The example in Figure 12.53 shows a bevel along each edge of the colored area. The file is 700 pixels wide by 8 pixels tall and is 987 bytes when saved to disk (.96 seconds to download). The bevel effect (see Figure 12.54a) is very easy to produce. Make a rectangular selection as wide as you wish the bevel to be and the height of the image. Press Command+J or Ctrl+J to make the

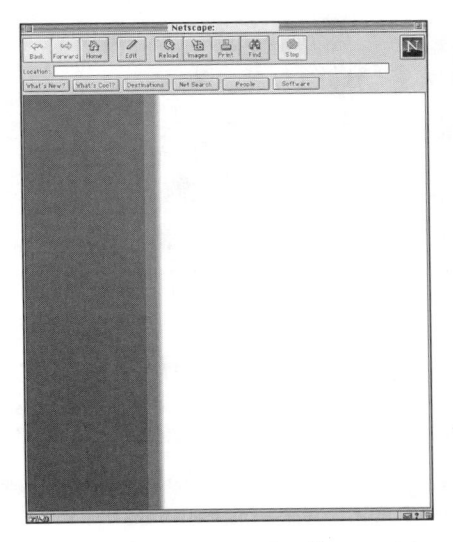

Figure 12.51 An example of how a wide tile, 700×8 pixels, produces a dramatic vertical background.

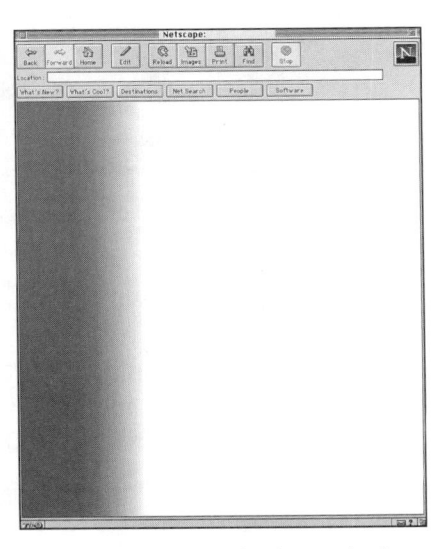

Figure 12.52 This wide tile is in the form of a gradient.

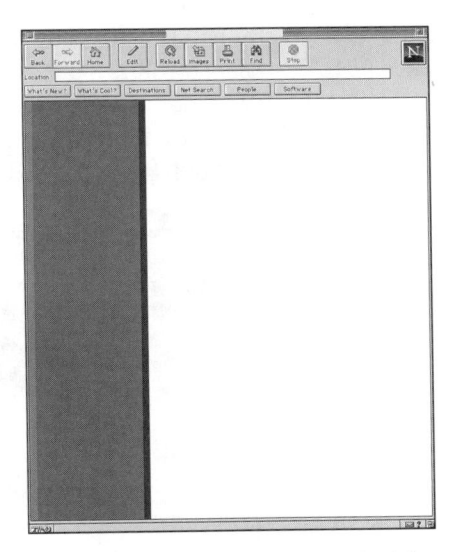

Figure 12.53 A lighter stripe on the left and a darker stripe on the right make this wide tile appear to be beveled.

selection into a layer. Duplicate this layer. Move the first layer so that it lines up with the rightmost edge of the colored area of the tile. Change its Blend mode to Multiply. Move the other layer so that it lines up with the leftmost edge of the tile. Change this layer's Blend mode to Screen. You can control the lightness or darkness of the bevel (see Figure 12.54b) by changing the Opacity of the layers. The lower portion of this figure shows a faceted effect achieved by duplicating layers and changing their Opacity in 20% increments.

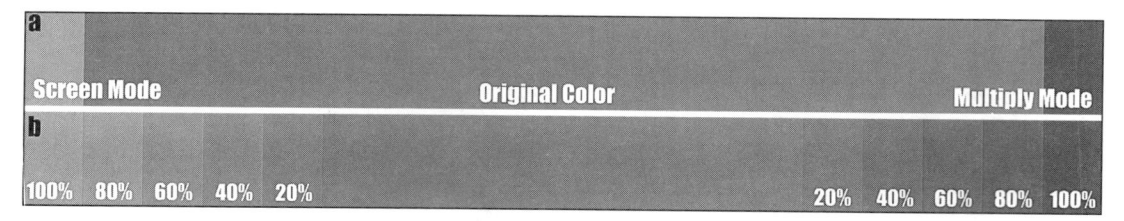

Figure 12.54 (a and b) Bevel effects are easy. Simply take a small rectangular piece of the tile and place it on a layer. For a lighter color, use the Screen mode. For a darker color, use the Multiply mode. Shades of light or dark are made by changing the layer's Opacity.

When you're using tiles of the sort shown in Figure 12.53, you can place beveled buttons on the colored area of the background tiles for a pleasing double-relief look (see Figure 12.55). We cover making beveled buttons later in this chapter.

Very Tall Tiles—Tiles that are a large number of pixels tall can be used to produce horizontal effects similar to the vertical effects made by very wide tiles. The only provision that needs to be made is that the content of the page not cover so much vertical area that a user needs to scroll far enough down to cause the second row of tile iterations to become visible. Careful planning of the page can overcome this in most cases.

In the example shown in Figure 12.56, a gradient is used on the tile. This is really the same tile used in Figure 12.52, but turned 90° clockwise. The tile is 8 pixels wide by 800 pixels tall. Saved to disk, it is 2,400 bytes (2.3 seconds to download). Another tile example is shown in Figure 12.57. It uses some of the ideas from the wide horizontal tiles to produce a decorative effect. The tile is 24 pixels wide by 800 pixels tall and is 2,600 bytes (2.5 seconds to download).

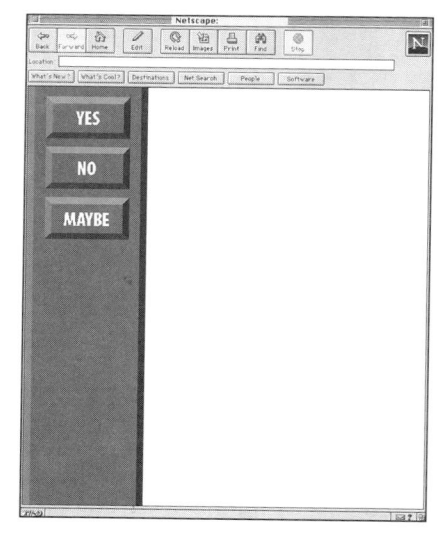

Figure 12.55 Add beveled buttons to a beveled background to enhance the dimensional look of a page.

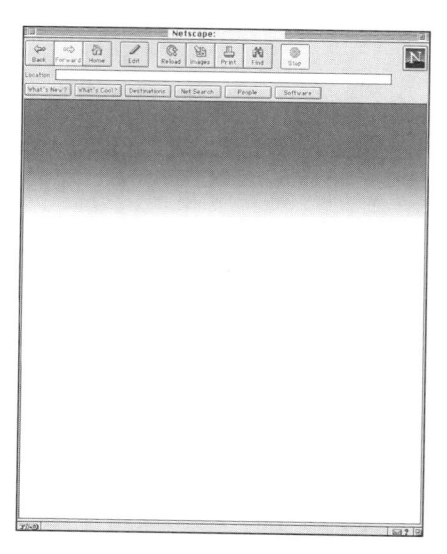

Figure 12.56 A tile that is narrow but tall gives a horizontal orientation to the background.

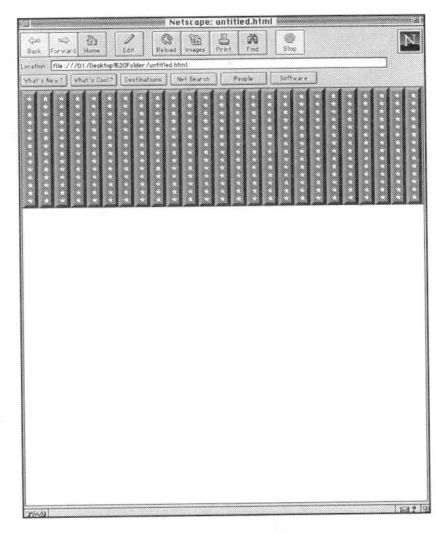

Figure 12.57 Another example of a tall tile, this one more elaborate to give a decorative feeling to the top of the window.

Tiles In Photoshop Using The Offset Filter

The Offset filter is bundled with Photoshop. It's one of those tools that does just one thing, but does it perfectly. As you'll see in this section, this filter can be combined with other Photoshop effects in a number of fascinating ways. The examples here are intended to give you an idea of the possibilities. We're certain that other ideas will occur to you as soon as you try these.

The Offset Filter With The Rubber Stamp Tool

We discuss using the Rubber Stamp tool with the Offset filter to make a seamless tile in the Rubber Stamp sections of Chapter 3.

The Offset Filter With The Paintbrush And Pen Tools

This technique creates linear effects that follow a diagonal. The effect is mysterious but very simple. It uses the Pen tool as a means of controlling the Paintbrush.

1. Begin with a small window. Draw a path with the Pen tool (see Figure 12.58).
2. Choose the Paintbrush tool and an appropriately sized brush. Stroke the path by clicking on the small icon, second-from-the-left, on the bottom of the Paths palette. (See Figure 12.59.)
3. From the Filter menu, choose Other|Offset. Offset the window by half of its vertical and horizontal size. Use the Wrap Around option. With the Pen tool, connect the ends of the previous paint stroke (see Figure 12.60).
4. Use the same Paintbrush to stroke this path (see Figure 12.61).
5. The pattern tile is now complete. Try it in a new window. First, Select All. From the Edit menu, choose Define Pattern. From the File menu, choose New. Specify a window that has the same resolution as the pattern tile and that has three to five times as many

856 Chapter 12

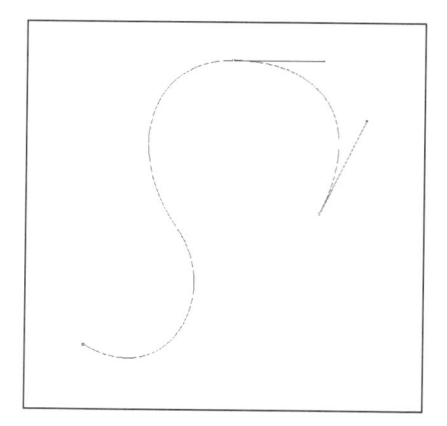

Figure 12.58 Draw a path with the Pen tool.

Figure 12.59 Stroke the path with a Paintbrush.

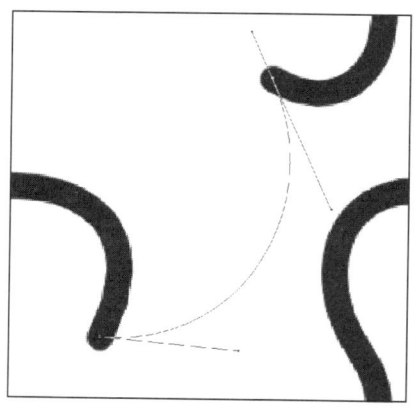

Figure 12.60 Use the Offset filter, and then connect the end of the stroke with a new path.

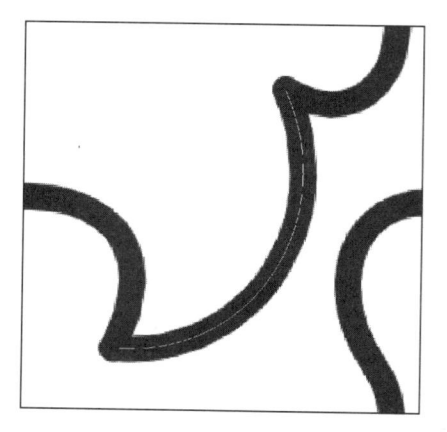

Figure 12.61 Your base tile looks like this.

Figure 12.62 Multiple iterations of your base tile produce this more-or-less diagonal texture.

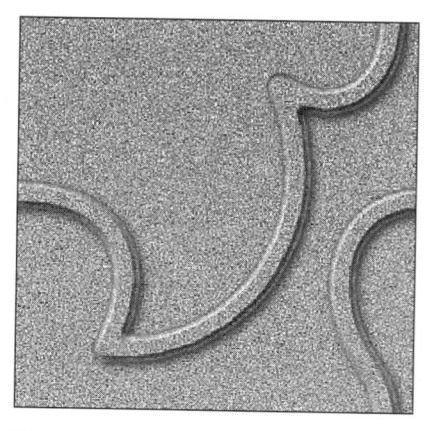

Figure 12.63 If you wish, you can apply embossing effects to your tile.

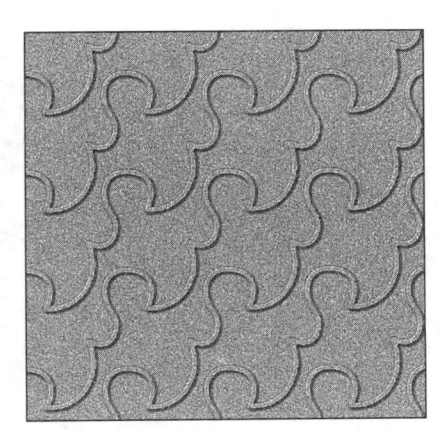

Figure 12.64 Multiple repeats of the tile result in this dimensional effect.

pixels in both directions. When the new window is open, Select All. From the Edit menu, choose Fill. Fill the window by using Pattern set to 100% Opacity and Normal mode (see Figure 12.62).

6. This simple black and white pattern can be further modified in a great many ways. One possibility is the low relief effect shown in Figures 12.63 and 12.64. We give complete instructions for this interesting dimensional effect later in this chapter.

The Offset Filter Used With Layers

Using this method gives results similar to those produced by the KPT Seamless Welder, but it allows more inventiveness and precision. It is particularly suited to photographic images that contain a well-defined subject surrounded by material of lesser importance. (Such an image is shown in Figure 12.65.)

1. After choosing the image from which the tile is to be generated, color correct the image and crop it. When cropping, it's useful to ensure that the number of pixels vertically and horizontally are even numbers. This image is 1,840 pixels wide and 1,264 pixels high. The offset numbers are 920 and 632.

2. Open the Layers palette. If it is not open, choose Window|Show Layers. Select All. Press Command+J (Mac) or Ctrl+J (Windows) to create an exact copy of the Background image on a layer. Select the Offset filter and enter the appropriate offset numbers (see Figure 12.66).

3. Click on the new layer thumbnail to select it. Set the Opacity of the layer to 40% to 50%. The change in Opacity is temporary—it will allow you to see the background through the pixels of the layer. (See Figure 12.67.)

4. From the Layer menu, choose Add Layer Mask|Reveal All. Choose a medium to large, soft-edged brush set to 100% Opacity. Be certain your Foreground color is set to black. Click on the layer mask thumbnail to make sure that you're painting on the mask and not the layer. Paint over the area of the central image that is the area to be eliminated from the layer (see Figure 12.68).

858 Chapter 12

Figure 12.65 The original photo from which the seamless tile will be generated.

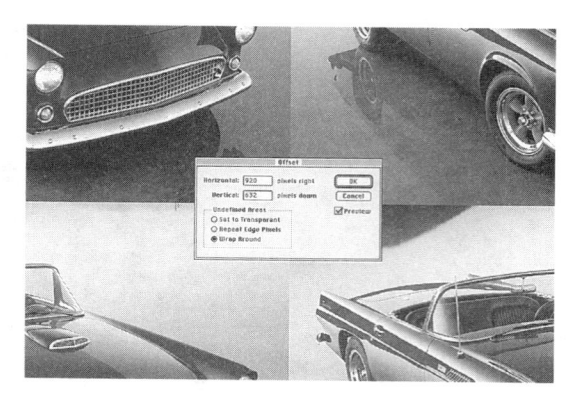

Figure 12.66 Put a copy of the image onto a layer. Offset the layer.

Figure 12.67 Set the Opacity of the offset layer to 40% to 50%.

Figure 12.68 Add a layer mask and paint the layer so that it vanishes over the central image on the Background layer.

Figure 12.69 Eliminate the joins from the offset layer.

Figure 12.70 Flatten the image and use the Offset filter again to check any edge joins.

5. Change the Opacity of the brush to 50% and choose a smaller size. Use this brush to touch up the transitions between the layer and the underlying image. Return the layer to 100% Opacity.

6. Use whatever method you think appropriate to eliminate the vertical and horizontal joins on all four sides of the central image. You can use the rubber stamp tool or the method used here, which is much simpler. With the Lasso tool, make a selection that includes most of the area where you see the abrupt change in tone on all sides of the figure. Feather this selection. The pictured example uses a feather of 10 on a 300 ppi image. Choose Filter|Blur|Gaussian Blur. Enter a high number (in this case 35 to 45 pixels radius). The filter will eliminate the lines. Next, from the Select menu, choose Modify|Expand, and expand the selection by the same amount you used to feather the selection. With this selection operating, choose Filter|Noise|Add Noise. The setting for the noise will be fairly low (5 to 15 pixels). Judge the appropriate setting by eye. The result of the two filters is shown in Figure 12.69.

7. Double-check to make sure that all the joins are perfect. Flatten the image and then run the Offset filter again with the same settings used before. You'll probably find that there are four areas—they are circled in Figure 12.70—that need to be touched up. These four areas are much easier to handle than the previous four. (After you have them in hand, your image should resemble that shown in Figure 12.71.)

8. Try out the tile as a repeating pattern. Select All, define the pattern, make a new window that is larger than the pattern tile, and then fill the new window with the pattern. This tile is shown with three repeats vertically and horizontally in Figure 12.72 and magnified in Figure 12.73.

Every photographic image you use to generate a tile with this method comes with its own problems. However, each image also brings its own special surprise. In this case, the intriguing multilevel feeling is underscored by the fact that some of the cars have shadows and some do not. The authors wish they could say that they foresaw how cool this effect would be, but....

Figure 12.71 The completed tile after all fixing is finished.

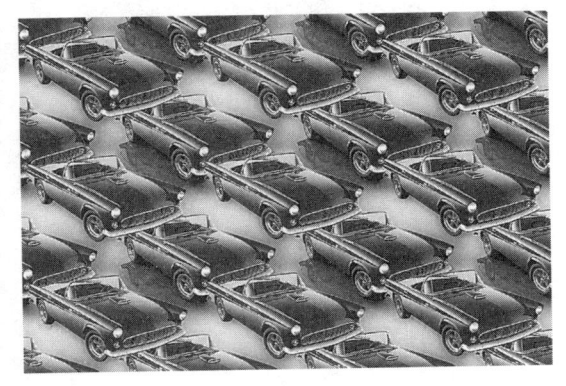

Figure 12.72 Try out a few repeats of the tile to see how it looks.

Figure 12.73 An enlarged detail of Figure 12.72.

Another example of this method is shown in Figures 12.74, 12.75, 12.76, and 12.77. The first of the figures is the original image, the second the pattern tile, and the last two magnifications of the pattern tile in use. As you can see, the main problem with this image was to fade the bottoms of the trunks of the palms. The Rubber Stamp tool set to 50% Opacity accomplished that task very fast. Also, the multitoned sky was selected using the Select Color Range command and then replaced with a single color. A small amount of noise inserted with the Add Noise filter completed the replacement of the sky.

Just to demonstrate the power of this technique, here are five more figures (Figures 12.78, 12.79, 12.80, 12.81, and 12.82). The original image is the first of these figures. It was chosen simply because it seems, at first glance, to be unpromising material for this kind of seamless tile. As you can see, it actually works very well indeed. Like most of the pattern tiles in this

Figure 12.74 The original image to be used to make the seamless tile.

Figure 12.75 The completed tile.

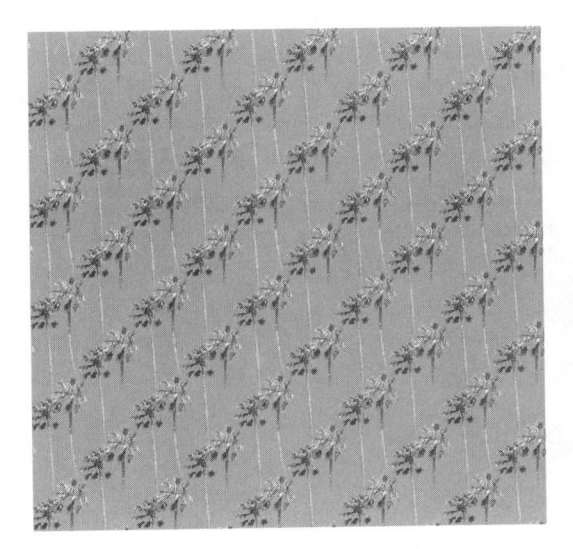

Figure 12.76 Multiple repeats of the tile.

Figure 12.77 An enlarged close-up of Figure 12.76.

Figure 12.78 Single photo source for a pattern tile.

Figure 12.79 The completed tile after the Offset filter with a layer mask.

chapter, it doesn't work particularly well as a background. There is too much contrast in the tile: Black text and white text would both be unreadable on this image tile. The fifth of the figures shows the tiled image screened back by 70%. Used in this way, text is completely readable. To screen back the tile, add a new layer and fill it with white. Change the Opacity of the layer to 70% or whatever number you feel is most appropriate for your tile.

Tiles With Terrazzo

Do you sometimes think to yourself, "If everybody knew how much fun Photoshop is, would I still get to use it as a work tool?" Many parts of Photoshop—the smoothness with which it

Figure 12.80 Four iterations vertically and horizontally.

Figure 12.81 An enlarged detail of Figure 12.80.

Figure 12.82 The same tile, screened back so that text will be readable when displayed upon it.

accomplishes its miracles, the clever features built into the program, the lack of the bugs that seem to bedevil other programs—are really enjoyable to work with. Just when you think it can't get any better, along comes a cute little filter package like Terrazzo by Xaos Tools. Terrazzo is a real kick (and is also now available for either Mac or Windows). Of course, it *is* a wonderfully useful utility for creating tiled patterns, but it's also a lot of fun. How could it not be? If you've ever enjoyed looking into a kaleidoscope, you'll understand Terrazzo's appeal. Terrazzo gives complete control over which part of the image will generate the tile and how large the area will be. Any one of 17 symmetries can be used and the tile can be applied back onto the original image (see Figure 12.83), using any one of nine Blend modes. The edges of the tile components can be feathered to produce a softened edge. You choose Terrazzo from the Filter menu. The dialog box and its expanded pop-up menus are shown in Figure 12.84.

PHOTOSHOP AND THE WORLD WIDE WEB **863**

Figure 12.83 Source image for Terrazzo.

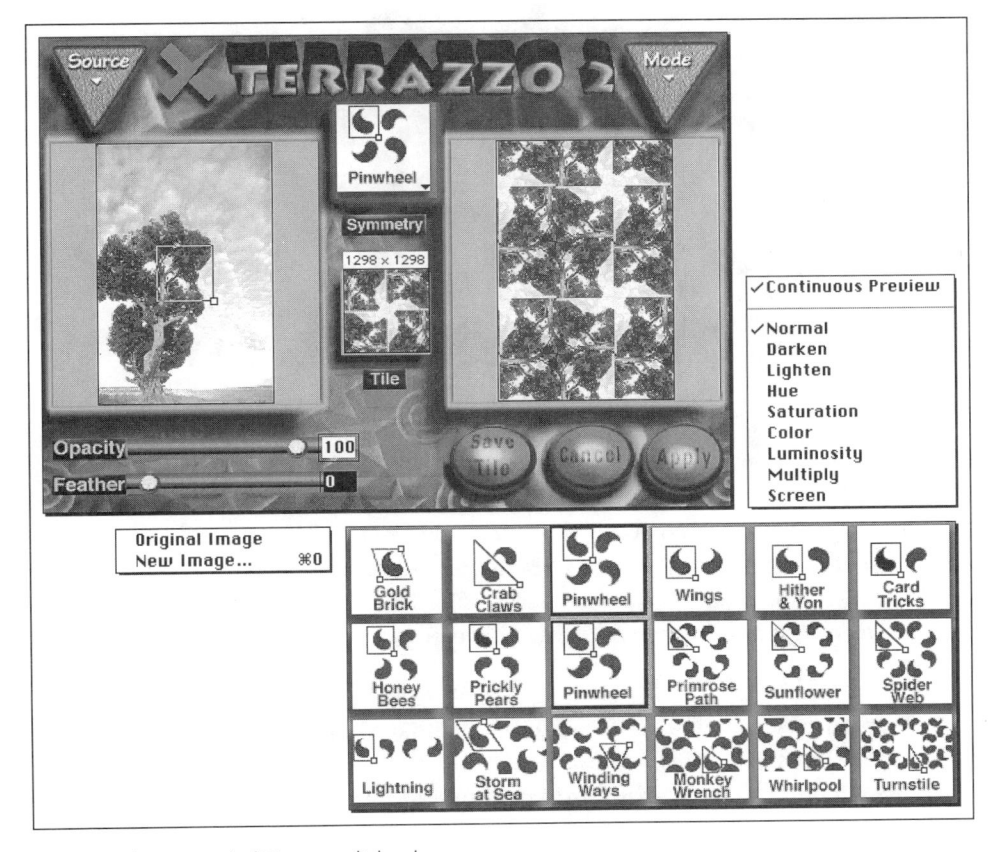

Figure 12.84 The expanded Terrazzo dialog box.

Figure 12.85 With the source file, choose the Whirlpool symmetry.

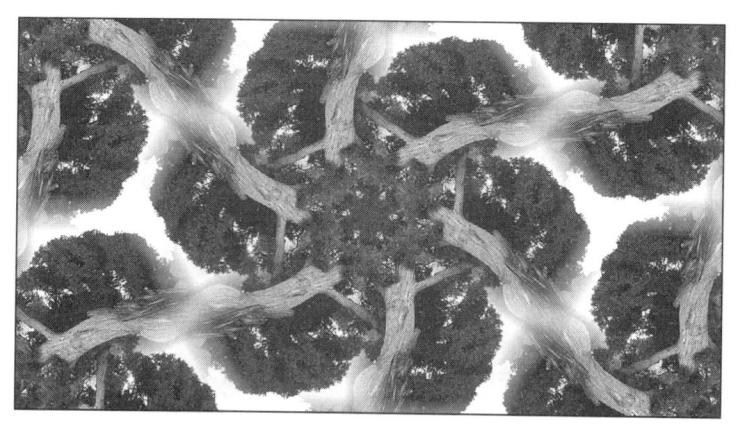

Figure 12.86 The tile saved as a file and opened in Photoshop.

Besides being able to apply the Terrazzo effect back onto the image, the button in the bottom center allows the tile to be saved as a separate file. Figure 12.85 shows an area of the image subjected to the Whirlpool symmetry, with a 30-pixel feather radius applied. When saved as a separate file, the generated tile is as shown in Figure 12.86. Figure 12.87 gives an idea how the tile looks in use. This is another tile that would have to be screened back or treated in some manner to lessen the contrast between dark and light areas. Otherwise, type placed on this tile would not be readable.

Seamless Tiles Using Illustrator

The capability to construct and use tile patterns as fills and strokes is one of the great strengths of drawing programs like Adobe Illustrator and Macromedia FreeHand. With Photoshop able to rasterize such patterns, these powerful vector programs can be used by Web designers.

Illustrator 7 ships with a large number of patterns. You can also find collections of intricate and beautiful Illustrator patterns as freeware on the Web. There is even a collection of Illustrator

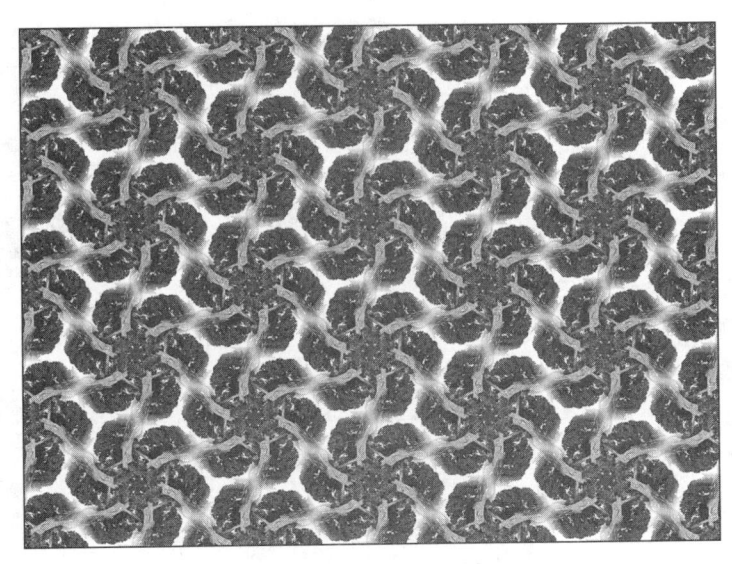

Figure 12.87 Multiple iterations of the tile show how the edges join perfectly.

patterns that ships with Photoshop. You can find them in the Goodies folder, inside the folder called Brushes and Patterns. The folder containing the patterns is called PostScript Patterns. You can open, or rasterize, Illustrator patterns such as these directly into Photoshop at whatever size and resolution you desire. For the patterns that are stored with the Illustrator Startup document, no single file can be opened. Moving the stored patterns from Illustrator to Photoshop is a simple procedure. First, open both programs.

> **TIP**
>
> It's really helpful to have a hotkey set up to switch back and forth between Illustrator and Photoshop.

In Illustrator, locate the Swatches palette. Click on the Pattern Swatches icon (the fourth from the left). This contains all of the patterns that are embedded in the Illustrator startup document. (See Figure 12.88.)

Illustrator 7 stores a copy of the original tile used to make this pattern. Stored, it's instantly available to be used as a fill or a stroke. Drag the pattern from the Swatches palette into a blank document. It re-creates its own tile, as shown in Figure 12.89.

You can magnify the pattern and edit it as shown in Figure 12.90. If you change the color of any of the corner areas, remember to do the same thing to all of the corners, or your pattern will not tile properly.

If you decide to use a pattern that isn't in your startup document—one that is in the Collector's Edition, for example—the process has an additional step. If your pattern doesn't fit into a perfect rectangle (it has pieces outside of the boundary), then you need to copy the bounding box and paste it in front of the pattern. Make sure that all four points on the bounding box

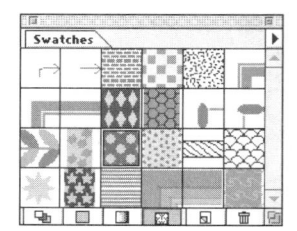

Figure 12.88 The Swatches palette in Adobe Illustrator.

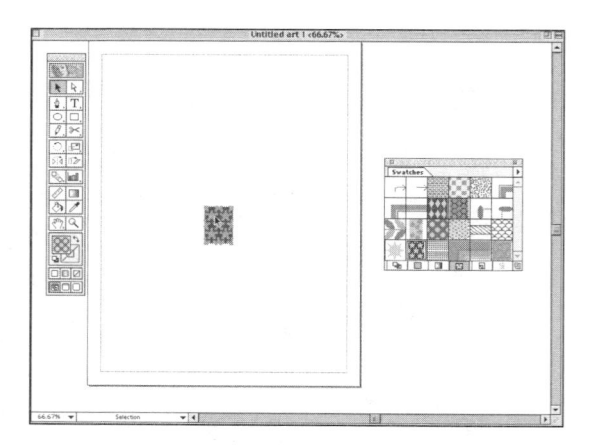

Figure 12.89 The Illustrator pattern dragged into a blank document.

corners are filled (selected). Choose Object|Masks|Make. The mask hides all parts of the pattern that extend past the bounding rectangle. With the mask in place, the exact dimensions of the tile are clearly visible (see Figure 12.91).

Select All and choose Edit|Copy. Switch to Photoshop. In Photoshop, select File|New. The dimensions shown in the dialog box will be those of the copied object that is now on the clipboard. Enter the resolution and mode you wish to use. Click on OK (see Figure 12.92).

Another dialog box appears. Select Paste As Pixels and click on the OK button (see Figure 12.93).

When the paste operation has concluded, the pattern tile is rasterized and ready to use. Figure 12.94 shows the tile window. Figure 12.95 shows a larger window with the pattern tile used as a fill.

Figure 12.90 The pattern is magnified and edited.

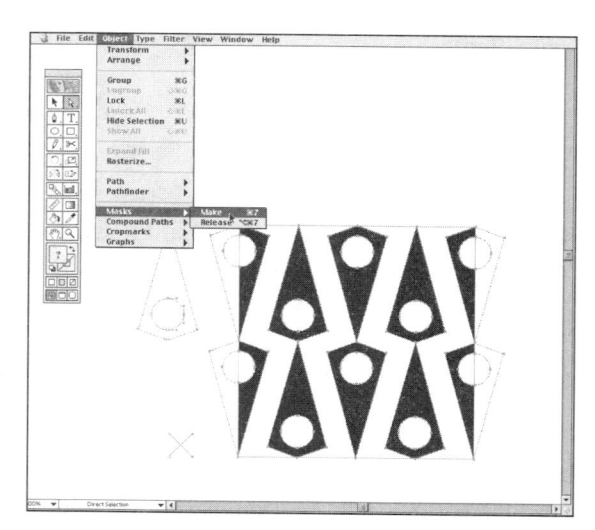

Figure 12.91 After masking, the pattern has been trimmed back to the edges of the bounding rectangle.

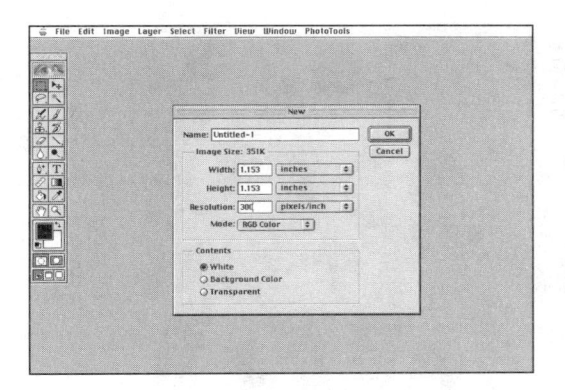

Figure 12.92 Copy the selected pattern. Switch to Photoshop. Choose New from the File menu.

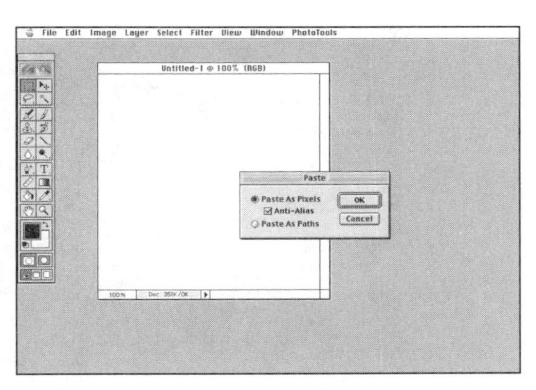

Figure 12.93 Paste the pattern as pixels.

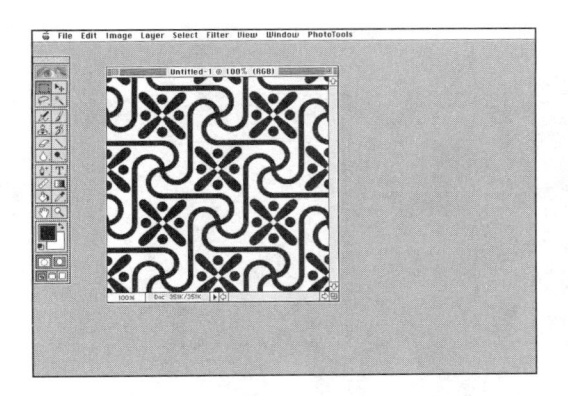

Figure 12.94 Photoshop will rasterize the pattern.

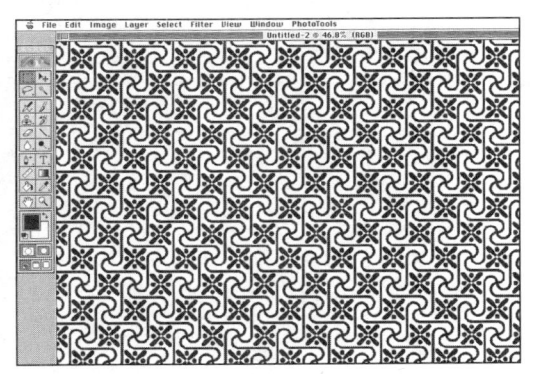

Figure 12.95 Select All and define the pattern. Multiple tiles give an idea how the pattern tiles fit together.

Sometimes it's necessary to remove the white background from a black and white pattern. Instead of pasting directly into the image window, press Q to enter Quick Mask, and then use the Paste command. The window will look somewhat like Figure 12.96.

Invert the Quick Mask by pressing Command+I (Mac) or Ctrl+I (Windows), as shown in Figure 12.97.

Press Q to exit Quick Mask. Your pattern will appear as a selection (see Figure 12.98).

Create a new layer (click on the New Layer icon at the bottom of the Layers palette). With the new layer selected, fill the selection with a color. The dark parts of the pattern are now independent of the background. (See Figure 12.99.)

A pattern like this is too bold to be used as a background. Here's an easy strategy for toning it down and making it more interesting than the original. First, fill the background with a different—and lighter—color. Next, use the Add Noise filter on the Background layer. Finally, change the Opacity of the pattern layer to something like 40%. The pattern is now complete. Flatten the image and use it as you wish. (See Figures 12.100 and 12.101.)

Figure 12.96 To remove the white background of a tile, copy it and then paste it into Quick Mask.

Figure 12.97 Invert the Mask.

Figure 12.98 Exit Quick Mask. Your image now consists of a selection.

Figure 12.99 Create a new layer and fill with a color.

Nonrectangular Graphics On The Web

A transparent GIF file is the only format that allows a nonrectangular shape to be placed on a Web page. However, the GIF format doesn't give you the opportunity to do complex shapes with variable transparency. For example, you might wish to show a simple shape with a drop shadow. For the shadow to look good, it must seem to blend in with the background of your page. For this to be convincing, variable transparency is required. Another example would be when you wish to present a silhouetted image with so much detail that saving it as a GIF file is out of the question. Your only option is the JPEG format. Unfortunately, JPEG doesn't support transparency.

Can these things be done? The short answer is no, not really. However, you *can* do a simulation of transparency effects that is indistinguishable from the real thing. In the following section, you'll learn the easy principles behind simulated transparency effects. You'll also learn a couple of other useful production techniques such as fast masking.

Figure 12.100 Fill the background with a light tone. Use the Add Noise filter on the Background layer. Change the Opacity of the upper layer to 40%.

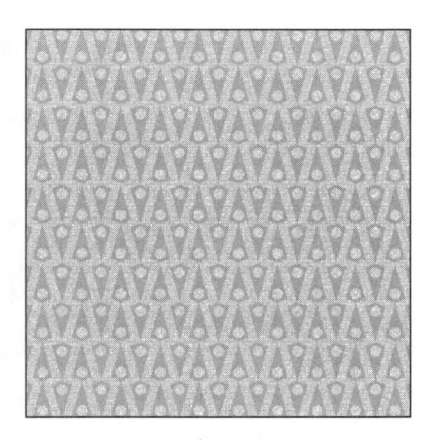

Figure 12.101 The pattern is now more muted and forms an interesting all-over texture.

A Fast Mask Technique For The Web

Nonrectangular photo images used on the Web are not usually presented as shapes with an exotic crop. More often, the subject of the photo is silhouetted and the surrounding area changed to transparent or filled with the color used for the background of the Web page. You can isolate, or *mask*, the subject of an image many different ways. Several ways are presented in various places within this book. This technique is very quick and produces good results without your having to spend a lot of time. The idea behind this technique is that Web graphics don't usually require the precision edges that are the norm for the print/prepress industry. Begin by color-correcting and cropping the image to be used. The sample image—RGB, shown here as grayscale—is shown in Figure 12.102.

Figure 12.102 The image for the fast mask example. From this image, you can generate 11 different channels.

First, let's examine the various available component channels of this image to determine if one is suitable for use as a starting point for the mask. With a well-defined image of this sort, we could make a selection with one of the selection tools, but instead let's make use of a more timesaving possibility:

1. Choose Image|Duplicate and make three new copies of the original RGB image. Convert the first to Grayscale mode, the second to CMYK mode, and the third to Lab mode. You can access the individual channels of the three color modes by clicking on the channel numbers on the Channels palette. Representations of the 11 channel possibilities are shown in Figures 12.103 (*Black* from Grayscale), 12.104 (*R* from RGB), 12.105 (*G* from RGB), 12.106 (*B* from RGB), 12.107 (*C* from CMYK), 12.108 (*M* from CMYK), 12.109 (*Y* from CMYK), 12.110 (*K* from CMYK), 12.111 (*L* from Lab), 12.112 (*a* from Lab), and 12.113 (*b* from Lab).

Figure 12.103 Grayscale.

Figure 12.104 The R channel from RGB mode.

Figure 12.105 The G channel from RGB.

Figure 12.106 The B channel from RGB.

Figure 12.107 The C channel from CMYK mode.

Figure 12.108 The M channel from CMYK.

Figure 12.109 The Y channel from CMYK.

Figure 12.110 The K channel from CMYK.

Figure 12.111 The L channel from Lab mode.

Figure 12.112 The a channel from Lab.

Figure 12.113 The b channel from Lab.

2. Of the available channels, the two that seem to most clearly differentiate the auto from the texture surrounding it are the Cyan and Black channels. The Cyan channel is probably the better of the two. Begin by Selecting All, copying the Cyan channel, and pasting it into a new document.

3. Choose Image|Adjust|Levels. Uncheck the Preview option. Now, hold down Option or Alt and move the rightmost slider on the top scale to the left. Your screen enters what is called Threshold mode. Move the slider until the shape of the car becomes substantially bleached out. Be sure not to push the slider so far that there is no difference between the central image and the textures around it. If needed, you can also move the left input slider (with the Option key or the Alt key held down) to darken the area around the car. Click on OK. If your video card will not support Video LUT, then leave the Preview on (see Figure 12.114).

4. With the Polygon Lasso tool, make a very quick selection of the nonwhite areas within the perimeter of the central image and fill the selection with white, as shown in Figure 12.115.

5. Use a large-end brush shape with the Pencil tool to add white to the areas of the tires and the shadowed areas beneath the car. The Pencil tool is used here because an anti-aliased edge is not wanted for this silhouette. You will be selecting the shape with the

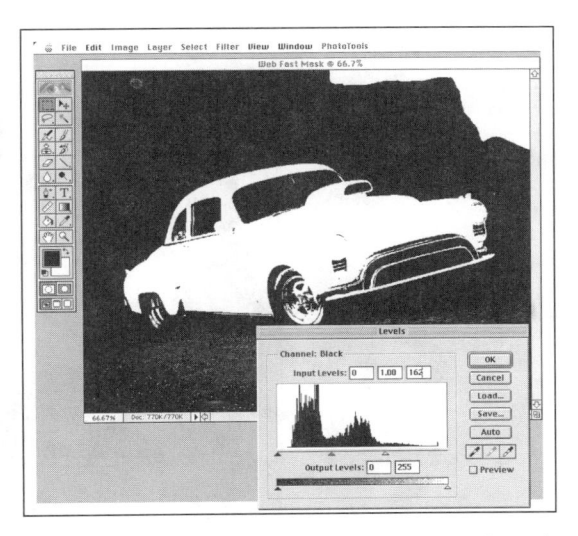

Figure 12.114 Use Threshold mode in the Levels controls to change the channel to a high-contrast image.

Magic Wand tool. Anti-aliasing will give you an edge that will be soft and difficult to select. (See Figure 12.116.)

6. Use the same brush and paint with black to create a line of contrast between the under part of the car and the light areas of the ground around the image. This ensures that when we select the white area of the car with the Magic Wand tool, the selection remains within the boundaries we wish (see Figure 12.117).

7. Set the Magic Wand tool to a Tolerance of 1 and turn off the anti-alias. Click within the white area to select the auto shape. Invert this selection (Select|Inverse) and fill with black (see Figure 12.118).

8. Select All and copy this image. Return to the original RGB photo and create a new channel. Do this by clicking on the New Channel icon at the bottom of the Channels palette (the icon just to the left of the trash icon). Paste the car mask into this channel.

9. Click on the top thumbnail of the Channels palette. Now, activate the mask channel by holding down Command or Ctrl and clicking on the thumbnail of the mask (Alpha 4)

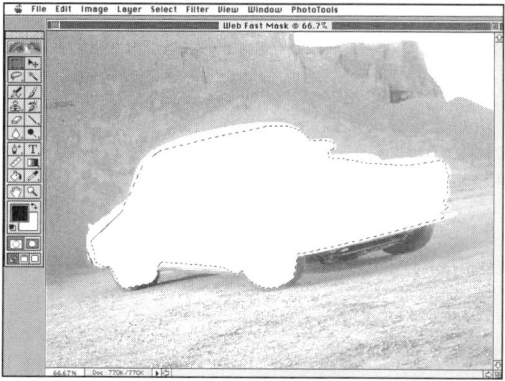

Figure 12.115 Make a quick Lasso tool selection and fill with white.

Figure 12.116 Use the Pencil tool to firm up the edges along the bottom of the car.

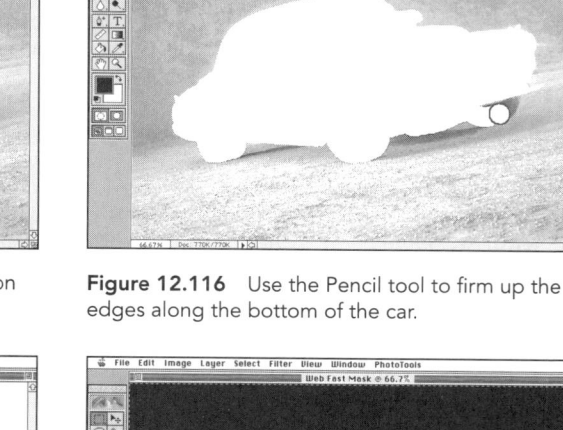

Figure 12.117 Add a black edge outside the car's lower boundaries to keep the Magic Wand from selecting outside the car.

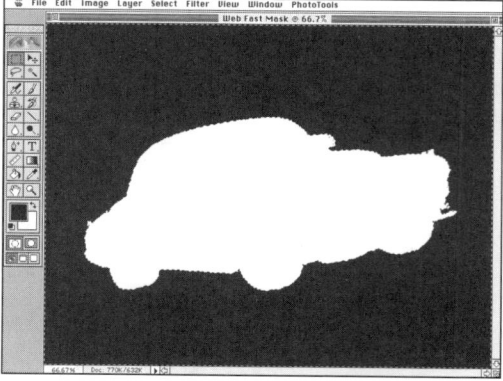

Figure 12.118 Select the shape with the Magic Wand tool, select the inverse, and fill with black.

on the Channels palette. Zoom in to the edges of the mask and correct any visible problems with the Lasso tool (set anti-aliasing to Off). When the selection has been corrected, press Command+J or Ctrl+J to place the car onto a separate layer. You can now fill the Background layer with a solid color or, by hiding the Background layer, you can export the image as a GIF89a file. (See Figure 12.119.)

10. Web pages that use graphics such as this automobile can have a problem. Having spent the time masking the car and to turning the background transparent, the designer forgets to crop the image (see Figure 12.120). Unless it is cropped, all of the useless information outside the crop line shown in the figure is still a part of the file and would have to be downloaded by the browser. Be sure to make your file as small as possible by remembering this important step.

More About Nonrectangular Shapes

Another method for making an image appear to be a cutout or a silhouette is to use, as the background color for the image, the same color used as the background for the browser window. The main difficulty with this is that different monitors have different gamma settings, and a neutral gray (192, 192, 192) on one monitor appears subtly different on another monitor. This leads to problems of the sort shown in Figure 12.121. The gray background of the beetle may have looked perfect against the gray background of the designer's browser. However, when the page is viewed on a different monitor, chances are good that there will be enough of a difference to cause visible lines between the two gray tones.

The solution to this problem is to lock in the background color by using a small single-colored background tile and to use, as the background color for the graphic, the same color used for the tile. In the layered document shown in Figure 12.122, the Background layer is filled with the same color as the small tile. The shadow layer is set to Multiply mode to ensure that it integrates with the background gray. When the background tile and graphic are used together, the result is as shown in Figure 12.123, which is a perfect merge of graphic with background that simulates the effect of a nonrectangular shape.

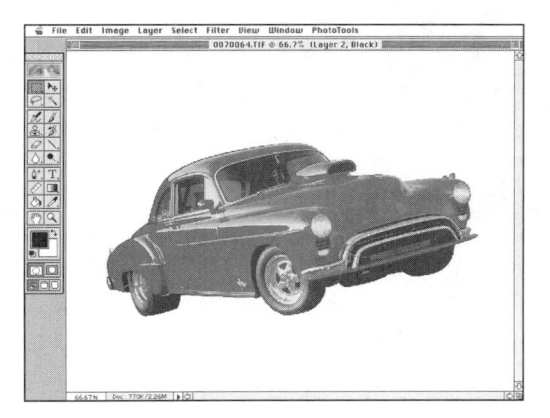

Figure 12.119 Activate the mask channel and place the selected car onto a new layer. Fill the Background layer with white.

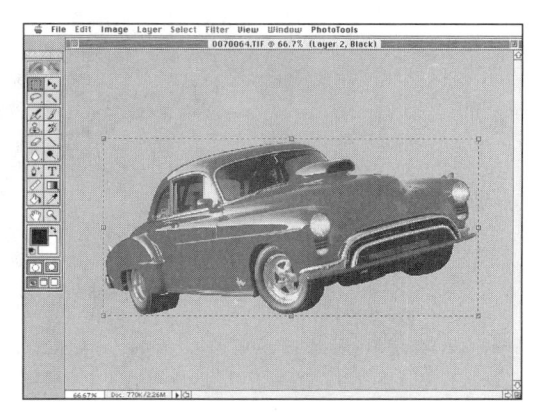

Figure 12.120 After eliminating the background, remember to get rid of all the space around the image by cropping.

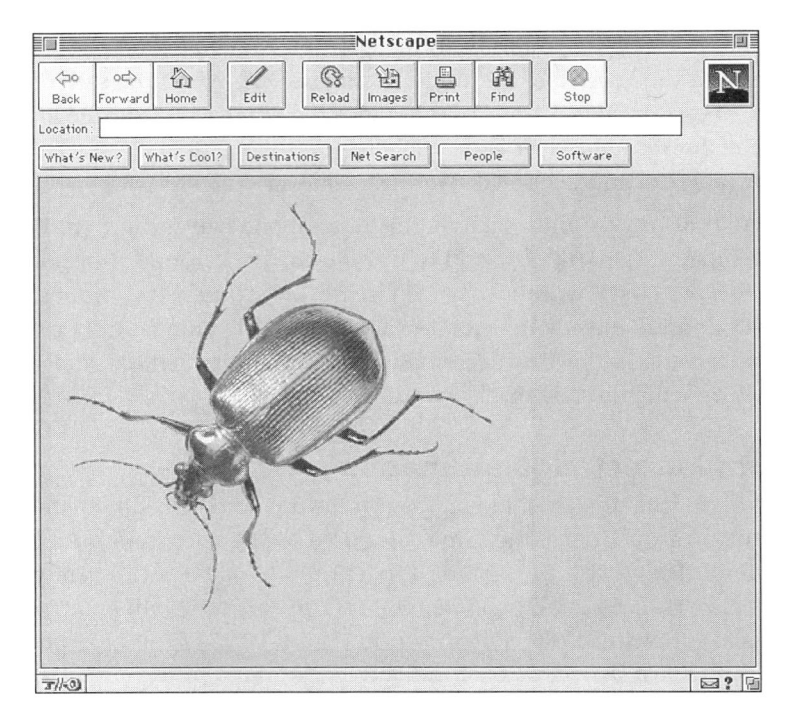

Figure 12.121 Code specified background colors can look different from monitor to monitor.

Figure 12.122 The background color of the large document is the same color as the small tile in the second window.

Figure 12.123 When the large file's background color and the identically colored tile are used together, there is no visible boundary.

By using these small, solid-colored tiles as backgrounds with the same background color for the photograph, a number of tricky-looking effects are possible. Two are shown in Figures 12.124 and 12.125. One is a silhouette that fades away along the bottom, the other is a vignette-edge effect. Neither of these is possible with the present capabilities of the JPEG or the GIF formats in HTML. Both effects are theoretically possible with the PNG file format.

Of limited use is a technique that simulates a vignette edge by applying the Dissolve mode to the edges of an image. The layered Photoshop document has a blurred or feathered edge applied to the central subject. This layer is then set to the Dissolve mode on the Layers palette (see Figure 12.126). The background is filled with any color useful as a possible transparent color or the layer is exported as a GIF89a file. The effect is as shown in the close-up in Figure 12.127.

Buttons, Arrows, And Display Type

The graphics on a Web page that act as link objects usually appear in the form of buttons, arrows, or text. When graphic objects are made into links, they often have a line drawn around them to indicate link status. The tag for the link (which is actually a one-line tag) can contain a switch to make the border equal to 0 pixels:

```
<a href="link.html"><img src="/filepath/file.gif" width="xxx" height="xxx"
align="center" border="0"></a>
```

Figure 12.124 An example of a silhouetted shape that fades out at the bottom.

Figure 12.125 A simulated vignette edge.

Figure 12.126 A vignette look-alike using the Dissolve mode.

Figure 12.127 Enlarged detail of Figure 12.126.

With the border set to 0 (invisible), it's important to give visual cues to the user that a graphic is a link. These cues can be in the form of shapes such as arrows, they can be in the form of shapes set off by drop shadows, or they can be in the form of shapes that are embossed. Four common shapes for link graphics are the rectangle, circle, letter form, and arrow. The arrow is the only one of the four that is, self-evidently, a link (see Figure 12.128).

Quick Drop Shadows

By making these shapes seem to float above the page with a drop shadow, link status is easier to imply (see Figure 12.129).

Making drop shadows in Photoshop is fairly simple. We'll assume that the graphic is as shown in Figure 12.128 and that the shapes are not isolated on a layer. The first part of the following set of instructions contains a useful tip for isolating shapes very quickly:

1. Begin with the shape(s) in a window set to the appropriate resolution and in Grayscale mode. With the Channels palette showing, drag the Black channel thumbnail onto the New Channel icon at the bottom of the Channels palette. Click on this layer (now titled Channel 2) and invert it (press Command+I or Ctrl+I). Click on the original channel's thumbnail to select it.

2. Command+click or Ctrl+click on the second channel's thumbnail. The black shape(s) become selected. Switch to the Layers palette. Make this selection a layer by pressing Command+J or Ctrl+J.

3. Duplicate this layer by dragging its thumbnail down onto the New Layer icon. Click on the Background layer to select it, and fill it with white. Hide the upper layer, then click on the lower of the two layers to select it.

4. Change the Opacity of the selected layer to 60%. Choose Filter|Blur|Gaussian Blur. Experiment with the Radius setting to achieve a diffused edge. Press V to select the Move tool. Drag this layer down and to the right, or press the Down arrow key five or six times followed by the Right arrow key five or six times.

Figure 12.128 These simple shapes are often used as navigation aids on a Web page. Only the arrow shape is an obvious button.

Figure 12.129 With a drop shadow, the viewer is alerted to the fact that these shapes mean something more than just decoration.

5. Make the upper layer visible. Flatten the image. Discard the extra channel, and save the image in an appropriate format (see Figure 12.129). If you're feeling pressed for time, you can also use the Layer Effects Drop Shadow.

Embossed Shapes

Embossing is another good way to indicate that a graphic is interactive. There are many ways to create an embossed effect. This Photoshop procedure may appear to be cumbersome, but it achieves very good results. It has the added advantage of not requiring any third-party filter effects. You can certainly use the Emboss Layer Effect, but you will get better results with more control by using our methods. Notice that the image is subjected to several filters and commands before the Emboss filter is used. If the Emboss filter is used before the others, the effects are likely to be disappointing. The preliminary work ensures that the shapes will look good when the final filter is applied to them.

1. Begin with the same grayscale document used for the drop shadow technique. With the Channels palette showing, drag the Black channel thumbnail onto the New Channels icon at the bottom of the Channels palette. Click on this channel (now titled Alpha 1) and invert it (press Command+I or Ctrl+I). Click on the original channel to select it. Command+click or Ctrl+click on the Alpha 1 channel. The shapes are now selected.

2. From the Select menu, choose Modify|Contract. Choose a number between 5 and 10. When the selection has contracted, click on the small icon that is second-from-left at the bottom of the Channels palette. Clicking here makes a new channel titled Alpha 2. Both of these channels will be used later in the embossing process. Deselect. All of this preliminary work simply provides some tools that will be needed later. The embossing procedure comes next.

3. Make sure that the original channel is active. From the Filter menu, choose Other|High Pass. Pick a setting that gives a semi-embossed effect without making large, black, empty areas in any sharp corners of the shapes. A setting of about 8.4 will work (see Figure 12.130).

4. From the Filter Menu, choose Stylize|Find Edges. The filter results are shown in Figure 12.131.

5. Choose Filter|Blur|Gaussian Blur. Experiment with the settings. If you look closely at Figure 12.131, you can see the small white areas at the corners of the shapes (artifacts of the High Pass filter) that need to be eliminated by the Blur filter. After the filter executes, the image should look similar to Figure 12.132.

Figure 12.130 The High Pass filter applied to the black shapes.

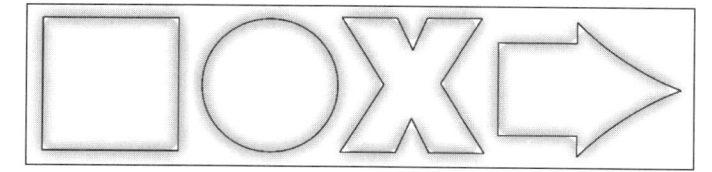

Figure 12.131 The same shapes after using the Find Edges filter.

Figure 12.132 The next step is to use the Gaussian Blur filter.

6. Open the Level dialog box (press Command+L or Ctrl+L). Move the midtone slider to the right to darken the image slightly. From the Filter menu, choose Stylize|Emboss. Experiment with the settings to change the direction of the light, the height of the emboss effect, and the amount of contrast between highlight and shadows. The height of the emboss effect should be about the same number of pixels used to contract the selection (above). After executing the Emboss filter, the image should resemble Figure 12.133.

7. Command+click or Ctrl+click on the thumbnail of the Alpha 1 channel. Press D to set the Foreground/Background colors to their defaults. From the Select menu, choose Inverse and press the Delete key. The background area fills with white, leaving the embossed shapes visible (see Figure 12.134). The shapes look fairly good, but we're about to make them look even better.

8. With the Eyedropper tool, select a medium tone from one of the embossed shapes. Command+click or Ctrl+click on the thumbnail of the Alpha 2 channel. Fill the selection with this medium tone (see Figure 12.135).

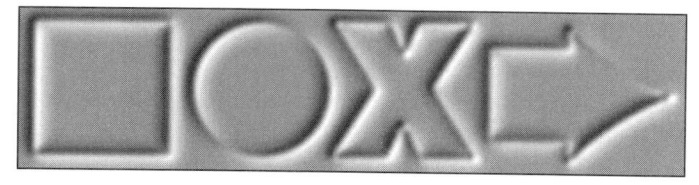

Figure 12.133 The Emboss filter.

Figure 12.134 After embossing, use Channel 2 to help get rid of the background.

Figure 12.135 Use a Channel 3 selection to fill the interior shapes with a single color.

9. The Foreground color is now the medium tone selected with the Eyedropper tool. The Background color is white. With the selection still active, choose the Linear Gradient tool. Set the Gradient tool's Opacity to 65% and the gradient type to Foreground to Background. Draw the gradient from bottom to top of the selected area. Deselect. The result of the gradient overlay on this center area is shown in Figure 12.136.

10. Set the Gradient Opacity to 45%. Pay attention now, this next bit is a little tricky. Command+click or Ctrl+click on the Alpha 1 channel. Hold the Command and Option keys or the Ctrl and Alt keys and click on the thumbnail of the Alpha 2 channel. This subtracts the area of the third channel's selection from that of the second. Draw a gradient from bottom to top of the selected area (the border within the shapes). Deselect. The result is shown in Figure 12.137.

A Few Niceties

To continue the process and to add more of a reflective effect to the shapes, follow these steps:

1. First, increase the contrast of the embossed shapes by choosing Image|Adjust|Auto Levels.

2. Select the inner shape (Command+click or Ctrl+click on Alpha 2). Use a soft paintbrush. Set the Foreground color to white and the Paintbrush Opacity to 50%. Click outside the selection on the far left edge of the window. Hold down the Shift key and click once again, this time on the far right edge of the window. A straight line will connect the two points, but will be visible only inside the selection. (Use the tick marks on the rulers to help align the brush so that the drawn line is perfectly horizontal.)

Figure 12.136 Draw a 65% opaque gradient over the inner shapes.

Figure 12.137 Add a 45% opaque gradient to the outer edges.

3. Select the outer border areas of the shapes as you did previously. Draw the same Paintbrush line, but slightly lower than the first and with the Opacity set at 40% (Figure 12.138).

You can make the embossed shapes appear to be a more organic part of the Web page if you fill the background of the page with the same color you used to fill the interior part of the embossed shape, as shown in Figure 12.135.

An attractive modification of the embossed shapes, which turns out to be a very simple effect, is to map a texture onto the embossed shape.

1. Begin with the image as it was in Figure 12.137 and execute the Auto Levels command. Create a new layer for this document and fill it with the texture of choice. The example shown in Figure 12.139 uses the Gray Marble texture from the Pixar 128 series (a commercially available set of 128 high-quality textures from Pixar, Inc.).
2. Change the Blend mode of this layer from Normal to Overlay. Flatten the image. (See Figure 12.140.)

No, you don't have to make more selections to get rid of the texture in the background area: The Blend mode does it for you. (Whoever said, "There ain't no such thing as a free lunch"?) Figure 12.141 shows the same set of shapes with a layer filled with a metallic-looking gradient and then changed to Overlay mode. It's the very same operation, but it achieves a very different look!

Figure 12.138 A single wide Paintbrush stroke seems to add reflectivity.

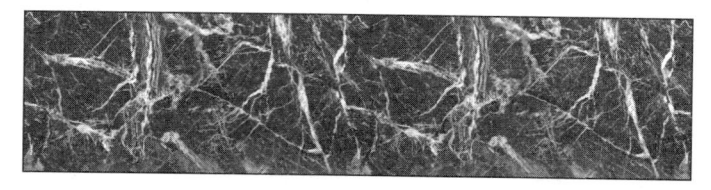

Figure 12.139 Add a new layer and fill it with a texture.

Figure 12.140 Change the mode of the layer to Overlay. It's magic!

Figure 12.141 As an alternative to the stone texture, fill the layer with a zippy gradient to get this effect.

The Easiest Dimensional Effect Of All

SF Deko-Boko is *mailware* software. On the bottom of the filter's interface window is a message from the programmer: "If you like Deko-Boko, send me a mail." Please do. This filter is wonderful. Deko-Boko is one of a series of filters called Sucking Fish Software. Some of its companion filters are: SF Inai-Inai-Bar, SF MagicalCurtain, SF Midnights TV, and SF Mr. Sa^Kan. These filters are widely available on Web servers with extensive shareware collections of Photoshop utilities. Most of them can be found on America Online, the Microsoft Network, and **www.shareware.com**.

This filter couldn't be easier to use. Open a small window in Photoshop and fill it with a color or a texture. In the case of Figure 12.142, the texture is pebbles in mortar, another of the Pixar 128 series. Under Filter, choose SuckingFishSeries|SF Deko-Boko (see Figure 12.143). Figure 12.144 was made with the default settings.

To add a touch of extra realism, carefully select the center rectangular area of the image. Now, draw a white-to-black gradient (Foreground to Background, Opacity 30%) along the course shown by the arrow in the small image on the right side of Figure 12.145.

Figure 12.142 Begin with a small window filled with a color or a texture.

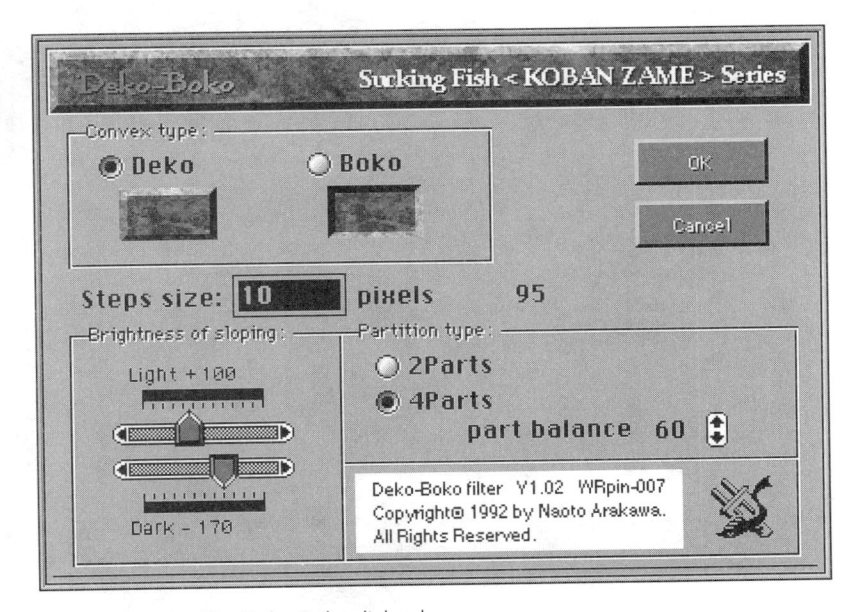

Figure 12.143 The Deko-Boko dialog box.

Figure 12.144 The filter applied to the texture.

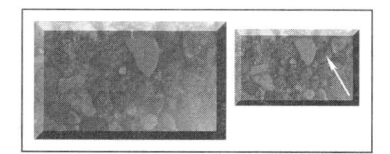

Figure 12.145 Add depth and shine by overlaying a 30% opaque gradient on the center area.

The Sucking Fish filters have been revised and issued as a commercial package under the name WildRiverSSK 1. The interface is sexier, more elaborate, and much more powerful (Figure 12.146 shows WildRiverSSK Deko-Boko's dialog window). Figure 12.147 shows what the filter can do with an empty, white window in Photoshop. The other parts of the WildRiverSSK set include Chameleon, MagicCurtain, MagicFrame, MagicMask, TileMaker, and TVSnow. Note that the lack of spaces in all of the filter titles—and the title of the filter set—is the choice of the software publisher. Makes you want to gasp for air, doesn't it?

Circular Shapes

Circular shapes with a three-dimensional look are among the most interesting buttons you can construct in Photoshop. You can use several simple techniques with Photoshop's built-in features and bundled filters. Other filters, particularly the KPT Spheroid Generator 3, produce spectacular and intriguing shapes.

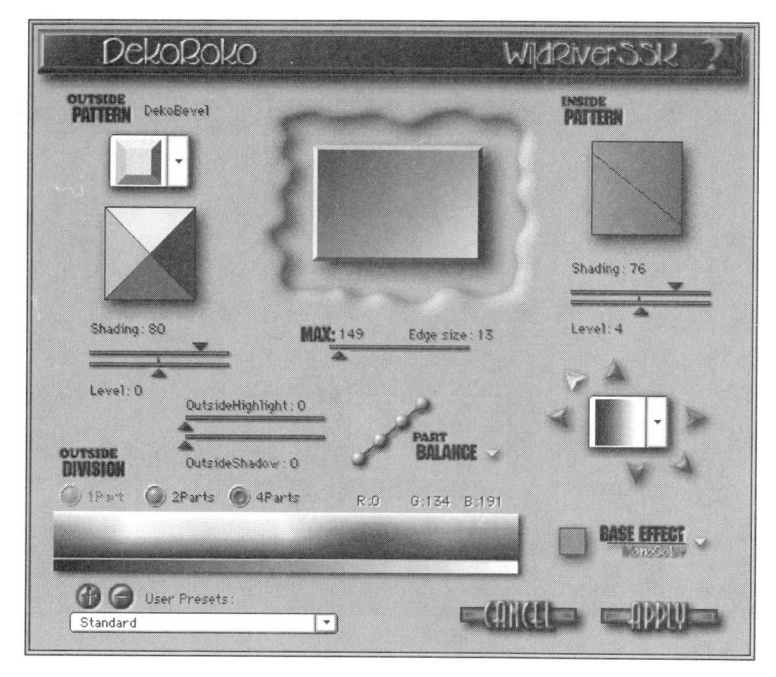

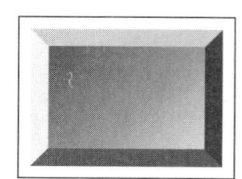

Figure 12.147 This button was generated from a blank white window.

Figure 12.146 The commercial version of Deko-Boko, WildRiverSSK DekoBoko.

KPT Spheroid Generator 3.0

The wide variety of filters usable within Photoshop produce some great effects with very little work. One of the most extraordinary is the KPT Spheroid Generator 3, one of the Kai Power Tools modules. Some designers find the interface for the Kai Power Tools intriguing, refreshing, and different. Others find it irritating, artsy-cutesy, and opaque. Despite differences of opinion, there is no denying the amazing results the KPT filters produce, and the Spheroid Generator is one of the best! The eight examples in Figure 12.148 were generated—using the Spheroid Generator presets—in five minutes. All of the examples in this figure have small drop shadows constructed as discussed previously.

Make Your Own Spheroids

Spherical—actually, these are hemispheres—buttons can be created in other ways if the KPT filters are not available to you. Here's a set of instructions for such a button that you can create using only Photoshop's bundled features. The eight stages of the button are shown in Figure 12.149.

1. Begin with a simple circular shape filled with a medium color (see Figure 12.149a). Be sure that this circular shape is on a separate layer and that the Preserve Transparency option for the layer is turned on.

2. Create a new layer. On this layer, make a rectangular selection and fill it with a light color. While the selection is still active, choose Filter|Noise|Add Noise to overlay the color with a noise texture (see Figure 12.149b). Deselect.

3. Press Command+T or Ctrl+T for Free Transform. Drag the center right-hand control point to the right, and press the Return key (see Figure 12.149c). This operation takes the noise texture and distorts it into a set of streaks.

4. Group the two layers into a Clipping group by pressing Command+G (Mac) or Control+G (Windows): The streaks on the top layer are trimmed by the boundaries of the circular shape (see Figure 12.149d). Hide the Background layer. From the Layers palette menu, choose Merge Visible.

5. Make the Background layer visible. Make sure that the top layer is selected. Hold down the Command key or the Ctrl key and click on the top layer's thumbnail on the Layers palette. This selects the circular shape.

Figure 12.148 Examples of presets from the KPT Spheroid Generator 3.

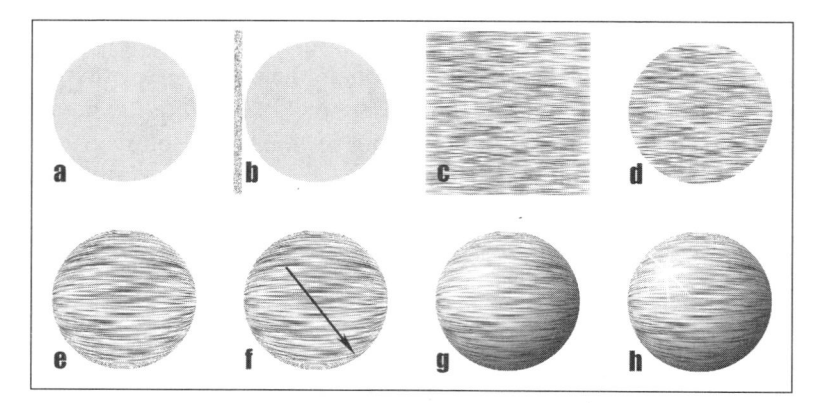

Figure 12.149 (a through h) Eight stages in creating a spheroid button from scratch.

6. From the Filter menu, choose Distort|Spherize. Make the Spherize settings 100% and Normal. Click on OK (see Figure 12.149e).

7. Make the Foreground color white and the Background color black. Select the Radial Gradient tool. Set the Opacity to 80%, the gradient type Foreground to Background, and the Blend mode to Hard Light. Draw the gradient using the same course as the arrow in Figure 12.149f. The result will be as shown in Figure 12.149g.

8. Add an optional specular gleam, if you wish, by choosing a starburst-shaped brush shape with the Paintbrush tool chosen. Click once on the highlight of the sphere (see Figure 12.149h).

The KPT Glass Lens Filter And Other Refinements

You can combine more elaborate spherical effects with the KPT Glass Lens 3 filter. Beginning with a simple circular shape, apply a variety of textures and distortions. The Glass Lens filter tops off whatever has gone before and leaves a pleasing, dimensional spheroid. The examples beginning with Figure 12.150 and ending with 12.159 are all examples of how this works. Figure 12.150 has the filter applied to a single-color circular shape. The following eight examples begin with gradients of one sort or another (KPT Gradient Designer 3), to which are applied distortion filters such as Wave, Twirl, and Polar Coordinates. The last example shows how, when text is placed on the button before the Spherize filter is run, the text itself becomes distorted and appears to conform to the surface of the spheroid. You can see these buttons in the Color Studio section of this book.

Very Low Relief

Expressive of the minimalist point of view, here is a severe and monochromatic relief effect that lends itself to the use of symbol fonts and very simple shapes. The effect is attractive and extremely easy to produce. An example—with two variations—is shown in Figure 12.160. For this effect to be most successful, you need to use a light-colored background.

1. Place the relief shape—our example uses the uppercase K from the Critters font—onto an independent layer. Duplicate the layer twice by dragging the layer onto the New Layer icon at the bottom of the Layers palette.

Figure 12.150 KPT Glass Lens filter applied to a single-color circular shape.

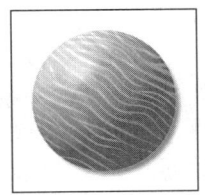

Figure 12.151 KPT Gradient, Ripple filter, KPT Glass Lens.

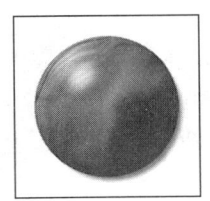

Figure 12.152 KPT Gradient, Wave filter, KPT Glass Lens.

Figure 12.153 KPT Gradient, KPT Glass Lens.

Figure 12.154 KPT Gradient, Polar Coordinates filter, KPT Glass Lens.

Figure 12.155 KPT Gradient, Polar Coordinates filter, KPT Glass Lens.

Figure 12.156 KPT Texture Explorer, KPT Glass Lens.

Figure 12.157 KPT Gradient, KPT Glass Lens.

Figure 12.158 KPT Gradient, Twirl filter, KPT Glass Lens.

Figure 12.159 Retroscan filter, added text, KPT Glass Lens, one click with a starburst-shaped Paintbrush.

Figure 12.160 (a through c) Three variations on a low relief effect.

2. Set Preserve Transparency to On for each of the layers, and set the Opacity for the two new layers to 80%. Set the Foreground color to RGB 197, 197, 197 (equivalent to 25% black). Fill the Background layer and the topmost layer with this color. (At this point, the window will look uninteresting. Persevere—it gets better quickly.)

3. Click on the second layer down to select it. Set the Foreground color to RGB 233, 233, 233 (equivalent to about 10% black). Fill the second layer with this color.

4. Select the third layer down. Set the Foreground color to RGB 162, 162, 162 (equivalent to about 40% black). Fill the third layer with this color. Note that the three color tones are 15% apart (10%, 25%, and 40%).

5. Now for the fun part. Select the Move tool. Click on the second layer's thumbnail to select it. Press the Up arrow key twice and then the Left arrow key twice.

6. Select the third layer. Press the Down arrow key twice and then the Right arrow key twice. Magic, huh?

The two variations shown in the example are simple enhancements. A is the original. B has had the Add Noise filter applied to the Background and to both of the offset layers. The result is a slight improvement in contrast. C has had the Add Noise filter applied to the topmost layer as well. Compared to the original, the difference is simply one of surface texture. None of the three is *better* than the others. All might profitably be used under different circumstances.

Sources For Small-Picture Shapes

There are, literally, thousands of collections of clip art that are available at very low cost. The ClickArt Image Pak (T/Maker Company), for example, sells 65,000 royalty-free images—indexed by subject—at a cost of about .0007¢ a file. The set ships on eight CD-ROM disks and includes hundreds of pictographic fonts, as well as high-quality clip art and color photographic images.

The Internet give you access to another useful image source—freeware and shareware fonts of the variety sometimes called pi, or picture, fonts. (The ubiquitous Zapf Dingbats is an example of such a font.) To give you an idea of the richness of this source as design material, we've included a set of figures showing some of the possibilities. Some fonts are commercial packages, some are shareware, and some are freeware. Examples of some of these fonts are shown in Figures 12.161 (Mayan Dingbats), 12.162 (Nahkt), 12.163 (Critters), 12.164 (Postage Stamps), 12.165 (SportsThree), and 12.166 (Monotype Xmas Pi).

Accessory Software

Beyond the preparation of specific graphics, two programs are excellent for making large-scale graphic/text documents for use on the Web. Some of these products are very new, but they will prove very helpful to Web designers. Because these software packages do tasks that would be difficult for Photoshop to handle by itself, it's appropriate to look at them here.

Figure 12.161 Part of the character set from the Mayan Dingbats font.

Figure 12.162 Part of the character set from the Nahkt font.

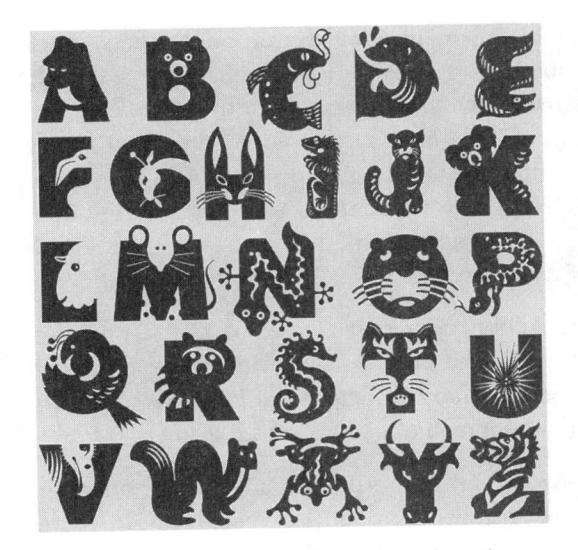

Figure 12.163 Part of the character set from the Critters font.

Figure 12.164 Part of the character set from the Postage Stamps font.

Adobe Acrobat

Acrobat was introduced by Adobe several years ago as a broad solution to document exchange across many platforms. Acrobat documents are called PDF (Portable Document Format) files and use a display model based on Display PostScript.

Figure 12.165 Part of the character set from the SportsThree font.

Figure 12.166 Part of the character set from the Monotype Xmas Pi font.

PDF documents have a range of features that make them ideal for electronic distribution. Each document can have its pictures and fonts embedded. Because of this and because of built-in properties of the display model, you can obtain excellent quality when printing the document. Documents can be annotated by the placement of Notes (small icons placed in the text which, when clicked, open to a small window containing more text). Inter-document and intra-document hyperlinks can be a part of each PDF file. Such links would include hypertext jumps from place to place in the same document, from one document to another, and even URLs. Document security can also be built into each PDF as it's created.

To make the PDF format more widely accepted, Adobe has released its Acrobat Reader royalty-free. With Reader, any user can open, view, search, and print a PDF document (printing can also be prohibited—it's one of the security options that may be included with a PDF document). The construction options for a PDF document are not available from within Reader.

Construction options are available with the Acrobat Exchange program. Exchange functions simultaneously as a reader, annotator, and link installer. Acrobat Exchange is not freeware, but is modestly priced. The most current version of Acrobat is Version 3, which allows a number of exciting possibilities for Web designers and for businesses that have an interest in what is being called *document repurposing*.

Acrobat ships with a plug-in for browsers that allows Acrobat to function as a kind of super helper application. The Acrobat browser interface opens inside the Navigator window and allows users to view multipage PDF documents from within the browser. Effectively, this places many graphically exciting documents—all constructed outside the limitations of HTML—within the browser for as few as five lines of HTML code. To illustrate how this will happen, a document is constructed in any software package. The source document can be Adobe PageMaker, Adobe FrameMaker, Adobe Illustrator, Macromedia FreeHand, Deneba Canvas, Microsoft Word,

Microsoft Excel, Microsoft PowerPoint, ClarisWorks, QuarkXPress, and so on. The document used as an example is a five-page QuarkXPress file. The file contains step-by-step instructions for a special edge effect using Photoshop's Quick Mask (described in this book in the "Quick Mask" section of Chapter 3). Every page contains a colored photograph and a small amount of text. The document deliberately uses a small physical page size—3.5×5 inches. Graphic size is usually a problem on the Web. Make the graphic too large, and it becomes too much of a hassle to download. Make it too small, and the viewer is unable to see relevant details. Acrobat, however, is able to display the document in a variety of display percentages such as 125%, 150%, 200%, and so on.

This document was put together with graphic files at a resolution of 72 ppi and saved as JPEG files. The process of conversion to the PDF format compresses any graphic files automatically. These placed files simply assist the process by performing the compression ahead of time.

Graphic files in any format can be used—TIFF, JPEG, EPS, and so on. Vector-based objects from Illustrator and FreeHand can also be used, but to display them at their best in the finished PDF file, these graphic objects should be rasterized into Photoshop and then reimported (see below).

With the QuarkXPress document completed, the conversion to Acrobat proceeds in this manner: Open the Chooser or go to Printer Setup in Windows. The Acrobat PDF Writer is one of the driver choices. Click on the icon to make it active. (See Figure 12.167.)

Choose Page Setup from under the File menu. The dialog box contains the usual size and orientation specifications as well as two buttons, Compression and Fonts (see Figure 12.168).

The Compression button opens the dialog shown in Figure 12.169, which gives a choice of settings for compressing placed graphics.

The Fonts button gives options for the embedding of fonts (see Figure 12.170). This option is, perhaps, one of the most useful features of Acrobat since the embedding of fonts in the document bypasses the problem of widely distributed users not having the same fonts that built the document.

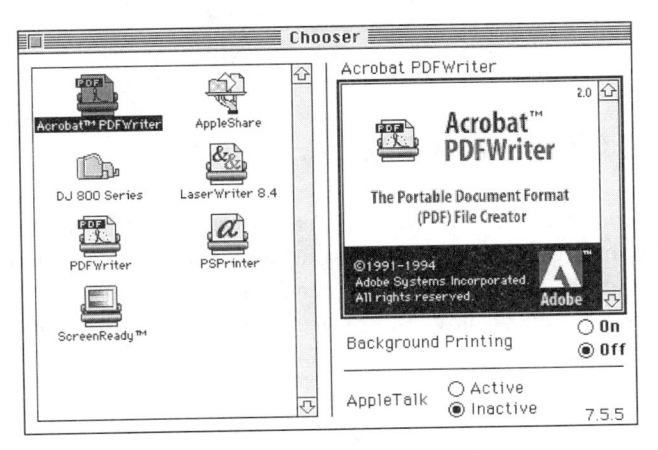

Figure 12.167 The Macintosh Chooser with the Acrobat PDF driver selected.

Figure 12.168 The Acrobat Page Setup dialog box.

Figure 12.169 The Acrobat Page Setup Compression settings dialog box.

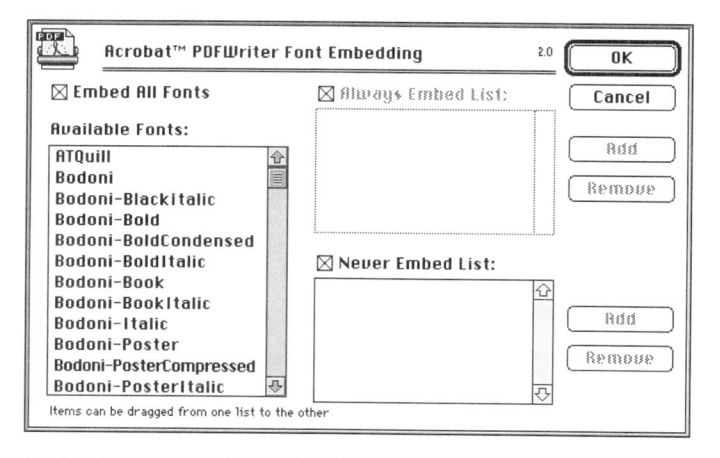

Figure 12.170 The Acrobat Page Setup Font Embedding dialog box.

When all the options are set, choose File|Print (see Figure 12.171). The options in the lower part of the box are the same as when printing to a hard-copy printer. The upper portion of the box gives options relevant to Acrobat. View PDF File opens the Acrobat application upon completion of the conversion and displays the new PDF document. Short DOS File Names ensure compatibility with cross-platform naming conventions. Prompt For Document Info is available only when View PDF is unchecked.

Figure 12.171 The Acrobat Print dialog box.

When these options are taken care of and the OK button is clicked, the dialog box shown in Figure 12.172 appears, which requests a name for the new PDF file and a place for it to be saved. The Acrobat driver then converts the document to the PDF format.

To use the finished PDF file, you must install the Acrobat 3 plug-in in the browser's Plug-Ins folder. To make a simple HTML page containing a link for opening the new PDF file (see Figure 12.173), use code approximately like this:

```
<html>
<body><center><A HREF="PDF_Sample.pdf">Click Here for Acrobat Sample
Document.<BR></center></body>
</html>
```

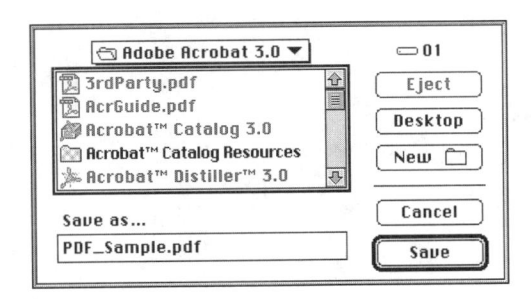

Figure 12.172 Naming the new PDF file before it is generated.

Figure 12.173 Link text in Netscape Navigator to display the PDF document.

With this document loaded into the browser, click on the hyperlink text. The PDF file loads into the browser window, along with all the Acrobat navigation controls (as shown in Figure 12.174). Download time for this document is, as you might expect, longer than for an HTML document with the same number of placed graphic files. However, Adobe has made use of *streaming* technology, which displays the first page of a multipage document as soon as it's received by the client computer. Succeeding pages download while the user looks at the information on the first page.

Document repurposing is a natural outgrowth of the print industry, with its millions of files already built in digital form. The ease of the Acrobat conversion, and the ease with which documents intended for one purpose can be placed onto the Web with very little work, makes Acrobat the program of choice for many businesses. The only undesirable aspect of the process is the need for a client/user to obtain the Acrobat plug-in for the browser. Although this isn't difficult—a Web site may even furnish a link directly to the Adobe site from which you can downloaded the plug-in—studies have shown that many users of the Internet don't take the time to download the plug-in and place it in the browser's Plug-Ins folder. Perhaps in the future, support for Acrobat might be built into the browser just as support for Java is. Or, perhaps, different strategies may develop for browser technology that may bypass the need

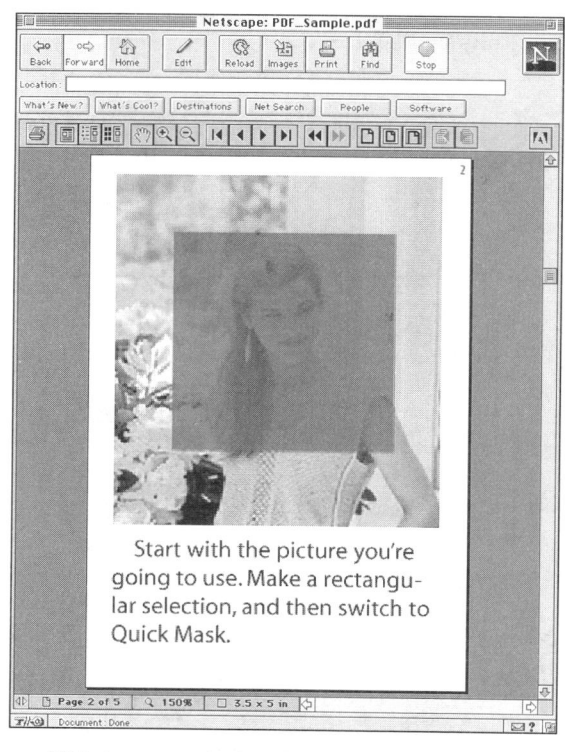

Figure 12.174 The multipage PDF document displayed in the Navigator window, complete with all of the Acrobat Reader navigation controls.

for third-party plug-ins. No matter the future, you owe it to yourself to become conversant with the Acrobat software, not only for its ease of cross-platform portability, but also for its use on the Web.

Preparing A Pre-Acrobat File

Files to be converted to PDF are often files that have already been used as prepress files. Photo information contained in such documents is in CMYK mode, is at a resolution of 266 to 300 ppi, and is in a file format such as EPS/DCS or TIFF. Open all the photo files contained in the document. Choose Image|Mode|RGB to convert the images from CMYK. (Intensify the colors if you wish—the Web is not concerned with printable colors and the saturation of your photo documents may be enhanced.) Choose Image|Image Size and change the resolution of the image to 72 ppi. Save this file in the JPEG format. Use Optimized Baseline and Low for quality retention. Replace the photo images in the original document with those you have modified in Photoshop.

If your file contains an Illustrator graphic, follow these steps for best use in Acrobat. Note that these instructions may seem a little involved, but they will make the difference between an acceptable document and one of very high quality.

1. Open the Illustrator file.
2. Select All, copy, and switch to Photoshop.
3. From the File menu, choose New. The size of the new image is shown.
4. Enter a title, make the resolution 72 ppi, and make the mode RGB.
5. Paste, using the Paste As Pixels option.
6. Leave this document open and return to the Illustrator document.
7. If any objects on the outer perimeter of the graphic are stroked objects, convert them to filled objects by using Object|Path|Outline Path.
8. Next, choose Object|Rasterize.
9. In the resulting dialog box, choose RGB for the Color Model, Screen for Resolution. Choose both of the checkbox options (Anti-alias and Create Mask). Click on OK.
10. When the graphic has been rasterized, click on the outer edge of the graphic to select the masking path.
11. Copy this path, switch to Photoshop, and then Paste. This time, choose the Paste As Paths option.
12. Save this path and make it into a clipping path.
13. Save the document as an EPS file with the clipping path you have saved.
14. Replace the original Illustrator file in the target document with the one you just saved from Photoshop.
15. Discard the original Illustrator file.

> **TIP**
>
> Sometimes it becomes necessary to adjust the color on a scan that—in the worst-case scenario—has been converted to Indexed Color mode and for which there is no longer an original to be rescanned. With such an image, a look at the histogram shows that there is very little information with which to make corrections and adjustments. To replace—with mathematically fictitious values that are nonetheless usable—those missing values, convert the file back to RGB mode. Now, choose Image|Image Size. Add one pixel to the number in the Horizontal Pixels data entry field at the top of the window. Click on OK. Open the same window (Image Size). Subtract 1 pixel from the Horizontal Pixels data entry field. Click on OK. Photoshop will use its Bicubic interpolation scheme and will replace the missing values in your image. You can then proceed with your image adjustment.

Adobe ImageReady

ImageReady is the newest addition to the Adobe family. This program is similar to a "lite" version of Photoshop, with the addition of some high-powered features for creating Web-optimized graphics. It's tightly integrated with Photoshop so that designers can easily work on an image in both programs. Layers, channels, and Layer Masks are retained in the "round trip." Figure 12.175 shows the basic interface, which, as you can see, looks almost identical to Photoshop's interface.

If you look carefully at Figure 12.175, you can see three documents that all look similar. ImageReady keeps the image in a window that accommodates two views—the original image and the optimized image (brought down in color to 2, 3, 4, 6, or 8 bits). You can duplicate either the original or the optimized image into another "double" window and easily compare how different your image looks in 256 versus 16 colors (or whatever other combo you want to try). You can also select the information to be displayed under the images. Figure 12.175 shows the file format, optimized file size, number of colors, and amount of applied dither in one window information area. The other one contains file size and download time at a selectable baud rate. Here's how the three windows shown compare:

Format	# Colors	File Size	Dither	Download	Baud Rate
GIF	128	54K	100%	20 seconds	28.8
GIF	128	66K	47%	24 seconds	28.8
GIF	32	34K	0%	13 seconds	28.8

You also have a choice of the RGB-to-Indexed Color conversion algorithm. You can select from Perceptual (attuned more to the Human Eye), Adaptive (conversion by popularity of the color), Web-safe palette (the 216 "common" colors, which are used in the 54K file above), or the Mac or Windows System colors. You can also define the matte color (the one to blend towards in semitransparent areas), and whether to allow transparency. Figure 12.176 shows a close-up of a window double so that you can actually read the information under it.

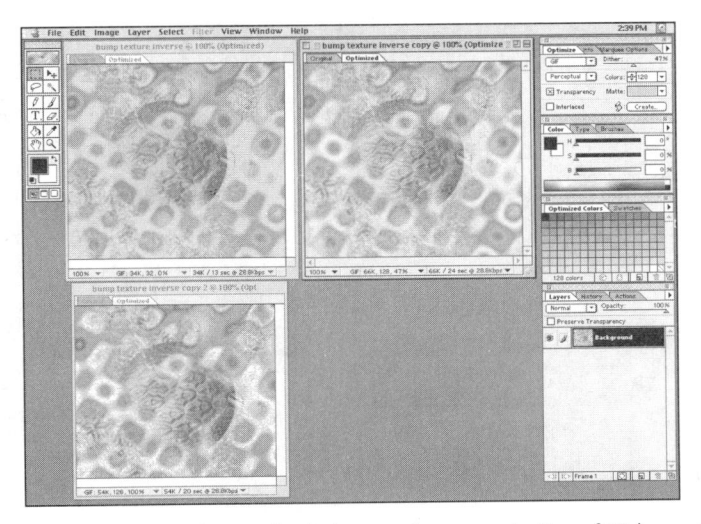

Figure 12.175 Adobe ImageReady is designed to help speed your production of Web graphics in an environment that is already familiar to most graphic artists.

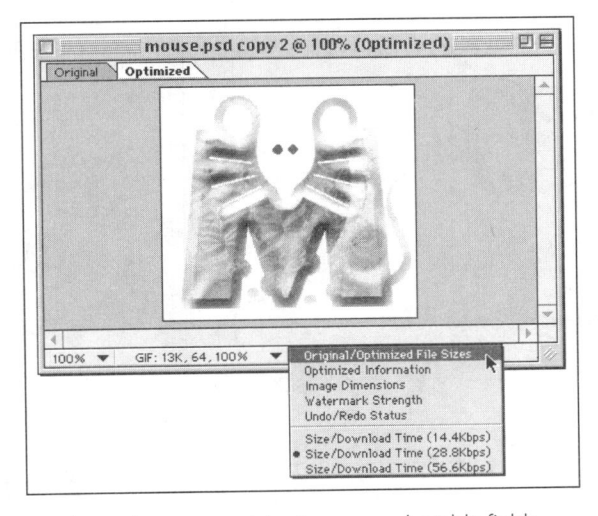

Figure 12.176 The Window information area contains two user-selectable fields.

Let's look at the top and palette sidebar menus. Figure 12.177 shows the File menu. Although it isn't enabled on this menu, you can open your Browser to view the optimized image (Preview In...), and you can hand off the image to another program for further editing (Jump To...). Figure 12.178 shows the Edit menu. In addition to the usual Edit menu options, you can save an HTML tag for a color or copy the HTML code that the program writes for an image. The Image menu (shown in Figure 12.179) has a number of unique options on it. You can Clip or Trim images and you can create and manage a Master palette of colors (to create the best general palette for a number of different images to use). The Layer (see Figure 12.180), Select, and Window menus have fewer options than the corresponding menus in Photoshop, but

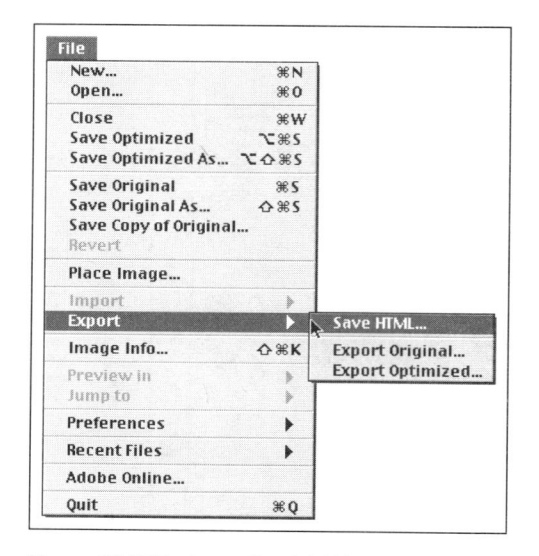

Figure 12.177 ImageReady's File menu.

Figure 12.178 ImageReady's Edit menu.

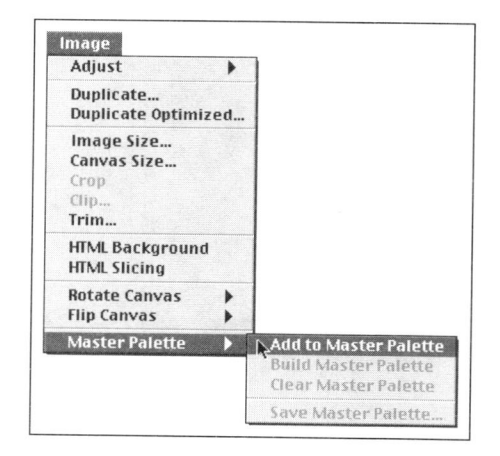

Figure 12.179 ImageReady's Image menu.

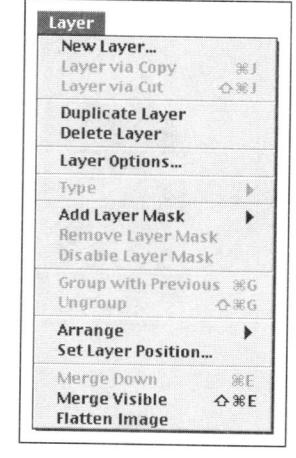

Figure 12.180 ImageReady's Layer menu.

contain most of the same items. You can point ImageReady to your Photoshop Plug-Ins folder. The View menu (see Figure 12.181) allows you to see what the image would look like in a browser on a 256-color monitor or in the "other" platform's gamma—on the Mac, it says "Windows Gamma" and on Windows it says "Mac Gamma."

As you can see, this is a program specifically created with the Web designer in mind. Everything is fashioned to make your task easier. The Layers palette is similar to Photoshop's, but it has some different options on the sidebar menu, as you can see in Figure 12.182. The Layer Options dialog box (see Figure 12.183) doesn't let you remove color areas, but it does let you create image maps.

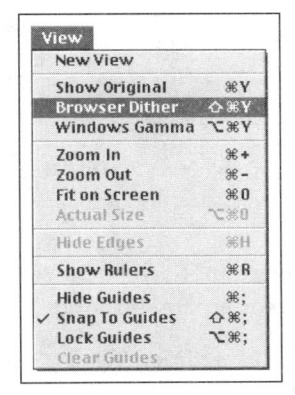

Figure 12.181 ImageReady's View menu.

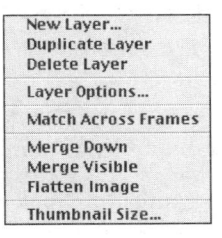

Figure 12.182 ImageReady's Layers palette sidebar menu.

An image map defines a clickable area on the image and attaches a URL to it. Finally, last in our whirlwind tour of ImageReady is the Optimized Colors palette (see Figure 12.184). This is the "heart" of the program's conversion magic. You can lock specific colors to protect them during conversion to less than 256 colors. When you sort by popularity, you can immediately see the trace colors in your image. By locking them, you are taking control over how your image is converted to lower color—in a very easy-to-use manner that still delivers a lot of power. Another interesting feature allows you to shift your image toward the 216 Web-safe colors. You can nudge your entire image in that direction or only try to bring selected colors into range.

ImageReady also makes it easy to create GIF animations. You create an animation by taking a picture of your image in a frame. You can stack as many layers as you want and turn them off and on. As you manipulate the image, you can put each version into its own frame. You can set the timing (or delay) by frame. In Figure 12.185, we've taken the letter "M" from the Critters font and embossed it as described earlier in the chapter. We then moved the mouse's eyes from

Figure 12.183 ImageReady's Layer Options dialog box.

Figure 12.184 ImageReady's Optimized Colors palette sidebar menu.

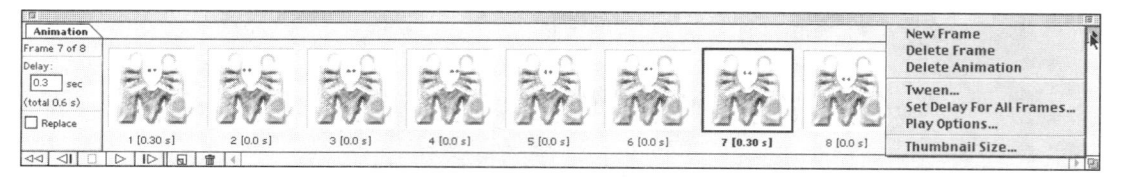

Figure 12.185 ImageReady gives you a great deal of control over the creation of an animation.

frame to frame. You also have the ability to *tween* motion—to move a ball from one side of the image to the other, for example, by simply creating the start and the end frame.

We could probably write an entire book about using ImageReady (and books probably will be written about it), but this isn't the time or place to delve more deeply into it. However, if you know Photoshop, you can easily learn ImageReady. The two programs are a very nice complement for each other.

Moving On

In this chapter, we explored a variety of issues that are specific to the Internet. The speed of the network connection and how that relates to the size of your graphic files is one issue. Another has to do with the limitations of the file formats that you can use on the Web. Your graphic files need to be as small as possible to minimize the download time for your viewer. Studies of Web users show that the average user's patience begins to grow thin at about 12 seconds into a download. A good strategy is to provide the user with something to do, something to look at, to make the wait worthwhile. You can do this using files saved with interlacement, or by using the LOW SRC technique.

Another way to keep your viewers interested is to make sure that your graphics are as clear and as attractive as possible. This subject, the adjustment and correction of photographic scans, is the only topic of concern to developers for the Web that we didn't cover in this chapter. For more information, turn to Chapters 2, 8, and 9. Apply the information learned in these pages to your Web photos to make them as appealing as you can. Pay particular attention to instructions for using the Unsharp Mask filter in Chapter 9. Knowledgeable use of this filter can make the difference between your images looking merely good and looking superb! Good enough, as the saying goes, isn't.

As we come to the end of our look at graphics on the Web, we also come to the end of the book. Photoshop is far too large for a single volume to cover it completely, but we hope we've covered Photoshop's most important and useful capabilities. We've also tried to give you a framework for working out your own solutions to image-editing problems. Should you run up against something that you can't solve, remember that you have the authors' email addresses listed in the book's Introduction. Possibly, we will meet again. Good luck!

WHAT'S ON THE CD-ROM

The companion CD-ROM included with your copy of *Photoshop 5 In Depth* contains software and teaching example files that you will be using while you work through the chapters. This appendix is meant to serve as your roadmap to this valuable addition to this book.

Practice Files

You will find the teaching example files in folders marked, appropriately enough, Chapter0*n*—for example, to find the file snowflke.psd for a Chapter 7 exercise, you double-click on the Chapter07 folder.

Where the chapter contains only practice files, it's this simple. However, where other resources may be involved, you may need to drill a little deeper into the CD-ROM's folder structure. For example, in Chapter 4, you need to use a particular resource for one of the examples—Brushes. To access this resource, take the following steps:

1. Click on the Chapter04 folder. Here, you will see two more folders—Chapter04 Brushes and Chapter 4 Practice files.
2. Click on the Chapter 4 Brushes folder.

Now you can access the files necessary to use this resource.

The following list shows the figures in the folders, and—where applicable—lists legal restrictions that you need to observe while using them.

Legal Image Restrictions

Chapter 1

Knothole.psd: Photograph by Sherry London; all rights given.

Bouquet.Psd: Photograph by Sherry London; all rights given.

Shrine.Psd: Photograph by Ed Scott; non-commercial use only.

Palace.Psd: Photograph by Ed Scott; non-commercial use only.

Table1.Psd: Photograph by Sherry London; all rights given.

Chapters 2 Through 6

All images, no restrictions.

Chapter 7

Flower.Psd—Photograph by Sherry London; all rights given.

Star.Psd—Image rasterized from Ultimate Symbol Collection; for non-commercial use only.

Texture.Psd—Created by Sherry London; all rights given.

Sunface.Psd—Image rasterized from Ultimate Symbol Collection; for non-commercial use only.

Zodiac.Psd—Image rasterized from Ultimate Symbol Collection; for non-commercial use only.

SnowFlke.Psd—Image rasterized from Ultimate Symbol Collection; for non-commercial use only.

Bluelady.psd—Created by Rhoda Grossman, Copyright Rhoda Grossman; you may use this ONLY for the purpose of completing the exercise (*absolutely* no reproduction rights given).

Fractal.Psd—Generated by Sherry London from KPT Fractal Explorer; all rights given.

Medalon.Psd—Created by Susan Kitchens; VIEW ONLY (no rights given).

Chapter 8
No example files needed.

Chapters 9 Through 11
All images, no restrictions.

Chapter 12
No example files needed.

Third-Party Software

The demo software provided on this CD-ROM has been organized into PC and Macintosh folders. Most of the software on the CD-ROM must be installed onto your computer's hard drive with an installation program. To install a specific application, navigate to its folder and run the installation program within.

For some of the applications, there's no need to run an installer; just drag the app's folder to your computer's hard drive.

Mac Software

Here's a rundown on the demonstration software that we have included on this book's companion CD-ROM:

Adobe After Effects—A demo of a program that allows you to take Photoshop or Illustrator images and animate them so that they move across the screen. Because Adobe After Effects is video compositing software, you can also layer Premiere files and add a variety of effects.

Adobe Illustrator—Demo of Adobe's top-notch vector drawing package. This program is the standard for professional computer illustration.

Auto/FX Demos

- *PageEdges*—Creates edge effects for use in a page layout program
- *PhotoGraphic Edges*—Creates interesting edge effects for images
- *Typo/Graphic Edges*—Creates rough and textured type effects
- *Ultimate Texture*—A collection of textures to apply to selections
- *Universal Animator*—A program to create GIF animations from any application
- *Webvise Totality*—A set of tools to help create images for the Web

Eye Candy—Demo of shadow, emboss, and glow filters from Alien Skin Software.

PlateMaker—A .PDF file that describes a plug-in for Photoshop that can help and vastly simplify the export of spot color images.

Web Actions—A collection of Actions that you can use to create special effects within Photoshop. Also included, information on how to get more Actions.

FourSeasons—A Photoshop plug-in that allows you to create realistic skies, clouds, and weather effects.

PC Software

Adobe After Effects—A demo of a program that allows you to take Photoshop or Illustrator images and make them move across the screen. Like the Mac version, this is video compositing software, so you can also layer Premiere files and add a variety of effects.

Adobe Illustrator—Demo of Adobe's PC version of the top-notch vector drawing package. This program is the standard for professional computer illustration.

Auto/FX Demos—

- *PageEdges*—To create edge effects for use in a page layout program
- *PhotoGraphic Edges*—Creates interesting edge effects for images
- *Typo/Graphic Edges*—Creates rough and textured type effects
- *Ultimate Texture*—A collection of textures to apply to selections
- *Universal Animator*—A program that allows you to create GIF animations from any application
- *Webvise Totality*—A comprehensive graphics compression and optimization set of tools to help create images for the Web

FourSeasons—A plug-in for the PC version of Photoshop that allows you to create realistic skies, clouds, and weather effects.

Web Actions—A collection of Actions that you can use to create special effects within Photoshop, along with information on how to get more Actions.

Eye Candy—A demo of shadow, emboss, and glow filters from Alien Skin Software.

PlateMaker—A .PDF file that describes a plug-in for Photoshop to help export spot color images.

COMMON PREPRESS TERMS AND DEFINITIONS

24-bit color

RGB monitors display 8-bit brightness values (256) for each of the monitor phosphors, red, green, and blue. The number of combinations that can be assigned to any monitor pixel is $256^3 = 16,777,216$, the total number of colors the monitor can display. An interesting fact that relates to this color number is that the human eye is capable of differentiating only about 2.4 million colors. Some of the colors the eye can see lie inside the RGB range, others outside. If you assumed that the visible colors are about 70% within the monitor range and 30% outside—those aren't the exact numbers—then your monitor can display 15.9 million colors that you cannot differentiate as separate tones.

Accurate Screens

Software program from Adobe Systems, Inc., a proprietary PostScript screening model based on supercells. Supercells simplify the creation of screen dots by rationalizing conventional screen angles with cell groups in which dots of the same percentage may be unlike each other and can be fitted to a raster grid in an integer relationship. For further information, consult *PostScript Screening: Adobe Accurate Screens* by Peter Fink, Adobe Press, ISBN 0-672-48544-3.

Amplitude modulated

Refers to conventional screen dots that increase in size with the increase of ink density requirements. More simply, as ink values become darker, larger dots are required to print them. Within the total range of values—theoretically 256—ink requirements, and indirectly tone requirements, modulate the amplitude of the dot. (See also *frequency modulated*.)

Art board

Bronze-age artifact used to mount unwieldy strips of type, artwork, and masks. The finished board was then photographed (see *line shot*), with the resulting negative used as a mask for making a printing plate.

Black

One of the process inks, added on press to improve the sharpness and purity of shadow tones, and to reduce the overall amount of ink required for color reproduction. (See also *GCR*, *UCR*, and *black generation*.)

Black generation

Process in which black ink is substituted for neutral tones produced by cyan, magenta, and yellow.

Blanket
In offset printing, ink is transferred from the plate to the offset blanket. The blanket transfers the ink to the press sheet.

Blown out
When highlight tones in an image have been too drastically lightened, they produce areas on a printed image in which there is no ink. These areas are said to be blown out. The effect is not attractive.

Blue
Beyond the color definition, *blue* is printer slang for cyan.

Blueline
Exposure of blueprint paper masked by plate-ready film produces a blue-toned simulation of the printed piece. The blueline is used for customer approval of a job and to test to see that imposition and work-and-turn backups are correct.

Brightness
Brightness is the amount of light seen reflected from an illuminated object. Brightness values vary with position and distance from the object being viewed. In computer terms, brightness is the generic term for the values between black and white. It is usually applied to a pixel. These two uses of the word are examples of one word describing similar phenomena within two visual paradigms: reflected light and emitted light.

Bump plate
Plate used to overprint an additional amount of ink on an already printed area in order to intensify the color.

Choke
Trapping term, indicating that a surrounding color/ink has slightly overlapped the object of a different color/ink that it encloses.

CIE
Centre Internationale d'Eclairage, the international color definitions standards committee.

Clipping path
Beziér outline saved with a Photoshop document that acts as a mask. Pixels within the perimeter of the path are visible, all others appear transparent. Used to make irregular-shaped photo images.

CMS
Color Management System, a system for harmonizing the color and color-handling characteristics of different digital devices. Such devices might include scanners, monitors, and color output devices. CMS strategies are usually based on an accurate analysis of the color throughput for each device.

CMYK
Cyan, magenta, yellow, and black, the four process color inks used for the great majority of color reproduction.

Color Sync
Integrated system-level color management software by Apple Computer, Inc. Designed to be used by software publishers who can tie into this built-in capability and use it for in-program color management.

Colorimeter
Device for accurately measuring the characteristics of colors.

Colorize
Term used in several ways, all of which indicate the addition or substitution of non-black colors when reproducing a monotone image.

Colortron II
Monitor calibration instrument by X-Rite, Inc. Can also be used as a colorimeter and as a densitometer. (See *densitometer* and *colorimeter*.)

Custom color
Four-color process printing achieves different colors by mixing tints on press. Custom colors are premixed to give a single solid color value as well as tints. Custom colors are often used for color values that cannot be produced by the four process inks.

Cyan
One of the four process color inks. Provides the blue component of color images.

DCS
Desktop Color Separation. File format designed by Quark, Inc. that separates the ink components of a CMYK document into four individual files linked to a master file. A newer format, DCS 2, allows the incorporation of CMYK and spot color data within the same file.

DCS 2.0
Extension of the DCS format that allows more than four files to be linked to the master file. This allows process color and spot colors to be saved within the same file.

Densitometer
Device used to measure the amount of ink coverage within a given area. Densitometers measure the difference between known input values and values that press conditions such as dot gain place on the press sheet.

Device profiles
Descriptive files that accurately describe the color throughput characteristics of digital devices within a color-managed environment.

Digital proof
Simulation of a print job based on a digital printer's interpretation of what the job will probably look like on press.

Dot gain
When liquid ink is applied to the press sheet, it spreads out slightly. This results in a darker tone. The difference between the dots on the plate and the dots of ink on the page, when measured in an area of 50 percent tone, is called dot gain.

DPI
Dots per inch. Clumsy, inelegant term that may refer to several different things. Other, more accurate terms have the advantage of a narrowly focused meaning. DPI is sometimes used to describe the pixel density of a CRT, more properly PPI (pixels per inch). The same term is used to describe the pixel density of a raster image file; the correct term is PPI (pixels per inch). DPI is also used to describe the resolution of an output device (here, the term is more or less accurate), as well as the output itself, which should be described in LPI (lines per inch).

Drum scanner
High-quality scanner/digitizer that uses vacuum tube photomultiplier sensors.

DTP
Desktop Publishing, the name given to microcomputer preparation of press materials. The more-or-less simultaneous introduction of the Macintosh computer by Apple Computer, Inc., the PostScript page description language and PostScript-driven printers, and Aldus Corporation's PageMaker program ushered in the era of DTP.

Duotone
When a grayscale image is printed with two inks, each plate of which is derived from a different interpretation of the image's gray values, it is said to be duotoned. Duotoning is used to colorize grayscale images or to extend the tonal range far beyond what can be achieved with a single ink.

Eight-bit color
System in which the total number of tones is limited to 256. The tones present can be grayscale or an adaptive sampling of colors from a color image.

EPS
Encapsulated PostScript, a file format in widespread use in the prepress community because of its ability to provide trouble-free output on PostScript devices. EPS files are capable of embedding screening information, tone controls, fonts, graphics, and clipping paths.

Film
Prepress files are typically output as thin sheets containing opaque black dots surrounded by areas of complete transparency. The black dots comprise the lithographic conversion of the computer data. For offset printing, a negative image on the film—the inverse of the values

manipulated on the computer—is used as a mask for making a plate. Some other kinds of printing require the film mask to be positive.

Film processor
Device in which film exposed by the laser assembly in an imagesetter is developed.

Flap
Associated with artboards, a flap is a sheet of transparent overlay material to which some element of the artboard page is attached. The flap is usually taped into place so that the element's placement is superimposed upon other artboard elements.

Flatbed scanner
Usually a low-end scanner that makes use of CCD (Charge Coupled Device) sensors. Flatbed scanners usually do not have the optical or color sensitivity of drum scanners. However, they are far less expensive.

Flood
When inks or transparent coatings are applied by a press over the entire surface of the press sheet, the coating is said to be flooded.

Frequency modulated
Screening system that uses small, uniform screen dots distributed at random. Density is achieved by increasing the number of dots—as opposed to amplitude modulated dots, which increase density by increasing the dot size. FM screening technology achieves a precision of detail that is far superior to AM screening.

GCR
Gray Component Replacement, black generation algorithm in which black is pumped into tones composed of the other three inks. This has the effect of purifying the color in areas of heavy coverage, making shadow tones more crisp and using less ink on press.

Grayscale
Photoshop display mode for working with monotone images. Grayscale is also a generic term indicating the manipulation of the proper subset of RGB values where R, G, and B are equal.

Halftone
When grayscale digital images are converted to output for press purposes, gray values are changed to screen dots. This process is called halftoning, and the word has been extended to describe the printing of monotone images.

Halftone cell
When a PostScript output device converts 8-bit information to screen dots, it does so by dividing its resolution by the requested line screen value. It then sets up a square area with the result number on each side (the cell). Screen dots are then constructed to fill percentages of the area.

Hexachrome
Ultra high-fidelity color printing process developed by Pantone, Inc. that increases the printable tone range by a large amount. The process uses four specially formulated process color inks (CMYK) and two additional ink colors, green and orange.

High contrast
By decreasing the number of values in an image, more weight can be given to those that remain. With this procedure, related values become farther apart, with noticeable difference between them. Detail is sacrificed for the purpose of image drama.

High-fidelity printing
One of several strategies devised by the printing industry to increase the tonal fidelity of color-image reproduction. The process nearly always requires the use of more than four inks. The Pantone Hexachrome method (see *hexachrome*) is one of these competing strategies.

High key
Image in which the majority of values present are very light.

Highlight dot
The small screen dots that represent very light tonal values.

Highlight dot fall-off
In offset printing, the mechanical process sometimes prevents very small highlight dots from printing. The range of tones from white to one of the low percentages—such as 5 percent—is called the highlight dot fall-off range.

Histogram
In digital photo manipulation schemes, histograms display the range of values in an image in what appears to be a miniature bar graph. This graph ranges the values from dark to light, and is called a histogram.

Hue error
Percentage of hue deviation from pure caused by a color's contamination with small amounts of other colors. Where process inks are measured for hue error, the contaminants for each ink are percentages of other inks. Yellow ink, for example, has a hue error that results from contamination of percentages of cyan and magenta.

Image contrast
Overall description of the range of values in a photo image. When the image contains a broad range of tones that are naturally distributed, the contrast is said to be good. When the image shows a range of detail but relatively few tones, the contrast is said to be poor.

Imposition
Refers to the process of separating sequential pages into a non-sequential order so that, as multiple pages are placed on a single press sheet, folding the press sheet results in the pages running in proper finished order. (See also *reader spreads* and *printer spreads*.)

Input value
When digital values are processed by an output device, they are said to be the Input values.

Interpolated resolution
When a raster image is resized, pixels must be added or subtracted. The process of calculating new values for pixels that must be added, or of deciding which pixels should be discarded, is called interpolating the resolution.

JPEG
Joint Photograph Experts Group, who formulated a compression method for stored or electronically transmitted photographic images for the purpose of decreasing their size.

Keyline
Term referring to the placement of elements on an artboard.

Knock out
When an area of one color needs to print within the boundaries of another color, but overprinting would result in an unwanted color, a space the shape of the first object is knocked out of the area of the second color.

Lab color
Color model used as the behind-the-scenes color space in programs such as Adobe Photoshop. The advantage of lab color is that it enunciates color values without reference to specific electronic or output devices. Because of this, it is said to be a device-independent color model.

Laminate proof
Color proof used to match values on press. This proof is usually made from the same film used for the plating. The four tones are laid atop each other in a laminating process. Laminate proofs are the current proof of choice for the printing industry.

Lightness
Lightness refers to the natural tones of a surface from which light is reflected. A white wall and a black fabric are examples of differing degrees of lightness.

Line art
Line art refers to print artwork that is usually non-photographic and composed of more-or-less simple shapes that are printed with one ink.

Line screen
Also known as *screen frequency*, line screen refers to the number of rows of screen dots in some unit of measurement. Smaller numbers indicate larger dots, and larger numbers indicate finer dots.

Line shot
When a finished artboard is converted to film, the process of photographing it is called a line shot.

Lossy
Refers to file compression methods that result in permanent data loss. Should not be used in polite company because it is an ugly, geeky word.

Low contrast
This term describes a photographic image in which too few tones are present to accurately show details in the image.

Low key
When the tones in a photographic image contain mostly dark tones, it is described as a low key image.

LPC
Screen frequency abbreviation; stands for *lines per centimeter*.

LPI
Screen frequency abbreviation; stands for *lines per inch*.

Magenta
The reddish component in four-color process printing.

Maximum black
When black ink is added to a color separation, this term expresses the highest allowable percentage with which the separation algorithm is governed.

Maximum shadow dot
Because press gain darkens an image, black inks are usually limited to an input percentage that is smaller than 100 percent (the maximum shadow dot), because the smaller percentage will grow, on press, to 100 percent.

Metallics
Specialty inks containing metal flakes that give a metallic surface texture wherever the ink has been applied.

Midtone
In photographic images, the midtones are the range of values that fall into the percentage range between 30 percent and 70 percent.

Midtone gain
Dot gain refers to the growth of the dot on press. The percentage of growth is at its highest for tones of 50 percent. Measurements of gain are always made on areas of 50 percent and are referred to as midtone gain.

Minimum highlight dot
Refers to the smallest dot that a press can actually reproduce.

Monitor calibration

Analysis by an external device of a monitor's display characteristics. After evaluation, calibration software then brings the monitor display into line with some predetermined standard.

Negs

Slang for the negative films used to make plates.

Neutral tones

Printed tones in which no colored inks predominate and which appear to be a uniform gray.

Offset

Presses that use a plate to transfer ink to a blanket, which then imprints the press sheet print by the process called offset. This differs from presses that imprint the press sheet directly from the plate.

Out-of-gamut color

On an RGB monitor, out-of-gamut colors are those that the monitor can display but which cannot be duplicated with process color inks.

Output value

This value is the measured result of an output device. System calibrations are always made by comparing this value to input values.

Overlay proof

Older proofing method in which clear flaps containing colored dots were carefully laid atop each other to emulate press output.

Overprint

When one color is printed atop an area of the press sheet already containing one or more inks, it is said to overprint.

Pantone

Company that has been responsible for vending a wide array of custom colors and a color matching system as a standard for the printing industry.

Perfecting press

Sophisticated press in which two offset blankets simultaneously imprint both sides of a press sheet.

Plate

The metallic sheet that contains the inking imprinter of the printed pages. The plate receives the ink from an ink font and either transfers the ink to a blanket or directly imprints the page.

Plugged

Refers to a press condition in which, for various reasons, too much ink is being applied. Image details become obliterated and letter counters become filled in.

PostScript
Page description computer programming language used to describe the objects on a page to an output device that controls the imaging assembly. PostScript is published by Adobe Systems, Inc. As a cultural achievement, it ranks with—and probably rivals—the much vaunted accomplishments of Johann Gutenburg, the inventor of movable type, which led to mass-produced books and widespread literacy.

PPI
Pixels per inch, a measurement of the resolution of a scanned image.

Prepress
Prepress refers to the preparation of materials for printing.

Press
Device for applying ink to paper for the mass distribution of printed material.

Press gain
Refers to the growth of screens dots on press as a factor of darkening.

Press misregistration
When a press sheet passes through several inking stations, the press sheet can become slightly misaligned with the press. This results in ink areas becoming inaccurately registered to each other.

Printer spreads
Refers to page sequence on a press sheet that results in sequential pages when the press sheet is imprinted on both sides and then folded to produce a multipage book.

Process color
Color reproduction is typically accomplished by mixing, on press, four primary tones that combine to produce thousands of other colors. The four primary tones are cyan, magenta, yellow, and black.

Proportional color reduction trapping
When colors are overlapped for trapping purposes, the zone of overlap usually shows up as a darker line. If the amount of ink is reduced proportionally within the zone of overlap, the trapping remains, but without the visually intrusive dark line.

Quadtone
Similar to a duotone, but produced with four inks.

Raster grid
On a PostScript output device, the raster grid is the theoretical grid on the image plane that defines the smallest mark the device can make. All output is composed of shapes built from these small, square-shaped marks.

Rasterize
Graphic shapes such as type are simply scaled versions of curve segments that outline an area. Rasterizing is the process where these segments are rationalized to a grid environment such as a pixel or the squares of a raster grid.

Reader spreads
Printed documents are often designed as spreads that, on the computer screen, resemble what the eventual reader will see. The pages of reader spreads are eventually taken apart and reassembled as printer spreads.

Red
Beyond the color definition, *red* is printer slang for magenta.

RGB
The pixels of a computer monitor use an additive color system to build up different colors using three primary colors—Red, Green, and Blue.

RIP
Archaic funeral monument inscription admonishing the departed to Rest In Peace. Also, the imaging computer associated with an output device that converts vector objects (and low-resolution raster objects) to a high-resolution raster configuration: *Raster Image Processor*.

Screen
Refers to the lithographic process of converting inks to small dots of various sizes that blend with the white of the page upon which they are printed to produce many degrees of a single tone.

Screen angle
Four-color process screens are imaged so that each ink's screen dots follow an angle that is different from the other three inks. Yellow is typically printed at 0°, black at 45°, and the remaining two at 90° − 15° = 75° and 0° + 15° = 15°.

Screen dot
Tiny spot of ink that represents some percentage of color density on a printed page.

Screen print
Screen printing is an ink application method using fine-mesh fabrics stretched over frames. The fabric is flood coated with a resist substance that fills in the spaces between the fabric threads. Later, parts of the resist are removed. The frame is then placed over the material to be printed, flooded with ink, and a wiper blade—similar to the windshield wiper blade on an automobile—passes across the fabric, forcing the ink through the mesh wherever the resist substance has been removed.

Separations
Color images, before they can be printed, are separated into four components—cyan, magenta, yellow, and black—so that the colors can overprint to produce the colors of the image when printed.

Shadow
The dark areas of an image.

Sharpen
When an image is prepared for printing, it is usually put through a process that artificially enhances edge contrasts to produce a clearer and more detail-laden image.

Sheet-fed presses
Presses through which pass pre-cut sheets of paper.

Spot
This term can refer to a lithographic dot. It also indicates an added color printed with a pre-mixed ink.

Spot function
When an RIP builds up screen dots, it can produce many dot shapes. The process of building dots that are square or round or oval or linear is called the RIP's spot function.

Spread
Two sequential pages in a printed presentation are called a spread. Even-numbered pages are on the left of a spread, odd-numbered pages are on the right.

Spread also refers to a trapping procedure where a color is artificially extended—spread—past its own boundaries.

Step wedge
One term describing a bar with discrete areas of ink percentages. For example, a step wedge might contain 10 sections, with each section 10 percent greater than its neighbor on one side and smaller than its neighbor on the other side.

Stochastic
From the Greek word *stochastikos*, meaning *skillful in aiming*. This term describes the random-appearing assignment of dot placement in an FM screen.

Stripper
Prepress technician responsible for the final assembly of elements from which a plate-mask film is to be made. You might want to make up your own print-specific fun definition. Your non-printing-industry friends will never believe you anyway. How about this one: print plant personnel who scrape the tea leaves from the bottoms of break-room cups to determine if tomorrow's large press run will be successful?

Surprint
Overprint.

SWOP
Specification for Web Offset Printing.

TIFF
Tag Image File Format. One of the oldest and most flexible of disk file formats used for images.

Tone
Word often applied sloppily to a range of color or grayscale values.

Touch plate
Plate used to supplement process color work by overprinting—often a tint—a spot color in an area where process colors cannot achieve a desired tone.

Transfer function
A set of values that can be embedded in an image file to override the controls of an output device that has been diagnosed as delivering faulty output.

Trapping
Refers to the process of deliberately making color areas overlap each other to counteract the gaps that can form due to press registration. (See also *choke* and *spread*.)

Tritone
Similar to a duotone, but using three inks.

TruMatch
Color-matching system based on colors that can be achieved by the four process inks.

Two-up, four-up, etc.
On a press, two-up or four-up refers to printing two or four of the same piece on one larger sheet so that the press sheet needs to pass through the press half as many times or a quarter as many times. This passes the responsibility for the number of needed pieces from the pressman to the bindery department in a print plant.

UCR
Under Color Removal, another black generation strategy that adds black and removes colored inks only in areas where the colored inks produce true neutrals.

Under Color Addition
In a GCR separation, this process subtracts black ink and pumps in more colored inks to produce richer dark tones that possess more detail.

Unsharp Mask
Photoshop filter that gives images sharpness lost in the digitizing (scanning) process. (See also *sharpen*.)

Value
What a photographer measures with a light meter in order to calculate the proper exposure for a camera shot.

Web press
Large, high-speed press used for large numbers of printed pieces such as newspapers. *Web* refers to the fact that paper is fed into the press as a continuous sheet from large rolls. The individual pages are cut apart and stacked at the finishing end of the press. Web presses often have two rolls of paper feeding into them—they are then called *double webs*—which are printed simultaneously front and back. The web sheet moves through the press at such a high rate of speed that it must pass through an oven to ensure that the ink is sufficiently dry before it reaches the finishing end.

Work and turn
When pages are to be printed on both sides on a non-perfecting press, the job is often worked two-up or four-up with, for example, one front and one back. After the first run is finished, the sheets are turned over and run through the press so that the front and back of the pages are printed on the appropriate place on the sheet's opposite side. With this procedure, the entire job can be done with a single set of plates. By contrast, printing all fronts in one run and all backs on another run would require two sets of plates and considerable extra make-ready expense.

WYSIWYG
Acronym from the early days of digital prepress. Stands for What You See Is What You Get, a bit of market hype that everyone learned soon enough was, to be charitable, wishful thinking.

Yellow
One of the process color inks. Contributes yellow and gold tones to a printed image.

PHOTOSHOP 5

KEYBOARD SHORTCUTS

*Photoshop 5.0 and keyboard shortcuts...
Very few software programs give you as
many ways to control the program!*

Some Photoshop users employ the keyboard with the virtuosity of a great pianist. They are the very fast workers, the ones who work with blinding speed. They are the users who make the image transformations look as if they were an animation sequence. If you want to become a fast user—a *really* fast user—start making an effort to learn the key commands listed on the following pages. You'll find that there are so many commands that you might wonder if anyone could learn them all. But persist: Before you know it, you'll remember many of them!

Bold = New to Photoshop 5

General Shortcuts	MAC OS	Windows 95/98/NT
show or hide all palettes	Tab	Tab
show or hide all but tool palette	Shift+Tab	Shift+Tab
toggle to Move tool	Cmd	Ctrl
toggle Precise Cursors	Caps Lock	Caps Lock
bring up Fill dialog	Shift+Delete	Shift+Delete
fill with foreground	Opt+Delete	Alt+Delete
fill with foreground using preserve transparency	Shift+Opt+Delete	Shift+Alt+Delete
fill with background	Cmd+Delete	Ctrl+Delete
fill with background using preserve transparency	Shift+Command+Delete	Shift+Command+Delete
fill from history	Cmd+Opt+Delete	Ctrl+Alt+Backspace
nudge selection mask 1 pixel	arrow key	arrow key
nudge selection mask 10 pixels	Shift+arrow key	Shift+arrow key
nudge layer/selection 1 pixel	Cmd+arrow key	Ctrl+arrow key
nudge layer/selection 10 pixels	Cmd+Shift+arrow key	Ctrl+Shift+arrow key
pan image (scroll both horizontal & vertical)	spacebar+Drag	spacebar+Drag
zoom in	Cmd+spacebar+Drag/Click	Ctrl+spacebar+Drag/Click
zoom out	Cmd+Opt+spacebar+Click	Ctrl+Alt+spacebar+Click
scale using center point (free transform)	**Opt+Drag corner handles**	**Alt+Drag corner handles**
skew using center point (free transform)	**Cmd+Opt+Shift+Drag side handles**	**Ctrl+Alt+Shift+Drag side handles**
scroll up one screen	Page Up	Page Up
scroll up 10 units	Shift+Page Up	Shift+Page Up
scroll down one screen	Page Down	Page Down
scroll down 10 units	**Shift+Page Down**	**Shift+Page Down**
scroll left one screen	**Cmd+Page Up**	**Ctrl+Page Up**
scroll left 10 units	**Cmd+Shift+Page Up**	**Ctrl+Shift+Page Up**
scroll right one screen	**Cmd+Page Down**	**Ctrl+Page Down**
scroll right 10 units	**Cmd+Shift+Page Down**	**Ctrl+Shift+Page Down**
move view to upper left corner	**Home key**	**Home key**
move view to lower right corner	**End key**	**End key**
increase text edit values by 1	Up arrow	Up arrow
increase text edit values by 10	Shift+Up arrow	Shift+Up arrow
decrease text edit values by 1	Down arrow	Down arrow
decrease text edit values by 10	Shift+Down arrow	Shift+Down arrow
adjust angle value in 15-degree increments	Shift+Drag in angle wheel	Shift+Drag in angle wheel
cancels out of pop up slider in mouse up mode	**Esc**	**Esc**
commits edit in pop up slider in mouse up mode	**Return**	**Enter**
pop up slider resets to prev in mouse down mode	**Hold Opt outside of slider rectangle**	**Hold Alt outside of slider rectangle**
change opacity of layers or brushes	number keys (2 = 20%, 4+3 = 43%)	number keys (2 = 20%, 4+3 = 43%)
set layer to next blend mode	**Shift++ (Plus)**	**Shift++ (Plus)**
set layer to previous blend mode	**Shift+- (Hyphen)**	**Shift+- (Hyphen)**
set brush or layer to Normal	**Opt+Shift+N**	**Alt+Shift+N**

Bold = New to Photoshop 5

General Shortcuts *(continued)*	MAC OS	Windows 95/98/NT
set brush or layer to Dissolve	Opt+Shift+I	Alt+Shift+I
set brush or layer to Multiply	Opt+Shift+M	Alt+Shift+M
set brush or ayer to Screen	Opt+Shift+S	Alt+Shift+S
set brush or layer to Overlay	Opt+Shift+O	Alt+Shift+O
set brush or layer to Soft Light	Opt+Shift+F	Alt+Shift+F
set brush or layer to Hard Light	Opt+Shift+H	Alt+Shift+H
set brush or layer to Color Dodge	Opt+Shift+D	Alt+Shift+D
set brush or layer to Color Burn	Opt+Shift+B	Alt+Shift+B
set brush or layer to Darken	Opt+Shift+K	Alt+Shift+K
set brush or layer to Lighten	Opt+Shift+G	Alt+Shift+G
set brush or layer to Difference	Opt+Shift+E	Alt+Shift+E
set brush or layer to Exclusion	Opt+Shift+X	Alt+Shift+X
set brush or layer to Hue	Opt+Shift+U	Alt+Shift+U
set brush or layer to Saturation	Opt+Shift+T	Alt+Shift+T
set brush or layer to Color	Opt+Shift+C	Alt+Shift+C
set brush or layer to Luminosity	Opt+Shift+Y	Alt+Shift+Y
set brush to Threshold (Bitmap Mode only)	Opt+Shift+L	Alt+Shift+L
set brush to Dissolve	Opt+Shift+I	Alt+Shift+I
set brush to Behind (on a layer only)	Opt+Shift+Q	Alt+Shift+Q
accept crop, transform or any dialog	Enter/Return	Enter
cancel cropping, transforming or any dialog	Cmd+. (Period)	Esc+. (Period)
exit type dialog from keyboard	Return	Enter
activate buttons in alert dialogs	1st letter of button (e.g., D=Don't Save)	1st letter of button (e.g., D=Don't Save)
snap guide to ruler	Shift+Drag guide	Shift+Drag guide
toggle guide orientation (H/V)	Opt+Drag guide	Alt+Drag guide
Help	Help key	F1
Image Size dialog	F11 with Default Actions loaded	F11 with Default Actions loaded
Revert	F12 with Default Actions loaded	F12 with Default Actions loaded

Palette Behaviors: Tools Palette	MAC OS	Windows 95/98/NT
access Adobe Online	Click on identifier icon	Click on identifier icon
Rectangular Marquee Tool	M	M
Move Tool	V	V
Lasso Tool	L	L
Crop Tool	C	C
Magic Wand Tool	W	W
Airbrush Tool	J	J
Paintbrush Tool	B	B
Rubber Stamp Tool	S	S
History Brush Tool	Y	Y
Eraser Tool	E	E
Pencil Tool	N	N

Bold = New to Photoshop 5

Palette Behaviors: Tools Palette (continued)	MAC OS	Windows 95/98/NT
Blur Tool	R	R
Dodge Tool	O	O
Pen Tool	P	P
Add Anchor Point Tool	+ (Plus)	+ (Plus)
Delete Anchor Point Tool	- (Hyphen)	- (Hyphen)
Direct Select Tool	A	A
Type Tool	T	T
Measure Tool	U	U
Gradient Tool	G	G
Paint Bucket Tool	K	K
Eyedropper Tool	I	I
Hand Tool	H	H
Zoom Tool	Z	Z
Cycle through Marquee tools	**Shift+M**	**Shift+M**
Cycle through Lasso tools	**Shift+L**	**Shift+L**
Cycle through Rubber Stamp tools	**Shift+S**	**Shift+S**
Cycle through Blur, Sharpen, & Smudge tools	**Shift+R**	**Shift+R**
Cycle through Toning tools	**Shift+O**	**Shift+O**
Cycle through Pen tools	**Shift+P**	**Shift+P**
Cycle through Type tools	**Shift+T**	**Shift+T**
Cycle through Eyedropper tools	**Shift+I**	**Shift+I**
Cycle through above tools	**Opt+Click in tool slot**	**Alt+Click in tool slot**
Swap Foreground/Background colors	X	X
Reset to default colors	D	D
Toggle Quick Mask on/off	Q	Q
Invert Quick Mask mode	Opt+Click on Quick Mask button	Alt+Click on Quick Mask button
Open Quick Mask Options dialog	Double-click on Quick Mask button	Double-click on Quick Mask button
Toggle Standard/Full Screen with menus/Full Screen	F	F
Toggle Menu when in Full Screen	Shift+F	Shift+F
zoom to 100%	Double-click Zoom tool	Double-click Zoom tool
zoom to fit in window	Double-click Hand tool	Double-click Hand tool

Palette Behaviors: Navigator Palette	MAC OS	Windows 95/98/NT
scroll viewable area of image	Drag view proxy	Drag view proxy
move view to new portion of image	Click in preview area	Click in preview area
view new portion of image	Cmd+Drag in navigator	Ctrl+Drag in navigator
Change zoom % and keep focus in zoom % text edit	Shift+Return	Shift+Return

Palette Behaviors: Info Palette	MAC OS	Windows 95/98/NT
show or hide palette	F8 (with Default Actions loaded)	F8 (with Default Actions loaded)
change unit of measure	Click on icon pop-up	Click on icon pop-up
change color mode readout	Click on icon pop-up	Click on icon pop-up

Bold = New to Photoshop 5

Palette Behaviors: Options Palette	MAC OS	Windows 95/98/NT
show Options palette	Double-click tool or press Return	Double-click tool or press Enter

Palette Behaviors: Color Palette	MAC OS	Windows 95/98/NT
show or hide palette	F6 (with Default Actions loaded)	F6 (with Default Actions loaded)
cycle through color bars	Shift+Click on color bar	Shift+Click on color bar
bring up Color Bar dialog	Cmd+Click on color bar	Ctrl+Click on the color bar
choose specific color bar	Control+Click on color bar	Right Mouse+Click on color bar

Palette Behaviors: Swatches Palette	MAC OS	Windows 95/98/NT
add foreground color as a new swatch	Click in empty slot	Click in empty slot
insert new swatch color	Shift+Opt+Click in palette	Shift+Alt+Click in palette
replace swatch color with foreground color	Shift+Click	Shift+Click
delete swatch	Cmd+Click on swatch	Ctrl+Click on swatch
choose swatch as foreground color	Click on swatch	Click on swatch
choose swatch as background color	Opt+Click on swatch	Alt+Click on swatch

Palette Behaviors: Brushes Palette	MAC OS	Windows 95/98/NT
show or hide palette	F5 (with Default Actions loaded)	F5 (with Default Actions loaded)
select first brush	Shift+[	Shift+[
select previous brush	[	[
select next brush	]	]
select last brush	Shift+]	Shift+]
create new brush	Click in empty slot	Click in empty slot
delete brush	Cmd+Click	Ctrl+Click
edit brush	Double-click on brush	Double-click on brush

Palette Behaviors: Layers Palette	MAC OS	Windows 95/98/NT
show or hide palette	F7 (with Default Actions loaded)	F7 (with Default Actions loaded)
show or hide layer	Click in Eye icon area	Click in Eye icon area
toggle show all layers/show just this layer	Opt+Click on Eye icon area	Alt+Click on Eye icon area
show/hide multiple layers	Click+Drag through Eye icon area	Click+Drag through Eye icon area
link layer to current target layer	Click in Link icon area	Click in Link icon area
turn on/off linking for multiple layers	Click+Drag through Link icon area	Click+Drag through Link icon area
create new empty layer	Click on New Layer button	Click on New Layer button
create new empty layers with Layer Options dialog	Opt+Click New Layer button	Alt+Click New Layer button
duplicate layer	Drag layer to New Layer button	Drag layer to New Layer button
delete layer using Warning Alert	Click Delete Layer button	Click Delete Layer button
delete layer while bypassing Warning Alert	Opt+Click Delete Layer button	Alt+Click Delete Layer button
create new adjustment layer with Adjustment Layer dialog	Cmd+Opt+Click New Layer icon	Ctrl+Alt+Click New Layer icon
toggle preserve transparency for target layer	/ (Forward Slash)	/ (Forward Slash)
load layer transparency as selection	Cmd+Click layer thumbnail	Ctrl+Click layer thumbnail
add layer transparency to selection	Cmd+Shift+Click layer thumbnail	Ctrl+Shift+Click layer thumbnail
subtract layer transparency to selection	Cmd+Opt+Click layer thumbnail	Ctrl+Alt+Click layer thumbnail

Bold = New to Photoshop 5

Palette Behaviors: Layers Palette (continued)	MAC OS	Windows 95/98/NT
intersect layer transparency w/selection	Cmd+Opt+Shift+Click thumbnail	Ctrl+Alt+Shift+Click thumbnail
select top layer	Shift+Opt+]	Shift+Alt+]
select next layer (up)	Opt+]	Alt+]
select previous layer (down)	Opt+[	Alt+[
select bottom layer	Shift+Opt+[	Shift+Alt+[
move target layer (up)	Cmd+Opt+]	Ctrl+Alt+]
move target layer (down)	Cmd+Opt+[	Ctrl+Alt+[
create layer mask with Reveal All / Reveal Selection	Click on Mask button	Click on Mask button
create layer mask with Hide All Hide Selection	Opt+Click on Mask button	Alt+Click on Mask button
lock/unlock layer and layer mask	Click Lock Layer Mask icon	Click Lock Layer Mask icon
open Layer Mask Options dialog	Double-click Layer Mask thumbnail	Double-click Layer Mask thumbnail
toggle layer mask on/off	Shift+Click Layer Mask thumbnail	Shift+Click Layer Mask thumbnail
toggle layer mask on/off	\	\
toggle viewing layer mask/composite	Opt+Click Layer Mask thumbnail	Alt+Click Layer Mask thumbnail
toggle rubylith mode for layer mask on/off	Shift+Opt+Click Layer Mask thumbnail	Shift+Alt+Click Layer Mask thumbnail
merge down a copy of current layer into layer below	Opt+Merge Down	Alt+Merge Down
merge a copy of all visible layers into target layer	Opt+Merge Visible	Alt+Merge Visible
merge a copy of linked layers into layer below	Opt+Merge Linked	Alt+Merge Linked
toggle Group with Previous/Ungroup	Opt+Click line between layers	Alt+Click line between layers
clear each Effect on layer one at a time	**Opt+Dbl-Click Effect icon**	**Alt+Dbl-Click Effect icon**
edit Layer Options	Double-click Layer Name	Double-click Layer Name
edit Adjustment Layer Options	Double-click Adustment icon	Double-click Adustment icon
edit Type Options	**Double-click Type icon**	**Double-click Type icon**
edit Layer Effect Options (last edited)	**Double-click Layer Effect icon**	**Double-click Layer Effect icon**

Palette Behaviors: Channels Palette	MAC OS	Windows 95/98/NT
target individual channels	Cmd+[1-9]	Ctrl+[1-9]
target composite channel	Cmd+~ (Tilde)	Ctrl+~ (Tilde)
show or hide channel	Click in Eye icon area	Click in Eye icon area
activate/deactivate channel	Click on channel	Click on channel
add/remove channel to targeted channels	Shift+Click on channel	Shift+Click on channel
create new channel	Click on New Channel button	Click on New Channel button
create new channel with Channel Options dialog	Opt+Click on New Channel button	Alt+Click on New Channel button
duplicate channel	Drag channel to New Channel button	Drag channel to New Channel button
delete channel using Warning Alert	Click Delete Channel button	Click Delete Channel button
delete channel while bypassing Warning Alert	Opt+Click Delete Channel button	Alt+Click Delete Channel button
create new spot color channel	**Cmd+Click on New Channel button**	**Ctrl+Click on New Channel button**
create new channel from selection	Click on Save Selection button	Click on Save Selection button
create new channel from selection with Channel Options	Opt+Click on Save Selection button	Alt+Click on Save Selection button
load channel as selection	Click Load Selection button	Click Load Selection button
add channel to selection	Shift+Click Load Selection button	Shift+Click Load Selection button

Bold = New to Photoshop 5

Palette Behaviors: Channels Palette (continued)	MAC OS	Windows 95/98/NT
subtract channel to selection	Opt+Click Load Selection button	Alt+Click Load Selection button
intersect channel with selection	Opt+Shift+Click Load Selection button	Alt+Shift+Click Load Selection button
load channel as selection	Cmd+Click channel thumbnail	Ctrl+Click channel thumbnail
add channel to selection	Cmd+Shift+Click channel thumbnail	Ctrl+Shift+Click channel thumbnail
subtract channel to selection	Cmd+Opt+Click channel thumbnail	Ctrl+Alt+Click channel thumbnail
intersect channel with selection	Cmd+Opt+Shift+Click thumbnail	Ctrl+Alt+Shift+Click thumbnail
edit Channel Options	Double-click Channel Name	Double-click Channel Name

Palette Behaviors: Paths Palette	MAC OS	Windows 95/98/NT
create new path	Click New Path button	Click New Path button
create new path with New Path dialog	Opt+Click on New Path button	Alt+Click on New Path button
duplicate path	Drag path to New Path button	Drag path to New Path button
delete path using Warning Alert	Click Delete Path button	Click Delete Path button
delete path while bypassing Warning Alert	Opt+Click Delete Path button	Alt+Click Delete Path button
convert Work Path into path item	Drag Work Path onto New Path button	Drag Work Path onto New Path button
convert selection into Work Path	Click Make Work Path button	Click Make Work Path button
convert selection into Work Path with Work Path dialog	Opt+Click Make Work Path button	Alt+Click Make Work Path button
convert path into selection	Click Load Selection button	Click Load Selection button
convert path into selection with Make Selection dialog	Opt+Click Load Selection button	Alt+Click Load Selection button
stroke path with foreground color	Click Stroke Path button	Click Stroke Path button
stroke path using Stroke Path dialog	Opt+Click Stroke Path button	Alt+Click Stroke Path button
fill path with foreground color	Click Fill Path button	Click Fill Path button
fill path using Fill Path dialog	Opt+Click Fill Path button	Alt+Click Fill Path button
load path as selection	Cmd+Click path thumbnail	Ctrl+Click path thumbnail
add path to selection	Cmd+Shift+Click path thumbnail	Ctrl+Shift+Click path thumbnail
subtract path to selection	Cmd+Opt+Click path thumbnail	Ctrl+Alt+Click path thumbnail
intersect path with selection	Cmd+Opt+Shift+Click thumbnail	Ctrl+Alt+Shift+Click thumbnail
edit path name	Double-click path name	Double-click path name

Palette Behaviors: History Palette	MAC OS	Windows 95/98/NT
toggle back/forward one step	Cmd+Z	Ctrl+Z
step forward	Shift+Cmd+Z	Shift+Ctrl+Z
step backward	Opt+Cmd+Z	Alt+Ctrl+Z
duplicate history state (other than current)	**Opt+Click on state**	**Alt+Click on state**
create new snapshot	**Click on New Snapshot button**	**Click on New Snapshot button**
create new document from state snapshot	**Click on New Document button**	**Click on New Document button**

Palette Behaviors: Actions Palette	MAC OS	Windows 95/98/NT
show or hide palette	F9 (with Default Actions loaded)	F9 (with Default Actions loaded)
new action and begin recording	Click New Action	Click New Action
new action and begin recording w/o dialog	Opt+Click New Action	Alt+Click New Action
selects multiple items of the same kind	Shift+Click	Shift+Click

Bold = New to Photoshop 5

Palette Behaviors: Actions Palette (continued)	MAC OS	Windows 95/98/NT
play action	Cmd+Double-click on action	Ctrl+Double-click on action
play single command	Cmd+Click Play button	Ctrl+Click Play button
stop action	Click on Stop	Click on Stop
record action	Click on Record	Click on Record
play action	Click on Play	Click on Play
toggle command on/off	Click on Checkmark icon area	Click on Checkmark icon area
toggle all other commands on/off for this action	Opt+Click on Checkmark icon area	Alt+Click on Checkmark icon area
toggle dialogs on/off for action	Click on Dialog icon area	Click on Dialog icon area
toggle all other dialogs on/off for this action	Opt+Click on Dialog icon area	Alt+Click on Dialog icon area
toggle all commands on/off for action	click Checkmark icon area for action	click Checkmark icon area for action
toggle all dialogs on/off for action	click Dialog icon area for action	click Dialog icon area for action
toggle all commands on/off for set	click Checkmark icon area for set	click Checkmark icon area for set
toggle all dialogs on/off for set	click Dialog icon area for set	click Dialog icon area for set
edit Action Options/Set Options/Command	Double-click item	Double-click item
expand/collapse hierarchy	Opt+Dbl Click triangle	Alt+Dbl Click triangle

Tool Behaviors: Marquee Tool (Rectangular/Elliptical)	MAC OS	Windows 95/98/NT
add to selection	Shift+Click then draw	Shift+Click then draw
delete from selection	Opt+Click then draw	Alt+Click then draw
intersect with selection	Opt+Shift+Click then draw	Alt+Shift+Click then draw
constrain to square while drawing	Shift+Drag	Shift+Drag
draw from center while drawing	Opt+Drag	Alt+Drag
constrain from center while drawing	Opt+Shift+Drag	Alt+Shift+Drag
move selection constrained to 45 degrees	Shift+Drag selection	Shift+Drag Selection
move selection while dragging with mouse down	spacebar	spacebar

Tool Behaviors: Crop Tool	MAC OS	Windows 95/98/NT
rotate cropping box	Drag outside cropping box	Drag outside cropping box
move cropping box	Drag inside cropping box	Drag inside cropping box
resize cropping box	Drag cropping handles	Drag cropping handles
constrain crop to square	Shift+Drag handles	Shift+Drag handles
resize crop from center	Opt+Drag handles	Alt+Drag handles
constrain crop from center	Opt+Shift+Drag handles	Alt+Shift+Drag handles
apply crop	Return	Enter
cancel crop	Esc/Cmd+. (Period)	Esc/Ctrl+. (Period)

Tool Behaviors: Move Tool	MAC OS	Windows 95/98/NT
move constrained to 45 degrees	Shift+Drag	Shift+Drag
copy selection	Opt+Drag	Alt+Drag
copy layer	Opt+Drag	Alt+Drag
select layer by name	Ctrl+Click	Right mouse click
select topmost visible layer	Ctrl+Opt+Click	Right Mouse+Alt+Click
link with topmost visible layer	**Ctrl+Shift+Click**	**Right Mouse+Shift+Click**

Bold = New to Photoshop 5

Tool Behaviors: Lasso Tool	MAC OS	Windows 95/98/NT
add to selection	Shift+Click then draw	Shift+Click then draw
delete from selection	Opt+Click then draw	Alt+Click then draw
intersect with selection	Opt+Shift+Click then draw	Alt+Shift+Click then draw
draw using Polygonal Lasso	Opt+Click/Drag	Alt+Click/Drag

Tool Behaviors: Polygonal Lasso Tool	MAC OS	Windows 95/98/NT
add to selection	Shift+Click then draw	Shift+Click then draw
delete from selection	Opt+Click then draw	Alt+Click then draw
intersect with selection	Opt+Shift+Click then draw	Alt+Shift+Click then draw
draw using Lasso	Option+Drag	Alt+Drag
constrain to 45 degrees while drawing	Shift+Drag	Shift+Drag

Tool Behaviors: Magnetic Lasso Tool	MAC OS	Windows 95/98/NT
add to selection	Shift+Click then draw	Shift+Click then draw
delete from selection	Opt+Click then draw	Alt+Click then draw
intersect with selection	Opt+Shift+Click then draw	Alt+Shift+Click then draw
add point	single Click	single Click
remove last point	Delete key	Delete key
close path	Double-click/Return	Double-click/Enter
close path over start point	Click on start point	Click on start point
close path using straight-line segment	Opt+Double-click	Alt+Double-click
cancel operation	Esc/Cmd+. (Period)	Esc/Ctrl+. (Period)
switch to Lasso	Opt+Drag	Alt+Drag
switch to Polygonal Lasso	Opt+Click	Alt+Click
increase Magnetic Lasso width	[(Open bracket)	[(Open bracket)
decreases Magnetic Lasso width	] (Close bracket)	] (Close bracket)

Tool Behaviors: Magic Wand Tool	MAC OS	Windows 95/98/NT
add to selection	Shift+Click	Shift+Click
delete from selection	Opt+Click	Alt+Click
intersect with selection	Opt+Shift+Click	Alt+Shift+Click

Tool Behaviors: Airbrush Tool	MAC OS	Windows 95/98/NT
paint constrained to horizontal or vertical axis	Shift+Drag	Shift+Drag
paint straight lines	Shift+Click	Shift+Click
toggle to Eyedropper Tool	Opt	Alt

Tool Behaviors: Paintbrush Tool	MAC OS	Windows 95/98/NT
paint constrained to horizontal or vertical axis	Shift+Drag	Shift+Drag
paint straight lines	Shift+Click	Shift+Click
toggle to Eyedropper Tool	Opt	Alt

Bold = New to Photoshop 5

Tool Behaviors: Rubber Stamp Tool	MAC OS	Windows 95/98/NT
paint constrained to horizontal or vertical axis	Shift+Drag	Shift+Drag
paint straight lines	Shift+Click	Shift+Click
specify clone origin	Opt+Click in document window	Alt+Click in document window

Tool Behaviors: Pattern Stamp Tool	MAC OS	Windows 95/98/NT
paint constrained to horizontal or vertical axis	**Shift+Drag**	**Shift+Drag**
paint straight lines	**Shift+Click**	**Shift+Click**

Tool Behaviors: History Brush Tool	MAC OS	Windows 95/98/NT
paint constrained to horizontal or vertical axis	**Shift+Drag**	**Shift+Drag**
paint straight lines	**Shift+Click**	**Shift+Click**

Tool Behaviors: Eraser Tool	MAC OS	Windows 95/98/NT
erase constrained to horizontal or vertical axis	Shift+Drag	Shift+Drag
erase straight lines	Shift+Click	Shift+Click
erase to History	**Opt+Drag**	**Alt+Drag**

Tool Behaviors: Pencil Tool	MAC OS	Windows 95/98/NT
draw constrained to horizontal or vertical axis	Shift+Drag	Shift+Drag
draw straight lines	Shift+Click	Shift+Click
toggle to Eyedropper Tool	Opt	Alt

Tool Behaviors: Line Tool	MAC OS	Windows 95/98/NT
draw constrained to 45 degree axis	Shift+Drag	Shift+Drag
toggle to Eyedropper Tool	Opt	Alt

Tool Behaviors: Blur Tool	MAC OS	Windows 95/98/NT
blur constrained to horizontal or vertical axis	Shift+Drag	Shift+Drag
blur in straight lines	Shift+Click	Shift+Click
toggle to Sharpen Tool	Opt	Alt

Tool Behaviors: Sharpen Tool	MAC OS	Windows 95/98/NT
blur constrained to horizontal or vertical axis	Shift+Drag	Shift+Drag
blur in straight lines	Shift+Click	Shift+Click
toggle to Blur Tool	Opt	Alt

Tool Behaviors: Smudge Tool	MAC OS	Windows 95/98/NT
blur constrained to horizontal or vertical axis	Shift+Drag	Shift+Drag
blur in straight lines	Shift+Click	Shift+Click
smudge using foreground colors	Opt	Alt

Bold = New to Photoshop 5

Tool Behaviors: Dodge Tool	MAC OS	Windows 95/98/NT
dodge constrained to horizontal or vertical axis	Shift+Drag	Shift+Drag
dodge in straight lines	Shift+Click	Shift+Click
toggle to Burn Tool	Opt	Alt
set Dodge to Shadows	**Opt+Shift+W**	**Alt+Shift+W**
set Dodge to Midtones	**Opt+Shift+V**	**Alt+Shift+V**
set Dodge to Highlights	**Opt+Shift+Z**	**Alt+Shift+Z**

Tool Behaviors: Burn Tool	MAC OS	Windows 95/98/NT
burn constrained to horizontal or vertical axis	Shift+Drag	Shift+Drag
burn in straight lines	Shift+Click	Shift+Click
toggle to Dodge Tool	Opt	Alt
set Burn to Shadows	**Opt+Shift+W**	**Alt+Shift+W**
set Burn to Midtones	**Opt+Shift+V**	**Alt+Shift+V**
set Burn to Highlights	**Opt+Shift+Z**	**Alt+Shift+Z**

Tool Behaviors: Sponge Tool	MAC OS	Windows 95/98/NT
saturate constrained to horizontal or vertical axis	Shift+Drag	Shift+Drag
saturate in straight lines	Shift+Click	Shift+Click
set Sponge to Desaturate	**Opt+Shift+J**	**Alt+Shift+J**
set Sponge to Saturate	**Opt+Shift+A**	**Alt+Shift+A**

Tool Behaviors: Pen Tool	MAC OS	Windows 95/98/NT
toggle to Direct Select Tool	Cmd	Ctrl
toggle to Convert Direction Tool	**Opt**	**Alt**
draw constrained to 45 degree axis	Shift+Click/Drag	Shift+Click/Drag
add/delete anchor points	**track over path/anchor points**	**track over path/anchor points**

Tool Behaviors: Direct Select Tool	MAC OS	Windows 95/98/NT
toggle to Convert Direction Tool	**Command over anchor points**	**Control over anchor points**
select multiple anchor points	Shift+Click	Shift+Click
toggle to Group Select function	Opt+Click	Alt+Click
duplicate path	Command+Opt+Drag	Control+Alt+Drag

Tool Behaviors: Add/Delete Anchor Point Tool	MAC OS	Windows 95/98/NT
toggle between add/delete anchor point	Opt	Alt

Tool Behaviors: Convert Direction Tool	MAC OS	Windows 95/98/NT
draw constrained to 45 degree axis	Shift+Drag	Shift+Drag

Bold = New to Photoshop 5

Tool Behaviors: Magnetic Pen Tool	MAC OS	Windows 95/98/NT
add point	single Click	single Click
remove last point	Delete key	Delete key
close path	Double-click/Return	Double-click/Enter
close path over start point	Click on start point	Click on start point
close path using straight line segment	Opt+Double-click	Alt+Double-click
cancel operation	Esc/Cmd+. (Period)	Esc/Ctrl+. (Period)
switch to Freeform Pen	Opt+Drag	Alt+Drag
switch to Pen	Opt+Click	Alt+Click
increase magnetic width	[(Open Bracket)	[(Open Bracket)
decreases magnetic width	] (Close Bracket)	] (Close Bracket)

Tool Behaviors: Type Tool	MAC OS	Windows 95/98/NT
designate type origin	Click or Click+Drag	Click or Click+Drag
designate type origin while over existing type	Shift+Click or Click+Drag	Shift+Click or Click+Drag
Re-edit existing type	Click on type in image	Click on type in image
toggle to Eyedropper Tool	Opt	Alt

Tool Behaviors: Type Mask Tool	MAC OS	Windows 95/98/NT
add to selection	Shift+Click then draw	Shift+Click then draw
delete from selection	Opt+Click then draw	Alt+Click then draw
intersect with selection	Opt+Shift+Click then draw	Alt+Shift+Click then draw
designate type origin	Click+Drag	Click+Drag

Tool Behaviors: Vertical Type Tool	MAC OS	Windows 95/98/NT
designate type origin	Click+Drag	Click+Drag
toggle to Eyedropper Tool	Opt	Alt

Tool Behaviors: Vertical Type Mask Tool	MAC OS	Windows 95/98/NT
add to selection	Shift+Click then draw	Shift+Click then draw
delete from selection	Opt+Click then draw	Alt+Click then draw
intersect with selection	Opt+Shift+Click then draw	Alt+Shift+Click then draw
designate type origin	Click+Drag	Click+Drag

Tool Behaviors: Measure Tool	MAC OS	Windows 95/98/NT
measure constrained to 45 degree axis		Shift+Drag Shift+Drag
create protractor	**Opt+Click+Drag on end point**	**Alt+Click+Drag on end point**

Tool Behaviors: Gradient Tools	MAC OS	Windows 95/98/NT
draw constrained to 45 degree axis	Shift+Drag	Shift+Drag
select foreground color	Opt+Click	Alt+Click

Tool Behaviors: Paintbucket Tool	MAC OS	Windows 95/98/NT
toggle to Eyedropper Tool	Opt+Click	Alt+Click
change color of area around canvas	Shift+Click outside canvas	Shift+Click outside canvas

Bold = New to Photoshop 5

Tool Behaviors: Eyedropper Tool	MAC OS	Windows 95/98/NT
select background color	Opt+Click	Alt+Click
toggle to Sampler Tool	Shift	Shift
delete Sampler	Opt+Shift+Click on sampler	Alt+Shift+Click on sampler

Tool Behaviors: Sampler Tool	MAC OS	Windows 95/98/NT
delete Sampler	Opt+Click on sampler	Alt+Click on sampler

Tool Behaviors: Hand Tool	MAC OS	Windows 95/98/NT
toggle to zoom in	Cmd	Ctrl
toggle to zoom out	Opt	Alt
fit image on screen	Dbl Click tool slot	Dbl Click tool slot

Tool Behaviors: Zoom Tool	MAC OS	Windows 95/98/NT
zoom out	Opt+Click/Drag	Alt+Click/Drag
actual size	Dbl Click tool slot	Dbl Click tool slot

Menus: File Menu	MAC OS	Windows 95/98/NT
New	Cmd+N	Ctrl+N
Open	Cmd+O	Ctrl+O
Open As	Cmd+Opt+O	Ctrl+Alt+O
Close	Cmd+W	Ctrl+W
Save	Cmd+S	Ctrl+S
Save As	Cmd+Shift+S	Ctrl+Shift+S
Save As a Copy	Cmd+Opt+S	Ctrl+Alt+S
Page Setup	Cmd+Shift+P	Ctrl+Shift+P
Print	Cmd+P	Ctrl+P
Preferences > General	Cmd+K	Ctrl+K
Quit / Exit	Cmd+Q	Ctrl+Q
New with Default Settings	Cmd+Opt+N	Ctrl+Alt+N
Preferences with Last Settings	Cmd+Opt+K	Ctrl+Alt+K

Menus: Edit Menu	MAC OS	Windows 95/98/NT
Undo	Cmd+Z	Ctrl+Z
Cut	Cmd+X	Ctrl+X
Copy	Cmd+C	Ctrl+C
Copy Merged	Cmd+Shift+C	Ctrl+Shift+C
Paste	Cmd+V	Ctrl+V
Paste Into	Cmd+Shift+V	Ctrl+Shift+V
Fill	Shift+Delete	Shift+Backspace
Free Transform	Cmd+T	Ctrl+T
Transform > Again	Cmd+Shift+T	Ctrl+Shift+T
Free Transform with Duplication	Cmd+Opt+T	Ctrl+Alt+T
Transform Again with duplication	Cmd+Opt+Shift+T	Ctrl+Alt+Shift+T

Bold = New to Photoshop 5

Menus: Image Menu	MAC OS	Windows 95/98/NT
Adjustment > Levels	Cmd+L	Ctrl+L
Adjustment > Auto Levels	Cmd+Shift+L	Ctrl+Shift+L
Adjustment > Curves	Cmd+M	Ctrl+M
Adjustment > Color Balance	Cmd+B	Ctrl+B
Hue/Saturation	Cmd+U	Ctrl+U
Desaturate	Cmd+Shift+U	Ctrl+Shift+U
Invert	Cmd+I	Ctrl+I
Levels with last settings	Cmd+Opt+L	Ctrl+Alt+L
Curves with last settings	Cmd+Opt+M	Ctrl+Alt+M
Color Balance with last settings	Cmd+Opt+B	Ctrl+Alt+B
Hue/Saturation with last settings	Cmd+Opt+U	Ctrl+Alt+U

Menus: Layer Menu	MAC OS	Windows 95/98/NT
New > Layer	**Cmd+Shift+N**	**Ctrl+Shift+N**
Layer via Copy	Cmd+J	Ctrl+J
Layer via Cut	Cmd+Shift+J	Ctrl+Shift+J
Group with Previous	Cmd+G	Ctrl+G
Ungroup	Cmd+Shift+G	Ctrl+Shift+G
Bring to Front	Cmd+Shift+]	Ctrl+Shift+]
Bring Forward	Cmd+]	Ctrl+]
Send Backward	Cmd+[	Ctrl+[
Send to Back	Cmd+Shift+[	Ctrl+Shift+[
Merge Down/Linked/Group	Cmd+E	Ctrl+E
Merge Visible	Shift+Cmd+E	Shift+Ctrl+E
New Layer without dialog box	Cmd+Opt+Shift+N	Ctrl+Alt+Shift+N

Menus: Select Menu	MAC OS	Windows 95/98/NT
All	Cmd+A	Ctrl+A
Deselect	Cmd+D	Ctrl+D
Reselect	Cmd+Shift+D	Ctrl+Shift+I
Inverse	Cmd+Shift+I	Ctrl+Shift+I
Feather	Cmd+Opt+D	Ctrl+Alt+D

Menus: Filter Menu	MAC OS	Windows 95/98/NT
Filter with the last settings	Cmd+F	Ctrl+F
Fade [Filter or last command]	Cmd+Shift+F	Ctrl+Shift+F
Last-used Filter with Dialog box	Cmd+Opt+F	Ctrl+Alt+F

Bold = New to Photoshop 5

Menus: View Menu	MAC OS	Windows 95/98/NT
CMYK	Cmd+Y	Ctrl+Y
Gamut Warning	Cmd+Shift+Y	Ctrl+Shift+Y
Zoom In	Cmd++ (Plus)	Ctrl++ (Plus)
Zoom Out	Cmd+- (Hyphen)	Ctrl+- (Hyphen)
Fit On Screen	Cmd+0	Ctrl+0
Actual Pixels	Cmd+Option+0	Ctrl+Alt+0
Hide Edges	Cmd+H	Ctrl+H
Hide Path	Cmd+Shift+H	Ctrl+Shift+H
Show Rulers	Cmd+R	Ctrl+R
Hide Guides	Cmd+; (Semicolon)	Ctrl+; (Semicolon)
Snap to Guides	Shift+Cmd+; (Semicolon)	Shift+Ctrl+; (Semicolon)
Lock Guides	Opt+Cmd+; (Semicolon)	Alt+Ctrl+; (Semicolon)
Show Grid	Cmd+" (Quote)	Ctrl+" (Quote)
Snap to Grid	Shift+Cmd+" (Quote)	Shift+Ctrl+" (Quote)
Zoom in without changing window size	Cmd+Opt++ (Plus)	Ctrl+Alt++ (Plus)
Zoom Out without changing window size	Cmd+Opt+- (Hyphen)	Ctrl+Alt+- (Hyphen)

Dialog Behaviors:	MAC OS	Windows 95/98/NT
pan image in document window	spacebar+Drag	spacebar+Drag
zoom in in document window	Cmd+spacebar+Drag/Click	Ctrl+spacebar+Drag/Click
zoom out in document window	Cmd+Opt+spacebar+Click	Ctrl+Alt+spacebar+Click
toggle Cancel to Reset for internal dialogs	Opt	Alt

3D Transform	MAC OS	Windows 95/98/NT
Select Tool	V	V
Direct Select Tool	A	A
Cube Tool	M	M
Sphere Tool	N	N
Cylinder Tool	C	C
Add Anchor Point Tool	+ (Plus)	+ (Plus)
Delete Anchor Point Tool	- (Hyphen)	- (Hyphen)
Pan Camera Tool	E	E
Trackball Tool	R	R
Hand Tool	H	H
Zoom Tool	Z	Z
toggle between Select/Direct Select Tools	Cmd+Tab	Ctrl+Tab
pan image	spacebar+Drag	spacebar+Drag
zoom in	Cmd+spacebar+Drag/Click	Ctrl+spacebar+Drag/Click
zoom out	Cmd+Opt+spacebar+Click	Ctrl+Alt+spacebar+Click

Bold = New to Photoshop 5

Type Dialog	MAC OS	Windows 95/98/NT
zooms in while in dialog	Cmd++ (Plus)	Ctrl++ (Plus)
zooms out while in dialog	Cmd+- (Hyphen)	Ctrl+- (Hyphen)
Cut copy and paste in the type dialog	Cmd+C, Cmd+X and Cmd+V	Ctrl+C, Ctrl+X and Ctrl+V
Left/Top text alignment	Cmd+Shift+L	Ctrl+Shift+L
Center text alignment	Cmd+Shift+C	Ctrl+Shift+C
Right/Bottom text alignment	Cmd+Shift+R	Ctrl+Shift+R
Increase text point size by 2 pt increments	Cmd+Shift+>	Ctrl+Shift+>
Decrease text point size by 2 pt increments	Cmd+Shift+<	Ctrl+Shift+<
Increase text point size by 10 pt increments	Cmd+Opt+Shift+>	Ctrl+Alt+Shift+>
Decrease text point size by10 pt increments	Cmd+Opt+Shift+<	Ctrl+Alt+Shift+<
Increase leading in by 2 pt increments	Opt+Down arrow	Alt+Down arrow
Decrease leading by in 2 pt increments	Opt+Up arrow	Alt+Up arrow
Increase leading by10 pt increments	Cmd+Opt+Down arrow	Ctrl+Alt+Down arrow
Decrease leading by 10 pt increments	Cmd+Opt+Up arrow	Ctrl+Alt+Up arrow
Increase kerning/tracking by 20/1000 em space	Opt+Right arrow	Alt+Right arrow
Decrease kerning/tracking by 20/1000 em space	Opt+Left arrow	Alt+Left arrow
Increase kerning/tracking by 100/1000 em space	Cmd+Opt+Right arrow	Ctrl+Alt+Right arrow
Decrease kerning/tracking by 100/1000 em space	Cmd+Opt+Left arrow	Ctrl+Alt+Left arrow
Increase baseline shift by 2 pt increments	Opt+Shift+Up arrow	Alt+Shift+Up arrow
Decrease baseline shift by 2 pt increments	Opt+Shift+Down arrow	Alt+Shift+Down arrow
Increase baseline shift by 10 pt increments	Cmd+Opt+Shift+Up arrow	Ctrl+Alt+Shift+Up arrow
Decrease baseline shift by 10 pt increments	Cmd+Opt+Shift+Down arrow	Ctrl+Alt+Shift+Down arrow
Move to the right one character	Right arrow	Right arrow
Move to the left one character	Left arrow	Left arrow
Move up one line	Up arrow	Up arrow
Move down one line	Down arrow	Down arrow
Move to the right one word	Cmd+Right arrow	Ctrl+Right arrow
Move to the left one word	Cmd+Left arrow	Ctrl+Left arrow
Select word	Double Click	Double Click
Select one character to the right	Shift+Right arrow	Shift+Right arrow
Select one character to the left	Shift+Left arrow	Shift+Left arrow
Select one word to the right	Cmd+Shift+Right arrow	Ctrl+Shift+Right arrow
Select one word to the left	Cmd+Shift+Left arrow	Ctrl+Shift+Left arrow
Select one line above	Shift+Up arrow	Shift+Up arrow
Select one line below	Shift+Down arrow	Shift+Down arrow
Select all characters	Cmd+A	Ctrl+A
Select characters from current insertion point	Shift+Click	Shift+Click
position type	drag type in image	drag type in image

Levels Dialog	MAC OS	Windows 95/98/NT
show clipping using video LUT	Opt+Drag sliders with Preview off	Alt+Drag sliders with Preview off

Bold = New to Photoshop 5

Curves Dialog	MAC OS	Windows 95/98/NT
add color as new point on curve	Cmd+Click in image	Ctrl+Click in image
add color as individual points for each curve	Cmd+Shift+Click	Ctrl+Shift+Click
move points	arrow keys	arrow keys
move points in multiples of 10	Shift+arrow keys	Shift+arrow keys
select next control point	Cmd+Tab	Ctrl+Tab
select previous control point	Cmd+Shift+Tab	Ctrl+Shift+Tab
add point	Click in grid	Click in grid
delete point	Cmd+Click on point	Ctrl+Click on point
select multiple control points	Shift+Click	Shift+Click
deselect all points	Cmd+D	Ctrl+D
Toggle grid between fine/coarse	Opt+Click in grid	Alt+Click in grid

Hue/Saturation Dialog	MAC OS	Windows 95/98/NT
move range to new location	Click in image	Click in image
add to range	Shift+Click/Drag in image	Shift+Click/Drag in mage
subtract from range	Shift+Opt+Click/Drag in mage	Alt+Click/Drag in mage
edit master	Cmd+~ (tilde)	Ctrl+~ (tilde)
edit individual colors	Cmd+1 - 6	Ctrl+1 - 6
slide color spectrum	Cmd+Drag on ramp	Ctrl+Drag on ramp

Layer Effects Dialog	MAC OS	Windows 95/98/NT
toggle effects without dialog on or off	**Opt+Menu item**	**Alt+Menu item**
move effect	**Drag in image**	**Drag in Image**
move effect constrained to 45 degree axis	**Shift+Drag in image**	**Shift+Drag in image**
drop shadow	**Cmd+1**	**Ctrl+1**
inner shadow	**Cmd+2**	**Ctrl+2**
outer glow	**Cmd+3**	**Ctrl+3**
inner glow	**Cmd+4**	**Ctrl+4**
bevel and emboss	**Cmd+5**	**Ctrl+5**

Gradient Dialog	MAC OS	Windows 95/98/NT
new gradient	Cmd+N	Ctrl+N
new gradient w/o options dialog	Opt+Click on New button	Alt+Click on New button
save gradient as map settings	Cmd+Opt+Click on Save button	Ctrl+Alt+Click on Save button
discontiguous selection of gradients in list	Cmd+Click gradient name	Ctrl+Click gradient name
contiguous selection of gradients in list	Shift+Click gradient name	Shift+Click gradient name

Lighting Effects	MAC OS	Windows 95/98/NT
clone light in Lighting Effects preview	Opt+Drag light	Alt+Drag light
delete light in Lighting Effects preview	Delete key	Delete key
adjust light footprint without affecting angle	Shift+Drag handle	Shift+Drag handle
adjust light angle without changing footprint	Cmd+Drag handle	Ctrl+Drag handle

INDEX

A

a lowly apprentice production, 508
    PlateMaker 2, 508
Absolute calculation, 698
Accented Edges filter, 467
Accessory software, 888
    Adobe Acrobat, 889–895
    Adobe ImageReady, 507, 896–900
Accurate Screens, 905
Acrobat (Adobe), 889–896
    preparing pre-Acrobat file, 895-896
Actions
    editing, 57–59
    getting complex with, 59–66
    limitations of, 53–54
    recording, 54–57
    saving and recalling, 66
Actions pack (KPT), 53
Actions palette, 52–66
Active node, 240
Actual Size, 222
Adam7 option, 842
Adams, Ansel, 575
Adaptive display, 821
Adding to selection, 324
Add Layer Mask command, 399
Add mode, 428
Add Node tool, 239, 241
Add Noise filter, 455–456, 474, 487, 510, 511, 888
Add to Selection, 327
Adjustment layers, 737, 738
    adding, 538–539
    advantages of using, 743
    creating, 739
    creating sepiatones, 753–756
    density masking, 750–753
    downside of, 742–743
    object masking in, 744–749
    stacking, 756–762
Adjustment options, 396
Adjustments, making, 738
Adjust menu, 692
Adobe
    Accurate Screens, 905

Acrobat, 889–896
    preparing pre-Acrobat file, 895-896
Gamma Utility, 35, 663
    installing and using, 519–526
Illustrator, 82, 190, 227, 228
    making parallel paths in, 258
    manipulating paths using, 255–262
    Object menu, 257
    seamless tiles using, 864–867
    text from, 195–199
ImageReady, 507, 838, 896–900, 899
monitor setup table, 685
PageMaker, 81, 585, 586
Paintshop 4, 763
Paintshop 5, 763
Photoshop 5, 738
Separation Table, 685
Adobe Online, 224
African-American skin tones, 701
Agfa, 78
Airbrush tools, 164–166, 625, 831
Aldus Gallery Effects, 30
Algorithmic painting, 439
Alien Skin, 2
    Black Box, 30, 497
    Eye Candy, 30, 53, 497
Alignment, 416–419
Alpha channels, 245, 298, 348
    filtering, 511
AM (Amplitude Modulated) screens, 641, 905
America Online, 883
Amount value, 545
Anchor points, 228
Andromeda
    Series I filter, 503
    Series III filter, 508
    Series IV Textures filter, 500
    Series V Shadows filter, 497
    Velociraptor, 509
Angled Strokes filter, 467
Angle value, 466
Animated GIF (Graphics Interchange Format), 833–837, 838, 899–900
Anti-alias fringe, 830–831
Anti-aliasing, 200–201, 830–831, 872

Anti-alias PostScript box, 10
Apple RGB, 664
Apply Image command, 5, 424–426
    blending, 438
    results, 438–439
    selections, 438
    source images, 437–438
Arbitrary Rotation, 85
Around Center, 474
Arrays, 227
Arrows, 875
Artboard, 358, 905
Artifacts, removing from scanned file, 94–102
Artistic filters, 461–465
ArtScan Pro (Jetsoft), 77–88, 103
    interface window for, 78
    tools palette, 85–88
ASCII files, 705
Asian skin tones, 701
ATR (Adobe Type Reunion), 35
Auto Balance tool, 88
Auto button, 558–559, 561
Auto Color Balance checkbox, 113
Auto Erase function, 167
Auto/FX, 506
    filters, 506
    The Ultimate Texture Collection, 500
    Typo/Graphic Edges, 494
    Universal Animator, 507
    WebVise Totality, 507
Auto Levels command box, 561
Auto-naming technique, 450
Auto Range Options dialog box, 559, 561, 562
Auto Select Layer option, 159–160
Avec, 78

B

Background, 359, 380
Background Line effect, 272
Background tiles, 846–868
Barco monitor, 9
Base color, 360
Bas Relief filter, 481, 482, 510
Batch scanning, 80
Baud rate, 819
Behind mode, 379

Beziér, Pierre, 227–228
Beziér curves, 227–228, 812
    corner nodes, 229
    smooth nodes, 229
Beziér paths, 227
Bicubic, 75
Biedny, David, 451
Big data, 21–28
Bilinear, 75
Binary encoding, 705
Bit depth, 820
Bitmap mode, 459, 625–651
    converting grayscale files to, 637–651
Black, 905
Black body, 523, 823
Black Box (Alien Skin), 30, 497
Black Generation, 671, 905
Black Ink Limit, 672
Black Ink setting, using, 519
Black Intensity sliders, 468
Black Level sliders, 485
Black Matte, 420
Blanket, 906
Blend color, 360
Blend If box, 392
Blend If sliders, 394–395
Blend modes, 359–376, 427–428, 430
Block option of Eraser tool, 168
Blown out, 906
Blue, 906
Blueline, 906
Blue-Screen filters, 505–506
Blur filters, 456, 465–466
Blur/Gaussian Blur, 101
Blur More filter, 466
Blur tool, 176–178
Border command, 141
Border filters, 506
Bounding boxes, 767
Boxtop Software
    ColorSafe, 507
    GIFmation, 507
    ImageVice, 507
    PhotoGIF, 506
    ProJPEG2.0, 840
    ProJPEG plug-ins, 506
Brightness/Contrast controls, 695

Brightness setting, 462, 906
Brightness values of Grayscale Channel, 296
Bring forward, 383
Bring to front, 383
Brush Detail, 462
Brush palette menu, 161
Brush Size, 160, 462, 463
    painting cursors, 14
    slider, 465
Brush Stroke filter, 467–468
Brush tool, 292
Brush Type pop-up menu, 463
Bump plates, 607–616
Burned out highlights, 530
Burn tool, 178–183
Buttons, 875

C

Calculating grayscale, 431–432
Calculating selections, 432–436
Calculations, 423–453
    on solids, 428–431
Calculations command, 5, 426–437
    blending, 438
    results, 438–439
    selections, 438
    source images, 437–438
Calibration, 659–660
    Adobe Gamma, 663
    and color reproduction, 653–735
    Colortron II, 661–662
    monitor control, 663–665
Camera ready, 626
Cameras, digital, 69
Candela, Ltd.
    ColorCircuit, 684–685
    ColorSynergy, 674, 675, 683, 685–686
Canon, 78
Caucasian skin tones, 701
CCD (charge-coupled device)
    costs of, 69–70
    general scan quality of, 69
CCD (charge-coupled device) sensors, 69, 109–110
CD-ROM drivers, 20
Central Point, 7–8

Centre Internationale d'Eclairage. *See* CIE (Centre Internationale d'Eclairage)
CE Software
    QuicKeys, 34–35, 120
CGSD, 500–501
Chalk & Charcoal filter, 482
Chameleon, 884
Channel Mixer, 698–699
Channel Options, 322
Channels, 295–355
    definition of, 295
    filtering, 510–511
    in making special effects, 328–330
    manipulating, 318–326
    purpose of, 296–318
        to hold selections, 297–300
        to represent color values, 307–314
        to represent ink, 315–316
        to represent moderators, or masks, for commands, 302–307
        to represent variable opacity, 300–302
Channel selections
    loading, 326
    saving, 322–325
Channels Palette menu, 318–322
    saving selection using, 298
Charcoal filter, 482
Charge-coupled device (CCD). *See* CCD (charge-coupled device)
Choke, 906
CHOPs (CHannel OPerations) command, 423, 439–451
    classic, 450–452
Chroma, 665
Chroma Graphics
    Chromatica filter, 503, 505
    EdgeWizard, 505
    MagicMask, 30, 505
    MagicMask 2, 504–505
Chrome filter, 481, 482–483, 510
CIE (Centre Internationale d'Eclairage), 906
Cinematte (Digital Dominion), 505
Circular shapes, 884
ClarisWorks, 891
Classic CHOPs, 450–452
Clear Amount slider, 469
ClickArt Image Pak (T/Maker Company), 888

Clipboard buffer, 5, 6
Clipping group, 382
    establishing, 383–384
Clipping paths, 227, 245, 249–250, 712–714
    defining, 714
    problems with poorly drawn, 715–716
    for rotated export photos, 721
    trapping with, 730–734
    tricks with, 720–723
Cloning tool, 185
Clouds and Difference Clouds filter, 60–66
Clouds filter, 456, 478, 510
CLUTs (Color look-up tables), 814, 822, 823
CMS (Color Management Systems), 653–654, 656, 906
CMYK color, 81, 907
CMYK documents, 295
    color channels of, 315–316
CMYK files, 103
CMYK format, 76
CMYK image, 134
CMYK mode, 182, 459
CMYK Preview option, 387
CMYK printer (MatchPrint or Digital Proof) Profile Generation, 679–680
CMYK Setup
    built-in options, 665–669
    ICC (International Color Consortium) Profiles, 674–687
Coded background color, assigning, 845–846
Color Balance dialog box, 694
Color calibration, 656
ColorCircuit (Candela, Ltd), 684–685
Color corrections methods, 691–700
    editable, 738–743
Color Depth setting, 822, 824
Color Dodge, 368–369
Colored Pencil filter, 455, 461
Color Halftone filter, 476, 510
Colorimeter, 9, 907
Colorimetric rendering intent, 654
Colorimetric translations, 654
Color Indicates, 322
Colorize, 907
Color look-up tables. *See* Cluts (color look-up tables)
Color-management software and controls, 2
Color Management Systems. *See* CMS (Color Management Systems)

Color manipulation filters, 502–504
ColorMatch RGB, 664
Color modes, 374
    and filters, 458–459
Color negative, 87
Color Picker, 322, 824, 829
Color Range dialog box, 156
Colors, 41
    background, 121–122
    foreground, 121–122
    out-of-gamut, 608–609
    and tone corrections, 738
ColorSafe (Boxtop), 507
Color Sampler tool, 219–220, 543
Color scans in preparing grayscale files, 568–575
Color separations, 526
    preparing to make, 687–688
    processing RGB (Red, Green, Blue) file intended for, 688–708
    saving/exporting your, 702–708
Color settings, 518–519
    installing and using *Adobe* Gamma utility, 519–526
ColorShop (Light Source, Inc.), 661
ColorSync, 656
    button, 2, 86, 907
    Control Panel, 524, 662
    Profile pop-up menu, 661–662
ColorSync/ICC dialog box, 81
ColorSynergy (Candela, Ltd), 674, 675, 683, 685–686
Color toning, 182
Colortron (Light Source, Inc.), 9
Colortron II (Light Source, Inc.), 661–662, 907
Colortron II (Light Source, Inc.), 661–662, 907
Colortron (Light Source, Inc.), 9
Color values, channel representation of, 307–314
Commands, channel representation of moderators or masks for, 302–307
Commands palette R.I.P., 66–67
Compression, LZW (lossless compression algorithm) method, 827–828
Concavity setting, 202
Concentric shapes, 212–215
Constrained Aspect Ratio (CAR), 144
Conté Crayon filter, 483
Contextual text help, 85

Contract command, 142
Contrast slider, 468, 485
Control buttons, 85
Control handles, 228, 229, 231–232
Control point, 228
Convolver (KPT), 492, 504
Copy command, 5
Copy-dot scanning, 634–635
Corel, 848
Corner nodes, 229
Corners, 719
Correction filters, 94–102
Corrupt fonts, 31
Craquelure filter, 490
Crop command, 157
Cropmarks/Release, 257, 260
Cropping tool, 157–159
Crosshatch filter, 468
Crystallize filter, 396, 476, 510
CSI PhotoOptics (Cytopia Software), 17, 35, 502
Cube shape, 210–211
Cumulative operations, 427
Curve controls, 541
Curve dialog box, 565
Curved shapes
    analyzing, 234
    drawing, 231–232
Curve Fit setting, 235–237
Curve grid, 539
Curves, understanding and customizing, 561–567
Curves Adjustment layers, 539, 740
Curves dialog box, 539, 562
Curve segments, drawing, 233
Custom, 823
Custom color, 907
Custom filter, 492, 513, 514
Custom inks, using, 580
Custom kernels, 504
Custom pattern, 645–647
Cutout filter, 461–462
Cyan, 907
Cybermesh, 502
Cylinder shape, 216–217
Cytopia Software
    CSI PhotoOptics, 17, 35, 502

D

Darken mode, 369
Dark Strokes filter, 468
Data, archiving your, 9
Data compression, 110–111
DCS (Desktop Color Separation) format, 707, 907
DCS 2 (Desktop Color Separation) format, 707–708, 907
DeBabelizer (Equilibrium Software), 837, 840
Deconstructed photo material, spot colors in, 616–620
Definition slider, 465
Defringe command, 419–420
De-Interlace filter, 491
Deko-Boko filter, 497
Delete command, 240
Delete layer, 390
Delete Node tool, 241
Delete Path menu command, 244
Deluxe Tutorial, problems with, 41–42
Densitometer, 527, 907
Density masking, 750–753
Density slider, 485
Desaturate command, 693
Descreening, 85, 99–102
Desktop Color Separation. *See* DCS (Desktop Color Separation)
Desktop Publishing. *See* DTP (Desktop Publishing)
Despeckle filter, 95–96, 475
Destination, 114
Device gamuts, 681
Device independent color, 656
Device Link Profile, 685
Device profiles, 907
Difference Clouds filter, 478
Difference mode, 371–372
Diffuse filter, 468
Diffuse Glow filter, 455, 469
Diffuse scatters filter, 485
Diffusion Dither, 640–641, 650–651
Digimarc filters, 493
Digital cameras, 69
Digital Dominion
    Cinematte, 505
Digital files, processing more-than-8-bit, 103–104

Digital Frontiers
    HVS Animator, 507
    HVS ColorGIF, 506, 838
    HVS JPEG, 506
    Web Focus, 506
Digital images, 70
Digital proof, 908
Digital trapping, 723
Digitizing, 69, 71
DIMM chips, 2
Direction, drawing curve segments that change, 233
Direction Balance slider, 467
Direct Select cursor, 271–272
Direct Select tool, 239–240
Disk compression, 35
Disk Defragmenter, 7–8
Disk error, 36
Displace filter, 469–470, 512
Displacement Maps folder, 469, 512
Display and cursors, 13–14
Display PostScript, 889–890
Dissolve mode, 362–363
Distance value, 466
Distort command, 407
Distort filters, 456, 469–474
Distortion slider, 470
Dithering, random, 641
Dither option, 203–204, 824
Document repurposing, 890
Dodge tool, 178–183
DOS Monitor Plus, 35
DOS Mounter 95, 35
Dot gain, 526–529, 908
Dots per inch. *See* DPI (dots per inch)
DPI (dots per inch), 908
Draw Net Selection button, 87
Drop shadows, 331–334
Drum scanner, 69–70, 908
    costs of, 69
Dry Brush filter, 462
DTP (Desktop Publishing), 908
Dual 180, 4
Duotone Curve dialog box, 581
Duotone mode, 459
Duotones, 575–583, 585–589, 908
    colorful, with Powertone by Intense Software, 592–597
    special effects in multichannel mode, 589–592

Duplicate command, 537–538, 838
Duplicate Layer command, 388–390
Duplicate Path command, 243–244
Duplicating layers, 264
Dust & Scratches filter, 97–98, 475–476
Dynamic Color Sliders, 11

E

Edge Brightness value, 467
Edge Contrast setting, 154–155, 237
Edge effect, 134
Edge enhancement with Find Edges, 351–354
Edge Intensity, 464
Edge Only option, 467
Edge Width slider, 467
EdgeWizard (Chroma Graphics), 505
Editable color corrections, 738–743
Edit/Fill command, 831
Edit/Transform/Transform Again command, 255
Eight-bit color, 908
Eismann, Katrin, 505–506
Elliptical Marquee tool, 51, 831
Embedded color-management system, 2
Embed Watermark filter, 493
Embossed effects, 335–341
Embossed letters, 338–341
Emboss filter, 486
Embossing, 879–882
Encapsulated PostScript. *See* EPS (Encapsulated PostScript)
Encoding pop-up menu, 704–705
EPS (Encapsulated PostScript), 908
Epson, 78
Equalize command, 692–693
Equilibrium Software
    DeBabelizer Toolbox, 507, 837, 840, 843
Eraser tool, 122, 168–169, 832
Eurostandard inks, 665
Exact, 823
Excel (Microsoft), 891
Exclusion mode, 372
Expand command, 142
Expert Silhouettes, 147–152
Export Clipboard preference, 10
Export dialog box, 685
Exposure times, 69

Extensis Software, 2
    MaskPro, 504, 718–723
    PhotoAnimator, 507
    PhotoFrame, 506
    PhotoTools, 194–195, 497
Extrude filter, 486
Eye Candy (Alien Skin), 30, 53, 497
Eyedropper cursor, 535
Eyedropper tools, 85, 122, 156–157, 219, 272, 696, 881

F

Facet filter, 476
Facini, Charles, 693
Fade command, 693
FastCore plug-in, 41
Fast Eddy (LizardTech), 838, 839
Feathering, 141, 154
50% Threshold option, 638
Fill Subpath Command, 248
Film, 908
Film Grain filter, 462
Film granularity, 547–552
Film processor, 909
Filter/Blur/Gaussian Blur filter, 859
Filter/Distort/Ripple effect, 132
Filter Factory, 514
Filtering channels, 510–511
Filter/Noise submenu, 95–96
Filter/Pixelate/Pointillize, 132
Filters, 7, 453–516
    and Color mode, 458–459
    combining, 510
    creating own, 513–514
    Foreground/Background colors, 455
    functions, 454–455
    keyboard shortcuts, 453–454
    managing, 515
    native, 461
        Artistic, 461–465
        Blur, 465–466
        Brush Stroke, 467–468
        Digimarc, 493
        Distort, 469–474
        Noise, 474–476
        Pixelate, 476–478
        Render, 478–480
        Sharpen, 480–481
        Sketch, 481–485
        stylize, 485–489
        texture, 490–491
        video, 491
    previewing effects, 459–461
    and RAM, 454
    removing old, 29–30
    and selections, 457–458
    and transparent layers, 455–456
Find Edges filter, 487
    edge enhancement with, 351–354
Finger Painting setting on Options palette, 175
Fixed Size, 144
Fixed Target size, 158
Flap, 358, 909
Flash 3 (Macromedia), 507
Flatbed scanners, 69, 909
Flatness setting, 714–715
Flatten Image command, 397
Flip horizontal command, 409–410
Flip Image button, 87
Flip vertical command, 409–410
Floating selections, 380–381
Flood, 909
FLO (Valis), 509
FM (Frequency Modulated) screens, 641, 708–709, 909
Focus tools, 176
Fonts, corrupt, 31
Foreground/Background colors, 121–122
Fragment filter, 476
Freeform Pen tool, 237
    drawing paths with, 235–237, 238
Freehand Graphics Inc.
    Spot Process, 624–625, 693
FreeHand (Macromedia), 82, 227, 632, 864
Free Transform command, 24, 250, 252–253, 410, 763–764
Frequency setting, 154
    on Options palette, 237
Fresco filter, 462
Fuzziness slider, 157

G

Gaebel Half-Tone Screen Determiner, 100
Gallery Effects filters, 37, 467

Gamma Utility (Adobe), 35, 663
    installing and using, 519–526
Gamut, 654
Gaussian Blur filter, 96, 102, 289, 344, 348, 466, 511–512
G3 chip, 4
GCR (Gray Component Replacement), 670–672, 909
General preferences, 10–11
Genesis, 501
GIF87a, 828–829
GIF89a, 828–829, 844
GifAnimator (Ulead), 507
GIF (Graphics Interchange Format), 820, 844
    animated, 833–837, 838, 899–900
    converting to, 820–833
    interlaced, 832–833
GIFmation (Boxtop Software), 507
GIF87s, 844
Glass filter, 470
Glass Lens filter (KPT), 886
Glass letters effect, 282–289
Glow Amount slider, 469
Glow effects, 270–271, 342–347
Glowing Edges filter, 487
Gradient Options palette, 203
    Dither option, 203–204
    Edit button on, 204
    Reverse option, 204
    Transparency option, 203
Gradients
    making new, 204–205
    masking with, 347–354
    need for in digital art, 207–218
Gradient shapes, 206
Gradient tool, 203–218, 348, 852
Grain filter, 455, 490
Graininess slider, 469
Graphic Pen filter, 483
Graphics computer operators, 517–518
Gray Component Replacement *See* GCR (Gray Component Replacement)
Grayscale, 518–575, 820, 823, 909
    calculating, 431–432
    converting RGB to, 54–57
Grayscale Channel, brightness values of, 296
Grayscale checkbox, 113

Grayscale files
    converting to bitmap mode, 637–651
    using color scans to prepare, 568–575
Grayscale image, processing, 531–541
Grayscale mode, 81, 318, 459, 659
Grids, 784
    creating, 784–785
    making visible, 788–789
    painting on, 785–787
    and positioning, 776–777
Grossman, Rhonda, 439
Grow command, 141, 156
GROWSTUB errors, 42
Guides
    creating, 779–780
    hiding and viewing, 781
    moving, 780–781
    removing, 781
    using, 778–784
    wish list for, 782–784
Guides and Grids, 16, 737

H

Halftone cell, 518, 909
Halftone Pattern filter, 483
Halftones, preparing, for printing, 526
Halftone screen, 641–645, 705–706
    bitmap conversion option, 647–649
Hand tool, 220–221
Hard drive, 8–9, 46
Hard Light mode, 366–367
Hewlett-Packard, 78, 663–664
Hexachrome process, 735, 910
Hex numbers, 846
HexWrench (Studion Soft Industries, Ltd), 735
Hide Selection, 404
High contrast, 910
High-fidelity printing, 910
High key, 910
Highlight Area slider, 464
Highlight dot, 910
    fall-off, 910
Highlights
    burned out, 530
    printing, 559
    specular, 559

Highlight Strength slider, 464
High Pass filter, 492–493
Hi-res color separation files, 200
Histograms, 553–554, 740–742, 910
Histograms/Curves dialog box, 87–88
History Brush, 168, 169, 172
History Options command, 169–170
History palette, 5–6, 42–52, 46, 169, 738
    and hard drive, 46
    menus and options, 43–45
    using, 47–52, 171–172
HTML (Hypertext Markup Language), 814
Hue, 182, 373
Hue error, 665, 666, 910
Hue mode, 373
Hue/Saturation controls, 695–696
Hue/Saturation layer, 739
Hue slider, 749
Human Software
    Otto Paths, 494
    Squizz, 509
    Textissimo, 494
HVS Animator (Digital Frontiers), 507
HVS ColorGIF (Digital Frontiers), 838

I

ICC (International Color Consortium) Profiles, 81, 654–656, 685
    exporting, 683–685
    within Photoshop, 686
Illustrator (Adobe), 82, 190, 227, 228
    making parallel paths in, 258
    manipulating paths using, 255–262
    Object menu, 257
    seamless tiles using, 864–867
    text from, 195–199
Image acquisition, 69–118
    basic scanning, 75–77
    cleaning original material, 93–94
    digital files, 103–104
    evaluation, 88–92
    interpolated sampling, 71
    photo CD, 109–118
    pixels, 70
    removing artifacts from scanned file, 94–102
    resolution, 70

sampling frequency, 70–71
scanner controls, 77–88
scanning software, 88
tonal corrections, 104–109
Image/Adjust/Invert command, 303–304
Image adjustment, 83
Image Balance, 485
Image Cache, 19–20, 47
Image contrast, 910
Image enhancement, 113–114
ImageExpress ScanPrepPro, 508
Image files, tagging your, 686–687
Image/Image Size dialog box, 74–75
Image manipulation, 737–809
    adjustment layers
        creating, 739
        stacking, 756–762
    creating sepiatone, 753–756
    density masking, 750–753
    editable color corrections, 738–743
    grids, 784–789
    grids and positioning, 776–777
    guides, 778, 784
    hue slider, 749
    making adjustments, 738
    mask layer, 743–756
    object masking, 744–749
    rulers, 778
    software for, 70
    transformations, 763–776
Image Pack file, 111
ImageReady (Adobe), 507, 838, 896–900, 899
Images
    evaluating, for scanning, 88–92
    strokes used to integrate two, 275–283
ImageVice (Boxtop Software), 507
Imposition, 910
Impressionist option, 172
Index Color mode, 83
Indexed Color, 507, 837, 838
Infinop, 843
Info button, 116
Initializing problems, 36–37
Ink, channel representation of, 315–316
Ink Colors, 665
Ink Outlines filter, 468
Inline graphics, 814

Input value, 911
Installation, 20–21
Intellihance (Extensis Software), 508
Intense Software
    PowerTone, 508, 592–597
    Powertone, 592–597
    Silvertone, 597
Interlaced GIF (Graphics Interchange Format), 832–833
Interlacing, 832–833
    alternative to, 844–845
International Color Consortium. *See* ICC (International Color Consortium) Profile
Internet, 811. *See also* World Wide Web (WWW)
Internet Explorer (Microsoft), 812
Interpolated resolution, 71, 634, 911
Interpolated sampling, 71, 73
Interpolation, 73
Intersect Selection command, 328
Intersect with selection, 325
Invert Adjustment layer, 739
Invert button, 86–87
Invert command, 502
Irrational tangent, 709

J

Jaz drive, 8
Jetsoft
    ArtScan Pro, 77–88, 103
        interface window for, 78
        tools palette for, 85–88
Joint Photographic Experts Group. *See* JPEG (Joint Photographic Experts Group) format
JPEG (Joint Photographic Experts Group) format, 705, 839–842, 844, 911

K

Kai Power Tools (KPT), 30, 500, 851, 885
    Actions pack, 53
    Convolver, 492, 504
    Glass Lens filter, 886
    seamless tiles with, 849–851
    Seamless Welder, 851
    Spheroid Generator 3.0, 338, 884–885
    Texture Explorer, 851
    Vortex Tile, 851

Keyboard shortcuts, 919–936
Keyline, 911
Kitchens, Susan, 452
Knock out, 911
Knoll, John, 502
Knoll, Thomas, 502
Kodak Access, 111
Krause, Kai, 423, 439, 450

L

Lab color, 911
Lab mode, 317, 459
Laminate proof, 911
LaserSeps Pro (Second Glance Software), 508, 623, 711, 712
Lasso tool, 143–146, 146–155, 831, 859
Layer/Disable Layer Mask, 402
Layered documents, 358
Layer Effects, 331, 412–415, 495
Layer flaps, 358–359
Layer Masks, 358, 398–404
    filtering, 511–512
Layer menu, 384–397
Layer/New/Layer
    via Copy command, 5, 404
    via Cut command, 5
Layer Options dialog box, 390–396, 898
Layer Palette trash icon, 540
Layers, 357–421
    duplicating, 264
    Offset filter used with, 857–861
    rearranging, using palette list, 382–384
Layers palette menu, 358, 359, 384–397, 898
    Blend mode, 359–376
    layers thumbnail list, 380–382
    opacity, 376–378
    preserve transparency, 379
    rearranging, using list, 382–384
Layers Palette Options command, 397
Layers thumbnail list, 380–382
Layer visibility, 381
L Channel, 317
Lens Flare filter, 478
Letters, embossed, 338–341
Levels, 740
Levels adjustment layer, 540

Levels command, 502
Levels controls, 104–108, 541
    understanding and customizing, 552–561
Levels filter, 502
Lighten mode, 370–371
Lighting Effects filter, 30, 478, 479
Lightness, 373, 538, 911
Light Source, Inc., 661
    ColorShop, 661
    Colortron, 9
    Colortron II, 661–662, 907
Line, Noise, Artifact Removal button, 87
Line art, 81, 625–651, 911
    interpolated samples for, 71
    processing scans, 626–637
    spot colors in, 616–620
Line screen, 84, 911
Line shot, 911
Lines per centimeter. *See* LPC (lines per centimeter)
Lines per inch. *See* LPI (lines per inch)
Line tool, 201–202, 832
Linked layers, 381
LizardTech
    Fast Eddy, 838, 839
    Planet Color, 837, 838
Load button, 558
Load Selection command, 142
Load Settings command, 87
Lossy, 912
Lost cursor, 36
Low contrast, 912
Low-end scanners, 76
Low key, 912
LPC (lines per centimeter), 84, 912
LPI (lines per inch), 912
Luminosity mode, 375
LZW (lossless compression algorithm), 703–704, 820, 827–828

M

Mac extension conflicts, 34–35
MacPaint, 122
Macro-manipulation tools, 250
Macromedia, 812, 848
    Flash 3, 507
    FreeHand, 82, 227, 632, 864
Mac System Color Picker, 10
MAC troubleshooting, 32–37
Magenta, 912
MagicCurtain, 884
MagicFrame, 884
MagicMask (Chroma Graphics), 30, 505
MagicMask 2 (Chroma Graphics), 504–505
MagicMask filter, 497, 884
Magic Wand tool, 155–156, 297, 625, 831, 872
Magnetic Lasso tool, 146, 152–155, 235–236, 504
Magnetic Pen, 504
    drawing paths with, 235–237
Magneto Optical disk, 8
Magnifier keyboard command, 37
Magnify Image Preview button, 86
Mailware software, 883
Make Selection command, 246–248
Make Work Path command, 245, 717–718
Marquee tools, 143–146, 850
Masked Areas, 322
Mask Incomplete Blocks, 486
Masking, 430–431
    with gradients, 347–354
Masking filters, 504–506
Mask layer, 358, 743–756
MaskPro (Extensis Software), 504, 718–723
Masks, 358
    channel representation of, 302–307
Mask technique, 869–873
Master Juggler, 35
Matting, 419–420
Maximum black, 912
Maximum filter, 493
Maximum shadow dot, 912
Measure tool, 219
Median filter, 97, 100, 476
Memory colors, 700
Memory leaks, 35–36
Memory setting, 18–19
Menu commands, keyboard equivalents for, 119–120
Merge Channels command, 320–321, 321
Merge Down command, 397
Merge Spot Channels, 318
Merge Visible command, 397
MetaCreations, 2
    Painter, 493
Metallics, 912
Mezzotint filter, 476, 485

948   *Microsoft*

Microsoft, 663–664
    Excel, 891
    Internet Explorer, 812
    Network, 883
    PowerPoint, 891
Microtek, 78
Midtone, 912
Midtone gain, 912
Minimum filter, 493
Minimum highlight dot, 529–531, 912
Mixed curve and straight-line shapes, drawing, 232–233
MMM
    HoloDozo filter, 501
    SISNIKK stereograms, 509
MMX chip, 40–41
Modems, 819
Moderators, channel representation of, 302–307
Modify command, 141
Moiré patterns, 85
    reducing, 512–513
Monitor calibration, 913
Monitor RGB, 665
Monochromatic noise, 474
Monroy, Bert, 451
Moody, Nathan, 451
Mosaic filter, 478, 487
Mosaic Tiles filter, 490
Motion Blur filter, 466, 489
Mouse problems, 42
Move tool, 5, 51, 140, 159–160
MovieFLO (Valis), 509
Multichannel mode, 318, 459
    duotone special effects in, 589–592
Multiple Master fonts, 278
Multiple Pages setting, 79–80
Multiple processor cards, 4
Multiple stroke effect, 273–275
Multiply command, 423
Multiply mode, 361, 364, 758
Multirotate Action, 773–776

N

Native filters, 453, 461
    Artistic, 461–465
    Blur, 465–466
    Brush Stroke, 467–468

    Digimarc, 493
    Distort, 469–474
    Noise, 474–476
    Pixelate, 476–478
    Render, 478–480
    Sharpen, 480–481
    Sketch, 481–485
    stylize, 485–489
    texture, 490–491
    video, 491
Navigator palette, 223–224
Nearest Neighbor, 75
Negative filter, 502
Negs, 913
Neon effect, using paths, 278–282
Neon Glow filter, 455, 462
Netscape Navigator, 812, 843
Network (Microsoft), 883
Neutral tones, 700–701, 913
New adjustment layer, 387–389
New Document command, 171
New Layer command, 385–387
New Layer dialog box, 390–396
New Path option, 243
New Selection, 326
Nikon, 78
Node Delete tool, 239
Node Edit tool, 239, 241–242
Nodes, 228
    active, 240
    corner, 229
    semi-active, 240
    smooth, 229
Node selections, transform commands and variability of, 251–262
Noise filter, 474–476
Noise textures, 849
Non-Linear history, 172
Nonrectangular graphics on the Web, 868–875
Nonrectangular shapes, 873–875
Normal mode, 362
Normal option, 144
Norton Directory Assistance, 34
Norton File Saver, 35
Norton Utilities, 7–8
Note Paper filter, 483
NTSC, 665
    Colors filter, 491

Numeric input fields, 84
Numeric Transform command, 763, 766–768, 767
Numeric Transform dialog box, 407–408

O

Object masking, 744–749
Objects, 767
Ocean Ripple filter, 470
OCR (Optical Character Recognition software), 80
Offset, 913
Offset filter, 493, 836
    with Paintbrush tool, 855–856
    with Pen tool, 855–856
    with Rubber Stamp Tool, 855
    Tiles in Photoshop, using, 855–861
    used with Layers, 857–861
Oil, mounting with, 94
Oil-mount fluid, 94
OneClick, 35
Opacity, 295, 376–378
    representation of variable, 300–302
Opacity slider, 164
Optical resolution, 634
Option/Alt key, 439
Option-Merge-Visible command, 397
Options palette, 139
    and Curve Fit setting, 235–237
    Frequency setting on, 237
Original material
    cleaning, 93–94
    type of, 83
Otto Paths (Human Software), 494
Out From Center, 474
Out-of-gamut colors, 608–609, 913
Output size, 114–115
Output value, 913
Overlay Edge, 467
Overlay mode, 364–365
Overlay proof, 913
Overprint, 913

P

Page Fault errors, in Windows 95, 41
PageMaker (Adobe), 81, 585, 586
Paint Alchemy (Xaos Tools), 499

Paintbrush tool, 166–167, 831
    Offset filter with, 855–856
    using *Illustrator* and paths to create new, 290–292
Paint Bucket tool, 202–203, 625, 692
Paint Daubs filter, 463
Painter (MetaCreations), 493
Paintshop 4 (Adobe), 763
Paintshop 5 (Adobe), 763
Paint tools, 122
Palette icons, 170–171
Palette Knife filter, 463
Palette list, rearranging layers using, 382–384
Palette pop-up, 821–823
PAL/SECAM, 664
Pantone, Inc., 735, 913
    HexWrench program by, 508
Pantone color selector, 580
Parallel paths, making, in *Illustrator*, 258
Parquet Tiling, 851
Paste command, 5
Patchwork filter, 490–491
Path-export file, 260
Path-manipulation capabilities, 269
Paths, 228, 812
    drawing with magnetic pen and Freeform pen tools, 235–237
    drawing with pen tool, 230
        analyzing curved shapes, 234
        curved shapes, 231–232
        curve segments that abruptly change direction, 233
        Freeform, 238
        with magnetic pen and Freeform pen tools, 235
        magnetic pen paths, 235–237
        mixed curve and straight-line shapes, 232–233
        rule of thirds, 234
        straight-line, 230–231
    editing, with Pen tools, 239–242
    manipulating
        in Illustrator, 255–262
        in Photoshop, 250–262
    neon effect using, 278–282
Paths palette, 164
    sidebar menu, 242–250
Pattern dither, 639–640

Patterns
- color mode sensitive, 800
- defining, from Transparent layer, 802

PDF (Portable Document Format) files, 889–890, 894
Pencil tool, 167, 565, 831, 871–872
Pentium platform, 4
Pen tool, 227–293, 625, 831
- Beziér curves, 227–228
  - corner nodes, 229
  - smooth nodes, 229
  - drawing paths with
    - analyzing curved shapes, 234
    - curved shapes, 231–232
    - curve segments that abruptly change direction, 233
    - editing, 239–242
    - freeform, 238
    - magnetic, 235–237
    - magnetic pen and freeform pen tools, 235
    - mixed curve and straight-line shapes, 232–233
    - rule of thirds, 234
    - straight-line, 230–231
- Offset filter with, 855–856
- paths palette, 242
  - sidebar menu, 242–250

Pen Width option, 235–236
Perceptual mapping, 656
Perfecting press, 913
Perspective command, 252–253, 407
Perspective Tiling, 851
Photo, creating old from new, 584
PhotoAnimator (Extensis Software), 507
Photo CD, 109–112
- correcting images, 117–118
- loading images, 112–116

Photo CD Pro scanner, 70
Photo CD scanner, 70
Photo Cell (Second Glance Software), 507
Photocopy filter, 484
PhotoExplorer (Ulead), 507
Photofilter, 503
PhotoFrame (Extensis Software), 506
PhotoGIF (Boxtop Software), 506
PhotoGlow filter, 497
Photographic image, trapping part of, 725–727
Photomultiplier vacuum tubes, 69
Photoshop, 70
- Color Picker, 10, 122, 580
- EPS format, 704–707
- platform for, 1–2
- Quick Mask program by, 891
- and RAM, 2–3
- speed of, 2

Photoshop 2, 450
Photoshop 2.5, 424
Photoshop 3, 423–424
Photoshop 4, 103
Photoshop 5, 103, 427, 738
Photoshop Channel CHOPs (Biedny, et al.), 451
Photoshop paths, making, in Illustrator, 259–262
PhotoTools (Extensis Software), 194–195
PhotoSpotCt (Second Glance Software), 508, 620–623
Pinch filter, 470
Pixar, 848
Pixelate filters, 476–478
PixelCraft, 78
Pixel Doubling option, 159
Pixel frequency, 71, 72–73
Pixels, 15, 70, 813
- changing number of, 74–75
- ratio of, per inch to line screen, 84
- size of, 70, 73

Pixels per inch. *See* PPI (pixels per inch)
Plain, solid-colored tiles, 847–848
Planet Color (LizardTech), 837, 838
Plaster filter, 484
Plastic Wrap filter, 464, 482–483
Plate, 913
Plugged, 913
Plugin Manager, 17
Plug-ins, 812
- and Scratch Disk Preferences settings, 16–18

Plug-Ins folder, 7, 453
PNG (Portable Network Graphics Specification) file format, 842–843
Pointillize filter, 129, 455, 478
Polar Coordinates filter, 456, 470–471, 886
Polygonal Lasso tool, 146, 871
Pond Ripples, 474
Pop-ups, 84
Poster Edges filter, 464
Posterization, 464
PostScript, 914

PostScript Color Management, 707
PostScript dots, 529
PostScript Level 2 Color Rendering Dictionary, 685
PostScript Patterns, 865
PostScript RIP (Raster Image Processor), task of, 626
PowerPoint (Microsoft), 891
Powertone (Intense Software), 592–597
Powertone-processed images, 592
Power Tools (Kai)
    Power Tools, 30, 851, 885
        seamless tiles with, 849–851
PPI (pixels per inch), 914
Prebuilt seamless tiles, 848
Precise cursor, 160
Preference file corruption, 29
Preferences, 16
    setting your, 9–20
Preferences tool, 88
Prefs button, 116
Prepress, 517–651, 914
    bump plates, 607–616
    color scans in preparing grayscale files, 568–575
    color settings, 518–531
    converting grayscale files to bitmap mode, 637–651
    curves, 561–567
    custom inks, 580
    duotones, tritones, and quadtones, 575–583, 585–589
    duotone special effects in multichannel mode, 589–592
    duotone with Powertone by Intense Software, 592–597
    levels controls, 552–561
    processing greyscale image, 531–541
    processing line art scans, 626–637
    spot color, 597–607
        in deconstructed photo material, 616–620
        third-party utilities, 620–625
    touch plates, 607–616
    unsharp mask filter, 542–552
Preserve Transparency, 379, 456
Press, 914
Press gain, 914
Press misregistration, 914
Pressure-sensitive digitizing tablet, 236
Preview button, 115
Preview icons, 37

Previous, 824
Printer spreads, 914
Printing highlight, 559
Print Size, 222
    changing values, 75
Process color, 914
Production filters, 508
Profile/Preview, 683
ProJPEG 2.0 (Boxtop Software), 840
ProJPEG plug-ins (Boxtop Software), 506
Propeller motion, 411
Proportional Color Reduction Trapping, 727–730, 914
PseudoColor filter, 503

Q

Quadruple processor cards, 3
Quadtones, 575–583, 585–589, 914
Quality, 83
QuarkXPress, 81, 585, 586, 891
Quick drop shadows, 878–879
QuicKeys (CE Software), 34–35
Quick Mask, 119, 122–137, 458, 867
    dialog box, 123–124
QuickTime, 20

R

Radial Blur filter, 466
Radius and Threshold values, 467
Radius PressView monitors, 9
Radius value, 545
RAM Doubler, 34
RAM (random access memory), 3, 37
    conserving, 5–6
    and filters, 454
Random dithering, 641
Raster, 813
Raster file, 813–814
Raster format, 70, 812
Raster grid, 914
Raster image files, 811
Raster Image Processor. *See* RIP (Raster Image Processor)
Rasterization, 70, 191, 915
Raster objects, 227
Reader spreads, 915

Read Watermark filter, 493
Red, 915
Red, Green, Blue. *See* RGB (Red, Green, Blue)
Reinfeld, Eric, 431
Relative calculation, 698
Relisys, 78
Render Clouds filter, 455
Render Difference Clouds filter, 455
Render filter, 478–480
Rendering intents, 654
Repeat Edge pixels, 470, 472, 473
Replace Color, 696–697
Rescreens, 99
Reset the Parameter, 37
Resolution, 70
Result color, 361
Reticulation filter, 485
Retroscan filter, 130
Reveal Selection, 404
Reverse option, 204
RGB (Red, Green, Blue) color, 81, 657–659, 915
    converting to grayscale, 54–57
RGB (Red, Green, Blue) file, processing, intended for color separation, 688–708
RGB (Red, Green, Blue) Input (monitor) Profile Generation, 675
RGB (Red, Green, Blue) mode, 83
RGB (Red, Green, Blue) printer (desktop printer) Profile Generation, 678–679
RGB (Red, Green, Blue)-to-Indexed Color conversion algorithm, 896
RGB (Red, Green, Blue) values, 518–519
Ricoh, 78
Ripple filter, 130, 468, 471–472
Ripple Magnitude slider, 470
RIP (Raster Image Processor), 915
Rotate 90° button, 86
Rotate 180° button, 408–409
Rotate Canvas, 4
Rotate 90° CCW button, 408–409
Rotate command, 406
Rotate 90° CW button, 408–409
Rotated export photos, clipping paths for, 721
Rotation tricks, 768–773
Rough Pastels filter, 464
Rough Pastels Texture controls, 465
Rubber Stamp Tool, 98–99, 183–190, 860
    Offset filter with, 855

Rubylith, 122–123
Rule of thirds, 234
Rulers, 776, 778
Rules and Guides shortcut keys, 778

S

Sample, 71
Sample depth, 83
Sampling, interpolated, 71, 73
Sampling frequency, 71, 73
Sampling rate, 70, 71
Saturated colors, 701
Saturation, 182, 373, 656
Saturation mode, 374
Save A Copy command, 397
Save button, 558
Save Selection command, 142
Save Settings command, 87
Saving files, 844
Saving Files dialog box, 12–13
Saving Files Preferences, 11–13
Saving paths, 714
Scale, 405–406
Scale dialog box, 267
Scan mode, 81
Scanned file, removing artifacts from, 94–102
Scanner Input Profile Generation, 676–677
Scanner noise, 30–31
Scanners
    controls of, 77–88
    costs of, 69
    hand-held miniature, 69
    low-end, 76
    optical precision of, 71
    precision of, 71
    types of, 69–70
Scanning
    basic, 75–77
    evaluating images for, 88–92
    software for, 76, 88
Scan type, 79–81
Scissors tool, 259
Scitex Continuous Tone format, 702–703
Scratch disks, 7–8
Screen, 915

Screen angle, 915
Screen command, 423
Screen dot, 915
Screening, 84
Screen mode, 364
Screen mode selectors, 137–138
Screen print, 915
SCSI devices, 30–31
SCSI hard drive, 8
Seamed tiles, 848
Seamless Patterns, 292
Seamless tiles, 848–854
    with Adobe Illustrator, 864–867
    with Kai Power Tools, 849–851
Seamless Welder (KPT), 851
Second Glance Software, 711
    Chromassage filter, 503
    LaserSeps Pro, 508, 623, 711, 712
    PhotoCell, 507
    PhotoSpotCT, 508, 620–623
Select All, 140
Select Color Range command, 141
    from Select menu, 156–157
Select/Inverse command, 140, 305
Selections
    adding to, 324
    calculating, 432–436
    holding with channels, 297–300
    intersect with, 325
    retrieving saved, 299–300
    saving, 298–299
    subtracting from, 324
Selection tools, 139–140, 143
Selective Color, 697–698
Select menu, 140–142
    select Color Range from, 156–157
Select None, 140
Semi-active nodes, 240, 252
Send backward, 383
Send to back, 383
Separations, 915
Separation Setup, 669–670
    gray component replacement, 670–672
Sepiatone, creating, 753–756
Service Packs, 3
SF Deko-Boko, 883

SF Inai-Inai-Bar filter, 883
SF MagicalCurtain filter, 883
SF Midnights TV filter, 883
SF Mr. Sa^Kan filter, 883
Shadow, 916
Shadow/Emboss/Bevel/Glow filters, 495–498
Sharpen, 78, 916
Sharpen button, 86
Sharpen Edges filter, 481, 542
Sharpen filters, 480–481, 542
Sharpening, 113
Sharpen More filter, 481, 542
Sharpen tool, 176–178
Shear filter, 472
Sheet-fed presses, 916
Show Tool Tips, 11
Sidebar menu, Paths palette, 242–250
Similar command, 141, 156
Single Image, 79
Single Row, 144–145
SISNIKK, 509
16-bit image, 105–106
16-bit mode, 109
Size slider, 462
Sketch filters, 481–485
Skew command, 252–253, 406–407
Skin imperfections, correcting, 189–190
Skin tones, 701
    strategies for realistic, 701
Smart Blur filter, 467
SmartSaver (Ulead), 507
Smooth button, 565
Smooth command, 141–142
Smoothness slider, 465, 470
Smooth nodes, 229
SMPTE-C (Society for Motion Picture and TV Engineers), 664
SMPTE-240M (Society for Motion Picture and TV Engineers), 664–665
Smudge Stick, 464
Smudge tool, 174–175, 287, 625
Snapping, 781–782
Snapshot, 171
Soften Blue Channel checkbox, 86
Soft Light mode, 366
SoftQuad, 848

Software

Software
    image-manipulation, 70
    scanning, 76, 88
Solarize filter, 488
Solids, calculations on, 428–431
Source, 114
Source images, 437–438
Spatter filter, 468
Special effects
    using channels to make, 328–330
    using Strokes On paths, 263–292
Specification for Web Offset Printing. *See* SWOP (Specification for Web Offset Printing)
Specification for Web Offset Publications, 665
Specular, 848
    TextureScrape, 848
Specular highlight, 559
Speed, 83
Sphere shape, 207–209
Spherize filter, 470, 472
Spheroid Generator (KPT), 338, 884, 885
Spheroids, making own, 885–886
Split Channels command, 319–320, 321
Split edge effect, 271
Sponge filter, 465
Sponge tool, 178–183
Spot, 916
Spot Channel, 318
Spot colors, 597–607
    in deconstructed photo material, 616–620
    in line art, 616–620
Spot function, 916
Spot Process (Freehand Graphics, Inc.), 624–625, 693
Sprayed Strokes filter, 468
Spread, 916
Squizz (Human Software), 509
sRGB standard, 663–664
Stained Glass filter, 30, 455, 491
Stamp filter, 485
Star border, 163
Step wedge, 916
Stochastic screens, 641, 708–712, 916
Straight-line paths, drawing, 230–231
Stripper, 916
Stroke command, 263
Stroke Length slider, 467
Strokes, used to integrate two images, 275–283

Strokes On paths, 263–292
Strokes On The Offset contour, 271–272
Strokes On waving lines, 274
Stroke Subpath command, 249
Studion Soft Industries, Ltd
    HexWrench, 735
Stylize filters, 485–489
Subtract From Selection, 324, 327
Subtract mode, 428
Sucking Fish collection, 497
Sucking Fish filters, 884
Sumi-e filter, 468
SuperMac/Radius, 659
Surprint, 916
Swatches palette menu, 822, 865
SWOP (Specification for Web Offset Printing), 916
    inks for, 665–666
System option, 822

T

Tables, 687
Tagged Image File Format. *See* TIFF (Tagged Image File Format)
Tamarack, 78
Tangent, 228
Target, 424–425
Terrazzo (Xaos Tools), 499–500, 862
    tiles with, 861–864
Text, 875
    from *Adobe Illustrator*, 195–199
Texture Channel, 511
Texture Explorer (KPT), 851
Texture Fill filter, 478, 479
Texture filters, 490–491, 499–501
TextureScrape (Specular), 848
Texturizer filter, 491
Third-party filters, 493–494
    blue-screen, 505–506
    border, 506
    color manipulation, 502–504
    favorite tricks, 509–513
    masking, 504–505
    production, 508
    Shadow/Emboss/Bevel/Glow, 495–498
    texture, 499–501
    3D, 501–502

type, 494
Web, 506–507
wild effect and NOC (Not Otherwise Classified), 509
Third-party spot color utilities, 620–625
3D filters, 501–502
3D Render filter, 478
3D Studio Max, 501
3D Transform filter, 480
Threshold mode for *Windows* users, 555
Threshold setting, 545
Thumbnail, 112
TIFF (Tagged Image File Format), 506, 703–704, 917
TileMaker, 884
Tiles
　in Photoshop, using Offset filter, 855–861
　in Terrazzo, 861–864
Tiles filter, 488
T/Maker Company
　ClickArt Image Pak, 888
Tolerance setting, 245
Tonal corrections, 104–109
Tone, 917
Toolbox, key commands for, 121–139
Tools palette, 119, 239
　ease in using, 120
Torn Edges filter, 455, 485
Total Ink Limit, 672
Touch plates, 607–616, 917
Toyo inks, 665
Trace Contour filter, 488–489
Transfer Function, 706, 917
Transformation command, 250, 737, 763–764
Transform commands, 404–410, 834
　keyboard shortcuts for, 764
　and variability of node selections, 251–262
Transform/Numeric Transform command, 250
Transparency & Gamut settings, 14–15
Transparency option, 203
Transparent layers, 455–456
Trapping, 723–734, 917
　with clipping paths, 730–734
　part of photographic image, 725–727
　Proportional Color Reduction, 727–730
Trash icon, 171
Trilinear array, 109–110
Tritones, 575–583, 585–589, 917

Troubleshooting, 28–42
　common concerns in, 28–32
　general strategies, 31–32
　MAC, 32–37
　Windows, 37–42
　Windows NT, 39–40
True Finder Integration, 35
TruMatch, 917
Turn Off Path, 244
TVSnow, 884
TWAIN (or Technology Without An Interesting Name) standard, 77
24-Bit color, 905
Twirl filter, 472, 886
Two-ink color image reproduction, 592–597
Two-up, four-up, etc., 917
TypeCaster (Xaos Tools), 494
Type 11 error message, 33–34
Type filters, 494
Type in Photoshop, 190–191
　Extensis PhotoTools, 194–195
　Gradient tool, 203–218
　Line tool, 201–202
　Paint Bucket tool, 202–203
　text from Adobe Illustrator, 195–199
　Type tools, 191–193
Type tools, 191–193, 831
Typographical errors, correcting, 190
Typo/Graphic Edges, 494

U

UCA (Under Color Addition), 917
UCR (Under Color Removal), 672–673, 917
Ulead
　GifAnimator, 507
　PhotoExplorer, 507
　SmartSaver, 507
　WebRazor, 507
Ultimate PhotoFusion filter, 505
The Ultimate Texture Collection (Auto/Fx), 500
Ultra High-Fidelity Offset Color Reproduction, 734–735
UMAX, 78
Under Color Addition Amount, 672
Under Color Removal. *See* UCR (Under Color Removal)
Underpainting filter, 465
Uniform, 822

Unisys Corporation, 820
    patented LZW (lossless compression algorithm), 820
Units and Rulers Preferences box, 15–16
Unsharp Mask filter, 4, 104, 372, 481, 542–545, 917
    using, on difficult photos, 545–552
Upgrades, 20–21
Use Diffusion Dither, 14
Use System Palette, 14

V

Valis
    FLO, 509
    MovieFLO, 509
Value, 917
Variations, 699
Vector artwork, importing, 794
Vector files, 812–813
Vector line art, 82
Vector shapes, 227
Vertigo Dizzy filter, 501
Vertigo HotTEXT, 494
Very wide tiles, 852–854
Video filters, 491
Video LUT Animation, 14, 743
View Gamut, 681
View/Print/Size, 222
Vignette edge, 132
Vivid Details TestStrip, 508
    PlateMaker 2, 508
Vortex Tile (KPT), 851

W

Watercolor filter, 128, 465
Water Paper filter, 485
Wave filter, 473, 886
Waving lines
    Strokes On, 274
    variation using, 274–275
Web, 822
Web filters, 506–507
WebFocus (Digital Frontiers), 506

Web graphics, 814
    essentials of, 812
Web press, 918
WebRazor (Ulead), 507
WebVise Totality (Auto F/X), 507
Wet Edges option, 166
What You See Is What You Get. *See* WYSIWYG (What You See Is What You Get)
White Intensity sliders, 468
White Level sliders, 485
White Matte, 420
White Point measurements, 523
White Point value, 522–523
Wide Gamut RGB, 665
Width setting, 154
Wild effect and NOC (Not Otherwise Classified) filters, 509
WildRiverSSK Chameleon filter, 503
WildRiverSSK set, 884
Wind filter, 489
Windows 95, Page Fault errors in, 41
Windows NT troubleshooting, 39–40
Windows RGB picker, 10
Windows System, 823
Windows troubleshooting, 37–42
Windows users, Threshold mode for, 555
Work and turn, 918
Work Paths, 242, 243
World Wide Web (WWW), 811–900
    nonrectangular graphics on, 868–875
Wrinkles, eliminating, 189–190
WYSIWYG (What You See Is What You Get), 918

X

Xaos Tools
    Paint Alchemy, 499
    Terrazzo, 499–500
    TypeCaster, 494

Y

YCC model, 110–111
Yellow, 918

Z

Zapf Dingbats, 888
ZigZag filter, 474
Zip drive, 8
Zoom commands, 222–223
Zoom tool, 221

What's On The CD-ROM

The companion CD-ROM included with your copy of *Photoshop 5 In Depth* contains a variety of software and teaching example files for PC and Macintosh platforms.

- Tutorials that include plenty of cool graphics
- Demo version of Adobe Illustrator for top-notch vectored drawings
- Adobe's demo version of After Effects which allows you to animate Photoshop and Illustrator images
- Demos and information on several Photoshop plug-ins including Eye Candy, FourSeasons, Page Edges, PhotoGraphic Edges, Typo/Graphic Edges, Ultimate Texture, Universal Animator, and Webvise Totality
- A collection of Actions that you can use to create special effects within Photoshop

System Requirements

PC:

Hardware:

- 486 or better
- Windows 95/98 or later, or Windows NT 4.0 or later
- 32MB of RAM

Software:

- Adobe Photoshop 5.0

Macintosh:

Hardware:

- PowerPC preferred
- Mac OS version 7.5 or later
- 32MB of RAM

Software:

- Adobe Photoshop 5.0